William F. Pinar
William M. Reynolds
Patrick Slattery
Peter M. Taubman

Understanding Curriculum

An Introduction to the Study of Historical and Contemporary Curriculum Discourses

PETER LANG
New York • Washington, D.C./Baltimore • San Francisco
Bern • Frankfurt am Main • Berlin • Vienna • Paris

Library of Congress Cataloging-in-Publication Data

Understanding curriculum: an introduction to the study of historical and
contemporary curriculum discourses/ William F. Pinar...(et al.).
   p.   cm.—(Counterpoints: vol. 17)
   Includes bibliographical references and index.
   1. Education—United States—Curricula. 2. Curriculum planning—
United States. I. Pinar, William. II. Series: Counterpoints (New York,
N.Y.) : vol. 17.
LB1570.U434   375'.00973—dc20   94-44009
ISBN 0-8204-2601-6 (Pbk.)
ISSN 1058-1634

Die Deutsche Bibliothek-CIP-Einheitsaufnahme

Understanding curriculum : an introduction to the study of historical and
contemporary curriculum discourses / William F. Pinar... - New York;
Washington, D.C./Baltimore; San Francisco; Bern; Frankfurt am Main;
Berlin; Vienna; Paris: Lang.
   (Counterpoints; Vol. 17)
   ISBN 0-8204-2601-6
NE: Pinar, William F.; GT

Cover design by James Brisson.

The paper in this book meets the guidelines for permanence and durability
of the Committee on Production Guidelines for Book Longevity of the
Council on Library Resources.

Printed in the United States of America.

Understanding Curriculum

An Introduction to the Study of Historical and Contemporary Curriculum Discourses

Preface and Acknowledgements   xiii

SECTION I: INTRODUCTION   1

Chapter 1: Understanding Curriculum: An Introduction   3
   I. Introduction: From Curriculum Development to
       Understanding Curriculum   3
  II. The Synoptic Text: Notes on a Genre   11
 III. Textbooks: "An Important Indicator"   16
 IV. Conceptions of Curriculum and Curriculum Specialists:
       Philip W. Jackson   25
          Mappings of the Field   28
   V. Mapping the Contemporary Field   41
 VI. Research   52
VII. Conclusion: Paradigm Wars   63

SECTION II: HISTORICAL DISCOURSES 1828-1979   67

Chapter 2: Understanding Curriculum as Historical Text:
**   Creation and Transformation, 1828-1927**   69
   I. Introduction: The Importance of History   69
  II. The Emergence of the Field in the Nineteenth Century:
       Faculty Psychology and Classical Curriculum Theory   70
 III. The Herbartians   78
 IV. Toward Child-Centeredness   83
   V. Scientific Curriculum Making for Social Efficiency   90
 VI. The Progressive Reform Movement   103
VII. Conclusion: A Major Retrospective   121

Chapter 3: Understanding Curriculum as Historical Text:
**   Crisis, Transformation, Crisis, 1928-1969**   124
   I. Introduction: The Tumultuous 1920s and 1930s   124

II.   The Eight-Year Study   133
III. The Synoptic Text   139
IV.   The 1940s: The Triumph of the Middle   142
V.   The 1950s: A Decade of Criticism, Conflict,
      and Reformation   151
VI.   The 1960s: Expansion, Conflict, and Contraction   159
         Structure of the Disciplines   159
         Curriculum Projects and Reports   162
VII. Curriculum Theory in the 1960s   168
VIII. Conclusion: Initial Stages of Reconceptualization   177

Chapter 4: Understanding Curriculum as Historical Text:
            The Reconceptualization of the Field 1970-1979   **186**
I.   Introduction: A Decade of Cataclysmic and
      Paradigmatic Change   186
II.   Popular Press   187
III. Humanism in the 1970s   190
IV.   Joseph J. Schwab   193
V.   Synoptic Textbooks and Other Developments   197
         National Institute of Education:
         The Curriculum Development Task Force   207
VI.   Tension in ASCD   208
VII. The Reconceptualization of the Curriculum Field   211
         Phenomenological, Political and Theological Discourses:
         The Work of Dwayne E. Huebner   213
         Transcendence and Politics:
         The Work of James B. Macdonald   215
VIII. The Conferences   218
IX.   Controversy   230
X.   Conclusion: A Reconceptualized Field   238

SECTION III: CONTEMPORARY CURRICULUM
             DISCOURSES 1980-1994   **241**

Chapter 5: Understanding Curriculum as Political Text   **243**
I.   Introduction: Curriculum is Political   243
II.   Reproduction Theory: Apple and Giroux   244
III. From Reproduction to Resistance: Apple, Giroux, Goodman   252
IV.   Pedagogy and Practice: Issues of Class, Race, and Gender:
      Carlson, Freire, Simon, Apple   260
V.   Criticism and Controversy   266
         Political Theory is Anthropocentric: C. A. Bowers   271
         Political Theory is Reactionary: Philip Wexler   276
         Political Theory is Voyeuristic: Elizabeth Ellsworth   279
         Problems of Agency and Resistance   281

VI. Discursive Shifts in Political Curriculum Theory:
McLaren, Ellsworth, Willinsky, Bowers   283
VII. Feminism, Semiotics, Poststructuralism, and the Coming
Crisis of Political Curriculum Theory   293
     The Constitution of Curriculum: James A. Whitson   297
     Knowledge as Social Practice: Social Practice as
     Discursive Formation   302
VIII. Conclusion: The Political Sector Divides and Disappears?   313

Chapter 6: Understanding Curriculum as Racial Text   **315**
  I. Introduction: Racial Theory is Autonomous   315
  II. Black Curriculum Orientations: William H. Watkins   319
  III. Multiculturalism: Cameron McCarthy   323
  IV. Identity and Repression: Castenell and Pinar   327
  V. Issues of Institutional Practice: Troyna, Hatcher, Sleeter   331
  VI. Racial Representations: Taubman, Edgerton, Whatley, P. Collins,
     Luttrell   335
  VII. Curriculum Politics: Young, Edelin, Gordon   346
VIII. Conclusion: The Significance of Race   · 357

Chapter 7: Understanding Curriculum as Gender Text   **358**
  I. Introduction: The Prevailing System of Gender   358
  II. Historical Background   359
  III. The Most Public Revolution   363
     The Reformist Position   365
     The Radical Analysis   366
  IV. Feminism, Gender Analysis, and the
     Reconceptualization   370
     The Late 1970s   371
  V. Conception, Contradiction, and Attachment:
     The Scholarship of Madeleine R. Grumet   376
  VI. Creating Spaces and Finding Voices:
     The Scholarship of Janet L. Miller   381
  VII. Teaching in the Patriarchal Wilderness:
     The Scholarship of Jo Anne Pagano   384
VIII. Feminist Pedagogy and Politics: An Overview   387
  IX. Gender Analysis and Male Identity   396
     Curriculum as Homosexual Text:
     The Scholarship of James T. Sears   396
     Profeminist Men: The Scholarship of Jesse Goodman   399
     Other Gender Analyses   400
  X. Conclusion: Isolation and Influence   402

Chapter 8: Understanding Curriculum as Phenomenological Text   **404**
  I. Introduction: A Poetic Activity   404

II. Critique of Mainstream Social Science: Aoki, Grumet, Jardine   410
    Phenomenological Foundations of *Currere*   414
III. Curriculum Language: Huebner and Smith   417
IV. Hermeneutics: Smith, Atkins, Reynolds, Martel, Peterat   422
V. Teaching: Aoki and van Manen   427
VI. Reading and Writing: Grumet, Hunsberger, van Manen   434
VII. The Secret Place: Langeveld and Smith   440
VIII. Temporality: Huebner and Lippitz   443
IX. Conclusion: A Discursive Shift toward Poststructuralism?   446

Chapter 9: Understanding Curriculum as Poststructuralist,
Deconstructed, Postmodern Text   **450**
I. Introduction: Language, Power, and Desire   450
II. Poststructuralism   452
III. Deconstruction   465
IV. Postmodernism   468
V. Poststructuralism and Curriculum Theory   475
    Desire and Identity: Peter Taubman   476
    Between Suicide and Murder: Jacques Daignault   480
    Poststructural Criticism of Traditional Curriculum Theory:
    Cleo Cherryholmes   485
    Arch-Writing on the Body: jan jagodzinski   490
    Above All a Matter of a Language: Clermont Gauthier   491
    A Taoist Connection: Wen-Song Hwu   492
    Poststructuralist Influences on Other Contemporary
    Curriculum Discourses   493
VI. Postmodernism and Curriculum Theory:
The Work of William E. Doll, Jr.   497
VII. Postmodernism, Feminist Theory, and Politics:
Lather, Giroux, Kincheloe, Steinberg, McLaren   503
    Post-formal Thinking:
    Joe L. Kincheloe and Shirley R. Steinberg   509
    The Postmodern Critical Theory of Peter McLaren   510
VIII. Conclusion: Post Poststructuralism?   514

Chapter 10: Understanding Curriculum as Autobiographical/
Biographical Text   **515**
I. Introduction: Three Streams of Scholarship   515
II. Autobiographical Theory and Classroom Practice   517
    Currere   518
    Voice   525
    Place: Joe L. Kincheloe and William F. Pinar   532
    Self as Discursive Formation:
    Poststructuralism and Autobiography: Daignault, Taubman,
    Grumet   536
    Dreams, Myth, and Imagination: Mary Aswell Doll   540

III.	Feminist Autobiographical Theory	544
	The Middle Passage: Grumet and Miller	548
	Autobiographical Reclamations of the Self:	
	Grumet and Reiniger	551
IV.	Studying Teachers' Lives	553
	Collaborative Autobiography:	
	Richard Butt and Danielle Raymond	554
	Personal Practical Knowledge:	
	F. Michael Connelly and D. Jean Clandinin	557
	Teacher Lore: William Schubert and William Ayers	561
	Biographical Studies: Ivor F. Goodson	563
V.	Conclusion: Not Pruned from the Disciplines	564

Chapter 11: Understanding Curriculum as Aesthetic Text   **567**

I.	Introduction: Not the Singing of Hymns	567
II.	Significance of the Arts: Broudy, Beyer, and Hamblen	569
III.	Aesthetic Knowing and Inquiry: Rosario, Vallance,	
	and Barone	571
IV.	Twentieth-Century Art and Curriculum Theory:	
	Ronald E. Padgham	576
V.	Art and Society: Landon E. Beyer	578
VI.	The Art of Curriculum and Teaching: Eisner, Vallance,	
	Figgins	581
VII.	Curriculum as Theater: Grumet, Figgins, Norris, Steinberg	589
	Figure/Ground in *Currere*:	
	The 1976 University of Rochester Theater Festival	591
	Reclamations	599
	Collective Creation	601
VIII.	Mind, Body, and the Postmodern: jagodzinski, Hamblen,	
	Sawada, Blumenfeld-Jones	601
IX.	Conclusion: Imagination and Wonder	604

Chapter 12: Understanding Curriculum as Theological Text   **606**

I.	Introduction: Historical Background	606
II.	Contemporary Concerns	612
III.	Moral and Ethical Dimensions: Huebner, Purpel,	
	Oliver, Gershman	627
IV.	Hermeneutics	638
V.	Liberation Theology: Kincheloe and Slattery	643
VI.	Eschatology, Cosmology, and Feminist Theology:	
	Slattery, Mitrano, Noddings	652
VII.	Conclusion: Between the Ideal and the Actual	659

Chapter 13: Understanding Curriculum as Institutionalized Text   **661**

Part One: Curriculum Development   **664**

I.	Curriculum Policy: Elmore, Sykes, McNeil, Page, Shulman	665

  II. School Reform: Sizer and Cheney   671
       Decentralization: Hans Weiler and David Tyack   675
       Curriculum in Restructured Schools:
       D. Tanner, McNeil, Cuban, Kirst and Meister, Weiler   679
 III. Curriculum Planning, Design, and Organization:
       Saylor, Alexander, Lewis, Egan, Noddings   684
       A Shift in the Field: Kieran Egan   690
       Caring: Nel Noddings   694
       The Core Curriculum: Goodlad and Su   697
  IV. Curriculum Implementation:
       Snyder, Bolin, Zumwalt, Fullan   699
       Three Major Approaches   699
   V. Technology: Saettler, Bereiter, Scardamalia, Bowers   704
       Visual Instruction   706
       Programmed Instruction   709
       Technology Education   717
  VI. Supervision: Sergiovanni, Smyth, Garman, Haggerson   720
 VII. Curriculum Evaluation: Scriven, Stake, Eisner   732
       Quantitative vs. Qualitative Methods   736
       Disciplinary Foundations   737
       The Artist as Curriculum Evaluator: Eisner   738
       Conclusion   742

       Part Two: Curriculum and Teachers   **744**
VIII. Pedagogy: Doyle, Shulman, Jackson, Cuban   744
  IX. Pre-service Teacher Education: The Holmes Group   755
   X. In-service Teacher Education: Aoki, Hargreaves, Fullan,
       and Jackson   763
       Teacher Lore: Schubert and Ayers   765
       Studying Teachers' Lives: Goodson   768
       Teacher Thinking and Development: Kincheloe, Smyth,
       Britzman, Carlson   770
       The Critical Thinking Movement: Ennis and L. Tanner   771
  XI. Textbooks: Venezky, Elson, Doyle   775

       Part Three: Curriculum and Students   **781**
 XII. School Lunch: Frederick Erickson and Jeffrey Shultz   781
XIII. Becoming Somebody: Philip Wexler and Nancy Lesko   785
 XIV. The Extracurriculum: Laura Berk   788
  XV. Conclusion   790

Chapter 14: Understanding Curriculum as International Text   **792**
   I. Introduction: Politics and Research   792
  II. Educational Outcomes   796
 III. Global Education   799
  IV. Japan   804

V.	Germany	809
VI.	The People's Republic of China	814
VII.	Africa	818
VIII.	Latin America	826
IX.	Selected Contemporary Discourses: Carson, Willinsky,	
	Gutek, Thelin	830
X.	Conclusion: Education for Global Survival	841

SECTION IV: CONCLUSION: POSTSCRIPT   **845**

Chapter 15: Understanding Curriculum: A Postscript for
the Next Generation   **847**

I.	Introduction	847
II.	The Curriculum Field Today: Problems and Possibilities	849
III.	What Is the Field Saying?	856
IV.	Conclusion	863
V.	Prologue	866

References   869

Subject index   1035

Name index   1117

Preface and Acknowledgements

This is an unruly book, a cacophony of voices. That is the reality and our stylistic intention. We walked a fine line, not wanting to submerge individual scholars and lines of discourse in *our* narrative. To do so would be to create a "master" narrative. What we have tried to do is represent the field as it is, not as we wish it to be, or even what it looks like from our point of view. Indeed, we have been quite explicit about our contributions and commitments so that the reader can factor these in his or her interpretation of our representation of the field.

How did we determine this representation of the field? That is, how did we decide which scholars, which discourses, were important? First, let us be clear we did not do it by surveying our colleagues in public and private elementary, middle, and secondary schools as to which curriculum books they read. That might be an interesting survey to make, but it would not constitute a representation of the field. To think so would be like suggesting that a portrait of the field of political science could be undertaken by surveying which political scientists and which streams of political science research and theory are read by politicians and voters. Or, it would be like suggesting that the field of medicine could be mapped by surveying the health habits of the population. All three—curriculum theorists, political scientists and physicians—might wish to influence our fellow citizens. But none would claim that what our fellow citizens read and do necessarily reflects the state of our respective fields.

So how do we determine this representation, paint this portrait? The answer is probably self-evident: we examined what is published by the scholarly presses and in the professional journals. Among the latter, we examined carefully *Curriculum Inquiry*, the *Journal of Curriculum Studies*, *Curriculum Perspectives*, the *Journal of Curriculum Theorizing* (now *JCT: An Interdisciplinary Journal of Curriculum Studies*), and the *Journal of Curriculum and Supervision*. We looked at selected issues of the *Harvard Educational Review*, *Teachers College Record*, *Educational Theory*, the *American Journal of Education*, *Phenomenology + Pedagogy*, the *Journal of Educational Thought*, and the *McGill Journal of Education*. We examined conference programs, especially those of the American Educational Research Association.

There is the question of time. Particularly in the writing of chapter 14, we knew we could not wait the customary two years between conference presentation and publication, given the rapidity of international developments. More specifically, the American field of curriculum is moving rapidly. We have feared that the discipline which, after ten years of study we are confident we see fairly clearly now, may not be the field emerging on the horizon.

Despite this problem of "lag," we are confident we have a recognizable portrait, even to our junior colleagues. Conscious, however, of this generational feature of a field's development, we conclude this book with "a postscript to the next generation."

There was the problem of gaining access to curriculum scholarship published outside the journals we chose to study. To compensate, I wrote 200 prominent curriculum scholars in 1987 requesting reprints of their articles and essays, to provide some protection against missing contributions not published in the journals we examined. Many responded generously. All of this does not add up to an infallible and statistically accurate picture of the field, but we are certain that, in general terms, with exceptions (one line of research may be overemphasized somewhat, another possibly underemphasized), we present here a comprehensive and accurate portrait of the field. What you will read is what the field is saying, or has been saying, during its more or less one hundred year history, emphasizing the past twenty years.

The curriculum field, after a period of stasis, is very much in motion now. Indeed, there is a veritable explosion in scholarly publication in the field. Moreover, the major categories by which we can understand contemporary work exhibit, in some cases, ever-increasingly porous boundaries. This somewhat fluid state acknowledged, I think we have a reasonable snapshot of the American curriculum field at this time. To characterize this representation as "comprehensive" means that we believe we have included the primary and much of the secondary scholarship in each sector. It is not to say that we have included all scholarship; we have omitted some work to maintain a narrative line. We have come as close to being encyclopedic as we dared. After all, we view this as an *introduction* to the study of curriculum. Students are encouraged to pursue ideas introduced in this volume by referring to original sources; serious students will do so. There are those who will regard this book as too complicated to function as an introduction. Our reply is that the field is now complex, and we have simplified its representation as much as we responsibly could. We believe advanced undergraduates and beginning graduate students can both profit from studying this introduction. For too long curriculum professors have patronized their students by assuming their ineptitude. Compared to the textbooks in other fields undergraduates have studied, i.e. physics, the curriculum field remains quite accessible.

There are many to thank for assistance in the production of this work. We wish to thank Janet L. Miller for her permission to use a draft of a co-authored (with Pinar) essay (which was never finished) as the genesis of chapter 7, and for her careful reading and critique of chapters 7 and 10. We thank Madeleine R. Grumet for her critiques of chapters 7, 8, 10, and 11. My thanks to Louis Castenell, Jr., Cameron McCarthy, and Susan Edgerton for their advice regarding chapter 6, to Kim MacGregor for advising me on the technology section of chapter 13, to Noreen Garman for advice regarding the supervision section in chapter 13, to Tony Whitson for helping with the sections reporting his work, to Karen Hamblen for reading chapter 11, and to Margo Figgins for suggestions regarding chapters 11 and 15. We wish to acknowledge Bill Schubert's non-competitive and generous support, as well as his advice regarding chapter 2. Thanks especially to Craig Kridel for reading the historical chapters. We thank all of those who responded generously to Pinar's letter of request for reprints. Many thanks go to Bill Doll for reading 7, 9, 10, and 14. Thanks as well to Elizabeth Adam Langlinais for typing first drafts of chapters 12 and 14, to Cheryl Friberg Slattery for her review of all chapters, and Wendy Taylor, Celeste Brinkhaus, and Wendy Hellenger, graduate students at the University of Southwestern Louisiana, for their research assistance on chapter 14.

I wish to acknowledge my reliance, especially in chapter 13, on the *Handbook of Research on Curriculum*, edited by Philip Jackson (1992c), published by Macmillan, and supported by the American Educational Research Association. Jackson, has, I think, made a very substantial contribution, both in his essay and in his editing, as the quality of essays is quite high, in contrast, for instance, to the superficiality of the curriculum pieces in Noel Entwistle's (Ed.), *Handbook of Educational Ideas and Practices* (Routledge, 1990). Serious students of the field are well advised to purchase their own copies of the Jackson handbook. Too, students should not overlook the recently published *The American Curriculum: A Documentary History*, edited by George Willis, et al. (Greenwood, 1993).

While the idea for the book and its organizational scheme are mine, this project has been a collaborative effort. Bill Reynolds developed the first drafts of chapters 2, 3, and 5; additionally he provided preliminary material for chapters 4 and 10. Peter Taubman worked on the second draft of chapter 7, redoing that first draft extensively. He also reworked my version of chapter 6, and took my fragment of chapter 9 and wrote a first draft. Patrick Slattery provided first drafts of chapters 12 and 14, and a first draft of the supervision section of chapter 13. I wrote all drafts of chapters 1, 8, 11, and 15, although Bill, Peter, and Patrick commented on these. I wrote the final draft of all chapters, although in chapters 9, 12, 14, and part of 7 much of their language remains intact. While each of us claims the perspective presented in this history and analysis of the field, responsibility for errors is mine alone.

This book presented a special problem for me regarding the reporting and referencing of my own work. There is a trend is recent scholarship to quote oneself, sometimes rather extensively. Indeed, reference lists appear on occasion to function as bibliographic introductions to the work of the author. Even more remarkably, two recent books (Giroux, 1992a; Apple, 1993) include interviews with the authors themselves as chapters! Given these practices, I suppose I ought not feel awkward about reporting my own efforts. The truth is that I have been very much involved in recent developments in the field, and for the sake of accuracy, modesty had to be suspended. I have tried to report carefully criticisms of my efforts, in part to avoid the appearance of self-promotion. Regarding a related matter, it is also true that I have not been timid in reporting the work of my friends (at the least I have been careful not to understate their contributions). For the sake of fairness I have worked hard to report appreciatively the work of my critics, as well as the very much larger number of scholars I do not know or with whom I have no particular history. Being conscious of these complications I believe to be the best protection against arguments ad hominem. Last but not least, the candid responses of more than a dozen anonymous reviewers provided additional insurance. Of course, you the reader must judge whether or not we have succeeded in being fair.

I wish to thank former and present LSU graduate students who have helped me in many ways. Among these are Margaret Sullivan (who also worked on permissions and the bibliography, in the latter task assisted by Mark Bernu, a Ph.D. student at Oklahoma State University), Gregory Nixon, Susan Edgerton, John Stier, Yonghwan Lee, John St. Julien (who read the technology section in chapter 13), Douglas McKnight and Anne Pautz (who read the second draft and final drafts, making extensive and useful comments; both helped faithfully with the bibliography while Anne helped with the section on Bill Doll in chapter 9 and with permissions), and Wen-Song Hwu. I would especially like to acknowledge the labor and friendship of Professor Hwu, who came to LSU for Ph.D. study by way of Bill Reynolds, when Bill taught at the University of Wisconsin-Stout. Wen-Song's summaries of well over one hundred journal articles and his companionship and his general help during the 1992-1993 academic year enabled me to maintain a focus that threatened to blur due to the sheer volume of labor. My thanks, Wen-Song. Finally, I thank Louisiana State University for a sabbatical leave during fall term 1991 when much was accomplished.

I began work on this project in 1981, when I first sensed that the movement known as the "Reconceptualization" had succeeded. The field had been reconceived from one with an essentially institutionalized aim to maintain practice (by improving it incrementally) to one with a critical, hermeneutical goal of understanding practice and experience. Other projects interrupted progress on this one, including the chairmanship of the Department at LSU in 1985, a post I resigned in 1991, in part to finish this project. By the middle of the decade I realized I would not finish this project without help, and I asked Bill Reynolds to join me. Bill worked closely with me during that initial period, and I am most grateful for his commitment and colleagueship.

My map of the field after the Reconceptualization is drawn incompletely in *Contemporary Curriculum Discourses*, published in 1988. In one sense that collection represents the "best of *JCT*," as most of the essays published in that book first appeared in *JCT* (first *The Journal of Curriculum Theorizing*, now *JCT: An Interdisciplinary Journal of Curriculum Studies*). Many of those papers were presented at the *JCT*-sponsored yearly conference, held from 1979-1982 at the Airlie House in Virginia, afterward at the Bergamo Conference Center in Dayton, Ohio. [The 1994 meeting will be held at the Banff Centre for the Arts, Banff, Alberta, CANADA.] In that collection I conceived of the major sectors of scholarship according to their theme, source, and apparent aspiration. These discourses included efforts to understand the curriculum historically, politically, aesthetically, phenomenologically, and from feminist perspectives. Omitted from this collection, partly due to space, were discourses that now are clearly major or emerging: race, autobiography/ biography, theology, postmodernism/poststructuralism, and international perspectives. Of course, the boundaries among these sectors is porous, more porous between and among some than others.

As the reconceptualist movement succeeded, it came apart. To the extent the movement was cohesive, it was opposition to the Tylerian tradition that held the movement together. Once that tradition had been displaced, the cohesion splintered. Now there is a certain "balkanization" in the field, a certain tendency for students and practitioners of each discourse to act as if his or her discourse of affiliation and labor is the most important. Such a tendency is "natural," of course, to some extent, but also false. This problem has led to a tendency in the field to ignore discourses, to fail to teach curriculum theory comprehensively. This book is an effort to correct this "balkanization." We hope it signals and supports a period of consolidation in the field, in which discourses can emphasize their intertextual complementarities. It must not be possible to study for the Ph.D. in curriculum without knowing all the major sectors of scholarship. To teach the field as if it were only political or institutional is irresponsible.

My sense is that the next "paradigmatic shift" in the field will represent not a shift in scholarly function for the field—as the Reconceptualization of the 1970s represented—but a shift to a more conceptually autonomous, intertextually complex effort to understand curriculum. The current state of curriculum discourses indicates a relative closeness to or dependency upon the sources of these discourses, sources in other fields. For example, ideas from postmodernism are "applied" or focused upon curriculum issues. The next stage will involve a relative movement away from sources, although historically informed students will not forget them, and the establishment of a conceptually autonomous discipline of curriculum theory, an idea sketched in chapter 15.

In addition to his support, I wish to acknowledge the editorial advice of Michael Flamini. It is difficult to imagine an editor as civilized and smart as Michael has been. And our special thanks go to Joe L. Kincheloe and Shirley R. Steinberg for inviting us to publish in their important series, for their insightful suggestions, and unwavering support. They are remarkable scholars, teachers, and friends.

Finally, I wish to acknowledge the mentorship and friendship of Paul R. Klohr. I met Paul in summer 1969 upon the recommendation of Donald R. Bateman. Don had been the inspiration in my senior year, teaching in an experimental program that focused upon urban education. Bateman taught me Freire, Mao, and black radicalism. He would continue as my mentor and friend. However, my focus would shift from English education to curriculum theory. On this occasion I wish to acknowledge Paul's influence on my hope for the field, a hope that was mostly a fantasy as I began working in 1972 at the University of Rochester. He helped me to plan the Rochester conference, which is generally acknowledged as the beginning of the movement to reconceptualize the field. He very much influenced my editing of *Curriculum Theorizing: The Reconceptualists* (1975d). Paul has never agreed with all that I have done. For instance, he has never seemed very interested in autobiography. Paul has disagreed with what he regards as my underinvestment in "practice." No doubt his enduring commitment to the schools and to practice has helped keep my drift away from the institution of schooling from being complete. Despite these disagreements Paul has been generous in his advice over the years, and I have eagerly sought it. This book is dedicated to him.

William F. Pinar
December 1994

SECTION I

INTRODUCTION

Chapter 1

Understanding Curriculum:
An Introduction

[T]he field of curriculum . . . resides at the very core of education.
(Elliot W. Eisner, 1984, p. 209)

Curriculum is a central concept in Anglo-Saxon (or English-speaking) educational studies; and . . . curriculum practice is integral to the modern institution of *schooling*.
(David Hamilton, 1990, p. 3)

Education functions, at least in secular societies, as a text that says something about the things society considers sacred.
(David Gordon, 1988, p. 446)

Whether the 1990s will be indeed prove to be a period of consolidation and integration, based on broadly humanistic approaches . . . remains to be seen. It would be a worthy agenda.
(William A. Reid, 1992, p. 177)

I
Introduction:
From Curriculum Development to
Understanding Curriculum

This is a different kind of textbook than students in curriculum courses typically read. It is different from introductory textbooks in other areas of education, such as educational administration or educational psychology, and it is different from textbooks in the social sciences such as psychology and sociology. True, like other textbooks, we wish to paint a portrait of what the field is like, to represent it as accurately and comprehensively as space will allow. However, unlike many other textbooks, we wish to preserve the individual voices of individual scholars as much as possible. It seems to us that most textbooks present a field of study as if it were an army of disembodied ideas, marching across the blank space of time, inevitably annexing unincorporated space, establishing cities of systematized thought. The truth is fields do not proceed that way. Fields are comprised of people, sometimes extraordinary, often ordinary people, whose job it is to write material that complies with the rules and principles other people—their predecessors—have established as reasonable. Fields, just like schools, are comprised of people, people with ideas. Both people and ideas change, often not very fast (or fast enough, some people think), but they do change. We want to portray this process of people-with-ideas changing, that is, the history of the field.

Quoting the scholars themselves. Those of us writing this book have backgrounds in literature and linguistics. We have always been very much interested in the concreteness of fictional characters who are living out their individual and collective dramas in novels and short stories. Our backgrounds in literature, and in literary theory, have helped us to see, as has much scholarship in areas such as the history of science (Kuhn, 1962), that fields are comprised of people with ideas, working on problems—theoretical and practical (although, as we will see, the distinction between these two realms is no longer self-evident in the curriculum field)—within institutional constraints. Fields develop over time, and specific ideas develop about what constitutes the appropriate ideas, the appropriate problems for students of the field to study. Traditions develop, including conventional notions of what ideas are important, which problems, theoretical and practical, are worth working on. In this textbook we will present the major traditions of the American curriculum field. But we will attempt to do so in ways that leave intact the voices of individuals working within, and sometimes on the margins of, these traditions. How do we think we can achieve this? We think that by including an unusually large number of quoted passages, that is, the words of the scholars themselves, we can preserve the voices of individual scholars, working together in, around, and against the traditions and conventions of the field. Now the "conventional wisdom" advises against such a strategy. Most established scholars would say that, for example, for Ph.D. students writing dissertations or assistant professors attempting to establish a line of research, such a strategy is ill-advised. Including a large number of quoted passages may suggest, they worry, an inability to formulate an autonomous point of view. However, establishing a line of research and formulating an autonomous point of view are not our concerns in this volume.

Each of us *has* an established point of view, Pinar in autobiography, Reynolds in that tradition of interpretation known as hermeneutics, Slattery in postmodernism and theology, and Taubman in gender analysis conducted in ways associated with poststructuralism. Because we have points of view, there is no need to establish one. The need here is to write a history of the field in which the individuals comprising the field do not disappear into *our* characterizations of their work. In fact we have worked to violate the history of introductory textbooks by preserving the individuality of scholars' voices. That is reason enough to quote extensively from others' work, including others' quoting of others' work (so-called secondary sources).

Preservation of individual identities is essential. There is an additional reason, however, to write a "person-centered" portrait of the field (Bullough, 1979b). We see the contemporary American curriculum field as seriously

balkanized, that is, divided into relatively separate fiefdoms or sectors of
scholarship, each usually ignoring the other except for the occasional criticism. The sense of a collective enterprise, of all of us working together,
despite serious differences in outlook and methods of working, is conspicuously absent at the present time. For example, it is possible to attend graduate school in curriculum studies in 1994 and never read work that understands curriculum in terms of race or aesthetics. Many curriculum specialists
—including the most prominent—are so caught up in their individual perspectives that they feel little obligation to present the perspectives of others with
whom they might disagree. That breakdown in the sense of collective effort
is a major problem facing the field today. It was a major motive for us to
write this textbook, in which *all* the major sectors of scholarship are
presented. It is this breakdown which prompted us to include an unusually
large number of quoted passages, despite knowing that reviewers might criticize this stylistic practice. However, we suffer this criticism gladly if we can
accomplish our aim. That aim is to present a mosaic, even if, at times, it will
sound (to change momentarily from a visual to an auditory image) like a
cacophony of individuals' voices so that the beginning student might see this
quilt, might hear this complicated symphony, that is the contemporary
curriculum field. True, the book may read like a Charles Ives' symphony—we
would be lucky if it read so pleasingly—but the preservation of individual
identities required us leave individual melodies in tact, even if it seems to
add up at times to what will sound to some as excessively contrapuntal.

We do not need another—to use a poststructuralist term—"master narrative" wherein individuals and individuals' lines of research disappear into the
author's line of reasoning or the author's ideological commitment. What we
do need is a vivid and audible sense of the hundreds of individuals who
spend their days working on curriculum issues and problems, theoretical and
institutional (although this distinction blurs too we discovered), so that the
individuality of these efforts, as well as their differences, their similarities,
their areas of intersection, and their points of divergence and even antagonism are preserved. We have worked to emphasize that fields of study are
comprised of actual living people, not disembodied ideas which appear out
of nowhere.

The era of "curriculum development" is past. There are those who will not
accept this argument. We predict that even a few of our friends will think
this is "master narrative," and that *any* effort to bring together differing
discourses in one book, different people in one room, is authoritarian or
patriarchal in principle. If they do, then these friends have forgotten that
there remains today what they would characterize as an intellectually inactive
and inert group of traditional curriculum specialists who teach traditional
synoptic textbooks—one, for instance, first written in 1954—portraying a
curriculum field that does not exist anymore. In effect, by teaching these out-
of-date but still-in-print books they silence the voices of many important, but
sometimes younger, intellectually more complex, scholars such as feminists,

poststructuralists, and phenomenologists. By bringing everyone into the same room we aspire to put an end to the exclusionary politics of traditional curriculum textbooks which repeat the litany, now without scholarly foundation, of curriculum objectives, design, implementation, and evaluation. These are no longer the major concepts of the day. True, they do retain a certain, very much reduced, institutional currency—that is, in the schools—and we will outline these traditional concepts, now understood sometimes non-traditionally, non-institutionally, in chapter 13. The main concepts today are quite different from those which grew out of an era in which school buildings and populations were growing exponentially, and when keeping the curriculum ordered and organized were the main motives of professional activity. *That was a time of curriculum development.* Curriculum Development: Born: 1918. Died: 1969.

From "development" to "understanding." We live in a different time. True, in science and mathematics education, traditional curriculum development still occurs, as these privileged areas still receive significant amounts of federal and private grant monies. [In the 1960s it was the space/military race with the Soviet Union that fed the irrational idea that mathematics and science are keys to national supremacy; now it is international economic competition.] However, the general field of curriculum, the field interested in the relationships among the school subjects as well as issues within the individual school subjects themselves and with the relationships between the curriculum and the world, that field is no longer preoccupied with development. As we shall see, the field today is preoccupied with *understanding.* To understand curriculum does not mean that many of us do not want to change curriculum, both theoretically and institutionally. In fact, surveying the literature of the field makes it clear: we want change. However, many degrees of complexity have entered our conceptions of what it means to do curriculum work, to be a curriculum specialist, to work for curriculum change. In general, we are no longer technicians, that is, people who accept unquestioningly others' priorities. However, it must be said here that there was always a wing of the field unhappy with its role of simply carrying out the policies of others. Before we were technicians, we were master planners, but that is relatively ancient history (pre-1950) as far as beginning students are concerned. We will review these phases of the field, in a broad sweep in this chapter (via the work of Philip Jackson, 1992a), and in more detail in chapters 2, 3, and 4. The contemporary field receives most of our attention. It is presented in chapters 5 through14. We end with what we characterize as "a postscript for the next generation," mindful that this book, this photograph if you will, is taken in time, and that already another era is on its way. You, the student who may someday become a curriculum theorist yourself, may wish or may be called upon, to articulate it.

The language of the field. To grasp the present era of American curriculum studies we believe it is necessary to think of what is written regarding curriculum as, in fact, writing. You might suggest that our English backgrounds are showing. But we are not retreating into English teacher roles. We are acknowledging that a field of study *is a field of study*, a tradition of language or discourse. A field is rooted in the world, of course, in that world it chooses to examine. It is influenced also by the entire world: history, politics, life, and death. To understand the contemporary field it is necessary to understand the curriculum field as discourse, as text, and most simply but profoundly, as words and ideas. By discourse we mean a particular discursive practice, or a form of articulation that follows certain rules and which constructs the very objects it studies. Any discipline or field of study can be treated as a discourse and analyzed as such. To do so requires studying *the language of the field*. Yes, the curriculum field is about what happens in schools, but in being about schools it employs and is comprised by the language which both reflects and determines what "being about schools" means. So to understand the field means that we need to attend closely to the language scholars working in the field use.

How can we focus on language? Again, we are left with the strategy of quoting rather often, so that you, the student, can appreciate exactly what an individual scholar has said, in her or his own words. As well, to help us focus on the language or discourse of the field, we decided to regularly include the titles of books and articles, as these make explicit the themes, the language, the discourse, in which the writer is working, and which help form, indeed, comprise, his or her understanding of what curriculum is, how it functions, and what it might be. At times this focus on titles and on language may make this textbook seem to be a bibliographic essay, that is a book about titles. That is partly true. To portray the discourses which comprise the contemporary field we must portray their expression in titles. Now titles do not always convey in simple fashion the main idea of the book or article, although they often imply it. Nor should our summarizing of titles and the ideas they imply be a substitute for reading the original book or article. Remember, this is an introduction to the field. It is not the field itself. Those who want to know more are encouraged, of course, to read the books and articles we report here.

Only secondary sources. In this sense this textbook is a map of the country of curriculum. If you want to know more about, say, New Orleans, you need to go there, not that being there is any substitution for reading about it. New Orleans is text, too. If you want to know more about poststructuralism, read the work we report in chapter 9 (especially the general introduction which comprises the initial sections of that chapter). Speaking of poststructuralism [a movement in French philosophy that, after influencing English departments in major ways over the past twenty years is now influencing curriculum scholarship], it is probably necessary to comment on another piece of "conventional wisdom," that of quoting original sources. Perhaps the most famous French poststructuralist, Jacques Derrida, has pointed out that there is no such thing as an "original" source. Another French poststructuralist, Michel Foucault, has argued relatedly that there is no "author." That is, any piece of writing, any author, is "filled" with the writings of others, and while a particular piece of writing, a particular author, achieves a singular identity, we must not mistake its singularity for absolute originality. All of us are indebted to others. You should read "original" sources. However, in the senses that Derrida and Foucault have written, "secondary" sources are also original, and quoting, say, "Dewey in Rippa," is not necessarily distorting or misleading. In fact, it underscores the poststructuralist insight that all of us are "in" others. None of us stands alone, or thinks only original thoughts, or does original actions. In fact, Dewey lives in Rippa today, just as this print lives in you, as you read.

Theory exists to provoke thinking. Just from that paragraph you can begin to see that this is not a book telling you what you should do with that seventh-grade American history curriculum dictated by the school district central office. True, there are still curriculum specialists who have much to say on day-to-day institutional matters in ways intended to make your functioning as a teacher smoother. However, much of what is written today in American curriculum studies is about understanding the problem of being a teacher of students in seventh grade from the variety of perspectives which make it problematic. That is, being a seventh-grade teacher is not primarily a matter of maintaining discipline, although, of course, for some it is. But that is not what is interesting about that situation. What is interesting is how your life history, politics, gender, race, and theology have come together in complicated ways to make a problematic situation. The field no longer sees the problems of curriculum and teaching as "technical" problems, that is, problems of "how to." The contemporary field regards the problems of curriculum and teaching as "why" problems. Such a view requires that we *understand* what was before considered only something to be solved. Now, the contemporary field is hardly against solving problems, but the view today is that solutions to problems do not just require knee-jerk, commonsensical responses, but careful, thoughtful, disciplined understanding. So why should a beginning or in-service teacher know this material? Our answer is that *conventional responses to problems of curriculum and teaching have clearly failed to solve those problems.* Writing behavioral objectives, evaluating with standardized tests, presenting material in linear, lock-step fashion, expelling unruly students: these solutions have failed. We would not suggest that the work reported in this volume "has the answers," although we think answers are certainly here. There are more questions, however. Not questions that simply leave you, the beginning student, feeling overwhelmed by the complexity of it all, but rather questions which will provoke you to reflect on what it means to educate, what it means to be educated, questions that might literally alter how you proceed, not only as a teacher, but perhaps as a person. That is the function of theory. It is not to find an eternal truth, to establish for now and evermore "what works," or what's right. Theory functions to provoke you to think.

To the instructor. There is another reason why students should read this material. This is a reason your university professor should know, and we address this paragraph to your university instructor. This reason has to do with professional conduct, professional obligation, of teaching what the field is. The contemporary field seems to say quite clearly that it is a fantasy to assume beginning students require "steps" to successful teaching, i.e. technical and behavioral forms of social engineering. The field has dismissed that approach to teacher education as well as to curriculum development. Our students should know the field as the field is now, not as it was when you were a graduate student. Frankly stated, it is a professional obligation to report to your students what the scholars in the field are thinking. To ignore poststructuralism, for instance, is little different than censorship, little different from an old Soviet-style refusal to report world news, simply because the Party insisted on its version of what reality was. The curriculum teacher, as well as the beginning or in-service teacher, may find poststructuralism—we take that because it is the most recent discourse and anonymous reviewers found it the most difficult to grasp—unhelpful or distasteful or not useful (we disagree with each of these judgments), but she and he is obligated to read what is being done in the name of poststructuralism. It is an important discourse in the American field today. Just as teachers in the schools may not wish to teach certain topics because they do not interest them, teachers in colleges and universities must teach all important sectors of the contemporary field, whether or not they disagree with them.

Back to you, a beginning student. We have a few tips on how to use this book, although your instructor will no doubt indicate how he or she wishes you to proceed, given the requirements of the course. We assume you will not be expected to memorize facts for recitation on a standardized examination. We assume that a minority of readers intend to become professional curriculum specialists. Given these assumptions, therefore, we advise you, upon your first acquaintance with the book, to scan the material, not allowing yourself to be tripped up over terms you do not immediately understand, such as "poststructuralism." They will become clearer by the last page. The point for you is not to grasp the material as its writers have grasped it. The point for you, a prospective or in-service teacher, is to allow yourself to be challenged by what you read, to employ the material to reflect on your own situation as student, as teacher, as a person. *The educational possibility for curriculum theory is to help you reflect more profoundly, and not without humor on occasion, on your individual, specific situation.* Be patient with material that is difficult to grasp; be patient with yourself. Tolerate material that seems irrelevant or just "way out." You are not obligated to agree with what you read, or, for that matter, to remember it. You *are* obligated as an educator to consider material which you may not like immediately, and to formulate some response, however negative. Your obligation is to reflect on your own situation, to formulate language to describe and understand that situation more carefully, more precisely, more fully. For many years we have been teaching curriculum theory to beginning students (22 years in Pinar's case), and we know this material can stimulate such reflection.

During your first read, your first scan, you might attend primarily to the italicized descriptors introducing many paragraphs. Generally, these convey the main point of the paragraph, or on occasion they comment on the main point rather than express it. As a descriptor catches your eye, move to the main text. Remember, reading a textbook can be like going on a date. On a first date you do not expect learn everything about your partner. Rather, you speak about that which captures your attention. As happens on later dates, on a second read you can attend more fully to the main text and begin to move through the entirety of the material.

Intertextual references. As you read you will discover that specific ideas and specific individuals sometimes appear in more than one section of a chapter; sometimes an idea or a person will appear in more than one chapter. We will help you locate these ideas by parenthetical references to other sections of the book (and, of course, via the subject and name indices at the back of the book). For example, in chapter 1 you will read about Franklin Bobbitt, Ralph Tyler, and Joseph Schwab as these three "giants" in the field represented long-term shifts in how curriculum is perceived as a field. While discussing them in that context, we will also point you to chapters 2, 3, and 4 where they appear in historical context. In those chapters we will also refer you back to chapter 1. We will "walk you through" the various discourses, the story of the field. However, as with any textbook it is up to you to refer to your situation, your own responses to what you have read, to formulate your own point of view regarding what you read. Again, we suggest that you do not try to memorize; rather, allow an impression to build, as the language of the field gathers itself into discourses.

Organization. We move next in this chapter to a consideration of this genre of writing, the textbook, known as the synoptic textbook, as it is said to summarize the field. Synoptic (or summarizing) textbooks have played an unusually influential role in the development of the American curriculum field, although, as we shall see, many synoptic textbooks today are not truly synoptic of the contemporary field. After a review of these textbooks, we will move to a consideration of the field's concept of what it is about, reviewing shifts in the field from, as we mentioned, Bobbitt (1920s), Tyler (1940s, 1950s), and Schwab (1960s, 1970s), to the group of curricularists who, in the 1970s, worked to reconceptualize the field from one focused on curriculum development to one focused on understanding curriculum. We conclude this chapter with a review of the major sections of contemporary scholarship, including contemporary conceptions of curriculum research.

After introducing the book and laying the basis for understanding the contemporary field in chapter 1, we move to consideration of scholarship which reviews the history of curriculum in the United States. Various dates are cited as beginning dates for the professional field of curriculum; we chose 1828 and the publication of the *Yale Report*, a choice which allowed us to anticipate the curriculum debates during the third quarter of the nine-teenth century, debates repeated in somewhat different forms in the 1980s. [We could have easily chosen 1918 and the publication of Franklin Bobbitt's *The Curriculum*.] Chapter 2 concludes with the publication of a major retro-spective on curriculum in 1927. Chapter 3 reports the developments between that date and 1969, when the traditional field was first pronounced to be in, and indeed went into, crisis. Chapter 4 recounts the decade in which the crisis was lived through, filled with controversy and debate, and when a new field, the contemporary field, first emerged. Chapters 5-14 report the major contemporary discourses of the 1980s and 1990s, concluding with a postscript to the next generation. It is a somewhat long story we report, although not literally longer than stories other fields—such as psychology—must tell. It can seem a complicated story, although by no means more com-plicated than the stories the, say, natural science disciplines like biology have to tell. Let us take a first step, focusing on the "conveyance" in which we will travel: the textbook, or, what is known in our field as the synoptic textbook.

II
The Synoptic Text:
Notes on a Genre

As years passed, everyday usage in education slowly corrupted "curriculum development" into a shortened term, "curriculum." This term was invested with renewed meanings, which served to alter that to which it referred in practice while elevating its symbolic potency.

(O. L. Davis, 1986, p. 86)

Students ought to have a clear picture of the genre in which this textbook appears. Synoptic texts provide encyclopedic portraits of the complex "socio-intellectual" community known as a field of study (Pagano, 1981; Schubert, 1980a; Schubert, 1986c). They do more, however, than simply represent or capture the field as it exists at the time the text was written. Synoptic texts also articulate that field and help determine what in the field is important. In shedding light on some areas of the field to the exclusion of others, they often present a part of the field as the whole field. In representing the field in a particular way they inadvertently give the impression that the field *is* their articulation of it. We are determined to avoid such misrepresentation.

The tradition of synoptic curriculum texts can be said to have originated in 1935 with the publication of Caswell and Campbell's *Curriculum Develop-ment*. The tradition continues to be a strong one today; note, for instance, the appearance of three synoptic texts in 1988 and 1989 (R. Doll, 1989; Ornstein & Hunkins, 1988; Wiles & Bondi, 1989). Each of these textbooks attempts to give historical treatment of curriculum issues, although in more than one instance such treatment is superficial at best. Attention to the history of the field is essential as it alerts scholars and schoolpersons that curriculum issues occur in historical time and in political context. Rarely are new curriculum proposals "new." For instance, the current wave of school reform (Fiske, 1991) echoes aspects of both the social efficiency and progressive movements of seventy years ago, as well as containing elements of nineteenth-century classicism, movements we will report in chapters 2 and 3. Historically informed curriculum scholars and practitioners can make more discerning choices as to their participation in politically-inspired "reforms." Furthermore, historically informed scholars are more likely to make contributions which will move the field forward. However, as Kliebard (1970, 1975a, 1975b, 1975c, 1986, 1987, 1992a) and others (Tanner & Tanner, 1990) have made plain, the traditional curriculum field had been notoriously ahistorical and atheoretical. These are not separate problems. Theoretical development requires understanding the history of the field. Due to the increasing significance of historical scholarship in the contemporary field, three chapters of this textbook are devoted to historical discourses. Students of the field need to understand that fields of study, including this one, are "socio-intellectual communities" whose systematic and formalized "conversations" accumulate and change over time (Pagano, 1981, pp. 171-184).

The American curriculum field has undergone a profound shift during the past twenty years, a fundamental reconceptualization of its primary concepts, its research methods, its status, and its function in the larger field of education. This shift—which we will term for convenience's sake "the Reconceptualization"—occurred during the decade of the 1970s; we examine that decade in chapter 4. Some have debated whether or not this shift was paradigmatic (see Brown, 1988). By paradigm we mean the constellation of rules, domain assumptions (Gouldner, 1970), theories, discourses, and values that govern and shape a discipline at a particular historical moment. In simpler terms, paradigm is a general "mind-set" or perspective which dictates, for example, in which directions research might go, what constitutes legitimate knowledge, and who is a legitimate speaker for the field. We would say that the curriculum field has experienced a paradigm shift similar, for example, to that undergone in the humanities during the previous two decades as those disciplines—especially literary theory—changed to include feminist scholarship and theory and continental philosophies. That is not to say that these changes did not contain within them elements of previous discourse systems. Indeed, we see, for example, in contemporary curriculum scholarship, echoes of earlier child-centered, progressive, and social-efficiency themes in several contemporary discourses. Phenomenological scholarship [chapter 8], for instance, captures child-centered concerns while political scholarship [chapter 5] recalls the work of George S. Counts. Racial scholarship [chapter 6] recalls the work of black historians and cultural theorists like W. E. B. DuBois and Horace Mann Bond, and in its central concepts—such as identity —reconfigures strands of political, phenomenological, poststructuralist, and feminist discourses. The interest in social efficiency lives still in many current institutional curricular schemes, as we will see in the section on school reform in chapter 13.

Perhaps the most serious problem today in American synoptic textbooks is their relative neglect of contemporary research and scholarship in the curriculum field (Rogan, 1991). Few textbooks available now—William Schubert's *Curriculum: Perspective, Paradigm, and Possibility* is a relative exception—seek to portray the contemporary field with any degree of comprehensiveness. Comprehensiveness means "having the attribute of comprising or including much of large content or scope;" it also is characterized by "mental comprehension; that which grasps or understands" (OED, 1979, p. 743). While several curriculum textbooks (Saylor, Alexander, & Lewis, 1980) mention scholarly developments since 1970, these developments receive insufficient attention. Even "state of the field" issues of scholarly journals, i.e. issues which attempt to assess the progress of the field, remain partial (see, for instance, McCutcheon, 1982). How can we account for this irresponsible neglect of contemporary discourses? We believe the answer has to do in part with the paradigm shift of the 1970s in which the American field was reconceptualized from a field preoccupied with curriculum development to the contemporary field in which understanding curriculum is the central aspiration. Such a shift does not occur without pain and anger. Why?

When a field shifts from one major paradigm to another, many scholars are left with allegiances to concepts no longer pertinent. There is a temptation to ignore contemporary developments and to retreat into a nostalgia for the field no longer present. Daniel and Laurel Tanner's (1990) *History of the School Curriculum* is an example. This book is an excellent if truncated history of the field, as it fails to record the paradigm shift of the 1970s. But for many scholars who have come of age during or after the Reconceptualization [1969-1979; see chapter 4], it is not simple allegiance to the past which is to blame for ignoring the present (Pinar, 1990); it is ideological commitments and the political struggle for ascendency in a field still in formation. However, for those curriculum specialists whose intellectual coming of age occurred during the earlier paradigm of curriculum development, it is not ideological commitment that clouds their vision. For these often older scholars, the Reconceptualization was experienced as a personal rebuke.

Generational conflict is not, we noted, the only reason for the failure to treat the field of curriculum comprehensively. Ideological and intellectual commitments sometimes lure scholars away from impartiality and comprehensiveness to narrowness and dogmatism. Political scholars have been criticized for ideological insularity; phenomenological and poststructuralist scholars sometimes view their traditions as complete in themselves (Pinar & Bowers, 1992). Feminist scholars sometimes regard gender as traditional Marxists viewed the means of production, the fundamentally constituent element of *all* understanding. While we cannot hope to persuade ideologues to treat all major contemporary discourses with fairness, we can make the effort to do so.

In this textbook we work to present impartially each of these sectors of scholarship. We aspire to point to a "common ground," maybe "a common faith" (Dewey, 1934a), in which different traditions and understandings can contribute to a comprehensive and inclusive understanding of the present stage of the American curriculum field. Such a project cannot, we believe, be likened to the authoritarian tendencies of so-called "master narratives" which pretend to establish final truth [see chapter 9]. Rather, we are engaged in an effort to present a detailed portrait of the field in which dissenting and disparate voices and traditions, grounded in history, can contribute to a more profound understanding of the contemporary curriculum field. Such an understanding would contribute to an improvement of the nation's schools if current power arrangements would permit curriculum theorists sufficient influence. The schools, to a considerable extent, are now in the hands of politicians, textbook publishers, and subject matter specialists in the university. Additionally, schools are, of course, subject to the great social and cultural problems of the day. Our influence as curriculum specialists, while potentially important, is in reality modest, as we shall see in greater detail later in this chapter. Indeed, it is reasonable to conclude that education professors are no more responsible for the present condition of the nation's schools than are business school professors for the state of the American corporation or professors of political science for the state of American politics.

Probably education professors did have more influence on the workings of the school in the past than they do today, as Philip Jackson's (1992a) seminal essay on this subject implies. Seventy years ago—during the time of Bobbitt, Kilpatrick, and Dewey—education professors did appear to exercise more influence on large-scale curriculum development projects than it is possible to imagine today. In this regard, Daniel and Laurel Tanner (1990) observe, in understated terms, what they characterize as "the teacher's shrinking space" (p. 305). "The role of teacher as curriculum maker," they note, "has not been reflected in pubic policy making in recent history" (p. 305). Quite so.

Of course, conflicting conceptions of the curriculum (Eisner & Vallance, 1974) have meant that various specialists worked in different directions, sometimes at cross purposes, thus undermining each others' efforts. However, politicians, parents, and socio-economic forces (such as the mass immigration of 1890-1930; the Great Depression) have probably always been more powerful in influencing the character of schools than have the curriculum proposals advanced by professors of education. John Dewey, the most important American philosopher of education, is said to have exerted little influence on educational practice in his day, despite public controversies accompanying the progressive education movement. Particularly since the 1970s, the influence of curriculum generalists has been limited. In fact, this limitation can be cited as one catalyst for the Reconceptualization of the American curriculum field in the 1970s.

The traditional field: Curriculum development. Perhaps because curriculum specialists did have greater access to the schools in the past, or at least wrote as if they did, their concerns were more focused on curriculum development in and for the schools. Their writing tended to be addressed to elementary and secondary teachers and administrators, as some writing still is. Relatively speaking, there was little sense of developing a field devoted to accumulation of knowledge and to the enhancement of understanding, a field at once theoretical and historical. Mauritz Johnson (1967) expressed succinctly this core idea of the traditional field: "The majority of educationists, education practitioners and scholars active in curriculum reforms are oriented toward improvement, rather than understanding, action and results rather than inquiry" (p. 267). This focus upon the school curriculum and its incremental improvement delimited the horizon of the traditional field. Consequently, we observe that *the paradigm of the traditional field was curriculum development.* [Other scholars—such as Laurel Tanner (1982)—employ the term "paradigm" in reference to the Tyler Rationale specifically; others would seem to regard this period as pre-paradigmatic (Rogan & Luckowski, 1990). The use of the term paradigm seems to us not entirely unreasonable to refer to the Reconceptualization.]

A review of the synoptic texts published during this early period [roughly 1920-1980] reveals their preoccupation with curriculum development: from the 1920s W. W. Charters' *Curriculum Construction* (1923) is illustrative; from the 1930s H. L. Caswell and D. S. Campbell's *Curriculum Development* (1935); from the 1940s Ralph W. Tyler's *Basic Principles of Curriculum and Instruction* (1949); from the 1950s Smith, Stanley, and Shores' *Fundamentals of Curriculum Development* (1957); from the 1960s Hilda Taba's *Curriculum Development: Theory and Practice* (1962); from the 1970s Daniel and Laurel Tanner's *Curriculum Development: Theory Into Practice* (1975). Even some number of scholars whose careers were lived out within this paradigm came to see it as limited, especially when associated with the "measured curriculum" (Klein, 1986), i.e. that curriculum which is then tested, resulting in a numeral grade which presumably measures learning. For such scholars, theory and practice became uncomfortably distant from one another. One major scholar termed her situation, in this regard, as "one foot in the camp of curriculum visionaries. . . . The other foot is in the real world where teachers and principals deal with day-to-day problems" (Berman, 1985, p. 66). These scholars can be said to have straddled the "generational divide" in the field (Klohr, 1992).

The reconceptualized field: Understanding curriculum. The major synoptic text of the 1980s is William H. Schubert's *Curriculum* (1986a). Note that "development" has been dropped from the title. Nor does "development" appear in the subtitle: *Perspective, Paradigm, and Possibility.* In the Schubert textbook, the exclusive attention to curriculum development has given way to representations of basic categories of curriculum development, i.e. selection of purposes, content or learning experiences, organization, and evaluation. These categories are still consistent with the Tyler Rationale (1949), the quintessential articulation of the curriculum development paradigm. True, in Schubert's textbook there are chapters devoted to inquiry and—for the first time in a synoptic text—to that scholarship in the 1970s which had functioned to reconceptualize the field away from curriculum development. However, the direction of the field's movement is not completely clear in Schubert's pluralistic scheme. The Schubert textbook reflects that the field was moving toward reconceiving its function from curriculum development—a function no longer politically or institutionally available to it—to understanding curriculum. In science and mathematics education, curriculum development remains. For curriculum generalists, however, those interested in the relations *among* the school subjects, and their relationships to non-institutionalized elements such as race and gender, the sphere of curriculum development is much reduced (Jackson, 1992a; Tanner & Tanner, 1990).

Indicative of this change is the perception of the phrase "curriculum development" itself. O. L. Davis (1986) has observed: "As years passed, everyday usage in education slowly corrupted 'curriculum development' into a shortened term, 'curriculum.' This term was invested with renewed meanings, which served to alter that to which it referred in practice while elevating its symbolic potency" (p. 86). *Understanding Curriculum: An Introduction to the Study of Historical and Contemporary Curriculum Discourses* reflects the shift in the definition from curriculum as exclusively school materials to curriculum as symbolic representation. Curriculum understood as a symbolic representation refers to those institutional and discursive practices, structures, images, and experiences that can be identified and analyzed in various ways, i.e. politically, racially, autobiographically, phenomenologically, theologically, internationally, and in terms of gender and deconstruction. We can say that the effort to understand curriculum as symbolic representation defines, to a considerable extent, the contemporary field.

We do include attention to curriculum development, not only in historical terms (as a relic of a past paradigm), but as a current institutionalized (or bureaucratic) function. However, this phase of curriculum no longer merits the title of a synoptic textbook. In the 1990s, it is appropriate to restrict curriculum development to only one, albeit lengthy, chapter in what we hope will signal a new generation of synoptic curriculum textbooks. Curriculum development and its constituent phases, such as curriculum policy, planning, supervision, and evaluation, will be elaborated in the chapter which depicts curriculum as institutionalized text [chapter 13]. Before we describe further the organization of this book, let us review two major studies which illustrate in detail these issues of synoptic textbooks and the field they try to summarize. The first study examines carefully a series of synoptic curriculum textbooks, the series in which this present book appears.

III
Textbooks:
"An Important Indicator"

The ethnocentricity of most of the texts is not confined to national, but also cultural, boundaries.

(John M. Rogan & Jean Luckowski, 1990, p. 26)

In an important study of synoptic curriculum textbooks, John M. Rogan and Jean Luckowski (1990) observe that textbooks constitute "an important indicator" (p. 17) of the field they reflect. The Rogan-Luckowski study and its sequel (Rogan, 1991) performed the significant service of focusing our attention on the discursive strategies employed in the major synoptic texts, and what those strategies indicate about the field they claim to represent. What sort of field did they find in their study of textbooks? "We suspect that the field is fragmented, and little in the way of consensus about what this required course should cover has been reached" (1990, p. 17). This is not a surprising finding, is it. Indeed, if a field had undergone a paradigm shift within the last twenty years, what would you, a beginning student, expect to find? Consensus? No. Fragmentation is precisely what one would expect.

If you could travel back in time to a period of paradigm stability, say in the 1940s and 1950s, you would expect to find a different kind of field reflected in textbooks. In fact, in those textbooks focused on the first paradigm of "curriculum development," of which the Tyler Rationale was the prototypical expression, there *were* a number of common themes. This is true even in textbooks that appeared after the Reconceptualization in the 1970s but did not acknowledge it. There was a certain consensus. How might we describe it? Rogan and Luckowski (1990) discovered that many textbooks conveyed the idea that the Tyler Rationale (1949) provides the paradigmatic questions of the curriculum field. The elements of the Rationale, i.e. objectives, learning experiences, organization, and evaluation, each enjoy a full chapter, even in relatively recent books by Schubert (1986a) and by McNeil (1985). Other texts, such as Tanner and Tanner (1980) and Miller and Seller (1985), devote a chapter, or at least sections of a chapter, to the development of the Tyler Rationale. Saylor (Saylor, et al., 1981) includes twelve observations on the power and impact of the Tyler Rationale, even citing Molnar and Zahorik's (1977) conclusion that the Tyler Rationale expressed fundamental assumptions regarding American culture. Additionally, Rogan and Luckowski (1990) observe that so-called alternative models, including those proposed by Miller and Seller [i.e.,Taba, 1962; Weinstein-Fantini, 1970], "are in fact variations on the ways and order in which Tyler's paradigmatic questions may be asked" (p.19).

In order to review at a glance the major thematics of the introductory curriculum textbooks Rogan and Luckowski studied, we reproduce their table on page 18 (1990, p. 19).

Reconceptualization ignored. Notice that the Reconceptualization of the curriculum field from curriculum development to understanding curriculum is ignored or, at best, underemphasized in these traditional curriculum textbooks. The only hint of the change in the field appears in the Eisner and Schubert books. In this regard, Rogan and Luckowski (1990) observe that, with the possible exception of Eisner (1985a), Schubert's *Curriculum: Perspective, Paradigm, Possibility* (1986a) is alone in its acknowledgement of "practical inquiry and critical praxis to the status of a paradigm" (p. 20). [Critical

Table 1. Selected curriculum texts and their major sections or units

Curriculum text	Major sections
R. Doll (1989)	Decision-making in curriculum improvement Processes in curriculum improvement
Eisner (1985)	Historical and contemporary social forces Definitions and orientations Evaluation and educational criticism
McNeil (1985)	Concepts of curriculum Curriculum development Managing curriculum Issues and trends Research, theory and curriculum
Miller and Sellers (1985)	Perspectives Practices
Saylor et al. (1981)	Perspectives and processes Purposes, designs, models Evaluation Planning and the future
Schubert (1986)	Perspective Paradigm Possibility
Tanner & Tanner (1980)	The search for rationale The new reformation—science and sentiment Crosscurrents in curriculum reform and reconstruction Improving the curriculum
Wiles & Bondi (1984)	Perspectives Procedures Practices Prospectives
Zais (1976)	Field of study Foundations Anatomy of a curriculum Design and engineering

inquiry is sometimes substituted for the effort to understand curriculum as political text, sometimes for the Reconceptualization generally. So-called "practical inquiry" is often associated with the Reconceptualization, but it is an idea that has been around for a very long time; see, for instance, Morrison, 1934; Taba, 1957, and other essays in the 1957 ASCD Yearbook.]

Additionally, Rogan and Luckowski (1990) note that in a number of other texts, the scholars and ideas associated with the Reconceptualization of the field during the 1970s are either completely ignored (cf. Wiles & Bondi, 1984; R. Doll, 1989) or are briefly acknowledged, and then only insofar as they contribute "to an ongoing debate on curriculum theory" (McNeil,1985; Saylor, et al., 1981; Rogan & Luckowski, 1990, p. 20). Galen Saylor, et al. (1981), for example, characterized the so-called reconceptualists as a "small but able group . . . [who] are to be encouraged in their work" (p. 267; quoted in Rogan & Luckowski, 1990, p. 20). Rogan and Luckowski note that "the reference is buried deeply within the text in a chapter devoted to implementation" (p. 20). They note that Daniel and Laurel Tanner attack the research program of the Reconceptualization [see chapter 4]. Tanner and Tanner make a strong case for a single paradigm, Rogan and Luckowski conclude. We would add that this paradigm is curriculum development.

Eisner critical of the Tyler Rationale. Rogan and Luckowski (1990) note that the Eisner (1985a) textbook did not accept the Tyler Rationale as a legitimate paradigm. "Like the critical theorists," Rogan and Luckowski continue, "he [Eisner] has more faith in personal and aesthetic concepts as a way to reformulate the curriculum." [We would add that critical theorists, until very recently, have shown very little faith in "personal and aesthetic" constructs; see chapter 5.] The Zais text (1976) is an overview of three curriculum models: 1) Macdonald's interactive model, 2) Johnson's systems model, and 3) Zais' own eclectic model. [You will be introduced to Macdonald's influential work in chapters 3 and 4; to Johnson's model in chapter 3; see also chapter 13 and this chapter.] Zais' model is patterned after the Tyler Rationale, while Macdonald's model represents one beginning, one source, "of a reconceptualist, critical paradigm" (1990, p. 20). "Zais' book," Rogan and Luckowski add, "betrays its datedness in this regard, published as it was at a time when interest in reconceptualizing the curriculum field was beginning to intensify" (1990, p. 20). It is clear, they conclude, that there is no one definitive way of developing curriculum or of engaging in curriculum inquiry. They assert that they would like to see texts explore in some depth and with some measure of understanding, the alternative positions that exist, the basis for their existence, and what curricular form they might take in practice. While several of the textbooks attempted this, most did not (Rogan & Luckowski, 1990). The failure of textbook writers to portray the field accurately, i.e. including its Reconceptualization, required the writing of *Understanding Curriculum.*

Rogan and Luckowski (1990) discuss their uneasiness regarding the Tyler Rationale as constituting a paradigm. Why would it not represent a paradigm? They answer that the Tyler Rationale "lacks any kind of a theoretical commitment illuminating the nature of curriculum" (1990, p. 21). Such a theoretical commitment, we would note, *is* absent in the Tyler Rationale, but predictably so. The paradigm of curriculum development is about procedure; it is fundamentally bureaucratic or institutional in conception and execution. The project to illuminate, to understand, represents the key to understanding curriculum studies since the 1970s. And so for Rogan and Luckowski, the Tyler Rationale, and by implication the fifty-year emphasis upon curriculum development, represent a "pre-paradigmatic stage" of the field:

> . . . it seems that the essential feature of the paradigm is the theoretical understanding of the nature of the phenomenon. Since the Tyler Rationale does not seek to develop a theoretical explanation of curriculum, we find it hard to view it as a paradigm. It seems to us that the Rationale has somehow been elevated far beyond its original intent. On the other hand, it is quite possible that some of the "alternative paradigms" articulated by Schubert do come closer to Kuhn's concepts of paradigm than the Tyler Rationale, since they do seek to illuminate the nature of curriculum. Nevertheless, it is our feeling that it might be closer to the mark to say that as a field, curriculum is without a paradigm rather than subject to competing paradigms. (Rogan & Luckowski, 1990, p. 22)

In a strict Kuhnian sense (in which "paradigm" refers to scientific fields exclusively), Rogan and Luckowski may well be right [see Brown, 1988]. The Tyler Rationale and the curriculum development concept of the field do not represent "paradigms" in the restricted sense of conveying a theoretical understanding of curriculum. However, in a non-specialized, non-Kuhnian, simple dictionary sense of the word paradigm as an "outstanding instance or example of a pattern," Tyler's work certainly qualifies. Our point is simply that the Tyler Rationale is by far the best-known expression of the traditional field's interest in development, and therefore qualifies as the quintessential instance of the traditional field's interest in procedure, in social engineering, that is, in curriculum as institutional text. Philip Jackson (1992a) appears to agree, in that he likens the Tyler book to a curriculum bible [see next section].

The notion of "orientation." During that period when the paradigm (or pre-paradigm) of curriculum development organized the field and the school curriculum represented the "pay off" of curriculum theory, theoretical positions were characterized as "orientations" to curriculum practice. However, in the reconceptualized, contemporary field, curriculum development occupies a smaller space. [Smaller but still significant; note the length of chapter 13, over half of which is devoted to scholarship on curriculum development.] Further, the function of curriculum theory is now to understand, not primarily to rationalize institutional maintenance or to guide incremental improvement, as the work of curriculum developers tended to do. Therefore, in the reconceptualized field "orientation" plays no role as an organizing concept for *Understanding Curriculum*. Rogan and Luckowski graphically characterize traditional textbooks' "orientations." We reproduce that chart (1990, p. 23) here.

Table 2. Selected curriculum texts and categorization of orientation

Curriculum text	Orientations to curriculum
R. Doll (1989)	Traditionalist Progressivist
Eisner (1985)	Cognitive processes Academic rationalism Personal relevance Social adaptation and social reconstruction Curriculum as technology
McNeil (1985)	Humanistic Social reconstruction Technological Academic subject
Miller & Seller (1985)	Transmission Transaction Transformational
Saylor, et al. (1981)	Subject matter/disciplines Specific competencies/technology Human traits/processes Social functions/activities Individual needs and interests/activities
Schubert (1986)	Traditionalist Social behaviorist Experientialist
Tanner & Tanner (1980)	Cumulative tradition of organized knowledge Modes of thought Race experience Experience Instructional plan Technological system of production
Wiles & Bondi (1984)	Knowledge product Experience Instructional plan
Zais (1976)	Program of studies Course content Planned early experiences

Table 2. (continued)

Curriculum text	Orientations to curriculum
Zais (1976)	Experiences
	Structured learning outcomes
	Plan of action

Traditional textbooks' treatment of history. In addition to the notion of orientation, the prominence of curriculum history is another feature of textbooks which Rogan and Luckowski examine. As you will discover, in the contemporary field, history is a major discourse or sector of scholarship. In the textbooks Rogan and Luckowski studied, the treatment of curricular history varied considerably. The most comprehensive treatment was found in Schubert's book. If Schubert's treatment of curriculum history is the broadest, the Tanners' treatment provides the most historical depth. [The Tanners' 1990 study of curriculum is organized historically. We found that book most helpful in writing this synoptic text; we recommend it to you.] The second unit of the Tanner and Tanner book, consisting of five chapters, is devoted to curriculum history. In the Miller/Seller and Eisner textbooks, the interest in curriculum history seems limited to its significance for the present. Four textbooks receive failing grades for their treatment of curriculum history: "Saylor's inclusion of historical background obscures our picture of it. . . . Neither McNeil, [R.] Doll nor Wiles and Bondi make serious attempts to introduce the history of curriculum" (Rogan & Luckowski, 1990, p. 26). In contrast to these traditional textbooks, we have devoted three chapters to curriculum history; additionally, several chapters (such as 5, 7, and 10) on contemporary curriculum discourses are organized historically.

International issues. While our focus is the American curriculum field, that field does not exist in isolation. National borders appear to be of decreasing importance in economic, political, environmental, and yes, curricular spheres. No synoptic textbook can afford to ignore international issues altogether. With the increasing internationalization of curriculum studies in mind, let us ask, with Rogan and Luckowski: How extensive are traditional textbooks' treatment of international themes and issues? Rogan and Luckowski (1990) found that only the Schubert textbook acknowledges the need to look beyond the borders of the United States. "The ethnocentricity of most of the texts," they lament, "is not confined to national, but also cultural, boundaries" (p. 26). Traditional textbooks have little to say about Africa or Asia, or the significance of global themes and international issues in general. One would expect a curriculum textbook "to provide an adequate, global, multicultural, historical framework that gives a balanced picture of both practice and ideology" (1990, p. 27).

One need not leave the borders of the United States to realize the centrality of multicultural concerns to American education generally, and to the

American curriculum field specifically. Debates over "the canon" have occupied center stage in public debates, with some contemporary conservatives fearing multiculturalism as their elders, in the 1950s, might have feared "creeping communism." Issues of racial inequality cannot be ignored by any student of curriculum. To study curriculum today requires understanding curriculum as racial text. That previous textbooks omitted this vital and highly significant sector of scholarship represents nothing less than an academic instance of racism (Castenell & Pinar, 1993).

Rogan and Luckowski's study of curriculum textbooks appeared at a crucial time, when the realization that the paradigm (or pre-paradigm) of curriculum development had given way to a paradigm of understanding, in which concerns of curriculum development are not only fewer and less important but are treated differently, and international and multicultural issues are moving toward center stage. Consequently, in order to reflect these developments, we include entire chapters outlining the efforts to understand curriculum as international and racial text [chapters 14 & 6, respectively].

Curriculum policy is another important area of contemporary scholarship. For instance, the *Handbook of Research on Curriculum* (Jackson, 1992c) included a major chapter on the subject (Elmore & Sykes, 1992). Regarding curriculum policy, Rogan and Luckowski (1990) observe that curriculum and policy questions and decisions intersect. Only five of the textbooks they examined devoted one or more chapters to an exposition of curriculum policy-making. McNeil's book contains the most comprehensive discussion of curriculum policy, while Wiles and Bondi's and R. Doll's books include more limited discussions of policy. Overall, the R. Doll book receives the poorest marks: "the text by Doll must be found to be lacking. Three major areas, history, orientations and philosophy, are all condensed into the first chapter. History is dealt with in a single six-page table!" (1990, p. 32). The Wiles and Bondi book perhaps ought not even be included in the category of synoptic text; "[it] is largely a handbook for managers in leadership roles, rather than a comprehensive text on curriculum in the mold of Schubert and Tanner & Tanner" (1990, p. 22).

An additional problem of the Wiles/Bondi text is that: "the book does not involve the reader" (p. 34). Of the Miller and Seller book, they conclude that "if its aim is to begin to engage its readers in actively contemplating such action [conducting curriculum practices from an integrated perspective], or even viewing action from different perspectives, it falls short of the mark" (p. 33). Regarding John McNeil's book, Rogan and Luckowski (1990) write: "McNeil's identified purpose is similar in many respects to Miller and Seller. . . . The orientation of the book is basically transmissional. . . . Nothing in the body of the text seeks to initiate or develop the deliberation which is the stated goal of the author" (pp. 33-34). The Schubert and Eisner books appear to receive the highest marks. Rogan and Luckowski write: "Along with Schubert, Eisner comes closest actually to engaging interested educators in active, reflective dialogue concerning curriculum" (1990, p. 35).

A relatively recent collection of essays which introduces students to the contemporary field (and which does not appear in the Rogan and Luckowski study) makes some effort to include reconceptualized scholarship, but appears to weigh too heavily traditional categories of planning, design, implementation, and evaluation. The categories of essays listed in the Gress (1988) collection are: a) definition and perspective, b) frameworks, c) curriculum planning and design, d) hidden curriculum, e) implementation, evaluation, and change, f) theory and research. Like the Schubert book, the Gress collection represents another transitional textbook, one foot in the traditional field, one foot in the reconceptualized, contemporary field.

The Rogan and Luckowski study represents a major accomplishment. It reminds us that introductory synoptic textbooks have indeed functioned as strong indicators of the curriculum field they represent, even when they misrepresent the field, as traditional textbooks now do. Thanks to the Rogan/Luckowski study, we now have a clear picture of the organization of synoptic texts written during the curriculum development paradigm (or, as they prefer, pre-paradigm or phase). The Schubert book emerges as the transitional text, written after the Reconceptualization, but with obvious ties to the traditional [pre-Reconceptualization] paradigm. As the only transitional text, and one which covers broadly curriculum history, it has secured for itself an important place in the history of curriculum synoptic textbooks. One purpose of *Understanding Curriculum* is to move beyond the transitional character of the Schubert book. Our aim is to reflect as comprehensively as possible the contemporary field, linking the field in place in the 1990s with the traditional field that has almost vanished.

So perhaps you, the student, can now appreciate why we have worked to present you with a clear picture of the genre in which this textbook appears. For curriculum specialists, it is an important genre because synoptic textbooks in this field do more than summarize their field, they indicate its nature, its function, and point to its future. Consequently, it is the professional responsibility of textbook writers to report all the major scholarship in their field, even if they disapprove of it. The suppression of knowledge cannot be tolerated in scholarly fields, especially in one which works to understand scholarly fields, and their relationships to history, society, and the individual person. Studying the genre of textbooks gives us one perspective on these matters. An examination of the work curriculum specialists do will provide another.

In the next section, then, in order to view from another perspective the link between the traditional and contemporary fields, we will move from a discussion of synoptic textbooks to the character of the curriculum field itself. We focus particularly on its function in education and society more generally, including what the function of the field means for the professional activities of those who work in the field. For these considerations we turn to a major study published in 1992, written by Philip W. Jackson of the University of Chicago.

IV
Conceptions of Curriculum and Curriculum Specialists:
Philip W. Jackson

> There is another possibility, of course, at least hypothetically, and that is to respond to current conditions by seeking to rejuvenate the field from within, which is what the reconceptualists have obviously sought to do and may be what those who are moving closer to practitioners are seeking to do as well. Can that be accomplished? Will either group succeed in recapturing the spirit of optimism and the sense of mission that clearly marked the first two or three decades of the emergence of curriculum as field of study?
>
> (Philip W. Jackson, 1992a, p. 37)

In a significant and clarifying essay, Philip Jackson (1992a) reviews concepts of curriculum and of the work of curriculum specialists which help us situate and introduce historically the contemporary project to understand curriculum. Because the essay helps to set the stage for understanding curriculum, we will report it in some detail. [Jackson's important essay and the research review he edits have been the subject of a special issue of an important scholarly journal; see Short, 1992.] By following Jackson's history of the field, which he organizes by focusing on its major contributors, the contemporary scene will come into sharper focus. But it is not just the present we see more clearly as a result of Jackson's scholarship, it is the relation between present and past that too becomes discernible.

To begin, Jackson reports that "both the state of affairs" and "recurrent mood" in the field today is "confusing" (p. 3), although we might point out that the clarity of Jackson's essay undermines that assertion. True enough, the field *is* complicated, much more complicated than it has ever been. It is not, we think, confusing. If we understand the field to be in a certain stage of development, i.e. relatively soon after its first paradigm shift in the 1970s, and if we appreciate the disciplinary sources for and functions of the scholarship in the curriculum field that has been conducted since the 1970s, linked with pre-1970s scholarship, then the picture that emerges of the field is quite clear. That is not to deny the complexity of the contemporary field. Clarity and complexity are not mutually exclusive, of course. We share Jackson's view: "Let our writing be as difficult as it has to be to deliver its message in full" (1990, p. 6). That point acknowledged, let us return to our story.

Definitional shifts. In his 1992 study, Jackson focuses on definitions of curriculum and definitional shifts during the history of the field. He begins by recalling that Harold Rugg, one of the most prominent members of the founding generation of the field [see chapter 3], called curriculum "an ugly, awkward, academic word" (quoted in Jackson, 1992a, p. 4). Aesthetic issues notwithstanding, a proliferation of definitions accompanied the rapid expansion of the field. In Latin, curriculum means "race-course" or "career." Cicero extended this meaning to "the course my mind runs on." Jackson

(1992a) lists characteristic definitions which span nearly a half a century. Curriculum has been defined as:

1. A course; a regular course of study or training, as at a school or university (OED).
2. A course, especially, a specified fixed course of study, as in a school or college, as one leading to a degree. The whole body of courses offered in an educational institution, or by a department thereof (Webster's New International Dictionary, 2nd edition).
3. Curriculum is all of the experiences children have under the guidance of teachers (Caswell & Campbell, 1935).
4. Curriculum encompasses all learning opportunities provided by the school (Saylor & Alexander, 1974).
5. Curriculum [is] a plan or program for all experiences which the learner encounters under the direction of the school. (Oliva, 1982) (Jackson, 1992a, pp. 4-5) [For another definitional review, see Portelli, 1987.]

Mature scholars and beginning students alike have bemoaned the plethora of definitions. We do not see this as a terrible problem. A complex field will use central terms in complex, sometimes even contradictory, ways. The multiplication of definitions is not an urgent problem to be solved. It is, rather, a state of affairs to be acknowledged. In a field comprised of various and autonomous discourses, it is inevitable.

Experience. From a comparison of dictionary definitions with those formulated by scholars who came to develop and study curriculum, it is obvious that the dictionary definitions were too narrow, too simple. Certainly they are accurate; they are, however, incomplete. The definition of curriculum has shifted throughout the history of the field, beginning with John Dewey and Franklin Bobbitt. Jackson (1992a) observes that Dewey accepted the customary definition, implying that curriculum is knowledge which, organized ordinarily along subject matter lines, ultimately must be mastered by students. However, Dewey did see a problem with the customary definition. It stipulated a difference between content and experience. In *The Child and the Curriculum*, Dewey (1902) wrote that "[the problem is] just to get rid of the prejudicial notion that there is some gap in kind (as distinct from degree) between the child's experience and the various forms of subject-matter that make up the course of study" (1902, p. 11; quoted in Jackson, 1992a, p. 6). Significantly, Dewey asserted that "the child and the curriculum are simply two limits which define a single process" (1902, p. 11; quoted in Jackson, 1992a, p. 6). Thus Dewey brings the concept of experience to the definition of curriculum, a concept operative in the field today. For some curricularists, however, "experience" and "curriculum" have sometimes been conflated, a practice that for some scholars has left curriculum defined, perhaps, too vaguely (Kliebard,1970,1975a).

Bobbitt's definition. Relying on Caswell (1934), Jackson (1992a) cites Franklin Bobbitt's *The Curriculum* (1918) as "the first text in what was soon to become a burgeoning field of professional activity" (p. 7). By the publication of this book, the concept of curriculum as educative experience was assumed. Bobbitt defined curriculum in two ways: "(1) it is the entire range of experience, both undirected and directed, concerned in unfolding the abilities of the individual; or (2) it is the series of consciously directed training experiences that the schools use for completing and perfecting the unfoldment. Our profession uses the term usually in the latter sense" (1918, p. 43; quoted in Jackson, 1992a, p. 7). Bobbitt expands the definition to include "out-of-school" experiences. This definition introduces a distinction between "directed" and "undirected" experience, the latter referring to "out-of-school" experience.

The curriculum of "out-of-school" experience, although mainly a figure of speech, has, as Jackson notes, been addressed by curricularists such as William Schubert (1986a) and Lawrence Cremin (1961, 1976). These scholars argue that various institutions, ranging from the church and temple to the media and business, from day-care centers to the family itself, have curricula and that the school curriculum often challenges these other curricula. To illustrate this point, think of fundamentalist Christian parents' reservations regarding the "secular humanism" of the public school curriculum, a topic we will explore in chapter 12.

Hidden, unstudied, null curriculum. Jackson notes that within twenty years after the publication of Bobbitt's *The Curriculum*, "definitions of the curriculum routinely included all of the experiences planned and unplanned, that occur under the auspices of the school" (p. 8). Later, definitions would expand further to include "unwanted outcomes of schooling" (p. 8), such as the hidden curriculum (Jackson, 1968; Apple, 1975a; McLaren, 1994), the unstudied curriculum (Overly, 1970), and the unwritten curriculum (Dreeben, 1976). Additionally, there have been definitions of the curriculum which emphasize what is not offered, i.e. the so-called "null" curriculum (Eisner, 1979; Flinders, Noddings, & Thornston, 1986) as well as the "out-of-school" curriculum (Schubert, 1981c). The null or unstudied curriculum consists of those topics not included in the official curriculum (Apple, 1993). The hidden curriculum is the ideological and subliminal message presented within the overt curriculum, as well as a by-product of the null curriculum. Is it an understatement to observe that curriculum is a variegated concept?

Making sense of definitional shifts. What sense can we make of these definitional diversities and shifts? One possibility, Jackson (1992a) answers, is that they add up to "conceptual progress" (Tanner & Tanner, 1980). Perhaps they in fact reflect a more sophisticated view of the curriculum (Zumwalt, 1988). Several scholars have judged controversies over definitions as "not a very productive enterprise" (Zais, 1976, p. 93; quoted in Jackson, 1992a, p. 10). Illustrative is John Goodlad's "impatience" (Jackson, 1992a, p. 10) with the proliferation of definitions. Goodlad (1979) complained:

Who is to say that one of these courses deserves the word "curriculum" attached to it and the others do not? That one is right and others are wrong? Yet this is the box we get ourselves into in attempting some single, proper definition of curriculum, a questionable activity in which curriculum specialists have far too long engaged. We need definitions, of course, to carry on productive discourse, but attempts to arrive at a single one have inhibited discourse. If someone wishes to define "curriculum" as a course of study, this is legitimate— and certainly not bizarre. Let us begin there and see where it takes us. If someone wishes to begin with curriculum as "the experiences of students," let us see where this carries us. But let us not begin by throwing out each definition and seeking only to substitute another that merely reflects a different perspective. We can readily see what a short distance this has taken us. (pp. 44-45)

Jackson expresses two reservations regarding Goodlad's view. First, he wonders how sound is the advice that one begins with definitions and moves on from there. Secondly, he suggests that instead of following a definition to see where it leads that "we ask not only where it *goes* but also where it *comes from* and *why*" (Jackson, 1992a, p. 11). [We do not see the Goodlad and Jackson positions as mutually exclusive. Definitions can be both beginning and end points, dependent upon the discourse and its functions.]

Definitions lodged in "rhetorical structures." Jackson concludes this consideration of definitions and definitional shifts by suggesting that students of curriculum think of definitions as lodged in "rhetorical structures" (p. 12) which attempt to persuade us to conceive of curriculum in particular ways. He points out:

We may disagree with that way of looking, but we nonetheless cannot avoid making use of the definition even while expressing our disagreement. Is it valuable, for instance, to think of there being something called a hidden curriculum? It may or may not turn out to be so, but even those who oppose the use of the term and who argue against it are momentarily caught in its ideational grasp. And so it is with all of the other ways of defining the word "curriculum." (Jackson, 1992a, p. 12)

This is a wise observation. While we may share Goodlad's impatience with the field's occasional obsession with a "correct" definition, we endorse Jackson's placement of definitional issues in larger concerns of meaning and interpretation. As we will see, the contemporary field can be grasped clearly if we appreciate the sources and rhetorical reasons why curriculum is defined within each sector of scholarship. These sources are at times disciplinary (i.e. curriculum as aesthetic text), at times interdisciplinary (i.e., curriculum as racial text). Definitions become intelligible as we grasp the rhetorical structure and direction of each sector. We will describe these later in this chapter, but now let us continue with our examination of Jackson's carefully reasoned argument.

Mappings of the Field

To illustrate more contemporary mappings, Jackson (1992a) turns to three curriculum texts: a synoptic text by John McNeil (1975) (which, as you may recall, Rogan and Luckowski included in their study), a collection of essays edited by Elliot Eisner and Elizabeth Vallance (1974), and a historical study by Herbert Kliebard (1986). McNeil (1975) lists four conceptions of curriculum: the humanistic, the social reconstructionist, the technological, and the academic. The last corresponds to what Bobbitt termed the "advocates of culture." The humanistic re-expressed much of the child-centered or individual-focused wing of Progressivism, as the social reconstructionist aimed to reform society via school reform. Eisner and Vallance (1974) listed five orientations, adding a "cognitive process approach" to McNeil's four, which they defined: "the cognitive process approach, curriculum as technology, curriculum for self-actualization [McNeil's humanistic] and consummatory experiences, curriculum for social reconstruction, and academic rationalism" (p. 3). Jackson quotes the definitions Eisner and Vallance provided for each of these terms:

> The *cognitive process orientation* to curriculum seeks to develop a repertoire of cognitive skills that are applicable to a wide range of intellectual problems. In this view subject matter, as typically defined, is considered instrumental to the development of intellectual abilities that can be used in areas other than those in which the processes were originally refined. . . . These abilities, it is argued, will endure long after the particular content or knowledge is forgotten or rendered obsolete by new knowledge. (1974, p. 19)

> The *technological orientation* to curriculum is one that is preoccupied with the development of means to achieve prespecified ends. Those working from this orientation tend to view schooling as a complex system that can be analyzed into its constituent components. The problem for the educator or educational technologist is to bring the system under control so that the goals it seeks to attain can be achieved. (1974, p. 49)

> In the [*self-actualization*] orientation to curriculum thought . . . schooling is to become a means of personal fulfillment, to provide a context in which individuals discover and develop their unique identities. Curriculum, in this view, is a pervasive and enriching experience with implications for many dimensions of personal development. (1974, p. 105)

> *Social reconstructionists* see schooling as an agency of social change, and they demand that education be relevant both to the student's interests and to society's needs. Curriculum is conceived to be an active force having direct impact on the whole fabric of its human and social context. (1974, p. 135)

> The major goal of *academic rationalists* as far as curriculum is concerned is to enable students to use and appreciate the ideas and works that constitute the various intellectual and artistic disciplines. Academic rationalists argue that ideas within the various disciplines have a distinctive structure and a distinctive set of contributions to make to the education of man (sic). Indeed, acquisition of these structures is largely what education is about. (1974, p. 161; all Eisner & Vallance passages quoted in Jackson, 1992a, p. 15)

Twelve years later Elizabeth Vallance would review their organization of the field, especially in light of changing political priorities in the schools and from her own evolving curriculum commitments. In her view, the self-actualizing perspective had lost the most currency in the intervening decade, in effect disappearing from the public discourse (Vallance, 1986). In light of this development, she drops self-actualization from the model and adds two others. The first she terms a "personal success" model, associated with the pro-business climate and policies of the United States during the early Reagan years. In this "personal success" orientation, "curriculum is seen as a means to an immediate practical end. The astonishing increase in numbers of students majoring in business, computer science, and engineering, and the concomitant decline in enrollments in the humanities and social sciences, bespeaks [this] orientation" (1986, p. 27). Her sympathies are not here, however, but rather with what she terms a "curriculum for personal commitment" (p. 29), an orientation which:

> encompasses academic rationalism and the self-actualizing perspective. . . . [It is] the conception of education that we may hope the *student* carries with him or her when formal schooling is finished. . . . It is the conception which sees the purpose of schooling as creating a *personal commitment to learning*. . . . I mean instead an underlying passion for the hard work and joys of intellectual exploration, whether it be in the humanities, mechanical engineering, nutrition science, or even curriculum theory. (1986, pp. 27-28)

It is important to note that Vallance relies on what she perceives to be occurring in schools (and society) in her alteration of her and Eisner's 1974 map of the field. To look to the schools to map the curriculum field is a discursive move only possible within the traditional paradigm. In the reconceptualized field, while much scholarship is about the schools, it is clear that the field of curriculum is comprised of what is published by curriculum scholars, not by institutional practices in schools. Contemporary curriculum discourses often have the schools in mind (or at the least in the back of their minds), but it is not to the schools but rather to the discourses themselves one must look if one maps the curriculum field.

Kliebard's mapping. Next, Jackson (1992a) moves to compare these orientations with the historical perspective of Herbert Kliebard. Kliebard (1986) identifies four "interest groups" during the early years of the field, "each with a distinct agenda for action" and each determined to influence the character of "the modern American curriculum" (Kliebard, 1986, p. xi; quoted in Jackson, 1992a, p. 15). The first of these Kliebard characterizes as "*humanists*," whom he describes as "the guardians of an ancient tradition tied to the power of reason and the finest elements of the Western cultural heritage" (1986, p. 27; quoted in Jackson, 1992, pp. 15-16). Clearly, these are equivalent to what Eisner and Vallance term "academic rationalists." Kliebard's second interest group is "*the developmentalists*," whom he describes as those who believed that "the curriculum riddle could be solved with ever more scientific data, not only with respect to the different states of child and adolescent development, but on the nature of learning" (1986, p. 24; quoted in Jackson, 1992a, p. 16). This group overlaps but does not coincide with Eisner and Vallance's cognitive skills and self-actualization orientations. Kliebard's third group is the "*social efficiency* educator," who, like Bobbitt himself, sought to apply "the standardized techniques of industry to the business of schooling" (1986, p. 28; quoted in Jackson, 1992a, p. 16). This group overlaps with both McNeil's and Eisner and Vallance's technology conception or orientation, and draws upon the latter's cognitive process orientation, insofar as academic skills are believed to have transfer value to other settings, such as work settings. The fourth group is comprised of the *social meliorists*, those who regard the curriculum as in the service of social reconstruction or, more simply, social improvement. Kliebard concludes, as we will see in more detail in chapter 2, that in "the end, what became the American curriculum was not the result of any decisive victory by any of the contending parties, but a loose, largely unarticulated, and not very tidy compromise" (Kliebard, 1986, p. 29; quoted in Jackson, 1992a, p. 16). The Kliebard map is linked to the discourses on the curriculum which, true enough, are linked to the school curriculum, but not in terribly "tidy" or self-evident ways. Especially today, the school is a world apart from the sphere of curriculum theory.

Jackson's skepticism. Jackson is skeptical of the value of these mappings for the contemporary field. He asks: "Who calls oneself a new humanist or a self-actualizer or a social reconstructionist, or an academic rationalist? The answer is, no one does" (Jackson, 1992a, p. 17). An additional problem, he continues, is the implication in these mappings that everyone should adopt one or another of these general views. He asks: "But does everyone? *Need* everyone?" (p. 17). Jackson asks, should educators feel compelled to study these "conflicting conceptions," to borrow the Eisner-Vallance phrase, what would be the point? There is no point, he answers: "most teachers and administrators *inherit* a curriculum when they accept their jobs and there is relatively little they can do to modify or change it globally. . . . There is little need for them to concern themselves with broad curricular issues" (Jackson, 1992a, pp. 17-18). While Jackson regards the mappings as "stereotypes" (p. 18), he does credit the mappers with acknowledging the tentativeness of their categories. Jackson is right that these maps of the field are of limited utility now. So far Jackson has clarified the definitional and mapping issue, no small achievement. To where does he turn next? From maps of the field he moves to the subject of what in fact curriculum specialists do.

What do curriculum specialists do? Jackson leaves definitional and associated issues of mapping to focus, in part three of his essay, on "professional issues," namely "divisions of labor within the field of curriculum" (1992a, p. 21). He answers the question of what curriculum specialists do: "The long-standing answer says that university-based specialists should be of direct, practical help to classroom teachers and school administrators as the latter go about the day-to-day business of trying to improve the curriculum of their schools. This is not to say that the specialists must actually *work* in schools. It is only to insist that what they teach and write should have clear relevance to the curriculum improvement efforts of practitioners" (1992a, p. 21). Here Jackson has articulated economically the relationship between theory and practice that has prevailed during the approximately sixty-year history [1918-1979] of the curriculum development paradigm (or pre-paradigm, in Rogan and Luckowski's term). Jackson then seems to acknowledge the paradigm shift when he writes:

> The more recent answer . . . calls for the university-based specialist to be doing something different, something other than serving the practitioner's need for technical help. . . . One possibility is for them to begin working even more closely with practitioners than they have in the past. Another possibility is for them to bring to bear on educational matters in general the outlooks of scholarly disciplines and political perspectives that heretofore have been overlooked or largely ignored. (Jackson, 1992a, p. 21)

At the beginning of his essay, Jackson claimed that the field is confused. Some curricularists are no doubt confused; Jackson is not. We would guess that those who report confusion tend to be those who are caught in the "generational divide" between the curriculum development paradigm and its shift in the 1970s to understanding. Jackson is not confused. He is quite clear what issues of theory and practice are at stake; he is quite clear regarding the inadequacy of traditional mappings of the field. The contemporary field is indeed organized exactly along the lines Jackson suggests. What are these? He points out that a large sector of the field remains interested in serving the daily and technical needs of those who work in schools. We see those who work within this sector as striving to *understand curriculum as institutional text*. They phrase their questions, approaches, and answers in the traditional discourse of curriculum development, although, as we shall in see in chapter 13, this discourse too is changing in response to the reconceptualization of the field.

[A paranthetical note on text: in employing the term text, as in institutional text, we acknowledge the fact that the field of curriculum as we know it and as it is communicated to you is composed of various discourses, i.e. specific language systems and traditions which have specific histories and political legacies. Furthermore, the term suggests issues involved in understanding curriculum that are otherwise ignored. For instance, how does one read or write curriculum, how has curriculum historically been written and read, what analytical tools may be brought to bear on reading a text? A textualist mapping of the field has links to poststructuralism, which we summarize in chapter 9.]

Other sectors of the reconceptualized field, Jackson observes, import the outlooks of scholarly disciplines and political perspectives. As the table of contents in this book indicates, a geography of the contemporary field must take into account the ways the arts, sciences, and humanities have addressed and influenced the interdisciplinary domains of race, gender, and politics. Such a geography also acknowledges the scholarship associated with phenomenology, poststructuralism, autobiography, aesthetics, theology, and international studies. Before we turn to this map of the contemporary field, let us return to the historical journey for which Jackson is our guide.

Bobbitt, Tyler, Schwab. Jackson traces conceptions of the field through the work of three historical "giants" in the field: Franklin Bobbitt, Ralph Tyler, and Joseph Schwab. Let us quickly follow Jackson's tracing, and then turn to mapping the contemporary field. Jackson tells us that Bobbitt saw his task, and that of the curriculum specialist, as reforming the curriculum of the schools. He recommended a general strategy for curriculum development, which we will examine in chapter 2, which starts, in Jackson's (1992a) words, "with a very broad, all enveloping conception of the activities in which humans engage and moves to progressively narrower and more concrete specification of what humans need to know in order to do [adult activities]" (p. 24). Bobbitt recommends that the process of curriculum development be led by educators, but that other groups in the community, including "salesmen, physicians and nurses, civic and social workers, religious workers," and others be included. Bobbitt acknowledged the scale of this ambition and counseled against moving more quickly than any specific community could accommodate (Jackson, 1992a). Clearly, Bobbitt's formulation of curriculum was as institutional text and curriculum development was to occur on a national scale. Recall that the 1920s were a period of immigration, unsteady but rapid economic expansion, and conservative national politics. Curriculum standardization and centralization were, at this time, goals, not oppressive realities.

The Tyler Rationale. From a consideration of Bobbitt, Jackson moves to Ralph W. Tyler. "If any single volume deserves to be called the Bible of curriculum making," Jackson begins, "it is certainly Ralph Tyler's *Basic Principles of Curriculum and Instruction.* . . . A more influential text within the field of curriculum would be hard to name" (1992a, p. 24). This thin book, which began as a syllabus for a course Tyler taught at the University of Chicago in the 1930s and 1940s (and published by the University of Chicago Press, first in 1949), "attempts to explain a rationale for viewing, analyzing and interpreting the curriculum and instructional program of an educational institution" (Tyler, 1949, p. 1). [Tyler's emphasis upon "rationale" helps explain why the contents of the book came to be referred to as the Tyler Rationale.] Tyler goes on to say that the book "outlines one way of viewing an instructional program as a functioning instrument of education" (p. 1). The heart of Tyler's "basic principles" consists of four questions (to which he devotes separate chapters), which as Jackson points out, "a goodly number of today's curriculum specialists, thanks to Tyler, probably know by heart" (Jackson, 1992a, p. 25). These four questions are:

1. What educational purposes should the school seek to attain? [Objectives]
2. What educational experiences can be provided that are likely to attain these purposes? [Design]
3. How can these educational experiences be effectively organized? [Scope and Sequence]

4. How can we determine whether these purposes are being attained? [Evaluation] (Tyler,1949; quoted in Jackson, 1992a, p. 25)

Do Tyler and Bobbitt agree? Jackson then compares the views of Tyler and Bobbitt: "In their conceptions of what a university-based curriculum specialist ought to be doing, Bobbitt and Tyler see eye to eye. They both agree that at least one job of such a specialist is to give advice to practitioners on how to revise the curriculum of their schools" (Jackson, 1992a, p. 25). This view, as Jackson has pointed out, represents the traditional conception of the field. "A second task," Jackson continues, "which both theorists endorse but in different ways, is to conduct studies that shed light on what should be taught or how various curricula could be evaluated. A third task is to train a cadre of specialists who will move to other university posts" (Jackson, 1992a, pp. 25-26). Jackson judges that both men wished "to bring some order and regularity to this complex task [of curriculum development]" (p. 26), what we have termed an administrative or managerial interest (Pinar & Grumet, 1988). Further, both Bobbitt and Tyler "are optimistic about the curricular benefits of empirical investigations of various kinds. For Bobbitt the chief form of those investigations should be studies of activities carried on within the society at large. Tyler calls for such investigations as well but also looks toward psychological studies of learning as a source of help. Both hope that such investigations will ultimately put the process of curriculum development on a firm scientific footing" (Jackson, 1992a, p. 26). Both Bobbitt and Tyler "share a spirit of practicality" (Jackson, 1992a, p. 26).

Does Tyler improve on Bobbitt? Jackson answers "yes." He judges that Tyler extended and refined Bobbitt's view by moving beyond Bobbitt's two-step model of (1) defining educational objectives and (2) devising learning experiences. Tyler added two additional steps, one involving the organization of learning experiences and the other requiring their evaluation. Tyler further refined the first step of formulating objectives by including the development of a school philosophy and for examination of psychological studies, both of which were to be used as screens to weed out unwanted objectives and to reduce their overall number. More than Bobbitt, Tyler was willing to accept a smaller stage for curriculum development and revision. The "space" in which university-based curriculum specialists can contribute to curriculum development had been reduced, partly due to the increasing influence of the political and corporate spheres. Politicians were less willing to leave curricular matters to the discretionary judgments of educators, and the textbook industry itself co-opted teachers' opportunities for the development of curricular materials. Both Bobbitt and Tyler "lie within the single tradition of curriculum specialist as advice giver to practitioners" (1992a, p. 27). Finally, Jackson wonders why Bobbitt and Tyler were so widely read. He looks for those rhetorical qualities of their books which might help explain their wide influence: "Most notable among these [rhetorical] qualities is the strong appeal to common sense" (p. 27). We would add that they were read because professors assigned them.

Schwab's proposals. Next Jackson turns to Joseph J. Schwab's famous four papers on curriculum. These papers, Schwab tells us, "propose alternatives to present or envisaged practices, discriminate possible consequences (good or bad) of alternatives, trace these consequences to their further probable effects, and in other ways contribute to the responsible deliberation necessary for defensible choices of new or altered practices" (1978, p. 320; quoted in Jackson, 1992a, p. 28). Do Schwab's four essays realize these aims? Jackson judges that "it would be a generous critic who said they did but a blind one who concluded they did not try" (Jackson, 1992a, p. 28). [Schwab's students have observed that his proposals are complicated by writing that is "at once a model of erudition and eloquence and, at the same time, . . . pedantic and convoluted" (Eisner, 1984, p. 203). To be enacted, Schwab's proposals would require related changes in teacher education and research, thus further reducing the likelihood of implementation (Shulman,1984). We attend in more detail to Schwab's influence on the field in a separate section devoted to him and his work; see chapter 4.]

Schwab's three questions. After Schwab declared the curriculum field "moribund" in 1969, a state, he asserted, in which "all fields of systematic intellectual activity" find themselves periodically, he proposed a solution. He advises the field to transfer "curriculum energies" from the "theoretic" to "three other modes of operation," which he calls "the practical, the quasi-practical, and the eclectic" (quoted in Jackson, 1992a, pp. 28-29). As part of this proposal, Schwab asks three questions, which Jackson (1992a) restates: 1) What is the "art of the practical"? and how does it relate to the curriculum? 2) What is the role of school-based curriculum-specialist who seeks to practice that art? 3) What is the role of the university-based specialist? (p. 29).

Deliberation. The first question is answered in the following terms. The "art of the practical" is the art of deliberation. Understood in terms of curricular affairs, this means that curriculum improvement will occur incrementally, rather than on, say, the grand scale that Franklin Bobbitt envisioned. Curriculum development and improvement "must be so planned and so articulated with what remains unchanged that the functioning of the whole remains coherent and unimpaired" (1978, p. 312; quoted in Jackson, 1992a, p. 29). Schwab proposed that each school assemble a team to take responsibility for curriculum development and revision. Periodically, this team would employ external consultants of two types: "professional academics" to serve as subject matter consultants, and social scientists, such as sociologists and psychologists, to offer advice regarding social and psychological concerns. Chairing this team would be a curriculum specialist trained for the task and who would occupy a new position within the school's governance system. The three responsibilities of the school-based curriculum chairperson would be: 1) monitor the activities of the group, 2) supervise curriculum development activities, especially the preparation of materials, and 3) assist in the team's formulation of its curricular values (Schwab, 1978; Jackson, 1992a).

Schwab: What curriculum specialists ought to know. Jackson moves next to Schwab's elaboration of the role of the university-based curriculum professor. The basic obligation of this individual is to prepare persons who would serve as school-based curriculum committee chairpersons, as described above. What these individuals will want to know includes:

> 1) skillful use of the rhetorics of persuasion, 2) experience in deliberation, 3) ability to read "learned" journals, 4) ability to guide teacher-colleagues in use of journals, 5) knowledge of curricular practices throughout the country, 6) knowledge of those behavioral sciences which contribute to guidance of educational practice, and 7) a "nodding" acquaintance with some of the academic fields from which school curricula are drawn. (Jackson, 1992a, p. 30)

For Schwab, the Ph.D. program in curriculum would include seminars and internship experiences, culminating in a dissertation which would be comprised of "a report, analysis, and assessment" of an internship in the office of a curriculum chairperson within an actual school. This scholarship "would inform, advise and refresh their former students working in the schools" (Schwab, quoted in Jackson, 1992a, p. 30).

Does Schwab improve on Tyler? That Schwab self-consciously linked his work to Tyler is evident from Schwab's own statement: "It will be clear from these remarks that the conception of a curricular method proposed here is immanent in the Tyler rationale," (1978, p. 320; quoted in Jackson, 1992a, p. 30). Jackson tells us that there are two differences between Tyler and Schwab, differences which Schwab regarded as weaknesses in Tyler: 1) Tyler's heavy emphasis upon defining objectives (for Schwab objectives are too vague to provoke deliberation, resulting in "delusive consensus," or false agreement), and 2) those who use Tyler's work are not trained in deliberation (Jackson, 1992a). Both Schwab and Tyler, again in Schwab's words, "insist on the practical and eclectic treatment of a variety of factors" (1978, p. 320; quoted in Jackson, 1992a, p. 30). What is the fundamental belief that both Schwab and Tyler share? Jackson tells us:

> Chief among the similarities is the fact that Schwab and Tyler share a common understanding of what they are about, one that Bobbitt shared as well. *All three seek to be of help to practitioners who want to improve the curriculum of the schools in which they work.* That is their chief goal. They have different ideas about how to get there, true enough, but there is no wavering in their pursuit of that overall mission. (Jackson, 1992a, p. 30, emphasis in original)

Jackson qualifies this judgment by saying that Schwab seems slightly more distant from "the day-to-day business of school affairs than either of his predecessors" (p. 30). Jackson notes that Bobbitt had an overarching vision, i.e. that something is wrong with schools which requires reform. He points out, however, that while Tyler does not hold as grandiose an ambition as does Bobbitt, Tyler does believe that a broad perspective is important. Jackson notes that Tyler recommends that every school develop its own set of objectives. In contrast, Jackson observes, Schwab does not talk about how the schools might undertake social reform on a grand scale. Nor does Schwab recommend that practicing educators occupy themselves with such broad issues. Instead, Schwab worries over spending time on statements of objectives at all. Formulating objectives is too easy, Schwab (1978) says. More important is to spend time problem-solving the "frictions and failures of the curricular machine" (1978, p. 315; quoted in Jackson, 1992a, p. 31). Regarding the scale of the task of curriculum development and revision, Jackson concludes, Schwab "seems to have drifted away from Bobbitt and Tyler rather than to have moved one step further in the same direction" (Jackson, 1992a, p.31). Schwab's work acknowledges the shrinking space for curriculum development, while retaining an institutional sense of curriculum work.

A tension in Schwab. Jackson identifies an important tension in Schwab. On the one hand, Schwab urges curriculum professors to abandon theory for more school-oriented and practical efforts. On the other hand, Schwab also invites curriculum professors to become more scholarly and intellectual, to read broadly, to educate themselves in the social sciences, and "to become critical essayists who comment insightfully on the social injustices and hypocrisies of the day as they bear on educational affairs" (Jackson, 1992a, p.32). Jackson then takes up these two "paths" as they are evident in the field today, noting two fundamental versions of what it means to be a curriculum specialist. One version he regards as "moving toward practice: the curriculum specialist as consultant" (p. 32). The other he regards as "moving toward the academy: the curriculum specialist as generalist" (Jackson, 1992a, p. 34). We will examine the former first.

Curriculum specialist as consultant. Jackson notes that a precedent exists for this version in the United Kingdom, where historically teachers have served as curriculum makers. Teacher groups and associations were very much involved with curriculum reform in the 1960s, in contrast to the American scene [see chapter 3]. In the United Kingdom, then, university professors played roles much like those Schwab recommended for American professors of curriculum [see Stenhouse, 1980; Reid & Walker, 1975; Goodson, 1983]. The contemporary American expression of engagement with schools, for which the British example is an antecedent, is one that blurs the traditional distinction between curriculum development and in-service training or staff development. [See the section on teacher development in chapter 13 for a description of this sector of scholarship.] For illustrations of this group, Jackson cites the work of F. Michael Connelly and D. Jean Clandinin (1988a), Freema Elbaz (1983), Robin Barrow (1984b), and Antoinette Oberg (1987). Jackson says about this group: "A sampling of books and articles written by adherents of a more practitioner-oriented point of view reveals plenty to write about after the goal of discovering general principles of curriculum has been abandoned. . . . The mixture of criticism and advice in Schwab's four essays is paradigmatic of this kind of writing" (p. 33). The difference between Bobbitt's vision of a nationwide program of curriculum development and reform, and Schwab's focus upon the constant need to fix broken curricular machinery reflects "a marked diminution in the scope of the curriculum specialist's mission that appears to have taken place during the intervening 50 years" (Jackson, 1992a, p. 34). While noting the continuities among Bobbitt, Tyler, Schwab, and the contemporary interest in curricular practice, Jackson does express a reservation regarding the work of those moving "closer to the practitioner":

> If the specialist brings no special knowledge or vision to the task of establishing the need for change, if he or she turns out to be only a facilitator of the change process without substantive involvement in the question of what needs changing and why, one then begins to wonder in what sense the label curriculum specialist is appropriate. Perhaps something like discussion leader or Schwab's term "deliberator," would be more suitable. . . . To give that [the visionary role of the generalist] up would indeed be to flee the field, though not quite in the way Schwab suggested. (Jackson, 1992a, p. 34)

Curriculum specialist as generalist. The second path the contemporary field is traveling Jackson terms as "moving toward the academy: the curriculum specialist as generalist" (p. 34). Schwab (1983) imagined that the curriculum generalist would study American government and society, including the character of daily life in America. The curriculum specialist as generalist might, for instance, study the intensity of competition in American life and ask how the schools might call its taken-for-grantedness into question. Racism and nationalism might legitimately preoccupy curriculum generalists. [As we will see chapters 5 and 6, they do.] Developments in the academic disciplines, as well as in society, which might be important for consideration in the formulation of curriculum, would also be appropriate for curriculum generalists to study (Schwab, 1983). Who would constitute the audience of these generalists' essays? Schwab tells us that in addition to the colleagues of curriculum professors, former students and the public at large might take an interest. Jackson then observes:

> In the late 1960s and early 1970s there emerged a group of curriculum professors whose writing sounded as though they had taken Schwab's advice to heart, even though his fourth essay [from which the preceding quote was taken] was not to appear for at least a decade and Schwab himself was to be among those with whom the group as a whole was said to differ. Some members of this group spoke of what they were doing as reconceptualizing the task of the curriculum specialists, particularly with respect to the role of theory in curricular affairs. (Jackson, 1992a, p. 34)

Jackson describes this group—the Reconceptualists—as exhibiting three salient features: 1) a dissatisfaction with the Tyler Rationale, 2) the employment of eclectic traditions to explore curriculum, such as psychoanalytic theory, phenomenology, existentialism, and 3) a left-wing political bias "that drew on Marxist and neo-Marxist thought and concerned itself with issues of racial and ethnic inequalities, feminism, the peace movement, and so forth" (1992a, p. 35). We will examine the history of the Reconceptualization in detail in chapter 4. Chapters 5-14 outline just how these "eclectic" traditions and interests in race, gender, and politics became formulated and expressed in the American curriculum field during the last 15 years.

A second wave of reconceptualization? Jackson quotes Pinar's 1988 observation regarding the Reconceptualization of curriculum studies: "While the academic field of curriculum studies has been reconceived, the major ideas which constitute the contemporary field of study have yet to make their way to colleagues in elementary and secondary schools. If there is a 'second wave,' such schools will be its site" (Pinar, 1988f, p. 13). Jackson asks why has the Reconceptualization not yet reached the schools. Will it in time? Should it be a matter of concern if school people do not read contemporary curriculum theory? The answer to these questions, Jackson tells us, depends upon one's view of curricular change, a matter that can be subdivided into three parts: 1) an idea of which changes are most needed, 2) understanding how changes might occur, and 3) a set of beliefs regarding the roles curriculum specialists might play in change. If, for instance, one regards the principal agents of change to be policymakers rather than practitioners, or if one's critique of the curricular status quo stops short of recommending change, or finally if one holds to any combination of these points of view, "it matters much less that relatively few practitioners are listening" (Jackson, 1992a, p. 36). Jackson continues:

> [There is an] additional consideration . . . related to the question of what practitioners are willing to read but bears even more directly on the future of curriculum as a field of study. It begins by asking whether curriculum change on a massive scale (Bobbitt) or even on the more modest scale of continuous tinkering (Tyler and Schwab) remains the issue it once was. There are signs that it is not. Certainly the days of nationwide curriculum reform that swept the country in the 1960s are long past. Similar movements in other nations seem to have ceased as well. . . . The activity of curriculum development in these specialized areas tend to be dominated by specialists in particular subject matter fields rather than by specialists whose domain of expertise is the curriculum in general or curriculum improvement across the board. (Jackson, 1992a, p. 37)

Here Jackson is acknowledging that the domain of curriculum development no longer belongs only or even primarily to curriculum specialists (in contrast to subject matter specialists, such as reading or science educators). The loss of this domain was gradual until the 1960s, when the Kennedy administration's national curriculum reform projects made clear that the traditional curriculum field was no longer the major player in curriculum development and revision on a national scale. [That story is told in chapters 3 and 4.] Here Jackson understands that curriculum development is no longer the paradigm of the field.

Recapture the optimism and sense of mission? Jackson concludes with consideration of another possibility, one which might recapture the excitement and sense of importance once associated with the traditional curriculum field. He holds out this possibility:

> There is another possibility, of course, at least hypothetically, and that is to respond to current conditions by seeking to rejuvenate the field from within, which is what the reconceptualists have obviously sought to do and may be what those who are moving closer to practitioners are seeking to do as well. Can that be accomplished? Will either group succeed in recapturing the spirit of optimism and the sense of mission that clearly marked the first two or three decades of the emergence of curriculum as field of study? (1992a, p. 37)

That is a question to which we hope the present work will constitute a partial answer.

Jackson has made three major contributions. First, he is the first major scholar to link the contemporary scholarship of the reconceptualized curriculum field to the major concerns of the traditional field, threading these carefully through the work of Bobbitt, Dewey, Tyler, and Schwab. [That he has chosen scholars all associated with the University of Chicago, the institution where his own career has unfolded, is forgivable given the indisputable significance of Bobbitt, et al.] Second, Jackson understands, as no major figure in the field has to date, that the "space" of curriculum development and revision has been reduced significantly over the field's seventy-year history, and that this reduced "space" is reflected not only in the diminishing scale of curriculum development and revision evident in the work of Bobbitt and Tyler and Schwab, but in the role of theory in the field. The role of theory has shifted from its status as the "tail" on the "dog" of practice to that of a more equal status. As Jackson notes, there are two paths taken in the contemporary field, one toward practitioners and the other toward the academy.

We believe this division is only apparent. It is not, finally, accurate to conclude that in the contemporary, reconceptualized field of curriculum, specialists are sometimes closer to schools or sometimes closer to the university. Our view is that contemporary scholars are simultaneously closer to both "practice" and closer to "theory." Note that those Jackson has associated as closer to practice have sophisticated theoretical understanding of their school-based research and practice (for example, Connelly & Clandinin; we might also include Butt, Schubert, and Shulman). Theoreticians perform "practical" work with enormous skill and realism (Grumet, 1988b; Miller, 1990a). We would say that the apparent distance between scholars and schools is just that, apparent. Even those who do not work in the schools are keenly aware of conditions in the schools. It is the relationship between scholars and teachers which has changed. In the curriculum development paradigm the relationship tended to be hierarchical, with the university professor as expert and the teacher as client. In the reconceived field the relationships are more collaborative (Miller, 1990a). In this changed relationship, theory and practice appear to be apart, but it is only apparent and, we believe, for the benefit of both:

> Too often, curriculum theory has been tainted with the self-conscious complexity of academic work, disdaining practical activity in order to maintain the class privilege that clings to the abstract in order to aggrandize its status. Although the field situation provides a context where curriculum theory and practice confront one another, our objective ought not to be to resolve their differences, reducing one to the dimensions of the other. No longer must contemplation be reserved for the privileged; rather, it becomes a mode of analysis which challenges unjust privilege. Theory must not reinforce class differences but help dissolve them. Theory must not hang alienated from practice in some timeless realm of unchanging, arrogant truth. *Rather, let us play theory and practice against each other so as to disclose their limitations, and in so doing enlarge the capacity and intensify the focus of each.* (Pinar & Grumet, 1988, p. 99; emphasis added)

Jackson's contribution to the curriculum field is considerably more extensive than this one—albeit highly significant—essay indicates. His 1968 book, *Life in Classrooms*, helped define thematically and methodologically much research conducted since. During the decade of Reconceptualization, his 1979 invited "state of the art" address to the American Educational Research Association expressed many of the tensions that shift provoked; we examine that address and responses to it in chapter 4. In chapter 13, we will examine his thoughtful reflections on teaching and "teacher development." Here, he has provided a sturdy historical and conceptual bridge between the field that exists in the early 1990s and the field that existed before the 1970s. We turn now to a geography of the field that exists today.

V
Mapping the Contemporary Field

> The concept "text" . . . is now understood in a very wide sense: social practices and institutions, cultural products, indeed anything that is created as a result of human action and reflection.
>
> (H. McEwan, 1992, p. 64)

We have summarized the shift from the traditional to the contemporary field from two points of view. The first took us on a review of the synoptic textbook; the second examined definitional and occupational shifts within the profession. From both viewpoints, we have seen that shifting historical conditions—specifically the shrinking domain of curriculum development as politicians, textbook companies, and subject-matter specialists in the university, rather than school practitioners and university professors of curriculum, exercised leadership and control over curriculum development—changed the occupational and definitional character of the field. In so doing, these changing conditions precipitated the paradigm shift the field underwent in the

1970s. Jackson outlined very briefly features of the reconceptualized field that resulted. Let us outline them now in more detail.

Historical scholarship. The study of curriculum history, of which Jackson's study is an excellent example, has emerged in the 1980s as one of the most important sectors of contemporary curriculum scholarship. This has been a rapid and recent development. As Kliebard (1992a) observes in his *Forging the American Curriculum,* "When I was a graduate student there was no such thing as a curriculum historian." [Herbert Kliebard, as well as Daniel and Laurel Tanner (1980; 1990), Ivor Goodson (1981a, 1983, 1988a, 1988b, 1989a, 1989b), Barry Franklin (1986), Steven Selden (1988), and Craig Kridel (1989; 1991) are among those whose scholarship has made history important to the contemporary field.]

Why was the traditional field ahistorical? The Tyler Rationale was finally procedural, and this bureaucratic interest has little need to consult history. Curriculum development itself was conceptualized according to protocol and orientation, often influenced by a scientific faith that the best was yet to come, i.e. that more effective knowledge awaited more refined and rigorous scientific experimentation. The administrative or managerial character of the field's origins cannot be overemphasized in this regard. William Reid (1986) notes:

> Curriculum, as a focus of academic activity, was first institutionalized in North America with the object of supplying school districts with educational leaders who understood how curricula could and should be improved, updated, or reformed. To this day, such aspirations are still at the heart of the curriculum enterprise. (p. 159)

This reformist orientation, linked with a faith in "progress," has led to an emphasis on the future (Longstreet & Shane, 1993), not the past. Reid (1986) writes that "curriculum study has tended not merely to be ignorant of, but even to be positively opposed to historical research, since the past has often been represented as a dark age best forgotten in the search for a brighter future" (p. 160). Even within this orientation, however, Reid (1986) believes that "history can be beneficial to a practically based conception of curriculum change" (p. 164). Also, Reid (1986) believes history has been underemphasized in curriculum studies because "most [curriculum scholars] have been raised in other disciplines" (p. 159).

One reason that historical scholarship has become important now, we believe, is that the cataclysm that was the Reconceptualization precipitated a crisis of identity for the field. We know we are a theoretical as well as practical field now, involved in the project to understand curriculum. What are the continuities and discontinuities between this "new" field and the traditional Tylerian field? If one distinguishing characteristic of the traditional field was that it tended to be atheoretical and ahistorical (Kliebard, 1970, 1992a), then *one distinguishing characteristic of the reconceptualized, contemporary field is that it is profoundly historical.* Scholars are acutely aware that curriculum work occurs in time, in history, and this self-consciousness regarding the historicity of curriculum work, theoretical or institutional, has helped support the increasing interest in historical studies of curriculum. We devote three chapters (chapters 2, 3, and 4) to an abbreviated history of the field from 1828 to 1979. While the contemporary discourses, reported in chapters 5-14, are organized topically, several are also organized historically, especially the chapters on politics, gender, poststructuralism, theology, and autobiography. In addition to historical treatments of the field, bibliographical (Schubert, 1980a), mentorship (Iverson & Waxman, 1981; Schubert, 1992a), and genealogical studies (Schubert & Posner, 1980; Schubert, et al., 1988; Pinar & Reynolds, 1992b) are now available. Historical scholarship receives institutional support from the Society for the Study of Curriculum History and the Museum of Education at the University of South Carolina. Recently, a significant new resource has been published. *The American Curriculum: A Documentary History*, edited by George Willis, William Schubert, Robert V. Bullough, Jr., Craig Kridel, and John Holton (1993), makes available to scholars primary source material documenting the history of curriculum in America. This material was not readily available before 1993. Each document is preceded by a brief introduction which places it in historical context. Clearly, understanding curriculum historically represents a major and dynamic sector of the contemporary field.

The categories of contemporary curriculum discourses we employ in this book did not come from a vacuum. As Jackson noted, they developed historically, out of the collapse of the traditional field, and out of the disputes which accompanied the struggles for influence and power that characterized the decade of actual paradigm shift, the 1970s [described in chapter 4]. The first "reconceptualist" discourses to appear in the 1970s were the political and autobiographical discourses, which vied head-on for a brief time for the ascendent position. Under the leadership of Michael W. Apple at the University of Wisconsin-Madison, the political sector triumpted early (by mid-decade), becoming the most important and voluminous sector by the end of the decade [see chapter 5]. Autobiographical work went into eclipse by decade's end, sapped by its defeat at the hands of Apple's Marxism and replaced partly by the emergence of feminist theory in the second half of the 1970s. However, autobiographical/biographical scholarship and theory have re-emerged with great energy in the last five years; we review it in chapter 10.

Feminist theory, through the energies of at least two theorists central to the autobiographical project in the 1970s, Madeleine R. Grumet and Janet L. Miller [see chapters 7 and 10], quickly emerged second to political scholarship in volume and importance. The effort to *understand curriculum as gender text* has become central to the contemporary project to understand curriculum, and we believe this sector is still ascendant, while the political sector enters a period of crisis. We review feminist and gender theory in chapter 7. In addition to its own autonomous history, racial scholarship grew out of political and gender scholarship; we locate it between politics and gender in chapter 6. It is this sector, once segregated into discourses on multiculturalism, that has moved with greatest energy and force, and promises to redefine the concepts central to the field as a whole.

Autobiographical scholarship engaged political work in the early 1970s, sometimes critically, sometimes sympathetically, but in general political scholarship ignored this engagement, concentrating instead on its own development, a self-chosen insularity which continues to the present-day [see Beyer & Apple, 1988]. From a political perspective, such a strategy has proved to be effective. As we have noted, Apple asserted leadership in the effort to *understand curriculum as political text,* to be joined by the end of the decade by Henry A. Giroux, who has now become better known outside the curriculum field [he has appeared on National Public Radio, for instance] than perhaps any other curricularist working in any discourse. As well, Giroux has become a kind of "lightning rod" within the field, drawing criticism from a wide variety of sources, although the differences between his work and Apple are not irreconcilable (Wexler, 1987; Apple, 1993). Giroux's former colleague, Peter McLaren, seems to have moved slightly away from Giroux's preoccupation with politics (which, too, has expanded recently to include considerations of race, gender, and postmodernism) toward a politicized postmodernism, or, probably more accurately, a postmodern politics [see chapters 5 and 9]. McLaren's recent scholarship personifies the crisis in the political sector. Philip Wexler has emerged as perhaps the most sophisticated critic on the Left of Apple and Giroux, and quite possibly the most sophisticated theoretician on the Left in the contemporary field. We examine the work of Apple, Giroux, McLaren, and Wexler, as well as that of many others—often Apple's students and colleagues—working to understand curriculum as political text, in chapter 5.

Another figure who came to prominence in the 1970s was Max van Manen, the University of Alberta phenomenologist, who was the second scholar to introduce this important European and now Canadian tradition of phenomenology to the American curriculum audience [Dwayne E. Huebner was the first; see chapter 3 and Pinar & Reynolds, 1992b]. After listening to van Manen speak at the 1976 meeting of the American Educational Research Association, James Macdonald pronounced him the "crown prince" of the field. Van Manen introduced his Ph.D. mentor at Alberta, Ted Aoki, to phenomenology, and Aoki quickly emerged as a major figure in *phenomenological curriculum theory.* Together Aoki and van Manen launched the phenomenological movement and nearly singlehandedly established it as a major (if still insufficiently acknowledged in the United States) contemporary discourse, as well as establishing the University of Alberta as the North American center for phenomenological studies in education. We report phenomenological scholarship in chapter 8.

Since the 1960s, Elliot Eisner's widely-read work has been critical of the Tylerian field, especially in the area of evaluation. His creation of a new aesthetic perspective in curriculum theory generally, and in curriculum evaluation more specifically, would receive a comprehensive exposition in 1979 with the publication of *The Educational Imagination.* His important and original contribution to the field is described in the chapter on *understanding curriculum as aesthetic text*, as well as in the section on curriculum evaluation in chapter 13, *understanding curriculum as institutional text*. Like Philip Jackson, Elliot Eisner is one figure whose influence spans more than one discourse and at least two generations.

Racial issues were conspicuously absent from reconceptualized curriculum theory in the 1970s and early 1980s, perhaps most noticeably so in the political sector where one would most expect them to surface. Instead, racial discourses were segregated in multicultural discourses, somehow not considered an integral part of the field in the 1970s and early 1980s. Not until the late 1980s did the political theorists discover race, but it was Cameron McCarthy's (1990) *Race and Curriculum* that placed the concept of race at center stage in the contemporary field. As we noted, discourses on the effort to *understand curriculum as racial text* are reported in chapter 6.

At the 1980 Airlie House Conference on Curriculum Theory and Classroom Practice, Jacques Daignault and Clermont Gauthier ridiculed talk of reconceptualization, calling it just another language game, another territorialization of the field [see Pinar & Reynolds, 1992b]. Their dramatic staging marked the emergence of *poststructuralism* in American curriculum studies, although Peter Taubman (1979, 1982) had quietly employed the work of Michel Foucault to frame gender identity and politics in the late 1970s. From different sources (Piagetianism, critical theory, and feminist theory, respectively), William E. Doll, Jr., Peter McLaren, and Patti Lather have worked to understand curriculum as postmodern text, a more inclusive term than poststructuralism, which refers more narrowly to a movement in French philosophy. While taking the field of American literary criticism "by storm" in the 1970s and early 1980s, poststructuralism and postmodernism are just now emerging full force in American curriculum studies, marked by the publication of major books by Cleo Cherryholmes (1988b), Patti Lather (1991), and William Doll (1993a), and a collection of essays edited by William Pinar and William Reynolds (1992a). This "frontier" sector is described in chapter 9.

There are chapters on two discourses many would not consider major sectors of scholarship at this time. We admit to advocacy by including them. We believe that the field cannot ignore *theological* and *international dimensions of curriculum*, and we think that these chapters will support that contention. We are not alone in characterizing the theological dimension as important (Short, 1991). There are antecedents to these discourses, of course. Suffice it to note here that long after abandoning the theology of his youth, John Dewey (1934a) wrote about religion and theorized "a common faith," a kind of secular democratic theology. And seven decades ago George Counts joined Dewey in declaring that international issues were of paramount importance to educators. Of course, comparative education as a separate field has a long and distinguished history. What we argue here is that pertinent international dimensions be incorporated into our field's project to understand curriculum, a judgment you will recall that is shared by Rogan and Luckowski (1990). Theological and international dimensions of curriculum are reported in chapters 12 and 14, respectively.

Scholarship that understands *curriculum as institutional text* is reported in chapter 13. Such work used to fill traditional textbooks in their entirety. While the domain of institutional scholarship, work conducted within the paradigm of curriculum development, has shrunk over the decades, it remains important, and we give it its due. Interestingly, the themes of this work reflect the thematic shifts in the field generally, and the reader will find considerable attention paid to autobiography, politics, and aesthetics, if in institutional and bureaucratic contexts. In the contemporary field, even the curriculum as institutionalized text is not narrowly conceived.

Other maps. Other maps of the field are available (Taylor, 1982; Reid, 1980b; Barrow & Milburn, 1986). Decker F. Walker and Jonas F. Soltis (1986) link the study of curriculum with aims, identifying three orientations: transmission, transaction, and transformation, terms with long histories [see Rosenblatt, 1938; Miel & Brogan, 1957, p. 87]. Another map, one that intersects with ours but focuses on modes of inquiry [see also Short, 1991] is one formulated by Nelson Haggerson (1988). Drawing on the work of James B. Macdonald (1975b), Haggerson employs multiple research paradigms to map the field. He lists four paradigms: 1) rational/theoretical, 2) mythological/practical, 3) evolutionary/transformational, and 4) normative/critical. The first is scientific and historical; the second is ethnographical and phenomenological; the third employs autobiography and hermeneutics; and the fourth relies on critical theory and hermeneutics. Both the third and fourth modes of inquiry seek "understanding" (p. 90). [Relatedly, Haggerson (1986) had earlier called for aesthetic reconceptualization of the professional literature.] George J. Posner has worked nearly alone developing a perspective associated with the mainstream social science and, later, cognitive science (Posner & Strike, 1976; Posner & Rudnitsky, 1986; Posner, 1979, 1982a, 1982b). Later, in a map of the field, Posner (1989) identifies the following areas: curriculum-research questions, studies of educational outcomes, studies of the curriculum development process, analyses of educational concepts and aims, studies of educational materials, studies of students, studies of schools and classrooms (table 1, p. 342). Despite the diversity of perspectives in the field, Posner believes that: "Through concentrated effort, coherent and cumulative curriculum theories and associated curriculum-research programs could evolve with the ultimate goal of improving the quality of the educational process" (1989, pp. 361-362).

Posner develops his 1989 map of the field more extensively in his 1992 synoptic textbook, *Analyzing the Curriculum.* Again acknowledging his intellectual debt to his mentor Mauritz Johnson (1967), Posner (1992) develops a synoptic text with traditional subheadings:

I.   Curriculum Documentation and Origins
    A.   Concepts of curriculum and purposes of curriculum study

B. Situating the curriculum
C. Theoretical perspectives
   1) traditional
   2) experiential
   3) structure of the disciplines
   4) behavioral
   5) cognitive
II. The Curriculum Proper
   D. Curriculum perspective and content: basic concepts
   E. Curriculum purpose and content: conflicting perspectives
   F. Curriculum organization: basic concepts
   G. Curriculum organization: conflicting perspectives
III. The Curriculum in Use
   H. Frame Factors
   I. Curriculum implementation: conflicting approaches
   J. Curriculum evaluation: basic concepts
   K. Curriculum evaluation: conflicting perspectives
IV. Curriculum Critique
   L. Reexamination and critique

Posner has expanded his view of the field in light of recent scholarship, but the book cannot be considered a comprehensive treatment, as it privileges the effort to understand curriculum as institutional text, only one sector of scholarship in the contemporary field [see chapter 13]. Still, Posner's analysis is intelligent and must be acknowledged.

Where the field is going? Finally, in chapter 15 we go beyond reports of scholarship to suggest what the next stage of the field's development may bring. To attempt such a speculation requires a certain hubris, we acknowledge. Further, we know that few will be pleased with this statement, at least initially. Most of us are too invested in our particular research programs, and the general political situation in the field seems too complex and too fluid to imagine some distanced distillation of where it all might be going and what might be its next stage of development. We attempt this statement, not expecting pledges of allegiance nor expecting it to advance our own particular theoretical positions. Rather, our intention here is to formulate as fairly as we can a view of where the field might be going. We do this by incorporating several important contemporary contributions so that the resulting configuration is not sheer eclecticism [which might be the case should we attempt fairness and comprehensiveness to a fault] or naked partisanship [employing what others have done only to advance our own specific causes]. Rather, we attempt an integrated statement which might move us slightly away from the field's sources in parent disciplines (i.e. social theory or phenomenology) and take a step more toward an intellectually autonomous field. We hope the effort will point to the order of theorizing and scholarship necessary to carry the field to the next stage of its development, a stage less directly attached to its sources in other disciplines and fields, and one more nearly reflective of the indigenous and extraordinarily challenging problems of understanding curriculum. Additionally, we are quite clear that this next stage will require the labor of those who are not yet on the scene, at least not conspicuously so. Our generation—we refer to those of us who have worked in this field for twenty years or more—may be too rooted in the past, and in those struggles which brought us to the present, to be able to carry off what will be necessary to take us to the next stage. It is, however, important to agree on the basic nature of this next stage, and the nature of the move required to take us there. Of course, we will not agree on its thematic contents, but we can encourage the order of scholarship that will be required in our students, at our conferences, in our journals, and in our classrooms.

We wrote this book partly because no one else in the field appeared willing to do so. As Rogan and Luckowski note, most synoptic textbooks simply ignore the Reconceptualization, and many prominent in the reconceptualized field ignore work outside their own sector of scholarship (Pinar, 1990). This book attempts to bring these together by being inclusive, although we admit—partly for reasons of space—not encyclopedic. Specifically, we will show how the Reconceptualization occurred. We will identify both its divergences from and continuities with the traditional field. In this sense *Understanding Curriculum*, we hope, will encourage a moment of consensus in the field, at least an acknowledgement of how the field looks at present, in its diversity. Our point now is that the new generation of curriculum students must be introduced to the field *as it is*. As strong as the Schubert (1986a) book is, the gap between it and the field is too great for it to claim to present an accurate picture. To Schubert's credit, the picture he does present is at least recognizable, in contrast to, for instance, the Ronald C. Doll (1989) and the Wiles and Bondi (1984) books, which represent only fantasies of what the traditional field would have been, had it survived. For students new to the field, this fantasy presents a distorted picture of the American curriculum field. Without supplementary readings reflective of the field as it is today, teaching these books is irresponsible.

While we use terms associated with poststructuralism in the organization of this book—terms such as "text" and "discourse"—we employ these suggestively. Certainly we are not claiming that the current field is primarily poststructuralist in orientation, although this discourse has now emerged as sufficiently important to merit a separate chapter. Nor will we argue that the field will become poststructuralist, or that it should. We use the terms "text" and "discourse" to focus on the language of the field, that is, the scholarly production of the field, to insist the field *is* its scholarly production. We have offered preliminary definitions of these terms and now we can comment in somewhat more detail on these as well as our use of the term "understanding."

Text. The concept of text implies both a specific piece of writing and, much more broadly, social reality itself. For example, one scholar notes that "the concept 'text' . . . is now understood in a very wide sense: social practices and institutions, cultural products, indeed anything that is created as a result of human action and reflection" (McEwan, 1992, p. 64). A term borrowed from poststructuralism, and more particularly from the work of Jacques Derrida, text implies that all reality is human reality, and as human reality, it is fundamentally discursive, a matter of language. In contrast to the phenomenological view (Pinar & Reynolds, 1992a) that language is derived from a more fundamental and prior substratum of preconceptual experience, the poststructuralist view is that all experience has been deferred (hence the famous construct *différance*) from original experience, and in this "gap" occurs language and history. Reading, in Derrida's words, "cannot legitimately transgress the text toward something other than it, toward a reference (a reality that is metaphysical, historical, psychobiographical, etc.) or toward a signified outside the text whose content could take place, could have taken place outside language" (Derrida, 1976, p. 158). There is, it is said, nothing outside text. In regard to the study of teaching, Joseph P. McDonald (1992) suggests that "we may do well to think of what we are observing as a kind of text" (p.16). And to understand curriculum—within which teaching is subsumed—implies the study of curriculum as text, the study of curriculum discourses.

Discourse. Discourse, as poststructuralists employ the term, communicates the social relatedness of the human world, and more specifically, our social relatedness as inscribed in and expressed through language. Once again we encounter the notion that the human world is a world of language. This idea regards the distinction between "theory" and "practice" as an apparent distinction only. Both are discursive realities. In this view, theory is practical. Practice is theoretical. And so the use of "discourse" and "text" implies that the curriculum field cannot be conflated with the school curriculum. From this perspective, the Tanners' (1990) recent *History of the School Curriculum* is mistitled; a more accurate title would be a *History of School Curriculum Discourses.* As they themselves note, we do not know with exactitude what went on in the schools. We do not know the verisimilitude between the scholarly discourse and the daily practices of those in schools (Short, 1985). As we have noted, the relationship of the curriculum field to what goes on in schools bears no greater correspondence than does the relationship of the field of economics to the American economy, or of political science to American politics, or of preventive medicine to the everyday nutritional practices of the general population. Scholarly fields develop for many reasons, of course, but certainly one of their raisons d'etre is to more deeply understand their domain of inquiry. The mass of citizens are quite free to ignore these understandings, as the case of cigarettes indicates in the field of medicine.

Understanding. Our use of this term points to hermeneutics [see chapters 8 and 12] and poststructuralism [see chapter 9] without suspending its commonsensical definition. Because the curriculum field is textual, comprised of a series of sometimes intersecting, sometimes separate discourses, understanding here invokes issues of interpretation and meaning. Hunter McEwan (1992, p. 64) writes that:

> it is in texts that meaning resides. . . . It is a characteristic of the creations of human communities [cf. curriculum]. . . .Meaning is a property of texts, and texts are more than just written documents. Human actions and practices, social institutions, cultural artifacts, and the products of artistic creation can also be considered as texts, or text-analogues, that are open to be read.

To understand curriculum, then, requires "reading"—i.e., interpreting—those discourses produced by the field. "Practice" itself is a text in this sense, and we have summarized those discourses which define themselves as "practical" in chapter 13, as communicating an understanding of curriculum as institutional text. Understanding is also political, implying transformation of those "discursive fields" which are curriculum and teaching as they are reinterpreted, that is to say, understood. While we are, as we acknowledged earlier, employing these terms suggestively, and not in any narrow or technical sense, they are discussed within their own traditions, i.e. phenomenology and poststructuralism, in chapters 8 and 9, respectively.

A changed status. What is the status of the curriculum field vis-a-vis other specializations within the broad field of education? While we cannot be precise in our answer to this question, we do know that its status has changed dramatically since the Reconceptualization. As we will explain in greater detail in chapter 3, the field had been in retreat since the national curriculum reform movement in the early 1960s. Other areas regarded it as conceptually underdeveloped. That view has changed during the past twenty years. As well, the "self-concept" of the field has changed. The pervasive sense of the field as atheoretical and ahistorical has been replaced by emphases upon theory and history, and, we might add, with a discernible sense of excitement. Despite important advances in educational psychology, for instance, we tend to see that field and others associated with the foundations of education as far behind the curriculum field in the complexity of understanding of their domain. We suppose they are weighed down by the formalism of mainstream social and behavioral science. Of course, the price we curricularists pay for our creative freedom is a fairly high level of speculative excess. It is a payment necessarily made, perhaps. In exchange for the tidiness of educational psychology, with its scientific status (however honorific), and relative prestige, we relish exploring those frontiers where the terrain of intellectual conduct, including the terrain of thinking, are not only unsettled, but unmapped as well.

Humanities and arts influential. What is distinctive about contemporary curriculum theory? In addition to its focus on curriculum, however broad and complicated its definition, and its explicit interest in the school as institution (the sphere of "practice"), the reconceptualized field is a rare area in the broader field of education in which the humanities and the arts, if we cannot say have triumphed, certainly have come to occupy a good deal of conceptual and methodological territory. Curriculum is not a stepchild of another field, as educational psychology can be said to be the stepchild of psychology or philosophy of education is of philosophy, although curriculum theory is in a stage in which its sources in other disciplines are clearer than what is yet to be made of them. The question we construe as the central curriculum question—what can be created of what we have been conditioned to be [what Pinar termed once the relationship of the knower to the known (Pinar, 1980b)]—turns out to be a question for the field in its present stage of development. Thus, we ask, what will be made of the sources which we use now, and to which we remain relatively close?

While the humanities, arts, and social theory have been formative in the reconceptualized curriculum field, the "scientific" influence has not disappeared. We will examine it historically in chapters 2, 3, and 4, and we will see its influence in the effort to understand curriculum as institutional text in chapter 13. In their review of the scientific tradition in curriculum inquiry, Linda Darling-Hammond and Jon Snyder (1992) usefully and succinctly summarize the influence of behavioral and developmental research on curriculum inquiry:

> Behavioral research has drawn our attention to the importance of environmental conditions and cues in the shaping of learning. Developmental research has described how cognitive strategies evolve through maturation and how this development can be supported through opportunities for active engagement with the environment. Research on cognitive structure has illustrated how perception and presentation influence information processing and interpretation. Cognitive scientists have extended this work to demonstrate how schema development and activation, along with conscious changes in information-processing strategies, can enhance learning. Over time, the distinctions among various research perspectives have become increasingly blurred. (Darling-Hammond & Snyder, 1992, p. 56)

Not only are distinctions among various scientific perspectives blurred, so are the boundaries of contemporary curriculum discourses themselves.

Boundaries are porous. Naturally, the boundaries of each sector of contemporary curriculum scholarship are somewhat porous. Work that elaborates, for instance, curriculum as political text, is now also interested in how curriculum is racial text or gender text. For the sake of convenience, however, we can distinguish work which seems to take the political dimension as the most important, with secondary interests in other areas acknowledged. Additionally, writers in certain sectors contest the very use of concepts in another. For instance, several feminist writers dispute that only neo-Marxist political scholarship is in fact political. We will be as faithful as space permits to these disputes. We do employ, however, the mainstream perceptions of these categories, that politics for instance includes gender but is also about more traditional issues, such as power, privilege, and social control. For the beginning student what is crucial to remember is that this geography must not be frozen in time; it too is changing. What will change the map is research.

VI
Research

Because of the problem of idiosyncrasy, however, no research finding and no theory will ever generalize to every setting and to every child.
(Robert Donmoyer, 1989, p. 264)

Despite the different forms it takes, all action research has a common intention: the belief that we may develop our understandings while at the same time bringing about change in concrete situations.
(Terrance R. Carson, 1990a, p. 167)

This paper will: . . . 5. provide no five except to agree with Jean Cocteau when he says, "angels fly because they take themselves lightly".
(Conrad P. Pritscher, 1988, p. 61)

Research in the contemporary field reveals the influences of the arts, humanities, and social theory. Quantitative research is relatively rare at this time (Grumet, 1990d). In this section we will review the defeat of quantitative research in the curriculum field and the victory of qualitative research, including action research, ethnography, and theoretical research. Relying on Joe Kincheloe's (1991a) portrait of critical research, we will outline the main requirements of contemporary curriculum research, although few scholars would subscribe to all of these requirements. Next we introduce ethnography, including an outline of "how to" plan such research. Finally, we sample theoretical research as illustrated in Peter McLaren's (1992a, 1992b) analysis of selected issues in ethnographic research in which he reconceives culture "as a field of discourse" (1991b, p. 151). Having provided an abbreviated and introductory tour of the illustrative forms of contemporary research in the field, we will conclude the chapter with a depiction of the "paradigm wars" which led to the present field.

After the defeat of "positivism" [the assumption that human experience can only be understood via research methods modeled after those employed in the natural sciences; there are problems in the use of that term; see Phillips, 1983; McHoul & Luke, 1988], research in American curriculum studies moved away from quantitative research, including the use of statistics, toward the humanities, aesthetics, and social theory. Research became increasingly "qualitative," an umbrella term which includes all non-quantitative work. In the proceedings of an important conference on the status of qualitative research held at Stanford University (and sponsored by Teachers College Press) in June, 1988, Elliot Eisner and Alan Peshkin (1990) observed: "We refer to the 'shift' from the quantitative to the qualitative by a host of distinguished American scholars. Shift does not accurately characterize the variety of circumstances that describe what may, in fact, represent a conversion by some of them and an embracing of both modes of inquiry by some others. Included in the list of such scholars are Lee Cronbach, Donald Campbell, Robert Stake, Egon Guba, and Philip Jackson, all of whom were trained to be quantitative researchers and gained considerable repute as such" (p. 7). [There are, of course, antecedents to contemporary qualitative curriculum research, especially with an interest in school improvement; see, for instance, essays in the 1957 ASCD yearbook: McKim, 1957; Taba, 1957; Miles, 1957; Frazier, 1957; Larson, 1957; Mooney, 1957.]

Others have noted this shift. Tracing the quantitative research tradition to Thorndike [see chapter 2], credited with starting the mathematization of human experience in educational research, Robert Donmoyer (1987b) observed: "[Q]uite clearly Thorndike's conception of educational research has been knocked off its pedestal"(p. 362). Debates over positivism continue, as evidenced by a special 1992 issue of the *Educational Researcher*. Note the titles of articles in that issue: Schrag's (1992a) "In Defense of Positivist Research Paradigms," Eisner's (1992a), " Are All Causal Claims Positivistic? A Reply to Francis Shrag;" Erickson's (1992) "Why the Clinical Trial Doesn't Work as a Metaphor for Educational Research," Popkewitz's (1992) "Cartesian Anxiety, Linguistic Communism, and Reading Texts," and Schrag's (1992b) "Is There Light at the End of this Tunnel?"

Issues of objectivity and subjectivity also continue to be debated. [See, for instance Eisner's (1992b) "Objectivity in Educational Research," in which he attacks the concept of objectivity.] Eisner (1992b) writes: "The upshot of my message is to urge that we recognize objectivity for what it is: a concept built upon a faulty epistemology that leads to an unrealizable idea in its ontological state and a matter of consensus . . . in its procedural state" (1992b, p. 14). Others argue that both objectivity and subjectivity are dead (Barone, 1992a). Egon Guba (1992) has become interested in what he terms relativism, which he distinguished from so-called "postpositivist" perspectives: "the relativist position has much to recommend it. . . . Relativism is not a presupposition of either the postpositivist paradigm (which currently enjoys hegemony) or of ideological oriented paradigms such as neo-Marxism, critical theory, feminist theory, and the like" (p. 17). What are the main points of contention in these debates? Positivism and quantitative research have tended to assume the following: 1) in the same circumstances many people will have the same experience; 2) the majority dictates reality; 3) the individual is omitted in understanding a situation, i.e. generalization rather than what is unique is important; 4) there is a tendency to treat subjects as means to ends; and 5) quantitative research pretends that objectivity, including political neutrality, is possible by eradicating subjectivity and ideology. These epistemological debates are now of peripheral interest to those of us who have moved beyond quarrels over quantitative and qualitative. For many of us at work in the field today, these debates have been over for twenty years.

Examples of action research. Indeed, qualitative research has extended to nearly all areas of educational research, including those spheres interested in the school, i.e. so-called "action research" in which researchers and teachers form collaborative relationships to make curriculum change. Action research is a prime example of that category of scholarship in the contemporary field which Jackson (1992a) has termed as moving closer to practitioners. [See the classic instance of this work, Carr & Kemmis' (1986) *Becoming Critical: Education, Knowledge and Action Research.*] Other titles which point to the range of topics studied from the point of view of action research include: Sanger's (1990) "Awakening a Scream of Consciousness: The Critical Group in Action Research," Rogers, Noblit, and Ferrell's (1990) "Action Research as an Agent for Developing Teachers' Communicative Competence," Allan and Miller's (1990) "Teacher-Researcher Collaboratives: Cooperative Professional Development," Dicker's (1990) "Using Action Research to Navigate an Unfamiliar Teaching Assignment," McElroy's (1990) "Becoming Real: An Ethic at the Heart of Action Research," Oberg's (1990) "Methods and Meanings in Action Research: The Action Research Journal," Cornett's (1990) "Utilizing Action Research in Graduate Curriculum Courses," McCutcheon and Jung's (1990) "Alternative Perspectives on Action Research," Boostrom, Jackson, and Hansen's "Coming Together and Staying Apart: How a Group of Teachers and Researchers Sought to Bridge the 'Research/Practice Gap,'" and Mishler's (1990) "Validation in Inquiry-guided Research: The Role of Exemplars in Narrative Studies." This last study focuses on narrative as a model for qualitative research, a model also employed by Connelly and Clandinin [see chapters 10 and 13]. [See Beattie, 1989, for a questioning of the "practical" and atheoretical character of action research.]

In addition to narrative theory, phenomenology (Carson, 1990a, 1992a; van Manen, 1991), poststructuralism (Gauthier, 1992), and political theory (Tripp, 1990) have spawned specialized versions of action research. For instance, phenomenologist Terry Carson (1990a) asks: "What kind of knowing is critical action research?" He answers: "Despite the different forms it takes, all action research has a common intention: the belief that we may develop our understandings while at the same time bringing about change in concrete situations" (1990a, p. 167). This belief is widely shared by action researchers working from a variety of theoretical perspectives. We would add that it is an essential feature of understanding as we have employed the term in the title of this textbook. Carson's phenomenological orientation becomes clear when he writes: "action research as a way of knowing becomes a hermeneutics of practice . . . the improvement of the quality of our life together" [rather than "improvements" in an incremental, bureaucratic sense] (1990a, p. 73). "How to" guides to action research are available. See, for example, Harry F. Wolcott's (1990) *Writing Up Qualitative Research* and Carson, Connors, Ripley, and Smits' (n.d.): *Creating Possibilities: An Action Research Handbook.* Action research is often reported in case study form, which presumably allows theoretical constructs to be expressed concretely (Donmoyer, 1987a; 1990a).

Because the humanities have been especially influential in the reconceptualized field, much contemporary scholarship resembles but does not coincide with research and scholarship conducted in the humanities, especially in the fields of literary criticism, aesthetic criticism, and history, and to a lesser extent, in philosophy (especially phenomenology) and religion (especially theology). Social theory has been influential as well, especially in the efforts to understand curriculum as political, racial, gender, and institutional text. Finally, interdisciplinary areas, including feminist theory and international studies, have influenced the character of contemporary curriculum research. Methodologically, anthropology has been influential, specifically via ethnography. While we leave more specific discussion of research traditions to individual chapters on specific discourses, we can summarize what many scholars tend to regard as characteristic of research in the reconceptualized field. Thomas Popkewitz (1988) summarizes essential elements of contemporary curriculum research when he writes:

> Understanding research . . . requires thought about the intersection of biography, history, and social structure. While we are immersed in our personal histories, our practices are not simply products of our intent and will. We take part in the routines of daily life, we use language that is socially created to make camaraderie with others possible, and we develop affiliations with the roles and institutions that give form to our identities. (p. 379)

Here we are pointed to efforts to understand curriculum as political text (social structure), as autobiographical/biographical text (life histories), as institutional text, and to their intersections. Relatedly, William Schubert has noted: "I wish to argue that practical curriculum inquiry offers a research perspective that more fully embraces the democratic and personal than does research as usually conceived" (Schubert, 1986b, p. 132).

Practical or theoretical research? As we will see, for at least one tradition—the poststructuralist—the distinction between theory and practice has disappeared [see chapter 9]. As Jackson (1992a) noted, both theoretical and practical orders of research are recommended by Schwab, and it appears the contemporary field has taken his advice. Schubert (1980b) has suggested: "Surely, the question is not whether theoretical or practical research should dominate educational inquiry; rather, it is now to generate a conscious sensitivity among those who create and use research so that they might discover the degree that each mode best serves particular research purposes" (p. 23). Anticipating the development of his teacher lore project [see chapter 10] almost a decade later, Schubert (1980b) concluded: "Finally, practitioners and scholars must inquire together to discover research modes that most productively serve the massive problems confronting the daily flow of students into schools. . . . This . . . should be a central aim of educational research as we enter the 1980s" (p. 23). Joining Schubert and others focusing on teachers' "lore" or "personal practical" knowledge as sources for understanding curriculum, Hugh Munby (1987) asserted: "Practical knowledge has considerable scope as a source [for] curriculum theory" (p. 10). Working from science education and an interest in constructivism [a theory which views knowledge as constructed not merely discovered], science educator Ronald Good points to the significance of context: "To go beyond the many faces (facades) of constructivism to the inner workings of curriculum and instruction is to recognize the importance of context. The context of real students with real curricula allows the faces to become recognizable" (Good, 1992, p. 6). [For one sketch of implications of constructivism for classroom practice, see Brooks & Brooks, 1993.]

So-called practical research has its drawbacks, however. Nancy King (1986) has observed: "Researchers are ordinarily under some pressure to provide answers or solutions to the problems confronting school systems. They may believe they do not have the time or the freedom to develop the deep understanding of curricular issues required to provide an adequate response to the problems of schools" (pp. 39-40). It is exactly issues of time and freedom that have persuaded some theoreticians to distance themselves from the schools (Pinar, 1992a). Even those who work in schools, who regard teaching as research but from the point of view of teachers (Grumet, 1990b), hold sophisticated theoretical positions (Grumet, 1988b). To sum up: in the contemporary field, theory and practice are often regarded as embedded in each other. Short, Willis, and Schubert (1985) conceive of "each individual developing the responsibility to ask fundamental curriculum questions about his/her own growth and its consequences for the growth of others that reconceives the *theory into practice* problem as *practice and theory* embedded in one another" (p. 66).

Contemporary scholars rarely regard theory as prescriptive. Such a view expresses a hierarchical expert/client relationship, a vertical power structure which often breeds teacher resistance to expert-originating prescriptions. For instance, Robert Donmoyer (1989) raised several questions in this regard:

> why scholars continue to complain that most curriculum theory and research are unusable; why those who look "behind the classroom door" discover that even when a curriculum theory has been adopted and translated into official policy it normally is not implemented by classroom teachers, and why even when teachers sincerely espouse a particular curriculum theory, the gap between their espoused theory and their theory-in-use often remains wide. (p. 257)

Because each school setting, indeed, each classroom is idiosyncratic, theory cannot be developed in the university, for example, and "applied" in a school. Due to this problem of idiosyncrasy, the distance between theory and practice, in Donmoyer's view, is not to be eliminated: "the gap is unavoidable . . . not a problem to be resolved" (p. 262). He is not suggesting that research is unimportant, only that: "Because of the problem of idiosyncrasy, however, no research finding and no theory will ever generalize to every setting and to every child" (p. 264). There can be little disagreement here.

The point of research. The point of contemporary curriculum research is to stimulate self-reflection, self-understanding, and social change. Simply put, practical or theoretical research is intended as much to provoke questions as it is to answer questions. As Joe Kincheloe (1993b) suggests: "Theorizing is a tentative process of reflection about one's experience for the purpose of becoming an author of that experience" (p. 20). Sixty years earlier Henry C. Morrison, a curriculum professor at the University of Chicago, understood that practice alone cannot stand.

> For a good many years, in attempting to study the fundamentals of our art, first with schoolmasters and teachers in practice and then with university students in education, I have chiefly been struck by their desire to be told "how to do it" and by their reluctance to believe that recipes cannot be written so that he who runs may read and run quickly, and with minimum effort, arrive at pedagogical efficiency. Parallel to this impatience of school workers themselves seems to be the impatience of people who introduce themselves as "practical" men and women and call for "something that our teachers can carry out. . . ." Far from the possibility of any such cut-and-dried conception of instructional processes is the principle that from day to day, from pupil to pupil, from district to district, the problem varies and must constantly be restated and solved anew. (p. 1934, p. iii)

Morrison then calls for a system of educational thinking based on a "valid *understanding* of what education itself is" (1934, p. iii).

Critical research. Critical research tends to be identified with political discourses [chapter 5], although there are links also with racial, gender, and autobiographical discourses [see chapters 6, 7, and 10, respectively.] Joe Kincheloe (1991a) summarizes basic assumptions of critical research in ways which incorporate the interests not only of the discourses above, but the phenomenological and poststructuralist discourses as well. Consequently, we will substitute "reconceptualized curriculum research" for "critical" to imply this broader association. To be considered "critical," research must meet, Kincheloe (1991a) tells us, five requirements. First critical research "must reject positivist notions of rationality, objectivity, and truth. Critical research will reject the positivist assumption that educational issues are technical rather than political or ethical in character" (Kincheloe, 1991a, p. x). We would amend this statement to acknowledge that for strands of discourses which understand curriculum as institutional text, a technical framework remains [see chapter 13]. Second, Kincheloe continues, to be "critical," research must incorporate the perspectives of those involved in school practice in the researcher's interpretation of their educational practices. Research must attempt to distinguish between ideologically laden interpretations and those which transcend ideological disfiguration. Critical research, Kincheloe tells us, attempts to analyze "false consciousness" [misunderstanding what is reality, especially political reality] while indicating strategies for overcoming its effects. Research critically examines those aspects of the dominant social order which block educators' efforts to pursue authentically educational (rather than political and economic) goals. For example, the destructive effects of social structure or of educational or governmental bureaucracy are analyzed and their effects strategically contested. Finally, Kincheloe insists that critical research always links theory and practice. One purpose of research "is to help guide the work lives of teachers by discovering possible actions they might take if they are to overcome the obstacles social structures place in their way" (Carr & Kemmis, 1986, pp. 129-30, 162; Kincheloe, 1991a).

Incorporating a phenomenological perspective, Kincheloe writes that a "critical constructivist researcher seeks to uncover . . . the phenomenological life history of actors in education settings" (p. 196). He goes on to suggest that the researcher as life historian employs "the interaction of: 1) the phenomenology of life history (the nature of the student's experience as a discrete phenomenon, i.e., lived events just as they exist); and 2) critical hermeneutics involving the interpretation of life history" (p. 196). In the following passage the interweaving of political and phenomenological perspectives in Kincheloe's notion of "critical research" becomes clear. He writes:

> The action researcher uncovers the student's perceptual organization of the information and gains insight into who the student really is by asking a series of questions of the student and of the information obtained: 1) What aspects of the student's life does he or she choose to remember and how does ideology affect the choices? 2) How do the narrative forms chosen to relate and catego-rize events reflect ideological formulas that unconsciously construct memory? 3) What are the competing forces that are structuring consciousness and what are the psychological "fault lines" formed by the clash of such forces? 4) How does the student's perceptual organization of his or her life history with the accompanying fault lines of ideology-conflict help construct the student's relationship with the school, the learning process in general? 5) How might the teacher researcher relate to school and to teachers if he or she had a similar life history? Such research promises to grant teachers a degree of empathy with students rarely achieved in educational settings. (p. 197)

Kincheloe concludes that: "Only when we as teachers are able to rescue wisdom from the cult of the expert will we control our own professional destinies and release our students from the burden of history" (1991a, p. 198). In Kincheloe's skillful summary, we see the reconceptualized field's insistence that research is not merely the accumulation of knowledge; it supports a wider and more just distribution of knowledge so that teachers and students alike may be emboldened and enlivened.

Ethnography. Once the sole province of anthropologists, ethnography has emerged as a major mode of research in the reconceptualized field of cur-riculum, as well as in the broader field of education (Heath, 1982, 1983; Simon & Dippo, 1986). Within ethnography are epistemological and methodological differences and controversies (Roman & Christian-Smith, 1987; Eisner & Peshkin, 1990). Here we will present an introduction to ethnography, inviting interested students to pursue the subject through addi-tional readings and coursework. [For one succinct review of issues in "critical ethnography," see Lesko, 1988a, pp. 30-33.] An accessible introduction to the subject is Walter Werner and Peter Rothe's (n.d.). *Doing School Ethnography*, published by the University of Alberta, Faculty of Education, Department of Secondary Education. Noting its Greek origins, Werner and Rothe define ethnography as "writing about people; *graphy* from the verb to write and *ethnos* from the nouns nation, tribe, or people. "We are defining ethnography," they continue, "primarily as descriptions of situations, whether classrooms, hallways, playgrounds, offices or parking lots, and the relation of such situations to the larger school and community context. We conceptualize a situation in terms of two interrelating structures: 1) personal interpretations held by individual participants, and 2) interpretations and rules of behavior shared and used within a group" (Werner & Rothe, n.d., p. 15). By what methodology does the ethnographic researcher portray these two interrelating and concurrent structures?

Ethnographic methodology. Werner and Rothe (n.d.) identify three phases of ethnographic methodology. First is what they term the "pre-entry," second is the "entry," and third and final phase is comprised of "follow-up procedures" (p. 20). As for the "pre-entry" phase, Werner and Rothe list the following procedures or steps:

> distribute statements regarding ethnographers' identities, organizational affiliations, and study goals: discuss with all involved parties. The study proposal includes: a) problems/questions, purposes of study; b) methodology for data collection, analysis and reporting; c) personnel needed or involved; d) budget; e) times for procedures and submission of reports. All of these activities are a part of negotiating entry. (p. 20)

Regarding the second phase, entry (or data collection), Werner and Rothe tell us that although there is overlap among participant observation, document analysis, interviewing, ethnomethodology, and conversational analysis, each can be discussed separately for clarity's sake. Once ethnographers start their research, they need to remember that people must be consulted and perhaps negotiated with regularly. Regarding the third and final phase, follow-up or data analysis and report, Werner and Rothe list the following constituent elements: a) description (situation from an insider's viewpoint), b) validation, and c) significance. Description is a compilation of data into an overall picture of the situation; validation is the acceptance which this description has for the participants (disagreement could provide an additional focus for study), and the significance is the meaning which the description has for future activities and policy planning [see pp. 20-27].

Other ethnographers have suggested that while the "insider's viewpoint" must be represented, the ethnographer's viewpoint must be clear as well. Harry Wolcott, author of the widely-read ethnography *The Man in the Principal's Office* (1973), wrote: "My tactic has been to avoid an advocacy position during fieldwork but to take a position in my subsequent writing" (1975, p. 119). The trend today may be to share that position taken subsequently with those described, including their response to the ethnographic position in the final report.

Ethnographic research activities. Among the various categories of research activities employed by ethnographers are participant observation, ethnomethodology [ethnomethodological techniques allow researchers to describe practical everyday rules, especially rules of language, ways individuals construct their everyday lives, document analysis, interviews, conversational analysis] (Werner & Rothe, n.d.), as well as ethnohistorical research, microethnographic work, linguistic investigations, and analysis of artifacts (Heath, 1982). Wilson (1977) included nonverbal behavior and patterns of action and nonaction in acknowledging the multimodal character of ethnographic research. While ethnographic research is complex, it is possible to summarize general features. For example, central to Werner and Rothe's view of ethnography are the following principles:

1. Interpreting the social world is inherently different from describing the physical world;
2. Interpreting is a temporal and cumulative process of understanding;
3. The interpreter is an important part in the outcomes of interpretation; and,
4. Interpretation is characterized by consensual guidelines. (p. 99)

Even as a beginning student, you no doubt have read ethnographic accounts of school life. Among those ethnographies you might wish to study are Gerald Grant's (1988) *The World We Created at Hamilton High,* Nancy Lesko's (1988a) *Symbolizing Society: Stories, Rites and Structure in a Catholic High School,* Philip Wexler (1992) *Becoming Somebody,* and, of course, Philip Jackson's (1968) classic *Life in Classrooms.*

Theoretical issues in ethnographic research. There are theoretical issues involved in ethnography which curriculum scholars have elaborated. Among these issues are political questions regarding the relationships among the ethnographer and those she or he studies. In this regard, Peter McLaren (1991b) has argued that:

> field relations and fieldwork must be extended beyond the prevailing humanistic *anthropologos* that informs their central axioms, and be taken seriously within the context of the following question: Under which conditions and to what ends do we, as concerned educators, enter into relations of cooperation, mutuality, and reciprocity with those whom we research? (p. 150)

Rather than turning toward phenomenology to answer this question, McLaren turns to postmodernism and politics. This "turn" is evident in his view that when ethnographic researchers enter the field, they are entering "a field of competing discourses that help structure a variegated system of socially constituted human relationships" (p. 150). That is, a school is not just a building occupied with people; it is an idea residing in and produced by historical traditions and configurations of thought, i.e. discourses. McLaren writes: "I am suggesting a radical reconceptualization of culture as a field of discourse" (p. 151). "As field researchers," he explains, "we both actively construct and are constructed by the discourses we embody in the metaphors we enact. . . . We are, in effect, both the subject and the object of our research" (p. 152). He asks that "field researchers act with the oppressed, not over them or on behalf of them" (p. 162). McLaren concludes that "a politics of field relations must be grounded in eros, in passion, in commitment to transform through a radical connectedness to the self and the other" (p. 163). It becomes quickly clear that research generally, and ethnography particularly, are not only technical activities that can be framed and pursued apart from politics, race, gender, phenomenology, and poststructuralism.

"Culture as a field of discourse." In an essay published a year later, McLaren extended his examination of ethnography as discourse and as linked to the body. He repeated his view of a year earlier: "The critical poststructuralist ethnographic practice I am both summarizing and advocating calls for a radical reconceptualization of culture as a field of discourse" (McLaren, 1992a, p. 80). McLaren calls for a:

> concept of the body as a site of cultural inscription . . . enfleshment, that is as a site where epistemic codes freeze desire into social norms. . . . We cannot separate the body from the social formation, since the material density of all forms of subjectivity is achieved through the "micropractices" of power that are socially inscribed into our flesh. (1992a, p. 81)

Further, McLaren says: "I would go so far as to say that theoretical knowledges constitute externalized metaphors of the body . . ." (1992a, p. 82). Referring to himself and to other white, male, middle class heterosexual researchers, McLaren observes that: "metropolitan intellectuals must persistently unlearn their privilege in the context of a neocolonial world in order to engage the truth of otherness" (1992a, p. 83).

McLaren both incorporates and worries over autobiographical dimensions of ethnographic research. For instance, on the one hand, he advises that: "The field researcher needs to share with his or her subjects the discourses at work that are shaping the field site analysis and how the researcher's own personal and intellectual biography is contributing to the process of analysis" (p. 84). Apparently appreciative of the influence of life history, he says a bit further that "our identities are constitutive of the literacies we have at our disposal through which we make sense of our day-to-day politics of living" (p. 85). However, so he is not misunderstood as endorsing autobiographical research, however, McLaren warned:

> But I would caution against often fashionable calls for auto-critique through more autobiographical and dialogical writing forms that demand writers acknowledge the biographical and sociological contexts surrounding their modes of analysis. Epistemologically, reflexive writing forms can fall into the trap of assuming that any text is really a description of the author's subject experience of whatever he or she is writing about. (p. 87)

He insists that ethnographic research remain, always, political: "As critical ethnographers, we must take human agency beyond the curator's display case where lost histories are contained, itemized, and made unimpeachable by the colonizer's pen and recover the meaning of identity as a form of cultural struggle, as a site of remapping and remaking historical agency within a praxis of liberation" (1992a, p. 90). McLaren's scholarship raises fundamental questions regarding the nature and conduct of ethnographic research while illustrating at the same time one form of contemporary theoretical research in the field. Additionally, as we will see in chapter 5, McLaren's recent scholarship expresses the coming crisis in political theory.

Theoretical research. Much research conducted in the contemporary curriculum field can be characterized as theoretical. At times this scholarship resembles research done in allied fields, such as literary theory and criticism, philosophy, theology, social and political theory, and aesthetic theory and criticism. Thus the research reported in contemporary political, racial, gender, phenomenological, poststructuralist, and theological discourses resembles (but does not copy) thematically and methodologically scholarship in its antecedent disciplines. For instance, concepts such as "hegemony" and "ideology" are borrowed from social theory and then "applied" to understanding curriculum as political text [see chapter 5]. Phenomenological concepts such as "lived experience" and "bracketing" are transported to the sphere of curriculum and pedagogy [see chapter 8]. Issues of poststructuralism are applied to an analysis of structuralism in traditional conceptions of curriculum theory and development [see chapter 9]. Concepts such as "liberation theology," "hermeneutics," "cosmology," and "eschatology" have been incorporated from theology [see chapter 12]. One form, therefore, of theoretical research is the application of concepts from the arts, humanities, and social sciences to curriculum. This proximity of much contemporary curriculum scholarship to its sources is perhaps a predictable aspect of the post-Reconceptualization stage of the field. Other forms of theoretical research have moved away from their sources in the arts, social sciences, and humanities; they have accomplished a relatively conceptual autonomy of their own. Certain scholarship in gender, poststructuralist, and autobiographic discourses is reflective of research that is more autonomously curriculum research, rather than, say, literary theory applied to curriculum. We will return to these issues regarding the field's development in the final chapter.

Make it meaningful. Toward what end is contemporary curriculum research directed? In contrast to the traditional field, the contemporary field is directed toward understanding curriculum. Such understanding is not positivistic, not a mathematicized copy of a reality "out there," somehow apart from the lives and language of those who conduct research and who are the subjects of that research. Rather understanding is a "reading" of reality that reinterprets that reality, and in that reinterpretation, changes both the interpreter and the interpreted. In this respect, the point of contemporary curriculum research is not different for the university scholar than it is for the practitioner. As one practitioner has written on this subject: "for the practitioner, adopting the interpretivist logic of justification for inquiry means foregoing the aspiration to *get it right* and embracing instead ideas of *making it meaningful*" (Greene, 1992, p. 39). University scholars working in the contemporary, reconceptualized field agree.

VII
Conclusion: Paradigm Wars

As you all know, the critics triumphed.
(N. Gage, 1989, p. 6)

We have reached the end of our beginning. First, we introduced you, the student, to this textbook, and made suggestions as to how you might proceed. Next, we reviewed the genre, the tradition, in which this synoptic textbook resides, a genre and tradition which gave you your first glimpse at the history and present state of the field of American (and to an extent North American) curriculum studies. Then we reviewed conceptions of curriculum and what these conceptions have implied for the work of curriculum specialists. This review, through the work of Philip Jackson, allowed us to introduce the rudiments of curriculum history so that you may situate the subsequent discussion of research in historical context.

In section II, we begin three chapters of historical discourses, starting in 1828 and ending in 1979. While not an official start of the contemporary field, the publication of the *Yale Report* in 1828 did signal an intensifying interest in curricular matters which would lead to the publication of Franklin Bobbitt's 1918 *The Curriculum*, often cited as the birth of the contemporary curriculum field. We conclude our abbreviated review of historical discourses with the decade of Reconceptualization, 1969-1979, which, due to its significance in the formation of the contemporary field, we report in some detail. We trust that you realize that the Reconceptualization of the field did not end officially in 1979; movements rarely have sharp beginning and end points. It is true, however, that with Joseph Schwab's 1969 charge of morbundity the crisis in the field intensified, and with Philip Jackson's 1979 "state-of-the-art" address at the American Educational Research Association meeting in San Francisco, attacks on the idea of Reconceptualization ceased [until recently; see Hlebowitsh, 1993]. We might surmise that traditionalists saw the futility of further critique, as the Reconceptualization was a *fait accompli*.

The three historical chapters are to be followed in section III by nine chapters depicting the major contemporary discourses, focusing on research conducted in these sectors from 1980 to present. As has become clear in this chapter, and will become clearer to you as you spend time with this book, the curriculum field of the 1990s is a very different one from the field in place thirty years ago. The contemporary field follows the paradigm shift from curriculum development to understanding curriculum, from a bureaucratic interest in institutional or school curriculum to an intellectual interest in understanding curriculum more broadly, including but not limited to the school curriculum. Accompanying that shift were what Gage (1989) has termed the "paradigm wars," wars between the scientific tradition and perspectives associated with interpretative (a vague term which includes phenomenology and autobiography) and critical (an equally vague term which includes politics, race, and gender) traditions. We conclude this chapter with a brief review of these paradigm wars, through the eyes of one of the most prominent exponents of a science of education, Nathaniel Gage (1963, 1972).

Gage's depiction of the paradigm wars. Gage's (1989) review of the "paradigm wars" and the retreat of mainstream social science in educational research begins with an impressionistic summary of criticisms of mainstream (quantitative) social science. The search for a scientifically-grounded way to understand and improve educational practice had led nowhere. Moreover, Gage continues, even if mainstream social science had succeeded, one writer said, it would have bred ideas that "can only be implemented in an authoritarian, manipulative, bureaucratic system" (Cazden, 1983, p. 33; quoted in Gage, 1989, p. 4). Scientific educational research was dismissed as "at best, inconclusive, at worst, barren" (Tom, 1984, p. 2), and "inadequate to tell us anything secure and important about how teachers should proceed in the classroom" (Barrow, 1984b, p. 213). Alan Tom (1984) claimed that the scientific research on teacher planning was doomed to fail because:

> the teacher may change objectives from month to month or from week to week; unforeseen events—a hot day or one student's open cruelty to another—may necessitate revising plans; the demands people place on the schools can change from year to year, from community to community . . . so that the teacher cannot necessarily construct his [sic] battle plan in 1984 for 1985, in September for May, on Monday for Friday, or during second hour for third hour. (p. 71)

In fact, because the complexity of human beings cannot be captured quantitatively, the concept of "social science" is at its root an oxymoron (Gage, 1989, p. 4).

A second and related criticism was formulated by those Gage (1989) terms the interpretivists. These critics called for a focus on the "immediate meanings of action from the actors' point of view" (Erickson, 1986, p. 120). So-called interpretive researchers emphasized the phenomenological or lived experience of the persons under study. A third criticism, Gage continues, was that of so-called critical theorists who argued that most educational research had been characterized by a merely "technical" orientation animated by efficiency, rationality, and objectivity. Critical research, as we have seen through Joe Kincheloe's (1991a) summary, focuses on the relationship of the school to society, especially the political and economic character of constructions of curriculum (Gage, 1989). Writing from an imagined future, Gage acknowledges: "As you all know, the critics triumphed" (p. 6). He continues: "What ended the interdisciplinary war and brought about the present productive harmony among the paradigms? To some degree, it was the dawning of the realization that, if the social sciences did not get together, they would perish" (p. 8). This is a view a number of observers have endorsed (see, for instance, Jacknicke & Rowell, 1987). But Gage does not seem satisfied that a negotiated settlement to the "paradigm wars" is guaranteed. He worries that the ascendent paradigms—in his terms the interpretivist and critical—might vanquish the scientific tradition. What will in fact happen? Gage (1989) writes:

> The answer to the future lies with us, with you. What you do in the years ahead will determine whether the wars continue, until one paradigm grinds the others into the dust. . . . We must hope our intellectual leaders . . . will keep us from getting bogged down in an intellectual no-man's-land. (p. 10)

Gage is writing after working for decades in the area of research on teaching, which we will examine briefly as it intersects curriculum [in chapter 13]. In that area, the scientific tradition was more highly developed than in the curriculum field. In fact, in curriculum, the scientific tradition has been rather completely defeated, perhaps more completely than the good of the field might suggest (Tanner, D., 1983), although political scholars tend to accept no terms except unconditional surrender (McLaren, 1992a, 1992b). The Reconceptualization of the curriculum field from a field preoccupied with curriculum development to a field concerned with understanding curriculum, informed by theory in the arts and humanities and by social theory, has been achieved. However, as Rogan and Luckowski's (1990) review of synoptic textbooks makes clear, there are scholars working today who have yet to appreciate that the shift has occurred. For instance, while Goodlad and Su (1992) acknowledge the reconceptualist movement, they seem to have overlooked that it succeeded rather than simply disappeared:

> For a decade beginning in the 1970s and extending into the 1980s, the views of the reconceptualists appeared to be the dominant theoretical position, virtually taking over the curriculum field and replacing the highly behaviorist-driven period that preceded. There was very little attention to the more traditional and conventional commonplaces of curriculum development and organization. Indeed, the reconceptualists eschewed these commonplaces in discourse dealing with the whole of education rather than with what large number of curriculum theorists had conventionally regarded as the domains of curriculum as field of study; the reconceptualists were succeeding in their stated intent. The vigor appeared to go out of the movement during the 1980s, but the fundamental concepts are too powerful and have too long a history simply to fade away. (Goodlad & Su, 1992, p. 338)

The vigor appeared to go out of the movement because the opposition collapsed. The Reconceptualization of curriculum has occurred. Despite the views of a very few that the future of curriculum studies is uncertain (Milburn, 1992), most scholars regard the present state of the field as vital, the future exciting. But we are ahead of ourselves. Now that you know the end of the story, we return you to the beginning.

SECTION II

HISTORICAL DISCOURSES
1828-1979

Chapter 2

Understanding Curriculum as Historical Text: Creation and Transformation 1828-1927

It is time to place historical study at the center of the curriculum enterprise.
(Ivor Goodson, 1989a, p. 138)

History should provide us with a sense of identity and collective conscience.
(Daniel & Laurel Tanner, 1990, p. 25)

I
Introduction:
The Importance of History

Centrality of history. The number of studies in curriculum history has exploded during the past two decades (Kliebard, 1970, 1979, 1986, 1987, 1988, 1992a, 1992b; Cremin, 1971; Curtis, 1989; Weldon, 1970; Franklin, 1977, 1979, 1980, 1986, 1988a, 1988b; Goodson, 1981b, 1983, 1984, 1989b; Pinar & Grumet, 1981; Kliebard & Franklin, 1983; Schubert, 1980a, 1986a; Selden, 1988; Kridel, 1979, 1989, 1990b; Tanner & Tanner, 1990; Tomkins, 1986; Schwartz, 1979b; Rosario, 1979; Glanz, 1990; Hamilton, 1989, 1990; Willis et al., 1993). These followed important studies that are now somewhat dated (Seguel, 1966). There are institutional histories as well, including histories of schools of education (Edwards, 1991). A field of study does not just "happen." A field evolves over time and involves the labor of many participants. To begin to understand curriculum comprehensively it is essential to portray its development historically. The ahistorical posture of the traditional field has meant that "curriculum [has been] practiced with urgency in a crisis atmosphere that excludes contemplation of its evolution" (Hazlett, 1979, p. 131). For instance, in the current wave of school reform, collaborative and small-group work is promoted with a naive enthusiasm, without realizing it is not exactly novel (see, for instance, Miel, 1952).

Scholars now appreciate that all curriculum courses must include a significant historical component. In this section we introduce you to historical discourses but by no means would we claim to have reported them in great detail. Indeed, the two chapters upcoming are very much abbreviated, even impressionistic; we want you to meet very briefly and in the most general terms the primary figures and ideas in the pre-contemporary field. [As mentioned, we will review the decade of Reconceptualization in detail.] Our hope is you will be persuaded to read the historical studies to which we refer in their entirety.

A socio-intellectual community. The American field of curriculum has now entered a time of serious historical reflection. In addition to the studies cited above, curriculum history has constituted significant portions of recent synoptic texts, as we saw in chapter 1 (Zais, 1976; Tanner & Tanner, 1980; Schubert, 1986a; R. Doll, 1989; Miller & Seller, 1985; McNeil, 1985). Schubert describes this genre of curriculum books—the synoptic text—as encyclopedic portraits of rapidly proliferating curriculum knowledge. Unfortunately, as we noted in chapter 1, few synoptic texts—Schubert's 1986 study is a relative exception—have managed to keep abreast of the swift progress of the field since 1969. A major function of the synoptic text is to introduce students to the field (Schubert, 1986a). We take seriously this function; we intend to fulfill it by utilizing a historical perspective throughout much of this text. As a teacher as well as a student, it is essential that you appreciate that all fields of study—not just this one—represent "socio-intellectual communities" whose systematic and formalized "conversations" accumulate and change over time (Pagano, 1981).

II
The Emergence of the Field in the Nineteenth-Century: Faculty Psychology and Classical Curriculum Theory

Isolation or the failure to achieve unity was . . . the greatest failure of traditional education.
(Daniel & Laurel Tanner, 1990, p. 57)

Little, if any, standardization of curriculum or uniformity of teaching methods prevailed [during the nineteenth century].
(Jeffrey Glanz, 1990, p. 150)

The birth of a field: 1828, 1893, 1918, 1923? Many scholars locate the birth of curriculum as a field of study in 1918 with the publication of Franklin Bobbitt's *The Curriculum* (Kliebard, 1975b, 1986; Giroux, Penna, Pinar, 1981; Jackson, 1992a). Bobbitt argued for the reform of existing curricula modeled after what were then contemporary scientific notions of organization and measurement. However, his book crystallized a field that had been developing for many years. The scientific movement in curriculum, and in education generally, was responding to the earlier dominance of faculty psychology [in which the mind was regarded as a muscle to be exercised by memorization and recitation]. Charles Eliot was perhaps most visible in promoting faculty psychology in school curriculum. This rationale was succinctly expressed in two documents, the Committee of Ten on Secondary School Studies (1893) and the Committee of Fifteen on Elementary Education (1895). Some locate the birth of the field with the publications of these statements. Others choose 1923 and the Denver curriculum revision project: "According to Cremin, if the curriculum field had a beginning it was at Denver" (Tanner & Tanner, 1990, p. 197).

British scholars tend to choose European origins. For instance, David Hamilton in his study of *Curriculum History* (1990) seems to locate the contemporary field in the movement from absolutism to the Enlightenment:

> Overall, the transition from the age of absolutism to the age of Enlightenment was marked, in curriculum terms, by four processes. First, continuous attention was given to the search for new knowledge. Secondly, repeated attempts were made to develop taxonomies of knowledge (e.g. the taxonomic initiatives of Carl Linneaeus, 1707-1778) that might accommodate such new knowledge. Thirdly, such taxonomic attention led to the fragmentation (or specialization) of knowledge, as in the individual of separate *subjects*. Finally, growing attention to the concept of academic freedom—particularly after the founding of Berlin University in the early years of the nineteenth century—fostered repeated revision in the curricula of schools and universities. (Hamilton, 1990, p. 36)

Here we can see the genesis of the very notion of curriculum development in the notion of "repeated revision." New knowledge requires constant curriculum revision. The fragmentation of knowledge into systematized and bureaucratized school subjects [the history of which has been an English and Canadian interest: see Ivor F. Goodson's Falmer Press book series on the history of school subjects (Goodson, 1981b,1983, 1984,1992b; see chapter 14) can be located three centuries ago as well. Additionally, we can see the interest in taxonomies developed by Bloom and Krathwohl in the 1960s [see chapter 3]. Other twentieth-century practices Hamilton (1990) locates in European history include the notion of a teacher-proof curriculum (approximately two centuries old; see Hamilton, 1990, p. 33) and the practice of concept-mapping in science education, often associated with the work of Joseph Novak [five centuries old; see Hamilton, p. 26; see Novak,1991; Wandersee, 1990b]. Reproduction theory (and curriculum as a means of social control) is linked to the Calvinists, so this major movement in contemporary political theory [see chapter 5] is not exactly new (Hamilton, 1989, p. 16).

Hamilton (1989) chooses two dates as beginning points for the curriculum field: 1582 and 1633. He tells us that these two dates represent the earliest sources for the use of "curriculum" in university records. The earliest source of "curriculum" in the records of the University of Glasgow [Scotland] is 1633; for the University of Leiden [Holland], 1582 (Hamilton, 1989, p. 43). He continues: "In the Leiden case, for instance, it was used in the form 'having completed the curriculum of his studies.' At Glasgow curriculum referred to 'the entire multi-year course followed by each student, not to any shorter pedagogic unit'" (1989, p. 45). While acknowledging the persuasiveness of these different British and American arguments, we choose

1828 and the publication of the *Yale Report* as a reasonable beginning point for our study of the contemporary American field of curriculum.

The publication in 1828 of the *Yale Report on the Defense of the Classics* communicates clearly the faculty psychology which rationalized the classical curriculum (Sloan, 1971). This faculty psychology was characterized by an emphasis on Greek and Latin as school subjects, and by an emphasis on memorization and recitation as instructional methods. [David Hamilton (1989) has argued that a "diversity of pedagogical thinking . . . suffused the recitation label" (p. 39).] Versions of both faculty psychology and the classical curriculum are discernible in the curriculum debates of the 1980s, nearly two hundred years later. Before we turn to descriptions of the *Yale Report*, faculty psychology, and classical curriculum theory, let us review briefly conditions in the schools during the nineteenth century.

General conditions during the nineteenth century. The public school developed first in the North; not until Reconstruction after the Civil War did public schools spread throughout the South. However, major cities throughout the nation did have public schools before the Civil War. While public schools appeared in New England early in the 18th century, coming as late as 1830 in New Jersey and Pennsylvania, and even later in Maryland, Virginia, and Georgia, the use of public money for schools was confined "to the education of the children of the poor" (Tanner & Tanner, 1990, p. 33). In 1827 a law was passed in Massachusetts that required every town having 500 families to maintain a high school. By 1850, northern states, as well as a few southern states, agreed that common or public schools, that is, publicly funded, tuition-free schools for all children, not just for poor children, were essential to the well-being of a society with universal manhood suffrage (Tanner & Tanner, 1990, p. 40).

Before 1840, the common school was characterized by the following: 1) children attended school sporadically, 2) teachers had no professional preparation and tended to regard teaching as temporary employment, 3) teacher turnover was very high, 4) the duration of the school year varied with the money available to pay the teacher, 5) schools were ungraded; children of every age, who used every variety of textbook, were crowded into one room under one teacher, and 6) there was no systematic supervision of teachers (Tanner & Tanner, 1990, p. 40). By current standards these are, to say the least, difficult conditions.

Additionally, throughout the nineteenth century up to 80 children, from age 2 or 3 to older than 20, were crowded together in one room with one teacher. Such class sizes received rhetorical support: "In general, the larger the classes the greater the improvement" (Bell, 1823, *Brief Manual of Mutual Instruction and Moral Discipline*, quoted in Hamilton, 1989, p. 75). Physical discomfort was high, particularly for the younger children, who had to sit still with nothing to do for hours at a time. Teachers relied heavily upon rote methods and upon older children to provide instruction for the younger ones. Illustrative of accepted instructional procedure during the early part of the century was the widespread teaching of reading by alphabet memorization (Yellin & Koetting, 1988). It was not until the 1830s that this a-b-c method of teaching reading was made illegitimate by Horace Mann, who advocated the whole-word method. A commonly accepted curriculum principle during the nineteenth century was that students should complete the study of a subject, or learn it completely, before beginning a new subject (Tanner & Tanner, 1990). William Russell, editor of the *American Journal of Education*, in a lecture before the first convention of the American Institute of Instruction, described a typical nineteenth-century elementary school: "We see usually a number of little sufferers, confined to one uncomfortable posture, for hours in succession" (quoted in Tanner & Tanner, 1990, pp. 47-48). Certain school arrangements, it must be admitted, have changed little in 100 years (Cuban, 1983).

Faculty psychology/mental discipline: The classical curriculum. In the United States faculty psychology (sometimes characterized as "mental discipline") constituted a major rationale for the classical curriculum. Presumably, the classical curriculum contributed to a child's mental discipline. Latin should be studied, this argument went, because its study develops the mental faculties, especially mental discipline. The mind was considered a muscle whose development depended upon simple but repeated exercises. [Think of working out with weights; repetition as well as weight itself builds biceps.] Additionally, the more difficult the curricular material—the heavier the weight in the analogy—the more rapid and extensively would the mental muscle develop. Comprehension was a secondary consideration. Memorization and recitation, like repetitions of muscular motions in a gymnasium, were thought to "pump up" the brain. This notion of mental discipline dominated curricular thought during this period (Rippa, 1988). As well, it permeated the allied areas of teaching methodology, curriculum building, and administrative organization, especially during 1860 to 1890 (Cubberley, 1934). While faculty psychology continued to influence curricular thought after 1900 (and in fact can be detected in 1980s curriculum debates), its "golden age" was 1860-1890.

Herbert Spencer: What knowledge is of most worth? Somewhat independent of the classical curriculum movement was a curriculum proposal advanced by Herbert Spencer, first in England. In 1860 Spencer published in the U. S. his famous essay "What Knowledge is of Most Worth?" Spencer insisted "that the only purpose of education was to prepare for complete living." His classification of life activities, in order of their importance, are as follows: 1) those ministering directly to survival, 2) those securing the necessities of life, contributing indirectly to self-preservation, 3) those which support the rearing and discipline of offspring, 4) those which support one's social and political relations, and 5) those which comprise leisure time, satisfying tastes and feelings (Tanner & Tanner, 1990; Hamilton, 1990, p. 38). Spencer insisted that children "should be *told* as little as possible and induced to *discover* as much as possible" (Spencer, 1860, pp. 124-125).

What was Spencer's significance? David Hamilton (1990, p. 38) tells us that three consequences followed. First, after Spencer came the notion that curriculum represented a selection from available knowledge. Second, curriculum was to be determined by reference to secular rather than spiritual purposes. Finally, through the construction and delivery of curriculum, the social progress of society can be promoted. Before the Enlightenment, curriculum was assumed to be a spiritual journey; afterward, curriculum denoted as means of social engineering and progress. In the *Yale Report*, we encounter a curriculum rationale based on faculty psychology, "a systematic and detailed psychological theory developed by some of Europe's outstanding Enlightenment thinkers" (Sloan, 1971, p. 244).

The Yale Report. Faculty psychology postulated three constituent faculties or powers. First was the presence of will or volition, that faculty which enables human beings to act. Second were the emotions, those affections and passions which enable human beings to experience pleasure and pain, love and hate. Third was the intellect, or understanding, which enables human beings to reason, to think, to make judgments, and comprehend meanings (Rippa, 1988, p. 198). There was a vast literature based on these fundamental notions. One of the most cited is *The Yale Report on the Defense of the Classics* (1828). Several historical studies cite this document (Kliebard, 1986; Sloan, 1971; Cohen, 1974; Rippa, 1988; Spring, 1986).

A "thoughtful, responsible attempt to consider the place of the under-graduate college in the totality of the American educational scene" (Sloan, 1971, p. 243), the *Yale Report* expresses two key concepts in faculty psychology: discipline and furniture. The aim of education is to expand the powers of the mind and to store it with knowledge. The former of these is perhaps the more important of the two. The primary aim in a curriculum, then, should be to call into daily and vigorous exercise the faculties of the student (Cohen, 1974). The *Yale Report* stated that schools should adopt course content and teaching methods which are most likely to teach the art of focus-ing the power of attention and directing the train of thought. Curriculum should arrange, in the language of the *Report*, the treasures which memory gathers (Cohen, 1974). Habits of mind, the *Report* continued, are not culti-vated hastily; they require lengthy and continuous application. It compared the development of mental powers to those of manual powers. The "muscles" of the mind require the same routinized exercise as do those of the body (Cohen, 1974). The school curriculum based on faculty psychology empha-sized the classical subjects and disciplines such as Latin and mathematics. These were to become organized arbitrarily into age-segregated groups, an administrative convenience which later led to elaborate schemes of psycho-social and cognitive development (Klohr, 1989). In a review of curriculum making during the nineteenth century, Harold Rugg (in NSSE,1927a) noted that instruction was organized around a dozen school subjects; it employed the reading and memorizing of textbooks. Textbooks were encyclopedic compendia of facts to be memorized, by means of which the mind became muscled.

Charles Eliot and the triumph of the classical view. Charles W. Eliot (1834-1926), President of Harvard University, was a visible scholar associated with the curricular ascendency of faculty psychology. During the last decade of the nineteenth century, the National Education Association (NEA) appointed three committees to make curriculum policy: the Committee of Ten on Secondary School Studies, the Committee of Fifteen on Elementary Education, and the Committee on College Entrance Requirements. Eliot was the chairman of the Committee of Ten. These reports cast a mold for the school curriculum out of which it has yet to break free. As Cubberly (1934) observed: "The committees were dominated by subject matter specialists, possessed of a profound faith in mental discipline. No study of pupil abilities, social needs, interests, capacities, or differential training found a place in their deliberations" (p. 543). In his proposal for reform, Eliot recommended a reduction in curricular time devoted to grammar and arithmetic so that the elementary-school program could be diversified. However, the outcome of the committee's deliberations was to afford these subjects even higher priority in the curriculum than they had before. In fact, grammar now topped what had become the official list of important school subjects.

The consequence of the report of the Committee of Fifteen on the elementary curriculum was to solidify the status quo. Additionally, it is also clear that the report established what would become an important precedent, strengthening the role of subject-matter specialists as curriculum makers. Educational leaders who were opposed to classicism were distressed. For instance, Francis Parker's (the "father" of progressivism) reaction to the report (Harris' Committee of Fifteen) was bitter. In protest, he demanded that a new committee be appointed. His calls went unanswered. Eliot, faculty psychology, and classical curriculum theory had triumphed in nineteenth century America (Tanner & Tanner, 1990). Loud echoes remain today.

School subjects as the "furniture" of the mind. Curriculum concerns during the "reign" of faculty psychology centered narrowly upon what subjects should comprise the "furniture" of the mind. This question was answered by Charles Eliot and the Committee of Ten on Secondary School Studies, which convened during 1892 and published their report a year later. The report identified basic categories of furniture or knowledge (such as English) but not how specific curricular items or pieces of furniture could be rearranged. The report, written largely by Eliot, outlined four courses of secondary school study, namely, Classical, Latin-Scientific, Modern Language, and English. The major differences among these four courses of study concerned language instruction. The Classical curriculum included three foreign languages, one of which could be a modern language. The Latin-scientific curriculum included two foreign languages and one modern tongue. The Modern Language curriculum included two foreign languages, both of which were modern. Finally, the English curriculum included one foreign language, either ancient or modern. The report of the Committee insisted that sufficient curricular time be allotted to ensure that each student "can win from it [the curriculum] the kind of mental training it is fitted to supply" (Krug, 1961, p. 88).

Teachers had to ensure continuity through each of the main subjects, namely, language, science, history, and mathematics. The Committee's work functioned to curtail curricular freedom: "The freedom to build a new curriculum continued during the early decades of the public high school but was sharply curtailed by the report of the Committee of Ten on Secondary School Studies in 1893. From that point the high school was dogged by college entrance requirements" (Tanner & Tanner, 1990, p. 32). Indeed, today the secondary school curriculum is the "tail" on the "dog" which is the college/university curriculum.

Mental exercise and balance. The reports of the Committees of Ten and Fifteen, clearly consistent with faculty psychology theory, prompted vigorous public and professional discussion. Among its most prominent critics were G. Stanley Hall, psychologist and President of Clark University, and, as we noted, Francis Parker, a highly visible and early progressive educator. Their time would come, but for now center stage belonged to the classicalists, among them William Torrey Harris.

William Torrey Harris (1835-1909), United States Commissioner of Education from 1889-1906, was another (along with Charles Eliot) leading proponent of the classical curricular view from the late 1860s until 1910 and was selected to serve on the Committee of Fifteen. Harris subscribed to a social philosophy of laissez-faire and to what is now sometimes termed the cult of the individual. The school was for him a force for social stability (Tanner & Tanner, 1990). He chaired the subcommittee which focused upon the correlation of subjects, a primary curriculum question within the classical view. The influence of Harris and faculty psychology was evident in the Report of the Committee of Fifteen. Curriculum organization was to be conducted "with a view to afford the best exercise of the faculties of the mind, and to secure the unfolding of those faculties in their natural order, so that no one faculty is . . . overcultivated or . . . neglected" (Harris, 1969, p. 4).

"Five Windows of the Soul." The Committee of Fifteen specified the necessary "furniture" for such mental development. Employing faculty psychology and mental discipline theory constituted an "objective and practical" method of curriculum selection, a far superior method to the "subjective basis so long favored by educational writers" (Harris, 1969, p. 5). [Attempting to discredit theoretical opponents via charges of subjectivism will enjoy a long life in curriculum studies, as you will see.] Harris developed his curriculum theory in his *Psychological Foundations of Education* (1898), in which he described "five windows of the soul." These windows "open out upon five great divisions of the life of man" (Harris, 1969, p. 321.) These windows consisted of arithmetic, geography, history, grammar, and literature. Harris' conservatism was

evident in his preferred instructional method. He strongly endorsed the textbook-recitation approach to teaching elementary-school science over the laboratory-experimental method. For Harris, the textbook was both the instructional method and the curriculum (Tanner & Tanner, 1990). His concept of the classical curriculum was shared by other members of the Committee of Fifteen, who recommended its installation in elementary schools.

This movement toward "method" was centuries in the making: "[Scholasticism gave way to] a general move among teachers to replace individual classroom example . . . by a generalized humanist curriculum. The individualism, verging on hero-worship, of early humanism gave way in the early sixteenth century to an ideology, routine, order and, above all, 'method.'" (Grafton & Jardine, 1986, p. 123; quoted in Hamilton, 1990, p. 19). For some readers the link between generalized method and humanism might seem odd, but recall that humanism has tended to focus on the abstract "man" rather than upon concretely-existing individual men and women. So situated, Harris' interest in method and upon textbooks is unsurprising and hardly novel: " 'Method' was the catchword of promoters of humanist education from the 1510s onwards. This practical emphasis on procedure signals a shift in intellectual focus on the part of pedagogic reformers, from the ideal end-product of a classical education (the perfect orator) to classroom aids (textbooks, manuals and teaching drills)" (Grafton & Jardine, 1986, p. 124; quoted in Hamilton, 1990, p. 23). With the loss of the individual we gain curriculum standardization and social control, neither original with nineteenth-century humanists like Harris nor with twentieth-century social engineers like Bobbitt. Rather than curriculum understood as an inner journey, we learned to consider curriculum as those policies and programs implemented institutionally. But we are ahead of our story.

The primacy of an administrative interest. Each of these committees—the Committee of Ten, the Committee of Fifteen, and a Committee on College Entrance Requirements formed in 1895—focused upon administrative issues, a focus which dominated curriculum thought for eighty years and still dominates curriculum practice. Curricular issues included a) the duration of each course, b) student age at which time each subject should be introduced, and c) the articulation of various grade levels of school subjects. These committees recommended modification of the academic nature of school subjects (N.S.S.E., 1927a, pp. 58-59).

The primacy of the administrative interest must be noted. Subjects were divided according to administrative convenience as much as to academic and disciplinary integrity of those subjects. Age segregation, the creation of the concepts of "junior high school" and "middle school," followed from administrative convenience. These arbitrary organizations of school life became rationalized in administrative theory and in various developmental psychologies, such as that of Piaget and Kohlberg. The arbitrary character of these administrative organizations becomes hidden in their common-sensical appeal (Klohr, 1989a). Further, curriculum scholarship itself has been shaped by administrative concerns. This explicitly administrative or bureaucratic scholarship will be presented in chapter 13, *understanding curriculum as institutionalized text*. What is one chapter in this synoptic text was the whole book 100 years ago. At the beginning of the twentieth century, classical curriculum theory, supported by faculty psychology, dominated. On the horizon, the seeds of reform were germinating in the work of those concerned with social efficiency on the one hand, and with the experience of the child on the other. More immediate, however, was the reaction of those educators known as Herbartians, who were to play a transitional role.

III
The Herbartians

> [Herbart held] that the mere memorizing of isolated facts, which had characterized school instruction for ages, had little value of either educational or moral ends.
>
> (E. Cubberly, 1934, p. 452)

This group of American educators adopted the pedagogical views of Johann Friedrich Herbart (1776-1841), a German philosopher, psychologist, and educator. Herbart taught at the University of Konigsburg, holding the same chair in philosophy once held by the great philosopher Immanuel Kant. Herbart's thought was influenced by Kant, Hegel, and Pestalozzi (Cubberley, 1934; Schubert, 1986a). Johann Heinrich Pestalozzi (Swiss educational reformer, 1746-1827) had regarded rote learning as mere "outward show." He viewed children's minds as active rather than passive, engaged in perception, analysis, and generalization (Tanner & Tanner, 1990). Influenced by these views of Pestalozzi, Herbart was instrumental in developing education into a distinct field with specific content and methodology (Rippa, 1988). He demonstrated his concept of education in *The Science of Education: Its General Principles Deduced From Its Aims*. Modern psychology as well as education can be regarded as indebted to Herbart.

Apperception. Herbart argued that the mind functioned through powerful ideas. These ideas were active forces. Learning, according to Herbart, occurred through the assimilation of dynamic ideas (Rippa, 1988). New ideas could be assimilated insofar as they were linked with ideas already learned. He employed the term *apperception* to refer to this process. In simple terms, Herbart argued that the mind apperceives or understands new knowledge based upon already acquired knowledge. He insisted that a teacher must engage the child's *apperceptive mass* in order for the child to learn new material. The teacher must work to develop this apperceptive mass so that the child could assimilate new ideas readily and effectively. You can see that apperception conflicted with the traditional notion of memorization. Herbart held "that the mere memorizing of isolated facts, which had characterized school instruction for ages, had little value of either educational or moral ends" (Cubberly, 1934, p. 452). Clearly, the Herbartians and the classicalists were not going to get along.

Herbart believed the point of education was the development of character. To develop character, Herbart emphasized first the principle of *concentration*, i.e. the value of locating a subject such as history or literature at the core of the curriculum, and second, the *correlation* of all subjects. The function of correlation and concentration was to cultivate unity in the curriculum. The five steps included: 1) preparation—the teacher calls previous learning experiences to the student's attention; 2) presentation—the new materials are summarized or outlined; 3) association—new information is compared with what is already known; 4) generalization—rules and general principles are derived from the new information; and 5) application—generalizations are given meaning by linking them to specific instances. (Herbart, 1895; Cubberly, 1934; Seguel, 1966; Rippa, 1988; Schubert, 1986a; Tanner & Tanner, 1990). It is important to remember that Herbart insisted that education was a moral enterprise (Schubert, 1986a). He aimed to nurture a knowledgeable human being whose purpose was ethical action in the affairs of life, a view that would resurface one hundred years later in moral [see chapter 12], political [chapter 5], gender [chapter 7], and phenomenological [chapter 8] discourses. Like Pestalozzi, Herbart believed that the individual was innately "good." Education had to elicit that inherent goodness.

Herbart's theories studied. At the time of Herbart's death in 1841 his theories exerted little influence (Dunkel, 1969a; Cubberly, 1934). Herbart's work would become influential as it became incorporated in the work of others. Tuiskon Ziller was one such individual. Ziller established a school at the University of Jena to study and apply Herbart's theory, and is credited with two contributions to Herbart's theory which typified the movement that became known as Herbartianism (Dunkel, 1969a). These were *concentration centers* and *cultural epochs.* Concentration centers organized curriculum by topics. In fact, an entire year's curriculum might, in the Herbartian scheme, explore one central topic.

The second notion, that of cultural epoch, has been discussed by several curriculum historians (Tanner & Tanner, 1980; Schubert, 1986; Kliebard, 1986; Seguel, 1966). Cultural epoch is the idea that children's individual development mirror the fundamental stages of human history, from its primitive epochs to more civilized ones. In the famous phrase, ontogeny is said to recapitulate phylogeny. That is, the developmental history of the individual repeats the evolutionary development of the entire species. This quasi-Darwinian theory would continue to hold currency for some well into the post-World War II period, notably in the work of Corrine Seeds, who influenced the U.C.L.A. Laboratory school (Klohr, 1989b). While these ideas seem eccentric to us today, at the time many took them utterly seriously. Even John Dewey—the great American philosopher—would find these ideas appealing, although he expressed a number of differences and reservations (see Kliebard, 1988).

Curriculum and species history. A major curriculum question arose from the presumed parallels between individual and species history. What curriculum would be suitable for those young children whose developmental states resemble those of uncivilized, primitive humans? When would children's apperceptive masses become ready for certain subjects? Would human history be a guide in answering this question? Do cultural epochs become concentration centers? (Dunkel, 1969a). A curriculum of cultural epochs would suggest study of nomadic peoples in the primary grades and a study of the industrial epoch in the upper elementary grades (Tanner & Tanner, 1990). These questions and others like them absorbed those educators loyal to Herbart's theory.

The principle that ontogenetic or individual development recapitulates phylogenetic or race development ignored the external influence of the environment on the child. That is, in this view the major influence of the child's development is the internalized history of the human species, not the nature of his or her present family or his or her school. Such an anti-environmental view would seem to negate the theory itself, as the theory depended upon the original imprinting influence of the various epochs. Despite this apparent contradiction, Herbartians enthusiastically adopted the culture-epochs theory. Why? There were three reasons: 1) It was a theory of history, and history was regarded as the subject with the most potential for character building; 2) culture epochs theory was thought to make curriculum integration easier—epochs could serve as "concentration centers" in the curriculum, and 3) neither the principle of the logical order of subject matter nor the principle of the psychological order of subject matter seemed adequate for curriculum making. The parallel between the evolution of the individual and the race appeared to be the most economical principle for connecting subject matter with the child (Tanner & Tanner, 1990). [Moreover, educators were not familiar with Carl Jung's concept of "cultural archetype," which he asserted permeated all of human history and culture. Today educators remain unaware of Jung's (1966, 1968, 1969) work, despite a general renaissance of interest in the Swiss psychoanalyst's contribution.]

The Ziller-Rein-Jena version of Herbartianism. Many Americans went to Germany to study Herbart's ideas during the final decades of the nineteenth century. Wilhem Rein's school at the University of Jena was a popular site for such study. Cubberly (1934) observed that a number of Americans, many of whom were graduates from the State Normal School in Normal, Illinois, traveled to Jena to study that Herbartian experiment. These Americans returned to the United States loyal practitioners of the Ziller-Rein-Jena version of Herbartianism (Cubberly, 1934). Among this group were Charles De Garmo, and Frank and Charles McMurry. The books these Herbartians published upon their return from Jena to the United States introduced Herbart's ideas to the American professional education audience (Cubberley, 1934; Seguel, 1966; Schubert, 1986a). Later president of the National Herbartian Society, Charles De Garmo wrote *Essentials of a Method*, published in 1889. De

Garmo's text was the first in the United States to advocate Herbart's concepts. Charles and Frank McMurry have been characterized as initiators of the curriculum field as well as key representatives of the Herbartian movement (Seguel, 1966). The McMurrys published *The Method of the Recitation* in 1897; Charles McMurry published his revised *The Elements of General Method* in 1903.

Note that the concept of method, not curriculum, preoccupied the Herbartians. However, the concept of method was extended broadly enough that it became nearly synonymous with the concept of curriculum (Schubert, 1986a). The McMurrys believed that related thinking was the highest stage of thinking. This view of cognitive development meant that subject matter specialists would play second to those interested in the overall relationships among individual subjects (Tanner & Tanner, 1990). These texts by American Herbartians cast a shadow on the field that would not be escaped for eighty years. Curriculum historian Mary Louise Seguel expressed this influence succinctly: "[These texts focussed] professional attention on technique or method of curriculum making" (Seguel, 1966, p. 40). It would not be until the 1970s that a field concerned with *understanding* curriculum in its various aspects—rather than curriculum as a field preoccupied with curriculum-making and development—would appear.

Herbartian organizations. The American Herbartians formed the Herbart Club (1892) which later became the National Herbart Society (1895-1899). The Society published five yearbooks. In 1900 the Society's name was changed to the National Society for the Scientific Study of Education (1900-1908); in 1909 it was changed again to the National Society for the Study of Education, the name which remains today. As the organization evolved over time and in concept, the interests of its members broadened beyond Herbartian theory. In fact, Herbart's ideas failed to interest a growing number of members (Tanner & Tanner, 1980). This development was not evident in the early yearbooks. The first yearbook (1895) was edited by Charles McMurry. Included in this volume is an essay by Charles De Garmo entitled "Most Pressing Problems Concerning the Elementary Course of Study." De Garmo discussed the Herbartian concepts of correlation, concentration of studies, sequence of studies, and the correlation of departments. In his essay Frank McMurry addressed the concept of concentration. Another American Herbartian who studied in Germany and a faculty member at the Illinois State Normal School, C. C. van Liew, discussed cultural epochs. Linda B. McMurry gave a "Plan of Concentration for the First Two School Years."

A University of Chicago professor (whose work would later dominate American philosophy of education for half a century) named John Dewey (1859-1952) provided an essay entitled "Interest Related to Will," included in the *Second Supplement to the Herbart Yearbook for 1895.* Later, as we noted, Dewey criticized many Herbartian concepts. At this time, however, he served on the executive board of the Herbart Society (Kliebard, 1988). The second yearbook of the Society (1896) focussed upon the theory of cultural epochs.

Illustrating both the importance of the Illinois State Normal School to the movement, as well as its national following, contributions were made by Levi Seely of the State Normal School of Trenton, New Jersey; Elmer Brown of the University of California; John Dewey; Louis H. Gabreath of the State Normal School of Winona, Minnesota; B. A. Hindsdale of Ann Arbor, Michigan; Charles McMurry, David Felmly, and C. C. van Liew of the Normal School of Illinois. The importance of this volume for the curriculum field was the increased emphasis given to the concept of curriculum. The cultural epoch issues debated in the volume quickly became characterized as curriculum issues. However, as an organizing concept for curriculum, cultural epochs became discredited, thanks in part to Dewey's criticism: "[E]ven psychologist and child-study advocate G. Stanley Hall endorsed the view, however Dewey ... took a dim view of the culture-epoch theory and abhorred its educational interpretation" (Tanner & Tanner, 1990, p. 102).

From method to curriculum. Herbart Society yearbooks continued to appear until 1899. The primacy of Herbartian concepts diminished during this period; however, the discussion of curriculum continued. For instance, in the third yearbook (1897), the editor, Jeremiah Henks, emphasized the importance of the school curriculum in the training of citizenship (Cremin, 1969), a theme which persists to the present day (Engle & Ochoa, 1988; Stanley, 1992b). In the fourth yearbook (1898) a preoccupation with history was evident. Given the centrality of concepts such as "cultural epochs" in Herbartian theory, history had always been regarded as a subject of paramount importance, especially by the McMurrys. Other Herbartians included literature as another primary school subject. The significance of science was debated as the yearbooks continued. By 1900 the themes of these debates had shifted from "method" to "curriculum" (Tanner, & Tanner, 1990).

The Herbartians vs. the Classicists. The Herbartians vocally opposed the "mental discipline" approach associated with "Dr. Harris' Report" (N.E.A., 1895) and the Committee of Fifteen. Their opposition is credited with undermining the dominance of the classical/mental discipline point of view. Even if that opposition seems to the contemporary reader as sometimes convoluted (Kliebard, 1986), one point of contention is clear. The Herbartians insisted that Harris had misunderstood and misused Herbart's conception of correlation. A Committee of Fifteen Subcommittee, the Correlation of Studies Subcommittee, stated that the curriculum involves the correlation of the student's course of study with the world in which he lives—his spiritual and natural environment (1895). The Herbartians (particularly Frank McMurry) angrily corrected the Subcommittee, noting that correlation involved the relation of subject to subject, or student to subject to the appropriate cultural epoch (Cremin, 1969). This confrontation signaled a decline in the importance in the classical position.

Herbartians' significance. What was the significance of the Herbartians? While Herbart's theories and the American Herbartian movement are interesting in themselves, their significance for the contemporary student of curriculum is their elevation of the concept of curriculum in educational theory and in educational debates. The Herbartians' interest in the individual school subjects and their interrelationships, i.e. correlation, remains today in notions of interdisciplinarity. Foreshadowing Dewey's concern for a holistic conception of cognition, i.e. a "complete act of thought," the Herbartians worked to establish relationships among the school subjects, rather than being content with their compartmentalization. The concept of cultural epoch suggests one thematized relationship. Finally, however, the Herbartians failed to reach consensus on what would constitute a concentrated or correlated curriculum. Although they never formulated one agreed-upon plan for unifying the curriculum, and although they failed to convince the Committee of Fifteen (including William T. Harris) about the need for curriculum synthesis, they did, as we noted, elevate the concept of curriculum to a new visibility and importance. The Herbartian movement was all but dead soon after the turn-of-the-century, making it a relatively short-lived reform movement in American education.

The Herbartian movement disappears. The Herbartian character of the Society weakened. *The Fifth Yearbook of the National Herbart Society* (1899), edited by Charles McMurry, contained essays such as "Significance of the Frontier in American History, "Medieval and Modern History in the High School," and "The Social Ends of Education." Appended was a lengthy supplement concerning commercial education. A heightened interest in history was still evident, but the general emphasis had shifted. Given the lack of interest evidenced by members of the Herbart Society in Herbart and his theories, it is not unsurprising that in 1900 the society changed its name to the National Society for the Scientific Study of Education, and that by 1906 the Herbartian movement in America had virtually disappeared (Tanner and Tanner, 1980; 1990). While helping to undermine classical curriculum theory and mental discipline (i.e. faculty psychology), Herbartianism functioned as a transitional theory toward child-centeredness.

IV
Toward Child-Centeredness

The common school is the embryonic democracy.
(Francis Parker, 1894, p. 423)

By the 1890s a movement appeared that rivaled Herbartianism in pedagogical popularity. That movement was known as child study. Although labeled a fad by some and as steeped in sentimentality by others, the child-study movement gained academic respectability after 1900, when it became associated with experimental psychology. In fact, as child study achieved academic status it lost its primary identification with educational issues (Tanner & Tanner, 1990).

Colonel Francis Parker (1837-1902), whom we have mentioned as a defeated opponent of the classical curriculum generally and of the Committees of Ten and Fifteen particularly, was instrumental in developing a curriculum emphasis upon the child. In a few years' time child study became a major orientation within the field. Having failed to loosen the grip of classical curriculum theory on educational leaders and practices, by the turn of the century Parker was involved in Herbart Society debates. From all accounts, these were rather heated. Parker defended the status of science as an important subject. He insisted, in reply to critics, that science was not his exclusive focus (Tanner & Tanner, 1980). [Having studied in Germany, Parker had observed that the Germans kept the study of science out of the elementary school for many years. The reason was, Parker believed, that the Germans were fearful that the study of science would lead children to search for truth. They would then begin to understand and doubt the perfection of Germany's present social structure and government. Herbartian Charles van Liew, who had also studied in Germany, generally agreed with Parker's explanation why science had been kept out of the German curriculum.] Science was not the center of Parker's curriculum organization; the child was. But Parker's view was not individualistic and asocial. In Deweyan fashion he believed that "the common school is the embryonic democracy" (Parker,1894, p. 423).

German elementary-school pedagogy had been influenced by Pestalozzi and Froebel (Tanner & Tanner, 1990), and Parker accepted their views. Over and over again, Parker emphasized that the child represented the curricular center in his educational theory: "Our McMurry friends persist in insisting that literature and history are the center of all educational movement. I repeat that the child is the center and educational values are to be determined by what the child needs" (Parker, quoted in Cremin, 1964, p. 82). Parker perceived no inherent tension between the child and the curriculum. Like Dewey, Parker viewed the child and the curriculum as two aspects of a unitary process (Tanner & Tanner, 1980). For instance, Parker was opposed to teaching geography via the disconnected morass of facts and statistics then reported in textbooks. Instead, he recommended that the children take field trips, make mud models, and draw sketches of the landscape to learn geography. Interestingly, Parker's school at Chicago escaped the organizational schemes requiring divisions between upper and lower schools. Parker's school exposed the arbitrariness of such organizational schemes while supporting a "community of scholars" notion, an idea which encouraged collaboration of teachers across grade levels (Klohr, 1989a).

Child study advocates further undermined the once invincible position of classical curriculum theory. Additionally, as the new century began, it became clear that the classical curriculum could not meet the needs of youth in the cities or in less populated and rural areas. As Daniel and Laurel Tanner (1990) point out, the Latin grammar school—the institution associated with the classical curriculum—was hardly a democratic institution. It seemed related more to ecclesiastical autocracy. Furthermore, in the Latin grammar school no provision was made for the education of girls [see chapter 7 for a brief history of co-education].

The academy differed from the Latin grammar school it followed. From its beginning, the academy was a dual-purpose institution, organized to prepare young people for the practical duties of life and for college. Over one hundred years earlier, Benjamin Franklin argued in 1749, in his *Proposal Relating to the Education of Youth in Pennsylvania,* for secular and practical education (Tanner & Tanner, 1990, p. 62). The contrast between the two types of institutions was quite evident in instructional method as well as curriculum content: "Whereas the only teaching tool in the Latin grammar school was the particular book being committed to memory by the students, globes, maps, charts, laboratories, and libraries were used as instructional resources in academies" (Tanner & Tanner, 1990, p. 64).

High schools. Academies became high schools, and from 1827 on, high-school programs expanded. High schools were attended by a relatively small proportion of the population; indeed, until 1930, most children had completed their education when they finished elementary school. Relatively few attended high school, and of these, in the period 1888-90, only 14.4 percent were preparing for college. Thus, the curriculum for more than 85 percent of the students was being ignored by the Committee of Ten to focus on the program for fewer than 15 percent. However, by the early twentieth century the high school would become more responsive to the diverse needs of the American population. The number of secondary curricula rapidly multiplied to attempt to meet expanding social needs (Tanner & Tanner, 1990), a trend criticized recently by some (Sizer, 1984, 1989).

Rural schools. What were rural schools like during the nineteenth century? From diaries, letters (Talley, 1991), and records, a picture becomes visible. Throughout the nineteenth century and in some cases into the twentieth century, rural schools—often one-room structures—held two terms: winter and summer. While schools preferred female teachers during summer terms when older male students typically stayed home to work in the fields, male teachers were regarded as necessary for winter terms. With no field work to do, older male students attended more regularly during the winter. It was commonly assumed that a male teacher was necessary to maintain discipline in a school attended by several large boys.

The board clerk in District #3, Township #11, of Clark County, Illinois, kept a record of every teacher hired between the fall of 1862 and the spring of 1879. During this seventeen-year period there were two terms each year, with thirty-four teacher contracts signed. Of these thirty four, twenty were signed by men, fourteen by women [in contrast to urban schools where women teachers soon constituted a majority]. All fourteen women teachers taught summer terms. Salary equity for men and women teachers would wait until the twentieth century. Over the seventeen-year period, the average monthly salary for male teachers was $33; for female teachers $17 (Theobald, n.d; Talley, 1991).

Child-centered reform. Child-centered advocates endorsed some aspects of the Herbartian curriculum. Recall that the Herbartians focused upon the subjects taught (emphasizing history and literature, and later science) and their interrelationships (correlation and concentration), and upon instructional methods (five in number), and steps that would make accessible this curriculum (apperception and cultural epochs). These notions served as a bridge of transition along which the child-centered reforms could move. Indeed, many of these child-study reformers were associated with the Herbartians. Perhaps the two most visible child-centered advocates were scholars to whom we have already been introduced. One was Francis Wayland Parker (1837-1902), the second was G. Stanley Hall (1844-1924).

Parker: Father of progressivism. As we have seen, Colonel Parker shared the Herbartians' opposition to the classical curriculum identified with William T. Harris. Parker borrowed from Pestalozzi [for method] and Froebel [for a conception of the child]. Froebel believed that play was the method of development and learning for children, a view he elaborated in his *The Education of Human Nature* (1826), in which he termed school for young children the *kindergarten*, a garden where children grow (Tanner & Tanner, 1990). In addition, Parker borrowed from Herbart the doctrine of concentration.

Parker published two influential works: *Talks on Teaching* (1883) and *Talks on Pedagogics* (1894). The latter gained national attention, perhaps the first such work to do so in the United States (Cremin, 1964). Parker asserted that school was not inherently boring and mundane and that students did not need to be rigidly controlled by strict discipline. Parker affiliated with the emerging Progressive movement. Indeed, John Dewey once characterized him as the "father" of the Progressive movement. The Progressive movement gathered strength during the last years of the nineteenth century, exerting considerable influence in the 1930's. [Progressivism will be discussed later in this chapter, and in chapter 3.]

Both in Quincy, Massachusetts as Superintendent (1873-1880) and in Cook County, Chicago, Illinois as principal of the Normal School, Parker argued the case of child-centered curriculum reform. In what became known as the "Quincy system," children learned to read, write, spell, and think simultaneously. Parker's progressive experiments attracted national attention and very mixed reactions. Not a few called him a charlatan. Overall, however, Parker's progressive and experimental methods were applauded in both the general press and professional literature of the day (Tanner & Tanner, 1990). Parker viewed his work in Quincy in the "spirit of study," as a search for the natural methods of teaching, not as a system or a method per se. He pronounced Quincy an educational breakthrough, rejecting, as it did, traditional education. Parker's curriculum experiments at Quincy have been characterized as "a milestone in curriculum development" (Tanner & Tanner, 1990, p. 93).

Parker's reputation took him from Quincy to Chicago in 1883 where he served as principal of the Cook County Normal School. In Chicago, Parker and his faculty formulated ideas for the "concentration" or unification of subject matter. "Economy of energy," wrote Parker, "is the intrinsic mark and sign of all progress" (Parker, 1894, pp. 25-26). Traditional education, Parker believed, had valued quantity above quality (Tanner & Tanner, 1990). The method of quantity was "word-cramming and word-recitation; of believing and conforming . . . the method that keeps the mind from looking outside a certain definite circle; the method of implicit belief" (Parker,1894, p. 408). Curriculum developers, Parker insisted, should build on the child's instinctive learning capabilities. Parker's curriculum theory, with its emphasis upon concentration, was indebted to Herbart's principles of correlation and concentration. In the preface to his *Talks on Pedagogics* (1894), he acknowledges this debt to Herbart and the Herbartians: "The psychology of Herbart, and the doctrine of Concentration enunciated and applied by his disciples, Ziller and Rein, have been a source of inspiration and a guide in the general direction of this work" (p. iii).

Not only was the general public's response to Parker's pioneering work varied, in academic and professional circles reaction was also mixed. Charles De Garmo, president of the Herbart Society, criticized Parker, arguing that the organizing principle was not the needs of the child "but at bottom the principle of philosophical unity that binds all nature into one" (De Garmo, 1895, p. 19). De Garmo's criticisms were motivated in part by self-interest; he wished to advance a curriculum plan of his own. He explained that he was opposed to the concept of concentration, yet he worried that when a subject becomes subordinate to another subject, it loses its identity. If that occurs, then the subject's own internal sequence or organizing principles will not be made apparent to the learner. Consequently, De Garmo concluded, *correlation* of the school subjects was preferable to *concentration* on one subject or topic (Tanner & Tanner, 1990). Parker was not persuaded.

Parker as a transitional figure. The child as the center of the curriculum and the Herbartian idea of concentration remained central to Parker's concept of curriculum reform. Given his location between the Herbartians and the Progressives to follow, Parker can be regarded as a transitional figure. He employed certain Herbartian ideas and methods but insisted that he was not a Herbartian. His work at Quincy and in Chicago anticipated the progressivism of John Dewey. Indeed, Parker sounds like Dewey when he writes that the school should be "a model home, a complete community, and an embryonic democracy" (1894, p. 450). This linking of democracy and education constitutes a major element of Dewey's educational philosophy and his curricular experiments. While Parker is rightly remembered for his child-centered emphasis, his enduring concern for curriculum, illustrated in his discussions of concentration, accords him important status in curriculum history (Cremin, 1964). Even so, he is remembered more as a champion of children and an advocate of child-centered methods than as a sophisticated curriculum theorist (Tanner & Tanner, 1990).

Hall: "Darwin of the mind." G. Stanley Hall (1844-1924) also occupied a transitional place between the Herbartians and the Progressive movement of the 1920's and 1930's. Like Parker, he regarded child study as a means of educational reform. Also like Parker, Hall borrowed from the Herbartians, agreeing at one point that "ontogeny recapitulates phylogeny" (Cremin, 1964, p. 104). For this reason Hall was referred to as "the Darwin of the mind" (Hall, 1923, pp. 357-360). In 1883 he founded the first psychological laboratory in the United States, at Johns Hopkins University. In 1887 he launched the *American Journal of Psychology*, the first such journal in the United States. Like many in his generation, Hall envisioned the coming of a new era in which the intellectual elite—especially social scientists like himself —would design a better social world. The leadership position he imagined for academicians generally, and for psychologists more narrowly, would replace that of church leaders. The psychologist, he wrote:

> is called today to be a sort of high priest of souls as in an earlier age the great religious founders, reformers, and creators of cults and laws used to be, for the day of great leadership in these fields seems to have passed. If he is concerned, as he should be, with the education of the race, nation or individuals, he is not content merely to fit into existing institutions as they are today but he would develop ever higher powers, which gradually molt old and evolve new and better institutions or improve old ones. (Hall, quoted in O'Brien, 1979, p. 34)

What role would education play in this vision of progress? Education, he wrote, is *"the* one and chief hope of the world" (Hall, quoted in O'Brien, 1979, p. 34). This faith in the progress and the role of social scientists and other experts—such as educators—in its design and execution have come under severe criticism [see Lasch, 1991].

Origin of "stage" theory. Hall's status as a leader of the child-study reform movement is unquestioned. His writings appeared widely, in such journals as the *American Journal of Psychology*, *Forum*, and *Pedagogical Seminary*. Both the *AJP* and *PS* were founded by Hall, the latter periodical publishing much of his child study. Under his leadership as President, Clark University became the visible center for research and publication in child-centeredness (Cremin, 1964, p. 102). The curricular influence of his work was recorded in the growing acceptance of a developmental scheme of "stages" in the child's evolution. Herbartian influences still detectable, Hall's concept of developmental stages helped legitimate administratively convenient school organizations by grade. Contemporary fascination with "stages" associated with the work of Piaget (1977) and Kohlberg (1981) and their employment in curriculum conceptualizations can be traced to Hall's concept of child development:

> One of its goals now near at hand, and which will involve considerable change both in regard to the method of teaching every subject in the curriculum and the age at which the different subjects can be most profitably taught, is the determination of nascent periods for both mental and muscular work. We shall very soon have curves of the years when many of the chief cultural-interests begin to culminate and decline. This will enable us to say definitely which are

premature and which are belated subjects. (quoted in Strickland & Burgess,1965, pp. 86-87)

The inter-related notions of gradedness and "stages" would become taken-for-granted educational knowledge.

A faith in experimental science. If Parker's criticism of the report of the Committee of Fifteen had been sharp, Hall's criticism of the report of the Committee of Ten was vehement. The very assumptions made by the Committee were anathema to Hall. That children should be made to fit the mold of pre-existing subjects and that all children should be taught in the same way inflamed Hall. In the name of child-centeredness and in the name of experimental science, he rejected these fundamental assumptions (Kliebard, 1986). In his "The Contents of Children's Minds" (1883), Hall employed measurement and other quantitative data to support his curricular position. For instance, the content of curriculum was to be based on derived data regarding child development as determined by questionnaire and inventory (Tanner & Tanner, 1990). It is important to note that so-called experimental science and the quantification of educational experience began in allegiance with broadly humanistic goals and specifically with child-centered emphases. Not until decades later, when measurement and quantification would seem to become ends in themselves, did experimental social and behavioral science oppose the goals and methods of broadly humanistic movements, such as Progressivism. While disagreeing on many issues, the Herbartians, the child-study advocates, and the social-efficiency reformers [who will try to combine business and behavioral science] all declared their faith in the power of experimental science, and more specifically, experimental psychology, to inform curriculum development and delivery. The multi-dimensional psychology of William James (reprinted, 1985), which included attention to the varieties of religious experience, was waived aside in the surging enthusiasm for the quantified and behavioristic educational psychology. Not until the Reconceptualization of the 1970's did non-measurable and non-observable traditions of psychology, theology, and philosophy re-enter curriculum discourse.

As a social Darwinian, Hall believed that social change occurred in slow, evolutionary fashion. Education could not accelerate changes in human nature, nor could it retard them. He believed that heredity, not environment, was the essential factor in producing the fit and the unfit. Insofar as his theory of curriculum development was supported by experimental psychology and rejected taken-for-granted assumptions upon which faculty psychology was predicated, it can be regarded as a radical-progressive idea. His rationale, however, for the individualization of education was conservative. Hall was interested in individualization because he saw it supporting the doctrine of laissez-faire. How so? For Hall, the purpose of individualization was not to provide opportunities for maximal development of each individual. Rather, it was to identify the gifted child. For Hall, unlike Parker, insisted that a child-centered curriculum was a laissez-faire curriculum. It was not to be directed to broad social needs and social development. By emphasizing individual values at the expense of social values, and by nearly ignoring the role of the school in social change, Hall's shadow would be cast far into the 1920s, influencing child-centered progressive educators who saw little need for social change. Other progressive educators, such as George S. Counts, would regard this laissez-faire view as disastrous (Tanner & Tanner, 1990).

Rice: School critic and originator of comparative studies. Another major voice of opposition to the classical position, and particularly to Harris, was that of Joseph Mayer Rice (1857-1934). Rice too had studied with the Herbartians in Germany, and visited many schools throughout Europe. Upon his return to the United States, he toured elementary schools in thirty-six American cities, reporting on what he observed in a series of nine articles for *The Forum*. These articles were a stinging indictment of the American public schools. Every aspect of the public system was criticized, especially the quality of the teachers he had observed. Despite intense counter-criticism from many school officials, including teachers, Rice continued his exposé of American schools.

Allowing that some schools were not as poor as others, he began comparative studies, then a new form of educational research. In fact, in addition to his reputation as a critic of American schools, Rice is remembered as the founder of comparative methodology in educational research (Kliebard, 1986). He is also credited with starting the testing movement in 1897. Convinced that opinions about educational achievement were only opinions, Rice tested the spelling ability of students in various schools in New York City. His methods of testing were simplistic, but more sophisticated methods were soon introduced, as testing gained credibility and popularity. In the following decade, Binet introduced the intelligence test and psychologist Edward Lee Thorndike developed the achievement test. Thorndike published *An Introduction to the Theory of Mental and Social Measurements* in 1904, and the American obsession with testing and measurement began (Nelson & Watras, 1981).

V
Scientific Curriculum Making for Social Efficiency

> Only as we list the errors and shortcomings of the human performance in each of the fields can we know what to include and to emphasize in the directed curriculum of the schools.
>
> (Franklin Bobbitt, 1918, p. 52)

As the first decade of the twentieth century closed, faculty psychology, weakened after battles with Herbartianism, fell victim to a triumphant experimental psychology. While Hall was instrumental in early skirmishes between the two forms of psychology, it was Edward L. Thorndike (1874-1949) who is most identified with the ascendancy of experimental psychology in education. Indeed, Elliot W. Eisner, himself a major figure on the contemporary scene (see chapters 1, 3, 4, 11, and 13) has observed that Thorndike and Dewey were the two most intellectually dominant figures in the field during the first several decades of the twentieth century. He further noted that given that Thorndike and Dewey dominated the intellectual tone and direction for inquiry into education, they also influenced the assumptions and practices of the curriculum field (Eisner, 1985a). This estimate of the scale of Thorndike's influence is shared by most educational and curriculum historians (Kliebard, 1986; Schubert, 1980a, 1986a; Spring, 1986; Rippa, 1988; Franklin, 1986; Krug, 1964; Seguel, 1966).

Thorndike and the triumph of experimental science. Thorndike was a student of William James. Like James, he discredited faculty psychology and mental discipline. James' experiments had failed to show any improvement in the faculty of memory as a result of memorization. Clearly, if memory could not be improved by memorizing it could hardly be rationalized as a major curriculum component (Kliebard, 1986). Thorndike continued James' attack on faculty psychology and promoted an experimental science of psychology no longer tied to philosophy (on which point he broke with his mentor). Thorndike found that no one discipline (be it Latin or Greek or mathematics or any other subject) was more likely than any other discipline to develop the mind. Rather than a matter of mental discipline, learning was subject, even task specific (Tanner & Tanner, 1990). To "prove" these views, the new science would adopt the research methods of the physical sciences, and thereby satisfy the demands of objectivity and verifiability. Education itself must be scientific as well, grounded in the foundation provided by the physical, biological, and social sciences, especially psychology (Clifford, 1962). Thorndike promulgated these fundamental notions successfully from his position at what was then (and would remain for more than half a century) the nation's leading center for research and graduate training in education, Teachers College, Columbia University in the City of New York. Thorndike had joined the Teachers College faculty in 1889, and remained there for the duration of his career.

Origin of behaviorism. Thorndike's major opus was *Educational Psychology*, published in 1913. It would influence the field for decades to come. In direct opposition to the mental disciplinarians, Thorndike advocated a stimulus-response behavioral psychology. He believed that scientific knowledge of stimulus-response behavioral patterns would enable educators to alter human behavior so that it would come closer to coinciding to humankind's fundamental aspirations: "It is a first principle of education—to utilize any individual's original nature as a means of changing him for the better—to produce in him the information, habits, powers, interests, and ideals which are desirable" (Thorndike, quoted in Rippa, 1988, p. 200). In prophetic words, Thorndike continued: "Education is a form of human engineering, and it will profit by measurements of human nature and achievement as mechanical and electrical engineering have profited by using the foot, pound, calorie, volt, and amphere" (Thorndike, 1922, p. 1). With these views behaviorist psychology was born.

By reducing each human action to its smallest unit, that of stimulus and response, Thorndike and later John B. Watson (Watson, et al., 1917), another major behaviorist, sought to establish the principles of human behavior that would permit its prediction. Experimentalism replaced speculation as Thorndike and Watson denied any role for consciousness in this new psychology (Nelson & Watras, 1981). Neither Watson nor Thorndike understood the "philosophical posture" (Clifford, 1968, p. 413). Watson (1917) wrote: "The problem of the schoolroom and of the laboratory is to find out what an individual can instinctively do and what he can be trained to do and the methods which will lead him most easily and quickly to a given set of ends" (Watson, Jennings, et al., 1917, quoted in Nelson & Watras, 1981, p. 63). This means-ends, calculative thinking would achieve widespread currency with those who understood curriculum as institutional text.

Response = learning. Thorndike's conception of the stimulus-response relationship was simple. He insisted that whatever behavior constituted the child's response to a particular stimulus indicated the content of that child's learning. In a phrase, response = learning. This conception of learning would permit the quantification of responses, i.e. learning, for scientific study. Human experience would then be mathematicized. The field of educational statistics appeared, applying statistical principles and methods so that responses could be judged for probability, compared, tabulated, ordered and correlated. The results would presumably give educators an improved, scientific basis for determining the effectiveness of teaching and learning (Seguel, 1966). This view of learning persists to the present day, sometimes in modified and more sophisticated forms. Behaviorism and its social engineering variations have been systematically rejected by many contemporary curricularists, for epistemological, political, and moral reasons which we outline in chapters 4, 5, 7, 8, and 9.

Mind as machine. For Thorndike and his growing number of experimental psychologist colleagues, the human mind was a machine with thousands, indeed, millions of individual connections, each containing a message which may have no logical relationship with other messages (Kliebard, 1986). [This concept of mind persists in modified form in contemporary conceptions of artificial intelligence.] For Thorndike, then, the human mind became a behavioral instrument which could be used to modify human nature and its environment (Rippa, 1988). To aid in this work Thorndike instituted the concept of psychological measurement, enabling educators to quantify the concept of intelligence. Individual pupil's potential for school success would then be predicted upon knowledge of these measures. Thorndike began teaching early versions of these ideas in 1901 in a child study course. This course involved the testing of "mental functions" and overall progress of children in the experimental schools at Columbia University. In 1902 he began teaching a course on educational statistics. His *An Introduction to the Theory of Mental and Social Measurements* (1904) became a bible to a generation of educators aspiring to establish a scientific practice of curriculum and instruction (Seguel, 1966).

Experimental science and social efficiency. Thorndike published more than five hundred books and articles by the end of his career (Clifford, 1962). His concept of mind, his experimental concept of psychology, and his faith in statistical research and measurement functioned to legitimate another emerging reform movement, the social efficiency movement. Faculty psychology was now buried and experimental psychology would marry social efficiency. Their "children" would be the schools our parents and we ourselves attended in the 1950s, 1960s, and 1970s, the curriculum we studied.

Thorndike's influence, then, has been enormous. What was he like? How did he live? A student of Thorndike recalls his mentor:

> From breakfast to dinner, Thorndike was a scientist concerned with the expansion and integration of knowledge. The second Thorndike came to life toward evening—Thorndike the inventor. Most of the materials he developed for schools he designed and constructed during the evening hours. That is what he did for relaxation, if one can call it that. (Travers, 1987, p. 47)

Unlike some ideologues today, Thorndike did not produce passive adherents to his point of view. His student recalls: "A few [of those who worked with Thorndike] were deeply influenced by him, but it was not the kind of influence that led to the establishment of a Thorndike school of psychology along connectionist lines. His influence came more in the message that in order to be a productive thinker, one had to be totally immersed in one's work" (Travers, 1987, p. 49). Evidence of this observation is that one of the great humanistic psychologists of the 1960s—Abraham Maslow—was a student of Thorndike's (Travers, 1987).

The junior high school. During this time of Thorndike's ascendency, the junior high school was born. The first junior high schools (initially called intermediate schools) were established in Berkeley, California, and in Columbus, Ohio, in 1909, and in Los Angeles in 1910. The appearance of the junior high school was foreshadowed by the recommendations of the Committee of Ten, who had recommended the introduction of secondary-school subjects in the 7th and 8th grades. Advocates argued that the junior high school was supported by the finding of G. Stanley Hall and others that early adolescence is a period of changing and emerging interests. There may have been an economic factor at work as well. In Columbus, for instance, junior high school teachers could be paid less than high school teachers because they were on the elementary-school teachers' pay scale. Many cities at this time had dual salary schedules. Regardless of the reason for their appearance, it is true that the curriculum of junior high schools could be more experimental than high schools. Beginning with the report of the Committee of Ten, high schools had their curriculum dictated by the colleges and universities. Junior high schools remained relatively free of that restraint (Tanner & Tanner, 1990).

The Committee on Economy of Time. Created by the National Education Association's (NEA) Department of Superintendence in 1911, the Committee on the Economy of Time studied ways to increase efficiency in the schools. The first task the Committee faced was to find out what in fact was being taught. From that investigation, recommendations were made. The result of the Committee's work was curriculum making by common denominator. To illustrate, in his report on arithmetic, Walter Jessup of Iowa State University noted that there was allocated no standardized amount of time for arithmetic instruction across cities. Jessup recommended that the time devoted to arithmetic in the various grades not exceed the median time expenditure throughout the country.

The Committee's second task was to recommend changes in the content of the curriculum based on the principle of social utility. Cremin (1961) noted the Committee had concluded what social utility was by defining the goals of education in terms of school practice as it was. By proposing a curriculum that would accommodate youngsters to existing conditions, little emphasis was placed on improving curriculum. This result was hardly progressive or Deweyan, however much it was construed as such in some circles. Daniel and Laurel Tanner (1990) characterize the Committee on the Economy of Time as "a reformist concept with a conservative outcome" (pp.185-187).

The eugenics movement. Imported from Great Britain where it was created by Charles Darwin's cousin, Francis Galton, the eugenics movement—which accepted the dominance of heredity over environment in human progress—gained a surprising number of adherents in the United States. The Galton Society, which counted among its members Thorndike and outright advocates of racism such as Madison Grant, endorsed biological determinism. Steven Selden (1988) reports that: "One early curriculum leader, for example, wrote of students of 'worm eaten stock,' and another, an early proponent of education for the gifted, supported 'eugenic marriages'" (p. 52). Unfortunately, the eugenics movement was not limited to just a few academic and educational leaders. During the 1920s the American Eugenics Society sponsored "Fitter Families" contests at state fairs across the United States; winners were presented with medals bearing the inscription, "Yea, I have a goodly heritage." Championed as two "new sciences," eugenics and education were regarded as interdependent. The field of education needed a scientific basis, and eugenics, its advocates insisted, was able to supply it (Selden, 1985). In the first decades of the twentieth century, eugenics advocates held posts in important agencies, such as the U. S. Bureau of Education and the National Educational Association (NEA), which in 1916 formed a Committee on Racial Well-Being (Selden, 1988).

Taylor and scientific management. If Edward Thorndike provided the psychological legitimation for the social-efficiency movement, Frederick Winslow Taylor (1856-1915) provided methodological guidance via his theory of scientific management. Taylor had devised this theory early in the twentieth century. It was predicated upon economic practice, more specifically the structure of the workplace. Labor had evolved from a nineteenth-century emphasis upon craft guilds, an economic structure which required a master craftsman who taught apprentices his knowledge of the total production process. By the twentieth century this structure was rapidly disappearing, replaced by large factories wherein labor was specialized and routinized. Accompanying such a division of labor was a call for "scientific" management to supervise and control the various divisions. In this new era of mass production, effectiveness and efficiency were paramount. Scientific management asserted it could guarantee them.

In this scheme, all managers were directed to accumulate knowledge of a specific division of labor by identifying and analyzing the various tasks or components of tasks involved. After each segment of the production/labor process had been broken into its constituent parts, it could be reconceived to assure its more effective execution. This process became known as "task analysis." Taylor stipulated: "The managers assume .. the burden of gathering together all of the knowledge which in the past has been possessed by the workmen; (knowledge of the entire production process) after which they (the managers) must classify, tabulate, and reduce this information to rules, laws, and formulae" (Taylor, quoted in Braverman, 1974, p. 112; Callahan,1962).

Goals and procedures. Essential to scientific management was the specification of the task to be performed. In his major work, *Principles of Scientific Management* (1911), Taylor characterized the "task idea" as the "the most prominent single element in modern scientific management." At least one day in advance, management must provide workmen complete instructions regarding each detail of the task to be performed the following day. Production goals as well as means (or procedures) to achieve those goals were to be made explicit (Taylor, in Braverman, 1974, p. 118). Managers who were to employ "task analysis" would write these instructions. Individual tasks would be divided into their smallest increments. Increments would then become sequenced as work instructions. It is easy to see how social-efficiency curricularists might apply these ideas to curriculum planning and delivery. Indeed, they did, and the legacy of their work and their influence remains today, as school subjects are sequenced and divided into parts.

Curriculum as assembly line. Social efficiency experts viewed their work as a "mission" (Kliebard, 1986). Rather than viewing curriculum as an opportunity to develop mental discipline, as "windows of the soul," or as organized around the needs, interests, and abilities of the child, curriculum became the assembly line by which economically and socially useful citizens would be produced. Social utility, for these reformists, became the sole value by which the curriculum would be judged (Kliebard, 1986). What was meant by efficiency? Certainly, discipline and hard work were meant. As well, it suggested notions of increased productivity and profits which mass production made possible. The idea of harmonious human relationships as necessary for the smooth functioning of the workplace was also included (Franklin, 1986), an idea even more emphasized during the 1980s when the corporation rather than the factory became the model for school reform (Fiske, 1991; Pinar, 1994).

As we noted at the beginning of this chapter, John Franklin Bobbitt's (1875-1956) *The Curriculum* (1918) is widely cited as the formal date of genesis of the curriculum field (Giroux, Penna, & Pinar, 1981; Tanner & Tanner, 1980; Schubert, 1980a, 1986a; Kliebard, 1979, 1986; Franklin, 1986). Although several of Bobbitt's main concepts were mentioned in William Chandler Bagley's (1874-1946) *The Educative Process* (1905), Bobbitt's text established them as "facts." In 1905 Bagley had asserted that the aim of education was the production of the socially efficient individual (Bagley, 1905), a position contradicting the classical/mental disciplinarian position that the mind developed as a muscle by memorization and recitation of complex subjects such as Latin. In 1905 Bagley's book did not spell the annihilation of the classical position. [Indeed, it will resurface, albeit, in different form, in the 1980s; see Bloom, 1987; Hirsch, 1987]. But by 1918 the social efficiency position was so plausible, however, it seemed to constitute a "fact."

Franklin Bobbitt. Awarded the Ph.D. degree from Clark University (where G. Stanley Hall was President) in 1909, Bobbitt began a long and illustrious career at the University of Chicago. In 1910 Bobbitt offered a course entitled simply "Curriculum," which appears to have met with great success (Kliebard, 1986). The "discursive shift" from method to curriculum was underway, and was further legitimized by the publication of *The Curriculum* in 1918. A second legitimizing event demarcating the formation of the curriculum field was the establishment in 1938, at Teachers College, Columbia University, of a Department of Curriculum and Teaching. This Department would play an important and historic role throughout the history of the field. The University of Chicago, Teachers College, Columbia University, and Ohio State University were to occupy institutional center stage in the history of the field during the first five decades of the century. [By the fifth decade the University of Wisconsin had become prominent as well.] Another important contribution to the development of the field at this time was the linking of curriculum and supervision by Hollis Caswell (1901-1988) [see chapter 3], a link which would later lead to the establishment of the Association for Supervision and Curriculum Development, now the largest professional organization of curriculum specialists (Klohr, 1989a) [see chapters 3 and 4].

Prior to the publication of *The Curriculum*, Bobbitt focused on ways to increase the efficiency of the school. In a 1912 article published in the *Elementary School Teacher*, entitled "The Elimination of Waste in Education," Bobbitt (1912) decried the fact that the typical school plant was used only

50% of the time. To increase efficiency and economy, Bobbitt advocated that schools should be kept open Saturdays, Sundays, and summers. In a 1915 article entitled "High School Costs," Bobbitt (1915a) reasoned that if the average cost of an English program is $50 per 1,000 student hours, and a particular school is spending $75 on an English program that is yielding only average results, then that program needs evaluation, i.e. revision. On the other hand, if only $30 is being allocated, perhaps the school is underinvesting in English. Like the work of the Committee on the Economy of Time, this is curriculum-making by common denominator. Bobbitt also wished to increase the efficiency of the school building by making it available to the larger community. In a 1911 article entitled "A City School as a Community Art and Musical Center," Bobbitt suggested that the top floor of the school could be used as an art museum; school could be used as community culture center. Schools should provide leadership in educating the public in profitable use of leisure time (Bobbitt, 1911). Indeed, Bobbitt argued in favor of making the school the recreation center for the city (Bobbitt, 1912).

School as preparation for the adult world. Although *The Curriculum* is the most cited and discussed of Bobbitt's work, his *What the Schools Teach and Might Teach* (1915b) is important as well. Published as one of twenty-five sections of the "Education Survey of the Cleveland Schools" conducted by the Survey Committee of the Cleveland Foundation, it specified what ought to constitute the curriculum in specific schools. Bobbitt became interested in the general relationship between the school curriculum and the so-called adult world. He came to believe that what was needed in schools was a curriculum that led directly to participating in the adult world (Schubert, 1980a). This notion of "life adjustment" was fundamental to *The Curriculum*, and it would influence curricular thinking for decades. The book had been written for use in teacher training institutions as an introduction to curriculum theory, for both prospective and practicing teachers. The influence of both Thorndike and Taylor in the book is evident. Bobbitt insists that effectiveness, efficiency, and economy are crucial concepts for the curriculum maker. His central tenet was that curriculum must directly and specifically prepare students for tasks in the adult world. The work of the curriculum maker became studying the adult world to determine the major tasks or activities comprising it. These tasks would then comprise the curriculum.

Task analysis. The parallel between Bobbitt's conception of curriculum analysis and development and "task analysis" as devised by Taylor for so-called scientific management is obvious. Bobbitt embraced the parallel, arguing that previous educational objectives were tantamount to no more than "vague guesses," and the means and methods used to achieve them were inevitably "vague guesses" as well (Bobbitt, 1918). In *The Curriculum* Bobbitt illustrates this so-called scientific curriculum making by elaborating, for example, a task analysis of the grammar curriculum. He cited a study regarding grammatical mistakes made by students. Their errors were counted and those made most frequently inspired the grammar curriculum. This study was entitled "A Course of Study in Grammar Based on the Grammatical Errors of School Children in Kansas City, Missouri"; its co-authors were W. W. Charters and Edith Miller. Charters would later become famous for the activity analysis procedure of curriculum construction.

Experience directed and undirected. Bobbitt used illustrations from other fields as well, including agriculture and vocational preparation. "Only as we list the errors and shortcomings of the human performance in each of the fields," he wrote, "can we know what to include and to emphasize in the directed curriculum of the schools" (Bobbitt, 1918, p. 52.) The concept of "directed curriculum" was crucial for Bobbitt, but as important as the directed curriculum was in the overall academic preparation of the child, it was not the complete curriculum. In addition to the directed curriculum, he asserted, there is "undirected experience." Bobbitt believed educators must be concerned with both realms. In his definition of curriculum, which we reviewed in chapter 1, he indicated why. The curriculum may, in his view, be defined in two ways: 1) it is the entire range of experiences, both directed and undirected, concerned in the unfolding of the abilities of the individual; or 2) it is the series of consciously directed training experiences that the schools use for completing and perfecting unfoldment. Bobbitt noted that our profession uses the term in the latter sense. Anticipating the contemporary field it would seem, Bobbitt (1918) speculated:

> But as education is coming more and more to be seen as a thing of experiences, and as work and play experiences of the general community life are being more and more utilized, the line of demarcation between directed and undirected training experience is rapidly disappearing. Education must be concerned with both, even though it does not direct both. (p. 43)

Task analysis applied. The curriculum of schools would encompass both orders of experience. In Bobbitt's view, the curriculum becomes a series of activities or experiences (the distinction between the two was not yet significant) the child undergoes on the way to attaining scientifically-determined objectives. Bobbitt refined this process in a number of works which followed. For instance, he applies these ideas of curriculum organization in *Curriculum Making in Los Angeles* (1922), where he enlisted the help of 1200 teachers to draw up lists of desirable traits. After consensus was reached, ten categories were listed, including, for instance, "physical efficiency," under which we find:

> 103. A continually maintained reservoir of vital energy as abundant of one's hereditary potentialities will permit. . . . 111. Ability to employ setting-up exercises for corrective or emergency purposes. (quoted in Kliebard, 1979, pp. 219-220)

His utilitarian orientation (to us it appears nearly an obsession) was further evident in his conclusion: "There is no sufficient warrant for teaching the growing citizens of this city at public expense to speak and write French" (quoted in Kliebard, 1979, p. 220). In *How to Make a Curriculum* (1924) his orientation is less theoretical than prescriptive and methodological. In fact, a 1926 book can be viewed as an application of the theoretical constructs developed in the 1918 book. In *Curriculum Investigations* (1926) Bobbitt continued his discussion of applications of the social-efficiency perspective.

Cardinal principles of secondary education. In addition to the publication of Bobbitt's *The Curriculum,* the year 1918 also saw the publication of *The Report of the Commission on the Reorganization of Secondary Education* (National Education Association, 1918). Five years in the making, the *Cardinal Principles of Secondary Education* was met with applause, in contrast to the previous and controversial report issued by the N.E.A., the Committee of Ten Report (1893). The Commission was chaired by Clarence Kingsley, a graduate of Colgate University and a teacher of mathematics at the Manual Training High School in Brooklyn, New York. The *Cardinal Principles of Secondary Education* provided additional support for the social-efficiency movement. Relatedly, it argued for increased emphasis upon vocational education which, by 1907, had become a dominant educational issue (Tanner & Tanner, 1990). The report represented "the capstone of the quarter century of furious efforts at educational reform that began with the Committee of Ten" (Kliebard, 1986, p. 113). As well, the report was significant for the developing curriculum field (Tanner & Tanner, 1980; Schubert, 1980a, 1986a; Cremin, 1955; Krug, 1966; Spring, 1986; Rippa, 1988).

A vocational emphasis. The report issued seven principles of education. These were: 1) health, 2) command of fundamental processes (i.e., basic skills), 3) worthy home membership, 4) vocation, 5) citizenship, 6) worthy use of leisure, and 7) ethical character. The impact of the report was enormous and twofold. First, the vocational emphasis in school curriculum was greatly expanded. Second, each of the seven principles could be analyzed in terms of tasks. The classical curriculum orientation was largely ignored in the enthusiasm for social efficiency (Kliebard, 1986). Sixty years later vocational (and economic) rationales for curriculum orientation remain commonsensical and taken-for-granted (Fiske, 1991).

How is this document remembered? Cremin (1955) declared that "most of the important and influential movements in the field since 1918 have simply been footnotes to the classic itself" (p. 307). In effect, the Report became the basis for curriculum development for years to come. In contrast to classical curriculum theory or child-centeredness, the Commission wrote: "Secondary education should be determined by the needs of society to be served, the character of the individuals to be educated, and the knowledge of educational theory and practice available" (Commission on Reorganization of Secondary Education, 1918, p. 7). The cardinal principles represented a partial declaration of independence by the high school from the domination of college-entrance requirements. Also of great significance is that the commission approached the problem of the curriculum through a study of adolescent and social needs rather than through Bobbitt's analysis of adult activities. The raison d'etre of the secondary school was not exclusively preparation for college or for careers, but to give reality to the ideal of democracy. This was the primary theme of the report and, not coincidentally, the primary theme of Dewey's (1916) *Democracy and Education,* published two years earlier (Tanner & Tanner, 1990).

The Commission promoted two principles regarding curriculum specialization and unification. First, the more the time for curriculum variables, the more purposefully should time be allocated to curriculum unification. Second, the more differentiated the curriculum becomes, the more important is the students' social interaction. The Commission endorsed the notion of teaching subjects variably, according to the needs and interests of pupils. In sum, it is clear that the Commission endorsed a notion of secondary education for all youth. That vision would influence developments in secondary school curriculum for the remainder of the century (Tanner & Tanner, 1990, p. 123).

Sociological determination of educational objectives. David Snedden was the "most eminent of the new breed of educational sociologists" (Kliebard, 1986, p. 112). Snedden became a visible proponent of social efficiency and more particularly of vocational education. In his *Sociological Determination of Objectives in Education* (1921), Snedden discussed the importance of determining objectives via scientific or empirical means rather than by reliance "on faiths and beliefs—often hardened into dogmas as to educational values, and the ex-parte creeds of subject matter specialists" (Snedden, 1921, p. 5). Like Bobbitt, Snedden considered job or task analysis as the primary means by which to determine curriculum. Given the necessary means, it would certainly be practicable to ascertain, with considerable precision, the quantity and kind of mathematical knowledge and skill required for the successful performance of the hundreds of vocations whereby people live (Snedden, 1921). Such sociologically derived data would determine curricular objectives. Also for efficiency's sake, Snedden advocated the division of children into specific groups. He distinguished between "normal" children and "variant" children and elaborated empirical means for establishing differing objectives for these groups. Later, in a number of articles, Snedden specified, in a detailed way, these so-called "case groups" and their respective curricula (Snedden, 1923, 1924, 1925). Snedden's work provided an additional and specifically sociological rationale for the social-efficiency movement.

W. W. Charters. Werret W. Charters' (1875-1952) *Curriculum Construction* (1923) represents a major statement of the social efficiency orientation. Charters was not an administrator like Bobbitt. Rather, he was a teacher educator who had, oddly it may seem, studied under Dewey at Chicago and who later claimed that Dewey had influenced him considerably (Seguel, 1966). [Dewey, however, expressed reservations regarding Charters' academic abilities and prospects.] Although the author of several articles and *Methods of Teaching: Developed from a Functional Standpoint* (1909), it was *Curriculum Construction* which established Charters' reputation as a nationally visible curricularist associated with the social efficiency movement (Seguel, 1966; Eisner, 1985a; Tanner & Tanner, 1980; Schubert, 1980a, 1986a; Kliebard, 1986; Franklin, 1986). His major contribution is the elaboration of a theory of activity analysis for curriculum development. Unlike Bobbitt, Charters viewed his method as providing the means but not the ideals of curriculum. However, like Bobbitt's work, Charters' functioned to shift the focus of curriculum theory from a preoccupation with content to a preoccupation with the means for determining that content. Method took priority over content, an important shift in curriculum theory that persists to the present day. Herbert Spencer's (1860) fundamental curriculum question—"what knowledge is of most worth?—became by the 1920s "by what means shall we determine what we will teach"? Professionals interested in curriculum were not taught to study the curriculum but rather how to develop curriculum. This organization of curriculum study around the concept of development shaped the field in profound ways. Not until the 1970's did the primacy of curriculum development as a category decline.

A procedure for curriculum development. Charters argued that curriculum was comprised of those methods by which objectives are determined. Thus, the content of curriculum is always methodological in nature. What was Charters' method of determining the curriculum? That method was activity analysis, a concept he borrowed from scientific management. Employing this concept, Charters elaborated a procedure for curriculum development:

> First, determine the major objectives of education by a study of the life of man [sic] in its social setting. Second, analyze these objectives into ideals and activities and continue the analysis to the level of working units. Third, arrange these in order of importance. Fourth, raise to positions of higher order in the list those ideals and activities which are high in value for children but low in value for adults. Fifth, determine the number of the most important items of the remaining list which can be handled in the time allotted to school education, after deducting those which are better learned outside school. Sixth, collect the best practices of the race in handling these ideas and activities. Seventh, arrange the material so obtained in proper instructional order, according to the psychological nature of children. (Charters, 1923, p. 102)

Charters had developed a basic procedure for curriculum construction, which he then applied to fields as varied as secretarial science, pharmacy, librarianship, veterinary medicine, teacher training, and those activities associated with being a woman (with curriculum development conducted at Stephens College, Columbia Missouri, at this time a women's college).

A well-known sociologist of education, Charles C. Peters, extended Charters' and Taylor's notions to curriculum development in Christian education: "We shall need to pick out a hundred, or a thousand best Christians and study their characteristics. We shall need to observe their habits, their ideals, their beliefs, their attitudes, etc., and compare these so as to ascertain what ones are common to all, or nearly all (and hence essential to Christianity) and what ones are merely accidental or personal" (quoted in Kliebard, 1979, p. 213). Not until the publication in 1949 of Ralph Tyler's *Basic Principles of Curriculum and Instruction* would a specific procedure be elaborated that would influence curriculum development activity on such a wide scale as did Charters'.

Accompanying the ascendancy of "scientific curriculum making" was the establishment of curriculum experts. As director of the educational research bureau at Ohio State University, Charters' oversaw a number of lucrative consultancies (Rosenstock, 1984). Experts were hired by states and school districts to assess the current state of curricula and to devise procedures by which curriculum could be developed scientifically. Texts specifying these procedures which focused upon particular levels of schooling (i.e. elementary, junior high, senior high) followed. [During the period 1910-1919 a total of 13 curriculum texts were published; during the decade of the 1920's that number jumped to 87.] School and specifically curriculum surveys, the most visible of which were conducted by Caswell and Campbell, were commissioned (Klohr, 1989a). The national interest in curriculum intensified.

Curriculum as a business plan. The social-efficiency movement's imprint on American educational debates is still evident in the 1990s. Striving to produce economically useful citizens remains the major political rationale for education funding, now set in a debate regarding international competitiveness [see chapter 14; Feinberg, 1993]. Still today one observes regular efforts to eliminate "waste" in education, to "streamline" the curriculum, to make the curriculum more like "business." While the social efficiency movement influenced the public discourse regarding education and curriculum, its actual imprint in the schools is less clear. However, the imprint of business language upon curriculum discourse has been significant (Cuban, 1984; Cremin, 1964). It is important to remember that democracy did not propel the scientific movement. Business and its own internal logic did. More studies [including surveys] had to be conducted as presumably more accurate methods of sampling and analyzing the data were being devised. Despite the large number of surveys and studies undertaken during the heyday of social efficiency, "the results were, for the most part, inconclusive and often contradictory" (Nelson & Watras, 1981, p. 64). Even when honestly attempted, the Taylor system was often quickly abandoned. The failure of Taylor's system, argued Bobbitt in *The Curriculum*, was that the planners themselves could not foresee all the contingencies of the tasks to be completed. By excluding the worker from participation in planning a key element, the human element was simply ignored (Nelson & Watras, 1981). In education as in industry, such a mistake is fatal (Brown, 1993).

VI
The Progressive Reform Movement

Nothing can be developed from nothing; nothing but the crude can be developed out of the crude—and this is what surely happens when we throw the child back upon his achieved self as a finality, and invite him to spin new truths of nature or of conduct out of that.

(John Dewey, 1902, p. 24)

Probably the best remembered reform movement of the first half of the present century is the Progressive education movement. Scholars trace the origin of this movement to three main figures: John Mayer Rice, Lester Frank Ward, and most commonly, John Dewey (Cremin 1964; Seguel, 1966; Tanner & Tanner, 1980; Schubert, 1980a, 1986a; Kliebard, 1982, 1986; Westbrook, 1991). All three exercised influence upon the character of this political and intellectual movement in American education, a movement whose influence on day-to-day classroom practice has always been debated. However, progressive education can be said to have been inaugurated in Quincy, Massachusetts, in the late 1870s, with the work of Colonel Francis Parker. Even during the time of the triumph of faculty psychology and the classical curriculum in the various NEA Committees, progressive ideas did circulate around the country. For instance, some superintendents advised teachers to "individualize" their teaching. Highly visible educators like Nicholas Murray Butler of Columbia and Charles De Garmo of Swarthmore endorsed curriculum reforms in favor of child-centeredness. Despite an apparent popularity of the progressive educational ideas with many teachers and their endorsement by renowned educators, traditional conceptions of education, i.e. classical curriculum theory with its profound faith in mental discipline, maintained its grip on the vast majority, especially school superintendents and school board members during the nineteenth century (Tanner & Tanner, 1990, p. 104).

As we noted earlier, John Mayer Rice's contribution consisted in part in establishing a climate for reform. In his series of studies of American schools, cited and described earlier (1893a, 1893b, 1912), Rice criticized the schools unrelentingly: "In 1892 Rice toured 36 major cities . . . only four of the 36 systems he studied were found to be progressive and scientific" (Doll, W., 1983a, p. 167). While he is remembered more as the originator of comparative methodology in educational research than as a precursor of American Progressivism, his innovative and biting studies of the schools helped set the stage for the movement (Cremin, 1964).

Ward: Nothing "natural" about the status quo. Lester Frank Ward (1841-1913) can also be regarded as a precursor to the progressive movement. His *Dynamic Sociology* (1883) argued against social Darwinism (the survival of the fittest), a view widely accepted during this period. Social Darwinism asserted that "the best" of the race would rise to the top. Therefore, an unequal distribution of wealth and power was "natural." Allowing this process to occur was termed "laissez-faire" politics. Ward asserted that the status quo in human affairs was not "natural" and thus was changeable. Indeed, Ward argued that human beings could create social change and that, in fact, the primary aim of education was the preparation of individuals to participate in social change. Ward viewed the American school system as a potential force for the improvement of society, a view adopted and developed by the Progressives, especially the Social Reconstructionists. [It is a view elaborated today by those who regard curriculum primarily as political text; see chapter 5.]

Ward is credited with having provided the theoretical underpinnings for progressivism by establishing a relationship between school and society, between democracy and education (Tanner & Tanner, 1980). Ward attacked the prevailing laissez-faire philosophy, and proposed instead a planned society. In this sense, Ward can be regarded as the architect of environmentalism in American education. He attacked the eugenics movement which considered heredity, not environment, as the crucial determinant of educational achievement. Ward's important but often overlooked work provided one basis for Dewey's experimentalist philosophy. He had written: "The present enormous chasm between the ignorant and intelligent, caused by the unequal distribution of knowledge, is the worst evil under which our society labors" (Ward, 1883, p. 602). It was Ward's book and his attacks on the status quo that helped to challenge and undermine laissez-faire as a social system (Tanner & Tanner, 1990).

Ward is nearly forgotten today. More than any other contemporary scholars, curriculum historians Daniel and Laurel Tanner have studied the contribution of Lester Ward. In addition to their characterization of Ward as the architect of environmentalism in American pedagogy and curriculum, they regard him as the creator of some of the field's most fundamental ideas about the curriculum. What do they make of Ward's relative invisibility? "[It] is partly because his contributions were underestimated and partly because his ideas were changed . . . through further development by Dewey" (Tanner, L. & Tanner, D. 1987, p. 538). They quote James Q. Dealey, Ward's colleague at Brown University, who wrote some ninety years ago: "Yet in future years. . . . Lester Frank Ward will surely be ranked high among America's masters of social science" (quoted in Tanner & Tanner, 1987, p. 546). If he is so ranked, the Tanners can take considerable credit for helping establish Ward's status in curriculum history.

John Dewey. John Dewey's (1859-1952) contribution to educational and curricular thought (1900, 1902, 1910, 1916) is incalculable. The student will observe his influence in those who espouse his views as well as those who oppose them. Dewey entered the curricular debates at the turn of the century with a thin book that is one of his more accessible writings, *The Child and the Curriculum* (1902). Many scholars assert that in this essay one finds Dewey's basic statement of curriculum theory (Kliebard, 1986; Schubert, 1980a, 1986a). In this early book, a certain Hegelian influence is discernible in his insistence that the dualism or dichotomy between the child and the curriculum is a false one (Kliebard, 1986). Apparent contradictions, or in Hegelian (and Marxian) terms, thesis and antithesis, can be unified to produce a higher order of reality, or synthesis. Dewey joined others in criticizing the classical curriculum of the nineteenth century. Curriculum must not be an "external annex to the child's present life" (Dewey, 1964, pp. 352-353). Dewey explained why he believed that some favor such a constricting conception of curriculum:

> We get used to the chains we wear, and we miss them when removed. . . . Unpleasant because meaningless activities may get agreeable if long enough persisted in. It is possible for the mind to develop interest in a routine or mechanical procedure if conditions are continually supplied which demand that mode of operation and preclude any other sort. I frequently hear dull devices and empty exercises defended and extolled because "children take such an interest in them." Yes, that is the worst of it; the mind, shut out from worthy employ and missing the taste of adequate performance, comes down to the level of that which is left to it to know and do, and perforce takes an interest in a cabined and cramped experience. (Dewey, 1902/1964, p. 355)

Routinization, memorization, and recitation characterized the classical curriculum for mental discipline. Dewey's criticism of the classical curriculum was insightful and unrelenting. He insisted that the child's experience must form the basis of the curriculum, and in so doing synthesize the apparent antagonism between the two.

Dewey did not advocate freedom without adult guidance. Later, many of those claiming to work progressively would forget Dewey's insistence that educational activity required careful pedagogical guidance. Dewey (1902) wrote: "Nothing can be developed from nothing; nothing but the crude can be developed out of the crude—and this is what surely happens when we throw the child back upon his achieved self as a finality, and invite him to spin new truths of nature or of conduct out of that" (p. 24). Partly in response to misunderstandings of Dewey's position on freedom, Harold Rugg and Ann Shumaker would emphasize: "We do not dare leave any longer to chance—to spontaneous, overt symptoms of interest on the part of occasional pupils—the solution of this important and difficult problem of construction of a curriculum for maximum growth" (Rugg & Shumaker, 1969/1928, p. 118).

Progressive movement launched. Some cite a second Dewey book as launching the progressive movement. In *The School and Society* (1899) Dewey asserts that schooling must be linked with society. Specifically, Dewey shared Ward's view that students ought to discuss, plan, and effect meaningful social change. Schooling which ignored this dimension produced egocentric individuals. This potential for "selfishness" worried Dewey considerably.

> The mere absorption of facts and truths is so exclusively individual an affair that it tends very naturally into selfishness. There is no obvious social motive

for the acquirement of mere learning, there is no clear social gain in success. . . . Indeed, almost the only measure for success is a competitive one, in the bad sense of that term—a comparison of results in the recitation or in the examination to see which child has succeeded in getting ahead of others in storing up, in the accumulating the maximum of information. (Dewey, 1959, p. 40)

Dewey worked to introduce a curriculum which would counter this tendency toward egocentricity.

School as community. Dewey proposed the idea of school as community. For Dewey, community denoted students involved in so-called "active occupations," not a vocational concept as one might easily misunderstand. Conducted in democratic and cooperative ways, these activities would revolve around the child's experience. The child's experience would be active rather than passive. Communication and ideas would be expressed relatively freely. The concept of school as democratic community might entail a school structured differently from its surrounding community, if the local environs lacked certain democratic qualities. This possibility marks an important distinction between Dewey and Charters. For the latter, the school should mirror the larger community for which students are being prepared. For Charters, the primary goal of schooling was the production of graduates who would "do well" in the larger society. If that larger society exhibited democratic qualities, then so should the school. If it did not, evidently the school ought not.

For Dewey, the ideal of democracy was supreme. Ensuring a democratic community within the school offered hope for democratic reform of society generally. Dewey wrote that:

When the school introduces and trains each child of society into membership within such a little community, saturating him with the spirit of service, and providing him with the instruments of effective self-direction, we shall have the deepest and best guarantee of a larger society which is worthy, lovely and harmonious. (Dewey, 1959, p. 49)

For Dewey "democracy [is regarded] as an *experience,* rather than simply as a form of government" (Tanner & Tanner, 1990, p. 113). This view has been linked recently to "communitarianism," associated with political philosophers such as Charles Taylor (1992). It is conspicuously absent in many schools today.

To improve society. It becomes clear that Dewey viewed the solution of social problems as a major focus of the curriculum. The goal of education was to improve society. This goal could not be reached, he insisted, unless the curriculum was constructed around the child. Dewey wrote:

I may have exaggerated somewhat in order to make plain the typical points of the old education: its passivity of attitude, its mechanical massing of children, its uniformity of curriculum and method. It may be summed up by stating that the center of gravity is outside the child. It is in the teacher, the text-book, anywhere and everywhere you please except in the immediate instincts and activities of the child himself. (1959, p. 52)

Dewey wrote these words while he taught at the University of Chicago. In 1896, two years after he came to the University of Chicago [from the University of Michigan], Dewey, in collaboration with Alice Dewey, opened an experimental or laboratory school. The term "Laboratory School" denoted the experimental character of the school, which began with 16 students and 2 teachers. By 1902 the School enrolled 140 children, 23 teachers and 10 assistants. By the time Dewey departed Chicago for Columbia University in 1904, the Dewey Laboratory School was the most "interesting experimental venture in American education; indeed, there are those who insist that there has been nothing to match it in excitement, quality, and contribution" (Cremin, 1964, pp. 135-136) [see also Tanner & Tanner, 1990, p. 130].

During his time in Chicago, Dewey worked with Jane Addams, a social reformer whose settlement house—Hull House—represented "an experimental bridging of class cultures" (Westbrook, 1991, p. 85). Dewey had lectured at Hull House for several years before his move to Chicago, and when he did move to the city he was warmly received by the reform community there (Westbrook, 1991). Jane Addams' educational ideas supported Dewey's educational theories. Both Dewey and Addams believed that learning is a continuous and vital process, not preparation for a life to come later. It was Jane Addams who declared that the traditional school was unsuitable for learning because it was disconnected from life (Tanner & Tanner, 1990), a view Dewey shared.

The Dewey School. Published records concerning the Laboratory School are available. One of the most interesting accounts is found in *The Dewey School: The Laboratory School of the University of Chicago* (1936). The authors, Katherine Camp Mayhew and Ann Camp Edwards, both teachers at the School, detailed the history and character of the curriculum. The authors identify two periods in the School's evolution. The first segment (1896-1898) was experimental in nature, guided by Deweyan principles of loyalty to the nature of children, "practical" acquaintance with various school subjects, and a concrete experience in the employment of scientific method. The second period (1898-1903) was characterized by revision of the curriculum based on analysis of what proved successful during the first period. The primary aim of the School was to foster "cooperative and mutually helpful living" (Mayhew and Edwards, 1936, p. 39).

This phrase, in Deweyan terms, meant the cultivation of social awareness and a democratic vision. The school became a home in which the curriculum was comprised of activities devised to develop social and community life. All activities were planned and conducted in the frame of children's native impulses. That is, curricular activities and problems were constructed and presented so that the child was encouraged to utilize creativity and acquire basic academic skills simultaneously. So conceived, subject matter became a resource, not the center of the curriculum. Children engaged in educational activity to develop their individual intellects so as to cultivate cooperative social relationships. In such a curriculum design, the responsibility of the teacher is magnified (Mayhew & Edwards, 1936; Tanner & Tanner, 1980; Kliebard, 1986; Schubert, 1986a). Educational activity was not justified according to some future dividend; each activity must be worthwhile in the present. Dewey insisted: "[E]ducation, therefore, is a process of living not a preparation for future living" (Dewey, 1964, p. 430).

What subjects should be required of all students? Harris and the classical curricularists had answered that Latin and other complex subjects, whose memorization and recitation would exercise the mind, should comprise the core of the curriculum. In contrast, Dewey answered that students should study those subjects that "deal directly with problems of health, citizenship, and the means of communication through the vernacular" (Dewey, 1902, p. 8).

Democracy and education. Dewey left the University of Chicago in 1904 for an appointment to the faculty of Columbia University's philosophy department. While at Columbia Dewey's attention somewhat shifted from educational to philosophical matters. However, this shift did not signify a loss of interest in education nor an end to his writing on the subject. In fact, his Chicago-period and Columbia-period writing formed the foundation for the Progressive movement (1897, 1899, 1900, 1902, 1910, 1916). His major work on education, *Democracy and Education* (1916), represented a "comprehensive synthesis of the ideas that Dewey developed during his Chicago period" (Kliebard, 1986, p. 85). Here Dewey argued that the school, an enlightened citizenry, and social change are interrelated (Tanner & Tanner, 1980). Dewey noted that a society embracing social change as an ideal requires certain forms of education:

> Particularly is it true that a society which not only changes but which has the ideal of such change as will improve it, will have different standards and methods of education from one which aims simply at the perpetuation of its own customs. To make the general ideas set forth applicable to our own educational practice, it is therefore necessary to come to closer quarters with the nature of present social life. (Dewey, 1916, 1966, p. 81)

Active occupations. In *Democracy and Education,* Dewey devotes a chapter to "Play and Work in the Curriculum" in which he explains his notion of "active occupations," which we introduced earlier. A central hypothesis was that life itself, and especially those occupations that served social needs, should constitute the focus of the curriculum. A second hypothesis was that freedom of expression was necessary for growth, but such expression must be guided by the teacher. For Dewey, "freedom and informality were means to intellectual development, not ends in themselves" (Tanner & Tanner, 1990, p. 130). The term "occupations" has been misconstrued sometimes to denote narrow technical activities. Yet Dewey was unequivocal in this definition of the term. "Active occupations" means "manual skill and technical efficiency" so that "immediate satisfaction [is] found in work. These things," Dewey continued, "shall be subordinate to education—that is, to intellectual results and the forming of a socialized disposition" (Dewey, 1966, p. 197). Daniel and Laurel Tanner (1990) comment on Dewey's views on social efficiency:

> Hence, in much of the literature in curriculum history the term social efficiency is interpreted in the narrow and evil sense as subordination of individuals to the demands of the industrial system and the authority of a ruling class. For Dewey there was another side to social efficiency—a side having a far different and broader meaning. It had an economic meaning ... a political meaning (being able to take a determining part in the political process and in the exercise of justice in daily life); and a sociopsychological meaning (complete development of personality—the recognition of the uniqueness of the individual as essential to the well being of a democratic society). "It must be borne in mind," wrote Dewey (1916, pp. 139-143), "that ultimately social efficiency means neither more nor less than capacity to share in a give and take of experience." (Tanner & Tanner, 1990, p. 24)

The Gary Plan. Perhaps the most widely known example of progressive experimentation was the Gary Plan. Dewey and his daughter Evelyn had applauded the Gary Plan in *Schools of Tomorrow* (1915). It was also praised by Dewey's disciples, most notably Alice Barrows and Randolph Bourne (who would break with Dewey over Dewey's support of American participation in World War I). In Barrow's words, the Gary Plan was evidence that "Dewey's philosophy could be put into practice on a large scale in the public schools" (quoted in Westbrook, 1991, p. 180).

Gary, Indiana, was an industrial city founded in 1906 by the U. S. Steel Corporation. School Superintendent William Wirt designed the plan which involved two platoons: one platoon of students filled classrooms for part of the school day, studying the school subjects. The other was involved in so-called practical activity, including working in school shops, exercising in the gymnasium, participating in fine arts activities, field trips, or meetings in the school auditorium. Later in the day, the platoons switched, so that each student experienced both sets of educational activities. This plan also allowed twice as many students to be enrolled as the classrooms could hold, an efficiency extended by keeping the school open at night for adult education (Westbrook, 1991).

Each school was organized as an "embryonic community." Work and study were done in physical spaces that were practical as well as intellectual. Physics laboratories, for instance, adjoined machine shops where practical application of scientific principles could be learned. To integrate the learning-by-doing and social aims of the schools in a practical way, children did the work of maintaining the physical plant. Students operated the lunchroom, ordered and distributed supplies, and did the accounting for the school administration. Younger children served as assistants to older students (Tanner & Tanner, 1990).

Superintendent Wirt valued the Gary Plan less as a participatory democracy than as a means by which children could be indoctrinated to the value of the work ethic. The platoon scheme functioned also as a means of cutting the costs of maintaining the expensive facilities the Gary Plan required. There is little evidence that the U.S. Steel Corporation exerted much direct influence on Wirt's program; the Corporation had no need to do so since Wirt's values were fully in accord with its own. Wirt's conception of social efficiency was not at all unlike that which Dewey attacked. Thus, the Gary schools proved that the progressive methods that emerged from Dewey's laboratory could be put to social uses quite different than those Dewey intended (Westbrook, 1991).

This was a problem that plagued the progressive movement, and in 1938 Dewey published *Experience and Education* to resolve these misunderstandings. As for the Gary Plan, it finally was judged negatively. A progressive who studied the Plan, Abraham Flexner, may have "set out to puncture the Gary bubble in the survey" (Cremin, 1964, p. 160). [According to Westbrook (1991), the bubble needed to be punctured.] Those elements of the Progressive movement that the work of John Dewey inspired were highly controversial. While this movement captured then and remains now in the popular imagination—conservative politicians still use the word as a slur—it is widely misunderstood. Dewey's ideas have been distorted to support an educational version of "laissez-faire" economics. The rigor, discipline, and complexity of his ideas are regularly overlooked. The Gary Plan was only one of numerous distortions of Dewey's curriculum theory.

The Progressive Education Association. To promote the educational ideas of John Dewey, the Association for the Advancement of Progressive Education formed in 1919. It had as its aim "the freest and fullest development of the individual, based upon the scientific study of his [sic] mental, physical, spiritual, and social characteristics and needs" (quoted in Saylor, Alexander, & Lewis, 1981, p. 241). The views of this association, later called the Progressive Education Association (PEA), were consonant with those of Dewey as indicated by their statement of principles (Cremin, 1964; Graham, 1967).

While the Association's views were Deweyan, the first honorary president was not John Dewey. Rather, it was the former President of Harvard University and chair of the Committee of Ten, Charles W. Eliot. Dewey himself declined to join (Schubert, 1986a). From the first meeting in 1919, the PEA was led by headmasters from small, private schools whose students came from the upper and upper-middle classes. They tended to be focused toward the elementary not secondary school. Craig Kridel (in press) tells us:

> Membership in the PEA during these early years was oriented as much toward ensuring that their students would enter the Ivy League schools as it was to attending to the interests and needs of the students. While this orientation would change, many of the schools who later participated in the [Eight-Year] Study would be these same private schools who led the organization during its first ten years. (p. 2)

What was the platform of the Progressive Education Association? The major planks in the progressive platform included: 1) the freedom to develop naturally; 2) interest should be the motive of all work; 3) the teacher is a guide, not a task-master; 4) the scientific study of pupil development should be pursued; 5) there must be greater attention to all that affects the child's physical development; 6) co-operation between school and home is necessary to meet the needs of child-life; and 7) the progressive school should serve as a leader in educational movements (Saylor, et al., 1981). Progressivism inspired reforms in many schools, especially in university laboratory and private schools. However, public schools also attempted progressive experiments. One such major experiment was conducted in the Detroit public schools. There the curriculum, as well as the process of curriculum construction, underwent significant revisions. Teacher involvement in this process had the consequence of a general faculty "revitalization" (N.S.S.E., 1927a). The progressive experiment would be reported in the Eight-Year Study, the results of which were published in 1942 [see chapter 3].

The Denver curriculum revision project. Other Progressive inspired curriculum reform efforts were made in the public schools of Burlington, Iowa; Winnetka, Illinois; Denver, Colorado; St. Louis, Missouri, and Los Angeles, California. The Denver project, known as the "Denver Plan," attracted considerable attention, as it included teachers in the process on a large scale (Pinar & Grumet, 1981; Tanner & Tanner, 1980; Kliebard, 1986; Hlebowitsh, 1993). Jesse Newlon, the Denver superintendent, had persuaded the Denver school board to support the project with the argument that he could "streamline" and make more efficient the curriculum of the Denver schools (Kliebard, 1979). As a result of this study—the Denver curriculum Project —Newlon is remembered today as a progressive administrator who understood the significance of teachers' collaborative participation in curriculum development. Newlon appointed committees of teachers to work with administrative and supervisory personnel. The committees on which teachers sat were also chaired by teachers. Working after regular school hours, these committees studied the professional literature. Newlon persuaded the school board to provide support and structure for the teachers' labor:

1) An appropriation by the Board for the curriculum revision project and at the end of 2 years a permanent department was to be established and given a budget;

2) Relief of teachers who served as members or chairs of curriculum revision committees from regular classroom work, with a few days to a few months release time;

3) Employment of specialists, nationally known for their contribution to problems of teaching in their own fields;

4) Arrangements with the University of Colorado and State Teachers College for professors of education to devote weekly time to general supervision of the curriculum revision work of more than 40 committees;

5) Provision of a clerical staff to support committee work. (Caswell, 1950; Hall & Lewis, 1925; Newlon, 1923a; Snyder, Bolin & Zumwalt, 1992, p. 419)

A professional library was established and a librarian was hired in 1923. In Denver, under the leadership of Jesse Newlon, curriculum revision was understood as an ongoing process. And teachers were central: "To Newlon, the personal growth and morale of teachers were as important as any specific outcomes of their curriculum efforts" (Snyder, Bolin & Zumwalt, 1992, p. 419). His point of view is indcated in the following statement taken from his Twentieth Annual Report to the Board (1923a):

> In organizing supervision the controlling principle is a consideration of ulti-mate rather than immediate results. The assumption is that the community can afford to wait two or three years in order to reap the results of this type of organization, rather than to attempt by more arbitrary methods to obtain rigid uniformity of practice at the expense of the teacher's initiative and resourceful-ness. (quoted in Snyder, Bolin & Zumwalt, 1992, p. 419)

By 1933, ten years after the Project was begun, curriculum development engaged teachers and students: "Where previously the course of study had been prepared by a committee of teachers for use by all, now teachers and pupils, planning in terms of their own situation and needs, developed units of study with a minimum of prescription by others" (Caswell, 1950, p. 419; quoted in Snyder, Bolin & Zumwalt, 1992, p. 419).

Even so, Superintendent Newlon concluded that the employment of teachers in curriculum revision did not obviate the need for curriculum specialists.

> There has come a general recognition of the importance of the teacher. It is evident, however, that other factors are equally essential. The policy of delegat-ing entirely to teachers the making of curricula would be fallacious as was the policy of leaving teachers entirely out of this process, and would likewise fail to take account of the indispensable contribution that must be made by research and by specialists who, by devoting their lives to the study of teaching in particular subjects, become authorities in their fields. (NSSE, 1927b, p. 240)

Superintendent Newlon—certainly a progressive but, not to be forgotten, also an administrator—employed the first district-wide curriculum administra-tor, A. K. Loomis, a doctoral graduate of Teachers College, Columbia University, in educational administration (Pinar & Grumet, 1981). In fact, the first generation of curriculum specialists were trained in departments of educational administration and those who held university appointments taught in departments of educational administration. The bureaucratic and administrative character of the curriculum development paradigm was estab-lished.

Newlon's progressive commitment to teachers' collaboration appeared to reach its limit when it intersected with the demands of the bureaucracy. His managerial interest is indicated in some of his overlooked (and often uncited) attitudes toward supervision. Despite teacher opposition to supervi-sion, particularly to the efficiency rating scales common in the 1920s, Newlon asserted the necessity of supervision and rating: "Many teachers resent supervision of any kind, and quite often these are the poorest and most talkative teachers in the school system." These teachers, Newlon complained, were unfortunately the very ones who were "accorded places of leadership in teachers' organization." [These teachers represented] "a menace to our profession, and their numbers should be eliminated" (Newlon, 1923b, p. 548; quoted in Glanz, 1990, p. 165). Despite the evidence, at least one contemporary scholar still characterizes Newlon as primarily democratic in his commitments (Hlebowitsh, 1993). Reality would appear to have been somewhat more complicated.

Progressive reform nationwide. Progressive reforms were widely conducted at university laboratory schools. Among those schools involved were those placed at the University of Chicago, Columbia University (the Lincoln Experimental School), Ohio State University, the University of Iowa, in Chicago (the Francis W. Parker School), at Teachers College Columbia University (the Horace Mann School), in McDonald County Missouri, in Brookline, Massachusetts (the Beaver County Day School), in New York (the City and Country School and the Walden School), and in Fairhope, Alabama (the School of Organic Education, where Marietta Johnson (Johnson, 1974; Lobdell, 1984), like Dewey, believed that the curriculum should involve the occupations and activities of interest to children) (Tanner & Tanner, 1990; see also NSSE, 1927a, NSSE, 1927b).

In Winnetka, Illinois, under the leadership of Superintendent Carleton Washburne, an especially memorable progressive experiment was attempted. There children were allowed to work on a unit as long as needed for mastery, a concept that came to be known as the "Winnetka Plan." The Winnetka Plan represented the first systemwide attempt to "individualize" the school curriculum. In contrast to the Winnetka Plan, the curriculum of the elementary division of the Lincoln School at Teachers College, Columbia University, also considered a progressive school, was organized around the "units of work." Operationally, however, the separate subject was still the basic curriculum unit (Tanner & Tanner, 1990).

Lincoln School. Illustrative of the range of curriculum reform progressives undertook was an experimental core curriculum at the Lincoln School. In 1937 a sizable grant from the Alfred P. Sloan Foundation to the Lincoln School made it possible to take large groups of students on trips to study the social and economic conditions of American life as part of the core curriculum. As preparation for "Living in the Machine Age," 50 ninth-graders lived for 8 days in the homes of rural New England farmers. There, away from New York City, they studied first-hand a less-mechanized society than their own. As part of their study of "economic and social planning in a democracy," 50 Lincoln School twelfth-graders toured the Tennessee Valley Authority and various other cooperatives in Georgia and Maryland.

Another such experiment included sending 15 eleventh-graders to Pennsylvania and West Virginia to study communities that were then being affected by unemployment in the coal and steel industries. What was the assessment of these expensive experiments? It was concluded that the groups who went on the trips achieved more understanding of relevant concepts and issues than the groups who remained at home; they also revealed greater sensitivity toward the social issues that were involved (Tanner & Tanner, 1990). In 1941 Teachers College merged the Lincoln School with the Horace Mann School, a subject-centered demonstration school, ending that particular progressive experiment. After the merger, the Horace Mann-Lincoln Institute of School Experimentation was established. Hollis Caswell was a key figure in this development.

At least one educational theorist thought that progressive schools were "altogether too timid" in their elimination of "useless" subjects from the curriculum. In an essay entitled "The Modern School," Abraham Flexner (1923)—who had studied the Gary Plan and worked at the Lincoln School—wrote that the goal of education was to develop in students the "power to handle themselves in our own world" (p. 98). According to Flexner, the curriculum of the modern schools should be organized around activities in four basic fields: science, industry, aesthetics, and civics, with science the central subject. Flexner also emphasized the importance of making explicit relationships among the four fundamental fields. He regarded the modern school as a center for scientific curriculum making, a truly experimental or laboratory school. Flexner wished to establish an experimental school which would function for education as the Johns Hopkins University Medical School had for medicine. The Lincoln School would be that school: "Emerson once remarked that every revolution is first a thought in one man's [sic] mind. Insofar as the Lincoln School wrought a revolution, Abraham Flexner was the man" (Cremin, 1961, p. 280).

Flexner was not alone in his criticism of progressive schools as too timid in their experimentation. Harold Rugg and Ann Shumaker, who in 1928 examined the curricula of more than one hundred so-called progressive schools, noted that relatively few had abandoned a school-subjects curriculum organization (Tanner & Tanner, 1990).

The "project method." As we have seen, the year 1918 is an important date in curriculum history. Bobbitt's *The Curriculum* was published, providing theoretical legitimation for an expanding and accelerating social efficiency movement. As well, 1918 saw the publication of the *Cardinal Principles*. As if that were not enough, that year *Teachers College Record* published William Heard Kilpatrick's (1871-1965) "The Project Method." Born in White Plains, Georgia, the son of a Baptist minister, Kilpatrick had received the A. B. and A. M. degrees from Mercer University, although most of his graduate work for the latter degree was done at Johns Hopkins. He took his Ph.D. at Teachers College, Columbia University in 1912 and immediately became a member of the faculty (Beineke, 1989).

Kilpatrick's 1918 essay "caused such an immediate sensation that the Teachers College Bureau of Publications was obliged to distribute an astounding 60,000 reprints" (Kliebard, 1986, p. 159). Critical of the social efficiency movement, worrying with Dewey that it would produce "selfish individualists" (Kilpatrick, 1918, p. 334), Kilpatrick wrote:

> We of America have for years increasingly desired that education be considered as life itself not as a mere preparation for living. The concept before us promises a definite step toward this end. If the purposeful act be in reality the typical unit of worthy life, then it follows that to base education on purposeful acts is exactly to identify the process of education with worthy living itself. (Kilpatrick, 1918, p. 323)

Kilpatrick's article was "read around the world as the concrete embodiment of Deweyan curricular philosophy" (Schubert, 1986a, p. 75).

Before projects were systematized into a "method" by Kilpatrick in 1918, they had been employed in the Dewey School before the turn of the century and in the Francis W. Parker School as early as 1901 (Tanner & Tanner, 1990). According to Kilpatrick, from the standpoint of theory, the concept of activity was methodological. Despite Kilpatrick's insistence that the project was a method and not a complete curriculum theory ["the activity conception by itself does not and cannot suffice for a complete curriculum theory" (Kilpatrick, 1936, p. 85)], in effect the project method was discussed as if it were a complete theory for curriculum development as well as a method. It would seem that the entire curriculum was to consist of a series of projects (Tanner & Tanner, 1990).

Kilpatrick's principle of curriculum organization. What was a project? For Kilpatrick, a project was "a whole-hearted purposeful activity proceeding in a social environment" (1918, p. 320). Would any activity be suitable as a project? Kilpatrick believed that although it was acceptable for the child to adopt the teacher's suggestion as his or her own, it was preferable for children to have practice in all four steps or aspects of any given project: purposing, planning, executing, and judging (Tanner & Tanner, 1990). For Kilpatrick, then, the "project method" was an organizing principle of the curriculum. Employing this method, curriculum makers and teachers would devise specific projects which would engage and further develop the inherent purposefulness of students.

Kilpatrick placed the "project method" in what was at that time considered a scientific paradigm. He insisted that the method employed the laws of learning, i.e. 1) readiness, 2) effect, and 3) exercise. In his conception of the project method, Kilpatrick combined Thorndike's educational psychology with Dewey's educational philosophy. He detailed usage of stimulus-response theories, arguing that "a more explicated reason for making the purposeful act the typical unit of instruction is found in the utilization of the laws of learning which this plan affords" (Kilpatrick, 1918, p. 323). Furthermore, Kilpatrick contended, "the wholehearted purposeful activity within a social situation as the typical unit of school procedures is the best guarantee of the utilization of the child's native capacities now too frequently wasted" (Kilpatrick, 1918, p. 334). Kilpatrick further elaborated the idea of the project method in his *Foundations of Method: Informal Talks on Teaching* (1925). He conceived of the curriculum as "a series of experiences in which by guided induction the child makes his own formulations. Then they are his to use" (Kilpatrick, 1925, p. 310). A basic curricular question—which projects are appropriate?—went unanswered.

The project method attracted attention among scholars as well as the educational public. This attention was not always completely favorable. For instance, some theorists worried that a curriculum comprised entirely of projects would be fragmentary and haphazard (Tanner & Tanner, 1990). A symposium on the "dangers and difficulties" of the project method was held at Teachers College, Columbia University, in the spring of 1921. In addition to concerns over the narrowness of a curriculum based on projects and the instrumental values it seemed to require, other questions were raised: 1) Would children select only manipulative (making and building) activities, many of which tended to remain at relatively low cognitive levels (in contrast with higher-level purposeful inquiries)? 2) Did the project method overemphasize the individual as it allowed students to select projects that did not relate to a common purpose and which ignored the socialization process? 3) How great would be the difficulty of obtaining materials that supported a given project? 4) How great is the danger of neglecting to extrapolate general ideas from project experiences—that is, failing to develop the capacity to think? These questions and others finally undermined the initial enthusiasm for Kilpatrick's project method, and it is now all but forgotten (Tanner & Tanner, 1990). Kilpatrick himself has been characterized recently as an "instrumentalist" (Stanley, 1992b, p. 61).

John L. Childs. Influenced by the work of Charles Pierce, William James, and particularly John Dewey, John L. Childs was another influential progressive educator who advocated child-centered education. Influenced also by the writing and mentoring of Kilpatrick, Childs believed that knowing was linked to activity (Watkins, 1990a). He argued: "experience is considered to be an active process of doing and undergoing and not primarily a cognitive affair" (Childs, 1931, p. 78). Despite his commitment to child-centeredness and the project method, Childs was not socially indifferent. In fact, he criticized public education for being insufficiently committed to social goals. Childs (1938) called for a definition of democracy which included economic justice and equality of opportunity. For him the central moral question of the day was how to restore (or create) significance and meaning in people's lives. Educators needed an "audit" of American civilization to identify unworthy cultural practices. Childs regarded many contemporary educational practices as nothing more than "animal training." What was necessary was a moral education that would respect human personality. [Moral education continues to be a theme in the 1990s; see chapter 12.]

Social efficiency and progressivism: Rival reform movements. The 1920's saw the appearance of two rival reform movements, the social efficiency movement identified with Bobbitt, Charters, and Snedden, and the Progressive movement identified with Dewey, Kilpatrick, Childs and others. Both groups justified their efforts by claiming social improvement, but their visions of social change and the methods employed to realize these visions differed. Boyd Henry Bode (1873-1953) criticized both movements in his *Modern Educational Theories* in 1927 (Kliebard, 1986). Like Dewey, Bode was trained as a professional philosopher. Also like Dewey, he chose to devote his career to the study of education. Bode criticized vehemently the social efficiency movement, attacking the work of Bobbitt, Charters, and Snedden. For instance, Bode accused Bobbitt of trivializing curriculum by reducing it to scientific technique:

> The determination to make every problem in education a problem to be solved by special scientific technique may easily result in a failure to appreciate the significance of the democratic movement. . . . When this happens scientific method becomes a means of opposing genuine progress. Refinement is no substitute for insight. (Bode, 1927, p. 78)

Bode's critique of Charters. A colleague of Charters at Ohio State University, Bode viewed unfavorably Charters' concept of "activity analysis," a popular idea and method of curriculum construction during the 1920's. Bode warned:

> There is a grave danger that the misconceptions of what may be expected from the method of activity analysis will interfere seriously with the usefulness of the method. It seems clear that the analysis of "jobs," such as bricklaying and plumbing, has led us astray by suggesting a false analogy between such jobs and the duties of life. Life undoubtedly consists of specific activities, if we mean that all activities are necessarily specific when we come to them. But if by specific activity (such as the duties of citizenship) is meant an activity that can be layed out in advance, at least in its main operations, like baking a pie from a recipe, then life clearly does not consist of specific activities. (Bode, 1927, p. 113)

Bode observed that activity analysis led to a curriculum of routinization in which tasks reduce the student to an automaton. He insisted that activity analysis could not provide any insight into the aims of education beyond a strictly vocational preparation (Nelson & Watras, 1981).

Bode's critique of Snedden. Bode's (1927) criticism of Snedden's *Sociological Determination of Objectives in Education* continued his attack on the social efficiency orientation. Bode insisted that relying exclusively on a scientific method for determining curriculum objectives guarantees trivialization. Bode declared that: "So long as we nurse the delusion that objectives can be got by 'sociological determination' we are obstructing the development that must come if education is to make its proper contribution to the advancement of democracy" (Bode, 1927, pp. 138-139). It was quite clear to Bode that neither scientific studies or scientific methods of constructing curriculum advanced the cause of democracy.

For Bode democracy was a process of continual social readjustment in the direction of a more complete and mutual recognition of private and collective interests. It was the aim of education to humanize the social order to make sure that the pursuit of self interest would not undermine social progress for others. He believed that progress did not result from doing the same things more efficiently, but from the creation of new standards. Additionally, Bode criticized Charters' and Bobbitt's faith in the capacity of the community to determine aims of education. Such a practice is full of danger, Bode worried, as the public is not sufficiently informed to make such curriculum decisions. Snedden's efforts to determine educational objectives sociologically required blind faith in the wisdom of consensus. In practice it was profoundly conservative, as the technique simply reflected taken-for-granted ideas and assumptions, or, at best, what people regarded as "good taste." Bode also cautioned that an overdependence on mental tests, which seemed to accompany practices of social efficiency, oversimplified intelligence (Nelson & Watras, 1981).

Bode's critique of Kilpatrick. Bode's criticism was not limited to the social efficiency advocates. Kilpatrick's "project method" also came under fire. Bode approved of the method's opposition to routinized and mechanical school work. However, he viewed Kilpatrick's method as evading the issue of direction. "The point is," writes Bode, "that the whole idea of the project method easily becomes a means of evading instead of facing the problem of educational guidance and direction" (Bode, 1927, p. 164). What should constitute educational direction? Bode wrote that:

> The purpose of a democratic program of education is primarily to secure the liberation of intelligence for the improvement of human life. This program requires first, a social program which clarifies the meaning of democracy, and secondly an organization of educational materials and methods so as to make the program effective. (Bode, 1927, p. 172)

The cultivation of children's intelligence was to enable them to reorganize and improve their social world. School subjects should function toward realization of this end (Cremin, 1964).

Bode allied with Dewey. Bode's differences with the social efficiency orientation are clear. His differences with Kilpatrick are perhaps less obvious but just as real. Curricular organization must reside in concepts of social intelligence and social change, not in techniques or methods. On this point Bode is allied with Dewey. Like Dewey, Bode worried that the project method might result in a curriculum built on "the quicksand of ephemeral interests" (Tanner & Tanner, 1990, p. 153). His influence was felt particularly at Ohio State University, where he foreshadowed later work by Laura Zirbes (1935) in elementary curriculum and Harold Alberty (1947) in secondary curriculum. Zirbes (1928 Ph.D. graduate of Columbia) and Alberty (1927 Ph.D. graduate of Ohio State) extended Bode's ideas, preparing a generation of curriculum specialists with strong theoretical interests (Schubert, et al., 1988). Among them would be Paul R. Klohr (1967a, 1967b), whose teaching influenced a number of those who, in the 1970s, would work to reconceptualize the field.

Dewey's democratic spirit extended to curriculum development. Dewey's work was extended specifically to curriculum development in Harold Rugg and Ann Shumaker's *The Child-Centered School* (1928), a work we mentioned earlier. This interpretative national survey of pedagogical innovations was conducted in the "Deweyan democratic spirit" (Schubert, 1986a, p. 77). Rugg and Shumaker (1928) found many child-centered schools lacking in faculty cooperation and in systematic attention to curriculum matters. They argued for a democratic model of curriculum development, advocating that teachers be integrally involved in all aspects of the curriculum construction process. Teachers who were involved themselves, they found, involved students in curriculum making, an extension of the democratic process of which they approved: "These schools believe that boys and girls should share in their own government, in the planning of the program, in administering of the curriculum, in conducting one's life in school" (Rugg & Shumaker, 1928, p. 57). According to Rugg and Shumaker, the process of democracy must extend to all aspects of school life, a Deweyan perspective shared by other Progressive theoreticians (Hopkins, 1929). Rugg would later become famous for his inclusion of aesthetic ways of knowing in curriculum conception and for the controversy generated by his social studies curriculum proposals (Schwartz, 1979a, 1979b; Rosario, 1988).

Counts' repudiation of social efficiency. George Sylvester Counts (1889-1974) was another important Progressive reformer. Counts had studied with Charles Judd and Albion Small at the University of Chicago. Let us focus for just a moment on Judd, a noteworthy figure himself. Judd had earned his Ph.D. in social psychology under Wilhelm Wundt at the University of Leipzig. He served as co-chairman of the Cleveland Study of 1915, the first survey of a large city school system in which "scientific instruments were used to gain comprehensive information about the structure and functioning of the system" (Tyler, 1987, p. 21). After the publication of *Introduction to the Scientific Study of Education* (1918), Judd became very much associated with the social efficiency movement. In fact, Judd was instrumental in bringing Bobbitt to the University of Chicago, regarding him as a kindred spirit (Kliebard, 1986).

One can imagine the shock to Judd and other social efficiency and scientifically oriented curricularists when Counts, who had completed a scientifically oriented dissertation, rejected this emphasis in his doctoral training for a career in "social analysis and criticism" (Cremin, 1964, p. 225). Perhaps the switch is not as surprising as it first seems, as another student of Judd—Ralph W. Tyler (who took his Ph.D. with Judd in 1927)—recalls his mentor as having a "strong social conscience. I always think of him [Judd] as an insightful teacher and a kindly mentor" (Tyler, 1987, pp. 23-24). Tyler will remember Counts as influencing his own development as a curriculum theorist, but that is another story [see chapter 3].

A theory of reproduction. Despite his beginnings in scientific curriculum making, Counts emerged as perhaps the first among Progressives to "reflect the uneasiness about American social structure and to direct that malaise to a critical examination of the schools" (Kliebard, 1986, p. 184). Possibly influenced by international critiques of capitalism during the 1920's (Cremin, 1964), Counts was critical of the use of mass production metaphors and techniques in education. [See chapter 14 for further mention of Counts and international issues.]

In *The Selective Character of American Secondary Education* (1922), Counts charged that the American schools served the monied classes at public expense, so that "misfortune, as well as fortune, passes from generation to generation" (Counts, 1922, p. 148). Furthermore:

> At the present time the public high school is attended quite largely by the children of the well-to-do classes. This affords us the spectacle of a privilege being extended at public expense to those very classes that already occupy the privileged positions in modern society. The poor are contributing to provide secondary education for the children of the rich, but are either too poor or too ignorant to avail themselves of the opportunities which they help to provide. (Counts, 1922, p. 152)

This "reproduction" theory of curriculum [in which the curriculum is alleged to reproduce the political and social status quo as a result of economic and ideological forces] would surface again in the 1970's [see chapters 4 and 5]. While at least one contemporary historian contests Counts' reproductionist account of the emergence of the high school (Angus, 1981,1988), for Counts, reproduction theory was self-evidently true.

Curriculum change alleged to be cosmetic. Counts' next major work, *The Senior High School Curriculum* (1926), reported the results of his 1923-1924 survey of 15 American secondary schools in several cities. Counts reported that although curricular innovations had been attempted, results were often disappointing. He found that in many schools existing curricula had been merely rearranged to comply with the seven aims of the *Cardinal Principles of Education*. In some cases existing courses were defended as already in compliance (Kliebard, 1986). Many curricular changes, Counts concluded, had been cosmetic. In general, American school curriculum had not been fundamentally reconceived to meet the true needs of American civilization (Counts, 1926; Kliebard, 1986).

Schools controlled by the privileged. In his *The Social Composition of Boards of Education: A Study in Social Control of Public Schools* (1927), Counts surveyed 1,654 school boards to construct a profile of their composition (Kliebard, 1986). Counts found that schools not only served the privileged, they were controlled by them as well:

> The persons who are chosen for membership on the more powerful boards of education are those who have attended our secondary schools and colleges and occupy the privileged positions in society. The occupations which they most

frequently represent are those of the merchant, the lawyer, the banker, the manufacturer, and the physician. From the ranks of the less favored classes few are chosen. (Counts, 1927, p. 83)

Counts concluded this study with his statement of hope that political and social considerations of educational policy will become evident to all concerned (Cremin, 1964; Kliebard, 1986).

Counts quickly became the major figure on the Left within the Progressive movement. While social reform was an important element of Dewey's curriculum theory, it represented the major and even exclusive element of Counts'. While Progressivism generally, and Counts' political curriculum theory specifically, would wane in the decades to come, political curriculum theory would reappear in the 1970s, this time explicitly identified with the work of Karl Marx. Curriculum as political text, its major theoretical antecedent being the work of Counts, constitutes a major contemporary curriculum discourse, as we will see in chapter 5.

VII
Conclusion: A Major Retrospective

The bearing of this discussion on curriculum-making is plain. The fundamental goals of education cannot be determined by scientific method.
(George Counts, NSSE, 1927b, p. 90)

NSSE Yearbook. The first major retrospective in the history of curriculum studies was published in 1927 as *The Twenty-Sixth Yearbook of the National Society for the Study of Education, Parts I and II.* Prepared under the leadership of Harold Rugg, it was produced by a committee representing the major curricular orientations. Social efficiency and Progressive reformers were well represented, as illustrated by those who served on the Committee. In addition to Rugg, William Bagley, Franklin Bobbitt, Frederick Bosner (an activity analysis advocate), W. W. Charters, George S. Counts, Stuart A. Courtis, Ernest Horn, Charles Judd, Frederick Kelly, William H. Kilpatrick, and George A. Works served on the Committee. The inclusion of social reformers such as Counts and Rugg helped legitimate their work in the field (Kliebard, 1986; Schubert, 1980a, 1986a). Part one of the *Yearbook*, entitled "Curriculum-Making: Past and Present," surveyed efforts at curriculum reforms in both public and private schools. Included in this part was a history of a "Century of Curriculum-Construction in American Schools." In part two, entitled "The Foundations and Technique of Curriculum-Construction," was an attempt to arrive at a consensus statement concerning the basic principles of curriculum making or, in the words of the *Yearbook*, a "reconstruction of the school curriculum" (NSSE, 1927b, p. xi). Because it attempted to encompass all curricular orientations, this consensus statement was "bland" (Kliebard, 1986, p. 182). Individual responses to the consensus statement disclosed the division among curricular orientations. Yet, the attempt at agreement on curriculum issues was admirable in itself. That effort, as did the *Yearbook* as a whole, conferred legitimacy upon the new field of curriculum.

Bobbitt changes his mind? Among the individual responses to the composite statement, perhaps Franklin Bobbitt's is the most surprising. It suggests a possible turn in Bobbitt's curriculum theory (Kliebard, 1986). As you recall, Bobbitt had been instrumental in developing the rationale and techniques of the curricular orientation termed social efficiency. Borrowing from scientific management, Bobbitt developed a "task analysis" to guide curriculum construction, insisting that the value of present educational activity was the vocational "pay-off" in the future. In 1927 he appears to change his mind on this point:

> In a very true sense, life cannot be "prepared for." It can only be lived. But, fortunately, living it provides the momentum which continues it on the same level. Living it in proper ways impels it forward along the lines desired by education, and nothing else will do so. Preparation for life is thus a by-product of life itself. (NSSE, 1927b, p. 43)

Here Bobbitt seems to reject scientific management, the ideal of an adult-centered school.

W. W. Charters prepared the briefest of responses: two paragraphs! Unlike Bobbitt, Charters gave no indication of altering his position. He still differed with those who would emphasize the needs and interests of the child: "Rather, I believe that the curriculum must be based upon the needs, interests and activities of both children and adults" (NSSE, 1927b, p. 71).

A skepticism regarding science. Counts' social reform emphasis, later to become known as "reconstruction" in educational philosophy (whose major proponent was Theodore Brameld; see Stanley, 1992b), included commentary upon the relative merits of science and philosophy to the curriculum enterprise. Counts viewed philosophy as crucial to the understanding and developing of curriculum: "The bearing of this discussion on curriculum-making is plain. The fundamental goals of education cannot be determined by scientific method" (NSSE, 1927b, p. 90). [This skepticism regarding social science in curriculum research would be elaborated again in the 1970s; see chapters 4, 8, 10.] Counts again stressed the social functions of schooling: "The school is an instrument for doing the difficult educational tasks, for anticipating the problems of the future, and for directing the course of social behavior" (NSEE, 1927b, p. 85).

Curriculum organization paramount. Charles Judd, the University of Chicago Department Chairman and advocate of social efficiency and scientific curriculum-making, summarized his position. "The reconstruction [of curriculum materials] here called for," he insisted in what to contemporary readers seems to be sexist language, "is not a task to be turned over to untrained and inexperienced girls of the type one finds in charge of elementary classes." He is just as dismissive of competing reform orientations, terming them "shallow." The primary job facing curriculum makers, he declared, involves organization: "The material of instruction needs to be amplified and rearranged and organized. The emphasis is on organization" (NSSE,1927b, p. 117).

Kilpatrick's progressive position remained unchanged. He acknowledged that he espoused a "curriculum theory widely different from that customarily followed" (NSSE, 1927b, p. 120). Kilpatrick's concerns were focused not upon curriculum content, but on issues located in a broad view of the educative process. From this perspective, "much of the scientific procedure is ruled out or relegated to a distinctly inferior position" (NSSE,1927b, p. 142).

The necessity of cooperation. The final response to the consensus statement came from the Committee Chair, Harold Rugg. His statement is important as it acknowledges the nascent stage of the new field in the mid-1920's and asserts the need for cooperation in curriculum making.

> The General Statement, therefore, in my judgment should have made more emphatic the doctrine that curriculum-making demands the cooperation of several specialists. This generalization has hardly been grasped at all as yet. Nevertheless, each of the tasks is important. Each demands specialized equipment. The day is past in which a single individual—be he professor, teacher, administrator, psychologist, sociologist or research specialist of whatever brand—can encompass all of these tasks singlehanded. (NSSE, 1927b, p. 162)

A field with a complex identity. The 1920s came to a close, then, with a historical study, a consensus statement, and a series of responses to that consensus statement. While the composite statement was "bland," it did present an effort to congeal curriculum knowledge. In so doing, it conferred legitimacy and identity to the new field. The Tanners (1980) observed that curriculum as a field of professional work emerged from this statement. That identity contained two elements: social efficiency and Progressivism (including social reform and child-centeredness). This complex, internally antagonistic identity would characterize the field in the decades to come, as we shall see in chapter 3.

Chapter 3

Understanding Curriculum
as Historical Text:
Crisis, Transformation, Crisis
1928-1969

Curriculum history is the collective memory of the field of curriculum. . . .
Curriculum history . . . helps us to understand the traditions that have defined
our professional and personal lives. This function is not just a practical affair—it
is a matter of feeling.

(Daniel & Laurel Tanner, 1990, p. 7)

[Curriculum theory] is disciplined by the vertical awareness of curriculum
theory as it has developed historically and by the horizontal awareness of man's
contemporary status of development in various formal disciplines.

(James B. Macdonald, 1967, p. 169)

I
Introduction:
The Tumultuous 1920s and 1930s

The 1920's was a decade of battle between two incompatible ideas, both of
which wanted control of the American school curriculum. Winning the first
round was the social efficiency movement, supported by a decade of public
enthusiasm for American business. Borrowing from scientific management,
social efficiency curricularists made task and activity analysis the primary
methods of curriculum construction (Bobbitt, 1918; Charters, 1923). The
Progressive dissent claimed democracy, social reform, and child-centeredness
as the fundamental ideas of curriculum construction (Dewey, 1916; Bode,
1927). While activists from these two reform movements cooperated in writing the *Twenty-Sixth Yearbook*, they failed to adjudicate their differences.

Social efficiency wanes, Progressivism ascendant. Just as the decade-long business expansion supported the ascendancy of social efficiency in curriculum,
the 1929 stock market crash and subsequent economic crisis undermined its
influence. Indeed, the social reform and social reconstruction elements of
Progressivism replaced social efficiency as the primary paradigm. Moved off
center stage by historical events, social efficiency advocates fought back. They

demanded scientific evidence to support the claims made by the Progressives (Schubert, 1986a). While Bobbitt's and Charters' scientific methods promised efficient management in a time of proliferating programs, they offered little solace to a nation in economic contraction and social crisis. While a revision of Charters' *Curriculum Construction* appeared in 1938, the 1930's belonged to the Progressives (Schubert, 1980a). The social efficiency orientation would have to wait until another period of economic expansion to reassert its claims. That time would come after World War II.

Dewey and curriculum reorganization. The title of Dewey's 1931 pamphlet underlined the mood of the country and the field. In *The Way Out of Educational Confusion*, Dewey blamed the curricular crisis upon rigid divisions among subject areas. He argued for a reorganization of subject matter based upon a study of the student. Such a curriculum "cannot fail . . . to awaken some permanent interest and curiosity. Theoretical subjects," he wrote, "will become more practical because [they become] more related to the scope of life; practical subjects will become more charged with theory and intelligent insight" (Dewey, 1964, p. 425). Lessening the sharp separation of subject areas received considerable emphasis in curriculum thought in the 1930s.

However, many writers focused upon curriculum correlation and integration, rather cosmetic versions of Dewey's views (Schubert, 1980a). For instance, L. Thomas Hopkins, in his *Integration: Its Meaning and Application* (1937), attempted to "investigate the concept of integration further" (Hopkins, 1937, p. v). "From the educational viewpoint," Hopkins writes, "integration must be the shorthand word to describe the process involved in this intelligent, ongoing, interacting, adjusting behavior" (Hopkins, 1937, p. 2). Hopkins argued that this process of continual interaction and adjustment among subject areas constituted the "building [of] an ideology that is more appropriate to our changing life" (Hopkins, 1937). This ideology reflects Hopkins' conception of the role and task of the curriculum-maker. Hopkins wrote:

> If [the curriculum maker] disapproves of existing forms of economic, business, recreational, political, or other activity because of their obvious disintegrative effects upon the young, [the curriculum maker] must then try to discover the deeper dynamics or orientations of these activities in order that he may get clues for their effective reorientation and integration. (Hopkins, 1937, p. 68)

This quoted passage is actually somewhat misleading of Hopkins' view. He was largely concerned with internal integration but generally omitted Dewey's idea of socially relevant problems. Hopkins was perhaps the most "child-centered" of all Progressives.

Dewey and Bode worried that the child-centered school often lacked any social direction. Some child-centered educators seemed to refuse the responsibility of providing educational direction, seeing teaching itself as a form of imposition. Certain child-centered educators, like Margaret Naumburg, the founder of the Walden School, in fact attacked Dewey's group psychology and social theory as leading to "a dull and gloomy picture, this Technological Utopia" (cited in Karier, 1967, p. 239). Naumburg's program was built upon the use of therapy, her faith in social engineering justifying intervention into the pupil's inner life. A therapeutic notion of education would resurface in the alternative schools movement of the 1960s (Nelson & Watras, 1981; Lasch, 1977; Glasser, 1969). Dewey believed that the fundamental misconception about the concept of growth is to regard it as having an end, instead of being an end (Callan, 1982). According to Dewey, when we view education as growth we come to see the child "intrinsically" rather than "comparatively." Dewey (1916) wrote:

> When we abandon the attempt to define immaturity by means of fixed comparison with adult accomplishments, we are compelled to give up thinking of it as denoting lack of desired traits. Abandoning this notion we are also forced to surrender our habit of thinking of instruction as a method of supplying this lack by pouring knowledge into a mental and moral hole with awaits filling. Since life means growth, a living creature lives as truly and positively at one. state as at another, with the same intrinsic fullness and the same absolute claims. (p. 51)

While Dewey was careful to define his terms, his concepts were often misconstrued. Israel Scheffler (1974) has pointed out that criticisms of Dewey have tended to take two contradictory directions. On the one hand, he has been castigated as an apostle of conformity who did not value individuality, and, on the other, he has been denounced as the champion of permissiveness in the classroom. These criticisms have very limited legitimacy as each is based on an incomplete picture of Dewey's educational thought. The former focuses on the idea of democratic socialization while the other concentrates exclusively on the abstracted idea of education as growth (Callan, 1982). The implications of Dewey's concept of experience would intrigue curriculum scholars for decades [see, for instance, Chiarelott, 1983a, 1983b].

Curriculum as political text. In many ways 1932 was the best year progressive education ever enjoyed; certainly it was the most hopeful year. However, these hopes would never materialize. Within ten years the Progressive Education Association would be a shadow of itself; membership would be down 50 per cent (Doll, W., 1983a). In 1932, however, progressive education was ascendent. In that year George S. Counts published a pamphlet comprised of three papers read at various educational meetings that year, papers that stirred excitement and controversy. These were entitled "Dare Progressive Education Be Progressive?," "Education Through Indoctrination," and "Freedom, Culture, Social Planning and Leadership." The resulting pamphlet was the famous *Dare the Schools Build a New Social Order?*

The child-centered and social wings of the Progressive movement went to war against each other. Viewing child-centeredness as a comfortable position compatible with the economic position of the privileged classes, Counts attacked: "The weakness of Progressive Education thus lies in the fact that it has elaborated no theory of social welfare, unless it be that of anarchy or extreme individualism. In this, of course, it is but reflecting the viewpoint of the members of the liberal-minded upper class" (Counts, 1932, p. 7). Counts was adamant that the problems of American education could not be solved by child-centered schools. To become truly progressive, Progressivism must articulate a social vision. This "politicization" of Progressivism frightened many, particularly as Counts refused to repudiate indoctrination. Many Progressives feared that espousing a social ideology would result in indoctrination. Counts agreed, arguing that indoctrination is both inevitable and positive. "All education," Counts declared, "contains a large element of imposition. . . . It is eminently desirable. The frank acceptance of this fact by the educator," he concluded, "is a professional obligation" (Counts, 1932, p. 12).

Ten fallacies. Counts identified ten fallacies underlying educators' opposition to imposition. One such fallacy foreshadows a criticism made in the 1970's of what at that time was traditional curriculum work, specifically the Tyler Rationale:

> My thesis is that complete impartiality is utterly impossible. . . . The school must shape attitudes, develop tastes and even impose ideas. Because what is known is too immense to be taught in schools, choices must be made. Whenever choices are made regarding curriculum, teachers, teaching methods, partiality is demonstrated. (Counts, 1932, p. 19)

Counts identified another fallacy, again foreshadowing contemporary curriculum debates, that curriculum without a social perspective leads to intellectualism and self-absorption. Educators have "the responsibility of bringing to the younger generation a vision which will call forth their active loyalties and challenge them to creative and arduous labors." Counts worried that a generation lacking such a vision is condemned to live "a life of absorption in self, inferiority complexes, and frustration. The genuinely free man," he concluded, "is not a person who spends the day contemplating his own navel, but rather the one who loses himself in a great cause or glorious adventure" (Counts, 1932, p. 23).

Reactions to Counts. Counts' *Dare the Schools Build a New Social Order?* was a call to arms. Reactions ranged from "inspiring!" and "stirring!" to "impractical" and "un-American." Counts split the progressive movement beyond reconciliation, and this polarization began the slow erosion and ultimate demise of education's most memorable era (Niece & Viechnicki, 1987).

Dewey's responded in 1933, in an address to the Minneapolis Department of Supervisors and Directors of Instruction. On that occasion Dewey made three recommendations: 1) teachers had an obligation to search for solutions to social problems; 2) the study of social problems should focus on what teachers know best, i.e. their local community; only then could the focus broaden to the nation; and 3) social objectives which might support teachers in social reform efforts ought to be formulated (Niece & Viechnicki, 1987). Clearly, Dewey supported the decentralization of authority, democratization of the workplace, redistribution of wealth, the strengthening of civil liberties, and the representative institutions essential to dissent and the diffusion of power (Westbrook, 1991; Schwartz, 1991). While his tone was calmer than Counts, Dewey was in general agreement that schools should function to change society.

Horace Mann Bond. Another notable scholar of the progressive period was Horace Mann Bond. While not directly involved with the Progressive movement, Bond's historical scholarship shared Counts' analysis of American education as reproductive of the political status quo (1934, 1939). Bond's Ph.D. dissertation (completed at the University of Chicago) on African-American education in Alabama received a best dissertation prize; in paperback form it was reprinted in the 1960s (Urban, 1989, 1992). At Dillard University in New Orleans, Bond designed the undergraduate curriculum, borrowing from the curriculum structure of the University of Chicago. As his biographer notes, however:

> Bond did more than borrow the Chicago curriculum for Dillard. He added an emphasis on the special contributions of blacks. . . . He also stressed the social sciences, since these areas of study both provided the means for analyzing the problems blacks faced and pointed the way to their possible amelioration. (Urban, 1992, p. 61)

Bond's scholarly career was perhaps surpassed by his accomplishment in administration (Urban, 1992). Bond served not only as Dean at Dillard, but as the President of Fort Valley State College in Georgia and of his own alma mater, Lincoln University in Pennsylvania. Additionally he served as Dean of Atlanta University's School of Education. Despite the demands of administration, Bond managed to publish studies of issues in black educational life (1959, 1972, 1976). Moreover, he traveled frequently to Africa during the 1940s and 1950s, striving to support educational, political, economic, and cultural relations between Africans and African Americans. Bond is also known as the father of Julian Bond, the brilliant civil rights activist of the 1960s. Horace Mann Bond's understanding of the profoundly conservative character of American education, particularly in the racial sphere, represents a significant moment in the advancement of curriculum knowledge. Bond's work foreshadowed the establishment in the 1990s of race as a central curriculum discourse.

Curriculum as labor toward realization of a social vision. The centrality of a social vision to education is evident in Bond's, Counts', and Dewey's conceptions of curriculum. Counts, for instance, cautioned educators against being content with giving children the opportunity only to study contemporary society. While study is essential, schools must go beyond contemplation. School "must become centers for building. . . . We should . . . give our children a vision of the possibilities that lie ahead and endeavor to enlist their loyalties and enthusiasms in the realization of the vision" (Counts, 1932). The influence of Counts within the Progressive Education Association was unmistakable, creating a division within the group which was never mended.

Responding to Counts' speech, the Association created a Committee on Social and Economic Problems, with Counts as chair. The recommendations issued by the Committee were never approved by the P.E.A.'s Board of Directors, but appeared separately, published in pamphlet form as *A Call to the Teachers of the Nation* (Tanner & Tanner, 1980). Another indication of Counts' divisive effect upon the Progressive movement was the tension felt in the John Dewey Society. This tension, expressed along institutional lines, centered on the issue of dogmatism and indoctrination. Counts' colleagues at Teachers College, Columbia University, tended to discount the Ohio State University group's critique of Counts' position as undemocratic (Foshay, 1991).

Unlike the clichéd image of the scholar as a socially weak if not passive figure, progressive scholars—led by John Dewey and George Counts—were authentic social radicals who expressed a deep commitment to social planning and, among other issues, public ownership of the means of the production. Furthermore, not only did the advocates of a new society battle the remnants of the once strong child-centered wing for leadership of the Progressive Education Movement, they also struggled against internal dissension while working to arouse support for their educational ideas among classroom teachers largely indifferent to the ideological dispute then raging between the two wings of the movement (Bowers, 1969). Other progressives, such as William Heard Kilpatrick, were pedagogical (rather than social) radicals who remained deeply skeptical of leftwing, especially Marxist, influences in the movement (Stanley, 1992b, p. 46). Despite important differences among progressives, they were courageous and committed to the reconceptualization of American education.

A vehicle to support Counts and his colleagues was established in 1934. Entitled *The Social Frontier*, this periodical argued for the "school's role in creating a new social order" (Kliebard, 1986, p. 196). Cremin (1961) noted: "*The Social Frontier* remained the only journal specifically addressed to teachers that openly and forthrightly discussed the ideological problems of an ideological age" (p. 232). In recounting the short history of *The Social Frontier*, Cremin observed that despite its fairly wide circulation, reaching some 5,000 subscribers, the magazine ran deficits. Overtures were made during 1937 and 1938 to the Progressive Education Association for sponsorship. After repeated refusals, the P.E.A. accepted in 1939 with the proviso that the name be changed to *Frontiers of Democracy* under a new editorial board. However, *Frontiers of Democracy* was to become a mere shadow of *The Social Frontier*. In the last issue (December 15, 1943), the editor, Harold Rugg, wrote a lengthy and bitter editorial in which he doubted the P.E.A.'s commitment to its professed principles (Tanner & Tanner, 1990). With the collapse of the P.E.A. some twelve years later, the John Dewey Society waged a losing battle to continue the publication (Tanner, D., 1991).

Struggles to survive. As we mentioned earlier, the rise of progressive education was short-lived. By the end of the 1930s the beginning of the end was evident. For example, the year 1940 was something of an "open season" on progressive education, as national magazines characterized the movement as "naively sentimental on the one hand, dangerously subversive on the other" (Cremin, 1961, p. 267). Another illustration of the demise of the progressive movement was the Association's inability to agree on a platform. In the absence of a platform to define its mission, the P.E.A. appointed a Committee on Philosophy of Education in 1938. Issued under the chairmanship of Harold Alberty of Ohio State as a special supplement to *Progressive Education* in May, 1941, the Committee's report is characterized by Cremin as "Deweyan from beginning to end" and as "the most fundamental statement of principles ever to issue from the PEA." However, the report was never formally adopted by the Association (Cremin, 1961).

The John Dewey Society met with the American Association of School Administrators (AASA) after World War II, but their program proved too controversial for the school administrators. The minutes of the meeting of the Society's Executive Board on November 10-11, 1947 in New York City, reveal that the Society was refused accommodation at the February, 1947 annual meeting of the American Association of School Administrators. The role of the John Dewey Society in seeking to save *The Social Frontier* and *Progressive Education* is "testimony to a courageous and unparalleled effort" (Tanner, D., 1991, p. 100).

Bobbitt vs. Counts: Social efficiency counterattacks. The internal divisions between child-centered advocates and social reconstructionists undermined the influence and effectiveness of the Progressive Education Association (Tanner & Tanner, 1980; Schubert, 1986a; Kliebard, 1986). The influence of the latter was sharply circumscribed, for several reasons. First, many educational administrators did not share the political vision of Counts and *The Social Frontier* (Kliebard, 1986). Second, many teachers were indifferent to the idea of working toward a new social order. Clearly, the labor required of teachers to participate meaningfully in social reconstruction was immense. Indifference, not laziness, explains why so few teachers chose to align themselves with Counts (Tanner & Tanner, 1980). Third, the "down but not out" social efficiency advocates challenged the political character of Progressive reform. On one occasion, Bobbitt characterized the social reconstructionist perspective as a "mere protective smoke-screen for a communistic offensive" (Bobbitt, 1934, p. 295; Kliebard, 1986, p. 197). This was nonsense. With the exception of Theodore Brameld, who would not become well-known until the 1950s, Counts, Rugg, Dewey, and other social reconstructionists were not, by any measure, Marxists or communists (Stanley, 1992b).

Dewey reviews social perspectives on schools. John Dewey was not silent during the controversies of the 1930's. In "Education and Social Change," which appeared in a 1937 issue of *The Social Frontier,* Dewey reviewed the range of positions regarding the social function of schools. Working to be inclusive of both camps, Dewey observed:

> There are those who assert in effect that the schools must simply reflect social changes that have already occurred, as best they may. Some would go as far as to make the work of schools virtually parasitic. Others hold that the schools should take an active part in *directing* social change, and share in the construction of a new social order. Even among the latter there is, however, marked difference of attitude. Some think schools should assume this directive role by means of indoctrination; others oppose this method. (Dewey 1939, p. 691)

While Dewey agreed that schools played an important role in social change, he disagreed with Counts and his followers that the schools could become the primary force in stimulating such change. What schools could do, he argued, was foster in students those attitudes and dispositions which would prepare and inspire them to participate in social change. "The problem will be," Dewey asserted, "to develop the insight and understanding that will enable the youth who go forth from the schools to take part in the great work of construction and organization that will have to be done." Progressive educators, he continued, will "equip them with the attitudes and habits of action that will make their understanding and insight practically effective" (Dewey, quoted in Ratner, 1939, p. 695).

In the decades to follow, educational reformers would often wonder how to reconcile the participatory and democratic schools that Dewey envisioned with the dominant and often authoritarian structures of a bureaucratic society. Dewey's own answer to this question is now clear: they cannot be reconciled. To achieve a decent and just society—one in which every person can fulfill his or her true potential—all institutions, not just schools, must support social cooperation and effective citizen participation (Schwartz, 1991).

Bode: Avoid an apolitical preoccupation with "pupil interest." Bode shared Dewey's and Counts' concern for social reform (Bullough, 1981). Perhaps he occupied a space between them, more politically radical than Dewey but less so than Counts, although still very much a "committed intellectual and academic" (Kridel, 1983, p. 92). In *Progressive Education at the Crossroads,* Bode (1938) reminded his readers that the progressive movement was inseparable from the cause of democracy:

> Democracy as a tradition encourages reliance on intelligence in matters of education; and education, in turn, becomes an instrumentality for bringing democracy to a clear consciousness of its meaning and purpose.
> This is the general direction in which progressive education must move if it is to remain faithful to its basic principles and ideals. The alternative is to keep rotating on the axis of "pupil interest." Progressive education has a unique opportunity of serving as a clearinghouse for the meaning of democracy and thus making a significant contribution toward bringing to fruition the great hope and promise of our American civilization. (p. 61)

Further: "[Progressive education] emphasizes freedom, yet it also attaches major importance to guidance and direction. . . . It places the individual at the center of the stage; yet it perpetually criticizes the competitive character of the present social order, which indicates that it rejects the philosophy of individualism" (Bode, 1938, p. 10). Finally, Bode asserted: "Progressive education has a unique opportunity to become an avowed exponent of a democratic philosophy of life, which is the last remaining hope that the common man will eventually come into his own" (Bode, 1938, p. 122).

Democracy __and__ child-centeredness. John Dewey and Harold Rugg were also concerned with the danger of "catering to student caprice" (Schubert, 1986a, p. 80). In what has been described as his most "important pedagogical work of the thirties" (Cremin, 1964, p. 236), Dewey, in *Experience and Education* (1938), worried that the division within Progressivism between child-centeredness advocates and social reconstructionists would only result in a stagnation of the movement. Dewey was troubled by a tendency toward "either-or" thinking, an acceptance of dualisms (Dewey, 1938, p.1). Also in this thin volume Dewey attempts to clarify popular misunderstandings of his previous work. For instance, he insists yet again that Progressivism must be committed to democracy as well as child development. As Gutmann (1987) has also noted, in Dewey's laboratory school the idea of creating an embryonic democratic society was tempered by the understanding that such an embryonic form could not be simplistically democratic; the school for instance, did not regard students as political and intellectual equals (Hlebowitsh, 1992).

Harold Rugg's and Ann Shumaker's *The Child Centered School* (1928) praised child-centered education because it developed tolerance, creativity, and supported the development of the child. Nevertheless, Rugg also promoted the use of controlled experiment and careful planning for the child-centered school (Nelson & Watras, 1981). Rugg developed what became the most widely adopted school texts in a Progressive vein. His elementary social studies series, entitled *Man and His Changing Society* (1929-1932), was widely adopted by school districts nationwide. However, like a fate to be met by another social studies series developed three decades later (*Man: A Course of Study*)[see later this chapter] Rugg's series also fell prey to right-wing political attacks. By the 1940s, the series was no longer adopted.

Kilpatrick retires. Other events marked the close of the 1930s. The well-known exponent of the "project method," William Heard Kilpatrick, taught his last class during the summer of 1937. Kilpatrick had been attracting classes of up to seven hundred students, filling the Horace Mann auditorium on the Teachers College campus in New York. He organized the meetings so that small groups of students discussed the topics and issues in the syllabus, and then reported conclusions and ideas to the larger meeting through elected spokespersons (Cottrell, 1987).

Kilpatrick, it becomes clear, had been a "larger than life" figure during his twenty-five years on the Teachers College, Columbia University faculty.

Indeed, a registrar at Teachers College once described Kilpatrick to a new student as the "man who looks like God and talks like God" (Beineke, 1989, p. 147). Kilpatrick's last class enrolled 622 students. At the last meeting of that class, one student rose and said, "We believe in what you are telling us, Dr. Kilpatrick, but how can we go back to our little towns and schools and implement your ideas?" Kilpatrick walked to the front of the platform and said, "I'll tell you how to implement what I have been telling you. You do what the greatest of all teachers said to do, 'I came that you might have life and that you might have it abundantly.' And those are my final words to you" (Beineke, 1989, pp. 148-149).

Teachers College, Columbia University. While Dewey taught in Columbia's Department of Philosophy, other important progressives taught at Columbia's Teachers College. Norman Cousins (1987) recalls what it was like to be a student at that great institution in the 1930s:

> It would be difficult to think of a school in the mid-thirties more drenched with a sense of living history than Teachers College. Teachers College was more than a graduate school at Columbia; it set the intellectual and philosophical tone for the University and, indeed, for a large segment of the national liberal community. [I remember] Harold Rugg surrounded by the inevitable cluster of students at the end of a lecture, then looking up and saying, "Good heavens, I was supposed to be at a faculty conference a half hour ago!" [There was] a visit to John Dewey at his home, talking about his view of the Trotsky assassination and about the Soviet purges. [One recalls] William Kilpatrick talking about the need to educate for world citizenship. . . . At a time when many intellectuals were giving up on American political and economic institutions and turning to the Soviet Union, the key figures of Teachers College—Counts, Kilpatrick, Guss, Childs, et al.—with the full backing of John Dewey, were redefining the nature and place of vital progressive social-democratic thought and action. . . . They were custodians of the American liberal tradition of Jefferson, Emerson, William James, and Oliver Wendell Holmes. (Cousins, 1987, p. 22, 24)

Clearly, Teachers College was a most remarkable institution during the 1930s.

II
The Eight-Year Study

I would like to place on the record the fact that my teaching in the Progressive Education Movement . . . was one of the finest experiences I've had in my life.
(James Michener, 1987, p. 10)

The Progressive Education Association conducted a comprehensive study and field experiment with secondary school curriculum during the 1930's known as the Eight-Year Study. This effort remains today as perhaps the major curriculum study in the history of the field. In April 1930, the P.E.A. met to discuss ways in which "the secondary schools of the United States might better serve all our young people" (Aikin, 1942, p. 1). Elementary schools were already undergoing experimental changes inspired by Dewey and others. The secondary schools were constrained by rigid college requirements. Understandably, secondary school officials were reluctant to experiment with curriculum when such experimentation might jeopardize their graduates' admission to colleges and universities. Too, the courses required for college entrance shaped most high school programs.

Commission on the Relation of School to College. The Progressive Education Association established the Commission on the Relation of School to College in October, 1930, with Wilford M. Aikin as chair. Funding for the project was provided by grants from the Carnegie Foundation and the General Education Board, eventually amounting to $70,000 and $622,500 respectively, large sums in Depression America (Kliebard, 1986, p. 214). For a year the Commission studied secondary schools; then it issued a statement wherein eighteen (18) areas which required "exploration or improvement" were identified (Aikin, 1942, p. 4). Most of these "areas" involved curriculum issues; five specifically referred to curriculum matters. For instance, the Commission questioned the "relevancy" of the traditional high school curriculum. Student centeredness was absent, noted by the Commission in language not unfamiliar to contemporary students of the curriculum: "There was little realization that much of the work of the classroom was meaningless to students and that they were doing the work assigned chiefly for the 'credit'" (Aikin, 1942, p. 7).

A second area requiring "improvement" concerned the "vitality and significance" of the curriculum. The Commission found the secondary school curriculum disjointed with subjects isolated from each other. Curricular continuity within subject fields and between grade levels was absent as well. The effect was a pervasive sense of purposelessness to school work. Yet, this state of affairs seemed to prod little analysis, a third area identified by the Commission: "Minor curriculum changes were frequently made, but there was little serious questioning of purposes, practices, or results. Lavish financial support and blind faith on the part of the people encouraged schoolmen to conclude that all was right with their world" (Aikin, 1942, p. 9). A final finding of the Commission concerned the relationship between secondary schools and colleges and universities, a relationship that was "unsatisfactory to both institutions" (Aikin, 1942, p. 10). In particular, college entrance requirements limited secondary school officials' capacity to correct those curricular problems identified by the Commission. Entrance requirements constituted a fundamental problem to be solved before meaningful curricular changes could be attempted.

Colleges cooperate. The Commission sought the cooperation of colleges and universities on this point. Their willingness to cooperate was crucial to the progressive reform of secondary schools. Colleges and universities were challenged to release secondary schools from unit entrance requirements. In 1932 the Commission received statements of cooperation from more than 300 colleges and universities. These post-secondary institutions agreed to release designated secondary schools from entrance requirements for a period of five years initially, and for a period of eight years beginning with the class entering college in 1936. These activities were supervised by the Directing Committee of the Commission. Participating secondary schools were self-selected, according to their willingness to participate in progressive experimentation. Initially, twenty-seven schools were chosen; two California schools were added later. Both private and public schools, large and small schools, and schools representing different sections of the United States participated in the Eight-Year Study (Aikin, 1942). Public schools famous for progressive reform, for instance Denver and Winnetka, Illinois, as well as laboratory schools, participated. The twenty-seven original schools were:

Altoona Senior High School	Altoona, PA
Baldwin School	Bryn Mawr, PA (metropolitan Philadelphia)
Beaver Country Day School	Chestnut Hill, MA
Bronxville Senior High School	Bronxville, NY (metropolitan New York City)
Cheltenham Township High School	Elkins Park, PA (metropolitan Philadelphia)
Dalton School	New York, NY
Denver High Schools	Denver, CO
Fieldston School	New York, NY
Francis W. Parker School	Chicago, IL
George School	George School PA (metropolitan Philadelphia)
Germantown Friends School	Germantown, PA (metropolitan Philadelphia)
Horace Mann School for Girls	New York, NY
John Burroughs School	Clayton, MO (metropolitan St. Louis)
Lincoln School	New York, NY
Milton Academy	Milton, MA (metropolitan Boston)
New Trier Township High School	Winnetka, IL (metropolitan Chicago)
North Shore Country Day School	Winnetka, IL (metropolitan Chicago)
Ohio State University Lab School	Columbus, OH
Pelham Manor Day School	Pelham, NY (metropolitan New York City)
Radnor High School	Radnor, PA (metropolitan Philadelphia)
Shaker High School	Shaker Heights, OH (metropolitan Cleveland)
Theodore Roosevelt High School	Des Moines, IA
Tower High School	Wilmington, DE
University High School	Chicago, IL
Windsor School	Boston, MA
Wisconsin High School	Madison, WI
Central High School	Tulsa, OK

Three schools were added by 1934: Eagle Rock High School, Los Angeles, CA; Friend's Central School, Overbrook, PA (metropolitan Philadelphia); and University High School, Oakland, CA. In 1936 the Pelham Manor Day School withdrew (Kridel, in press).

Evaluation. The schools undertook curriculum revision in 1933; an evaluation staff was formed in 1934. Each school "developed its own plans and decided for itself what changes should be made in curriculum organization and procedure" (Aikin, 1942, p.15). Director of Research for the Evaluation Staff (not the entire study as is commonly misunderstood) was Ralph W. Tyler. As we noted earlier, Tyler had been a student of Charles Judd at the University of Chicago, graduating with the Ph.D. in 1927. Tyler would become the single most visible name in American curriculum studies.

From the outset Tyler was a proponent of the scientific study of education. This orientation made his selection appropriate, given the importance of evaluation in the study. One evaluative mode was the analysis of objectives, a mode endorsed by Tyler. Participating schools identified ten major objectives. The evaluation committee, headquartered at Ohio State University, would then work to ascertain what progress students were making toward realization of these goals. Characteristic goals included social sensitivity, aesthetic appreciation, physical health, building a philosophy of life, and a general broadening of interests.

The birth of behavioral objectives? The means by which progress toward the attainment of these goals would be evaluated became a prime concern. During the course of seven years the evaluation committee "devised about two hundred tests that were used experimentally, refined and tried out again and again" (Aikin, 1942, p. 90). In volume III of the five volume series describing the Eight-Year Study, entitled *Appraising and Recording Student Progress*, Tyler discussed measurement devices: "Any device which provides valid evidence regarding the progress of students toward educational objectives is appropriate. . . . The selection of evaluation techniques should be made in terms of the appropriateness of that technique for the kind of behavior to be appraised" (Smith & Tyler, 1942). Stating objectives in terms of behaviors as a first step in curriculum making would imprint the future course of the field (Kliebard, 1986, p. 220).

Ten years later Tyler would formalize the process in his famous *Basic Principles of Curriculum and Instruction* (1949). Employed in the 1930s to evaluate the progressive Eight-Year Study, the emphasis upon behavior and objectives would, in thirty years time, become taken-for-granted in the curriculum field:

> The idea that educational outcomes needed to be defined in terms of identifiable behavior and in operational terms was the keystone of Tyler's Eight-Year Study. Tyler's rationale is depicted by a triangle, at the apex of which are the objectives that lead to the development of learning experiences, which in turn lead to evaluation of the extent to which objectives were realized. (Madaus & Kellaghan, 1992, p. 121)

As Travers (1983) notes, "the simplicity of the formula, and its appearance of logicality, gave it instant appeal across the country" (p. 152). Not until the Reconceptualization of the 1970's would its status be challenged.

Study ignored in face of World War II. Although participating schools attempted many curricular innovations, the results were far from revolutionary. Graduates made a negligible impact on the colleges which they later attended. The experiment did establish one significant fact—namely, that there is no one fixed pattern for a high-school curriculum required for college success. The impact of the Study was limited due to circumstances quite beyond its control: World War II (Kliebard, 1986). As Harold Alberty (1947) observed: "Unfortunately the reports of the study came at a time when the entire nation was involved in a death struggle against totalitarianism. Consequently it did not receive the attention it deserved. The impact upon the rank and file of secondary schools was very slight indeed. Teachers, by and large, went on assigning daily lessons from textbooks" (p. 287; quoted in Kridel, in press, p. 2). The final five-volume report of the Study was published in 1942 and 1943. Included in this set were *The Story of the Eight-Year Study* by Wilford Aikin, *Exploring the Curriculum* by Giles, McCutchen, and Zechiel; *Appraising and Recording Student Progress* by Smith, Tyler, and the evaluation staff; *Did They Succeed in College?* by Chamberlin, Chamberlin, Drought, and Scott; and *Thirty Schools Tell Their Story*.

Over 2000 students identified by teachers, headmasters, principals, and directors were followed into college and university. Fourteen hundred seventy-five were included in the follow-up study (Kridel, in press). Aikin (1942) summarized the findings:

> First, the graduates of the Thirty Schools were not handicapped in their college work. Second, departures from the prescribed pattern of subjects and units did not lessen the student's readiness for the responsibilities of college. Third, students from participating schools which made most fundamental curriculum revision achieved in college distinctly higher standing than that of students of equal ability with whom there were compared. (p. 117; quoted in Kridel, in press, p. 6)

Additionally, students from more experimental schools outperformed students from less experimental schools even when economic disadvantages were present:

> It is of considerable interest that one of these most experimental/most effective schools was located in an area characterized by poverty and predominantly populated by low socioeconomic students. Despite these disadvantages, students from this school outperformed students from more advantaged environments but less experimental schools. (Synder, Bolin & Zumwalt, 1992, p. 422)

This result should have been a victory for those who sought to break the yoke of college domination. No notable or lasting changes in the national pattern of college-entrance requirements emerged from the Eight-Year Study, despite the fact that the study indicated that success in college is not dependent on credits earned in high school in the traditionally prescribed subjects. In fact, one finding of the Eight-Year Study is that integrative approaches to the curriculum produced superior results (Kliebard, 1987; Tanner & Tanner, 1990). Another result of the Study was the production of curriculum design models with the assistance of consultants such as Harold Alberty of Ohio State University. These design models and the changes in school structure required to support them represent antecedents to certain contemporary school improvement efforts, such as Theodore Sizer's Coalition for Essential Schools [see chapter 13].

One curriculum historian suggests that it was the sense of adventure and genuine experimentation that represents the lasting significance of the Eight-Year Study (Kridel, in press). Aikin (1942) described the 1933 meeting of faculty and administrative staff from the participating schools:

> Everyone had a strong sense of sharing in a great adventure; few anticipated fully the hard work, the problems, the discouragements, and the eventual satisfactions which were to come. No one present at the first conference (in 1933) will ever forget the honest confession of one principal [from Francis W. Parker High School] when she said, 'My teachers and I do not know what to do with this freedom. It challenges and frightens us. I fear that we have come to love our chains.' Most of us were just beginning to realize that we were facing the severest test of our initiative, imagination, and wisdom. No one of the group could possibly foresee all the developments ahead, nor were we all of one mind as to what should be done. (p. 16; quoted in Kridel, in press, p. 10)

It was the spirit of the Study that was crucial for those who were involved (Kridel, in press). This spirit was not regarded as limited to the schools which participated:

> The most important result of this happy situation, if and as it is realized, will be, of course, the freeing of the teachers and administrators, not in thirty schools only, but in all our secondary schools, to work away at the improvement of their programs, in whatever ways their combined thinking, experience, and experimentation may suggest, untrammeled by artificial restrictions from "above." They will still be handicapped, as the Thirty Schools were, by school and community mores, by budgetary limitations, and by their own inertia and disagreements; they will make their grievous mistakes, as the Thirty Schools did; but they will in the end, like the Thirty Schools, make highly significant gains—to be realized in the fuller and happier living of oncoming generations of American boys and girls. (Chamberlin, Chamberlin, Drought, Scott, 1942, p. xxii; quoted in Kridel, in press, p.12)

Teaching in a progressive school. The Eight-Year Study afforded a general view of progressive schools. What was it like to teach in one? The widely read novelist and writer, James Michener (1987), recalled teaching in a progressive school:

> I would like to place on the record the fact that my teaching in the Progressive Education Movement at both the George School in Pennsylvania and the experimental school in Greeley, Colorado (at the Colorado State College of Education) was one of the finest experiences I've had in my life. I saw that the very best of contemporary education, conducted in a no-nonsense way, prepared my students for a 100% success rate in taking College Boards, and watched with delight as my graduates earned highly successful places for themselves in both later college life and adult performance. I have always viewed with mild amusement the loose charges that Progressive Education was a failure or that it promoted laxity in either study or morals. My classes, if I say so

myself, were among the best being taught in America at that time, all with a far above average model of deportment and learning. And through the years my former students constantly wrote to me that they evaluated those years in the same way. A failure? One of the greatest successes I've known. As to the effect on me: it made me a liberal, a producer, a student of my world, a man with a point of view and the courage to exemplify it. I wish all students could have the experiences mine did. I wish all teachers could know the joy I found in teaching under such conditions. (p. 10)

Clearly, the progressive era was an exciting time for teachers as well as students.

III
The Synoptic Text

The subject matter specialist became something of an anathema within professional curriculum circles.

(Herbert M. Kliebard, 1979, p. 223)

Caswell and Campbell's Curriculum Development. Of significance to the curriculum field during the 1930's was the appearance of the so-called "synoptic text," examples of which we examined in chapter 1. Hollis L. Caswell and Doak S. Campbell's *Curriculum Development* (1935) established a tradition of synoptic texts in the American curriculum field. [Caswell pioneered statewide programs of curriculum development in the 1930s (Tanner & Tanner, 1990).] These comprehensive introductory texts would dominate the field for decades to come (Schubert, 1980a), up to the present time (Tanner & Tanner, 1980; McNeil, 1985; Schubert, 1986a). Recently, these texts have failed to keep abreast of the rapidly changing field, a problem we lamented in chapter one.

Hollis Caswell founded a genre of scholarship in the curriculum field. What was he like as a teacher? Arthur Foshay (1987), a former student of Caswell, recalls:

It was the summer of 1945 at Teachers College, Columbia University. I looked through an open door into a spacious office. Seated at an orderly desk at the far end was the man I had come from California to see—Hollis L. Caswell. He was reputed to be the leader in curriculum development in the country. I wanted to study with him, to become acquainted with his approach to curriculum problems. I was not to be disappointed. In the course of time, he became my advisor, mentor, colleague, and friend.... Education, he obviously believed, had to deal not only with cognitive development, but also with the solving of social problems and the building of civic morality. His extensive work on state and city curriculum programs during the heart of the Great Depression of the Thirties had no doubt deepened these convictions of his.... The difference between Caswell and the others of that time—such people as George Counts and Harold Rugg—was that Caswell got into the field and made things happen. [Referring to a course in 1946 taught by Caswell assisted by William Alexander, Foshay tells us that Caswell insisted]: "the individual school is the unit for curriculum development." Caswell's emphasis on action led him to

emphasize cooperative action research, which places the teacher at the center
of school experimentation, and offers a consultant to help the teacher to
design the research and evaluate the consequence. (pp. 76-78)

Despite these progressive features of Caswell's view of curriculum development, he maintained some distance from the movement itself. He had not,
for instance, been a member of the Progressive Education Association.

In addition to Foshay, William Alexander, Marcella Lawler, Alice Miel, A.
Harry Passow, and Galen Saylor were all students of Caswell. His influence
over important curriculum scholars was wide. Foshay (1987) tells us that
Florence Stratemeyer's *Developing a Curriculum for Modern Living* (1957) was
the result of "pressure" from Caswell for two years. The notion of building a
curriculum in light of "persistent life situations" which became the theme of
that book can be found in a 1929 publication of Caswell's. However, no
acknowledgement of Caswell's contribution appears in the Stratemeyer book.

In addition to intellectual influence, there was institutional influence:
Caswell formed the first Department of Curriculum and Teaching in 1938, at
Teachers College, Columbia University. Foshay (1987) credits Caswell with
inventing the field of curriculum development with his innovative state and
city curriculum development programs. Also among Caswell's achievement
was the establishment of the Horace Mann-Lincoln Institute of School Experimentation, an institution we noted in chapter 2.

Upon Caswell's death in 1988, curriculum historian Barry Franklin (1989)
wrote an obituary. Noting that Caswell had been a doctoral student of
George Strayer at Teachers College, Franklin (1989) reminded us that
Caswell participated in and championed the school survey, a favorite efficiency oriented practice of early school administrators. Despite this enthusiasm and his work with Strayer, "Caswell did not exactly embrace the efficiency tradition" (Franklin, 1989, p. 1). Caswell judged scientific curriculum
makers as excessively preoccupied with the use of predetermined objectives.
He believed it was necessary to address the educational and social problems
associated with the transformation of the United States into a modern,
urban, and industrial society.

Unlike Bobbitt, Charters, and other social efficiency advocates who viewed
the emergence of corporate capitalism as a sign of progress, Caswell was less
optimistic. For example, the courses of study that resulted from the Virginia
state curriculum revision of the early 1930s, for which he served as a consultant, appeared, at least from the stated objectives, to acknowledge the
exploitative and inegalitarian features of industrial capitalism. Central to
Caswell's thinking was his view that Americans were living in an increasingly
interdependent world. "If a more democratic world was to really emerge
from this 'United Nations' War,'" he wrote in a 1943 article, "then it was critical that the ideas of 'imperialism' and 'racial differentiation' which fueled
authoritarianism be eradicated from our ways of thinking" (quoted in
Franklin, 1989, p. 2). As Franklin's commentary makes clear, Caswell was a
far-sighted curriculum scholar.

Theoretical eclecticism established. The Caswell and Campbell textbook represented a movement toward theoretical coalescence, a negative aspect of which was the establishment of "eclecticism in curriculum development" (Kliebard, 1986, p. 222). Caswell and Campbell found a field in disarray and attempted to conceptualize a coherent view of curriculum development (Seguel, 1966, p. 163). Quite aware of the limited appeal of social reconstructionism for school administrators, Caswell and Campbell de-emphasized this segment of the field in their text, making the textbook more palpable for school administrators. The text "leaned toward Dewey and progressive thought," however, emphasizing the importance of attending to pupils' interests and experience in curriculum construction (Schubert, 1986a). The social emphasis in the text was limited to a call for schools to cooperate with other social institutions in rediscovering and redefining democratic ideals (Seguel, 1966).

Caswell and Campbell's *Curriculum Development* included units on the "Challenge of Contemporary Life to the School, The Social Responsibility of the School, Significant Influences on Curriculum Development, Concepts of the Curriculum, Principles Basic To Curriculum Development, Aims of Education, Scope of the Curriculum, Pupil Purposes, The Unit Basis of Organizing Instruction, The Course of Study, and Administrative Considerations in Curriculum Development." Caswell and Campbell composed a conceptual framework and fit into it coherently almost everything in curriculum making that had come before (Seguel, 1966). A review of the book, which appeared in the *Curriculum Journal* in 1935, worried that such a synoptic text lacked a point of view, a concern which has persisted to the present time. Seguel has defended the synoptic text, arguing that they should not be polemical (Seguel, 1966), not represent a particular perspective (Schubert, 1986a). Caswell and Campbell produced a second synoptic text, a collection of articles entitled *Readings in Curriculum Development* (1937). Collections of articles or essays have also persisted as a common form of publication in the field.

Crisis and transformation. The currents of curriculum scholarship moved tumultuously during the 1930s, understandable perhaps for a field with such close ties to popular culture, a culture in social, economic, and political crisis during that decade. Within curriculum, the social efficiency movement declined in importance, but the decline would be for a short term. Progressivism moved center stage but foundered over its own internal divisions between the social reconstructionists and the child-centered advocates. The social reconstructionists took a strong position morally and theoretically, but they produced resistance to social reform in the field's constituencies, i.e, school teachers and school administrators. The consequence of this crisis was eclecticism, resurfacing after its appearance in *The Twenty-sixth N.S.S.E. Yearbook* and in Caswell and Campbell's *Curriculum Development* and *Readings in Curriculum Development.* Synoptic, eclectic books created a centrist position which functioned to consolidate a field threatening to break into unyielding orientations and interest groups. The price of this fragile coalition was theoretical eclecticism and blandness which lay the ground—as would become clear—for a triumphant return of social efficiency and scientism a decade later.

A second generation accepts theoretical eclecticism. Another instance of theoretical eclecticism in the field at this time is the establishment early in 1936 of the Joint Committee on Curriculum, a small federation of curriculum specialists interested in summarizing the "state of the art" in curriculum development. This group represented what Kliebard (1979) has characterized as a "second generation of curriculum specialists" (p. 223), among whom were university leaders such as Henry Harap of George Peabody College (now a part of Vanderbilt University), Laura Zirbes of Ohio State University [see Reid, T., 1993], and school leaders such as Edith Bader of the Ann Arbor (Michigan) Public Schools and Prudence Cutright, the assistant superintendent of the Minneapolis Public Schools.

From their association came *The Changing Curriculum*, in which they advocated a view of the curriculum as "functional," that is curriculum designed around the needs and interests of children or around categories of life activities. Thus the Joint Committee accepted an eclectic model of curriculum, combining aspects of both social efficiency and progressivism. However, they did not accept curriculum organization around the school subject and academic disciplines. Indeed, Kliebard (1979) reports that the "subject matter specialist became something of an anathema within professional curriculum circles" (Kliebard, 1979, p. 223). That would, in twenty-five years time, change rather completely.

IV
The 1940s: The Triumph of the Middle

Ralph W. Tyler was a prophet of evaluation.
(James O'Shea, 1985, p. 450)

America's preoccupation with World War II precluded a sustained support for curricular experimentation. The agenda of the social reconstructionists lost what remained of its mass appeal. The theoretical eclecticism associated with the appearance of the synoptic text, which had surfaced in the 1930's, cemented its position in the field. Theoretical eclecticism was institutionalized in the field with the founding, on January 1, 1946, of the Association for Supervision and Curriculum Development (ASCD). This organization was formed in 1943 in the merger of the National Education Association's Department of Supervisors and Directors of Instruction with the independent Society for Curriculum Study.

ASCD committed itself to promoting the cause of a functional curriculum, developed by the Joint Committee ten years earlier. Chapters and articles in ASCD's publications, such as *Educational Leadership* and the yearbooks, emphasized democratic—rather than administrative—means of changing the curriculum. Teachers were regarded as central to the curriculum development process, partly in loyalty to progressive ideas of democracy, and partly to the legacy of social efficiency, a marriage reminiscent of Jesse Newlon's 1923 Denver curriculum reform project [see chapter 2]. In its early decades of existence, only the 1956 ASCD yearbook, *What Shall the High School Teach?*, deviated from the mainstream ASCD publications. That volume included a historical analysis by Lawrence Cremin, and a chapter by Arno Bellack which rejected ASCD's eclecticism in favor of a curriculum design based on the intellectual resources of the culture. Kliebard (1979) commented: "By 1956, however, the directly functional curriculum which had been a cornerstone of ASCD ideology was under serious attack from academic critics, and the respectability that Bellack accorded to a curriculum organized around the fields of knowledge was not especially welcome in ASCD circles" (Kliebard, 1979, p. 225).

Three types of synoptic texts. During the 1940s synoptic texts became differentiated into three distinct types (Schubert, 1980a). The first type restricted its focus to elementary schools; the second type examined curriculum concerns appropriate for secondary schools; and the third purported to depict curriculum issues for both elementary and secondary schools. Three books illustrate these three types of synoptic curriculum texts, all three of which remain very much in the curriculum development tradition. J. Murray Lee and Dorris Lee (1940, 1950, 1960) wrote *The Child and His Curriculum* which focused upon the child as organizing center of the curriculum. For the Lees, the teacher became a "guide to the learning experiences of child" (Lee & Lee, 1960, p. v). Thus the child-centered orientation remained an important force in the 1940s. A secondary curriculum text, Harold Alberty's (1947, 1953, 1962) *Reorganizing the School Curriculum*, was dedicated to Alberty's mentor, Boyd Bode, and reflects Bode's thought (Schubert, 1980a). Alberty argued that the high school should "play a significant role in perpetuating, refining, and reinterpreting our democratic way of life" (Alberty, 1947, p. vii). While emphasizing the so-called foundations of curriculum development, Alberty did include a section on "the curriculum in action," surveying experimentation efforts and curriculum trends. Also included were a "how-to" section on "preplanning for learning" as well as a section on audio-visual materials, which were by then readily available in many schools. Alberty's unique contribution was his curriculum design for achieving general education.

Illustrative of the third type, both elementary and secondary curriculum, are two texts. The first is J. Minor Gwynn's (1943, 1950, 1960, 1969) *Curriculum Principles and Social Trends*. The book demonstrates the eclectic synoptic genre instituted by Caswell and Campbell. The Gwynn book is encyclopedic, beginning with an historical overview of the "evolution of the curriculum," and discussing all facets of curriculum development and pertinent social factors as well. Importantly, Gwynn espouses a centrist position:

[The book] describes numerous curricular experiments which have been conducted in various schools and school systems. It relates all curricular developments and experiments to current social trends, and it constructively discusses those developments and experiments and trends. It integrates good practice and sound theory; it tells how and why. It takes a middle of the road position between extreme progressivism and extreme fundamentalism. (Gwynn, 1943, p. vii)

Gwynn's widely read text solidified the centrist, theoretically eclectic position. The middle had triumphed.

"Persistent life situations." A second text illustrative of the third type of synoptic text is *Developing a Curriculum for Modern Living* by Florence B. Stratemeyer, Hamden L. Forkner, Margaret G. McKim, and A. Harry Passow (1947, 1957). In this volume the concept of "persistent life situations" was elaborated. Stratemeyer wrote: "A curriculum which has maximum meaning for learners develops as learners and their teachers work together on the problems and interests of everyday living" (Stratemeyer, 1957, p. 115). Persistent life situations are "those situations that recur in the life of the individual in many different ways as he grows from infancy to maturity" (Stratemeyer, 1957, p. 115). This notion became in this text an umbrella under which traditional design aspects of the curriculum, such as scope, sequence, continuity, balance, and depth, were situated. "Persistent life situations" might have originated as a response to the common criticism during the 1940's that "schools had little influence on the lives of youth; educational activities begun in school were usually dropped when students left school" (Tanner & Tanner, 1980, p. 387). Linking traditional curricular concerns with a notion of "life situation" might enable the teacher to link school knowledge with everyday life.

Decreased scholarly production during World War II. Understandably, the production of curriculum synoptic texts decreased during World War II. For instance, while 80 curriculum books were published during the decade, only 13 were published during 1943-1945 (Schubert, 1980a, p. 99). School subjects were influenced as well by the War. Mathematics courses began to employ military examples. Social Studies courses focused on wartime aims. As the War drew to a close, the curriculum reflected speculation concerning international relations in the post-war era (Kliebard, 1986). The release of the results of the Eight-Year Study had been ill-timed and consequently largely ignored. Social efficiency advocates would recognize and seize their opportunity.

The 1945 N.S.S.E. Yearbook. In 1945, the National Society for the Study of Education, which had produced the landmark 1927 *Yearbook* on curriculum, published its *Forty-Fourth Yearbook.* Part one was entitled *American Education in the Postwar Period: Curriculum Reconstruction.* Two curricularists involved in the project would emerge with heightened visibility and influence: Ralph W. Tyler and Hilda Taba. Tyler chaired the committee that prepared the report.

Taba wrote an important section entitled "Problems in Curriculum Reconstruction," her specific area of interest being "General Techniques of Curriculum Planning." The subtitle of reconstruction as well as the content of the Yearbook disclosed that the reform impulse continued to constitute the raison d'etre of the field.

In his introduction, Tyler argued that too often efforts to reform the curriculum resulted in an overcrowded curriculum with subjects' boundaries blurred. Often an elective system was developed which left "students having to make the selections the staff were unable to make" (NSSE, 1945, p. 4). Tyler argued that the next step of curriculum change would involve "careful selection and elimination" (NSSE, 1945, p. 4). Taba, who would publish an influential synoptic text in 1962, discussed the selection and organization of learning experiences, focussing upon planning specific units of study. This language would be used by Tyler later in the decade in his *Basic Principles of Curriculum and Instruction* (1949). Taba's emphasis, as well as that of the *Yearbook* in general, was changing school curriculum so that it might become more functional and useful to the nation's youth, a view which resurfaces from time to time [see, for instance, Wilcox, et al., 1984].

Curriculum ought to reflect students' outlook. Reports of special commissions on education and curriculum were again published during the 1940's. One example of this genre in this decade is the report of the Special Committee on the Secondary School Curriculum prepared for the Youth Commission. In *What the High Schools Ought to Teach*, the authors argued that a majority of students required an education not specifically directed toward college admission or a specific vocational role. The secondary curriculum ought to reflect the outlook of the majority of students, a view consistent with the "life adjustment" emphasis being taken up by synoptic text writers. The concept of "general education" became linked with "life adjustment" during this period.

The famous "redbook" report of the Harvard Committee on the Objectives of Education in a Free Society, entitled *General Education in a Free Society* (1945), also argued that the majority of high school students were not being well served by extant curricula. Introduced by James B. Conant, who would later become visible in teacher education, the report alleged that "instead of looking forward to college, three-fourths of the students now look forward directly to work" (Harvard Committee on Objectives, 1945, p. 8). The Committee called for a general education which provided knowledge of natural science, social science, and the humanities (Committee, 1945, p. 58). Such knowledge would be taught in ways that non-college bound students could learn. General education, the argument continued, would help produce an educated citizenry capable of making wise decisions in a democratic society. The "redbook" was widely discussed in professional journals and conferences, but it had little, if any, effect upon high school curricula in the country at large.

Social efficiency as "life adjustment." During these years immediately after World War II, the social efficiency movement reclaimed lost status and power. This time it eschewed its explicit embrace of scientific management and American industry for a concept called "life adjustment education" (Kliebard, 1986, pp. 240-270). The surface parallels between the earlier view of curriculum preparing students for productive vocational lives and this view of adjustment to life are self-evident. Richard Hofstadter, in his widely read *Anti-intellectualism in American Life* (1963), characterized "life adjustment education" as a movement stemming from the wide sweep of progressive educational reforms beginning before the twentieth century. In fact, the term was first used in 1945 by a vocational educator in connection with the neglect of the majority of high-school youth who were not going on to college. Life adjustment never became a "movement," yet the label was used by such historians as Arthur Bestor in his attack on the field of education six year later (Tanner & Tanner, 1990).

At the 1947 National Conference on Life Adjustment Education, educators expressed concern for the "general track" student, the student who neither aspired to college nor had chosen a specific vocational track. Their dilemma was linked to enrollment problems, and specifically a dropout problem. The report, entitled *Life Adjustment Education for Every Youth*, worried about low school enrollment. In 1940-1941, the year of highest school enrollments, only 73% of the high school age children were enrolled in schools (United States Office of Education, 1948). For the years 1943-1944 "only seven out of ten enter senior high school and fewer than four of them remain to graduate" (United States Office of Education, 1948, p. iii). For those enrolled in school, over half were not well served by college-bound curriculum or vocational programs. Charles Prosser composed what became known as the Prosser Resolution, demanding that the U.S Commissioner of Education and the Assistant Commissioner for Vocational Education call a series of conferences to address the problem (United States Office of Education, 1948).

Life adjustment conferences. The call was answered. Five regional conferences were scheduled under the joint direction of the Division of Secondary Education and the Division of Vocational Education. The first was held in April, 1946; the second was held in Chicago in June; the third was held in Cheyenne in September; the fourth was held in Sacramento the same month; and the fifth was held in Birmingham in November 1946. Participants reached consensus regarding life adjustment education, elaborating nine points. First, it was concluded that, at the present time, there was inadequate life adjustment education. Second, it was argued that public opinion could be enlisted to support life adjustment education. Third, the curriculum lay in the provision of educational experiences based on the diverse needs of secondary-school aged youth. Fourth, to so provide, teachers had to develop a broadened viewpoint and a genuine desire to serve all youth. Fifth, in this national effort, local resources had to be employed maximally. Sixth, the so-called practical arts, functional experiences in home and family life, in health and physical fitness, and civic competence, had to be provided in all secondary schools. Seventh, supervised work experience was essential for the life adjustment of youth. Eighth, it was resolved that the number of small school districts represented an administrative barrier to life adjustment curriculum reform. Finally, it was resolved that an intimate, comprehensive, and continuous program of guidance and pupil personnel services had to underlie all efforts to provide life adjustment education (U.S. Office of Education, 1947, p. 17).

Life adjustment's contributions. Life adjustment curriculum reform stimulated a large literature. Two Commissions on Life Adjustment Education convened for three years (Tanner & Tanner, 1980, p. 386). The movement made two contributions to curriculum reform: it extended the concept of curriculum beyond school subjects specificity, and it stimulated genuine concern for the drop-out rate in the nations' schools. There is no evidence, however, that life adjustment views actually brought about many major curricular changes. The movement did support the addition of guidance counselors and the elimination of very small schools. On the other hand, its rhetorical successes provoked the reappearance in the 1950s of a reform movement that had been relatively silent regarding curriculum reform for fifty years. The 1950's would witness the resurgence of the mental disciplinarian and classical curriculum orientation [see chapter 2 for a review of these terms]. In addition to these more public debates regarding the school curriculum, a major step was taken in the progress of the curriculum field as an academic discipline. That step was taken at the 1947 University of Chicago Curriculum Theory Conference.

University of Chicago Curriculum Theory Conference. The University of Chicago Curriculum Theory Conference was held on October 16 and 17, 1947. This conference is appraised by many scholars as a "benchmark in the field" (Klohr, 1974a; Miller, 1979a; Pinar, 1974c). "That is not to say," writes Paul R. Klohr, "that there were not efforts that approached the level of theory before this time, but rather to underscore that this was the first to emphasize curriculum theory as theory" (Klohr, 1974a, p. 6). Conference proceedings were published as *Toward Improved Curriculum Theory* (1950), edited by Virgil Herrick and Ralph Tyler.

In a preliminary overview section, Herrick and Tyler discussed the threefold tasks of a "defensible curriculum theory" (Herrick & Tyler, 1950, p. 1). First, curriculum theory should identify the critical issues or points in curriculum and their underlying generalizations. Secondly, curriculum theory must identify relationships which exist between these critical points and their supporting structures. Thirdly, defensible curriculum theory must suggest and forecast the future of approaches made to resolve these issues. Consistent with the field's identity at this time, most papers focussed upon curriculum development. Papers by Herrick and B. Othanel Smith, however, "clearly suggested the need for new paradigms for curriculum theorizing" (Klohr, 1974a, p. 6).

Education in a transitional period. In his "Social Perspective as the Basic Orientation of the Curriculum," B. O. Smith identified five tasks of education in a transitional period. Smith first argued for a "new frame of acceptance," i.e. a value orientation adequate for the age. Second, Smith argued for collective social goals which conferred meaning upon individual effort and achievement. Third, curricularists must draw upon a conceptualization of human nature based upon psychological and social theory, one which conveyed, in Smith's words, "new insight into personal and social actions and accomplishments." Fourth, he called for a new pattern of thinking regarding social policies and actions, to replace current linear, compartmentalized thinking, which result in rigid boundaries between disciplines (Pinar, 1974c). In his "The Concept of Curriculum Design," Herrick listed eleven propositions regarding curriculum design. He pointed to a need for seeking new directions, asking new questions. Herrick called for analysis of curriculum decisions and curriculum approaches and orientations via examination of their underlying assumptions.

Tyler's basic principles. These contributions were overshadowed by Ralph W. Tyler's "The Organization of Learning Experiences," a paper which would become a chapter of the single most influential curriculum text ever written: *Basic Principles of Curriculum and Instruction* (1949), which we reviewed in chapter 1. Tyler's eighty-three page book was the syllabus of a course he taught at the University of Chicago: Education 360, Basic Principles of Curriculum and Instruction. In the introduction Tyler stated his intention to "help the student of education to understand more fully the kinds of problems involved in developing a curriculum and plan of instruction and to acquire some techniques by which these basic problems may be attacked" (Tyler, 1949, p. 1). As we saw in chapter one, Tyler's book established a tradition of research and teaching about curriculum which would remain unchallenged for twenty years. In it Tyler extended and developed concepts linked with his evaluation work with the Eight-Year Study.

The administrative and managerial origin and motive for this work are significant in understanding its structure and content. Structurally, the rationale is a linear, administrative procedure for curriculum development. The steps are: 1) the selection and definition of "learning objectives," discussed in the chapter entitled "What Educational Purposes Should the School Seek to Attain?"; 2) the selection and creation of appropriate learning experiences, discussed in the chapter entitled "How Can Learning Experiences be Selected which are Likely to be Useful in Attaining these Objectives?"; 3) the organization of learning experiences to achieve a maximum cumulative effect, described in the chapter entitled "How Can Learning Experiences be organized for effective instruction?"; and 4) the evaluation of the curriculum so that revisions become discernible, described in the chapter entitled "How

Can the Effectiveness of Learning Experiences be Evaluated?" These four principles stimulated "the format of curriculum guides, teachers' editions of schoolbooks, lesson plan books, evaluation instruments by accrediting agencies, course syllabi, and many curriculum books that appeared in the 1950s and 1960s" (Schubert, 1980a, p. 110). The simplicity and functionality of the Tyler Rationale were compelling for many educators. One prominent curriculum historian points out that all the essential elements of the Tyler Rationale were derived from predecessors' works, including those of Dewey, Rugg, the Eight-Year Study, and Taba's 1945 work (Tanner, 1982).

There would be, eventually, many criticisms of the Tyler Rationale, especially in the 1970s (Kliebard, 1975c). [It would be defended as well (Hlebowitsh, 1993); see chapter 4.] To illustrate the range of this criticism that would come in thirty years, let us look briefly at a criticism of Tyler's emphasis upon objectives from a scholar interested in cognitive psychology: "Clearly, the teacher who aims for a transformation of cognitive structure is concerned with *how* the child thinks and not solely with the product of his thinking. The teacher, so guided, cannot enter the instructional situation with predetermined behavioral objectives for the students; objectives must arise out of the situation in which, first, what is possible has been revealed" (Noddings, 1974, p. 364). The Tyler procedure is not a teacher's statement of curriculum development; it is a bureaucrat's.

Ralph Winfred Tyler. Inevitably, figures who are widely criticized are also highly visible. Ralph W. Tyler is perhaps the most influential figure the field has known. Who was this man who first came on the curriculum scene with his evaluation work on the Eight-Year Study, and then crystallized a half-century of curriculum development thought in one thin book which sold over 85,000 copies during 36 printings and was translated into 7 foreign languages? As we noted earlier, Ralph Winfred Tyler received his doctoral education at the University of Chicago, one of the three great institutions in American curriculum studies during the first half of the twentieth century. [The other two were Teachers College, Columbia University, and Ohio State University.] Tyler has indicated that as a graduate student the ideas of George S. Counts were among the most influential factors in his Ph.D. education. He pointed to Counts' (1927) article in the *Twenty-Sixth Yearbook* of the National Society for the Study of Education, entitled "Some Notes on the Foundation of Curriculum," as delineating a series of topics in which three of the categories (curriculum-making and the nature of the society, curriculum-making and the organization of knowledge, and curriculum-making and the nature of the learner) ultimately became the sources of what twenty years later came to be called the Tyler Curriculum, Instruction, and Evaluation Rationale. A fourth category, curriculum-making and the scientific method, made the deepest impression on Tyler's future intellectual stance. Counts had argued in 1927 that the relation of the scientific method to the construction of curriculum had been and was the central question of importance in the domain of constructing an institution that would address the needs of each individual (O'Shea, 1985). Clearly, it was Counts' categories of curriculum construction, not his social reconstructionism, that influenced Tyler during his graduate study in the 1920s.

Tyler's argument for a shift from child-centeredness to more generalized behaviors as goals of education was a response to the 1912 research based on the principle of generalization in learning that was formulated by his mentor, Charles W. Judd. Tyler's dissertation seemed to reflect a Juddian focus, as indicated in its title: "Statistical Methods for Utilizing Personal Judgments To Evaluate Activities for Teacher Training Curricula" (O'Shea, 1985, p. 448). Perhaps the most lasting influence on the theoretical development of Tyler at the University of Chicago was the work and teaching of W. W. Charters, the great social efficiency curricularist. Tyler took three seminars in techniques of curriculum construction from Charters. He also worked as a statistical technician on the Commonwealth Teacher Training Study, which was directed by Charters.

After receiving the Ph.D. degree in 1927, Tyler's first appointment was to the faculty of the University of North Carolina at Chapel Hill, where he remained for two years. From Chapel Hill Tyler moved to Columbus and Ohio State University, during which time he published 59 articles, 25 of which were published in the Ohio State University journal, *The Educational Research Bulletin,* and 8 of which published in the *Journal of Higher Education,* a publication instituted by W. W. Charters in 1930 when Charters himself was on the faculty at Ohio State. The principles Tyler identified in *Constructing Achievement Tests* (1934) have served as the basis for most of the major efforts in evaluation since 1934. Tyler has been termed "a prophet of evaluation. . . . All educational evaluation is a commentary on Tyler's work of the 1930s" (O'Shea, 1985, pp. 450-451).

When Ralph Tyler joined the faculty at Ohio State in September 1929, he was assigned an office across the hall from Boyd Bode, the prominent professor of philosophy of education whose work we reported earlier. He became a friend of Bode; they often walked together to the faculty club for lunch. Bode recommended that Tyler be asked to draw up a design for the comprehensive evaluation of the Eight-Year Study, a job, which, of course, launched his career. In the Eight-Year Study evaluation, Hilda Taba was in charge of evaluation in the social studies; Bruno Bettleheim, a refugee from a Nazi concentration camp, took charge of the evaluation of art programs. Others working with Tyler on the Eight-Year Study who would become major figures included Benjamin S. Bloom, Lee J. Cronbach, and Herbert Thelen (O'Shea, 1985).

In January 1938, University of Chicago President Robert M. Hutchins invited Tyler to accept the dual position of chairman of the department of education and the university examiner. Tyler reminded Hutchins, who had been a vocal critic of the progressive education movement, that he was director of the evaluation staff of the Eight-Year Study, but this fact was evidently of no consequence. Tyler became chair at age 36, following former chairs of the department such as Francis W. Parker, John Dewey, and Charles H. Judd.

In 1952, Tyler became chairman of a planning committee that sought to establish a unique research center, whose original and continuing purpose was to support better research in the behavioral sciences. This research center became the Center for Advanced Study in the Behavioral Sciences at Stanford University. In October 1953, Tyler was chosen to become the first executive director; he would remain in this position until his retirement in 1967.

The 1940s end. The 1940's ended quite differently than they began. Progressivism had occupied curriculum center stage as the decade opened. The Eight-Year Study promised a revolutionary revision of secondary school curricula. However, World War II functioned to erase Progressivism's influence, and the post-war era began with the partial reappearance of social efficiency, this time in the guise of "life adjustment" education. The life-adjustment movement would prove to be short-lived, and the functionality of social efficiency asserted itself simply and forcefully in the Tyler Rationale. As the history of curriculum reform has already suggested, even while one orientation occupies center stage, forces gather on the periphery waiting for their moment of ascendancy. The 1947 University of Chicago Conference "Toward Improved Curriculum Theory" both signaled and authorized such possibilities even while it heralded the triumph of Tyler and curriculum functionality. It would take two decades, however, for conditions to favor the realization of those possibilities for a fundamental Reconceptualization of the field.

V
The 1950s: A Decade of Criticism, Conflict, and Reformation

Our schools must return to the traditional task of formal education in Western civilization—transmission of cultural heritage, and preparation for life through rigorous intellectual training of young minds to think clearly, logically, and independently.

(Admiral H. Rickover, 1959, p. 18)

It can be said that curriculum has a long past but a short history.

(Daniel Tanner, 1982, p. 412)

Dewey dies. The 1950s saw criticism of American schools and their curricula on a scale not seen again until the 1980's. We can distinguish between two periods of criticism, one beginning in 1950, and the other starting after the Soviet satellite launching in 1957. Before we turn to these curricular debates, let us note that John Dewey, the giant of philosophy of education and of curriculum theory, died early in the decade. Distinguished American philosopher Richard Rorty (1991) has written about Dewey:

John Dewey died in 1952. No American intellectual of the next four decades has managed to fill his shoes. Henry Steele Commager said of him, "no public issue was clarified until he had spoken"—the sort of thing that once might have been said of Jean-Paul Sartre in France or Bertrand Russell in Britain, and today might be said by Germans of Jurgen Habermas. What is most admirable in Dewey, what makes him a paradigm to be imitated, is not his criticism of a stitched-together monster called "liberal realism" but his tone—that extraordinary combination of courtesy and passion, decency and romance, loyalty and skepticism. Dewey remains the best person an American intellectual can take as his or her model. (pp. 13, 15)

Students' reminiscences afford us a portrait of what Dewey was like as a teacher. From one student, Earl K. Peckham of Montclair State College (quoted in Williams, 1982), we glimpse this scene:

About thirty-five years ago, one evening in a classroom in Macy Hall, Teachers College, Columbia University. Dewey was speaking slowly and very carefully, also in simply constructed sentences, which was typical of his style. I was listening intently to a point. Many of the class seemed to have left the area of thought. Dewey himself seemed to have left, to have gone into his own world. I felt that I was with him regardless of the seeming absence of other members of the class. He hesitated after his point was made, and he looked at me through his thick bifocals. I said to him in a too loud, nervous voice, "Doesn't emotion play a part in this thought process?" His stare fixed on me. I was embarrassed. He was silent—then he walked slowly over to the window and looked into the night, for the better part of two minutes. Then he looked back and fixed his stare on me (at least that is how I felt) and he said in a very slow and almost inaudible voice—but he knew I heard and he seemed to me not care if anyone else heard or not—"Knowledge is a small cup of water floating on a sea of emotion." (p. 127)

Another student, John C. Thirwall of City College (City University of New York) (quoted in Williams, 1982), recalls:

In 1932 I was an English graduate student at Columbia. Ashley Thorndike was then Chairman of the English Department and every graduate student took his Shakespeare course, which came at 2 p.m. in a lecture room holding over 100—on the 6th floor of Philosophy Hall. One day, promptly at 2 p.m., Professor Dewey shambled in, sat down at the desk and proceeded to read a long list, marking absent each one, since there was no reply from a crowded room. At 2:20 Thorndike strode into the room, gawked at Dewey a moment, then tapped him on the shoulder, saying: "John, you are one flight up." None of us laughed as Thorndike proceeded to read the proof sheets of his Shakespearean comedy. (p. 157)

The classical curriculum orientation returns. In the 1950s, the life adjustment movement came under attack by a twentieth-century version of the nineteenth-century classical curriculum/mental disciplinarian orientation. Life adjustment prodded the academic community [those with faculty appointments in science, social science, humanities, and the arts] to take a serious look at what was going on in elementary and secondary schools. A series of attacks on pubic schools and upon education professors would characterize the decade, with historian Arthur Bestor perhaps the most vocal critic. What became clear was that high schools and colleges were now populated with faculties holding quite differing views on what the curriculum should be. When the decade ended, the battle ended. The academicians would win hands down; they have been consolidating their position ever since (Kliebard, 1987). Opposed by a loose but effective coalition of politicians, arts and sciences scholars, and the business community, the professional education community would lose control of curriculum development by the 1960s.

One restatement of the nineteenth century classical view was made by University of Chicago President Robert Maynard Hutchins. In his *The Higher Learning in America*, Hutchins identified "classics" of Western civilization to be installed in schools as a "great books" curriculum: "How can we call a man educated who has never read any of the great books in the Western world" (Hutchins, 1936, pp. 78-79). When he first published the book, Hutchins succeeded in attracting only a "small coterie of followers" (Kliebard, 1986, p. 258). The classical curriculum perspective would reappear in the 1980s in Mortimer Adler's *Paideia Proposal* (1982), in Allan Bloom's *Closing of the American Mind* (1987), and E. D. Hirsch's *Cultural Literacy: What Every American Needs to Know* (1987). Political and racial responses to these formulations of the classical orientation are articulated in chapters 5 and 6.

Anti-intellectualism? As we mentioned, one of the most vocal critics of life adjustment education was a history professor at the University of Illinois, Arthur Bestor. In his *Educational Wastelands: The Retreat from Learning in our Public Schools* (1953), Bestor charged that life adjustment education represented anti-intellectualism. Echoing nineteenth century voices of Charles W. Elliot and William Torrey Harris [see chapter 2], Bestor (1953) insisted: "The nation depends on its schools and colleges to furnish this intellectual training to its citizenry as a whole. Society has no other institutions upon which it can rely in this matter. If schools and colleges do not emphasize rigorous intellectual training, there will be none" (p. 14). Bestor's attacks were wide-ranging, although he was enough of a scholar to recognize that his criticism of life-adjustment education had no relation to the work of John Dewey (Kliebard, 1987). This struggle over the American school curriculum would continue throughout the decade. Admiral Hyman Rickover joined Bestor in leading the classical charge against life adjustment, a losing position defended most prominently by Harold Hand (Kliebard, 1986), a professor of education at the University of Illinois.

Life adjustment–a functional curriculum? The title of William F. Featherstone's classic statement of the life adjustment education position implies its orientation—*A Functional Curriculum for Youth* (1950). Featherstone defined the concept of the functional as:

> education for use rather than for mere possession; education for a reasonably direct and obvious contribution to the improvement of daily living here and how; education for all aspects of an individual's necessary and inescapable involvement in community life—his role as a person, as citizen, as homemaker, and as general beneficiary of the cultural heritage. (Featherstone, 1950, vii.)

Rejecting the classicist orientation, Featherstone insisted that the nation's schools needed a realistic curriculum. Employing this basic idea he constructed models of curriculum development and planning. Featherstone and the life adjustment advocates would lose this argument for two reasons. The first reason for the decline of the life adjustment orientation could be found in the curricular proposals themselves. As Kliebard observed (1986), these proposals were of such scope and magnitude that the classicist opposition felt forced to defend the importance of the disciplines. Had the life adjustment advocates been satisfied with the notable gains that had been achieved—namely the increased attention given to vocational education, an emphasis upon utilitarian outcomes for school curriculum, and the substitution of life adjustment themes for conventional subject disciplines —they might have solidified their position in preparation for even greater gains later. However, their unlimited ambition combined with a specific event to defeat their movement.

Sputnik. The specific event in question was the launching of the Soviet satellite in 1957. The Sputnik satellite launching created a national reaction that propelled curriculum discussion forward to an immediate and enduring obsession with science and technology. Simply stated, the Soviet success cast doubt on the quality of the American educational system. If our schools were strong, the public press demanded to know, why had the Soviets defeated us in the race to travel in space? Admiral Hyman Rickover led the charge in his *Education and Freedom* (1959) and *American Education–A National Failure: The Problem of Our Schools and What We Can Learn from England* (1963). Rickover's charges will ring familiar to today's reader, as they have been employed by politicians—such as William Bennett—who blame the schools for military (as in the case of Sputnik) or economic (as in the case of Japan and the U. S. trade deficit) setbacks. [See chapter 14 for further discussion of international economic competition and curriculum.]

In *Education and Freedom,* Rickover (1959) accused the American public of indifference to intellectual achievement and excellence. He insisted that Americans valued athletic over academic accomplishment, (a point with which few curriculum scholars would take issue). He argued that schools must help children of varying abilities understand the complexity of the world. Here his agenda seemed to overlap that of the life adjustment advocates. However, the curricular means by which Rickover intended to achieve these ends were quite different: "Our schools must return to the traditional task of formal education in Western civilization—transmission of cultural heritage, and preparation for life through rigorous intellectual training of young minds to think clearly, logically, and independently" (Rickover, 1959, p. 18). His call echoes the nineteenth century classicists and anticipates the traditionalists of the 1980's: Bennett, Hirsch, and Bloom (although there are distinctions among the proposals of these three]. The life adjustment movement waned.

Bloom's taxonomy. The national debate over the American school curriculum seemed to be reflected in increased scholarly production in the field. Next in influence to Ralph Tyler's *Basic Principles of Curriculum and Instruction* might be Benjamin Bloom's *The Taxonomy of Educational Objectives, Handbook I: The Cognitive Domain* (1956). The book became known simply as "Bloom's Taxonomy." Bloom developed a classification scheme for behavioral objectives in the so-called cognitive domain. This work reformulated the scientific model first elaborated in Tyler's 1949 book, focusing particularly on the area of objectives. Countless students were required to memorize the taxonomy; countless teachers were required or encouraged to write objectives within the guidelines Bloom established. Taxonomies for other domains, including the affective (Krathwohl et al., 1964) and psychomotor, were to follow in the 1960s. The work of both Tyler and Bloom was technical and scientific; it adapted well to changing curriculum rhetoric. For instance, both the Tyler Rationale and Bloom's taxonomy were embraced by both life adjustment advocates and subject-centered critics (i.e. those espousing the academic disciplines as curriculum content) who ascended to power after the Sputnik satellite launching.

"Heyday of the synoptic curriculum text." Increased scholarly production was reflected in the publication of synoptic texts. In fact, the 1950s have been characterized as the "heyday of the synoptic curriculum text" (Schubert, 1980a, p. 130). Several popular texts first issued during the 1940s were reprinted during the 1950s. Among these, as we noted, were Lee and Lee's *The Child and His Curriculum* (1950), Gwynn's *Curriculum Principles and Social Trends* (1950), and Alberty's *Reorganizing the High School Curriculum* (1953). Several influential texts appeared, the first of which was the famous Smith, Stanley, Shores volume entitled *Fundamentals of Curriculum Development* (1950, 1957). Encyclopedic in scope, this widely-read book depicted six major areas: 1) social diagnosis for curriculum development, 2) basic curriculum issues, 3) principles and procedures of curriculum development, 4) patterns of curriculum organization, 5) human relations in curriculum development, and 6) the curriculum and social reintegration. Smith, Stanley, and Shores assumed that curriculum is determined by society. Technical aspects of curriculum development—such as planning and design—mirrored steps outlined by Tyler. The discussion of curriculum organization included sections on the subject curriculum, the activity curriculum, the core curriculum, and unit organization. As well, this synoptic book included a section on curriculum theory, a subject regularly included in synoptic texts that would follow.

Harold Spears' *The Teacher and Curriculum Planning* (1951), as the title indicates, also included teachers as integral to curriculum planning. In fact, Spears argued that teachers' involvement was a prerequisite to curriculum development and implementation. Spears observed: "The point of emphasis throughout the book is the teacher, for it is well recognized that no school program is going to succeed unless teachers have had an active part in its planning" (Spears, 1951, p. 3). In this synoptic text, 62 principles were listed relating to the meaning, foundation, study, and administration of the curriculum. Spears' book is largely forgotten today, but not J. Galen Saylor and William Alexander's *Curriculum Planning for Better Teaching and Learning* (1954, 1966, 1974, 1981). Still in use in the 1980s, this synoptic text even outlasted that other classic of the 1950s, the Smith, Stanley, Shores volume. Like Spears, Saylor and Alexander focused on teachers' involvement in curriculum planning. It included a historical section and reflected the Tyler Rationale: curriculum was regarded as the planning of learning opportunities. We will examine the book more closely on the occasion of its second edition in 1966, later in this chapter.

Against recipes? These texts reflected the mainstream, commonsensical thinking of the field during the 1950s. Thousands of teachers, curriculum administrators, and professors understood the field through these books. Despite the omnipresence of the Tyler Rationale, quiet voices suggesting alternatives began to be heard. P. T. Pritzkau's *Dynamics of Curriculum Improvement* (1959) departed from the mainstream. It represented "a stance that might be labeled existentialist and provided a departure from the usual generalizations found in many of the synoptic texts, especially those that utilized the guideline or recipe notion of principles" (Schubert, 1980a, p. 143). Pritzkau's book was not widely read or discussed. The book is noteworthy because it anticipates the interest in Existentialism found in the work of Maxine Greene, Madeleine Grumet, and William Pinar.

Other voices foreshadowing the 1970s Reconceptualization were being raised at Teachers College, Columbia University. There, a course in curriculum theory taught by Dwayne Huebner and Arno Bellack relied on non-Tylerian foundations. First offered in 1957, this course on curriculum theory was part of the doctoral core in the Department of Curriculum and Teaching at Teachers College, not only the first department in the field [1938], but at this time probably the premier department as well. Bellack approached curriculum problems through analytic philosophy and Huebner worked through phenomenology and political science. Ten year later Huebner would introduce these traditions to the field at large (Huebner, 1967).

No language of protest–yet. Characterized as "humanistic" by one commentator (Huber, 1981), another series of educators began to develop critiques of mainstream curricular thought and work from alternate foundations. While no "language of protest" (Huber, 1981, p. 18) was produced during this time (that would wait twenty years until the Reconceptualization), curriculum understood from perspectives associated with the humanities and with studies in creativity and self-reflection were under development by scholars such as Ross Mooney and Paul Klohr at Ohio State University and Elliot W. Eisner at Stanford University. Ross Mooney wrote prolifically during the 1950s, expressing views of the curriculum grounded in creativity research. Setting aside a technical or social agenda, Mooney believed the supreme obligation of the educator was the creation and valuing of the self.

Huber (1981) observed: "[Mooney's] view of the individual influenced his view of the curriculum field. He saw curriculum building as a 'creative process' in which the curriculum builder is both rational and poetic" (p. 18). Mooney's ideas were reflected in the work of his colleague at Ohio State, Laura Zirbes, who developed proposals for elementary curricula.

Laura Zirbes. Laura Zirbes had joined the Ohio State faculty in 1928 [see chapter 2] to help build an elementary program to rival that of Teachers College, Columbia University. She established an elementary demonstration school which joined the new secondary laboratory school unit in 1932 to become University School, perhaps the most experimental institution in the Eight-Year Study. Zirbes was an extraordinarily powerful teacher who challenged legions of graduate students to rethink, re-vision, and reimagine. She also committed herself to research and writing, often employing her own classroom as a laboratory. [Tony Reid, her 1993 biographer at the University of South Carolina, identified over one hundred entries in her bibliography.] Of all aspects of her work, she wished to be remembered for her enduring interest in the relationships between creativity and curriculum. She and Mooney were collaborators on a theory of creativity long before the notion became fashionable in the 1960s and 1970s (Zirbes, 1959). President Harry S. Truman, in conferring upon her the Woman of the Year Award in 1948, called her an outstanding "teacher of teachers."

Faint voices and the National Defense Act. These voices, faint in the din of 1950s debate over life adjustment, intellectual rigor, and military/space competitiveness, would become louder two decades later. Indeed, it was the impact of these debates on the field during the 1960s which would set the stage for the Reconceptualization of the 1970s. The National Defense Act (1958), which would greatly influence school curriculum and the curriculum field, made federal money available for curriculum development. However, the National Defense Act funds were not channeled to curriculum specialists. Kliebard observes: "Their credibility impaired by the excesses of life adjustment education, professional educators were no longer to be given free rein in curriculum matters" (Kliebard, 1986, p. 267). This event would undermine the mainstream curriculum field, especially as federal grant monies grew more crucial to university budgets. Any specialization deemed unworthy of leading the major federally funded curriculum reform movement became vulnerable to attacks from competing specializations, such as educational psychology, educational administration, and educational foundations. As well, by the late 1960s enrollments in curriculum courses began to level off and, in some regions of the country, decline.

Cold war military research, the science establishment. The major recipient of the National Defense Act funds was the National Science Foundation. Given that "the major influence over federal policy regarding education in the 1950s was the scientific establishment, which was supported by and had intimate connection with cold war military research" (Spring, 1989, p. 65), this development was unsurprising. What was surprising and important was the selection by N.S.F. of disciplinary specialists to lead curriculum development initiatives. Illustrative of this development was the establishment, by the National Science Foundation, of the Physical Science Study Committee (PSSC), chaired by Jerrold Zacharias, a professor of physics at the Massachusetts Institute of Technology. The work of this committee would widely influence school science curriculum. The Act also funded initiatives in mathematics and foreign language. Funds were also provided for the "improvement of guidance and testing programs directed principally at discovering and developing the talents of our most academically able youth; and for the training of highly skilled technicians in the fields that were deemed essential for our national defense" (Tanner & Tanner, 1980, p. 520). The impact of this Act and the consequent "curriculum reform movement" would undermine the traditional focus of the field on development and planning. These spheres of responsibility had been given to disciplinary specialists. The consequences of these developments would be enormous for the field. However, like an extinguished star in another galaxy, it would take time for practicing curricularists to realize their taken-for-granted light source was gone.

Conant's comprehensive high school. The 1950s drew to a close with the publication of James Bryant Conant's influential *The American High School Today* (1959). Supported by the Carnegie Corporation, Conant worked to establish a concept of the comprehensive high school. Such a school would include college preparation, general education, and vocational training. He argued that small rural schools should be consolidated so that economies of scale could be effected. Curriculum requirements for the high school diploma were specified: four years of English, three or four years of social studies (including two years of history, one year of which ought to be American history, and a senior-year course in civics or government), one year of mathematics, and one year of science. Conant argued against rigid tracking; however he did allow for programs designed for the "development of marketable skills" (Conant, 1959, p. 51). Provisions for highly gifted students —perhaps three percent of the student population—should be made. Each school principal was advised to maintain an academic inventory, a record of those programs offered to talented seniors (approximately the top fifteen percent of each graduating class) and post-graduation destinations of this population, specifically four-year or two-year colleges. The inventory would be published each year. Conant also gave specific curricular advice for foreign language, science, reading, social studies, summer school, and even homeroom. Conant's book was widely read and his proposals widely accepted, many becoming common practice in secondary schools across the U.S.

Toward paradigm shift. The importance of the synoptic text was well established by mid-century. These texts—reflecting mainstream knowledge of curriculum—regarded teachers as central to the curriculum planning and development process. However, the curriculum debates of the early 1950s, the attacks on the schools which intensified as a result of the Sputnik launching in the latter part of the decade, and the ensuing National Defense Act all functioned to undermine the roles of both teachers and curriculum specialists in curriculum development specifically and in curriculum affairs generally. The disciplinary leadership of the curriculum reform movement of the 1960s would underscore this significant development. A decade later, a weakened field would undergo that cataclysm known as "paradigm shift" (Kuhn, 1962).

VI
The 1960s: Expansion, Conflict, and Contraction

Designing curricula in a way that reflects the basic structure of a field of knowledge requires the most fundamental understanding of the field. It is a task that cannot be carried out without the active participating of the ablest scholars and scientists.

(Jerome Bruner, 1960, p. 32)

The events of the 1950s—the defeat of the life adjustment movement, the national debates over curriculum, the Sputnik launching and the National Defense Education Act—led to a decade in which the field appeared to expand. During the early 1960s enrollments in curriculum courses continued to increase on the whole, federal funding for education generally and curriculum specifically increased, the traditional American faith in education as a means to national prosperity remained substantially unshaken by the space race setback. The National Curriculum Reform movement was joined by other projects funded by Washington, including the Elementary and Secondary Education Act of 1965 (Schubert, 1980a). Two hundred ninety-four curriculum books were published during the decade (Schubert, 1980). Yet, the intellectual and political power of the field had been undermined by the selection of disciplinary specialists to lead the National Curriculum Reform movement. Not until the end of the decade would the field go into crisis.

Structure of the Disciplines

The Woods Hole Conference. The first major event of the decade was a conference held at Woods Hole on Cape Cod, Massachusetts and attended by psychologists, scientists, and mathematicians (not by curriculum specialists). The Woods Hole Conference was organized by the National Academy of the Sciences and supported by the National Science Foundation, the Air Force, the Rand Corporation, the U.S. Office of Education, the American Association for the Advancement of Science, and the Carnegie Corporation (Tanner & Tanner, 1980, p. 523). A curriculum manifesto for the 1960s which would frame the National Curriculum Reform Movement followed.

That curriculum manifesto was Jerome S. Bruner's *The Process of Education* (1960). In this enormously influential book, Bruner outlined a curriculum theory based on the notion of disciplinary structure. Bruner argued that each discipline exhibited a particular structure which could be made accessible to the student. Understanding a discipline's structure enabled the student to understand how a discipline worked: how it understood its problems, what conceptual and methodological tools it employed to solve those problems, and what constituted knowledge in the discipline. Students' understanding of disciplinary structure would enable them to learn essential disciplinary knowledge, regardless of their cognitive level. Bruner's theory echoed certain Herbartian ideas [see chapter 2]. In one sense the structure of disciplines theory implied that children assimilate ideas (structural characteristics of the disciplines) which form an understanding (or apperceptive mass) which enabled them to acquire more sophisticated knowledge later. The Herbartian interest in subjects as the fundamental organizer of curriculum resurfaced in the contemporary, psychological language of the Bruner text.

Shifting the leadership of national curriculum reform away from the curriculum field to disciplinary specialists found its theoretical justification in Bruner's curriculum theory. Bruner (1960) observed: "Designing curricula in a way that reflects the basic structure of a field of knowledge requires the most fundamental understanding of the field. It is a task that cannot be carried out without the active participating of the ablest scholars and scientists" (p. 32). Teachers and students were to be included in the curriculum development process, but in collaboration with (and often only assisting) disciplinary specialists. Bruner theorized the importance of the student in *Toward a Theory of Instruction* (1966). He acknowledged that "curriculum reflects not only the nature of knowledge itself but also the nature of the knower and of the knowledge getting process" (Bruner, 1966, p. 72).

A decade later Bruner would do a complete about-face. The social, political, and racial crisis of the 1960s persuaded him that the curriculum must address issues other than those associated with the structures of academic disciplines. In 1971 he wrote:

> We shall kill ourselves as a society and as human beings, unless we address our efforts to redressing the deep, deep wounds that we inflict on the poor, the outcast, those who somehow do not fit within our caste system—be they black or dispossessed in any way. . . . I would be quite satisfied to declare, if not a moratorium, then something of a de-emphasis on matters that have to do with the structure of history, the structure of physics, the nature of mathematical consistency, and deal with it rather in the context of the problems that face us. (Bruner, 1971, p. 21)

Bruner would appear to break rather completely from his early 1960s work on the structure of the disciplines, exploring in the 1980s topics concerning meaning and the self (Bruner, 1983,1986; Bruner & Weisser, 1991).

The San José State Conference. A structural theory of the curriculum was elaborated at a 1963 Conference on the Structure of Knowledge and the Curriculum held at San José State College (now University). The proceedings, published as *The Structure of Knowledge and the Curriculum* (1964) and edited by G. W. Ford and Lawrence Pugno, attempted to "map" fundamental concepts and methods of inquiry for specific disciplines. Perhaps the most systematic attempt to do so was made by University of Chicago Professor Joseph Schwab, whose work became central to the contemporary field, as we saw in chapter 1 [see also chapter 4]. In the "Structure of the Disciplines: Meanings and Significances," Schwab (1964b) asserted that there were three "major but related sets of problems which define the area called the structure of the disciplines" (p. 10). First was the problem of determining the membership and organization of the disciplines, including identification of particular disciplines and their relations to one another. Second was the problem of identifying the particular structure and limits of the disciplines, structures Schwab term "substantive." Third was the problem of the "syntactical structure of the disciplines," which included the "canons of evidence and proof" and "how they can be applied" (p. 14). Schwab cautioned (1964b) against dogmatic adherence to disciplinary structures in curriculum development:

> We may, if we like, choose but one of several pluralities of bodies of knowledge. But if we do, let it be taught in such a way that the student learns what substantive structures gave rise to the chosen body of knowledge, what the strengths and limitations of these structures are, and what some of the alternative structures are which give rise to alternative bodies of knowledge. (p. 29)

Astute critics of the 1960s curriculum reform movement have understood that military and nationalistic objectives were buried in erudite discussions of the structures of the disciplines. In the Bruner/Schwab scheme, learning was to serve as a means for further specialized learning. The long-range purpose, however:

> was neither personal development nor social reform but national power. We were a warfare state seeking international supremacy in military-related scholarship. Paradoxically, the disciplinary doctrine was focused on an abstract view of knowledge to the neglect of applied knowledge. Without practical application the possibilities for transfer were limited. (Tanner & Tanner, 1990, p. 178)

Unfortunately, astute critics were few in number and lacked influence in the 1960s, and in the avalanche of money and prestige accompanying the structure-of-disciplines approach, mainstream curriculum specialists simply tried to stay upright on the slopes.

Structure of disciplines orientation becomes taken-for-granted. The Fifth Annual Phi Delta Kappa Symposium on Education Research held in 1963 at the University of Illinois also focused upon questions of structure, the disciplines, and knowledge. The proceedings appeared as *Education and the Structure of Knowledge* (1964), edited by Stanley Elam, editor of *Phi Delta Kappan*, and introduced by B. Othanel Smith (who also chaired the conference). Smith explained that the purpose of the conference was to explicate the meaning of the phrase "structure of the disciplines," and to determine its impact upon education. "Structure of the disciplines" had become commonplace, a taken-for-granted "fact." It too would depart center stage, although it would still be discussed by a few subject matter specialists into the 1980s

(Kantor, 1983). However, in the early 1960s, many students and scholars of curriculum embraced the concept [see, for example, Lowe, 1969].

Curriculum Projects and Reports
In 1962 the National Committee of the National Education Association's Project on the Instructional Program of the Public Schools reported on those curriculum projects informed by disciplinary structure. Entitled *Curriculum Studies in Academic Subjects*, the authors of the report note that teachers had been pressured to teach the structure of disciplines. In this report ASCD pleaded guilty to the charge that professional educators had failed to keep school curricula paced with the findings of university researchers in the arts and sciences: "To some extent these pressures have come from the realization that, with the decline in participation by academic scholars in planning the school program, the schools have lagged in introducing findings of recent scholarship" (Fraser, 1962, p. 3).

The Report describes curriculum projects in several subject areas, including science, mathematics, English, foreign language, and social studies. Most National Science Foundation support went, predictably, to curriculum projects in the sciences and mathematics. Military and space competitiveness did not suggest massive investments in the humanities and social sciences, and this logic was reflected in funding decisions. Curriculum projects in English and the social studies represented a small fraction of the total federal investment in curriculum reform (Tanner & Tanner, 1980). The Physical Science Study Committee (PSSC) became the archetype of curriculum reform informed by the structures of the disciplines orientation. In addition to physics curriculum reform, similar efforts were conducted in biology (BSCS) and Chemistry (Chemical Bond Approach Project). The curriculum proposals and accompanying teaching materials of the BSCS Committee emphasized relationships among scientific concepts, an orientation not fundamentally dissimilar from that of the structure of the disciplines orientation (Tanner & Tanner, 1980).

New math. The National Science Foundation also funded the Mathematics Study Group (SMSG), the main purpose of which was the improvement of mathematics curricula via the improvement of college-oriented textbooks. The SMGS and the College Entrance Examination Board's Commission on Mathematics emphasized both the introduction of modern mathematics and "a deeper treatment of traditional mathematical topics within the course structure" (Fraser, 1962, p. 33-34). These emphases supported the theoretical wings of the mathematics field. They precipitated debates, lasting for the duration of the decade, between those who advocated the teaching of the so-called "new math" and those who wished to focus upon basic skills. Other curriculum reform projects funded during this period are listed in *New Curricula* (Heath, 1964), and also in secondary sources (Tanner & Tanner, 1980; Schubert, 1980a, 1986a). The specific projects are probably less important to remember than the general influence of the "structure of the disciplines" orientation upon the nation's schools and upon the curriculum field during the 1960s.

Man: A course of study. In the late 1960s and early 1970s the National Science Foundation invested nearly $5 million in the development of an upper elementary social studies curriculum called *Man: A Course of Study* (MACOS). MACOS provoked a major debate among educators and policy-makers, in which its opponents argued that it indoctrinated students in ethical relativism and legitimated antisocial behavior. Not a few of its opponents judged it as an attempt to undermine the moral fiber of American youth (Schaffarzick, 1979; Boyd, 1979, p. 91; Elmore & Sykes, 1992).

ASCD describes projects. Illustrative of the influence of the "structure of the disciplines" orientation is the (Gilchrist, 1963) *Using Current Curriculum Developments*, published by the Association for Supervision and Curriculum Development (ASCD). Forty-six curriculum projects and thirty-three studies are described; eighty-one references to source materials are listed. Trends, issues, and problems within specific curricular areas are summarized. The "structure of the disciplines" orientation is evident in the opening essay by Helen Heffernan and William M. Alexander. Other essays describe developments in specific subject areas.

Goodlad and Tanner criticize curriculum reform. Among the curriculum projects of the period reviewed in John Goodlad's *School Curriculum Reform in the United States* (1964) are those of the Mathematics Study Group, the Physical Science Study Committee, the Biological Sciences Curriculum Study, the Elementary School Science Project, the High School Geography Project, the Anthropology Curriculum Study Project, and the Commission on English and the Foreign Language Program. Goodlad criticized the curriculum reform movement for underemphasizing the humanities and the social sciences. Goodlad observed that little attention was paid to the unity of the overall curriculum. Setting the movement in historical context, Goodlad hinted at the decade to come:

> The current curriculum reform movement is partly a reaction to perceived curricular excesses of the 30's and 40's. To the extent that this reaction to child-centered and society-oriented theories is itself perceived to be an overemphasis on subject matter in determining curricular ends and means, today's movement already is breeding tomorrow's counter-reaction. (Goodlad, 1964, p. 87)

Daniel Tanner (1966) also expressed concern for the taken-for-grantedness afforded the structure-of-the-disciplines approach: "Curriculum theorists are expressing deep concern over the tendency to focus on the discrete disciplines without [attending to] their interrelationships in the development of the total curriculum" (p. 370).

In another article published five years later, Tanner (1971a) identified four inadequacies of the structures of the discipline approach. First, he expressed a concern that the spirit of "each discipline for itself" would function to contribute to the problem of course proliferation. Second, the premise that the curriculum should consist entirely of knowledge which comes from the disciplines undermines the status in the curriculum of many vitally important studies such as literature, the fine and performing arts, and vocational education. Third, Tanner noted that many fields of knowledge are multi-disciplinary in nature, a fact necessarily obscured in a structure-of-the-disciplines approach. Finally, the multi-disciplinary nature of various fields of knowledge requires interdisciplinary applications of knowledge to problem-solving in the social, public world.

Dewey evident in 1960s curriculum reform? In *The Changing School Curriculum* (1965), Goodlad, and co-authors Renata von Stoephasius and M. Frances Klein, summarized the structure-of-the-disciplines approach as "updating and reorganizing those academic disciplines that are considered basic in the precollegiate curriculum" (Goodlad, et al., 1965, p. 10). The authors observed: "The ends and means of schooling are derived from organized bodies of knowledge. Further, curriculum is planned by physicists, mathematicians, and historians, and students are encouraged to think like these scholars" (pp. 14-15). Despite the structure-of-the-disciplines emphasis, the authors insisted that Dewey and Progressivism had not been rejected. They pointed to the reliance upon disciplinary "principles"—such as structure—rather than upon facts, the decided preference for learning via problem-solving rather than by precept, and an apparent appreciation for individual differences.

Other important curriculum scholars disagreed, arguing that the apparent similarities between Bruner's ideas and those of Dewey were just that, apparent. More important were differences between the two. Burner must be understood as addressing himself to learning within individual academic disciplines such as science and mathematics; Dewey, in contrast, was interested in social problem-solving as a task for which the school must prepare the new generations (Tanner & Tanner, 1990).

A curriculum to embody the unpredictable. Continued emphasis upon the disciplines is evident in *New Curriculum Developments*, edited by Glenys Unruh (1965) for ASCD's Commission on Current Curriculum Developments. Contributors urged curriculum change in various curricular areas, including the arts, English, foreign languages, health and physical education, mathematics, science, social studies, and vocational education. A cognitive organization of subject matter was advanced by Robert Gilchrist and Donald Snygg in their essay entitled "The Case for Change." Gilchrist and Snygg suggested that a new concept of cognitive organization was required—one more sophisticated than stimulus-response (s-r) theories of learning—if the curriculum was to embody the unpredictable (Unruh, 1965). The pace of conferences and publications continued to be swift. Papers from the ASCD Seminar on Strategy for Curriculum Change, edited by Robert Leeper, were published as *Strategy for Curriculum Change* (1965b). In a notable closing essay entitled "Proposals of Strategies: A Summary," Kimball Wiles suggested a series of seven questions raised during the seminar. These included questions concerning the local staff's commitment to change, the local communities' role, in-service patterns, the role of supervision, alternative patterns of curriculum design, the role of the scholar, and the role of teacher education institutions in curriculum change (Wiles, 1965, pp. 72-75).

Many of the aforementioned publications represented the profession's effort to keep abreast of rapid and pervasive curriculum change. Change was monitored and managed. There were efforts to understand curriculum reform as well, to situate it in larger concepts and currents. One such effort was John Goodlad's *School, Curriculum and the Individual* (1966). In this study of "the interwoven nature of these threads in curriculum fabric: society, institutions and individuals," Goodlad included a section on "Curriculum as a Field of Study." Included in this section was a review of the state of the field, a practice to be repeated regularly during the 1970s. Goodlad's prescription for the field included more rigorous conceptual development, including devising theoretical constructs which would demonstrate how the values and expectations of various individuals and groups were influential in constructing and delivering the curriculum. As well, "studies are badly needed to show with rigor and precision how best to arrange material in a field for effective learning" (Goodlad, 1966, p. 137).

Goodlad argued that taxonomies of educational objectives in the affective and psychomotor domains required development and implementation. Studies isolating and comparing process-product factors were needed. Finally, studies of teacher-pupil relationships were advised. Goodlad concluded that the increasing interest in curriculum as a field and in curriculum problems should lead to: "conceptual schemes which separate logical from empirical questions and point to appropriate sources of data; theoretical constructs which lead to meaningful, cumulative empirical research; curricular practices which stem from answering appropriate questions with tested data selected from pertinent sources" (Goodlad, 1966, p. 138). Goodlad's agenda for the field was a research agenda, a major shift from the traditional emphasis upon curriculum development and other concerns linked to "practice." It was an agenda to be adopted by the field in the decade to follow.

Behavioral objectives. While objectives had been important to curriculum conceptualization for forty years, during the 1960s behavioral formulations of these objectives became preferred. This development has been linked to federal funding of curricular initiatives: "With the growing demands for government accountability in society at large came increased demands for curricularists to pre-specify what they planned to achieve, to directly strive to obtain it, and to prove that they did. Hence behavioral objectives arrived on the scene" (Schubert, 1980a, p. 176). A preference in many schools for behavioral or so-called performance objectives remains discernible today, despite their controversial status (Macdonald & Wolfson, 1970; Popham, 1970).

Behavioral objectives established measurable goals and outcomes for curriculum, a means for quantifying these outcomes. Curriculum was then

said to be "accountable." This goal was widely sought through such administrative approaches to programs as P.E.R.T.—program evaluation and review
technique. School administrators were taught how to "P.E.R.T." curriculum
to make curriculum more "accountable." Perhaps the classic statement of
behavioral objectives was Robert F. Mager's *Preparing Instructional Objectives*
(1962). This thin text found its way into many teacher preparation programs
for years. Mager elaborated three objectives: a) the student will be able to
identify from a list of educational objectives those stated in performance
terms; b) the student will be able to identify—within each objective—that
which defined minimally acceptable performance; c) the student will be able
to select appropriate text items to measure the performance objective
(Mager, 1962). Mager's concept of objectives echoes the social efficiency
advocates of the 1920s: "When clearly defined goals are lacking, it is impossible to evaluate a course or program efficiently, and there is no sound basis
for selecting appropriate materials, content, or instructional methods"
(Mager, 1962, p. 3).

A taxonomy of the "affective" domain. Accompanying this emphasis upon
behavioral formulations of educational objectives and activity generally was
the ascendancy of educational psychology in schools of education. Many
argued that educational psychology represented the foundational discipline
of all education specializations, including curriculum. The Mager text
reflected this viewpoint, as does the conceptualization of human feeling as an
"affective domain" which can be expressed behaviorally. Following his 1956
taxonomy of objectives in the cognitive domain, Benjamin Bloom—with
David Krathwohl and Bertram Masia—developed a *Taxonomy of Educational
Objectives: Handbook II: The Affective Domain* (1964). Krathwohl, Bloom, and
Masia acknowledged that the "affective domain" is less susceptible to a
taxonomy than the cognitive domain, and that they are less satisfied with the
result. However, they view the taxonomy as framing research in the area
(Krathwohl et al., 1964). The taxonomy arranged human feeling into a hierarchical order, providing illustrative objectives for each of the five classifications: receiving or attending, responding, valuing, organization, and characterization by a value or value complex (Krathwohl et al., 1964). What was
claimed as the educational significance of this effort? Krathwohl (1964) wrote:

> The actual sharing in the process of classifying educational objectives would
> help the members of the group clarify and tighten the language of educational
> objectives. We are aware that all too frequently educational objectives are
> stated as meaningless platitudes and clichés. . . . If, however, educational objec-
> tives are to give direction to the learning process and to determine the nature
> of the evidence to be used appraising the effects of learning experiences, the
> terminology must become clear and meaningful. (Krathwohl, 1964, p. 4)

"Mastery learning" introduced. Taxonomies were one application of behavioral formulations of learning and curriculum. The concept of "mastery
learning" also grew out of this "movement toward behavioristic objectives
and accountability" (Tanner & Tanner, 1980, p. 422; Schubert, 1980a, p. 177;

1986a, pp. 350-351). Perhaps the first discussion of "mastery learning" surfaced in John Carroll's "A Model of School Learning" (1963). Later, this concept would be attached to the concept of "competencies" which framed many teacher education programs early in the 1970s. The simplicity of the model was appealing. Learning, it was asserted, is a simple function of the amount of time during which the pupil engages in educational activity (Carroll, 1963). Applications of behavioral educational psychology—such as performance objectives, taxonomies, time on task, mastery learning—would prove influential in curriculum studies during the decades to follow.

A second major application of behaviorism to education was published in 1965: Robert M. Gagné's *The Conditions of Learning*. Drawing heavily on Edward Thorndike [see chapter 2] and behavioral psychologist B. F. Skinner, Gagné described varieties of learning and specified those conditions which made them possible. According to Gagné, the major types of learning included: 1) signal learning, 2) stimulus response learning, 3) chaining, 4) verbal association, 5) multiple discrimination, 6) concept learning, 7) principle learning, and 8) problem solving (Gagne, 1965, pp. 31-32). In a chapter entitled "Learning Decisions in Education," Gagné discussed those decisions which affected planning for learning in light of behavioral objectives, in language reminiscent of Mager's book. Gagné (1965) wrote: "Analysis of a topic begins with the statement of the terminal objective—the performance or performances one expects the student to be able to exhibit after the learning topic has been completed" (p. 245). Six factors in educational decisions were identified: 1) learning objectives, 2) the structure of knowledge to be learned, 3) motivation, 4) conditions of learning, 5) the transferability of knowledge, and 6) assessment (Gagne, 1965, p. 263). Gagné seemed to believe that if these factors were present "anyone could learn anything." These ideas would be extended to issues of curriculum planning and design in a volume published nine years later (Gagné, 1974).

In that book, entitled *Principles of Instructional Design*, Gagné and Briggs (1974) applied the "system approach" to the design of instruction. Consistent with the work of Bloom, Tyler, and Mager, they outlined and provided elaborations of various stages in designing instructional systems. These stages included: 1) the system level, comprised of the a) analysis of needs, goals, and priorities and b) the analysis of resources, constraints, and alternative delivery systems, and the determination of scope and sequence of curriculum; 2) the course level, in which course structure and sequence are determined and course objectives analyzed; 3) the lesson level, wherein performance objectives are defined, lesson plans or "modules" are prepared, materials are developed and/or selected and students are assessed; and 4) the system level most broadly speaking, including attention to teacher preparation, formative evaluation, field testing, summative evaluation [see chapter 13 for a discussion of these evaluation terms], and installation and diffusion [referring to the widespread adoption of curricular designs after their complete and thorough testing]. Gagné and Briggs's work illustrated the emphasis upon assessment characteristic of behavioristic curriculum emphases. This work was accepted by those who endorsed behaviorism (Schubert, 1980a). It was very effectively criticized by the distinguished Canadian (but British born and Oxford educated) curriculum theorist Robin Barrow (Barrow, 1984b; see pp. 100-107), who, like R. S. Peters (1974; see chapter 4), insisted that learning theory has little to offer education in general, and curriculum theory in particular: "In 1959 David P. Ausubel took the view that the study of growth and development could offer 'only a limited number of very crude generalizations and highly tentative suggestions' (Ausubel, 1959, p. 245). In my view that was a very fair summary of the situation" (Barrow, 1984b, p. 108).

VII
Curriculum Theory in the 1960s

> As the school places priority upon . . . creating, loving, knowing, organizing, and other process skills, they will orchestrate more beautifully the components of tomorrow's world.
>
> (Louise M. Berman, 1968, p. 191)

While chapters on curriculum as a field and on curriculum theory appeared in synoptic texts of the period, George Beauchamp's *Curriculum Theory* (1961) was devoted to the subject exclusively, if from a scientific perspective. Beauchamp dedicated the book "to the hope that we may move forward with a science of education" (Beauchamp, 1961, p. v). Beauchamp conceived of curriculum "as a written document" (Beauchamp, 1961, pp. 101-103; Tanner & Tanner, 1980, p. 22). The major function of curriculum theory, according to Beauchamp, was to "give meaning to the various facets of curriculum activity in light of our present knowledge, the values we bring to bear upon problems, and the assumptions or hypotheses that may be evoked" (Beauchamp, 1961, p. 60). Beauchamp hypothesized four specific functions of curriculum theory. The first function concerned curriculum development, especially those decisions which dictate selection and content, scope, and sequence, or objectives. The second function provides applications of theory in practice. The third function brought to curriculum problems the knowledge of other disciplines. Finally, Beauchamp viewed the task of curriculum theory as developing "theoretical deliberations about curriculum" (Beauchamp, 1961).

Clearly, Beauchamp's conception of curriculum and curriculum theory was influenced by the Tyler Rationale. However, Beauchamp's work was more narrowly scientific and might be characterized as positivistic (Schubert, 1986a, p. 131). Beauchamp credited the 1947 University of Chicago Curriculum Theory Conference as initiating his curriculum theory. Others would dispute this view of the Conference (Klohr, 1974a; Miller, 1979a; Pinar, 1974c). Publishers were, at first, not very interested in Beauchamp's book-length manuscript. He published it himself. However, by 1975 the book had enjoyed a third edition, justifying Beauchamp's investment. [In 1981 it was reprinted by a commercial house.] The book was the first to appear with

"Theory" in its title. It would not be the last. [Relatively few in the field extended interest in Beauchamp's pioneering work; for an example see Kimpston and Rogers' (1986) "A Framework for Curriculum Research."]

Mauritz Johnson's model. An influential curriculum model in the "scientific" tradition was that formulated by Mauritz Johnson at the State University of New York at Albany. [We have acknowledged Johnson's influence on the work of his most prominent student, George J. Posner (1992) of Cornell University.] Johnson's (1967) model characterized curriculum as the output of the curriculum development system, ". . . a structured series of intended learning outcomes" (p. 129). Johnson's model defined curriculum in terms of objectives and emphasized the concept of learning, an emphasis which Dwayne Huebner (1966b), among others, criticized.

Other definitions of curriculum which emphasized intentions did not share Johnson's engineering orientation. Alice Miel (1968a), for instance, defined curriculum as intended opportunities for engagement. Gordon Mackenzie (1964) conceived of curriculum as engagement as well, focusing not on intentions but on upon the classroom experience. Johnson's emphasis upon intended learning outcomes would be all but forgotten in the Reconceptualization of the field during the 1970s.

Embracing the disciplines and democracy. Broudy, Smith, and Burnett's *Democracy and Excellence in American Secondary Education: A Study in Curriculum Theory* appeared in 1964 as a synoptic text that "went far beyond the encyclopedic treatment of usual synoptic texts to build theoretical perspectives from which further curriculum thought could be generated" (Schubert, 1980a, p. 186). This study combined an interest in the disciplines with an interest in democracy. The prototypical curriculum design proposed in this text is reminiscent of the classical/humanist position advocated by Eliot [see chapter 2]. Broudy, Smith, and Burnett called for one curriculum without electives for all students. They argued for the elimination of vocational education. They identified five categories of knowledge which, they argued, redefined the traditional disciplines. First was symbolics (English, foreign language, mathematics); second was basic science (general science, biology, physics, chemistry). Third was developmental studies (evolution of the cosmos, evolution of social institutions and of human culture). Fourth was the category of exemplars (art, music, drama, literature); fifth was what the authors termed molar problems (social problems) (Broudy, Smith, Burnett, 1964, p. 247; Tanner, D., 1972, p. 359). This curriculum design focused upon the disciplines, if reordered, rather than, say, upon the socialization of the child. The capstone of the proposed design was the course in molar problems, centering on problem-solving:

> One cannot repeat too often that the outcome is not the *solution* of these social problems, but rather the achievement of an intelligent orientation toward them and a disposition to ask the right questions, or at least to recognize the right ones when others ask them. For such learnings all men, if not equally apt are, at least, legitimate candidates. (Broudy, Smith, Burnett, 1964, p. 243)

In this 1964 study we observe curriculum theory functioning as a guide to the development, selection, and organization of content. Curriculum theory was an ideal "for use in the development of the secondary curriculum" (Broudy, Smith, Burnett, 1964, p. 9). Consistent with this view, Broudy, Smith, and Burnett clarified the theoretical base which undergirded their curriculum design.

Meaning: A source for content. Trained as a professional philosopher, Philip Phenix investigated the disciplines in his *Realms of Meaning* (1964). Here, however, we see a new approach to defining the role of the disciplines as a source of curriculum content. Phenix noted that the disciplines-centered orientation: "simply argues for the exclusive use of the materials that have been produced in the disciplined communities of inquiry by men [sic] of knowledge who possess authority in their fields" (Phenix, 1964). Phenix argued that education must be grounded in the search for meaning, proposing that curriculum be organized in interdisciplinary ways, providing both for depth in the individual disciplines but also for correlation and integration among them: "Hence, a philosophy of the curriculum requires a mapping of the realms of meaning, one in which the various possibilities of significant experience are charted and the various domains of meaning are distinguished and correlated" (Phenix, 1964, p. 6).

Phenix derived six patterns of meaning from distinctive modes of human understanding. The realms included: symbolics (ordinary language, mathematics as well as nondiscursive symbolic forms such as gestures and rituals); empirics (including the sciences of the physical world, of living things, and of human culture); aesthetics (music, visual arts, dance, literature); synoetics (including the Michael Polanyi's idea of "personal knowledge" and Martin Buber's idea of the "I-Thou" relationship, signifying relational insight or direct awareness); ethics (personal conduct and decision-making); and synoptics (meaning that is integrative, for instance history, religion, and philosophy (Phenix, 1964). Phenix emphasized the importance of interdisciplinary learning.

Disciplines as communities of discourse. Arthur King and John Brownell brought a significantly new dimension to the continuing concern with the role of the disciplines in curriculum development in *The Curriculum and the Disciplines of Knowledge: A Theory of Curriculum Practice* (1966). They defined a discipline as that body of ideas which emerged from the work of a "corps of human beings with a common intellectual commitment who make a contribution to human thought and to human affairs" (p. 68). Disciplines are "communities of discourse" which ought to be made accessible to all: "We have in effect argued that liberal education, traditionally considered suitable only for the elite of society, belongs to all. All students—children or adults—are worthy of encounters with the disciplines of knowledge" (King & Brownell, 1966, p. 213). King and Brownell insisted that both curriculum and curriculum theory must be rooted in the disciplines, but they anticipated later work in their redefinition of disciplines as "communities of discourse" (Pagano, 1981).

Curriculum: A social laboratory. Herbert Thelen, a group dynamics specialist at the University of Chicago who had worked with Tyler on the evaluation of the Eight-Year Study, linked his concept of curriculum to social relations, conceiving of the classroom as a social laboratory. In his *Education and the Human Quest: Four Designs for Education* (1960), Thelen elaborated four models of education with curricular implications. The first model was that of personal inquiry, defined as a quest for selfhood or integration. Thelen described the personal quests of the gifted child, the anti-social child, and the culturally deprived child, each requiring individualized instruction. A second model was group investigation. Characterizing human beings as essentially social, he conceived of the individual person as one who "builds with other men the rules and agreements that constitute social reality" (Thelen, 1960, p. 80). In the classroom, for instance, social order is developed and maintained by the formulation and enforcement of "house rules." The point of such rules is to permit inquiry. A third model Thelen characterized as a reflective action quest. In this model the group is viewed as "transacting business with the environment both in order to change the environment and in order to learn the skills and insights for changing the environment" (Thelen, 1960, p. 83). Thelen distinguished his position from Counts' reconstructionism [see earlier in this chapter] when he declared: "The school is not out to change society, but only to produce enlightened citizens who will act intelligently" (Thelen, 1960, p. 84). Such citizens, in Thelen's view, would rationally institute changes. The final model was that of skill development, which is "subsidiary to and facilitative of the other kinds of inquiry" (Thelen, 1960, p. 86). In these proposals Thelen showed the significant relationships among assumptions, curriculum, instruction, and learning environments (Schubert, 1980a, p. 181). In this respect, Thelen contributed importantly to a growing knowledge of curriculum theory.

New questions arise. In 1961, a three-day curriculum conference had been sponsored by Teachers College, Columbia University, the Department of Curriculum and Teaching. The meeting was attended by two hundred educators interested in curriculum and representative of the various academic disciplines. Speakers were asked to examine a "frontier" area in an effort to crystallize concepts (Passow, 1962). The proceedings, including portions of subsequent discussions, were published as *Curriculum Crossroads* (1962). Particularly notable in this collection was Dwayne Huebner's "Politics and Curriculum." Huebner, who would serve—at times it would seem against his will—as an intellectual parent of the Reconceptualization of the field during the 1970s, discussed the use of political science in investigating curriculum problems. His theme distinguished his paper from the others presented at the Columbia conference as it examined curriculum in terms of democratic ideology, control of resources, power, and slogans. Huebner's major student, Michael W. Apple, would extend these themes in the decade following [see chapters 4 and 5]. Significant in the early 1960s, however, was Huebner's insistence that the curriculum field permit the use of all major disciplinary systems, not only behaviorist psychology: "By utilizing concepts rooted in political science, the curriculum worker may find new questions for dealing with his age-old problems" (Huebner, 1962, p. 95). Huenber's attention to curricular language would provide the foundation for understanding curriculum as text and discourse [Huebner, 1966b, 1969, 1974; see chapter 8].

Humanistic voices are heard. The 1962 Yearbook of the Association for Supervision and Curriculum Development (ASCD) would become a classic. Entitled *Perceiving, Behaving, Becoming: A New Focus for Education*, this volume brought to the study of curriculum humanistic or so-called third force psychology, an orientation which would later influence reconceptualized curriculum scholarship. Both Carl Rogers and Abraham Maslow, two prominent humanistic psychologists, contributed papers to the volume. Rogers' paper, entitled "Toward Becoming a Fully Functioning Person" and Maslow's, entitled "Some Basic Propositions of a Growth and Self-Actualization Psychology," serve as excellent examples of a conception of psychology alternative to mainstream educational psychology, and more narrowly, to behaviorism, which had dominated the school curriculum so thoroughly at the time. Their pioneering work would be acknowledged and extended in the humanistic movement in the field later in the 1960s and during the early 1970s [see chapter 4].

A pioneer in search of theory. University of Wisconsin curriculum specialist Virgil Herrick mentored two major intellectual parents of the Reconceptualization, Dwayne Huebner and James B. Macdonald. In 1965 a collection of Herrick's essays was published as *Strategies for Curriculum Development*. These essays demonstrated the emergence of alternative curriculum conceptualizations, specifically alternative conceptions of curriculum theory, planning, and organization. Herrick wrote: "There is more than one base upon which curriculum structures can be erected. Our almost exclusive preoccupation with subject matter gives rise to the danger that we will fall behind in creative, imaginative thinking about different ways in which an educational program can be planned" (quoted in Macdonald et al., 1965, p. 70).

   Herrick explored the problems of subject centeredness in his discussion of "organizing centers." Such centers involved an organization of activities and behavior of children around centers or focal points of interest and attention. Herrick elaborated the qualities of sound organizing centers; they were: significance (centers that both develop and broaden certain understandings, skills and value referents of intrinsic interest to students), accessibility (ideas are made intellectually and physically accessible), breath and scope (moving several curricular areas together, focussing upon significant life problems), organizing and relating (utilizing learning that has previously occurred, and group work), and development (providing for further learning). The editors suggested that teaching was an emphasis throughout Herrick's work: "The analysis of the teaching operations should be central to the development of curricular and instructional theory and practice and . . . research and theorizing which disregard the central operations of teaching are doomed to early extinction despite their popularity" (quoted in Macdonald, 1965, p. vii). A critical response to the structure-of-the-disciplines approach was underway. Nine years later Robert Starratt would attack the concept directly (Starratt, 1974).

No consensus on curriculum theory. The ASCD Commission on Curriculum Theory—its members included Arno Bellack of Teachers College, Columbia University, Paul Klohr of Ohio State University, Paul Komisar of Temple University, Elizabeth S. Maccia of Ohio State University, and B. Othanel Smith of the University of Illinois—held a seminar on curriculum theory in Chicago in 1965, with twenty curricularists attending the seminar. Three papers were presented; they were "Content Analysis of Significant Theories" by James McClellan and Paul Komisar, "Methodological Considerations in Theory Building" by Elizabeth Maccia, and "Significant Elements in Curriculum Theories" by B. O. Smith. The papers were never published as a collection. ASCD had hoped for a consensus on the nature of curriculum theory from this seminar. Its other major commission (on instructional theory), chaired by Ira Gordon, issued such a consensus report entitled *Theories of Instruction* (Gordon,1968). That group had chosen a "scientific" base for theory development in instruction. Gordon wrote: "It offers the challenge of careful assessment, logical analysis, and empirical pursuit of understanding" (quoted in Macdonald & Leeper, 1968, p. xi). In effect, members of the Commission on Curriculum Theory were unwilling to adopt an exclusively "empirical" or "scientific" framework for theory development in curriculum, a view articulated twenty years later by Canadian theorist Robin Barrow (1984b): "The view that curriculum theory should concern itself with empirically-based prescription for practice is evidently misplaced, and the idea that curriculum planning should involve instructional prescriptions of a specific kind is to be resisted" (1984b, p. 145). This view of the ASCD Commission in the 1960s would set the stage for a reconceptualized field of curriculum informed not by mainstream social science, but rather by literary theory, aesthetics, phenomenology, theology, race, feminist and social theory.

Humanities enter the picture. In 1965 ASCD's Commission on Curriculum Development sponsored a conference on "The Role of the Humanities in Current Curriculum Developments," published as *The Humanities and the Curriculum* (1967). The humanities were a neglected curricular area, particularly since World War II. The editor, Louise M. Berman, concluded the collection with an essay entitled "Toward a Sharper Focus on the Humanities," summarizing the conference. In that essay, Berman recognized that learning opportunities must provide access to the "essence of experience," which meant a new concern for ethical, social, intellectual, and aesthetic values, not merely the content of academic disciplines.

This conference suggested that the reign of the structures of disciplines orientation was beginning to be seriously questioned. Berman can be credited with recognizing new priorities that were emerging in the curriculum field. Her *New Priorities in the Curriculum* (1968) evidenced a humanistic orientation in which the curriculum would be characterized as perceiving, communicating, loving, knowing, decision making, patterning, creating, and valuing (Berman, 1968). To support these curricular priorities, Berman drew upon "third force" psychology (including Maslow, Rogers, Allport, Fromm) and existentialism (Kierkegaard, Sartre). The epilogue to this volume is as engaging today as it was twenty-one years ago. In it Berman insisted that curriculum is marching to the beat of a drummer fifty years past; the melodies of the present were only "slightly changed variations of old themes (Berman, 1968, p. 191). Berman (1968) wrote: "Our hypothesis is that as the school places priority upon developing a setting where children and youth have the opportunity to experience and verbalize the meanings of creating, loving, knowing, organizing, and other process skills, they will orchestrate more beautifully the components of tomorrow's world than if they did not have such new priorities established in the curriculum" (p. 191). Against the backdrop of Beauchamp and even Bruner, Berman's work represented a courageous call for "new priorities."

In the widely read and widely quoted *Life in Classrooms* (1968), Philip Jackson examined elementary school classrooms as a site of curriculum. Jackson argued that classroom life had received insufficient attention. His study included summaries of the socialization literature and examination of group formation and evaluation. Jackson was convincing in his argument that the day-to-day life of children in schools influenced teaching and learning. Jackson's study aroused interest in the "hidden curriculum," a central concept of politically oriented curriculum scholars of the 1970's, and provoked a scholarly interest in classroom life which continues today. The book is a classic in the field.

Federal Legislation. In 1958 the federal government had responded to the perceived education crisis provoked by the Soviet Sputnik launching by massive funding. In 1965 the federal government intervened again through passage of the Elementary and Secondary Education Act (ESEA), legislation consisting of six major titles. Title I focused on the so-called disadvantaged child. It was to address the special needs of educationally disadvantaged children. This title received 78% of the $1.25 billion initially appropriated (Spring, 1989). Funds were employed to improve educational programs for this group. Title I became the major education component of President Lyndon B. Johnson's "War on Poverty" (Spring, 1989). Title II focussed on library resources, providing funds for acquiring library materials, including textbooks and other instructional materials. Title III provided funds for Projects to Advance Creativity in Education (PACE), establishing centers for promoting educational innovation. Title IV provided funds for educational research, establishing Research and Development Centers at universities in several regions of the U.S. Title V funded further development of state education departments, a move designed to allay fears of a "federalization" of education (Spring, 1989). Despite the large appropriation, no funding was provided directly to support the essential theoretical work which might have coordinated and integrated the hundreds of specific curricular projects spawned by the detailed legislation.

Synoptic texts continue. The tradition of synoptic texts continued in the 1960s. New editions of previously published texts appeared (i.e. Lee & Lee, 1960; Alberty & Alberty, 1962; Gwynn, 1960; see Schubert, 1980a, pp. 178-179). New and influential synoptic texts were also published. As we shall see, these were often general in focus (addressed to problems of the curriculum across the grades) as well as specific to elementary, junior, and senior high school. Kimball Wiles' *The Changing Curriculum of the American High School* (1963) was a typical synoptic text of the period. Wiles described the "process of change," in which he presented a method for advocating and accomplishing curriculum change. From his perspective in the early sixties, Wiles forecast what the American high school would be like in 1985. He foresaw seminars in the various disciplines, buildings and classrooms of variable shape and size, and enormous federal support. His forecast has proved to be less than accurate.

Taba's modification of Tyler. Hilda Taba's *Curriculum Development: Theory and Practice* (1962, reprinted 1972) was a widely-read synoptic text which proposed a theoretical base for curriculum development. In Taba's view, there was "a strong tendency to assume that the theoretical foundations of our current curriculum are sound and that the difficulties occur chiefly in translating theory into practice" (Taba, 1962, p. v). Taba was disturbed by the lack of "systematic thinking about curriculum planning" (Taba, 1962, p. 3). Planning, she argued, should include consideration of the demands of society and culture, the learning process, the development of the individual, and the specific characteristic and unique contributions of the disciplines (Taba, 1962). A critical aspect of her proposals involved a modification of the Tyler Rationale, regarded largely as a linear process moving from statements of purpose through learning experiences to evaluation. Taba conceived of the process as more nearly circular with the emergence of new purposes and goals during the process. This modification was more in accordance with Dewey's conception of purpose as arising out of transactions between teachers and students. In this sense, evaluation becomes "formative" rather than exclusively "summative" [see chapter 13], i.e. utilized in the process of curriculum planning and instruction rather than at its conclusion. Again we observe in Taba's volume the eclectic character of the synoptic text. She used a wide range of sources including conflicting curriculum reform notions from Dewey to Tyler, her former colleague. She included influences from the structures of the disciplines proposals as well as taken-for-granted emphases upon objectives. Taba's textbook was influential and widely used in curriculum courses during the 1960s and into the early 1970s.

Curriculum development remains as a focus. In 1966 J. Galen Saylor and William Alexander contributed to the synoptic textbook tradition with the re-publication, i.e. the second edition, of their *Curriculum Planning for Modern Schools*, also a widely used text. Again in this volume curriculum is conceptualized in terms of curriculum planning and development. The book is divided into five sections, illustrative of this concept: 1) the process of curriculum planning; 2) the determinants of the curriculum; 3) the bases for curriculum planning; 4) organization of the curriculum and instruction; 5) procedures for curriculum planning (Saylor & Alexander, 1966). In the section on organization the authors reported various curriculum projects underway in selected subject areas, reflecting the national emphasis upon discipline-based curriculum development. As well they discussed plans for individualizing the curriculum. Concluding the book is a discussion of the roles of various persons and agencies in curriculum planning. So conceived, the book reflected the typical concerns of the curriculum field at mid-decade. It would be revised twice more (and retitled), once in 1974 and finally in 1981.

The "death" of the curriculum field. What came to be perceived by many as the "death" of the traditional field occurred in 1969 with Joseph J. Schwab's "The Practical: A Language for Curriculum," first published in 1969, later reprinted widely, by, among others, the National Education Association (1970) and by Arno Bellack and Herbert Kliebard in their collection *Curriculum and Evaluation* (1977). In this, the first of a decade of attacks on the traditional field, Schwab made three charges. First, he declared that the curriculum field was "moribund." Second, he argued that the field had reached that point due to an "inveterate and unexamined reliance on theory." Third, Schwab declared that the field would experience a "renaissance" only if the energies of the field were diverted from theoretical concerns to the practical, the quasi-practical and to the eclectic. Schwab insisted that a flight from the field's appropriate subject—practice—was a sign of the crisis.

Schwab identified six types of flight which characterize a moribund field. First is flight from the field itself. Included in this flight is the appearance of others, outside the field, working on the field's problems, a probable reference to the leadership of the national curriculum reform movement being given to arts and sciences scholars rather than to curriculum specialists. A second kind of flight was "upward" to discourse about the field, illustrated by "exploitation of the exotic and fashionable in the curriculum field." Third was a flight downward, characterized by practitioners returning to the subject in a state of innocence. To look at the field with a "new" and "pristine" eye was the chief feature of this type of flight. Schwab suggested that this was the only type of flight not evident in the current crisis. Fourth was a flight to the sidelines to the role of observer, commentator, historian, or critic of the contributions of others to the field. Schwab suggested that the curriculum literature abundantly illustrated this type. Fifth was a marked preservation or repetition of old and familiar knowledge, and meanings in new languages which add little or nothing to the field. Schwab "recoiled from listing the persons and books who and which simply repeated the Tyler Rationale, behavioral objectives or arguments over Dewey." Sixth was an increase in contentious and "ad hominem" debate.

Schwab argued for eclectic methods in curriculum, a central place for the "practical," a need for social science theories, a necessity for the practical arts and a commitment to deliberation if the field were to emerge from the present crisis. He also discussed the need for new journals to provide a forum for debate in the field. Finally, he argued that teacher preparation programs should teach deliberation, a prerequisite for exercise of the "practical arts." Schwab (1970): "By means of such journals and such an education, the educational research establishment might at least find a means for channeling its discoveries into sustained improvement of the schools instead of into a procession of ephemeral bandwagons." Schwab is the one of the "giants" of the field whose contribution Philip Jackson (1992a) considered in his historical study, which we reviewed in chapter 1. We will focus on Schwab's significance in more detail in chapter 4.

The field in crisis. Schwab's charge of moribundity would be repeated two times more during the 1970s. His particular analysis of the crisis would not be widely shared, although it has inspired a line of research termed "personal practical knowledge" [see chapter 10]. Others would view the field as insufficiently theoretical and excessively practical. What would be shared was the view that the field had lost its legitimacy. The Tyler Rationale, conceived first as a rational scheme for curriculum development, had become a rationale for narrow, behavioristic conceptions which reduced curriculum to objectives and outcomes. The field had, in effect, broken down internally. But it also had broken down externally, as the leadership of the national curriculum reform movement indicated. As well, demographic trends reduced student populations by the end of the decade; indeed a teacher surplus would occur in most school subjects by the early 1970's. Thus as enrollment in curriculum courses dropped, federal funds were directed elsewhere, and as internal doubt grew over the traditional Tylerian paradigm, it was not surprising that the field went into a kind of cardiac arrest. What would be surprising would be those who arrived to revitalize the patient. Before we tell this story [in chapter 4], we conclude with developments in the 1960s.

VIII
Conclusion: Initial Stages of the Reconceptualization

Curriculum theory should be committed, not neutral.
                                        (James B. Macdonald, 1967, p. 168)

The central focus of American education must be on the individual.
                                        (Elsie J. Alberty, 1967, p. 208)

Early internal challenges to the Tylerian paradigm emerged from humanistic psychology identified with Abraham Maslow, Gordon Allport, Erich Fromm, Carl Rogers, and Erik Erikson. Humanistic psychology waned in influence by the end of the decade, to re-emerge in altered form in some early 1970's work. Humanistic psychology, specifically that of R. D. Laing, provided a non-behavioristic base to the early effort to reconceive the field (Huber, 1981).

The 1963 ASCD Yearbook was entitled *New Insights and the curriculum* and focused upon the child as an individual. The book was dedicated to "help us develop new insights and to push our thinking beyond the traditional frontiers" (Frazier, 1963, p. iii). The next year James B. Macdonald discussed the relationship between society and the individual, and specifically the ways in which society defined individuals. He called for a new image which could shape schools in general and the curriculum in particular. He called those schools which recognized a new image of children as self-actualizing as "reality-centered." This early essay would mark the beginning of his enormous contribution to the Reconceptualization of curriculum. Macdonald (1964) wrote:

> We simply mean that the school does not exist primarily to inculcate our cultural heritage, not principally to develop role players for society nor primarily to meet the needs and interests of the learners. The school exists to bring learners in contact with reality, of which our society, ourselves, and our cultural heritage are parts. (p. 47)

Clearly, Macdonald challenged the supremacy of the structure-of-the-disciplines in the constitution of curriculum. In addition, he challenged both the socially and psychologically oriented curricularist, positing another concept in which these become elements. The point of this concept is to rationalize a curriculum in which the student can be free to develop his or her own thinking and values, and to encourage creative responses to reality (Burke, 1985). It was frontier work which would be continued and extend over the remaining twenty years of his important career.

Macdonald challenges structure of the disciplines movement. The proceedings of ASCD's Tenth Curriculum Research Institute were published in 1966 as *Language and Meaning*, edited by James B. Macdonald and Robert Leeper. In this collection, the human aspects of schooling were emphasized as a counterpoint to the taken-for-grantedness of the discipline-centered and scientific orientations of the period: "Language, after all, is the vehicle by which most teaching is accomplished. Meaning is the human goal of learning, the ultimate test of any curriculum change" (Combs, quoted in Macdonald & Leeper, 1966, p. v). Macdonald's essay, "Learning Meaning and Motivation: An Introduction," discussed the problems associated with the structure-of-the-disciplines movement and urged a concern for the person. He challenged directly the former:

> There is, after all, no reason to suspect that the reformulation of content alone in the schools will suffice to counter the loss of self, the dehumanization and

depersonalization of people living in a technological society such as ours. Further, there is no reason to suspect that the structure of the disciplines can by magic of organization reduce the threat of nuclear holocaust, bring justice and equality to all people or provide a basis for freedom from poverty for all. (Macdonald & Leeper, 1966, pp. 5-6)

This challenge would constitute the thematic heart of the Reconceptualization of the 1970s.

The primacy of the person. A second major statement by Macdonald on the primacy of the person was published in *Precedents and Promise in the Curriculum Field* (1966), edited by Helen F. Robison of Teachers College, Columbia University. Dwelling on the theme of dehumanization, Macdonald advocated a person-oriented curriculum:

> We will create our own image of ourselves through the ways we structure and relate to our own world. This image is in dire peril of becoming characterized by a partially ordered and conditioned set of regimented performances in the modern age. What we must strive for is to make men what they ought to be—complete human beings. (Macdonald, quoted in Robison, 1966, p. 52)

The current school structure was dehumanizing. What was necessary was a reconceptualization of what school and curriculum could be, the cultivation of self-conscious and complete human beings. Again, Macdonald had sounded a challenge that would be repeated over and over again ten years later.

The Ohio State University Conference. A major curriculum conference was held in 1967 at Ohio State University, chaired by Paul R. Klohr (Klohr, 1967a, 1967b, 1967c; Alberty, 1967, Duncan & Frymier, 1967; Huebner, 1967; Mooney, 1967b). This conference has been regarded as a major step toward Reconceptualization of the traditional field by several scholars (Pinar, 1974c; Miller, 1979a). Proceedings were edited by Klohr and published in *Theory Into Practice*. Klohr (1967b) wrote: "The individuals who planned the Ohio State University Curriculum Theory Conference . . . were determined, if possible, to examine curriculum theory in the making" (p. 165). In addition to Huebner's groundbreaking paper on temporality [see chapter 8] which introduced phenomenology to the field, Macdonald's paper was also noteworthy. Here he delineated between "framework" and "engineering" theories at work in curriculum. Framework theorists were said to interpret curriculum issues by means of "aesthetic rationality," a concept Macdonald borrowed from Herbert Marcuse (1966), the well-known critical theorist widely read during the 1960s. Macdonald argued that aesthetic rationality pointed to the human capacity to cope rationally with the world on an intuitive basis. The individual must return to the world as experienced for insights which enabled one to transcend one's present systems of thought and to move to new paradigms or fresh perspectives.

The danger of curriculum engineering. Macdonald focussed on the danger of the engineering theorists, predominant at that time. In this 1967 statement, one finds the heart of the political theory so influential in the decades to follow. Macdonald's concern foreshadowed those of nearly an entire generation of curricularists: "The danger of our present 'systems approach' to human behavior is that as we gain greater control over ourselves, the systems concept will become so useful in solving our problems of efficiency and effectiveness that we shall be in grave danger of losing contact with reality through 'aesthetic rationality.'" Further: "Schooling will be reduced to objectification of this systematic process [efficiency and effectiveness]. This process is already demonstrable in other aspects of our society. It is especially obvious in the realm of our national economic security policies" (Macdonald, 1967, p. 168). The "systems approach"—another characterization of the Tyler Rationale and its behavioristic offspring such as performance objectives—would not prove popular due to its success but due to its failure. The more it failed, the more its use was intensified. The objectification process, including the objectification of students into categories (gifted, etc.), of the interpersonal process [commodification, see chapter 5] would indeed permeate educational institutions.

The central question. Calling for a very different field, Macdonald (1967) began by acknowledging that curriculum theorizing is "a challenging undertaking" (p. 166). At this stage, and quite beyond mainstream thinking of the period, Macdonald discerned that "there appears to be framework theorists and engineering theorists. Both may be needed" (p. 166). Framework theorists are those interested in larger, non-technical issues, and he identified himself with this group: "This paper will focus upon theory as the development of frameworks from which designs can be generated rather than theory as the testing of designs," which represented a form of "technological rationality" (p. 166). In technological rationality:

> phenomena are identified as separate objects (always in transaction or flux); common qualities are abstracted, related to one another, and put into a system. The danger of using technological rationality in human behavior is that, in our desire to gain control, understand, and predict, we may (and perhaps already have) come to see ourselves as objects or the representation of these objects that we find useful for our purposes. . . . We will then become what Marcuse called one-dimensional. (pp. 166-167)

Macdonald then introduced the notion of "aesthetic rationality [which] is meant here to mean man's [sic] capacity to cope rationally with the world on an intuitive basis—to return to the world for insights which will enable him to transcend his present systems of thought and move to new paradigms . . . or fresh perspectives" (p. 167-168). In contrast to technological rationality, which is "closed," aesthetic rationality "is a rationality of means applied to ends which are always open" (p.168). Macdonald (1967) then moved directly to the field of curriculum:

> Obviously, if education is to escape a similar entrapment (as weapons delivery system locks us into nationalism, and an arms race), theorizing in curriculum

must remain broad enough in scope to include the use of aesthetic rationality—this means specifically, that the systems metaphor is not enough and must be used carefully. . . . The central question is whether theory and theorizing are neutral or committed. Yet, its [curriculum theory's] central utility may well be the creation of forms which lead to interpreting curriculum phenomena, not so much to solving curriculum problems by applying scientific generalizations. At present, the most appropriate role for curriculum theory is probably an interpretive role. . . . Theory in curriculum has an essentially heuristic role. Curriculum theory should be committed, not neutral. It should be committed to human fullness in creation, direction, and use. All of man's rational potential should be committed to the processes and goals in curriculum theorizing. . . . Curriculum theorizing is an act of disciplined thinking. It is disciplined by the vertical awareness of curriculum theory as it has developed historically and by the horizontal awareness of man's contemporary status of development in various formal disciplines. . . . Rather than place emphasis only upon the discipline of technical reason, curriculum theory should be disciplined by the total rational potential of man [sic], both aesthetic and technological. (pp. 168-169)

It was a major paper, one which went beyond public curriculum debates (although correctly locating them in national defense issues) to the very character of thought employed in curriculum research. He rejected rationalistic and technical systems of theorizing as distortive and finally inhuman, endorsing an aesthetic rationality which holds political, historical, and technological potential. Note that Macdonald suggested an interpretative role for curriculum theory, one that in fact the field would take up a decade later, i.e. the project to understand—not only develop—curriculum.

Dwayne Huebner: Modes of relationship and language. Another speaker at the Ohio State Conference was Teachers College, Columbia University Professor Dwayne E. Huebner. Trained at the University of Wisconsin by Virgil Herrick (as was Macdonald), Huebner would also lead the way toward Reconceptualization. After completing a statistical dissertation, Huebner experienced an intensifying dissatisfaction with his own education and the education of those around him. He committed himself to study theology and philosophy, and to bring aspects of those fields to curriculum (Huber, 1981). In a 1963 essay entitled "New Modes of Man's Relationship to Man," Huebner worked to shift curricular attention away from the disciplines' structures to how persons are in relation to each other. He relied on third-force psychology and existentialism, and foreshadowed several themes he and others would take up later. Among these, as we noted, was the matter of curriculum language. Huebner worked to "make the educator aware of his limited, and limiting thought patterns and language systems for shaping values and legitimizing action" (Huebner, 1963, p. 162).

In his 1966 "Curriculum as a Field of Study" Huebner advanced four radical propositions. First, he argued that conceptions of curriculum tended to be tied to "technique" and not linked to the human spirit. Second, the field suffered from an overdependence upon values conceived as goals or objectives. Furthermore, the field suffered from an overdependence upon learning as the primary expression of human temporality [see chapter 8 for a discussion of Huebner's articulation of curriculum as concern for temporality]. Third, correction of this conception of curriculum could be achieved partially by the design of an educative environment conceived as valued educational activity. Fourth, Huebner insisted that curriculum design was inherently a political process by means of which the curricular worker sought to attain a just environment. Like Macdonald and Eisner, Huebner (1966a) endorsed art as a model of curriculum theory and design:

> Is it possible, now that we are partially freed from vision-hindering busywork, that we can begin to make efforts to grasp the overall design of curriculum and to see how man's evolving techniques can be made subservient to man's evolving spirit? Educational environment and activity in the schools are symbolic of what man is today and what he wants to be tomorrow. The design of these symbols is a great art. The study of curriculum should be a preparation for this artistry. (p. 112)

Huebner's contribution. Huebner studied marginalized traditions for a new language for curriculum. The titles of his essays during the 1960s illustrate his search: "Politics and the Curriculum" (1962), "Curriculum as a Field of Study" (1966a), "Curricular Language and Classroom Meanings" (1966b), "Curricular Concern for Man's Temporality" (1967), "Implications of Psychological Thought for the Curriculum" (1968), "Language and Teaching: Reflections in the Light of Heidegger's Writing About Language" (1969). Like Macdonald, Huebner created a literature quite different from the dominant "scientific" orientation, drawing upon language analysis, existentialism, phenomenology, theology, and political science. As these titles indicate, his scholarly range was broad; his focus traversed the daily exigencies of the classroom to fundamental questions regarding the character of the curriculum field (Huebner, 1991, 1963). Huebner's interest in political theory was passed on to his most prominent student Michael W. Apple, who would become one of the leading politically oriented curriculum theorists of the 1970s and 1980s [see chapters 4 and 5]. Huebner and Macdonald would continue to be influential in the 1970s, as we shall see.

Mooney and creativity. Others were working out of the mainstream also. As we have noted earlier, Ohio State University Professor Ross Mooney studied creativity in teaching, research, and curriculum. Among his essays are "Creation and Communication" (1961), "Creation and Teaching" (1963), "Nurturing the Educational Researcher as a Creative Artist" (1965), "Creative Integration" (1966), "Creation: Contemporary Culture and Renaissance" (1967a), "Perspectives on Ourselves" (1967b) (presented at the 1967 Ohio State University Conference), and "Three Moments in Crisis" (1969). In these essays Mooney explored the various ways educators could support creativity in the curriculum. Like the great literary critic Norman O. Brown, Ross Mooney articulated a view of life against death, arguing that the school must exhibit structures which support life, rather than unconsciously expressing death (Huber, 1981).

Klohr's influence. Ohio State University Professor Paul R. Klohr, as we observed, participated in the ASCD Commission on Curriculum Theory (1965), and chaired and edited the proceedings of the 1967 Ohio State Curriculum Theory Conference. Among his published works are "Use of Design Element in Curriculum Change" (1965), "Problems in Curriculum Theory Development" (1967b), "Curriculum Workers in a Bind" (1969a), and "Seeking New Design Alternatives" (1969b). Klohr's remarkable scholarly range (Kridel, 1990a) and unusually committed teaching would produce many students involved in various ways with the Reconceptualization (Schubert, et al., 1988).

Eisner: Curriculum as aesthetic text. Stanford University Professor Eliot W. Eisner was instrumental in creating a literature we have termed "curriculum as aesthetic text" (see chapter 11) and in qualitative evaluation (see chapter 13). His 1971 "How Can You Measure a Rainbow?" summarized the growing skepticism toward the prevailing behavioristic orientations to curriculum, teaching, and evaluation. Eisner noted that testing, grading and measurement do not exhaust the idea and means of evaluation. This early work would develop into a major perspective on curriculum evaluation and theory (Willis, 1978; Eisner, 1979, 1985a, 1985b, 1991a). In the 1990s, with Macdonald deceased, Klohr retired, and Huebner having left the field for religious education (as of this writing he teaches at the Yale University Divinity School), Eisner remains the sole major figure from the 1960s still actively at work today.

Greene: The importance of the arts and humanities. Teachers College, Columbia University Professor Maxine Greene, who first joined that institution to edit *Teachers College Record*, taught "philosophy of literature; the arts and American education; philosophy, literature and the visual arts; criticism and contemporary art forms" (Greene, 1975a, p. 297). Her early work, typified by *The Public School and the Private Vision: A Search for American in Education and Literature*, investigated the possibilities of the school's role in American culture. "We will," Greene (1965a) wrote, "continuously seek the angles of vision that may help us see the school somewhat more clearly and understand a little more about its role in American life" (p. 8). That role, as she suggested in her 1965 "Real Toads and Imaginary Gardens," concerned a lack of meaning, both in school and in the culture at large. She argued that the humanities, and in particular the study of literature, might help students confront meaninglessness, especially that meaninglessness associated with the triumph of science and the decline of religion. While never associating herself with the Reconceptualist movement [see chapter 4], Greene's work would significantly influence it.

Kliebard criticizes the traditional field. A major commentator on the field and soon to become its most eminent historian, Herbert M. Kliebard discussed the fragmentation of knowledge and bureaucracy. In "Structure of the Disciplines as an Educational Slogan" and "Bureaucracy and Curriculum

Theory," Kliebard criticized the use of scientific management and the disciplines approach in curriculum. He questioned the "product" orientation associated with the former. Kliebard observed that the dominant metaphor for curriculum theory in the early twentieth century was borrowed from corporate management (Kliebard, 1970, 1975a). In particular, he examined the influence of scientific management upon curricularists such as Bobbitt. This influence had resurfaced in the 1960s and would continue into 1970s.

Kliebard (1975a) criticized the curriculum field for its ahistorical perspective. In other disciplines, he noted, progress is achieved through "dialogue" between contemporary practitioners and their historical predecessors (Huber, 1981). The field of curriculum lacked this dialogue. It is "characterized by an uncritical propensity for novelty and change rather than funded knowledge or dialogue across generations" (Kliebard, 1975a, p. 41). The field's ahistorical posture permitted bureaucratized, standardized, and fragmented curriculum conceptions to be promoted as "new." Kliebard (1975a) advised: "The work of the next fifty years in the curriculum field is essentially developing alternatives to the mode of thinking and the limited framework that have so clearly dominated our first fifty years" (p. 49). Those committed to a Reconceptualization of the field in the 1970s took his advice very seriously indeed.

The first stage of Reconceptualization. The decade of the 1960s was dominated by federal funding and disciplinary leadership of a national curriculum reform movement. Bruner and others developed a coherent curricular view based on the disciplines, one based in inquiry and possibly not wholly in dispute with the Deweyan progressive emphasis of thirty years earlier [although this, as we noted, was contested by some scholars]. The scientific/behavioral wing of the field developed strongly, although, as we have seen, several individuals labored in relative isolation to challenge the taken-for-granted conceptions of curriculum and instruction. Macdonald, Huebner, Kliebard, Eisner, Greene, Berman, and Klohr opposed behaviorism, scientism (a reduction of forms of knowing to quantifiable ones), dehumanizing technology, and an oppressive, alienating bureaucratization of the schools. These curricularists first attacked behavioral objectives, then bureaucratization, the disciplines-centered orientation, and quantified, standardized evaluation and measurement of learning (Huber, 1981). This challenge—largely uncoordinated—represented the first stage of the Reconceptualization, as the traditional field, for a few, became static and limiting.

The traditional paradigm begins to come apart. The challenge to the mainstream field moved beyond a few solitary and courageous individuals and, indeed, became widespread when certain political and cultural events occurred during the 1960s. The civil rights movement, the student opposition to the Vietnam War, and the development of the so-called counter culture would support serious challenges to both the disciplines orientation and that of the behavioral managers. This challenge appeared first in the popular press, with the appearance of widely read books by John Holt, Ivan

Illich, Jonathan Kozol, Herbert Kohl, and others, and in an increasing interest in third-force psychology (especially that associated with Maslow and Rogers), and political theory (especially that which was associated with Marx). An alternative schools movement developed, reminiscent in some ways of the progressive movement thirty years earlier.

C. A. Bowers [a major political theorist; see chapter 5] linked the alternative school movement of the 1960s and the work of the child-centered progressives by alluding to Freud and Rousseau: "In the earlier phase of the progressive education movement, Freud provided psychological justification for an educational experience that maximized opportunities for the free expression of the child. But just as the child-centered phase of the earlier progressive movement broadened its ideological base by incorporating those elements of Rousseau's thinking that reflected the American liberal's commitment to freedom and equality, the alternative-free school movement of the 1960s fused A. S. Neill's Freudian-based pedagogy with the 'return to nature' philosophy of Rousseau" (Bowers, 1984, p. 20). For curriculum scholars, Freud would prove more interesting than Rousseau, but in the 1970s, Marx would prove more interesting for many than either. The traditional field of curriculum development would be first challenged, and then reconceptualized. The "moribund" curriculum field would become revitalized, and in a surprising way.

Chapter 4

Understanding Curriculum as Historical Text: The Reconceptualization of the Field 1970-1979

The main thrusts in curriculum development and reform over the years have been directed at microcurricular problems to the neglect of macrocurricular problems.
(Daniel & Laurel Tanner, 1975, p. ix)

What has now become decisive for society is the centrality of *theoretical* knowledge, the primacy of theory over empiricism.
(Daniel Bell, 1973, p. 343)

The new epoch is long overdue.
(Herbert M. Kliebard, 1975c, p. 83)

I
Introduction:
A Decade of Cataclysmic and Paradigmatic Change

In retrospect, the highwater mark of positivism and structuralism in American curricular thought was the 1960s (Cherryholmes, 1988b). The structure of the disciplines had triumphed, supporting a proliferation of curricular and instructional schemes influenced often by behaviorist psychology. In the 1970s the curriculum field underwent a profound change. We would term this change "paradigm shift." Others might argue that the decade represented only a reassertion of earlier dormant interests. Certainly, the themes of much 1970s scholarship can be linked to the interests of the Progressives in the earlier part of the century, although there were important differences (Stanley, 1992b). So-called humanistic approaches and the initial interest in autobiography can be linked to the child-centered Progressives, and others might point to nineteenth-century Romanticism as antecedent (Willinsky,1987, 1990b). The explosion of Marxist, neo-Marxist, and other political perspectives onto the curriculum scene recalled the earlier interests of George Counts and the social reconstructionists, but, in their adherence to Marxian categories, differentiated themselves from Counts' work (Stanley, 1992b). While these themes echo earlier ones, their function during the

1970s was to reconceptualize the character of the American curriculum field, both conceptually and methodologically. The field would shift from a primary and practical interest in the *development* of curriculum to a theoretical and practical interest in *understanding* curriculum.

By the early 1970s, it is clear that the field was "up for grabs." Schwab's declaration that the field was "moribund" struck a deep chord. Indeed, variations of the charge would be repeated throughout the decade: Huebner in 1975 termed the field dead (Huebner, 1976); Pinar in 1978 termed the field arrested (Pinar, 1979c). In his foreword to Daniel and Laurel Tanner's (1975) *Curriculum Development: Theory into Practice*, Arthur W. Foshay traced the 1970s situation to the 1950s: "The curriculum field was driven into disarray with the collapse of progressive education during the Fifties" (Foshay, in Tanner & Tanner, 1975, p. vii). The Tyler Rationale had reached the end of its utility, partly for conceptual reasons, and partly for historical ones. Critics of the rationale pointed to its technicism [i.e. its emphasis upon procedure to the exclusion of ethics, etc.] and its political naiveté (see, for example, Kliebard, 1975c). Historically, as we have seen in the previous chapter, the field was bypassed during the National Curriculum Reform Movement of the 1960s. That blow to the prestige of the traditional field, coupled with declining enrollments, politically ascendant departments of educational administration and educational psychology, the replacement of retiring curriculum generalists with subject matter specialists (such as science educators), and the paradigm instability within the field itself (i.e. dissatisfaction over the Tyler Rationale) all sent the curriculum field in crisis.

History supported the Reconceptualization of the field in another way. The world-wide student revolution of the 1960s, in the United States linked especially to the anti-war and the civil rights movements, reached beyond even those profound issues to challenge conventional ideas of American culture generally. In addition to political and racial dissent, the 1960s gave rise to the so-called counter culture, to notions of cultural revolution, enacted perhaps most seriously in the Peoples Republic of China under the leadership of Mao Zedong [see chapter 14]. Nearly every discipline associated with the social sciences underwent self-critique [see, for example, Gouldner, 1970]. The curriculum field would be no exception. Over 400 books of curriculum scholarship were published in this tumultuous decade (Schubert, 1980a), a decade of cataclysmic, contentious, and paradigmatic change (Klohr, 1980; Bullough, 1979a; Miller, J., 1979a; Vallance, 1980b; Purpel, 1981).

II
Popular press

It is not possible to spend any prolonged period visiting public school classrooms without being appalled by the mutilation visible everywhere—mutilation of spontaneity, of the joy of learning, of pleasure in creating, of sense of self.
(Charles Silberman, 1970, p. 10)

A number of popular books on education would influence, if indirectly, the field and the direction it would take through its crisis. One such book was written not by an educator but by a journalist and sociologist, Charles Silberman who, in the late 1960s, was a member of the Board of Editors of *Fortune* magazine. The book—*Crisis in the Classroom: The Remaking of American Education*—was produced for the Carnegie Corporation and appeared in *The Atlantic Monthly* magazine in a prepublication serial which included sensation-making titles such as: "Murder in the School Room" and "How the Public Schools Kill Dreams and Mutilate Minds." Both the book and the articles were widely read.

Earlier in the decade Silberman had been an advocate of the structures-of-the-disciplines approach [see chapter 3]. In *Crisis in the Classroom* Silberman's views had changed considerably. Human spontaneity and the joy of learning —that is, their absence in the schools—concerned Silberman in *Crisis in the Classroom*, not the structural verisimilitude of the school subjects and the academic disciplines. He wrote:

> I am indignant at the failure of the public schools themselves. It is not possible to spend any prolonged period visiting public school classrooms without being appalled by the mutilation visible everywhere—mutilation of spontaneity, of the joy of learning, of pleasure in creating, of sense of self. The public schools, those "killers of the dream," to appropriate a phrase of Lillian Smith's—are the kind of institution one cannot really dislike until one gets to know them. (Silberman, 1970, p. 10)

Unlike the decade to follow [the 1980s], the crisis was not one of falling test scores. In the early 1970s the crisis was one of meaning. Education was in need of a "remaking," and Silberman viewed the curriculum as one area in need of dramatic change. [Ironically, the Carnegie Foundation, which supported Silberman's proposals, had, in the preceding decade, supported James B. Conant's reform of the American high school, which led to many of the same problems Silberman discovered in his study [see Conant, chapter 3]. The Tyler Rationale, in which curriculum became a means to achieve ends or objectives, had become self-evident to practicing educators. Silberman termed the result a confusion of means and ends, illustrated pointedly in the "tyranny of the lesson plan." He charged: "[The lesson plan] encourages an obsession with routine for the sake of routine. School is filled with countless examples of teachers and administrators confusing means with ends, thereby making it impossible to reach the end for which the means were devised" (Silberman, 1970, p. 125).

In a three-chapter section of *Crisis in the Classroom*, Silberman outlined the nature of the remaking that public education required. In the case of the elementary school, the "open classroom" was recommended. Silberman recalled English primary schools and in particular the Plowden Report (1963) on the state of primary schools in England. This report, named after the committee chair, endorsed "informal education" or "open education" (Barth, 1972; Featherstone, 1968). Widely read in the United States (Tanner &

Tanner, 1980), the Plowden Report advocated the "open classroom" concept. Silberman joined this movement, claiming that "informal education can work as well in the United States as it does in England" (Silberman, 1970, p. 266). Reminiscent of the views of the child-centered Progressives, informal education advocates challenged the dominant structure-of-the-disciplines approach, which, by the late 1960s, conceived of instruction in behavioristic terms.

Reminiscent of Dewey, Silberman insisted that childhood should be treasured for its own sake, and not only as a time of preparation for later life (Silberman, 1970). This view is expressed in his more general recommendation for secondary schools:

> Somewhat bolder attempts were made to humanize the schools as a whole—for example, by cutting the number of required classes, leaving students with a third more of their time unscheduled to be used for independent study, for taking more elective courses, for fulfilling some course requirements outside the classroom, or for relaxation and leisure. (Silberman, 1970, p. 337)

While his ideas have been characterized as "sketchy and impressionistic" by Laurel and Daniel Tanner (1980, p. 504), Silberman's book both alerted the American public to deepening problems in American education and to the possibility of humanistic—rather than technical—reform.

Recall that Huebner, Macdonald, Eisner, Klohr, and others in the 1960s questioned the taken-for-granted emphasis upon the structure-of-the-disciplines approach. Their work anticipated Silberman's charges in the 1970s. Their courage and questioning were part of a wider cultural and academic reassessment of mainstream approaches. Erich Fromm situates this interest historically:

> There is the threat of mankind's [sic] physical existence by nuclear war, and the threat to his spiritual existence by increasing automatization, bureaucratization and alienation of man. Against this threat to man a new wave of humanist thought and feeling is moving. The representatives of the new humanism are still in the minority in their respective camps. Yet their voice is heard with ever-increasing clarity. (Fromm, quoted in Huber, 1981, p. 59)

Many of the issues humanists such as Fromm raised would be extended by those curriculum specialists working to rethink their own field. External to the Reconceptualization proper, however, humanism surfaced in several curriculum writings. One should not confuse this humanism with the classical humanist approach discussed in chapter 2 which emphasized recitation and memorization for the development of mental discipline. The humanism which surfaced in the 1970s was quite different, as suggested by its primary descriptors: "humanistic education, affective education, personalized education, values clarification, etc." (Schubert, 1980a, p. 243; for instance, see Glasser, 1969; for a review see Simpson, 1986). Values clarification in particular appealed to many classroom teachers, and several elaborations of the process were published [see, for instance, Casteel & Stahl, 1975; Hall, 1973]. The various humanistic approaches to the classroom have also been criticized from a variety of perspectives, but perhaps most memorably by Robin Barrow (1984b).

III
Humanism in the 1970s

> The pervasive emphasis on cognition and its separation from affect poses a threat to our society in that our educational institutions may produce cold, detached individuals, uncommitted to humanitarian goals.
>
> (Gerald Weinstein & Mario Fantini, 1970, p. 27)

The Association for Supervision and Curriculum Development (ASCD) entitled its 1970 Yearbook *To Nurture Humanness*. In this volume the editors (M. M. Scobey and G. Graham) called for education for tranquility and self-actualization, the latter of which was made famous by humanistic psychologist Abraham Maslow (1968). Self-actualization represented one form of humanistic development, a concept which received varied treatment in the volume. One essay was written by Arthur Foshay of Teachers College, Columbia University, who explored making curriculum development more humane in his "Curriculum Development and Humane Qualities." To achieve more humaneness would require individualization of instruction both in the students' pace and style of learning. Curriculum development must proceed by perceiving that human beings "act as wholes in an endlessly complex fashion" (p.150). Foshay insisted that humane curriculum development must be "tentative, interactive, take into account individual strengths, be cooperative and at the same time rigorous" (Foshay, 1970, p.151). In this essay are several elements of the humanistic position: persons as holistic and in a state of becoming or growing, the necessity of interaction with the environment for learning and knowledge creation, the importance of dialogue for both the exchange and growth of knowledge, and the centrality of acknowledging and fostering individuality (Schubert, 1980a).

Another illustrative title in this genre was *Toward a Humanistic Education: A Curriculum of Affect* (1970) by Gerald Weinstein and Mario Fantini. Funded by the Ford Foundation, this study decried the overemphasis upon exclusively cognitive elements in the traditional school. In this vein, Weinstein and Fantini (1970) charged that: "The pervasive emphasis on cognition and its separation from affect poses a threat to our society in that our educational institutions may produce cold, detached individuals, uncommitted to humanitarian goals" (p. 27). To meet this threat Weinstein and Fantini proposed a "three-tier" curriculum, an idea borrowed from Bruce R. Joyce (1966). The first tier would be comprised of the basic "building blocks" for the intellectual development of the child (i.e., reading, writing, and computation). The second tier would be developed from the latent talents and abilities of the individual student. Weinstein and Fantini characterized this tier or mode as the personal discovery tier. The third tier would consist of "group inquiry curriculum," dealing with societal problems and issues that "were related to the self and exploration of self and others—not in the sense of individual problems but in terms of the thread of commonality that runs through these personal issues" (Weinstein & Fantini, 1970, p. 30). These three tiers would, presumably, correct the imbalance in the curriculum toward the cognitive.

One of the most serious and important collections of curriculum scholarship was published by *Teachers College Record* in 1971, edited by Frank Jennings. Each of the major essays was written by faculty of Teachers College, Columbia University; several pieces remain examples of exemplary theory and scholarship today. Robert McClintock (1971) convincingly questioned the primacy of instruction in educational models and pointed to the significance of study. Lawrence Cremin's (1971) "Curriculum-Making in the United States" focused on William Torey Harris but travels a one-hundred year time span in noting that twentieth-century curriculum-making, in failing to study its own history, tended to repeat itself. Douglas Sloan (1971) clarified college curriculum debates, focusing on the 1828 *Yale Report*. Maxine Greene's (1971, 1975b) "Curriculum and Consciousness" is a virtuoso performance of possibly the most important philosopher of education of her generation. Philip H. Phenix's (1971) "Transcendence and the Curriculum" is a seminal statement of the effort to understand curriculum as theological text. Essays by Ralph F. Goldman, William H. Weber, and Harold J. Noah on "Some Economic Models of Curriculum Structure" and by George La Noue on "The Politics of Education," in which he discusses, among other issues, the notion of vouchers, concluded this lasting contribution to curriculum theory by members of the Teachers College faculty.

The future. The interest in humanism was broad, ranging from studies of possible futures to organizational change. Futurism or future studies occupied several scholars in curriculum during the 1970s. Illustrative of this interest in American curriculum studies was Harold G. Shane's (1977) *Curriculum Change: Toward the 21st Century*, in which he called for a "human needs" curriculum to serve persons of all ages (p. 11). Another expression of the interest in the future was Jack R. Frymier's (1973) edited collection entitled *A School for Tomorrow*, in which he compared the school to an Army tank: "The public school is something like an Army tank: it possesses fantastic power and has extremely thick walls, but it is very vulnerable in spots, is extremely slow moving, and requires tremendous amounts of support and fuel" (pp. 6-7). Included in the collection is his (1973) "A School for Tomorrow," and the continuation of his 1967 work with James Duncan [see Frymier, Wilhour, & Rasp (1973)]. Sometimes speculation regarding the future seems bittersweet in retrospect: "Carefully designed experimentation and curriculum studies will increase, with teachers enjoying released time, a lessened work load, or paid summer employment in setting up studies and evaluating outcomes" (Cook, R. & Doll, R., 1973, p. 469).

Willis Harmon (1972) also sketched broad trends in society, politics, and knowledge in an essay which organized David Purpel and Maurice Belanger's 1972 collection of essays entitled *Curriculum and Cultural Revolution* (Purpel

& Belanger, 1972a). Following the Harmon essay, Purpel and Belanger (1972b) sketched implications for curriculum in their "Toward Humanistic Curriculum Theory." This volume reprinted several influential essays including Joseph Schwab's (1970, 1972) "The Practical: A Language for Curriculum," Fred Newmann and Donald Oliver's (1967, 1972) "Education and Community," and Lawrence Kohlberg's (1966, 1972) "Moral Education in the Schools: A Developmental View." Purpel and Belanger included "state-of-the-art" essays by Michael Scriven (1972), Jane Roland Martin (1972), Joseph C. Grannis (1972), Zvi Lamm (1972), and Carl Rogers (1972). The division of essays into sections entitled "school and society" and "the development of self-awareness and personal growth" would constitute the two basic thematic movements in the Reconceptualization, which would begin in May, 1973 at the University of Rochester conference. The proceedings of this conference would also feature the notion of "cultural revolution" in its title (Pinar, 1974c).

Also reflecting the decade's interest in change, John I. Goodlad (1975) published *The Dynamics of Educational Change: Toward Responsive Schools*. In his introduction, Samuel G. Sava claimed that "this study goes beyond the passive, hands-off investigation of a natural system at work in the formulation of an active, interventionist strategy for producing change" (p. xv). Goodlad underlined this point early on, writing that he is most "concerned with dynamics of educational change and improvement—not with description of what reconstructed schools should look like" (p. 2). In Goodlad's view, for change to occur, an "ecological model of education is needed. . . . The entire ecosystem is now polluted by overlap, duplication, jangled communication lines, and the general dysfunctionality of institutional overload" (p. 203). He asserted that "ecological thinking embraces the whole: the impact of pupils on teachers as well as the reverse; the impact of teachers on teachers, the use of resources, the relationship among all these" (p. 206). Rejecting the input-output model associated with behaviorist psychology, he offered what he characterized as a "responsive model." Rejecting also the tradition of social efficiency, Goodlad asserted: "Schools are not factories. Their worth is found in the quality of life sustained there" (p. 216).

Other titles published during the decade illustrate the character of this humanistic emphasis. In his edited *Curriculum Handbook: The Disciplines, Current Movements, and Instructional Methodology*, Louis Rubin (1977) restated the traditional curriculum question "what knowledge is of most worth" in generational terms: "What shall we tell the children?" (p. 1), the communicative aspect of which was developed by Margaret Ammons (1969, 1973). In his *Adventuring, Mastering, Associating*, Alexander Frazier (1976) foreshadowed what would become an intense interest in the late 1980s in "collaborative learning" (p. 131). Jack Frymier's (1977) elaborate *Annehurst Curriculum Classification System* was an effort to individualize the curriculum by creating curriculum units or modules accessible to each teacher. Eva Baker and W. James Popham (1973) were interested in *Expanding Dimensions of Instructional Objectives* to "humanize" educational objectives (in part by identifying so-called affective objectives), attempting to demonstrate that instructional technology can have a positive impact on classrooms. Aimed at the schools, these humanistic proposals extended the curriculum development paradigm into the 1970s, until the influential essays of Joseph J. Schwab signalled the end of an era.

IV
Joseph J. Schwab

> It was this practical trait of Schwab's personality, one that led him always to commit himself to action, that was the primary motivation of all that he was to attempt.
>
> (Ian Westbury & Neil J. Wilkof, 1978, p. 18)

As we saw in the last chapter, Schwab's characterization of the curriculum field as moribund sent shock waves through the field. He had written: "The field is moribund. It is unable, by its present methods and principles, to continue and contribute significantly to the advancement of education" (Schwab, 1970, p. 1). His indictment and his recommendations regarding how the field should proceed would, as we saw in chapter one, have enormous influence. Schwab had declared:

> There will be a renascence of the field of curriculum, a renewed capacity to contribute to the quality of American education, only if curriculum energies are diverted from theoretic pursuits . . . to three other modes of operation. These other modes, which differ radically from the theoretic, I shall call, following tradition, the *practical*, the *quasi-practical*, and the *eclectic*. (Schwab, 1970, p. 2)

We summarized Schwab's argument in chapters 1 and 3. Suffice to say here that his 1969 declaration (published again in 1970) that the field was moribund signalled the decade of Reconceptualization. His work will continue to be discussed in the literature for years to come [see, for instance, Eisner, 1984; Shulman, 1984; Pereira, 1984; Jackson, 1992a). Who was this man whose single essay set in motion the collapse of the traditional paradigm and helped establish the contours of the new one?

In their introduction to Schwab's collected essays, Ian Westbury and Neil J. Wilkof (1978) summarize Schwab's career. Joseph J. Schwab was born on February 2, 1909; he died on April 13, 1988. For nearly fifty years, Schwab worked at the University of Chicago and lived in Hyde Park. Originally from Columbus, Mississippi, Schwab entered the university at only 15 years of age, graduating in 1930 with a baccalaureate in English literature and physics. In the fall of 1931 he began graduate work in biology, receiving his doctorate in genetics eight years later. He left Hyde Park for a year in 1937 to accept a fellowship in science education at Teachers College, Columbia University, where he explored the emerging field of psychometrics and assisted in curriculum development while completing a doctorate in education. In 1938 he returned to the University of Chicago as an instructor and examiner in biology in the undergraduate college of the university. In 1974 he retired from the university as professor of education and the William Rainey Harper Professor of Natural Sciences. Subsequently he became a fellow at the Center for the Study of Democratic Institutions in Santa Barbara, California, an independent institute founded by Robert Maynard Hutchins [see chapter 3], the president of the University of Chicago from 1929 to 1951 (Westbury & Wilkof, 1978).

Schwab was influenced by a number of significant figures. First, he was influenced by Hutchins, Adler, and others at the University of Chicago who were interested in "Great Books," a version of nineteenth-century classical curriculum theory. Schwab was influenced also by Sewall Wright, a pre-eminent biostatistician in his day, and by Irving Lorge at Columbia, a major figure in the new field of educational measurement. With this background, Schwab was able to follow in the work being done by Louis L. Thurstone, the first university examiner. As an examiner in biology he worked in the late thirties with Thurstone's successor, Ralph W. Tyler. He acquired Tyler's concern for the articulation of courses and curriculum with testing procedures, with its implied concern for curriculum development. During this same period, Schwab made his mark as a teacher in the undergraduate college by introducing discussion methods into the undergraduate program, an innovation when introduced to the classical curriculum of the University of Chicago. By 1940 Schwab believed in discussion teaching, in the potential importance of the Great Books, and in the significance of science for general education; indeed, he was passionately concerned with the relationships among science, values, and education—the subject of his first published paper on education (Schwab, 1941/1978). At this early stage he lacked a coherent framework within which to place his ideas and concerns. Richard McKeon, a professor of philosophy who had been Dewey's student and colleague at Columbia and who was interested in hermeneutics, persuaded Schwab that reading a text requires concern for both the text itself and for the interpretive strategies which the interpreter brings to the text. Schwab would come to believe that a curriculum which uses interpretation as its core method entails a focus on *both* the semantic problems inherent in the work being read *and* on the consciousness of students as readers (Westbury & Wilkof, 1978).

Schwab's contact with McKeon enabled him to articulate his concerns as a teacher of biology and his interest in the potential of the "Great Books" as resources for liberal education. In Schwab's (1978) "The Nature of Scientific Knowledge as Related to Liberal Education," he developed a preliminary taxonomy of the varieties of scientific enquiry which he offered as a "prefatory guide to the curriculum-planner in his choice of materials and subject matters and as an aid in the analyses of scientific research which he and his students do" (p. 81). This paper complemented his (1978) "What Do Scientists Do?" By the late 1940s Schwab was studying Dewey. In 1948 he read the biological works of Aristotle to prepare the index of these works for the "Syntopicon" of the *Great Books of the Western World,* the last of Hutchins' and Adler's projects associated with the Great Books. In addition, he was beginning to investigate psychology and psychiatry. In 1949 Schwab was appointed to the university's Department of Education where Ralph Tyler, the chairman of the department and Schwab's long-time colleague from the university examiner's office, encouraged him to turn his attention to the formal study of the rationale for liberal education.

In Schwab's "Criteria for the Evaluation of Achievement Tests: From the Point of View of the Subject-Matter Specialist" (1978), with its emphasis on process, communication, and the need to define problems through a search for ways of articulating and expressing experience, we see the influence of Dewey:

> a more valuable kind of test would be one whose items would serve to suggest to the teaching staff alternatives or additional aims of education which deserve consideration. And still more valuable would be a test which would disclose the unknown and unanticipated consequences (in addition to those intended) which any effective curriculum inevitably must produce upon its students. (1978, p. 277)

Over and over Schwab stressed the indeterminacy of what we think we know and the necessity of searching for ways of giving form to the "shadowy and incomplete condition" (p. 278) which is the human world. Also in this paper Schwab explored how a text can be used in a concrete situation. Westbury and Wilkof note: "It was this practical trait of Schwab's personality, one that led him always to commit himself to action, that was the primary motivation of all that he was to attempt" (p. 18).

In an essay he wrote in 1951, "Dialectical Means vs. Dogmatic Extremes in Relation to Liberal Education," Schwab (1978) employed the forms of analysis and argument that McKeon (and, from a different tradition, Dewey) had taught him. Schwab's method consisted of a comprehensive mapping of a territory of a given subject matter by means of a set of *topics* or *commonplaces* which ordered the elements that a teacher might need to consider as one sought to plan one's curriculum. In "Eros and Education" (1978), we see Dewey's emphasis on the roles of continuity and growth in experience, although Schwab's views on this topic are filtered through both the psychoanalysis that Schwab was undergoing in these years and his reading of Aristotle's biology. The aim of a liberal education is not to "destroy the mammal within us." Rather, the aim, Schwab tells us, is to harness Eros through reasonableness so to employ its energy for intellectual purposes and, conversely, enjoy to the fullest the capacities for feeling and action Eros makes possible (Westbury & Wilkof, 1978).

Schwab (1964a, 1964b, 1964c) was widely regarded as a spokesman for the discipline-based teaching of science in the schools. His essay "The Concept of the Structure of a Discipline" and his contributions to two widely read symposia on the subjects of the structures of disciplines became basic texts for the structuralists in schools and colleges of education (Cherryholmes,

1988b). Westbury and Wilkof (1978) tell us, however, that Schwab did not identity himself with the structure-of-the-disciplines movement, despite his writings on the subject. They point to the opening paragraphs of "Education and the Structure of the Disciplines" (1978), wherein Schwab stipulates: "before, indeed, we ask what "structure' is—there is a prior question: What relevance may the structure of disciplines have for the purposes of education? Why should the curriculum maker or the teacher be concerned with the structure of the discipline with which he or she works?"

Westbury and Wilkof (1978) believe these questions indicate that Schwab's primary commitment was to science seen as a distinctive model of inquiry. Schwab's other major essay from this period, "What Do Scientists Do?" (1978) described those semantic clusters associated with the process of scientific inquiry. Like his other projects, this one had to do with the need to order the boundaries of the interpretative task. The underlying model of knowledge reflected in "What Do Scientists Do?" resembled in spirit the hermeneutical sociologies of such scholars as Mannheim, Dilthey, and Habermas (Westbury & Wilkof, 1978). [See chapters 8 and 12 for further discussion of hermeneutics.]

As Schwab achieved visibility during the 1960s as a theorist of the structures-of-the-disciplines movement, he was working at the Jewish Theological Seminary's Melton Research Center where he was seeking to understand not only psychological theories of growth and development but also the place of tradition and community in the formation of character, subjects seemingly far apart from his research on the structures of the disciplines. His *College Curriculum and Student Protest* (1969) is an impassioned book that takes as its pretext the student protest movement but has as its most basic aim a restatement of Schwab's views regarding the nature of liberal education. His primary focus here was a description of the relationships between the curriculum in its institutional aspects and the characterological development of the person.

As we have seen in "The Practical: A Language for Curriculum" and "The Practical: Translation into Curriculum," Schwab sought to formulate the nature of appropriate deliberation about curriculum problems, the contribution to the field for which he is perhaps most remembered today. He also wrote during this period about what he saw as the corruption of the field of education by psychology, a subject other curriculum theorists would pursue [see Huebner, 1966b, 1967, 1968; Barrow, 1984b]. Schwab accused educators and curriculum scholars of "doctrinaire adhesion" to educational psychology, which resulted in single-minded and simplistic views of what the subject matter of education might be. In *College Curriculum and Student Protest* he attacked political science for its attempts to reduce the complexities of political life to regression equations. In the famous "practical" essays he emphasized the concreteness of curriculum deliberation:

> The curriculum constructed of these particulars will be brought to bear, not in some archetypical classroom, but in a particular locus in time and space with

smells, shadows, seats, and conditions outside its walls which may have much to do with what is achieved inside. Above all, the supposed beneficiary is not the generic child, not even a class or kind of child out of the psychological or socio-logical literature pertaining to the child. The beneficiary will consist of very local kinds of children and, within the local kinds, individual children. (Schwab, 1978, pp. 309-310)

Throughout his career as a teacher and a scholar, Schwab's attention was captured, not by a classroom in the abstract, but to *this* particular classroom, a careful examination of the characteristics of the students he taught *this* semester, and always a concern for the here-and-now of the next class, in *this* course, in *this* program. Westbury and Wilkof (1978) conclude: "He was from the beginning of his career his own man, argumentative, critical, dominat-ing" (p. 36). As Jackson's (1992a) analysis suggests, Joseph J. Schwab is one of the most brilliant and influential minds the curriculum field has known.

V
Synoptic Textbooks and Other Developments

Curriculum is not a process. . . . [It] represents a set of *intentions*, a set of intended learning outcomes.
(George J. Posner & Alan N. Rudnitsky, 1986, p. 14)

It should be evident that [Kieran] Egan (1982) was entirely correct when he pointed out that [Decker] Walker (1976) was simply mistaken to say that "curriculum problems are practical not theoretical ones." Such a remark takes us back to a simple-minded and false dichotomy between theory and practice.
(Robin Barrow, 1984b, p. 260)

[The 1970s are a] decade of curriculum crisis.
(William A. Reid, 1978, p. 1)

Textbooks written during the 1970s differed somewhat from those of the two decades preceding (Schubert, 1980a). The texts of the 1970s (cf., Bell, 1971; Firth & Kimpston, 1973; Saylor & Alexander, 1974; Tanner & Tanner, 1975; Unruh, 1975; Zais, 1976; Hass, 1977; McNeil, 1977; Gress & Purpel, 1978; Taylor & Richards, 1979) did not contain "massive lists of principles or guide-lines that served as prescriptions for practice" (Schubert, 1980, p. 249). Instead, these textbooks contained more analysis of curriculum concepts; several included extensive sections on curriculum history (Tanner & Tanner, 1975; Zais, 1976; Davis, 1976, 1986). Books emphasizing the traditional focus on curriculum development were published, of course; for example, Jon Schaffarzik and David H. Hampson (1975) edited a collection examining *Strategies for Curriculum Development*, a book for beginning students focused, as the title suggests, on curriculum development and design. In Great Britain, Philip Taylor, founding editor of the *Journal of Curriculum Studies*, and Colin M. Richards edited *An Introduction to Curriculum Studies* (1979) which emphasized the same categories: development, design, and evaluation.

Notably, many textbooks and essays emphasized notions of change, innovation, and improvement in institutional practice (Schubert, 1980a). They seemed to communicate a sense of the future that was uncertain and rapidly changing (cf., Saylor & Alexander, 1974; Beck, Cook & Kearney, 1973; Billett, 1970; Burns & Brooks, 1970; Egan, 1978; Feyereisen, Fiorino, & Nowak, 1970; Foshay, 1970; Frymier & Hawn, 1970; Frymier, 1977; Goodlad & Klein, 1974; Goodlad, 1975; Hass, Bondi, & Wiles, 1974; Hicks, Houston, Cheney, & Marquard, 1970; Holt, 1978; Inlow, 1973; Lee & Lee, 1972; Morley, 1973; Oliver,1977; Talmage, 1975; Trump & Miller, 1972; Turner, 1971). We turn now to a brief review of several of the more important publications of the decade.

In his *Secondary Curriculum: Theory and Development*, Daniel Tanner (1971b) insisted on the need for developing a balanced and coherent curriculum: "The curriculum is more than the sum total of the separate disciplines that comprise the course of study" (p. xi). Part one of this textbook depicts the history of educators' efforts to reconceive the teaching-learning process so that the traditional emphasis on memorization and recitation of information is replaced in favor of understanding (i.e. the theoretical movement in the field from classical curriculum theory to progressivism). Part two investigates curriculum reform in the various disciplines and subject fields. As well, Tanner studied the theoretical foundations of curriculum construction as they have been influenced by sociopolitical forces. In part three Tanner anticipated many concerns that curricularists would have twenty years later regarding the increasing use of technology in the classroom:

> It is ironic that the devices and systems of technology, which give promise to freeing man [sic] to become more human, also portend a danger of diminishing our humanity. In education, we have made the error of seeking to use the devices and systems of technology to restrict our notions of human behavior. We become less tolerant of ambiguity, digression, divergence, and expressions of feeling—all characteristically human qualities. (p. 403)

[See chapter 13 for a discussion of technology in the curriculum.]

Also early in the decade a collection of essays appeared that spanned the temporal and thematic range of the field from 1920 to 1970, a kind of summary of the wisdom of the traditional field. Introducing his edited collection of *Approaches in Curriculum*, Ronald T. Hyman (1973) acknowledged that "the Tyler formulation has crystallized to become *the* rationale. . . . Recently there have appeared some published doubts" (pp. 7-8). Included were essays expressing the historical and thematic range of the traditional field by distinguished contributors to the field, many of whom the reader will recognize from earlier chapters: 1) The Subject Matter of Education (John Dewey), 2) The Essentials of the Activity Movement (William Heard Kilpatrick), 3) Developing a Curriculum for Modern Living (Florence Stratemeyer), 4) The Case for the Common Learnings Course (Harold C. Hand), 5) Encounter: A Theory of the Curriculum which Affirms the Centrality of the Communities of Discourse (Arthur R. King, Jr. and John A. Brownell), 6) What Knowledge is of Most Worth? (Arno A. Bellack), 7) Integrative Education for a Dis-inte-grated World (Gene Wise), 8) Relevance and the Curriculum (Lawrence E. Metcalf & Maurice P. Hunt), 9) High School Student Protest and the New Curriculum Worker (John S. Mann), 10) Communication: A Curriculum Focus (Margaret Ammons), and 11) New Curriculum Designs for Children (Louise M. Berman). Among these chapters we find John Steven Mann's—a Marxist scholar—article on student protest, certainly a "doubt" cast on the presumed political neutrality of the Tylerian Rationale. [Mann's career would be a relatively short one, but his scholarship was influential—and not only in the political sector; see his elaboration of curriculum criticism reprinted in 1975 in Pinar's edited collection of *Curriculum Theorizing*. His teaching would be influential also; two of his students at the Johns Hopkins University would become prominent scholars in the field: George Willis and William E. Doll, Jr.]

A concern for the social, characteristic of the scholarship of John Steven Mann and others involved in the Reconceptualization, was first expressed early in the decade as an acknowledgement of the American social crisis requiring an ameliorative response in the school curriculum. To put the mat-ter differently, rather than rethink the traditional paradigm and its claim to political neutrality, politics and the social were "added on" as another curric-ular problem to which the school must respond in the traditional way, i.e. via curriculum development. Illustrative of this discourse was a book written by B. O. Smith [of Smith-Stanley-Shores (1957) fame] and Donald E. Orlosky. Smith and Orlosky (1975) introduced their study by reflecting on the Ameri-can bicentennial:

> As the nation approaches its bicentennial celebration it faces a situation of increasing peril, a situation of which it is scarcely aware, and yet one that rivals in gravity of its ultimate consequences the discrimination against minorities and the hazards of environmental disruption. It is the breakdown of the processes of socialization resulting in an increasing dissipation of the produc-tive potential of youth and their moral fiber. . . . The discourse set forth in the following chapters faces this problem from the standpoint of both the adult world and the school. (p. iii)

Other examples of books published during the 1970s which focused on social change include C. A. Bowers, Ian Housego, and Doris Dyke's (1970) edited collection entitled *Education and Social Policy* and William van Til's (1971) edited collection entitled *Curriculum: Quest for Relevance*, the contents of which also reflect a concern for the turmoil of the period.

The influence of behaviorism. The behavioristic orientation continued to influence curriculum textbooks and curriculum practice. Perhaps the best-known example, as we noted in the previous chapter, was R. F. Mager's *Preparing Instructional Objectives*, reprinted in 1975. His emphasis upon the link between performance and objectives had much in common with "training programs in such areas as business, industry, and the military" (Schubert, 1980a, p. 255). Other examples of this continuing influence of behaviorism were "competencies, computerization, systematic needs assessment, attempts to combine elements of the humanistic with the behavioristic, and much rhetoric from systems theory and management theory" (Schubert, 1980, p. 255). The influence of behaviorism was seen in several academic and professional journals in the field which "published material of that genre with considerable exclusiveness" (Schubert, 1980, p. 256). Robin Barrow (1984b) spoke for many curriculum scholars when he wrote: "The long-standing grip of behaviorism on psychological study, and indirectly on education, particularly in North America, is hard to understand. The obvious inadequacies of behaviorism have time and again been exposed, but still the grip strangles" (p. 135). Indeed.

One sophisticated example of an approach to curriculum design influenced by the work of Mauritz Johnson (1967) and by aspects of behaviorism was *Course Design: A Guide to Curriculum Development for Teachers* written by George Posner and Alan N. Rudnitsky (1978; 2nd edition,1982; 3rd edition, 1986), an extension of Posner's earlier work [see Posner & Strike (1976) "A Categorization Scheme for Principles of Sequencing Content"]. Posner and Rudnitsky (1986) prefaced their book by noting that it is "intended for secondary and postsecondary teachers and teachers in training, it presents the skills and concepts of curriculum development and applies them to actual course planning" (p. xiii). An extension of Mauritz Johnson's (1967) model, Posner and Rudnitzky's book guided the reader through the steps one might take in constructing a course design. Each chapter is divided into categories, and these categories are subdivided again, and sometimes once again. Each chapter begins with what the reader should know by that chapter's conclusion. For instance, the list from chapter 2 includes: 1) comprehend the meaning and significance of "intended learning outcome;" 2) generate one or more "central questions" for a course, teaching strategies, materials, activities, and other initial ideas; 3) develop a tentative course outline; 4) generate one or more "central questions" for a course; 5) distinguish intended learning outcomes (ILOs) from teaching strategies, materials, activities, and other initial ideas. . . . 11) use flowcharts and conceptual maps to identity ILOs for a course (p. 14). For Posner and Rudnitsky (1986),"curriculum is not a process . . . [it] represents a set of *intentions*, a set of intended learning outcomes" (p. 14).

Restating Tyler's four questions as "modules," John D. McNeil's (1976) *Designing Curriculum: Self-instructional Modules* represented a simpler instance of behaviorism in curriculum design: module 1) the design and selection of learning activities, module 2) deriving objectives, module 3) selecting among educational objectives: defensible choices, and module 4) evaluating the effectiveness of the curriculum.

Elliot W. Eisner. While behaviorism continued to surface in the curriculum literature of the 1970s, its influence slowly began to wane. For instance, Elliot Eisner's work, based on aesthetics, continued to grow in influence during the 1970s. In *Confronting Curriculum Reform*, Eisner (1971b) and contributors discussed the 1960s curriculum reform movement. In Eisner's (1971b) view, "students of curriculum have an unparalleled opportunity to study phenomena that are truly indigenous to the field of education" (p. 11). In 1974, with his student Elizabeth Vallance, Eisner identified five conflicting conceptions of curriculum in a collection of essays with the same title (Eisner & Vallance, 1974), a book we examined in chapter 1. The decade would end with the publication of Eisner's (1979) *The Educational Imagination,* the most complete and mature articulation of his position to that time. In that volume he developed his notions of educational criticism and connoisseurship, concepts which we will examine in chapters 11 and 13. While not affiliated with those working to reconceptualize the field, his continuing criticism of scientism in education, and his development of an aesthetic concept of teaching and curriculum evaluation functioned to help overturn the traditional field. While reconceiving the curriculum field's disciplinary foundations—from the sciences to the arts—Eisner has been unwavering in his focus on and interest in everyday curriculum issues associated with the school. In this sense, he has one foot planted in each paradigm, development and understanding.

A.E.R.A. During this period of upheaval in the field an influential "special interest group" (SIG) in the American Educational Research Association (AERA), named the "Creation and Utilization of Curriculum Knowledge" (Short, 1973), was formed. The initial group was comprised of forty-five curriculum researchers whose purpose was to "foster excellence in curriculum inquiry, generally" (Short, Willis, & Schubert, 1985, p. 2). Edmund Short organized the group, with Paul R. Klohr as co-chair, because he was concerned that curriculum theory dominated the A.E.R.A. division B (Curriculum and Objectives) conference program, and that this theory was only "indirectly related to the needs of the practitioner" (Short, Willis, & Schubert, 1985, p. 2). Short explained:

> A few signs of interest in redirecting some of the scholarly work in curriculum toward the needs of the practitioner were beginning to appear. . . . I thought this tendency needed encouragement, perhaps through an organizational effort within A.E.R.A. that might help legitimate this kind of work and might stimulate some new ideas on the subject. (Short, Willis, & Schubert, 1985, p. 3)

Short appears to have been correct, as membership in the SIG grew to 316 scholars by 1978. By the early 1990s this SIG's name had been changed to "critical issues in curriculum." The name of the curriculum division—Division B, Curriculum and Objectives—of the American Educational Research Association had been changed as well. Reflecting the Reconceptualization of curriculum was the disappearance of the Tylerian emphasis upon objectives in favor of a more paradigm-appropriate term Curriculum Studies.

Sponsored and prepared by the American Educational Research Association, a collection of essays examining traditional curriculum questions by many distinguished curriculum scholars appeared in 1977. Edited by Arno

Bellack and his former student [at Teachers College, Columbia University] Herbert M. Kliebard, the collection was entitled *Curriculum and Evaluation*. The first section contained essays on the question: How should curriculum problems be studied? It included contributions by Mauritz Johnson, Jr., George A. Beauchamp, Joseph J. Schwab, Ralph W. Tyler, Herbert Kliebard, Dwayne Huebner, and Kenneth Charlton. The second section focused on the question: What purposes should the curriculum serve? Answers were provided by Harry Broudy, Robert M. Gagné, Richard Peters, William K. Frankena, Paul Hirst, and Arthur G. Wirth. The third section asked: How should knowledge be selected and organized for the curriculum? Essays were written by John Dewey, Joseph J. Schwab, Florence Stratemeyer, Arno Bellack, Maxine Greene, Michael F. D. Young, and Neil Keddie. The fourth section, also modeled on the Tyler Rationale, asked: How should the curriculum be evaluated? Essays by Lee Cronbach, Michael Scriven, Robert E. Stake, Urban Dahllof, Decker Walker and Jon Schaffarzick, David Cohen, and Michael Apple provided responses. Reflecting the decade's interest in reform, the final section asked: How should the curriculum be changed? Israel Scheffler, John Goodlad and Maurice N. Richter, Jr., Eric Hoyle, Michael W. Kirst and Decker Walker, Seymour B. Sarason, Elizabeth Vallance, and Herbert Kliebard provided answers. A bibliographical essay by Linda McNeil, a graduate student at that time at the University of Wisconsin-Madison, concluded the collection. [For reports of McNeil's subsequent work, see chapters 5 and 13.]

Paul Hirst and R. S. Peters. In Great Britain, philosopher of education Paul H. Hirst (1974) published his *Knowledge and the Curriculum: A Collection of Philosophical Papers*. In contrast to curriculum studies in the United States, curriculum theory in the U.K. was linked more with philosophy and less with institutional practice. Indeed, the two spheres tended to operate rather independently. In the United Kingdom, then, the function of curriculum theory was the function of philosophy, and within philosophy the tradition known as linguistic or concept analysis (Lawton, et al., 1978). This British tradition in philosophy regarded philosophical problems as logical problems, to be solved through the clarification of concepts [see also Barrow, 1976a, 1982b]. Hirst (1974) wrote: "Philosophy, I shall take it, is above all concerned with clarification of the concepts and propositions through which our experience and activities are intelligible" (p. 1). "[Curriculum is] . . . a programme of activities designed so that pupil will attain by learning certain specifiable ends or objectives" (p. 2). For Hirst, "First there can be no curriculum without objectives" (p. 3). Hirst's work "is important because he quite rightly points to the need for a definition of liberal education consistent with current philosophical work and capable of enabling individuals to live rationally in contemporary society" (Schilling, 1986, p. 14). Another British philosopher of education, R. S. Peters (1975), was visible in British curriculum theory in the 1970s. The goal of curricular breadth, central to R. S. Peter's (1975) conception of education, figured prominently in British debates regarding the curriculum. Scholars such as J. P. White (1973) and Paul Hirst (1974) argued that a curriculum in the secondary school should reflect the broad range of humankind's aesthetic and intellectual achievements. Such a curricular emphasis can be criticized as restricting the opportunities for specialization. Because they focused on logical clarification of curriculum goals, British philosophers of curriculum have been criticized for failing to attend to issues concerning the experience of curriculum in the schools (Callan, 1982). That criticism would not be made of Lawrence Stenhouse, also working in Great Britain during the 1970s. Accomplished in what Schwab had termed the practical arts, Stenhouse (1971) was working on his famous Humanities Project, which influenced research in curriculum evaluation and in teacher development [see chapter 13]. Stenhouse's work (1975, 1980) was read widely in the United States, while the work of Hirst and Peters was not. [It was read seriously, however, by American philosophers of education.] Robin Barrow's work might be said to extend this tradition in the contemporary field. Finally, let us note that in the 1970s in Great Britain at the University of Birmingham was a scholar who would be among the first to extend Schwab's work, especially Schwab's emphasis upon deliberation. That scholar, who would become well-known in the United States, was William A. Reid.

Deliberation and change. In a collection of essays edited with the American curricularist Decker F. Walker, the title of which indicated the decade's preoccupation with change, Walker and William A. Reid (1975) presented *Case Studies in Curriculum Change: Great Britain and the United States*. The foreword to the collection was written by Joseph J. Schwab. The intellectual debt to Schwab is made clear from the outset. The editors wrote: "Especially we would like to record our indebtedness to the work of Schwab [which] has emphasized the importance of collecting data on the curriculum as it exists" (p. ix). Conceiving of curriculum as institutional text, "the studies offer descriptions of a variety of phases in planning and implementation" (p. x). In a historical study, Lynn W. McKinney and Ian Westbury (1975) wrote of "Stability and Change: The Public Schools of Gary, Indiana, 1940-1970" in which they found that maintenance and change were the two primary functions of the managerial structures which permeated the schools. [Recall that Gary, Indiana was the site of the famous progressive experiment: the Gary Plan. See chapter 3.] McKinney and Westbury came away with a deepened appreciation that understanding curriculum maintenance and change was essential to curriculum planning for innovation, a conclusion not dissimilar from the one reached by Larry Cuban (1979) in his study of curriculum change and stability. In a study of "Curriculum Development in an Art Project," Decker F. Walker (1975) concluded that curriculum developers should stop trying to replace the "natural" process of curriculum planning by artificial prescriptions. They should accept "deliberation" as one of the essential features of curriculum planning. Finally, resources of science and rationality ought to be organized by curricularists to improve the quality of deliberation and making it more effective.

In his study of "The Diffusion of Keynesian Macroeconomics through American High School Textbooks, 1936-70," Herbert W. Voege (1975) was interested in how knowledge is diffused from one institutional level to another. His study of Keynesian economics suggested that the time required for the entry of a leading idea into the high school curriculum may be as long as 25 years. In the concluding essay, "The Changing Curriculum: Theory and Practice," Reid (1975) suggested that the essays contribute "to the theory of curriculum design and diffusion" (p. 240). He advised: "The most urgent need is for curriculum theory that will help us to make good use of human resources" (p. 253). However, perhaps "negotiation should replace deliberation at times" (p. 255). Finally, pointing away from a bureaucratic perspective: "Indeed, planning itself should take the form of an educational experience" (p. 256). Here we have a mix of administrative and theoretical interests in curriculum.

In his *Thinking about the Curriculum: The Nature and Treatment of Curriculum Problems*, William A. Reid (1978) extended this theoretical perspective on curriculum development drawn from Schwab's work, emphasizing even more the centrality of deliberation to curriculum development. For Reid, central to the field is an appreciation that "curriculum tasks are practical tasks" (p. 14). However, thinking about curriculum as a practical field involved an apparent problem, in so far as "thinking is associated with theorizing, and theorizing, it is claimed, is inappropriate to practical tasks. . . . Theory might be useful in carrying out those curriculum tasks that can be thought of as 'proactive:' where we can take an initiative, relatively free from constraint" (p. 14). Further: "Curriculum problems are practical problems which are moral rather than technical in nature" (p. 29).

In Reid's view, the 1970s were a "decade of curriculum crisis" (p. 1) and deliberation was key to working through the crisis, i.e. solving curriculum problems and improved decision-making. Reid emphasized that curriculum problems are not exclusively "rationalistic" dilemmas, but are ones that require the full range of human capacities. In his final chapter entitled, "Rationalism or Humanism: The Future of Curriculum Studies," he appeared to endorse a position of humanism, linking it with the Reconceptualization in American curriculum studies: "In Pinar's terminology, the long dominance of the 'traditionalist' is coming to an end. . . . The future lies with the 'reconceptualists'. . . . The intention or the interpretation may be exaggerated, but new positions are being taken up, and the lines are being drawn very largely in terms of the great coalitions of rationalism on the one side and humanism on the other" (1978, p. 97).

Robin Barrow. Another important curriculum theorist has worked from the British tradition. British born, Robin Barrow teaches in Canada, as of this writing at Simon Fraser University in Vancouver, British Columbia, the same institution where the distinguished theorist Kieran Egan teaches [see chapter

13]. Barrow's scholarly production is prodigious (1975, 1976a, 1976b, 1978a, 1978b, 1980, 1981a, 1981b, 1982a, 982b, 1984a, 1984b, 1990). Because much of his scholarship falls outside the American mainstream, and the new American field has not proven interesting for him (1984b, p. 259), his contribution tends to be overlooked by Americans. This is unfortunate for several reasons. First, Barrow's scholarship is among the most literate and intelligent in the field. Second, he not only criticizes much of the traditional field—especially its reliance upon educational psychology, upon models and diagrams—he demolishes it. Unlike Reid, Barrow has not been influenced by Schwab, and his interest in practice (and deliberation more specifically) seems rather slight. To put the matter another way, Barrow appears to have sufficient respect for practitioners that he has no interest in usurping the discretionary judgement practitioners must exercise. Third, from an American point of view, Barrow's scholarship reveals the limitations of the British overreliance upon philosophy and especially upon ordinary language analysis which has so influenced Anglo-American philosophy.

As we noted, Barrow works from the British view that the curriculum theory is a subset of philosophy of education:

> The message then and the message now is simple: until philosophy becomes an integral and directing force in our educational thinking, until we become motivated more by a genuine desire for understanding and wisdom than by a desire for accolades and for practical success, we shall continue to make the sorts of errors referred to above, and we shall continue to fail generations of individuals in respect of education, with dire consequences for the state as a whole. (Barrow, 1990, pp. 178-179)

Here Barrow is dismissing traditional curriculum theory in the United States, with its emphasis upon curriculum development, and its corresponding fondness for models, diagrams, and procedure. Barrow may be at his best when he makes fun of this tradition:

> When a diagram is appropriate for the wiring circuit of a hi-fi perhaps, for depicting human veins, or for an automobile engine, it offers a very accurate pictorial representation. To use a diagram to summarise one's interpretation of T. S. Eliot's *The Waste Land*, besides being almost certainly inadequate, is to suggest that a poem can profitably be treated like the cross-section of a motorbike engine. (1984b, pp. 59-60)

Barrow dismisses the Tylerian emphasis upon objectives, design, implementation and evaluation. Instead of responding to Tyler directly, Barrow concentrates on Pratt's (1980) adaptation of Tyler's rationale [see Barrow, 1984b, p.41 ff.]. He is especially critical of the scientific pretensions of the traditional field: "Perhaps it is not in itself a crime of major significance to talk of 'models,' but it is misleading in that it implies clear distinctions . . . where they do not exist. . . . The too easy use of diagrams serves likewise to reinforce the idea that we are dealing with a relatively precise domain comparable to that of the natural sciences" (1984b, p. 56). The reliance upon educational psychology and upon Piaget and Kohlberg (Barrow, 1984b, pp.

113-114) is also dismissed: "there is very little of importance for educators that can be gained from the study of such things as learning theory, child development and personality" (1984b, p. 97). The very institutional characterization of curriculum is eliminated: "It should be evident that [Kieran] Egan (1982) was entirely correct when he pointed out that [Decker] Walker (1976) was simply mistaken to say that 'curriculum problems are practical not theoretical ones.' Such a remark takes us back to a simple-minded and false dichotomy between theory and practice" (1984b, p. 260).

Here we see a reconceptualization underway but on quite a separate track, as it were, not widely read by the Americans, and made from very different disciplinary foundations. After doing away with the traditional field, where does Barrow return? He returns to Britain: "What is crucially missing from all curriculum designs is a recognition that the whole operation can only make sense, let alone be successfully carried out, in the light of a clear articulation of the central educational concepts" (1984b, pp. 63-64). He quotes Hirst (1980) that curriculum theory is the formulation of general principles for practice, that is, rational and defensible statements of what we ought to do and what we do (1984b, p. 261). We can almost hear Barrow recasting Henry Higgins' infamous question "why can't a woman be more like a man?" into "why can't a North American be more like an Englishman?" An Oxford-educated [Barrow read classics there] Englishman, to be sure. In fairness to Barrow, it becomes clear his purpose is broadly educational, not narrowly philosophical: "the point of this exercise is not to study philosophy of education, but to ensure that the students really do articulate full and coherent conceptions of their own" (1984b, p. 266). Reservations regarding Barrow's fidelity to philosophy aside, we cannot argue with the view that: "Surely the essence of the educated mind is a breadth of understanding" (1984b, p. 35). And for Barrow understanding incorporates mind and heart. As he tells us: "I write from passion. Passion for reason" (1990, p. 2).

Mastery learning continues. Back in the United States, "scientific" efforts continued, unmindful of Barrow's insight. Perhaps most notable was Benjamin Bloom (1976), who theorized that learning time and quality of instruction are "alterable conditions" (Tanner & Tanner, 1990, p. 295). Bloom stated that "most students can attain a high level of learning capacity if instruction is approached sensitively and systematically, and if students are helped when and where they have learning difficulty, if they are given time to achieve mastery, and if there is some clear criterion of what constitutes mastery" (quoted in Tanner & Tanner, 1990, p. 295). Bloom's theory that much student failure can be corrected by adjusting the conditions of teaching and learning in school is generally congruent with progressivist theory. His mastery plan was, however, primarily appropriate for hierarchical or sequential subject matter, and not as useful for, say, poetry and creative writing. Mastery of one unit was the basis for later ones. Mastery learning has been linked with behavioristic psychology and the accountability movement. Daniel and Laurel Tanner (1990) comment:

This [linking] is indeed regrettable. . . . Developmental psychology provides the basis for Bloom's theory, but mastery learning becomes behavioristic in application. Bloom leaves the question of what should be taught open, as well he should; his is a theory of learning, not of curriculum. (pp. 295-296)

The Tanners are correct.

National Institute of Education: The Curriculum Development Task Force
Established in 1972, the National Institute of Education convened a Curriculum Development Task Force in 1975. Jon Schaffarzick and Gary Sykes' (1979) *Values Conflicts and Curriculum Issues: Lessons from Research and Experience* contains several products of that task force. The titles of the collected essays reflect the range of the Task Force's interests. Schaffarzick (1979) wrote "Federal Curriculum Reform: A Crucible for Value Conflict," a history of federal curriculum reform in the 1960s, including attention to the MACOS project [see chapter 3], and to the question of what role NIE should play in curriculum development efforts. For Schaffarzik the central curriculum value conflict involved what to include in the school program. The task force commissioned two historical studies: Larry Cuban's (1979) "Determinants of Curriculum Change and Stability, 1870-1970" and Herbert M. Kliebard's (1979) "Systematic Curriculum Development, 1890-1959." Ralph W. Tyler (1979) identified those "Educational Improvements Best Served by Curriculum Development," Decker F. Walker (1979) summarized "Approaches to Curriculum Development," Nel Noddings (1979) described "NIE's National Curriculum Development Conference," and Gary Sykes (1979) reflected on "Government Intervention in the School Curriculum: Floating like a Bee, Stinging like Butterfly."

Tyll van Geel (1979) reviewed "The New Law of the Curriculum," in which he concluded:

> One of the most striking features of the new curriculum law is the degree to which it reveals the increased centralization in the control of the program of the public schools. With the entrance of such new participants in the curricular decision-making system as the federal courts and Congress, and with increased activity on the part of state legislatures and state courts, control of the curriculum is no longer so purely a local affair as it once was. (p. 62)

William Lowe Boyd (1979) analyzed "The Changing Politics of Curriculum Policy Making for American Schools," noting that: "Currently, the accelerated pace of social change has exacerbated the tension between old and new ideas, between accepted and minority cultural values, and has dramatically politicized curriculum policy making" (pp. 75-76). Further: "Indeed, to date the controversy over MACOS presents perhaps the most dramatic instance of public reaction against the efforts of the professional reformers" (p. 91). He concluded: "If there is one proposition about curriculum politics that is clear, it is that the school curriculum becomes an issue in communities and societies that are undergoing significant social change. . . . Curriculum policy making ... generally is characterized by the ... mundane strategy of disjointed incrementalism" (p. 80). Boyd believed that increasing politicization of education meant that "contemporary reforms will make future reform still more difficult to obtain" (p. 1). This collection remains important today, documenting further the shrinking space for traditional curriculum development.

VI

Tension in ASCD

An unconnected discipline may not be worth doing.
(Landon E. Beyer, 1983, p. 88)

To understand more fully the conditions present at the beginning of the Reconceptualization, let us examine the tension, indeed, the critical upheaval that erupted in the major professional association to which most curricularists belonged in 1969. The Association for Supervision and Curriculum Development (ASCD) had been viewed, since its founding in 1946 [see chapter 3], as the professional "home" for most individuals concerned with the curriculum field. Its strength rested on its efforts to bring together professors of curriculum, school district curriculum supervisors, school administrators, and teachers. ASCD's journals and yearbooks, as well as its annual conventions and state affiliates, sought to find a common ground among all professionals concerned with curriculum.

To be sure, there had always been a certain, if often unspoken, tension among members of the Association. Were the college and university scholars too theoretical, too influential? Were the "real needs" of supervisors and school people being met? (Firth, 1986). Tension notwithstanding, year after year publications reporting a wide range of curriculum issues were published and widely distributed. Many of these publications aimed to break "new ground." Yearly conferences were held in major American cities, and state affiliates sponsored local workshops and other training activities designed to translate "theory into practice." Approximately one hundred "invited" professors of curriculum had met since 1959 prior to ASCD national conferences to discuss significant problems and issues. Considered as an informal honorary society, the "professors of curriculum" regarded ASCD as its constituency. In general, then, ASCD functioned as the broad-based professional curriculum community. The American Educational Research Association (AERA) did not yet occupy center stage, as it came to do in the 1980s and 1990s.

The 1969 Chicago Conference. Acknowledging this central role in the curriculum field ASCD had played, it is suggestive of the paradigm shift of the 1970s to examine two events in the history of this professional association in 1969 and 1970, the 1969 Chicago and the 1970 San Francisco national conferences (Klohr, 1992). The 1969 Chicago conference was held in the

Hilton Hotel in the spring following the nationally televised and widely reported summer riots that had accompanied the Democratic Party National Convention held in Chicago in 1968. The Hilton Hotel sat opposite Grant Park where Chicago Mayor Richard Daley had ordered Chicago police to suppress protesters of the Democratic Party's support of the Vietnam War. Memories of the turbulent summer before were fresh.

Within ASCD, with the sanction from its Executive Committee, a group of approximately ten had invited disenchanted citizens to attend the conference to "sensitize" participants to those in society whose needs the public schools were failing to meet. Before the conference began and during the first several hours after, a rather pervasive fear swept Executive Committee members and a few early-arrival members of the Association: "things could get out of hand." The invited visitors arrived by bus and pressed those in charge (namely, the Executive Committee) to give them priority in the conference program. Shifts in the planned program were made; meeting room assignments were changed. A continuing open session was announced and space given for the visitors; conference members were invited to engage in dialogue.

As hours passed, the ASCD President, a nationally recognized school district staff member, Muriel Crosby, viewed herself and her Executive Committee as being held hostage to demands that had not been "democratically" presented. Several members proposed that the Chicago police might be brought in to insure the conference would proceed as planned, without disturbance. Others, including the majority of the Executive Committee, believed that there was no apparent threat or any move to disrupt. In their view, the disenfranchised visitors should be made a part of the ongoing general sessions and small-group discussion. The President, who was to have presided at the entire conference, abruptly left Chicago, feeling that the Association had "caved in" to outsiders (ASCD *Update*, 1993, p. 4).

The President-Elect, Alexander Frazier, a professor at Ohio State University, took over as the presiding officer, and the conference proceeded as scheduled. There were no disruptions. However, at the open business meeting, tension spilled over. A number of vocal individuals asserted they had not been heard. The presence of disenfranchised visitors forced the issue: could ASCD meet new social and cultural realities? The old issue surfaced again, this time fueled by these events: were (more conservative) school people adequately represented in the administration of ASCD? Some saw the tensions of this conference, symbolized by the president's departure from the conference, as indicating that ASCD could no longer serve as a common meeting ground for curriculum professionals.

The 1970 San Francisco Conference. It was becoming clear that the conceptual and instrumental "tools" provided by the traditional paradigm of curriculum development no longer adequately addressed rapidly changing social and cultural realities. Somehow, the traditional paradigm attempted to insulate itself from these indications of "cultural revolution." A second event which illustrates cultural and generational tensions building in the curriculum field was the 1970 national conference of ASCD. In March 14-18, 1970, ASCD convened its 25th annual conference in San Francisco, far from the Chicago setting and memories of riot-torn Grant Park, far from the tensions and splits within the Executive Committee and the Association membership. ASCD President Alexander Frazier (1970), presiding at the conference, called for a time of healing and for "moving on" to consider "Tomorrow's World," the conference theme. A convention center workers' strike delayed the opening session, but the entire conference focused on how the curriculum might become more responsive to the pervasive changes taking place in American society and culture. Recall that San Francisco and the Bay Area were widely viewed as the center of the so-called counter-culture.

The conference program represented an attempt to bring racial and ethnic issues to the various sessions. A distinguished black educator, Samuel D. Proctor (1970) of Rutgers University, opened one general session with his address on "Education for Social Change." A Chicano theater group brought music and drama to one session to emphasize the richness and special problems of living in two cultures. Theodore Roszak (1970), at that time writing his analysis of American culture which became, in 1972, *Where the Wasteland Ends: Politics and Transcendence in Postindustrial Society*, spoke at the second general session. Roszak described his concept of "rhapsodic intellect" (i.e. a search for larger, deeper meanings, somewhat akin to Michael Polanyi's notion of "tacit knowing") which he asserted would involve a "revolution of consciousness." Roszak expressed doubt such a cultural move could occur without a major shift in our thinking about education. In addition to these sessions, which for most conference participants represented a markedly different conference experience, a general session devoted to the arts was held. The School of Creative Arts at San Francisco State University presented its version of what it might mean to "think" in a different mode—the imaginative realms of the poet and the artist.

These details of the San Francisco conference function as a photographic image of the major cultural and social shifts underway in the 1970s and which surfaced in the professional association of most curricularists. These two conferences underscored the cracks in the then-current paradigm of curriculum development. As the events of the Chicago conference imply, the American curriculum community was not well prepared for these shifts. Prevailing conceptual tools were not adequate, and new ones had not yet been formulated.

The 1975 Yearbook. ASCD did make efforts during the decade to respond to changing conditions. The 1975 ASCD yearbook [*Schools in Search of Meaning*] was a concise and accessible statement by curriculum scholars concerned with political and socioeconomic issues. Coedited by James Macdonald and Esther Zaret, the yearbook contained writing by Huebner, Apple, Mann, and Macdonald, all of whom would appear soon after in Pinar's (1975d) *Curriculum Theorizing: The Reconceptualists*, as well as writing by William Burton and

Esther Zaret. The basic stance of the yearbook contributors was clear: to find meaning in America in the 1970s, curricularists must be aware of the role that schooling played in maintaining the status quo of the working and ruling classes. Tracking and grading, for example, communicate to students their places within society. Schools were said to "domesticate" their political consciousness. The authors pointed to the necessity of further analysis of curriculum based on class interest, a position still promoted by Apple (1992a). They advocated the continual asking of the questions, "In whose interest in this being done?" and "Who decides?" (Miller, 1979a, p. 38). Concluding the yearbook were steps educators could take toward political action, such as convening small groups of students to teach the tools of dialectical analysis (Miller, 1979a).

By the end of the decade ASCD occupied a more modest role in the professional life of curriculum scholars than it had at the beginning of the 1970s. In a belated effort to attend to the Reconceptualization, ASCD sponsored, at its 1981 St. Louis national meeting, a debate between Ralph W. Tyler and William F. Pinar, the two individuals identified most with the competing paradigms. Also at this meeting Pinar met with Gordon Cawelti, ASCD Executive Director, and other officials regarding ASCD's acquisition of *The Journal of Curriculum Theorizing* (*JCT*) which Pinar had established three years earlier to support the scholarship of the new scholars. [Negotiations broke down over the issue of editorial control.] However, this belated effort to be responsive to developments in the scholarly field of curriculum came too late to allow ASCD to take a major role in the Reconceptualization. By the early 1990s, the honorary group called the "professors of curriculum," who by this time were meeting at both ASCD and AERA conferences, voted to consider meeting at the Bergamo Conference, the annual meeting associated with those who had reconceptualized the field. While a majority of the group voted to continue meeting only at AERA and ASCD conferences, the vote, compared to the near monopoly role ASCD had played twenty years earlier, would serve to highlight the dramatic change in the curriculum field itself. But we are ahead of our story. Let us turn now to developments internal to the decade-long movement to reconceptualize the field.

VII
The Reconceptualization of the Curriculum Field

A third group of individuals look upon the task of theorizing as a creative intellectual task which they maintain should be neither used as a basis for prescription or as an empirically testable set of principles and relationships.

(James B. Macdonald, 1975b, p. 6)

The movement to reconceptualize the field was sometimes incorrectly termed "reconceptualism," a term indicating greater thematic cohesion among participants than was accurate. Those involved in the movement came to be termed "reconceptualists," a problem to which Pinar contributed when he subtitled his 1975 collection *Curriculum Theorizing: The Reconceptualists* (1975d). Robert Graham (1991) characterized the book as a "broadside" (p.121) against the Tylerian paradigm dominant in the field from 1950-1970. Pinar's four essays in that collection—"Sanity, Madness, and the School," "The Analysis of Educational Experience," "*Currere*: Toward Reconceptualization," and "Search for a Method"—Graham depicts as "individual bullets from a sniper's rifle of a guerrilla band of self-styled reconceptualists" (p. 121).

A number of studies have detailed the history of the Reconceptualization (Huber, 1981; Miller, 1979a; Schubert, 1980a, 1986a; Mazza, 1982; Benham, 1981; Feinberg, 1985; Pinar, 1988d, 1988f; Jackson, 1992a; Lincoln, 1992). A summary will suffice here. We can begin by recalling that during the 1960s Dwayne E. Huebner and James B. Macdonald questioned the basic assumptions of the traditional field [see chapter 3]. These two scholars were among those "several lone individuals critical of the Tylerian mainstream of the field who worked to legitimate conceptions of curriculum derived from philosophy, aesthetics, and theology" (Pinar, 1988f, p. 3; see Kliebard, 1975c).

Reconceptualization defined. What was the Reconceptualization? Pinar answered the question in the preface to the 1975 collection. His characterization of the traditional field would be debated into the 1990s (Hlebowitsh, 1991, 1992, 1993). In 1975 he insisted the distinction was a simple one.

> Before I continue, let me clarify what I mean by "traditional curriculum writing." I mean the work of Professor Tyler, and all the work that falls under his considerable shadow. . . . This genre constitutes the heritage of the contemporary curriculum field, and it is a field characterized by . . . the concrete ever-changing tasks of curriculum development, design, implementation, and evaluation. The bulk of this writing has one essential purpose; it is intended as guidance for those who work in the schools. Understandably, this writing has been largely atheoretical; being directed at school people who want to know "how-to," it has had to be "practical." . . . While it is true that the themes of these books differ—from "humanizing" the curriculum, to organizing it around the structures of the disciplines—the function of these books is basically the same. They are intended to guide practitioners. (Pinar, 1975d, pp. xi, xii)

Where was the "crack" in the wall of the traditional field? Following Macdonald, Pinar mapped two non-traditional orders of work in the field, both much smaller in volume and visibility. The second order of work [the first being Tylerian] was conducted by a second group whom Pinar termed "conceptual-empiricists." He suggested that their "work differs from the traditionalists, often both in theme and function. This group tends to be steeped in the theory and practice of present-day social science. . . . Like most work in contemporary social and behavioral science it investigates 'phenomena' empirically, with an eye to the goal of prediction and control of behavior" (p. xii). In the third group he found the beginnings of the Reconceptualization:

The purpose of this [reconceptualist] work is not to guide practitioners, as it is with the traditionalists, and to some extent with the conceptual-empiricists. Nor is it to investigate phenomena with the methods and aims of behavioral and social science. . . . The function of this work would appear to be understanding, and this understanding is of the sort aimed at and sometimes achieved in the humanities. The humanities fields that have been influential thus far are history, philosophy, and literary criticism. Hence the dominant modes of inquiry for this group have been historical, philosophical, and literary. (1975d, p. xii)

Twenty years ago, when the contemporary field was still embryonic, it was clear that *understanding*—not curriculum development—would typify the primary modes of scholarship and pedagogy in the reconceptualized curriculum field.

Phenomenological, Political and Theological Discourses: The Work of Dwayne E. Huebner

In several important essays published during the 1970s, Huebner continued to lay important groundwork for reconceptualizing the field [see White (1980) and Plantinga (1985) for summaries of Huebner's work]. It was Huebner who argued for the necessity of moving beyond so-called scientific and so-called empirical language in the explanation of educational phenomena, heresy in the field in the 1960s. There exists, he insisted, a need to examine curriculum historically, with the present situation very much linked to both the past and the future, also a view the majority of curricularists found eccentric at best. Huebner advanced the notion of curriculum as praxis, i.e. curriculum as involving thought and action, a foreign language before Reconceptualization but the "daily tongue" afterward.

Reflective of this work, which we summarized briefly in the previous chapter, is "The Tasks of the Curricular Theorist" in which Huebner (1975d) made three points that would be developed in the decade after the Reconceptualization. First, he noted that curricularists operated in human history, with other human subjects, in actual human environments. This complexity could be seen in the individual biographies of students and educators. Second, the curriculum theorist was responsible through language and through environmental design to generate new language and environmental forms. Huebner's notion of environment included the school building, materials, and people—all that affects educational experience. Third, Huebner argued that in praxis, through engagement and work in the world, was where education occurred. Huebner wrote:

What are the tasks of curriculum theorists? As is true of all theorists his [sic] task is to lay bear the structure of being-in-the-world and to articulate this structure through the language and environmental forms he creates. His responsibility is for the forms he creates and uses, that they may be controlled by him rather than controlling him. (Huebner, 1975d, p. 269)

The political interest indicated in the last sentence is developed further in his "Poetry and Power: The Politics of Curricular Development" (1975e).

Here Huebner expressed his view that educators are lost, that they will remain lost as long as they accept the promise of a "quick fix" through slogans and bandwagons, as long as *they* do not act to change the educational world. Such action, Huebner is careful to point out, requires risk-taking. Huebner (1975e) advocated three rights: 1) there must be "unconditional respect for the political, civil, and legal rights of the young as free people participating in a public world" (p. 276); 2) the student has "the right of access to the wealth in the public domain—I mean primarily the knowledge, traditions, skills that shape and increase a person's power in the public world" (p. 276); and 3) the right of "each individual, regardless of age, to participate in the shaping and reshaping of the institutions in which they live" (p. 279). Huebner (1975e) concluded: "The school is but a manifestation of public life. As educators we must be political activists who seek a more just public world. The alternative of course is to be school people—satisfied with the existing social order—the silent majority who embrace conservatism" (p. 280).

Huebner's rejection of the traditional role of curriculum developers in favor of politically inspired actors engaged in seeking "a more just public world" would inspire a generation of curriculum scholars. The contemporary efforts to understand curriculum politically, phenomenologically, and theologically [see chapters 5, 8, and 12], can be traced to Huebner's groundbreaking scholarship in the 1960s and 1970s. In the preface to his essays in Pinar's (1975d) *Curriculum Theorizing: The Reconceptualists*, Huebner reflected on his own journey:

> Throughout this contact with diverse philosophical and theological traditions, the basic operating assumptions of curriculum thought bothered me. How could one plan educational futures via behavioral objectives when the mystical literature emphasized the present moment and the need to let the future care for itself? The thread that ran through my questions and my searching was an intuition that an understanding of the nature of time was essential for understanding the nature of education. . . . The journey has been lonely at times, but the direction feels right even though it seems veiled in a "Cloud of Unknowing." I am convinced that the curriculum person's dependency on scientific thought patterns, even though they have not found their way into practice as they should, has broken the linkage with other very great and important intellectual traditions of the East and the West which have profound bearing on the talking about the practice of education. (Huebner, 1975a, p. 215)

Among the traditions on which Huebner called were phenomenology and theology, the former of which he had introduced to the field in 1967 [see chapters 3 & 8]. Huebner's (1970) assertion of self-definition would thematize the reconceptualized field. First, he claimed the concrete, institutional interest Schwab had claimed: "I am a curriculum person. I happen to be concerned with the nitty gritty of schooling: what goes on in classrooms" (p. 169). Second, he pointed to language and discourse, both of which would preoccupy the contemporary field, when he wrote: "We have oversimplified the relationship between the design of educational environments and the language with which we talk about them" (pp. 178-179). Huebner's work would help alter the path of contemporary studies, a path partly in the everyday life of schools and partly in theoretical issues of language, discourse, and textuality.

Transcendence and Politics: The Work of James B. Macdonald

Like Dwayne Huebner, James B. Macdonald's work provoked the Reconceptualization, influencing an entire generation of curriculum scholars (Searles, 1982; Holland & Garman, 1992). Like Huebner, Macdonald received his Ph. D. in education from the University of Wisconsin-Madison, advised by Virgil Herrick. Macdonald's first university position was as Assistant Professor in Curriculum and Extension at the University of Texas-Austin during the 1956-1957 academic year. From 1957-1959 he served as Assistant Professor in Elementary Education at New York University. From 1959-1963, Macdonald was Associate Professor and Director of School Experimentation and Research at the University of Wisconsin-Milwaukee. He was a Professor in the Department of Curriculum and Instruction, and Department of Educational Policy Studies at the University of Wisconsin during the period 1963-1966. From 1966-1972 Macdonald served as Professor of Curriculum and Social and Philosophical Foundations of Education at the University of Wisconsin-Milwaukee. From 1972 until his death on November 21, 1983, Macdonald was Distinguished Professor of Education at the University of North Carolina at Greensboro (Brubaker & Brookbank, 1986). Macdonald's contribution was acknowledged by an international conference in his honor (Apple, 1985a; Grumet, 1985; Huebner, 1985; Molnar, 1985; Pinar, 1985; Spodek, 1985; Burke, 1985; Wolfson, 1985a, 1985b). At that conference Pinar hinted at the scope of Macdonald's significance:

> It will be hard for the curriculum field at large to see the importance of what James B. Macdonald has done. The field at large has tried not to see this work at all. It has not understood it, except for a primitive awareness that Macdonald's work was critical of mainstream curriculum theory and practice. . . . Jim was "a" if not "the" major theoretician of [the reconceptualist] movement. (1985, p. 43)

In an autobiographical reflection which prefaced his essays collected in *Curriculum Theorizing: The Reconceptualists* (1975d), Macdonald wrote:

> Personally, my own work in the field in retrospect is best explained to myself as an attempt to combine my own personal growth with a meaningful social concern that has some grounding in the real world of broader human concerns. Thus, education has served as a societal pivotal point to explore myself and the broader human condition in a meaningful context. (1975a, p. 3)

In a seminal paper first published in 1971 entitled "Curriculum Theory," James Macdonald foreshadowed the movement to reconceptualize the field by laying out three categories of curriculum theorists, a scheme Pinar employed in his mapping of the field (1975d; Giroux, Penna, & Pinar, 1981;

Pinar & Grumet, 1988). Extending the notion of "framework" theorist that he had developed in 1967, Macdonald wrote that:

> One group (by far the largest) sees theory as a guiding framework for applied curriculum development and research and as a tool for evaluation of curriculum development. . . . A second "camp" of ofttime younger (and far fewer) theorizers is committed to a more conventional concept of scientific theory. This group has attempted to identify and describe the variables and their relationships in curriculum. The purpose of this theory is primarily conceptual in nature, and research would be utilized for empirical validation of curriculum variables and relationships, rather than as a test of the efficiency and effectiveness of a curriculum prescription. A third group of individuals look upon the task of theorizing as a creative intellectual task which they maintain should be neither used as a basis for prescription or as an empirically testable set of principles and relationships. The purpose of these persons is to develop and criticize conceptual schema in hope that new ways of talking about curriculum, which may in the future be far more fruitful than present orientations, will be forthcoming. At the present time, they would maintain that a much more playful, freefloating process is called for by the state of the art. (Macdonald, 1975b, p. 6)

After a decade of Reconceptualization, this third group would come to dominate the field.

In a major paper delivered at the 1973 University of Rochester Curriculum Theory Conference [the 1970s curriculum conferences as indices of Reconceptualization will be discussed later in this chapter], entitled "A Transcendental Developmental Ideology of Education" (1974), Macdonald began by citing the limitations of developmental models in curriculum and in education generally. In the context of a reference to Freire [the Brazilian theorist who would inspire two decades of American political theory in curriculum; see chapters 5, 12, and 14], Macdonald pointed to the development of the autobiographic (which he termed romantic) and the political discourses (which he linked with earlier reconstructionist discourses) which would become influential in the Reconceptualization. Macdonald (1974) wrote:

> We still do not generally recognize this radical thrust in curriculum thinking, but the growing edge of writing in the past five to ten years leans toward a resurgence of romanticism and a renewal of past reconstructionist terms of the radical tradition. Neither . . . is the same as its predecessor. (Macdonald, 1974, p. 87)

Macdonald goes on to note that the political or radical criticism of the autobiographic emphasis upon the individual asserts that it is a conservative reassertion of the status quo, i.e. of conservative political theory. He (1974) wrote:

> . . . a radical ideology claims that liberal developmental ideology and romantic ideology are embedded in the present system. That is, the emphasis upon the individual and his unfolding or developing necessitates acceptance of the social structures as status quo in order to identify in any empirical manner the devel-

opment of the individual. Thus, developmental theory is culture and society bound, and it is bound to the kind of a system that structures human relations in hierarchical dominance and submission patterns and alienates the person from his activity in work and from other people (p. 88).

However, like the developmental/psychological view, the radical perspective was flawed as well.

Yet I find this [radical] view limiting in its materialistic focus, and I suspect that it is grounded fundamentally in the Industrial Revolution and reflects the same linear rationality and conceptualizing that characterizes the rise of science and technology. . . . The world today is not the same, and a different reading of history is needed to help make sense of the contemporary world. . . . The radical-political perspective as a home for curriculum thinking does not adequately allow for the tacit dimension of culture: it is a hierarchical historical science that has outlived its usefulness both in terms of the emerging structure of the environment and of the psyches of people today. (Macdonald, 1974, pp. 89-90)

This critique of Marxism would become loud with the arrival of poststructuralism in the field not ten years later (Taubman, 1979, 1982; Daignault & Gauthier, 1982).

Then Macdonald the visionary surfaced. He (1974) wrote that "today's technology is yesterday's magic" (p. 91). He continued:

technology is in effect an externalization of the hidden consciousness of human potential. Technology . . . is a necessary development for human beings in that is the means of externalizing the potential that lies within. Humanity will eventually transcend technology by turning inward, the only viable alternate that allows a human being to continue to experience oneself in the world as a creative and vital element. Out of this will come the rediscovery of human potential. (Macdonald, 1974, p. 91)

Political and economic analysis cannot, to borrow Jean-Paul Sartre's concept, "totalize" culture, society, and history. Rather, political and social theory represents:

. . . a radical social adjunct to conceptual culture. Now we are facing the opening of doors of perception in human experience, not as the minor mystical phenomena that have appeared throughout history, but as a large-scale movement of consciousness on the part of our young. A multimedia world is perceptual, not linear, in the utilization of concepts, but patterned concepts are received upon impact as perceptual experience. The psychological attitude born in this culture is a psychology of individuation, not individualism or socialism. . . . Thus the conscious attitude of integration is one of acceptance, of ceasing to do violence to one's own nature by repressing or overdeveloping any part of it. This Jung termed a "religious" attitude, although not necessarily related to any recognizable creed. (Macdonald, 1974, p. 92, p. 98)

Macdonald's thought represents a major contribution. First, we have a rather full curricular view here, one which is rooted in the historical world, as well as in the history of curriculum discourses. It contains within it the major theoretical elements of the field's history, and it has made them over in a view of complexity and moral power. Second, as Melva Burke (1985) has chronicled, Macdonald's career spans what we might tentatively call the four theoretical movements of the field: scientific thinking, personal humanism, sociopolitical humanism, and transcendental thought. For Macdonald curriculum theory was fundamentally a creative act. Perhaps his view is summarized in his statement that "curriculum is an exciting venture for persons whose dispositions lead them in this direction. There is an article of faith involved . . . [because it is] 'the study of how to have a world'" (Macdonald, 1975b, p. 12).

In a videotaped autobiography Macdonald identified four stages of his development. The first stage was scientism, which he eventually felt excluded too much—especially affect. From scientism Macdonald moved to what he termed person-centered humanism, and third to what he termed sociopolitical humanism. His fourth and final stage was transcendentalism, with its significant secular and religious implications and its need for cultural revolution. He believed that each stage was necessary and important to his study of what he considered the key question in curriculum: How shall we live together? (Brubaker & Brookbank, 1986; Macdonald, 1986)

The pathbreaking work of Huebner and Macdonald not only challenged the traditional field during the 1960s and 1970s, it suggested a thematic route for Reconceptualization in the 1970s. Its thematic outlines would be political, autobiographic, and would include European traditions such as phenomenology and theology. What sounded like "faint voices" in the 1960s and like sheer speculation in the very early 1970s would turn out to be "fact" by 1980. This swift movement from the traditional field to the reconceptualized one would be marked by a series of annual conferences. To these meetings we turn next.

VIII
The Conferences

The curriculum of domination is political; subtly or blatantly, by commission or omission, it teaches racism, sexism, classism.
(Donald R. Bateman, 1974, p. 61)

Relating the self to itself is no easy matter in a culture that systematically erodes subjectivity. Part of the cure entails getting back to the body, relating self to self.
(William J. Pilder, 1974, p. 120)

The University of Rochester Conference (1973). The conference which would signal that the Reconceptualization of the American curriculum field was underway was held in Rochester, New York, May 3-5, 1973, sponsored by the University of Rochester's College of Education, the dean of which was James I. Doi. With the assistance of Paul Klohr, William Pinar invited those whose work he considered to contain the major thematic and methodological elements of a possible reconceptualization of the curriculum field. These scholars included Robert Starratt (1974), Donald Bateman (1974), Maxine Greene (1974), Dwayne Huebner (1974), James B. Macdonald (1974), William J. Pilder (1974), and Pinar (1974c) himself. Punctuating these general sessions were small-group sessions, in which participants worked through, in their own terms, the significance of the papers. These small groups were led by Charles Beegle (1974), Paul R. Klohr (1974b), Eleanore E. Larson (1974), William T. Lowe (1974), Robert L. Osborn (1974), Francine Shuchat-Shaw (1974), and George Willis (1974). The essays and reports on the small groups (written by the leaders) and the general-session papers given by those listed above were edited by Pinar and published the following year as *Heightened Consciousness, Cultural Revolution, and Curriculum Theory: The Proceedings of the Rochester Conference* (Pinar, 1974c). The theme of the conference was "heightened consciousness and cultural revolution," terms that Pinar (1988f) later admitted "make one wince today" (p. 3). This theme, however, did link curriculum with developments in the political and cultural spheres, and this linkage continued, if in different form, throughout the 1970s and in the field today.

Approximately one-hundred scholars from the United States and Canada came to Rochester, New York that May. In addition to the general sessions attended by all, the registrants met in small groups to discuss the issues speakers had raised. Paul Klohr, who chaired one of the small groups, described the sense of the conference:

> We can see something of the personal struggle involved, the despair, the paradoxes, the excitement, the unfinished questions yet to be faced. Sensing this struggle gives us courage to try to make the pilgrimage ourselves. Not all of us will finally want to do this, but some will. What more can one ask but that those who do want to join hands and move ahead? The road is far from clear, but the Rochester conference points out some directions. (Klohr, 1974b, p. 173)

Klohr's comments captured the sense not only of the Rochester conference, but foreshadowed the remainder of the decade as well. The traditional paradigm of the field had broken down, and a sense of being "adrift" would pervade the field for several years, the present residue of which is a sense of confusion (Jackson, 1992a), for those living in the "generational divide." This resulted in part from the uncertainty as to what form the Reconceptualization would take. Indeed, some questioned if the field would survive at all. The field did survive, of course, and it emerged from the 1970s a revitalized and considerably more complex field than it was in May, 1973. The Rochester Conference would be the first in a series that would be sponsored by various universities until 1978, when the establishment of *JCT* (at first *The Journal of Curriculum Theorizing*, now *JCT: An Interdisciplinary Journal of Curriculum Studies*) would initiate a series of conferences organized by the editors of the *Journal*, conferences chaired by William F. Pinar and Janet L. Miller, editor and managing editor, respectively, of the *JCT* [see Pinar (1980a); Reid (1980a) for a discussion of the role of journals in the curriculum field.]

The Rochester conference bears closer scrutiny as it expressed what would become the major themes of the Reconceptualization. Pinar (1974c) summarized these themes in the preface to the proceedings:

> Four issues . . . kept making themselves heard, and I comment impressionistically and briefly. a. *Confidence in schools as liberating institutions.* Pilder is unequivocal that schools are hopeless. . . . Bateman seemed similarly unhopeful; schools are extensions of the oppressive, totalitarian capitalist superstructure, and as such can only be expected to continue sexism, classism, and racism. Huebner seems similarly pessimistic. . . . b. *Shape of future reform.* In part it must be theoretical, involving a reworking of the language we employ to describe phenomena associated with curriculum. It must be political. . . . It must as well be psychological. . . . c. *Commitment to public education.* Pilder's paper clearly undercuts the traditional commitment to public educational institutions. Although other papers were not explicit, one sensed a frustration, at times almost a hopelessness, at the possibility of significant reformation. . . . d. *Future of "scientism" in the field of education.* It is not that the speakers dismissed scientism; they ignored it. (p. xi)

The reconceived field would move ahead in a direction quite different from the painful path public schools took in the 1970s and 1980s, and in ways not inspired by mainstream social science, but by scholarship associated with the humanities, the arts, and social theory.

Schwab's emphasis on the practical is criticized. In a tense atmosphere of high expectation, Robert Starratt gave the first paper on Thursday night, May 3. In this overview of the field, he responded pointedly and persuasively to Schwab's criticism of the traditional field. Starratt (1974) disagreed "with Schwab's conclusion that we ought to call a moratorium on theoretical speculation and devote our attention to dealing with more practical affairs, like the maintenance and improvement of existing institutions and practices" (p. 24). He continued:

> Schwab's documentation of the incompleteness of contemporary theory leads him to recommend a moratorium on theory. It leads me to the opposite recommendation. . . . Our educators need . . . more stimulation to reflect upon the nature of man [sic] and society so that they can perceive the underlying significance of the confusing circus of daily experiences they face. The one-dimensional and fragmented theory we suffer with at present seems to require a much larger effort to develop a comprehensive theory, rather than a need to flee the task of theory in desperation and immerse ourselves in the perhaps more satisfying but shortsighted tasks of solving immediate problems. (p. 25)

Further, Starratt argued that Schwab's recommendation that curriculum scholars move directly into the arena of pragmatic problem-solving in the schools, conducting much more empirical research on what actually goes on in classrooms, is like asking architects to leave the drawing board, replace them with hammers and saws, and become carpenters, construction foremen, and building contractors. Starratt insisted: "The political negotiation and management of educational programs is the job of teachers, administrators, and central office supervisors, not of curriculum theorists. They may and should be consulted, but they should not be called on to perform the tasks of front-line personnel" (1974, p. 25).

Starratt also criticized Schwab's emphasis upon incremental reform. He wrote:

> Besides confusing the roles of theoretician and practitioner, this suggestion could be dangerously shortsighted. When one becomes engaged in identifying and repairing frictions and failures in the school organization and programs, it tends to absorb all of one's attention. . . . The practitioner whose immersion in the immediate task of keeping the ship afloat has little time to engage in frontier research. . . . Were curriculum theorists to abandon their proper role and engage in the practical problems of maintenance and incremental institutional reform, schools could blindly drift into obsolescence at a time when our planetary survival may depend on the development of a whole new set of cultural attitudes and a different sense of national purpose. While acknowledging the accuracy of Schwab's criticism of the many shortcomings in curriculum theories, I strongly oppose his recommendation that curriculum theorists abandon theory and divert their efforts to the realm of the practical. On the contrary, his critical analysis of the limitations of current theory should spur efforts to develop . . . more comprehensive curriculum theory. (p. 27)

Starratt's criticism and Schwab's proposals intersected with Kliebard's (1970) characterization of the traditional field as atheoretical. Both Starratt and Kliebard provided important support for the development of a sophisticated theoretical wing of the field that would emerge from the 1970s movement to reconceptualize the field. [See also Butt (1980) for a critique of Schwab.]

Curriculum as political text. One strand of theory central to the field by the end of the decade of Reconceptualization was that strand which understood curriculum as political text. Donald Bateman summarized the state of political scholarship at this early stage in a ringing indictment of the political status quo. After a scathing review of the "teacher proof" aspects of the national curriculum reform movement in the 1960s, Bateman reviewed sympathetically the "neo-Romantic" criticism written by John Holt, Paul Goodman, and others. He went on to charge:

> we begin to see that the central and primary theme of our age is domination: domination of the poor by the rich, Blacks, browns, reds, and yellows by whites, women by men, students by teachers. It is called neocolonialism, imperialism, racism, classism, sexism, all different though alike, related and interrelated in obvious and subtle ways. (pp. 58-59)

Further, he employed Freirean [the internationally acclaimed Brazilian educator Paulo Freire mentioned earlier; see chapters 5, 12, and14] language to assess the political role of the school:

> The pedagogy of domination mythologizes reality; the pedagogy of liberation demythologizes it. There is no way to be neutral, no way to be apolitical. . . .
> Schooling is not neutral politically; it takes place in an institution designed and

operated by those in power, to serve those who will come into power, to teach each child to accept his preassigned place. (p. 60)

Next, in one sentence Bateman would anticipate political scholarship for the next twenty years: "And so the curriculum of domination is political; subtly or blatantly, by commission or omission, it teaches racism, sexism, classism" (p. 61). Like the political scholars [see chapter 5] who would follow him, Bateman denounced humanistic education as insufficiently political:

> Racism, sexism, classism—those deeply internalized social values—are at the root of our problems. They are deep in our psyches, and they cause our liberal reforms to fail because they treat the symptoms and not the causes. Even humanistic education, which has always seemed so attractive, from the early writing of Holt to the later ones of Maslow, tacitly accepts the class system with its racism, its gross commercialism, its male chauvinism, its institutional violence, its imperialistic wars—accepts them by failing to mention them, by pretending to be apolitical. (p. 64)

In terse and dramatic words, Bateman told the audience assembled in Rochester that:

> The channeling of children into the labor market, and the concomitant domestication that justifies it, is as much a part of America as mom and apple pie, but the myths weaken a little as the demythologizing proceeds from Watergate to the analysis of the sexist and racist content of curricula, and though our schools and colleges, our reformers and leaders, our journalists and curriculum developers seem committed to the preservation of the status quo, knowledge is available; it is our task, each one of us, to come to grips with what is known, to take a stand. (p. 66)

The demise of the progressive dream. William J. Pilder, an Ohio State Ph.D. who had studied with Alexander Frazier and Paul Klohr, read perhaps the most moving paper, entitled "In the Stillness is the Dancing." In this address on Saturday morning which concluded the three-day meeting, Pilder (1974) proclaimed that the progressive dream was over. He wrote: "The falling apart is a scaling down of expectations, the end of the progressive dream. The time is now to stop thinking and talking about using curricula in schools to accomplish major social change. The time is now to begin living the changes" (p. 118). Critical of the conference theme, Pilder expressed his skepticism that incorporating issues of consciousness and cultural revolution could revitalize either the sphere of theory or that of the school: "Keeping curriculum theory together with consciousness and cultural revolution can only perpetuate the illusion that something important is being done if school curricula are related to the latest happenings available in the media" (p. 118). Pilder proceeded: "Relating the self to itself is no easy matter in a culture that systematically erodes subjectivity. . . . Part of the cure entails getting back to the body, relating self to self" (p. 120). The passage that Pilder envisioned included a "middle way" between uncritical acceptance of the status quo and exploration of so-called alternative realities. To travel such a passage requires faith. Pilder wrote: "The development of this [faith] dimension involves a journey inward and a subsequent struggle to integrate what is seen with how the self relates with consensus reality. Integration is constantly threatened by temptation toward withdrawal or identification" (p. 124), a view which would be elaborated a decade later by Christopher Lasch (1984) in his study of "the minimal self." In a voice filled with emotion, Pilder concluded:

> Here, then, is my despair as a professional: human survival cannot depend on social programs directed at present institutional structures. Personal consciousness development and subsequent cultural transformation cannot be programmed in mechanistic fashion; a curriculum for consciousness development and cultural change is a blatant contradiction. From the ashes of despair a Phoenix stirs—a single hope. The process that brings me to this loss of confidence in programs, in professional reality, in views of all kinds is a wave of transformation in my personal life and in the culture at large. This is my hope: a kind of zero point, a carefully held difference between the contraries of identification with professional expectations and withdrawal inside a self-process. I try to walk the tightrope between rigidity and chaos and dance between the demons of professional identification and self withdrawal. (pp. 125-126)

Pilder declined to continue walking such a tightrope. He departed the field within a year after reading this dramatic paper to study Jungian psychoanalysis in New York.

The Rochester conference both launched the Reconceptualization and expressed its major themes, that is, to understand curriculum one must comprehend it as political, historical, and autobiographical text. While the Rochester conference conveyed a sense of the intersections of these projects, indeed a sense of the fundamental interconnectedness of these theoretical interests, subsequent conferences revealed antagonisms not evident in May, 1973. Reflecting on the conferences, Pinar (1988f) indicated that "almost as soon as the conferences began, internal divisions [in the movement to reconceptualize the field] appeared" (p. 3). The basic division occurred between "Marxists of various orientations and interests and those who were interested less in macro-structural issues and more interested in the individual" (p. 3). This division took institutional form, as the Marxists tended to be associated primarily with the University of Wisconsin-Madison and with Teachers College, Columbia University secondarily, while those interested primarily in the individual were associated with the University of Rochester, and Ohio State University secondarily. Identifying the organizers of the yearly conference reveals this institutional as well as thematic aspect of this division within the movement to reconceptualize the field of curriculum.

Klohr's depiction of the Reconceptualization. In 1974 the conference was organized by Timothy Riordan, an Ohio State Ph.D. [as was Pinar]. It was held at Xavier University in Cincinnati, Ohio. Even by this early date a discernible sense was clear that a movement was developing within the larger, traditional field. Paul Klohr, who had been involved in theorizing the thematic elements of the Reconceptualization with Pinar, identified nine themes common to those who were coming to be known as "reconceptualists." Klohr (1974a) listed the following "reconceptualist" articles of faith:

1) A holistic, organic view is taken of humankind and his or her relation to nature; 2) the individual becomes the chief agent in the construction of knowledge; s/he is a culture creator as well as a culture bearer; 3) the curriculum theorist draws heavily on his/her own experiential base as method; 4) curriculum theorizing recognizes as major resources the preconscious realms of experience; 5) the foundational roots of their theorizing lie in existential philosophy, phenomenology and radical psychoanalysis, also drawing on humanistic reconceptualizations of such cognate fields as sociology, anthropology, and political science; 6) personal liberty and the attainment of higher levels of consciousness become central values in the curriculum process; 7) diversity and pluralism are celebrated in both social ends and in the proposals projected to move toward those ends; 8) reconceptualization of supporting political-social operations is basic; and 9) new language forms are generated to translate fresh meanings—metaphors for example. (pp. 5-6)

Klohr was careful to note that these themes do not appear in toto in the work of any one individual. However, "they do appear time and time again as one examines a collection of reconceptualist writing" (Klohr, 1974a, p. 5). The 1975 conference was organized by University of Virginia Professor Charles Beegle, also an Ohio State Ph.D. The major emphasis at this conference was on humanistic themes, including attention to autobiography and the individual, although "political themes were just barely secondary" (Pinar, 1988f, p. 4). The 1976 conference was held at the University of Wisconsin-Milwaukee, chaired by Alex Molnar, a Wisconsin Ph.D. At this conference, political and social themes predominated. Selected presentations, edited by Molnar and his colleague John Zahorik, were published by the Association for Supervision and Curriculum Development (ASCD) in 1977 as *Curriculum Theory*. In her forward to the volume, ASCD President Elizabeth S. Randolph indicated the political nature of the work:

Throughout the book the contributors to *Curriculum Theory* challenge us to look at the real purpose of education, whether it is to maintain the social structure as it has existed or to improve the existing social structure by providing an educational environment that maximizes human potential. Several writers strongly urge us to reexamine the values implicit in our curriculum, to redefine these or other values and make them explicit. (Randolph in Molnar & Zahorik, 1977, p. iv)

"Critical" and "post-critical" reconceptualists. In addition to tensions that intrinsically belong to different positions, i.e. an emphasis upon "self" or society, additional tension was generated by the introduction Pinar wrote to his 1975 *Curriculum Theorizing: The Reconceptualists*, in which he characterized political scholarship as "critical," and autobiographical scholarship "post-critical," a characterization employed later to a somewhat different end by Philip

Wexler (1988b). Pinar (1988f) reflected on this development thirteen years later:

> In that volume [the 1975 collection] I differentiated between critical and post-critical theorists, placing the Marxists in the former and those of us interested in the individual and related concerns in the latter. Of course, it was implicit the post-critical theorists were somehow more advanced, psychologically if not theoretically, and it takes little imagination to conjure up the response of Mike Apple and the ranks of Wisconsin- and Columbia-trained Marxists. (p. 4)

In a public letter to Pinar, William Burton (1974) argued that Pinar's definition of post-critical, i.e. a concern with transcendence and consciousness, a movement away from criticism of the status quo toward creation of a new order—obscured and minimized the importance and necessity of political criticism and action. Furthermore, Burton claimed that the existential phenomenology in which Pinar's work was situated represented an evasion of the political oppression of the 1970s. For Burton, Pinar's approach to curriculum represented a dead-end (Burton, 1974; in Miller, 1979a). Pinar replied that all political acts require the self, and that recognition of self and one's place in the world becomes political, as self-understanding involves political and social understanding and action (Pinar, 1974d, quoted in Miller, 1979a). This correspondence illustrates the disagreements and tensions between "critical" and "post-critical" scholars. Political scholarship dominated the 1977 conference, organized by Richard Hawthorne, a Wisconsin Ph.D., and held at Kent State University in Ohio.

A Marxist threat? In 1979, Pinar attempted to adjudicate the disputes over the "critical" designation by emphasizing the democratic and inclusive character of the movement. In effect, he invited the disenchanted Marxists to participate in the process of definition of the Reconceptualization:

> Those reconceptualists who have refused to acknowledge the reality and promise of the Reconceptualization have done so, in part, in protest of the process of being defined by another. Such protest is healthy, but its time is now past. The Reconceptualization, I am suggesting, is fundamentally a dialectical relation among knowers, knowing, and the known. Its thematic character must and will be identified and constructed through the discourse and scholarship of its participants. To imagine it a finished product, a doctrine, is to miss its point. What is essential about the Reconceptualization—as the literal definition of the word denotes—is its constant redefinition. Thus the question that serves as a title to this paper [What is the Reconceptualization?] is a question that serves to invite your participating in its answering. For it is ourselves who shape our relations among each other, to colleagues in other disciplines, to the American public. The order of contribution to that pubic and its educational system is contingent in inescapable ways upon the quality of our own self-constitution. We cannot expect to meaningfully participate in the transformation of the nation and its educational institutions if we fail to authentically participate in the constitution and transformation of ourselves and our work. (p. 102)

Pinar believed that both political and autobiographic discourses were central to the curriculum field that would emerge after the final collapse of the traditional field. The animosity of the Marxists toward the emphasis upon the individual raised fears that the reconceptualist movement itself was at stake. Pinar (1988f) reflected:

> To whatever extent these conferences were a movement that would reshape curriculum studies theoretically and methodologically, they could not, if they were to survive, be viewed as completely or even primarily identified with Marxist orientations, however crucial these were to the theoretical development of the field. . . . My concern was just how much "space" (to borrow a poststructuralist term) these analyses ought to occupy, at least on the conference program. (Pinar, 1988f, p. 4)

JCT is launched. The 1978 conference returned to Rochester, however this time held at the Rochester Institute of Technology, and chaired by Ronald Padgham, a professor of fine arts and University of Rochester doctoral graduate. That same year Pinar began publication of *The Journal of Curriculum Theorizing* (now *JCT: An Interdisciplinary Journal of Curriculum Studies*), working closely with Janet L. Miller, who has remained as Managing Editor since 1978. [Pinar retired as editor in 1985, replaced by William M. Reynolds. Jo Anne Pagano was named Editor-in-Chief of the renamed *JCT* in 1990. Pagano also chairs the yearly conference.] In 1978 *JCT* editors undertook sponsorship of the annual conferences, organized during the early years by Miller and Pinar. From 1979 through 1982 they were held in northern Virginia at the Airlie Conference Center. Afterward, the meetings were moved to the Bergamo Conference Center in Dayton, Ohio, supported in part by the University of Dayton. The 1994 conference was held at the Banff (Alberta, Canada) Centre for the Arts.

Apple's rejection of traditional curriculum questions. Michael Apple would become one of the major figures in the movement to reconceptualize the field, although he disavowed any affiliation with the movement. However, it is indisputable that his work functioned to reconceptualize the field. In a statement introducing his essays collected in *Curriculum Theorizing: The Reconceptualists*, Apple (1975b) wrote:

> I would like to begin by affirming the fact of being an educator but by rejecting the comforting illusion that the types of questions that are commonly being asked by curriculum workers and other educators are fruitful. In fact, it seems to me that many of the modes of activity, the forms of language, the basic ideologies, even the things we do that supposedly "help" kids are in need of radical (in the sense of going to the very root of an issue) rethinking. For one thing, there is no educational poetry, no disciplined esthetic sense; yet we misconstrue education if we think of it as engineering (though part of it is, to be sure). Furthermore, [education] . . . is ultimately a moral activity. As such it cannot be understood without recourse to, and thus must be held accountable to, ethical principles and obligations of justice and responsibility to other persons. (p. 89)

Apple continued by calling for research that examined curriculum underneath the bureaucratic surface of schools. In his prefatory statement were several notions that would thematize his research for the next fifteen years, including ideology, instrumentality, the situatedness of curriculum in the larger society, and community. At the same time, the influence of his doctoral mentor at Teachers College, Columbia University—Dwayne E. Huebner—is evident in this passage, with its emphasis upon language.

> The usual questions that school people are so fond of asking—better management systems, behavioral objectives pro and con, "affective" education, and so forth—are ultimately false issues. Their roots lie in ideological rules that are dialectically related to social and economic forms. . . . For example, the dominant consciousness in advanced industrial societies is centered on a vulgar instrumentality—a logical structure that places at its foundation the search for certainty, order . . . the cooptation of significant social dissent, process/ product reasoning, therapy to treat surface symptoms rather than basic structural change, and the search for even more efficient instrumentality. . . . Educational criticism, hence, becomes cultural, political, and economic criticism as well. Without the latter, the former is impotent. Second, the setting of educators within more basic social groups means that extensive investigations are required to demonstrate to other educators and a concerned citizenry the concrete linkages between personal, social, and economic injustice and education's models of inquiry, of talking about schooling, of "helping" children, and so forth. . . . Here, I am not speaking of new ways of talking, but, if I may borrow from Wittgenstein, of new forms of life, new ways of being with students, with each other. New ways of talk can only emerge with students, with each other. New ways of talk can only emerge from the dialectic of language and the generation of altered community. And this can only be generated if the negativity of the existing community is *shown*. (1975b, pp. 89-90)

Marx as a source of curriculum theory. Finally in this 1975 autobiographical statement, Apple pointed to Marx as the source for what he termed a strategic curriculum theory. He wrote:

> I must reject any false posturing of certainty. . . . What we can do is be guided by an insight of Marx in arguing that specific steps will become clearer only when the ways are illuminated that institutions now function to deny "freedom," to destroy or degrade meaning, to unduly dominate the intersubjective and intrasubjective relations of a society. From this negation can emerge a positive vision. . . . One has no choice but to be committed. (Apple, 1975b, pp. 92-93)

Students' rights. In addition to Bateman (1974) and Apple (1975b), John Steven Mann and Alex Molnar (1975) advanced a view of curriculum as political, focusing on students' rights. Molnar (1975) reflected on both that interest, and Mann's influence in his own political movement toward Marxism.

> While I was working with Jim [Macdonald] I got involved with ASCD and the Radical Caucus. My contact with the caucus and my friendship with Steve Mann, more than anything else, challenged the humanistic orientation of my

thought. Discussions, arguments, criticism, and reflection helped me make connections between what I had read of Mao, what I was learning with Jim, and my reality as an educator. This process resulted in my rejection of the flabby humanism that has become so characteristic in the dialogue and practice of many educators. . . . "On Student Rights" is an experimental piece that, while fundamentally sound, is flawed in at least two aspects. First, like a good deal of analysis referenced in Marxism-Leninism, it fails to account for the significance of the spiritual dimension in human affairs. Secondly, it does not clearly avoid the trap of advocating social change through the activities of schools. . . . Perhaps everything I write is an experiment, an attempt to understand better who I am and what my commitments must be. (p.166)

[Parenthetically, Molnar would achieve public visibility briefly during 1989 when he appeared several times on the Cable News Network (CNN) expressing opposition to the American war against Iraq. He has been less visible in curriculum field.]

Neo-Marxist curriculum theory not social reconstructionism. Mann, who would soon leave the curriculum field to work in the labor movement, and Molnar argued that schools refused to sanction students' political struggle for social justice. "We assert . . . that it is both the right and responsibility of young people, as citizens and as students, to study and engage in progressive social action as part of their education" (Mann & Molnar, 1975, pp. 167-168). Distinguishing their view from the social reconstructionism associated with Counts, Rugg, and Brameld [see Stanley, 1992b and chapter 5], Mann and Molnar asserted that "social reconstructionists fail to recognize that oppression and exploitation are a fundamental characteristic of class structure in the United States and cannot be altered by tinkering with the schools" (p. 170). They concluded:

> To talk of student rights and responsibilities as we have is to see the teacher as an organizer who must identify allies among his fellow teachers, the students, and community members to develop a program organized around issues specific to his situation, guided by the principles of dialectical analysis. (pp. 171, 172)

To speak of "organizing" and "principles of dialectical analysis" is, of course, familiar Marxist discourse, and Counts and Rugg (but not Brameld) distanced themselves from Marxism (Stanley, 1992b). In the 1970s, political scholars would not distance themselves from Marxism; indeed, they would embrace it.

In Canada. At the University of Alberta in Edmonton, Max van Manen and Ted Aoki (1981) were developing a phenomenological program of studies in curriculum and pedagogy. In 1979 Aoki published a widely-read monograph which functioned to support the movement to reconceptualize curriculum studies in North America. Entitled *Toward a Curriculum in a New Key*, Aoki's (1979) paper called for a multi-perspectival approach to curriculum development and evaluation: "we need to seek out new orientation that allows us to free ourselves of the tunnel vision effect of mono-dimensionality" (1979, p. 4). Commenting on developments in the American scene, Aoki observed:

> In curriculum inquiry, there is an array of orientations. . . . First there is the empirical analytic in which explanatory and technical knowledge is sought. This research mode is familiar to us as "science." Second, there is the situational interpretative inquiry orientation in which research is conceived as a search for meaning. . . . Such an account is called phenomenological description. Third, there is a critical inquiry orientation. (Aoki, 1979, p. 7)

Aoki aligned himself with second orientation, which he and van Manen would help develop—with their students—into a major contemporary discourse [see chapter 8].

Also in this 1979 monograph, Aoki responded to Schwab's challenge to the curriculum field. As did Robert Starratt (1974) at the Rochester conference, Aoki criticized Schwab's apparent atheoretical posture [which Schwab himself would correct in his final and fourth paper, published in 1983; see Jackson, 1992a and chapter 1]. Aoki's phenomenological orientation was clear when he wrote: "I concur with him [Schwab] that the practical day-to-day world of curriculum development merits intensive attention. I feel, however, that *merely moving to the practical is not sufficiently fundamental.* . . . An authentic radical departure calls for not only a lateral shift to the practical but also a vertical shift that leads us to a *deeper understanding of the program developer's theoretic stanc*e" (p. 51). Aoki's embrace of a perspective that was at once theoretical and practical would anticipate the reconceptualized field of the 1990s. [Indeed, Aoki continues in 1993 to be a pivotal figure in the field, 7 years after his retirement. Now invited to teach part-time at various universities (including the Universities of Lethbridge, Calgary, Victoria, British Columbia, Alberta, and Louisiana State University, among others) and working with the British Columbia Teachers Federation, Aoki remains a theorist and pedagogue of subtle brilliance and international importance (his accomplishment has been recently recognized by the awarding of honorary doctorates by the Universities of Alberta, Lethbridge, and British Columbia, an honor few curriculum theorists have enjoyed), linking theory with institutional practice, participating in various conferences (and instrumental in planning the 1994 Bergamo at Banff Conference), and intellectually, moving into poststructuralism without relinquishing his sophisticated phenomenology. As we will see in chapters 8 and 9, there are "through lines" from phenomenology to poststructuralism.]

The thematic characteristics of the American reconceptualization were not limited to the North American continent. Curriculum theory was just underway in earnest in the United Kingdom (Lawn & Barton, 1980) and Australia (Marsh, 1987; see also Musgrave, 1979, for a history of Australian school curriculum). As Jackson (1980a) and others would observe, scholarship in the United Kingdom, France, and Germany provided sources for American neo-Marxist scholarship; scholarship in Holland, France, and Germany provided sources for the development of phenomenology; and in the Nordic countries a similar movement was evident (Kallos & Lundgren, 1979; Lundgren, 1979, 1983; Harbo, 1983; see also Gudem, 1992). Freire's (1968) radical pedagogical work in Brazil a decade earlier would inspire hundreds of scholars worldwide to link literacy, culture, and politics. We examine the situation in Latin America in chapter 14, *understanding curriculum as international text.*

IX
Controversy

It is a mistake to see them [reconceptualists] as representing a movement that offers a new conception of curriculum inquiry.

(Robin Barrow, 1984b, p. 259)

How this "emancipation" will derive from reconceptualist ideology is never made clear. We are simply expected to accept the notion that the curriculum field, and indeed the entire culture, will be emancipated somehow by the new alchemists and concierges of countercultural ideology who call themselves reconceptualists.

(Daniel & Laurel Tanner, 1981, p. 390)

To retreat, as the Tanners have done, into a nostalgic affirmation of the familiar is not to enrich curriculum dialogue. Nor is it to chart a path to effectual research.

(Maxine Greene, 1979, p. 25)

Creators in any field threaten the established order. . . . As a result, creators in a field arouse fear of the unfamiliar and the unknown in those who cling to the traditional.

(Ronald E. Padgham, 1983, p. 132)

Existential, Marxist, or conservative, curriculum theories are all refusals of the common order. They express longing for coherence, for passion for identity, for nature and spirituality. And they all locate what they seek beyond what goes on in schools. Predicated on loss, these curriculum theories replicate the rupture in human consciousness that strands us on one side, longing for the other.

(Madeleine R. Grumet, 1990c, p. 196)

A paradigm shift does not occur painlessly. Scholars who lived their entire careers according to one paradigm do not accept passively claims that their paradigm is disappearing. So, in addition to controversy within the reconceptualist group, considerable controversy erupted from the traditionalist camp. By mid-decade it became clear to everyone in the field that the movement to reconceptualize curriculum was gaining strength. For instance, in 1978 Pinar was invited to deliver the first "state-of-the-art" address to the curriculum division of the American Educational Research Association (AERA). Pinar would represent the reconceptualist movement while John McNeil, from the University of California at Los Angeles, would represent the traditional viewpoint. Maxine Greene, the distinguished philosopher of education whose work had been employed by many reconceptualists, would act as respondent. Several hundred scholars were in attendance at this event, held in 1978 in Toronto. Pinar (1979c) asserted that the traditional field was "arrested," repeating Schwab's 1969 and Huebner's 1975 charge that the traditional field was moribund. He relied on Habermas' theory of knowledge and human interests to suggest differences among traditional, conceptual-empirical, and reconceptualist curriculum research [see also Macdonald, 1975c]. Pinar (1979c) concluded his assessment:

> The production of curriculum knowledge is important to the advancement of the field. However, if this production does not originate in an emancipatory intention but in a static one—such as an essentially atheoretical accumulation of a "body of knowledge," or the application of theory . . . to practice . . . then no fundamental movement . . . can occur. The state of the field is arrest. For movement to occur, we must shift our attention from the technical and the rational, and dwell on the notion of emancipation. Not until we are in emancipatory relation to our work will we devise theory and formulate strategic action which will . . . "improve" the nation's schools. (p. 11)

John McNeil (1978) worried that "the field suffers from the belief that there can be no objectivity in selecting and interpreting data from which educational purpose can be derived" (p. 23). He seemed to call for a de-emphasis of political considerations, or at least a separation between politics and curriculum development. He concluded:

> Just as some artists . . . have been able to separate their political beliefs and causes from their art . . . so, too, some curriculum specialists at all levels must not be instruments in behalf of special interests or national policy, but instead maintain credibility as curriculum inquirers, systematically studying a range of meanings that have implications for what should be taught and subsequently presenting new goals for consideration. (McNeil, 1978, p. 23)

Traditionalists are enraged. As long as the movement to reconceive the field appeared marginalized in conferences attended mostly by those committed to the movement, the threat to the traditional field seemed to be contained. When the mainstream research association (AERA) invited a leader of the movement to deliver the first major statement on the state of the field, the situation for traditionalists became critical and intolerable. Not long after the Toronto meeting they responded. Daniel and Laurel Tanner spoke for traditionalists in their "Emancipation from Research: The Reconceptualist Prescription," published in the *Educational Researcher* in 1979 (reprinted in 1981). The Tanners linked the reconceptualists with the "radical countercultural rhetoric of the 1960s" (1981, p. 382), and asserted that "just as paranoid phraseology characterized the rhetoric of student demagogues and radical critics of the 1960s, so paranoid phraseology suffuses much of the reconceptualists' 'theoretical writing'" (1981, p. 383). The Tanners would expect that reconceptualists "would translate their concern into an actual undertaking: the development of reformist curricula" (p. 384). "However," they continued, "this appears not to be the case; reconceptualists show surprisingly little interest in the curriculum" (p. 384). [Add "develop-ment" to this sentence, and the nature of the paradigm shift which the Tanners were fighting is clear.] They asserted: "It favors mystical illumination ('heightened consciousness') over reason and is therefore not curriculum knowledge but a promiscuous enthusiasm for whatever advertises itself as counter to our culture" (p. 385). Further, the Tanners asserted that theory in a "reconceptualist" sense was not theory. "Reconceptualism is an attempt to substitute a radical critique of society for a curriculum theory, and this is testimony to its atheoretical character. . . . A doctrine is not a theory" (p. 386). Referring to the reference to emancipation in the final paragraph of Pinar's 1978 state of the field address, the Tanners wrote:

> How this "emancipation" will derive from reconceptualist ideology is never made clear. We are simply expected to accept the notion that the curriculum field, and indeed the entire culture, will be emancipated somehow by the new alchemists and concierges of countercultural ideology who call themselves reconceptualists. (p. 390)

A second attack. At the second "state of the field" address to the curricu-lum studies division of the American Educational Research Association, held in San Francisco in 1979, Philip W. Jackson delivered a second attack against the reconceptualist movement, entitled "Curriculum and Its Discontents." Here, however, the rage of the first response of traditionalists, exemplified by the Tanners' attack, took a more complex form, both emotionally and intellectually. Jackson (1980a, 1981) began by recalling Schwab's declaration of the field as "moribund" in 1969, and Huebner's 1975 (published in 1976) "The Moribund Curriculum Field: Its Wake and Our Work." Jackson (1980a, 1981) commented:

> For all its starkness, Schwab's health bulletin did contain a ray of hope, though its light was faint indeed. As we know, the word moribund allows within its meaning for the possibility of a miraculous recovery, but as we also know, the chances of that happening are mighty slim. . . . The field of curriculum may not have been completely gone at the time Schwab took its pulse, but if we were to believe his prognosis, its end was close at hand. . . . [Huebner] went on to assure his readers that there could be no hope of renaissance. . . . Huebner, like Schwab, found it useful to muse on the question of whether the curriculum field was alive or dead. Also like Schwab, he arrived, with some waffling I fear, at a gloomy conclusion. (1981, pp. 389-369)

Next he turned to Pinar's assessment, the 1978 "state of the field" address to the Toronto meeting of the American Educational Research Association which the Tanners had found so infuriating.

> In 1977 and again in 1978, William Pinar . . . delivered two papers at the annual meeting of the AERA, each of which helped to keep alive the question of the curriculum field's state of health. . . . Pinar's 1977 pronouncements could hardly be called gay spirited. If not overly mournful, they were at least draped in black. By last year, however, in his state-of-the-art address to Division B [curriculum] of AERA, Pinar was in a more cheerful mood. In his remarks he

made no mention of death and dying. Instead, he described the state of the field as being "fragmented and arrested.". . . Perhaps I have become hypersensitive . . . through exposure to the views already discussed, but Pinar's words suggest the most final of all diagnoses: a cardiac arrest. Thus, the thanatotic fantasy, which Pinar had entertained earlier which seems to have captured the imagination of Schwab, Huebner, and others, was gone perhaps but not forgotten. (1981, pp. 369-370)

Jackson complained: "My impatience with this lugubrious talk about the curriculum field's last gasps should be obvious by now. . . . What . . . is the reality behind the metaphor?" (pp. 370, 373). "Who are these people whom I have labeled 'discontents' in the title of this paper?" (p. 374). Among those Jackson listed in answer to his question are Pinar, Schwab, and Eisner. He then summarized what he took to be their common critique of the field:

> 1) The Tyler rationale is out-of-date, and we have little or nothing to replace it with. 2) Our present ways of thinking and talking about schools and schooling do not do justice to the complexity and dignity of the human condition. 3) The control of curriculum is in the hands of technologists, test makers, textbook publishers, and school administrators. 4) Our schools are losing sight of humanistic values and goals. 5) Curriculum workers have little to offer teachers that is of direct help to them. 6) The aesthetic, ethical, and spiritual dimensions of the educational experience are being ignored. 7) Our schools are damaging too many students, particularly to children of the poor and oppressed minorities. (Jackson, 1981, pp. 375-376, numbers added)

Jackson then worried that his efforts at humor may mislead the reader into thinking that he did not regard these issues as important: "In truth, I see most of the items pointing to serious problems that are worthy of our genuine concern" (p. 376).

Jackson continued, summarizing the sources for Reconceptualization and noting the Marxian tendency in some segments of reconceptualist scholarship.

> The proposed shift in scholarly allegiance is away from what is increasingly referred to as "mainstream social science" . . . toward a wide assortment of intellectual traditions that have not heretofore been drawn upon heavily by persons interested in educational and curricular topics. These comprise, in the main, existential, phenomenological, and Marxist thought, but they also include, somewhat less prominently, the contributions of literary critics, psychoanalysts, and even a philosopher of science or two. The key ideas being drawn upon are distinctly European in flavor, with French and German influences predominating. Besides Marx and Freud, others that are frequently cited in this literature include Heidegger, Husserl, Merleau-Ponty, Sartre, Schutz, Gramsci, Polanyi, and Habermas. Taken as a whole, the ideological bias of the sources drawn upon most heavily is decidedly left of center. (pp. 376-377)

Jackson observed also that the second general proposal of the Reconceptualization involved a shift in the relationships between university professors of curriculum and school personnel, a shift which moved in two directions, one closer to practice, and the other apparently more distant. Here, thirteen years before the appearance of his historical study we reviewed in chapter 1, Jackson discerned the complication of the theory-practice relationship that the Reconceptualization entailed.

"Bracing," but. . . . Finally, Jackson expressed his view of these "discontented" scholars: "It should come as no surprise, then, if I were to sum up what has been revealed already and what has yet to come with a single wishy-washy word, ambivalence. That's how I feel toward the discontents" (pp. 378-379). He concluded:

> Finally, I sense a youthfulness in this body of curricular writings that is at once bracing and disconcerting. I need hardly explain the bracing quality, for that is what youthfulness is all about. It's full of life, feisty, and has a sparkle in its eye. What I find disconcerting about this quality, however, is that it seems to be conjoined with a spirit of intergenerational conflict that diminishes its initial attractiveness. Perhaps this, too, is an inevitable aspect of youthfulness, but I suspect it's not. My suspicion returns my thoughts to the deathbed metaphor and to Pinar's talk of becoming an heir. The occupant of that bed, come to think of it, cannot be just any aged person. It almost has to be a relative, and probably a parent at that. An ancient fantasy, Freud reminds. As common as acne among the young. Enough talk about my own ambivalence. I suspect that many of the discontents feel it as well. (p. 380)

Pinar replies. In 1979 and again in 1980 Pinar replied to these critics, emphasizing the importance of scholarly dialogue which promotes movement in the field, rather than simple confrontation that ends in angry silence. He observed that:

> Conversation cannot occur unless the participants are willing to maintain a minimal civility, a pedagogic orientation, and a willingness to be changed by the other. With such conditions present, a vital conversation, indicative of a vital field, can occur. I, for one, am open to being influenced by my critics. And so I invite Daniel Tanner, Laurel Tanner, and Philip Jackson to critique my writing once again, or other reconceptualist writing, but with one stipulation: that they cast their critiques in terms that I and others can use. This openness, it seems to me, is a prerequisite for not only individual development, but—writ large—the advancement of the field as well. Those of us who care for the field will cultivate it. (Pinar, 1980d, 1981, pp. 397-398)

Additionally, Pinar acknowledged that the term "reconceptualization" was an umbrella term of convenience:

> Reconceptualization . . . describe[s] a fundamental shift—a paradigm shift—in the orders of research conducted by diverse curricularists, the common bond of which was opposition to the traditional field. Because the term reconceptualization is historical in nature, the duration of its appropriateness is limited. . . . Where the field will stabilize and what will constitute the next major paradigm remain open questions. (1980d, 1981, pp. 394)

Maxine Greene responds. In a letter to the editor of *Educational Researcher*, in which both the Pinar and the Tanners' articles had appeared, Maxine

Greene (1979), herself a respondent at the 1978 "state-of-the-art" session which had provoked the Tanners' article, commented: "to retreat, as the Tanners have done, into a nostalgic affirmation of the familiar is not to enrich curriculum dialogue. Nor is it to chart a path to effectual research" (p. 25). Regarding Jackson's (1980a) "state of the art" address, Greene (1980) wrote:

> Jackson speaks of the shift in scholarly allegiance from one intellectual tradition to another, and I understand the ambivalence of his response. Unlike Jackson, however, I do not believe all this to be merely a journey among appealing fictions; nor do I believe it to be a mindless acquiescence to "life in the world". . . . Yes, indeed, there is bad faith. And yes, there is a degree of elitism in the academic character of the talk that has been going on. It helps to be moved to collective self-reflection; and I think Jackson's article may well have that effect. (pp. 174-175)

Jackson replies to Greene. Jackson (1980b) replied to Greene's criticism of his paper:

> My aspirations in writing "Curriculum and Its Discontents" were really quite modest. In the first part of the essay, I was only trying to reveal how enduring and insidious the mixed metaphor of a dying curriculum field has become. (I admit to trying to have some innocent fun in the process, at the expense of three of my friends—Schwab, Huebner, and Pinar). In the second half, I sought to map what I perceived to be the dominant positions of those who are calling loudest for a change in curricular thought and practice. Following that, I confessed to my own ambivalence about some of these newer trends. Nothing very profound about the whole thing. I am quick to admit, though I am grateful for having been welcomed and made to feel at home in Professor Greene's upwardly mobile literary salon, I really don't belong there. . . . Professor Greene begins her accusation with the charge that I do not get to the heart of the matter, that I do not "have a clear sense of the actuality the metaphors [the dying field of curriculum] obscure." Fair enough. I plead guilty. But who, I wonder, does possess the clear sense that I lack? Not, I fear, Professor Greene. . . . Finally, Professor Greene takes me to task for being too harsh with some of the folks I have called the Discontents. . . . She seems to think that I dismiss all such efforts as little more than "a journey among appealing fictions." Maybe I should have been clearer on that point, for I did not intend to leave such an impression. . . . My only concern is with the rigor of thought. (pp. 176-177)

Other responses. In another letter to the editor of the *Educational Researcher*, James Finkelstein and Ray Williams (1979) pointed to an epistemological conflict: "the Tanners' inability to identify a reconceptualist theory is due to their, and other critics' preconceived notion of what is to count as valid knowledge" (p. 24). Another observer of the controversy, Jean King (1981), shared Pinar's reflection on the paradigm controversy. She advised:

> If our goal is understanding . . . then we will approach the work of other curricularists gently. . . . Only when we have succeeded to the best of our ability in understanding the text . . . will we "violate" the text to ask questions it does not, in and of itself, raise. Such understanding, a product of a just approach to the text, creates justice in the process. (p. 172)

Ronald Padgham (1983) found the tone of the Tanner article quite under-standable: "Creators in any field threaten the established order. . . . As a result, creators in a field arouse fear of the unfamiliar and the unknown in those who cling to the traditional" (p. 132).

The decade ends. The decade ended, then, in attacks on the movement to reconceptualize the field, but as the 1980s would show, the attacks came too late. In retrospect, we can say that by 1980 the Reconceptualization had occurred. That is not to say that traditional work did not continue, or that work representative of mainstream social science did not appear after 1980; both did. It is to say, however, that by 1980 the field's focus had discernibly shifted from curriculum development to an effort at understanding. As an institutional index of the paradigm shift, the professional allegiance of curriculum professors had shifted from the Association for Supervision and Curriculum Development (ASCD) to the American Educational Research Association (AERA), implying movement from incremental, "practical" curriculum development to research to understand curriculum. The compo-sition of AERA meeting presentations reflected the themes and the interests of the Reconceptualization. These are important indicators of the paradigm shift. Curriculum development as a topic virtually disappeared, and papers exploring political, gender, phenomenological, and aesthetic themes became common. While the nation's schools slipped further into the hands of the business community, the politicians, bureaucrats, and the social engineers, the scholarly field of curriculum detached itself, and concentrated on understanding curriculum in all its complexity, relying on intellectual sources quite distant and apart from social engineering and conservative business politics. In 1992 Yvonna Lincoln reflected on the decade.

> What began [in the 1970s] as a radical but small group of critics of contempo-rary curriculum theory has now become a groundswell. Scholars writing about curricular matters today cannot avoid taking into account one or many of the critical schools of curriculum discourse. As a result, the reconceivers of the curriculum studies are not just postulating that a new world could exist but also creating it—voice by voice, criticism by criticism, scholar by scholar. (Lincoln, 1992, p. 94)

In retrospect. Writing in the 1990s, one scholar argued that Tyler was misconstrued during the decade of Reconceptualization. Peter S. Hlebowitsh (1991) noted that the core of the criticism of the Tyler Rationale character-ized Tyler as working in the tradition of Bobbitt's efficiency/production model. This view, he believes, was mistaken. In contrast to Bobbitt, Tyler (1949) argued for a small number of objectives framed at high levels of generalizability; formulated mediating elements (i.e., the philosophical screen) in the process of considering objectives as insurance against the mechanical treatment that indeed typified Bobbitt's approach to curriculum making. Tyler also warned, Hlebowitsh tells us, against undue specificity in the definition and measurement of behavioral objectives; moreover, the rationale need not be used in a step-wise or rigidly linear fashion. Based on a manufacturing model, Bobbitt advocated hundreds of objectives for which he framed no mediating factors. Hlebowitsh did admit that Tyler's characterization of learning as "process of changing the behavior patterns of people" is a definition that would support the connectionist patterns of learning conceptualized by behaviorists. Further, Hlebowitsh conceded, Tyler's suggestion that the construction of objectives could be elicited from the relationship between present conditions and desirable norms appeared to suggest that learning was a narrow process requiring the elimination of ambiguity and variance. True enough, instructional behaviorists have misused the rationale in exactly this manner.

Hlebowitsh (1991) complained about Pinar's focus on the administrative function of traditional curriculum development:

> Pinar seems to give improper emphasis to the character of Newlon's [see chapter 2] influence by highlighting the administrative imperative rather than the mandate to perform participatory curriculum revision. . . . The four questions in the rationale signal, according to Pinar (1975d), a "managerial concern with smooth operations." The charge of "smooth operations," which implies a kind of reductionism and efficiency function, is peculiar because the rationale is a guiding framework for curriculum change. (pp. 93-94)

Hlebowitsh (1991) concluded:

> The Tyler rationale works in the tradition of Dewey by framing curriculum work as an inquiry process that supports the consideration of ends as open points for deliberation, but that nevertheless upholds sources demanding sensitivity to the nature of the learner, the values and aims of the society and the reflective reformulation of the subject matter. . . . [The rationale] is not a mechanism of social efficiency and is not an administrative procedure anchored in a technocratic rationality. . . . Unfortunately, many of these curricularists have not made their case, as Tyler did, for a practical theory that informs and guides the argumentation and the *conduct* of schooling. (pp. 97-98)

Hlebowitsh's careful effort to redeem the Tyler Rationale has not been a solitary one. Distinguished Canadian scholar Kieran Egan (1992) argues the same case: "Tyler's work is based in Dewey but as been debased by those who have employed it for efficiency schemes" (p. 91). The debate over Tyler's Rationale is far from finished. Here may we suggest that the matter does point out that caution can be a casualty in the heat of argument and debate, particularly when that debate is over the nature of one's work and one's field. Graham (1992) understood this when he noted:

> It is clear that the kind of hornet's nest *currere* [Pinar's autobiographical theory which challenged the traditional field; see chapter 10] stirred up in the field involved more than an argument over the adequacy of the conceptual lenses one wore to examine curricular phenomena, but in fact addressed a series of sensitive issues that struck at the heart of professional reputations, at political and social ideologies, at aspirations for education, and indeed at permutations of all three. (p. 31)

Now that the Reconceptualization is a historical fact might be the time for that reflection and understanding which can bring healing to the wounds that were suffered twenty years ago.

X
Conclusion: A Reconceptualized Field

The future lies with the reconceptualists.
(William A. Reid, 1978, p. 97)

By the early 1980s, the movement to reconceptualize the curriculum field lost the cohesive bonds that maintained the coalition during its first years of struggle and enthusiasm. Opposition to the traditional field was no longer powerful enough a force for coalition, as the movement had succeeded in delegitimating the ahistorical, atheoretical field of the pre-1970 period. With the continued resistance of Marxist scholars to a multi-perspectival conception of reconceptualization and curriculum, with the emergence of autobiographical studies as a major force in the field, with the concurrent expansion of existential and phenomenological scholarship (Pinar & Reynolds, 1992a), with the burgeoning of feminist theory, and the appearance of poststructuralism in curriculum studies, the original reconceptualist movement can be said to have disappeared. Its success was its demise as a movement. The Reconceptualization had occurred.

As the American public schools moved to right during the 1970s, the Silberman report was forgotten. After a relatively brief moment of humanism, some educators turned to stage theories in child development (such as Piaget's) as curriculum theories, which, of course, they were not. In the aftermath of curriculum retrenchment of the back-to-basics movement, by the end of the decade mainstream psychological researchers turned once again to higher-order thinking. Early in the 1980s, with the election of Ronald Reagan, another conservative reaction chilled the schools. A series of national reports called for educational retrenchment by reducing the curricular prerogatives of the high schools and streamlining the school curriculum to so-called essential subjects or academic basics. Statewide minimum-competency testing mushroomed, and teachers responded to intensified public pressure by teaching-to-the-tests (Tanner & Tanner, 1990; for an analysis of competency-based education see Magnusson & Osborne, 1990). By 1980, however, the curriculum field had separated from the schools, and was traveling on its own, rather different, path.

From the vantage point of the early 1990s, it is clear that the American curriculum field was reconceptualized swiftly and rather completely. Replacing the nearly exclusive preoccupation with curriculum development and design were scholarly efforts to understand curriculum. These efforts can be characterized now by the framing of their interest to understand curriculum, i.e. understanding curriculum as political text, as phenomenological text, as autobiographical text, and the other major sectors of scholarship we report in the upcoming chapters 5-14. Finally, in chapter 15, we will speculate about what might comprise the next stage of paradigmatic evolution in the effort to understand curriculum. Next, however, we turn to a review of the major contemporary curriculum discourses. The most voluminous of these is also the one at most risk, and to this discourse we turn first: understanding curriculum as political text.

* * *

Note: The account of the Chicago and San Francisco ASCD conferences was written from notes taken in an interview with Paul Klohr on October 12, 13, and 14, 1992, at his home in Columbus, Ohio. Klohr had been a member of the ASCD Executive Committee in 1969 when Muriel Crosby served as President. Crosby served on the central office staff of the Wilmington, Delaware Public Schools and was a recognized authority on supervision. Alexander Frazier of Ohio State became President in 1970. Other members of the Executive Committee that year were: John Greene, Director of Instruction, Baton Rouge, Louisiana Schools; Joyce Cooper, University of Florida; Ronald C. Doll, Richmond College of the City University of New York; Alvin Loving, Sr., University of Michigan; and Glenys S. Unruh, Assistant to the Superintendent for Curriculum, School District of University City, Missouri. After this October interview, the *ASCD Update* published (January 1993) a similar account of the 1969 Chicago Conference.

SECTION III

CONTEMPORARY CURRICULUM DISCOURSES 1980-1994

Chapter 5

Understanding Curriculum
as Political Text

Curriculum . . . is the social product of contending forces.
(Michael W. Apple, 1988a, p. 201)

Developments in the curriculum do not occur in a vacuum.
(Daniel & Laurel Tanner, 1990, p. 20)

Schools mirror the surrounding society and many people want to be sure that they continue to do so.
(John I. Goodlad, 1984, p. 161)

I
Introduction:
Curriculum is Political

The systematic effort to understand curriculum as political text asserted itself in the curriculum field in the 1970's. In contrast to the earlier efforts of Counts and Rugg [see chapter 3], the political scholarship in the 1970s was avowedly Marxist and neo-Marxist in nature (Stanley, 1992b). While we will review the appearance of reproduction theory in the 1970s, we will focus on events since 1980. For details of prior and related developments in the 1930s, 1960s (for instance, the foundational work of Macdonald and Huebner), and the 1970s (including the disputes between politically-oriented and phenomenological/autobiographical scholars), see chapters 3 and 4. [See also William B. Stanley's (1992b) *Curriculum for Utopia: Reconstructionism and Critical Pedagogy in a Postmodern Era*, for an accessible and detailed summary of the linkages between 1930s reconstructionism and progressivism, and Marxist curriculum scholarship in the 1970s and 1980s. Developments in Britain also influenced American theorists, especially the work of Bernstein, 1977, Whitty & Young, 1976, and Willis, 1977, 1981; for other developments, see, for instance, Barton & Walker, 1981; Barton & Walker, 1984; Barton, Meighan & Walker, 1980.] In this chapter we focus upon selected developments during the past decade in that strand of curriculum research which has labored to understand curriculum as political text.

Curriculum is political. Termed variously as the new sociology of curriculum, radical or critical curriculum theory, politically oriented curriculum theory, this large body of work has swiftly become (during the past twenty years) the most voluminous body of scholarship in the curriculum field today. From a somewhat narrow thematic beginning, political theory has extended its range of interests far beyond commonsensical concepts of the political [see, for instance, the notion of child development reconstructed in light of political and feminist theory, Kaufman & Kaufman (1980)]. Despite its broad range, it is possible to summarize its contributions. Certainly, one of its contributions is an almost taken-for-granted view that curriculum can be understood in any comprehensive sense only if it is contextualized socially, economically, and politically (Carlson, 1992a). Put simply, curriculum cannot be grasped unless it is viewed in context: "the isolation of curriculum from its multiple, interacting contexts is an absurdity" (Cornbleth, 1988, p. 85).

Today no serious curriculum scholar would advance the argument that schools in general and curriculum in particular are politically neutral. Yet the political neutrality of school curriculum was a commonplace assumption in the pre-1970s literature. That the idea is largely discarded today represents one testimony to the influence of this body of curriculum scholarship. While there are many differences among political theorists, differences which have led to lively and sometimes contentious exchanges, it is possible to speak very generally about what they tend to share. Political theorists tend to view American society as rife with poverty, homelessness, racism, and political oppression. While they tend to blame these problems on the economic system, i.e. capitalism, they do regard the schools as participating in this general system of injustice and suffering. There is a visionary element among politicial theorists, as they tend to call for an empowered citizenry capable of altering their circumstances in favor of a more just society. The school in general, and the curriculum in particular, play important roles in both oppression and reform. First, we will turn to the role of curriculum in oppression, elaborated nearly twenty years ago as reproduction theory.

II
Reproduction Theory

The hidden curriculum deals with the tacit ways in which knowledge and behavior get constructed, outside the usual course materials and formally scheduled lessons. It is part of the bureaucratic and managerial "press" of the school—the combined forces by which students are induced to comply with the dominant ideologies and social practices related to authority, behavior and morality.

(Peter McLaren, 1994, p. 191)

Reproduction or correspondence theory. The first step in the effort to understand curriculum as political text involved the concept of reproduction or correspondence. In their widely read *Schools in Capitalist America*, Bowles and Gintis (1976) regarded schools as functioning in the stratum of superstructure, a stratum determined by society's economic base. Strike (1989, p. 26) portrays this relationship as follows:

Consciousness
Superstructure
Institutions

. . . .

Relations of production
Base
Material productive forces

Causality occurred unidirectionally, from base to superstructure. Elements in the base account for elements in the superstructure (Strike, 1989, p. 26). In classic Marxian terms, the base determines the superstructure. Congruent with this model, Bowles and Gintis argued that schools prepare students to enter the current economic system via a correspondence between school structure and the structure of production. They wrote:

> The structure of social relations in education not only inures the student to the discipline of the workplace, but develops the types of personal demeanor, modes of self-presentation, self-image, and social class identifications which are the crucial ingredients of job adequacy. Specifically, the social relationships of education—the relationships between administrators and teachers, teachers and students, and students and students, and students and their work—replicate the hierarchical divisions of labor. Hierarchical relations are reflected in the vertical authority lines from administrators to teachers to students. Alienated labor is reflected in the student's lack of control over his or her education, the alienation of the student from the curriculum content, and the motivation of school work through a system of grades and other external rewards rather than the student's integration with the process (learning) or the outcome (knowledge) of the educational "production process." (Bowles & Gintis, 1976, p. 131)

Relying on this principle of correspondence, Apple (1979a, 1979b, 1979c) and Giroux (1981a, 1981b, 1981c) argued that schools functioned to reproduce the class structure of the workplace (Liston, 1986). While originating outside the curriculum field (as was typical during this early phase of reconceptualization), the principle of correspondence was an important first step in understanding curriculum as political text.

Ideology. A second concept imported from other fields aided politically oriented curriculum scholars to advance their argument (Shapiro, 1982a). Louis Althusser's (1971) understanding of ideology provided another major concept in curriculum scholarship. McLaren (1989) explained:

> Simply put ideology refers to the production of meaning. It can be described as a way of viewing the world, a complex of ideas, various types of social practices, rituals and representations that we tend to accept as natural and as common sense. It is the result of the intersection of meaning and power in the social world. Customs, rituals, beliefs and values often produce within individuals distorted conceptions of their place in the sociocultural order and thereby serve to reconcile them to that place and to disguise the inequitable relations of power and privilege; this is sometimes referred to as "ideological hegemony." (p. 176)

Other scholars have emphasized the phenomenological character of ideology. For instance, Kickbusch and Everhart (1985) insisted:

> ideology is not only theoretical or abstract, as in an idea or patterns existing outside of the individual. Rather, it is "lived," in that an ideology is also a set of representations and actions which, together with ideas, constitute the standards influencing concrete social relationships among people and a material world. (p. 283)

Only a critical stance offers, it was argued, any hope of undermining the reproductive force of ideology. The absence of a critical stance fosters "the illusion among the unprivileged that choice and openness are the same as social power" (Kickbush, 1986, pp. 138-139).

A system of representations. Ideology has been regarded as the first key concept in the movement to understand curriculum as political text. Rejecting what some characterized as more "vulgar" interpretations of the base/superstructure relationships in Marxian theory, Althusser argued that the relation of the economic base to the institutions of society cannot be reduced to any linear cause/effect determinism (Giroux, 1983a, p. 79). Institutions are termed "ideological state apparatuses" by Althusser (1971), who claimed that institutions functioned to subjugate the working class. Giroux (1983a) interpreted the Althusserian conception of ideology for curricularists:

> First, it [ideology] has a material existence: rituals, practices, and social processes that structure the day-to-day workings of schools. . . . Second, ideology neither produces consciousness nor a willing passive compliance. Instead it functions as a system of representations, carrying meanings and ideas that structure the unconscious of students. (p. 81)

The concept of ideology became central in understanding curriculum as political text, with curriculum itself conceptualized as an ideological mystification. Both Apple and Giroux described how both the content and form of the curriculum were ideological in nature (Apple, 1990a; Giroux, 1981c). Generally, the ideas and culture associated with the dominant class were argued to be the ideas and content of schooling. Dominant culture was described as those "social practices and representations that affirm the central values, interests, and concerns of the social class in control of the material and symbolic wealth of society" (McLaren, 1989, p. 172). Ideology, like reproduction theory and other major concepts in the effort to understand curriculum as political text, would soon be reconsidered by political theorists themselves:

> The point that educators forget at their peril is that ideologies both constrain and enable the project of empowerment. To claim that ideologies merely distort and falsify consciousness can only continue to cause the categories of critique, struggle, and transformative practice to further dissolve under the overbearing weight of a Marxism that lacks a programmatic discourse of hope. (McLaren, 1989, p. 179)

Reproduction contradicted. By the early 1980s the largely economic version of reproduction (correspondence) was criticized by many of those same scholars who had embraced it in the 1970s. Now reproduction theory was characterized as deterministic and simplistic (Giroux, quoted in Olson, 1981), as lacking a cultural analysis (Apple, 1979a, 1979b, 1980), as lacking an adequate theory of agency (Strike, 1989), and as basically mechanistic (Giroux, 1983a). In an essay entitled "Contradiction and Reproduction in Educational Theory," Bowles and Gintis themselves criticized their earlier work (Bowles & Gintis in Barton, Meighan & Walker, 1980):

> The most critical [problem] is simply this: by standing in our approach as the *only* structural link between education and the economy and by its character as an inherently *harmonious* link between the two, the correspondence principle forced us to adopt a narrow and inadequate appreciation of the *contradictions* involved in the articulation of the educational system within the social totality. (Bowles & Gintis, 1980, p. 53)

Bowles and Gintis acknowledged that their earlier argument missed certain essential aspects of reproduction. They will not be the only Marxist scholars to engage in self-criticism, as we shall see.

Four types of social practice. Bowles and Gintis theorized four types of social practice. First is the appropriative, the goal of which is the creation of useful projects. The second was the political, the goal of which is the transformation of social relations. Third was termed the cultural, which is said to transform the tools of discourse. Fourth was the distributive, which alters the distribution of power and income (Bowles & Gintis, 1980; see also Liston, 1988). Sites and practices "add up" to what Bowles and Gintis term a "contradictory totality" (Bowles & Gintis, 1980, p. 56). This mixing of sites and practices was said to produce two dynamic tendencies with distinct consequences: reproductive and "contradictory" (and undermining) effects (Liston, 1988, p. 54). Bowles and Gintis acknowledged that their earlier work (1976) failed to account for this fundamentally contradictory character of social relations. Schools were said to exhibit these contradictory tendencies. Suddenly, with this theoretical movement, the stage was set for "resistance theory." Before describing resistance theory, however, let us continue with our review of the major concepts associated with the reproduction phase of political curriculum theory.

The Frankfurt School. Earlier, in reporting the notion of ideology, we saw the use of the word "critical" as essential in undermining the reproduction of ideology. This word can be traced to critical theory, a stream of Marxian scholarship and theory associated with the Frankfurt School. More than Michael Apple, Philip Wexler was influenced by the Frankfurt School, which pointed to the sphere of culture, and not just to material production or to the economy, to theorize the nature of society. Wexler noted that: "The Frankfurt School analysis of culture was also used to establish the view of education as a site for reproduction" (Wexler, 1987, p. 40).

Among those associated with the Frankfurt School are Theodor Adorno, Walter Benjamin, Jurgen Habermas, Max Horkheimer, and Herbert Marcuse, all of whom were cited by politically oriented curriculum scholars, especially by Giroux and Wexler. What was the intent of the Frankfurt School? The hope of those associated with the Frankfurt School was to help establish a critical social consciousness able to penetrate existing ideology, support independent judgment and be capable, as Adorno put it, of maintaining the freedom to envision alternatives (Held, 1980). The Frankfurt School's interest in social consciousness provided a conceptual "seed" for the move away from mechanistic reproduction to resistance in the 1980s. Giroux (1983a) regarded the Frankfurt School as fundamental to understanding curriculum as political text:

> I argued that the foundation for a radical theory of schooling can, in part, be developed from the work of the Frankfurt School and the more recent literature on the hidden curriculum. Whereas the Frankfurt School provides a discourse and mode of critique for deepening our understanding of the nature and the function of schooling, critiques of the hidden curriculum have provided modes of analysis that uncover the ideologies and interests embedded in the message systems, codes and routines that characterize daily classroom life. (p. 72)

While Giroux would emphasize the usefulness of the Frankfurt school in providing a means of critique, Wexler would focus more upon the School's theorization of culture and history. This difference in emphasis would lead Wexler to criticize (with then Ph.D. student Tony Whitson, 1982) Apple's and Giroux's use of major concepts such as ideology and hegemony, and then to issue a sharp and more definitive denunciation of Giroux and Apple some ten years later (Wexler, 1987). Given Wexler's importance, we will review his work in more detail in this chapter and in chapter 13.

The hidden curriculum. The hidden curriculum was another important conceptual tool for politically oriented curriculum scholars in the 1970s, first popularized by Philip Jackson (1968, 1970) and recently reformulated as "curricular substructure," also by Jackson in the 1990s (Jackson, Boostrom & Hansen, 1993, p. 14 ff.). The concept refers to those unintended but quite real outcomes and features of the schooling process (Dreeben, 1976; Apple, 1975a, 1990a; Giroux, 1983c; McLaren, 1989). The "hidden curriculum" is distinguished from the "overt" curriculum, or the planned curriculum, including objectives. McLaren (1989) defined the concept in this way:

> The hidden curriculum deals with the tacit ways in which knowledge and behavior get constructed, outside the usual course materials and formally scheduled lessons. It is part of the bureaucratic and managerial "press" of the school—the combined forces by which students are induced to comply with the dominant ideologies and social practices related to authority, behavior and morality. (pp. 183-184)

Michael W. Apple, as we have seen [in chapter 4] among the first to assert curriculum as political text in the 1970s, defined the hidden curriculum in a way which pointed to the concept of hegemony, another important notion for politically oriented curriculum scholars.

> The hidden curriculum in schools serves to reinforce basic rules surrounding the nature of conflict and its uses. It posits a network of assumptions that, when internalized by students, establishes the boundaries of legitimacy. This process is accomplished not so much by explicit instances showing the negative value of conflict, but by nearly the total absence of instances showing the importance of intellectual and normative conflict in subject areas. The fact is that these assumptions are obligatory for the students, since at no time are the assumptions articulated or questioned. (Apple, 1975a, p. 99)

The silence and marginalization of ideas and voices both in the academic disciplines and in society would become significant ideas in both political and feminist theory a decade later.

Curriculum reproduces social stratification. The concept of the hidden curriculum became taken-for-granted curriculum knowledge, widely cited by those who insisted that the curriculum preserved social stratification, as well as other stratifications, especially those of class, race, and gender (Apple, 1982b, 1990a; Aronowitz & Giroux, 1985; Beyer & Apple, 1988; Giroux, 1981a, 1983a, 1988b; Giroux & Purpel, 1983; Giroux, Penna & Pinar, 1981; Oakes, 1985; Shapiro, 1981, 1983a; Sharp, 1980; Shor, 1986; Weis, 1988). The scholarship on the hidden curriculum inspired a range of studies, including investigations of school programs found to function in ways not always evident.

Illustrative of this research was a study by Robert V. Bullough, Jr., Stanley L. Goldstein, and Ladd Holt (1984) who found technical rationality or "technomindedness" embedded in five different programs: 1) GEMS or Goals-Based Educational Management System, a behaviorally oriented program for assuring competence in basic skills, 2) Individually Guided Education (IGE), a similar approach to curriculum design with a focus on prescription of individual objectives for each student, 3) Art Is Elementary (AIE), an arts program designed to provide activities and skill development in a number of the arts, 4) Experience Based Career Education (EBCE), an alternative-school approach intended to give students practice in "real-world" jobs as part of their educational programs, and 5) the Democratic School Project, an effort to define and realize democratic principles in an urban high school. Their analysis followed from their earlier examination of teachers' work to establish a curriculum management system (NEMS) (Bullough, Goldstein, & Holt, 1982). Despite the apparent diversity of these programs, upon closer scrutiny, all were found to have hidden within them modes of technical rationality, one mode of the dominant ideology. [See Olson, 1989b, for a non-political commentary on technical rationality.] Even apparently progressive programs were found to reproduce the dominant ideology.

Another study linked to the assumption of a hidden curriculum is Gaskell's (1986) case study of vocational teaching in one high school. Gaskell explored the ways teachers actively reproduced the social relations of the workplace in their classrooms, even as they presumably searched for "new curriculum ideas that will better meet the changing requirements of the labor market and the school" (p. 417). By examining the ways teachers explained their approach to their subject matter, she studied how reproduction of class and gender relations occurred through vocational schooling. Gaskell (1986) also attempted to account for what seemed a widespread curriculum change (in vocational areas) away from the traditional business skills toward a "life skills" emphasis (p. 419), an effort to make students employable, i.e. more acceptable to potential employers. Everywhere researchers looked, it seemed, schools were busily reproducing the status quo, even when they claimed to change it.

Hegemony. A major concept employed in understanding curriculum as political text was hegemony (Apple, 1979c), borrowed from the Italian Marxist Antonio Gramsci (1971), who borrowed the term from Marx and Engels (1974). Gramsci emphasized "the role of the superstructure in perpetuating class divisions and preventing the development of class consciousness" (Carnoy, quoted in Apple, 1982a, p. 86). Gramsci employed hegemony in two senses: first, hegemony referred to a process of domination whereby the ruling class is said to exercise political control through its intellectual and moral leadership over allied classes (Gramsci, 1975). [This is the sense in which Marx and Engels employed the term.] Second, hegemony referred as well to the use of force and ideology in the reproduction of class relations (Aronowitz & Giroux, 1985, p. 88). Thus hegemony is understood to occur via the use of force and via the shaping of human consciousness.

Philip Wexler and Tony Whitson (1982) criticized the prevailing use of hegemony in political scholarship. They contended that:

> the concept of hegemony has been distorted. . . . When radical pedagogy fails to produce its intended outcomes, and when that failure cannot be attributed to a neglect of ideology or to the repressive use of force, then "hegemony" is invoked as a residual explanatory variable, a sort of "dummy coefficient" standing for the "totality of lived relations" which results in ruling class domination. (Wexler & Whitson, 1982, p. 31)

Quoting Chantal Moufé's definition of hegemony as "the ability of one class to articulate the interests of other social groups to its own," Wexler and Whitson (1982) argued that hegemony is not "a separate weapons system in a capitalist arsenal, deployed alongside and in addition to ideology, culture and coercive power. Hegemony is a situation or outcome, achieved through ideological (as well as coercive) practices. . . . Hegemony is not an 'element' of ideology" (p. 32). They continued that:

> The concept of hegemony that is used by the radical educationists (Apple, 1979b; Sharp, 1980; Giroux, 1981a) points either toward the exclusion of the

culture of dominated groups from the schools, or to the depth and intensity of the transmission of class cultures as school knowledge, or even to how dominant ideologies are imposed. But questions of the development of an oppositional alternative, analysis of methods of incorporative accommodation, and the fundamental issue of the totalizing articulation of classes and social practices, are all reduced to a new dichotomy: "reproduction/resistance." In the past, the bourgeois antinomy individual/society worked to preclude an analysis in terms of social relations. The same type of dichotomous reification is now reasserted in the language of Marxism. . . . One cannot imagine a classroom where the teacher attempted to practice Cherryholmes's (1980) curriculum of "critical discourse". . . . It must occur in the context of compulsory school attendance—a counterfeit of the social relations of non-dominated discourse. Where coercion is so fundamental to the situation, any pretended denial of that social reality can only be an exercise in ideological self-delusion, a double-think redefinition of terms, by which coercion is rationalized and its incompatibility with the interactional norms of symmetry and non-domination goes unnoticed. It becomes an unintended training in the separation of the ideal from the actual. In this way, the present is maintained. (p. 39)

Wexler and Whitson (1982) concluded: "What we have attempted here should not be read as an appendix to the current litanies of political pessimism. . . . For a counter-hegemony is not simply opposition, either at the level of cultural intent or social organizational infrastructure. A counter-hegemony means the reorganization of all these elements around the new cultural vision of a genuinely different way of life" (p. 41). The articulation of that "cultural vision" would await the publication of Wexler's important *Social Analysis of Education* (1987).

Despite Wexler and Whitson's cogent criticisms, mainstream political scholars continued to employ hegemony as they had, to refine the basic "base/superstructure" model of reproduction that had been accepted during the 1970's. Relying on Raymond Williams (1976), Apple declared that the concept of hegemony captures the complexity of processes of "saturation." In particular, Apple drew upon Williams' concept of "selective tradition" to point to the ways in which curriculum functions to privilege certain sets and orders of knowledge over others (Williams, quoted in Apple, 1990a). Other politically oriented scholars relied on this concept in their analysis of cultural reproduction (Dale, 1976; Apple, 1982b, 1986, 1990a; Giroux, 1980a, 1980b, 1981a, 1981b, 1983a, 1988b; McLaren, 1989; Sharp, 1980).

Deskilling and teacher autonomy. How did teachers participate in cultural reproduction? The answer appeared to reside in the issue of teacher autonomy. Michael W. Apple and Kenneth Teitelbaum (1986) asked: "Are teachers losing control of their skills and curriculum?" They seemed to answer yes, focusing on what they saw as a progressive separation of conception from execution in the history of teaching in the United States. Relatedly, Goodman (1988) declared that accountability and pre-packaged curricula disenfranchised teachers from their own occupation. However, Martin Lawn (1987) argued, the issue of teacher autonomy is not a simple one. Apparent independence may be only an indirect form of social control. He believed that teacher unrest in Great Britain and the need to alter the nature of control in education produced an administrative and political solution which reproduced the structure of colonial government by "indirect rule." From Lawn's perspective, this reproduction of colonial rule enabled "the Board of Education to continue operating the education system inexpensively and efficiently, from its points of view, but with a lighter hand, yet retaining its options for direct control" (p. 228). Regardless the subject of investigation, political theorists saw the reproduction of the status quo, despite apparent efforts to make change. [The focus upon deskilling would change to reskilling by the early 1990s; see Kanpol, 1993.] Teachers were, it seemed, unwitting victims in a hegemonic process that appeared overwhelming.

Reproduction: A discourse of despair? By the late 1970s, Henry Giroux and other political scholars came to worry that an overreliance upon the concept of reproduction risked a "discourse of despair." If reproduction occurred as incontestably as Bowles and Gintis and many critical curriculum scholars of the 1970s insisted that it did, there was little hope for significant change, aside from alterations in the economic base, i.e. socialism. The concept of ideology portrayed teachers and students as accomplices in the reproduction of the ruling class. Hegemony seemed to suggest that no escape was possible, as consciousness itself was saturated, "forged into the cognitive chains which bind the minds of the working class" (Strike, 1989, p. 137). The work of those politically engaged scholars who linked social action to consciousness, imagination, and the human will was overlooked (Littleford, 1979, 1980, 1982, 1983; Whitt, 1981). Absent such links and any theory of cultural change (Wexler, 1982a, 1982b, 1988a), it appeared that reproduction theory lacked a concept of agency. Soon it would be repudiated. In the early 1980s, reproduction theory gave way to resistance theory.

III
From Reproduction to Resistance

One of the major tasks of the curriculum field is to demonstrate in consistent fashion the process of self-criticism and self-renewal.
(Henry A. Giroux, 1980c, p. 27)

In his widely read *Learning to Labor*, Paul Willis (1981) introduced the concept of resistance to an eager audience now disenchanted with reproduction theory. Willis observed that the working class boys he studied resisted both the official and hidden curriculum of their English secondary school. The roots of this resistance, he wrote, "are in the shop-floor cultures occupied by their family members and other members of their class" (Giroux, 1983b, p. 283). Willis' concept of resistance allowed political theorists to view the process of reproduction as contestable, thereby correcting the non-dialecticism of the Bowles and Gintis 1976 thesis which they had embraced so uncritically.

The early 1980s saw considerable discussion of resistance theory. Particularly during the period 1980-1984 several scholars discussed and developed resistance theory [for example, see Anyon, 1979, 1988; Apple in Olson, 1981; Apple 1982a, 1982b; Apple & Weis, 1983; Giroux, 1981a, 1983a, 1983b]. Henry Giroux cited resistance theory as important insofar as it corrected the failure of both conservative and radical curriculum theory. Conservatives, he alleged, tended to view oppositional behavior via psychological categories such as deviate, disruptive, and inferior. Radical theorists had overemphasized economic and cultural determinants. Put differently, in radical curriculum theory was an "underemphasis on how human agency accommodates, mediates and resists the logic of capital and its dominating social practices" (Giroux, 1983b, p. 282). Giroux characterized the reproduction theory of the 1970s as a "discourse of despair."

In his introduction to Giroux's *Ideology, Culture and the Process of Schooling* (1981a), Stanley Aronowitz advocated resistance as a positive step for radical educators. Radical educators, he argued, should concentrate on the "cracks and disjunctions created by oppositional forces" (in Giroux, 1981a, p. 31). Doing so would permit the contestation of power in the schools. Giroux asserted that struggles could be waged over administrative and curricular issues. Reproduction failed to inspire struggle; it was, in Giroux's words, a "myth of total domination" (Giroux, 1981a, p. 99). As we have observed, political scholars would prove to be resourceful when their current theories appeared to collapse from within; they would denounce theories they had once held, and greet with enthusiasm the arrival of new, superior ones. The 1980s model would be resistance theory, and it would be announced at a dramatic conference in Toronto, Ontario, Canada.

The Conference at the Ontario Institute for Studies in Education. A special issue of *Interchange*, edited by Paul Olson and published in 1981, illustrated the rapid shift from reproduction to resistance theory. A collection of papers from the conference held at the Ontario Institute for Studies in Education in Toronto, the issue was entitled "Rethinking Social Reproduction." In his introduction, Olson noted that "social constructivists" wished now to integrate knowledge of hegemony with strategies designed to counter it (Olson, 1981). In his essay entitled "Reproduction, Contestation, and Curriculum: An Essay in Self-Criticism," Michael Apple noted that his previous work lacked analysis which "focused on contradictions, conflicts, mediations and especially resistance—as well as reproduction" (Apple, quoted in Olson, 1981, p. 35). He cautioned his audience, however, that it is not enough to conduct research into resistance; one must actually resist, in practice.

In Giroux's "Hegemony, Resistance, and the Paradox of Educational Reform," the outline of his scholarly agenda for the decade was evident. Discussing the assets and liabilities of reproduction theory, he praised resistance theories, which "perform a theoretical service" (Giroux, quoted in Olson, 1981, p. 13). These theories demanded analyses of those social practices which constitute the class-based experiences of day-to-day existence in schools. He called for the development of a notion of radical pedagogy based on the pioneering work of Paulo Freire (1971). "At the core of radical pedagogy," Giroux insisted, "must be the aim of empowering people to work for change in the social, political, and economic structure that constitutes the ultimate source of class-based power and domination (Giroux, quoted in Olson, 1981, p. 24). [Curiously, the concept of empowerment—in 1981 used by relatively few radical curriculum theorists—would become an educational cliché by the 1990s.] For Giroux, however, resistance theory would turn out to be a transitional concept to the notion with which he is associated today: critical pedagogy.

Toward a focus on race, class and gender. In 1982 Michael Apple published two works examining issues of reproduction and resistance. In his introduction to *Cultural and Economic Reproduction in Education,* Apple distinguished between two forms of reproduction theory, that which focused on economic or macrostructural issues and that which concentrated on cultural or microstructural matters. According to Apple, the school curriculum belongs to the latter category. Again acknowledging difficulties with "pure" reproduction theory, Apple suggested that resistance and reproduction theory are intertwined, that studies inspired by this synthetical view would point to struggles in specific places. He alluded to issues of race, class, and gender, foreshadowing his own scholarly agenda for the decade. In a second essay entitled "Curricular Form and the Logic of Technical Control," Apple outlined the pervasiveness of resistance. He alluded to developments such as poststructuralism, which in this essay he depicted favorably, an attitude that would change later. Concluding the essay was a discussion of curricular sites of resistance. Despite increasing state control, Apple declared, there are moments of individual resistance. Teachers' resistance was said to be never "far from the surface" (Apple, 1982b, p. 269).

The question became: what is the status of these resistances? Were they in fact counter-hegemonic? Or did they function to reproduce the status quo? Willis noted, for instance, that the resistance of his "lads" functioned reproductively: their resistance to mental labor functioned to reproduce their entrapment in the working class. In another 1982 work, Apple continued his examination of resistance theory and in particular the possible reproductive consequences of resistance. Apple worried that even the terrain of resistance could be viewed as determined by the interests of capital, not by those resisting (Apple, 1982b). Despite resistance, Apple concluded, reproduction proceeds. In fact, he continued, reproduction will continue "as long as the penetrations into the nature of work and control generated by working-class youths and their parents are unorganized and unpoliticized" (Apple, 1982a, p. 108). Only two years after its introduction, then, resistance itself seemed in danger of being swallowed by reproduction. Apple (1992a) would eventually retreat to versions of 1970s reproduction theory.

Taking human agency seriously. Two noteworthy efforts to understand the curriculum as political text appeared in 1983: Henry A. Giroux's *Theory and*

Resistance in Education: A Pedagogy for the Opposition and Michael W. Apple and Lois Weis' *Ideology and Practice in Schooling.* In both books one can still discern some movement away from reproduction theory. For Giroux resistance pointed to possibilities of oppositional pedagogy (1983a). He called for a reformulation of the relations among ideology, culture, and hegemony, one which would "make clear the ways in which these categories can enhance our understanding of resistance as well as how such concepts can form the theoretical basis for a radical pedagogy that takes human agency seriously" (Giroux, 1983a, p. 111). Apple and Weis also discussed the movement beyond simple reproduction theory, stating that "hegemony is not and cannot be fully secure" (Apple & Weis, 1983, p. 28). Their view that the cultural sphere was relatively autonomous led them to move beyond resistance to a belief in the possibility of meaningful intervention in the schools. However, they cautioned that this action must be a kind of praxis and that the connections between the schools and the larger society must be made.

The focus on agency and the political action it implied raised hopes. Hopes turned quickly to frustration, as the gap between the conservative, Reagan America of the early 1980s and radical rhetoric of political curriculum theory seemed large indeed. Worrying that political theory was rhetorical only, George Wood (1983) observed "that while Giroux and his colleagues have made great strides towards once again politicizing schools, there is still additional work to be done if educators are to be involved in building a new social order" (p. 56). Wood continued: "Giroux's work while important and useful is, by design, incomplete. . . . Primary among shortcomings of resistance theory is its translatability. . . . How does this work translate to practicing teachers?" (p. 69). He concluded: "Giroux and others have made an important contribution. . . . What is now necessary is to move beyond interpretation to change" (p. 71).

For Wood one form of such change was his establishment of the Institute for Democracy in Education at Ohio University in Athens. The work of the Institute included summer institutes at which "action-guides" were put into practice, resulting in, for example, the elimination of ability-grouping in a middle school. Other illustrations included high school students' involvement in community action projects such as fasts for African famine, and the utilization of alternative sources in American and world history classes. Additionally, a project employing Appalachian culture and cultural history as subject matter in English and social studies was proposed (Wood, 1986, 1988a). A few years later, Wood resigned his full-time faculty position [he remains part-time, 1993] at Ohio University to work directly in the schools.

Research is political. The rhetoric of political action entered the discourse on research. Patti Lather (1986a, 1986b) argued for the involvement of the subjects of research "in a democratized process of inquiry characterized by negotiation, reciprocity, empowerment—research as praxis" (p. 257). Lather expressed concern regarding the possibility of a new orthodoxy in political curriculum studies, a concern others would share (Pinar & Bowers, 1992).

She cautioned: "Rather than establishing a new orthodoxy, we need to experiment, document, and share our efforts toward emancipatory research"
(1986a, p. 272).

Lather's was the most visible scholarship linking politics and research, but
it was hardly alone. For instance, Andrew David Gitlin (1990; Gitlin, Siegel, &
Boru, 1988) argued on behalf of "educative research," a dialogical approach
to research that attempted to develop voice as a form of political protest.
[Voice has been an important feminist and autobiographical concept; see
chapters 7 and 10.] Relying on the teachers' writing in his research, Gitlin
(1990) described how the use of personal and school histories, along with a
peer evaluation model, supported a question-posing process that could lead
to the development of teachers' voices. Gitlin's work has been criticized by
Patti Lather [see chapter 9].

Worrying that too much political research was excessively theoretical, Jesse
Goodman (1991a) called for political writing that was less abstract and
rhetorical:

> In calling for more detailed illustrations of people working in classrooms and
> schools as a basis for analytical and theoretical discourse, it is not being
> suggested that curriculum theorists provide "cookbook" descriptions of "how it
> should be done". . . . [Readers of classroom-focused research would] apply what
> is vicariously experienced to one's own particular situation and limitations. (pp.
> 69-70).

Here Goodman is worrying that in political theorists' rejection of "technical
rationality" (including the specification of teacher behavior by objectives)
they had failed to provide any concrete help to teachers at all.

Cornbleth (1991) complained that typical political scholarship studies
curriculum in relation to sociocultural dynamics such as economic and
gender elements, but overlooks the more immediate setting. Against reproduction theory, she insisted that contextual elements were multidimensional,
fluid, and intersecting. Further, she complained that the concept of "hidden
curriculum" labeled more than explained. Forego that concept, she advised,
and examine directly a) the constraints and opportunities as well as the seemingly contradictory messages that are communicated by curriculum practice
and the school milieu, and b) how these are mediated by students. Political
research must, she concluded, emphasize the relational nature of social reality. There must be sufficient attention paid to curriculum practice
(Cornbleth, 1991).

Critical pedagogy in an elementary school. A number of political scholars
accepted the challenge issued by Lather, Gitlin, and Cornbleth that political
research be classroom focused and itself democratic. One major study that
exemplified these ideals was conducted by Jesse Goodman (1992), who studied an alternative school in Bloomington, Indiana—the Harmony School—
which seemed to institutionalize many aspects of a critical pedagogy. [For an

early description of this school, see Baron (1979)]. Goodman (1992) was careful to avoid the abstract discourse of many critical theorists; his writing is accessible, consistent, and, for many, convincing.

Goodman begins by noting that the ideology of bourgeois individualism —which asks us to be self-sufficient, industrious, and materialistic—reveals itself to be isolating and conforming. Reviewing the early writings on democracy and individuality/community in the United States, Goodman (1992) argued that individualism is a construction of the power elites and that "elementary schools play an important role in supporting and promoting individualism within the United States" (p. 22). He notes that the ideals of Dewey in building a critically democratic, participatory society have either been misinterpreted or ignored, although they continue to live, Goodman suggests, in more contemporary theorists like Freire, and in progressive curriculum theorists working today. In Goodman's view, interdependence should be emphasized, though not imposed: "While recognizing the need to deliberately promote a moral agenda that accentuates community values in our society, we must also hold children's individuality, self-confidence and participation in their own education in high esteem" (1992, p. 29). Goodman understands that the researcher, himself, by assuming a seemingly neutral posture, expresses an implicitly political posture. Goodman attempts, instead, to "develop a methodology in which the observer is located directly within a socio-political context and is self-reflexive about his or her situatedness within such a context" (Giroux & McLaren in Goodman, 1992, p. xiii).

Goodman and his graduate students attempted to circulate among Harmony's students and faculty, taking notes, etc. while being explicit about the purpose of their research and the kinds of practices for which they were watching. Goodman refused, however, to locate himself within any single characterization and declared that "the theories themselves are better off referred to in the plural (feminisms, phenomenologies, Marxisms, postmodernisms)" (p. 43). He proposes instead to become aware of the "modes of thinking" found in educational perspectives, myths, and rituals. He tells a thoroughly documented story of the year spent at Harmony, the people and the situations encountered, and the methods of response and guidance used by administrators and teachers. Overall, the hierarchical structure he found there was more like an inverted pyramid than the usual top-down one. Rules, power, and philosophical assumptions were not assumed and seemed always open to negotiation, including with students. There were differences among those in the school, and while the negotiations may have become time-consuming, an acceptance of difference and a readiness to deal with each situation on its own terms avoided the dehumanization of bureaucracies: "Bureaucracies are formed on the premise that organizations should be governed by an elaborate and formal system of written regulations" (p. 73) Bureaucracies evolve, Goodman reminds us, into impersonal control systems which may be "personal", "bureaucratic", or "technical" (p. 77). Harmony attempts instead to develop a "society of intimates" among the staff and students. The power structure is always open to negotiation. In fact, it is in this negotiation itself that the medium becomes the message: "Perhaps the most important strategy used to develop this power structure within Harmony was an emphasis on the social bonds among the students and between students, teachers, and administrators." This social bonding was fostered through several different means: "establishing a collective identity among the children, teaching students the value of collective responsibility, and consciously reducing the stratification between teachers and students" (p. 95).

Goodman's examples take the form of vignettes of conflict and coopera- tion, or tales from Harmony. Not all tales end satisfactorily of course, but the process always seemed revelatory. Goodman and his team's recording of these incidents seemed to have become part of the tale in that they "provided these individuals with a lens through which they could see themselves, become aware of new ideas, or recognize concepts that they were intuitively acting upon but that lacked clear articulation" (p.179.) One of his suggestions for the future is a greater collaboration of critical scholars in education and the teachers in the school. This interaction would become part of the curriculum. This aspect of Goodman's work points to his differences with Apple and Giroux, both of whose work he had criticized as excessively abstract, too far removed from the everyday life of schools.

The Harmony curriculum, though giving the students much more freedom than most public schools, also gave them more responsibility. In this, the school remains teacher-centered, as Goodman explains. Public schools are not really teacher-centered at all, but system-centered. Inter- actionist teachers are necessary, he felt:

> Because of the strong individualistic messages children in our culture receive, it is important, whenever the opportunity arises, that children be asked to consider a connectionist rationale for learning and going to school. This ratio- nale emphasizes the view that children need to learn to achieve not just some individual goal but a form of social responsibility. Children need to be exposed to the view that the reason for learning is to nurture their intellectual talents for constructing our society into a more democratic, just, and caring place to live. Students need to hear that democratic societies cannot grow and develop (let alone survive) unless their citizens are well informed and have the educa- tional abilities and sensitivities needed to critically examine the world in which we live. Students need to be repeatedly asked to consider the viewpoint that their learning is not just for their own benefit, but for the democratic well- being of our society (and the world) as a whole. (p. 126)

Goodman closes his study of the Harmony School with several observa- tions and suggestions. Although he acknowledges the necessity of developing a discourse separate from the mechanical metaphors of the superstructure, he warns once again that the language of critique has often become so abstract that its impact is greatly limited: "Whether it is found in sociology, literary, or educational discourse, the intellectual elitism that is embedded in much of this language of critique significantly undermines its own liberatory intentions" (p. 167). As an alternative, he proposes what he terms "an educational language of democratic imagery." [Goodman's position is not unlike Thomas Barone's (1993a, 1993b) notion of critical storytelling; see chapter 11.]

Concluding, Goodman notes that, although the school sought diversity and though there were many individual differences within Harmony, to an outsider the school population may have seemed somewhat homogeneous. This may have helped the growth of the school's essence, what Goodman called "a subtle, delicate, and loving spirituality. . . . The key to what makes Harmony a meaningful democratic alternative is the spiritual nature of its enterprise" (p. 178). Lastly, he suggests that the way to overcome the pessimism of the times is for such schools themselves to be liberated from their isolation. Such contemporary progressive schools could contact each other forming networks. Another alliance could be with university theorists, but Goodman avoids any patronizing words:

> Although we do not want to suggest that the theory making that these teachers were clearly engaged in is inferior to the scholarly theorizing that occurs in colleges and universities, there is valuable substance in this scholarship. For instance, given the values of caring and social responsibility that guide the experiences inside of Harmony's walls, it seems to us that the recent scholarship in feminist pedagogy might be particularly useful. (p. 179)

Goodman's study models what it calls for: an accessibly written story filled with democratic imagery. It also points to a diversification in scholarship the political sector, but before we describe these discursive shifts let us conclude our review of the resistance phase of political theory.

Beyond resistance. The concept of resistance would continue to appear in political analyses of curriculum, but after 1985 it became a point of departure rather than arrival. For instance, Geoff Whitty called for a movement away from reproduction theory and academic critique generally to radical intervention. He warned against romanticizing the resistances of the working class, even those which are not reproductive. What was important, he argued, is the elaboration of intervention strategies:

> What the American worker increasingly recognizes is that whether or not particular aspects of education are ultimately reproductive or transformative in their effects is essentially a political question concerning how they are to be worked upon pedagogically and politically, and how they become articulated with other struggles in and beyond the school. (Whitty, 1985, p. 90)

This is a theme Apple's work would repeat throughout the decade, despite its quixotic character in a nation which overwhelmingly re-elected Ronald Reagan President in 1984. Perhaps it is unsurprising, then, that while acknowledging the importance of struggles in the larger society, the focus of political scholars narrowed further during the second half of the 1980s to aspects of institutional practice. This smaller sphere would also escape their influence, as the schools became locked more tightly in a grid comprised of increasing political, economic, and bureaucratic pressures.

IV
Pedagogy and Practice: Issues of Class, Race, and Gender

[Critical scholars] need to be closely connected to feminist groups, people of color, unions, and to those teachers and curriculum workers who are now struggling so hard in very difficult circumstances to defend from rightist attacks the gains that have been made in democratizing education and to make certain that our schools and the curricular and teaching practices within them are responsive in race, gender and class terms. (Michael W. Apple, 1986, p. 204)

Transformative intellectuals. By 1985 scholarly efforts to understand curriculum politically began to turn away from reproduction and resistance theories to issues of political and pedagogical practice. This shift away from resistance theory was evident, for example, in the work of Henry A. Giroux, which, beginning in 1985, moved to questions of literacy, the liberal arts, and transformative or critical pedagogy (Giroux, 1988d). In his 1985 co-authored (with Stanley Aronowitz the first author) *Education Under Siege* [and reissued in 1993 as *Education Still Under Siege*], Giroux discussed reproduction and resistance insofar as they led to radical action. In the field of curriculum a "language of possibility" was necessary. Educators must become transformative intellectuals rather than "skillful technicians." What is now necessary was to "link emancipatory possibilities to critical forms of leadership by rethinking and restructuring the role of curriculum workers" (Aronowitz & Giroux, 1985, p. 142.) This move toward emphasizing the agency of teachers and students was heard by receptive ears. For instance, Dennis Carlson (1987) worked to establish the basis for a view of teachers as an important force for transformative change in the schools:

> Only by critically reflecting on their own roles in the schooling process, theorizing about what could be, and working to promote specific changes consistent with a broad vision of a just society, can teachers expand and realize their capacity to challenge the status quo in ways that are transformative rather than merely reformist. (p. 307)

Teachers in crisis. In *Teachers and Crisis: Urban School Reform and Teachers' Work Culture,* Carlson (1992b) summarized critical social theory and pedagogy while focusing on the teacher. He moved from a general description (for instance "crisis tendencies in urban education") to site-specific description (for instance, "role formalization and 'playing the game' in urban schools") to descriptions of the social malaise generally and finally to suggestions for actions to be taken (beyond the crisis in urban schooling). Carlson outlined the discourse of the conservative reaction of the 1980s: the "top-down," "one best way" bureaucratization of the school system led to an era of "basic skills," with the consequence of an alienation of students and a demoralization of teachers. This was especially visible in urban public schools, where basic skills and standardized testing were emphasized in response to high dropout rates and apparently inadequate preparation for college or employment. Carlson suggested that the conservative reaction of the 1980s represented a backlash to gains by liberals in the 1960s. Carlson observed the value-laden character of conservative discourse, built around patriotism, success, competition, order, and found there old discourses of patriarchy and mercantile control. Liberal discourse remained undertheorized: "Liberalism thus faces a difficult task of delivering on all of its promises because it fails to account for power relations that impinge upon the educational site and that serve to maintain dominant forms of school organization and control, pedagogy, and curriculum" (p. 238). Carlson dismissed alternative discourses, including "vulgar" Marxism such as reproduction theory, "vulgar" pragmatism" (p. 224), Weberian theories of control, the pessimism and rationalism of the Frankfurt School, and poststructuralism.

Carlson then moved to sketch an alternative democratic-progressive discourse. He offered no concrete proposals, but, rather, a discursive direction:

> Critical literacy has been used within the progressive, democratic Left discourse in education to imply a capacity for self-reflexivity—the deliberate, discursive reflection on experience and identity construction within a culture in which one is positioned as a classed, raced, and gendered subject. (p. 241)

[Here we note what will increasingly typify political scholarship, an effort to incorporate autobiographic, biographic, and poststructuralist concepts such as identity to reanimate political discourse.]

Carlson advised that students become aware of the sources of their anger (through discussion and autobiographical writing) and then work to construct a unified front to create solutions. He cautioned: "Self-reflexive, dialectic thinking about social reality and identity construction is not easily taught in a society that actively discourages individuals from raising these difficult questions about purpose, identity construction, and the making of culture" (pp. 244-245). Carlson looked to a rebirth of trade unionism as a political force, and a decentralization of authority which would encourage difference, and other popular movements (such as Jesse Jackson's Rainbow Coalition) to defeat the Reagan-Bush "authoritarian populism" (p. 251). An opening for this Leftist democratic-progressive revival would come, Carlson speculated, as "the contradictions endemic to urban schooling in advanced capitalist America . . . lead to deepening crisis in the years ahead" (p. 253). Clearly, the crisis deepens for those in the schools, but the evidence that this will lead to a Leftist revival is thin at best. And, one must recall, the Right rose to power in the U.S. in part due to the failures of the Left.

Action, practice, and cultural politics. The shift toward a rhetoric of action and practice that Carlson's work would summarize and advance was discernible a few years earlier in Giroux's many journal articles (1985a, 1985b, 1987, 1988a, 1988b, 1989), emphasizing always the importance of transformative struggle, both in school and in society generally. Books published in the late 1980s, *Schooling and the Struggle for Public Life: Critical*

Understanding Curriculum

262

Pedagogy in the Modern Age (1988a), *Teachers as Intellectuals: Toward a Critical Pedagogy of Learning* (1988b), and *Critical Pedagogy, the State and Cultural Struggle* (1989) (the last title co-authored with Peter McLaren) emphasized critical or transformative pedagogy. Pedagogy was to be distinguished from teaching (McLaren, 1989). Roger Simon (1987) explained:

> "Pedagogy" [implies] . . . the integration in practice of particular curriculum content and design, classroom strategies and techniques, and evaluation, purpose, and methods. All of these aspects of educational practice come together in the realities of what happens in classrooms. . . . Talk about pedagogy is simultaneously talk about the details of what students and others might do together and the cultural politics such practices support. In this perspective, we cannot talk about teaching practices without talking about politics. (p. 370)

Scholars working in other areas adopted this concept of pedagogy, including some of working in teacher education (Gordon, 1986). Giroux and McLaren (1986) themselves outlined a teacher education curriculum that "links the critical study of power, language, culture, and history to the practice of a critical pedagogy, one that values student experience and student voice" (p. 213). For Giroux and McLaren, teacher education was another form of cultural politics. The use of this phrase—cultural politics—both recapitulated the cultural (rather than economic) emphasis of the Frankfurt School (and represents an intersection with the work of Philip Wexler) and foreshadowed a discursive shift toward a poststructuralism in which theory *is* practice.

Freire's influence. Freire's work, which had been influential in the late 1960s and early 1970s (Gordon & Weingarten, 1979), re-emerged as central to political curriculum scholarship during the past ten years (Bolin, 1985; Shor & Freire, 1987a, 1987b; Wallerstein, 1988; McLaren & Leonard, 1993). In his *The Politics of Education* (1985), *A Pedagogy for Liberation: Dialogues on Transforming Education* (1987) with Ira Shor, and *Freire for the Classroom* (Shor & Freire, 1987a), critical pedagogy was promoted. Among those Freire influenced was George Wood (1988b), whose interest in transformation led, as we noted earlier, to establishment of the Institute for Democracy in Education at Ohio University. [By mid-decade Giroux had established a Center for Cultural Studies at Miami University in Oxford, Ohio.] Peter McLaren's *Schooling as Ritual Performance* (1986b) and *Life in Schools* (1989; revised and reissued in 1994) made Freirean suggestions to teachers attempting resistance in their own schools. Freire's ideas extended to other, more specialized spheres. For instance, Marilyn Frankenstein (1983) extended Freirean ideas to the teaching of mathematics: "Critical mathematics education can challenge students to question these hegemonic ideologies by using statistics to reveal the contradictions (and lies) underneath the surface of these ideologies" (p. 329). She argued that a concept of mathematical literacy as inspired by Freire's work "is vital in the struggle for liberatory social change in our advanced technological society" (p. 315). Freire's globally significant career is important for other sectors of the field. A collection of essays (McLaren & Leonard, 1993) honoring Freire's contribution appeared late in 1993. [See his influence in theological and international discourses, chapters 12 and 14, respectively.]

A pedagogy of possibility. One of the most notable of the secondary figures in Giroux's critical pedagogy group is Roger Simon of the Ontario Institute for Studies in Education. Simon (1987) advocated "a pedagogy of possibility," one which is "not yet but could be if we engage in the simultaneous struggle to change both our circumstances and ourselves" (p. 382). In describing what it is like to be *Teaching Against the Grain*, he (1992a) extended critical pedagogy as a "project of possibility." Such a project was interested, he insisted, in how the substance of schooling might be recast in ways that focused teaching on the problem of reconstituting a progressive moral project for education as social transformation. Required was a "social vision on which a pedagogy of possibility might be founded" (p. 6), and schools and other sites of cultural production are central to the struggle to establish such a vision. Simon wanted to "specify how a practice of pedagogy might be conceptualized that would help establish concrete forms of hopeful practice" (pp. 6-7). He concluded with thoughts on how a critical "pedagogy of remembrance" might be conceived, as part of a new long-term effort to rethink the ways educational practices are involved in production of social memory and historical sensibility (Simon, 1992a). Here, in notions of "remembrance" and "memory" we are moving from the traditional Marxism of the reproduction phase to a more complex (as we will see, perhaps an unmanageably complex) view that incorporates elements of poststructuralism and psychoanalysis (Kincheloe & Pinar, 1991).

Voice. Political scholars have insisted that teachers' and students' voices have been silenced as conservatives have attempted to insure curriculum dissemination without "distortions," a version of so-called "teacher-proof" curricula. For McLaren and Giroux, critical pedagogy is expressed, in part, through voice, through stories that teachers and students tell each other. Voice becomes a key element in critical pedagogy as "it alerts teachers to the fact that all discourse is situated historically and mediated culturally" (McLaren, 1989, p. 229). Voice is said to refer to the "cultural grammar" and "background knowledge" teachers and students employed to understand experience (McLaren, 1989, p. 230). McLaren distinguished between teacher and student voice:

> A student's voice is not a reflection of the work as much as it is a constitutive force that both mediates and shapes reality within historically constructed practices and relationships of power.... Teacher voice reflects the values, ideologies, and structuring principles that teachers use to understand and mediate the histories, cultures, and subjectivities of their students. (McLaren, 1989, p. 230)

Voice is important to the projects to understand curriculum as gender [chapter 7] and as autobiographical/biographical text [chapter 10], although not exclusively as an instrument and expression of political struggle and conflict.

Textbooks and collective action. Apple's work during the mid-1980s shifted also from reproduction and resistance to pedagogy and politics, especially as understood in terms of race, class, and gender. In his early 1980s work, clearly class was the linchpin of his analysis; race and gender were conceptually subservient. However, we must credit Apple with a relatively early (in the nearly all-male political sphere at least) acknowledgement of what now is a central feature of curriculum scholarship: gender. For instance, in 1982 Apple (1982c) wrote: "What I do want to argue quite strongly, however, is the utter import of gendered labor as a constitutive aspect of the way management and the state have approached teaching and curricular control. It is the absent presence behind all our work" (p. 17). His interest in gender, while subservient to class, antedated other political theorists' incorporation of the concept [see Apple, 1983]. Apple's scholarship during this time did emphasize political and pedagogical struggle (Apple & Teitelbaum, 1986; Apple, 1987a; 1987b, 1988; Apple & Ladwig, 1989).

In 1984 Apple called for a long-term politically grounded ethnographic investigation that followed a curriculum artifact, such as textbook, from its writing to selling. In his 1986 *Teachers and Texts: A Political Economy of Class and Gender Relations in Education,* Apple examined the textbook industry, particularly as it perpetuated the "selective tradition." He called for political and pedagogical action by critical scholars, teachers, students and parents. Apple argued that the effort to democratize the curriculum must be a collective one involving all interested parties:

> [Critical scholars] need to be closely connected to feminist groups, people of color, unions, and to those teachers and curriculum workers who are now struggling so hard in very difficult circumstances to defend from rightist attacks the gains that have been made in democratizing education and to make certain that our schools and the curricular and teaching practices within them are responsive in race, gender and class terms. After all, teaching is a two-way street and academics can use some political education as well. (Apple, 1986, p. 204)

Relatedly, Kenneth Teitelbaum (1990) studied those textbooks used to challenge dominant ideology. Socialists adopted these materials during the first two decades of this century. Illustrative themes in these materials included: class consciousness, social interdependence, and the benefits of cooperative social and industrial relations. [For a summary of research on the textbook, including scholarship outside Marxism and critical theory, see chapter 13.]

Larger struggles. In essays published in 1988, Apple extended his analysis of curriculum as political text to include race. In "Race, Class and Gender in American Education: Toward a Nonsynchronous Parallelist Position," Cameron McCarthy [Apple's Ph.D. student] and Apple called for theoretical work that demonstrated how "race, class and gender interact, and how economic, political and cultural power act in education" (McCarthy & Apple in Weis, 1988). [Description of scholarly efforts to understand curriculum as racial text appear in the next chapter.] They pointed as well to a shift in strategies for fundamental change in curricular content, pedagogical practices and social structures (McCarthy & Apple in Weis, 1988).

Landon Beyer [an early Ph.D. graduate with Apple at Wisconsin] and Apple's edited collection *The Curriculum: Problems, Politics and Possibilities* (1988) focused on issues of political and pedagogical agency. Fundamental to these issues was the concept of praxis, which involves "not only a justifiable concern for reflective action, but thought and action combined . . . by a sense of power and politics. It involves both conscious understanding of and action in schools on solving our daily problems" (Beyer & Apple, 1988, p. 4). Praxis implies "critical reflective practices that alter the material and ideological conditions that cause the problems we are facing as educators in the first place" (Beyer & Apple, 1988, p. 4). In his "The Politics of Pedagogy and the Building of Community" (1990c), Apple continued this emphasis upon collective and concrete action, narrating episodes from his "Friday Seminar" held at the University of Wisconsin in Madison. He reminded his students that educational politics are inseparable from national politics: "I am constantly reminded of how important it is that we participate in those larger struggles as well" (Apple, 1990c).

The dominance of Apple and Giroux. The effort to understand curriculum as political text shifted from an exclusive focus upon reproduction of the status quo to resistance to it, then again to resistance/reproduction as a dialectical process, then again—in the mid-1980s—to a focus upon daily educational practice, especially pedagogical and political issues of race, class, and gender. The major players in this effort continued to be Apple and Giroux, Apple through his voluminous scholarship and that of his many students [see Schubert, et al., 1988, pp. 173-174] and Giroux through his prodigious scholarly production. By decade's end, three other scholars would become major contenders in controlling the conversation among political theorists: C. A. Bowers, Philip Wexler, and Peter McLaren.

Bowers, Wexler, McLaren. Who were these three scholars? Before reviewing their work separately, let us introduce each institutionally. *Bowers*: affiliated with the University of Oregon until recently [when a funding crisis resulted in the closing of his department and his transfer to Portland State University], Bowers' scholarship has been known more by a foundations rather than curriculum audience, until his sharp attacks on Giroux, McLaren, and Apple (Bowers, 1980, 1981, 1986, 1991a, 1991b, 1993). As we will see, his scholarship holds considerable significance for curriculum theory. *Wexler*: before moving to the University of Rochester, Wexler had taught in the sociology department at the University of Wisconsin, where he formed a lasting friendship with Apple [Apple & Wexler, 1978; see Apple's goodnatured introduction to Wexler' attack on him (in Wexler, 1987); and also Apple, 1993]. As we observed earlier, Wexler (Wexler & Whitson, 1982) entered the conversation early on, criticizing Apple's and Giroux's employment of the crucial term "hegemony." He would enter the conversation again, even more dramatically, in the 1987 book we will describe in the next section. *McLaren*: a doctoral graduate of the Ontario Institute for Studies in Education affiliated with the University of Toronto, Peter McLaren first moved to Miami University of Ohio, where he worked closely with Henry Giroux. In recent years McLaren has moved somewhat away from Giroux theoretically; institutionally they have separated: Giroux moved to Pennsylvania State University in 1992 and McLaren to the University of California, Los Angeles in 1993. These three scholars—Bowers, Wexler, and McLaren—threaten to upstage Apple and Giroux, despite conciliatory efforts (Apple, 1993). [Giroux's (1992a) strategy is to leave the curriculum field in search for a broader constituency, i.e. "cultural workers," and for the interdisciplinary field of cultural studies (Giroux & McLaren, 1994).] However, as we will see in a later section, in so doing they may signal the collapse of this sector as the field has known it. Before examining the coming crisis of political theory, we move next to the controversy which has accompanied this sector of scholarship. Indeed, more than any other contemporary curriculum discourse, we can say that political theory has been a lightning rod of criticism, criticism from within as well as outside its ranks.

V
Criticism and Controversy

The new sociology of education is historically backward-looking and ideologically reactionary, although its ideals combine the values of the New Left and traditional socialism.
(Philip Wexler, 1987, p. 127)

The desire by the mostly White, middle-class men who write the literature on critical pedagogy to elicit "full expression" of student voices . . . becomes voyeuristic when the voice of the pedagogue himself goes unexamined.
(Elizabeth Ellsworth, 1989, p. 312)

Reading at times like a poster about the circus coming to town, Aronowitz and Giroux's (1991) enticing phrases seem to be left to others to enact . . .
(John Willinsky, 1992b, p. 345)

Where's your data? One major critique of political scholarship appeared in 1988. In his *Capitalist Schools: Explanation and Ethics in Radical Studies of Schooling,* Daniel Liston—himself an insider to political theory as a student of Apple's at Wisconsin—alleged numerous weaknesses in Marxian analysis of schooling. Specifically, Liston criticized the purposes and methods of explanation, justification, and empirical validation in radical scholarship. After analyzing the work of Bowles and Gintis (1976, 1980), Giroux (1981a, 1983b), Apple and Weis (1983), Apple (1980, 1982a, 1982b) and Wexler (in Barton, et al. 1980), Liston criticized what he termed the "facile functionalist" assertions found throughout these works. He observed that the fundamental base/ superstructure model was assumed, not explained. Additionally, no empirical evidence was presented in these works to support the model. Liston (1988) charged: "Marxist explanations of public schools, while critical of functionalist approaches, nevertheless rely on functionalist assertions and ignore rigorous empirical assessments of these claims" (p. 10).

Liston was interested in ethical as well as methodological problems in the effort to understand curriculum politically. He noted that "freedom was and still remains the central ethical standard" in radical thought (Liston, 1988, p. 143). However, the major scholars seem to be unaware that Marx himself viewed concepts of justice and equality as problematical. Liston argued that "Marx viewed (and a consistent Marxist tradition would construe) justice as a deficient standard. Marx criticized capitalism morally but his standard was freedom (not justice), a standard embedded in the naturalist ethic" (Liston, 1988, p. 168). Marx's primary concern was freedom. Yet, Liston observed, Marxist scholars often based their criticisms of the status quo on notions of justice: "Marxist educators claim that the structure of the larger socioeconomic system is unjust and that the schools contribute to the reproduction of the unjust system" (Liston, 1988, p. 123).

If Marxist criticism of the status quo cannot be based on a concept of injustice, upon what can it be based? "What is the basis of condemnation? The basis exists, I believe, in Marx's notion of freedom" (Liston, p. 1988, p. 136). Liston asserted that those Marxists who currently employed standards of justice in their arguments "must at least recognize and appraise the merits of Marx's own critique of these standards" (Liston, 1988, p. 143). Further, he advises radical scholars to "revise the basis of their critiques or argue against Marx's position" (Liston, 1988, p. 143). Liston made clear that his critique was a "friendly" one: "Without enhanced explanatory claims or moral justification it does not seem likely the radical tradition will convince reasonable skeptics. I hope it does. Without convincing these skeptics it will inevitably fail. I hope it does not" (p. 174).

Monumental in its speciousness? Liston's claim of "friendliness" was rejected, at least by one major theoretician. Peter McLaren portrayed Liston's effort as having resurrected "an old and theoretically threadbare Marxian orthodoxy" (McLaren, 1990, p. 1). In his view, Liston's call for empirical validation represented a return to an epistemological position radical scholars long ago rejected, i.e., a "stance of objectivity and . . . the scientific goal of Truth" (McLaren, 1990, p. 8). Liston's logic was characterized as "reductionist" (McLaren, 1990, p.4). Recent debates regarding poststructuralism made it "difficult to remain sympathetic to Liston's penchant for causal mechanism and his reduction of ideology to flow charts and empirically based formulae" (McLaren, 1990, p. 5). Further, McLaren characterized Liston's treatment of Giroux's scholarship as "monumental in its speciousness" (McLaren, 1990, p. 7). Liston's analysis can be likened to "what Sartre called 'bad faith,' a kind of ritualistic blood-letting, an exaggerated self-flattery, and an inflated moral righteousness that is damaging to the book's intent and purpose" (McLaren,

1990, p. 7). McLaren would seem to be casting Liston as a more old-fashioned Marxist than his academic father [Apple]; certainly he is staking his claim to what he believes is a politically progressive poststructuralism, as we will see later in this chapter and in chapter 9.

No moral foundation. Another major criticism of the effort to understand curriculum as political text concerned its lack of a moral foundation. Writing also as politically engaged scholars (whose work we have mentioned already), Landon Beyer and George Wood (1986) argued that critical scholars "have not taken seriously enough the need for a set of moral principles and convictions that can be used to critique current educational theory and practice. . . . This has resulted in a premature applause for alleged resistances to ideological domination" (p. 1). In other words, the resistance phase of political theory would seem over-strategic and over-pleased with itself, lacking a sober, moral foundation. "Our concern," they continued, "with the field of social reproduction stems from what we see as an alarming lack of productive debates among proponents and between adherents to that orientation and others" (p. 1).

Beyer and Wood (1986) located the absence of a moral foundation partly in a problematical identification of radical scholars with the working class [see also Wexler, 1987, p. 181, for another analysis of the same problem.] They pointed out that both Willis and Apple expressed an identification with the working class. Willis had applauded the ideological "penetrations" of the "the lads" because these working-class boys occupied a subordinate, exploited-class position. [For a gender analysis of political rhetoric see Pinar, 1994.] Illustrative perhaps of what for Beyer and Wood was a dishonest identification with the working class, Apple (1985) approved of some form of "vocational education" because the working class was skeptical of the educational value of academic knowledge.

The problem with Willis and Apple's reasoning, Beyer and Wood continued, "is that it reduces moral issues to questions of social acceptability, where 'acceptablility' is defined in terms of the working class. . . . This leads to moral relativism based on social sentiment" (p. 4). Moral principles, in contrast, operate as "a means of overriding actions based on self-interest or social convenience" (p. 5). They concluded that:

> the cause of this identification [with the working class] . . . is a replacement of the foundations of positivism . . . with a new foundation, namely, the "dictatorship of the proletariat". . . . This reliance on a new foundation may have come about because of the entrenched nature of the older epistemological tradition with its search for absolute certainty. (p. 7)

From the Beyer/Wood critique, it seemed as if the work of Apple, Giroux, and other political theorists was morally rudderless, substituting a fashionable but phoney identification with the working class to advance their strategic position as middle-class academicians. This latter charge had been made earlier by Pinar (1981b, also 1994) and would be taken up by Wexler (1987). [Issues concerning morality are also associated with the effort to understand curriculum as theological text, as we shall see in chapter 12.]

Incidentally, that same article of Apple's of which Beyer and Wood were so critical, also pointed to what Apple (1985b) regarded as the inattention to context which characterized 1980s classical curriculum theory, especially the work of Mortimer Adler. Recall we discussed Adler in the section on Joseph J. Schwab [see chapter 4], as an influential philosopher who worked closely with University of Chicago President Robert Maynard Hutchins in the promotion of a "Great Books" curriculum. Adler had entered the curriculum debates of the 1980s during the same period when others [for example, Hirsch and Bloom] were arguing on behalf of perennial knowledge. In 1985 Apple had criticized these efforts as ignoring social context. The criticism did not go unanswered:

> I would suggest that the tone of [Apple's, 1985b] "Old Humanists and New Curricula" is impertinent. It stretches credulity to believe that [Mortimer] Adler, as a student and philosopher to the human condition, can fail to know or care about the context in which education, or any other human enterprise, occurs. (Gray, 1985, p. 323)

From outside the Marxist camp as well as from within it, criticism of political scholarship intensified.

Concepts problematical? Concepts basic to the project to understand curriculum as political text have been criticized as problematical. In this regard, distinguished philosopher Kenneth Strike (1989) has said of the reproduction theorists that "the drive to epistemological suicide is strong" (p. 151). Other scholars have focused in their critique on particular concepts used by those who understand curriculum as political text. In addition to the Wexler/Whitson (1982) critique of "hegemony," Dale (1986) criticized Apple, Giroux, and Wexler also for their too loose usages of the notion of ideology: "the concept of ideology changes, like a chameleon, depending upon the context in which it appears" (p. 241), and further, "the arguments against a base-superstructure study of ideology are weak" (p. 255). Dale (1986) insisted that "the concept of ideology [should] be restricted to just those beliefs and ideas that 1) are false, 2) contribute to the reproduction of production relations and class domination, and 3) are determined and explained by the production relations" (p. 257).

Not only political theorists' use of "ideology" came under fire; so did what had become the almost taken-for-granted notion of a hidden curriculum. For instance, tracing the concept back to Philip Jackson (1970) and Robert Dreeben (1976), Lakomski (1988) insisted that there is "no evidence of the . . . hidden curriculum" (p. 451). Relatedly, other scholars have examined the learning theory which they found embedded in the concept of hidden curriculum. That embedded theory of learning is a simplistic one of internalization without agency or complexity. Avi Assor and David Gordon (1987) observed: "we have a learning theory which concentrates on a redundancy principle and at the same time does not seriously consider other well-known learning factors" (p. 329). Referring to Jackson (1968) they noted: "It is these elements of repetition, redundancy and ritualistic action which later on in the chapter Jackson calls 'the hidden curriculum'." Referring to Dreeben, Apple, Giroux, and Anyon, Assor and Gordon (1987) advised: "this one-factory theory [redundancy] is inadequate and should be revised to include two additional factors: a) student's internal cognitive structures and organizational capacities, and b) reward value of the learned material" (p. 338).

Even the concept of resistance theory came under fire. At least one scholar was worried that this term was employed without rigor. George Wood (1984) wrote: "In fact, much of the resistance theory tends to glorify the oppositional behavior of students regardless of the consequences" (p. 231). Another scholar has criticized the failure of critical scholars to adequately distinguish between science and scientism, resulting in failure to understand the dangers and potential of both. Peter Hlebowitsh (1992) complained: "But the distinction between science and scientism in the curriculum, which Dewey understood, seems to have been lost by critical curriculum theorists who continue to claim that the notion of curriculum as a problem-solving process is part of a technocratic rationality" (p. 80). Given the range and power of criticism, it may seem surprising that political scholarship continued at all. It would not continue unchanged.

"Closet" liberals? Like Liston (1986), C. A. Bowers (1987) and Kenneth Strike (1989) alleged that Marxist scholars had abandoned Marx. More specifically, Bowers and Strike concluded that radical scholars were moving away from Marxism toward liberalism: "Marxism has been decisively rejected. It appears that no alternative hard core is on the horizon, unless it is some variety of liberalism" (Strike, 1989, p. 166). Among those whose work Strike discussed included Apple, Bowles and Gintis, Giroux, Willis, Levin and Carnoy, McLaren, and Dale. Strike described the movement of these efforts to understand curriculum as political text, a movement which increasingly exhibited "idealist and indeed liberal terms" (Strike, 1989, p. 160). The emphasis upon cultural autonomy characteristic of radical scholarship after 1985 represented, for Strike, an "abandonment of the core of the Marxist program" (Strike, 1989, p. 155). Marx's labor to substitute materialism for idealism had been forgotten, apparently, by those who claim the heritage. Strike (1989) concluded: "Finally, the fact that many of those who gave us the Marxist critique of schooling seem to have lapsed into liberal construction is at least a piece of evidence that allows us to see Marxism as a degenerative research program. It suggests that the problems generated by a Marxist research program cannot be solved without abandoning the program's central assumption" (p.167). Strike's criticism of political scholarship has also been criticized (Crittenden, 1991).

Political Theory is Anthropocentric: C. A. Bowers

One of the most vociferous critics of Marxist scholarship has been C. A. Bowers (1980, 1981, 1984, 1986, 1987; 1991a, 1991b, Pinar & Bowers, 1992). His critiques have spanned a fifteen-year period and a wide range of issues. While Bowers' criticism of political theory has occasionally sparked a return volley (McLaren, 1991e), his contribution more generally has, unfortunately, been overlooked and undervalued by the American field. Ignoring scholarship which political theory opposes has been one of its strategies over the past twenty years, a strategy that has helped lead to the current balkanization of the American field. Bowers' scholarship is significant, and careful, respectful attention to it by the curriculum field is long overdue.

In one of his first critiques, a study of "cultural reproduction" as metaphor, Bowers (1980) observed:

> While Marx was unable to shed much of the traditional mental template that stamps his work as the product of a particular historical and cultural period, his followers, including Apple, have been even less successful in avoiding a thought process that organizes reality into rigid categories and linear causal relationships. In the writings of Apple, as well as those of Bowles and Gintis, socialism and capitalism are clearly organized into the rigid categories of right and wrong, truth and falsity, salvation and perdition (p. 278)

Anticipating Wexler's (1987) and Strike's (1989) critique, Bowers argued in 1980 that political scholars were not as radical as they alleged. Rather, these self-proclaimed radicals were trapped in cognitive patterns dominant in Western culture since the Enlightenment. Consequently, many of the major concepts associated with political scholarship are plagued by flaws in Western rational logic, rendering the concepts almost politically meaningless. Political theory seemed so unself-critical that Bowers admitted (1980) that "the analysis of curriculum as a form of cultural reproduction is based on such a basic truism that one can only wonder about the excitement it has produced in certain quarters" (p. 280). Others might agree (Tanner & Tanner, 1990, p. 20; Goodlad, 1984, p. 161).

Perhaps even more damaging to Apple's work, Bowers (1980) detected that:

> The deep structure of Apple's metaphor of equality—the coding of reality into either-or categories, the preeminence given to theoretical-abstract thought over pretheoretical experience, the image of equality that is based on an image of atomistic-voluntaristic individualism, the anthropocentric universe—seems to imply the hegemony of Western cultural episteme. (p. 282)

Furthermore, Bowers insisted: "To imply, as Apple does, that the overturning of capitalism will lead to a state where we are free of hegemony is tantamount to saying that we can live without mental templates and without language systems" (pp. 286-287). In a work six years later, Bowers turned his attention to the privileged roles that critical pedagogy also afforded to the notion of reflective thought. Bowers (1986) complained: "The emphasis on the authority of reflective thought, the power of theory to guide action, and the view that the future can only be controlled as the past is destroyed represents, to reiterate, the relativizing of all forms of authority except the reflective judgment of the individual" (p. 230). The political theory of both Apple and Giroux were found to be naively recapitulating Cartesian assumptions regarding the relations of mind and matter, thought and action. How could politically progressive curriculum theory emerge from such profoundly conservative modes of analysis?

In his *Elements of a Post-Liberal Theory of Education,* Bowers (1987) critiqued the work of Paulo Freire upon which much of the transformative or critical pedagogy literature rests. Freire's work shared four basic assumptions with liberalism, according to Bowers. These assumptions included: 1) change is inherently progressive; 2) the individual is the basic social unit "within which we locate the source of freedom and rationality" (p. 2); 3) human nature is basically good or at least changeable via environmental manipulation; and 4) rationality is "the real basis of authority for regulating the affairs of everyday life" (p. 2). Bowers concluded that Freire's version of Marxism is more appropriately characterized "as a form of democratic humanism, an ideology which would be scorned as a form of revisionist liberalism in those countries that rely upon a more scientific Marxism as a basis of their social organization" (p. 37). Here Bowers' criticism may be directed more specifically at political theorists' appropriation of Freire's work than at Freire himself. It was the political theorists who had made so much of Freire's radical credentials, not Freire himself.

The Promise of Theory. In an important work entitled *The Promise of Theory: Education and the Politics of Cultural Change,* C. A. Bowers (1984) outlines his own political theory. He began by identifying three groups of educational practitioners and theorists at work today. The first and most politically powerful was the liberal technocratic group, interested in incremental reform. The second, neoromantic reformists, advocated progressive free schools, reminiscent of the child-centered progressives during the 1930s. The third were the neo-Marxist critics, such as Apple and Giroux. Provocatively, Bowers argued that all three groups "are following the same cultural map and are committed to the same trajectory of cultural evolution. In identifying their basic value orientation we shall be mapping essential characteristics of our modernizing form of consciousness" (p. 14).

Regarding liberal-technocratic educators, Bowers noted that they "produce curriculum material that give the appearance of individualizing the learning of information that is increasingly one-dimensional" (pp. 14-15). Noting that this program of reform was profoundly conservative, Bowers observed that: "Liberal-technocratic educators possess a high commitment to improving the effectiveness of classroom instruction, which they see as necessitating more effective teacher control over classrooms" (p. 15). Bowers insisted that "neo-Marxists are grounded in the same traditions of thought that lead the liberal-technocrat to give theory a preeminent role in directing practice" (p. 15).

Another distinguishing characteristic of the liberal-technocratic educator's pattern of thought is the belief that change, based on abstract ideas and theory, is progressive, a belief embedded in the use of measurements to validate increasing levels of efficiency and predictability [see also Lasch, 1991]. Essential to the liberal/technocratic view is that their major concepts (freedom, equality, individualism are key liberal metaphors; measurement, efficiency, system are key technocrat metaphors) are understood as culture free and context-independent. Therefore, it is clear that the liberal-technocratic pattern of thought "equals abstract thought with power, organizes experience into component parts, views the reorganization of components into new systems as essential for asserting rational control, determines success on the basis of efficiency, which can be measured, and views change as the normal state of affairs" (pp. 18-19).

Neoromantic educators inadvertently further the power of liberal-technocratic educators. Without realizing the consequence of their action, Bowers believes that "neoromantic educational reformers, with their back-to-nature orientation, were contributing to relativizing those areas of culture that might have served as points of resistance to the growing imperialism of a technological social order" (p. 23). Here Bowers is not suggesting that alternative-free schools promote authoritarianism. Rather,

> it is more a question whether the values of freedom, equality, and individual centeredness, when made the starting point of the educational process, are allowed to overpower curricular and pedagogical practices that develop the intellectual discipline necessary for resisting authoritarianism in its more modern forms. (p. 23)

Here Bowers is implying that the radicals' dismissal of all traditionalism left a vacuum of power and morality which might have combatted the rise of Right and the dominance of the liberal/technocratic view, still in place in the schools.

The myth of progressive change. Bowers' critique of political scholars focused especially upon what he regarded as the Marxist antipathy toward the past and the uncritical assumption that change is progressive:

> The basic question pertains to why neo-Marxist educational theorists have taken most elements of the cultural modernization for granted. This intellectual bias has resulted in the nearly total failure of the neo-Marxist educators to consider the claims that history makes on us, including the continuities that ought to be maintained. The belief that rational thought or theory is the chief means not only of grasping the nature of reality but also for directing the course of change is fundamental to the neo-Marxist educators' modernizing orientation. This [Freirean] stance appears naive when we consider how reason itself is shaped by the unconscious history embedded in the language through which we derive the cognitive maps that serve as the basis of the rational process, but it nevertheless provides an important clue to the deep antipathy that Marxist educational theorists feel toward the past. . . . At the center of the new mythology . . . [for the Marxists] is the belief that change is progressive. (pp. 24-25)

While varying in many respects, all three groups—neo-Marxists, alternative-free school advocates, and liberal-technocratic educators—share a confidence in their ability to condition students to expect change, in self-realization and expression as the highest forms of humanity, in an anthropocentric view of the universe, and in a rationalized, social engineering orientation toward existential and social problems (although some alternative-free school advocates would depart company with the others on this last issue). Each of the three groups failed to take into account that "individuals" do not exist as represented by the folklore of bourgeois individualism. Notions of "self-realization," "self-expression," "self-determination"—employed by all three groups to communicate different pedagogical claims on behalf of individual freedom—carry certain tacit assumptions about self-formed, self-contained, volitional beings. Given this notion of the individual, traditional mores, responsibility to a larger social entity, and historically-grounded knowledge are naively regarded as sources of oppression and self-alienation.

Bowers' five propositions. Next Bowers moves to formulate his own view. First, he wants us to realize that "a society that values individual freedom and equality . . . must ensure that each individual be educated to exercise communicative competence" (p. 28). Bowers then outlines five propositions which would characterize a curriculum for communicative competence. The first is that "social reality is shared, sustained and continuously negotiated through communication" (p. 35). The second proposition is that "through socialization the individual's intersubjective self is built up in a biographically unique way, and it serves as the set of interpretational rules for making sense of everyday life" (p. 36).

The third proposition asserts that "much of the social world of everyday life is learned and experienced by the individual as the natural, even inevitable order of reality. This natural attitude toward the everyday world is experienced as taken for granted. . . . The cultural unconscious" (p. 39). The fourth proposition is that "the individual's self-concept is constituted through interaction with significant others: the individual not only acquires the socially shared knowledge but also an understanding of who she/he is in relation to it" (p. 40). Bowers recalls that Nietzsche believed that our interpretations of everyday life were hardly just simple expressions of objective knowledge and understanding as they were interwoven with the deeply rooted psychological processes of identity maintenance. Bowers notes: "This connection between self-identity and the socially derived knowledge codes . . . means that individuals have a degree of ego-investment in maintaining those definitions and assumptions upon which their self-concept is based" (p. 42).

The fifth proposition is that "human consciousness is characterized by intentionality; it is the intentionality of consciousness that insures that socialization is not deterministic. . . . Phenomenologists have suggested that human consciousness should be understood as a verb" (p. 42). In other words, socialization becomes sedimented as the individual's intersubjective self, helping to comprise the existential experience of the individual. Acquired symbolic codes, in effect, "become powerful shapers of the individual's freedom, identity and sense of ontological groundedness, and the forms of alienation that will be experienced" (pp. 46-47).

Bowers is explaining here how intellectual development is intimately related to freedom in its existential and political senses:

> Existential choice is thus expanded in proportion to the complexity of the symbolic code the individual acquires. A complex symbolic world provides the means for choosing among different interpretational schemes, as well as imagining future possibilities that would result from different scenarios . . . what cannot be imagined cannot be chosen. (p. 47)

In these passages Bowers is integrating political theory, phenomenology and psychoanalysis in a subtle and complex curriculum theory.

Bowers is careful to avoid lapsing into the abstraction of reproduction and resistance theory; he returns to the concrete, to the everyday, to the symbolic, existentially embodied. Reflective thought and political action do not become pledges of rhetorical allegiance; they are situated in classroom life. He writes that the individual derives from cultural traditions that are sustained via language of everyday conversation:

> A theory of education that is grounded in an understanding of how our patterns are acquired will enable the teacher to understand which "moves" in the language game of socialization are likely to bind the student to the world of taken-for-granted belief and which "moves" enable the student to obtain conceptual distance necessary for reflective thought. (pp. 49-50)

Here we hear echoes of discursive analysis which other political theorists—most notably Peter McLaren—will take up later.

A curriculum for communicative competence. Next Bowers (1984) formulates questions which recognize that the teacher can change the process, and thus the outcome, of socialization. The first question is: "does the content of the curriculum reflect what the student already experiences as taken for granted?" (p. 57). The second question: "is the content of the curriculum represented as reified reality?" (p. 60). The third is: "what are the areas of audible silence in the curriculum?" (p. 63) The fourth is: "is the curriculum characterized by a limited or complex language code?" (p. 65). The fifth is: "Does socialization involve using the legitimation process to make students feel powerless?" (p. 66). The sixth is: "does the curriculum contribute to social stratification and inequalities of opportunities?" (p. 68). The seventh is: "what is the influence of the purposive-rational system of thought on the liberalizing potential of school knowledge?" (p. 69). Bowers believes that the tradition of grounding the educational process in the student's experience, which he traced to Locke, Pestalozzi, and, in this century, to Dewey, failed to explain how cultural codes are internalized into consciousness and experienced by both students and teachers in commonsensical understandings of the world. Without the insight, Bowers continues, derived from the more contemporary work in cultural linguistics, phenomenology, and the sociology of knowledge, grounding education in the student's experience risks reinforcing mutually-shared, taken-for-granted attitudes. In light of this view, how should the curriculum be appraised? Bowers (1984) writes:

> The curriculum, whether it deals with the nature of work, time, metaphorical thinking, poverty, or ways of knowing, should be judged, in part, on the basis of whether it helps the student understand how the content area relates to the broader, overarching belief system of the culture and that influences the existential questions faced in the course of everyday life. The question of whether the curriculum assists students in identifying the more important features of the cultural territory can also be approached in terms of whether the curriculum enables the student to deal with the paramount political themes and issues. . . . If the curriculum is designed to reinforce the taken-for-granted beliefs that represent historically outmoded ways of responding to today's problems, the curriculum will serve to undermine the student's growth in communication competence. (pp. 80-81)

Bowers identifies three principles of a curriculum for communicative competence: the first principle involved "utilizing students' phenomenological culture" (p. 86). The second principle required the "use of historical perspective to de-objectify knowledge" (p. 87). The third principle involves "incorporating a cross-cultural perspective" (p. 92). Bowers concludes:

> Ultimately, one must ask the question whether the socialization process in the classroom contributes to the student's ability to understand the conceptual foundations of the major problems confronting society. Communicative competence . . . thus becomes the test of the adequacy of the theories that guide our approach to the education of teachers. (p. 114)

Here the political theory of Habermas, phenomenology and anthropology are interwoven in a sophisticated analysis of curriculum.

Bowers has done much more than to establish himself as an astute critic of the work of Michael Apple, Henry Giroux, and other Marxist theorists. In *The Promise of Theory* he has formulated a sophisticated and relatively comprehensive theory of curriculum that has incorporated in its general principles and propositions essential features of at least two of the major sectors of contemporary curriculum scholarship: the political and the phenomenological. It is a considerable achievement which political theorists have yet to acknowledge.

Political Theory is Reactionary: Philip Wexler

Perhaps the most brilliant and caustic critic of political analyses of curriculum is Philip Wexler, himself an "insider" to debates regarding base/superstructure, ideology, hegemony, etc. (Wexler, 1976). Wexler had taken his Ph.D. in sociology at Princeton University and taught in the Department of Sociology at the University of Wisconsin-Madison [where, as we noted, he collaborated with Apple; see Apple & Wexler, 1978] before moving to the University of Rochester's Graduate School of Education and Human Development at the end of the decade. We have already reviewed his critique (with, at that time, his Ph.D. student Tony Whitson) of the use of hegemony in political scholarship. In his *Social Analysis of Education: After the New Sociology* (1987), Wexler charted the rise and fall of the so-called "new sociology." [The "fall" may have been somewhat premature, although not mistaken.]

Central to Wexler's analysis is the linkage of academic work to social movements outside the academy. He pointed out, for instance, that the "new sociology" arose in the aftermath of the radical student and civil rights movements of the 1960s. Wexler charged that radical critics romanticized that movement. Political scholarship "neglected its own historicity," and following the decline of the 1960s student radicalism, it appeared as a post-movement discourse which "recapitulates that defeat, restating it abstractly and obsessively" (pp. 4, 27). Politically oriented scholarship, then, amounted to little more than "a displaced imitation of it [the student movements of the 1960s], an attempt culturally to recapitulate the practical historical course of the movement, *in theory*" (Wexler, 1987, p. 26).

Radical scholarship did express, Wexler suggested, a "renewed but idealized interest in collective mobilization and social change" (Wexler, 1987). However, such change would occur within institutions and within professional roles. Wexler (1987) stated: "In this view, the new sociology of education is a rationalized cultural representation of identity politics: it is part of a *post-*'movement' effort to create a meaningful professionalism that is consonant with the ideal of a defeated social movement" (p. 27). In this respect, politically oriented scholars were committed to their own professional advancement, which they mistook for political activism [see also Pinar, 1981b, p.440]. Their activism constituted the "cultural formation of an identifiable social group which is engaged in sociocultural action on its own behalf." Consequently, "Left professional middle class institutional intellectuals became a socially residual remnant, rather than the institutional vanguard of an ascendant social class segment" (Wexler, 1987, p. 123). These are vicious charges: that Apple and Giroux have exploited defeat of the student movements of the 1960s in order to advance their own professional careers, and in so doing, are reproducing the conservative status quo.

Reactionary? Furthermore, Wexler alleged, the primary concepts employed to understand curriculum politically—reproduction and resistance—represented a "combination of functionalist structuralism and romantic individualism" (Wexler, 1987, pp. 16, 42). In consequence, "the new sociology of education is historically backward-looking and ideologically reactionary, although its ideals combine the values of the New Left and traditional socialism" (p. 127). The history of the effort to understand curriculum as political text can be located in the social path of its producers, i.e., the so-called "new sociologists" of curriculum. That path leads from:

ideology-critique to awareness of systematic reproduction through the accumulation of cultural capital; and then from idealized and socially displaced individual cultural resistance to the dissonant bifurcation between idealized social
mobilization and an unconscious politics of internally exiled speech. (Wexler,
1987, p. 45)

From Wexler's point of view, Apple's and Giroux's work is not only reactionary; it is schizophrenic.

Theories of reproduction should be discarded, Wexler continues, replaced
with studies of "historical movements in society and education" (p. 88) in
which social movements are not only the key social actors in identity formation, "but also construct the social setting in which identities are formed" (p.
412). Wexler argues for social analysis to appropriate poststructuralist literary methods due to the importance of signs, symbols, and texts in the emerging postmodern, information-based society. Wexler writes that the heightened power of imagery, symbols, and systems of signification in postmodern
society creates a context in which "literary theory displaces social theory" (p.
149). For the first time in political theory, a rather full-blown discursive shift
toward poststructuralism has occurred. Wexler will retreat somewhat from
this 1987 position [see Pinar & Reynolds, 1992b, pp. 244-245], but McLaren
will move in to explore the political possibilities of poststructuralism. In
1987, though, Wexler clearly embraced poststructuralism and, to a certain
extent, feminist theory as solutions to the overwhelming problems of
political theory.

A progressive poststructuralism. While the "new sociology" may have become
trapped in the progressive-liberal paradigm, there is a possibility of escape.
Certain strands of feminist thought and poststructuralism point to social
movements and change that might inspire collective mobilizations. Particularly literary "textualism" is "potentially transformative . . . the starting point
for a counter-practice" (Wexler, 1987, p.180). Additionally, poststructuralism
might free political scholars from "a socially inauthentic identification with
'the working class' or with the triadic oppressed groups of 'class, race and
gender'" (Wexler, 1987, p. 181), a point Landon Beyer and George Wood
had made a year earlier. Wexler (1988b) notes:

> The sad irony of that critical and radical tradition is that in its major accom-
> plishment of exposing the false objectivity of abstracted empiricism and in its
> correct attempt to politicize educational analyses, it forgot the institutional,
> culturally structured, collective, ritual, and rhetorical or "poetical" character of
> everyday life in school and in society. It forgot the core of the social. (p. ix)

Wexler (1987) insists we were undergoing "the emergence of a qualitatively new social formation" (p. 152) typified by the "rise of informationalism" (p. 153) in which both the production and distribution of information
increasingly determine the organization of social relations, the networks
within which power is wielded, and the processes of individual and collective
identity formation. Wexler continues: "Neither the schools as organized for

most of the postwar period nor as they now are now being restructured by conservatives help develop individuals with the skills and identities which will be 'functional' for the developing postmodern society" (p. 413). Wexler's analysis of the present organization of school and identity formation will be reported in chapter 13.

Unsurprisingly, responses to Wexler's work have been mixed. While a South African critic has praised Wexler's argument as "genuinely novel" (Muller, 1989, p. 77), another reader, this one affiliated with University of Wisconsin, attacked. In his review, Hunter (1991) alleged that:

> the density, obtuseness, and disorganization will confirm the view that radical theories are incoherent, contribute nothing to the study of education, and that their democratic pretensions are belied by their coded, exclusionary language. The inaccessible style and near incoherence of much of the book is disconcerting. (p. 411)

Further, he insisted that "Wexler's argument about the class identity of the new theorists not only reduces an intellectual current to its class interest thereby underestimating its intellectual project, but is more finger pointing than analysis" (p. 415). This is rather venomous language. It is reminiscent of another critique, that time directed at Giroux, made by another Wisconsin graduate student ten years earlier (McNeil, 1981; later this chapter).

Hunter noted that Wexler did not incorporate gender, race, or nationality as critical determinants of identity formation, elements central to Apple's 1980s scholarship. Despite these criticisms, Hunter (1991) did find some merit in Wexler's work:

> Still his perspective is useful because programmatically it underscores the need to describe and analyze institutional developments like schooling as part of large socio-historical patterns. . . . Wexler's challenge to study changes in education as an integral aspect of the rise of commodified informationalism is one well worth addressing (p. 420)

Given the significance for the field and the threat to political theory postmodernism and poststructuralism now pose, Hunter's praise seems mild indeed.

Political Theory is Voyeuristic: Elizabeth Ellsworth

A revised version of a presentation made to the *JCT*'s Tenth Conference on Curriculum Theory and Classroom Practice (the 1988 Bergamo Conference), Elizabeth Ellsworth's "Why Doesn't This Feel Empowering? Working Through the Repressive Myths of Critical Pedagogy" critiqued both the conceptual structure and daily practice of critical pedagogy, that branch of political theory associated with Henry A. Giroux. Ellsworth pointed out that critical pedagogy should not be confused with feminist pedagogy, which "constitutes a separate body of literature with its goals and assumptions" (Ellsworth, 1989, p. 298). The key terms of critical pedagogy— "empowerment," "student voice," "dialogue"—represented "code words" and a "posture of invisibility" (p. 301). Relying upon a decontextualized and universalistic conception of reason, critical pedagogy led to "repressive myths that perpetuate relations of domination" (pp. 298, 304). Critical pedagogy, she continued, left the structure of domination and authoritarianism in place. In Ellsworth's (1989) words: "[critical pedagogy] fails to challenge any identifiable social or political position, institution or group" (p. 307). The "utopian goals" of critical pedagogy are unattainable.

In working with participants in Curriculum and Instruction 607 at the University of Wisconsin-Madison, Ellsworth conceived of her role as interrupting institutionally imposed limits on "how much time and energy students . . . could spend on elaborating their positions and playing them out to the point where internal contradictions and effects on the positions of other social groups could become evident and subject to self-analysis" (p. 305). This position was in contrast to that of critical pedagogy, which Ellsworth viewed as enforcing rational deliberation (p. 305), a charge not unlike that made by Bowers. Further she alleged that critical pedagogy—here she quotes Freire, Shor and Giroux—fails to question its own stance of superiority of teachers' understanding over students' (p. 307). Ellsworth was skeptical of critical pedagogy's claim of "emancipatory authority," judging the goals for which such authority is utilized remain "ahistorical and depoliticized" (p. 307). "Empowerment," she insisted, was defined so broadly that it failed to challenge specific social or political groups or positions. This failure represented critical educators' inability to confront the paternalism of traditional education (p. 307). Ellsworth went on to criticize the concept of "student voice," as it was discussed in the critical pedagogy literature, relying on her experience in her course to suggest its flaws. From a gender perspective, for instance, she noted: "the desire by the mostly White, middle-class men who write the literature on critical pedagogy to elicit 'full expression' of student voices . . . becomes voyeuristic when the voice of the pedagogue himself goes unexamined" (p. 312).

Concluding, Ellsworth noted that as long as critical pedagogy failed to understand issues of trust, risk, fear and desire, especially as these are expressed through issues of identity and politics in the classroom, its "rationalistic tools will continue to fail to loosen deep-seated, self-interested investments in unjust relations of, for example, gender, ethnicity, and sexual orientation" (pp. 313, 314). After critiquing critical pedagogy's ahistorical use of "dialogue" and "democracy," Ellsworth suggested a "pedagogy of the unknowable" (p. 318), in which knowledge was understood as "contradictory, partial and irreducible" (p. 321). Reflecting on her own teaching Ellsworth (1989) wrote:

> A preferable goal seemed to me to become capable of a sustained encounter with currently oppressive formations and power relations that refused to be theorized away or fully transcended in a utopian resolution—and to enter into encounter in a way that owned up to my own implication in those formations and was capable of changing my own relation to and investments in those formations. (p. 308)

Ellsworth advocated labor toward a position informed by feminism and poststructuralism (p. 304) in which none of us is permitted to be "off the hook." Ellsworth's criticism provoked considerable comment and controversy (Tierney, 1993a, p. 10; Bryson & de Castell, 1993a; Edelsky, 1991, p. 5), as suggested by letters published in the August 1990 issue of the *Harvard Educational Review*, and by the attention given to it by William B. Stanley (1992b) in his history of political scholarship.

Giroux replies. Giroux replied to Ellsworth one year later. Politically he characterized Ellsworth's criticism of critical pedagogy as "a crippling form of political disengagement" (Aronowitz & Giroux, 1991, p. 132). He continued that Ellsworth: "degrades the rich complexity of the pedagogical processes that characterize the diverse discourses in the field of critical pedagogy. In doing so, she succumbs to the familiar academic strategy of dismissing others through the use of strawman tactics and excessive simplifications that undermine the strengths of her own work and the very nature of social criticism itself" (p. 132). For Ellsworth (1990b), Giroux's counterattack was not persuasive. As she entitled her response, "the question remains." William Stanley (1992b) has come to Giroux's defense in his exchange with Ellsworth. However, Ellsworth's criticisms were not the only ones Giroux's work would encounter.

Problems of Agency and Resistance

Referring to Giroux's *Theory and Resistance*, Paul Smith (1988) noted that while Giroux is not completely uncritical of the Frankfurt School, its influence on his work is considerable. What Giroux took from the Frankfurt School was primarily a dissatisfaction with the more economistic orthodoxies of traditional Marxism. After Adorno, Giroux argued that struggle did not take place only, or even primarily, in the context of the labor process; rather, the sphere of struggle was ideology and culture. In a scheme in which culture not economics is primary, education is crucial, a point Wexler (1987, 1990) made as well. Smith praised Giroux's efforts to construct a notion of human agency which privileged the ability to resist those institutions of social control that sometimes seem impervious to change, such as schools. Further, Smith praised Giroux's attention to a wide range of crucial pedagogical issues in ways that made change seem possible. It is on this point of the possibility of change and resistance, so central not only to Giroux's work but to many political scholars, that Smith raised questions.

Smith noted that Giroux's language appeared to suggest that what might be termed a "will to resistance" was simply empirically present in the everyday lives of oppressed groups. After Marcuse, Giroux often stated that the "individual's sedimented history" by which he meant the person's lived experiences, conscious and unconscious, were implicated in the whole of cultural and social history. Given the status Giroux afforded this notion of "sedimented history" and its inescapable relation to a notion of human agency, Smith noted that:

Some account must be given of the way in which ideology reaches into the "subject"—specifically, into the "subject's" unconscious. In other words, ideology's work in the realm of the unconscious needs to be reckoned with, since resistance involves not just conscious self-constituting acts, but also the agent's individual history. . . . Thus the unconscious comes to be equivalent, in Giroux's lapsus, to "unconsciousness." This scarcely allows the drawing of psychoanalytic work into a radical problematic, as Giroux claims. Rather, it returns psychoanalysis to an older epistemology relying on a strict conscious/unconscious opposition. All the dialectical tampering in the world won't be able to remove such an opposition from its metaphysical problematic or hide the fact that it basically ignores almost a century of psychoanalytical theory. . . . Such a view would minimally require a conception of the mediating function of the unconscious. . . . The unconscious . . . the site where social meanings and practices are negotiated *prior to* and *simultaneously with* any activity of the conscious agent. Thus, to account for human agency and its actions—resisting or passive—in the face of ideology, social theory must begin to apprise itself of what it has to say about their shared problematic—the place of the "subject" within structures of power and domination. (Smith, P., 1988, pp. 68-69)

The place of the subject within structures of power and domination, then, refers to unconscious content of the individual as well as social and institutional structures. The complexity of agency within social and psychological determination (what Giroux terms "sedimented history") appears to leave little hope for the transformation which critical pedagogy demands. Other scholars have noted this disturbing reality (Senese, 1991). The human subject will not change easily.

Earlier, other doubts had been raised regarding Giroux's notion of agency and its adequacy to support resistance. Linda McNeil, worked at the Wisconsin Center for Public Policy when she attacked Giroux, asked: "Are present teachers to come to new awarenesses on their own? If so, would this be individually or collectively? If not, are they to gain new insights from outside experts like Professor Giroux" (McNeil, 1981, p. 206). Further:

Giroux has attempted to break out of the chicken-and-egg question of whether social change depends on school reform or school reform on social change. But I am not sure that many of the teachers I have observed would appreciate having the whole burden of both placed on them. The hostility to theory as such which prevails in contemporary public life is really directed against the transformative activity associated with critical thinking. (p. 209)

Giroux (1981d) counterattacked, complaining that in McNeil's critique: "critical inquiry gets reduced to an advertisement for her own ideological wares." Furthermore, McNeil's conceptual tools are inadequate: "The mentality of the critique that McNeil provides is structuralist. Schools are viewed as overpowering institutions that reduce teacher behavior to a feeble echo of the institutional demand for social order" (p. 212). Here Giroux is attacking the reproduction theory to which Apple [and many of his graduate students, such as McNeil] had returned by mid-1980s. Giroux concluded: "In short, the assumptions at the core of McNeil's perspective represent a problematic that diminishes human agency and consciousness while at the same time empowering the ideological and material constraints that exist in schools with a force that makes them appear overwhelming" (p. 217). The debate between reproduction and resistance theory appeared to reached a stalemate. In fact, the effort to understand curriculum as political text would enter a fourth phase: one of discursive shifts leading to a fifth, possibly final phase.

VI
Discursive Shifts in Political Curriculum Theory

[Border pedagogy] attempts to link an emancipatory notion of modernism with a postmodernism of resistance.
(Stanley Aronowitz & Henry A. Giroux, 1991, p. 18)

I see great virtue in Green politics and many challenging ideas emerging from the new frontiers of science.
(Noel Gough, 1989a, p. 26)

Peace education is the exploration of a possible life together.
(Terrance R. Carson, 1992a, p. 113)

On the surface, it might appear that the voluminous literature critical of political scholarship might itself portend a coming crisis for this entire sector of contemporary curriculum scholarship. While it is true that this criticism has raised damaging, unanswered questions, in general it has also focused attention on this work, raising its visibility and contributing to a sense of its centrality to the contemporary curriculum project. A crisis would appear to be coming, however, a crisis that does not follow only from the criticisms we have reported in the previous section. The crisis of political theory has to do with its very conception of itself and the world. Basic questions regarding the adequacy of Marxism, neo-Marxism, and critical theory have been raised by poststructuralism and feminist theory, as Stanley (1992b) recognized and has attempted to repair. As the recent work by Peter McLaren illustrates, postmodernism and poststructuralism may not be readily incorporated, despite Stanley's (1992b) efforts to demonstrate that they can be. Before we turn to this coming crisis for political scholarship, let us turn first to a phase of continued expansion of this sector of scholarship. During this most recent period, new areas have been incorporated, such as popular culture and ecological concerns, and new concepts appeared.

Popular culture. Perhaps the most important hint of the move away from reproduction and resistance theory to an interest in cultural politics was research on so-called popular or everyday—rather than "high"—culture (Allen, 1987). Now decrying that the old reproduction and resistance models were limited and limiting, Giroux et al. (1989) argued that schooling must be "analyzed as part of a complex and often contradictory set of ideological and material processes through which the transformation of experience takes place" (p. 1). In this view, educational practice became both a "site and a form of cultural politics" (p. 11). Such practice enabled teachers and students to "intervene in the formation of their own subjectivities and to be able to exercise power in the interest of transforming the ideological and material conditions of domination into social practices that promote social empowerment and demonstrate possibilities" (Giroux et al., 1989, p. 11). One expression of this rapidly developing interest in popular culture was research in media.

Some recent work suggests an all-inclusive notion of resistance theory as cultural politics. Peter McLaren and Richard Smith (1989), for instance, examined "Televangelism as Pedagogy and Cultural Politics." Another instance of the burgeoning interest in popular culture was the work of Alan Wieder (1988). Working to capture images of popular culture, Alan Wieder (1988) published photographs of children which made visual and concrete the differences among race, class, and gender. Perhaps the important example of the emphasis upon popular culture was the work of Elizabeth Ellsworth (1984, 1986, 1987a, 1987b, 1987c, 1987d, 1988; Ellsworth & Whatley, 1990), which insightfully analyzed educational film for often latent, sometime explicit, political content.

For example, in her "I Pledge Allegiance: The Politics of Reading and Using Educational Films," based on a study of 30 classical educational documentaries drawn from a three-year investigation of a sample of 150 educational films produced for classroom use between 1930-1965, Ellsworth (1991) found that: "educational documentaries encourage students to enter into a particular type of allegiance to the authority of the Academic Expert as constructed in these films. Specifically, they offer a viewing experience that attempts to make pleasurable the position of subject of paternalism" (p. 41). Here Ellsworth is reconstructing a psycho-social process of political passivity, even infantilization. Furthermore, she continued:

> educational documentaries invite students to see themselves in *relation* to the "outside" world . . . to "make sense" of and use an educational documentary on its own terms, the viewer must at least temporarily and imaginatively align her/himself with the specific set of power relations that underpin the logic of the film's use of available film forms and styles. (p. 42)

Students are seduced into accepting the film's construction of the world as natural. Ellsworth concluded:

> An expert has solved problems for the student viewer, who is therefore no longer threatened by the consequences of ignorance or misunderstanding about this particular issue. Positive outcomes are certain, progress is insured, and nothing can stop viewers from becoming safer, happier, or richer. The power that the father/patriarch/teacher/mythical norm has over the viewer is only benevolent. (p. 57)

Ellsworth's sophisticated analysis incorporates not only the critical theory that had informed political theory, but feminist theory as well, emphasizing the psycho-social and gendered elements of domination. In this regard, her scholarship undermined and replaced the reproduction/resistance emphases which had typified political theory since the early 1970s.

A border pedagogy. In their *Postmodern Education: Politics, Culture and Social Criticism,* Aronowitz and Giroux (1991) joined Ellsworth in pointing to popular culture as an central feature of postmodern education. In such education the curriculum "can best inspire learning only when school knowledge builds upon the tacit knowledge derived from cultural resources that the students already possess" (Aronowitz & Giroux, 1991, p. 15). Giroux updated the notion of "critical pedagogy" to include the teaching of popular culture as a form of postmodern resistance. In a postmodern world Giroux's notion of "critical pedagogy" became "border pedagogy." In this new work, critical pedagogy is updated to include terms linked with postmodernism such as territorialization:

> In short, the notion of border pedagogy presupposes not merely an acknowledgement of the shifting borders that both undermine and reterritorialize different configurations of power and knowledge; it also links the notion of pedagogy to a substantive struggle for a democratic society. It is a pedagogy that attempts to link an emancipatory notion of modernism with a postmodernism of resistance. (Aronowitz & Giroux, 1991, p. 118)

However, the tension between the postmodern notion of struggle as discursive and the modernist political notion of struggle as involving "action," as in the streets, is neither acknowledged or resolved. Attempting to accommodate these tensions by their juxtaposition, Giroux borrowed additional terms of the discourses on postcolonialism [see Willinsky (in press) later in this chapter].

Counter-text, counter-memory. Border pedagogy was said to function as "counter-text" and "counter-memory." According to Giroux, it is time to blur such boundaries and incorporate knowledge forms and content from formerly marginalized discourses. It was time to "redefine the complex, multiple, heterogeneous realities that constitute those relations of difference making up the experience of students who often find it impossible to define their identities through the cultural and political codes of a single, unitary culture" (Aronowitz & Giroux, 1991, p. 120). Popular culture became one means to promote this "counter-text." Popular culture provided students with an identity, which, according to Aronowitz, was rapidly disappearing among working class children. Especially for such children, the cultural identity communicated with the so-called "Great Books" of Western Culture was fantasy. The popular culture of the working class served as one important instance of "counter-text" in the school curriculum.

Popular culture, Aronowitz continued, expressed an "aesthetic of pleasure" in contrast to the schools, which are "institutions of deprivation" (Aronowitz & Giroux, 1991, p. 183). Popular culture afforded credibility to cultural difference by making the everyday life of students an integral part of the curriculum. With the emphasis upon popular culture, what had been termed "critical pedagogy" shifted from an emphasis upon the "demystification of domination" toward "the politically strategic issue of engaging the ways in which knowledge can be remapped, reterritorialized, and decentered in the wider interests of rewriting the borders and coordinates of an oppositional cultural politics" (Aronowitz & Giroux, 1991, p. 119).

In its latest formulation, critical pedagogy became "border pedagogy," and with this concept came a notion of "counter memory." What is counter-memory? "[Counter-memory represents] a critical reading of how the past reads the present and how the present reads the past" (Aronowitz & Giroux, 1991, p. 124). Relying also on Arac, Giroux argued that counter-memory contested current concepts of truth and justice, enabling us to understand and alter the present via a changed relationship to the past (Arac, 1986, in Aronowitz & Giroux, 1991, p. 124). Counter-memory provides a possibility of "solidarity within difference" (p. 126).

The canon. An example of curriculum as "counter memory," Alan A. Block (1992) examined a number of radical novels which, in most instances, are no longer in print. In *Anonymous Toil: A Re-evaluation of the American Radical Novel in the Twentieth Century*, Block (1992) argued for the inclusion of the twentieth century radical novel in the literature curriculum. His intent was "to reclaim a vast body of abandoned American literature and to expose the ideological category by which that originary exclusion had been effected" (p. 119). In fact, the literary productions Block studied—associated with the socialist and communist movements in America—became marginalized because mainstream literature constructed them as "radical." He characterized mainstream literature as a social form which produced and reproduced the reality to those values associated with the mainstream, dominant culture.

Block returns the radical novel from its constructed marginalization to the specific historical settings and conditions which it portrays. In so doing he shows how it had been separated from these historical conditions and then appraised next to a literature—traditional canonical literature—which also had been removed from its political and historical setting. So removed, the classification of one genre against another served to perpetuate the dominance of one set of values over another. Block concluded:

> Literature as both social practice and form is the site and product of such cultural contention, the battleground and the spoils of the victor, wherein could be found the result of the struggle for the language forms by which a particular group makes sense of its circumstances and conditions of life. . . . The radical novel is an ideological creation of the dominant culture. (p. 121)

Such reading and investment permit teachers and students to "give voice to unrealized possibilities" (Giroux & Simon, 1989, p. 25). Popular—not high—culture becomes the curriculum.

The significance of Block's scholarship is twofold. First, he portrays the process by which the canon—the traditional curriculum of literary education—is formed and reinforced by the intentional exclusion of alternative ways of seeing. [See Taubman 1993a—reported in chapter 6—for a discussion of the canon in terms of multicultural debates.] Block regards literature as the product of hegemonic forces and an important site of political struggle. Through this struggle certain forms of consciousness, related psychologies, and their literary representations, are made seem to seem "natural," at least to those who accept uncritically the dominant culture. Block (1992) argued for the inclusion of the radical novel in the literary curriculum not only as a representation of alternate consciousness but as exemplars of the methods by means of which dominant hegemonic forces operate in the curriculum generally.

Second, Block argued that the exclusion of the radical novel may be understood as central to the processes of the production and reproduction of that educational ideology which govern schools today. Debates over political correctness and multiculturalism may be framed as parallel phenomena to the exclusions mainstream literature made to create the radical novel. In like fashion, the school silences and marginalizes those voices not reproductive of dominant curricular assumptions and practices. In more recent work, Block (1993) has continued to pursue popular culture as one complex site in which curriculum may be comprehended as political text. This interest has led to him study reading education, situating the "whole language" approach to reading in Deweyan pragmatism and autobiography (Block, forthcoming).

The new literacy. Not only literature but the notion of literacy itself has become politicized, as we see in the work of the Director of the Centre for the Study of Curriculum and Instruction at the University of British Columbia, John Willinsky. A doctoral graduate of Edgar Friedenberg (formerly famous in the United States for his *The Vanishing Adolescent* and *Coming of Age in America*) and Michael W. Apple (who served as the external examiner at Dalhousie University in Halifax, Nova Scotia, Canada), John Willinsky (1984, 1987, 1990c, 1991b, 1992a, 1993a) has detailed historically the rise of a "new literacy" in reading and writing curriculum:

> The New Literacy consists of those strategies . . . which attempt to shift the control of literacy from the teacher to the student; literacy is promoted in such programs as a social process with language that can from the very beginning extend the students' range of meaning and connection. (1990c, p. 8)

Willinsky cites the National Writing Project, "writing across the curriculum," whole language approaches to reading instruction, reader-response theory, and political curriculum theory as instances and inspirations of new literacy curricula. In the new literacy are conjoined understandings of curriculum as phenomenological, autobiographical, political, postmodern, racial, and gender text [see Delgado-Gaitan, 1988; Edelsky, 1991; Freire & Macedo, 1987; Giroux, 1988d; Lankshear, 1993; Luke, 1988; McLaren, 1991e; McLaren & da Silva, 1993; and Yellin & Koetting, 1988].

The ecological crisis. The focus of political theory expanded further still, from the social world to the planet earth. The ecological crisis received increasing attention in recent years (Krall, 1979, 1981, 1988b; Gough, 1989a, 1989b; Starratt, 1989; Beegle, Bentley, & Bash, 1987; Bowers, 1993), despite its relative underemphasis in the political literature (Pinar & Bowers, 1992). For a political theory grounded in Marxism, this may have been no mere oversight. Aronowitz himself noted: "Marx had no doubt that the progressive mastery of nature was a presupposition of human emancipation" (Aronowitz, 1990, p. 1974). Predictably, perhaps, Marxist scholars of curriculum have tended to understudy the contemporary ecological crisis.

A long-time student of the ecological crisis and its implications for educational theory and practice, C. A. Bowers (1987, 1991a, 1993) has taken Marxists to task for their failure to attend to this urgent issue. For instance, he (1987) pointed out:

> The problems of inequality and restricted individual empowerment are not nearly as important as the cultural roots of our alienation from nature. Regardless of how our agenda for social reform is framed, the bottom line has to do with reversing the global ecological deterioration we are now witnessing. (p. 159)

Moreover, the failure of Marxist theorists goes beyond overlooking the crisis; it occurs in uncritically reproducing that structure of thought which has led to the current crisis. Bowers (1991a) wrote: "The problem with the Giroux-McLaren interpretation of a critical pedagogy is not so much that they missed the most fundamental event of our epoch, but that they continue to promote the modernizing ideology that is a major contributing factor to the crisis" (p. 250). Bowers (Pinar & Bowers, 1992) and several other scholars have been working to develop an ecological perspective.

In her "Ecology and Equity: Toward the Rational Reenchantment of Schools and Society," Ruthanne Kurth-Schai (1992) argued that the "primary barriers on the path to equity were philosophical rather than material or technical in nature" (p. 147). What is needed, she insisted, is "a moral and conceptual vision in which connections between social and environmental oppression are acknowledged and addressed in an integrated manner. This is the project of rational reenchantment: promoting social and environmental justice by transcending the constraints of dualistic thought" (pp. 147-148). The Australian curricularist Noel Gough would seem to agree. In sketching elements of an "ecopolitical paradigm," Gough (1989a) wrote: "I see great virtue in Green politics and many challenging ideas emerging from the new frontiers of science" (p. 26). Other scholarship which incorporates ecological knowledge in curriculum studies includes that of Paul Theobald and Dale Snauwaert (n.d.), who examined the educational perspective of Wendell Berry. Berry promoted the importance of being connected to the land—to place—as necessary for the accomplishment of one's humanity. Berry posited, Theobald and Snauwaert tell us, an "ecological" conception of human nature, in which a concept of personhood is constructed, not only socially, "but ecologically, in dialectical relation to one's geographical space" (p. 2). Berry's perspective may best be described as "ecological" (p. 18). This focus on ecological considerations may well intensify in coming years.

Peace education. Recently, there has appeared political scholarship which has developed largely outside the spheres of Marxism and critical theory. One example of such work is peace education, especially as it has developed at the University of Alberta under the leadership of Terrance R. Carson. Peace education promotes not only peace on macropolitical levels but on micropolitical levels of everyday human relationships in schools. Grounded in phenomenology, influenced by action research, Carson's work illustrates how political initiatives can be based on hermeneutics, not class analysis. Peace, Carson (1992a) tell us, "is known primarily by its absence, and it is this absence that gives meaning to the project of educating for peace" (p. 102). Relying on the tradition of action research established by Carr and Kemmis (1986) and on also the work of Habermas (1970), Carson established a "collaborative action research group" (p. 106) in 1988, which participants named CARPE (Collaborative Action Research in Peace Education). The goals of the group included: 1) to understand more completely the meaning of peace education, 2) to develop the practice of peace education in participants' respective teaching settings, and 3) to work to transform the places where participants teach into place that "reflect peaceful structures (i.e., places where human rights are attended to, conflicts are resolved nonviolently, etc.)" (p. 107).

As the group worked, four questions arose: 1) how can we discover hope after all?; 2) what to do when the global encounters the local?; 3) what is a project anyway?; 3) what is a community? In working through these basic questions, the group came to conclude:

> Peace education casts politics, pedagogy, and what it means to be a teacher in a different light. . . . [Yet] peace is better known to us as the insistent question of our time, not as a potentially clear course to be followed through an unfolding spiral of action and reflection such as that suggested by Carr and Kemmis. . . . Peace education is the exploration of a possible life together. (pp. 111-113)

For Carson, then, peace education requires a hermeneutics of interpretation, a practice of interpretation and reinterpretation, thoughtfully grounded in practice. It is not, then, another subject. Peace education is not about "trying to implement some-thing, but to unfold a possibility" (Carson, 1992a, p. 113).

Place. Another concept that has emerged in recent political theory is that of place. Joe L. Kincheloe and William F. Pinar (1991) introduced the notion of place as one organizing idea for political, autobiographical, racial, and gender issues in curriculum, illustrating the concept through studies of the American South. [Leslie Roman has used the South, specifically the "embattled reactionary politics of Louisiana" (1993, p. 73), to inform her view of politics and race. For a more complex view of the South in general

and Louisiana in particular, see Kincheloe, Pinar, & Slattery (in press) as well
as Kincheloe & Pinar (1991).] In *Curriculum as Social Psychoanalysis: Essays on
the Significance of the Place* (1991), Kincheloe and Pinar formulated the
outlines of a southern curriculum predicated on a concept of place. Pinar's
(1991) essay in that volume is a depiction of interdisciplinary southern studies programs (at the Universities of Mississippi and South Carolina) which, in
his judgment, expressed, in curricular form, repressed historical and cultural
elements of the South. When such elements surface and are re-integrated
culturally and politically, Pinar believes, blocks to the development of intelligence will be removed. Via this process of cultural renewal, the general
educational level of the South might be raised. Employing the South as illustration, Kincheloe and Pinar argued that the major contemporary curriculum
discourses—the political, the autobiographical, the phenomenological, and
the gender-focused—can be linked in a curriculum theory of "place."

They suggested that a curriculum theory of place is rooted in a Haber-
masian notion of social psychoanalysis and a related literary conception of
"place." It is psychoanalysis, argues Habermas, which serves as a paradigmatic
example of a science incorporating self-reflection (Habermas, 1970). As new
information and its interpretation alter the state of the interpreter, psychoanalysis moves beyond traditional hermeneutics. The world of appearances
has been bracketed by the psychoanalyst, as he or she attempts to bring to
the patient's awareness the hidden meanings and functions of symbolic
expression. Therapy enjoys success as it makes these unconscious processes
accessible to and understood by the analysand (Held, 1980). In this way
psychoanalysis becomes a politically progressive form of social science.

Just as psychoanalysts maintain that the individual's world of superficial
appearances disguises the psychic malformations which influence behavior,
progressive social theorists contend that the social facade that constitutes
everyday social life shields the social malformations which serve to shape
events (Gibson, 1986). In the attempt to remedy these distortions, psychoanalysis and progressive social theory (in the Frankfurt School tradition)
proceed in parallel fashion. The labor of the individual to gain freedom from
a distorted and undermining past has its parallel in the political activity of
groups committed to simultaneous social and self critique (Giroux, 1983a).
Both the psychoanalyst and the progressive social theorist appreciate the
necessity of self-understanding in the cultural and educational renewal of
individuals, groups, and nations. In each sphere the "psychoanalyst" concentrates on the influence of past events on present everyday life. The psychoanalyst interrogates the past as childhood, the social theorist as historian. A
critically inspired school curriculum becomes, in this sense, a form of social
psychoanalysis (Kincheloe, Pinar & Slattery, in press).

Certain literary theorists and artists have complained that too many characters and scenes achieve significance via stereotypes (Welty, 1977). They
have alleged that the structural elements of fiction—such as character, plot,
scene—are lifted from geographical setting, and so lifted they obscure the
power of place. Such works move away from specificity as they aspire to

archetypical universality. Political curriculum theory has exhibited similar tendencies, as Pinar observed (1981b). Great value has been derived from such universalistic analysis (Pinar, 1988f), but the effects of politically oriented scholarship can be reactionary when abstracted from history and social movement (Wexler, 1987). Political curriculum theory is more likely to function progressively when it is grounded in the particularity of place. A concept of place brings the particularistic into focus; it locates understanding of the individual and the psychic as well as those social forces which are expressed in and through him or her. Without place, our appreciation of the particular tends towards vagueness and depersonalization. Place embodies the social and the particular.

The effort to achieve a curricular synthesis arises out of the theoretical tension between autobiography and Marxism in curriculum studies. Self and situation are in principle a unity (Pinar & Grumet, 1981). As Kincheloe and Shirley Steinberg (1993) note: "Power manifests itself not through some explicit form of oppression, but via the implicit reproduction of the self" (p. 300). Kincheloe and Pinar argue that their collection of essays (Kincheloe & Pinar, 1991) illustrates these themes by focusing on the place called the South and the unique distortions remaining from its history. Employing a synthesis of self and situation, the individual and the social which they characterize as social psychoanalysis, Kincheloe and Pinar (1991) explore the possibility of cultural and educational renewal which might be stimulated by a social psychoanalytic southern studies.

However, the concept of place is not only associated with the South or the field of curriculum theory. In the appendix to *Curriculum as Social Psychoanalysis* are listed regional study centers throughout the world. Related scholarship in other fields, such as American studies, has been developing. For instance, in "Beyond the Scared and the Profane: Landscape Photography and the Sense of Place," Timothy Davis (n.d.) wrote: "Further development of a cooperatively evolved, inhabitant-based paradigm that preserves cultural differences and multiple voices through various combinations of verbal and visual imagery offers unsurpassed potential as a highly evocative and ethically desirable approach to studying the human experience of place" (p. 28). Here we discern the same suspicion of abstraction and that appreciation for the local in all its complexity that inspired the Kincheloe/Pinar work. [For different account of this concept, emphasizing its autobiographical features, see chapter 10.]

Citizenship and pubic policy. For political scholars, citizenship has also become an important concern, as it expresses civic and political obligations and possibilities in a time of neo-conservatism (Cherryholmes, 1980; Starratt, 1989; Stanley, 1992b, pp. 68,76-77, 78-81, 87-88, 91-92, 113; Gordon, 1985). Of course, for decades citizenship has been of interest to social studies educators, such as Shirley Engle. From a liberal perspective, Engle and Ann Ochoa (1988) have argued for a curriculum for democratic citizenship. The Engle/Ochoa curriculum proposal focused on those dynamics and complexities of decisions people must make in the course of their civic lives and the impact of these decisions on the development of democratic institutions. The curriculum they propose would presumably help expand the intellectual powers of citizens as they face environmental, institutional, cultural, and social problems.

Citizenship has been another medium of the political struggle for justice, which, as Walter Parker (1986b) has pointed out, has customarily been treated without attention to theory, history, or social context. Parker (1986b) notes: "To seek virtue and with it justice is to understand that the individual and the community must be known simultaneously" (p. 291). Giroux has located justice in public policy debates over public expenditures. In "Educational Leadership and the Crisis of Democratic Culture," Giroux (1992b) wrote:

> The money and missiles sense of reality must be challenged through a different vision of public life; a vision which demands a reallocation of resources away from the killing machines of the defense industry to programs that insure that every child in this country as the opportunity for gaining access to a free and equal education; a vision that sees public schooling in this country has an essential institution for reconstructing and furthering the imperatives of a democratic and just culture. (p. 19)

In 1993 in the United States, we see both significant reductions in the federal military budget, with attendant base closings and employment declines in the military-industrial sector. In Michigan and in other states, schools close early in the spring and fail to open as scheduled in the fall due to declining tax revenues (Schmitt, 1993; Celis, 1992).

The abstract character of political theory itself may work against the cultivation of democratic citizenship within the professional spheres of education. In this regard, Goodman (1991b) has worried that political scholars have retreated from effective participation in the public sphere [see also Bullough, 1988; Konopak, 1989; Lasch, 1984; Fraser, 1994], in part due to the specialized language of political curriculum theory. He suggests (1991b):

> it is worth emphasizing that the development of this language [of imagery] alone is not enough of a response to the need for connecting scholarly analysis to the practices of those administrators, teachers, and students who work in our schools. . . . [As] part of a broader political effort . . . we need to make our voices heard in other arenas of discourse. For example, our voices should be heard in committee hearings when state legislators are considering "education reform" bills. (p. 70)

Goodman is suggesting that political theory must move beyond its own rhetoric, and participate in the everyday political world of the schools, a view Thomas Barone seems to share [see chapter 11].

In another study focusing on public policy, Douglas Noble (1992) looked at the New American Schools Development Corporation (NASDC), established by President George Bush to funnel corporate funds into innovative designs for "new American schools" (p. 1). [NASDC received $50 million of the $500 million gift to public education made by Walter Annenberg *(New York Times*, 1993).] Such schools are to prepare American youth for the new world order which, according to Noble, amounts to the pursuit of unfettered competitive advantage for American corporations in the global economy, coupled with the promotion of a strong U. S. military presence worldwide. Principal corporate members of the NASDC board were prominent advocates for this "geostrategic" view (p. 4). Noble (1992) characterized NASDC members as on the cutting edge of "wholesale corporate dismemberment," cutting jobs, failing to invest long-term in their corporate infrastructure for sake of short-term gains. Noble argued that these corporate leaders have brought their disinvestment agenda with them; they are now directing it, in a case of mistaken identity, toward the schools. In meetings of the President's Educational Policy Advisory Committee, chairman O'Neil exhorted its members repeatedly, with exasperation, to "pressure the system," to "catalyze" action, to "force change," to "leverage" urgency, to "explode the bomb, a reference to NASDC being education's "Manhattan Project" (p. 9). Noble (1992) concluded:

> [NASDC] members have been most explicit, of course, about their need for a skilled workforce to remain competitive. Yet this rationale makes bewilderingly little sense, in light of their access to a global workforce and their termination of thousands of highly skilled workers, and in light of recent studies that contradict their earlier claims about "skill gaps" and skill shortages. . . . [NASDC members'] emphasis throughout will be on efficiency and productivity and competitiveness, not because they need the schools to be more efficient or productive or competitive, but because this is the only posture, the only game, they know (p. 10).

A Ph.D. graduate of Rochester where he worked with Philip Wexler, Noble is observing—through a more explicit political lens—what the *New York Times* education editor Edward Fiske noted, namely that the current wave of school reform in the United States began with the right and with the business community more generally. Fiske (1991) argued that contemporary school reform amounts to a shift from the factory model [see chapters 2 & 3] to the corporate model [see school reform in chapter 13]. For this reason alone curriculum theorists might be wary of their participation in reform initiatives (Pinar, 1992a, 1994).

VII
Feminism, Semiotics, Poststructuralism, and the Coming Crisis of Political Curriculum Theory

> As I have argued throughout this essay, class relations, even when more elegantly treated, may not tell all. But to push them once more to the sidelines would be a tragedy of immense proportions.
>
> (Michael W. Apple, 1992a, p. 145)

[W]hat we, sociologically, have to come to study as "the social" was a construction of some radical bourgeois *men*. In psychoanalytic terms, these radical bourgeois *men* encountered a Significant Other which they sought, in important terms, to socialize and to civilize; to model (in Marx's famous phrase) after their own image.

> (Philip Corrigan, 1989, p. 66, emphasis in original)

The dialogue between critical theory and postmodernism produces a theoretical hesitation, a theoretical stutter.

> (Joe L. Kincheloe & Shirley R. Steinberg, 1993, p. 298)

Freedom, therefore, becomes something that must be won within discourse.

> (Peter McLaren, 1991a, p. 248)

Despite strong echoes of apparently discredited reproduction and resistance theories, in the early 1990's there is evidence of shifts in the scholarly effort to understand curriculum as political text. Perhaps as a result of new intellectual movements and "new historical actors" (Aronowitz, 1990, p. 105), politically oriented scholars are rethinking, perhaps against their will, the future of this important sector of curriculum scholarship. Feminist theory, ecological movements, and poststructuralism (especially with its emphasis upon the discursive character of social reality) call into question conventional Marxisms (Shapiro, 1988b). The response of politically oriented scholars has not been uniform; it is often changing, sometimes ambivalent. The status of the concept of class permits us to gauge the shifting ground of political theory. Recall that class has functioned as a major concept in understanding curriculum as political text. Summarizing research regarding the role of class in education, William B. Stanley (1992a) observed:

> It is also clear that one's class position has a powerful effect on the quality and level of education attained. . . . Lower class children generally require more educational assistance, yet they typically receive less than their more affluent counterparts. What remains in dispute is the extent to which the existing class structure is more a natural reflection of human abilities or the artifact of unequal economic, cultural, and political power. Until this [elimination of discrimination according to class and culture] occurs, we should remain skeptical regarding the conservative (functionalist) assertions regarding the inevitability of our present class structure. (pp. 204-205)

In general, class analysis has been central to the kind of political analysis that typified scholarship in this sector during the 1970s and early 1980s. Among writers for the general public, class analysis—especially when linked with race—remains key [see Kozol, 1991].

Decline of class analysis. As we have seen, political scholars moved to studies of race, class and gender in the aftermath of the collapse of reproduction and resistance theories. By the mid-1980s, however, "race" and "gender" had become relatively autonomous sectors of scholarship [see chapters 6 and 7], leaving "class" to the politicists. Yet a major theoretician—Stanley Aronowitz— has declared that even the emphasis upon class analysis on the Left has proven to be relatively unfruitful in its explicative power. Only ten years earlier Willis' *Learning to Labor* (1981), which typified class analysis in the post-reproduction phase, dominated discussions among leftist curriculum theorists. Why the relatively rapid decline of class analysis? Aronowitz tries to account for this development. The first problem with class analysis has been with socialism itself. Aronowitz points out that in socialist countries, political and economic control has not been held by the working class. Additionally, there has been a failure of working class revolutions to materialize, in either so-called advanced countries (such as in the United States) or in the third world. History itself, then, has undermined class analysis as a primary category of social and educational analysis. Aronowitz declares it is time to move on: "Marxism retains its force to the extent that it insists upon the importance of theory taking the point of view of human emancipation, but which does not hold to a particular doctrinal canon" (Aronowitz, 1990, p. 168). While Aronowitz welcomes a new face for political curriculum theory, Michael Apple does not.

Apple: "A tragedy of immense proportions." Indicative of the sharp decline in the importance of class analysis is Michael Apple's (1992a) appeal to the field to maintain a class perspective. Apple (1992a) writes of "my feelings of discomfort with certain aspects of postmodernism as it has been incorporated into the theoretical discourse in education" (p. 130). He worries that the field has moved too quickly away from class analysis, and in so doing, risks the "loss of collective memory" (p. 130). Yet, Apple is unwilling to dismiss poststructuralism and postmodernism. He writes: "*If this remains sufficiently political,* it can lead to a salutary focus on how power works in every day life without having to reduce it always to the working out of, say, larger economic forces. I take this as a gain, if we do not use it to ignore the economic and the structural dimensions of a society" (p. 145, emphasis added). The possible contribution of poststructuralism acknowledged, Apple returns to his deeper concern that class will be shelved in the field's fascination with textuality and discourse. Apple (1992a) concludes:

> As I have argued throughout . . . class relations, even when more elegantly treated, may not tell all. But to push them once more to the sidelines would be a tragedy of immense proportions, not only to the vitality of the community of researchers in education, but to the millions of children for whom class exploitation and domination are facts of life. (p. 145)

Apple's appeal to not forget the last fifteen years of political scholarship is the not the first time he had responded to the appearance of poststructuralism and postmodernism in American curriculum studies. [For a history of poststructuralism in North American curriculum studies, see Pinar & Reynolds, 1992b.] In a 1982 essay discussing the distinction between economic and cultural reproduction, Michael Apple appeared to advocate the employment of poststructuralism to further political understanding: "In this regard, our analysis could profit immensely from the incorporation of the work of people such as Barthes, Macherey, Derrida, and other investigators of the process of signification and impact of ideology on cultural production" (Apple, 1982b, p. 265). Such an incorporation would acknowledge the primacy of cultural over economic considerations in political analysis (Wexler, 1987). The political struggle is said to have shifted from the economic to the symbolic (Aronowitz, 1990). On this occasion, then, Apple had joined Aronowitz, Giroux, McLaren, and Wexler (and later, Whitson, Stanley, Kincheloe, and Steinberg) in suggesting that poststructuralism can be politically progressive. Warren Crichlow agreed: "While postmodern politics of representation may not in themselves have an effective theory of political action and movement, I agree . . . that the undeniable political import of these practices are their 'denaturalizing critique' of prevailing cultural representations" (Crichlow, 1990, p. 9).

Another theorist of race is less than enthusiastic. Cameron McCarthy, introducing his "Slowly, Slowly, Slowly, the Dumb Speak: Third World Popular Culture and the Sociology of the Third World," dissented:

> As an Afro-Caribbean writer, I find myself, perhaps, permanently out of sync with radical and social science accounts of the human condition which marginalize third world people. . . . We are simply deprived of structural positions to speak within . . . the new wave strategies of periodization associated with postmodernism and poststructuralism now being forced marched into the field. (McCarthy, 1988b, p. 8)

We will examine racial theory (some of which has been influenced by poststructuralism) in chapter 6.

In other recent work (1990b; 1992b), Apple seemed more favorable to aspects of poststructuralism. In "The Text and Cultural Politics," Michael Apple (1990b) writes: "I shall caution us against employing overly reductive kinds of perspectives and shall point to the importance of newer forms of textual analysis that stress the politics of how students actually create meanings around texts" (p. 4). Continuing his 1985 attack on Hirsch and other classical curriculum theorists, Apple (1992b) argues that a common culture: "requires not the stipulation and incorporation within textbooks of lists and concepts that make us all 'culturally literate,' but the creation of the conditions necessary for all people to participate in the creation and re-creation of meanings and values" (p. 10).

Other recent scholarship in the political sector reveals this apparent shift. In *Working Class Without Work: High School Students in a De-Industrialized Economy*, Lois Weis (1990) argued: "We are no longer an industrial society characterized by the primary struggle between capital and labor. Rather, we are moving into a post-industrial era, one that is, by necessity, characterized by struggle over the symbolic realm of information and the production of culture more generally" (p. 9). In his critique of political curriculum scholarship, Philip Wexler (1987) endorsed a social analysis of the symbolic:

> This new social theory [symbolic theory] is critical now simply because it de-reifies processes of signification or meaning production in knowledge and culture, although in a commodity society, de-reification is a cardinal form of

social criticism. It is socially critical not only because it describes the transition to a new type of post-industrial/post-structuralist, semiotic or as, Baudrillard (1981) disparagingly calls it "semiurgical society." (pp. 126-127)

How would research be conceived that acknowledges these developments? One illustration might be found in the work of one prominent member of a second generation of political scholars, James A. Whitson.

The Constitution of Curriculum: James A. Whitson

After completing an undergraduate degree in Asian Studies at Harvard University, Tony Whitson studied law at the University of Wisconsin-Madison. After practicing public interest law in Madison, he began graduate studies in Curriculum and Instruction at Wisconsin. He followed Wexler to the University of Rochester, where he completed the Ph.D. in 1985. His work (1988a, 1988b, 1991a, 1991b, 1992a, 1992b) embodies and illustrates the discursive shifts in the political sector. Indeed, one constant theme in Whitson's work is the discovery, in one particular conflict after another, that the very notion of a political sector of scholarship, or the dichotomy between political and non-political aspects of curriculum, is an artifact of discursive practices that conceal as much as they reveal. His perspective is decisively informed by his view of curriculum inquiry as the study of *Bildung* (formation) and *Bildungsprozess*—encompassing the range of process in what Grumet aptly refers to as our "coming to form." Whitson is interested in the complex process in which a society "comes to form" in the formation of its participants just as they, in turn, "come to form" within the formation of their society. Whitson's appreciation of curriculum as *Bildung* is closely related to the critical and social psychology of Philip Wexler.

Heteroglossia. Wexler's influence can also be seen in Whitson's emphasis on those material, semiotically structured, discursive practices through which interpretations of educational realities are not only manifested, but effectively imposed (cf., e.g., Wexler 1981, 1982b). In an important essay, Whitson (1988a) focused on the political discourse of those advocating educational "reforms" which would impose limitations on curriculum, ostensibly for the sake of promoting educational "effectiveness." Such "effectiveness" is presumably promoted by preventing the intrusion of "political" elements, and by supporting parental "choice" of a "non-political" but educationally "effective" curriculum. Whitson argued that the contradiction between what these reformers claim that they are doing and what is actually being done is indicated by the very discourse in which they make such claims. While they claim to be taking a stand against "political" contamination of an ideally non-political (privately chosen and educationally effective) curriculum, it is they in fact who are carrying a program of crippling educational effectiveness of the curriculum by promoting and defending the exclusion of materials and activities on political, not educational, grounds.

Whitson insists that these reformers' discourse produces it own theory of knowledge, learning, and meaning which is determined solely by their political agenda, and has no basis in any other social, psychological, or educational reality. While pretending to defend education against politics, they impose a thoroughly political theory of education to rationalize their censorial debasement of the curriculum. Beyond issues of curricular inclusion or exclusion, education is corrupted by the theory of knowledge, learning, and meaning that is implicit in their discourse of "non-political" curriculum reform.

Whitson's essay also deals with what he takes to be the corrupt theory of education to be found in the work of E. D. Hirsch and others who have been championed by conservative educational "reformers." In his critique of the theoretical presupposition implicated in their politically determined discourses, Whitson makes use of the concept of heteroglossia, which points to the inclusion of conflicting voices. Whitson analyzes current school reform, and particularly reform initiated from right-wing interests which attempts to remove dissident voices from the curriculum, sometimes via censorship [see also Littleford, 1983].

By what means is such a monolithic, single-voice curriculum defended by conservatives? Positivism [see chapter 1] is one fundamental characteristic of conservative ideological practices. What is positivism? Whitson explained that positivism represents that line of reasoning, that logic, that language in which dualisms are created. Whitson employs censorship as an example. The Supreme Court ruled that materials could be removed from a school, from its library, without that action being construed as censorship. The Court ruled that only an object which happened to house the idea was removed when a certain book was removed, but not the idea. In so ruling, the Supreme Court conferred upon parents the power to exclude certain school materials, and this power is perceived as "choice." This reasoning depends upon the exclusion and muting of discordant voices in favor of a certain "order." Conservative reformers claim that the curriculum they favor is non-political, which means that they accept their culture as dominant. Other cultures and voices are flattened out and muted; some reforms—such as those of E. D. Hirsch—claim that all minorities need to be inculcated into the main-stream culture so that they can participate fully. Hirsch and others believe that only then can "effectiveness" be achieved. Unfortunately, in such a "non-political" curriculum of "effectiveness" students receive only that information which serves to legitimate and make "natural" the power relationships they encounter day-to-day.

Whitson asked how can we break from the reproduction of the status quo to a more open, even free society, in which students learn to navigate through more than one discourse in an effort to communicate and make decisions—their own decisions? To answer he points to Bakhtin's notion of heteroglossia, defined as the inclusion of all conflicting voices. Whitson argues that students must confront controversial ideas outside of their prior knowledge and experience. Through this confrontation students alter their conceptions of their self and their surroundings. Students must not simplify alternative expressions and new experiences to readily accessible forms which might fit easily into their existing world views. In other words, to minimize "difference" in what one encounters means to homogenize experience. One assimilates new knowledge to prior knowledge, and nothing gets changed. Whitson advocates entering "otherness" so that prior experience and knowledge offer little help in understanding the "new." Only in the space of "otherness" can dialogue be authentic, and from authentic dialogue can come new understanding.

For Whitson (1993) heteroglossia is not a political program. Rather, it is a fundamental condition of language in modern society. Heteroglossia is not introduced in Whitson's work as a method or strategy for promoting a political agenda. It is the condition of the linguistic world which must be taken into account for any understanding of what must constitute competence (seen as the not-politically-defined goal of education) within that world. It is because of the heteroglossic character of society that there can be no valid rationale for the restricted curriculum, except as a political rationale for a politically restricted curriculum supported even at the cost of sacrificing educational competence and understanding.

Constitution and curriculum. Whitson also employs this analysis in a monumental study of the discourses revealed in legal conflicts over First Amendment rights and the curriculum. Referring to Supreme Court decisions affecting curriculum, Whitson (1991b) wrote:

> My point here is that sophisticated academics are not the only ones making and using theories of curriculum and teaching. Insofar as classroom realities may be transformed through the application and influence of the theories that support legal and political decision, it is important that judges, lawyers, and politicians not be left on their own, theorizing in the dark without the benefit of what is known and understood by those actually engaged in education. (p. 120)

This aspect of Whitson's project would seem to be in general agreement with Strike's (1985) insistence that issues of censorship are more complex than commonly understood, with Grabiner's (1983) criticism of earlier of Supreme Court rulings on affirmative action, and related scholarship on the American Constitution and education (Grabiner & Grabiner, 1987).

Whitson's exposition and analysis (1991a) began from the vantage point of the situation after *Hazelwood v. Kuhlmeier*, 484 US 260 (1988; see also Konopak, 1989):

> *Hazelwood* was the case involving a Missouri high school principal's action in blocking publication of stories in the student newspaper. The Court ruled that, because the student newspaper was part of the school curriculum, the principal could exercise control over its contents without violating students' First Amendment rights. (p. 2)

Whitson recounts how this decision marked a drastic change from the legal situation for students and teachers claiming First Amendment protection against censorship, for the curriculum as well as other avenues of communication in the schools. Noting that the rationale for this decision depends on a presupposition concerning education as well as jurisprudence and political theory, Whitson embarked upon a book-long analysis of how the First Amendment right to "freedom of speech" for students and teachers as (apparently) opposed to the rights of state, local, or school authorities has been construed within discursive practices that have been engaged in social, political, historical, and social-scientific, as well as educational and legal, struggles and controversies. He proposed to "begin with the practical problems of how to interpret 'the freedom of speech' that the Constitution guarantees for students in specific concrete situations," but then he immediately noted that: "We cannot pursue that question very far, however, without confronting questions about 'speech' and 'freedom' generally, and about how to understand and interpret the meaning of such phrases in the Constitution, its texts and its contexts" (pp. 8-9).

Whitson argued that the Supreme Court does not work from some originary ahistorical and nondiscursive truth of the Founding Fathers but, instead, in the context of historical and political forces at work at the time. Until the conservative retrenchment, the ongoing conflict between "formalism"—e.g. conformity to the letter of the law (as in the "separate but equal" dogma justifying segregation)—and "realism"—e.g. the recognition of the material reality of the actual situation—appeared to be moving toward the realist camp. From the Social Darwinsim of the late nineteenth century to the watershed 1954 case of *Brown v. Board of Education, Topeka,* 347 US 483, in which school segregation was overthrown, the Supreme Court is regarded as both reflecting the tenor of the times and helping to prod "paradigm shifts" in knowledge.

Whitson goes on to perform a "doctrinal analysis of Supreme Court precedents." After reviewing past and present pertinent cases, he found that, although the Justices published several conflicting opinions in recent education-censorship decisions, they were in agreement on the following doctrinal propositions:

> 1) that the political socialization of students is an important, and constitutionally legitimate, purpose for the public schools; and 2) that although censorial exclusion of some undesirable influences may be justified by the school's mission as a socializing agency, the First Amendment nevertheless imposes limits on the school officials' discretion in controlling influences to which students may be exposed. (p. 71)

The overt doctrinal disagreement occurred "over criteria for recognizing violations of 'the freedom of speech'" (p. 113). "Liberal" Justices assumed freedom required an openness to other ideas and influences. Other Justices insisted that, despite censorship, the students still had their right to *free* expressions (of inculcated values) and that the local authorities should be *free* to act without interference from the courts. Whitson concluded that "at the end of our 'doctrinal reading' of the cases, the nature of the broader inquiry confronts us, more than ever, as an enigma" (p. 115). For this reason, Whitson outlined "approaches to interpretation." Here he compares what he terms the objective subjectivism of Hirsch [that is, subjective preference stated as objective truth] to the relativism of Gadamer and the more politically-oriented work of Habermas. To avoid the "nihilist challenge" of the relativists (p. 123), Whitson turned to the ideas of the former judge and legal scholar Jerome Frank who understands socialization to be necessary and proper in education:

> But Frank has also indicated that the effects of at least some prejudices on fact interpretation should be nullified by the "antiseptic effect" of "the sunlight of awareness." And here we have a role for legal scholarship, informed by relevant discoveries of social scientists, which might even contribute to "increasing judicial justice" (including protection of "the freedom of speech"). (p. 127)

Next, Whitson works with a structural-semiotic and hermeneutical interpretation of Supreme Court decisions. Instead of doctrines, history, or paradigms, Whitson examines the *discourses* on freedom of speech. To illustrate, Whitson analyzed the semiotic structures of the discourses to indicate the regions in which interpretive meaning can be said to reside. He found that the conservative judges interpret the freedom of speech as *expression*, that is, the freedom of individuals to express *through* them a previously socialized range of appropriate ideas. More liberal judges understand "free speech as action in which the participants in purposeful communication can make use of the creative powers of language to produce new meanings constituted within the speech activity itself" (p. 198). Additionally, Whitson compared education as expression, and education as action—each representative of different ideas of the student's subjectivity. Though elucidating the discourses behind the pronouncements of the Judiciary, the structural approach fails to reveal any way such discourses can be made commensurable.

His final approach, in the last chapter, he terms "post-structuralist reinterpretations," in which the incompatible discourses above are revealed to be interdependent. He writes: "Although each discourse structurally denies any recognition of the other, each is ultimately dependent on the logic of the discourse that it would deny" (p. 211). And, further, Whitson finds that "deconstructive criticism will not discredit either the 'action' or 'expression' discourse in favor of its rival; rather, deconstruction shows how each conceals the common metaphysical commitments upon which both discourses depend" (p. 211). The chief "metaphysical commitment" turns out to be a faith in the entity of a non-discursive self which must either be socialized into the democratic community (expression) or must be socialized into acting from open critical agency (or action). Like his mentor Wexler, Whitson moves toward poststructuralism to provide a means of adjudicating these legal and curricular issues.

Whitson cites Derrida [see chapter 9] in the quest for textual meaning as indicating meaning's deferral and non-presence because the thing-in-itself can never be known without an intervening sign, which also must be interpreted. Meaning is in the interpretation. This is not relativism, Whitson insists. Moreover, he adds that "it is a mistake to fear deconstruction as the cause of nihilism, which results rather from the faith that our only alternative is unrealizable objectivism" (p. 229). Whitson turns to "non-structuralist (Peircean) semiotics" to develop a pragmatic orientation to interpretation:

> The pragmatic orientation makes possible a synthesis of semiotics and hermeneutics. Hermeneutical phenomenology regards the horizons of cognition as pragmatic in this sense, and semiotics can be used as a means for describing aspects of those horizons. This makes possible a more articulate reflection on the transformations that enable any "fusion of horizons" to occur. (p. 244)

Peircean pragmatism, Whitson believes, avoids both nihilism and the assumption of an originary transcendental signified by seeking a *telos*, as opposed to an *arche*. It is a dialogic, finally, of "power" (p. 272). This is the place for the oft-mentioned social science researcher and this includes the voice of curriculum theorists and teachers:

> A corollary . . . is that the general discourse on students' First Amendment rights requires input from the education community (no less than from legal scholars and social scientists) as to what we know about factors affecting the freedom of a student's speech, and the scope of protection required for implementation of the student's First Amendment interests. Furthermore . . . in our own professional domains we should be promoting First Amendment protections where they may be required beyond the scope of protection by the Court. (p. 274)

To work dialogically for telos requires elements of *heteroglossia* and, more importantly, *Bildungsprozess*:

> the telos of a developmental or formative process: with an understanding of the textual nature of meaning in interpretive discourses, the political community will recognize that in the process of its own self-formation, it is necessarily both interpreting and influencing the self-formation process of the more specialized interpretive communities, as well as the *Bildungsprozess* of each individual student in the district schools. (p. 277)

With such a circular dialectic between agency and community, between socialization and free-choice, Whitson suggests that we, and our students, may maintain the "freedom to become ourselves" (p. 277). Whitson's final words appear to move him toward autobiographical theory. Without question, Whitson's scholarship is work of remarkable scope and complexity. Like Wexler's, it requires a field that recognizes the significance of theory.

Knowledge as Social Practice: Social Practice as Discursive Formation

Knowledge is power. Recent efforts to understand curriculum as political text acknowledge that in a post-industrial society the production of symbols—information, images (TV, film), signs (including advertising)—rather than the production of material products represent the major mode of economic production. As we noted, Aronowitz has suggested that a curriculum which takes this fundamental shift into account might become a curriculum of popular culture in which the processes of symbolic production become central. Aronowitz's concept of popular culture contrasts with that of popular cultural criticism, which was recognized by some as an "educational wolf in sheep's clothing in the late 1960's and 1970's and quickly rejected as yet another hegemonic ploy, a co-optation of the culture of youth by the dominant culture" (Block & Reynolds, 1991). Instead, Aronowitz's curriculum is one of popular cultural production, in which students would write, produce and perform their own ideas. Such a curriculum would function as a counter-text (Aronowitz & Giroux, 1991). Wexler's (1987) sense of such a curriculum is similar, if more complex:

> The most difficult path, and the most promising, is to actively appropriate the awareness that historical change brings to the surface: awareness of the deeply socio-political concrete character of knowledge, science, and education, and the asking of what that now implies for public school practice. In the semiotic even more than industrial society, knowledge is power. (p. 192)

Knowledge is social practice. Knowledge is power; it is also a social practice. Recently, Wexler has continued his study of systematized knowledge as social practice. In his "Cultural Change, Science, and the University," Wexler (1990) argued that "social science can also be seen as the institutionalization of the specific historic cultural practices of social groups as the subjects of social movements" (p. 83). Just as corporatism has eliminated certain institutional boundaries in the service of more technologically efficient solutions to problems of production, traditional disciplinary and academic boundaries have blurred in recent theory. Wexler (1990) noted:

> It is not certain what forms this deinstitutionalization, decomposition, or dereification of institutionalized and legitimate knowledge will take. . . . [Poststructuralism can be] seen as an aspect of a new social formation that I call the "semiotic society." A society of informational corporatism encourages the revolt against the essentialized knowledge of both western science and European humanism. . . . The process of movement of culture is the basic constituent of knowledge which is its representation. *Not social organization, but social movement is the basis for the categories and criteria of legitimate thought.* (pp. 86, 89)

In this view curriculum *is* power, not only reproductive of power. It is social movement. In a more profound sense than politically oriented scholars understood twenty years ago, Wexler explains how curriculum is political text.

Women as "other." For the politically-focused curriculum scholar working in the 1970s and early 1980s, feminism was initially subsumed in class analysis, but the sector of feminist scholarship soon broke away from its subsidiary status. In the 1990's, feminist theory and gender research are one of the most vital sectors of curriculum scholarship. As we have seen in the controversies section, feminist theory has criticized Marxism (Ellsworth, 1989, 1990;

1992; see also Grumet, 1988b; Lather, 1987, p. 33], arguing that sexism was historically prior to capitalism and class struggle and exploitation, and is thereby more fundamental. Aronowitz summarized the feminist critique of political scholarship: "The feminist critique of Marxism is fundamentally oriented to the issue of women as the otherness of civilization" (Aronowitz, 1990, p. 92), an accurate but incomplete synopsis. Marxists have attempted to include considerations of gender since early in the resistance theory stage (Apple, 1982c, 1983, 1986, 1990b; Giroux & McLaren, 1989; Aronowitz & Giroux, 1991; Giroux et al., 1989; Weis, 1990; Wexler, 1987).

Identity. Another theme of recent political criticism has been identity. In "Working-Class Identity and Celluloid Fantasy," Aronowitz (1989) described the development of identity, particularly in the working classes. He linked identity development with popular culture and curriculum, contending that a major purpose of schooling is the denial of identity, an idea Pinar sketched earlier (Pinar, 1975a). For Aronowitz, school functions "to strip away what belongs to the student, to reconstitute his/her formation in terms of the boundaries imposed by the hegemonic intellectual acting for the prevailing social order" (Aronowitz, 1989, p. 200). He emphasized that those students who succeed do so at the cost of their ethnicity, race and sex, all of which are stripped away. For working-class students, "submission to the curriculum" signifies social mobility aspirations (Aronowitz, 1989, p. 200). Other critical scholars turn to the concept of "subject" to incorporate feminist criticism [see Ellsworth, 1989] and aspects of postmodernism [see Martusewicz, 1992]. In this regard, Hammer and McLaren (1991) warned that:

> one [must be] attentive to the dangers inherent in vulgar Heglianism which universalizes the concept of liberation through a conception of an androcentric, autonomous, Cartesian subject. We argue that critical pedagogy needs to appropriate a reading of the dialectic which avoids a masculinist conception of the self and Eurocentric and patriarchal narratives of emancipation based upon a vulgar Hegelian confrontation with and negation of the Other. (p. 45)

However, this acknowledgement is insufficient for many feminist theorists.
    Other scholars find this area of identity and "subject position" underdeveloped by critical scholars. In addition to Paul Smith's critique of Giroux's work, a Ph.D. student of Philip Wexler at Rochester, Stephen Appel (1992), agreed that an important area of analysis not developed by political curriculum theory is that of the actual processes of identity or subject formation. To accomplish such a description of these process, Appel believes that psychoanalysis, with its emphasis on the unconscious, must be introduced into political curriculum theory to address this underdevelopment. Psychoanalysis had been introduced earlier [see Louise Tyler, 1986; Grumet, 1976b; for a much earlier introduction, George H. Green, 1922.] As we see in chapters 7 and 10, psychoanalysis has influenced contemporary feminist and autobiographical scholarship.

An incorporating concept. Critical pedagogy has tried to be flexible, incorporating areas where it is vulnerable (Ellsworth, 1989, 1990), such as gender, race, and postmodernism. A 1989 essay entitled, "Critical Pedagogy and the Postmodern Challenge: Toward a Critical Postmodernist Pedagogy of Liberation" is illustrative. Here, Peter McLaren and Rhonda Hammer (1989) work to extend critical pedagogy to include postmodernism. They begin by pointing out that a key feature of postmodernism is that meaning has been severed from representation. Put simply, the image has become detached from the reality to which it presumably referred. [See chapter 9 for an elaboration of this idea.] In the sphere of subjectivity this has meant that "the alienation of the subject associated with modernism has been replaced by the fragmentation of the subject" (p. 31). Given this historical and cultural setting, then, the postmodern challenge for the critical educator is "to take a stand on issues of human suffering, domination, and oppression . . . to live with courage and conviction with the understanding that knowledge is always partial and incomplete" (p. 32).

Central to a postmodern critical pedagogy is an elaboration of the relationship between the self and other. A pedagogy of "difference" is one in which the "Other" is neither exoticized nor demonized, "but rather seeks to locate difference in both its specificity and ability to provide position for critically engaging social relations and cultural practices" (p. 34). Summarizing, McLaren and Hammer (1989) stated:

> Critical pedagogy is essentially a hybrid pedagogy . . . [it] is ethically rooted in addition to being theoretically grounded; the ethical stance it assumes calls for us as teachers, parents, students, and administrators to be held accountable as critical citizens to transform the maldistribution of wealth and resources, the pauperization of children, and the feminization of poverty caused by existing economic structures. (p. 40)

This concept of critical pedagogy, they continued, "has made it more urgent for critical educators to develop a theoretical basis for a feminist pedagogy" (p. 41). Endorsing the pioneering feminist theory of Mary Daly (p. 42; see chapter 7 and Reiniger, 1982; 1989) they write: "To respond to the challenge of the colonization of women in the present historical juncture, and in the North American context in particular, educators must find a way of making female voices heard in classrooms" (p. 46). The theoretical task involves in part the development of "a critical language that enables us to both identify ourselves and recreate ourselves as active subjects in history and distinguish our real needs from manufactured desire" (p. 49). In what they term "the postmodern era of neo-capitalism" (p. 50), critical pedagogy "must become a theoretical and strategic method of uncovering the manner in which ideological contradictions are resolved at the imaginary level in the individual subject; it must also becomes a means of politically contesting the structures of domination within consumer capitalism" (p. 50). Finally :

The critical pedagogy of which we speak works against the conflation of description with representation, information with knowledge, language with reality, and the institutional and power arrangement such conflation serves. . . . The job of the critical educator in the postmodern era is . . . to construct an emancipatory curriculum which legitimates the postmodern condition of mass culture in order to help students both criticize and transcend its most disabling conditions. (pp. 54-55)

McLaren and Hammer demonstrate that "critical pedagogy" is a flexible idea indeed, here filled with poststructuralist and postmodern notions. As we will soon observe, McLaren's scholarship is noteworthy for embodying the coming crisis of political theory, a crisis of overextension, overincorporation, and the incommensurability of poststructuralism and critical theory.

That old ghost "resistance." Just ten years ago, reproduction theory had been dismissed as reductionistic and simplistic, replaced by dynamic resistance theory. In the early 1990's, resistance theory is now dismissed as simplistic in a postmodern world with new historical agents and the integration of marginalized discourses. Just as Apple and Giroux repudiated reproduction theory ten years ago, a second generation of politically oriented scholars now attack resistance theory. A Ph.D. graduate of Apple's at Wisconsin, Leslie Roman, for instance, insisted that the concept of resistance romanticizes the "potential of specific instances of working class practices to create emancipatory social transformation (Roman & Christian-Smith, 1988, p. 143). Aggleton (1987) and Whitty (1985) decried resistance theory for reducing the "intentions" and behaviors of social actors into a single structuralist typology or "grammar of challenge" (i.e. contestation and resistance). Additionally, in resistance theory is a risk of "class essentialism" (Roman & Christian-Smith, 1988, p. 143). Finally, in those studies of popular culture in which resistance theory plays a role, there is a tendency to "pay homage to a productivist logic in Marxism, a logic which treats the domination of women by men as either secondary to or as a consequence of the exploitation of workers (usually presumed male) in the sphere of commodity production and waged work" (Roman & Christian-Smith, 1988, p. 144).

What else is wrong with resistance theory? In his study of teacher resistance, Barry Kanpol (1991) suggested that "a missing and key concept [is] group solidarity" (p. 135). Kanpol claimed to observe teachers acting to subvert the dominant ideology of competition, taken-for-granted concepts of success, prejudice, and authoritarianism. Teachers in Kanpol's (1991) study, in part, "acted in unison and sustained with them the intersubjective consciousness that had to do directly with traces of transformation in their personal, political resistances" (p. 146).

Political curriculum theory had been constituted, in its earlier phases, by reproduction and resistance theory. Clearly these theories have been repudiated. Critiques of individualism and passivity (Giroux's "discourse of despair") have been replaced by notions of solidarity, agency, identity, and popular culture. What is next for this overextended sector of scholarship?

Will it continue in any recognizable form? One scholar who works to builds bridges between the earlier phases and the present crisis is Joe L. Kincheloe.

A powerful tool? Kincheloe's postmodern political theory. Joe Kincheloe (1993b; Kincheloe & Steinberg, 1993) is convinced that postmodernism can be employed to promote political change. Kincheloe's synoptic scholarship illustrates well the current expansive, incorporating phase of political theory, including its efforts to domesticate and thereby employ postmodernism. Kincheloe's (1993b) postmodern political view is informed by liberation theology (p. 72), a theory of place and difference (p. 69, p. 215), feminist and gender theory (pp. 154-155; p. 214), Jungian synchronicity (p. 171), ecology (p. 172), popular culture (p. 85), qualitative research (p. 91), and shows the influence of Henry Giroux and especially Peter McLaren.

This influence is evident in Kincheloe's framing of postmodernism in his *Toward a Critical Politics of Teacher Thinking: Mapping the Postmodern* (1993b). On the one hand postmodernism appears as ominous: "The postmodern pedagogical mission involves rescuing meaning even as we understand its destruction by the postmodern information landscape" (1993b, p. 85). On the other hand, postmodernism is worthy of occupying the curricular center: "At the center of the postmodern curriculum is a study of media that analyzes not only the effects of television, radio, popular music, computers, and such, but also teaches postmodern forms of research such as semiotics, film analysis, and ethnography" (p. 91). [See chapter 1 for a discussion of Kincheloe's useful summary of contemporary curriculum research.] For Kincheloe, perhaps postmodernism is simultaneously a threat *and* a possibility, another expression of political oppression *and* a tool for progressive change:

> When postmodernism is grounded on a critical system of meaning that is concerned with questions for the purpose of understanding more critically oneself and one's relation to society, naming and then changing social situations that impeded the development of egalitarian, democratic communities marked by a commitment to economic and social justice, and contextualizing historically how world views and self-concepts come to be constructed, postmodernism becomes a powerful tool for progressive social change. (1993b, p. 5)

Here the qualifications of postmodernism are numerous, implying a risk for the political project if postmodernism is not carefully circumscribed. Despite these efforts to incorporate postmodernism, it would appear to represent a threat to the political project. In a somewhat more recent essay, written with Shirley Steinberg (Kincheloe & Steinberg, 1993) and focused on cognitive theory, Kincheloe's qualifications of postmodernism appear to be fewer. Its incorporation in his and Steinberg's view of "post-formal thinking" is rather complete [see chapter 9].

The crisis of political theory. Probably the work of no political scholar exemplifies the crisis of contemporary political curriculum theory more than the recent work of Peter McLaren. McLaren has attempted to incorporate into his political pedagogical perspective more aspects of postmodernism than another other major scholar, although Giroux has made considerable efforts as well. The decentering consequences of postmodernism and poststructuralism undermine what many see as the latent authoritarianism of the political perspective, including its thinly concealed self-righteousness and its employment of class guilt (manipulated by a false identification with the working class) to enlist loyalty (Beyer & Wood, 1986; Wexler, 1987). In undermining this central psycho-dynamic of Marxist curriculum theory, postmodernism threatens the political enterprise as the field has known it for the last twenty years. Whether it portends the collapse of this sector—certainly Apple's appeal to return to class analysis cconcern on this scale—or foreshadows its reconceptualization away from reliance on reproduction and resistance toward poststructuralist categories such as identity and subject formation as central organizing ideas, remains to be seen.

These tensions and questions are evident in a provocative essay entitled "Decentering Culture: Postmodernism, Resistance, and Critical Pedagogy" written by Peter McLaren (1991a). McLaren (1991a) writes:

> This essay is intended to provide teachers with an introduction to the topic of culture written from a post-structuralist theoretical perspective. I will address five interrelated movements in the debate over culture: culture and the age of postmodernism; culture as a form of discourse; culture as plurivocal; culture as resistance; and cultural politics as the discourse of the other. (pp. 231-232)

Culture, McLaren explains, can be conceived as "a contested terrain that serves as the loci of multivalent voices and power" (p. 283). For McLaren, a central question in contemporary scholarship concerns the role of schools in shaping student identity.

Moving beyond the old dualisms of thought/action, theory/practice, scholarship/the real world common to earlier phases of political scholarship, McLaren endorses "a radical reconceptualization of culture as a field of discourse or text, [that is] to speak of culture as a discourse is to situate discourses in what [Michel] Foucault calls a discursive field" (p. 235). What is the import of such a view? Culture as a discursive field comprised of diverse voices hardly supports a national curriculum, for example, presumably not even a national curriculum that carefully reflected that diversity. Nor, he continues, is culture, even the culture of sexism and patriarchy, unitary. McLaren (1991a) writes:

> culture is not seamless or all of one piece. For instance, if we look at the culture of patriarchy, we notice it is not monolithically repressive. Not everything about patriarchy is oppressive, since cultural spaces do open up where oppressive discourses can and have been contested by women. . . . Discourses are struggled over and resisted. (p. 240)

Feminist scholars may not accept this assessment of patriarchy in which its benign nature is indicated by the permission its extends to women to speak.

McLaren returns to the consequences of his view of culture as a diverse discursive field, in which voice and identity become central concepts. What does this view offer teachers? McLaren (1991a) writes:

A critical pedagogy should speak against the notion that all cultural realities need to follow one dominant narrative or that all diverse cultural realities need to be given voice, since it is obvious that many of these realities harbor racist, classist, and sexist assumptions. The key here isn't to insist simply on cultural diversity, transforming culture into a living museum of contemporary choices (e.g., pluralism) but a critical diversity. A critical diversity means that choices need to be seen as social practices which are themselves historically and socially constructed and teachers need to distinguish cultural choices as liberating or oppressive. Freedom, therefore, becomes something that must be won within discourse, and not sought outside of the social practices which anchor it, as though freedom can somehow be found outside the materiality of the social world, as in some metaphysical meadow. . . . Teachers must decide which discourses are to be hacked out from a thicket of possibilities, and which are to be discarded, which discourses need to be denaturalized and democratized, and which need to be opened up as potential points of resistance and political struggle. (pp. 247-248)

In this passage McLaren is travelling far outside the world of Willis' (1981) lads, a world of class conflict, the sabotage of institutional authority, and the old Marxist fondness for general strikes and barricades in the streets. For more economically and class oriented Marxists such as Apple, McLaren must indeed appear to be "in some metaphysical meadow." From a poststructuralist perspective, however, he is quite right. Serious struggle and resistance are not about misbehaving in classrooms; rather, they require facing one's self as a "discursive position," in which various discourses and practices intersect and diverge, reflecting and creating a political location, with its own set of limitations and opportunities. Understood poststructurally, political struggle *is* discursive; it involves destabilizing patterns of thought which cannot, finally, be separated dualistically from physical behavior or "action."

In this regard, McLaren (1991a) understands that "to act ethically means to act with a certain narrative identity. . . . Personal history takes the form of a political project by extending ethical responsibility to include a collective history. The narrative self is forever in crisis because it refuses to reduce the Other to any representation [sic] form" (p. 251). However, that said, McLaren now steps back toward class struggle and historical inevitability. McLaren (1991a):

We . . . must not reject the dream of totality outright. While there may be a number of public spheres from which to wage an oppositional politics, and while the micropolitical interests of groups that fleck the horizon of the postmodern scene may have overwhelmingly separate and distinct agendas, I believe that we should—all of us—work together towards a provisional and perhaps even ephemeral totality to which we can all aspire. . . . We need to struggle to free ourselves from the bondage of discursive determinations and produce ourselves through the act of imagining other "selves" we could become. We need a plurality of possibilities of what we might become by recovering who we once were, what we are at present, and how we might position ourselves and (through what discourses) to become otherwise. . . . We need to change reality rather than simply change our conception of reality, although the latter is certainly a prerequisite to the former. . . . In psychoanalytic terms, we might fear that our own ignorance of the contradictions which inform us as human subjects may lead to a "return of the repressed." (p. 252)

At the end, for now, McLaren has returned to more familiar epistemological ground for political scholars. The notion of culture as a discursive field has receded somewhat, and he has reintroduced the dualism between "reality" and "our conception of reality." In the world understood discursively, no such simple distinction exists, nor did it seem to for McLaren in earlier paragraphs. We are not suggesting that the problem is McLaren's; it cannot, for example, be simply understood as his inconsistency. Rather, it is the problem—indeed the crisis—of contemporary political curriculum theory: how to reconcile a view of politics that, finally, has strikes and street barricades in mind, with a more complex view in which what we think and what we do, i.e. the realm of the symbolic, in a semiotic society, represent the location of political action, not the streets.

To assert its own authoritativeness and moral and political self-righteousness, Marxism requires its proponents to insist *they* understand history; *they* embody morality and ethics; *they* dictate strategy. This self-righteousness—which is not altogether absent in McLaren's work—still runs the considerable risk of dogmatism. McLaren may be understood as not only taking the most risks, he may also, perversely it may seem, be acting prudently. Probably the old-style Marxism cannot remain in power in the American curriculum field. That may represent a "tragedy of immense proportions" (Apple, (1992a), although this judgment represents a minority opinion to be sure. McLaren's work, a poststructuralist critic might say, returns at its end the political hubris, the self-conferred moral high ground, while allowing to an extent what traditional Marxism, with its dualisms between thought and action, theory and practice, the real world and what professors say, cannot: that is, a playing field in which conversation, or, the rhetorical tradition (Bridges, 1991; see chapter 6), is the rule of the game. This is not a step away from the world, as Sears (1992b) misunderstood. It is an acknowledgement of the world. McLaren's recent work has become central to the project to understand curriculum as political text. In it the challenges posed by postmodernism and poststructuralism may be resolved, and they may not. The future of this sector is clearly at stake.

For one with considerable intellectual property (i.e. cultural capital) assets in the field, such risk is not prudent. For Apple, a judicious use of aspects of poststructuralism is recommended. More important is not to forget the power of class, of traditional Marxists' emphases on reproduction. The radical in the field twenty years ago, Apple has positioned himself, or as a Marxist might say, history has positioned him, as a conservative. Giroux has remained faithful to the spirit of resistance theory, still extolling struggle, urging his audiences—with doses of inspiration and guilt—to overturn the evil empire. His recent work has become theoretically more diverse, incorporating insights from African-American feminism as well as poststructuralism to formulate a complicated grammar and vocabulary of resistance, now involving "border crossings." In perhaps the most sophisticated fashion, Wexler incorporates poststructuralism as a discursive aspect of a new social configuration. Returning always to society and history understood in a fairly rigorous, unyieldingly Frankfurt School perspective—laced with feminism, semiotics, and poststructuralism— Wexler's work remains the best contemporary example of a thoroughly political perspective, more complex than Apple's, whose economistic tendencies pull him toward a reductionistic emphasis upon class and artifacts, such as textbooks. Due to its theoretical diversity yet relative simplicity, and to its volume, the work of Giroux has emerged as the most visible scholarship in this sector. Bowers' occupies a stimulating but unpopulated position, inspired by phenomenology, critical theory, existentialism, and ecological theory. McLaren has moved the farthest away from the political perspective of the 1960s; he has traveled in the postmodern/poststructuralist universe, but to date he manages to return to what remains a recognizable political perspective. How he moves next may determine not only whether he follows Giroux in visibility and influence, but where political discourses themselves move next.

The 1990s viewed from the late 1970s. A scholar whose work was important in the reproduction theory literature in the late 1970s [see Anyon, 1979] has returned after some absence to political debates. Jean Anyon's response points to the tensions in the political sector, which revolve primarily around poststructuralism and feminist theory. In her analysis of what she characterizes as "The Retreat of Marxism and Socialist Feminism: Postmodern Theories in Education," Anyon (1992) appears to decry the discursive shifts in the political sector during the decade. Referring to the first major explanation of poststructuralism for curriculum studies—Cherryholmes' (1988b) *Power and Criticism*—Anyon (1992) complains:

> Cherryholmes's text [1988b] exhibits fundamental characteristics of a method of thinking and valuing he seeks to transcend; he fails to enact the basic theoretical premises he adopts. His text exemplifies a fundamental problem of postmodern approaches: basic theoretical premises that are advanced are not carried out in practice. (p. 16)

Referring to Patti Lather's book-length exposition of postmodernism, Anyon (1992) judges: "Lather's research and pedagogy (that is, her practice) does not meet the theoretical hopes she has for it" (p. 19). Other feminists influenced by poststructuralism are apparently victimized by that influence:

> When we read postmodern accounts of analyses of the "local," such as Ellsworth's of classroom dynamics and institutional racism, we are reading accounts that have been fictionalized. . . . I would argue that in Ellsworth's case, an assumption of the systematic nature of oppression in our society, based on

one or more "grand narratives" of some sort, influenced the decisions she and her students made. (p. 22)

Anyon continues: "Ellsworth's practice is informed by more than the theoretical premises on which she attempts to base it. While the theory makes the impossible demand to 'stay local,' in fact her analysis was substantially more global" (p. 23).

Next, Anyon turns to Giroux: "Giroux marginalizes others' voices" (p. 26). Referring to postmodern theories, especially those of Giroux and McLaren, Anyon (1992) writes: "the theory serves primarily the interests of those who produce it" (p. 30). "Useful theory," she goes on, "would be neither total . . . nor completely ad hoc and applicable to only one locale. . . . Janet Miller's recent work (1990) exemplifies the use of middle-range theorizing in an attempt to develop personal agency in teachers" (p. 32). [We have mentioned Miller's work in chapter 4; see chapters 7 and 10 for reports on her feminist and autobiographical theory.] Returning to the old dualism between theory and practice, Anyon (1992) reminds: "theory must make recommendations capable of enactment. . . . It is now more than ever before politically imperative that our scholarly work be socially useful" (pp. 33-34). Anyon's dismissal of recent developments in political theory provides another measure of how far that sector has traveled in the last decade.

Not a crisis? In contrast to Anyon's essay, William B. Stanley (1992b) wrote a detailed and sympathetic history of the effort to understand curriculum as political text, linking it with reconstructionism [see chapter 3], and concluding with attention to the role poststructuralism might play in political curriculum theory (or critical pedagogy, the term associated with the work of Giroux and McLaren especially, but which Stanley adopts). Stanley (1992b) makes three related points regarding the function of poststructuralism for political theorists, namely that 1) it is not nihilistic and not antagonistic to the political project; 2) further, that poststructuralism contributes to a more sophisticated understanding of "our sociocultural environment and how it is constructed" (p. 205); and 3) poststructuralism can contribute to counter-hegemonic praxis, i.e. to resistance to the status quo. Relying on Whitson (1991; see our report on his work earlier in this chapter and in chapter 9), Stanley (1992b) defines textuality, a concept central to poststructuralism, as referring "to the material nature of our human existence as manifested in our institutions, discursive practices, and power arrangements [;] each of these operate in the textual context of diverse and dynamic structural systems of signs and codes" (p. 205).

Such a concept of "text" points to "structures of human agency" (p. 205) as well as to "the more general deterministic structures (e.g., language) within which agency is exercised" (p. 205). So understood, Stanley insists, poststructuralism invites us to focus on apparent oppositions between human agency and social structures, oppositions which become sites for resistance, or counter-hegemonic praxis. Central to Stanley's concept of a pedagogy for social transformation is the concept of phronesis, which he defines as "a fundamental human interest which encompasses all dimensions of human thought and action, including a basic ethical dimension, a quest for the good or human betterment" (p. 215). Acknowledging the tendencies in social reconstructionism, and by implication in political curriculum theory, to verge "on becoming an authoritarian form of social engineering" (Stanley, 1989), Stanley (1992b) believes that "a reconceptualized reconstructionist approach to critical pedagogy" could avoid this danger by focusing upon phronesis. Such "competence for practical judgment" (p. 218) is fundamentally ethical as well as political; it acknowledges that "praxis is textual in the sense that, as human subjects, we are largely formed by language, and language is the medium for all praxis" (p. 219).

Phronesis requires resistance to domination and oppression; poststructuralism requires us to "heighten our sense of humility . . . we should [act] with caution and restraint" (p. 220). He concludes by reaffirming the utopian character of political work, quoting McLaren that "with dreams we can do wonderful things" (quoted in Stanley, 1992b, p. 222). Stanley's cautious and detailed study sympathetically tries to mend the irreparable rifts others, such as Anyon, see in the political movement. While a considerable contribution to curriculum history, we suspect his effort to accommodate the threat poststructuralism poses to political theory cannot succeed.

VIII
Conclusion: The Political Sector Divides and Disappears?

There is a danger that social theorists will be reduced to mere curators of various discourses.
                                                          (Peter McLaren, 1986, p. 392)

Righteous indignation became routinized, professionalized, and in so doing, underwent an odd transformation. Back in the 1930s a magazine editor wondered aloud if there was a typewriter at the *Partisan Review* with the word *alienation* on a single key. Right now I'm on the lookout for a typewriter that has *counterhegemonic cultural production* on a single key.
                                       (Henry Louis Gates, Jr., 1992, p. 186; emphasis in original)

The systematic effort to understand the curriculum as political text has asserted itself forcefully since the 1970's. The traditional notion that curriculum development, evaluation, etc. could be conducted in a politically neutral fashion quickly became one conceptual casualty of this effort, as was the taken-for-granted assumption that schools functioned as avenues of upward social and economic mobility. The rejection of these mainstream and common-place ideas of the traditional curriculum field was accompanied by the building of a relatively elaborate conceptual edifice, among the foundations of which were notions of reproduction, resistance, ideology, hegemony, the key concepts of the first two phases of development in this sector, roughly the period of 1970s and into very early 1980s. As the effort grew voluminous and more complex, so did the range of its interests, incorporating notions of critical pedagogy and literacy as well as issues of race, class, and gender in the 1980s. The next phase, punctuated by heated controversy and criticism from inside and well as outside the sector, was marked by continued incorporation of nearby terrains, including hostile ones, such as feminist, racial, and poststructuralist and postmodern discourses. As the sector expanded, it became divided, and, some would say, self-enclosed.

Apple appeared to retreat to an earlier stage of class emphasis, while Giroux attempted to revive resistance theory with poststructuralism and African-American feminism. Wexler declared their work reactionary, ruling that the rhetoric of reproduction and resistance theory acted out a dead 1960s student movement and ignored movements in history and society since that time. Wexler's own theory, rooted in social and historical analysis traceable to the Frankfurt School, incorporated poststructuralism as a discursive formation of a new social movement. Bowers formulated a sophisticated theory of curriculum as communicative competence which political scholars have yet to address. McLaren has moved farthest into poststructuralism, returning, perhaps not altogether intact, to resistance theory, and thereby embodying the coming crisis of political curriculum theory.

How will political theory be political without Marxism or the Frankfurt School (i.e. critical theory) as its foundations? The coming crisis of political curriculum theory concerns the challenges poststructuralism entails for political theory's very conceptual, epistemological, and moral composition. For mainstream political theorists, politics and power remain important categories, however routinized and professionalized these categories have become, as Gates (1992) complained. Others have simply replaced these Marxian notions with concepts associated with studies of race and gender. To these discourses we turn next.

Chapter 6

Understanding Curriculum
as Racial Text

The old Marxist and neo-Marxist orthodoxies of class and economic primacy in education debates are rapidly being replaced by the new pan-ethnic-cultural orthodoxies of racial origins and racial identity.

Cameron McCarthy & Warren Crichlow (1993, p. xiv)

Race, class, and gender are *relations* that have to do with how people define themselves and how they participate in social life. They are not *mere* theoretical categories.

(Roxana Ng, 1993, p. 51)

Racial classification is a matter of *identity*.

(Michael Omi & Howard Winant, 1983, p. 49)

We are not, in fact, "other".

(Toni Morrison, 1989, p. 9)

I
Introduction: Racial Theory is Autonomous

Race autonomous. There are those who would subsume the subject of race within that of the preceding chapter on politics. Among these would be those theorists and scholars who tend to insist that the political character of curriculum is its most significant feature. Our view is that "race" must be regarded as an autonomous concept in the effort to understand curriculum. It is true that each discourse identified in the thematic organization of this book intersects with others. Of course, political considerations are important in the *racial* constitution of curriculum. For instance, the exclusion of third-world literature from school literature courses reveals a political aspect of canon formation. The battle over the canon involves aesthetic issues as well as historical and psycho-social ones. However, there is an autonomous domain of race which cannot be reduced to these related discourses and issues. The power and complexity of scholarship on race and curriculum recommends its status as a major contemporary curriculum discourse. In this chapter we will focus primarily upon race as related to the experience of African-Americans, given the centrality of that experience to the constitution of the American nation. At the same time, it must be acknowledged that Native Americans, Asian-Americans, Chicano/Chicana and Latino/Latina

Americans are also central, and this fact is acknowledged in the scholarship [see, for instance, Aoki, 1993a; Au, 1980; Delgado-Gaitan, 1990; Deyhle, 1986a, 1986b; Dumont, 1972; Erickson & Mohatt, 1982; Fillmore & Meyer, 1992; Gibson, 1982; Krall, 1981; McLaughlin, 1993a; Perez, 1993; Ryan, 1989; Tierney, 1993b; Walsh, 1991].

The effort to understand curriculum as racial text may well develop, as William Watkins (1993) suggests of "black curriculum orientations," both autonomously and intertextually, i.e. "as both a part of and separate from the mainstream curriculum movement" (p. 321). Certainly racial theory must not be viewed as a form of intellectual segregation: "We should not revive the belief that some people are, by virtue of their background, culture, status, religion, or race, peculiarly suited for a life of scholarship in some specialized area. We must forge an intellectual community transcending boundaries of ethnicity" (Hamerow, 1993, p. A36). The effort to understand curriculum as racial text would appear to be such an intellectual community, simultaneously separate and integrated within the field at large.

The concept of "race." Race is a complex, dynamic, and changing construct. Like gender, race is not a biological given, and the cultural weight it has been made to bear is out of all proportion to any biological or morphological differences among groups of people. As Anthony Appiah (1985) has observed: "Every respectable biologist will agree that human genetic variability between the populations of Africa or Europe or Asia is not much greater than that within those populations" (p. 21). Or, as Henry Louis Gates, Jr., (1985) noted: "Race, as a meaningful criterion within the biological sciences, has long been recognized to be a fiction. When we speak of 'the white race' or 'the black race,' 'the Jewish race,' or the Aryan race,' we speak in biological misnomers and, more generally, in metaphors" (p. 4). These metaphors and "misnomers" not only have resulted in massive suffering and oppression but have also been used to organize the "white" world, including the American school curriculum and the curriculum field.

Racial categories, for all their historical pervasiveness, have not been fixed through time. Those identified as "people of color" have changed according to political circumstance. For instance, before the American Civil War southern Europeans, Jews, and even the Irish were considered "non-white" (Omi & Winant, 1983). The racial category of "black" grew out of slavery. "Whites" collapsed the diversity of African—and native—peoples into monolithic, racialized categories:

> By the end of the seventeenth century, Africans, whose specific identity was Ibo, Yoruba, Dahomeyan, etc., were rendered "black" by an ideology of exploitation based on racial logic. Similarly, Native Americans were forged into "Indians" or the "red man" from Cherokee, Seminole, Sioux, etc. people. (Omi & Winant, 1983, p. 51)

In nineteenth-century California, the arrival of large numbers of Chinese provoked a "crisis" of racial classification. In *People v. Hall* (1854), the

Supreme Court of California ruled that the Chinese should be regarded as "Indian" and thereby ineligible for those political rights afforded to whites (Omi and Winant, 1983). In the United States the grouping of individuals into blacks and whites has been and continues to be central in shaping American society and the curriculum as well. It is impossible to understand curriculum without understanding the centrality of race in the construction of the American identity.

Race marginalized. Before the Reconceptualization of the curriculum field in the 1970s, race was regarded as marginal to the effort to develop curriculum, as perusal of the historical discourses [see chapters 2, 3, 4] will indicate. It is now reasonable to argue that race has become central to the field, a status also supported by the intensity of public debate over multiculturalism. Until recently, however, even politically oriented curriculum scholars have tended to overlook race, ascribing to it marginal status. Cameron McCarthy, one of the theorists whose scholarship has been instrumental in moving racial theory to centerstage, observed:

> American curriculum theorists and sociologists of education have been far more forthcoming in their examination of how the variables of class and, more recently those of gender, have informed the organization and selection of school knowledge and the production and reproduction of subcultures among school youth [than they have been in their examination of race.] (McCarthy, 1988a, p. 265)

And there may have been an additional problem:

> The old left critique of the commodity has a usefully confining tendency: it sets up a cunning trap that practically guarantees that the marginalized cultures it glorifies will remain marginalized. They knew just how to keep us in our place. And the logic was breathtakingly simple: if you win, you lose. (Gates, 1992, p. 184)

Separated now from the effort to understand curriculum as political text, where it was undertheorized and perhaps, if Gates is right, exploited, race is moving to center stage in curriculum discourse. Certainly the public interest in and debate over multiculturalism have no doubt helped to support its growth in the curriculum field. What signs indicate this growth? There are many. In addition to its place in this textbook as a major sector of curriculum scholarship, a review of race and related issues was included in the 1992 *Handbook of Research on Curriculum* (Fillmore & Meyer, 1992; Strickland & Ascher, 1992). An important new collection of essays edited by Cameron McCarthy and Warren Crichlow (McCarthy & Crichlow, 1993), entitled *Race, Identity, and Representation in Education,* promises intensified interest. Racial discourses can be regarded as occupying an expanding space between political and feminist theory, intersecting with both but independent of each.

Economic substructure. This movement has not occurred without struggle, sometimes struggle with apparent friends. McCarthy points out that radical educational theorists and researchers such as Berlowitz (1984), Bowles and Gintis (1976), and Nkomo (1984) locate problems of race within social and economic structures of capitalism. Curriculum reproduction theorists [see chapter 5] understand schools' social function as reproductive of dominant values, not only through curriculum content, but via grouping procedures, faculty hiring patterns, and differential school funding. The theoretical point McCarthy makes is that this entire genre of curriculum theory [the effort to understand curriculum as political text] locates understanding in an economic substructure, from which class is derived, and from class, other elements such as race. In these conceptualizations race is relegated to a status of "episodic" and epiphenomenal rather than determining. McCarthy (1988a) summarized the neo-Marxist position:

> Racism as an ideology fulfills capitalism's economic requirements for superexploitation and the creation of a vast reserve army of labor. Racial strife disorganizes the working class and hence weakens working-class resistance to capitalist domination. Schools, as apparatuses of the state, both legitimize racial differences in society and reproduce the kind of racially subordinate subjects who are tracked into the secondary labor market. (p. 271)

As have feminists, racial theorists decline to function as a subservient element of Marxism and political theory.

Racism preceded capitalism. McCarthy has identified several weaknesses in the neo-Marxist view. First, he notes that locating racism within capitalism is historically and empirically inaccurate. He points out that forms of racism, such as slavery, antedated capitalism. Slavery occurred in ancient Greece, for instance. Second, racial and class interests do not necessarily coincide; further, forms of racism persist in so-called post-capitalist countries. Third, McCarthy argues that subsuming race into class and into the economic substructure trivializes the power of the school in both the reproduction and transformation of race relations. Fourth, neo-Marxist scholarship tends to characterize racial groups as monolithic, blurring significant differences within and among racial groups (McCarthy, 1988a).

McCarthy distinguishes Marxist cultural theory from neo-Marxist theory, suggesting that the former communicates a more complex understanding of the interrelationships among economic, political, and racial issues. This position—known as the parallelist position—is identified with the 1983 work of Michael Apple and Lois Weis. Apple and Weis criticized the tendency of neo-Marxist scholarship to bifurcate economic structure and culture. For example, for neo-Marxists race is reduced to class; for so-called liberal theorists the problem of race is reduced to prejudice and other socio-cultural values. McCarthy notes that Apple and Weis construe race as a social process interwoven with other social processes, especially with class and gender. Pedagogical and political work in one sphere is said to influence processes in others (Omi & Winant, 1986). This more complex Marxist view of race is well expressed by Peter McLaren and Michael Dantley (1990):

Racism must be seen as a set of structured social practices which reproduce themselves through individuals who are imprisoned by historically conditioned regimes of discourse, by market-logic interests, and by interests of dominant groups. Racism, therefore, must be described as structured (through historically and ideologically loaded discourses, social practices, relations of production, gender, and social class) and as structuring (through the individual's active, yet often contradictory, participation in these discourses, relations, and practices) while it often is simultaneously destructured (through both formal and informal resistance to these discourses, relations, and practices). (p. 37)

Nonsynchrony. While approving of the parallelist position as an advance over liberal and neo-Marxist positions, McCarthy expresses a reservation. He suggests that this position is "additive," meaning that race is merely added to class and gender. The dynamics of "tension, contradiction, and discontinuity in the institutional life of the school" are overlooked (McCarthy, 1988a, p. 274). To correct this problem, McCarthy draws upon Hick's thesis of "nonsynchrony." Hicks (1981) argues that race, class, and gender function in contradictory fashion in daily life; they do not reproduce themselves in any simple manner. McCarthy (1988a) charged:

The fact that the principles of selection, inclusion, and exclusion that inform the organization of school life have been hitherto understood primarily through class and socioeconomic paradigms says more about the biographies of mainstream and radical neo-Marxist theorists than about the character of schooling. (p. 277)

With Wexler (1987) then, McCarthy locates the effort to understand curriculum as political text, with its attendant privileging of socio-economic elements—and until recently the relative absence of racial elements—in the biographies of political scholars themselves.

In this critique McCarthy challenges the assumption embedded in much political scholarship that it is comprehensive. McCarthy and others, through their critique of neo-Marxist scholarship and their conceptualization of curriculum as racial text, have established this sector of scholarship as autonomous. Its concepts are essential to any serious effort to understand curriculum. Any comprehensive theory of curriculum must include race, and its concepts—such as multiculturalism, identity, marginality, and difference—as fundamental. While the political sector enters a period of crisis, racial theory is ascendant. Let us continue our review of this work by surveying the major black curriculum orientations.

II
Black Curriculum Orientations

Black curriculum theorizing . . . is inextricably tied to the history of the Black experience in the United States.

(William H. Watkins, 1993, p. 322)

In an important essay published in the fall 1993 issue of the *Harvard Educational Review*, William H. Watkins (1993) summarizes black curriculum orientations and situates them historically. Watkins employs the notion of curriculum orientation which he links with the work of Schubert (1986a), Giroux, Penna, and Pinar (1981), Kliebard (1987), and Eisner and Vallance (1974). However, the notion of curriculum orientation derives not only from antecedent formulations within the field but also from "complex overlapping historical forces" (p. 323). Watkins lists the following six orientations: functionalism, accommodationism, liberalism, reconstructionism, Afrocentrism, and Black Nationalism.

Functionalism. This orientation characterized black education in the eighteenth and early nineteenth century. Functionalism is an orientation characterized by self-effort, religious altruism, and "the involvement of benevolent Whites" (Watkins, 1993, p. 323). One such benevolent person was Sarah Grimke, who admitted that: "The light was put out, the keyhole secured, and flat on our stomach before the fire with spelling books in our hands, we defied the laws of South Carolina" (Birney, 1885, pp. 11-12; quoted in Watkins, 1993, pp. 323-324). Watkins notes [as had Bullock (1967) earlier] that there may have been sufficient permissiveness in slave society to permit limited education to occur. Such education was shaped by the conditions of slavery and directed to basic human survival: "This preparation for life is at the center of the functionalist curriculum. Consistent with colonial education, functionalism is typically basic, largely oral, and frequently includes folklore as part of its curriculum" (Watkins, 1993, p. 324). Such education can be likened to early colonizing efforts in British West Africa (Fafunwa, 1974), for instance. Slavery in the American South made educational efforts colonial in character. Even as informal Black education became more formal, functionalism remained a significant orientation.

Accommodationism. Watkins (1993) tell us that while functionalism is "linked to the limited and rudimentary interaction of an earlier period, accommodationism was a more widespread and politically charged curriculum for the emerging late nineteenth and early twentieth-century racially segregated, industrial nation" (p. 324). More than any curriculum orientation, accommodationism is unmistakably linked with an imposed racial agenda (DuBois, 1903; Watkins, 1993). Often termed the "Hampton-Tuskegee" model, this curriculum emphasized "vocational training, physical/manual labor, character building . . . and racial subservience" (Watkins, 1993, p. 324). It was promoted by northern corporate interests (Berman, 1980; King, 1971; Watkins, 1993). Accommodationism is associated with Booker T. Washington whose famous 1895 speech to a mostly white audience in Atlanta offered a palpable platform to corporate and other conservative interests (Anderson, 1988; Harlan, 1983; Watkins, 1993). "Offering agricultural education, vocational training, and character building as centerpieces," Watkins tells us, "this orientation is sharply distinguished from the liberal, progressive, and more militant outlooks" (p. 325). The accommodationist curriculum aimed for incremental black progress without militancy, and appeared to accept the notion of a "backward race" (Watkins, 1993, p. 326). Directed especially at southern rural blacks, the model was later exported to Africa (Watkins, 1989c, 1993). Another proponent of accommodationism, Thomas Jesse Jones, was judged an "evil genius of the Negro race" by W. E. B. Dubois (DuBois, 1919; Watkins, 1993, p. 327). Watkins explains that "Jones was not only an important curriculum theoretician and ideologist, he was also corporate America's point man in Black education" (p. 327). Linked with colonialism, segregation, and submission, accommodationism remained the educational and social policy of the South for decades (Watkins, 1993).

Liberal orientations. Watkins indicates that liberal orientations were "more hopeful" and coincided with the optimism that in part characterized progressivism during the final decades of the nineteenth and the first decades of the twentieth century. The influence of missionary philanthropists is evident here. While not opposed to industrialization, they pressed for improved social conditions. During this period a number of black colleges were established, including Fisk University, Talladega College, Morehouse College, Shaw University, and others. Watkins (1993) tells us that while "not unaffected by the racial and paternalistic attitudes of their times, the missionary community derived a liberal education curriculum that borrowed from the traditions of humanism, such as altruism, free expression, and the unfettered intellectual development of the individual" (p. 328). He continues:

> Black liberal education differed little from traditional liberal thought. A clear connection to Deweyan themes is evident. The curriculum was designed to develop the students' analytical and critical faculties, and to help students become worldly, tolerant, and capable of significant societal participation. Black liberal education placed much significance on leadership. It strove to educate teachers, preachers, civil servants, and others who would be committed to the ideals of the liberal democratic state; these ideals encompassed gradual change, electoral politics, and planned societal transformation. (Watkins, 1993, pp. 328-329)

Black nationalism. The liberal faith in progress and change has not been shared by nationalists and separatists, whose views first appeared at the end of the eighteenth century. Nationalist and separatist "views were linked to international slavery, colonization, the debasement of Africa, and the mistreatment of African peoples scattered throughout the world" (Watkins, 1993, p. 329). Important twentieth-century nationalists and separatists included Marcus Garvey, Noble Drew Ali, Elijah Muhammed, and Malcolm X. Pan-Africanists such as Bishop Turner and Marcus Garvey supported return to Africa, whereas others believed cultural revitalization could occur only where Africans had been transported, such as the United States (Watkins, 1993). Separatists such as Black Muslims, Malcolm X, and the Republic of New Africa share certains views with Pan-Africanists and Black Nationalists. Separatists call for the establishment of a parallel society. Watkins (1993) reports that the separatist platform of the Nation of Islam advocated a program of black-owned business, a separate black educational system modeled after the University of Islam, and an end to black participation in American electoral politics (Essien-Udom, 1962), all of which is aimed at cultural revitalization and independence. The black studies curriculum movement of the past twenty-five years represents one programmatic expression of the nationalist orientation (Watkins, 1993, 1989b).

Afrocentrism. Afrocentrism [see also chapter 14] reclaims the significance of Africa not only in the history of African-Americans, but in the history of the world. Ancient Egyptian civilization has become an important reference point (Asante, 1987; Watkins, 1993). Included in this remembrance of the African contribution is a reconsideration of Anglo-American epistemological theories as the only appropriate models of inquiry:

> Eurocentric analysis is viewed as linear. Rooted in empiricism, rationalism, scientific method and positivism, its aim is prediction and control. . . . African epistemology, on the other hand, is circular (Asante, 1987) and seeks interpretation, expression, and understanding without preoccupation with verification. (Watkins, 1993, p. 331)

Afrocentrics such as Asa Hilliard, et al. (1990) identify six areas in which the Eurocentric curriculum has failed: 1) the history of Africa before the slave trade is omitted; 2) the history of the people of the African diaspora (including, for instance, the Fiji, the Philipines, Dravidian India) are ignored; 3) cultural differences rather than similarities among Africans in the diaspora are underlined; 4) the struggle against racism is insufficiently communicated; 5) analyses of the global systems of racial oppression are undertaught; and 6) the history of the peoples of Africa is omitted (Watkins, 1993, pp. 332-333). Other Afrocentrics assert that African ways of knowing must be communicated, and devaluations of blacks implied by bureaucratic designations like "at-risk" must cease (van Sertima, 1990; Asante, 1987; Watkins, 1993). Additionally, Afrocentrics promote the teaching of the work of lesser-known African-oriented scholars such as Cheikh Anta Diop, Yosef ben Jochannan, Chancellor Williams, J. A. Rogers, Walter Rodney, Eric Williams, and others (Watkins, 1993, p. 332).

Social reconstructionism. Watkins (1993) explains that while "Afrocentrics are very provocative, in general they don't challenge the contemporary or historic economic arrangements of society" (p. 332), the agenda of social reconstructionists [see chapters 2 & 3; Stanley, 1992b]. One of the major progressives and social reconstructionists, Harold Rugg, expressed interest in black educational issues (Rugg & Withers, 1955, pp. 264-280; Watkins, 1993, footnote 14, p. 333). Additionally, Watkins (1993) tells us, the platform of social reconstructionism, i.e. "the ideals of a collectivist, egalitarian, reformed society found some support among the politically conscious Black intelligentsia" (p. 333). Further, black radicals during the 1930s and 1940s such as A. Philip Randolph (founder of the Sleeping Car Porters Union) and Angelo Hearndon (active in southern sharecroppers unionization movements) were very much concerned with educational issues in ways consistent with the social reconstructionists (Watkins, 1993, p. 333). Despite the absence of formal ties between social reconstructionists and black intellectuals and radicals, an ideological affinity is unmistakable. W. E. B. DuBois, "the preeminent twentieth-century Black educator" (Watkins, 1993, p. 333), advocated views indistinguishable from those of social reconstructionists such as Rugg and Counts (Marable, 1986). Indeed, in an earlier essay, Watkins characterized DuBois as a "black social reconstructionist" (Watkins, 1989a).

While Watkins subtitles his essay "a preliminary inquiry," this modesty does not blur his accomplishment. In an accessible and organized way which will prove highly useful to a curriculum audience generally undereducated regarding racial issues and racial theory, Watkins outlines the major historical movements in black curriculum in the United States over the past three hundred years. It is a considerable achievement, and one which also functions to elevate Watkins' status to that of a major scholar and theoretician in the contemporary field. Next, we review the debates regarding multiculturalism, relying on the work of another major figure: Cameron McCarthy.

III
Multiculturalism

> Our failure to understand how racism undergirds educational institutions will ultimately lead to further racial polarization.
> (Louis A. Castenell, Jr., 1992, p. 5)

> The curriculum should be reformed so that it will more accurately reflect the history and cultures of ethnic groups and women.
> (James A. Banks, 1993, p. 4)

A curricular truce? Cameron McCarthy views multiculturalism as representing a "curricular truce" between liberals and Black radicals. For McCarthy, multiculturalism absorbed that Black activism aimed at restructuring schools, re-expressing activism as so-called "non-racism." Multicultural education represents an effort to acknowledge cultural diversity in the curriculum. Despite its noble intentions, it is problematical. McCarthy (1993a) characterizes multicultural education as a "contradictory and problematic 'solution' to racial inequality in schooling" (p. 225). McCarthy reviews the history of multicultural education, beginning with its assimilationist antecedents during the 1950s and 1960s. Multiculturalism, McCarthy tells us, was replaced by a so-called pluralist model that advocated cultural diversity. Multiculturalism, in McCarthy's words, "disarticulated elements of Black radical demands for restructuring of school knowledge and rearticulated these elements into more reformist professional discourses around issues of minority failure, cultural characteristics, and language proficiency" (1993a, p. 228). Multicultural proponents emphasize: a) cultural understanding, b) cultural competence, and c) cultural emancipation.

Cultural   understanding   and   competence. Cultural   understanding,   as expressed in curricular documents such as those published by the Wisconsin Department   of   Education   (1986),   is   presumed   to   lead   to   cultural "enrichment," which encourages, presumably, the elimination of racial prejudice. The cultural understanding model assumes that individual attitudes are central in the reproduction of racial prejudice. Unfortunately, cultural understanding programs, including those which utilize so-called sensitivity training, have resulted in modest or no significant measured reduction in white prejudice. One possible explanation for this failure may reside in the tendency of cultural understanding models to overstate ethnic differences, thereby contributing to the perpetuation of racial and ethnic stereotypes (McCarthy, 1990). Models of cultural competence arose, in part, from the failure of cultural understanding models. Multicultural curriculum theorists such as James Banks (1981, 1987) argued that students must demonstrate cultural competence in the language and cultural practices of groups other than the one in which they hold exclusive or primary membership. Cultural competence models support bilingual and ethnic studies, the objective of which is the preservation of cultural diversity. The American Association of Colleges for Teacher Education (AACTE) endorsed this model in 1973 in an often cited report entitled "No One American Model." Teachers are urged to facilitate the cultivation of ethnic identities and to communicate knowledge of "different" cultural groups. Unlike the cultural understanding model (in which white students were the main audience), the cultural competence model focuses upon minority students. The curricular interest here is the development of competence for the "public" sphere, i.e. white mainstream culture. Somehow minority students must balance their ethnic origins and identities with competence in mainstream society (McCarthy, 1990; Lucas, Henze, & Donato, 1990). Issues related to notions of ethnicity and identity will be examined later in this chapter.

McCarthy observes that the cultural competence model goes beyond simple multicultural awareness and individual attitudinal adjustment. This model is critical of the culturally disadvantaged model of mainstream programs such as Headstart because such programs presumably locate the problem in blacks themselves. Instead, cultural competence proponents, in McCarthy's (1993a) view, "valorize minority cultural heritage and language" (p. 236.) The cultural competence model does function in an affirmative manner. Yet, it also undermines as it supports minority efforts to become competent in a majority world. In so doing it commits minority youth to incorporation and assimilation (McCarthy, 1990).

Cultural emancipation. As do the cultural understanding and cultural competence models of multicultural education, the cultural emancipation model affirms minority identity. Like the cultural understanding model (and even like cultural deprivation models), the cultural emancipation model notes the value of positive self-concept for minority students, a state enhanced, presumably, by studying minority history and culture. There is an additional claim associated with this model: improved academic achievement should enable minority youth to succeed in the labor market. Like the social reconstructionist views of Rugg and Counts [see chapter 3], proponents of the emancipatory model believe that profound shifts in the economic and social spheres will accrue from improved academic achievement. Summarizing, McCarthy (1993a) writes:

> As we saw, each of these approaches represents a subtly different inflection on the issue of what is to be done about racial inequality in schooling. Thus proponents of cultural understanding advocate sensitivity and appreciation of cultural differences—a model for racial harmony. Cultural competence proponents insist on the preservation of minority ethnic identity and language and "the building of bridges" between minority and mainstream culture. Finally, models of cultural emancipation go somewhat further than the previous two approaches in suggesting that a reformist multicultural curriculum can boost the school success and economic futures of minority youth. (p. 242)

McCarthy characterizes this last approach as a "language of possibility," a language not evident in earlier assimilationist discourse. Further, implicit in this model is an enlargement of school curriculum to include the history and experience of minority and other marginalized groups. Finally, this model points to the economic and public sphere generally, well beyond the confines of the classroom. However, the emancipatory model fails to acknowledge the racial inequality in those spheres. Indeed, implicit in all models of multicultural education is a naive assumption that academic achievement guarantees economic achievement.

Multiculturalism: A postmodernist project? Multiculturalism has also been understood as a postmodernist project. In this regard, Bridges (1991) writes: "What troubles us [conservatives] about multiculturalism is its inevitable association with the agenda of postmodernism" (p. 3). Bridges discusses the rhetorical tradition in Western thought, i.e. the view that there are (at least) two sides to every question, that any question is best understood by one who can argue both sides with equal effectiveness. In this rhetorical tradition, content, i.e., the subject matter of knowledge, occurs in the context of advocacy and disputation. Within this context, no absolute certainty or final proof is ever possible. The goal of inquiry, understood rhetorically, is not objective truth, but reasonable belief, the state of being persuaded. Due to its very incorporation of a multiplicity of conflicting viewpoints [this definition recalls Whitson's work on heteroglossia; see chapter 5], rhetorical culture seemed unemployable to seventeenth-century intellectuals as a framework from which to impose ideological order on the warring religious and political factions of that age. This recognition led the seventeenth century to embrace the logic of Cartesian dualism, giving rise to natural science [see Doll, W., 1993a]. Bridges reminds us, then, that the Enlightenment project started as a rejection of rhetorical conceptions of reason and knowledge. It is unsurprising that multiculturalism has created controversy, especially among political conservatives who see their task as the defense of the Enlightenment project of reason and order. Bridges (1991) explains:

> The controversy over multiculturalism has raised educational and political issues that in fact can be resolved only by explicit appeal to and use of the resources of the rhetorical tradition. In this sense, multiculturalism is the particular program of educational reform most clearly and directly linked to the more general and long-term task that faces us: the rediscovery and revival of rhetorical culture. If we are troubled by multiculturalism, then, it is not surprising. What at first appears to be a welcome and relatively unproblematic program of curriculum reform becomes, upon second glance, the first item of an agenda of epochal cultural transformation. (p. 7)

Also informed by postmodernism are discourses on postcolonialism and multiculturalism. Illustrative of this work is John Willinsky's (in press) study entitled "After 1492-1992: A Post-Colonial Supplement for the Canadian Curriculum." Here Willinsky—known for his work on literacy [see chapter 5]— discusses multiculturalism as a "valuable starting point for a global process of decolonization" (p. 9). However, undermining multiculturalism as a postcolonial initiative is that "it has suffered from tendencies to a) treat cultures other than the dominant one as both exotic and monolithic, b) represent these cultures through food-and-festival events, and c) regard racism as an isolated matter of individual ignorance among certain segments of the population" (p. 9). [See Willinsky, 1992a, 1992b, 1992c; see also chapter 14.] As is evident, multiculturalism has been criticized by those on both the Left and the Right.

No relationship between education and economic advancement? There are additional reasons why multiculturalism and the project to understand curriculum as racial text prove disturbing to American political conservatives. One of the great myths employed by conservatives is that everyone enjoys the opportunity to improve his or her social and economic position. This apparently does not hold true for African-Americans. Troyna (1984) and Blackburn and Mann (1979) found no necessary relationship between education and economic advancement. Troyna found that race and social networks, rather than educational accomplishment by itself, were linked with employment prospects. In this regard, Crichlow (1985) concurs that despite adequate educational backgrounds, blacks continue to suffer high rates of unemployment.

Furthermore, as Andrew Hacker (1992) has noted, while increased education does tend to increase incomes for blacks, academic achievement does not bring pay equity with whites at similar academic levels. Hacker (1992) wrote: "Even worse, black college men end up just a few dollars ahead of whites who went no further than high school. . . . There is little evidence that spending more years in school will improve [blacks'] position in relation to whites" (p. 96). Troyna and Williams (1986) argued that multicultural curriculum reorganization has failed to correct racial inequality in schools. In one study, black parents, by being unemployed, underemployed, and suffering multiple forms of discrimination, and by speaking informally of these experiences in daily life, communicated to their school-aged children that academic, success guarantees little. Therefore, the economic expectations of African-Americans may be cause rather than consequence of Black school failure (Ogbu, 1990). A similar phenomenon occurred in the Mexican-American community (Ogbu & Matute-Bianchi, 1986). Such findings cast doubt on the emancipatory claims of multicultural curricularists (McCarthy, 1990; Troyna, 1984).

An enormous responsibility? Unfortunately, McCarthy has also observed, multicultural approaches to curriculum reform fail to provide explanations or "solutions" to persisting problems of racial inequality in school. All three approaches, he believes, depend on changing values and attitudes. Common to these approaches is an emphasis upon the "individual." McCarthy (1993a):

> Schools, for example, are not conceptualized as sites of power or contestation in which differential interests, resources, and capacities determine maneuverability of competing racial groups and the possibility and pace of change. . . . In abandoning the crucial issues of structural inequality and differential power relations, multicultural proponents end up placing an enormous responsibility on the shoulders of the classroom teacher in the struggle to transform race relations in American schools and society. (p. 243)

Typically, the classroom teacher has not been prepared multiculturally (Sizemore, 1990).

Put another way, past approaches have tended to favor "building bridges" from marginalized groups to mainstream society rather than a collective minority identity politics focused on change in the current structure of race relations in schools (McCarthy, 1993a). A notion of "collective minority identity politics" suggests a more fundamental reconceptualization of curriculum as racial text than multicultural approaches have exhibited. We turn next to issues of identity, politics, and representation.

IV
Identity and Repression

The issues of culture and identity must be seriously incorporated into a nonsynchronous approach to racial domination in schooling.
(Cameron McCarthy, 1988a, p. 276)

The trauma of racism is, for the racist and the victim, the severe fragmentation of the self.
(Toni Morrison, 1989, p. 16)

One of the challenges in dealing with racial issues . . . is for whites . . . to think of ways in which racism has been a limiting factor in their lives.
(Keith Osajima, 1992, p. 92)

A repressed American identity. "We are what we know." Linking knowledge and identity, Castenell and Pinar (1993) argue that Americans are also what they do not know. If what Americans know about themselves—American history, American culture, the American national identity—is deformed by absences, denials, and incompleteness, then the American identity—both as individuals and as Americans—is fragmented. A fragmented self, they argue, represents a repressed self. Such a self lacks full access both to itself and the world. Repressed, the self's capacity for intelligence, for informed action, even for simple functional competence is impaired. Its sense of history, gender, and politics is incomplete and distorted. Denied individual biography and collective history, African-Americans have been made appendages to European-Americans (Bulhan, 1985). The American identity is not comprised of timeless traits; it is comprised of "the changing products of politics and history" (Scott, 1991, p. B2).

Knowledge and ourselves. Linking debates regarding the "canon" with questions of self, identity, and difference enlarges the curricular debate from an exclusive preoccupation with equity or with multiculturalism to include debates regarding the relationship between knowledge and ourselves. In this regard, the "Eurocentric" character of school curriculum functions not only to deny "role models" to non-European-American students, it denies self-understanding to "white" students as well (Castenell,1990). The American identity is not exclusively or even primarily an European-American. Fundamentally, it is an African-American. For this point Castenell and Pinar refer not only to well-publicized demographic trends (minorities are predicted to constitute the majority perhaps by midpoint in the twenty-first century); they refer to the American past and the present. To a still unacknowledged (by European-Americans) extent, they observe, the American nation was built by African-Americans. African-Americans' presence informs every element of American life. The concept of "white" is predicated upon an excluded, racialized "other." For European-American students to understand who they are, they must understand that their existence is predicated upon, interrelated to, and constituted in fundamental ways by African-Americans (Goldberg, 1990).

The American self not exclusively European. The American self denied and repressed "acts out" repression via imperialism in foreign policy and political, economic, and cultural repression domestically. The refusal—sometimes unconscious, sometimes not—to incorporate African-American knowledge into the mainstream curriculum is a psychoanalytic as well as a political process of repression. Understanding curriculum as racial text suggests understanding education as a form of social psychoanalysis (Kincheloe & Pinar, 1991). The school curriculum communicates that which we choose to remember about our past and that which we choose to believe about the present. It also might elicit what we have forgotten, and in so doing might crack the walls of repression and allow a more accurate memory of the past to surface. Understanding the past accurately might allow us then to grasp the present. How do representations of race and difference communicate a sense of the American identity? The American identity is constructed partly by denial, by maintaining fictions. The American "self" is not exclusively or even primarily European. That delusion represents a fantasy, a flight from historical and cultural reality (Castenell & Pinar, 1993; Baldwin, 1985).

Willful aggression toward Blacks? The absence of African-American knowledge in many American schools' curriculum is not simple oversight. Its absence represents an academic instance of racism, or in Houston Baker's apt phrase, a "willful ignorance and aggression toward Blacks" (quoted in Castenell & Pinar, 1993, p. 1). Just as African-Americans have been denied their civil rights in society generally, they have been denied access to their history and culture in school. Not only African-Americans have been denied, however. Institutional racism deforms white students as well. By refusing to understand curriculum as racial text, (white) students misunderstand they are also racialized, gendered, historical, political creatures. Such deformity occurs—for most "whites"—almost "unconsciously." Many European-American students and their parents—and many curriculum specialists—would deny that curriculum is racial text. Such denial is done "innocently"; it represents an instance of repression in its psychoanalytic sense (Castenell & Pinar, 1993). In social terms, psychological repression expresses itself as political repression (Schwartz & Disch, 1970; Kovel, 1971).

The 1980's: Triumph of "superego?" Castenell and Pinar employ Freudian imagery of the self to frame the racialization of political and curricular debates. During the decades of the 1980s, they suggest, the businessman represented the American prototype. Lee Iaccoca, Donald Trump, Michael Milken were among the most admired: white, male, savvy, shrewd, devoted to the bottom line. If this prototype represented the American ego: realistic, adaptive, adjusting in self-profiting ways to "reality," then African-Americans represented the "id," pleasure-seeking, unpredictable, accomplished in athletics and the arts. European-American culture projected African-Americans as the "id" (West, 1988), and in classical Freudian style, maintained relative repression of the "pleasure principle" so that—presumably—ego stability could be maintained. Those elements of American life which could be said to represent the "superego," fundamentalist religious groups, were permitted by the "business" ego to grow in size and influence. Those groups marginal to this version of the "ego"—African-Americans, other marginalized ethnic groups, women, children, gays—were undermined, via public policy and in political practice (Castenell & Pinar, 1993).

Christopher Lasch (1984) has argued that the conservative political prescription for schools and society during the 1980s can be characterized as "superego" in nature. Illustrative of this "superego" voice are slogans such as "more homework," "just say no," "work harder!" Conservatives insisted that the problem with American society was simple laziness (not their own of course), and in this simplistic analysis African-Americans were assigned a major blameworthy role. Liberals continued to call for rational deliberation, incorporating aspects of the unconscious (African-Americans in the parallel) into the conscious ego (mainstream society), but in controlled and planned ways (cf. the liberal conceptualization of an orderly, incremental civil rights movement). Race is now "deeply imbedded . . . in each voter's conceptual structure of moral and partisan identity" (Edsall & Edsall, 1991, p. 53).

Castenell and Pinar employed Lasch's analysis to make their point that the question of school curriculum is also a question about the self, the American self. For them, understanding curriculum as racial text means understanding the United States as fundamentally a racialized place, as fundamentally an African-European place, and the American identity as inextricably African-American as well as European, Latino, Latino/Latina, Native American, and Asian-American. Debates over the canon are also debates over the constitution of the American self and the constitution of the public sphere (Pinar, 1988b).

No "black" without "white." Historically European-Americans and African-Americans are two-sides of the same cultural coin, two interrelated narratives in the American story, two interrelated elements of the American identity. Projected as "other" and repressed, African-Americans' presence in the American, indeed, "Western" self has been grasped, perhaps most precisely, by Frantz Fanon (1963, 1967, 1970). Like James Baldwin (1971) and others, Fanon understood that "white" is a fabrication made possible by the construction of the concept "black." For Fanon, there can be no "black" without "white" and vice versa. One cannot understand the identity of one without appreciating how it is implied by the other. So it is that European-Americans cannot hope to understand themselves unless they are knowledgeable and knowing of those they have constructed as "different," as "other." The sequestered suburban white student is uninformed unless he or she comes to understand how he or she is also—in the historical, cultural, indeed psychological sense—African-American. Because "white" does not exist apart from "black," the two co-exist, intermingle, and the repression of this knowledge deforms us all, especially those who are white. All Americans can be understood as racialized beings; knowledge of who we have been, who we are, and who we will become is a story or text we construct. In this sense curriculum—our construction and reconstruction of this knowledge for conversation with the young—is racial text (Castenell & Pinar, 1993).

Cultural literacy. During the past decade much has been made of the failure of public-school students to learn even the most elementary and necessary facts regarding their history, geography, and culture. Cultural literacy is a non-controversial requirement for any citizenry. What becomes controversial is the composition of such literacy. In the popular press voices express views of cultural literacy that are informed by, primarily, Eurocentric and patriarchal knowledge systems. Few would contest that American students must know and understand the European antecedents of contemporary American culture. However, this knowledge ought not be used as a defense against "otherness" and "difference," a denial of what we might term our cultural unconscious (Castenell & Pinar, 1993). Put another way, "neglecting the experiences of African-American people in the curriculum is not only detrimental to African-American children, it is also a great source of the miseducation of other children who continue to be poorly prepared for a multicultural world" (Boateng, 1990, p. 77).

V
Issues of Institutional Practice

Racist behavior may be partially suppressed inside the school but only to be driven outside the school gates.
(Barry Troyna & Richard Hatcher, 1992, p. 199)

Curricula . . . shapes thoughts and feelings about "self" and about one's own and others' cultures.
(Ellen Swartz, 1992, p. 85)

[A] predominantly white teaching force in a racist and multicultural society is not good for anyone, if we wish to have schools reverse rather than reproduce racism.
(Christine E. Sleeter, 1993a, p. 157)

Issues of institutional practice are varied, including school desegregation (Dentler, 1991; Willie, 1991b), school reform (Comer & Haynes, 1991; Jones-Wilson, 1991), teacher education (Garibaldi, 1991b), specific curricular issues (Pearson, 1991; Banks, 1991; Stewart, 1991; Gordon, 1993; Kincheloe, 1993a), and reports of successful programs (Lomotey, 1990c; Sizemore, 1990; Ratteray, 1990, Hale-Benson, 1990), including anti-racist initiatives.

Efforts to combat the racial miseducation of children have been varied, worldwide, and interdisciplinary (Romer, 1992; Lomotey, 1990a). Recently in Great Britain, in their investigation of *Racism in Children's Lives: A Study of Mainly-White Primary Schools*, Barry Troyna and Richard Hatcher (1992) report that the "common view," or "contact hypothesis," is that racial prejudice and discriminatory social practices are "dispelled by the positive experience of white and black children being together in school." Unfortunately, the evidence does not support this view. They write:

On the contrary, it reveals that "race," and racism, are significant features of the cultures of children in predominantly white primary schools. By far the most common expression of racism is through racist name-calling. . . . It is in general the most hurtful form of verbal aggression from other children. (1992, p. 195)

Troyna and Hatcher's theoretical assumption is that racist ideologies are not simply passively received. Rather, they are employed by children in ways which help the children to make sense of their material and cultural circumstances.

Given this assumption and their findings, what do Troyna and Hatcher suggest that schools can do? The first step, they suggest, is to recognize that racism is an important issue in predominantly white primary schools. School officials ought to be aware, however, that attempts to address this issue can easily remain on the surface:

> a school policy may be effective in reducing racist behaviour within the school, but on its own it may do nothing to challenge the roots of racist behaviour within what we have called children's thematic and interactional ideologies. Racist behavior may be partially suppressed inside the school but only driven outside the school gates. (1992, p. 199)

Troyna and Hatcher express skepticism regarding the efficacy of multicultural education as a curricular strategy through which racism and racist incidents in school might be ameliorated. What are implications of their research for dealing with race in the curriculum?

Troyna and Hatcher (1992) reach several conclusions:

> The first is the centrality of the personal experience of the child. . . . In order to respond to the real meanings of "race" in children's lives, the curriculum needs to open itself up to engage with the full range of children's experiences . . . [including] other sources of children's racial experience: adult world (family, street, neighborhood) and television. (p. 201)

Additionally, they identify mutually dependent elements of school policy. First, a clear and firm policy must be in place in order to deal with racist incidents, a policy which includes seriously listening to complaints of black children and to white children too, understanding the "social meanings of racist behaviour within children's cultures" (p. 204). Second, a school policy must be in place in order to deal with other forms of oppressive behaviour (such as disabilities, etc.). Third, a curriculum (both formal and informal) needs to be devised that addresses issues of "race" in association with related forms of inequality and injustice, both within children's worlds as well as in the wider society. "Anti-racist education," Troyna and Hatcher (1992) explain, "should facilitate children's recognition that racist behaviour trades on and helps to reinforce much broader patterns of discrimination.... Our evidence demonstrates that racism in mainly white primary schools is more prevalent, more complex and more entrenched than many educationists care to admit" (p. 204).

From racial issues in mostly white British primary schools let us move to issues in native education in North America. In his "Islands of Remorse: Amerindian Education in the Contemporary World," Richard Courtney (1986) asked why does Amerindian education seem to nearly inevitably fail? Courtney identified six factors which, in his view, characterize the Amerindian world view: 1) life is seen as a whole rather than in parts; 2) human beings in mundane, everyday life are viewed as highly active in spiritual life and not as passive; 3) the arts are considered expressions of the spiritual world rather than as simply personal expressions; 4) time is not experienced in linear fashion; 5) learning occurs in social settings as lived, rather than via formal programs in schools; and 6) religious beliefs, attitudes, and mores comprise a world view that is fundamentally different from that of the white culture. For example, among the Tewa of New Mexico, ritual drama unifies intellectual and emotional experience into an active metaphors which frame reality. Such a use of drama is paralleled by the work of Dorothy Heathcote, a well-known modern drama educator, who effectively employed improvisation as a significant method of learning. Courtney (1992) reports a University of Calgary experiment in Amerindian education to support the view that the creative arts generally, and spontaneous drama particularly, can help provide meaningful educational experience among native peoples.

Test-taking and Navajo students. Other research (Deyhle, 1986a) points to a "clash of cultures" in schools. In a study of Navajo students, Deyhle (1986b) found that an assessment of learning through individual assessment—considered standard practice in school—was culturally incongruent with Navajo experience and expectations. Test-taking itself, Deyhle reminds us, is a cultural activity; it depends on the acceptance of two specific values, including the value that achievement is an individual accomplishment, and, second, that the individual should display that accomplishment. In Deyhle's study, white students shared these values, the Navajo students did not. For Deyhle (1986b), this finding raises an important policy question: can or should schools enculturate students more effectively into the values required by testing, or can and should the forms of testing themselves be changed? Christine Sleeter (et al., 1992) is clear what the answer to that question should be: "Schools should concentrate on changing themselves, developing the capacity to serve all students, instead of consistently trying to change the nature of the students" (p. 181).

Non-Innu standards. Other research on native education reveals that schools bring in the larger society, complicating natives' school experience. In his study of native education, Ryan (1989) found that the school employed perpetual observation, evaluation, documentation, punishment, and reward to "normalize" the Innu, to ensure that they abide by non-Innu standards. This process, however, created negative self-images among the young Innut he studied. Ryan (1989) concluded that changing the classroom environment to match the local cultural milieu, a strategy that a number of researchers and others associated with minority education recommend, will do little to alleviate difficulties in Native education, for such a tactic does not address those basic components of the problems associated with cultural assimilation that originate in white society.

Another example of scholarship focused on institutional practices attends to the role of parents and other family members in children's success at school. In her *Literacy for Empowerment*, Concha Delgado-Gaitan (1990) writes that school success for many minority children is dependent on the ability of the schools to incorporate the parents and the culture of the home as an integral part of the school curriculum. She reports research [the Portillo study] that shows how "some families, schools and one community defy the stereotypic constraints and become empowered by their collective work toward building educational opportunity for Mexican children in the home and the school" (p. 1). Research that focuses upon family and school cooperation in the education of minority children is important, as afterward, she feels, "families and the schools will have a stronger basis for communicating with each other and literacy can be better understood in relation to the home-school communication that questionably empowers all those involved in the process" (p. 169).

Other research focused upon the institution reveals how racial relations are reproduced and resisted. Carl Grant and Christine Sleeter (1986) report a ethnographic case study of "Five Bridges Jr. High School" which examined race, class, gender, and handicap disability, showing how inequality and the status quo are perpetuated. In her "Schooling and Cultural Production: A Comparison of Black and White Lived Culture," Lois Weis (1983) explored the "lived culture" of black students in community college (p. 235). She found that black students "drop out and blame themselves. . . . Not only is the underclass reproduced, but the potential for transformative political activity is minimized" (p. 256). How might reproduction of racism be interrupted? Resisting racism requires authentic dialogue in classrooms, according to Lisa Delpit (1988). Delpit (1988) concluded that "teachers must teach all students the explicit and implicit rules of power as a first step toward a more just society" (p. 78). Further: "The dilemma is not really in the debate over instructional methodology, but rather in communicating across cultures and in addressing the more fundamental issue of power, of whose voice gets to be heard in determining what is best for poor children and children of color" (p. 94). One instance of a curriculum designed to give voice to children is Louise Derman-Sparks' (1989) *Anti-bias Curriculum: Tools for Empowering Young Children*, published by the National Association for the Education of Young Children. What might characterize such anti-racist curriculum? We may speculate that "it emphasizes experience, critical self reflection, and personal growth through self education. . . . [It will] emphasize peer learning and cooperation using media that stimulate all the senses, feelings, and emotions" (Butt, 1985a, p. 30).

As Troyna and Hatcher's (1992) work suggests, even the voices of racist white children need to be heard if anti-racist education is to be non-superficial. Studying children's books which express racially problematical views, Joel Taxel (1986) advised: "Rather than attempting to suppress these, and even blatantly racist (and sexist) books, we would be far wiser to incorporate them into multidisciplinary units of study designed to explore the evolution of racial and gender-related attitudes" (p. 277). Other research seems to support this general view that anti-racist teaching requires listening to a range of expression without, as the teacher, hiding behind the pretense of neutrality. In evaluating a lesson on India, for instance, Jeffcoate (1981) tells us: "It is indisputably important that teachers should 'come clean' on salient social and moral issues. It is equally important, as a matter of rights as well as tactics, that pupils who have views on these same issues should have some kind of classroom forum for expressing and exploring them" (p. 14).

Richard Butt (1988) tells us that "educating ourselves beyond racism" might emphasize the personal nature of racism and prejudice: "I have tried to show that the way out of this negative cycle is through *inter-relationship*" (p. 2). Such inter-relationship is not only intersubjective; it requires the collaborative efforts of scholars, teachers, students, and their families. The range of research on institutional practice underlines the need for change in the nature of the school and in the academic field of curriculum. In this regard, understanding curriculum as racial text "would require a genuinely independent educational studies with the time and resources to pursue serious and controversial political issues" (Hartnett & Naish, 1987, p. 369). The reconceptualized curriculum field labors to become such a field, one in which race is now a central discursive element.

VI
Racial Representations

For Black culture is not what you see; it's what you don't see.
(Russell H. Coward, Jr., n.d., p. 215)

Can the language of multiculture begin with a recognition of the ambivalence of meaning and the detours of representing identities that are already overburdened with meanings one may not choose but, nonetheless, must confront and transform?
(Deborah P. Britzman, et al., 1993, p. 189)

Identity and Curriculum Politics. In a provocative essay entitled "Canonical Sins," Peter Taubman (1993a) alleges that canonical conservatives are guilty of idolatry, of fixing selected "classics" in an ahistorical realm in which "they are worshipped for their embodiment of the Western metaphysic" (p. 36). He characterizes canonical radicals as heretics, as they seek "to stretch the canon's boundaries to include non-canonical texts to dissolve those boundaries altogether" (p. 36). Both radicals and conservatives, he suggests, might be guilty of a decontextualism. He suggests:

> Perhaps both discourses [radical and conservative] do violence to the quirky and unique ways books move through our lives, flatten out our private relationship to reading, and force us to read and hear a prior discourse in the words which meet our eyes and ears and the intentions which move our hand to pull down the volume from the shelf. (Taubman, 1993a, p. 36)

He proceeds by asking, with Foucault, "how is it, given the mass of things that are spoken, given the set of discourses actually held, a certain number of these discourses are sacralized and given a particular function? Among all these narratives, what is it that sacralizes a certain number and makes them begin to function as 'literature'?" (p. 38). Toni Morrison answers the question politically. "Canon building," she writes, "is Empire building. . . . Canon defense is national defense" (p. 8). [For a discussion of canonical issues in English departments, see McGee, 1993.]

A discursive unconscious. Taubman (1993a) regards the knowledges of marginalized groups as a kind of discursive unconscious, and this realm, he suggests, is "fueled by Desire in the Lacanian sense." From Freud and Lacan, he continues, we have learned that:

> the unconscious is formed by the No! which separates mother and child and introduces the paternal or patriarchal realm of language. . . . I am suggesting that the formation of the canon introduced a No! into the individual's relationship to reading and thus opened the space for a canonical unconscious, one structured by the canon but not articulated by its discourse. (Taubman, 1993a, pp. 41-42)

Taubman sketches pedagogical as well as curricular implications of his view of the canon, worrying that the demise of the traditional canon may result in a "new canon," which in turn would produce its own canonical unconscious. He worries also, as does Henry Louis Gates, Jr. (1990), that a radical interest in the margins, in the molecular and in dispersion rather than unification [those radical discourses associated with post structuralism; see chapter 9] risks undermining the political initiatives of marginalized groups. Taubman (1993a) writes:

> The fetishizing of the molecular in particular is a denial of difference. Each unique molecule is finally the same since no identity lasts long enough for difference to exist. I suspect such a fetishizing of the molecular and the temporal reflects the fear of any real relationship between reader and reading, reader and text. (p. 48)

Race and Representation. Susan Edgerton (1993a) understands that marginality is created by centrality (and vice-versa), that marginality "lives within the very language/world that makes it necessary and that it must oppose" (p. 36). [For another study of marginality, see Hudak, 1993.] Marginality can suggest invisibility, as portrayed in Ellison's (1952) *Invisible Man*. By the end of the novel, the Invisible Man notes he is "invisible, not blind." Others so marginalized may internalize their social invisibility, may suppress their interior life, indeed their humanity. Edgerton quotes from the Ellison novel: "Already he's learned to repress not only his emotions but his humanity. He's invisible, a walking personification of the Negative. . . . The mechanical man!" Hidden perhaps not only to himself, the African-American is hidden to "White" America. Again, Edgerton quotes from the Ellison novel: "You're hidden right out in the open. . . . They wouldn't see you because they don't expect you to know anything, since they believe they've taken care of that" (quoted in Edgerton, 1993a, p. 64). The second novel Edgerton consults—Toni Morrison's (1987) *Beloved*—enables her to depict how the fantasies of European-Americans become realized in the marginalized "other." Edgerton quotes from the Morrison novel:

> White people believed that whatever the manners, under every dark skin was a jungle. Swift unnavigable waters, swinging screaming baboons, sleeping snakes, red gums ready for their sweet white blood. In a way, he thought, they were

right. The more colored people spent their strength trying to convince them how gentle they were, how clever and loving, how human, the more they used themselves up to persuade whites of something Negroes believed could not be questioned, the deeper and more tangled the jungle grew inside. But it wasn't the jungle Blacks brought with them to this place from the other (livable) place. It was the jungle whitefolks planted in them. And it grew. It spread. In, through and after life, it spread, until it invaded the whites who had made it. Touched them every one. Changed and altered them. Made them bloody, silly, worse than ever they wanted to be, so scared were they of the jungle they had made. The screaming baboon lived under their own white skin; the red gums were their own. (quoted in Edgerton, 1993a, pp. 71-72)

In this passage the inextricability—psychologically and culturally—of whites and blacks is vividly portrayed. This inextricability is not only an empirical historical fact, it is a psychological reality. European-Americans are also what they displace onto others, and their self-repression requires repression of the "other." The dynamics of racism are complex, much deeper than a catalog of attitudes which workshops might change. The very complexion of one's skin, the nature of one's blood, one's view of the world are all experienced racially. These dynamics cannot be decreed away; perhaps, as Edgerton suggests, "love in the margins"—a notion rooted in poststructuralism and psychoanalysis—might make them visible.

Images of racism. Making the dynamics of racism visible is one essential function of scholarly efforts to understand curriculum as a racial text. Warren Crichlow (1990) writes in this regard: "Our collective efforts to contextualize racism and social and structural oppressions of all kinds begin with interrogating how these forms of oppression are already inscribed in prevailing modes of representing truth and knowledge in textbooks, policy and teaching, and in the curriculum and the wider culture" (p. 13). One such inscription occurs in educational films. In *The Ideology of Images in Educational Media: Hidden Curriculum in the Classroom,* edited by Elizabeth Ellsworth and Mariamne Whatley (1990), seven scholars show how educational films, videos, and photographs convey sexist, elitist, and racist messages via their ostensibly neutral media conventions. [We have examined Ellsworth's scholarship in chapter 5; we will return to it in chapter 7.]

Photographic images. Another such form of inscription is photographic images reproduced in textbooks. Such images become representations of identity, especially when reprinted in textbooks. Because photographs appear "objective," they can communicate a sense of truth that, say, a drawing might not. In her study of photographic illustrations of black people in college-level sexuality textbooks, Mariamne Whatley (1993) reports that while images of black people were intended to be positive, negative patterns or themes were discernible. Characteristic of these negative themes were: blacks as "exotic," blacks as "sexually dangerous," and also blacks as asexual. The photographs she studied functioned to communicate a sense of "difference," of blacks as "other." A message of racial tolerance seemed merely tacked on.

Whatley (1993) notes that blacks have been construed historically as "other" in Eurocentric culture. She suggests that this construction of "other" or "exotic" is evident in sexuality textbooks, albeit in subtler forms. In one 1985 book a photograph is captioned: "What is attractive? Ideas about beauty differ from culture to culture. The So of northeastern Uganda consider neck-rings and a hole in the lip to be attractive" (Allgeier & Allgeier, 1984, p. 179; in Whatley, 1993, p. 92). Whatley observes that an embedded assumption here is that readers will regard the So as unattractive. Another schoolbook containing a photograph of an African woman distinguished only by a large ornament on her forehead is captioned: "There is great diversity in the culturally-defined images of what is beautiful" (Schultz, 1984, p. 86). These and other photographs are intended to teach multiculturalism to escape ethnocentrism. Nonetheless, white western culture is clearly the norm; all else is "other" (Whatley, 1988).

Pimps and prostitution. Illustrative of the theme of "sexually dangerous," Whatley found that textbook sections on prostitution portrayed only blacks. One photograph is captioned: "A street pimp with his fancy car" (Meeks & Heit, 1982, p. 273; in Whatley, 1993, p. 96). The prostitutes were white, expressing the American myth of the black man as dangerous, as a threat to white women. In another textbook a photograph was captioned "Many streetwalkers are managed by pimps" (Allgeier & Allgeier, 1984, p. 468; in Whatley, 1993, p. 96), expressing a fear of black men's sexual power. Whatley notes that one caption under a photograph of a white prostitute and a black pimp may be construed as a warning to black men: "Prostitutes are more likely to survive the fast life than are their pimps" (Geer, Heiman, & Leitenberg, 1984, p. 481; in Whatley, 1993, p. 96). A variation on the theme of "sexually dangerous" occurs in a section on sexually-transmitted diseases, wherein a full-page photograph of a crowded street scene is dominated by two black women in the foreground. Facing this photograph is the title page for the chapter: "sexual diseases." The myth of sexual disease transmitted from blacks to white is hardly a recent one; in a 1909 article in the *Journal of the Southern Medical Association* syphilis among blacks is regarded as: "A very real menace to our White boys and through them after marriage to our innocent daughters also. For despite our best efforts many boys are going to sow wild oats" (Sutherland, 1909, p. 217; in Whatley, 1993, p. 97). In textbook sections on AIDS, the worldwide origin of the disease in Africa is overemphasized.

The rape myth. The theme of blacks as "sexually dangerous" extends the Castenell-Pinar (1993) observation that in contemporary "white" American culture, African-Americans are, in Freudian terms, the "id." One form this projection or fantasy takes involves the long-standing and powerful myth of rape. White women and men have feared black men for centuries (Jordan, 1971). However, rape statistics indicate that at least 90 per cent of sexual assaults involve same-race rapist and victim (Whatley, 1988, 1993). How are we, then, to understand the persistence and intensity of the rape myth?

Psychoanalytically, fear is sometimes inverted desire, and Pinar (1991) has speculated—after Eldridge Cleaver (1968)—that the pervasive fear that African-American men will rape European-American women might represent a denied and displaced (onto "white" women) homoerotic attraction of white men to black men. Aside from these possible inter-racial sexual dynamics (West, 1988; Carby, 1993, p. 245), the fear has, more importantly, also justified white violence against black men. In the realm of popular culture, the singer Michael Jackson is said to appropriate these dynamics for his own gain:

> By physically transforming himself into a Diana Ross look-alike, Michael Jackson situates himself in the tradition of black women's blues. The thematic concerns of his music often take up the question and consequences of being sexually renegade, i.e. "bad"; however, Jackson ultimately represents the black male reversal of all that was threatening to patriarchy in black women's blues music. Where the black women singers affirmed the right to self-determination, both economically and sexually, Jackson taunts that he is "bad" but asks for punishment. Jackson toys with the hostility associated with sexual oppression, but, rather than unleashing it, he calls for the reassertion of a patriarchal form of authority. (Willis, 1990, p. 88)

[For other racial analyses of popular culture—for instance, the film "Grand Canyon"—see Carby, 1993; Giroux, 1993a.]

A form of erasure. In other textbooks that Whatley examined, photographs appeared to desexualize blacks. In those photographs expressing sexual intimacy, one text exhibited eight photographs of white couples, none of blacks. In another textbook 12 photographs are printed of nude adults alone, in groups or in couples; none of these is black. In textbook sections featuring photographs of homosexuals and lesbians, no blacks were to be found. Whatley depicts this presentation of blacks as asexual as a "serious form of erasure, because, in this culture, to be sexually active, desirable, and desiring is to be validated as a person" (1993, p. 99). The alternative to sexually dangerous blacks appears to be desexualized or asexual blacks. Further, black men are assumed to be absent fathers in the textbooks Whatley studied. One textbook contained three photographs of black fathers with their children compared to only one of a white father and his child. Another photograph of a black father and child carries the caption: "The number of men heading single families is increasing dramatically" (Greenberg, Bruess, & Sands, 1986, p. 436; in Whatley, 1993, p. 100). The issue of young single mothers, Whatley notes, is linked with the sphere of individual solutions: black fathers should stay at home. Racism, structural inequalities, and inadequate governmental policies go unanalyzed in these textbooks. Whatley concludes that gains in sexuality textbooks have been accomplished: once not represented at all, blacks now receive "token" representation. Many photographs tell us less about black sexuality and more about white stereotypes and fantasies regarding it. For instance, the black woman is rarely represented; the emphasis in these textbooks is on the black man. And the black man, Whatley concludes, is imagined in polarized fashion. On the one hand he is viewed as sexually dangerous, as a pimp, or, on the other hand, as asexual parent. The range of sexual identity and expression assumed for whites seems disallowed to blacks.

AIDS education. Brenda Hatfield (1993) examined an example of racial representation in the electronic media, namely in an educational film on the AIDS epidemic, produced by and for an African-American student audience. Hatfield learned that student viewers were "critically concerned" over what appeared to be their roles as carriers and victims of the disease. Student responses included: "It makes it look like only black people have it. If whites see it, they might say 'oh only blacks have AIDS.' On tv always lots of things about Black people. Like they are the only ones to get the virus, use drugs and stuff. Act like they are the only ones to have the problem" (quoted in Hatfield, 1993, p. 116). Statistics indicate otherwise: of the infected population 57% is White, 27% Black, 15% Hispanic, 1% others (Hatfield, 1993).

Super(white)woman. There were positive aspects of the film, Hatfield found. Students liked the presentations of "rap" in the film. One wrote: "What I like about the film, I have never seen in a film like this before. They have new changes such as rap, and someone dressed represented AIDS" (p. 119). Unfortunately, the film featured only male rappers. Females were assigned to background positions in the dance routines only indicating, Hatfield (1993) writes, "their subordinated gendered positions" (p. 119). Further:

> African American females were stereotyped in roles of anguish, suffering, and singing the hymns. Ironically, the strongest character in the play among all of the roles was a female, but this powerful role figure was depicted as a super-natural white female. In this case, the message of white racial domination is clearly signified above Black characterizations in the film. (p. 119)

As we see, gender considerations are very much intertwined with race. [For an analysis of another film on AIDS, see Ellsworth, 1990a, pp. 22-23.]

Gender, race, and class. Racial theory itself is gendered, although that fact has not always been fully acknowledged. Patricia Hill Collins (1993) has called for "breaking the silence on gender in African-American studies" (p. 127). She acknowledges that the survival of African-American Studies Departments on predominantly white campuses has required the elevation of the category of race over class and gender. The external threat to African-American Studies has undermined diversity and dialogue among black intellectuals. Collins asks "can African-American Studies accommodate the scholarly diversity essential for producing analyses of Black life and culture responsive to race, class and gender?" (p. 130). If the answer is to be an affirmative one, then the silence on gender must be broken. Gender must join class and race as a major analytical category of research in African-American Studies. Gender, race, and class can be considered interlocking dimensions of African-American experience. After listing the contributions and directions feminist research in African-American Studies might take, Collins posed a "final question."

> How [might] Black feminist thought produce unique analyses that neither confirm, complement nor challenge existing African-American Studies paradigms but instead produces something that is entirely new? Reconceptualizations of rape, violence and the overarching structure of sexual politics; of power, political activism and resistance; of the relationship among work and family; of homophobia and its impact on the interlocking nature of race, class and gender oppression are all neglected topics explored in Black feminist thought. (Collins, 1993, p. 138)

A gendered racialized identity. The relationships among gender, race, and class raise crucial theoretical questions, not only within African-American Studies, and not only within the sector of scholarship on race, but across curriculum studies as well. These are questions of identity, which get framed differently according to which dimension one emphasizes. For example, being black and female represents a double discrimination. In her study of black girls' "place" in schools, in desegregated classrooms specifically, Linda Grant (1984) discovered that social rather than academic skills are emphasized for black girls, particularly in classrooms taught by European-American teachers. Further, she found that black girls' everyday schooling experiences are more likely to nudge them toward conformity with stereotypical roles of black women than toward alternatives. These roles include service to others and the maintenance of peaceful social relations among diverse persons rather than developing one's own skills. Summarizing another study that examined gendered racism, Deem (1980) wrote: "I have described a group of black girls whose acute awareness of their double subordination as women and black was accompanied by a refusal to accept the 'facts' of subordination for themselves" (p. 13). In other studies as well, we observe layered representations of gendered racialized identity. First, we explore fictionalized, gendered racial identity.

"Here's reality; where's the fiction?" Jewelle Gomez (1993) begins by noting that imaginary representations of idealized figures are essential to cultural life. Oddly enough, Gomez reports, heroic black women characters are difficult to find in that genre she terms "fantasy fiction." Certainly, historical figures are not uncommon, as Gomez's survey of them reminds us. In fact, she writes:

> African history has provided the role models for an expansion of what heroism can be. But few of us have taken the cue. When this store of wealth has been exploited, it has generally been white male writers who bleach the history of Dahomean Amazons and turn them into Wonder Woman and Queen Hera. It is clear that the history of African women has many epic figures for those interested in the fantasy genre. But why have so few Black women writers been intrigued by this genre of this history? (Gomez, 1993, pp. 145-146)

One answer might reside in European-American representations of heroism, typically male. Typically, women are portrayed as deferential and dependent, mere appendages to male conquering heroes. Further, Gomez (1993) continues, those women who are independent are characterized as "bitch" (p. 146). And, to take this analysis a step further, Gomez concurs with Barbara Christian's analysis:

> The stereotypic qualities associated with lesbian women: self-assertiveness, strength, independence, eroticism, a fighting spirit, are the very qualities associated with us (meaning black women in general). Qualities that we have often suffered for and been made to feel guilty about because they are supposedly "manly" rather than "feminine" qualities. (quoted in in Gomez, in 1993, pp. 146-147)

These are the charges leveled at the "bitch;" the same words are accolades for the male hero.

An identity of spirit, strength and eroticism. This sexism is reflected, Gomez (1993) asserts, in creative thinking and writing. Black women have suffered the inability to see themselves as the center of anything, even of their own lives. Black men sometimes resent black women's efforts at autonomy. Gomez lists examples of female heroism in science fiction, noting that these works replace images of black women as passive victims with representations of an identity comprised by "fighting spirit, strength, eroticism" (p. 151). In an argument that could include representation generally, Gomez insists that fictional representations affect everyday experience, including how we think about ourselves and the world. Gomez (1993) concludes:

> While critics have often neglected to scrutinize fantasy or science fiction or place it within the context of literary and social constructs, the genre—like any other popular art form—is very intimately related to the sensibilities of the broad-based populace. It can be a barometer of our secret fears, and secret dreams: dreams of solidarity, strength or heroism. And we, as a people, should be acutely aware of just how powerful dreams can be. (p. 152)

No single, universal mode of women's knowing? From the world of fiction let us return to the specificity of the present-time to examine a different order of identity representation. In her "Resisting Racial Awareness: How Teachers Understand the Social Order from their Racial, Gender, and Social Class Locations," Christine E. Sleeter (1992b) reports that as white women, not a few of whom have arrived in the middle class from working class origins, many teachers already have considerable knowledge about social and racial stratification in America. She adds that this knowledge tends to be fairly conservative. Sleeter (1992b) describes her study:

> In this paper, I will use data from a two-year ethnographic study of 30 teachers, 26 of whom are White, who participated in a staff development program in multicultural education, to illustrate how social class and gender life experiences inform White teachers' understanding of the social order that they use to construct an understanding of race. (p. 7)

What did she learn? Sleeter (1992b) writes: "Teacher educators who work with teachers in multicultural education need to confront teachers' political perspectives, doing so in a way that accounts for, rather than dismisses, the experiential basis of those perspective" (p. 30).

From teaching we move to learning in Wendy Luttrell's (1993) "Working-Class Women's Ways of Knowing: Effects of Gender, Race, and Class." Luttrell describes how black and white working-class women define and claim knowledge. Based on participant observation in adult education classrooms and in-depth interviews outside school, Luttrell found that these women's experience challenged those feminist analyses which posit a single, universal mode of women's knowing. Before describing differences among these women, Luttrell described similarities. Both black and white working-class women tended to share similar conceptions of knowledge and a similar framework for evaluating their claims to knowledge. Both differentiated between that knowledge associated with school and textbooks and that knowledge associated with living, with experience. Both groups tended to share ideas regarding their commonsensical abilities to take care of others. That is, their ideas of knowing and knowledge were situated in community, family, and in work relationships. They cannot, Luttrell asserts, be judged by ordinary academic standards. Moreover, "their commonsense knowledge cannot be dismissed, minimized, or taken away" (p. 154).

Common sense and "real intelligence." Both black and white women appeared to accept the stratification of class. They accepted a taken-for-granted distinction between common sense and intelligence. While white working-class women described themselves, their mothers, their aunts and sisters as exhibiting common sense, they regarded only certain aspects of common sense as "real intelligence"—aspects associated with men's work and men's activities. Even when referring to skilled manual work as requiring "real intelligence" they were not referring to skilled manual work required of women working in factories; they were referring to men's manual labor. One woman commented: "Now just because we're going to school and getting educated, we shouldn't forget that people, like my husband, who work with their hands, are just as important as college professors and just as smart" (p. 165). The black women interviewed did not emphasize the intelligence required to do manual work, perhaps, Luttrell speculates, because black men have had, historically, limited access to the crafts. Further, unlike the white women interviewed, the black women did claim "real intelligence" for themselves. They credited their domestic, caretaking work as requiring "real intelligence." One woman reported:

> I got a sister I think she is smart, real intelligent. All of them is smart, but this one is special and she do the same kind of work I do but she's smart. She can hold onto money better than anyone. It look like anything she want she can get it. . . . Anytime she or her children need something, she can go and get it. But she has a husband that help her, not like my other sisters or me. Her

husband is nice to her and both of them working. But even that, it take a lot of intelligence. (quoted in Luttrell, 1993, p. 169)

Further, the necessity of dealing with racism requires "real intelligence." A woman named Kate reported: "I'll tell you what takes real intelligence—dealing with people's ignorance. . . . You see and watch people. It's a feeling you have to have because not all white people are the same. I sure know that 'cause I worked for different ones, you know, taking care of their children, and I've seen different things" (p. 169). Resisting racism requires intelligence.

Luttrell (1993) concluded that differences between white and black working-class women's understandings of knowledge suggest that women do not share a single view of their identities as women. They do share a sense that the organization of knowledge—organized as academic expertise and as men's competence—undermines their power in negotiating the world. Luttrell concluded that women do not all experience the work of being a woman in the same way. As a result, it is impossible to identify a single mode of knowing. To appreciate why certain forms of knowledge appear more amenable to women, it is necessary to look more closely at the ethnic, class, and race-specific nature of women's experience, as well as the values that are promoted in each educational context.

"Race" an economic category? Luttrell's research points toward the specificity of the relations between identity and knowledge, and especially toward the non-synchronous complexity of race, class and gender. Her study undermines the feminist claim that women's gendered experience is more fundamental than their racial or class experience. This view is contested in a study entitled "Racism and the Limits of Radical Feminism." While presenting radical feminism as monolithic, Murphy and Livingstone (1993) make important points pertinent to identity and representation. Provocatively, they assert that "race" is a social—and economic—question; upon analysis, it falls apart as a category. The distinction between black women and women of "color" (a more inclusive category, including Asian, Hispanic, Native American, and third-world people generally), for example, does not hold:

> (i) Black does not designate a color. Africans are no more Black than Eskimos are white; and people of color may be "blacker" (i.e. darker) than Black people. (ii) Black does not designate a culture. Black people may be of Caribbean or English culture, as may people of color have a culture which is Indian, English, or anything else. (Not to mention the fact that never is any "culture" homogeneous.) (iii) Black does not designate a "race." A Black person or person of color may be of "mixed race." (Murphy & Livingstone, 1993, p. 185)

They point out that such efforts to differentiate racially are "products" of racism. What underlines the gradations of color is nothing biological; it is political: "Those who are the most resistant tend to be painted the blackest, and those who are more easily 'integrated' are given a lavishing of White" (p.

185). To whatever extent there is a black culture, they continue, it is created through the struggle against racial oppression.

Ethnicity a "white" concept? The concept of ethnicity, Murphy and Livingstone insist, is a "white concept." [This point of view is not shared by, for instance, Alma Young (1993) whose views are summarized later in this chapter.] They write: "Black culture is the culture of resistance and rebellion—whatever form this may take. . . . *Ethnicity* turns what is essentially an economic question about racism into a problem of culture" (p. 185). In this sense, multiculturalism becomes an instance of Fanon's concept of cultural mummification:

> Multi-culturalism tries to resurrect an old culture, a culture from the past, from a different setting: a mummy to mummify. It takes what it supposes to be Black people's culture, separates it from its living historical context, and offers it, like a drug, to Black people, to make them placid and inert. (Murphy & Livingstone, 1993, p. 186)

This is also a view not universally shared, as we will see.

Written in the United Kingdom for a British audience, the Murphy-Livingston article functions to remind us that issues of racial identity and representation are not exclusively American, although given the American history of slavery and racial segregation, they may prove more intractable for us than for many other nationalities. Within the U.S. context, groups without a history of slavery fare better in schools. For instance, Ogbu and Mattute-Bianchi (1986) found that "Chinese immigrants are successful in American schools because their culture is compatible with the culture of the school" (p. 104). Even immigrant groups—such as the Punjabis—whose culture is not necessary compatible with the culture of school sometimes fare well "because they have deliberately decided . . . to do well in school" (Ogbu & Mattute-Bianchi, 1986, p. 104).

Other groups—Mexican Americans, for instance—experience such bitterness, frustration, resentment, and distrust of the dominant Anglo culture that the identity they construct adversely affects school performance. The "fault" is not with Mexican-Americans, according to Ogbu and Mattute-Bianchi (1986):

> Our argument is that the school failure of Mexican-Americans, especially among the older children, is due, in part, to inadequate effort or low academic effort syndrome, resulting from sociocultural factors created by caste-like barriers. . . . Upwardly mobile Mexican-Americans learned that assuming a "Spanish" identity made movement possible from a stigmatized caste to a neutral social position. (pp. 116-117)

Difference. A fragmented American identity suppresses difference. As Cornel West (1988) writes: "white supremacist logics are guided by various hegemonic Western philosophies of identity that suppress difference, heterogeneity, and multiplicity" (p. 23). The concept of curriculum as racial text supports complexity. One element of that complexity—as we have seen—is that of representation, including how images of racial identity are portrayed in curricular materials such as textbooks. Obviously, these can convey racial stereotypes, despite the intentions of their producers. The complexity of racial identity—its singularity, diversity, and historicity—is illustrated in the importance of gender. Issues of "breaking the silence" within the African-American community, issues between and within white and black working class women, as well as vignettes of fictional and historical figures, all speak to this complexity, and suggest, most elementally, that representations of racial identity might be most progressively produced from within racialized communities. Representation becomes important, then, not only because it reflects identity at a particular historical conjuncture; it is important because it also creates that identity. Understanding curriculum as racial text implies, in part, that we teach ourselves when we teach textbooks. The identities we represent to children are those we wish (as a nation) to become and to avoid as well as those which we are and have been. The complexity of these issues makes unsurprising that representations of difference have led to contentious curriculum politics. To this subject we turn now.

VII
Curriculum Politics

A curriculum that teaches people to think about difference—not as a biological essence but as a historically created and changeable identity—is a democratic curriculum.

(Joan W. Scott, 1991, B2)

More interesting are the ways in which teachers and students are implicated in resistances to "knowing".

(Susan H. Edgerton, 1993b, p. 233)

Any discussion of curriculum reform must address issues of representation as well as issues of unequal distribution of material resources and power outside the school door.

(Cameron McCarthy, 1993b, p. 291)

Cultural pluralism and ethnicity. Roger Collins (1993) has pointed out that during the decade of the 1980s, the United States absorbed the second largest wave of immigration in the nation's history. During previous waves of immigration—primarily European—there was consensus upon the assimilation model. For other ethnic and racial groups—Collins lists Blacks, Hispanics, and Native Americans—this model has not functioned. Despite efforts to assimilate, significant segments of these populations met and continue to meet discriminatory mistreatment. Due to insufficient rewards, relinquishing the group's cultural identity came to seem unwarranted. Assimilation came to be replaced by the idea of cultural pluralism. The cultural pluralism model permits ethnic groups to retain certain elements of their native culture. It implies a multiplicity of subcultures within society linked in various ways with the mainstream culture. Of course, there are contentious disputes regarding which elements of native culture are to be retained, which relinquished. Additional questions concern the constitution of "subculture." Does this concept include only blacks, Native Americans, and so on, or for instance, do Louisiana Cajuns qualify? Do homosexuals also constitute a subculture? Despite these complications, Collins (1993) concludes clearly the cultural pluralism model is more sophisticated than the assimilation model.

A culture of power. The second question concerns the nature of integration with mainstream culture. Collins (1993) employs the term "culture of power:"

> . . . to draw attention to the premise that certain ways of self-presentation, certain ways of talking, interacting, writing, etc., can serve to facilitate or hinder an individual's chances for success within "mainstream" institutions. When an institution is dominated by individuals from the majority culture, facility with that culture, the culture of power, can contribute to a minority person's chances for success. Often, the failure of the culture of home advocates to acknowledge the importance of minority students' access to the culture of power leads to minority parents' resistance to a curriculum and instruction that promotes, exclusively, the culture of home. Cultural pluralism, however, does not view the cultures of power and of home as mutually exclusive. (p. 199)

Other scholars appear skeptical. In Felix Boateng's view, it is not limited access to and competence in the culture of power which limits African-American success:

> One of the most injurious of these factors [contributing to poor academic performance of African-American children], and the one that seems to have the most damaging impact, is the continuous deculturalization of the African-American child, and the neglect of African-American cultural values in the curriculum. (Boateng, 1990, p. 73)

One distressing example of deculturalization is provided by Carlos E. Cortes (1986):

> "I will not speak Spanish at school," wrote the young Mexican-American boy. The words increasingly covered the chalkboard, as he repeated and repeated the teacher-imposed penance. The punishment: to write that sentence 50 times after school. The crime: having been caught speaking Spanish with his Latino classmates during recess. (p. 3)

Racism and xenophobia, not cultural competence, would seem to be the issues here.

Assimilation with sacrifice? In Collins' essay we discern a notion of American identity in which the integrity of its marginalized cultural elements is honored. At the same time, the expediency of acquiring modes of self-presentation palpable to the mainstream white culture—the "culture of power" in Collins' essay—is accepted. Identity here becomes a mediation between native and acquired cultures. There is the implication that assimilation can occur without sacrifice of native cultural integrity (Deever, 1991). As Derrida put it, the point is "to speak the other's language without renouncing [one's] own" (Derrida, 1986, p. 333). Certainly here is a different representation of difference than Murphy and Livingstone posit. That is, for Collins and Young representations of race do have cultural referents, not simply political or economic ones. Additionally, in the Collins' view, curriculum and instruction are conceived as mediating the difference between native and acquired (dominant) culture.

Ethnicity as "conscious togetherness." Glazer and Moynihan (1975) regarded ethnicity as conceptually autonomous, at least as important as concepts of class and gender. Ethnicity may be autonomous (a view Murphy and Livingston would dispute), but its intensity varies according to group. Recently, for instance, the experience of ethnicity appears to be waning among European-Americans (Hacker, 1990). For blacks, the opposite may be true. What is ethnicity? Is it racial? For Alma Young (1993) the distinguishing characteristic is not racial (in a biological sense) but behavioral: "An ethnic group may well include people of differing phenotype; and a recognized phenotype may create an identity that has marked behavioral consequences" (p. 210). In contrast to van de Berghe's (1981) socio-biological view of ethnicity as innate, Barth (1969) views as crucial the subjective interpretative experience of ethnic classification. Shirley Brice Heath (1982) suggests a cultural definition: "Cultural learning includes all the learning that enables a member of a family and community to behave appropriately within that group, which is critical to one's self-identification and whose approval is necessary for self esteem" (p. 146).

Cultural learning intersects with Young's notion of "conscious togetherness." The content of both concepts derives, in part, from racism, and from others' prejudices. Young quotes Kilson: "so much of what it means to be Black in America is intricately linked to white society, and the formation of Black ideas, values and institutions occurs in complex dialectical interaction with this society" (quoted in Young, 1993, p. 213). Language (including dialect) is said to be the fundamental medium through which ethnicity is expressed; children are deculturalized if the dialect of their home and community is not acknowledged in the school (Boateng, 1990). Aware of the significance of cultural self-affirmation, Young reminds the reader of the tradition of "self-help" in the African-American community:

> We must continue to draw upon our own resources, the most basic of which is the special value structure that has sustained us. Those values include the primacy of the family, the importance of education, and the necessity for individual enterprise and hard work. We need to renew our commitment to those historic values as a basis for action today. (Young, 1993, pp. 219-220)

Self-help is not enough. Self-help, Young adds, is not enough. She recalls the definition of ethnicity as learned behavior, behavior not only learned internally within African-American society, but as responses to others outside that society. She argues that racism must be interrupted by governmental policies and programs for job creation, restoration of the physical infrastructure of Black neighborhoods, and the development of human resources (education, training, and health). Both self-help and governmental intervention against racism will enable African-Americans to compete more effectively in the marketplace. She adds: "Only then will African-Americans be able to create a stronger sense of community and cultural identity. That greater sense of self will help us to struggle against the injustices to which all African-Americans are exposed" (Young, 1993, pp. 220-221). Relatedly, Ogbu (1992) has argued that the black middle class must not dissociate itself from black youth. He suggested:

> The involuntary minority middle class does not provide adequate concrete evidence to the youth and less successful that school success leads to social and economic success in later adult life. The involuntary minority middle class must rethink its role vis-a-vis the minority youth. What is needed is for the middle class to go beyond programs, advocacy, and institutional representation to reaffiliate with the community socially. (p. 13)

"There is no safety." Within black or white, across black and while, we are not, finally, insulated from each other. In this regard, Peter Taubman (1987) reports that James Baldwin told him that "there is no safety." Taubman interprets Baldwin's statement as suggesting that "we cannot hide from ourselves, cannot hide from our individual and collective histories and cannot hide from the truth" (p. 1). Baldwin's *oeuvre* has been communicating this fact, says Taubman, that in the effort to achieve safety "we have denied who we are as a nation." Who we are as a nation is fundamentally an African-European (as well as Hispanic, Asian, and First Peoples') nation, and this knowledge has been denied and repudiated. Part of what it means to understand curriculum as racial text is the necessity of incorporating denied and repudiated knowledge into our narratives we tell about ourselves, as individuals and as a nation. Continued denial of our complex identity and continued exclusion of those knowledges which both constitute and accompany those identities risk the "abyss." As Baldwin wrote more than twenty years ago: "If we do not now dare everything, the fulfillment of that prophecy, recreated from the Bible in song by a slave is upon us:

> God gave Noah the rainbow sign,
> No more water,
> the fire next time.
> (quoted in Taubman, 1987, p. 8)

The American dream. Taubman agrees with Castenell and Pinar (1993) that the American dream is quite literally a dream, an escape from reality. It is a dream, for Baldwin, that is profoundly Eurocentric and white supremacist. For the dreamers, to challenge this definition of America is to invoke a panic. For reality would jar dreamers from their sleep, and they would understand that they are "white" only because they have created "black."

[Likewise, "heterosexual" depends upon the construction of "homosexual." In Baldwin's *Giovanni's Room* (1956/1968) the gender parallel is indicated.] This theme runs throughout Baldwin's writing, argues Taubman, and it is only the dreamers whose American dream functions to deny this fact. To awaken means to face the truth about the American past and present, and such truth cannot be faced if it is not taught, if it is not communicated in the American school curriculum. Baldwin: "whoever cannot tell himself the truth about his past is trapped in it, is immobilized in the prison of his undiscovered self. Whoever cannot face the truth cannot love" (quoted in Taubman, 1987, p. 24).

"Double consciousness." While African-American knowledge must be incorporated in the mainstream school curriculum, it must not become diluted there. Consequently, separate departments of black studies [see Diawara, 1993; Collins, P., 1993] need to be maintained in order to honor the civil rights struggles out of which that field developed, and to maintain a separate space in which African-American self-critique and understanding can proceed without the undermining participation of even well-intended whites. DuBois' concept of the psychic duality of African-Americans, of a "double consciousness," suggests the importance of an academic "safe haven" for a divided self to engage in healing, understanding, and to advance.

History with a critical edge. Joe L. Kincheloe's interest in multiculturalism is evident in his work on place (Kincheloe & Pinar, 1991; see also Steinberg, 1992b]. Kincheloe (1993a) argued that black history be taught with a "critical edge." When black history is taught as a series of isolated events or organized around brief personality profiles—for instance, Booker T. Washington as a "credit to his race" (p. 251)—black history ignores the fundamental question: what does it mean to be an African-American? Historically, this question of identity would include, for example, a black perspective on the Age of Discovery. Kincheloe (1993a) comments:

> The rote-based memorization of the "discoveries" of Columbus, Cortes, Balboa, DeGama, et. al. would give way to a thematic conceptualization of the reasons for European expansionism and the effect of such actions on African, Asian, and Native American peoples. . . . The study of the Age of Exploration would lead naturally into an examination of colonialism and its effect on the daily events of the late twentieth century. Thus, questions generated by Black history would fundamentally change what mainstream educators and standardized test makers have labeled "basic knowledge" about Western civilization. (Kincheloe, 1993a, p. 252)

A tendency for virus-like mutations. Like Cameron McCarthy (1993a), Kincheloe (1993a) criticizes mainstream multicultural approaches as depicting racism as an attitude to be changed. Like McCarthy, Kincheloe notes that such a characterization hides the "social relations of domination in which racism is situated." A critical black history would reveal these social relations, for instance, the ways in which racism has exhibited a tendency for virus-like mutations. From the segregation of the first half of this century racism now tends to hide in institutional policies, policies which pretend to be racially neutral but in their repudiation of affirmative action function to discriminate against African-Americans. An equally significant feature of a critical black history is its capacity to support an Afrocentric vision. Kincheloe argues that those who are subjugated must establish their own visions, not copy those of dominant groups. In this respect, the power of black history is in its truthtelling. He writes: "As it removes history from the afternoon shadows cast by dominant culture, its truth-telling reshapes the present as it creates new visions of the future" (Kincheloe, 1993a, p. 256). Such self-representation of the future allows knowledge to support self-generated identities, allows difference itself to support an identity with a "critical edge," rather than one experienced as a powerless and devaluated marginality. Kincheloe (1993a) concludes:

> Critical Black history at its essence is concerned with repressed memory, subjugated knowledge and the influence of such repression on the life of the present. The power of the memory of repression is nowhere better represented than in the Afro-American experience—among those who have been denied a useful past. Memory finds itself intimately connected to the present as its cultivation helps liberate the knowledges of peoples long separated from their pasts. With oppressed groups memory engenders consciousness which leads to panoply of possible futures. (p. 259)

Afrocentrism. In "Afrocentrism: Capitalist, Democratic, and Liberationist Portraits," Alan Wieder (1992) reports three major criticisms of Afrocentrism, namely that it is: 1) a historical distortion, 2) a divisive curriculum, and/or 3) a race-driven curriculum. Afrocentrism is, as Watkins (1993) explained, a broad and diverse movement that promotes the inclusion of African and African-American history and culture in the school curriculum. Wieder (1992) identifies three different emphases within the Afrocentric movement, the first being capitalist Afrocentrism, a version which addresses the racial disparity that exists in American education and society at the present time. James Comer, a professor of psychology at Yale, is associated with this educational view which focuses on economic disparities between blacks and whites in America. [Comer's "major experiments" in the New Haven, Connecticut schools has been mentioned favorably by the important literary theorist, Henry Louis Gates, Jr., 1992, p. 125.] A second version is what Wieder terms democratic Afrocentrism; Michael Harris and Joyce Braden Harris are associated with this emphasis, which focuses upon the democratic heritage of African and African-American culture. Harris (quoted in Wieder, 1992, pp. 36-36) has written: "Black speech has a collective orientation based on African communal values. Speakers who are able to use the rhythm of the ancestors to verbalize the Black condition become folk heroes to African-Americans."

Ramona Edelin's (1989) "Curriculum and Cultural Identity," is a proposal for an Afrocentric curriculum that is twofold. First, she calls for: 1) an Afrocentric curriculum that reasserts the African-American democratic cultural integrity of the past; and 2) African-American participation and involvement in present educational policy and decision making. Edelin's Afrocentrism does not settle for a "piece of the American pie;" she insists: "No! As we have said many times, in many contexts, once we get into the mainstream, the mainstream will change" (1989, p. 43).

The third version Wieder (1992) identifies is Liberationist Afrocentrism, a Marxist formulation that is presented in Marvin Berlowitz's book *Racism and the Denial of Human Rights: Beyond Ethnicity*. This view echoes the emancipatory multiculturalism that McCarthy, and the social reconstructionism that Watkins, identified. Wieder (1992) concludes that each of the Afrocentrism presented promotes a different outcome. It is a capitalist Afrocentrism which promotes making the "American Dream" accessible to African-American children. A democratic Afrocentrism would provide the African/African-American democratic roots to promote democracy in the United States and throughout the world. Finally, liberationist Afrocentrism promotes educational and occupational excellence for all, including African-Americans, European-American, and man/woman.

Anthony Appiah (1992), a major scholar associated with Afrocentrism, has examined Africa as a European construct. He suggested that very invention of Africa (as something more than a geographical entity) must be appreciated as fantasy associated with European racialism. In other words, Appiah is suggesting there is no "Africa." Even the notion of Pan-Africanism is predicated on the European fantasy of the African, a fantasy founded not on any genuine cultural commonality but on the very European construction of the Negro. The category of Negro is at root a European product manufactured by whites to dominate Africans. Appiah (1992) noted that Africans do not share a common traditional culture, a common language, a common religious or conceptual vocabulary. Moreover, Africans do not even belong to a common race. What Africans do share is a certain contamination by Europe so that Africans themselves are complicit in the manufacture of Otherness. While focused on Africa, Appiah's provocative view echoes those of Baldwin and Morrison, reviewed earlier in this chapter.

Give leadership. As McCarthy (1993a) has noted, a language of "possibility" and "hope" characterizes radical approaches to a multicultural curriculum. Beverly Gordon (1993) located these in African-American cultural knowledge, "because it is born out of the African-American community's historic common struggle and resistance against the various oppressive effects of capitalism and racism" (p. 265). In her "Toward Emancipation in Citizenship Education: The Case of African-American Cultural Knowledge," Gordon provided an abbreviated history of this knowledge. Afterward, she suggested that:

> a major shortcoming of the African-American intelligentsia . . . has been their failure to take the work . . . [of] Booker T. Washington, W. E. B. DuBois, Kelly Miller, Carter G. Woodson, and William T. Fontaine . . . [and] synthesize it into a body of knowledge and to make it the basis of a common intellectual heritage

that would give leadership and direction to the African-American community. (1993, pp. 275-276)

African-American scholars, she continued, must return to this legacy, to the whole of African-American traditions, history, and cultural thought and construct an African-American mode of rationality independent of Western European domination. African-American knowledges need to be synthesized in what she terms an "African-American epistemology." Gordon (1993) concluded:

> Emancipatory pedagogy requires the reconceptualization of knowledge into new forms of ideology, paradigms, and assumptions that can help illuminate and clarify African-American reality. Emancipatory pedagogy also requires counter-indoctrination against the blind acceptance of the dominant culture's concepts and paradigms. Emancipatory pedagogy is the freeing of one's mind to explore the essence and influence of the African-American race through the world, and the ability to pass on that information as a foundation upon which to build. (pp. 277-278)

Gordon's argument does not represent simply another effort to justify the teaching of African-American history in the schools. Instead, she is arguing that teachers and teacher-educators must be knowledgeable in black scholarship and that the varieties of African-American experience must be explored in classrooms, utilizing an emancipatory pedagogy: "Citizenship education then ideally becomes education for informed political awareness, and in the practice of critically analyzing reality, and not simply a process of rote indoctrination" (Gordon, 1985, p. 19).

A border pedagogy. The notion of an emancipatory pedagogy is, of course, associated with the scholarship of Henry A. Giroux and Peter McLaren [see chapter 5]. Recently, McLaren (1993a, 1993b) and Giroux (1992a) have extended their notion of a critical or emancipatory pedagogy to include the struggle against racism. Giroux, for example, examines what he characterizes as a "discourse of possibility" in the writing of African-American feminists. In this work, he argues, there is an effort to articulate the notion of voice as related to the formulation of identities lived in cultural difference. Also in the work of African-American feminists he discerns an attempt to express voice historically. These elaborations of voice understand that racial identities are specific historical and social constructions.

Whiteness creates itself as a norm to privilege its own power. The white majority or dominant category tends to forget that it is constructed via its process of marginalizing African-Americans. By positing universality for itself, the Eurocentric mainstream in the U.S. constructs a cultural apartheid. This psycho-political process is played out, as we noted earlier in the chapter, in contemporary curricular debates regarding the constitution of "general education, a "core curriculum," and perhaps most broadly, the composition of an "American identity." Black feminists have established that any analysis of race must include analysis of the ways whites conceal their own historical and cultural identity while devaluing the identity of other racial groups. Identity itself, then, becomes fluid, constructed in the play of self and other, and can be situated in the culture and history of African-Americans. Thus situated, subjectivity is reclaimed as the fascination with the (white) "other" diminishes. African-American education becomes a key in the reformulation of identity. The aspiration is to paint portraits of African-American subjectivity and voice that escape, in Giroux's (1992a) words, an essentialist and stereotypical reading. Castenell and Pinar (1993) would add that European Americans must study such portraits and come to identify with them, not to erase "difference" but incorporated to understand the African-American presence as culturally omnipresent and determinant. As McCarthy and Crichlow (1993) observe: "[R]acial difference is the product of human interests, needs, desires, strategies, capacities, forms of organization, and forms of mobilization" (p. xv).

White is a color. As Leslie Roman (1993) has pointed out, white is a "difference," an identity, a color. In this regard, James Scheurich (1993a) asserts: "We need to make White racism a central, self-reflective topic of inquiry within the academy" (p. 9). [For responses to Scheurich's view see Allen, 1993; Sleeter, 1993b; see also, Scheurich, 1993b.] In a like vein, Peter McLaren (1993a) argues that educators must work to give white students a sense of their own identities as white. By examining their history and experience as ethnic, white students "are less likely to judge their own cultural norms as neutral and universal" (p. 139). What is the role of educators in such a multicultural view? McLaren (1993a) answers that "educators need to stare bodily and unflinchingly into the historical present and assume a narrative space where conditions may be created where students can speak their own stories, listen loudly to the stories of others, and dream the dream of liberation" (p. 142). For McLaren, then, the possibility of multiculturalism is the possibility of liberation, but this is a sense of liberation quite different from the earlier scholarship of various political scholars [see chapter 5]. For McLaren, the liberational possibility of multicultural education resides not in class analysis nor in conventional political action. Rather:

> The rhythm of the struggle for educational and social transformation can no longer be contained in the undaunted, steady steps of the workers' army marching toward the iron gates of freedom but is being heard in the hybrid tempos of bordertown bands; in the spiralling currents of an Aster Aweke Kabu vocal, in the percussive polyrhythms of prophetic Black rap, in meanings that appear in the folds of cultural life where identities are mapped not merely by diversity but through difference. (p. 143)

In this McLaren essay, postmodernism [see chapter 9] meets political theory at the intersection of multiculturalism. For further elaboration of McLaren's views on multiculturalism, see Estrada & McLaren, 1993.]

Toward a non-synchronous identity. In "Separate Identities, Separate Lives," Peter Taubman (1993b) examines approaches to multicultural and anti-bias education in terms of identity. To do so he has defined three separate but intersecting registers through which the construction, function, and meaning of identity are expressed. The first register he terms *fictional* "because identity emerges here primarily as a construct of language and certain pre-verbal relationships and as an artifice imposed on the plenitude of the individual" (p. 288). This register can be explored through the post structuralist work of Lacan, Foucault, and Derrida. In this register, Taubman tells us, "occur the attempts to endlessly evoke and utter the unutterable, to map the uttered and to expose the absence under the fading presence of the word" (p. 288). The second register he terms the *communal;* in this register "identity is activated and given meaning by and through the group" (p. 288). In this register, identity functions as pretext for reflection and action. The third register Taubman calls the *autobiographical,* wherein "identity emerges as a personally meaningful and continually developing aspect of one's Self, as a private center of being or as an autonomous subject capable of excavating his or her own history in the service of transcending it" (p. 288).

Identity-in-motion. Taubman criticizes mainstream approaches to multicultural and anti-bias education as being frozen in the second register. He suggests that:

> Blackness or Afro-Americanness rather than an identity-in-motion which can be used to illuminate experience and serve as a ground for action and reflection, becomes a fixed and sedimented identity over which may be erected a monumentalized history and culture, one in which the process of memorializing history forgets it. For example, in the monumentalizing of Martin Luther King, Jr., his possibility-in-the-present is forgotten. (pp. 299-300)

When the identity-in-motion becomes frozen, it becomes severed from the fictional and autobiographical registers. The person disappears into a Lacanian dialectic of alienation. He illustrates this danger by recounting the widely reported dispute which occurred in New York between a Korean grocery store owner and a Haitian customer. "The trap in this dynamic," Taubman argues, "was that the identities-in-motion lost dialectical tension with the other registers and became immobile" (p. 300). Consequently:

> neither group could possibly attain the gaze desired nor could either group become more than what the gaze of the other returned to them. No member of either group could be seen as what the member wanted to be seen as, since each member embodied the group and thus would always remain less than what he or she was, while thinking he or she was more. (Taubman, 1993b, p. 300)

Oppression as origin and horizon of identity. After criticizing the conservatives, Taubman turns to the radicals, those who espouse "empowerment" and who focus upon those non-synchronous racist, classist, and sexist dynamics which operate in the school to produce knowledge and identity. Taubman regards this view as incomplete. The identities implicit in radical approaches to multiculturalism remain immobilized "because the approach posits oppression as the origin and horizon of the identity. . . . One's identity is determined along an axis of oppression. . . . The communal register is severed from the autobiographical register" (p. 303). What is absent in this approach is a creative tension between the fictional and autobiographical registers which functions to mobilize the identity of the oppressed and/or oppressor, thus transforming it into an identity-in-motion "which could be used to illuminate the dynamics of oppression and investigate one's own being as well as the relationships one has with others" (p. 303). Taubman quotes Jessica Benjamin: "Once we understand submission to be the desire of the dominated as well as their helpless fate, we may hope to answer the central question, how is domination anchored in the hearts of those who submit to it?" (quoted in Taubman, 1993b, p. 303). [For a discussion of Taubman's essay see Edgerton, 1993b, pp. 221-222.]

Booker Peek answers that question by pointing to the internalization of the dominant culture's view of African-Americans as inferior, a view not unlike DuBois' notion of "double consciousness." Not until African-Americans, via political education, can repudiate this internalization, can education proceed: "Again, speaking of academic success in terms of skills education, the basic barrier is that our political education is not what it should be. That is, in order for the skills education to take on meaning—to take on a significant form—the political education must change" (quoted in Lomotey, 1990b, p. 18).

Identity and difference. As research reported in this chapter makes clear, when we acknowledge we are racial creatures, that we are what we know and what we do not know, we acknowledge that curriculum is racial text. In its representations of race, difference, and identity, the school curriculum communicates images of who we are, as individuals and as civic creatures. As Americans we live a complex, non-synchronous identity. We Americans are multicultural, multi-classed, and multi-gendered. Despite this fundamental truth, various elements in the American national character continue to be devalued, indeed repressed. Morrison: (1992) makes this point vividly: "certain absences are so stressed, so ornate, so planned, they call attention to themselves; arrest us with intentionality and purpose, like neighborhoods that are defined by the population held away from them" (p.11). Not only the repressed suffer—although surely their suffering is the greatest, the most intolerable. However, European-Americans suffer as well. In their ignorance that they are racial creatures, that their knowledge is racial knowledge, indeed that their material and cultural wealth is in significant measure the product of "others," especially African-Americans, they forget history and politics—and themselves. They have lost touch with reality, their own and others. They cannot grasp that they "have been shaped and transformed by the presence of the marginalized" (Carby, 1989, p. 39).

What does understanding curriculum as racial text imply for African-American scholars? One answer is provided by the distinguished philosopher Cornel West, who suggests that:

Black cultural workers must constitute and sustain discursive formations and institutional networks that deconstruct earlier Black strategies for identity formation, demystify power relations that incorporate class, patriarchal, and homophobic biases, and construct more multivalent and multidimensional responses that articulate the complexity and diversity of black practices in the modern and postmodern world. (West, 1990, p. 105)

In West's statement we see clearly how poststructuralist categories—such as deconstruction—can inform racial theory and produce political strategy.

VIII
Conclusion: The Significance of Race

Examining race relations is critical not simply for an understanding of social life as it is expressed in the margins of industrial society, but ultimately for an understanding of life as it is expressed in its very dynamic enter.
(Cameron McCarthy & Warren Crichlow, 1993, p. xxi)

Marginality and homelessness are not, in my opinion, to be gloried in; they are to be brought to an end, so that more, not fewer, people can enjoy the benefits of what for centuries been denied the victims of race, class, or gender.
(Edward Said, 1993, p. 314)

Once we get into the mainstream, the mainstream will change.
(Ramon Edelin, 1989, p. 43)

The American cultural identity has been predicated upon exclusions, and in the imagery of an intrapsychic politics of the self is replicated the politics of repression evident in the public sphere. These politics of identity are represented in textbooks specifically and in the curriculum generally. Clearly, the theoretical research conducted in this domain has important implications for curriculum theory and inquiry generally. First, it becomes apparent that the construct of identity becomes increasingly powerful as formulating a site of intersection between private and public experience. In the concept of non-synchronous identity can be located the pedagogical possibilities of anti-racist education. Second, race represents a quintessential instance of social construction of reality, the primacy of discursive formations over biological "fact." This scholarship hints at a concept of curriculum which constructs as well as reflects exchanges of power between generations and groups. Third, anti-racist education resides at the heart of education, as it requires commitments to justice, freedom, and diversity to be enacted in the context of daily institutional life, rather than murmured as a litany for a world yet to come. Anti-racist, postcolonial education might function as an "encroachment on the hegemony of the disciplines" (Willinsky, 1993b, p. 7). The psycho-political dynamics of race intersect with another important effort to understand curriculum, as McCarthy and Crichlow note (1993, p. xxvii). To the effort to understand curriculum as gender text we turn next.

Chapter 7

Understanding Curriculum
as Gender Text

If sexism refers to the response of society to a particular sexual identity, gender refers to that sexual identity as it is experienced, acknowledged, and owned by the individual.

(Madeleine R. Grumet, 1988b, p. 45)

We need to be sure we do not become "good wives" of a Marxist patriarch.

(Patti Lather, 1987, p. 33)

Current constructions of difference across diverse disciplines have unsettled notions of social and cultural identity that are widely used and circulated in education. For example, this work calls into question separate and fixed categories of identity, such as gender, race, and sexuality.

(Elizabeth Ellsworth & Janet L. Miller, 1992, p. 2)

I
Introduction: The Prevailing System of Gender

In chapter 4 we learned how the Reconceptualization of the field was in part a response to the field's internal crisis and to the social and political movements that shook American society during the 1960s. Incorporating strains of continental philosophy, particularly phenomenology, hermeneutics, existentialism, Marxism, and critical theory, inspired by the civil rights and anti-war movements, and by leftist critiques of both the 1950s and 1960s, also influenced by counter-cultural interests such as Eastern religions and other efforts to achieve "heightened consciousness," and rooted in various schools of psychoanalytic thought, the Reconceptualists brought a complex and inter-disciplinary critique to a field disintegrating in the hands of traditionalists and positivists. Autobiographical, phenomenological, and neo-Marxist analyses refocused the curriculum field on lived experience, on individuals' life histories, on the socioeconomic construction of the individual and society, on self and consciousness, and generally on the myriad of ways we as subjectivities are produced and reproduced within a capitalist system. Simply stated, the new curriculum theory focused on educational experience not as it was planned by technocrats, but rather as it is lived, embodied, and politically structured. The Reconceptualization, as we saw in chapter 4, refocused the field from developing curriculum, a bureaucratic function, to understanding curriculum, an intellectual, academic, as well as practical and political project.

Since its beginnings, organized schooling in the United States and the national conversation on education have been concerned with gender, although appreciation of this historical fact is rather recent (Leach, 1990). In other words, schooling and the discourses on schooling have been informed historically by the meanings we have given to the division of human beings into male and female (Tyack & Hansot, 1990) and to those attitudes and discourses that prompt us to divide the world according to biological and hormonal differences we mark as sexual (Butler, 1990). Concerns with gender have taken many forms in education, from questions regarding the value of coeducation to debates regarding the differences and similarities between females and males; from criticism of institutional sexism and heterosexism to analyses of the way gender permeates our concepts of knowledge and our ways of knowing.

The prevailing system of gender. To understand curriculum as gender text is to investigate the relationships between curriculum and gender. It is to subject the curriculum and its discourses to feminist analysis, radical homosexual or gay analysis (or queer theory; see Britzman, 1994; Brysmt de Castell, 1993; Doty, 1993), and gender analysis (this last phrase subsuming the first two), which are concerned with the unequal ways people are regarded due to their gender and sexuality, and the ways we construct and are constructed by the prevailing system of gender. Understanding curriculum as gender text appeared during the 1970s, although, as we noted, gender has always been central to the organization of schooling and the national conversation regarding education.

In this chapter we will summarize the history of discourse on gender, framing it in larger debates over the status of women in society. We review the feminist revolution in the 1960s and 1970s, summarizing the major points of view. We then recall the emergence of feminist theory and gender research in the curriculum field which appeared during the Reconceptualization in the 1970s. In the second half of the chapter we will review examples of contemporary efforts to understand curriculum as gender text. Efforts to understand curriculum as gender text have proliferated during the past decade, so much so that this sector of scholarship has become one of the important discourses in the field today.

II
Historical Background

Where the sexes are separate, methods of instruction . . . gravitate continually towards extremes that may be called masculine and feminine. The masculine extreme is mechanical formalizing in its lowest shape, and merely intellectual training in its highest side. The feminine extreme is the learning-by-rote system on the lower side and the superfluity of sentiment in the higher activities.
(William T. Harris, quoted in Tyack & Hansot, 1990, p. 103)

According to David Tyack and Elisabeth Hansot (1990), the Puritans grouped together boys and girls in the primary schools in the seventeenth century in New England. These dame schools [schools in which women taught the rudiments of reading in their homes] and later summer schools employed women teachers and served as early child care centers. Only boys attended winter schools and these were taught by men. By the early nineteenth century academies for girls appeared. Advocates of educational equality such as Judith Sargent Murray, Emma Willard, Mary Lyon, Catherine Beecher, and Benjamin Rush agitated for the establishment of girls' schools which emphasized serious academic training. The central argument in the movement for women's education was that females were just as competent to pursue advanced study as males. However, these early advocates also insisted that the aim of this additional schooling was to produce "sober and rational wives and mothers" (Tyack & Hansot, 1990, p. 40). Implicit in these arguments was the assumption that such schooling would be directed to middle-class, white females.

Coeducation. During the first half of the nineteenth century, public elementary schools began to admit girls and to hire more women teachers. According to several historical studies (Tyack & Hansot, 1990; Grumet, 1988b; Sklar, 1976; Schwager, 1987), the admission of girls and the hiring of female teachers was in large part economically expedient since the schooling of boys and girls could be centralized in one building and the cost of hiring female teachers was much less than the cost of hiring male teachers. The increase in the number of female teachers may also have resulted from the shift in economic production from the home to the factory, making it possible and necessary for single females to leave the home and look elsewhere for employment. The pervasive ideology of mothers as inculcators of republican virtues also supported the movement of women into teaching, even though those women tended to be single. Although were regional differences existed, by 1870 some 59% of all public school teachers were women and by 1850 "girls and boys went to school in roughly similar proportions" (Tyack & Hansot, 1990, p. 50). It is important to remember that "school" refers here to elementary school. At this time, only a small percentage of high-school-aged boys and girls attended high school.

Girls better mothers? Boys less unruly? The discourse on coeducation during the first half of the nineteenth century consisted mainly of those who argued that mixed schooling, as it was then termed, would benefit all students. Presumably it would make girls better mothers and boys, when confronted with girls, would presumably cease acting in an unruly fashion. Furthermore, it was argued, female teachers would civilize the classrooms and add a maternal and moral dimension to teaching. Others warned that mixed schools would lead to a blurring of the separate spheres for men and women, and that girls and women were simply not equipped for the rigors of advanced schooling or for teaching boys. Although the assumptions regarding gender and the differences in pay and power between males and females spoke loudly, it was not until the second half of the century that concerns about gender and schooling became explicit (Tyack & Hansot, 1990).

A male-centered curriculum. Several scholars (Tyack & Hansot, 1990; Tyack, 1974; Grumet, 1988b; Douglas, 1988; Schwager, 1987; Sklar, 1976) have studied the American educational scene during the second half of the nineteenth century in terms of gender. What emerges from these accounts is a complex picture. By the end of the century graded public schools were coeducational, but graded private schools in the Northeast and the South remained mainly single sex. The teacher workforce was comprised primarily of unmarried female teachers who worked at lower wages than male teachers. The administration was overwhelmingly male. African-American schools in the South where legal segregation, and in the North where de facto segregation, prevailed, served both sexes and hired large numbers of women. Particularly in the South Jim Crowism, entrenched racism, and the white male fear of black, male teachers as role models resulted in fewer black men hired as teachers. Designed by male administrators, the curriculum was overwhelmingly male centered; it banished the body and the vibrant intimacy of a real family (Grumet, 1988b); it represented the values and interests of white, Anglo-Saxon, Protestant, middle-class males (Tyack & Hansot, 1990). Attending schools in numbers increasingly equal to that of boys, girls tested better than the male student body in all subjects, including mathematics. Girls stayed in school longer than did boys. Recall that only a small percentage of middle class, white pupils attended high school. During this period, the discourse on education as it related to gender issues was split into two opposing viewpoints.

William T. Harris (again). The first viewpoint was represented by William T. Harris [see chapter 2] who had represented the cause of classical curriculum theory, based on mental discipline, so effectively for a quarter of a century. Regarding the gender question, Harris argued that coeducation was healthy for both sexes, since it balanced their opposite temperaments and softened their complementary differences. Harris stated: "Where the sexes are separate, methods of instruction . . . gravitate continually towards extremes that may be called masculine and feminine. The masculine extreme is mechanical formalizing in its lowest shape, and merely intellectual training in its highest side. The feminine extreme is the learning-by-rote system on the lower side and the superfluity of sentiment in the higher activities" (quoted in Tyack & Hansot, 1990, p. 103). For these reasons, Harris opposed separate sex education, and his views intersected with arguments regarding the economic efficiency of coeducation.

Dall, Anthony, Stanton, Alcott. Harris' influential views were supported and extended by advocates of women's rights who viewed coeducation as a step toward equality in the workplace in public life. Catherine Dall, Susan B. Anthony, Elizabeth Cady Stanton, and Louisa May Alcott argued first that coeducation was a "must" if equality of schooling was to be achieved since single sex schools meant separate and unequal education. They argued also that coeducation would lead to the same opportunities later in life for both women and men. Illustrative of these nineteenth-century feminists was Louisa May Alcott. Signing her letters "yours for reform of all kinds," the famous New England novelist and thoughtful schoolteacher in the mid-nineteenth century was quite clear about the value of co-education (Laird, 1991). Educated in an experimental community of New England's most prominent intellectuals, the Transcendentalists [see Griffin, 1993], Alcott promoted ideas of co-education in her fiction as well as in her everyday life. Her *Little Women* (1896) was a "classic . . . narrative of experimental coeducation . . . [and] along with her other popular novels for children, provided her only available medium for practical philosophizing about education and childhood" (Laird, 1991, p. 276). Alcott's portrait of the reconstructed school/family is Plumfield, "a happy home-like school" (Louisa Alcott, 1896, quoted in Laird, 1991, p. 277).

G. Stanley Hall (again). On the other hand, influential educators such as Edward Clarke of the Harvard Medical School and G. Stanley Hall, President of Clark University [see chapter 2], warned that coeducation was dangerous to both boys and girls. They insisted that it distorted and deformed the biological, and therefore "natural," natures of male and females. Referring only to middle-class, white women, Clarke and Hall suggested that mental, let alone physical, exertion by women would reduce their reproductive and maternal capacities. Conversely, schools with a large number of female students and teachers would, according to Hall and Clarke, "feminize" male students. Clarke's and Hall's views embodied a larger movement that emerged at the end of the nineteenth century in response to the increasing demands of suffragettes and, not incidentally, to the advocates of immigration, industrialization, and imperialist expansion. Perhaps the movement was best expressed by Theodore Roosevelt who applauded Hall's views and "the barbarian virtues" necessary for a nation to fight (Tyack & Hansot, 1990, p. 161). Despite this reaction, by the end of the century coeducation was "the basic way to organize gender relations in the high schools, as in the elementary grades" (Tyack & Hansot, 1990, p. 164). Included in that organization was the continued difference between male and female teachers in terms of pay, power, and prestige, a difference sustained in part by what Grumet refers to as the "cult of motherhood" (1988b, p. 43).

An increasing regulation of gender. During the first half of the twentieth century coeducation in public schools (but single sex education in private schools) remained the dominant pattern in the United States. Within the public schools, however, occurred an increasing differentiation between males and females. The emergence of organized sports, home economics, shop or industrial arts, tracking, and sex education or health classes supported this differentiation. This production of the differences between males and females represented an increasing regulation of gender (Carlson,

1992c). For example, according to Pronger (1990), Kett (1977), and Tyack and Hansot (1990), organized sports arose in schools in the early twentieth century as a response to three rather different problems: first, to the male counter-culture which consisted of male gangs, truants and drop-outs, second, the unruliness of adolescent boys generally, and third, the fear that boys were becoming feminized due to the absence of male role models at home and at school.

In fact, Pronger (1990) suggests that the entire structure of sports in the schools and in society generally was and is "masculine" in nature (competitive, violent, and disproportionately performed by males) and produces a particular version of maleness and femaleness, a version which glorifies the former at the expense of the latter. Athletics, according to Pronger, also served in the schools to monitor sexuality since athletic success was conflated with male heterosexuality in numerous ways. For example, threats of being called a "sissy," "faggot" or "girl" were (and still are) used to motivate athletic success while policing male sexuality. Homosexuality became the unutterable in male sports at the very time that lesbianism became associated (although unacknowledged publicly) with female sports. The cult of masculinity that influenced male administrators and which was institutionalized in male sports was also a response to what was seen as an ideology of maternalism in the schools (Grumet, 1988b). Sports in the high school, particularly football, compensated for the fear that schools were too feminine. As the emphasis on sports grew, however, girls, unable to find the same sense of glory and prestige in sports that boys did, were sidelined to the roles of spectators and cheerleaders. Assumed differences between the sexes in part became unified and solidified by sports programs (Tyack & Hansot, 1990).

Boys go to shop, girls to home economics. Differences between girls and boys were underlined in other ways. Directing boys into shop [industrial arts] and girls into home economics classes reinforced and rearticulated assumed gender arrangements as did tracking [see chapter 13], which sent girls to commercial programs and boys to college. Sex education or health classes often promoted a sexual double standard and Victorian morality (Tyack & Hansot, 1990). During the first half of the twentieth century, coeducation continued to typify the general organization of gender in schools. Women gained rights for which they had been struggling (among them the right to vote). Women's colleges saw their enrollments increase. Accompanying these gains was an increased regulation of the gender system, a system which feminists would systematically critique in the second half of the century.

III
The Most Public Revolution

Part of the problem is that women's studies . . . are grounded in advocacy movements . . . The educational challenge in the foreseeable future will be to teach people to acknowledge and understand their own passions, their own advocacy positions, without becoming reduced to them.

(Jo Anne Pagano, 1992, p. 150)

During the 1960s and 1970s there occurred what Juliet Mitchell (1971) characterized as "the most public revolutionary movement ever to have existed" (p. 13). At first called the "women's liberation movement" and later "feminism," this movement embodied and reformulated the revolutionary programs advanced during the previous decades, particularly the 1960s (Mitchell, 1971). The discursive territory staked out for this new movement by theoreticians such as de Beauvoir (1974), Friedan (1981/1963), Millett (1971), Morgan (1970), Greer (1970) and Firestone (1972) was that of women's oppression. In this project, women's oppression marked the starting point to analyze and transform prevailing social conditions. Patriarchy, the entire system oppressing women, would, in the 1970s, became the subject of feminist analysis and critique. That analysis and critique powerfully affected not only the national conversation on education, but contemporary curriculum discourses as well. Feminist theory became integral to the reconceptualized curriculum field in the United States by the mid-1980s.

In more general terms, the feminist or "sexual political" analyses and critiques conducted during the 1970s which addressed schools and education did so on two distinct and complementary levels. On one level, criticism took the form of analyzing sexism and gender-stereotyping embodied in such aspects of schooling as its physical setting, textbooks, rules and norms, classroom interaction, official and unofficial policies of the school. The concern here was equity. Jaggar (1977) termed this approach the "liberal approach," Kliebard (1970) termed it the "ameliorative approach," and Tyack and Hansot (1990) called it a "reformist approach." On the other level, the analyses and critiques of the 1970s examined the ways gender differences were produced and maintained in society and in the schools, including the ramifications for education, educational research, and notions of knowledge and of the relationship between the knower and the known. This orientation was more theoretical and akin to what Jaggar (1977) and Firestone (1972) termed "radical feminism." This latter orientation eventually gave rise to gender analysis and was in the 1970s influential in the Reconceptualization of the curriculum field (Mitrano, 1979a, 1981; Wallenstein, 1979a, 1979b, 1980; Pinar, 1981a, 1983a, 1983b, 1988d; Miller, J.L. 1979a, 1979b, 1980, 1982a; Grumet, 1981; Taubman, 1982). In its emphasis upon the production and reproduction of gender, this version of feminist theory resembled reproduction or correspondence theory in political curriculum studies.

In radical feminist analysis, recommendations called for a radical change in the gender system through the transformation of "individual consciousness." Liberal analyses revealed institutional sexism and seemed contented with more incremental changes, that is the establishment of a meritocratic, gender-neutral school with equality between the sexes and a truly identical coeducation. More radical analyses challenged the social and educational production of gender and sexuality, sought changes closely allied with other political movements—particularly those with anti-racist, anti-imperialist, anti-capitalist agendas—and fiercely challenged what they articulated as a patriarchal and misogynist society.

The Reformist Position

In the 1970s, liberal or reformist feminist analyses of education critiqued the ways that sexism laced the schools, especially patterns of sexual discrimination. An impressive body of literature identified gender stereotyping in many of the curriculum materials to which students were exposed (U'Ren, 1971; Fisher, 1974; Joffee, 1974; Women on Words and Images, 1974; Steffere, 1975; Trecker, 1977; Frasher and Walker, 1975; Braverman, 1974; Federbush, 1974; Brannon & David, 1976; Walum, 1977). These writers found that girls were depicted overall much less frequently than were boys. When portrayed, they often appeared as passive, other-directed, manipulative, delicate, dependent, cautious, and lacking initiative, imagination, and even personhood. They found as well that males were often fixed in competitive, aggressive, and psychologically rigid but superior positions. In addition to addressing gender-stereotyping in textbooks, the liberal feminist critique also began to critique the promulgation of heterosexual relationships (Lehne, 1976). When depicted together, females appeared dependent, males independent, females dangerous and manipulative, males gullible and childlike. The entire taken-for-granted model of opposite sexed relationships was permeated with an ideology of romance and mystery (Greer, 1970; Christian-Smith, 1987,1988; Goodman, 1991b; Sapon-Shevin & Goodman, 1992).

Sexual stratification also began to be addressed in the 1970s. Girls were directed frequently into home economics courses and boys to courses which were profession oriented (Frazier & Sadlek, 1973; Bull, 1974), a variation on the theme common earlier in the century. Athletic programs were analyzed in terms of their biases against women (Walum, 1977) and their adverse effects on men (Coleman, 1976). The domain of classroom interaction was analyzed in terms of gender-stereotyping in the classroom. For example, researchers found that teachers pay more attention to boys than to girls (Sears & Feldman, 1974; Serbin & O'Leary, 1975).

Sexual inequality. Liberal feminist criticism in the 1970s also addressed the stratification of authority. Whereas in the U.S. in 1973 some 66 percent of elementary and secondary teachers were women, only 19 percent of elementary school principals were women, 5 percent of junior high school principals were women, and one percent of senior high school principals were women. Clearly, power in the schools continued to be held in the hands of men. The models of power to which students were exposed relegated women to low-status positions. The liberal feminist critique of schooling revealed pervasive institutional sexism and countless discriminatory practices.

In its subsequent recommendations liberal feminism assumed a sex-role socialization model. Such a model suggested that by changing external gender structures to make them more equal, children could take what was best from traditionally defined male and female roles and develop their own full, perhaps androgynous potential (Bem, 1975). This reformist approach relied on mainstream social science methodologies and established political avenues, including legislative strategies, for change. Perhaps the greatest political achievement liberal or reformist feminist critics enjoyed in the 1970s was Title IX of the 1972 Education Amendment which barred federal funds to any public educational institution that practiced sexual discrimination. Unfortunately, Title IX languished under the Nixon, Ford, Reagan and Bush administrations. Nevertheless, it did help to support an increase in girls' participation in competitive sports and a desegregation of prevocational and vocational classes (Tyack & Hansot, 1990).

These liberal analyses and critiques suggested that the solution to sexual inequality was equity in the treatment of women and men and an equitable division of resources, including power. What was not specifically addressed by this criticism were those structures of knowledge that held and continue to hold privileged positions in the school curriculum. Furthermore, the 1970s criticism was ahistorical and atheoretical in that it did not call for revolution in the larger society as much as it called for specific changes in the school. Reformist criticism did not offer a historical perspective on the ways gender has been produced and maintained inside and outside the schools as much as it offered a picture of the asymmetrical ways schools treated male and females. This is not to suggest the liberal critique was or is illegitimate. If the liberal/reformist agenda had been acted on, a major step in the affirmation of human rights generally, and in the eradication of sexual prejudice more specifically, would have been taken by now. However, the reforms enacted left relatively undisturbed structures of power, forms of knowledge, ways of knowing, and gendered structures of consciousness privileged in schools, curriculum discourses, and in society at large that produce and are produce by the current gender system.

The Radical Analysis

In the 1970s radical feminists turned their attention to that system they termed patriarchy. Analyses of patriarchy by feminists such as Adrienne Rich (1976), Mary Daly (1973), Germaine Greer (1970), Kate Millett (1971), Robin Morgan (1970), Ti-Grace Atkinson (1974), Shulamith Firestone (1972), Jill Johnston (1974), Phyllis Chesler (1978) and Juliet Mitchell (1971), coupled with the analysis of radical educators such as Paulo Freire, informed a more radical critique of gender arrangements in education. In 1975, Florence Howe documented the hierarchical structure of schools, including institutions of higher learning; Kantner (1975) explored the evolution of that model and in particular what she saw as the institutionalization of the "masculine ethic of rationality" (toughminded, analytic, cognitive, and unemotional). Such a hierarchy, according to Daniels (1975), could be seen as a world organized both formally and informally to maintain the dominance of males. Formally, as Roby (1973) documented, the barriers against women were great. Informally, the hierarchy dominated by men continued to discriminate systematically against women (Harris, 1970). Men maintained control by employing an inflexible system biased toward behaviors and activities exhibited more often by men than by women (Astin & Bayer, 1973), behaviors and attitudes which included competitiveness (van den Berghe, 1976), and a split between personal and public worlds (Rich, 1975). To rise in the academic hierarchy required a commitment to "hard" as opposed to "soft" research, and research per se, as opposed to teaching. The dichotomy between "soft" and "hard" research perpetuated, according to Carlson (1972), the functional myth that emotionalism, expressivity, and the imaginative and intuitive apprehension of the world were signs of weakness and lacked "truth." Rich (1975) saw the hierarchical structure of academia and the consequent emphasis on individual achievement and self-interest as creating isolation and functioning to undermine any sense of collective interest. These critiques of the 1970s revealed the sexual roots of the fundamental structures of educational institutions, including the very structures of knowledge themselves.

Feminist critique of the academic disciplines. In the 1970s radical feminist critics began to speak of a reality interpreted by men in institutions of higher learning. These descriptions of reality—constituent to a large extent of our public knowledge of ourselves and the world—had been compartmentalized into disciplines and claimed objectivity. During the 1970s each of the academic disciplines came under scrutiny by feminist critics (e.g. Weisstein, 1971; Tennov, 1976; Daly, 1973; Rubin, 1975; Millman, 1975; Kantner, 1975; Carroll, 1976). Several conclusion were reached: 1) the research methodologies of these disciplines were found to prevent certain kinds of information; 2) whole areas of inquiry related to women continued to be overlooked or trivialized; 3) generalizations to both sexes were made based on the study of men only; 4) research itself, while claiming objectivity, was revealed to be value-laden; 5) knowledge was seen to be treated as something external to human consciousness; 6) the difficulty of introducing new ideas was exacerbated because extant knowledge and modes of inquiry produced knowledge consonant with what was already accepted and with the methodology itself; 7) knowledge was revealed as knowledge of men, not of human beings; 8) women were devalued in all the disciplines; and 9) a dualistic perspective, highly rational and technological, was revealed to guide much research.

Women's studies. Partially in response to these findings but also created as an alternative to the hegemony of patriarchy in institutions of higher learning, women's studies program appeared in the 1970s. These programs attempted, in part, to redefine and reconstruct the academic disciplines. According to Peggy McIntosh (1986), Director of the Wellesley College Center for Research on Women, during the 1970s more than one-hundred projects investigated the redesign of the academic disciplines. In the 1980s, an interest in curricular change through women's studies was articulated by McIntosh (1986), Gerda Lerner (1986), Mary Kay Tetreault (1985) and Schuster and van Dyne (1985). These approaches to curriculum reformation began in the 1970s as an ordering of stages through which disciplines would pass and as a conscious attempt, as Kay Boals (1976) wrote, to "demystify the dominant other" and "remythologize one's own tradition" (p. 199). We can see how far and how swiftly these curriculum analyses proceeded in a recent statement of Jo Anne Pagano (1992), in which she noted: "Part of the problem is that women's studies . . . are grounded in advocacy movements. . . . The educational challenge in the foreseeable future will be to teach people to acknowledge and understand their own passions, their own advocacy positions, without becoming reduced to them" (p. 150). Only from a position of relative security, even victory can a warning about ideological reductionism be made. It could not have been made 20 years ago.

Stage theory was exemplified by McIntosh's (1986) analysis of phases in curriculum change in history. Stage one, she said, is "womanless history." Stage two is "women in history" where women exist as exceptions. Stage three is "woman as problem" in history. Here the barriers and structures that have kept women out of history are examined. Stage four is "women's lives as history" in which pedagogical methods become less hierarchical and the construction of knowledge through the lens of gender is investigated. Stage five is a radical transformation based on holism and affiliative modes of knowing and relating. Contemporary feminist theorists, such as Pagano, can be associated with stage five.

Essentialism. The 1970s also saw the beginnings of divisions within radical feminist theory that would further subdivide in the 1980s. The basic division in the 1970s occurred first as a split between lesbian and heterosexual feminists over the definition of "woman." Later it emerged in a theoretical division between essentialists and social constructionists. According to Chodorow (1978):

> The essentialist position [posed] male-female differences as innate. Not the de-gendering of society, but its appropriation by women, with their virtues, is seen as the solution to male dominance. These virtues are uniquely feminine, and usually are thought to emerge from women's biology, which is seen as intrinsically connected to or entailing a particular psyche; or a particular social role such as mothering; or a particular body image (more diffuse, holistic, non-phallocentric); or a sexuality (not centered on a particular organ and its goals; at times lesbianism). In this view women are intrinsically better than men and their virtues are not available to men. (p. 52)

The essentialist position, prominent in the 1970s work of Mary Daly and Adrienne Rich, also emerged in certain theories of feminist teaching in the 1980s, including the work of Culley and Portuges (1985) and Judith Ramond (1980). These feminist educators advocated an approach to teaching and education deeply anchored in female anatomy and essentialist arguments (Taubman, 1986). This approach would inform certain streams of feminist thought in the 1980s as exemplified by the influential book *Women's Ways of Knowing* by Belenky et. al. (1988), by Nel Noddings' influential work on a pedagogy of caring (1984), and in Carol Gilligan's formulation of women's moral development (1982).

Social construction of gender. Opposed to gender essentialism were those radical feminists who advanced a position which argued that gender was socially constructed and/or produced by particular familial arrangements. In the 1970s the position was forcefully articulated by Nancy Chodorow (1978) whose *The Reproduction of Mothering: Psychoanalysis and the Sociology of Gender* would profoundly influence feminist theory in the 1980s, including feminist curriculum theory. Chodorow situated the persistence of sexism in the different psychic structures of males and females, structures created by asymmetrical child-rearing patterns, namely that women as mothers raised both males and females. The fact that women are primary caretakers fixes the configuration of the oedipal crisis and, according to Chodorow, produces an asymmetry in male and female experience which ensures an asymmetry in gender relations. Chodorow opposed essentialism:

> To speak of difference as a final, irreducible concept and to focus on gender differences as central, is to reify and deny those processes that create the meaning and significance of gender. To see men and women as qualitatively different kinds of people . . . is to reify and deny relations of gender, to see gender differences as permanent rather than created. (1978, p. 67)

In a general way, Chodorow spoke for socialist and Marxist feminists, who located the construction of gender in the nexus of economic, cultural, and political forces in society. One could also hear the voices of French feminists, some of whom argued, following structuralism and poststructuralism, that discourse as well as nondiscursive practices constituted gender (Kristeva, 1986; Martusewicz, 1992; see chapter 9). However, the essentialist position also existed among French feminists (Cixous, 1986).

Feminist men? The 1970s not only witnessed many changes precipitated by feminism but also saw the emergence of gay liberation and men's liberation, and with these the emergence of radical homosexual or gay (now queer) analysis. Writers such as Joseph Pleck and Jack Sawyer (1974) advocated a movement of "feminist men," and took up the critique proposed by the women's movement, analyzing such concepts as "masculinity," "male sex-roles," and "homophobia." Both reformist and radical voices in the gay liberation movement and the emergence of a radical homosexual analysis (Hocquenghem, 1978; Mieli, 1977) broadened the area addressed by feminist theory by raising questions about male homosexuality and masculinity generally. In so doing, they extended the terrain on which "the most public revolutionary movement ever to have existed" lay claim.

During the latter half of the 1970s, then, the revolution which originally focused only on women's oppression came to include a radical analysis of and attack on the entire gender system. That analysis and attack grew, multiplied and differentiated during the 1980s. It permeated several academic disciplines, particularly those associated with the humanities and, to a lesser extent, the social sciences. In the late 1970s this analysis surfaced in the curriculum field during the Reconceptualization (Pinar, 1983a, Miller & Pinar, 1982). Indeed, that analysis and attack were in part constitutive of that moment.

IV
Feminism, Gender Analysis, and the Reconceptualization

> While the sociology of curriculum has carefully studied the role of the school in maintaining dominant social arrangements in societies characterized by strong class and racial divisions, it has only lately acknowledged that gender is an equally important dynamic in society.
>
> (Linda Christian-Smith, 1987, pp. 365-366)

As we saw in chapter 4, by the mid-1970s the Reconceptualization splintered between those who explored the individual's lived experience and those who explored the sociopolitical determination of that experience. It soon became apparent, however, that although compatible with aspects of feminism, the Reconceptualization's thematics were not immune to the dilemma Adrienne Rich articulated when she said that humanism too often meant the study of man, that is men. Neither the phenomenological/autobiographical nor the neo-Marxist camp seemed any more responsive initially to the feminist project than traditionalists. Referring to the political camp, Linda Christian-Smith (1987), a Ph.D. graduate of the University of Wisconsin [the institution most prominently linked with Marxism in the field], has noted: "While the sociology of curriculum has carefully studied the role of the school in maintaining dominant social arrangements in societies characterized by strong class and racial divisions, it has only lately acknowledged that gender is an equally important dynamic in society" (pp. 365-366).

In the late 1970s, however, feminism erupted within the Reconceptualization and began to change not only that movement but what would become the contemporary field. Curriculum theorists such as Madeleine Grumet, Janet Miller, and Sandra Wallenstein launched a critique that established feminist theory as a central discourse in the field. Peter Taubman introduced poststructuralism in his investigations of gender theory, and radical homosexual analysis or gay analysis informed William Pinar's gender scholarship that appeared at the end of the 1970s. A sector of scholarship which was responsibly reviewed in the early 1980s in an article of fewer than ten pages (Pinar & Miller, 1982) now [1993] requires a lengthy chapter in this synoptic textbook. The development of the effort to understand curriculum as gender text has been swift and dramatic.

Differences. Before reviewing the early "reconceptualist" work on gender, we must address the question of how these theorists' work differed from the work of educators not identified with the curriculum field but who brought to their exploration and critique of education analyses of gender. In what ways was the work of feminist curriculum theorists and other curricularists involved in gender analysis different from those liberal and radical feminists discussed earlier? The answer is threefold. First, those who analyzed curriculum in gender terms brought to their project a historical perspective on education. Radical feminists outside the curriculum field showed, in their critique of schooling and education, no awareness, for instance, of the Progressive tradition [see chapters 2 and 3] or of those insights and understandings educators and curriculum theorists more specifically had brought to the study of education. Those questions posed by feminist theorists were thus situated differently from those questions posed by feminists working outside the field. Second, curricularists who incorporated feminist, homosexual and other gender perspectives in their work turned these analyses on the field of curriculum itself so that, for example, not only were the Tyler Rationale and other traditional concepts subjected to analysis [see Macdonald & Macdonald, 1988], but so were contemporaneous curriculum concepts and schools of thought, such as the neo-Marxist body of scholarship (Pinar, 1983a, 1994). Feminists working outside the curriculum field saw, of course, no need to address such field-specific issues. Third, those scholars who, in the late 1970s, were influenced by and receptive to feminist theory not only introduced feminist understandings to the project of reconceptualizing the traditional field, they also introduced to feminist theory a range of discourses that had initially constituted the Reconceptualization (Johnson & Pinar, 1980). The result was a richer and more powerful Reconceptualization of the curriculum field, as well as a richer, more complex gender analysis of curriculum.

The Late 1970s

Barbara Mitrano. The first works written by feminist Reconceptualists drew links between feminism and the Reconceptualist project and critiqued the concerns, assumptions, and methodologies of traditional curricularists. For example, in 1978, Barbara Mitrano argued in her *Feminism and Curriculum Theory: Implications for Teacher Education* (published in 1981) that mainstream methodology and the ways knowledge is conceptualized and surveyed reflected patriarchal attitudes which Collins (1974) characterized as objective, rational, linear, logical, dissecting, cool, expedient, aggressive, hierarchical, exclusive, and goal-directed. Based on her understanding of feminism and women's experience as gendered, Mitrano argued for the importance of circular, mystical, unifying, emotive, reflective, communal, and inclusive educational orientations. For Mitrano, reconceptualized curriculum theory intersected with feminist theology:

> Feminist theology and curriculum theory have more in common than phenomenological method. These commonalities deal with certain themes: self, transcendence, education, and praxis. For some curriculum reconceptualists, education is a searching for an affirming of self. The meeting of this self is a spiritual experience. Its manifestation take place in a world in which one of the most fundamental aspects of one's experience is one's sexuality. (1981, p. 4)

Mitrano argued that the Reconceptualists' privileging of self-reflection, phenomenological understanding, autobiographical research generally and Pinar's method of *currere* in particular [see chapter 10], all required the centrality of gender.

Sandra Wallenstein. Sandra Wallenstein pointed to the complementarity between feminist theory and Reconceptualist curriculum theory:

> Both fields evolve in response to the same source, disillusionment with life the way it is. They also display similar patterns of adoption in their stages of development as revolutionary theories. . . . An understanding of how feminist principles when put into action differ from patriarchal organizational principles, could add a new dimension of depth to curriculum theory. (1979a, p. 7)

Wallenstein's 1979 "Notes Toward a Feminist Curriculum Theory" linked autobiographical work, *currere* specifically, with feminist theory and practice. In "The Reflexive Method in Curriculum Theory: An Autobiographical Case Study" (1979b), Wallenstein not only provided a case study of the method of *currere* but also pointed to several directions in which explorations of gender issues within education might lead. These included: 1) a historical analysis of gender relations within schools, and in curriculum theory, 2) a socioeconomic analysis that would examine relations among gender, work status, and income, and 3) a psychological analysis with respect to sexual relations and body consciousness. By the early 1990s, feminist curriculum studies exhibited all three concerns which Wallenstein foresaw a decade earlier. Her work was important for three reasons. It located the centrality of gender in autobiographical theory, thereby adding a profoundly important dimension to the reflexive method. It positioned *currere* within the feminist project, thus extending *currere's* theoretical elaboration beyond autobiography, phenomenology, and psychoanalysis to feminist theory. Finally, in its very form, Wallenstein's work remained congruent with the feminist project of revealing the personal as political, a clear challenge to traditional and to neo-Marxist studies in the field of curriculum.

Janet L. Miller. Janet L. Miller' work in the late 1970s made links between feminist theory and those curricularists who privileged autobiography and the study of the individual's educational experience. Following a feminist critique of patriarchal modes dominant at that time in the curriculum field, Miller argued for an integration of emotion and intellect as well as an examination of the curricular forms that distort and deny women's educational experience. She would write fifteen year later (Miller, 1992b) that equity was not enough. Feminist theory requires that one change the very character of educational institutions, of the academic disciplines and their representative curricula. In her early work (1980), Miller excavated the unconscious ways she and other female teachers internalized patriarchal assumptions about who they were as women and teachers.

Miller established a lineage with other women curriculum theorists and philosophers of education whose work had influenced her. Particularly, she acknowledged the work of Maxine Greene (Miller, 1977). Miller reminded curricularists that Greene's important contribution (1973, 1975a, 1975b, 1978, 1988a) focused on the complicated situation of women in education, including related aesthetic and political dimensions of women's pedagogical work, arguments for self-reflectiveness, wide-awakeness, and social transformation. Greene's elaboration of multiple realities and landscapes from which we know and reconstruct our worlds encouraged Miller and many others to name themselves and to tell their stories of resisting the patriarchal forms of schooling and traditional curriculum theory. While situated in philosophy of education, Maxine Greene's remarkable scholarship inspired a generation of curriculum theorists, especially women working in the field (Jacobs, 1991). Miller's early contribution is interwoven with Greene's in several respects.

Questions raised. As feminist theorists such as Miller, Wallenstein, and Mitrano introduced to the curriculum field feminist analysis of educational experience and of the field itself, and feminist educators and theoreticians outside the field began to subject education to gender analysis, certain questions and concerns arose. They might be summarized as follows: 1) If feminist analysis challenged patriarchy, its biological determinations and its definitions of "man" and "woman" and sexuality yet still anchored its critique in a dualistic gender system, did it perpetuate the very gender system it sought to dismantle? 2) Did the identity of women and men pre-exist their formation within an oppressive gender system? If so, was there an essential identity and if not, was there any identity other than those identities based on oppression? 3) Could anyone talk about "woman" or only women, and if the latter, was that talk any less constraining than other talk of "woman?" 4) Were the identity categories presumed necessary and foundational for the feminist project also a constraint on the space feminism aimed to open? 5) Did the radical homosexual critique and radical feminist analysis drag with them the chains of an oppressive gender system? 6) What were the consequences of an analysis and critique anchored in a fixed identity? These questions had implications for the Reconceptualization of the curriculum field, for as feminist analysis helped articulate that Reconceptualization, it might be bringing with it several of the very assumptions, approaches, and concepts it opposed. Furthermore, the lingering question of what to do about the education of males, particularly heterosexual males, emerged, since maleness and masculinity were increasingly foreclosed as sites of possible insight and change.

Peter Maas Taubman. It was to these questions and concerns specifically that Peter Taubman turned in his doctoral research at the University of Rochester at the end of the decade. *Gender and Curriculum: Discourse and the Politics of Sexuality* introduced to the American curriculum field the work of Michael Foucault (Pinar & Reynolds, 1992b), which Taubman employed to analyze contemporary configurations of sexuality, especially the categories of "man," "woman," "heterosexual," "homosexual," and "lesbian" and the ways these identities formed within the prevailing gender system and within those movements such as feminism and radical homosexuality which sought to dismantle that system. By investigating the ways both the prevalent discourses on gender and sexuality and the then current "sexual political" discourses in particular formed the discursive system which created the domain of sexuality, Taubman tentatively mapped the dangers and possible culs-de-sac within feminist and radical homosexual analyses. Following Foucault, he concluded his investigation by suggesting three strategic possibilities for bringing about the transformation of the dominant sexual grid. These included a detotalization and deconstruction of sexuality, a temporary reclaiming of the fixtures "women," "lesbian" and "homosexual" for political purposes, and a radical nominalism. Taubman's work raised several important questions but these would be ignored until the end of the 1980s when post structuralism became established as a compelling sector of curriculum scholarship.

Madeleine R. Grumet. The most important feminist work in the 1970s was Madeleine R. Grumet's "Conception, Contradiction, and Curriculum" presented at the Airlie conference on curriculum theory in October, 1979. Her paper would profoundly influence the work done subsequently. Grumet began that paper by stating her project: "to draw that knowledge of women's experience of reproduction and nurturance into the epistemological systems and curricular forms that constitute the discourse and practice of public education" (1979b, p. 3). Grumet stated that as human beings and teachers we are all inextricably involved in the project of reproducing ourselves and our present relationships with one another as well as our primordial relationships.

Locating the roots of epistemological categories of subject/object in the psychosocial dynamics of the family, using object relations theory, the sociological analysis of Nancy Chodorow, and highlighting the inferential nature of paternity, Grumet first explored the subject/object scheme that "permits us to analyze, criticize...and transform the subject/object relations that organize curriculum and the disciplines" (p. 11). She argued, following Chodorow, that the asymmetry of childrearing practices was intimately related to different epistemologies:

> Whereas constructivism mirrors the configurations of the symbiosis of the mother/child bond, and the extension of that continuity beyond the oedipal crisis in the mother/daughter relationship, the tenuous father/child bond and harsher repression of the mother/son preoedipal bond reflect the dyadic structure of materialist and idealist epistemologies. (pp. 15-16)

These masculinist epistemologies are also, Grumet argued, compensations for the inferential character of paternity.

Grumet suggested that curriculum can contradict both biological constraints and the culture that gives meaning to them and structures us as persons. Thus curriculum offers men a way to contradict the cultural imperatives of repressing the maternal and privileging materialist and idealist epistemologies consistent with their need to deny relation and emphasize differentiation and distance. On the other hand, it offers women a way to transcend the lure of the preoedipal symbiosis. Unfortunately, traditional curriculum, according to Grumet, often simply reflects masculinist epistemology by emphasizing control, and is oriented "toward a subject/object dyad in which subject and object are not mutually constituting but ordered in terms of cause and effect, activity and passivity" (p. 22). On the other hand, Grumet criticized alternative educational strategies which reproduce a preoedipal symbiosis and represent a retreat from the public and the political. For Grumet (1979b) a feminist curriculum theory offered the possibility of transcending and contradicting those curricular programs and epistemologies which reproduced those intrapsychic structures developed in culturally constructed asymmetries in parenting and childrearing.

Madeleine Grumet's contribution to the Reconceptualization of the curriculum field and to educational theory generally has been immeasurable, but "Conception, Contradiction, and Curriculum" was especially significant. In that one paper Grumet introduced and elaborated a rich and multifaceted feminist analysis which she further developed in the 1980s, culminating in the publication of *Bitter Milk: Women and Teaching* (1988b). Grumet's 1979 presentation inaugurated a veritable explosion of feminist and gender analyses of curriculum.

William F. Pinar. By the late 1970s, Pinar had incorporated the radical homosexual analysis of Guy Hocquenghem (1978) and his own investigation into the construction of sexuality generally and of masculinity particularly into his ongoing study of autobiography and of curriculum theory. The outlines of what would become his essay "Curriculum as Gender Text: Notes on Reproduction, Resistance and Male-Male Relations" (1983a, 1994) emerged in his earlier work on gender, notably his (with Lee Johnson) "Aspects of Gender Analysis in Recent Feminist Psychological Thought and Their Implications for Curriculum" (1980) and, with Janet L. Miller, "Gender, Sexuality, and Curriculum Studies: The Beginning of the Debate" (1982), and the "Corporate Production of Feminism: The Case of Boy George" (1983b, 1994). In his early gender work Pinar called upon men to work to understand their oppression of women by studying their oppression of each other, arguing that the dynamic of the former is inextricably interwoven with the dynamic of the latter. Borrowing from feminist theory generally, and from Chodorow's elaboration of object relations theory more specifically, Pinar argued that the patriarchal codes embedded in the curriculum as well as neo-Marxist reproduction and resistance theory were caught in a culturally constructed oedipal drama that not only produced stunted, sexist males and females, but also made loving relationships between men and between men and women unlikely:

> We men are at war with each other, on battlefields, in corporate meeting rooms, in lecture halls, all symbolizations of and abstractions from the father wound and the mother repudiation. Homosexuality becomes the site of the

politics of the concrete, of the body, the potential politics of authentic solidarity and mutual understanding. Let us confront each other, we the circumcised wounded ones, not on the battlefield as abstracted social roles and political pawns of the Father, but in bed, as embodied, sexualized beings fighting to feel what we have forgotten, the longing underneath the hatred. (1983a, p. 34)

Pinar's work on male-male relations, the social construction of homosexuality, heterosexuality, and of masculinity foreshadowed a body of work which examined the curriculum from the point of view of males generally and gay men specifically (Goodman 1987, 1991b; Goodman & Kelly, 1988; Sears, 1987a, 1987b, 1988a, 1988b, 1989a, 1989b 1990a, 1990b, 1992a; Sillin, 1992; Pinar, 1994). By suggesting that men could not become "feminist men" without "denying [their] gender specific life histories" (1983a p. 27) and that they could not "usefully appropriate feminist understanding and substitute it for their own" (p. 27), Pinar created a space in which men in the following decade could investigate their own lives through the lens of gender theory.

One can see in this early work on gender carried out by these "reconceptualist" curriculum theorists the outlines of analyses that, during the 1980s, constituted the effort to understand curriculum as gender text. Neither feminist analysis, nor gay analysis nor gender analysis has been a monolithic enterprise; all three in the 1980s supported an enormous range of scholarship. Concerns, practice, and discourses often overlapped. Appreciating that any attempt to impose a metanarrative upon this diverse body of work is at best tenuous and at worst might be seen as a phallocentric maneuver, we will, nonetheless, attempt to review, sometimes only impressionistically, certain currents within this complex sector of scholarship.

V

Conception, Contradiction, and Attachment: The Scholarship of Madeleine R. Grumet

In schools we become civilized by denying attachment.
(Grumet, 1988b, p. 181)

Psychoanalysis, phenomenology, autobiography, political and feminist theory inform the work of Madeleine R. Grumet. As you read passages from her major essays, note how she juxtaposes the immediacy and concreteness of everyday life with the complexity of theory. Grumet's scholarship is among the most exciting and sophisticated in the field today. In this chapter we will review her feminist theory, saving for subsequent chapters (8, 10, and 11) her phenomenological, autobiographical, and aesthetic scholarship. Despite this division, it will be clear to the careful reader that her work achieves an integration of all of these discourses. To begin, let us review her analysis of the "look," which for Grumet is a feminist and political as well as phenomenological event.

Knowing resides in intersubjectivity. Grumet postulates the "look" as one way to emphasize the intersubjectivity of the human world, "a direct passage between persons" (p. 96). "That is not to say," she writes, "that our minds created the world but that the world we know is the one we share with others" (1988b, p. 95). The genesis of knowing resides in intersubjectivity and, specifically, in the primordial relationship of infant and mother. While parenting and pedagogy are not isomorphic, Grumet believes that each affects the other. For both, the look is an index of the complex of relations that prevail in both parenting and pedagogy. The look of parenting and pedagogy, however, differs, as Grumet explains.

Touch. Grumet tells us that the look of parenting includes touch; it recalls the symbiosis of the infant-mother relationship and the tactile quality of that relationship. The look of teaching rejects touch. Grumet notes that the teacher is "untouchable" (p. 111), apart from the student, invulnerable. Further, the intersubjective character of the classroom is disguised by the traditional seating pattern of rows. Grumet writes:

> By arranging students in rows, all eyes facing front, directly confronting the back of a fellow's head, meeting the gaze only of the teacher, the discipline of the contemporary classroom deploys the look as a strategy of domination. (1988b, p. 111)

The gaze of the teacher is often impersonal and determining, just as is the look of her supervisor, ordinarily a male administrator who, for the sake of evaluating her teaching, "observes" her. Women came to classrooms as victims of the look, pornography being the most obvious. Is teaching an avoidance of the look? "Dreading the objectification of the look, prohibited from extending touch, the female teacher turns to talk to assert her subjectivity" (p. 113). While the predominance of teacher talk in classrooms is most readily traceable to traditions of Greek rhetoric and Christian liturgy, it is also traceable to the psychodynamics of the look. In such a view, (female) teacher talk represents the "sending out of waves of words to ward off the look that surges toward us in the stillness of the silent classroom" (p. 113). In this regard, avoidance of the gaze of male students may help account for the female teacher's tendency to call on boys more frequently than on girls. For Grumet, then, the look expresses the subjectivity and specificity of a particular relationship (as in a parent-child relationship), while the gaze appears objectifying and impersonal.

Must pedagogy preclude reciprocity? Parenting permits reciprocity because it occurs over time. Grumet writes: "The history of the parent/child relation is one of exchanged glances. The child will walk many miles and make many visits to understand the look under which he has stood" (p. 116). The adult returns to his or her parents repeatedly, in part to study again the gaze under which he or she has come of age. And in old age, as the bodily decline reverses the relations of dependency, "the adult who was once the child is now the overseer within whose gaze the aged parent sees his former power and possibility" (p. 116). Denied such duration and intimacy, pedagogy precludes reciprocity. Further, for those teachers who regard the curriculum as prohibition, as denying access to the world as lived, as intersubjective, the look is bloodless. Grumet concludes:

> When curriculum is alive, it invites the student to reappropriate it as she reclaims her identity from its origin in her parents' look, grasping and dislodging and reclaiming its perspective. When the curriculum is a dead sign, all of us, teachers and students, stumble under its empty stare. (1988b, p. 116)

Trapped in transference Grumet explains that transference—a psychoanalytic concept which refers to the reproduction of past emotional patterns in present relationships—denotes the displacement of original, often traumatic feelings that are transferred from those first associated with them to the psychoanalyst. One of the projects of psychoanalysis is the disclosure and analysis of the transference relationship, permitting the analysand (or patient) to travel back to possibly blocked, repressed experience. Grumet extends the concept of transference beyond psychotherapy to the relationship between student and teacher. Speaking of teachers Grumet writes: "We expect them to know and, in that knowing, to confer knowledge and power on us" (1988b, p. 122). This expectation to know derives from original dependence upon the parent, usually the mother, and becomes transferred to teachers. However, the medium of dependence—language—is the symbolic order, associated with the father. Grumet draws upon Lacan's assertion that language is always the "other" and that at the basis of self formation is an estrangement—the other, a "not-self." Grumet notes:

> The language of the other is the basis of the self, and the desire for the other is always a desire to appropriate that power and to undo the alienation that is the basis of ego identity. . . . We enter the symbolic order in an action of desire that can never be fully gratified. (p. 125)

Facing front. Because language—the symbolic order—cannot ever restore the sense of self apart from the other, "all symbolic activity," Grumet explains, "is motivated and outstripped by desire" (p. 125). She continues:

> Now we have arrived back in the classroom, facing front, eyes on the instructor. What funds our attention is hope. We expect to grow into a self within his look. But we always suspect that he is actually looking not at us but at another whom we do not know but who is finally more powerful and compelling than we. (p. 125)

Traditional teaching, because it tends to focus primarily, sometimes exclusively, upon the curriculum as object, curriculum as textbook, focuses on the symbolic, phallic order created by men, rather than the concrete, embodied world of children created by women. Traditional teaching assumes that the student's understanding is misguided and inadequate; rarely is the student's reading the subject of classroom discourse. Indeed, it is the lived experience of students—linked as it is to the text, mediated and expressed through language—that is missing from the traditional classroom. Of traditional teachers Grumet writes:

> For the first time I understand that when they are ripping me off they themselves are struggling to recover their losses. Must we perpetuate this economy? Must we observe the golden rule of pedagogy and withhold from others what has been withheld from us?" (128)

If teaching carries with it the teacher's as well as the students' transferences, we must become aware of the original look under whose gaze we first came to form, to identity. To learn to teach, then, requires studying the transferences operative in classrooms. Grumet advises that we:

> build our pedagogies not only around our feeling for what we know but also around our knowledge of why and how we have come to feel the way we do about what we teach. Then, perhaps, teaching the text may lead us to devise new forms of knowing that will not compel our students to recite the history and future of our desire. (p. 128)

Other people's children. "Curriculum," Grumet asserts, "is our attempt to claim and realize self-determination by constructing worlds for our children that repudiate the constraints that we understand to have limited us" (p. 169). A yearning for affiliation has become associated with weakness and with the family, especially with women. As Grumet explains in her gender history of American public schools, women embraced the public world, the symbolic order, as a defense against the constraining, enforced intimacy of the nuclear family. Indeed, the public world becomes embraced more adamantly to forget how much we miss the intimacy of the mother-child bond. Referring to the feminist political theory of Jean Elshtain (1981), Grumet explains:

> The history of political thought stresses this repudiation of the essential connections within which our humanity evolves. The male repudiates those feelings and actions that he associates with femininity in order to achieve maleness; the female repudiates her mother in order to participate in the public world. Politics repudiates the family. Ethics repudiates the experience of the body, of particular persons, and of intimacy as it strives to construct a logical argument to support autonomy and differentiation. (p. 170)

We are not common. Parents have been, in general, excluded from curriculum decision-making, an exclusion justified on the grounds that their interests are too parochial and self-interested. The vision of a "common culture" has been somehow a vision bleached of particularity, including the specificity of ethnicity and family. Somehow that which we experience and live in our everyday lives is not "common." Indeed, "common culture" always implies a rejection of contemporary life. Grumet notes:

> Because the common culture is always anywhere other than this world, its curriculum rarely speaks to a world children know, a world accessible to their understanding and action. It is a curriculum that controls through mystifica-

tion, encouraging placid passivity. . . . Power wears many masks, and if in some countries it appears as the Church or the Party, or even the People; here it is the Common Culture. (pp. 171-172)

In the common culture our children become "other people's children." They lose the intimacy and specificity that characterize the parent-child bond in the name of the meritocracy; they gain anonymous labels such as "gifted" or "disadvantaged," bureaucratic designations designed to transport our flesh and blood into a bloodless public sphere:

> Few of us would excuse our own children from their futures with the grace and understanding we extend to other people's children. Other people's children are abstract. They are reading scores, FTEs, last year's graduating class, last week's body count. (p. 173)

A curriculum for one's own child, Grumet observes, would be a conversation in which our son's and/or daughter's response is a necessary, welcomed, and prominent feature. Curriculum decisions for one's own children involve parents' and children's participation. Parents and children would join teachers in the interpretation of educational experience, in making choices regarding "next steps." Such parental participation goes beyond the traditional politics of "local control;" such participation brings parents into the daily life of classrooms. Parental "participation would interrupt the march to the common culture without necessarily shifting the whole parade to another destination" (p. 174).

[Other scholars have noted that the school violates the intimacy of the child/parent bond. For example, the Schuberts have suggested that "the parent-child relation is a microcosm for curriculum theorizing" (p. 61); however, "the institution of schooling as we know it runs counter to the natural curriculum relationship that is symbolized in the parent-child dialogue" (Schubert, Schubert, & Schubert, 1986, p. 71).]

Caring in the classroom. Referring to Nel Noddings (1984) groundbreaking work on caring, Grumet substitutes relationship for rules. So understood, caring is not simply a moral attitude; it is an event. Caring becomes situated in concrete human relationship. Women teachers' complicity with those patriarchal institutions known as schools allows them to relinquish the specificity of caring to relatively anonymity of teaching. Women, Grumet suggests, "must make peace with the women who teach our children and acknowledge our solidarity with the mothers of other people's children if we are going to reclaim the classroom as a place where we nurture children" (p. 179). For in schools, Grumet asserts, feeling and passion are consigned to domesticity, to the home, and the classroom is designed to be purged of such "contaminants." Grumet reminds us: "But attachment and difference never disappear just because we declare them invisible. They always seep back in" (p. 181). Schools may have been designed as neutral places, but neutral places they have never been; always they have been places where some people's children are subordinate to other people's children. By remaking the school as places of caring and duration, other's people's children may become our own. For Grumet, attachment need not be price of civilization; instead, it must be the medium through which civilization is cultivated and transformed.

An important work of conception, Grumet's *Bitter Milk* stands as one of the most important books in the field in the past thirty years. A masterful and synthetical work, *Bitter Milk* links autobiography, phenomenology, psychoanalysis, political and feminist theory in a mature, sophisticated, and provocative work of curriculum theory. Grumet's accomplishment provides inspiration for other curricularists struggling to understand curriculum as a gender text. Feminist theorists have completed studies not only psychoanalytic in nature but historical, social, and cultural as well. These analyses exemplified the relational complexity to which Grumet's work pointed. They implied possible reformulations and reconstructions not only of individuals' roles as educators but to their subsequent relationships to students, to colleagues, to communities, to families and friends, as well as to the texts and discourses expressing these relationships. All curriculum scholars who have worked on issues of gender are indebted to Madeleine R. Grumet, whose *Bitter Milk* staked out the territory which other theorists have now begun to explore.

VI
Creating Spaces and Finding Voices:
The Scholarship of Janet L. Miller

We are on the edge, not quite knowing what holds back the sound, what prevents the total shattering of our silences.
(Janet L. Miller, 1982a, p. 5)

During the 1980s Janet Miller, working with autobiography, explored the relationships among gender identity, the self, and others. In "The Sound of Silence Breaking" (1982a), she wrote: "The dream is recurring: the quiet is everywhere. It surrounds my classroom, penetrates the halls of the building in which I teach. I wait with my students for the voices, horrified that they might scream in rage, trembling that they may never whisper" (p. 5). This silence is the silence of women's experience, the splitting off of women's lived worlds from the public discourse of education. In the early 1980s feminist curricularists remain "tentative, passive, anxious to please, defensive, angry" (p. 5). In this situation, Miller asked: "how much [does] it take to break silence?" (p. 5).

Silence broken. Janet L. Miller's lyrical and powerful scholarship helped break the silence. In 1982 she reported the emerging discourse on gender and sexuality so that "feminist pedagogy and curriculum [may] . . . reciprocate, inform, and alter one another" (p. 5). Reviewing recent work by Grumet, Pinar, Taubman, and Wallenstein to illustrate an "evolving feminist pedagogy" (p. 10), Miller noted that "breaking silence with my students creates a way for me to ground my fears of the unnatural silences and to focus my voice, my energies upon the articulation of our work together" (p. 10). It was not only her work, however, which her autobiographical voice helped to advance during 1980s.

Perhaps more than any other major feminist theorist, Janet Miller has focused upon "our work together." This acknowledgement of the presence and conservation of others is paralleled by her collaborative work with students. Increasingly her scholarship has focused on the ways these issues of voice, community, and selfhood are present in her dialogues with other women who teach (1986, 1987c). Of central concern have been the possibilities and the contradictions that emerged in feminists' attempts to develop collaborative and dialogical relationships with their students and colleagues (1990a). Her work during the 1980s underlined her observation early in the decade that "the sound of silence breaking is harsh, resonant, soft, battering, small, chaotic, furious, terrified, triumphant. The tentative first murmurs are becoming a chorus" (1982a, p. 11).

In her 1986 "Women as Teachers: Enlarging Conversations on Issues of Gender and Self-concept," Miller sought conversation among those women who have broken the silence on gender. By interviewing women who teach, Miller sought "the enlargement of my understanding of how my own dichotomous feelings might reflect perceptions shared by other women who choose teaching as a profession" (1986, p. 111). These interviews, conducted with women who had been teaching from 2 to 22 years, were open-ended and conducted over a two-year period. Miller found that many women entered the teaching profession because teaching did not appear to require sacrifice of the traditional feminine role. However, she found that for many women the nurturing aspects of teaching conflicted with the concept of professionalism. Miller observed:

> Thus, attempts to professionalize teaching seem to have simply reinforced the internalized conflicts of many women who are encouraged to move beyond the confines of "women's work," and yet who still are being molded by external definitions of their profession. . . . The overwhelming majority of the women with whom I have spoken thus far, however, still are questioning their roles as teachers in light of what seems to be merely personal or, at best, cultural preference. (pp. 117, 118)

Miller found that her conversations with women teachers released them from an "encapsulation" in those "fragmentations they experience as representative of the larger social imbalances of control and power" (p. 112). It is to issues of fragmentation and power that Miller turned next.

"Toward the integration of fragmented selves." In "The Resistance of Women Academics: An Autobiographical Account" (1983a), women's conversation is clearly underway; the sound of a chorus is unmistakable. Here Miller speaks to the dilemma of women working in academe. This is a dilemma at once political and psychological, as this essay makes clear. It is both, insofar as the

university requires conduct, in both teaching and research, that is male-identified, requiring some degree of women's self-alienation. Moreover, it is a code of conduct which takes advantage of women's conditioning, specifically the feminine capacity for nurturing and giving. Resisting such a code might imply repudiation of these qualities, but Miller makes clear that the self-reflective study of her educational experience allows the feminist researcher to move through this psychopolitical labyrinth, preserving her nurturant capacities while developing autonomy, independence, and a critical posture. Miller reflected:

> I float, then; at times, I become enmeshed in habitual response or protective withdrawal. I know that much of the new academic journey for women is uncharted, and it is easy to remain in fragments, unwilling and unable at times to muster the energy required for synthesis. The very ways of knowing are strange, alien, and frightening. The vision is gaining substance, however; as we continue to understand ways in which we may resist the infiltration, in our minds and hearts, of oppressive conceptions of ability and desirability of action, we continue to move toward the integration of fragmented selves. Ultimately, it is through our individual and collective wholeness that we might conjoin our work and our selves in truly becoming knowers in our worlds. (1983a, p. 109)

Gaining a sense of ourselves. In "Women as Teachers/Researchers: Gaining a Sense of Ourselves," Miller (1987c) suggested that:

> If a teacher sees herself as an active agent within her own classroom, conducting her own research and thus making her own informed pedagogical decisions, she may apply the criteria of awareness and equity both to her students and herself as knowers, and, in so doing, she indeed may be gaining a sense of herself. (p. 57)

Convinced that long-term investigations into such issues are necessary in order "to bring into view sides and facets that are normally turned away and unseen" (de Beaugrande, 1988, p. 258), she joined five classroom teachers to investigate possibilities of integrating feminist perspectives on research methodologies into enactments of teachers-as-researchers. In this ongoing investigation into collaborative inquiry as a form of feminist research and theorizing, group members challenged not only their taken-for-granted conceptions of research, teaching, and curriculum, but also those political and social constructs said to guide their notions of collaboration, of subjectivity, and of schooling generally. Working together to challenge issues of hierarchy and imposition in collaborative inquiry, group members understood that finding voices and creating spaces were not definitive, boundaried events but rather constantly emerging and contradictory processes (Miller, 1990a).

In *Creating Space and Finding Voices*, Janet Miller's emphasis includes not only the quest to integrate the fragmented parts, the contradictions within the self, but also explorations of ways in which those fragmentations and contradictions reflect and frame social, cultural, and historical constructions, positionings, and representations of women and men, and their work as teachers, researchers, and curriculum creators. The emphasis in *Creating Spaces and Finding Voices* is less on forging a unified whole, either within collaborative communities or within individuals, and more on exploring the connections that are possible among those fragmentations and differences.

The significance of Miller's work includes the grounding of the autobiographical method in feminist theory, legitimating collaborative research, and extending her unique perspective to other areas, such as the teaching of English (1992d), early childhood education (1992c), teacher education and development (1990a, 1990b, 1992a, 1992e), all the while influencing considerably the contours of contemporary feminist theory (1992b, 1993a, 1993b; Ellsworth & Miller, 1992). Miller's collaborative research has inspired a wave of interest in collaboration [see for instance, Petra Munro and Janice Jipson 1991], and in so doing, lays to rest forever the old Marxist charge that autobiography is solitary, apolitical, and undertheorized. Janet Miller's accomplishment is enormous.

VII
Teaching in the Patriarchal Wilderness:
The Scholarship of Jo Anne Pagano

> We represent, stand in for, those traditions within which we live as exiles. These traditions are the houses our brothers have built for themselves in their exile from the maternal body. They are at home there. We are political and epistemological refugees.
>
> (Jo Anne Pagano, 1990, p. 9)

In 1988, "The Claim of Philia" catapulted Jo Anne Pagano into prominence. That paper began with the problem of teacher authority. Where, Pagano wondered, do teachers derive the moral authority to change students' lives? She rephrased the problem as an investigation of why and how women teachers remain complicit with patriarchal structures of schooling. Women, Pagano reasoned, remained complicit with patriarchy, its authoritarian structures and posture, its totalizing discourses and its bodiless, abstract versions of knowledge to the extent that they deny their connectedness not only to their students but also to their own autobiographies and to their own authority.

Following Grumet, Pagano warned against celebrating "the amorphous thoroughly individualized, subjective, male-romanticized, theatricalized version of the female" (Pagano, 1988a, p. 527). Rather, Pagano argued, there was no conflict between nurturance and authority, between paternal and maternal power. Authority, she continued, arose from the affiliation one had with one's students, not from the Law. The Law provided paternal power, but it had to be worked through by women teachers, contradicted, and finally employed in the service of the claims of Philia: affiliation. Pagano identified two steps:

We must recognize that this has been our first step; we must acknowledge our power, our paternal authority. . . . We can either stop there, secure in our positions as father surrogates, or we can truly aim for power, the power which must be taken, cannot be conferred, by understanding and celebrating the contradictions in our lives. Analyzing these contradictions will take us to the second step—contradicting patriarchal culture. (Pagano, 1988a, p. 526)

Pagano (1988b) observed that the art of teaching involves the art of conversation, the subtleties and intricacies of which, she notes, women novelists are well accomplished. Further, the art of teaching, when it is practiced by women and when it is practiced in the teaching of women, must labor to produce difference by acknowledging what women know. Either women are locked out of scholarly discourses or are plagiarists, Pagano says, as the discourses women teach are not their own.

The important themes in this early essay were elaborated throughout the 1980s. These themes—women's relationship to their own intellectual development, the ambivalent relationships women and women teachers have to males and to patriarchy, the constitution of women's authority in a world constituted by asymmetrical gender arrangements—are woven together in her book *Exiles and Communities: Teaching in the Patriarchal Wilderness* (1990). In that carefully reasoned work, Pagano argued that teaching was a morally charged and politically infused endeavor that for women was complicated by gender. Since, as she wrote, knowledge is power, and those who possess it are powerful and those who define what it is are the most powerful, teaching is inherently involved with questions of power. *Exiles and Communities* addresses ethical questions of education, questions of knowledge and power, of authority and of the relationship between the individual and the community. It explores alternatives to those methods, assumptions, and goals which preserve male authority. Further, the book explores how women teachers can build communities in the wilderness, a wilderness which is androcentric, but it is also "symbolic of the powerful devouring mother" (1990, p. 9).

The book is autobiographical even when it does not seem so. Regardless how abstract, Pagano's conversations with various philosophers, novelists, and curriculum theorsts are all autobiographical. Her narratives have as much concern, she asserts, for the kitchen as they do for the office and the seminar room. Her students, her colleagues, and her friends wander in and out of these conversations. In this respect, Pagano notes, when one speaks to oneself, one is speaking to someone else. For Pagano, as it is for Grumet and Miller, connection, community, and attachment are essential to the feminist project. Pagano notes: "Our intellectual work ought to give point to and signify those attachments. Our attachments ought to give point to that work" (p. 39).

Against sentimentalization and essentialism. Pagano warns that connection and attachment should not slip into sentimentality, nor be claimed as inherently or exclusively feminine. For Pagano original knowledge is knowledge of connection, of the symbiotic attachment to the mother, but this fact does not make such knowledge essentially feminine. In this view discourse becomes a compensation for the absent mother. What interrupted the symbiotic relationship to the mother, and thrust the infant into the symbolic, compensatory register? Pagano explains:

> [The phallus is] . . . the symbol of difference. The possessor of the phallus interrupts, breaks communion. At the same time that the phallus stands symbolically for the mother's absence, it becomes a symbol of power, the power to possess the mother . . . even when he who possesses the phallus is denied the original object. He can only generate symbolic substitutions. (p. 4)

Not only sons create substitutions, that is, language, for the lost mother. Daughters join sons in coming to form through language.

Resettling disciplinary communities. In coming to form, bringing oneself to presence via language, women encounter themselves as Other. It is in this sense that women are exiles. Through community, that is through the establishment of attachments and the conversations which sustain these attachments, feminist educators might move through the symbolic register, discovering themselves and their students as subjects and agents, rather than as Other. In this regard, Pagano asserts: "The task I see for feminist theory in education just now is one of making conversation with our professions and with our history within them. We can theorize our vulnerability as practitioners of our disciplines and as teachers, speak our exile and, in doing so, resettle our disciplinary communities" (p. 14). In such resettlings, however, women do not seek that superiority characteristic of patriarchy. She writes: "[Women] do not want the power to oppress, to maim, and to silence" (p. 14). The power women seek is to speak women's voices, women's experience:

> If we women are to find our voices, we must insist on describing the claiming the difference produced in experience and on naming and claiming the original connection denied and forbidden in patriarchal discourse. (14-15)

That connection and difference "open the world to the moral imagination and to humane practice" (p. 156).

Without question the works of Grumet, Miller, and Pagano are central to the feminist project to understanding curriculum as gender text. These three theoreticians have served as pioneers. They have staked their claims—the claims of all women—bravely. Their work remains as some of the most sophisticated theory in the field. The feminist project is not one of self-aggrandizement, however. The inspiration of and collaboration with others are primary aims. It is unsurprising, then, that during the 1980s other important voices came to articulate gender issues. Among these scholars were Nel Noddings, Florence R. Krall, Elizabeth Ellsworth, Meredith Reiniger, Magda Lewis, James and Susan Macdonald, James Sears, Linda Christian-Smith, Jesse Goodman, and others.

VIII
Feminist Pedagogy and Politics: An Overview

Concern for our children is extended through empathy with other maternal thinkers for all children.

(Nel Noddings, 1992b, pp. 67-68)

Through such shared struggles in the classroom women might embrace for themselves the politics of autonomy and self determination rather than reject it as a liability.

(Magda Lewis, 1990, p. 487)

In the 1980s feminist scholarship expanded, as did political theory, into related areas. The work moved from the more general to the more specific, although "global" and "local" movements occurred in much of the work simultaneously. Thematically, feminist theorists took interest in language, the natural environment, feminist pedagogy, and popular culture. Early in the 1980s, the focus remained broad. Illustrative of a general focus on sexism is an article by James B. Macdonald and Susan Colberg Macdonald [regarding Macdonald's significance for the field see chapters 3 and 4] who sketched the outlines of the relation between gender and curriculum in general terms. They pointed to the scale of the problem of sexism and the links among sexism, world armament, and the environmental crisis. The Macdonalds connected politics, economics, and culture with the production of gendered personalities in the family and the school. They distinguished between the "agentic" or agency-oriented personality (typically male), and the "communal" one (typically female), concepts which generally parallel the gender distinctions drawn by object relations theorists (Grumet, 1988b). These psychoanalytic theorists typify contemporary man (in countries like the U.S.) as achieving independence at the price of relationship and intimacy, and the contemporary woman as sometimes submerged in relationship at the cost of independence and autonomy. These psychological constellations of self formation support and express political inequalities.

The Macdonalds (1988) argued that sexism permeates all aspects of the school, including its organization, status hierarchy, and curriculum. They noted that concepts such as behavioral objectives, behavior modification, competency analysis, instructional systems, and so on, support agency-oriented value orientations. The so-called hidden curriculum reproduces familial sex-role stereotyping at worst, and fails to challenge the gender status quo at best. No aspect of school life seems to escape these influences. What course of action is possible? The Macdonalds suggested that "social engineering" was inappropriate and ineffective. Rather, incremental social action, taken in individual ways according to what is possible at each institutional site, offers hope for long-term change. In addition, scholarship (especially theoretical work) is necessary to justify and explicate what must be done. The Macdonalds suggested that the school must be reconceived to support a concept of "sociability" or community, in which patterns of independence, relationship, and intimacy could be lived by both sexes within the institution. At stake, the Macdonalds insisted, is not only gender equity in the school but the survival of the planet.

Internalized misogny. Illustrative of a more specific and radical focus is the scholarship of Meredith Reiniger, who employed the "meta-ethical" feminist language of controversial theologian and feminist theorist Mary Daly (1978). Reiniger studied autobiographical material written by her high school English students and by herself for traces of internalized misogyny, which she found configured according to individuals' life histories as well as more general patterns of woman-hating (Reiniger, 1982, 1989). Reiniger's path-breaking effort to introduce feminist perspectives into analyses of students' self-perceptions foreshadowed what would become a feminist insistence upon the gender contextualization of analyses of daily classroom life (Berlak, 1989; Ellsworth, 1989).

Florence R. Krall. The ecological dimensions of feminist theory and the potential sources of knowledge in non-Western myths and matriarchal religions found expression in the 1980s in the highly suggestive and lyrical work of Florence R. Krall. Creating a new form of curriculum inquiry in which feminist themes, ecological metaphors, and autobiographical methods were linked, Krall (1981) shared segments of her journals and her interactions with students as they explored the interrelationships between the Navajo and their reservation home:

> [This work] continues my struggle to describe and interpret the underlying meaning that flows from an "ecological" curriculum in which students explore . . . their "lived experience" of the Navajo. (p. 165)

In this and other work Krall enlarged the concept of the mytho-poetic (Macdonald, 1988; Haggerson, 1991) mode of theorizing in which issues of self, other, and curriculum are portrayed. By disclosing the physical as well as psychological journeys undertaken by her and her students, Krall connected lived experience and adventure with academic structures, and in so doing, moved beyond the physical and metaphoric containment of the patriarchal institution (Krall, 1979; 1988a, 1988c, 1989, 1990, n.d.).

In a voice remarkable for its directness, simplicity, and lyricism, Krall remembered (1988a) her time as a department chairperson. In "Behind the Chairperson's Door: Reconceptualizing Woman's Work," Krall wove the everyday and the mundane with the poignant, even—when she evokes the natural world, as she often does in her work—with the sublime. Images of sunlight, birds, and a moth are juxtaposed to academic sexism, pettiness, triviality, and inanity:

> The [chairperson's] door behind which I sit opens into a small office with one wall of southern-facing windows. From my desk, I witness the progression of seasons: clouds building over the mountains to sudden, summer showers; leaves dusting the lawn autumn yellow: drab-coated gold finches, backdropped by

winter snow, feeding on dry catskins, spring greening, succession; years blending into an eternity. (p. 496)

Section titles include "the phone is ringing," "someone is knocking," and "opening the door." The work of administering is juxtaposed with the struggles of everyday life. The phenomenological dictum "back to the things themselves" is evident here, as well as a feminist manifesto for women's solidarity. Krall (1988a) concludes:

> The seasons are too short. But, out of the litter of summer's bloom will sprout new forms. The door of my office is open and departmental life seeps in. Perhaps I'll move my desk so that the two horizons can blend and I can meet both worlds full force as I would the tree falling toward me in the forest, with full awareness, awakeness, and responsiveness. . . .
>
> If I am establish a new covenant between us [i.e., colleagues], I must first emancipate myself from repression and tyranny, both from within and without. I am filled with passionate desire and fierce patience, anxious to get on with it but able to wait. The work of further reconceptualization lies before me. But for one brief moment I stand on the tower top looking at a realm of possibilities. (p. 512)

Krall's original synthesis of feminist, autobiographical, and ecological interests remains a poignant and powerful contribution to contemporary curriculum theory. In a profound sense, she achieved what James B. Macdonald dreamed when he asked us to imagine curriculum as a creation of a vision, as building a world [see also Krall, 1988c].

Others explored the links between gender and nature. In 1986 Steven DeMocker examined the concept and practice of "outdoor education" from gender and specifically feminist perspectives. He studied the history of the concept of "nature" in the West, noting that men have traditionally conceived of the "outdoors" in role terms such as frontiersmen, explorers, and conquerors, what he termed a "masculinized heroic." DeMocker argued that organized wilderness activities by and for women represent an opportunity to reconceive not only outdoor education but the humankind-nature relationship itself in more cooperative, non-adversarial, and loving modes: "The broader implication for human consciousness may be the possibility of recognizing in Nature a non-exploitative, genuinely liberative paradigm on which to base human social relations (DeMocker, 1986, p. 12).

Caring, voice, and solitude. A feminist notion of humane social relations is also found in Nel Noddings' (1981, 1989, 1992a, 1992b) interest in nurturance, caring, and women. Early on, Nel Noddings (1981) introduced a theory of ethics based on a model of maternal care and nurturance. [Pinar (1981a) suggested gender implications embedded in Noddings' work, implications which Noddings later made explicit (1989). Noddings was not alone in this interest; Ava McCall (1989) has also raised questions regarding conceptions of nurturance and caring in teacher education.] Later, "In Search of the Feminine," Noddings (1985) made the case for studying the history of the feminine. More recently, Noddings (1992) continues to employ feminist theory and her notion of caring in a fundamental reformulation of curriculum design. She points out that: "Concern for our children is extended through empathy with other maternal thinkers to concern for all children" (1992b, pp. 67, 68). We review Noddings' feminist curriculum design in chapter 13. Noddings' scholarship is sophisticated and wide-ranging, of importance to many working not only in feminist theory, but in school reform and moral education as well.

Other feminist research labored to develop a notion of feminist pedagogy. For instance, theoretical research into issues of feminist pedagogy and conceptions of "maternal practice" conducted by Susan Laird (1988, 1991) presented particular analyses of the ways in which the dominant gender culture influences our perceptions and expectations of our roles as students and teachers. Relatedly, Kathleen Casey (1990; see also chapter 10) addressed the specific social contexts in which teachers work; she delineated ways in which those contexts frame teachers' differing conceptions of feminism and of mothering as well as of curriculum and teaching. Geraldine Joncich Clifford (1987), the distinguished biographer of Thorndike (Clifford, 1962), reviewed historical links between mothering and teaching. Other contemporary scholarship integrates life history and politics [see also chapter 10]. For instance, in "Teaching as 'Women's Work': A Century of Resistant Voices," Petra Munro (1992) notes that: "When curricular practice is seen and remembered as fluid and embedded in lived experience, these women [that she studied] not only subvert traditional forms, but deflect the standardization of curriculum which has traditionally functioned as a form of control" (p. 15). Feminist pedagogy in general and Petra Munro's work more specifically reconceives the Marxist conception of resistance. Munro (1992) argues that:

> resistance is not an "act" but a movement, a continual displacement of others' efforts to name our realities. This is a resistance born out of survival, an attempt to stay real and claim the realities of our lives as women, as teachers an as women who choose to be teachers. (p. 16)

Ann Berlak (1989) contributes to feminist pedagogy by examining her own teaching. Via reflective journal writing, including detailed journal entries on her current teaching practices, and via examination of notes on her teaching, Berlak worked to uncover traces of unconscious and unintended imposition of her beliefs on her students. By focusing on inequalities perpetuated by social structures, including those of race, class, and gender, Berlak exhibited her commitment to emancipatory pedagogy by autobiographically laying bare traces of inequalities in her own teaching practice. Such willingness, indeed courage, to examine their own practices characterizes a number of contemporary feminist curriculum scholars. Continuing to argue against the dichotomies of research and practice, emotion and intellect, public and private, these scholars are extending the concerns of the autobiographers by incorporating reflexive inquiry into their current theorizing and research initiatives. In this regard, Susan Stinson (1988) critiqued the traditional curriculum of dance education as patriarchal, i.e. as replicating dualisms of mind and body, feeling and thinking. She argued for a curriculum that enables dancers and dance educators to link dance to the larger project of transcending masculinist dualisms. Collaboration has now been joined by solitude as a feminist concept (Wear, 1993). [Solitude and solidarity have long been modes of women's political and spiritual work; see Meehan, 1993.] In this regard, Delese Wear (1991) writes:

> Perhaps what some of us can do . . . is . . . stalk those moments of solitude often wedged in dailiness. We're far more than what we see of ourselves reflected in others; learning how and where to look for ourselves, to "dive deep" and still surface, seems to be what we must learn to do as we, too, stand here ironing. (p. 183)

Relatedly, Atkins (1991) insists that "without solitude and silence, we don't give ourselves much chance of creating a vocabulary that can sustain us" (1991, p. 202).

In the late 1980s, other feminist curriculum theorists focussed on sexual concerns of women, among them sexual harassment and related forms of misogyny (Brodkey & Fine, 1988; Linn, et al., 1992). As the decade progressed, curriculum theorists continued to focus on their own practices as teachers and researchers, and to theorize ways to make teaching and research more democratic, less hierarchical, and more collaborative. This work often referred to the influential volume *Women's Ways of Knowing: The Development of Self, Voice, and Mind* by M. F. Belenky, et al., (1988), and relied on the concept of voice, a concept which, unlike those associated with masculinist epistemologies, used the metaphors of listening and speaking rather than visual metaphors. That concept was also given prominence in Carol Gilligan's widely-cited *In a Different Voice* which appeared in the middle of the decade. In part, the concept of voice allowed curricularists to investigate the ways patriarchal structures, research methods, and teaching techniques silence, exclude, distort, and misrepresent women's educational experience. In this regard, Valerie Walkerdine (1985) found that the success of "girls who did well at school [was] attributed to hard work, diligence and not brilliance" (p. 18).

Feminist curriculum theorists also addressed issues of race and class. For much of the 1970s feminism had failed to take into account the problematics of race and class, although neo-Marxist and socialist feminists such as Juliet Mitchell had attended to the latter. With increasing awareness of race and class, however, it became more difficult to assume a homogeneous group called "women" (Luttrell, 1993; see chapter 6). Reflecting a wider focus of the feminist project, several scholars introduced issues of race as they struggled to find more democratic, collaborative, and connected ways of knowing. One such theorist who came to prominence by the end of the decade was Elizabeth Ellsworth.

Feminist pedagogy. As we saw in her critique of critical pedagogy in chapter 5, Elizabeth Ellsworth acknowledged the contradictions that emerge in authentic attempts to enact reciprocal and non-impositional forms of curriculum, pedagogy and research within such hierarchical and often authoritarian settings such as universities. Ellsworth's focus has included examining possibilities and limitations of deconstructing and reconstructing power relations in university classrooms in ways that are linked to specific and contextually defined political agendas. Acknowledging that local configurations of power cannot be severed from their larger social, economic, and historical contexts, Ellsworth (1989) has argued that within specific sites such as classrooms, larger struggles and relations of power are present and get played out. Concluding a study of educational films, she explained:

> While the conventions of educational films invite students to take up social and ideological positions of the white, male, middle-class scientist/problem solver, critical educators can construct other social positions within their classrooms, which are real material sites of social relations. (1990a, p. 24)

Elizabeth Ellsworth has extended and illumined feminists' insistence on contextualization as a requisite element of critical analyses as well as their insistence on active attempts to overturn oppressive pedagogical stances and curricular forms. In the early 1990s, she (Ellsworth, 1993) would subject tenure to feminist analysis, employing a self-reflective, self-critical, and socially contextualized mode of inquiry. Additionally, [see chapter 5], Ellsworth contributed to the understanding of the politics of popular culture, specially the politics of educational films (1984, 1986, 1987a, 1987b, 1988c, 1987c, 1987d, 1988, 1990a). The work of Elizabeth Ellsworth is multi-faceted and innovative, always extending beyond itself toward the frontier of the field, earning her the reputation of the one of the most provocative and revolutionary theorists at work today.

Jean Erdman (1990) has questioned those definitions of community which emerged from women's differing social and economic settings as she worked to construct possibilities for feminist teaching as one form of community. [For another exposition of community as a feminist issue, see Beck, 1992.] While recognizing the structural inequities that risk making such "emancipatory" work open to "malefic generosity" (Freire, 1968), many feminists believe that through self-reflexive and social inquiry, it is possible to disrupt established meanings, value and power relations. By examining their origins in life history, making explicit whose interests they support, and by analyzing how they are susceptible to change, feminists wage a multi-front struggle for gender justice (Weedon, 1987). Feminist scholars working in universities as well as other educational settings such as elementary or high schools, child-care facilities, latch-key children's programs, or home education services understand that their positions can be "actively utilized (rather than transcended) as a location for the construction of meaning, a place from where meaning is constructed, rather than simply the place where a meaning can be discovered . . . or as a locus of an already determined set of values" (Alcoff, 1988, p. 434; see also Alcoff & Porter, 1993). Such realizations inform the work of those contemporary feminists who develop research, curriculum theory, and teaching strategies.

Magda Lewis (1988, 1990) emphasized students' and teachers' experiences and voices as she argued that theories neither confine nor emancipate unless the practices of confinement and emancipation are embodied in how lives are lived, decisions made and actions taken. In "Interrupting Patriarchy: Politics, Resistance, and Transformation in the Feminist Classroom," Lewis (1990) tells stories of teaching strategies employed to subvert the gendered status quo of classroom interaction between women and men. Among the subjects she taught was date rape. The "No Means No" campaign was sometimes interpreted by men as "No means tie me up" or "No means dyke." Lewis (1990) recalled the massacre at the University of Montreal on December 6, 1989, when 14 women were murdered by a young man screaming "you bunch of feminists." In teaching women she finds that women exhibit a "woman-as-caretaker" ideology even when men are not in attendance, although even more so when they are: "For women, overt acts of violence, like the one that occurred at the University of Montreal, are merely an extension of their daily experiences in the psychological/social/sexual spaces of the academy" (p. 485). Lewis' stories of teaching do not, however, represent a model:

> My intent, rather, has been to articulate how, at particular movements in my teaching, I made sense of those classroom dynamics that seemed to divide women and men across their inequalities in ways that reaffirmed women's subordination, and how making sense of those moments as politically rich allowed me to develop an interpretive framework for creating a counter-hegemony from my teaching practice.... Through such shared struggles in the classroom women might embrace for themselves the politics of autonomy and self determination rather than reject it as a liability. (1990, p. 487)

Lewis has pointed to the ways women and their work, however construed, have always been central to the conditions under which men have created the symbolic order, in spite of women's exclusion from that order. We must all work together, Lewis has insisted, to transform the discourse that encases such relationships. She questions:

> how we might consider the possibilities for as well as the constraints on self-critique as a form of pedagogy in a context where, despite our struggles to the contrary, we continue to invest ourselves and each other—those with whom we share our classrooms—with discourses that in speaking, silence ... in raising issues of power, reinforce it ... and in seeking to give voice, withhold it. (1990, p. 2)

Deborah Britzman (1989) highlights the processes of intersubjective critique among herself and her students; she focuses on ways in which she works with students as well as on ways in which students work with her to reproduce and challenge traditional relations of power and authority. Britzman conceptualizes curriculum as relational and, thus, as necessarily infused with a diversity of cultural expressions and productions which enabled students and herself as teacher to construct their educational and lived worlds.

Feminist ethnography. Leslie Roman has studied the dilemmas of feminist researchers who wish to employ naturalistic field-work approaches. Many feminists judge that these approaches enable them to contextualize their research in the classroom as well as homes, workplaces, and leisure settings of students' and teachers' lives, but they do not wish to enact those positivistic presuppositions which Roman argued are embedded in naturalistic ethnography. In developing a critical as opposed to a naturalistic ethnography, Roman described the social and political functions of ethnographic research when it is guided by a feminist materialist epistemology. Roman claims that a critical ethnography encourages women to develop their own perspectives from which to study and change the world, while acknowledging subtle differences and commonalities in their experiences of oppression (Roman & Christian-Smith, 1988; Roman & Apple, in Eisner & Peshkin, 1990).

As the 1980s drew to a close intense debates began to appear among feminist curriculum theorists regarding the possibility of dialogue among the various "voices" raised in classroom settings and in curriculum discourse. How was it possible to truly allow everyone's voice to be heard equally? How could the patriarchal push for closure, totalization, and for monologue be resisted both in schools and in research, but also in oneself? These questions seem to inform a good deal of feminist analysis in the curriculum field during the latter half of the 1980s. In this analysis one can also see an increasing attention to the formation of identity. It became increasingly clear during the 1980s that it was not enough to talk about women or men; one had to address the racial, class, sexual, and embodied dimensions of identity too. From this understanding it was only a short step to acknowledge the provisionality of identity, the role of difference, and other questions that had been circulating within poststructuralism and postmodernism.

Identity and popular culture. The turn to research on identity and its construction was helped by the attention feminist curriculum scholars began to give to how gender is constructed in schools. For instance, Roman and Christian-Smith's analyses of the politics of popular culture (1988) defined and located gender within a set of asymmetrical power relations between men and women as well as among women at a given historical conjuncture. They pointed to ways feminists might analyze how gender ideologies and forms of representation are constructed in the production and consumption of contemporary popular culture. Roman and Christian-Smith's *Becoming Feminine* highlighted the debates that continue to surround gender as both construct and category of critique. Feminist curriculum scholars combat ahistorical and essentialist interpretations of both curriculum and human nature. At the same time, they extend their investigation into the construction of gender ideologies as these are expressed in the daily educational experience of students and teachers. Lois Weis also considered constructions of gender ideologies, especially as they intersect with class and race (1988, Weis & Fine, 1993). She explored critically a variety of educational issues and policies, including school dropouts (1989a) and current reform efforts (1989b).

Nancy Lesko's (1984, 1988a, 1988b, 1994) studies of adolescents and the cultural themes of individualism and community emerging in their interpersonal relationships and in their experience of schooling hold considerable significance for curriculum scholars [see also Hudak, 1993]. Employing semiotics and a Foucauldian analysis, Lesko located adolescent sexualities historically and socially; she argued against the alleged gender, race, and class neutrality of adolescent literature and schooling practices. [See chapter 13 for further discussion of Lesko's work.] Linda Christian-Smith's work on adolescent romance fiction illustrated this absence of neutrality. In one essay she studied how femininity is constructed discursively. Employing a sample of 34 adolescent novels written from 1942-1982, Christian-Smith found that adolescent female readers are prepared as "future keepers of heart and hearth" (1988, p. 77). In "Gender, Popular Culture, and Curriculum: Adolescent Romance Novels as Gender Text," Christian-Smith (1987) explored how domestic and romantic concerns structure girls' decisions about their futures: "The novels are structured around a dominant model of femininity, the 'good girl,' who is characterized by filial obedience and adherence to traditional romantic conduct centering around males' control of interactions" (p. 365). In both Lesko's and Christian-Smith's work, feminist theory problematizes what were taken-for-granted concepts in the traditional field.

The focus on how gender is discursively and non-discursively constructed and the incorporation of poststructuralist and postmodern critiques into feminist curriculum analysis are clear in the work of Rebecca Martusewicz (1992) and Patti Lather (1991a). Martusewicz examined what it meant to be an educated women, a woman teacher, and a woman researcher. Rather than using an autobiographical approach, as for example in the case of Janet Miller, Martusewicz employed poststructuralist approaches. Influenced by the work of French poststructuralists and feminists as well as the work of Valerie Walkerdine (1985, 1988), a British scholar influenced by Foucault and feminism whom we mentioned earlier, Martusewicz argued for an understanding of curriculum that would emancipate men and women from those discourses that have tied them to the "truth of woman," an elaborate fiction spun in culture. She suggested: "to live as feminist educators is to live a tension between a critical theoretical space and an affirmative political space. It is within this in-between, this 'elsewhere' that we must seek the educated woman" (1992, p. 155).

Good wives. Patti Lather (1987) argued that gender is central to both understanding and changing the work lives of teachers, emphasizing that gender is not subservient to class, as it is in the effort to understand curriculum as political text. She put the matter bluntly: "We need to be sure we do not become 'good wives' of a Marxist patriarch" (1987, p. 33). To bring gender to the forefront is to empower women teachers, to tap their estrangement and sense of relative deprivation, in the name of transformation. Lather has perhaps done more than any contemporary scholar to date to introduce to feminist theorizing the concept of the postmodern. Her work at the end of the 1980s and the beginning of the 1990s has focused attention on "women's estate" in a postmodern culture. Lather's early work focused many feminists' theorizing on the processes of research, per se. To approach research as praxis requires that one attempt to conduct research as a democratized process of inquiry characterized by an emphasis upon negotiation and reciprocity between the researchers and the researched. Such a research orientation could illuminate "awareness of the contradictions hidden or distorted by everyday understandings" (Lather, 1986a, p. 259).

As Lather moved into poststructuralist frames of inquiry, she questioned not only concepts basic to positivist ways of knowing—such as neutrality, objectivity and "observable facts"—but also the impositional tendencies inherent within attempts at transparent description, "clean" separation of the interpreter and the interpreted, and placement of the researcher at the center of research processes (1986b, 1989). Lather in Pinar & Reynolds, 1992b). Her *Getting Smart* has attracted considerable attention in the curriculum field, particularly among feminist curriculum theorists and others interested in postmodern gender analysis. The introduction of postmodern discourses to the examination of gender has helped expand the contemporary field to include postmodern gender analysis alongside psychoanalytic and Marxist feminist analysis. That inclusion was also supported in the 1980s by the body of curriculum theory written by men, addressing issues associated with homosexuality and masculinity more generally.

IX
Gender Analysis and Male Identity

For those students in your school who have been the butt of locker room jokes, who have lost the significance of pink triangles and the struggles of the Mattachine Society and the Daughters of Bilitis in the dustbins of history, and who have never been exposed to positive gay and lesbian role models, I ask that our existence be recognized.

(James T. Sears, 1983, pp. 96-97)

The pedagogical environment . . . has as its central business the production of compliant heterosexual identities, largely by means of demonizing homosexuality.

(Simon Watney, 1994, p. 175)

The real question isn't whether an individual is male or female, but what perspective teachers have toward gender identity and sexual/social roles. In influencing children's views of society, a teacher's perspectives are more significant than his or her sex.

(Jesse Goodman, 1987, p. 52)

Curriculum as Homosexual Text: The Scholarship of James T. Sears
The most visible male scholar working to understand curriculum as gender text (and more particularly, as homosexual text) is James T. Sears. [While the

most visible, Sears is not the only curriculum scholar interested in homosexual issues; see, for instance, Pinar, 1983a/1994; Sillin, 1992; Tierney, 1993a, 1993b; McLaughlin & Tierney, 1993.] The range of Sears' research is indicated in the following titles: "Sexuality: Taking off the Masks" (1983), "Growing Up Gay: Is Anyone There to Listen?" (1988a), "Playing Out Our Feelings: The Use of Reader's Theater in Anti-Oppression Work" (1989a), "Impact of Race and Gender on Growing Up Lesbian and Gay in the South" (1989c), *Growing Up Gay in the South* (1990a), "Teaching for Diversity: Student Sexual Identities" (1991b), "Lesbian and Gay Men in Education" (1991), and *Sexuality and the Curriculum* (1992a).

Often employing empirical data and analyses, Sears' early scholarship exhibited an activist bent. In works such as "Growing Up Gay: Is Anyone There to Listen? (1988a) and "Peering into the Well of Loneliness: The Responsibility of Educators to Gay and Lesbian Youth" (1987a), Sears argued that educators have a social responsibility to promote human dignity, a responsibility which entails supporting the struggle for social justice for gays and lesbians. "This means," Sears asserted:

> providing a learning environment which is free from physical and psychological abuse, portraying honestly the richness and diversity of humanity, fostering an understanding of human sexuality, integrating homosexual themes and issues in the curriculum, counseling young people who have or may have a different sexual orientation, and supporting gay and lesbian teachers. (1987a, p. 1)

In support of his argument, Sears examined and refuted three interrelated expressions of homophobia, i.e. that homosexuality is a sin, an illness, and a crime. He admonished educators:

> For those students in your school who have been the butt of locker room jokes, who have lost the significance of pink triangles and the struggles of the Mattachine Society and the Daughters of Bilitis in the dustbins of history, and who have never been exposed to positive gay and lesbian role models, I ask that our existence be recognized. And for those who have been taught that homosexuals are sinners, criminals or neurotics, I ask that educators work to destroy these myths. (1983, pp. 96-97)

Sears established the Lesbian and Gay Studies Special Interest Group in the American Educational Research Association. He formed a not-for-profit corporation to sponsor and disseminate research of interest to the lesbian, gay, and bisexual communities as well. Other examples of Sears' activism include the development and publication of *Empathy*, an interdisciplinary journal devoted to ending oppression based on sexual orientation, and the passage of a student sexual orientation resolution by the Association for Supervision and Curriculum Development. As part of Sears' study of growing up gay in the South, he conducted empirical research on southern guidance counselors' and prospective teachers' attitudes regarding homosexuality. Sears found that "many counselors expressed alarmingly negative attitudes and feelings" regarding homosexuality. While most guidance counselors

knew or suspected homosexual students, fewer than one-quarter of counselors provided these students with information regarding homosexuality.
Those minority of counselors who work with gay youth report that the majority of these students suffer greater psychosocial difficulties than do their
heterosexual classmates. Sears concluded:

> Training counselors to work effectively with homosexual students should be a
> high priority for school districts, counseling associations, and university gradu-
> ate programs. An integrative and ongoing set of programs jointly sponsored by
> these groups may be the most effective. Such workshops ought to include
> participation by gay youth. (p. 27)

With *Growing Up Gay in the South* (1990a), Sears shifted his gay-activist
stance to a more critical perspective of homosexual research. In "On
Conducting Homosexual Research," Sears challenges the uncritical adoption
by many scholars of "canons of gay liberation." He denounces the cult of
"political correctness" in the homosexual community. The canon of essentialism—"I just am"—permeates gay and lesbian communities and much of the
scholarship devoted to this topic, according to Sears. Scholars who fail to
heed the party line often find themselves criticized by certain segments of
gay liberation. Sears writes:

> The identities of the new Advocate Man or Amazonian Woman born out of the
> struggles of Stonewall, nourished through homosexual culture, protected in
> homosexual communities, and maturing during the AIDS crisis are dependent
> upon these orthodoxies. Challenging these orthodoxies questions the legiti-
> macy of these identities and threatens the existence of homosexual communi-
> ties. These sexual identities and the communities which have given them mean-
> ing have served us well, but as social artifacts, they also pose problems. One is
> confusing social artifacts with sexual destinies. (1990b, pp. 15-16)

Sears' research on how young people make meaning of the differing intersections of racial, gender, social class, and sexual identities lies at the heart of
Growing Up Gay in the South. This shift from the primacy of sexual orientation
to the construction of human identities is significant; it mirrors a similar shift
in feminist theory. In studying the impact of southern culture on these various identities, Sears found that certain regional characteristics such as those
associated with religion (especially fundamentalism), family, "honor" and
tradition, influence a young person's idiosyncratic understanding of sexual
feelings and gender arrangements. Based upon these case studies, Sears
(1990a) concluded that sexual orientation itself is fictive:

> Gay identity, like Southern identity, is an elaborate social fiction. The mind of
> the South, like the homosexualization of America, transforms contempt into
> distinction and refashions exiles into champions. This dusting of reality by the
> wings of a fairy seduces us into believing that our differentness is our special-
> ness. But, to borrow a phrase from Buckminster Fuller, differentness is verb—it
> energizes the journey of our spirit but it is not our spirit. As human beings we
> are all bestowed with the gift of the differentness: sexual, racial, gender,
> regional, and so forth. These differences are the portals toward knowledge-of-

being; they allow us to see the world upside down; they are the moon and the stars that allow us to chart our journey. (pp. 438-439)

Sears' scholarship and activism stand nearly alone in their important contribution to understanding male homosexual issues. With time this essential aspect of the project to understand curriculum as gender text will no doubt develop further, quite possibly under Sears' leadership. However, this work is not without controversy.

During the summer 1993 term, Sears offered a course on Christian fundamentalism at the University of South Carolina. Known in the state and especially among Christian fundamentalists for his homosexual scholarship and advocacy, Sears' course "raised a furor" (*Out*, 1993, p. 12). Governor Carroll Campbell of South Carolina and 46 state legislators asked University President John Palms to cancel the course. The University held firm, but the controversy underscores how contentious curriculum debates can become. Not only multiculturalism and racial theory can be exploited by politicians to ignite public opinion; gender theory can as well.

Profeminist Men: The Scholarship of Jesse Goodman

Gender analysis aimed at uncovering the construction of male identity was carried out in the 1980s by Jesse Goodman who has studied preservice male elementary schoolteachers. [We described Goodman's study of the Harmony School in chapter 5.] After reviewing studies of male socialization and gender identity, Goodman (1987) conducted case histories of nine men preparing for elementary schoolteaching. He created three categories by which he typified these men. Rick and Sam are traditionalists, expressing traditional ideas of gender identity and roles typically assigned to men and women. Both men saw their ability to maintain discipline in the classroom as special strengths. Both men favored equal-pay for equal-work, but both preferred men in leadership positions, while preferring women to remain in the classroom and the home. Tom, Frank, and Mike were characterized by Goodman as neo-traditionalists. These men regarded the women's movement as a positive force; they agreed that sexism was a pervasive social fact. However, gender issues were specific to women, according to these neo-traditionalists; traditional concepts of men and masculinity went unquestioned. Goodman observed that while these three men accepted the feminist movement, they failed to address gender issues in the curriculum. Bill represented a "new direction." Older than the other men, Bill had been influenced by the anti-war movement of the 1960's, as well as by the women's movement and by Eastern philosophies. Bill wanted his students to understand a "complete and holistic view of what it means to be a human being" (p. 50). He encouraged girls in this third-grade class to participate in traditional "all-boy" activities; he encouraged boys' participation in what are often considered girls' pursuits, such as sewing. Goodman concluded: "Although Bill was a unique preservice teacher, his beliefs and actions are noteworthy. While small in numbers, the perspectives of individuals like Bill reflect an important shift in social perceptions within our schools and society" (51).

Goodman concluded this study by observing that the mere inclusion of men in elementary education hardly guarantees:

a healthier, more balanced view of occupational roles to the children in our society. . . . The presence of men such as Rick and Sam would serve as a regressive force. . . . The real question isn't whether an individual is male or female, but what perspective teachers have toward gender identity and sexual/social roles. In influencing children's views of society, a teacher's perspectives are more significant than his or her sex. (p. 52)

Profeminist teachers. In a related study, Goodman and Tom Kelly (1988) worked to lay the ground for inquiry and understanding of profeminist teachers and the roles they might play in the struggle to create a non-sexist society. Profeminist men, Goodman and Kelly tell us, are those teachers not content to simply "cheer women on." Rather, "profeminists oppose, reject, and actively work within their own context against patriarchal practices in society" (Goodman & Kelly, 1988). Their study was organized into three sections: 1) a discussion of the notion of patriarchy and the feminization of teaching, 2) a discussion of the concept of feminist pedagogy; and 3) sketching implications for profeminist teachers.

Goodman and Kelly begin by observing that teaching during the American colonial period was considered men's work. These men tended to hold other occupations (such as preaching and farming); they held teaching jobs when not otherwise occupied. These male teachers were left to their own devices. Goodman and Kelly report that during this period when teaching was a man's occupation, the teacher was perhaps more autonomous than during any subsequent period (1988, p. 3). As Grumet has also observed, by the mid-1800's the teacher corps was female, a majority that grew to 90% by the 1930's. Goodman and Kelly note that "as women filled the classroom of our schools, teachers' professional status and autonomy diminished" (p. 3).

Goodman and Kelly summarized the literature on feminist pedagogy. A feminist teacher, they conclude: 1) is a feminist advocate who presents her/himself as a collaborative co-learner rather than a detached, authoritarian figure, 2) affirms student "empowerment" by respective students' personal knowledge, interests, and experience, 3) supports a cooperative vs. competitive learning environment, 4) considers feminist perspectives in the curriculum, including attention to history, race, and class, 5) emphasizes both emotional and intellectual development, and 6) recognizes the importance of praxis, i.e. acting in the world upon one's beliefs. Goodman and Kelly conclude that profeminist teachers are potentially a powerful force. They need to develop support systems, and in particular, profeminist men need to promote "more communication and support among men" (p. 11).

Other Gender Analyses

Marxists such Michael Apple and Henry Giroux incorporated gender analyses in their effort to understand curriculum politically [Apple as early as 1982]. While neither scholar directly investigated the construction of masculinity or, more generally, gender, both articulated an anti-patriarchal stance as part of their political theory. Giroux (1992a) has drawn on the work of African-American feminist theorists to support his postmodern notion of "bordercrossings." Michael Apple and Susan Jungck (1990) studied ethnographically a computer literacy curriculum to illuminate processes of rationalization, deskilling, and intensification in teaching. They found that teachers often employed a prepackaged curriculum which left them bored and "other-dependent." At the same time, these teachers employed the computer literacy curriculum for their own purposes, in order to solve problems provoked by schedule and work load generally. This complex response by teachers cannot be understood, Apple and Jungck assert, without understanding the gendered realities of teachers' labor.

Feminist analysis was also employed by Peter Taubman in his "The Silent Center: An Essay on Masculinity" (1986). He took the generic "man" in its particularity to reveal the tragic picture of men presented in those metanarratives that speak about men, employing the work of Nancy Chodorow (1978) to explore what it has meant in our culture to be a man and in turn how this meaning of masculinity has informed our conceptions of curriculum. In working to understand not only the construction of masculinity, "men" and "women" but also sexuality itself—issues addressed in Taubman's early work—several contemporary curricularists studied the entire enterprise of sex education to determine what versions of sexuality, men, and women have been promulgated in the schools.

Sex education. Sex education is, obviously, an important curricular area where gender theory surfaces explicitly. One scholar of sex education programs has noted that "failure to recognize the social and historical dependency of sex allows for the reification of our conceptualizations of sex into objective elements of a fixed and socially independent human nature" (Diorio, 1985, p. 246). One area, for instance, in which this essentialist view of sexuality surfaces is in much recent literature on sex education and adolescent pregnancy (Diorio, 1985). In this regard, in "Redirecting Sexuality Education for Young Adolescents," Jesse Goodman (1991b), alleges that:

> the dominant sexual scripting encouraged in the United States is counterproductive to the well-being of most of our adolescents. Conventional sexual scripting severely limits the information available to most young people, and it creates an oppressive atmosphere of isolation and mistrust. . . . This scripting needs to be . . . challenged in middle school human sexuality classes. (p. 20)

Goodman describes a sex education class at Harmony School [see chapter 5]. There he found that the teacher (whose name was Ursina) took the class "well beyond the physiological focus of conventional middle and high school sexuality classes and directly confronted the conventional sexual attitudes that most adolescents receive in American schools and society" (p. 20). Curricular problems in this area are not new. For instance, Michael Imber (1982) tells us the story of the social hygiene movement's attempt to introduce sex education into the curriculum of American public schools during the period 1900-1917. There were sex education opponents eighty years ago also.

Recently this area has received book-length attention in *Sexuality and Curriculum: The Politics and Practices of Sexuality Education*, edited by James T. Sears (1992a), which challenges mainstream sex education. In this collection, sexuality is treated historically (Carlson, 1992c), legally (in terms of censorship) (Whitson, 1992a), autobiographically (Sapon-Shevin & Goodman, 1992) and in terms of teaching (Fonow & Marty, 1992), all of which contribute to a revision of traditional sex education theory. The importance of this book and of sexuality education in general is underlined by the AIDS epidemic. Proposals for AIDS education (Sloane & Sloane, 1990; Silin, 1992) as well as articles depicting the realities of AIDS have appeared recently.

Another controversial aspect of sexuality and the curriculum concerns homosexuality, as our review of Sears' scholarship reminds us [see also Tierney, 1993a, p. 49 ff.]. In its 1992 version, California's health curriculum framework included references to sexual orientation. It included four references to "homosexuality" and in a passage regarding the family, same-sex parents were mentioned. In California, the issue of including information regarding gays, not only in sex education and health education courses, but across the curriculum, is regarded by some as a civil rights issue. A student at Palto Alto (California) High School named Jim reports that he knows that Walt Whitman, Emily Dickinson, and Alexander the Great were all gay. But this important fact "is never mentioned. It's just a totally ignored point. It emphasizes the loneliness [gay kids feel]" (Heyser, 1992, p. 10E). The issue is a political issue, one contested by various conservative and religious groups. How it will be resolved, in California and in the nation as a whole, is far from clear. To support progressive curriculum reform, universities may need to institutionalize gay studies. A number of scholars believe that gay studies are an important counterpart to feminist theory and women's studies (Mohr, 1989).

X
Conclusion:
Isolation and Influence

Feminist thought to date operates in relative isolation from other eddies of curriculum theory and practice, but its ripples will have profound . . . influence.
(William F. Pinar & Janet L. Miller, 1982, p. 222)

Feminist scholars work to bring together domains of experience and understanding that history and culture have kept apart.
(Madeleine R. Grumet, 1988c, p. 538)

In the late 1980s and 1990s, those scholars committed to understanding curriculum as gender text have explored the frontiers of gender, politics, and culture as articulated in our conversations with the young, that is, in the curriculum. Sophisticated gender curriculum theory—such as that of Grumet, Miller, and Pagano—questions the very categories employed in this textbook. For Grumet, for instance, the effort to comprehend the curriculum politically is a gender project, and vice versa. She would contest as well the compartmentalization of autobiographical, aesthetic, and phenomenological discourses, as her work incorporates these discourses into a conceptually autonomous and coherent curriculum theory. Grumet's own words economically express what is *au fond* the feminist, gender project: She writes:

> Feminist scholars work to bring together domains of experience and understanding that history and culture have kept apart. For what it means to teach and learn is related to what it means to be male or female and to our experience of reproduction and nurturance, domesticity, sexuality, nature, knowledge and politics. (Grumet, 1988c, p. 538)

What Pinar and Miller wrote in 1982 remains true in 1994: "Feminist thought to date operates in relative isolation from other eddies of curriculum theory and practice, but its ripples will have profound . . . influence" (p. 222). Perhaps no other single discursive configuration in the field circulates these traditional concepts into a kaleidoscopic theoretical whole as effectively as that sector of scholarship which labors to understand curriculum as gender text. As the 1990s unfold, feminist curriculum theorists and others committed to gender analysis will no doubt continue to confront the ways all of us, especially students perhaps, are affected, often in brutal ways, by the gender system that forms and deforms us. It is urgent work which continues to situate the effort to understand curriculum as gender text at the center of the field.

Chapter 8

Understanding Curriculum
as Phenomenological Text

Curriculum is to be thought of . . . as meaning and as lived in.

(John Steven Mann, 1975, p. 147)

An educated person, first and foremost, understands that one's way of knowing, thinking, and doing flow from who one is. Such a person knows that an authentic person is more than a mere individual, an island unto himself or herself, but a being-in-relation with others and hence is, at core, an ethical being.

(Tetsuo Aoki, 1988b, pp. 8-9)

I
Introduction: A Poetic Activity

At the outset, let us acknowledge that phenomenologists would probably not use the notion of "text." For phenomenologists, experience and its conceptualization are distinguishable modalities. First is experience; language and thought follow. The poststructuralist notion of text, in which experience and thought are interwoven, is in fact a response to the phenomenological distinction between the two. At the conclusion of this chapter, we will focus on the links and discontinuities between phenomenology and poststructuralism. For now, note that a phenomenologist would simply entitle this chapter "understanding curriculum phenomenologically," or perhaps, simply, understanding curriculum, as the notion of understanding is a hermeneutical one [i.e. a process of interpretation; see the sections on hermeneutics later in this chapter and in chapter 12], requiring phenomenological inquiry. Because phenomenology contributed to certain strands of feminist theory (namely, the work of Madeleine Grumet and Janet Miller) and is inextricably linked with poststructuralism, we situate it between the two. However, the effort to understand curriculum phenomenologically is an autonomous and important curriculum discourse which, like the others we have identified, no responsible scholar can ignore.

Phenomenological curriculum theory. What is phenomenological inquiry? George Willis, who has worked on this question for a number of years (Willis, 1979), has answered that phenomenological inquiry is aesthetic and pre-hermeneutic, although he amends this (Willis, 1991). While phenomenological inquiry is accurately classified as a form of interpretive inquiry, it is that form of interpretive inquiry which focuses on human perception and experience, particularly on what many would characterize as the aesthetic qualities of human experience: "In its most basic form, phenomenological inquiry investigates the distinctly human perceptions of individual people and results in descriptions of such perceptions which appear directly to the perceptions of other people" (Willis, 1991, pp. 173-174). In its contemporary forms, however, one cannot separate phenomenology and hermeneutics.

What is the history of phenomenological inquiry? Among the "the earliest and most original studies," Willis (1991) cites three:

> The first study, by Pinar and Grumet (1976), cuts into the onion intuitively but does not sufficiently use the empirical knife when necessary to cut cleanly. The second study, by van Manen (1978-1979), quickly and roughly slices empirically through the entire onion, but disregarding what this knife reveals, it then keeps on both empirically and intuitively peeling away the separate halves in search of an essential center. The third study, by Willis and Allen (1978), cuts cleanly into the onion empirically but not sufficiently deeply to reveal much more than can also be revealed by the intuitive knife alone. (p. 179)

In these judgments one finds the problems of phenomenology: it can seem "messy," not clean and rigorous as statistical studies have been alleged to be; it can seem mystical, aspiring to a truth that seems religious in nature, accessible only to those who believe. And when accessible, it can be superficial, risking a restatement of cultural clichés. We believe it is none of the three, although specific studies may suffer one or more of these problems. Phenomenology is a disciplined, rigorous effort to understand experience profoundly and authentically. In this effort, phenomenology becomes quite complex. Further, it is hardly monolithic; there is a wide range of phenomenological methodologies and themes. For example, several scholars emphasize the hermeneutical or interpretative aspect of phenomenological inquiry; others strive to honor a philosophical tradition of phenomenology; still others work in the space between phenomenology and poststructuralism.

While there are important differences among phenomenologists, for present purposes it is legitimate to conclude the following. The phenomenologist rejects both rationalism [in which the "bottom line" of reality is logic] and empiricism [as elaborated in twentieth century mainstream social science, the "bottom line" of reality is its mathematical representation in statistics] because they fail to account for the world as experienced by the human being. More specifically, both rationalism and empiricism fail to depict thought as it occurs in lived or "inner" time. The phenomenological investigator questions how phenomena—"the things themselves"—present themselves in the lived experience of the individual, especially as they present themselves in lived time. Consciousness becomes a major category for the phenomenologist. However, as Maxine Greene has observed, this term does not suggest introspection. Greene (1973) explained that human consciousness moves *toward* the world, not away from it. The term consciousness speaks to the multiple ways in which objects, events, and other human beings are presented via the distinctly human processes of perceiving, judging, believing, remembering, and imagining. Phenomenologically understood, consciousness is characterized by intentionality: it is always *of* something which, when apprehended, relates to the act of consciousness involved as the meaning of that act.

While grounded in the world, phenomenological research is a "poetizing activity" (van Manen, 1984a, p. 2), an aesthetic rendering of experience, as Willis (1981) noted above. Working phenomenologically is rigorous; it requires a profound sense of what is competent and practical in educational conduct, and a sense of political consequence. One of the most prominent contemporary phenomenologists, Max van Manen (1984b), observes:

> The increasing bureaucratization of pedagogic institutions and the technologiz-
> ing effect of educational research and knowledge forms tend to erode our
> understanding and praxis of pedagogic competence in everyday life. It is in this
> sense that phenomenological research has radical consequences. . . .
> Phenomenology responds to the need for theory of the unique. . . . It is
> thoughtful learning which is at the heart of our pedagogic competence. (p. 19)

Just as feminist theory implies a politics of curriculum, so does phenomenology.

The lifeworld and one's biographic situation. As van Manen's comment makes clear, phenomenological scholarship is not mystical, not removed from the world. As Greene (1973) explained, the phenomenological concept of consciousness refers to an "experienced context" or lifeworld. The phenomenologist postulates his or her lifeworld as central to all that he or she does—including research and teaching—and as a consequence focuses upon the *biographic situation* (Pinar, 1994; see chapter 10) of each individual. Ordinarily the individual is unaware of his or her lifeworld; he or she is immersed in it. In this state, one adopts the natural attitude, taking for granted the reality and legitimacy of daily, practical life. The edges and boundaries of this atti-
. tude constitute the locations of self-reflexivity, of consciousness, necessary in order to reflect on or, in phenomenological terms, "bracket" the taken-for-granted. The great phenomenological philosopher, Martin Heidegger, conceived of difficulties or problems as occasions for becoming aware of the boundaries or horizons of the natural attitude. As Greene (1973) has observed, ordinary perception has to be suspended for questions to be posed. The individual has to be "shocked" into awareness of his or her own perception, into a recognition that one has constituted one's *own* lifeworld.

Characteristics of phenomenological research. As a beginning student, you may be a bit mystified at this juncture. You may appreciate the prospect of basing notions of curriculum and teaching upon your life as you live it, as you experience it. But how would such a notion be developed? What would be its characteristics? van Manen observes that phenomenology comprehended intellectually differs from phenomenology understood "from the inside."

With Maurice Merleau-Ponty [along with Edmund Husserl, Martin Heidegger, and Alfred Schutz, the fourth great philosopher of phenomenology], van Manen asserts that phenomenology can only authentically be understood by "doing it."

With that caveat, van Manen (1984a) sketches the following characteristics of phenomenological research: 1) Phenomenological research investigates lived experience. The phenomenological investigator studies the lifeworld as it is immediately experienced, presumably before we conceptualize it; one seeks to live in and report a deeper layer of experience than is accessible to most in the everyday "practical" world. The phenomenologist seeks a more direct experience of and encounter with the world. 2) Phenomenological research seeks the essence of experiences, employing an "eidetic reduction" to "bracket" the "natural attitude," or to reflect on one's taken-for-granted, commonsensical view of things (McEwen, 1980). These Husserlian notions point to what a phenomenon is, that which makes it "be." Thus phenomenological research is not interested in the frequency of events or their contiguity to other events; phenomenological research seeks instead the experience and meaning of events. Van Manen (1984a) makes this distinction by suggesting that phenomenology does not ask "how" questions, but rather "what" questions, as in what is the nature of the experience of learning? 3) Phenomenological research is the conscious practice of "thoughtfulness." van Manen writes that "thoughtfulness" characterizes phenomenology perhaps more aptly than any other single word. Thoughtfulness is defined as "minding," a "heeding," for Heidegger an "attunement" to what it feels like and means to be alive. Phenomenological pedagogy becomes an expression of thoughtfulness. 4) Phenomenological research does not produce knowledge for knowledge's sake; rather it produces knowledge to disclose what it means to be human. The phenomenological researcher works to comprehend the meaning of being in the world, as man, woman, child. Such comprehension requires knowledge of historical, cultural, and political traditions. [In this regard, McEwen (1980) postulates an "intentional" geography which would stress subjectivity and inter-subjectivity, especially attitudes, values, and beliefs, in the phenomenological study of that school subject.] 5) Phenomenological research always embodies a poetic quality. John Ciardi (1960) has explained that a poem cannot be reduced to a summary, to a capsule meaning, but rather, to understand a poem is to participate in "how a poem means." Likewise, phenomenological research cannot be reduced to "results." Like poetry, phenomenology attempts an incantational, evocative speaking, a primal telling, wherein the phenomenologist aims to utilize the voice to present an original singing of the world (van Manen, 1984a). We may say that phenomenological language "sings" the world.

Phenomenological research methodology. How is phenomenological research conducted? Polakow (1984a) described phenomenological research as involving the careful exploration of densely textured moments which point beyond the immediacy of the context in which they occur. Van Manen identified what he terms as four "procedural activities" to guide such exploration. First, the phenomenological investigator chooses a phenomenon which interests him or her in a serious way and simultaneously pulls him or her into the world. Authentic phenomenological research is not narcissistic nor is it idealistic in the classical philosophical sense. Serious phenomenological research attunes and pulls the investigator and the student more deeply into the world. Second, the phenomenological researcher investigates the identified phenomenon as it is lived, not merely as it is theorized. Third, the phenomenological researcher reflects upon the essential themes or structures which characterize the phenomenon (Barritt, et al., 1984). Finally, the researcher describes the phenomenon via the art of writing (van Manen, 1984b). Robert Burch (1989) summarizes: "[Phenomenology] seeks a transcending theoretical understanding that goes beyond lived experience to situate it, to judge it, to comprehend it, endowing lived experience with new meaning" (p. 192).

An outline for conducting phenomenological research. van Manen (1984b) outlines a methodology for "doing" phenomenology:

A. Turning to the Nature of Lived Experience
   1. Orienting to the phenomenon
   2. Formulating the phenomenological question
   3. Explicating assumptions and preunderstandings
B. Existential Investigation
   4. Exploring the phenomenon: generating "data"
      4.1 Using personal experience as a starting point
      4.2 Tracing etymological sources
      4.3 Searching idiomatic phrases
      4.4 Obtaining experiential descriptions from subjects
      4.5 Locating experiential descriptions in literature, art, etc.
   5. Consulting phenomenological literature
C. Phenomenological Reflection
   6. Conducting thematic analysis
      6.1. Uncovering thematic aspects in lifeworld descriptions
      6.2. Isolating thematic statements
      6.3. Composing linguistic transformations
      6.4. Gleaning thematic descriptions from artistic sources
   7. Determining essential themes
D. Phenomenological Writing
   8. Attending to the speaking of language
   9. Varying the examples
   10. Writing
   11. Rewriting: (A) to (D), etc. (van Manen,1984b).

Not every phenomenological curriculum theorist follows this procedure precisely, although in the phenomenological studies described in this chapter you will notice various elements of this procedure. Certainly van Manen's outline is a useful one for beginning students who wish to investigate this way of understanding curriculum.

The range of phenomenological curriculum research. The categories of curriculum research which have been explored phenomenologically are often quite unlike those pursued by mainstream educational research. A few categories follow closely from primary phenomenological texts, for example those which dwell on issues of language, temporality, and consciousness. Other categories are more typically associated with curriculum, such as teaching and reading. Such topics are treated differently, however, from the mainstream research literature, and from other curriculum research traditions. For instance, van Manen is interested in the *tone* of teaching, rather than in, for example, behavioral objectives or in teachers as a socioeconomic class with political interests. For him, the point of research is to attune or orient ourselves to children and teaching. Greene explored the role of *wide-awakeness* in teaching and learning. Grumet is interested in reading as an *embodied* activity. Aoki, Greene, Grumet, Pinar, and van Manen have explicated phenomenological critiques of mainstream educational research. Sometimes unusual topics are explored. For instance, consider the following themes: the "secret place" (Langeveld, 1983a, 1983b), pain (Raffel, 1984), loyalty (Moore 1984), the joke (Karatheodoris, 1984), the child prodigy (Allen, Bonner, & Moore, 1984), and adolescence as metaphor (Michalko, 1984). Vangie Kelpin (1985) has written on an aspect of pregnancy in her "Ear on the Belly: A Question of Fetal Monitors." David W. Jardine (1990) has written "On the Humility of Mathematical Language." Clearly, there is a thematic distinctiveness to much phenomenological curriculum scholarship.

Much of this research has occurred at the University of Alberta, the center for phenomenological studies in education in the Western hemisphere. Under the leadership of Ted Aoki, Max van Manen, Kenneth Jacknicke, and Terrence Carson, among others (Pinar & Reynolds, 1992c), phenomenology has been institutionalized at the University of Alberta, especially in the Department of Secondary Education. Chair of the Department from 1977 through 1985, Aoki's contribution was central, so much so that his retirement from that office was acknowledged in an international event honoring his accomplishment [see Carson, 1987; Pinar, 1987; Werner, 1987; Jacknicke, 1987; Martel, 1987; Bath, 1987; Aoki, 1987a]. A partial list (in chronological order beginning with the most recent) of the titles of Ph.D. dissertations completed in that Department reveals the range of phenomenological doctoral research conducted there, many under the academic supervision of those four men. You will notice that van Manen and Carson are Ph.D. graduates of the Department, having both worked with Aoki: *Justice in Evaluation: Participatory Case Study Evaluation* (Bath, 1988), *A Critical Understanding of Technology and Educational Development: A Case Study of the Korean Educational Development Institute* (Sung, 1986), *The Meaning of Morality and Moral Education: An Interpretative Study of the Moral Education Curriculum in Korea* (Oh,

1986), *Understanding the Meaning of Teacher Competence: An Interpretative Study of a Teacher Education Curriculum in Korea* (Hur, 1986), *Curriculum Orientation within Religious Education Programs for Catholic Secondary Schools* (van Damme, 1985), *A Hermeneutic Investigation of the Meaning of Curriculum Implementation for Consultants and Teachers* (Carson, 1984), *Social Worlds: British Columbia Social Studies Curriculum Unit "Developing the Tropical World" as Reflected Through the Writings of George Herbert Mead and Alfred Schutz* (Harrison, 1984), *Toward Understanding the Lived-World of Lebanese Muslim Students and their Teachers* (Fahlman, 1984), *Toward Understanding the Lived World of Three Beginning Teachers of Young Children* (Turner, 1984), *Re-Searching the Teachers' Perspective of Curriculum: A Case Study of Piloting a Home Economics Curriculum* (Peterat, 1983), *Re-Searching the Meaning of Consulting in Continuing Teacher Education through Phenomenological and Critical Inquiry Orientations* (Favaro, 1982), *A Study of Perspective in Social Studies* (Werner, 1977), and *Toward a Cybernetic Phenomenology of Instruction* (van Manen, 1973). Phenomenological research is sometimes found in traditionally conservative departments, for instance, in the Department of Educational Psychology at the University of Alberta (Daniel, 1991).

Phenomenological Themes. We organize the remainder of our study of curriculum as phenomenological text in the following way. First, we will summarize phenomenological critiques of mainstream social science. This critique will include attention to the phenomenological notion of lived experience and to issues of self-report. Next we "backtrack" a little, and review Huebner's groundbreaking work in the 1960s and 1970s toward the reconceptualization of curricular language. As we also saw in chapter 4, Huebner's pathfinding scholarship thirty years ago helped made possible some of the work being done now, for instance, David Smith's rehabilitation of the concept of the practical. Following is a discussion of hermeneutics which in contemporary phenomenological research functions as medium of political work. Next are phenomenological depictions of teaching or pedagogy, followed by research on reading and writing. Concluding the chapter are reviews of scholarship concerning two important phenomenological themes, the secret place and temporality. Let us turn first to the phenomenological critique of mainstream social science, a tradition of research in which rationalism and empiricism dominate.

II
Critique of Mainstream Social Science: Aoki, Grumet, Jardine

The rules for the understanding of meaning are constructed actively by those who dwell within the situation.

(T. Aoki, 1988a, p. 411)

Several phenomenological scholars have critiqued mainstream social science. Ted Aoki (1988a) characterized mainstream social science, especially quantitative educational research, as exhibiting an instrumentalist interest in control. That is, "empirical-analytical" social science identifies concepts or "variables" and investigates their interrelations statistically. The truthfulness of the "facts" and "generalizations" produced are said to constitute their usefulness. Aoki notes that this "empirical-analytic" tradition implies a radical separation of person and world, in sharp contrast to both phenomenological and aesthetic modes of knowing. This separation permits and supports a view of the manipulability of "objects," including students, in the world. Because "subject" and "object" are separate domains, the "empirical" researcher understands "objectively" or definitively. [Autobiographical research aspires to understand the experience of the individual from the point of view of that individual—see chapter 10; political curriculum theory insists "objectivity" is a political and epistemological impossibility, given that neither knowledge or the processes of knowledge production are politically neutral—see chapter 5.] A related assumption of the "empirical-analytic" tradition is that all of life can be explained, if not with certainty, at least with probability. Thus the prediction of events—both human and "natural" (say earthquakes)—is a realistic scientific goal (Aoki, 1988a). For teachers this view gets expressed as certainties regarding "what works," apparently regardless of the socioeconomic conditions of the students, the historical moment, and the geographic-cultural "place" where the class occurs (Kincheloe & Pinar, 1991).

Skepticism regarding prediction. Pinar (1988c) also challenged this general view that human conduct can be predicted. Relying on the work of Bauman (1978), he noted that if human conduct could be regularized, then the costly "scientific" research mounted in the social sciences would have succeeded. It is because human beings exhibit will, imagination, and the capacity to choose in light of their own "horizons" (a phenomenological idea) that mainstream social science research has not succeeded in its aspiration to predict with certainty. He observed that there are profound ethical questions for those who make the attempt. In education, the empirical-analytic tradition has found various expressions, including management by objectives, competency-based education, criterion-based testing, and behavioral objectives in which students become categories. Aoki (1988a) summarized: "It is an objectified world within which even people are transformed into objects, their subjectivities reduced out" (p. 410). Van Manen (1988) observed that mainstream research lacks connections with a "practical pedagogic orienta-. tion to children in their concrete lives" (p. 438). From the phenomenological tradition, mainstream social science is epistemologically impossible and ethically unimaginable.

First-order and second-order experience. Phenomenology advises social science to recall its "lived" origins and foundations. Merleau-Ponty asserted: "The whole universe of science is built upon the world as directly experienced and if we want to subject science to rigorous study . . . we must begin by re-awakening the basic experience of the world in which science is the second-order experience" (Merleau-Ponty, quoted in Aoki 1988a, p. 410). This declaration sets the stage for the phenomenological project, a project which explores and articulates that "first-order" experience of which Merleau-Ponty speaks, from which the academic disciplines and school curriculum are derived. Phenomenologically then, the curriculum researcher studies those who live within the "here and now" of a situation. The "life situation" is portrayed in ways which reflect an "insider's" experience. The central interest, Aoki (1988a) says, "is in communicative understanding of meanings given by people who live within the situation. The rules for the understanding of meaning are constructed actively by those who dwell within the situation" (p. 411).

Situation, a phenomenological concept, denotes those elements of a setting which are organized by the intentionality (the horizon of perceptions and understandings) of the individual or group. The forms of knowledge generated by (post-Husserlian) phenomenological research are not nomological (i.e. facts, laws, scientific theories) but rather meaning situationally understood and communicated. Reality is no longer "out there," separate from the observed. Reality becomes an intersubjective construct to be formulated and negotiated intersubjectively. From this perspective, the reality of classroom life is viewed as the construction of those who dwell within those situations (Aoki, 1988a). [Curriculum evaluation (Aoki, 1986a) has been influenced by these points of view—see chapter 13. It has developed along separate but not unrelated lines; see, for instance, the work of Elliot W. Eisner, although he is not regarded as a phenomenologist.]

Other critiques of empiricism. The epistemological assumptions of mainstream social science have also been criticized by Madeleine R. Grumet, the important feminist theorist whose scholarship we examined in the preceding chapter, work which reveals phenomenological influences. Grumet (1976a) argued that so-called "empiricism" discounts the distortions inherent in laboratory settings. Instead, it concentrates solely on behaviors that are quantifiable, and in so doing, upon passive, manipulable "subjects" who have surrendered their capacities to direct their own conduct, report their own experience. Phenomenological research is less concerned with behavior than it is with an individual's or group's understandings of and attitudes toward behavior. Grumet quotes Alfred Schutz to communicate this concern:

> Meaning does not lie in experience. Rather, those experiences are meaningful which are grasped reflectively. That meaning is in the way in which the Ego regards its experience. The meaning lies in the attitudes of the Ego toward that part of its stream of consciousness which has already flowed by. (Schutz, quoted in Grumet, 1976a, p. 37)

David W. Jardine (1987) provides a phenomenological critique of the notions of reflection and self-understanding in Piagetian theory, a critique which underlines points of divergence between mainstream social science and phenomenology. Jardine (1987) argues that Piaget's claims regarding the self-sufficiency of scientific discourse:

tend . . . to close off that discourse from the whole complex of human life out of which that discourse has emerged. Of course, it is not closed off in fact. . . . In spite of the rich manner in which Piaget describes the developmental emergence of scientific discourse out of sensorimotor, preoperational, concrete-operational, and eventually, formal-operational actions of the subject, what seems to emerge out of all of this, where all of this seems to be heading, is toward an idealized caricature of the nature and place of science. (p. 11)

Jardine goes on to point out that the developmental accomplishment of scientific discourse in Piaget's schema involves an orientation to an ideal of explicit interpretation, a compensation for the natural tendency of thought to operate implicitly or unconsciously. One of the principal processes in the achievement of scientific discourse is the process of reflection. However, Jardine argues that reflection, in a Piagetian sense, becomes an abstraction, and as such, it is a feature of the development of cognition. Jardine (1987) summarizes:

Formal logic is, in a peculiar way, exemplary of the pinnacle of self-awareness, since with formal logic, the operations performed on an object and the object of those operations are identical. It seems, then, that the notion of self-under-standing begins to dovetail with a notion of self-explicitness. (p. 14)

Self-understanding in Piagetian theory, then, is not simply an explicitness regarding one's interpretation such that understanding can be assured; it is the developmental achievement of a "decentered subject" (Piaget, quoted in Jardine, p. 15). Self-understanding in Piaget's version of scientific discourse requires, then, the methodical reconstruction of one's place in the world such that, that place becomes indistinguishable from any other place, given that one is referring to "others" who are at the same developmental level. In contrast to this scientific version of self-understanding are those principles involved in a phenomenological notion of practical self-understanding. Jardine (1987) identifies the following principles:

1) Practical self-understanding and reflection are localized and concrete in two different senses: a) they are embedded in a . . . particular biography (or life-history) . . . b) my beliefs, understandings and the like are not in question or at issue "in general," or "in theory," but in the midst of a concrete context, and a localized set of practices, such as the practice of teaching. 2) Practical self-understanding and reflection require the cultivation of an experience of ownership and appropriation. 3) [They] . . . are temporal and contingent. 4) [They] . . . are occasional. More often than not, one does not produce self-understanding ex nihilo as some self-generated, theoretical exercise, but in confrontation with others whose beliefs, attitudes or understandings are differ-ent from my own. (pp. 16-18)

In these four statements, Jardine (1987) summarizes the main distinctions between mainstream social science and phenomenology. Phenomenology embraces the world as we live it, but in the process, invites us to change the way we live. Our taken-for-granted notions of self-understanding, reflection, and practical competence are all reconceived in phenomenological inquiry.

Phenomenological Foundations of *Currere*

One form of curriculum research that incorporates the phenomenological critique of mainstream social science is *currere*, a phenomenologically related form of autobiographical curriculum theory. Grumet cited *currere* as a method and theory of curriculum which escapes the epistemological traps of mainstream social science and educational research. *Currere* focuses on the educational experience of the individual, as reported by the individual. Rather than working to quantify behaviors to describe their surface interaction or to establish causality, *currere* seeks to describe what the individual subject him or herself makes of these behaviors. As Harré and Secord suggested, the "most profound discoveries of social psychology will be made by those who, while playing a part, filling a role and so on, can be their own audience" (Harré & Secord, quoted in Grumet, 1976a, p. 38). Husserlian phenomenology undergirds the method of *currere*, particularly the emphasis upon the reciprocity between subjectivity and objectivity in the constitution of experience and meanings. *Currere* shares phenomenology's interest in describing immediate, preconceptual experience, and then makes use of the phenomenological processes of "distancing" and "bracketing" required to do so. The notion of "constitution," central to both *currere* and to Husserlian phenomenology, is founded on Brentano's formulation of "intentionality," as a fundamental structure of consciousness. Intentionality specifies that all consciousness is consciousness of something, and so the subject, as subject, is accessible to oneself via the object intended. Grumet (1976a) noted:

Objective constitution is the life of the subject; knowledge of self becomes knowledge of self as knower of the world, not just as a passive recipient of stimuli from the objective world, not as an expression of latent subjectivity, but as a bridge between these two domains, a mediator. The homunculus of educational experience resides in each cognitation. (p. 38)

Consciousness not passive. Edmund Husserl (1962, 1964, 1970) rejected the determinism which undergirds so-called empiricism, portrays consciousness as the passive recipient of sense impression. Husserl rejected as well philosophical idealism which, while denying knowledge of the world to human beings, consoled them with the definitiveness of the constructions of their own minds. Instead, he wished to understand those events belonging to human encounters with the world. Husserl explained:

When phenomenology examines objects of consciousness—regardless of any kind, whether real or ideal—it deals with these exclusively as objects of the immediate consciousness. The description—which attempts to grasp the concrete and rich phenomena of the cogitations—must constantly glance back from the side of the object to the side of consciousness, and pursue the general existing connections. (Husserl, 1964, quoted in Grumet 1976a, p. 39)

Currere draws support for its focus upon lived experience from Husserl's conviction that only in the immediacy and intensity of encounter can certainty reside. To that end Husserl formulated a system of disciplined

reflection to assess the adequacy and fullness of this certainty, a system designed to produce knowledge grounded in the lived experience of the subject.

Lived experience. What is the character of lived experience? Husserl postulated a series of "now-points," each expressing horizons of past and imminent nows, passing into retention or portension. Merleau-Ponty (1962, 1963) pointed to this prereflective flow of now-points:

to return to things in themselves is to return to that world which precedes knowledge, of which knowledge always speaks, and in relation to which every scientific schematization is an abstract and derivative sign language, as is geography in relation to the countryside in which we have learnt beforehand what a forest, a prairie or a river is. (Merleau-Ponty, 1962, quoted in Grumet 1976a, p. 40)

Unlike mainstream educational research which focuses upon the end products of the processes of consciousness as described by Husserl, those end products we call concepts, abstractions, conclusions, and generalizations we, in accumulative fashion, call knowledge. *Currere* seeks to slide underneath these end products and structures to the pre-conceptual experience that is their foundation. *Currere* is designed to act as the phenomenological *epoché*, slackening "the intentional threads which attach us to the world and thus bring them to our notice" (Merleau-Ponty, 1962, quoted in Grumet, 1976a, p. 41).

Distancing and the immediacy of experience. Through the practice of the method of *currere*, the researcher attempts a phenomenological description of both subject and object, requiring knowledge of self as knower of the world, attempting to trace the complex path from preconceptual experience to formal intellection. As formulated and practiced by Pinar and Grumet (1976), *currere* does not constitute a reflective retreat from the world, but a heightened engagement with it. As a research methodology, *currere* has employed literature as a foil for the reflection of the investigator. As a reader, the research recreates what the writer has created, and in so doing, creates another world, drawn both from the substance of his or her experience and fantasy and from the literature itself. This conscious and explicit participation in an aesthetic experience—it becomes like an archeol-ogy—illustrates the reciprocity of objectivity and subjectivity in the student's and teacher's experience of the curriculum. It extends to both student and teacher the artist's awareness that subjectivity transforms the objectivity it seeks to describe. In this way, phenomenology and the aesthetic process share that distancing from the everyday and the familiar in order to see them with a freshness and immediacy which is like seeing them for the first time. The autobiography this form of phenomenological curriculum research produces asks questions like Husserl's. For instance, to what extent does reflection, even the rigorous and disciplined reflection of *currere*, deform experience to fit preexistent categories? Does the prolonged and profound

practicing of the distancing required by phenomenological research in general and by the method of *currere* in particular loosen the bonds of commitment and action that bind us to the concrete, public world? Can the reflecting self be split off rather than continuous with the public, acting self? Do multiple social roles shred the self into situation poses strung along a temporal chain? (Grumet, 1976a)

Grounded in context. Grumet reminds us that quantitative methodology avoids these questions. Indeed, such questions become disguised by the atomization of the lived situation into quantifiable variables, and by a series of controls that creates an unreal world as a backdrop for another unreal variable. *Currere*, in contrast, is grounded in context. The method of *currere* offers the opportunity to study both the individual's lived experience and the impact of the social milieu upon that experience. It seeks to depict and reflectively comprehend the impact of milieu as well as the subject's past upon the educational experience of the individual in the present. In contrast to the conventional empirical-analytic paradigm of educational research, *currere* returns to the experience of the individual, searching for those qualities which disqualify them for consideration in the mainstream behavioral sciences: its idiosyncratic history, its preconceptual and lived foundations, its contextual dependency, and its capacity for freedom and intelligence in choice and action.

The importance of self-report. Pinar and Grumet were not the only scholars who linked phenomenology and autobiography. For instance, Ronald J. Silvers (1984) stressed the importance of self-report in the teaching of phenomenology. He viewed biography as the "locus of experiences of self." To teach phenomenological reflection, Silvers suggested, the following features of such reflection must be understood: 1) It includes commitment to non-objectifying interpretive analysis for the recovery of existential meanings. 2) This commitment is made manifest in the introduction of personal experience and sentiment through the biographical narrative. 3) The biographical narrative is the initial point of a reflectivity upon our own consciousness and its embeddedness in our language. 4) Reflectivity upon language brings attention to one's own discourse as an expressive movement of "reflective discourse." 5) Reflective discourse is made possible by an absence of a pre-structure and the presence of an uncertainty in the direction of the eventual theoretical formulation beyond the personal of the biographical narrative. 6) Participating in self-reflection as a joint communicative movement is found in a dialectic of meditation as a tension between the solitary movement of reflective thought and the social movement of communication (Silvers, 1984).

Currere as autobiographical self-report communicates the individual's lived experience as it is socially located, politically positioned, and discursively formed, while working to succumb to none of these structurings. It is, in an essential way, phenomenological in character. However, it is not exclusively

phenomenological. We will examine *currere* as autobiographical theory in chapter 10.

III
Curriculum Language: Huebner and Smith

Educational activity can symbolize the meanings felt and lived by educators.

(Dwayne E. Huebner, 1975b, p. 227)

When they focus on the illumination of the lived experience of teachers, curriculum workers are concentrating their attention on what is, in actuality, the operating curriculum in every school.

(J. Timothy Leonard, 1983, pp. 24-25)

As we noted, Dwayne Huebner was the first to introduce phenomenology to curriculum studies at the 1967 Curriculum Theory Conference held at Ohio State University [see chapter 3]. In that early work on temporality, Huebner examined the significance of language in the field [a continuing concern for Huebner; see, Huebner, 1993 and chapter 15; also see Dobson, Dobson, & Koetting, 1987]. Huebner argued that curriculum language was constrained by two myths embedded within it: that of learning and purpose. Learning he identifies with educational psychology and the empirical-analytic tradition; as such it becomes a technical term of control (Huebner, 1975b). He traced the then ubiquitous use of learning in curriculum conceptualizations to traditional curriculum thought. As we noted in chapter 3, Tyler conceived the problems of curriculum as being only four: the formulation of objectives or purposes, the selection of learning experiences, the organization of these learning experiences, and their evaluation. Huebner argued that "learning" and "objectives," or purposes need to be replaced:

the language of learning and purpose must be cast aside and new questions asked. To do so the curriculum worker must confront his reality directly, not through the cognitive spectacles of a particular language system. One is then forced to ask, "What language or language system can be used to talk about these phenomena? His reality must be accepted not his language; for many language systems may be used for a given reality. (Huebner, 1975b, p. 221)

The phenomenological distinction between language and reality, between lived experience or preconceptual experience, is evident here. Huebner then replaced learning and purpose with the following: "The central notion of curricular thought can be that of valued activity.' All curricular workers attempt to identify and/or develop 'valued educational activity'" (Huebner 1975b, p. 222).

Huebner's five value frameworks. Huebner then explicated five "value frameworks" curricular workers might use to assess the value of particular educational activities: the technical, the political, the scientific, the aesthetic, and the ethical. The technical he associates with the Tyler Rationale and its

successors, the political with bureaucratic and community politics [which anticipates the work of his most prominent student, Michael Apple; see chapter 5], and the scientific with quantitative research. The aesthetic and ethical frameworks reflect a rudimentary phenomenology of curriculum. The aesthetic value of educational activity has three dimensions, Huebner maintained. First is the element of psychical distance. Because the aesthetic object is removed from the daily, practical world, it becomes possible to achieve perceptual distance from it. Huebner suggests that its spontaneity is evident:

It is spontaneity captured, normally lost in the ongoing world. Because of aesthetic distance, the art object, in this case educational activity, is the possibility of life, captured and heightened and standing apart from the world of production, consumption and intent. The art object has beauty. Educational activity can have beauty. (Huebner, 1975b, p. 226)

The second dimension is wholeness and design: "Educational activity may thus be valued in terms of its sense of wholeness, of balance, of design and of integrity, and its sense of peace or contentment" (Huebner, 1975b, p. 226). Here Huebner anticipates the evaluation work of Elliot Eisner [see chapter 13]. The third dimension:

. . . is that of symbolic meaning. The esthetic object, indeed educational activity, may be valued for the meanings that it reveals, and may be valued for its truth. Educational activity is symbolic of the meanings of the educator, as an individual and as a [spokesperson for men and women]. . . . The meaningless-ness and routine of much educational activity today reflects the meaningless-ness and routine of a mechanistic world order. In the rare classroom is the possible vitality and significance of life symbolized by the excitement, fervor, and community of educational activity. Educational activity can symbolize the meanings felt and lived by educators. (Huebner 1975b, p. 227)

The ethical dimension. The ethical dimension of educational value refers to the sense in which educational activity is a human encounter among persons. This encounter is judged according to ethical categories. Ethically, then, "metaphysical and perhaps religious language become the primary vehicle for the legitimation and thinking through of educational activity" (p. 227). Employing phenomenological language, Huebner (1975b) observed that:

For some, the encounter of man with man [sic] is seen as the essence of life, and the form that this encounter takes is the meaning of life. The encounter is not *used* to produce change, to enhance prestige, to identify new knowledge, or to be symbolic of something else. The encounter *is*. In it is the essence of life. In it life is revealed and lived. The student is not viewed as an object, an *it*; but as a fellow human being, another subject, a *thou*, who is to be lived with in the fullness of the present moment or the eternal present. From the ethical stance the educator meets the student, not as an embodied role, as a lesser category, but as a fellow human being who demands to be accepted on the basis of fraternity not simply on the basis of equality . . . The fullness of educational activity, as students encounter each other, the world around them,

and the teacher, is all there is. The educational activity is life—and life's
meanings are witnessed and lived in the classroom (pp. 227-228).

Toward reconceptualization of curricular language. In the 1960s, as we saw in
chapters 3 and 4, Dwayne Huebner challenged the dominance of the Tyler
Rationale and the atheoretical and ahistorical tradition it had spawned.
Huebner urged a critique of conventional curricular language to lead to a
new language, which in turn, would lead to new conduct in classrooms. This
critique would be phenomenological in nature. Huebner quoted Karl Jaspers
approvingly: "We become aware of the fact that in cognition we have moved
in categories which, even in their totality, are like a fine filigree with which
we grasp what at the same time we conceal with it" (Jaspers, 1959, pp. 38, 79,
quoted in Huebner, 1975b, p. 233). From this awareness the curriculum theorist and classroom teacher might view educational activity ethically and
aesthetically as well as technically. Huebner (1975b) explained:

present curricular language is much too limited to come to grips with the problems, or rather the mysteries, of language and meaning of the classroom. The
educator must free himself from his self-confining schemas, in order that he
may listen anew to the world pounding against his intellectual barriers. The
present methodologies which govern curricular thought must eventually give
way (p. 235).

Written in 1966, these words anticipated the Reconceptualization of curriculum studies of the 1970s, a major element of which was the phenomenological movement. This movement would indeed create a new language, one
which took as a central tenet Huebner's Heideggerean view (Heidegger,
1962) that speech is the human being's reply as he or she listens to the world.

The practical. Huebner laid the groundwork for a phenomenological
reconceptualization of curricular language. One salient illustration of this
revision of conventional language concerns the crucial concept of the
"practical." Working twenty years after Huebner's landmark scholarship,
David G. Smith took the Husserlian notion of "eidetics" and rethought the
concept. Recalling Schwab's 1969 call for studies of the practical [see chapters 3 and 4], he insists that it does not imply "nuts and bolts technical know-
how of mindless practice." Quoting Schwab, Smith agrees that the practical is
"a complex discipline ... concerned with choice and action." What is
needed, Schwab declared, is "a totally new and extensive pattern of empirical
study of classroom life as a basis for beginning to know what we are doing,
what we are not doing, and to what effect" (Schwab, quoted in Smith, 1988a,
pp. 417-418). Phenomenologically understood, empirical research does not
imply quantitative research. Etymologically, "empirical" (from the Greek
empiria) means to acknowledge one's experience as the basis of knowledge.
Experience is a complicated term with a long history. Phenomenologically,
however, it refers to that which is "lived," not merely that which can be
observed and measured. Phenomenologically conceived, empirical research
"has to do with the whole person standing in the whole of life trying to make

sense of his/her experience of it all in its wholeness" (Smith, 1988a, p. 418). Consequently, claims to truth are always partial and incomplete. Their partiality and incompleteness are not liabilities, but the characteristics of the uniquely specific and individual character of experience and knowledge.

Critical of political analysts for being too restrictive in their views, David Smith (1988a) argued that curriculum research must—in addition to social critique—make explicit the character of day-to-day life, as it is experience of and lived by those in classrooms. He suggested that most educators are blind to the specific character of their daily lives, a blindness tantamount to inno-cence: "The root of injustice is not moral error but blindness" (Gadamer, quoted in Smith, 1988a, p. 419). Curriculum research must restore vision and bring knowledge to the innocent, in order that they might "love." [See Noddings, 1981; Pinar, 1981a; Edgerton,1993a]. Smith quotes Goethe: "We only understand what we love" (p. 420). The agenda of curriculum research must include developing insight into the character of our daily lives, as "lived."

Autobiography and dialogue. The autobiographical work of Pinar and Grumet (1976) would seem to provide such insight. While praising this schol-arship as "helpful" in "revealing the sorts of personal struggles many of us face," Smith (1988) criticized *currere* as overinterested in exploration and expression of the individual self and underinterested in dialogue and in the experience of others. Other phenomenologists—such as Aoki (1988a)—have praised autobiographical research as legitimately phenomenological. Grumet herself has both detailed the relation of autobiography to phenomenology and written one of the most complex and accomplished phenomenological curriculum studies to date (Grumet, 1976a, 1988a).

After criticizing both political and autobiographical studies as insufficient, Smith outlines his own view of "experimental eidetics." He explains *eidos*, derived from Plato and Husserl, refers to "that which is present behind appearances, yet which gives appearances their uniqueness, vividness and detail" (p. 421). Rejecting Platonic idealism, Smith affirms the Heideggerean view of language as expressing an implicit ontology. Thus Smith views concepts and events and so-called facts as "somehow uniquely expressive of something which makes them possible, rather than as things final and discrete in their own right" (Smith, D., 1988a, p. 421).

The present as past and future. Heidegger's student, Hans-Georg Gadamer (1960, 1976, 1980), accepted this view of language but grounds it in history. Gadamer viewed historicity as fundamental to human experience. Further, understanding this historicity is prior to understanding ourselves. For Gadamer, and for Smith, understanding is dialectical in nature, requiring elucidation of past, present, and future. Smith (1988a) writes "when I look at a classroom situation, I do not see it as 'present,' I see it as 'presently' expressing its history while at the same time as embodying within itself a sense of hope for the future" (p. 422). Such hope is frustrated in schools,

according to Smith, when teachers and others accept the language of conventional curriculum experts as definitive truth rather than as interpretations. The pretense at definitiveness characteristic of positivistic curriculum language precludes conversation, dialogue, debate and allows "only a mindless, ritual acting out of the working of other people's minds. . . . That is a form of madness" (p. 422).

To take seriously the classroom in a phenomenological sense is to portray the specificity and concreteness of our daily lives. To do so requires viewing the everyday in its eidetic quality, i.e. as referring to "something else" as well as to itself. Heidegger believed that the everyday "speaks" to us, suggesting who and what we are as human beings. Gadamer asserts that our language tells us who we are now, and who we were once and who and who we hope to become.

David Smith undertakes to illustrate these ideas by describing a grade five social studies class in British Columbia. After telling us about the class, Smith (1988a) summarizes the distinctive qualities of viewing curriculum conceived as phenomenological text:

> . . . the curriculum enterprise, at bottom, is not simply a technical, up-front, visible, manipulative enterprise performed by experts, be they teachers, planners, or politicians. Rather, all those manifest activities are eidetic: they are visible expressions of an invisible life which makes them possible. Making articulate that invisible life is the poetic art of phenomenological description. . . . An attention to the eidetic quality of our life together is an attempt to bring into the center of our research conversation everything that we are, as a way of reconciling in the present moment our ends with our beginnings. Where will such a conversation "get us?" In a sense it will not "get us" anywhere. (pp. 434-435)

Language as "home." Conventional speech, for Heidegger, was tantamount to chatter, an evasion of important matters. David Smith regards much educational language similarly. Mainstream instructional literature expresses a concept of language as a "tool of communication," a skill. Such a conception does not permit one to utilize language to orient oneself toward the world, indeed to find a home. Like Huebner, Smith views the traditional language of the curriculum as instructional text (i.e., that of objectives, and competencies) as having little to do with the lived experience of children or, for that matter, with the lived experience of teachers. He suspects many teachers make a "schizophrenic compromise" whereby they use educational jargon with the principal and other supervisors but drop it when they re-enter the life of classrooms. Smith views the task of the teacher as recovering those forms of life, and specifically those language forms, which enable him or her to be with children in a more livable way. The saddest teachers, Smith tells us, are those who never appreciate the difference between formal curricular goals and the only goal of any phenomenological significance, namely, learning to live together in the house of being, which is language itself (Smith, 1983a).

The middle way. This last line derives from Heidegger's assertion that to reflect on language means to dwell in language as an abode for humanity. Smith (1983a) understands "abode" as a place where one lives; in its earlier Anglo-Saxon form, as meaning to speak in order to reach an abode, a home. Such speaking takes us "in the middle of things," that place "between" human beings as mortals and the voice of language itself, the *logos*. Smith observes, with Heidegger, that language is where we live, our abode. Authentic human speaking is original, non-reproducible, and unfinished. Smith (1983a) worries that educators' language has been alienated from lived experience to such a degree that the art of hearing profound messages and calls, uttered in the midst of our teaching, has been lost. The alienation of language reduces all our doing and all our speaking to power negotiations which stifle and suffocate teachers and students alike. If we are to live at all, Smith tells us, if we are to speak phenomenologically, we must learn how to allow the voice of language itself to speak through us. To speak authentically again. Living in language, in the power of language itself to shape us and mold us, is for Smith the only authentic living. Phenomenological pedagogy might allow us to live together with the young in the house of being.

Another instance of the phenomenological reformulation of mainstream curricular language can be found in Aoki's (1993a) *In the Midst of Slippery Theme-Words: Toward Designing Multicultural Curriculum.* Conventional curriculum design was a pseudo-scientific term serving the bureaucratic function of program planning [see chapter 13], but he locates the problem of curriculum design in poetical, not in bureaucratic, language. Aoki (1993a) asks:

Can designers of Japanese Canadian curricula . . . participate in the creation of a minority curriculum language that, I believe, only minorities can speak and understand? Such a language would be, I suspect, neither the language of the dominant culture nor the Japanese language of our heritage, but one that grows in the middle. (p. 99)

Here the great phenomenologist is moving toward poststructuralism while still profoundly grounded in the lifeworld.

Clearly, to work phenomenologically is to dwell with language in ways so that the problems of the everyday world become different problems, and the classroom becomes a different reality. Indeed, to enter phenomenological language is to become a different reality oneself. However, phenomenological study changes not only oneself; it changes the world. In contemporary phenomenology, hermeneutics has expressed explicitly such political and social themes.

IV
Hermeneutics: Smith, Atkins, Reynolds, Martel and Peterat

Hermes and I found each other, I suspect, because of a mutual recognition that identity means nothing without a set of relations, and that the real work of our

time may be defined by an ability to mediate meaning across boundaries and differences, whether those boundaries and differences be concerned with gender, race, or ideas.

(David G. Smith, 1991a, p. 203)

The coupling of . . . "play" and "hermeneutics" is meant to indicate that there is a deep natural affinity between the phenomenon of play and the character of hermeneutic understanding.

(David W. Jardine, 1988d, p. 23)

Hermeneutics involves the study of the methodological principles of inter- pretation. It recalls the Greek god Hermes, who was the interpreter, and so the creator of language, between mortals and the gods. The "hermeneuticist" is such a messenger, as she or he labors to interpret other texts, often ancient, sometimes sacred, for our understanding in the present. Hermeneu- tics has a long history, especially in theology [see chapter 12]. Hermeneutical problems have preoccupied philosophers as well as theologians, and in the present century, have become important for social scientists and literary crit- ics as well as curriculum theorists. In phenomenological curriculum study, hermeneutics has functioned to enlarge the phenomenological endeavor to include the social negotiation of meaning, as well as individual attunement to truth.

For example, in his "Hermeneutic Inquiry: The Hermeneutic Imagination and the Pedagogic Text," David G. Smith (1991a) locates hermeneutics in society, suggesting "a link between social trouble and the need for interpreta- tion" (p. 188). The hermeneutical task is not a technical one, solved by logic; rather, it is born in the midst of human struggle and enables us to ask "what makes it possible for us to speak, think, and act in the ways we do." Smith sees the aim of interpretation not in an infinite regress or relativization "but human freedom, which finds its light, identity, and dignity in those few brief moments when one's lived burdens can be shown to have their source in too limited a view of things" (p. 189). Further, the significance of the hermeneu- tic imagination may be to "to problematize the hegemony of dominant culture in order to engage it transformatively" (p. 195). In the phenomeno- logical discourse on hermeneutics, phenomenology becomes explicitly politi- cal: "Pedagogy is concerned with mobilizing the social conscience of students into acts of naming and eradicating the evils of the times" (p. 196).

What is implied by the study of hermeneutics? Smith (1991a) tells us that we must work to grasp a sense of how language works, what drives it, what are its predispositions in terms of metaphor, analogy, structure, and so on. Such understanding of the history and dynamics of language is necessary for the work of the interpretive imagination, because in a deep sense our language contains the story of who we are as a people: "It is reflective of our desires, our regrets and our dreams; in its silences it even tells us of what we would forget" (p. 199). Smith understands hermeneutics not "as another self- defining imploding discourse within a universe of other discourses. Far more important is its overall interest in the question of human meaning and of

how we might make sense of our lives in such a way that we can go on" (p. 200). Odd in light of his earlier criticism of *currere*, Smith (1991a) closes with a brief autobiographical statement, recognizing that all

> writing is in a sense autobiographical. . . . Hermes and I found each other, I suspect, because of a mutual recognition that identity means nothing without a set of relations, and that the real work of our time may be defined by an ability to mediate meaning across boundaries and differences, whether those bound- aries and differences be concerned with gender, race, or ideas. (Smith, 1991a, pp. 202-203)

Our singular identities will always and only be a part of the story, he cautions, unless we can reinterpret the presence of an Other, a presence that is always a part "of the story of our shared future" (p. 203).

Elaine Atkins (1988a) has also discussed a reframing of curriculum in terms of hermeneutics. She explained: "The hermeneutic tradition focuses on knowledge as a coping-with, rather than as a mirroring-of, reality and defines understanding as a form of practical reasoning and practical knowl- edge" (p. 437). Noting that Hans-Georg Gadamer was Heidegger's most important successor, and that Richard Rorty (1979, 1989) and Richard Bern- stein (1976) have been two of this tradition's most influential American interpreters, Atkins (1988a) summarized:

> Hermeneutical phenomenology depends upon the concepts of historical consciousness, phronesis, dialogue, interpretation, community, and language. Heidegger, Gadamer and Rorty all share a belief in the historicity of human life and cultures and in the rootedness of truth, knowledge and morality in tradi- tions and social practices. (p. 438)

So framed, "understanding can never be bracketed or separated from a concrete cultural/social situation" (p. 439), as quantitative social science attempts to do. "The goal is not," Atkins (1988a) continued, "a commensura- tion of theories, but, in Heidegger's words, 'finding a footing,' or, in Wittgenstein's, 'finding one's way about'"(p. 439). Human understanding, then, occurs in actual, lived situations. Understanding comes through language within a tradition: "In Gadamer's account, phronesis is a form of reasoning, concerned with choice and involving deliberation" (p. 442). For Atkins, then, hermeneutics leads the curricularist back to Schwab who, as you will recall, was also influenced by hermeneutics. Atkins (1988a) asserts: "hermeneutics leads us to reframe curriculum theory in terms of practice, deliberation and choice" (p. 447). Atkins (1988b) concludes: "To a field that has always been concerned with moral choice, scientific method, and aesthetic sensibility, the pragmatic-hermeneutical approach to understanding has much to offer" (p. 83).

Brent Davis (1994a, 1994b) hermeneutically investigates the teaching of mathematics, drawing upon biology, ecological thought, and mathematics as well as phenomenology. He employs metaphors and images of post- Darwinian evolutionary theory as starting places to interrogate the taken-for-

granted conceptions of personal cognition, social interaction, and collective knowledge which give form to conventional mathematics teaching. Davis' work develops around the notion of "mathematics teaching as listening," and its centerpiece is a phenomenology of listening that invokes Merleau-Pony's conception of our "double embodiment" (i.e., our bodies are simultaneously biological and lived phenomenological structures) to critique and offer an alternative to patterns of teaching action that are founded on more isolated and fragmented conceptions of the subject.

Reynolds' phenomenological hermeneutics. In another hermeneutical study, William M. Reynolds (1989) presented an analysis of conservative and critical traditions in curriculum theory, employing a method developed by Paul Ricoeur (1981) for reading literary texts. The conservative texts Reynolds chose were *Nation at Risk* (NCEE) and *The Paideia Proposal* (Adler, 1983). The two examples of the critical tradition were Pinar's *Sanity, Madness, and the School* (1975a) and Apple's "Curricular Form and the Logic of Technical Control" (1982d). Reynolds' analysis moves from a naive reading to explanation to understanding, a sequence suggested by Ricoeur. With Gadamer, Reynolds suggests that prejudicial understandings cannot be eliminated in encountering texts, but that the reader should be willing to listen to the text to determine what is new.

From a naive reading Reynolds proceeds to the explanation phase. Here texts are explicated according to composition, genre, and style (Reynolds, 1989, pp. 84-89). In this phase resides the crucial step between a naive reading and an in-depth understanding. A structural analysis of the texts functions as the objective validation procedure. The third phase of the reading is a process of appropriation and self-understanding. This phase is made possible only due to mediation, different for each reader. Reynolds believes that theoretical texts, like words of fiction, posit possible worlds in which the self can be clarified, where the reader might dwell. Reynolds (1989) states that:

the authentic "I" or the "I" that I really am becomes in essence clarified. Through the recognition of the "not-I" of the text world and my reflection on the disparity between the "not-I" of the text world and the appearance of that to the self I am able to, by recognition of the "not-I," further distinguish my authentic self. (p. 127)

Reynolds concludes his study discussing the use of metaphoric language. He suggests that it might be useful to reflect on curriculum theory as story, fable, or parable. What began as a study of language and self-understanding concludes with an emphasis on language, suggesting new directions for curriculum theory, directions which intersect not only with Aoki's work, but with the emphasis upon narrative found in Claudinin, Connelly, and Goodson [see chapter 10].

In keeping with the Ricoeurian project, as we noted, the Reynolds' study is a documentary of the growth of self-understanding which emerges from a fusion of horizons with the texts. A perceptive review of the book summa-

rizes the major issues Reynolds (1989) elaborates. David Kennedy (1991) wrote:

As such, [Reynolds' book] is a personal testament about one sensitive man's journey through the bleak, confusing, and emotionally exhausting terrain of most contemporary educational practice, and the capacity of curriculum theory to help him understand this journey. The personal level of the text is a reflection on the author's search for self among the barbaric, soul-murdering constraints of the typical classroom, where he spent nine years, and then among the "powerful and attractive voices" of the academy, where he shares with the reader his struggle not to lose his own voice. This is a major subtext of the book. . . . It is a story about a serious academic's quest to find his own critical voice and in finding his own critical voice, to find his identity. (p. 160)

Finding one's own voice is, hermeneutically speaking, a public quest, involving questions of theory and practice, a dualism that disappears in phenomenological hermeneutics. Aoki (1984a, 1989c) has pointed to this hermeneutical development:

One of the promising re-understandings of "practice" views practice as *praxis*, wherein even the notion of theory requires a reunderstanding. I see at this time two major interpretations of praxis—one, in tune with the critical social theory of the neo-Marxist persuasion, and the other, hermeneutic praxis which seems to flow out of the existential posture of Heidegger and Gadamer. I note that at this cutting edge, forceful work is ongoing. (1986a, p. 4)

Aoki (1984a, 1989c) formulates a view of praxis that offers an existential view of thought-full-of-action and action-full-of-thought. For Aoki, reflection requires probing beneath language and action to the motives and assumptions that underlie them: "Reflection is not only oriented toward making conscious the unconscious by dis-covering underlying assumptions and intentions, but it is also oriented towards the implications for action guided by the newly gained consciousness and critical knowing (1984a, p. 77). As Robert K. Brown (1991), a student of Aoki's contribution, has noted: "For Aoki, to be alive is to dwell in tension. It is to be aware and open to the anxiety that exists in venturing forth into new frontiers of existence and to use that tension as a compelling force for creative interaction with the world" (p. 71). We can see, then, that hermeneutics as the study of interpretation moves between the individual in society and the world in the text. In curriculum, hermeneutics is the site of political, social, and institutional interests of the effort to understand curriculum as phenomenological text. This interest is reflected in a series of other studies, whose titles illustrate the range of the discourse. For instance, in his "Questioning Curriculum Implementation: Scenes From a Conversation," Terrance R. Carson (1992b) studied curriculum implementation as a hermeneutical process. In the field of home economics, Francine Hultgren (1985) reported "A Hermeneutic Approach: Reflecting on the Meaning of Curriculum through Interpretation of Student-Teaching Experiences in Home Economics." Reynolds (1993) explored the meaning of compassion. Shigeru Asanuma (1986a) underlined intentionality,

reflection, and intersubjectivity in understanding curriculum, noting that phenomenology allows aesthetic and ethical dimensions to be explored. Given this view of curriculum, other hermeneutical scholars have turned to social and political issues, including race (Barber, 1989, p. 228), the street children of Latin America (Aptekar, 1989), and sexism (Martel & Peterat, 1988). This topic we examine next.

Two studies of sexism underline the differences between political and feminist theory and phenomenological-hermeneutical scholarship that focuses on political and gender issues. In their "A Hope for Helplessness: Womanness at the Margin in Schools," Angeline Martel and Linda Peterat (1988) write: "Women are marginalized . . . marginality is a hope for social transformation" (p. 132). In an earlier article on the same subject, Martel and Peterat (1988) located sexism in language. It is language which shapes consciousness and embodies in us a particular view of the world. Martel and Peterat reconceived the feminist question: what do we do about the power which language commands of our lives? They answered: "Action is needed, but consciousness must precede, a more and more limpid, crystalline consciousness rejoining our language with our being" (p. 18). In addition to textual interpretation, hermeneutics has become a social, political form of contemporary phenomenological curriculum theory.

Such an agenda for phenomenology and hermeneutics was suggested by Dennis Carlson [see chapter 5] early in the 1980s: "Schooling involves learning the particular modes of being-in-the-world which sustain a fundamentally conservative conception of the individual and his or her relation to the larger society and act to preserve rather than challenge existing capitalist structures and social relations" (1982c, p. 207). Hermeneutical phenomenology is not usually associated with struggles against sexism or homelessness. With what category is it most commonly associated? Probably the notion of pedagogy or teaching is the best-known theme of contemporary phenomenology.

V

Teaching: Aoki and van Manen

Persons whose lives are embedded in gratitude for the gift of life and its possibilities can use conversation to share insights acquired in solitude, to transcend the mundane and humdrum and to become more caring human beings.
(Louise Berman, 1991, p. 138)

Teaching is fundamentally a mode of being.
(Tetsuo Aoki, 1986b, p. 8)

Phenomenologists insist that teaching is an orientation toward being. In a fundamental sense, such teaching is an "engagement of self-reflection." The teacher's phenomenological relationship to his or her subject matter is not to a field as objectified knowledge but to the possibilities inherent in subject matter for phenomenological knowing (Silvers, 1984). A distinction between teaching as "doing" and teaching as "being" is observed. A focus upon the

latter permits the teacher to understand that how he or she experiences not only subject matter but students, colleagues, and even himself or herself. All of these relationships are communicated to and learned by the students during the lived experience of teaching (Cunningham, 1979). Van Manen insists that "pedagogy is neither a question of process nor an issue of content. . . . [Pedagogy] constantly and powerfully operate in between" (van Manen, 1988, pp. 444, 446).

Aoki (1984a, 1984b, 1984c) has criticized educators who view the notion of "practice" as synonymous with that of "technique" and associate "competence" with that of instrumental action. Lost in the efficiency-based curriculum world is the lived-world of teachers and students. Curriculum-as-plan is the world of educational administrators and curriculum designers. Teachers are seen as officials. Such a view, Aoki insists, forgets "what matters deeply in the situated world of the classroom is how the teachers' doings' flow from who they are. . . . Teaching is fundamentally a mode of being" (1986b, p. 8). Juxtaposed to curriculum-as-plan is that of curriculum-as-lived-experience. Aoki contends that for a teacher to dwell in such a state is to dwell "in the zone of between" (1986b, p. 9). Dwelling between horizon of curriculum-as-plan and the horizon of curriculum-as-lived-experience, the teacher is asked to listen to both simultaneously: "This is the tensionality within which [a teacher] dwells" (1986b, p. 9). Aoki writes:

An educated person, first and foremost, understands that one's way of knowing, thinking, and doing flow from who one is. Such a person knows that an authentic person is more than a mere individual, an island unto himself or herself, but a being-in-relation with others and hence is, at core, an ethical being. (1988b, pp. 8-9)

An educated person, Aoki continues, "guards against disembodied forms of knowing, thinking, and doing that reduce self and others to things, but also strives . . . for embodied thoughtfulness that makes possible living as human beings (1990a, p. 114). Finally, an educated person enters the pedagogical relationship by acknowledging humbly "the grace by which educator and educated are allowed to dwell in a present that embraces past experiences and as possibilities yet to be" (1990a, p. 114). One must "be ever open to the call of what it is to be deeply human and, heeding that call, to walk with others in life's ventures" (1990a, p. 114). Aoki's lyrical and insightful evocation of teaching is phenomenological scholarship at its best.

A lived relation between adults and children. Max van Manen, the other major phenomenologist, views the point of research as orienting its readers pedagogically to children. The Dutch phenomenologist Langeveld likened research to a puzzle, each research report carrying the caption: "can you find the child." Van Manen agrees, and he worries that much research functions to cut off the "ordinary" relations adults have with children. Conventional research tends to objectify children, converting them into categories and jargon. Phenomenological research takes as its task the restoration of the

"ordinary" or "lived" relation, a relation, van Manen says, which might involve a "biographic seeing of the child's experience." For instance, van Manen describes a child skipping rope in this way:

I see a child skipping rope in the street, and I pause and smile. I see a youthful bounce, the commanding rhythm of a rope—and perhaps a memory. I recognize this rhyme. Times do not change. When the child stops, I still feel the snap against my feet. Regret fills me. I wish I could revisit the old school playground. But then I come to myself. My childhood place is thousands of kilometers away. It is not likely I would see it again as I knew it. I turn away from that child and resume my walk. I saw a child, a rope, a game. Sight and sound collaborated to make me feel the rope against my feet. Then I saw regret, nostalgia. Then I went on my way. (van Manen, 1986 in 1988, p. 439)

Van Manen's phenomenological description. The biographic seeing is incomplete, however, omitting the child's experience. How would that experience be understood phenomenologically? The phenomenological curricularist might describe how the child's body feels as he or she skips, the texture of the rope, the feel of the air, the rhythms of skipping songs, the sensation of the ground, and the experience of others skipping and turning the rope. The teacher will see the student via the pedagogical relationship the teacher has with him or her. Van Manen describes a teacher's "eye," i.e. a pedagogical seeing, phenomenologically:

The teacher sees Diane skipping rope. He sees much more than a passerby can see, for he has known her for more than a year. She skips away from the other children, and he wonders what it will take for Diane to become one of them. She is academically the best achiever of her class, but her achievements are not the product of some irrepressible raw intelligence. Diane earns her accomplishments with a grim fervor that saddens the teacher. She has an overachieving mother who fosters ambitious goals. Diane's mother intends to have herself a gifted daughter. Diane complies. She earns her mother's favor, but at the price of childhood happiness, her teacher thinks. As he sees her skipping, he observes her tenseness and contrasts it with the relaxed skipping of the others. It is the same tenseness that betrays her anxiety with every assignment, every test. Diane marches rather than skips through the hoop of the rope. The teacher also sees how Diane's eyes are turned to a half dozen girls who skip together with a big skipping rope. One of the girls returns her glance and gestures for Diane to come. Diane abruptly stops. The rope hits her feet and she turns toward the school door. What does the teacher see? A lonely girl who can relate to classmates only by constantly measuring herself by competitive standards. If only she could develop some personal space, some room to grow and develop social interests just for herself, away from her mother. The teacher is hopeful, for in Diane's eyes he has spotted desire—a desire to be accepted by her classmates. (van Manen, 1986 in 1988, p. 440)

From the singular to the universal and back again. Van Manen alleges that graduate study steeped in traditional curriculum thought and research tends to lead the sensitive pedagogue away from the sensitivity and insight evident in the above observation, away from concrete knowing to an abstraction

from, and categorization of, the "lived world." "Where," van Manen asks, "is the connection [in conventional graduate study in curriculum] with the everyday lifeworld which . . . used to be invested with a pedagogic interest (p. 441)?" Further, van Manen alleges that the cult of the practical (convention- ally understood as efficiency, not as portrayed by fellow phenomenologist David Smith) results in a confusion of what is possible with what is desirable. Phenomenological pedagogical theory begins with the single case, moves to the universal, and returns to the single instance. Van Manen (1988) postu- lates four conditions as necessary for what he terms a "pedagogical textual- ity," what might be described as a curriculum true to the lifeworld of those who attempt to teach and study it. First, the text (or curriculum) must be *oriented*. That is, the educator must self-consciously examine how he or she "observes, listens, and relates to children" (p. 449). The phenomenological educator develops an orientation that is "reflexive" and "ontological," meaning that theory is inseparable from life as lived. If we are researchers, van Manen emphasizes, we must be researchers oriented to the classroom in a pedagogical way. Second, the text must be *strong*. The educator uses his orientation as a resource for constructing pedagogical understandings and he or she strengthens this resource in the very practice of pedagogy and research. Thus the educator does not treat his teaching as one approach among many. Van Manen quotes Nietzsche on this point: "Every strong orientation is exclusive" (quoted in van Manen, 1988, p. 450). Third, the text must be *rich*. "The educator who is oriented in a strong way to the world of real children develops a fascination with real life" (p. 450). Such a fascination allows for and produces multiple meanings of events, meanings explored with children via anecdote, story, and other forms of phenomenological description. Fourth, the text must be *deep*. van Manen quotes Merleau-Ponty to make this point: "Depth is the means that things have to remain distinct, to remain things, while not being what I look at present" (quoted in van Manen, 1988, p. 451). Rich descriptions lay bare "meaning structures" beyond what is experienced in sensory and immediate ways.

In a more recent work, van Manen (1991) employs a notion of "tact." In his *The Tact of Teaching: The Meaning of Pedagogical Thoughtfulness*, van Manen (1991) lists a number of qualities of pedagogical thoughtfulness. For instance, he tells us that phenomenological pedagogy is sensitive to the context of life stories. Further, it asks us to reflect on children's lives. What is the meaning of the notion of "tact?" He tells us that tact means the practice of being oriented to others; to be tactful is to "touch" someone. He goes on to elabo- rate: tact preserves a child's space, protects what is vulnerable, prevents hurt, make whole what is broken, strengthens what is good, enhances what is unique, sponsors personal growth and learning. How does pedagogical tact do what it does? He answers that tact is mediated through speech, silence, the eyes, gesture, atmosphere, and example. Tact, van Manen (1991) contin- ues, gives new and unexpected shape to unanticipated situations, and in so doing, leaves a mark on the child. As he has not in earlier works, van Manen added a section in the final chapter on "the relation between pedagogy and

politics" and notes: "Thus, pedagogical tact requires of us a certain worldliness, and the moral fibre to stand up for political views in which we believe"
(p. 213). [For one discussion of tact, see Rudd, 1993.]

Hope and stability. Another theme of phenomenological research on teaching is that of hope and stability. In one study we are told that:

curriculum workers need to appreciate this hope/stability tension as a central
feature in the lifeworlds of teachers. It is central to understanding how teacher
agency completes a curriculum invention—that shapes its potential at the point
where the invention [such as computer-assisted instruction] is brought from the
outside, as abstraction, to the inner and social fabric of practice. Consequently,
the notion of hope/stability may be central to our understanding how curriculum forms change and how they persist (Parker, 1986a, p. 30).

In another study, Margaret Olson (1989) discussed "making the classroom
one's own, implying a search for comfort" (p. 178). The phenomenologist
looks not for the efficient employment of classroom resources but rather to
questions regarding "the nature of pedagogical space" (p. 178). Olson (1989)
explains:

It is a shared space. The contents of the room hold personal meaning for all
who inhabit it. . . . The presences of teacher and students pervade the space,
not as isolated individuals, but as a mingling of thoughts and actions, each
enhanced by the other. (p. 183)

Lived meaning. Another phenomenological theme points to lived meaning, and teaching as dwelling in the lived. What does this mean? Mikio Fujita
(1987) answers:

First, lived experience is characterized by immediacy, vividness, or presentness,
in which there is no separation into subject and object. Secondly, lived experience is a unit as a whole; it has already an articulated structure. Thirdly, lived
experience always has the sense of lasting importance and significance. Lived
meaning is what can be remembered vividly, even in the future, with its impact
and import, even though the precise interpretation of the original experience
may change through time. (pp. 4-5)

Fujita (1987) explains: "Lived meaning is the voiceless voice, unheard cry,
speechless words, shapeless expression, that is growing in the experience of
a person. . . . Dialogue is the soil of lived meaning" (p. 15). In such a view,
what is childhood?

Childhood is not an underdeveloped adulthood, perhaps like summer is not an
underdeveloped autumn. . . . It seems far more important to foster lived meaning of ourselves and others even in a seemingly "primitive" stage than trying to
run up the steps of developmental stages. I wish to call such a study of lived
meaning semiogenetics. (Fujita, 1987, p. 18)

In his studies of teaching, David Jardine (1988c) points to the importance
of waiting, listening, attending" (p. 298). In a view of teaching influenced by
Heidegger [see also Gotz, 1983], Jardine (1988a) writes:

The children all around us, then, are not given objects with certain properties, but persons about whom and with whom we must decide how to live our lives. . . . This is the sphere of practical understanding, the sphere of living our lives together with children and thoughtfully asking after what is best for them and for us, deciding . . . what should we do? (p. 185)

How does mainstream teacher education look in light of this view? David Smith (1988b) comments:

The most remarkable thing about contemporary North American teacher education may be that, in the name of concern for children, we have banished children . . . under a dense cover of rationalistic, abstract discourses about cognition, development, achievement, etc. (p. 175)

In another phenomenologically inspired effort to rethink teacher education, Basil Favaro (1981) suggested *Recasting a Program in Teacher Education from a Critical Perspective.* However, Favaro does not intend Marxism by the use of the concept of critical: "By 'critical' is meant bringing from concealment that which is implicit, dis-closing what is usually taken for granted in such a way that what is hidden becomes significant." Favaro (1981) draws on Habermas, but his proposal does "not suggest abandoning the objectivist and hermeneutic levels" (p. 1). Indeed, for Favaro to be critical means to be phenomenological.

Ceremonies, celebrations, and atmosphere. As we have noted, phenomenologists often do not concern themselves with taken-for-granted bureaucratic matters. Indeed, at times phenomenological themes seem rather far apart from those traditionally associated with the school as institution. The scholarship of Otto Bollnow is illustrative.

In reflecting on ceremonies and celebrations in the school, Otto Bollnow (1989d) suggests: "ceremonies and celebrations are not just minor matters; rather, they prove the Heideggerian thesis that the primary unlocking of the world is found fundamentally only by way of *pure* moods" (p. 64). [For a different view of school ritual, see Lesko, 1988a.] What is it about ceremonies and celebrations that might allow the experience of pure moods? Bollnow (1989d) explains: "A typical feature of festive celebration is extravagance and boisterousness. People feel themselves freed from and lifted above the limiting structures of everyday life" (p. 72). Once released from the taken-for-granted limits of everyday life, one is free to explore:

If wandering can make claim to great . . . pedagogical significance, then it is given this meaning through deep, far-reaching changes and rejuvenations of consciousness which the person experiences in wandering and which are similar in some ways to the experiences of festive celebrations. (p. 74)

Bollnow (1989a) has also written on the notion of "pedagogical atmosphere," by which he means "all those fundamental emotional conditions and sentient human qualities that exist between the educator and the child and which form the basis for every pedagogical relationship" (p. 5). In discussing

the pedagogical atmosphere from the point of view of the educator, Bollnow (1989c) points to what he terms educational love (which is neither eros nor charity), a notion which incorporates patience, hope, serenity, humor, and finally, goodness: "goodness does not relax the situation by lowering the demands; instead, it accompanies the other, especially the younger and more vulnerable person, with a requirement of strictness and a sensitive watchfulness" (p. 62). Writing of the pedagogical atmosphere from the perspective of the child, Bollnow (1989b) notes: "These impulses of a child's trust require special and cautious care, even when, from the perspective of the adult, these impulses appear excessive, for this trust is truly a foundation that must exist if the child is to develop properly" (p. 15). Trust is essential to the educational process "for there is a lasting significance of the atmosphere of security and cheerfulness" (p. 16). In a pedagogic relationship of trust Bollnow (1989b) tells us, there is "the sense of "morning-ness" (p. 22). He concludes: "But as Goethe saw so sharply, awe and respect come to the person not from within, but rather it is carefully nurtured through a long and protracted process of education and socialization" (pp. 34-35).

Another interesting example of phenomenological scholarship on teaching is a conversation among five educators regarding *Education for Being*. Ted Aoki recounts, in his preface to the book (Berman, et al., 1991), that the title—"Education is Being"—is recorded on a banner mounted outside the Institute for Education of the University of Heidelberg, Germany. Aoki writes:

For myself, these voices do not blend in a closure; rather, they celebrate openness to openness—there is distinct resistance on their part to be brought to a closure. I liken these five voices not to a symphonic harmony of oneness, but, as in certain Bach fugues, to a polyphony of five lines in a tensionality of contrapuntal interplay, a tensionality of differences. (Aoki, in Berman, et al., 1991, p. xiii)

Among the themes of this book are: toward curriculum for being; the person as significant, education as journey, language as meaning, knowledge as personally constructed, and the teacher as pilgrim. The hermeneutical process is evident in the conversation among the participants. Francine tells her listeners: "My knowing has been revealed in my power to be" (p. 16). Mary: "I do not completely understand this text I teach, but there seem to be some irreducibles: an elemental belief in freedom, a desire for grace, and a yearning for community" (p. 67). Jessie: "Whatever characterizes the next detour I take or the next pictures I find within, I feel certain that music will continue to be an accompaniment that helps bring together the internal (self) and external (others) aspects of my life" (p. 91). Diane: "Looking back I see that it has always been in connection with others that I am transformed. . . . I am a woman defined within relationships; relationships that I care about and, therefore, that constitute me" (p. 115). Louise: "Persons whose lives are embedded in gratitude for the gift of life and its possibilities can use conversation to share insights acquired in solitude, to transcend the

mundane and humdrum and to become more caring human beings" (p. 138).

The increasing political sensitivity of phenomenology is evident in a postscript:

> We have an ethical concern related to Heidegger (quoted often in this book). In the process of our inquiry we became aware that his political affiliations and activities were incompatible with his concern for Being. We abhor his politics. We share his expressed concern for Being. This issue confirms the value of a groups such as ours which created a space for us to ponder the tensions in people's lives. (p. 190)

Phenomenological scholarship on teaching invites you to teach as a mode of relation to yourself, to others, to subject matter. A contemplative and meditative self-reflexivity is required, as the quoted passages above imply. In the phenomenological world, modes of being rather than sets of behavioral skills characterize the effort to understand curriculum and teaching. Unsurprisingly, phenomenologists have also explored reading and writing as meaningful ways of being in the world, not as sets of behavioral skills. To reading and writing we turn next.

VI

Reading and Writing: Grumet, Hunsberger, van Manen

> A text speaks to us in a manner that shows us how we are in the world.
> (Max van Manen, 1985, p. 22)

> In phenomenology the concern is to understand . . . what difference reading makes in our lives.
> (Margaret Hunsberger, 1988, p. 211)

> Writing is the substance of education.
> (Alan A. Block, 1988, p. 47)

A phenomenology of reading requires returning that activity to the subjectively embodied person (Greene, 1974, 1975b; Grumet, 1988a). Grumet employed Merleau-Ponty's concept of "body subject" to rescue reading from a dualistic and idealistic epistemology. "Bodyreading" is Grumet's concept for embodied reading, an act which requires what Ricoeur termed "sense" and "reference," i.e. what one knows and how one lives. "Sense" refers to the "what" of the text. "Reference" is "what the text is about." Ricoeur employed these categories to repudiate idealism, what Sartre described as taking the word for the world. We are "in the world," influenced by situation and influencing situations," Grumet (1988a) explains. "Bodyreading," is strung between the poles of our actual situation, crowded as it is with our intentions, assumptions, and position, and the possibilities that texts point to" (p. 455).

Mainstream reading research and instruction is "decentered," guilty of idealism, obsessed with procedure and protocol, seemingly unaware that all

symbolic systems, including language, are aspects of lived worlds [see Heap, 1980]. Merleau-Ponty maintained that:

words, vowels, and phonemes are so many ways of "singing" the world, and their function is to represent things not, as the naïve onomatopoetic theory had it, by reason of objective resemblance, but because they extract, and literally express, their emotional essence. (quoted in Grumet, 1988a, p. 455)

Like language, curriculum is a "moving form," according to Grumet (1988a) "conceived as an aspiration, the object and hope of our intentionality, it comes to form and slips, at the moment of its actualization, into the ground of our action" (p. 455). It is this movement which Merleau-Ponty and Ricoeur recover for language and reading.

Bodyreading: A recovery of what is absent? A certain sadness is associated with bodyreading, Grumet (1988a) believes. The notion implies an integration and concreteness now lost, an idea consistent with Heideggerean phenomenology. Psychoanalytic theories of language also suggest this sense as they postulate desire as the precondition of symbol formation. Psychoanalytically then, to read, to write, indeed to speak and even to think, is to acknowledge the presence of an absence. Bodyreading may be such a concept, devised to recover what is absent; perhaps that is the mission of reading, phenomenologically conceived. As Jacques Lacan insists, language is a sign of estrangement, an expression of desire, predicated upon loss.

Grumet uses psychoanalytic and feminist theory to situate the reading debate between phonics and sight words. Grumet believes that in spite of the highly organized nature of phonics instruction (with its repetitious drill sequences), the recitation of sounds it requires is reminiscent of the echolalia that is the babble of infants. The highly inflected, immediately echoed preoedipal speech of mother and child is "the mother tongue," sounds which express intimacy without denotative meaning. Grumet (1988a) describes the differential course of speech development for boys and girls:

Girls, permitted to sustain the original identifications with their mothers, need not repress sound and touch as significant ways of being attached to the world. . . . To be male is to be, in effect, no mom, and that early identification as well as the sensual modalities that dominated it are repressed so that an identification with a father whose presence and relation depend more on sight than on sound or touch can be achieved. Surrendering the detail, the intimacy and texture that touch and sound provide, sight provides us with a view and privileges the structural relations of abstract and rational thought that accompany literacy. (p. 463)

The world as answer to the body's question. Grumet agrees with Merleau-Ponty that the world is the answer to the body's question: "One's own body is the term, always tacitly understood in the figure-background structure, and every figure stands out against the double horizon of external and bodily space" (quoted in Grumet, 1988a, p. 465). In this phenomenological sense the world arranges itself around our hopes, needs, and possibilities, real and

imagined. The meaning of a text is the possible and actual ground of thought and action; it is what the reader makes out of what she finds when she reads. Meaning in this sense is not *in* the text.

Grumet cites several projects which speak to the experience of reading. The Bay Area Writing Project and its associated projects appear to engage teachers in ways which bring attention to the experience of writing. Writing enables the reader to see the omissions, contradictions, and contingencies hidden or partially hidden in the text. The reader-response research done by David Bleich (1978) illustrates how students draw from their own store of associations to constructively read the text. In literary theory Terry Eagleton (1983) portrays a "writable" text, one characterized by what Barthes termed double signs, revealing their provisionality, materiality, and historicity. Eagleton explains:

The "writable text," usually a modernist one, has no determinate meaning, no settled signifiers, but is plural and diffuse, an inexhaustible tissue or galaxy of signifiers, a seamless weave of codes, and fragments of codes, through which the critic may cut his own errant path. There are no beginnings and ends, no sequences which cannot be reversed, no hierarchy of textual "levels" to tell you what is more or less significant. All literary texts are woven out of other texts, not in the conventional sense that they bear the traces of "influence" but in the more radical sense that every word, phrase or segment is a reworking of other writings which precede or surround the individual work. There is no such thing as literary "originality," no such thing as the "first" literary work: all literature is intertextual. A specific piece of writing thus has no clearly defined boundaries: it spills over constantly into the works clustered around it, generating a hundred different perspectives which dwindle to a vanishing point. The work cannot be sprung shut, rendered determinate, by an appeal to the author, for the "death of the author" is a slogan that modern criticism in now confidently able to proclaim. (Eagleton, quoted in Grumet, 1988a, pp. 467-468)

Intertextuality. While this view may seem extreme given many assumptions of mainstream English teachers, it does function theoretically to return texts to teachers and students. Intertextuality is an invitation to employ multiple texts, spliced, interwoven with commentary and question, all of which constitute the curriculum. Intertextuality is congruent with the word processor, not with "some video version of the questions at the end of the chapter, but the presentation of text that can disappear at the touch of the delete button" (Grumet 1988a, p. 468). Derrida's work speaks to the experience of reading also, in Grumet's view. Deconstructionism [see chapter 9] declares meaning an "alias", a false construction devised to disguise the plurality of meanings that is a text. For Derrida, meaning is provisional, lively, fluttering. For Roland Barthes (1975), it is sensual. The text is an invitation to pleasure, and reading is a multiple expression of intentionality.

To be with the one I love and to think of something else: this is how I have my best ideas, how I best invent what is necessary to my work. Likewise for the text, it produces in me the best pleasure if it manages to make itself heard indi-

rectly; if, reading it, I am led to look up often to listen to something else. I am not necessarily *captivated* by the text of pleasure; it can be an act that is slight, complex, tenuous, almost scatterbrained: a sudden movement of the head like a bird who understands nothing of what we hear, who hears what we do not understand. (Barthes, quoted in Grumet 1988a, pp. 468-469)

Margaret Hunsberger (1985a, 1985b, 1988, 1989, 1992) is perhaps the most prominent phenomenologist of reading. In her "The Time of Texts," Hunsberger (1992) criticizes mainstream conceptions of time as "segmented, invariant, and linear" (p. 64), noting that school time does not necessarily coincide with our experience of time as lived. To illustrate the lived experience of time while reading, Hunsberger converses with readers. Through this conversation she describes "entering the world of the text." Hunsberger concludes: "Reading gives us an opportunity to experience time in various ways, to start difficult but significant thinking, to glimpse not-time, and to stretch our imaginative limits" (p. 91). In an earlier study, Hunsberger (1985a), writing on the experience of re-reading, tells us: "Re-reading can be a way of moving ourselves forward, of deepening our understanding" (p. 161). Reflecting on oral reading she believes that what is essential to re-reading occurs in readers' interaction and sharing, a point made as well by Grumet and Pinar (1992). In her study of "Students and Textbooks," Hunsberger (1989) notes: "The interpretation of text . . . is concerned fundamentally with the relationship between reader and text" (p. 115). However, reading is a fundamentally social process, and "in an interpretive community the teacher is spared the burden of always being right" (p. 125); students become more active and engaged. Reading has also been studied by Robert K. Brown (1991), who portrayed phenomenologically a remedial reading program in the context of a major study of Aoki and van Manen. On the teaching of English as second language, Angéline Martel (n.d.) wrote: "Perhaps E.S.L. should be based, not on hopes of equality, but on differences, in an effort to dwell in the uniqueness of the individual while giving him/her the tools to live in the larger community" (p. 10). [For another engaging study of E.S.L., see Sauvé, 1991.] Understood phenomenologically, reading is an embodied being-in-the-world, with others.

Dennis Sumara (1992a, 1992b, 1993, 1994a, 1994b, in press) has worked to define a new location for curriculum theorizing by studying shared readings of literary texts. Situated in the hermeneutic phenomenological tradition, his work provides interpretations of the experience of reading within school contexts. Sumara wishes to render visible the largely invisible architecture of human/textual/contextual relations which emerge from the location announced by the presence of a literary text. His work has helped to discredit the idea of reading as *transaction* wherein literary meaning is conceptualized as a "third thing" existing between reader and text; rather, reading is understood as a form of "embodied action" whereby all of the constituent parts of a curriculum that include literary texts "co-emerge" through their relations with one another. Sumara has described these

embodied curricular relations as a continually evolving interaction between "us/not-us."

When reading is so understood, it becomes clear that the literary text is not simply transposed onto already-existing relations. Instead the literary text, when included in the "not-us" world of the classroom in which the student and teacher must interact, influences and alters *all* of the existing curricular relations. In addition, these shared literary relations, he suggests, function as a type of literary anthropology where what the reader has to say about the literary text is far less interesting than what the literary text announces about the reader. For Sumara, then, the hermeneutic tradition of self-interpretation in relation to the lived experience of reading with others becomes a way to learn about the complexity of ever-evolving curricular relations.

Writing. Writing is experienced in distinctively phenomenological terms as well. Van Manen (1989), in his "By the Light of Anecdote," defends the anecdotal phenomenological tradition in which he situates his work: "For some, such as Strasser (1969), the products of the Utrecht School suffered from a lack of philosophical rigor or sophistication, thus yielding a soft, anecdotal form of phenomenology" (p. 233). Van Manen believes that the power of the anecdote concerns its capacity to amplify the phenomenological and hermeneutic quality of human science text. Central to his interest is a methodological notion of seeing the process of human science research as intrinsically textual or a writing activity (van Manen, 1984b, 1984a, 1986, 1989). In fact, van Manen (1989) regards the "practice of research as a form of writing" (p. 237). He recalls Sartre, whom he regards as a phenomenologist "who stood and acted in the middle of the hustle and bustle of social and political life." For van Manen, "writing [is] thinking. . . . Writing is a kind of self-making or forming. To write is to measure the depth of things, as well as to come to a sense of one's own depth" (p. 238). Invoking this example, van Manen lists five aspects of writing. First, "writing separates us from what we know, yet it unites us more closely with what we know" (p. 238). Second, van Manen notes that phenomenological "writing distances us from the lifeworld, yet it also draws us more closely to the lifeworld" (p. 239). Third, van Manen believes that "writing decontextualizes thought from practice and yet it returns thought to praxis" (p. 239). Fourth, "writing abstracts our experience of the world, yet it also concretizes our understanding of the world" (p. 240).

Finally, van Manen notes that:

writing objectifies thought into print and yet it subjectifies our understanding of something that truly engages us. . . . The writing of the text *is* the research. Writing exercises the ability to see. . . . The methodology of hermeneutic phenomenology is more a carefully cultivated thoughtfulness than a technique. (pp. 240-241)

To further develop the notion of writing phenomenological thoughtfulness, van Manen defends the anecdote:

Anecdote can be understood as a methodological device in human science to make comprehensible some notion that easily eludes us. . . . [It is] analogous to the use of metaphor. Anecdotes are a special kind of story; they resemble mini-stories possessing a rhetorical quality that moves them more closely into the direction of *sayings* and *proverbs* on the one hand, and *poetic fragments* on the other hand. (p. 243)

"In the raindrop is the ocean" is an old saying the wisdom of which van Manen seems to share: "The paradoxical thing about anecdotal narrative is that it tells something particular while really addressing the general or the universal" (p. 247).

Phenomenological writing cannot be interested in purely hypothetical problems; it always derives from and returns to the world:

And so, because of the nature of its object of study—the pedagogical situa-tion—phenomenological pedagogical research cannot be interested in its ques-tions merely out of purely academic or intellectual curiosity. Pedagogy does not just want to know how things are; pedagogical research always has an inherent practical intent because sooner or later this knowledge figures in how one must act. (p. 250)

Finally, the power of anecdotes is that they resist escaping the world into abstraction: "anecdotes, like pedagogical situations, are always concrete and particular" (van Manen, 1989, p. 251).

Another instance of phenomenological scholarship in which writing is understood as not literal or technical is that of Minerva Lopez-Caples (1989), who suggested that "children fictionalize themselves first in play, then in oral storytelling, and in literate societies, through creative writing" (p. 101). Lopez-Caples (1989) believes that through play, storytelling, and writing, the child can re-experience him or herself as whole:

I believe that our first child-self . . . is one joyfully unconscious, loved and accepted, and nourished, centralized and attended to consistently, predictably, and eternally. As we begin to discover the contradictions between this inter-nally contained reality and what actually happens to self in the world, anxiety and uncertainty develop. . . . This resolution [of this tension] we find . . . through a search for the achievement of self-knowledge. (p. 103)

It is through a return to origins that the child can heal: "In the imaginative act of self-fictionalization, the child probes for a kind of truth. . . . Eventually, he or she may discover . . . a personal memory of historical proportions. It will be then that he or she will glance up at the sky and see the sun and perhaps not be so afraid anymore" (p. 104). Reading and writing, then, are modalities of self-creation, self-understanding, and self-presentation in an intersubjective, layered, textured world. It is a world from which one might retreat from time to time, to find a secret place where the scale of things conform more closely with one's intimate and private world. As we will see, this secret place is not only literal. One can be in the midst of people and activity and still be tucked safely away in one's secret place.

VII

The Secret Place: Langeveld and Smith

The playground is also a place for understanding what is happening to children. It is a child's place, a place for being able to act like a child, and a place for seeing what matters to children.

(Stephen J. Smith, 1988, p. 2)

In this section we will not only report Langeveld's fascinating exposition of the "secret place," but other phenomenological research which seeks to articulate those secret margins of lived experience, i.e. ordinarily inaccessible to the technical world of everyday institutional life. [For additional information regarding this influential Dutch pedagogical theorist, see van Manen, 1980]. Langeveld observed that children are not formed by the public world, including the school, alone. They are drawn, he wrote, by their own world. "To create these worlds, a formal curriculum is not sufficient: "They also need freedom and openness to the beckoning of that which is as yet undetermined and uncertain." That which is undetermined and uncertain, that which is mysterious, constitutes the "secret place." The secret place is a physical place, but its importance resides in its function for the child. Here the child can withdraw from a public world he or she does not yet comprehend. Here he or she can think about that world, and perhaps observe it.

Solitude and safety. The secret place is characterized by indistinct boundaries. Indeed, the child may lose himself or herself in the experience of the secret place. Langeveld approves of this possibility, regarding it as complementary to a public world, especially the school, that is characterized by systematization, explicitness, and order. In contrast, the secret place is construed by fantasy and creative imagination. It is laced with qualities of a waking dream, a mood, a feeling that is evoked again and again, comforting the visitor and owner of the secret place. Words are often unnecessary. Speech is said to occur in the deep silence of an a priori understanding of self and place. The tone of voice may change into the tonality of intimacy. In the secret place the child finds solitude and safety. There the distinctions between outer and inner world may melt into a single, unique secret world of the child. Space, emptiness, and also darkness reside in the same realm; time seems to stand still, or else it disappears: both feel the same (Langeveld, 1983a, 1983b).

Langeveld asserts that we are lonely only in the world. In the reality of worlds we create we feel at home, grounded. In the secret place we feel no anxiety; all is protected. It represents a state of innocence, and contrasts sharply with the exactness and objectivity of the school class. In the secret place, in lived space, phenomena present themselves to the child with immediacy. Here the eidetic image, sensory illusions, and dream images intermingle with the physical attributes of the, say, attic. The body feels at home, not too small compared to adult bodies, not too slow compared to adult pace

and rhythm. Space is the right scale, as it is created by the occupant of the secret place. Langeveld believes that adults who are whole retain this sense of "secret place" because this sense conveys aspects of what is essentially human. As adults, however, the secret place is no longer so secret; ordinarily it is shared with loved ones: the home, the studio, the workshop, the neighbor-hood pub. Educators, too, must share a fundamental understanding of this indeterminate place and must not fall into the mistake of viewing the whole world as the institution of school. Much is to be learned outside of the school-world (Langeveld, 1983b).

As we indicated, the "secret place" is a figurative as well as literal concept. Figuratively speaking, another secret place can be the playground, outside the usual locus of institutional curriculum, the classroom. As Jardine (1988b) has noted: "Play can be understood . . . as the exploration of possible worlds of meaning" (p. 34). Possible worlds may contain hidden danger and the risk of injury that can accompany play. For another phenomenological scholar (Fischer, 1989), injury itself is a category of study. Others focus on the risk, not the injury. Stephen J. Smith (1988) discusses this risk on the playground:

Ignored by those for whom children are of little consequence or those who are too preoccupied with adult concerns to be much bothered with things that matter to children, taken for granted by those who take children for granted and prefer to see their effective removal from the adult world, the playground is also a place for understanding what is happening to children. It is a child's place, a place for being able to act like a child, and a place for seeing what matters to children. (p. 2)

Smith recalls a knock on his door by a neighborhood child, whose knock-ing, seeking a playmate, obligates him to look out for him. The neighbor-hood boy, Stephen, is asking:

not only for a response that is mindful of the dangers to which he is exposed, but for a response that is mindful of his being a child and of the obligation that this fact places on me as an adult. How should I respond? Whatever I do, I am already responsible for the risky texture of his life. (p. 5)

How does Smith frame his responsibility? "I help the child by being with him or her in such a way that risks are seen where, without my help, danger might lurk" (p. 9). From this deeply felt sense of responsibility for the child, Smith moves to a "secret place" of the playground: "Might I suggest that being present pedagogically has to do with encouraging the child with a mindfulness of how the child encounters the world. It has to do with seeing risk as the child may come to see it" (p. 11). Speaking to other teachers, Smith (1988) says:

we [must] care for the risky nature of their activity, their playground activity in particular, by reawakening to the world which the child sees. Helping and encouraging the child's efforts, becoming mindful of how the playground

appears, and seeking to make this activity a common encounter, are the determinants of this pedagogic atmosphere. These are the atmospheric conditions of our responsibility for children on playgrounds and the dimensions of our thinking about how children can learn to become responsible themselves for the riskiness of everyday life. (pp. 13-14)

In a similar study, Smith (1989) describes risk not as a negative attribute of children's playground activity, but more positively as those challenges and adventures to which children can actively respond:

Risk refers to something that is being accomplished by children, some intended activity which expands their sense of the world. . . . I present an understanding how we can bring an underlying sense of security to children's feelings for the playground and for the risks that can be taken there. (Smith, 1990, p. 71)

In another study, Smith (1989) reflects on his child undergoing heart surgery: "The important thing is that we attend to the child's experience and that we who are reflectively engaged in his daily life learn how to speak up for the child during his hospitalization" (p. 162). This statement—and Stephen Smith's work generally—is reminiscent of child-centered progressivism in the 1920s. Yet, it is expressed in language and communicates a world-view that is rather different. Not based in psychoanalysis or developmental psychology, Smith's attentiveness to the child is rooted in a phenomenological appreciation of the power of the parent-child bond, a bond that seems to have a mystical as well as psychological content.

The notion of "secret place" is not only what is overlooked in the bustle of daily activity or a literal place children go, it can be a creative act of making some place hidden, making a secret. Reflecting on "creative concealment" among children and adolescents, Kenneth Stoddart (1989) asserted: "Indeed, in the presentation and preservation of a self, what is hidden is as crucial as what is revealed" (p. 163). He continued: "Indeed," it is the case that optimism regarding children's progress to competent adulthood can be generated by suspending interest in the *that* and *what* of their concealment and addressing instead the *locales* they choose" (p. 168). Sometimes the use of devices creates the insularity that makes for a secret place. Studying "The Walkman and the Primary World of the Senses," Rainer Schonhammer (1989) suggested:

an important aspect of the alteration in the subject-world-relationship of a Walkman user [is that] lived space loses its familiarity, [it] is somehow split into two. The familiar environment in which one lives and moves takes on a strange character when one is separated from the acoustic part of it. . . . [A] Walkman user [is] being present and absent at the same time. (pp. 133-134)

Whether in secret or public places, the phenomenological student is acutely aware of time. Time, however, is not that which is recorded on clocks and watchfaces. Rather, to be attuned to time is to reside in one's lived time, in one's lived space, an embodied temporality.

VIII
Temporality: Huebner and Lippitz

Human life is never fixed but is always emergent as the past and future become horizons of present.

(Dwayne E. Huebner, 1975c, p. 244)

A fundamental phenomenological concept and one which has received elaboration as a curricular concept is that of temporality. Dwayne Huebner first identified and explicated this concept's significance for understanding curriculum in 1967. Huebner relied on Heidegger's articulation of the concept. After rejecting "learning" as the key concept for curriculum, Huebner reconceived the field's interest in "purposes," "goals," and "objectives" as a concern for temporality (Huebner, 1975c). To explicate temporality, Huebner referred to Heidegger's *Being and Time*. For Heidegger time is a fundamental aspect of Dasein: "Dasein's totality of being as care means: ahead-of-itself-already-being-in (a world) as being-alongside (entities encountered within-the-world). . . . The 'ahead-of-itself' is grounded in the future. In the 'Being-already-in . . . ,' the character of 'having been' is made known. 'Being-alongside' becomes possible in making present" (Heidegger, quoted in Huebner, 1975c, p. 243). Huebner (1975c) explained:

[The person] does not simply await a future and look back upon a past. The very notion of time arises out of man's [sic] existence, which is an emergent. The future is man facing himself in anticipation of his own potentiality for being. The past is finding himself already thrown into a world. It is the having-been which makes possible the projection of his potentiality. The present is the moment of vision when Dasein, finding himself thrown into a situation (the past), projects his own potentiality for being. Human life is . . . a present made up of a past and future brought into the moment. . . . Human life is never fixed but is always emergent as the past and future become horizons of present. Education recognizes, assumes responsibility for, and maximizes the consequences of this awareness of man's temporality. (p. 244)

For Huebner this responsibility or concern must take curricular forms which "make possible those moments of vision when the student, and/or those responsible for him, project his potentiality for being into the present, thus tying together the future and the past into the present" (Huebner 1975c, p. 246).

Pinar (1992b) drew upon Huebner's concern for temporality in his phenomenological meditation on death and dying. He wished to "write about death, our deaths. Death which can seem so distant, but which can be so close at hand. Indeed, death here and now, in the midst of lights and life" (p. 92). Acknowledging his father's death a few months before, Pinar (1992b) recalled those who have participated in the curriculum field in time past:

A thought, a field, a relationship is never ours alone; it is theirs as well. (Rugg is here, in imagination.) To "let me be" can mean to permit some space of separa-

tion, of solitariness, of freedom, but they will not let us be completely. Nor do or should we wish to be free of them, for they are our origins, their flesh is our flesh, and to be truly free of them, is to lose them, and to lose ourselves. Let me be, blessed spirit, but do not leave me (p. 93)

Pinar went on to tell the story of Ingmar Bergman's 1972 film entitled "Cries and Whispers" in which a dying woman—the character's name is Agnes—comes alive the night after her death. Pinar noted:

A dead woman resurrects our hope. Through suffering and dying and witness-ing, Agnes . . . comes to express hope and life. There is death and then there is resurrection. In life there are thousands of deaths and rebirths, and the embod-ied intellect seeks transcendence of its past and entries into its future. We can take courage and comfort from Agnes' story as it portrays life from death. (p. 98)

Pinar (1992b) concluded:

Just as those who have died before us whisper and cry as we speak our time, our place, ourselves, those who have not yet appeared and those who are appearing—our children—speak in our voices. Our children provoke our parenting, permitting us to reexperience our own childhood. . . . The very fact of children testifies to our dying and to their birthing and gives urgency and immediacy to our pedagogical relationships to them. . . .

Cries and whispers of the dead who live; cries and whispers of she who dies, who is resurrected, whose death testifies to life. A phenomenology of death might . . . enable us to affirm those who have gone before us, those who, like us, are dying now, and those children born and unborn who bring life to our dyings, all of us, past, present, future, blessed by death, blessed by life. (p. 100)

Piaget's and Langeveld's views of time. In another phenomenological study of temporality, German phenomenologist Wilfried Lippitz (1983) contrasted Jean Piaget's view of time with that of Dutch phenomenologist Langeveld, whose reflections on the notion of "secret place" we reviewed earlier. Lippitz observed that for Piaget the development of the concept of time in the child is a special instance of the general development of intelligence. Indeed, time cannot be said to exist for the child, Piaget believed, until the age of operative intelligence, except as it is experienced in action. Lippitz asserted that Piaget is conscious of the child's "prereflective" experience of time, but does not view this prereflective dimension as foundational to all modes of experience in the world. For Piaget, prereflective experience is noteworthy only insofar as it anticipates rational, cognitive development. The child's sense of time does not belong to the sphere of his characteristic representational activity. Time is an intellectual construct, valid always and everywhere, requiring the concept of constancy of the velocity of the measur-ing instruments. For Piaget, then, time is "clock" time (Lippitz, 1983). [Earlier in the chapter we summarized Jardine's analysis of Piaget's concept of self-understanding. Piaget's stature and influence as well as his scientific commitments make him of special interest to phenomenologists.]

For Langeveld time is not a cognitive structure in itself. Rather, time is a fundamental structure of the lifeworld. In prototypical phenomenological fashion, Langeveld suggests that the concept of time for the child involves the child's attempt to fit him or herself into the temporal schema erected by adults: the primary analog for time is a lived directedness toward that which is coming in the future. This experience of time has little to do with the clock. In the course of education adults gradually but inexorably super-impose this "measuring tape" of time on the phenomenological experience of the child. With the continual aid of adults, the life of the small child must adapt him or herself to the adult's mechanical temporal schemes. At an early stage the child experiences the adult situation of being bound by time. Langeveld insists, then, that the child experiences time profoundly, and in multiple forms. He identifies an experience of anticipation, an experience of the present, and an experience of the past. Fundamentally then, there is an experience of duration. The experience of lived time cannot be reduced to clock time (Lippitz, 1983).

Exemplary incidents. To describe lived (*gelebter*) and experienced (*erlebter*) time, Langeveld relies (like van Manen) on anecdotes which, in the phenomenological view, portray "exemplary" and "typical" incidents in which time is discernible. He then employs these incidents as occasions of under-standing time for the child and as a fundamental structure of existence. A phenomenological method apprehends the fundamental structures of the lifeworld, such as time, from a distance, in this instance, from the memory of childhood. Memory must produce a precise observation and description, both of which are then examined intersubjectively, via conversation with others. This method avoids both mere replication of lifeworld processes and a complete reconstruction of those processes according to re-established elements of consensual knowledge. The phenomenologist begins with lived contexts, as in the case of Langeveld's use of anecdote as the starting-point of his interpretation of time for the child. He does not resort to a pre-given, abstract definition of time. Indeed, the phenomenologist strives to begin and end in concreteness. But as wedded to concreteness as phenomenological understanding is, it, in Husserlian fashion, claims to represent general understanding of which the concrete is an instance, however essential an instance. Lippitz (1983) asserts that the structures of the lifeworld have a pre-personal, pre-subjective character. They are experienced personally, and reconstituted personally, in body and mind. Likewise, general structures of the lifeworld, such as time, in principle cannot be adequately grasped by concepts. These structures are prior to language. Language itself, including phenomenological description, is grounded in prepredicative, unthematized, lived processes.

Modes of waiting. Another temporal theme in phenomenological research is that of waiting. Reflecting on this theme, Mikio Fujita (1985) notes: "Waiting occupies a significant place in the experience of parents and educators. . . . Waiting is a far from trivial matter in our day-to-day pedagogic lives" (p. 107). Fujita suggests that there are two aspects or qualities of waiting: "'what is waited for' (its explicitness may vary) and 'how we wait' (whatever its hue and nuance may be)" (p. 108). We can see that we are far from a mechanical or clock-time world here. Instead we are in the life-world, where time is lived, i.e. experienced, not counted: "The notion that waiting is nothing but boredom is only pertinent to the mechanical world, whereas the opposite notion that waiting is vitally important is pertinent only to the world of becoming" (p. 113). Waiting as a means of experiencing time underlines the lived experience of temporality in a phenomenological understanding of the lifeworld.

IX
Conclusion: A Discursive Shift toward Poststructuralism?

Phenomenology got out of hand and climbed down below the severed head when Husserl wasn't looking.

(David Jardine, 1992b, p. 129)

Phenomenology does not represent merely another "approach" to curriculum, merely another orientation or perspective. One cannot "try on" phenomenology or easily invoke it on specific occasions. One cannot because phenomenology is not only another language system, it suggests altered relationships to language itself. The phenomenological task is to live so that language becomes visible, becomes, in Heidegger's term, a "lens." To become distantiated from language to permit such a relationship requires an "ontological" shift, back from the everyday and the taken-for-granted, to the preconceptual, to the body. Some scholars point to the intersections between phenomenology and other traditions in curriculum thought, intersections which might serve as correctives to the narrowness of traditional curriculum theory. In this regard, Leigh Chiarelott (1983a) argued (not unlike Huebner) that in traditional curriculum development:

We have [had] to accept a very narrow view of experience in our design and development of curriculum. . . . A major next step is the continued analysis and criticism of theories of experience and the synthesis of both phenomenological and pragmatic perspectives. (p. 39)

The phenomenological research agenda—in itself and in collaboration with other traditions such as Deweyan pragmatism—holds enormous promise for understanding curriculum as a lived text. At the same time it frightens conservative students of curriculum, who tend to react to the language and the topics as esoteric. For those with intellectual courage, however, the phenomenological path offers rewards commensurate with the apparent risk, as we believe the studies described in this chapter illustrate. Phenomenology promises not only a revised curriculum; phenomenology promises a revised way of life.

Poststructuralism contests phenomenology. As we will see in the next chapter, poststructuralism contests the ontology and epistemology of phenomenology. For instance, the binary distinction between experience and language, experience and conceptualization, is denied. The phenomenological dictum that the conceptual sphere rests upon and derives from a preconceptual, antepredicative sphere is denied by poststructuralists. To be described, even "dumb" experience, Derrida insisted, becomes discourse. Original purity of experience cannot be achieved; while it is implied, it does not exist as text. In the beginning was flesh, but the flesh became word. Lyotard wrote:

> In so far as this life-originating world is ante-predicative, all predication, all discourse, undoubtedly implies, yet is wide of it, and properly speaking nothing may be said of it. . . . The Husserlian description . . . is a struggle of language against itself to attain the originary. . . . In this struggle, the defeat of the philosopher, of the logos, is assured, since the originary, once described, is thereby no longer originary. (quoted in Descombes, 1980, p. 16)

Lyotard does not deny that experience and discourse are distinguishable. He does insist that for "dumb" experience to speak—in language, in the look, in the gesture—it becomes discourse. Discourse includes meaning latent in experience but perhaps not yet articulated.

Language occupies the space of separation. For poststructuralists, then, meaning is discursive. Meaning can represent only approximations of original experience. Language is said to occupy the space between experience and the word, or logos. Lacan (1977) located metaphor exactly at the point where meaning is produced out of non-meaning. Merleau-Ponty anticipated this view: "It is true that we should never talk about anything if we were limited to talking about those experiences which we coincide, since speech is already a separation. . . . [But] the primary meaning of discourse is to be found in that text of experience which it is trying to communicate" (1962, p. 388). Discourse as speech or writing occupies that space which separates us, that space which is termed the "social." Thus "the word" is inextricably human, inextricably political, as Foucault documented in his studies of the discursive systems associated with madness, sexuality, and knowledge (Foucault, 1979, 1980a, 1980b). Merleau-Ponty anticipated this view also: "in the use of our body and our sense in so far as they involve us in the world, we have the means of understanding our cultural gesticulation, in so far as it involves us in history" (1962, p. 82).

Husserl's phenomenology attempted to order and stabilize the flux of experience via the eidetic reduction, by bracketing that flux and discerning its essences (Caputo, 1987). Heidegger invoked deconstruction to violate the everyday, the taken-for-granted sphere we construct and employ to evade the ontological facts of our fallenness, our being-toward-death. In *Being and Time*, deconstruction functions to disrupt mindless tradition and thus acts in service of the recovery and retrieval of Being. Deconstruction functions in the hermeneutic circle to set free the primordial (Caputo, 1987). In this movement Heidegger sets the stage for Derrida. Derrida radicalizes deconstruction so that hermeneutics itself is deconstructed. For Heidegger "understanding" sets free what is hidden from view by overlays of tradition, prejudice, and evasion. "Interpretation" represents movements toward such understanding. For both Heidegger and Husserl, phenomenological understanding moves from originary experience through language and back again. For Heidegger, originary experience does not preclude the linguistic. He acknowledges discourse as an essential constituent element of the "there." Interpretation is the conceptual working out of preexistent understanding, coming to know what we "knew" already, albeit obscurely. Empirical "proofs" have no place in hermeneutical understanding; to know phenomenologically is to allow to unfold what is already present but not yet seen (Caputo, 1987).

Fragility and contingency. Derrida repudiates Heidegger's epistemology; he has no interest in the language of "homecoming," "mystery," "unfolding," and "Being." He views Heidegger's epistemology as nostalgia for a time past, a time that never was. Derrida insists that hiding in the mist of nostalgia is a metaphysics of order in which the reality of flux becomes tamed and distorted. He suspects any moves that slow the movement and arrest the play of language and experience. Caputo observed that Derrida is more faithful to Nietzsche than to Heidegger, insisting that we always remain aware of the fragility and contingency of what we think and do (Caputo, 1987). David W. Jardine's (1992a, 1992b) work has moved out from phenomenology toward poststructuralism, and it resides somewhere between the two. It expresses phenomenological themes, in deconstructed fashion, indicating its recent movement toward poststructuralism. In *Speaking with a Boneless Tongue,* Jardine (1992b) writes playfully but with insight: "Phenomenology got out of hand and climbed down below the severed head when Husserl wasn't looking" (p. 129). For Jardine, phenomenology is both embodied and political: "Hope and despair," Jardine tells us in another place, "[are] the moods of colonialism" (p. 162). However, he is not seduced by a poststructuralist hunger for moving on for the sake of moving on: "If home is abandoned altogether—if we all get caught up in 'leaving'—our care for and devotion to the conditions, sources and intimate dependencies of renewal and generativity are also abandoned" (p. 177). Jardine lives on the edge of phenomenology, in the margin of poststructuralism, a space into which the "old master" of phenomenological curriculum theory—Ted Aoki (1993a)—has also moved recently. That these important figures are redoing phenomenology in light of poststructuralism suggests that this sector too may soon undergo dramatic discursive shifts.

Understanding curriculum as deconstructed text acknowledges knowledge as preeminently historical. Here, however, history is not understood as only ideologically constructed, rather as a series of narratives superimposed upon each other, interlaced among each other, layers of story merged and separated like colors in a Jackson Pollock painting. The stories we tell in schools, formalized as disciplines, are always others' stories, always conveying motives and countermotives, dreams and nightmares. To understand curriculum as deconstructed (and deconstructing) text is to tell stories that never end, stories in which the listener, the "narratee," may become a character or indeed the narrator, in which all structure is provisional, momentary, a collection of twinkling stars in a firmament of flux. Into the flux in chapter 9.

Chapter 9

Understanding Curriculum as Poststructuralist, Deconstructed, Postmodern Text

I believe, however, that I was quite explicit about the fact that nothing of what I said had a destructive meaning. Here and there I have used the word deconstruction, which has nothing to do with destruction. That is to say, it is simply a question of (and this is a necessity of criticism in the classical sense of the word) being alert to the implications, to the historical sedimentation of the language we use—and that is not destruction.

(Jacques Derrida, 1972, p. 271)

I have tried to find passages between the variable and the invariable, between both: not from one to the other, but passages at their absolute difference, the *différance* between death, twice evaded.

(Jacques Daignault, 1992a, p. 201)

[Postmodern curriculum is] a fascinating, imaginative realm (born of the echo of God's laughter) wherein no one owns the truth and everyone has the right to be understood.

(William E. Doll, Jr., 1993a, p. 151)

I
Introduction: Language, Power, and Desire

For the past two decades poststructuralism, deconstruction, and postmodernism have generated debates which "dominated the cultural and intellectual scene throughout the world" (Best & Kellner, 1991, p.1). To understand curriculum as poststructuralist, deconstructed, and postmodern text is to engage modes of cognition (Pinar & Reynolds, 1992a), methods of critique and analysis (Cherryholmes, 1988b), and versions of contemporary culture and history (Jameson, 1991), which challenge and subvert not only the central themes, organizing metaphors, and discursive strategies constituting Western thought and informing the Enlightenment project, but all that is modernism itself, including those perspectives and cultural structures associated with modernism. Because poststructuralism, deconstruction, and postmodernism are complex and far-ranging movements with which beginning curriculum students may not be familiar, we will devote the first four sections of this chapter to summarizing these movements before moving to the work of those curricularists whose scholarship has been influenced by them.

Definitions. Although the three terms—poststructuralism, deconstruction, postmodernism—have been employed interchangeably (Sarup, 1989), initially poststructuralism referred to those theoretical movements emerging in France which had grown out of and then opposed structuralism as well as the humanism which structuralism had challenged earlier (Descombes, 1980). Originally a Heideggerean concept, deconstruction was elaborated by Derrida into a rigorous method of analysis. It came to achieve a distinct identity as a "theory of philosophical discourse" (Descombes, 1980) and a "form of commentary" (Said, 1990b). It is often construed as one among many methods of analyses within poststructuralism and is thus often subsumed in the term poststructuralist. Postmodernism initially referred to radical innovations in the arts, in technology, and in science (Best & Kellner, 1991). Recently it has been used to refer to an epistemic and cultural break with modernism. In this version of postmodernism, deconstruction and poststructuralism are subsumed as theoretical and cognitive modes consistent with the cultural logic of the postmodern (Rosenau, 1992; Flax, 1990; Jameson, 1991; Doll, W., 1993a, Willinsky, 1991a, forthcoming).

Although "poststructuralism" and "deconstruction" continue as terms to refer to diverse and at times conflicting discourses and practices, it would appear that postmodernism has become the term which subsumes the other two and is most frequently employed by theorists (e.g. Rorty, 1989; Habermas, 1981; Flax, 1990) who wish to refer simultaneously to a paradigm shift in the academic disciplines and to a new cultural landscape. Postmodernism, then, refers simultaneously to a cultural and political movement, and to an historical moment. Due to its inclusiveness, postmodernism may be characterized by dissension rather than consensus (Bérubé, 1991), and therefore to some extent not only is protean *and* empty as a category, but also by its own logic runs the risk of subverting its usefulness as a descriptive term. Particular writers and intellectuals have been associated with the three "movements," although many of these would contest the labels applied to them. Poststructuralism has frequently been linked with Foucault, Lacan, Deleuze, Guattari, Kristeva, and Derrida. Deconstruction has been associated, obviously, with Derrida, but also with De Man and Hartman. Postmodernism has been linked with Lyotard, Rorty, Baudrillard, and Jameson but also, due to its subsumption of deconstruction and poststructuralism, the writers associated with these terms. In discussing curriculum as poststructuralist, deconstructed, and postmodern text, we will report the various ways curriculum theorists have used these terms, keeping in mind that there are distinctions between the terms and their uses, and the fields of phenomena which result from the organizing force of the terms. We also advise the reader to keep in mind the inherent limitations of an introductory study, such as this one, of what are clearly complex discursive and cultural movements now dramatically affecting the field of curriculum (Pinar & Reynolds, 1992a).

Overview. Before turning our attention to the work of those theorists who understand curriculum as poststructural, deconstructed, and postmodern text, it may be helpful to gain an overview, however partial, of poststructuralism, deconstruction, and postmodernism. In presenting such an overview, we hope that you will not only be better prepared to encounter curricularists who work in these modes but will also, perhaps, be inspired to engage the questions and challenges raised by poststructuralism, deconstruction, and postmodernism. However, it is important to note that these theories, questions, and challenges are only partially addressed and met by curriculum theory in its current stage of formulation. At its most general level, poststructuralism, deconstruction, and postmodernism share a rejection of structuralism, humanism, and modernism, a repudiation of the ways various academic disciplines have "traditionally" presented their versions of reality.

Poststructuralism denies all appeals to foundational, transcendental, or universal truths or metanarratives. There is the sense that our current historical situation constitutes a radical break with the period characterized as modernism or the Enlightenment. Above all, there is an attention to language, power, desire, and representation as discursive categories. To achieve a fuller understanding of these movements, let us approach them separately. This approach initially involves focusing on the distinguishing features of each movement. We will conclude our discussion of poststructuralism, deconstruction, and postmodernism by surveying the questions and challenges they have posed to curriculum theory.

II
Poststructuralism

We believe only in totalities that are peripheral.
(Gilles Deleuze & Félix Guattari, 1977, p. 42).

In *Modern French Philosophy*, Vincent Descombes (1980) locates the emergence of poststructuralism in France in the 1960s as a response to the intellectual scene in Paris. In its very name poststructuralism reveals its ties to structuralism, and indeed poststructuralism is a response to those theories which purported to discover invariant structures in society, the human psyche, consciousness, history, and culture. Poststructuralism, then, is both an assault on structuralism and also an outgrowth of it. It continues the attack on humanism—including phenomenology and existentialism—that structuralism had launched as well as certain echoes of themes within structuralism, for instance, the approach to language in terms of discourse or discursive systems.

What is structuralism? Although opinion varies regarding the definition of structuralism [Culler (1976) suggests any attempt at definition would lead to despair], most scholars agree that it is a method of analysis and a philosophical orientation which privileges structures, systems, or sets of relations over the specific phenomena which emerge in, are constituted by, and derive their identity from those structures and sets of relations (Norris, C., 1991; Cherry-holmes, 1988b; Martusewicz, 1988, Eagleton, 1983). For example, whereas a phenomenologist might describe education as it is experienced by an individual student or teacher, a structuralist might analyze education in terms of underlying structures that are invariant and that shaped the experience of individuals regardless who they are [for instance, reproduction theory]. Put simply, while structuralism has sought to identify "the system" that creates meaning, poststructuralism has sought to repudiate, dismantle, and reveal the variance and contingency of "the system." Perhaps it is not surprising that the decade of the 1960s, which had just witnessed political movements which focused on identifying "the system" and then attempted politically to dismantle it, would also be the era of structuralism's greatest triumph and the beginning of its demise at the hands of poststructuralists. In many respects structuralism was a response to existentialism and phenomenology, but in a more general way what all of these shared was the question of what is reality.

How is reality meaningful? For the existentialist, reality is the meaning freely given to it by a sovereign consciousness; it is the meaning I choose to give it. The origin of meaning, then, is the subject, individual consciousness or the "I." For Sartre, consciousness, the "pour soi" or "for-itself" freely chooses to give meaning to the "en soi" or the "in itself," that is, what is not consciousness. Since I am the origin of meaning, I am responsible for the reality of the world I choose and thus am responsible for the world. If I choose to know that suffering exists, I am responsible for that suffering.

A phenomenological critique of existentialism. Phenomenologists saw existentialism as maintaining the Cartesian dualism of subject/object in the "for-itself" and the "in-itself," and then smuggling in a kind of idealism by positing the freedom of a sovereign consciousness as the origin of meaning. To respond to what they saw as the Sartrean duality between subject and object, they offered a program which would "describe precisely what lies between the 'for-itself' and the 'in-itself,' between consciousness and the thing, freedom and nature" (Descombes, 1980, p. 56). To achieve such a description they introduced the idea of perception to replace the sovereign freedom of consciousness. Perception implies the body, and with the introduction of the body, they hoped to restore the material world to the question of what constitutes reality and meaning, and thus bridge the divide between consciousness and things. As Grumet (1988a) reminds us, Merleau-Ponty regarded the world as the answer to the body's question. With the introduction of the body, consciousness is said to be "grounded," always contextualized. Since, unlike the sovereign freedom of the consciousness asserted by existentialists, the phenomenological "I perceive" is incarnate, the unity of subject and object is established. The task for phenomenology is to describe this unity, as we reviewed in the preceding chapter.

For phenomenology, meaning can only be "for myself." Descombes explains:

> In more general terms, phenomenology maintains that the only meaning which "being" can have for myself is being for myself. Consequently we must include the actual conditions under which the object is given to us in our definition of it. Just as the trip to the holiday home is part of the holiday, the route toward the object is part of the object. This is the fundamental axiom of phenomenology. And so, perspective, for example, should not be considered as the perceiving subject's point of view upon the object perceived but rather as a property of the object itself. (Descombes, 1980, p. 64)

That object is the "object itself" as it emerges in the body/subject's perception. To describe the thing itself, to follow the phenomenological call back to things themselves, is to describe the situation in which the perceiving subject is. A description of lived experience—of the meaning into which the "for itself" and the "in itself" or the subject and object have been temporarily synthesized—is necessarily a unique description, since what is described is based on my experience at this particular moment under these particular circumstances. Thus meaning is always meaning for myself, although it is given in the inextricable, seamlessly woven relationships between the perceiver—the body/subject or embodied consciousness—and the world. The gestalt that is formed in this contingent synthesis of subject and object becomes the object for study or reflection. This is a reflection carried out by "bracketing" or distancing oneself from commonsensical descriptions or socially accepted interpretations or even those assumptions we tacitly hold, and by fully experiencing what it is we are experiencing here and how. It is this kind of reflection which allows one to describe the unity which constitutes the phenomena of phenomenology, a unity finally equivalent to the meaning given back to myself.

Let us pursue one example of such an approach. For an existentialist the meaning of a text is the meaning I, in my sovereign freedom, choose to give it. Just as, for example, Jean Genet turned his criminal status into a form of sainthood, so I choose the meaning of a text and am responsible for it. For the phenomenologist, at least those in the tradition of Merleau-Ponty, the meaning of the text is a product of an embodied and concrete here-and-now, and one stripped of the taken-for-granted meanings of the text. To be more specific, the meaning of, let us say, a chapter in *The Scarlet Letter* is my experience of it: the clock ticking, a sign carrying the memory of childhood evoked by a sentence about Hester Prynne, a yawn, a tension inscribed at the thought of a quiz, a sadness over the plight of Pearl and my own guilt over my own child, the turned head recalling the chores yet to be done, and the narrative sense unfolding, which evokes the public world, the community of readers. The text and the reader become one inextricable gestalt in which either text or reader may be temporarily foregrounded. From this gestalt meaning emerges, and it is this meaning that phenomenology attempts to describe, and it is this meaning that constitutes the essence of an object no longer severed from a subject.

Between subject and object. We can see in phenomenology's attempt to bridge the split between subject and object a response to the dilemma unsolved by existentialism and implicit in humanism—the dilemma of the increasing humanizing of the world. As the world becomes more human, more a creation of human subjectivity, any objective way of confirming or affirming this subjectivity disappears. The subject becomes increasingly alone, angst-ridden in its insubstantiality. Although Sartre tried to give this sovereign subjectivity a heroic glow, the anguish, despair, and forlornness he describes in "Existentialism and Humanism" are states resulting from the subjectivizing or humanizing of the world. Phenomenology's attempt to solve the dilemma by locating meaning in *neither* the subject *nor* the object but in between the two, in a somatized or embodied gestalt, seemed to halt the shrinking of the world into solipsism and the expansion of the subject into idealism.

However, phenomenology revealed two vulnerabilities we can glimpse in the following passage quoted from Merleau-Ponty's *Phenomenology of Perception*:

> [If] the person who experiences something knows at the time what he is experiencing . . . then the madman, the dreamer or the subject of perception must be taken at their word and we need merely confirm that their language in fact expresses what they are experiencing. (quoted in Descombes, 1980, p. 79)

The first vulnerability is contained in the notion of experience. If, as phenomenology posits, being and meaning are neither in consciousness nor in the thing itself, neither in the subject nor in the object but in the body/subject's lived experience, then the following question arises: is the object of reality different for each perceiver, as phenomenology's insistence on particularity would suggest? Or, is there a reality which exists in-itself, outside of perception or the body/subject's lived experience? If the former is true, then phenomenology is reduced to a kind of somatized idealism. If the latter is true, then phenomenology is still left with the subject-object dualism it sought to bridge. The second vulnerability is revealed in the word "merely" in the Merleau-Ponty passage, for the implicit assumption here is that language is a transparent medium which simply presents experience. These vulnerabilities would be explored by structuralism and poststructuralism.

Structuralism as response to phenomenology. In many respects structuralism was a response to the implicit idealism of phenomenology. Certainly, as Descombes points out (1980, p. 71), phenomenology represented a reformed idealism since it suggested an embodied idealism, and thus allowed for the incompleteness, partiality, and contingency of objects/perceptions/perceives. Nevertheless, it was an idealism, and to this structuralism responded.

In some of Merleau-Ponty's writing one can hear strains of structuralism. For example, he wrote: "The presence of structure outside us in natural and social systems, and within us as symbolic formation points to a way beyond the subject-object correlation which has dominated philosophy from Descartes to Hegel" (quoted in Descombes, 1980, p. 73). Such a comment implies that the ways the perceiving subject organizes perceptions and meanings are not a result of a unique situation arising in the here and now. Rather, the organization of perception and meaning are linked to certain structures shared by a community or social system and internal to human perception. Since the meaning of the object would be, in part, determined by these, the phenomenon's reality or essence would *not* be *only* what appeared to me in my particular situation. Reality would also be a result of structures out there, exterior to me, or invariant structures internal to me. In either case, the particularity of my experience would be negated or at the very least compromised, and perceiving or embodied consciousness would be displaced by impersonal structures. These are the structures structuralism sought to define, and in so doing it challenged the humanism of both existentialism and phenomenology.

Invariant structures. If for existentialists meaning is chosen freely by a sovereign subject's consciousness and for phenomenologists meaning is a result of the body/subject's world of the "I perceive," for structuralists meaning resides in those invariant structures, systems, and sets of relations that purportedly constitute objects or the content of the structured relations. The preeminence given to the subject within humanism is rejected for the preeminence of structures, systems, and sets of relations which "are not structures of some ineffable reality which lies behind them and from which they are separable" (Caws, 1988, p. 28). Structures, themselves, constitute reality. Jean Hyppolite described the area as a "transcendental field without subjects" (quoted in Descombes,1980, p. 77). For example, the existentialists' chosen meaning for a text or the meaning that emerges from the phenomenologists' reading of a text is replaced by a meaning which is made possible by the invariant structures within the text [see Frye, 1957] or the cognitive structures of the reader [see Piaget, 1975]. The subject of meaning is replaced by the "system."

Three kinds of structuralism. Descombes distinguishes among three kinds of structuralism. The first is a method of structural analysis which antedates the movement called structuralism and which can be found in any number of Western discourses (for instance, those of Kant, Marx, and Freud) which claim to discover and explain invariant structures in and constitutive of the human psyche, nature, society, indeed, of reality itself. This form of structuralism assumes language to be a transparent medium which simply reveals or mirrors the structures found "out there" or "in the mind." The second kind of structuralism, suggests Descombes, is indebted to Saussurean linguistics, and at times merges with semiology (the theory of the sign). It is this structuralism which, according to Descombes:

demonstrates that a certain cultural content (kinship system, or myth) is a "model" of that structure, or, as it is also known, a "representation" of it. . . . This content is isomorphic to a number of other contents "so that" structure is precisely that which holds good in an isomorphism between two sets of contents. (p. 86)

In other words, the content of stories from different cultures or different communities may differ, but the structure—such as "the heroic quest"—is invariant and gives meaning to what otherwise would be chaotic, dispersed, and meaningless events. The third kind of structuralism Descombes distinguishes as a philosophical orientation not only critiqued phenomenology, as the second structuralism did, but also semiology. Rarely does it attend to "structures." It is this third form of structuralism which can be regarded as sliding into poststructuralism. For example, the deconstructive loosening of the signifier from the signified, or the Foucauldian analysis of the construction of figures, such as the adolescent, implicitly challenge structuralism and semiotics.

In general, however, structuralism attempts to stop the hemorrhaging of subjectivity into the world. Not only would reality and meaning be found in and established by invariant structures, but the subject itself, and human consciousness generally, would be construed as products of invariant structures. What distinguishes the structuralist move (here we refer to Descombes' second structuralism, from those theories which posit, for instance, a "collective unconscious," or Kantian categories of thought, or classical Marxist structures, or classical behavioral paradigms or cognitive stages—all of which deny or limit subjectivity) is not only the more technical definition of structure. Important here is that structuralism turns to language as the medium through which structures reveal themselves. Language becomes for structuralism the field of investigation.

Saussure. What allows this turn to language is the linguistic theory of Ferdinand de Saussure (1959). Certainly Saussure's influence on structuralism was broad. For our purposes, four central concepts merit attention for their role in the evolution of structuralism and poststructuralism. First, Saussure believed language should be studied synchronically, not diachronically. That is, it should be approached not in terms of its history but in terms of its extant structures. Second, Saussure argued that languages are systems of signs which consist of a signifier and a signified. The signifier is the sound or spoken word and secondarily its written representation. The signified is the concept which the signifier signifies. Note that the signified is not an object or external referent. The relationship between the signifier and signified is culturally determined, but it is also arbitrary. Third, Saussure suggested that what makes it possible for a relatively small number of "linguistic elements to signify a vast repertoire of negotiable meanings" (Norris, 1982, p. 25) is difference. The user and receiver of the sign have the capacity to distinguish one signifier from another. Meaning is generated not by a correspondence between words and things or an intrinsic or necessary correspondence between signifier and signified, but by the sign's and the signifier's relationships to and difference from other signs and signifiers (Caws, 1988). As Saussure explained: "Signs define one another neutrally by means of their differences from one another. . . . 'The' and 'this' are meaningful only in so far as they are implicitly distinct from 'a' and 'that'" (1959, p. 59). Often, the relationships Saussure found in language were dualisms or binary opposites (such as male/female, up/down, light/dark, absence/presence), and these were construed as foundational structures that helped determine or constitute difference and thus meaning.

Langue and parole. Saussure distinguished between what he called "langue," that is language, and what he termed "parole," that is speech. "Langue" refers to the total collectivity of signs that make up any natural language, for example, French or English. This totality makes communication possible, yet cannot be possessed by any one individual. Philip Thody (1977) has described "langue" as "a corporate and virtually anonymous treasure which enables communication to take place. It can never have more than a potential existence in any actual speaker" (p. ix). "Parole" is the concrete embodiment of "langue," its empirical reality. Peter Caws (1988) suggested that "if it were not for language, parole would be a series of meaningless noises; if it were not for parole, language would be a series of mute abstractions" (p. 67). Therefore, what the individual says derives its significance from "langue" because it is not only constrained by the codes, rules, sets of relations, and structures within "langue," but also it derives its meaning from them. And so Saussure could say:

> The signifier, though to all appearance freely chosen with respect to the idea that it represents, is fixed, not free with respect to the linguistic community that uses it. The masses have no voice in the matter, and the signifier chosen by language could be replaced by no other. This fact, which seems to embody a contradiction, might be called colloquially "the stacked deck." We say . . . "choose!" but we add, "it must be this sign and no other." (Saussure, 1959, p. 71)

Consequences of Saussurean theory for structuralism. There were several consequences of the Saussurean linguistic theory for structuralism. Language became a field of study, semiotic structures or systems of signs became gateways to meaning, which itself became defined by difference and discoverable structures, and finally, traditional ways of articulating knowledge, history, and culture were exploded to reveal deep structures which called into question the taken for granted distinctions between, for instance, fact or fiction, rationality and irrationality, primitive and civilized, myth and reason. Several scholars have noted the structural equation of reality and language. Terry Eagleton writes that within structuralism "reality is not reflected by language but produced by it" (1983, p. 108). Citing Henri Lefebvre, Eve Tavor Bannet asserts that the central tenet of structuralism is that language "as a system defines society as a system and also the forms of thought it brings into accord, because it engenders mental structures and social structures" (1989, p. 3). Perhaps those working within a structuralist framework expressed this point best. Lacan said that the unconscious was structured like a language. He stated also that "it is the world of words which creates the world of things . . . the things originally confused in the *hic et nunc* (i.e. here and now) of the all-in-the-process-of-becoming" (Lacan, 1977, p. 39). Or, hear the early Foucault discuss knowledge: "Knowledge is that of which one can speak in a discursive practice and which is specified by that fact" (Foucault, 1972, pp. 182-183).

To understand the structuralist equation of language and reality more fully let us recall a passage from Aldous Huxley (1970):

> Every individual is at once the beneficiary and the victim of the linguistic tradition into which he has been born. The beneficiary in as much as language gives access to the accumulated records of other people's experience, the victim in so far as it confirms him in the belief that reduced awareness is the only awareness and as it bedevils his sense of reality so that he is all too apt to take his concepts for data, his words for actual things. . . . Most people, most of the time, know only [that awareness which] is consecrated as genuinely real by the local language. (p. 74)

A world woven by language. As it merges with semiology, structuralism takes as its field the world "consecrated as genuinely real" by language and attempts to describe how that world has been and is woven by language. What is important to understand is that this semiotic structuralism, after equating reality, thought, and the world with language, investigates this new and all encompassing territory in order to discover the structures or systems revealed in language and that are taken as constituting reality. The subject, object, and meaning are construed as emerging from and created by structures and systems revealed in language which is taken finally as a coded system of signs, the decoding of which will only reveal the structures that make the code possible. Since the construction of the world, reality, meaning, and the subject (i.e., individual consciousness) occurs within the codes of language, within the systems revealed by language, the speaking subject is displaced by a subject spoken by language. Codes, structures, and systems replace the sovereign consciousness, the body/subject of humanism.

No preconceptual experience. Now we can return to the second vulnerability of phenomenology. For phenomenology, language is expressive. The lived experience of the body subject, the "things themselves," are expressed in language. But this implies that words are merely the wings of our intentions, that the reality anterior to or behind or underneath language is already not only capturable in language but necessarily fitted for it. The subject awaits the "right words" to convey his experience. For structuralists, however, the Saussurean lesson was that language is already systematized, coded, and structured. The meaning that phenomenology asserts originates from the subject is already conditioned, constrained, delimited, and, ultimately, constructed. There is no "preconceptual" experience.

The meaning we ascribe to experience emerges in and is formed by language. There is always that small elision between the sensation, the sense we have, and the words or signs which give it shape or meaning. We push back the darkness or gap between the unutterable "nothingness" of sensation with the being of language. But language is a system, and so the invariant structures revealed by it predetermine the meaning that emerges. Phenomenology is accused by structuralism not only of idealism but also of naiveté for not taking into account the "prison house" of language.

The structuralists' task was to articulate the invariant structures revealed in language and the subject. Such a task was comparativist in nature and challenged the humanist and Enlightenment projects which saw history as progress and placed "man" at the center of creation and privileged rational thought and Western culture over myth and so-called primitive cultures. As we noted, structuralists viewed history synchronically or ahistorically. Norris (1982) explained:

> History was to be seen as a series of shifting configurative patterns, the "meaning" of which becomes increasingly opaque with time. . . . Historical understanding is only possible in so far as it adopts a synchronic standpoint, "classes of dates each furnishing an autonomous systems of reference." (p. 78)

Lacan and the de-centered subject. We have seen how structuralism de-centered the subject, sovereign consciousness, and "man" as the origin of meaning. Lacan continued this decentering by construing the unconscious and the conscious mind as products of language, of the symbolic. He argued that desire, and subjectivity generally, were only excesses squeezed out by the rigid constraints of language. We may say that the child has a pervasive but unutterable need for maternal love, for nurturance, for a sense of oceanic connectedness. This "need" can only be expressed in language as a demand which can never capture the felt reality of the need. When the demand colonizes, stakes out, and articulates the need, an "excess" is produced which Lacan labels as "desire." In its very being the subject is displaced and alienated within language.

Not only is the subject overthrown by structuralism, but taken-for-granted distinctions—such as fact/fiction, rational/mythic—are also challenged. Levi-Strauss and Michel Serres would articulate deeper structures beneath these dualisms which would subvert them. For instance, Serres revealed the steam-driven engine as the structuring metaphor in a variety of nineteenth-century discourses, ranging from Freud and Nietzsche to Marx and Zola. To discover inter-expressive structures in a variety of texts normally consigned to separate categories is to annul the difference between, in this case, fictional and non-fictional discourses (Descombes, 1980). By revealing the isomorphic structures of a variety of sign systems once grouped into myth and reason, structuralism argued that the real was not rational, that the real was both rational and mythic and the taken-for-granted distinctions between the two were themselves part of a system of myths. Reduced to sign systems, "the opposition between truth and error, or alternately between science and fable, which is at the root of positivism," were under the systematizing work of structuralists, made to appear "crude and "superficial" (Descombes, 1980, p. 91).

Poststructuralism attacks structuralism. The attack on the subject, on humanism, and on the Enlightenment project constituted the more radical aspects of structuralism, and this would be incorporated in poststructuralism. There were, however, more conservative aspects of structuralism and these would be attacked by poststructuralists who came to accuse structuralism of linguistic idealism, ahistoricism, and most importantly, a misunderstanding of language. If, as structuralism maintained, underlying structures constituted reality and meaning, then what was the relationship between the human mind and systems of meaning? Structuralism suggested that the human mind itself was structured in a way that corresponded to the structures "out there." Descombes noted:

> In order to account for [the] unity of all culture which would emerge at the end of structural analysis, we would have to postulate, Levi-Strauss tells us, an "unconscious activity of the human mind," one which would consist in the application of the structures to the ever-diverse contents supplied by human experience. (Descombes, 1980, p. 102)

Poststructuralists accused structuralism of neo-Kantianism, only a partial break with humanism, since it reproduced the humanist notion of an unchanging human nature.

Since structuralism chose to examine systems synchronically, it was attacked for being ahistorical. Poststructuralists, particularly Michel Foucault (1970, 1972, 1973, 1978, 1979, 1980, 1986a, 1986b), argued that structuralism's attempt to "establish a system of homogeneous relations: a network of causality that makes it possible to derive each of them, relations of analogy that show how they symbolize one another, or how they all express one and the same central [structure]" (pp. 9-10) did not take into account the sociopolitical construction of such systems. More significantly, the fact was ignored in structuralism that the underlying systems which structuralism articulated were themselves caught up in language. This blindness to its own involvement in language constituted the most important accusation poststructuralists leveled against structuralism. Poststructuralists charged structuralism with failing to take seriously the idea that nothing lies underneath language. According to poststructuralists, the systems and structures structuralism worked to reveal are themselves caught up in language and exist on the flat surface of language along with all else, and beneath which there is—well, one cannot say, except in language. The concept that was the signified in Saussurean linguistics is itself articulated in language and does not deserve any more of a privileged or foundational status than do structures or systems. Thus, for poststructuralists, the signifier is freed from the signified to become a free-floating signifier which can be defined only by other signifiers. "Concept," "structure," "system" become simply other signifiers deriving their meaning from yet other signifiers. Wrenched free from the ground or foundation of the signified, the signifier circulates and the ground or foundation disappears. One result is that words such as "meaning", "subject," "object," "true," and so on lost their tacitly assumed value and substance, and remained only as arbitrary valorizing terms to organize and legitimate (or delegitimate) signifying chains or discourses.

Discourse. Next we focus on the term "discourse," an important term in poststructuralism and in the organization of this textbook. As you note from the table of contents and chapter 1, we have organized curriculum scholarship into discourses. How did this term emerge in poststructuralism? At the most general level, discourse, according to Foucault, is a discursive practice which itself forms the objects of which it speaks. It consists of words spoken or written which group themselves according to certain rules established with the discourse, and certain conditions which make their existence possible. For Foucault, discourse is an anonymous field in that its origin or locus of formation is neither a sovereign nor a collective consciousness. It exists at the level of "it is said." It indicates certain circumscribed positions from which, he writes, "one may speak that which is already caught up in the play of exteriority" (Foucault, 1972, p. 122). Because discourses can cut across normally accepted unities such as the academic disciplines or books, one can speak, for instance, of a psychological discourse, a medical discourse, a curriculum discourse, or one can speak of a discourse on madness or sexuality. Not only does discourse form the objects of which it speaks, it also disperses the subject of sovereign consciousness into various subject positions. The assumed unity of the Self or the "I" of consciousness becomes a position attached to and retrospectively formed by the discourse surrounding it.

If this delimitation of language into discourses sounds like structuralism, it is not surprising. Foucault's early work and indeed much of poststructuralism is tied to the movement it followed. The difference, however, between the structuralists' set of relations, structures or systems, and the theory of discourse, is that the former are seen as foundational and invariant, while the latter proposes that discourse is historically and socially contingent, and that the analysis of discourse must remain at the level of the signifier. To analyze a discourse is not to say what it means but to investigate how it works, what conditions make it possible, and how it intersects with non-discursive practices.

The "adolescent." To give one example, during the late nineteenth and early twentieth century certain psychological, juridical, and medical discourses intersected under particular social conditions resulting in a discourse in which emerged the full-blown figure of the adolescent, a figure without existence prior to these discursive and non-discursive operations. This discourse produced the object or figure about which it spoke and continued to speak with increasingly prolixity. Thus an analysis of the discourse on adolescence would proceed at the level of reconstituting the discourses which constructed the concept of "adolescent" and investigate their formation. An example from curriculum would be the social construction of the "gifted," a category created by tests and measurements as, in part, a means of racial segregation, especially in the South.

From a "depth" to "surface" model. In focusing on discourse or the signifier, now uncoupled from the signified, poststructuralists moved from a depth model of understanding phenomena to a surface model or horizontal plane. Rather than attending to an underlying meaning or system, poststructuralists investigated how discursive formations formed, and how they form the very figures that emerge within them. For example, the meaning of "play" cannot be discovered through a phenomenological reduction, nor can it be found in a transcultural system whose invariant structure is based on the binary opposition "play" and "work." Rather, "play" is constructed by a variety of discursive formations and practices that are inserted into non-discursive practices. The meaning of "play," whether located in the body/subject or in a particular system, loses its position as something real and anterior to discourse; it is replaced by a surface or horizontal analysis of how it is discursively formed under particular conditions.

Power. There are multiple consequences of the move to poststructural analysis, but the one that is perhaps the most important concerns the notion of power. Traditionally power has been equated with knowledge. "Knowledge is power," Bacon asserted. But this equation implied that knowledge requires an undistorted view of how reality is. Knowledge is construed as a representation of the real, of reality as it "really" is. For poststructuralists, discourse, which includes knowledge, does not *represent* reality. For poststructuralists, discourse *constructs* reality. The question is then shifted from who has knowledge/power to how, and under what conditions, particular discourses come to shape reality. The concept of "homosexuality" is pertinent here. Foucault argued that "homosexuality" and the figure of the "homosexual" were discursively produced at the intersection of various discourses, ranging from the medical to the juridical. Consequently, the concept of the "homosexual" and the related notion of the "heterosexual," became real. Rather than reflecting a pre-existing reality—after all, the full range of sexual expression has been available to each individual since the beginning of recorded history—the concept created the reality.

No origins, no foundations, no totalizing concepts. If power, as poststructuralists suggested, was a function of discourse, then the very ability to define or unify or totalize phenomena was an act of power, as was any appeal to transcendental signifiers, metanarratives, foundations, or origins. To illustrate, Foucault attacked historical notions such as "the spirit of the age" or the "face of an era" as providing any basis for periodizing history. Even more broadly, Foucault attacked the very concept of "sexuality" as a transhistorical, transcultural category. Kristeva (1980) challenged Lacan's notion of the phallus as a transcendental signifier whose absence or presence solidified a system of sexual differentiation. Deleuze's attack on totalities and metanarratives is suggested by his comment that:

> We believe only in totalities that are peripheral. And if we discover such a totality alongside various separate parts, it is a whole of these particular parts but does not totalize them; it is a unity of these particular parts but does not unify them; rather, it is added to them as a new part, fabricated separately. (Deleuze & Guattari, 1977, p. 42)

In this passage we see clearly the poststructural move to treat reality as constructed and comprised by discourse that exists on a horizontal plane on a depthless surface.

What is the color of black? As a final example, issues of race are often taken—especially by racists—as fixed, as based on "biology" or "genetics." The assumption is often that "black" or "white" refer to antecedent conditions, usually biological, that they express essential qualities, that they derive their meaning from an invariant transhistorical system which is glued together by the binary opposition black/white. Poststructuralists insist that the figures of "black" or "white" are discursively formed. They take seriously Jean Genet's response to an actor who asked him to write a play for an all-black cast. Genet replied: "What exactly is a black? First of all, what is his color?" (Genet, 1978, p. 1). Poststructuralism would seem to take this comment as its beginning for understanding how "blackness" is constructed in particular discourses and how those discourses are selected, organized, and inscribed in a particular society. This view has influenced the discourse on curriculum and race, as we saw in chapter 6.

Any appeal, then, to unities, totalities, origins, metanarratives, and first principles is regarded by poststructuralism as a discursive strategy used to legitimate and perhaps disguise the exercise of power. At its most general level, poststructuralism attacks not only essentialism, universalism, transcendentalism, and humanism, but the very idea of a Western logos as well. It mounts this attack at the level of discourse where it works to reveal the oppression of specific discursive practices, such as discourses on sexuality and race. Dispersion and multiplicity replace unity and totality. Or, to put the matter another way, the assumed truth of constructions is deconstructed. One does not ask, for instance, what is the Good, the True, the Beautiful, or, what is "woman," the "self," or what is a "homosexual?" Instead one investigates the various discourses which created each of these by articulating them as somehow essential and universal truths. We can see emerging in this attack an "enemy" whose identity becomes explicit as we turn to the work of deconstruction, associated with the name of Jacques Derrida. That "enemy" is Western thought itself, and the primacy given to "reason" as a way of grasping reality and truth.

If, as Levinas wrote, "The idea of truth as a grasp on things must necessarily have a non-metaphorical sense somewhere" (quoted in Young, 1990, p. 13), then poststructuralism can be regarded as an attempt to discursively map how this "somewhere," or to employ a term associated with poststructuralism, this "other," is constructed by the intersection of discursive and non-discursive practices, such as jails, schools, and hospitals. It will be left to Derrida and deconstruction the task of taking on directly that thought whose a priori is the truth of reason. Derrida challenges the Western logos and the privileged position philosophy has "claimed as the dispenser of reason" (Norris, 1982, p. 18). Indeed, Derrida challenges the privileged position of reason itself.

III
Deconstruction

Il n'y a pas de hors-texte.
(Jacques Derrida, 1967, p. 227)

Before we outline deconstruction, we will suggest how it differs from post-structuralism, under whose label it is often subsumed. In many respects deconstruction incorporates the insights of poststructuralism. In its equation of reality with language, in its attack on origins, totalities, universals, and metanarratives, in its claims about the ways power functions, and in its claims that structures—so central to structuralism—are never closed systems, deconstruction is an instance of poststructuralism. Where deconstruction may be regarded as differing from poststructuralism is that it radicalizes certain post-structural insights and incorporates certain phenomenological ones.

Interpretations of interpretations. Perhaps more than anyone, Jacques Derrida has worked to think through the uncoupling of the signifier from the signified (Norris, 1982). For poststructuralists such as Foucault this uncoupling resulted in the freeing of discursive phenomena which could then be freshly analyzed in terms of those discourses which had formed them. But in mapping these discourses poststructuralists had to delimit the discursive territories appearing as that map and then to interpret them. As Foucault himself said, there are only interpretations, and interpretations of interpretations. To interpret, however, is to make meaning, to make sense of something. To describe the discourse on the "adolescent" must require something other than reproducing all the words of that time. It must involve selecting and systematizing, based on a priori assumptions that discursive structures are immanent within language itself, a move representing a turn back to structuralism, or that they emerged for the poststructuralist in the experience of language, which would represent a move back to phenomenology. Neither of these moves could be accommodated by a poststructuralism which saw itself as breaking with both structuralism and phenomenology.

"There is no outside text." It is at this point that Derrida's deconstruction enters. If indeed the signifier is uncoupled from the signified and the former is allowed to move freely while the latter becomes only another signifier, any move to draw a boundary around a group of signifiers, any move to map a discursive territory is an arbitrary act of power. It is an unacknowledged one-

upmanship carried out with the intent of subverting hierarchies. Although he uses the term "discourse," Derrida moves the focus to "text" at the very moment he states "Il n'y a pas de hors-texte" (1967, p. 227; quoted in Whitson, 1991c, p. 78) which, as Whitson points out, is accurately translated as "there is no outside text" (p. 78). Reality itself is text and constituted in intertextuality. There is only the free play of the signifier, a play called to a halt by any imposition of a period whose placement will constitute an act of power and meaning. Meaning then, if it is not to be continually deferred, is always a result of a "will to power" which cannot appeal to anything outside itself, not even reason.

As several scholars have noted (Descombes, 1980; Norris, 1982; Sarup, 1989), Derrida is playing a tricky game, for if there is nothing but the free play of the signifier, if meaning is always deferred except when power intercedes with its unacknowledged a priori, how do we ever emerge from the Heraclitean flux of language to make sense of the world? Before we see how Derrida responds to this question, it is necessary to recall that historically, in Derrida's view, this question has been answered by a recourse to reason, and it is reason itself—as it has been articulated by Western philosophy—that Derrida will try to subvert. We have seen that structuralism claimed reason was not synonymous with the real or the true, since, for instance, myths and dreams also reveal what is real and true. But structuralism's claim that beneath reason, myth, and dreams, lay discoverable structures did not overthrow the sovereign position of reason; it merely widened its purview. To challenge reason would appear to be an impossible task, since, as Derrida noted:

> it is only to itself that an appeal against it can be brought, only in itself that a protest against it can be made; on its own terrain, it leaves us no other recourse than to stratagem and strategy. . . . Only able, as soon as it appears, to penetrate at the interior of reason, the revolution against reason has only ever the limited scope of what is called—precisely in the language of the Ministry of the *Interior*—unrest. (quoted in Descombes,1980, p.138)

An attack from the inside. Derrida, then, chooses to attack reason from the inside, but to do this he must also speak the language of reason, while at the same time maintaining a certain distance from it. Derrida will continually point out, from within reason, its contradictions and blind spots, including the ways Western philosophy has reduced by fiat the multiplicity of meaning to "one" meaning, i.e., the "right" meaning (Descombes, 1980, p. 140). Furthermore, he will seek to show the fallacy in reason's assumption that its own a priori's are synonymous with being or reality. But to talk of fallacy—the false and the true—is to again appeal to reason. So, Derrida continually points out the difference between being and its representation in reason by recourse to the term *"différance"* which connotes both difference and to defer. He will, on the one hand, point out the difference between any reason or logic which pretends an identity between itself or its a prioris and truth, reality, and being, while, on the other hand, he will defer the meaning of these, so that he himself will not fall into the traps within which reason is caught. For instance, he will attack binary opposites for their hidden privileging of one term over the other, e.g. male and female are not symmetrical opposites.

To ravel and unravel. As Allan Megill (1985) has suggested, Derrida is like Homer's Penelope, who by day ravels her tapestry—Derrida speaks from within reason—and by night unravels it. Derrida's work demonstrates the "equivocity" and "heterologicity" of western reason. Ravelling and unravelling discourse, Derrida entangles and disentangles the central threads running through the tapestry of logocentric or Western thought. From the point of view of deconstruction, meaning, like a flat stone skipped across water, skims over the surface of language, leaving only traces and ripples. There is only the continual deferral of meaning which perhaps comes closest to being suggested in James Joyce's (1939) *Finnegan's Wake.* For Derrida, meaning and sense occur fleetingly, unless they are tyrannically imposed. As he has observed: "I am taking the risk of not meaning anything," which, to follow him, could mean that he means nothing or that he means some one thing. It is this problem that returns us to the question posed earlier: how, given the free play of the signifier, do we make sense or meaning?

First, we could simply say stop. We could simply claim that it will be the last words which will cement meaning. Such is the exercise of power. Poststructuralism maps this response and deconstruction subverts it. Second, we could surrender to a kind of infinite dispersion of meaning, never stopping but giving ourselves up to a kind of semiotic flow in which we become "nomads" carried along by flows of desire and intensities in a linguistic wilderness. Such is the answer suggested by Deleuze. Or third, we could answer with a kind of radicalized phenomenology, suggesting that the "being" and "meaning" phenomenology claims as anterior to language be replaced by language and evocation. The world I encounter is already a discursive text with no original meaning and only evokes a response which is a further articulation of it. For instance, to read a novel is not to establish its original meaning—this would be akin to the first response mentioned earlier —nor is it to drift through it in a semiological flow. Rather, it would be to articulate what the text evoked and when asked to state what that articulation meant, to state at each interrogation, "I meant exactly what I said." The world as textualized does not mean but evokes.

History. Deconstruction challenges meaning that operates in either a circular or linear fashion, resulting in some final meaning or truth. Such a view has radical implications for history, for historically speaking, history has been the agreed-upon meaning we give to past experience. Derrida comments: "The word 'history' has no doubt always been associated with a linear scheme of the unfolding of presence, where the line relates the final presence to the originary presence according to the straight line or the circle" (quoted in Megill, 1985, pp. 297-298). He continues: "History in all its forms, in so much as it aims to capture, to *re*flect, to *re*construct, to picture or express the real in the form of presence, to re-present, to make present again a present which is now present-in-the-past, has always been the principal support of metaphysics" (quoted by Carroll, 1978, p. 443).

History, then, is characterized as an impossible undertaking to capture an original past reality which cannot be captured. More importantly, history has suppressed difference. For Derrida, history will always be subject to difference in that it will always be different from what it seeks to express or represent, and its meaning will always be necessarily deferred. Such a challenge results not in negating history but in replacing the meaning of history with the history of meanings (Descombes, 1980; Young, 1990). The result is that we must now talk of histor*ies* rather than history.

There is much more to be said regarding deconstruction (for instance, its notions of the simulacrum and of writing), and poststructuralism (its articulation in the work of Kristeva and Deleuze, for example), but limitations of space require us to summarize the salient challenges these "movements" have posed to Western thought, including the challenges to curriculum theory which we will survey momentarily. It is difficult, perhaps impossible, after encountering poststructuralism and deconstruction, to take for granted the unity and autonomy of the self, of systems and structures, the phenomenological claims to present a prediscursive reality, the claims of humanism, the truth (Marxist or otherwise) of history, the traditional ways of conceiving power, the possibility of a final or true or original meaning, or finally any thought which is based on or posits universals, foundations, origins, absolutes or essences, or that does not take its own language into account. There are repudiations of poststructuralism (Brodribb, 1988, 1992), but the scope of its influence suggests that its consequence for curriculum theory is still in an early stage.

IV
Postmodernism

[As a kid] I imitated Humphrey Bogart's kiss, but I didn't feel it. Only later did I realize that perhaps Bogart didn't feel it either; he was merely kissing the way the director said he should. So there I was imitating a kiss that was never real.
(Jerry Mander, 1978, p. 236)

Within the last decade poststructuralism and deconstruction have come to be seen as part of a larger movement, parts of a new historical period termed postmodernism. Postmodernism articulates many of the ideas advanced by poststructuralism and deconstruction, including: the death of the subject, the repudiation of depth models of reality, metanarratives, and history itself, the illusion of the transparency of language, the impossibility of any final meaning, the movement of power as it represents and discourses on the objects it constructs, the failure of reason to understand the world, the de-centering of the Western logos and with it the "first world," the end of belief in progress, and the celebration of difference. [We should note here that there is also a "constructive postmodernism," associated with postmodern theologians such as David Ray Griffin (1988b, 1989, 1990; see chapter 12; see also Jencks, 1987, and Kung, 1979, 1981)]. These notions associated with poststructuralism and deconstruction come to intersect with certain social and cultural conditions and attitudes judged to be qualitatively different from modernism. They have come to comprise the postmodern period.

The postmodern period summarized. The conditions and attitudes which are characterized as postmodern may be summarized as follows: 1) television and the electronic media and the image industry (including advertising as well as film) solidified their dominance in representing the world and result in an increasing move from print to image culture; 2) there occurred an explosion in information and a concomitant rise of information technologies; 3) global or multinational capitalism moved unopposed to a preeminent position as the world economy; 4) nature appears dead in the complete humanization of the world; 5) the state and the economy grow more fully integrated; 6) terms such as "ironical," "cynical," "fragmented," even "schizophrenic" come to describe the psychosocial tone of the period; 7) the introduction of new technologies support poststructural and deconstructed notions of the subject, time, and history; and 8) concepts of high culture and low culture conflate and hierarchies of aesthetic taste are debunked. If we review these conditions associated with postmodernism, we can say that it is characterized by the "end of." Indeed, Fredric Jameson says as much when he writes:

> These last few years have been marked by an inverted millenarianism, in which premonitions of the future, catastrophic or redemptive, have been replaced by the sense of the end of this or that. . . . Taken together, all of these perhaps constitute what is increasingly called postmodernism. (quoted in Herron, 1987/88, p. 61)

The end of history, meaning, and the subject come to characterize a radical break with ways of knowing and being which constituted modernism, now itself seen as at an end. Poststructuralism and deconstruction claim to represent an end to the Enlightenment project, but how are these theoretical movements expressions of the experience that we are living through at this particular postmodern moment? With what does postmodernism replace modernism?

There is only now. To answer these questions let us begin with a slogan graffitied over walls in New York's East Village in 1980. It read: "Everything that has ever happened is happening now!" At first glance, such a statement appears ludicrous. We know that what happened yesterday or one hundred years ago is not happening now. But if we think poststructurally, we can read in such a statement the suggestion of a postmodern sensibility, for what we know of the past can only be that which exists now and what we know can only be known through current representations. If everything we "know" about the American Civil War, for example, consists of all we can say about it after all we have read, heard, or seen about it, then what we know is already caught up in the problems of language and representation which poststructuralism and deconstruction have demonstrated are incapable of expressing "the real." To put a slight spin on Derrida's comment: history becomes the re-presentation of the present disguised as the past. There is only the now, a flattened present in which or on which circulate a variety of versions of itself. [For a related discussion on eschatology, see chapter 12].

In such a present we lose our moorings, lose a sense of what has happened or is happening. No one seems capable of grasping what "is really going on," in part because there are so many versions of what is indeed happening, in part because the present seems too complex, and in part because any attempt at metanarrative or totalizing description is suspect. Our postmodern inability to grasp an ultimate truth may not be a great loss. As Lyotard (1989) observed:

> The nineteenth and twentieth centuries have given us as much terror as we can take. We have paid a high enough price for the nostalgia of the whole and the one, for the reconciliation of the concept and the sensible, of the transparent and the communicable experience. . . . Let us wage war on totality. (pp. 81-82)

An imagistic world overloaded with information. One worry associated with the postmodern condition is that we have more information about everything than ever before. Certainly those who work in schools and universities appreciate the intensifying pressure to read and know more and more. However, this sense is not limited to, although it may be more intense in, schools and universities. This explosion in information itself functions to undermine our sense of control, of knowing where we are in time. First, there is so much information that it becomes impossible to "stay on top of it all," but perhaps more importantly, information itself increasingly replaces any traditional understandings of it. As several observers have noted (Postman, 1985; Mander, 1974; Jameson, 1991; Hertzgaard, 1989), television and newspapers increasingly present information but do not appear to make sense of it, or even to discriminate between bits of information (Lasch, 1984). The evening newscast moves instantly from statements and images of war, to a local murder, to the love life of a celebrity, to a stock market downturn, to a commercial for diapers, to a coming attraction for its own next piece of information. Such a stream of images and information—not logically sequenced or summarized or interpreted—resembles the freely moving, free floating signifier Derrida describes.

Not only history but the representation of the present itself is said to become meaning-less. This "crisis" of representation and history is exacerbated by the loss of faith in public leaders to articulate believable versions of what is happening. As Hertzgaard (1989) put it, Ronald Reagan's success was in large part attributable to his ability to articulate a soothing and understandable story about the unfolding of world events, although Hertzgaard goes on to show that his story was a fantasy constructed by the collusion of the press and by Reagan's staff. But is a story possible that is not fictional? The postmodern answer suggests there is an increasing awareness that there are only fantasies, fictions, versions of reality which claim to represent nothing but themselves.

Pastiche. So the present becomes an eternal present, but itself seems incapable of representing itself to itself, except in terms of the "imitation of dead styles" (Sarup, 1989, p. 133), what Jameson describes by using the terms "pastiche" and "simulacrum." Jameson defines "pastiche" as being like parody, only a parody that lacks any antecedent motive for satire. He writes that pastiche is:

> the imitation of a peculiar or unique, idiosyncratic style, the wearing of a linguistic mask, speech in a dead language. But it is a neutral practice of such mimicry, without any of parody's ulterior motives, amputated of the satiric impulse, devoid of laughter and of any conviction that alongside the abnormal tongue you have momentarily borrowed, some healthy linguistic normality still exists. Pastiche is blank parody. (Jameson, 1991, p. 17)

Several examples of pastiche may help clarify the idea. First is the dominance of a retro-fashion movement in which styles themselves are based on imitations of previous styles, styles such that in 1992 platform shoes herald the return of the 1970s look, which was billed as a return of the 1940s look. Or think of the nostalgia film or the return of the 1960s fashion stripped of any statement that was made by the original fashion. To take another example, the skits on "Saturday Night Live" which present television episodes emptied of the meaning the initial episodes may have had and bereft of any critique of the form itself, so that only an empty form, now decontextualized, is represented.

The simulacrum is "the identical copy for which no original ever existed," which exists in a culture where "image has become the final form of commodity reification" (Jameson, 1991, p.18). We can read in this comment the poststructural and deconstructionist repudiation of any signified behind or beneath the signifier translated into cultural description. Substituted for the now discredited attempt to represent "reality" is the postmodern representation of only other representations for which no anterior reality exists. Thus we see in the postmodern era a proliferation of theme parks which reconstruct, for instance, colonial villages, or Disney versions of older historical and architectural styles, or we see the "historical" docu-drama which produces historical images for which no real signified exists except in the form of other signifiers or interpretations. Or, to take another example, in his seminal critique of television, Jerry Mander (1974) recalls: "[As a kid] I imitated Humphrey Bogart's kiss, but I didn't feel it. Only later did I realize that perhaps Bogart didn't feel it either; he was merely kissing the way the director said he should. So there I was imitating a kiss that was never real" (p. 236).

There are only copies. In Mander's comment we can discern the concepts of pastiche and simulacrum, concepts which inform Jean Baudrillard's (1988) sense that we live in a simulated or hyper-real space in which, for instance, a simulated environment becomes more real than a landscape, "a hallucinatory resemblance with itself" (quoted in Best & Kellner, 1991, p. 119). Joe Kincheloe (1993b) notes: "The world is not brought into our homes by television, as much as television brings its viewers to a quasi-fictional place—hyperreality" (p. 84), a place which "celebrates the look" (p. 88). Feuerbach could write in 1843 in *The Essence of Christianity* that "our era prefers the image to the thing, the copy to the original, the representation of reality, appearance to being" (quoted in Sontag, 1978, p. 153). Today the "thing", "original," and "reality" themselves no longer serve as foundations, against which their copies can be compared. Today there appear to be only copies, there is only, according to Guy DeBord (1990) "the society of the spectacle" in which history and events are created by the media and cease to exist the moment the media stops reporting them. Given an uninterrupted and meaningless flow of imagistic signifiers, we become dislocated, unable to find an orientation or at a loss, as Jameson puts it, to "position ourselves within this [postmodern space] and cognitively map it" (1987, p. 33). The proliferation of video players and video disk cassettes in classrooms may represent this interest in cognitively mapping images, and suggests the impossibility of such mapping.

The subject is lost. Not only are history and perspective lost under such conditions but the individual subject is also lost, not only to others but to him or herself. Modernist depth models for self-understanding, for example, the Freudian model of latent and manifest content or the existential model of authenticity and inauthenticity, are replaced by multiple selves, multiple intelligences, multiple surfaces, fragmentation, and a sensibility which describes itself in terms such as "cool," "hot," "down", "up," " high," "low," and "flat" but not in terms which recall a notion of the subject as having historical or emotional depth and substance. The assumed unity of the subject is replaced with multiple identities and differences, for example, a specific gender, race, class, sexual orientation, physical ability, with various lifestyles, and with a variety of consumer options. At the same time, we are bombarded by the media with various and ever-changing representations of "ourselves."

The loss of our foundations, of the concept of "original," of a fixed unchanging perspective, of a unified self, or in other terms, the loss of history, meaning, subjective experience, and collective identity is in the postmodern period compensated for, replaced with, and exacerbated by endless commodification and consumption. It is here that we can begin to see the relationships several writers (Baudrillard, 1988; Jameson, 1991; Lyotard, 1989; DeBord, 1990) have described as existing between postmodern culture and global or transnational capitalism which in large part depends on the increasing appetites of various publics for new commodities. In postmodernism these commodities emerge as images, information, and ultimately as culture itself, which as Jameson points out, no longer stands as a realm outside the economic system: "We must . . . affirm the dissolution of an autonomous sphere of culture throughout the social realm, to the point at which everything in our social life . . . can be said to be 'cultural'" (p. 48). History, meaning, indeed the world now appear as cultural commodities in the forms of information and images, in the consumption of which is said to now constitute our freedom, ideas we have seen in the works of Philip Wexler and Peter McLaren.

To emphasize this point let us first recall Jerry Mander's comments. He observed:

> The environment in which we live has been totally reconstructed solely by human intention and creation. . . . Living within artificial, reconstructed arbitrary environments that are strictly the products of human conception, we have no way to be sure that we know what is true and what is not. We have lost context and perspective. What we know is what other humans tell us. (1978, pp. 67-68)

Such a world suggests in one sense the triumph and completion of the modernist project which sought to establish complete human control over nature and reality. It is also a world constructed by our very representations of it. In a world that is constituted by simulacra the question is how these copies of the world without an original are presented to us. The descriptions of postmodernism claim that they are constituted by the media and technology, and then literally sold back to us. Thus the often-heard comment about some scenic beauty, "it is as pretty as a picture," implies that not only the signifier has become a signified but that we purchase an image of an experience which does not exist except as the picture, and which is given precedence over it. As Mark Poster commented: "'reality' is constituted in the 'unreal' dimension of the media. In this domain, there are no longer pure acts, only linguistically transformed representations, which are 'acts' themselves" (quoted in Lather, 1991a, p. 21). Under such conditions where "reality" is constructed, packaged, and sold, values such as truth, beauty, and goodness are replaced by marketability and efficiency. Within postmodernism it becomes impossible even to talk of the "market," for like "belief," such a totalizing concept has been discredited. The turn to marketability as a criterion for judging value is, as we have seen, part of what Jameson calls "the cultural logic of late capitalism" (1991a). The turn to efficiency as a legitimizing value is, at least according to Lyotard, a result of the postmodern collapse of science into technology.

Science: One narrative structure among many. For Lyotard, postmodernism is characterized by the discrediting of the great master narratives, but he goes on to derive implications from this insight for science. He begins by tentatively distinguishing between narrative knowledge and scientific knowledge. He goes on to suggest that it is to the latter that an appeal is made when people are confronted with the apparent death of truth and meaning. According to Lyotard, science is immune to poststructuralism and deconstruction, which apply only to narrative knowledge. Following philosophers of science such as Feyerabend, Lyotard claims that scientific knowledge cannot know itself to be true or claim for itself true knowledge outside of an appeal to narrative knowledge, which it considers no knowledge at all (Sarup, 1989, p. 122). Science finds its truth in the production of and legitimation by technology. For example, western science privileges itself over "witchcraft" by pointing to the technologies it has produced or by pointing to its own internal system for making truth claims. The latter is discredited once we ask poststructurally who determines the truth of such a system, now cast as one narrative structure among many. The former results in the rise of technological efficiency as one of the supreme values in a modern era.

Furthermore, Lyotard claims that in an age dominated by the computer, knowledge itself becomes that which can be stored as information. But, as Baudrillard points out: "Information dissolves meaning and the social into a sort of nebulous state leading not at all to a surfeit of innovation but to the very contrary, to total entropy" (Baudrillard, 1983, p. 100; quoted in Best & Kellner, 1981, p. 118). Information itself becomes a principal commodity in the postmodern period. It is sold back to the public in the now well known form of "info-tainment" or as "sound bites." Or it is stored in information or data banks access to which is limited to the rich and powerful (Lyotard,1989). In an information society, as Jameson reminds us, a premium is placed on briefing and instant recognition, so that efficiency and speed combine to strip away meaning and reflection (Jameson, 1991, p. 146). We can see in this proliferation of technologies, information, and images not only the increased commodification of the world but also the replacement of values such as the good, the true, and the meaningful with criteria of marketability and efficiency.

Interesting or boring? In the postmodern moment traditional notions of beauty or aesthetics have also been discredited and exploded, not only by poststructuralism and deconstruction, but also by the enormous expansion of "mass culture" which now comes to include everything. Whereas in modernism, art may have been construed as a space from which one could critique the bourgeoisie or the institutionalization of art or as a compensation for the injuries of life under capitalism, in postmodernism art has emerged as a "grab bag or lumber room of disjointed subsystems and random raw materials and impulses of all kinds" (Jameson, 1991, p. 31). Art is now dispersed, to be rewrapped as simply another aspect of mass culture which can then be described. Replacing a discussion of the beautiful are aesthetic reactions such as "interesting" or "boring," the former suggesting the deconstructionist notion of an evocative text, the latter, suggesting a kind of avoidance behavior which can now be articulated.

Another way to think of postmodernism and the discourses which inform it is to recall Plato's simile of the cave found in *The Republic*. In a cavern deep beneath the surface of the earth sat prisoners, fixed by chains, who saw reflected on the cave walls shadows of wooden figures which in toto represented a reality which existed outside the cave, and which was only knowable by those lucky enough to escape the cave and who upon reaching daylight could see the True, the Good, and the Beautiful, and thereby became enlightened. Postmodernism suggests a slightly different version of the cave. Now there is no outside. We wander aimlessly within, disoriented, and dislocated, still taking the shadows of our own imitations as constituting history, meaning, and the subject. We gaze at the shadows and affirm our freedom and individuality by constantly consuming ourselves in newer and newer forms.

Conclusion. For some theorists postmodernism, poststructuralism, and deconstruction lead only to a surrender to the moment, a "free play" of desire, a celebration of the now (Baudrillard, 1988). For others they lead only to a terminal passivity (Habermas, 1981, 1990). For still others they open possibilities for criticizing the theories, programs, institutions, and practices that are held responsible for the brutalization of contemporary life. What all these critics share is the sense that modernism—with its investment in meta-narratives, science, and humanism—is at an end. The challenges posed by poststructuralism, deconstruction, and postmodernism have profoundly shaken the way we conceive of ourselves and the world.

We have provided this overview of poststructuralism, deconstruction, and postmodernism in the hope that you will be better prepared to engage those curricularists who work with such theories and descriptions. To understand curriculum as poststructuralist, deconstructed, and postmodern text is to respond to the challenges of poststructuralism, deconstruction, and post-modernism. Obviously, many of the ways curriculum has been understood—for instance, as phenomenological, autobiographical, political, gender, and racial text—have been called into question by the theories and description we have summarized here. Curriculum theorists have responded first by summarizing the implications of these movements for traditional curriculum concepts. Other theorists abandoned traditional logic, and have attempted to enter a poststructuralist space. In the next section, we review of the work of both.

V
Poststructuralism and Curriculum Theory

Teaching provides access to various forms of discourse . . . which enable individuals to define themselves in ways that defy the state's classification of them. From a Foucauldian vantage, such self-definition is tantamount to the exercise of freedom.
(Aimee Howley & Richard Hartnett, 1992, p. 281)

To live is to read texts, but to be alive is to write them. Reading is the process by which a reality is consumed; writing is the very production of that reality.
(Alan A. Block, 1988, p. 23)

Desire and Identity: Peter Taubman

The first curriculum theorist in North America to introduce poststructuralism to the curriculum field was Peter Taubman. Taubman's doctoral dissertation was entitled *Gender and Curriculum: Discourse and the Politics of Sexuality.*
The dissertation was completed in 1979 at the University of Rochester; it was
published in its entirety by *The Journal of Curriculum Theorizing* (1982). In this
work Taubman investigated not only the dominant discourses on gender and
sexuality—the discursive grid which formed the taken-for-granted figures of
"man," "woman," "heterosexual," "homosexual," and "lesbian," as well as
"sexuality" itself—but also those oppositional discourses or "sexual political"
discourses which opposed and sought to dismantle that grid. To carry out
such an investigation he relied extensively on the work of Michel Foucault.
Taubman's central thesis was that those oppositional discourses variously
grouped under the labels of "feminism" and "radical homosexual analysis"
were themselves inextricably linked to those same oppressive discursive
systems they sought to dismantle. He explained:

> The task is to analyze the way "sexuality" in its broadest and most specific
> senses has been produced and re-produced, divided up and re-divided,
> employed and de-ployed in both the movements to alter society and the
> individual and the movements to resist that alteration, in the analyses that
> explain phenomena, in terms of their "sexual" roots and those which neglect
> "sexuality". . . . The domain in which I wish to situate this investigation . . . is
> broadly speaking the domain of language. (Taubman, 1979, p. 40)

It is not surprising, then, that to conduct such analysis, Taubman turned
to the work of Michel Foucault. After outlining that work and in so doing
introducing Foucault's oeuvre to the curriculum field, Taubman mapped the
ways gender and sexuality had been historically constructed, focusing particularly on the ways nineteenth and twentieth-century psychoanalytic and medical discourses constituted the figures of "woman" and the "homosexual," and
the ways twentieth century sociology and psychology produced versions of
gender and sexuality, particularly in their notions of sex roles and
androgyny, that were oppressive, even dangerous. Up to this point,
Taubman's work represented an extension of Foucault's *History of Sexuality*
(volume 1), but in the second half of the dissertation he mapped the various
ways oppositional discourses reified and essentialized their own versions of
"man," "woman," "homosexual", "lesbian," and "sexuality," so that they
brought with them the very grids they sought to oppose. It is this mapping
which constitutes the originality of Taubman's research.

Taubman deconstructed the assumed unity of feminism, a deconstruction
that would be echoed in later work by poststructuralist feminist curriculum
theorists who would then speak of "feminisms" rather than feminism. Surveying the differences among various feminist discourses he concluded that
"theoretical consistency or continuity cannot be used . . . as a criterion for
establishing the unity of 'sexual politics'" (p. 169). He then deconstructed
any notion of original tradition in order to make suspect any unity assumed

in the terms "sexual politics," "feminism," or "radical homosexuality," and he suggested that such an assumed unity is itself dangerous, since it functioned to turn the "multiplicity and dispersion of the resistances and challenges to the original grid of sexuality in on itself, and works to colonize it by articulating what sexual politics is aside from these resistances and challenges" (p. 173).

Surveying the oppositional discourses, Taubman found in them reasons for both optimism and despair. On the one hand, he suggested, they have de-centered "man" and made him an "other." They have made speak the silent center of heterosexual maleness which has historically organized the "other" around itself. They have created a space which can be articulated without recourse to static and foundational categories, and they have re-articulated historically oppressed figures, so there is a continual opening for a positive construction of women, men, lesbians, homosexuals, and sexuality. On the other hand, Taubman worried, there are dangers inherent in anchoring any new discourse in reified or essentialist figures. If, he wrote:

> it is imperative that the principles of integrity, wisdom, justice, dependability and psychic power be re-animated, if it is important that new Selves be articulated, and if new subject positions are to be opened up ... then to link this morality, these principles, these Selves, these positions ... to "woman," to anchor them in "woman" is to replace one privileged center with another; it is to replace a destructive male/female duality with the other side, which becomes the only side, yet which bases that only side on a final difference. (1979, p. 186)

Following Foucault, Taubman argued that in the gay and homosexual liberation movements the very sexuality that is and the very "homosexual" who is liberated are already formed by the grid these movements seek to dismantle.

Strategic essentialism. Taubman did not deny the necessity of anchoring, at least provisionally, new discourses in re-articulated figures. He stated that "to sever the anchor points from the discursive field which stands in opposition to the traditional organization of sexuality would ... centrifugalize this field" (p. 206). In other words, the themes and practices of oppositional sexual discourses would be pulled back "into a variety of discourses that have traditionally assumed an adversary position ... within society but have not focused their critique on the organization of sexuality" (pp. 206-207). The paradox that arises because "the re-articulated figures of the 'lesbian,' 'homosexual,' and 'woman,' as well as the 'heterosexual' and 'man,' are integral to the dismantling of the dominant organization of sexuality and yet serve to maintain the outlines of that organization" (p. 208) would be rephrased in later debates conducted by feminist theorists over essentialism versus constructionism.

Taubman provided no answers to the paradox but he did suggest three strategies. The first he called poetical, consisting of a Derridean-Deleuzian deconstruction of totalities which foreshadowed the postmodern turn. Here sexuality emerges as "intensities, dispersed whisperings, connections, co-minglings, communions and juxtapositions of de-gendered bodies and pleasures" (p. 208). A second strategy consisted of a "temporary reclaiming of the figure 'woman,' 'lesbian,' and 'homosexual'" (p. 208). This prefigured, for example, Spivak's "strategic essentialism" (1989,1990). The last strategy, which Taubman termed the ethical, referred to a radical nominalism which consisted in the refusal to "impose totalities, a refusal to impose on the manifest an interpretation of its hidden 'truth'" (p. 208).

Taubman's scholarship constituted a poststructural analysis of gender at a time when education, and especially curriculum, was being critiqued extensively in terms of gender. Not only did it raise questions that would be addressed later by feminists working in the curriculum field, but indirectly, through its reliance on Foucault, it challenged the phenomenological, autobiographical, and neo-Marxist work which at that time dominated the Reconceptualization of the curriculum field.

Soon after completing this doctoral dissertation, Taubman left the curriculum field to study acting in New York City, but he returned in 1985, and since then has published four essays which continue to explore curriculum and gender from poststructuralist perspectives. In a 1986 review of Culley and Portuges' *Gendered Subjects: The Dynamics of Feminist Teaching*, he argued that a feminist pedagogy must resist essentialist and separatist arguments, and instead incorporate a gender analysis which was informed by poststructuralist insights (Taubman, 1986). The essay, however, which most clearly returned to a poststructuralist understanding of curriculum was "Achieving the Right Distance" (1990, reprinted, 1992).

The right distance. Employing Lacanian theory but also noting its structuralist assumptions, Taubman presented an analysis of the identity of a teacher. First, he sketched the distinctions Lacan made between the Real, the Imaginary, and the Symbolic. Oversimplified, the Real is the unutterable which presses forward within and without the subject. The Imaginary consists of the visual and acoustic images which form the ego and its objects, and the Symbolic is the discursive system which locks the ego and the world into place. For Lacan, the infant is a chaotic, fragmented, pulsating field which congeals and finds unity and ego in the gaze of the Other. This "mirror stage," as Lacan termed it, creates a self, or ego, which is at bottom alienated since it is captured and given form by another. With the introduction of the Symbolic, the subject is solidified as that ego, and gendered. The Real is squeezed into the Imaginary, and then further condensed in the Symbolic. The part of oneself that is not synonymous with either the Imaginary or the Symbolic is repressed and forms the unconscious, but it exists there as already structured, like a language. Mistakenly, we take the alienated ego for the subject, when in fact the real subject lies in the unconscious.

Taubman suggests that the identity of a teacher, like Lacan's ego, is initially formed in the gaze of someone else, and so informed by what being a teacher meant consciously and unconsciously to the person in whose gaze one becomes a teacher. This identity is then condensed in the Symbolic when one enters the field of teaching. Taubman explains:

[Teachers] come to be within a complex dynamic. Their initial sense of themselves as teachers, given to them by another, is already a fiction. . . . Embedded
in the assumed identity are often emotional sediment left by the relationships
with the original namer, associations with the term itself, and introjected ideals
of a teacher. (1990, p. 123)

This imaginary identity and its emotional make-up, according to Taubman,
is reformed by the intrusion of the Symbolic in the form of institutional practices and demands:

Thus we see the stereoscopic image of teachers sequestered in their rooms,
acting out the imaginary behind another image of teachers unable to articulate
their view in any meaningful way, behind finally a last image of teachers reshaping their own submerged practice in the language of information conveyance
or transmission—that is the public language of the school. (1990, p. 124)

Taubman pointed out that teachers often act out the Imaginary through
transference. Following Felman's (1982) application of Lacan to pedagogy, he
suggested that for new teachers the student often becomes the Other, or the
screen onto which are projected the unconscious emotions and images
whose origin is the initial relationship with the one in whose gaze they
became teachers. At times this transference opposes the Symbolic, as for
example when teachers wish to become friends with students. At other times,
it dovetails with the Symbolic, as for example when teachers wish to be the
Master. The Symbolic itself constructs the relationship between teacher and
student as one of distance and generally, according to Taubman, it is this
relationship which holds true in most classrooms.

Next, Taubman looked at the "desire" of the teacher in terms of Lacan's
analysis of desire, an analysis we described earlier. Taubman argued that the
need "to be loved by—to be like—to be one with the Other [in whose gaze we
just became teachers] and to be what the Other desires" (p. 126) may on the
one hand be congruent with but nevertheless alienated in the demand
expressed in the Symbolic realm of the school as "lesson plans, goals and
objectives" (p. 127). Further:

When subtracted from need, desire results which is displaced into a desire to
be the Master, to know the field, to have the answer. To compensate for the
unconscious and forever unsatisfied need, the student, knowledge and the privileged position as the one who knows are substituted. . . . The desire of the
Master then is for students who do not know, for more knowledge . . . and for
greater privilege. . . . The desire to be, to know, to have is an unending desire
that works in the direction of increasing distance between teacher and student.
(1990, p. 127)

If the beginning teacher or the teacher who renounces the figure of the
Master did not develop an identity in the gaze of the Other congruent with
being the Master, then the need may become a demand "expressed as caring,
helping or engaging students" (p. 127). The desire that results, according to
Taubman, "when the latter is subtracted from the former is displaced into

the desire to be the student, to know the student, to have the student" (1990, p. 127). Taubman suggested that the "right distance" between these two poles of being the Master or dissolving all distance between teacher and student can be found between Lacan's return to the unconscious to recuperate "full speech" and Plato's philosopher who after seeing the ideal forms outside the cave becomes the master. In arriving at a provisional midpoint as the "right distance," Taubman's analysis appeared more indebted to Lacan's structuralist approach than to poststructuralism. However, Taubman concluded his study by suggesting that the ideal of Lacan's formless unconscious is similar to Plato's ideal form, and he deconstructs the very structures implicit in Lacan's and Plato's formulations.

Nevertheless, one can still detect in Taubman's work, both in his earlier discussion of discourse and his more recent use of Lacan, a pull toward structuralism. In his last two essays [1993a, 1993b; see chapter 6], however, "Canonical Sins" and "Separate Identities, Separate Lives," both of which addressed multiculturalism, Taubman worked poststructurally. In the former he analyzed both the traditional literary canon and oppositional canons to reveal their discursive formations. In the latter he employed poststructuralism as a balance to multicultural theories which anchor their discourses in reified identities, and to existential perspectives. He went on to argue, however, that these identities and perspectives must be employed to keep poststructuralism from falling into a linguistic idealism.

Between Suicide and Murder: Jacques Daignault

To understand curriculum as deconstructed text, that is, as one understood from a perspective which clearly rejects any hint of structuralism, we must turn to Jacques Daignault. Daignault is the major curriculum theorist in North America working in a deconstructed, poststructural mode. More than any other scholar, he has worked and played not only with the insights provided by poststructuralism and deconstruction, but also within the languages and currents of these movements. His understanding of the work of Lacan, Foucault, Derrida, Deleuze, and Serres is unmatched in the field at this time. The form of his own writing is a testament to this understanding of poststructuralism.

To appreciate Daignault's oeuvre requires considerable knowledge of contemporary French philosophy. His writing, relying as it does on allusions to the work of other poststructuralist theorists, on references to musical theory, on anagrams, puns, linguistic arabesques, and neologisms, can prove difficult for the beginning student. It is necessary, however, to persevere, for Daignault brilliantly explores the spaces, the gaps, the "in-betweens" and the differences within language, thought, the subject, and our ways and modes of conceiving ourselves and curriculum. He also attempts to articulate the passages across these spaces and between these differences. "I am trying," he writes, "to save difference itself . . . the passage itself" (Daignault, 1992a, p. 196). The significance of this work is immense, as Daignault is attempting to articulate the very movements of thought itself as it thinks itself in the relationships of teaching and learning.

Terrorism and nihilism. To begin our discussion of Daignault's work, we look at two terms which appear often: terrorist and nihilist. Following Serres (1983), Daignault argues that "to know is to kill" (1992a, p. 199), "that running after rigorous demonstrations and after confirmations is a hunt: literally" (1992a, p. 198). He quotes Serres: "From Plato and a tradition which lasted throughout the classical age, knowledge is a hunt. To know is to put to death. . . . To know is to kill, to rely on death. . . . The reason of the strongest is reason *by itself.* Western man is a wolf of science" (1992a, p. 198). Knowledge—understood poststructurally as the reduction of difference to identity, the many to the one, heterogeneity to homogeneity—is violence. This violence results from competition between ideologies or doctrines, and from "the radical transformation of what exists in conformity with what we believe it ought to be" (quoted in Hwu, 1993, p. 132). For Daignault, as for Serres, to know is to commit murder, to terrorize. Nihilism refers to the abandonment of any attempt to know. It is the attitude which says "anything goes" or "things are what they are." It is to give up, to turn one's ideals into empty fictions or memories, to have no hope. Daignault (1983) calls for us to live in the middle, in spaces that are neither terroristic or nihilistic, neither exclusively political nor exclusively technological. The former leads to terrorism, as it regards education as primarily an opportunity for power. The latter leads to technological manipulation, regarding education as primarily an opportunity for efficiency and manipulation.

Thinking is a passage. For Daignault "thinking happens only between suicide and murder . . . between nihilism and terrorism" (1992a, p. 199). What does this suggest? Thinking is a passage, but this passage is always in danger of being defined and known; it is always prey to the wolf. It is thinking or the passage which constitutes the "excluded third or middle" in the dualism of terrorism and nihilism. "Even the middle," Daignault writes, "attracts new people committed to reducing it to a matter of knowledge, to a new epistemological stake: the wolf's place" (1992a, p. 199). The only way to avoid this fate is to allow thought to think itself, to go beyond or to disrupt dualism, and to think the difference between them. It is to introduce paradox. It is not to stop defining, but to multiply the definitions. It is to invite a plural spelling, to experiment, to problematize. As Daignault explains: "I have tried to find passages between the variable and the invariable, between both: not from one to the other, but passages at their absolute difference, the *différance* [here he uses Derrida's term] between death, twice evaded" (p. 201). He is simultaneously teasing us and being utterly serious when he writes: "Do not expect me to know what I am talking about here; I am trying to think. That is my best contribution to the composer's creativity" (p. 4).

A matter of absolute speed. Much of Daignault's work involves attempts to portray thinking "between," and "thinking difference," that is, to articulate passages. In these attempts he follows Deleuze's move to liberate difference and to combat totalizing modes of thought. Daignault follows Nietzsche as well: "to translate life in joyful wisdom, gay knowledge. Thinking maybe" (1992a, p. 202). Rather than represent a totalized knowledge, rather than being the wolf, he will "stage this knowledge through a passage-way" (1983, pp. 7-13), and perform it by thinking aloud: "To be meaningful is not to say the truth, but to succeed in the 'performance'" (quoted in Hwu, 1993, p. 140). It is important to reiterate that thinking as Daignault theorizes it does not refer to a mental activity, as scientists and logicians might conceive it, or as a process of transcription of thoughts into words. Thinking is not representational, Daignault insists, though, that "is not to say that I do no want any more to use words to write and concepts to think!" (quoted in Hwu, 1993, p. 152). Rather, he wishes to articulate the space between words and concepts by, as Marcel Proust suggested, writing "in a sort of foreign language within our own language" (quoted in Hwu, 1993, p. 159). Quoting Virginia Woolf approvingly, he wishes to "spread [himself] out like a fog between the people that I know best" (1987, p. 27). He wishes to think the middle which, quoting Deleuze: "has nothing to do with an average; it is not a centrism or a form of moderation. On the contrary, it's a matter of absolute speed. Whatever grows from the middle is endowed with such a speed" (1987, p. 27). This thinking the middle will be a lightning flash, a performance that will be "staged."

Staging performance. How then does Daignault stage his performances of thinking about education? To begin, he states that: "The history of arts and the history of sciences are a struggle against prejudices and clichés of an age, while it seems the history of education is an irreducible struggle to find the best prejudices and clichés" (1992a, p. 209). This "irreducible struggle" is the Platonic struggle to find the best or truest copy, but Daignault knows quite well, following Derrida, that there are only copies of the traces of simulacra. What is curriculum, or what should it be? Daignault notes that educational researchers and practitioners are usually the ones who answer this question. In "The Language of Research and the Language of Practice: Neither One Nor the Other: Pedagogy" (1988), Daignault addressed the issue of whether or not there can be a dialogue between these two groups: "To worry about differences between the language of research and practice is to be concerned about the lack of common language, then of a dialogue, of a collaboration, of an involvement and finally of a real improvement in education" (1988, p. 1; quoted in Hwu, 1993, p. 164).

Daignault believes there can be dialogue, but that it must avoid the trap of terrorism or nihilism. If dialogue is reduced to knowledge, then terrorism results. If it is reduced to prejudices and clichés, to the popular forms of expression which confirm the a priori held by those to whom it tries to speak, nihilism will result. How then can one speak, not the language common to both researchers and practitioners, but a difference between the two that will subvert the dualism itself and yet honor the "surface differences" between both? He tells us: "Differences between the language of practice and the language of research are not reducible at the surface level. . . . Nevertheless, language is language. At some level, there are no differences between languages" (quoted in Hwu, 1993, p. 166).

Where is the space that is neither terroristic nor nihilistic? Daignault answers this question by way of an analogy to a poem by Frank O'Hara. In the piece, a poet visits his friend, a painter. The poet notices that in the painting on which his friend is working are sardines. "You have sardines in it," he says. "Yes, there is indeed something there." The poet leaves, but days later returns to find the sardines gone from the painting. He leaves again, goes home, and thinking about the color orange, composes. O'Hara writes: "One day I am thinking of a color: orange. I write a line about orange. Pretty soon it is a whole page of words, no lines. Then another page. There should be so much more, no, of orange, of words, of how terrible orange is and life. Days go by. It is even in prose, I am a real poet. My poem is finished and I haven't mentioned orange yet. It's twelve poems. I call it 'Oranges.' And one day in a gallery I see Mike's painting, called 'Sardines'" (quoted in Hwu, 1993, p. 165). By way of this story, Daignault is suggesting that we can write something about teaching, the teacher, and education entitled "Teaching" without saying a word *about* these. This something he calls pedagogy (quoted in Hwu, p. 166), which operates in the space between practice and theory, and between what is and what ought to be, and which is the "excluded third."

The gap that is curriculum. In the same way that he approaches the "gap" between theory and practice, Daignault tries to think the "gap" that is curriculum, and this "thinking is the incarnation of curriculum as composition" (quoted in Hwu, 1993, p. 172). By phrasing curriculum as thinking Daignault implies his opposition to any reification or belief in representational thought, for curriculum as thinking is always moving, diversifying, or to use Deleuzian terms, is "nomadic", a bit like Joyce's "riverrun." Curriculum does not exist, it happens. In "Curriculum Beyond Words, with Words," Daignault wrote that "curriculum is beyond words, that is what I say; with words, that's what I do" (quoted in Hwu, 1993, p. 143). Certainly this is a provocative and enigmatic statement. Let us approach it by recalling Daignault's idea of curriculum as composition, and in so doing examine several terms Daignault employs—namely "composition," "notes," "expressibles," "expresseds," and "expressings"—while remembering his reference to O'Hara's story about the poet composing a poem called oranges (quoted in Hwu, 1993, pp. 170-171).

Intensities: From the virtual to the actual. For Daignault "notes" are composed of an "expressible," an "expressed," and an "expressing." Following Deleuze, Daignault equates the "expressible" with the virtual, and the "expressed" with the actual. Let us move slowly here. The virtual is similar to the poststructuralist deconstruction of Plato's transcendental Idea into simulacra (a copy for which the original does not exist). These simulacra or concepts of the virtual are equated with expressibles which do not, strictly speaking, exist, but only make themselves felt in sense experience, and in the experience of meaning. They may appear as intensities to the five senses.

There are a multiplicity of expressibles but they make themselves felt depending on the sensitivity of the body to the intensities of experience and a linguistic openness to intensities of meaning. Recalling O'Hara's story, the expressibles are the orange or oranges to which the poet was sensitive, but which, strictly speaking, do not exist but subsist in experience and in-sist in language. The expressible can never "be," except in language. They take form as "expresseds." The "expresseds" for Daignault are "what is actualized in the idea" (quoted in Hwu, 1993, p. 170). It is "any institutional symbol" (p 170). In terms of the O'Hara story, the expressed would be the "Oranges," expressed by the poem with this title. It is a synthesis of expressibles within language. While the expressible is a result of sensitivity to intensities, the expressed is the result of the degree of openness to language. Traditionally, curriculum is approached as a linear correlation between a virtual and an actual, an expressible and an expressed. There is an expressible and it is expressed. There is the idea and curriculum is its representation. Such an approach would say that O'Hara's poem "Oranges" is nonsense because the poem never discusses oranges. Such an approach is bodily insensitive to the intensity of expressibles, and it is closed to language. Such an approach falls prey to the illusion of representation. O'Hara's poet's composition is roughly—only roughly—analogous to curriculum as Daignault conceives it, i.e. an expressible sensed in a sensitivity to intensities and the expressed result- ing from an openness to language. The difference lies in Daignault's notion of expressing.

Provocations and scandals. For Daignault the expressing "is nothing but the dynamics of an analyzer and a synthesizer" (quoted in Hwu, 1993, p. 171). Synthesizing requires the synthesis of intensities which are realized by expressibles on the body or in meaning. Analyzing requires the deconstruc- tion of the expressed. This analysis can take the form of a provocation or a scandal. Or it could be "a play on words—anagrams, homophones, porte- manteau words, etc. . . . It [expresseds] shakes and usually release[s] hidden or forgotten meanings" (quoted in Hwu, 1993, pp. 171-172). The expressing which he also calls "composing" is the lightning flash of synthesizing and analyzing, of making "sense" of expressibles, articulating expresseds and exploding expresseds into expressibles. Traditional ways of understanding curriculum slow this process down such that the expressible is expressed in a reified expressed, which is seen as reflecting a reified expressible. Much of Daignault's work, as we can see, is an attempt to release expressibles, just as O'Hara's story can be seen as a way of disturbing our taken for granted ideas of the poem, or oranges, or writing.

Curriculum, then, like the oranges of the poem, is beyond words yet insists and subsists in language: "curriculum is beyond words, that is what I say" (quoted in Hwu, 1993, p. 143). And it operates in words as an expressing, "with words, that is what I do" (p. 143). Curriculum understood as composition allows us "a participation" in "continuing creation" (p. 171). It is an intransitive verb like Joyce's "riverrun." It also allows us to problematize the idea of the subject which Daignault sees as existing in the frontier between an expressing and a composer (i.e. personal style). "The subject of education," he explains, "grows through such a process of composition, toward a continual problematization of the ego" (p. 172).

In his most recent paper, Daignault (1992b) speaks of serenity. Daignault defines serenity as inner peace, which he believes is also a concern for others. He writes that: "serenity is not happiness, at least not the child's one, but the comeback of happiness: in spite of suffering" (p. 2). Further, he tells us that "serenity [is] a victory over the feelings of active violence (hatred and its manifestations) and passive [violence] (indifference and its manifestations). A frail victory, however" (p. 7). Serenity helps dispel suffering by lending it a particular meaning, in making a link between the singular nature of a peculiar suffering and truth. Serenity releases suffering from ponderousness by providing it the grace of meaning. Daignault works to weave his academic work with caring for others: "I personally teach, take a lot of notes and make others take notes too, so I am well placed to understand how these notes show concern for others. I am therefore more comfortable about showing mine" (p. 15).

By attempting this summary we inflict an injustice to the creative provocativeness of Jacques Daignault's oeuvre, a provocation which disrupts taken-for-granted notions of theory and practice, the subject, and the ways we conceive curriculum and ourselves. His work, as it attempts to portray thought thinking itself, offers us understandings of curriculum and teaching which open up multiple meanings, allows us to break out of frozen ways of thinking in order to think through and between dualisms, and to move through to the other side of prejudices and clichés of education. Daignault's writing functions to affirm creativity, vitality, and uniqueness. Here we have discussed only a fragment of a considerable body of scholarship, which we have perhaps, from its point of view, turned into a static "expressed," stripped of its playfulness, tenderness, and flashes of joy. We hope not.

Toward the conclusion of his "Traces at Work from Different Places," Daignault (1992a) writes: "I do write. I teach too. I try to think of teachers I know and to look for words that could dress their wounds" (p. 213). The words he finds are often elliptical, but as he thinks them for us he helps us compose our own unfinished, unbegun poems, to articulate the passages between terrorism and nihilism, between murder and suicide. To think, perhaps.

Poststructural Criticism of Traditional Curriculum Theory: Cleo Cherryholmes

While Daignault's work, and to a lesser extent, Taubman's, constitute the major contributions in the project to understand curriculum as poststructuralist text today, during the late 1980s and early 1990s others made efforts to bring poststructuralist, deconstructionist, and postmodern insights to bear on the field of curriculum. The most important of these is the work of Cleo Cherryholmes. In his *Power and Criticism: Poststructural Investigations in Education* (1988b), Cherryholmes not only summarized, in an accessible way, the ideas of Foucault, Barthes, Derrida, and other poststructuralists, but he employed these ideas to critique several traditional curriculum discourses. Cherryholmes begins by defining structuralism as a "method of study" (p. 16), a key element of which is that all phenomena are characterized by an underlying structure [for contrasting concepts of structure, see van Manen (1979) and Stone (1979)]. In addition to influencing several disciplines, structuralism operates in education in those proposals, in that research, and in those programs that are conceived and legitimated by order and rationality. Cherryholmes identifies three well-known educational arguments as structuralist: 1) Tyler's famous basic principles of curriculum and instruction, 2) Bloom's 1956 classification of educational objectives in the *Taxonomy of Educational Objectives*, and 3) Schwab's 1983 extension and application of Tyler's basic principles (Cherryholmes, 1988b).

The structuralism of Tyler's rationale. The structural characteristics of Tyler's principles [also known as the Tyler rationale; see chapters 1 and 3] included:

1) Curricular meaning is determined by relationships among steps in the process. 2) Individual steps do not have educational significance apart from the system in which they are located. 3) The design process is ahistorical in that origins of objectives, learning experiences, and evaluation are discussed and analyzed in terms of the immediate situation and not historically. 4) Teachers and students are decentered and not at the center of meaning and curriculum because meaning is determined by relationships among objectives, learning experiences, their organization, and evaluation. 5) The design process gives the appearance of ideological neutrality. 6) The four steps of curriculum design define and regulate the curriculum—they constitute its reality. 7) The steps determine how curriculum is transformed. 8) Tyler's rationale posits a series of binary distinctions: purposeful/purposeless, organization/disorganization, evaluation/nonevaluation, legitimate educational purposes/illegitimate educational purposes, accountability/nonaccountability, continuity/discontinuity, sequence/nonsequence, and integration/nonintegration. (Cherryholmes, 1988b, p. 25)

Cherryholmes tells us that Tyler's "basic principles" appealed to the field because they "promised order, organization, rationality, error correction, political neutrality, expertise, and progress" (p. 26).

The structuralism of Schwab's "The Practical 4." Schwab's "The Practical 4," written in 1983, is, in Schwab's words, a "practical paper on the practical" (Schwab, 1983, p. 239; quoted in Cherryholmes, p. 26). Schwab defined curriculum as "what is successfully conveyed in differing degrees to different students, by committed teachers using appropriate materials and actions" (1983, p. 240; quoted in Cherryholmes, 1988b, p. 26; see chapter 4). He identified four commonplaces of education: teacher, student, what is taught, and the milieu of teaching. The problem becomes the monitoring of curriculum, a problem he proposes to solve by creating curriculum committees to evaluate and correct the curriculum. About Schwab's proposal Cherryholmes writes: "Schwab's 'The Practical 4' follows clearly in the Tyler tradition and is so acknowledged by Tyler himself" (Cherryholmes, 1988b, p. 27). What are the structural elements in Schwab's work? Cherryholmes identifies the following:

1. It [Schwab's proposal] emphasizes relationships among students, teachers, content, and setting in watching and correcting the curriculum.
2. Students and teachers are decentered because curriculum is centered on relationships, such as those among legitimated knowledge, appropriate actions, and communal decisions that are external to individual students and teachers.
3. Curricula do not exist beyond what is explicitly part of the curricular system that is systematically conveyed to students.
4. Curriculum analysis and correction deal with what is in place at a given point in time and not with historical analyses of how things got that way.
5. The curriculum is conceptualized in terms of binary distinctions: what is successfully conveyed/what is not successfully conveyed, committed teachers/uncommitted teachers.
6. The curriculum and the processes by which it is evaluated and corrected is ideologically neutral; it is a professional exercise based on professional expertise. (pp. 27-28)

Cherryholmes concludes that Schwab's essay "clearly illustrates continuing structural influences on curricular discourse in the 1980s" (p. 28).

The structuralism of Bloom et al.'s taxonomy. Bloom, Engelhart, Furst, Hill, and Krathwohl's *Taxonomy of Educational Objectives: Cognitive Domain* (1956) begins with a dedication to Ralph Tyler. The volume seeks to construct a taxonomy of educational objectives. What is a taxonomy? "A taxonomy must be so constructed that the order of the terms must correspond to some 'real' order among the phenomena represented by the terms . . . [and be] validated by demonstrating its consistency with the theoretical views in research findings of the field it attempts to order" (Bloom, et al., 1956, p. 17; quoted in Cherryholmes, 1988b, p. 27). The taxonomy that Bloom and his colleagues constructed include: 1) knowledge, 2) comprehension, 3) application, 4) analysis, 5) synthesis, and 6) evaluation.

To what use would the taxonomy be put? Cherryholmes identifies five "guiding principles" (p. 29) which indicates possible employment of the taxonomy: 1) the taxonomy indicates how teachers differentiate among student behaviors; 2) it is logical and internally consistent; 3) it communicates contemporary psychological knowledge; and 4) the taxonomy is descriptive, conveying educational objectives neutrally (Cherryholmes, 1988b). What are the structural characteristics of Bloom et al.'s work? Cherryholmes lists them:

1. The particular form of the taxonomy is arbitrary.

2. The value of each educational objective is determined by the relationships to and differences among other objectives.
3. It asserts a number of binary distinctions, for example, comprehension, knowledge, application/comprehension, analysis/application, synthesis/ analysis, evaluation/synthesis, and implicitly subject-centered learning/ student-centered learning.
4. Teachers and students are decentered because educational value and meaning is authoritatively located in structures external to individuals.
5. It is ideologically neutral, designed to "be a purely descriptive scheme in which every type of educational goal can be represented in a relatively neutral fashion" (Bloom, et al. 1956, p. 14; quoted in Cherryholmes, 1988b, p. 30).

Next Cherryholmes contrasts these major structuralist proposals in the field to "thinking about education poststructurally" (p. 31).

Cherryholmes on Foucault and Derrida. To contrast poststructuralism and structuralism, Cherryholmes focuses upon Foucault and Derrida. He notes that Foucault denies the political neutrality assumed in structuralism, asserting instead that all knowledge-producing enterprises are political. Further, not only is "truth" political, it is historically relative. Derrida's work, Cherryholmes continues, focuses more on the construction of text. Describing Derrida, he writes: "[Derrida] shows that meanings are dispersed and deferred and that rhetorical claims often diverge from logical argument. Meanings are in constant play. . . . The structure . . . is illusory, because it is a product of history and power (Foucault) and is analytically unstable (Derrida)" (1988b, p. 47). With these points in mind, Cherryholmes (1988b) concludes that the work of Tyler, Schwab, and Bloom, et al. rests on unstable category distinctions, has embedded within it ideology while denying ideological content, advances non-linear structures as linear, promotes educational decision-making separate from ethics, and ignores the political character of all argumentation. From a perspective associated with poststructuralism, their work is not to be taken seriously.

How are curriculum materials viewed poststructurally? From a Foucauldian point of view, textbooks are political, material products which represent specific political ways of viewing reality, ways informed by the political and economic position of those who support textbook production. [See chapters 13 and 14 for further discussion of textbooks; see also chapter 5.] From a Derridean perspective, the structure, coherence, rational sequence, and meaning of textbooks are fictions. Cherryholmes contrasts the two traditions: "Structuralism shows meanings to be decentered and external to the individual. Poststructuralism shows meanings to be shifting, receding, fractured, incomplete, dispersed, and deferred" (p. 61). Cherryholmes views the curriculum field from this perspective. In its turbulence the field would seem to be something of a poststructural phenomenon itself. Cherryholmes contrasts curriculum with other academic disciplines, and finds the following differences which account for the seeming difference in stability between curriculum and other fields of education, as well as between curriculum and the arts and sciences disciplines:

> curriculum is neither historically situated in the tradition of an academic discipline nor constrained by a concrete situation. The complexity of the demands thrust upon the study and practice of curriculum contribute to its looseness, its thrashing about, its contradictions, and its lack of a center, grounding, and foundations. (Cherryholmes, 1988b, p. 148)

The norm for curriculum is conflict and instability. Cherryholmes then observes that the apparent stability of other disciplines is just that: apparent. Citing Kuhn's work on paradigms shifts, Cherryholmes (1988b) notes that other disciplines, especially scientific ones, are buffeted by political and economic events external to them. Perhaps, the complexity of curriculum is not so atypical:

> The absence of foundations is simply more noticeable in curriculum than in academic disciplines and other areas of professional education. The norm for curriculum, then, is not consensus, stability, and agreement but conflict, instability, and disagreement, because the process is one of construction followed by deconstruction by construction. (p. 149)

He forecasts that if the curriculum field moves to a poststructural attitude, practitioners might avoid the false hope and goal of certainty and stability. "The possibility of such [a poststructural] understanding," Cherryholmes believes, "brings with it the promise of increased freedom . . . and more power to create our societies and schools rather than the other way around" (p. 149).

Cherryholmes wants to incorporate aspects of poststructuralism into what he terms "critical pragmatism" (1988b, p. 150 ff.). "Critical pragmatism", he writes, "results when a sense of crisis is brought to our choices, when it is accepted that our standards of beliefs, values, guiding texts, and discourses-practices themselves require evaluation and reappraisal" (1988b, p. 151). Such a view of curriculum theory and practice follows from adoption of "poststructural insights" (p. 151). Such a pragmatism is not bounded by conservative, conventional mores; rather, it is "radical, visionary, and utopian" (p. 151). He concludes:

> If we can be critically pragmatic in the construction, deconstruction, construction . . . of how we live and together build communities using our best visions of what is beautiful, good, and true, then the unreflective reproduction of what we find around us, including some of its injustices, might be tamed and changed a bit. (1988b, p. 186)

A political potential for poststructuralism is elaborated by others in the field as well, as we have seen in chapter 5 and will review in the final section of this chapter. Cherryholmes' book links poststructuralism with the tradition of the field, and in so doing performs a valuable service.

Arch-Writing on the Body: jan jagodzinski

Six aesthetic layers. jan jagodzinski's [sic] (1992) remarkable work exemplifies several poststructuralist characteristics, including imagistic reorderings of words intended to challenge taken-for-granted decodings. For instance, jagodzinski employs lower case letters to spell his name and to refer to himself ("i"), spells woman "wo(man)" to indicate man's origin in the womb, uses the word "gaia" for earth to indicate that the planet is a living entity. jagodzinski identifies six layers of what he terms aesthetically embodied skin, through which the curriculum is felt. These include 1) line, 2) color, 3) texture, 4), size, 5) mass, and 6) space. He suggests that a radical restructuring of the curriculum might support the dismantling of male dominance and technical rationality via these six aesthetic layers [see also chapter 11].

Line. Of "line," jagodzinski begins by asserting that rhythm, followed by movement, is fundamental to human experience. He continues: "the spatial-temporal experience of 'line' is continually informed by the body's negotiation between becoming *lost* and finding a *direction*" (jagodzinski, 1992, p. 160). Such negotiations or journeys, he writes, are characterized by "ambiguity, paradox, and above all, surprise" (pp. 160, 161). Line becomes "directionality" (p.161), "a criss-cross informed by both the feminine and masculine presence" (p. 161). However, in institutional settings, for instance, in curricular form, lines are employed as maps, a fact forgotten by the institution. The map becomes reality: "Curricular outlines as maps are the necessary starting point. It is only when the journey is plotted with precision that they become programs of repression" (p. 162). He concludes his discussion of line by advising us: "Educationally, we must recognize that all lines are bridges to new directions" (p. 161).

Color, texture, size, mass, and space. Color is defined by jagodzinski as the "lived experience of mood" (p. 162). He notes that in large organizations many remain camouflaged, "true colors are rarely shown; they are repressed" (p. 164). Texture, he continues, "is the conversation with 'things' to enable tone to know them intimately" (p. 165). Texture is worn like a skin, embodied in its patina. In terms of human skin, i.e., wrinkles, "texture is therefore an understanding of our waste and decay" (p. 166). In schools, texture speaks to "the need for recognizing the distinctive style that has emerged" (p. 167). Size represents the "lived experience of scale" (p. 168), and involves questions of design and theater, efforts to reach out to a wider audience" (p. 168). Mass is "the lived experience of gravity, informed through the binary oppositions between gravity (permanence) and lightness (moveability)" (p. 171). Curriculum might lighten, jagodzinski tells us, its current structure. Space is defined as "the lived experience of the cosmos" (p. 175), and in this sense curriculum represents "the architecture of a culture" (p. 175). Through arch-writing on the body, out of ourselves, jagodzinski tells us, "a new visionary myth" (p. 181) will be born. This work seems to reflect a phenomenological postmodernism, an embodied but dispersed subject, whose fundamental experience is aesthetic. It is a memorable contribution.

Above All a Matter of Language: Clermont Gauthier

Clermont Gauthier examines issues of theory, practice, and research in logical fashion, but it is a logic, it would seem, transported from a poststructuralist space. Epistemologically, Gauthier works poststructurally, viewing concepts as *machinism*, "that is a meeting, a closeness between independent heterogeneous elements" (1986, p. 25). It is a discourse of difference between elements. Like psychoanalysis, Gauthier regards traditional conceptions of education as based on "lack" (p. 32). He prefers to conceive of education "as a *machinic* production formed of meetings of breaks and of flow" (p. 34). Like Lyotard and Deleuze, Gauthier wants to avoid prescriptions, i.e., the "watchword" (p. 34). There are, however, escapes or passages in watchwords. He quotes Deleuze and Guattari: "There are passwords in the watchword. Words that are like a passageway, components for passage, while the watchwords mark stops, stratified organized compositions" (quoted in Gauthier, 1986, p. 35). For Gauthier, education is "a process of infinite connection" (p. 37), a series of passageways.

Poststructuralist action research. We have reviewed action research earlier [see chapter 1]; here we view it poststructurally. In his "Between Crystal and Smoke: Or, How to Miss the Point in the Debate about Action Research" (1992), Gauthier tells us that "there are only theoretical problems," exploding the binary opposites theory and practice, thought and action. In contrast to the taken-for-granted attitude that "action research" occurs only in the schools Gauthier asserts: "[action research] can take place anywhere: in one's office, in one's mind." Other explosions of taken-for-granted conceptions of action research include: "there is no such thing as a theoretical problem . . . action research is not really concerned with groups . . . [it] is based upon opinions" (p. 193). And Gauthier makes the quintessential poststructuralist assertion: "action research is above all a matter of language" (Gauthier, 1992). Like crystal and smoke, Gauthier's analysis is symmetrical and hierarchical while simultaneously being unstable, asymmetrical and uncontrollable.

When we read poststructuralist curriculum theorists like Daignault, jagodzinski, and Gauthier, we confront writing that disturbs the usual linear logic we have come to accept as being synonymous with rationalistic curriculum theory. Conservatives are apt to dismiss these scholars' work as nonsense. That would be a mistake. Rather, we should read their work as perhaps a kind of poetic theory. These theorists seek to dissolve, explode, and deconstruct the taken-for-granted and reified forms of curriculum research that are frequently mistaken for the reality of educational experience they pretend to map.

A Taoist Connection: Wen-Song Hwu

After summarizing structuralism, poststructuralism, and poststructuralist curriculum theory, especially that of Jacques Daignault, Wen-Song Hwu (1993) sketches possible links among poststructuralism, Chinese Taoism, and Zen. He notes, for instance, that, like poststructuralism, Taoism and Zen are paradoxical in nature. Lao-tze says that "one who knows does not speak; one who speaks does not know" (quoted in Hwu, 1993, p. 182). Zen appears to be antimetaphysical, yet Zen masters often make statements heavy with metaphysical content. Both Taoist and Zen masters employ language in ways that are not dependent upon extra-linguistic referents but rather upon internal linguistic conditions. Hwu tells us that Confucius has to employ language to tell us that "words are unnecessary" (1993, p.185). That is, language does not exhaust meaning, and requires us to say "you know what I mean." Of course, language as paradox and as implicated with power are important ideas in poststructuralism. Hwu (1993) explains:

> Reflections on language and discourse led to Foucault's connections among language, knowledge, and power, to Derrida's attack on dualism and his critique of logocentrism, to Deleuze's fourth dimension of language, to Lyotard's comments regarding the "language game," and to Serres' dialogue in an information society. The intellectual is no longer commissioned to play the role of the advisor to the masses and critic of ideological content, but rather to become one capable of providing instruments of analysis. (p. 185)

Hwu cites Deleuze's notion of "hammering" and Daignault's writing about curriculum with words, beyond words to explicate a passage oscillating among different discourses.

The fluid character of reality is evident in both Western and Eastern traditions. Hwu (1993) tells us: "For Taoism and deconstruction, a text does not fix a state of affairs; nothing is fixed and every interpretation transforms the reading perspective" (p. 187). History and meaning are not constituted by any principle of continuity; but "instead they rejoin above and beyond ruptures and discontinuities" (p. 188). Treat any order with suspicion, as a power play or arbitrary statement of preference. This multiplicity of forces, or:

> the multiple being of force, Taoism observes, is "wu-wei"—an act without activity. These forces are unfolded on the surface of internal depth and then folded under the surface; any given perspective can be only be validated by reverting to still other perspectives. (pp. 188-189)

Hwu goes on to link Serres notion of "noise" which implies that birth comes from chaos and to his concept of Hermes and the "parasite" as pointing to the uncertainty of being and the pervasiveness of indeterminacy: "This thinking parallels Lao-tze's concept of 'wu,' the fathomless form, the formless foundation of all forms" (p. 189).

Hwu notes that in poststructuralism the notion of identity is displaced by that of difference, undermining that autobiographical scholarship which rests on a foundation of an authentic self. Such an idea is simply a story one tells oneself about oneself, an aesthetic illusion created by narrative. He quotes Deleuze:

> No longer are there acts to explain, dreams or fantasies to interpret, childhood memories to recall, words to signify; instead, there are colors and sounds, becoming and intensities. . . . There is no longer Self that feels, acts, and recalls; there is a "glowing fog, a dark yellow mist" that has effects and experiences movements and speeds. (quoted in Hwu, 1993, pp. 195-196)

Hwu argues that while psychoanalysis is false and narratives about the self are illusory, still we live as if our experience were true. The point is, he continues, is to be playful about the stories we tell, recalling their illusory character and mystifying functions. What is curriculum theory in this poststructuralist world? Hwu (1993) answers:

> Therefore, the role of curriculum theorizing is not to formulate a global analysis of the ideologically coded. . . . Curriculum functions to displace discursive practices, such as self-formation, sense-making, historical awareness . . . [and explore] the possible connections among those fragmentations and differences. . . . Theory does not express, translate, or serve to apply practice: it is practice. (p. 198)

Hwu's explication of poststructuralism and its relation to certain Eastern traditions is a provocative effort to extend the boundaries of our understanding.

Poststructuralist Influences on Other Contemporary Curriculum Discourses
Some of the work done by curricularists that has incorporated aspects of poststructuralism, deconstruction, and postmodernism has done so from other theoretical perspectives and allegiances within the curriculum field (Weill, 1992). Perhaps these scholars have been persuaded by poststructuralist thought to rethink their own assumptions regarding, for instance, the "self," or perhaps "race," since unifying notions such as these have been problematized by poststructuralism and deconstruction. We have examined some of this work earlier in other contexts; here we take note of this scholarship as it has been explicitly influenced by poststructuralism.

A deconstructing autobiography. In "Autobiography and the Architecture of Self," Pinar (1988e, 1994) rethinks notions of authenticity, self, and autobiography itself through poststructuralist ideas. Pinar's autobiographical practice had been, in large part, an attempt to reclaim an authentic self from the frozen and false forms individuals take on in schools as they "educate" and are "educated." This reclamation was carried on through the autobiographical method of *currere* [see chapters 8 and 10], much indebted to phenomenology, existentialism, and psychoanalysis. To reclaim an authentic self would require the investigation of experience—educational experience—autobiographically. But such work is implicated in all the problems that, according to poststructuralism, phenomenology raised but failed to answer. Pinar's essay represents a rethinking of these problems, beginning by asking "is there an authentic self?" (1988e, p. 7; 1994). His reading of Nietzsche leads him to the conclusion that there are only fictive selves. In a Nietzschean sense, the self is an aesthetic creation, and the means by which the self is planned and "built" are story-telling and myth-making. However, Nietzsche was not trying to destroy these fictions and simply replace them "with a world of Dionysian immediacy and sensuality" (p. 15), although he wished to live in that world too. Rather, and here Pinar quotes Allan Megill: "Nietzsche envisages not the destruction of the conceptual world but rather . . . its deconstruction—that is, its transportation into a realm of aesthetic illusion and play" (Megill, 1985, quoted in Pinar, 1988e, p. 16).

This distinction between destruction and deconstruction recalls our earlier discussion of the deconstructive turn, as well as Daignault's maintaining of concepts and dualisms but thinking their difference. Pinar suggests: "Only via deconstruction can a reformulation of self begin, a self not frozen and overtly fixed psychologically or socially, capable of perceiving and processing new information about constantly adjusting notions of reality, the future and the past" (p. 19). But is this self that emerges an "authentic one"? Pinar turns next to Foucault and, following him, suggests that "it is not an authentic self that is obscured and distorted" by discursive practices. Rather, as we have seen, "objects" and "figures," including the "self," are discursively formed through processes of exclusions and the active working of power as it constructs these. Schools construct and maintain selves which are reified, excluding selves which the institutions regard as marginal. Pinar suggests keeping conscious "that which is excluded . . . and in suspension marginalized elements . . . [can be] kept alive. Alive, they sustain . . . life" (p. 22). In part, then, Pinar suggests allying one's self with "possibilities, exclusions, and repressions" (pp. 22-23).

Keep moving. Still, one must deconstruct the reified or frozen selves, and Pinar turns to Derrida for a method. He writes that "Derrida supplies a method of thinking and a method of participating in the architecture of self that makes complex and ever-shifting order of Nietzschean chaos" (1988e, p. 25). This method constructs only to deconstruct, a method that recalls Daignault's analyzing and synthesizing. The point is to keep moving: "Autobiography takes this task seriously, as it is the task of self formation, deformation, learning and unlearning" (p. 27). One way to keep moving is to understand that the stories we tell, however provisional, always exclude other stories, which may also be true. It is not enough to simply "tell our stories" or relate our "biographical themes." We must understand that this is only substituting "a false stability and unity of self for a false unity of text" (p. 29) or what is "out there." Pinar explains: "We are not the stories we tell as much as we are the modes of relation to others our stories imply, modes of relation implied by what we delete as much as what we include" (p. 28). If we can carry out this process, finding in ourselves that which is included and excluded, we may be able, as Nietzsche said, "to experience the history of humanity as a whole as [our own] history" (quoted in Pinar, 1988e, p. 30). In this essay Pinar incorporates poststructuralist insights into his ongoing autobiographical project (1994). From a poststructuralist perspective, however, fundamental questions remain: who is performing the construction and deconstruction of the self architecture? That is, who and where is the subject? What is the body?

Identity is not a fiction: Grumet. Other curricularists, working autobiographically, have rejected the dispersion of the subject into subject positions within discourse. For example, Madeleine Grumet notes that:

> Under the canopy of poststructuralism, sociologists, as well . . . as some humanities scholars, have justified readings of autobiographical narratives which erase the subjectivity of their authors. Claiming that identity is a fiction [they] attribute our scribbles and fantasies to the determination of . . . codes. I would be naive if I refused to admit influence in what we notice, what we choose to tell, and in how and why we tell what we do. Nevertheless, autobiographical method invites us to struggle with all those determinations. (1990b, p. 324)

In another place Grumet makes fun of the structuralism in poststructuralism:

> Displacing Marxist correspondence theories with a discursive model of the immaculate conception, they [contemporaries theories of the text] truly argue that words create consciousness. Experience is reduced to genre as we stroll through our lives narrating someone else's story. (1990c, p. 189)

Poststructuralism does appear in Grumet's work via references to Foucault and to Lacan, but this appearance owes much to articulations of poststructuralism by French feminists. [See chapter 10 for a description of Grumet's autobiographical theory; see chapter 7 for her feminist theory.]

Reclaim "woman" from male discourse: Martusewicz. In her essay "Mapping the Terrain of the Post-Modern Subject," Rebecca Martusewicz (1992) not only summarizes much poststructuralist theory but pays particular attention to French feminist poststructuralists and to feminist curriculum theorists who work poststructurally. In her essay she reviews structuralism, including major concepts associated with Saussure, Levi-Strauss, Barthes, Lacan, and the early Foucault. From structuralism she moves to the poststructuralist theory of Derrida, and to the poststructuralist implications of Lacan's work. This sets the stage for her discussion of French poststructuralist feminism. Reviewing Cixous, Irigaray, and Kristeva, Martusewicz describes the effort to reclaim "woman" from male discourse and locate her in desire and difference. The "feminine" is not, she tell us, the reverse of "masculine." Indeed, poststructurally it represents a denial of the concept of identity (a phallic principle) and the assertion of a multiple, indeterminate female subject. She writes: "The interest in this work by the French feminist writers is to 'forge the antilogos weapon,' to take apart the dominant male discourses that define woman according to man's image of himself, and to articulate woman's difference in and through language" (p. 145). Martusewicz goes on to address some of the criticism leveled against French feminist poststructuralists, particularly the charges that the "focus on language as the foundation of women's oppression . . . is not sufficiently grounded in material reality" and the assertion that "écriture feminine" is essentialist (p. 145). She attributes these criticisms to misinterpretation, that is, to the neglect of the material reality of discursive systems, and to the lack of recognition that women's bodies are a "source of metaphor for multiplicity and difference" (1992, p. 145). After summarizing Foucault's later work, particularly his understanding of knowledge, power, and gender as analyzed from a feminist perspective, Martusewicz moves to the work of Valerie Walkerdine (1985, 1988), Jennifer Gore (1989), and Nancy Lesko (1988a, 1988b), all of whom incorporate Foucauldian analysis in their work. She concludes her essay by answering her own question—what does it mean to be an educated woman?—with a statement that echoes Daignault. She writes: "To live as feminist educators is to live a tension between a critical theoretical space and an affirmative political space. It is within this in-between, this 'elsewhere,' that we must seek the educated woman" (p. 155).

Between poststructuralism and postmodernism: Whitson. We conclude this section on the effort to understand curriculum as deconstructed text with a brief discussion of "Post-structuralist Pedagogy as Counter-Hegemonic Praxis (Can We Find the Baby in the Bathwater?)," by Tony Whitson (1991c). In one sense Whitson's essay stands between poststructuralism and postmodernism in that it criticizes the latter while finding value in the former. Whitson begins by trying to sketch what postmodernism is and cites Giroux's observation that "postmodern criticism offers a combination of reactionary and progressive possibilities" (p. 2). Whitson goes on, however, to suggest that what several writers—among them Giroux, McLaren, and Lather—have found as progressive possibilities within postmodernism are really insights gained from feminism, poststructuralism, and anticolonialism. What, if anything, does postmodernism add?

Whitson critiques Lyotard and Rorty, often seen as exemplary postmodern theorists, for their collusion with capitalism and the status quo. He offers as one illustration, for instance, Rorty's statement that "in my view we should be more willing than we are to celebrate bourgeois capitalist society as the best polity actualized so far, while regretting that it is irrelevant (sic) to most of the world's population" (quoted in Whitson, p. 6). Whitson also argues that postmodernism's assault on metanarratives or *grand récits*, while often used to define postmodernism, smuggles in its own *grand récit* with modernism as the villain. Finally, he argues that postmodernists such as Rorty and Lyotard have been "actively complicitous in articulating places for themselves within the hegemonic structure" (p. 15), an allegation which recapitulates the claim that one aspect of hegemony is its location of "the opposition within the total ideological and sociopolitical structure in places where the opposition may be harmless or even supporting to the structure's viability" (p. 14). [Recall the Wexler/Whitson (1982) elaboration of hegemony in chapter 5.] In sum, then, Whitson claims that postmodernism—stripped of feminism, poststructuralism, etc.—is either a vacuous term or "outright nihilistic with regard to claims of truth as well as moral and political claims" (p. 9). If, as Giroux says, postmodernism offers both progressive and reactionary possibilities, it must either import principles for counterhegemonic practice from outside itself or it is politically and ethically neutral.

Whitson refutes charges that poststructuralism abandons any ground for political action or moral judgments. Rather he finds in poststructuralism a recognition that "phenomenological and existential structures of human agency are no less essential than the more impersonal, deterministic structures with which they are interwoven to form the textual fabric of historical existence" (p. 3). This "textuality" he sees as the object of a poststructural analysis can be embedded in a counterhegemonic practice. That is, Whitson thinks a counterhegemonic practice is unlikely without the insights of an at least tacitly poststructural understanding. It is interesting to note that the examples to which Whitson refers are analyzed by what he calls a "structuralist analysis." Whitson regards as one of the virtues of poststructuralism that it can make use of the analytical techniques developed by the structuralist. These techniques might be used with a praxis that is poststructural, however, in several respects, e.g. to disrupt structures in flux and perhaps displace them with more satisfactory (aesthetically, politically, etc.) structures (Whitson, 1993). As we noted in chapter 5, William B. Stanley (1992b) has relied on Whitson's analysis in his attempt to rescue political theory from the challenges posed by poststructuralism, mainly by insisting upon their compatibility.

Our summary of the effort to understand curriculum as deconstructed text is necessarily incomplete; this area is developing rapidly and in the gap between writing this chapter and its publication, important work may appear. Certain scholars incorporate poststructuralism in work that we locate in other discourses, such as the scholarship of Susan Edgerton [see chapter 6]. And there are several others, some of whose scholarship we will review shortly, who use theories of poststructuralism to extend their current work, or include in their work cultural descriptions of, or assume we are living in, a postmodern era. The term "postmodern" appears frequently in their work, and, as we shall see, these scholars are often concerned with modernism and its composition. Whitson's essay occupies the space at the end of this section as it points to differences between poststructuralism and postmodernism, and attempts to state its political potential.

VI

Postmodernism and Curriculum Theory: The Work of William E. Doll, Jr.

A new sense of educational order will emerge, as will new relations between teachers and students, culminating in a new concept of curriculum.

(William E. Doll, Jr., 1993a, p. 3)

Our survey of the effort to understand curriculum as postmodern text begins with William E. Doll, Jr., whose scholarly career began in studies of Progressivism (1983a), moved to Piaget (1980, 1983a, 1983b), and finally, in its third phase, to postmodernism (1988, 1989, 1993a) and its implications for the school curriculum. Anticipating his most recent work, Doll (1983a) wrote ten years ago that:

> [progressivism was] continually struggling to soften or humanize the harsher aspects of this industrial-technocratic model. Finally, it may be seen to contain the seeds for a new educational model, a model able to flourish not under industrialism but under post-industrialism, a model which considers humankind not in mechanistic terms but in biological, living-organism, terms. (p. 167)

This model Doll discovered in the "new science," especially the mathematical chaos theory of Ilya Prigogine, work that led Doll (1986) to envision a transformative curriculum. In his most recent and comprehensive work, *A Post-Modern Perspective on Curriculum* (1993a), Doll speaks directly to the differences between modernism and postmodernism, and in so doing very usefully summarizes the meaning of postmodernism. Additionally, Doll's book traces postmodernism's development through twentieth-century science, a link no other curriculum theorist has elaborated so completely. The scholars whose work we will discuss toward the end of this chapter also discuss differences between modernism and postmodernism, but they do so from the positions of prior political allegiances. While Doll is interested in articulating a postmodern curriculum, other scholars—we think here of Giroux, McLaren, and Lather—are more concerned with incorporating postmodernist ideas into their already developed notions of critical pedagogy, and in Lather's case, feminist theory.

Megaparadigmatic changes. William Doll introduces his project by proposing that the "megaparadigmatic" changes that postmodernism is bringing to all the disciplines will dramatically affect the curriculum, the confluence of many disciplines, to such an extent that a "new sense of educational order will emerge, as will new relations between teachers and students, culminating in a new concept of curriculum" (Doll, 1993a, p. 3). This new order will be more complex, pluralistic, and unpredictable. In such an order teachers and students will emerge as "individuals interacting together in the mutual exploration of relevant issues" (p. 4); traditional methods of evaluation and assessment will become obsolete, replaced by a focus on dialogue and the quality of inquiry. "Finally," he writes, "curriculum will not be viewed as a set, a priori, course to run, but as a passage of personal transformation" (p. 4).

To explicate such a transformation, Doll provides a detailed overview of the modernist paradigm, "developed over the past three to four hundred years" (p. 4). He focuses on science which he sees as a key discipline around which the postmodern paradigm will develop. He then turns to the "metaphorical application of postmodern characteristic to the curriculum" (p. 12), challenging the " 'machine and productivity' language that now dominates curriculum discourse" and replacing it with the language of "development, dialogue, inquiry, transformation" (p. 13). He inscribes the writings of John Dewey, Jean Piaget, and Jerome Bruner into a postmodern vision of curriculum. Finally, he offers his vision of curriculum, one exemplifying the postmodern paradigm as it replaces the Tyler rationale.

Premodern, modern, postmodern. Using science as an organizing frame, Doll divides the history of Western thought into three megaparadigms: the premodern, the modern, and the postmodern. The premodern he regards as existing up to the seventeenth and eighteenth centuries, and as being characterized by closure, stasis, a belief in cosmological harmony and a living universe, a sense of balance and proportion (as criteria of beauty), a fear of limitless process, and a belief that the individual was equivalent to his or her role and should carry that role only. During the seventeenth and eighteenth centuries this cosmology gave way to "a new mathematical and mechanistic cosmology—a scientific one—begun by men like Nicolaus Copernicus, Tycho Brahe, Johann Kepler and Galileo Galilei" (p. 20). This cosmology was characterized by a quest for control and prediction, mathematical and mechanistic models, a belief in progress, a vision of the universe as comprised of dead particles, a Lockean view of the mind, a radical separation of objective and subject realities, and the personal from the public. On one level, Doll cautions, the modernist paradigm was not a closed vision, for it held out a belief in progress, both politically in terms of human rights, and materially in terms of material well-being:

> But at a deeper level, the vision was a closed one. Descartes' methodology for right reason was as certain and dogmatic as the scholastic one it replaced, and Newton's mechanistic science was predicated on a stable, uniform, cosmological order. The centerpiece of this vision, cause-effect determinism measured mathematically, depended on a closed, non-transformative, linearly developmental universe. (p. 21)

The last megaparadigmatic change—postmodernism—Doll sees as occurring in the twentieth century, and as being characterized by open systems, indeterminacy, the discrediting of metanarratives, and a focus on process. Doll goes on to critique Descartes who "bequeathed to modernist thought a method for discovering a pre-existent world, not a method for dealing with an emergent evolutionary one" (p. 32). Using Serres, whose work we have reviewed earlier (and whose influence on Daignault we have acknowledged), Doll shows that Descartes and other modernist theorists positioned scientific rationalism as the wolf, as the reason outside of which existed nothing to which one could appeal for truth claims. A further critique follows of Newton's world view which sees reality as simple, orderly and observable.

> The real "peculiarity" of Newton's metaphysics, though, lies . . . in our wholesale acceptance of it as the "natural" order of the universe. We consider chaotic or complex order, indeterminacy, transformation, internal direction and self-generation as unusual . . . because they violate our "natural" acceptance of

Newton's world view. . . . It is Newton's metaphysical and cosmological views
. . . that have dominated modernist thought so long, providing a foundation in
the social sciences for causative predictability, linear ordering, and a closed . . .
methodology. These . . . are the conceptual underpinnings of . . . scientistic
curriculum-making. (p. 34)

The concept of an abstracted uniform order is the dominant organizing
principle in the modernist paradigm and it has given rise to the following
beliefs: 1) that change is uniform, incremental and follows a linear sequence,
2) for every effect there is an a priori cause since we live in a closed mechanistic universe, 3) time is cumulative, linear and sequenced, and 4) individual
atoms are arranged in linear order and form larger building blocks. Arguing
that modernism with its emphasis on "right reason" and its concrete embodiment in industrialization gave rise to views of curriculum which have dominated education until recently, Doll critiques the techno-rationality and scientism of these views, especially the work of Tyler, Bobbitt, and others whose
work recapitulates the modernist paradigm. Much of this critique parallels
Cherryholmes's critique, although in Doll the target is modernism, while in
Cherryholmes it is structuralism.

Doll argues for a replacement of the modernist paradigm—whose canonical model for science has been physics—with a postmodern paradigm which
would use biology "with its concepts of complexity . . . and network relations" (p. 67) and chaos theory, particularly as developed by Ilya Prigogine,
the Nobel-Prize winning theorist of irreversible thermodynamics, as heuristically rich metaphors for curriculum thought and development. Doll employs
Piaget's biological constructivism (not his stage theory) as an example of
theory which privileges open-ended process, the role of perturbation and
confusion in disrupting structures, interactionism, non-linear transformation,
and self-generation. Through Prigogine he argues for the "fecundity" of
chaos. Prigogine's "chaos theory" is a theory of orderly disorder. As Katherine Hayles (1990) has noted:

It can be generally understood as the study of complex systems, in which . . .
non-linear problems are considered in their own right. . . . Chaos is seen as
order's precursor and partner. . . . The focus is on the spontaneous emergence
of self-organization from chaos. (p. 9)

Patterns do not emerge in behaviors or movements but in the abstraction
of these onto a "phase space" graph "that correlates the movement's variables
into a single point and looks at these points over periods of time. . . . It is in
these abstract relationships that the patterns emerge" (Doll, 1993a, p. 91).
Movements are unpredictable, creation is continuous, and the very modes of
measuring these movements are themselves relative. To take one example of
the latter point, if we measure the coastline of Britain in terms of miles it is
shorter than if we measure it in yards or inches, and the coastline is always
changing (Hayles, 1990). Following Prigogine, Doll argues that "creativity
occurs by the interaction of chaos and order, between unfettered imagination and disciplined skill" (Doll, 1993a, p. 88). We see here certain resem-

blances to Taubman's notion of the teacher creating him or herself some-where between Lacan and Plato, and to Daignault's notions of "expressibles," "expresseds," and "expressing." In the work of Taubman, Daignault, and Doll, the teaching moment seems to take form in the interplay between order and chaos, closure and openness, form and freedom.

The metaphors found in Piaget's and Prigogine's work leads Doll to view curriculum as characterized by disturbance, perturbation, creation, and trans-formation. He goes on, however, to reinterpret the work of Bruner, Dewey, and Whitehead, finding in their writings rich metaphors for a postmodern vision of education, and an implicit break with modernist views of knowl-edge, learning, and a fixed universe capable of being grasped by a subject separate from them. Several implications for curriculum are found in Bruner's thesis that humans tend to organize experience "narratively" not logically, in Dewey's focus on experience as the primacy of our being, and in Whitehead's claim that reality lies in process itself (and not some reference point outside the process). Doll observes:

> The Tyler, Taylor and behavioral movements have not dealt with the *ferment*, but rather have denied, bypassed or overlooked it. However, in this *ferment* or—in Schön's *messes*, Prigogine's *chaos*, Dewey's *problems*, Piaget's *disequilibrium* or Kuhn's *anomalies* lie the seeds not only of development and transformation, but of life itself. (p. 148)

Here the first fifty years of curriculum development are reconceptualized; Tyler the modernist is replaced by Doll the postmodernist.

In the final section Doll presents his vision of a postmodern curriculum, influenced by Richard Rorty and Milan Kundera, a vision which posits "a fascinating, imaginative realm (born of the echo of God's laughter) wherein no one owns the truth and everyone has the right to be understood" (p. 151). In this realm, inhabited more by generative metaphor than by scientific facts, Doll lays out an alternative to the Tyler rationale. Doll's postulates "four Rs." A postmodern curriculum, he says, should be rich, recursive, relational, and rigorous. *Richness* provides depth to a curriculum, creating "layers of mean-ings . . . multiple possibilities or interpretations. . . . Curriculum needs to have the right amount of indeterminacy, anomaly . . . chaos, disequilibrium, dissipation, lived experience" (p. 176). He continues: "The concept of devel-oping richness through dialogue, interpretations, hypothesis generation and proving, and pattern playing can apply to all we do in curriculum" (p. 177). *Recursion* is the process of reflecting on one's work—"to explore, discuss, inquire into both ourselves as meaning makers and into the text itself" (p. 178), in an ongoing transformative process: "Recursion aims at developing competence—the ability to organize, combine, inquire, use something heuris-tically" (p. 178). *Relations* has two foci. Pedagogically it refers to connections within a curriculum's structure, while cultural relations grow:

> out of a hermeneutic cosmology—one which emphasizes narration and dialogue as key vehicles in interpretation. Narration brings forward the concepts of history . . . language . . . and place. . . . Dialogue interrelates these three to

provide us with a sense of culture that is local in origin but global in interconnections. (p. 180)

We must attend to the cultural relationships which influence the foundation of our views and thus break free of modernism's privileging of the individual severed from relations with others and the eco-system. Finally, *rigor* which "keeps a transformative curriculum from falling into either 'rampant relativism' or sentimental solipsism" (p. 181) is redefined in a postmodern curriculum as mixing indeterminacy with interpretation. In dealing with interpretations we must always be aware that "all valuations depend on (often hidden) assumptions. . . . Rigor . . . means the conscious attempt to ferret out these assumptions . . . as well as negotiating passages between these assumptions, so that the dialogue may be meaningful and transformative" (p. 183).

In his most recent work, Doll (1993b) discusses the significance of paradox in the new paradigm, shifting the focus from the separation of subject and object initiated by Descartes' mind-body split, to a focus of reintegration of the teacher with learner, the text with reader. He notes the paradox "that neither is the other, yet neither is without the other. Each needs the other for its own sense of being" (1993b, p. 286). This shift changes curriculum's focus to the "dialoguing, negotiating, interacting" (p.286) inherent in the postmodern view. He explains:

> These are words which imply (and use) indeterminacy, openness, self-organization. They are the words of a transformative curriculum, of a *currere* oriented curriculum, one focussing not on the external attributes of the racecourse but on the *process* of traversing the course, of negotiating with self and others. (p. 286)

This view also encourages the role of playfulness in the classroom, especially in the process of making meaning by the student: "Play deals not with the present and foundational but with the absent and the possible. Its very nature invites dialogue, interpretation, interaction. Its free-flowing form encourages participation. All of these activities are essential to meaning-making" (p. 286). Play becomes an agent of change: an "advantage of play, once one is attuned to its nature, is that its freedom allows one to challenge and explore in a non-hostile and non-threatening way" (p. 287).

In a work in preparation, Doll explores the unexamined assumption of control which currently operates in the modernist curriculum. The metaphor he uses to discuss how control has operated since the beginning of the modern era is that of a ghost which haunts the curriculum: "control is actually embedded in the concept of curriculum" from its very first educational usage. "Control is not only the ghost in the clock of curriculum—to use the predominant modernist, mechanistic metaphor—it is the ghost which actually runs the clock. It is time to put this ghost to rest, let it retire peacefully to the 'land of no return' and to liberate curriculum to live a life of its own" (Doll, in prep.). In order to exorcise this ghost, Doll proposes a hermeneutic influence in curriculum, providing a multi-focussed approach with concepts of community and the new theories of complexity providing provocative ground for development of curriculum in the postmodern era.

In William E. Doll's (1993a) *A Post-Modern Perspective on Curriculum*, we can see the emergence of a curriculum theory which incorporates convincingly several of the central characteristics of the postmodernism we discussed at the beginning of this chapter. The critiques of linear time, of reality as finally representable, of modernism, and of techno-rationality are all evident in Doll's vision. We can also see the postmodern emphasis on flux, randomness, multiple interpretations, variancy, indeterminacy, and fluid relationships. More than any other scholar, Doll reviews these major concepts associated with postmodernism and formulates clearly and accessibly a postmodern curriculum theory. His accomplishment is great. Tyler has now not only been rejected; his basic principles have now been replaced.

VII
Postmodernism, Feminist Theory, and Politics:
Lather, Giroux, Kincheloe, Steinberg, McLaren

It is clear that postmodernism can easily degenerate into another master narrative.
(Patti Lather, 1991b, p. 165)

The paradisiacal representations of public education from within the frameworks of the nostalgic modernist's "lost organic whole" and the critical-radical pedagogue's "utopia" respectively project a unified and disciplining (read terrorist) system and a totality soon to be united though presently overcome by (class, gender, and race) divisions.
(Kiziltan, Bain, & Canizares, 1990, p. 368)

The intellectual is no longer commissioned to play the role of advisor to the masses and critic of ideological content, but rather to become one capable of providing instruments of analysis.
(Wen-Song Hwu, 1993, p. 185)

Several prominent political scholars have engaged postmodernism, poststructuralism, and deconstruction, expressing various positions toward these developments, as we noted in chapter 5. For instance, while Michael Apple (1982c, 1983, 1992a, 1992b) has indicated ambivalence (although recently expressing only alarm), Philip Wexler (1987) argued poststructuralism itself ought to be regarded as a contemporary political practice. Joe Kincheloe (1993b) appropriated postmodernism as a tool for progressive political change. In chapter 5 our interest was the significance of poststructuralism and postmodernism for political theory; here we attend to the influence of political theory on understanding curriculum as postmodern, poststructuralist, deconstructed text.

In *Getting Smart: Feminist Research and Pedagogy With/in the Postmodern*, Patti Lather (1991a) employs feminism, neo-Marxism, and poststructural theory to investigate the postmodern period in which we are living, a moment characterized by, as she says, "a technology of regulation and surveillance" (p. ix), and to "take advantage of the range of mobile transitory points of resistance inherent in the networks of power relations" (p. ix) in an effort to develop a critical social science. Lather's focus is on research and teaching, more specifically how these can more effectively contest relations of domination. She states that her three aims are to develop a critical social science, to contribute to liberatory education and to "explore the implications of feminism, neo-Marxism and poststructuralism for developing inquiry-approaches in the human sciences" (p. xvii). Such a project raises three questions. First, if the postmodern is characterized by the discrediting of metanarratives and if poststructuralism and deconstruction constitute a challenge to notions of identity and the subject, how does Lather employ Marxism and feminism? Second, what would a postmodern liberatory pedagogy and critical inquiry look like? Third, how does Lather distinguish between postmodernism and poststructuralism? Let us take the last question first.

Aspects of the postmodern. Like Doll, Lather divides history into the premodern, the modern, and the postmodern. Briefly she characterizes the modern as a period of the triumph of secular humanism, nation-state capitalism, scientific rationality, liberal democracy, and Enlightenment discourses. The postmodern she describes as being characterized by a new view of history as non-linear, cyclical, indeterminate, and contingent. The present is represented in the fictional guise of the past. In the postmodern period, the individual is decentered, culturally inscribed and constructed, relational and displaced by the unconscious which itself is always transforming. Materially, the postmodern age is characterized by nuclear power and micro-electronic global capitalism. Lather goes on to describe two facets of postmodernism's influence on authority and knowledge. The first, which she sees as negative, champions a neo-Nietzschean collapse of meaning, nihilism, schizo-cynicism, and consumerism. The second, a positive aspect, she describes as affirming participatory, dialogic, and pluralistic structures of authority. It is non-dualistic and non-hierarchical and supports the construction of multiple sites from which the world is spoken.

With this characterization of postmodernism in mind, Lather distinguishes between poststructuralism and postmodernism in the following way: "I sometimes use 'postmodern' to mean the larger cultural shifts of a post-industrial, post-colonial era and 'poststructural' to mean the working out of those shifts within . . . academic theory. I also, however, use the terms interchangeably" (p. 4). We might recall here Whitson's criticism that the critiques lodged against modernism could be made from within modernism itself, and that postmodernism without poststructuralism is a vacuous term. Lather accepts Jameson's description of the cultural logic of postmodernism but strives to find within it, via poststructuralist Marxism and feminism, a way to contest that culture.

A post-Marxist space. Lather is well aware that the crisis in representation and the attack on metanarratives challenge Marxism, as we saw in chapter 5. She writes: "To move from establishing the 'real' to how what we see is constituted by our very pursuit of it is to move into a 'post-Marxist space'" (p. 25). Her view is that the decentering of Marxism is not anti-Marxist but rather the repositioning of Marxism as one discourse among many. The discursive strategies of Marxism can be reinscribed in a postmodern analysis. Additionally, Lather suggests that feminism can engage in a dialogue with postmodernism to their mutual benefit. She writes that, on the one hand, feminism "displaces the articulation of postmodernism from the site of the fathers and opens up the possibility of a heteroglot articulation premised on multiplicities and particularities" (p. 27). On the other hand, she continues:

> postmodernism offers feminism opportunities to avoid dogmatism and the reductionism of single-cause analysis, to produce knowledge from which to act, and to diffuse power as a means to take advantage of the range of mobile and transitory points of resistance inherent in the networks of power relations. (p. 39)

Following Spivak (1989) and Fuss (1989), Lather sees essentialism as a strategic possibility deployed as a deconstructive device. Nor does Lather fall into the trap of making poststructuralism the theory and feminism the practice. She argues with Kipnis' (1988) statement that "feminism is, at this particular historical juncture in North American culture, 'the paradigmatic discourse of postmodernism'" (p. 27). Ultimately for Lather, Marxism, feminism, and poststructuralism can problematize one another "in the struggle to do cultural change work in a post-foundational context" (p. 31).

Women's self-knowledge. Rejecting notions of the "self" as a stable authentic essence and replacing it with one which posits the self as constructed by diverse discursive and non-discursive practices, Lather works to understand and research what women's self-knowledge and self-possession mean. She suggests: "De-centering is not so much the elimination of the subject as it is the multi-centeredness of action, a re-conceptualization of agency from subject-centered agency to the plurality and agency of meaning" (p. 120). Much of Lather's book lays out the main lines of postmodernism as these are formed by the inter-discursive encounters among feminism, Marxism, and poststructuralism. Central to her work are the implications she draws for research and pedagogy. As an example of her own attempt to "write science differently" (p. 123), and to engage in a postmodern liberatory research, Lather presents her treatment of a "data base" which consisted of "interviews, research reports, journal entries, and my own insights/musings collected over the course of a three-year inquiry into student resistance to liberatory curriculum in an introductory women's studies course" (p. 123). The presentation of her research is staged as a multi-layered text consisting of *a realist tale*, i.e. one presumably representing reality; *a critical tale*, i.e. one which seeks to reveal counter-hegemonic knowledge of the ways hegemonizing discourses work; *a deconstructionist tale* which "foregrounds the unsaid in our saying . . . and creates stories that disclose their constructed meanings" (p. 128); and *a reflexive tale*, one which brings "the teller of the tale back into the narrative, embodied, desiring, invested in a variety of often contradictory privileges and struggles" (p. 129).

Lather (1991b, 1989) points out that all research, even emancipatory or critical research, represent forms of knowledge and discourse that are inventions about the researchers. All research, she insists, also represents definitions, categorizations and classifications of the researchers themselves. All forms of research, she asserts: "elicit the Foucauldian question: how do practices to discover the truth about ourselves impact on our lives?" (p. 167). Referring to Ellsworth's (1989) work [see chapters 5 and 7], "we come to see that the discourses of emancipation are as much a part of Foucault's 'regimes of truth' as not" (pp. 160-161). Referring to Andrew Gitlin's (Gitlin et al., 1988) work, she argues that by not including his own teaching as an object of study and defining his role as "consultant and troubleshooter" reproduces the very "cult of expertise" Gitlin wishes to undermine. "It is clear," Lather (1991b) concludes, "that postmodernism can easily degenerate into another master narrative" (p. 165).

Lather has been criticized by one Marxist-Feminist as uncritical of postmodernism (Roman, 1993). Her work has also come under fire by one political theorist. In a recent work, Henry Giroux (1993b) accused Lather of "traces of racism and theoretical vanguardism" (p.184). While in his text he does not mention Lather by name, in the footnote (#23) following the quoted passage he writes:

> The ways in which binary arguments can trap a particular author into the most superficial arguments can be seen in a recent work by Patti Lather. What is so unusual about this text is that its call for openness, partiality, and multiple perspectives is badly undermined by the binarisms which structure its arguments. See Patti Lather, *Getting Smart* (New York, Routledge, 1991). (Giroux, 1993b, p. 188)

How Lather's work is guilty of these charges is left unspecified.

Lather's understanding of postmodernism appears strong. First, the research is a multilayered interpretation, not of a foundational reality, but of various interpretations. Second, each tale is allowed to problematize the next so that the subjects of the research as well as the researchers themselves are dispersed throughout the text. No one voice "sums it all up." Third, a variety of discourses, the feminist discourse of the women's studies course itself, the Marxist and feminist discourses of the critical tale, the poststructuralist discourse of the deconstructionist tale, and the autobiographical of the reflexive tale reveal the ambiguities in each and complicate each other. Fourth, its purpose is to understand more effectively how to create counter-hegemonic discourses. Finally, by acknowledging the multiple ways we are constituted in society, this research seeks to affirm differences without opposition. While Lather's work does not directly investigate the postmodern cultural landscape, that landscape is always apparent in her references to technologies of surveillance, the electronic media's construction of the subject, the images promulgated by the media, and phenomena such as post-feminism and heated consumerism.

It is in the most recent work of Henry Giroux, Joe Kincheloe, Shirley Steinberg, and especially Peter McLaren that we can see the full-blown influence of political theory on postmodernism, as well as an effort to articulate a postmodern political theory of pedagogy and curriculum.

A politics of the postmodern. In several essays and in his book, *Border Crossings: Cultural Workers and the Politics of Education*, Henry A. Giroux (1992a) attempts to preserve the emancipatory potential within modernism and combine it with aspects of postmodernist, feminist, and post-colonial discourses to extend his earlier [see chapter 5 for a review of this work] efforts to elaborate a critical, liberatory pedagogy. As he puts it: "The varied discourses of postmodernism, feminism, modernism and postcolonialism provide diverse but theoretically provocative and valuable insights for educators and cultural workers to construct an oppositional discourse" (1992a, p. 21). To identity those aspects of postmodern discourses which are valuable, Giroux begins with a summary of the characteristics of modernism and postmodernism. He divides the modern into social, aesthetic, and political modernity. Social modernity, according to Giroux, is characterized by a doctrine of progress, confidence in the beneficial possibilities of science and technology, a concern with quantifiable time, and a cult of reason and pragmatism. Aesthetic modernity has a dual character. On the one hand it offers a tradition of the avant garde's disgust with and opposition to bourgeois values. On the other hand, it privileges "high culture" over and against "popular culture." It is these two areas of modernism that have been attacked by postmodern and postcolonial discourses. For Giroux, social and aesthetic modernity combined to create the Eurocentric, white supremacist culture of modernism, which perpetrated "rationales of domination, subordination, and inequality" (1992a, p. 22). The third area of modernity he terms "political modernism," and he views this realm as offering possibilities for democratic revolution. This last area, as it has often been defined by liberal political theorists, has preserved or counted on certain ideas of rationality, reason, and the agency of the subject that have been severely criticized by feminist and postcolonial theory. Giroux is sensitive to this criticism. He works to make his own political theory more inclusive of feminist discourse, and he incorporates the voices of African-Americans, particularly African-American women.

Just as he wishes to preserve certain insights and possibilities historically associated with modernism, Giroux also wishes to identify the politically progressive elements of postmodernism and feminism. He argues:

At stake here is an attempt to provide a political and theoretical discourse
which can move beyond a postmodern aesthetic and a feminist separatism in
order to develop a project in which a politics of difference can emerge within a
shared discourse of democratic public life. (1992a, p. 6)

To identify progressive elements of postmodernism, Giroux appeals to the
political modernist criteria of justice, democracy, and human rights. Those
elements or aspects of postmodernism which Giroux identifies as regressive
are much the same ones that Lather criticized: heated consumerism, celebration of an apolitical popular culture, and the cultivation of an ironical or
cynical stance. Those aspects he finds progressive include: popular culture as
"worthy of serious and playful consideration" (p. 27); the "de-naturalizing" of
the world so that we do not measure our social, cultural, and political
discourses against some "natural" or foundational order or reality; the
location of aspects of reality in discursive practices which can then be opened
and thus become sites for action; the attention to "the relationship between
power and culture" (p. 23); the emphasis on multiplicity and difference such
that various histories and voices, previously silenced or ignored, can be
heard; and finally, its production of new forms of knowledge that contest the
modernist constructions of knowledge. Giroux distinguishes between those
feminisms which champion essentialism and separatism, and those that have
interacted with postmodernism, to the benefit of each. These, according to
Giroux, "provide postmodernism with a politics" (p. 33). He does not distinguish between progressive and regressive elements in black feminist theory.
He finds the work of theorists such as bell hooks [sic] (1992a) crucial in
articulating a critical pedagogy.

An ambitious undertaking. What Giroux has attempted in several essays and
in *Border Crossings* is to interweave various strands of modernist political
thought, postmodern feminist thought, postmodern critiques (particularly
those of Lyotard and Foucault), and postcolonialist theory, especially as
articulated by African-American feminism. This is an ambitious undertaking,
as it demands a continual subversion of one's position. Provisionality,
process and transformation are all key to Giroux's successful completion of
his emancipatory project. As for pedagogy, Giroux thinks in terms of
"cultural workers," who, using the insights gained from Giroux's interweaving of different theoretical stands, must work to "extend . . . the democratic
principles of liberty, equality, and justice to the widest possible relations"
(1992a, p. 246).

Clearly, Giroux's interest in postmodernism concerns its political potential. As John Willinsky (1992b) notes in his review of Aronowitz and Giroux's
Postmodern Education: "Aronowitz and Giroux take only from postmodernism
the elements which might serve their notion of a radically democratic education" (p. 344). Further, although Giroux allies himself with some of the
marginalized groups Foucault, Derrida, and Deleuze championed, he does
not discuss the construction of those identities, nor does he engage in a
deconstruction of his own discourse [see also Ellsworth, 1990b]. Despite

these weaknesses, Giroux's work remains significant for its call to teachers to investigate the culture of the postmodern moment and for its commitment to a more democratic and just society which might be achieved through a pedagogical project involving insights from feminism, postmodernism, modernism, and postcolonialism.

Post-formal Thinking: Joe L. Kincheloe and Shirley R. Steinberg

We reviewed Joe Kincheloe's postmodern political theory in chapter 5; here we focus upon the theory of post-formal thinking, formulated by Shirley Steinberg and Kincheloe, and published in the fall 1993 issue of the *Harvard Educational Review* [a notable issue for curriculum theory as it contained as well William H. Watkins' (1993) "Black Curriculum Orientations: a Preliminary Inquiry"; see chapter 6]. Like Kincheloe's (1993b) *Toward a Critical Politics of Teacher Thinking*, the Kincheloe/Steinberg essay stakes its interest in postmodernism as politically useful. Also like the Kincheloe book, this essay is remarkably synoptic, informed by diverse traditions, focused by postmodern political theory and by an interest in cognitive theory [see also chapter 13 for references to situated cognitive theory]. Here we will focus on how the postmodern curriculum discourse itself has been influenced not only by politics (as in Giroux's case), but as well by developmental and cognitive theory.

Kincheloe and Steinberg (1993) begin stating that:

> we have sought a middle ground that attempts to hold the progressive and democratic features of modernism while drawing upon the insights postmodernism provides concerning the failure of reason, the tyranny of grand narratives, the limitations of science, and the repositioning of relationships between dominant and subordinate cultural groups. (p. 296)

In this list we see the influences of postmodernism and poststructuralism on several contemporary curriculum discourses. Kincheloe and Steinberg focus upon their impact on what they term "a new zone of cognition—a *post-formal* thinking" (p. 297). What is post-formal thinking?

Kincheloe and Steinberg (1993) answer by outlining its antecedent, i.e. formal thinking, which they link with Piaget and with "a Cartesian-Newtonian mechanistic worldview that is caught in a cause-effect, hypothetico-deductive system of reasoning" (p. 297). [In this sentence we hear William Doll's (1993a) characterization of modernism.] Kincheloe and Steinberg (1993) go on to underline the absence in formal thinking of concerns of power relations, a taken-for-granted assumption that "facts" must "fit in" a theory, that contradictions must be resolved or eliminated, and that formal operational thought represents the highest level of human cognition. They cite the work of Jean Lave (1988) and Valerie Walkerdine (1984, 1988) as indicative of recent efforts to formulate "a post-Piagetian cognitive theory" (p. 297). Piaget himself (Piaget & Garcia, 1989) anticipated post-formal thinking, although stopped short of a "socio-cognitive theory" (p. 297) that politicizes cognition. Such theory draws upon but moves beyond the work of Howard Gardner (1983, 1989, 1991).

Post-formal thinking "can change the tenor of schools and the future of teaching" (Kincheloe & Steinberg, 1993, p. 301) by: 1) supporting an emphasis upon self-reflection for both students and teachers, 2) ending the privilege of "white male experience as the standard by which all other experiences are measured" (p. 301), 3) refusing to take for granted the "pronouncements of standardized-test and curriculum makers" (p. 301), and 4) emphasizing understanding rather than memorization and recitation. Post-formal thinking emphasizes "the origins of knowledge" (p. 302), "thinking about thinking—exploring the uncertain play of the imagination" (p. 303), "asking unique questions—problem detection" (p. 304), "exploring deep patterns and structures—uncovering the tacit forces, the hidden assumptions that shape perceptions of the world" (p. 305), "seeing relationships between ostensibly different things—metaphoric cognition" (p. 307), "uncovering various levels of connections between mind and ecosystem—revealing larger patterns of life forces" (p. 309), "deconstruction—seeing the world as a text to be read" (p. 310), "connecting logic and emotion—stretching the boundaries of consciousness" (p. 311), a "non-linear holism—transcending simplistic notions of cause-effect process" (p. 313), "contextualization" or "attending to the setting" (p. 314), "understanding the subtle interaction of particularity and generalization" (p. 315), and "uncovering the role of power in shaping the way the world is represented" (p. 316). Post-formal thinkers, Kincheloe and Steinberg tell us, "are able to understand the way power shapes their own lives" (p. 317). Concluding this strongly synoptic study, Kincheloe and Steinberg acknowledge that the notion of post-formal thinking itself is a social construction, "for it also emerges from a particular historical and social location" (p. 317). As a heuristic, the term functions as "mere starting point in our search for what constitutes a higher level of understanding" (p. 317).

Here we can see how postmodernism is being altered by other discursive projects within the field as it incorporates the concerns and themes of those projects. In the Kincheloe/Steinberg essay, for instance, cognitive theory reconfigures postmodern and poststructuralist interests in marginality, history, and power. Several features of post-formal thinking are indeed straight out of French poststructuralism (i.e. deconstruction), but others may in fact be antagonistic to that oeuvre (holism). The point here is not to make such observations in order to legitimate certain themes while rejecting others; rather it is to make note of how scholarly traditions from other disciplines are reconfigured when they are appropriated by curriculum theory. We will have more to say about this matter in chapter 15.

The Postmodern Critical Theory of Peter McLaren

When we come to the work of Peter McLaren, we encounter the fullest response to postmodernism from a political perspective, as we observed in chapter 5. McLaren not only describes postmodern culture, he clearly defines a kind of postmodern critical theory which can oppose what he sees as the "disintegrating" (1993a, p. 119) postmodern culture of the United States. There is little positive in McLaren's characterization of the postmodern:

[I] am using [postmodern] to refer to the material and semiotic organization of society, primarily with respect to . . . visual culture and the homogenization of culture. That is, I am referring to the current tendency toward desubstantialized meaning or "literalness" of the visual in which students seem unable to penetrate beyond the media bloated surface of things. (1991c, p. 145)

For McLaren the postmodern condition is a pathological condition. We have been reduced to "semiotic orphans, clinging to the underbelly of consumer society" (1991c, p. 146), which is marked by "a rapture of greed, an untempered and hyper-eroticized consumer will, racing currents of narcissism, severe economic and racial injustices, and a heightened social paranoia" (1993a, p. 118). Living in a state of historical amnesia, we have lost any real sense of what democracy is. He complains bitterly that "the American public has preferred a vision of democracy that is a mixture of Sunday barbecue banality, American Gladiator jocksniffery, AMWAY enterprise consciousness, and the ominous rhetoric of 'new world order' jingoism" (1993a, p. 118). Television's spectacles and representations of other spectacles become the ground on which we base our decisions about public and private life. Our "media" or "image" society, according to McLaren, offers us a depthless fragmented surface, which is only unified by its flow of images, all of which are consumed equally, draining the maps themselves of any real meaning. As spectators receive the images, the cultural dominants penetrate their bodies without even passing through their minds. For McLaren, this "marks the penetration of information technology within the body and the psyche" (1991c, p. 153). [For earlier studies of television, visual culture, and curriculum see McLuhan, 1962; Miel, 1962, pp. 72-78.]

A confusion of image and reality. In "The Spectacularizing Subjectivity: Media Knowledges and the New World Order," McLaren and Hammer (1992) suggest that the postmodern is characterized "by a confusion of the image and reality, and the loss of everyday history, the leeching out of any moral sense or political agency from the individual whose subjectivity is increasingly constructed through the media, and by the media's reduction of "the historical present to a collage of images, a symbiotic coupling of machine and body, a new cult of the simulacrum" (1992, p. 58). When one adds to this characterization of the postmodern McLaren's description of social and economic realities—poverty, homelessness, racism, sexism, homophobia, and the harshness of everyday life—the picture that emerges of the postmodern period is bleak indeed. McLaren views two possible responses that postmodern theory provides. One, following Teresa Ebert (1991), is "ludic postmodernism." This is characterized by the theories of writers such as Derrida, Lyotard, and Baudrillard, all of which McLaren regards as playfully subverting any political action by turning politics into textual practice. He asserts:

While ludic postmodernism may be applauded for attempting to deconstruct the way that power is deployed in cultural settings, it ultimately represents a form of detotalizing micropolitics in which the contextual specificity of difference is set up against the totalizing machineries of domination. (1993a, p. 124)

For McLaren (1991f)—as for other major postmodern political theorists [see, for instance, Kincheloe, 1993b, p. 85)—"ludic postmodernism" surrenders any possibility of political transformation because it "reflects . . . an epistemological relativism that calls for a tolerance of a range of meaning without advocating any one of them" (p. 11). McLaren argues that a "ludic postmodern theory" coupled with postmodern culture provides a space for the political right to advance. With the right's claims to truth, morality, and a unified culture, as well as its appeal to nostalgia, it can offer an illusory balm to those struggling through the postmodern moment. Further, as "ludic" postmodern theory cuts itself off from a more "total" critique, it ends up complicitous with the consumer culture by turning out ever new fragments of interpretations to be consumed.

A resistance postmodernism. As an alternative to "ludic" postmodern theory, McLaren proposes "resistance" postmodernism. This notion insists that differences are "situated *in* real social and historical conflicts and not simply over abstract differences or *between* semiotic contradictions" (p. 12). McLaren seems to be calling for a kind of Foucauldian analysis, but one which would pay more attention to non-discursive practices or the material conditions of discursive practices. Following Ebert, McLaren (1991f) writes: "To view difference as simple textuality, as a formal, rhetorical space in which representation narrates its own trajectory of signification, is to ignore the social and historical dimensions of difference" (p. 12). McLaren (1986a) insists that political activists must employ only an oppositional postmodernism. Otherwise, "there is a danger that social theorists will be reduced to mere curators of various discourses" (1986a, p. 392).

McLaren uses "resistance" postmodern theory to analyze, for example, the media's treatment of the Gulf War, the construction of the body, and multiculturalism. Regarding the Gulf War, McLaren analyzed how the media not only, in his view, "sold" the war but also created a particular subjectivity which would be disposed to "buy" it. He and Rhonda Hammer argued: "CNN's spectacularization of the Gulf War managed to position the viewer so that to be against it was to be 'biased' and to be in favor of it was to be 'objective.' Its narrative apparatus with its apparent realism . . . not only restructured our feelings surrounding the historical conditions being played out but through strategies of induction and disinformation was also able to mobilize particular economies of affect" (McLaren & Hammer, 1992, p. 53).

Media literacy and enfleshment. McLaren and Hammer went on to suggest a need for media literacy which would incorporate the insights of "resistance" postmodern theory. Such media literacy would analyze the media's construction of subjectivities and "objective" realities, investigate the ways capitalism is able to "insinuate itself into social practices and private perceptions through various forms of media knowledges" (p. 60), and reveal the withdrawal of a democracy whose after-image is spectacularized television. Further, they insisted that:

> A critical media literacy recognizes that we inhabit a photocentric, aural and televisional culture in which the proliferation of photographic and electronically produced images and sounds serves as a form of media catechism—perpetual pedagogy—through which individuals ritually encode and evaluate the engagements they make in the various discursive contexts of everyday life. (p. 61)

In "Schooling and the Postmodern Body" McLaren (1991c) turns his "resistance" postmodern analysis on the ways subjectivity is constructed "by the media, by leisure activities, by institutions such as the family and by cultural forms such as rock n' roll and music videos" (p. 165). McLaren calls this construction "enfleshment." He criticizes "ludic" postmodernism for its dissolution of the subject in the text, and he proposes that the subject can be understood as a body/subject [phenomenological language emerges here] that is partially constructed by discursive practices, but also formed by non-discursive practices, e.g., television. Furthermore, McLaren argues for the reclaiming of "modes of resistant subjectivity." Thus subjectivity emerges for him not only as subject position in discourse but also as self-conscious agency. He writes: "We must not forget that we can act in ways other than we do" (1991c, p. 162).

McLaren's use of the body/subject, reminiscent of Merleau-Ponty, raises the issue of experience and its relation to language. Is McLaren proposing, after all, a mixture of phenomenology and Marxism dressed up in postmodern clothes? In "Critical Pedagogy, Postcolonial Politics and Redemptive Remembrance," McLaren (1991d) states that language is constitutive of subjectivity, and that "experience is an understanding constructed largely linguistically. . . . No experience is unmediated" (p. 10). McLaren asserts that the task of critical pedagogy is:

> to provide students the discursive . . . means to understand ideological dimensions of their experiences, deep memories, psychological blockages and passionate investments in everyday life and relate these to material and symbolic structures of power operating in the larger contexts of social life. (p. 10)

This call for a kind of "archeological analysis" of the self is reminiscent of Pinar's "architecture of the self" (1988e, 1994). One difference between the two notions, however, is that McLaren's primary allegiance is to a political program carried out in the public sphere, a conception of politics which Pinar worries is antiquated. More than Giroux, McLaren problematizes his own discourse, and in so doing demonstrates discursively a politicized postmodernism. How the incorporation of postmodernism will play in a modernist political agenda remains a question, as we saw in chapter 5.

VIII
Conclusion: Post Poststructuralism?

Oscar Wilde once quipped that when good Americans die, they go to Paris. I think in Paris, when good theories die, they go to America.

(Henry Louis Gates, Jr., 1992, p. 186)

The effort to understand curriculum as poststructuralist, deconstructed, postmodern text has burst onto the scene since the 1980s, provoking responses from a number of other discourses within the field. Many questions remain, of course, and several directions appear in which one might pursue such an understanding of curriculum. For instance, as yet there has been little effort to map contemporary curriculum discourses employing a Foucauldian analysis. Cherryholmes has done much to discursively analyze traditional curriculum discourses, but no one as yet has examined, from points of view associated with discursive analysis, the contemporary, reconceptualized field. [While we have employed poststructural terms such as discourse and text in the organization of this book, we have not attempted to map the field poststructurally.] Questions of the subject, of agency, of the relationship between the narrator or subject of an autobiography, and the text of that autobiography, warrant further exploration. The definition of postmodernism remains unfinished.

If the discourses of phenomenology, autobiography, feminism, multiculturalism, politics, and poststructuralism are all simply different discourses which construct different objects or "figures" of study, then what are the relationships among them all, and what criteria might one employ to choose one over the other at any particular moment? Poststructuralism, deconstruction, and postmodernism may have signaled the death of a particular historical period, and more narrowly, particular ways of understanding curriculum, and in so doing they may have ushered in a period in which possibilities for understanding curriculum in ways as yet not conceived will increase exponentially. Despite the heuristic potential, we must be careful not to expect too much or become too devoted. As Henry Louis Gates, Jr., quipped: "Oscar Wilde once quipped that when good Americans die, they go to Paris. I think in Paris, when good theories die, they go to America" (Gates, 1992, p. 186). We must remain faithful to *our* field and its questions, not become disciples of a new French testament.

The curriculum discourse to which we turn next values skepticism as well. Its skepticism is not just toward poststructuralism (although poststructuralism has been taken very seriously there as well), but toward all of one's academic experience. Perhaps the central question is: what does curriculum have to do with my life? The project to understand curriculum as autobiographical/biographical text explores that question and how it might be answered.

Chapter 10

Understanding Curriculum as Autobiographical/Biographical Text

Autobiography becomes a medium for both teaching and research because each entry expresses the particular peace its author has made between the individuality of his or her subjectivity and the intersubjective and public character of meaning.

(Madeleine R. Grumet, 1990b, p. 324)

Education is both intensely personal and intensely political.

(Jo Anne Pagano, 1990, p. xiv)

All experience is the product of both the features of the world and the biography of the individual. Our experience is influenced by our past as it interacts with our present.

(Elliot W. Eisner, 1985c, pp. 25-26)

There is no better way to study curriculum than to study ourselves.

(F. Michael Connelly & D. Jean Clandinin, 1988a, p. 31)

I
Introduction: Three Streams of Scholarship

The systematic effort to understand curriculum as autobiographical and biographical text has its roots in the 1970s [see chapter 4], specifically with the publication of "*Currere*: Toward Reconceptualization" (Pinar, 1974b, 1975e) and *Toward a Poor Curriculum* (Pinar & Grumet, 1976). In that volume William F. Pinar and Madeleine R. Grumet introduced an autobiographical theory of curriculum, denoted by the Latin root of curriculum, "*currere*," meaning to run the course, or the running of the course. Pinar and Grumet elaborated a method by means of which students of curriculum could sketch the relations among school knowledge, life history, and intellectual development in ways that might function self-transformatively. Although not widely read upon its publication, *Toward a Poor Curriculum* has been characterized recently as a "tour de force" by Robert Graham (1991). Graham writes "if not precisely a *Principia*, the book's exploration of the existential, phenomenological and psychoanalytic bases for *currere* is an intellectual *tour de force* and must on all accounts be reckoned with" (1991, p.129). In 1976, however, for the traditional field the appearance of the book was a "non-event." Pinar and Grumet's establishment of autobiography as major curriculum discourse was elaborated in their subsequent works (Pinar, 1975b, 1975c, 1978b, 1981b, 1988c, 1989, 1994; Pinar & Grumet, 1981, 1992; Grumet, 1978, 1981, 1988b, 1988c, 1990a, 1990b, 1990c, 1990d, 1991, 1992). Autobiography is very much visible in the related work of others (Miller, 1979b, 1983a, 1988; 1990a, 1992a, 1992b, 1993a, 1993b); Wallenstein, 1979b; Meath-Lang, 1980, 1981, 1990a, 1990b, 1992, 1993; Meath-Lang & Albertini, 1989; Reiniger, 1982; Butt, 1985a, 1986, 1989, 1990, 1991; Butt & Raymond, 1986, 1988, 1992; Butt, Raymond, & Yamagishi, 1987, 1988; Butt, Townsend, & Raymond, 1990; Clandinin, 1985, 1986; Connelly and Clandinin, 1988a, 1988b, 1990, 1991; Goodson, 1981a, 1992a; Schubert & Ayers, 1992; Krall, 1988c; Daignault, 1987, 1992a; Nixon, 1992; Edgerton, 1991, 1992; McLaughlin & Tierney, 1993; LeCompte, 1993; Foster, 1993a; Rice, 1993). In some cases the significance of *currere* has gone unacknowledged. The earliest formulations of autobiography were linked with disputes with politically oriented scholars [see chapter 4] and quantitative researchers [against which it is still being defended; see LeCompte, 1993; Lincoln, 1993]. Illustrative of this general dispute was Beyer's (1979b) specific criticism of David Bleich's (1978) autobiographical or subjective criticism as ignoring the politics of estrangement. The autobiographers were not silent. Autobiographical scholars [see, for instance, Pinar, 1981b] insisted that political theory was abstract and obliterated the individual. [For a British view of this dispute, see Wankowski & Reid, 1982.] In this chapter, however, we focus upon developments during the 1980s.

Three major streams of scholarship. Also attacked by conservative curriculum scholars as "mystical alchemy" and "emancipation from research" (Tanner & Tanner, 1979, 1981) and more recently as "solipsistic and purely personal" (Gibson, 1991, p. 498), the effort to understand curriculum as autobiographical and biographical text has emerged as a major contemporary curriculum discourse. At present we can identity three streams of scholarship linked to autobiographical and biographical research. Of course, like streams the work of these scholars overflows their banks, occasionally merging with the themes, methods, and aspirations of others' work. Acknowledging then, the porous nature of these boundaries, we identity the following categories of scholarship which understand curriculum as autobiographical and biographical text. The first stream of scholarship we shall term autobiographical theory and practice. Major concepts in this stream include *currere*, collaboration, voice, dialogue journals, place, poststructuralist portraits of self and experience, and myth, dreams, and the imagination. The second stream we characterize as feminist autobiography, major concepts of which include community, the middle passage, and reclaiming the self. The final major category of studies are those efforts to understand teachers biographically and autobiographically, including collaborative biography and autobiographical praxis, the "personal practical knowledge" of teachers, teacher lore, and biographical studies of teachers' lives.

There is interesting and important autobiographical theory and practice which appear in other chapters. See, for instance, chapter 11 for the work of Margo Figgins, who employs autobiography in theater and teacher education (Figgins, 1992), chapter 6 for the work of Peter Taubman (1993a, 1993b) and Susan H. Edgerton (1993a), both of whom employ autobiography to understand racial issues. As we will see in chapter 13, autobiography has become important to recent approaches to teacher education, both pre-service and in-service, the latter of which appears to have been renamed teacher development.

Autobiography has historical antecedents, of course. Curriculum historian David Hamilton (1990; see chapter 2) tells us that the link between curriculum and life history was obvious to the Calvinists, who "already had a fondness for using 'curriculum' in the form vitae curriculum ('course' or 'career' of life)" (p. 28; see Daignault, 1987). First published in 1678 (Hill, 1988), John Bunyan's *Pilgrim's Progress* can be appreciated, in part, as an early effort to understand curriculum as autobiographical text. Hamilton (1990) notes:

> Christian's progress (i.e. his journey) follows a Calvinist pattern in that it takes place across well-mapped terrain and is directed, ultimately, towards a pre-ordained destination (i.e. aided by the Calvinist doctrine of predestination). Nevertheless, Christian's progress was also an open journey, or an open course through life (or curriculum vitae). (p. 34)

A sense of educational journey would lie dormant during the curriculum development era of the field, but it would be rearticulated during the Reconceptualization in the 1970s. [See Abbs (1974) for an early British statement of the uses of autobiography in education; see the autobiographical statements by the contributors to Pinar's (1975d) *Curriculum Theorizing: The Reconceptualists* for one illustration of the role of autobiography in the Reconceptualization; see especially Huebner (1975a, 1993) for his thirty-year interest in the notion of educational journey.] And during the 1980s efforts to understand curriculum autobiographically and biographically proceeded rapidly, often overlapping, frequently pointing to distinctive understandings of the relations between life history and educational experience. We begin our survey of this sector of contemporary American scholarship by describing its origins in the development of *currere* in the 1970s at the University of Rochester.

II
Autobiographical Theory and Classroom Practice

Currere is a reflexive cycle in which thought bends back upon itself and thus recovers its volition.

(Madeleine R. Grumet, 1976b, pp. 130-131)

Teachers struggle to find their voices in these journals as students simultaneously search for theirs. It is appropriate that, in writing, teachers and students journey together.

(Bonnie Meath-Lang, 1990b, p. 16)

Like a thief at the gates, the unconscious slips through the cracks of conscious control.

(Mary Aswell Doll, 1982, p. 198)

Currere

Contemporary efforts to understand curriculum as autobiographical and biographical text originated in the 1970s with the formulation of the concept of *currere* (Pinar, 1974b; Pinar & Grumet, 1976; see Pinar, 1994). *Currere* is the Latin infinitive of "curriculum," meaning:

> to run the course: Thus *currere* refers to an existential experience of institutional structures. The method of *currere* is a strategy devised to disclose experience, so that we may see more of it and see more clearly. With such seeing can come deepened understanding of the running, and with this, can come deepened agency. (Pinar & Grumet, 1976, p. vii)

The earliest expression of interest in autobiographical method can be traced to "Working from Within" (Pinar, 1972). In this article Pinar quotes the abstract expressionist painter Jackson Pollock to suggest that teachers and students might work from inner sources of insight and imagination. Recalling Pollock, Pinar writes: "Like some modern painters, my students and I have come to feel that we rarely need to refer to subject matter outside ourselves. We work from a different source. We work from within" (Pinar, 1972, p. 331).

Sanity, madness, and the school. Early expressions of autobiographical method seemed to suggest withdrawal from the public world as means of rediscovering both the private and public worlds. Such a strategy derived from Pinar's analysis of the ways schools make children mad (Pinar, 1975a). In "Sanity, Madness, and the School," written in 1972 (published in 1975), Pinar identified twelve intersecting effects of traditional schooling. These include:

1. hypertrophy or atrophy of fantasy life;
2. division or loss of self to others via modeling;
3. dependence and arrested development of autonomy;
4. criticism by others and the loss of self-love;
5. thwarting of affiliative needs;
6. estrangement from self and its effect upon the process of individuation;
7. self-direction becomes other-direction;
8. loss of self and internalization of externalized self;
9. internalization of the oppressor: development of a false self-system;
10. alienation from personal reality due to impersonality of schooling groups;
11. desiccation via disconfirmation; and

12. atrophy of capacity to perceive esthetically and sensuously. (1975a)

Pinar concluded that "we graduate, credentialized but crazed, erudite but fragmented shells of the human possibility" (p. 381). An autobiographical method for curriculum research had not yet been formulated. However, Pinar set the stage for its development in his final paragraph:

> an intensive adherence to one's "within" forms the basis of renewal strategies. What configurations this loyalty to one's subjectivity must take, and what such configurations mean for theorists of the process of education are not yet clear. To these questions we must proceed next. (1975a, p. 382)

The question of self-renewal was examined in its cultural sense in the context of *Heightened Consciousness, Cultural Revolution and Curriculum Theory*, the title of the 1973 University of Rochester Conference [see chapter 4 for the significance of this meeting] and the published proceedings (1974c). Finding encouragement in North American subcultural movements devoted to "heightened consciousness and cultural revolution," Pinar listed two next steps:

> 1) Continued, more detailed explication of the phenomena of cultural revolution and heightened consciousness. . . . Development of linkages with related disciplines, partly with psychoanalysis and psychology, but possibly as well with literature and philosophy; and 2) the design and evaluation of experimental curricula which will attempt to explore the inner life, hence to underscore and possibly aid in an ontological shift from outer to inner. The sketch of one such curricular proposal, although still in an inchoate stage, is my notion of a psychosocial-based humanities curriculum, with opportunities for intense interpersonal encounter, for solitude, as well as for study in traditional areas of humanities: literature, music, dance and so on. (Pinar, 1974c, p. 15)

Search for a method. In "Mr. Bennet and Mrs. Brown" Pinar (1974a) continued movement toward an autobiographical method. Here he criticized the curriculum field as "arrested," a critique he will repeat in the first state-of-the-art address to the American Educational Research Association (Pinar, 1979c; see chapter 4). Despite a historical emphasis upon the "individual" in the field, Pinar alleged that the word amounted to only a slogan, an abstraction emptied of concrete life. The field of curriculum, he continued, had forgotten the existing individual. In its preoccupation with the public and the visible, with design, sequencing, implementation, evaluation, and in its preoccupation with curricular materials, the curriculum field ignored the individual's experience of those materials: "It is not that the public world—curriculum, instruction, objectives—become unimportant; it is that to further comprehend their roles in the educational process we must take our eyes off them for a time, and begin a lengthy, systematic search of our inner experience" (Pinar, 1974a, p. 3). Such a search would require a method.

The method. Pinar framed the search for a method by noting: "I am lost in a world not of my making, in a personality not of my making. How to constitute the already constituted?" (1978b, p. 104). Studying the school curriculum, he suggested, can function to answer those questions. To do so requires shifting one's focus upon the "biographic functions" (1978b, p. 112) of specific events. Initially, he posited intellectual development and "biographic movement" as parallel; later he would regard their relationship as more complex (1994). Discerning "biographic function" is like peering into darkness. Pinar wrote: "The blind spot notion has to do with my experience of biographic and intellectual movements as steps. There is always a next step, although it may be veiled. It's as if it is a dark spot to be illumined, and once illumined, the step may be taken" (1978b, p. 112). Pinar's "next step" was the formulation of a method.

Pinar posits four steps or moments in the method of *currere*. These are 1) regressive, 2) progressive, 3) analytical, and 4) synthetical. These depict both temporal and reflective movements for the autobiographical study of educational experience and suggest the modes of cognitive relationality between knower and known that might characterize the structure of educational experience (Pinar & Grumet, 1976; Pinar, 1994). Stated simply, *currere* seeks to understand the contribution academic studies makes to one's understanding of his or her life. The student of educational experience takes as hypothesis that at any given moment he or she is in a "biographic situation" (Pinar & Grumet, 1976, p. 51), a structure of meaning that follows from past situations, but which contains, perhaps unarticulated, contradictions of past and present as well as images of possible futures. In 1975, however, he emphasized the sense of one's life or biography as linear. Pinar suggested:

> I can see that this has led to that; in that circumstance I chose that, I rejected this alternative; I affiliated with those people, then left them for these, that this field intrigued me intellectually, then that one; I worked on this problem, then that one. . . . I see that there is a coherence. Not necessarily a logical one, but a lived one, a felt one. The point of coherence is the biography as it is lived. . . . The predominant [question] is: what has been and what is now the nature of my educational experience? (Pinar & Grumet,1976, p. 52)

In the regressive step or moment Pinar posits one's "lived" or existential experience as "data source." To generate "data" one free associates, after the psychoanalytic technique, to recall the past, and enlarge—and thereby transform—one's memory. To do so one regresses: "One returns to the past, to capture it as it was, and as it hovers over the present" (1976, p. 55). In the progressive step Pinar looks toward what is not yet the case, what is not yet present. He notes that the future—like the past—inhabits the present. Meditatively the student of *currere* imagines possible futures. In the analytical stage the student examines both past and present. Etymologically, *ana* means "up, throughout"; *lysis* means "a loosening." The analysis of *currere* is like phenomenological bracketing; one distances oneself from past and future so to be more free of the present. He asks: "How is the future present in the past, the past in the future, and the present in both?" (Pinar & Grumet, 1976, p. 60). What is this temporal complexity that presents itself to me as my present? In the synthetical moment—etymologically *syn* means "together"; *tithenai* means "to place"—one re-enters the lived present. Conscious of one's breathing, one asks "who is that?" Listening carefully to one's own voice one asks: what is the meaning of the present? Pinar concludes:

> Make it all a whole. It, all of it—intellect, emotion, behavior—occurs in and through the physical body. As the body is a concrete whole, so what occurs within and through the body can become a discernible whole, integrated in its meaningfulness. . . . Mind in its place, I conceptualize the present situation. I am placed together. Synthesis. (Pinar & Grumet, 1976, p. 61)

Robert Graham's *Reading and Writing the Self* (1991) investigated the scholarship that the formulation of *currere* had provoked. Among this scholarship is that of Shigeru Asanuma, who in 1983 pointed to "Seikatsu Tsuzurikata," meaning the recording of one's life experiences, an autobiographical tradition born out of political oppression in Japan before Word War II. Asanuma observed: "This writing project shares the basic components similar to those of Pinar's autobiographical method" (p. 11). Later, Asanuma (1986a) studied autobiographical method in Japanese social studies education and (1986b) autobiographical scholarship as it linked with phenomenological curriculum theories. In the 1970s, however, Pinar and Grumet pursued the roots of *currere* in phenomenology [see chapter 8] and psychoanalysis.

Psychoanalytical foundations of currere. Madeleine R. Grumet described *currere* as an attempt to "reveal the ways that histories (both collective and individual) and hope suffuse our moments, and to study them through telling our stories of educational experience" (Grumet, 1981, p. 118). Further, the method of *currere* represents a wrestling of individual experience: "from the anonymity and generalization that had dominated social science and even literary interpretation in the heyday of structuralism and systems theories and returning it to the particular persons who lived it" (Grumet, 1981, p. 116). Grumet studied the foundations of *currere* in psychoanalysis, phenomenology, and existentialism (1976b, 1992). This scholarship makes clear that the apparent simplicity of autobiography—as employed in the method of *currere*—is just that: apparent. Psychoanalytically, *currere* as interpretation of experience involves the examination of manifest and latent meaning, conscious and unconscious content of language, as well as the political implications of such reflection and interpretation. In this regard, Grumet writes that *currere* "is what the individual does with the curriculum, his active reconstruction of his passage through its social, intellectual, physical structures" (1976b, p. 111). In so doing, *currere* discloses new structures in the process of naming old ones. However, *currere* is not psychotherapy.

> *Currere* is not a form of therapy designed to treat symptoms. It cannot employ self-reflection to the degree that psychoanalysis does to free the subject from the chains that objectivize him by liberating him from behaviors overdetermined by unconscious impulses, defenses or repetition compulsions. Habermas maintains that in the analytic situation the very understanding of the causal

connections in one's own life history dissolves them. The self that was the object of its history regains subject status in self-formative process. While *currere* cannot share the magnitude of this claim, it can adopt both its developmental goal and methodological assumptions that by bringing the structures of experience to awareness, one enhances the ability to direct the process of one's own development. (1976b, p. 115)

The point, Grumet notes, is not to attempt to merely talk about education; it is to intensify one's experience of education.

Regression in the service of the ego. In psychoanalytical terms, *currere* represents an alternation of primary and secondary processes, unmediated experience and one's reconstruction of same. It represents an extension of "ego structure" via conversation of ego with nonego. Nonego is understood here as both external (including the school curriculum) and internal (including both personal and in the Jungian system, collective unconscious). In the practice of *currere*, the self-scrutinizing eye is not as relaxed as it might be in a psychoanalytic setting. Still, the subject employs a relaxed, permissive minding, much like Kris' (1952) notion of regression in the service of the ego. Grumet views *currere* as acknowledging Habermas' claim that the public language has driven ideas and impulses undermining its order out of its grammar and into the fragmentary language of the dream and the unconscious. Any authentic public political opposition requires political struggle in the terrains of character and identity. In this regard Grumet conceives of *currere* as parental in its function:

> The function of *currere* in even the elementary grades would serve to reinforce the dialectical relationship of the family and the school. By attending to the young student's experience of the curriculum, *currere* repeats the processes that Frankenstein (1966) calls the maternal and paternal principles. . . . As *currere* simultaneously acknowledges the student's experience and encourages him to distance himself from it *currere* is repeating the patterns of ego development initiated in the infant's early object relations. (1976b, p. 128)

Currere reminds the child that he or she is distinct from the nonego, the curriculum. Of course, the point is not to cultivate an adversarial relationship between the school and the child, but to establish sufficient distance so that the child will not be subsumed in the school or, alternately, submerged in his experience. The structures of the school and the school subjects are understood as distinct from the student, but linked to his lived experience, "so that he can make use of them without giving himself up to them" (1976b, p. 129). *Currere* encourages an alternating rhythm of incorporation of nonego by ego with that of a distantiation from the ego's introjected contents. Grumet summarizes: "*Currere* is a reflexive cycle in which thought bends back upon itself and thus recovers its volition" (pp. 130-131). As Robert Graham (1989) has observed: "Autobiography has everything to learn from psychoanalysis" (p. 101).

While Pinar has been his own respondent in his practice of *currere*, Grumet employed *currere* in teacher training seminars [see this chapter], in supervision (1979a), and in theater workshops [see chapter 11]. In contrast to psychoanalysis, Grumet discourages a friendship transference; from the beginning the student is taught to become his own mirror. Additionally, while in psychoanalysis the analyst may insist that the analysand confront obstacles to the flow of his free association, in *currere* there is no attempt to draw material from the student's resistance. Further, *currere* does not proceed with the powerful transference and countertransference characteristic of the psychoanalytic process. Grumet notes:

> While it is not possible to claim that transference does not take place at all within the writings and responses in the practice of *currere* or within any teaching situation for that matter, awareness of the phenomenon may deter its development. . . . Sensitivity to the projections and blocks that appear in counter-transference is heightened in the respondent who has himself been the subject of *currere*, if not psychoanalysis. (p. 139)

Grumet reminds her readers that *currere* does not aspire to alter basic personality tendencies; it offers to students and teachers a method by means of which greater access to their lived experience of schools can be accomplished (Pinar & Grumet, 1976). Grumet's theorization and employment of *currere* underline its social character and political potential.

Collaboration. Currere may seem solitary work, and it can be. Indeed, Pinar asserts it must be, at least occasionally. This aspect of *currere* has led to misunderstandings of autobiographical work as solipsistic and asocial:

> Such a perspective [*currere*] on curriculum is interesting, but in terms of the idealized civic mission of the school, which Dewey was committed to fulfilling, the premium placed on the self-encounter appears to come at the expense of the collective-encounter so obviously valued by Dewey. (Hlebowitsh, 1992, p. 76)

Pinar has acknowledged as well that the individual is a social process, that individual identity is, in Grumet's (1990b) word, a "chorus." Other scholars underline the collaborative character of autobiographical/biographical research, among them Nel Noddings (1986), Janet L. Miller (1990a, 1992e), and Richard Butt and Danielle Raymond (1992). Noddings viewed such research as one in which all participants regard themselves as members of a community. She wrote: "we approach our goal by living with those whom we teach in a caring community, through modeling, dialogue, practice and confirmation" (p. 502). Janet Miller agrees that collaborative relationships with teachers need to be of "long duration in order to take into account the complex constraints of those who want to uncover as yet unrecognized forms of oppression" (Miller, 1990a, p. 153). Through the use of autobiographical journals and through collaborative efforts to understand lived experience, Miller illustrates the necessity of collaboration and the social nature of autobiographical research. Describing her report of collaborative work with graduate students, Miller explained:

This narrative, then attempts to brings teachers' voices to the center of the dialogue and debate surrounding current educational reform, teacher educa- tion restructuring efforts, and research on teachers' knowledge. Our group's exploration of the possibilities of collaborative and interactive research as one way in which we might "recover our own possibilities" are at the heart of this chronicle. (Miller, 1990a, p. 10)

Her description of a collaborative research group (including a school psychologist, a first-grade teacher, a department chairperson, a special educa- tor, a science teacher, and the professor) illustrates vividly the lived character of autobiographical teacher research. The process of creating an interpreta- tive community in which lived experience can be discovered, expressed, and interpreted is one, in Miller's phrase, of "creating spaces." Such spaces must accompany the effort to understand curriculum as autobiographical text.

Also illustrative of the autobiographical interest in collaboration is Janet Miller's (1992a) discussion of her relationship with Katherine, the first-grade teacher from the teacher-researcher group reported in *Creating Spaces and Finding Voices*. Miller focuses upon their concurrent struggles to examine and analyze, from feminist perspectives, the nurturing and caring stereotypes associated especially with early childhood education. Miller discusses the ways in which Katherine's struggles informed her own attempts to preserve the nurturing and connected aspects of her work while, at the same time, chal- lenging essentialized versions of women as teachers. In another essay, Miller (1992d) reflects on the ways in which she herself was prepared as a teacher of English, initiated into the canon, and kept ignorant of the ways in which the teacher role and their content are gendered, raced, and classed.

Public and private. The categories of public and private, important in Miller's earlier work, surface also in her teacher research. The fissures, she writes, which appear between public and private are "artificial distinctions that separate us from ourselves and from the relationships in which knowl- edge about self and our worlds are generated" (Miller, 1990a, p. 172). Collaborative efforts such as those Miller describes offer the possibility of passages back and forth between private and public; such passages permit an envisioning and sharing of possible worlds for teachers and those with whom they work in schools (Miller, 1990a). Voice emerges as an important concept not only in the effort to understand curriculum as autobiographical and biographical text, but in feminist and political theory as well (Ellsworth, 1989) [see chapters 5 and 7]. As the title of Miller's award-winning study suggests— *Creating Spaces and Finding Voices* (1990a)—"voice" is a major concept in the autobiographical literature also. Miller, Noddings, and Hogan all agree that time, relationship, space, and voice are prerequisites for collaborative work (Connelly & Clandinin, 1990). Deborah Britzman has explained:

Voice is meaning that resides in the individual and enables that individual to participate in a community. . . . The struggle for voice begins when a person attempts to communicate meaning to someone else. Finding the words, speak- ing for oneself, and feeling heard by others are all a part of this process. . . .

Voice suggests relationships: the individual's relationship to the meaning of her/his experience and hence, to language, and the individual's relationship to the other, since understanding is a social process. (quoted in Connelly & Clandinin, 1990, p. 4; see also Apple, 1988b)

We shall review Grumet's reservations concerning the concept of voice in the next section of this chapter. For Janet Miller (1990a), the concept is also problematized. She rejects a fixed notion of voice that implies that, once "found," one is always able to articulate oneself, to pronounce one's identity, and to be heard:

> However, in openly grappling with the possibility of imposition and in presenting the many voices, the multiple positions and changing perspectives from which each of us speaks, I have tried to point to the ways in which each of us shared in the formation and constant reformation of our collaborative processes. . . . We have begun to hear our multiple voices within the contexts of our sustained collaboration, and thus recognized that "finding voices" is not a definitive event but rather a continuous and relational process. (p. x-xi)

To conduct studies which support the articulation of "voice" requires a collaborative research protocol, a community of affiliation (Pagano, 1990), a lived space where teachers' voices may be expressed (Miller, 1990a). As Britzman (1991) notes:

> No psychometric measures distance the researcher from the teacher. Indeed, it is for researchers to narrate and interpret the words of others and render explicit their own process of understanding. This type of knowledge production requires the researcher to be sensitive to representing the voices of those experiencing educational life as sources of knowledge, and to be committed to preserving their dignity and struggle. (p. 51)

As William Ayers (1990), a student of student voices [and of teaching; see Ayers, 1993], emphasizes: "life-history is always collaborative, negotiated, co-constructed" (p. 274). Using the contexts of the teacher-researcher collaborative, Miller (1992a, 1992b) continues to address tensions among curriculum discourses, teachers' daily lives, her daily life and commitments as a curriculum theorist, and the possible actions and theories that can be constructed out of those tensions.

Voice

As we have seen, the concept of voice is central in several strands of autobiographical and biographical scholarship. Janet Miller, D. Jean Clandinin, and F. Michael Connelly all emphasize the concept of voice. Grumet has expressed a reservation concerning the concept. She acknowledges that she is less than comfortable "with voice as a metaphor for feminist theory and pedagogy" (1990a, 277). In the 1970's the notion of "voice" enabled Grumet "to differentiate my work from male work and my text from male text" (Grumet, 1990a, p. 278). Grumet suggested: "Drawn from the body and associated with gender, voice splinters the fiction of an androgynous speaker as we hear rhythms, relations, sounds, stories, and style that we identify as male or female" (Grumet, 1990a, p. 278).

However, there may be limits. Voice may not only express the self-affirmative, self-differentiating complexity that is a woman's voice. Indeed, in the gaze of an objectifying, voyeuristic male, voice may be defensive. Grumet observes:

> If the voice is the medium for the projection of meaning, then woman as a meaning maker is undermined by the visual emphasis on her body as an object of display and desire. . . . If he projected the gaze as accuser or interrogator, she receives it, and I suspect, uses speech to deflect it. Teacher talk is then a defensive move deployed to assert her subjectivity in the face of the objectifying gaze. (Grumet, 1990a, p. 279)

Grumet locates this defensiveness in the fantasy of objectification, deflected and reorganized as a projection of maternity. Voice may represent a male narrowing of woman's possibility, a reduction of freedom to social role. She worries: "burdened by nostalgia, the maternal voice in educational discourse is prey to sentimentality and to an audience that consigns its melodies to fantasy, no matter how compelling" (Grumet, 1990a, p. 281). Can women escape the objectifying gaze of male subjectivity which reduces the woman to "woman?" Grumet suggests that a route out may be found in the very same location, the "voice," although understood multivocally. She asserts: "One escape is found in the chorus that is our own voice. . . . We need not dissolve identity in order to acknowledge that identity is a choral and not a solo performance" (Grumet, 1990a, p. 281).

A more complex notion of voice. To elaborate such a construction of voice, Grumet theorizes a more complex notion of voice. She identifies three elements or parts to educational voice: situation, narrative, and interpretation. She explains:

> The first, situation, acknowledges that we tell our story as a speech event that involves the social, cultural, and political relations in and to which we speak. Narrative, or narratives as I prefer, invites all the specificity, presence, and power that the symbolic and semiotic registers of our speaking can provide. And interpretation provides another voice, a reflexive and more distant one. . . . None is privileged. (Grumet, 1990a, pp. 281-2)

Grumet's elucidation of voice is heuristically rich. Understanding the autobiographical voice as the site for society, culture, and politics, a "site" which can be reflexively reconfigured via interpretation of voice, offers both political program and pedagogical process to a feminist notion of voice [see also Munro, in press].

Children's voices. William Ayers has argued: "What is missing in the research literature is the experience of crisis, is the insider's view" (Ayers, 1990, p. 271). By insider Ayers means the student, and in particular the urban elementary school student. Ayers wants to understand how such children understand their situation. Other questions include: "How do they survive, construct a meaningful universe, live with dignity or at least some sense of personal worth? What are their aims and how do their goals change over time? What voices do they attend to? (Ayers, 1990, p. 271). Missing in the scholarly research, Ayers insists, is "understanding the situation from within" (Ayers, 1990, p. 272). [A recent review of research on student experience supports Ayers' contention; see Erickson & Shultz, 1992, and chapter 13.] To correct this omission, Ayers suggests that scholars work with children to "convey their lives as they present them, to portray the world with immediacy as they see it, to create a monograph on meaning in which these youngsters are conscious collaborators" (Ayers, 1990, p. 272). Ayers notes: "This leads us to autobiography as story-telling" (p. 272). Among the problems in utilizing autobiography in conveying the lived experience of young children is a fundamental one: "how to convey a sense of individual life and collective design, of local detail and general structure, of personal integrity and social dimension" (p. 274). He continues: "The value of engaging these problems lies in the fact that autobiography is an act of self-creation and potentially of transformation" (Ayers, 1990, p. 274).

Ayers sees two audiences for this effort to understanding curriculum as autobiographic text. The first are the children themselves and their families. The second are educators, policy-makers, and other stakeholders in schools. Two audiences may require two distinct forms: monographs for scholars and interested educators, and child-autobiographies accessible to ten-year olds. Ayers concludes:

> Autobiography is one way to expand the natural history of children in schools. It can be an antidote to arid research and empty promises. It contributes more details, more instances, more cases. Reaching for wholeness is finally its own reward. It must begin with humility and more than a little awe. (Ayers, 1990, p. 275)

Ayers' project promises to add significantly to our understanding of how curriculum is experienced by those who live it day by day. It is a project that has been pursued by Paula Salvio with older students.

Undergraduate voices. Paula Salvio reports her autobiographical work with 25 undergraduate women in 1989, whom she asked to write a series of autobiographical narratives about educational experiences they regarded as "artistic." Salvio discovered that the narratives indicated that students reject aesthetic experiences in their lives. She observes: "Just as art is marginalized in schools . . . so its political and epistemological significance is marginalized in our lives" (Salvio, 1990, p. 283). She links aesthetic experience with:

> the meanings that are generated through intimate social relationships. In such relationships, as in aesthetic experience, the look, the touch, the distance we keep from one another and the objects framing our lives are all meaningful, and this meaning is grasped in a moment. (Salvio, 1990, p. 284)

In other words, Salvio regards that knowledge acquired via aesthetic experience can provide an understanding of the inner life.

To be like her and him. Such an understanding of inner life is suggested in the journal entries of one student. A physics major, Mary writes:

> Even though I strive for the power my father seemed to possess, I cannot escape the love and respect that I have for my mother. A part of me wants to be like her. If I could only be like her and have beauty and expression; while still being able to achieve my father's science and freedom, and power. (Salvio, 1990, p. 286)

Locating academic interests in life history and in the relationships with one's parents enables one to understand that academic work is also profound psychological labor. The autobiographically informed teacher supports awareness of this process. Salvio (1990) comments:

> Here, Mary's struggle to individuate from her mother is expressed as a desire literally to escape the feelings of love and respect she has for her. She contemplates the possibility of transgressing the limits of maternal knowledge, so she can attain the power, knowledge and freedom that circulates in the realm of her father. (p. 286)

To read against the text. Salvio regards the pedagogical challenge in student autobiography as creating a context in which students can identify and then investigate those epistemological assumptions which underlie their narratives. She writes: "When I ask students to 'read against' a text I invite them to move beyond an obvious, seemingly reasonable meaning to uncover the pedagogical, political, and epistemological meanings that are so often masked by convention" (Salvio, 1990, p. 287). "Threshold autobiography" is the term Salvio employs to depict this form of student autobiography, "for the writer inscribes into the curriculum her process of becoming" (288). Such autobiography:

> casts the questions, life-stories, pain, and desire that characterizes the journey for self-knowledge into an expressive form which captures the life feeling. Placed within the context of feminist studies, student autobiography is a provisional symbol of the writer's search for self-knowledge and of the epistemological forms she transgresses to attain it. (Salvio, 1990, p. 288)

Salvio's subtle pedagogical work expresses important elements of autobiographical understanding, among them the porous boundaries between self and knowledge, and the power of self-reflexivity in intensifying the educative process.

Voices of women teachers. In addition to theoretical studies of voice, and the reporting of the voices of children and undergraduate students, scholars have labored to report the voices of women (Miller, 1990a; Grumet, 1990a; Munro, 1992; Ellsworth, 1993; Pagano, 1988a, 1990; Reiniger, 1982). Important to this project has been the research of Kathleen Casey (1990),who has reported narratives of women teachers, including four groups. The first group was comprised of secular Jewish women who have been, at some time in their lives, active in the Old and New Left, and who have taught in urban public schools. The second group was comprised of Catholic religious women, who have taught in parochial schools and who have participated in a ministry concerned with social justice. The third group was composed of retired European-American women, who attended normal schools and taught before they were married, then returned to college for degrees, and taught in public schools when their own children left home. These were women who made "inconspicuous" contributions to a number of political causes. The fourth group was comprised of African-American women who demonstrated a life-long commitment to the black community, and who have taught in urban public schools. Casey observes that these voices have not exactly dominated the research literature. These voices which capture the "lived" quality of teaching, exhibit—in her judgment—considerable psychological sophistication. One woman reported:

> I have never in my life liked this school system, where I have been treated so much like a child. And it certainly was from the very start an *enormous* rage in my heart, strictly personal rage at how I was treated. From the first time that I went to get certified and was shouted at by matrons and you know had to carry your urine sample in and I mean the whole thing the impersonal debasing way in which you were treated. It enraged me. (quoted in Casey, 1990, p. 306, emphasis in original)

This narrator reflects on the infantilization of women teachers:

> On the whole, elementary school teachers do not have much solidarity. They would bitch and complain about the principal, and if I would speak up at a meeting in which we were all together, they would never back me up. They easily fell back into the pattern of thinking of themselves as children, and she was Momma. Or Pappa. (quoted in Casey, 1990, p. 306)

Other women expressed a sense of solidarity with students:

> And the reason I left that school was that I didn't agree with a lot of the philosophy in the school. I really believe that a school is a place where people come together, and form some kind of community and it's *not* a prison, and if it's likened to anything it's likened to a family rather than a prison. And, my experience in that school was that it was *much* closer to a prison. And I was not into prison ministry at the time! So I decided, I will get out of here. (quoted in Casey, 1990, p. 308, emphasis in original)

Another woman cannot tolerate that misunderstanding of children typical in a masculinist school:

> I left teaching because I got tired of trying to change the system. You know, I couldn't do it. And I couldn't fight any longer. I couldn't stand to watch the injustice against the kids, and I felt there was a lot of oppression. Toward children. And *because* of that, I wanted to stay in it, so that there'd at least be a *few*

voices, because the, some of the teachers I worked with were *super*, super people, you know, and were for the children. It doesn't make any sense to me if you're in the teaching and really not for the kids. It seemed like the hierarchy, you know, the *administrative* people in the education system, were just so *blind*, to who the children were. (quoted in Casey, 1990, pp. 308-309, emphasis in original)

Casey gives each women her "space" and "voice." One woman describes teaching literacy in a prison:

> There is not one reason why people go to prison. These guys have basic serious problems. It's not just that they did a purse snatching or an armed robbery. You know, these guys have real learning problems. And what these guys needed was, you know, they needed mothers. You know, they needed warm tender, loving care, which, of course, that was impossible to give them. They were so needy. They needed so many things. (quoted in Casey, 1990, p. 316)

In each of these passages a voice of teacher-as-mother is evident. Versions of this and other metaphors await documentation. Casey (1990) concludes:

> I have tried to show the ways in which ordinary women teachers have actively constructed meaning out of their own lived experiences. This curriculum theorizing will, hopefully, inspire other educators in their own reflections on such crucial issues as nurture, authority, and dependence. (p. 319)

These issues are indeed crucial and Casey's research accomplishes their portrayal in the lives of ordinary woman teachers. It is a considerable achievement and an important contribution to the field. As we saw in chapter 7, Grumet takes nurture to be a central issue in understanding women and teaching. As we saw also in that chapter, Jo Anne Pagano developed feminist understandings of authority and dependence. Casey's studies create vivid views of these issues, as they are lived and reported by women.

Dialogue and academic journals. While others have worked in this area (Roderick, 1984), the pre-eminent curriculum scholar in the classroom use of autobiography in journals is Bonnie Meath-Lang (1980; 1981; Meath-Lang, Caccamise, & Albertini, 1982). Meath-Lang (1992) has argued that curriculum study based on lived experience becomes pedagogically crucial in the face of a popular culture that devalues the life-story and appropriates it through the tabloid impulse and political inauthenticity. Well aware of the 1970s Reconceptualization of the field, Bonnie Meath-Lang (1992) took very seriously the call to return to the use of "life material" as a data base for research questions pertaining to social and language-related aspects of schooling. Working at the National Technical Institute for the Deaf, Meath-Lang (1990b) employed dialogue journals with deaf students and second-language learners. She conceived of dialogue journals as consonant with reconceptualized curriculum theory, specifically with its autobiographical methods and political ideals:

> Teachers struggle to find their voices in these journals as students simultaneously search for theirs. It is appropriate that, in writing, teachers and students

journey together. On the way, as I hope these texts demonstrate, both see greater control, complex structuring, and real fluency emerge; all characteristics that some people assume deaf students and non-native speakers cannot achieve. (p. 16)

In the biographies written by her students in academic journals, Meath-Lang (1992) found a growing sensitivity to the modes of description, as well as a heightened skepticism surrounding biographical language in both classroom contexts and popular literature. To provide support for collective skepticism, Meath-Lang (in press) worked to form writing communities: "I have argued that the formation of writing communities through dialogue journals ⟵ results, in effect, in reconceiving the curriculum; for student and teacher writing—and writing acts—*become* the curriculum" (p. 5). She presents two arguments for the use of dialogue journals in language classes: 1) dialogue journals encourage students to attempt a greater variety of language functions, that is, use of the language for different purposes and audiences, and 2) they encourage students to assume greater responsibility for control of successful communication in their own languages (Albertini & Meath-Lang, 1986). In Meath-Lang's and John Albertini's experience, dialogue journals create a conversant curriculum of activity, retrospection, and introspection: "The marriage of curriculum theory and language study is in itself a dialogue, only beginning; supported in structure by the voices of bewildered, brave people—some of them silent" (p. 198).

Meath-Lang's work with dialogue journals has persuaded her that the notion of access needs reconsideration. In "The Risk of Writing Outside the Margins: A Re-examination of the Notion of Access," she writes: "It is imperative that we begin to work on our institutions to broaden the notion of access and make access an inclusive term—inclusive of the pedagogical access students on the margins need, and access to experience marginalized students can offer us" (1993, p. 378). Harry Lang and Bonnie Meath-Lang (1991) see three major themes regarding deaf students' learning in postsecondary environments: 1) the affirmation of reflective and phenomenological orientations in learning and in research on learning, 2) the influence of feminist inquiry on the construction of knowledge, especially in young adults, and 3) the more careful examination of the role of social and political consciousness in intellectual development. Such orientations become even more important in the 1990s:

> Despite technological advances, social change, and increasing acceptance of sign language communication alone and in various combinations with oral/aural communication, the isolating effects of deafness remain, particularly for learners in high-pressure mainstream settings. As a consequence, teachers and support personnel in postsecondary programs need to understand deafness in a fuller educational sense, interacting with the words and presence of deaf people. (p. 84)

Meath-Lang (1990) reminds us: "Lonely, grieving, and marginalized persons are accustomed to silence. It is, to use Ted Aoki's metaphor, the dwelling-place of much of their experience" (p. 12). Meath-Lang is not hinting at sentimentality or patronization. Silence can be a opportunity for self-encounter and self-nurturance, as feminist theorists [see also Wear, 1993] have suggested:

> Further, a respect for authentic silence must be nurtured in schools, and in a sense that silence can convey disapproval of bigotry, aesthetic appreciation, and a profound empathy that might be shared. . . . In trying to establish a community of inquiry in classrooms, we cannot avoid life-issues, the sources of pain, confusion, and estrangement. There are political forces which would sever these issues from the curriculum, maintaining that explorations of life and death detract from family primacy, basic skills, and content mastery. We are often preoccupied, however, as I was last spring, with challenges, griefs, and desires of others, searching voices echoing others past. Our students are preoccupied no less than we. Learning to respond and choosing our responses to life, death, disability, and loss are the most basic skills of all. (pp. 15-16)

How can dialogue journals support such fundamental and human explorations and skills? Meath-Lang and Albertini (1989) advise:

> The dialogue journal should be used selectively, between partners and with classes where a certain level of commitment, reciprocity, and disclosure is understood and enacted. The dialogue journal may also be one strategy for dialogic classrooms, where authority is decentered in the interest of each student making a genuine, critical offering of perspective to a classroom community. (p. 11)

The dialogue these journals support is not completely open-ended, certainly not without aim. Authenticity, clarity, exploration of academic issues, and self-definition characterize the pedagogy of dialogue journals:

> To be authentic teacher-writers, our own voices must be examined, expressed, heeded, and continually clarified. Our students' voices in writing must be elicited, discussed, and honored, thoughtfully and, in the best sense of the word, critically. Indeed, as in the case of those of us working with deaf students, voice must be defined and redefined—perhaps even identified as a presence *with* the student, in the student's terms. And these tasks must be conducted with risk and with resoluteness. (p. 13)

Bonnie Meath-Lang's work with dialogue journals must be regarded as one of the most thoughtful examples of autobiographical theory and practice available today.

Place: Joe L. Kincheloe and William F. Pinar

In addition to voice, community, and gender, the concept of "place" has emerged as crucial to understanding curriculum autobiographically and biographically. [See John S. Lofty's (1992) *Time to Write* for a description of the influence of place and time, in this instance, on learning to write.] This question of place has been taken up by Joe Kincheloe and William Pinar (1991) in their collection *Curriculum as Social Psychoanalysis: The Significance of*

Place, a work we reported briefly in chapter 5 as a political concept. Here we examine its autobiographical aspects. In *Curriculum as Social Psychoanalysis*, seven writers examine issues of curriculum as related to "place," and in particular, the "place" that is the American South. [See also Adams, 1992.] Quoting the southern writer Eudora Welty, Kincheloe and Pinar note that place and human feeling are intertwined. When events take place, they achieve particularity and concreteness; they become infused with feeling. Fiction—novels, short stories—express daily human experience, situated in concrete places with specific characters. Kincheloe and Pinar (1991) write: "place is the life-force of fiction, serving as the crossroads of circumstance, the playing field on which drama evolves" (p. 4). Place and time are inter-twined: "Place is place only if accompanied by a history" (p. 8).

Displacement. Susan Huddleston Edgerton (1991; see also chapter 6) writes autobiographically of her childhood in northern Louisiana, attempting to situate her understanding of the South as place in her life history and in her reading of the autobiography of Maya Angelou (Angelou, 1969, 1976; O'Neale, 1984). She shares a fundamental experience of displacement and "otherness" with Angelou, despite their racial difference. She appreciates certain positive elements of the Southern experience: "nature, smells, risk taking, and music" (p. 96). In the distinction between alienation and angst, Edgerton distinguishes her experience from Angelou's. Edgerton explains:

> Alienation is estrangement, a sense of lost connection, displacement in the midst of place. Angst is not so much a result of being disconnected as being dissatisfied with the connection. . . . The alienated are, I believe, closer to having a sense of the social construction of alienation-producing circumstances. Clearly, what Angelou experienced was alienation. . . . While some of my nega-tive experience of the South is tied to alienation—discomfort with Southern sexism, racism, and fundamentalism—my most embedded experiences . . . are closer to angst. . . . Our difference functions as a foil, forcing me back onto myself. (pp. 96-97)

Kathleen P. Bennett employed autobiography in her course "Schooling in Appalachia." By reading Appalachian fiction and writing autobiographically, Bennett taught a heightened sense of place, and of self. One student explored these aspects of her identity in a final paper:

> My background in teaching is as strong as is my Appalachian background. . . . My grandmother's love of drama was recreated in me; my mother's drive and determination have been passed on to me; and my great-uncle's practical approach to problem solving is beginning to come my way, too. I am an Appalachian, born and bred. (quoted in Bennett, 1991, p. 119)

An autobiographical understanding of pedagogical practice is clearly informed by the complexity of place.

Willie Morris and southern ghosts. Joe L. Kincheloe (1991b) draws upon the autobiography of Willie Morris, whose "sensitivity is innocently phenomenological, as he responds poetically to the southern ghosts that haunted his mind and body" (p. 123). Kincheloe characterizes Morris as a student of southern traditions, constantly linking his life history to a history of place. The southern sense of place is sharp, as suggested in the following conversation between a young Mississippian and a Harvard student, taken from Morris' *Terrains of the Heart*.

> Where are you from? the Mississippian asked.
> What do you mean?
> Well, where are you from? Where did you go to high school?
> The other man mentioned an Eastern prep school.
> But where did you grow up? Where are your parents?
> Well, my father is in Switzerland, I think, and my mother is asleep in the next room.
> (Morris,1981, pp.30-31, quoted in Kincheloe, 1991b, p. 132)

The Mississippian realizes: "For the first time in my life, I understood that not all Americans are *from* somewhere (quoted in Kincheloe, 1991b, p. 132, emphasis in original).

Kincheloe summarizes Morris' autobiography of the southern place. First, Morris recounts the mindless racism and attendant acts of racial violence that characterized his childhood in Mississippi. Second, Morris reports the religious tyranny of school teachers and Sunday School teachers as they imposed a fundamentalist Christianity by fear and rote memorization. Third, Morris depicts the sexism of the southern place, and in particular the struggle to become a "good old boy." Fourth, Morris describes an elementary and secondary education so ritualized and obsessive that knowledge of the "outside" world was suppressed. Fifth, Morris tells how forms of "dominant culture" were communicated as prerequisites for entry into the middle class. Finally, Kincheloe tells us that Morris—despite the injustice and tyranny—felt so linked with Yazoo, Mississippi, that escape seemed impossible (Kincheloe, 1991b). Morris does leave, and when he returns he feels estranged:

> I look back and saw my father, sitting still and gazing straight ahead; on the stage my friends' fathers nodded their heads and talked among themselves. I felt an urge to get out of there. *Who are these people?* I asked myself. What was I doing there? Was this the place I had grown up in and never wanted to leave? I knew in that instant, in the middle of a mob in our school auditorium, that a mere three years in Texas had taken me irrevocably, even without me realizing it, from home. (Morris, 1967, pp. 179-180, quoted in Kincheloe, 1991b, p. 142, emphasis in original)

Kincheloe concludes that without autobiographical self-remembrance, Morris might not have understood how Mississippi remained in his soul:

> Without self-understanding, however, he could not see the connections between himself and Mississippi; he had to transcend it to find it. He had to transcend it to find himself. The southern curriculum must confront the source of modern alienation by using its social psychoanalytical methodology. (p. 145)

Southern studies. Pinar (1991) employed the work of literary theorist and historian Lewis Simpson (1983) in his study of "place," suggesting that the South has repressed memory and history in its denial of its status as, in Simpson's phrase, the "garden of chattel." Pinar argues that what the Southern literary renaissance achieved in the early decades of the twentieth century must now be achieved in Southern mass culture, namely a restoration of memory and history of the southern place so that it can be understood as distinctive historically and culturally. He suggests a program of interdisciplinary southern studies, organized thematically around race, class, and gender, employing autobiography, which could:

> provide an interesting study . . . of presentism, solipsism, political passivity and ethical relativism. An interdisciplinary program in southern studies would be taught with the aim of reexperiencing denied elements of the past, which, when critically reintegrated, might help provide a psychology of social commitment, as well as remove "blocks" to the development of intelligence. . . . Given the southern penchant for narrative and for place, political and cultural histories of the South can usefully and congruently be situated in life histories of individual students. . . . Individual autobiographical work needs to be complemented by group process. (Pinar, 1991, p. 180)

An example of situating life history in the cultural context of the South, Patrick Slattery and Kevin Daigle (1992) explored "Curriculum as a Place of Turmoil" in twentieth-century Louisiana fiction. The apparently divergent life histories of Jane Pittman in Ernest Gaines' (1972) *The Autobiography of Miss Jane Pittman* and Walker Percy's Tom More in *The Thanatos Syndrome* (1987) are juxtaposed in their struggle to break free from the bondage of southern social boundaries. Slattery and Daigle proposed that the barrier of the Mississippi River that separates Jane's world of slavery in Pointe Coupee Parish from Tom's world of malaise in the aristocracy of Feliciana Parish is actually the force that unites them. Slattery and Daigle concluded:

> What we have seen in both novels is a working metaphor for the current debates over curriculum development. Both Tom and Jane overcame the impositions and pomposity of standardized compartmentalized structures as they endured the turmoil in their respective places in history. May we hear the tales of the troubled hearts that flow together in the telling, unleveed and unlocked, in contrast to the Mississippi River which is bounded and confined. And just as the Mississippi ennobled Jane Pittman in the midst of racial strife in Pointe Couppée and emancipated Tom More in the midst of the malaise of Feliciana, may the experience of school curriculum emancipate those persons who meander in our places of education. (1992, p. 41)

Place is a concept that might prove suggestive for scholars of other regions of the U.S.A. and the world. It becomes an important focus of autobiographical/biographical studies, concretizing such research not only in "culture" but in specific places. For instance, Florence R. Krall (1982, 1988a) has written of "place" far from urban areas. She suggested: "It may in the end be the wild places that hold the key to creative self-realization and biospheric harmony.

Out of 'brute' experiences, we may yet come to . . . meaning" (p. 77). Just as for the phenomenologist the "secret place" is a figurative as well as literal concept, so for the autobiographer does the notion of place enjoy multiple meanings, literal and symbolic.

Self as discursive formation: Poststructuralism and autobiography
In his seminal exemplification of curriculum as deconstructed text [see chapter 9], Jacques Daignault (1992a) portrays experience understood in a non-linear autobiographical sense. The study, itself a series of "traces" of other, longer studies, begins autobiographically. He remembers the sound of the clapper, a contraption employed by the elementary school teacher to bring silence to a room filled with children. Daignault remembers:

> I was not yet accustomed to the confusion of the cries, laughter, and children's tears in the schoolyard, to the roaring of short and irregular steps in the corridors and on the terrazzo stairs, or to the crescendo of tables and chairs "gnashing their legs against the hardwood," but I started to fear and hate school: the sound of the restraining "clapper." Maybe I did not even hear it. The silence that fell then, sharp, yet reverberating drier and harder than the ebony or oakwood from which it was nevertheless emanating. More unbearable silence, the unforgettably stern look of the regulating authority that was in my first teacher's hands. (1992a, p. 195)

Noise and silence. Daignault's scene captures the suffocation of silence brought by the repression of the body, of young children's bodies, clapping them into silence, into submission. Yet, the screams of the children in the playground are not a preferable option; Daignault's vignette reminds us that school creates unacceptable scenes through noise and silence. The social construction that is the school brings too many children together with adults forced into regulatory positions, pushing the children themselves either into exaggerated rebellions or unchildlike submission. Daignault employs his body to fight its subjugation:

> I had to break that silence. At 5 years of age, I did not find anything better than the wheezing of asthma. This produced the desired reprieve. Peace in my room. Pleased to be there, I found that time stopped, that the regimentation of school vanished, once I was no longer subjected to it. . . . I was perfectly happy. (1992a, p. 195)

Perfect happiness does not last, of course. Daignault tells us:

> But there is no stopping progress. Medical marvels put an end to my escape mechanism. Progress imperatively brought me back into the reality of life: school. . . . I was forced to adapt myself to school routine. I learned gradually to compensate for the tediousness that school inspired. Practicing a musical instrument made me hear a new art of rhythm and rest, of time and silence. I have not forgotten the tactile pleasure of fingering a guitar nor the whispering created going up and down the strings. (1992a, p. 195)

"My link in language." From age 5 we are brought to the present of a man almost middle aged, for whom the body is a trace of experience, the same body that shouted in the schoolyard and wheezed to escape the dulling routine of the school day. The stillness of his room, the peace and happiness of solitude, takes him back to origins, to his mother's body, to the world, the world of flux and permanence. The project of education, in one sense, is not in the schoolyard, not in the school room, but in his room, at rest. Daignault writes:

> Today, neither wheezing nor playing guitar, I know another rest: soundless whispering and a quiver of eternity. Fetal reminiscence of world filtered from the womb. I prick my ears toward the origin of my ignorance: the questionnaire of the being, the answer of which is in a constant state of flux. Wheezing and whispering move into my soul unformed "expressibles." I am discovering in my skin a new body and with my ears a new soul: my audiotactile body is my soul, the undying trace of my education. My link in language is in transition. I am confident. The next century is ours. (1992a, p. 196)

Deconstructing a discursive self. Embedded in Daignault's assertion is that understanding curriculum as deconstructed text will involve a reconfiguration of the self—some poststructuralists assert a displacing of the self (Hwu, 1993). Daignault's confidence ("the next century is ours") is not generational, nor is it historical in a Marxian sense. Rather, through autobiographical traces Daignault understands that the stasis of the Western, some would add "male," self, can be "worked through," or surpassed. This process of "deconstruction," of analytically depicting the structures of the self, enables the individual to reconfigure these structures, and emerge from the current cultural crisis—which is also a crisis of the self—in life affirmative ways. It is through language, however, that Daignault the deconstructionist finds his "passage." To repeat his assertion: "My link in language is in transition. I am confident" (p. 196). It is via autobiographical remembrance, which for Daignault in this essay involves recalling the publication of his Ph.D. dissertation in which letters move from publication to publication, across oceans, moves he portrays anagrammatically. Crucial to understand here [see chapter 9 for a more detailed explanation of deconstruction] is that a simultaneously playful and disciplined reordering of language functions to transport the player to new "locations," to see new configurations of reality. Because for the poststructuralist reality is discursive, a view disputed by at least one major autobiographical theorist as we shall see momentarily, the transformation of reality is discursive. Daignault's brilliant essay illustrates these ideas and themes as he works through the main ideas in his work and his life, not in linear fashion, but in recursive ways which dissolve that which it repeats. Daignault asserts: "The individual is, in fact, the meeting between an I that is cracked and a Me that is dissolved" (p. 209). And such a meeting can become style in one's writing. In "Autobiography of a Style," Daignault (1987) suggests that "style is the presence of oneself in his or her text" (p. 7). He continues: "Let us suppose the style to which I refer is mine. Then biography of a style which is mine becomes "autobiography of a style" (p. 8). Further: "Style is always autobiographic and self-educative. I can't imagine working on style . . . without becoming someone else" (p.18).

An architecture of self. As we noted in chapter 9, William Pinar worked on the edge of poststructuralism in his "Autobiography and the Architecture of Self" (1988e), in which he returned to a central question in autobiography, namely, is there an authentic self? After reviewing phenomenological and psychoanalytical answers to this question, he turns to a Foucaldian idea, an "archeology" of self. In such a view, quoting Bertrand Russell: "The things one says are all unsuccessful attempts to say something else" (in Pinar, 1988e, p. 13). That is, what one says, who one is, "contains" what one does not say, who one does not seem to be. An "architecture" of self hides as well as expresses elements of the person. How one judges the architecture of the self depends upon the historical moment. Employing Christopher Lasch's (1984) provocative characterization of the current crisis in the West [in which the self has collapsed onto itself, dissociated from the public sphere], Pinar suggested:

> As a moment, or series of moments in the deconstruction of an overly-determined public (probably male) ego, [a] Heideggerean regression to a preindividual preoedipal merging with the Source is developmentally useful, perhaps even necessary. Only via destruction of the false self can the buried, authentic self be revealed. Laing understood that breakdown, even madness, can represent a necessary means to sanity in some cases. For the architect of self, should he judge his current edifice obscuring its foundation in ways that keep him in ignorance of himself, such a study is advised. For the already broken-down, another order of work is appropriate. (1988e, p. 21)

In a view associated with poststructuralism, the structures of the self become open to revision, especially through writing. Pinar suggests that "writing . . . becomes a kind of architecture, that space and those movements of mediation which give and take form to formlessness" (1988e, p. 27). Agreeing with Derrida that writing enables the individual to separate from the merging with situation that occurs in speech, from an over-reliance on presence, Pinar observed: "Speech like poetry and music can hover close to the Heideggerean 'ground of Being,' but writing, and in particular, the craft of autobiography, can soar, and from the heights, discern new landscapes, new configurations, especially those excluded by proclamations of Government, State, and School" (1988e, p. 27).

The gaze in the mirror. In this 1992 study of identity and teaching [which is examined as poststructuralism in chapter 9], Peter Taubman (1992) remembers turning to his mother—a teacher herself—for advice about teaching. As a beginning step, she suggested that he stand in front of their hallway mirror, practicing what he would do in front of his classes during the first weeks of school. He describes these practice sessions as the beginning of his sense of his identity as a teacher:

So I stood there, hearing myself talk about phrases and clauses, gerunds and participles, listening to myself ask questions, modulating and projecting my voice. I stood there watching my reflection smile and nod, gesture and pause, as I adjusted to the image projected back to me. And all the while in the shadows of the living room behind me, I could see in the mirror my mother, sitting quietly, nodding and prompting. It was during those fall evenings, in front of the mirror, that a loose sense of myself as a teacher emerged. (1992, p. 217)

Taubman tells us that, in a Lacanian view, identity as a unified "me" congeals during the mirror stage, that is, in seeing oneself in the face of the "other," especially the primary caretaker, often the mother. Because the "I" comes to form in the presence and reflection of another, identity is inextricably linked to someone else. There is no private "I."

Identity is alienated. Taubman concurs with Lacan, and suggests that his identity as a teacher which began in his mother's gaze was indeed "alienated," i.e. linked with the "other." He explains: "I was a teacher, which meant I was consciously and unconsciously assuming and assimilating what it meant consciously and unconsciously to my mother to teach and what others who were called teachers consciously and unconsciously meant by that term" (p. 218). Specifically, for Taubman becoming a teacher meant (in 1969) losing his long hair, which was exchanged for the teaching contract. Taubman remembers specific episodes in his teaching life in which he moved between an identity as teacher as public official, the one who "knows," and teacher as private person, the one who imagines and desires. These two general poles of identity pull the individual, on the one hand, toward the institution, and on the other, toward the students. He suggests:

there are two choices open to those who teach and thus two poles as regards the distance or closeness between teacher and student. One may become a master and thus remain castrated, forever separated from those one teaches, alienated both from oneself and one's students, and lost in a house of mirrors. Or one may flee from any identity as teacher and sink into the inarticulate realm of the unconscious, lost forever in the Other and renouncing any distance whatsoever. (1992, p. 223)

Taubman finds his way to a "midpoint" between the two poles, what he terms a "dialectic . . . whose endpoints must be attended to but not submitted to" (p. 232). At the crossroads of intimacy and distance, public good and private desire, teachers and students meet.

In each of these three studies autobiography is employed as discursive practice portraying identity through language. Indeed, the self which autobiography is said to communicate is a discursive self. As a discursive self, the position of the subject becomes problematical:

Self-reflexiveness becomes not just possible but necessary, since one of the central implications of poststructuralist perspectives is that there is no privileged position from which one can speak without one's own discourse being itself put into question. (Elbaz & Elbaz, 1988, pp. 127-128)

In this sense, the effort to understand curriculum autobiographically becomes a series of discursive moves to reconfigure semantic and lived structures not only associated with the past, but with the structuring of the present.

"Some cultural behemoth." Madeleine Grumet criticizes this general view—often associated with the work of Michel Foucault—that identity is discursive, and that the analysis of educational experience must focus upon the language rather than the experience of the autobiographer. The great autobiographer complains:

> It is fashionable these days to view all writing as the imprint of some cultural behemoth, striding through consciousness, literature, or criticism toward a compelling, if undetermined, destination. According to this deconstruction we, scribbling in our diaries, or squinting at our word processors, merely imagine that we are composing the original word that brings a new thought to expression. All language is social, all thought historical, all form predetermined, all invention shared, all intention sabotaged. (Grumet, 1990b, p. 321)

Grumet describes her own journal-keeping, rebuking the poststructuralist view as she evokes the texture of everyday life. Such writing is "both inner and outer, personal and public, spontaneous and considered, mind and body" (p. 322). It is always related to a conversation, real or imagined. Journal-keeping brings everyday experience to life. Grumet tells us: "my journals are about . . . moments of being in the world that I want to save" (p. 322). She recalls employing journals with student teachers to study educational experience: "We turned to autobiography to recover human feeling and motivation for studies of education that had become anonymous and quantitative" (p. 322).

Identity a fiction? Grumet rejects the view associated with poststructuralism that experience is discursive formation. She finds overdeterministic the discursive view of experience as linguistic: "Under the canopy of post-structuralism, sociologists, as well, I must admit, as some humanities scholars, have justified readings of autobiographical narratives which erase the subjectivity of their authors. Claiming that identity is a fiction, postmodernists attribute our scribbles and fantasies to the determinations of genres and codes. I would be naive if I refused to admit influence in what we notice, what we choose to tell, and in how and why we tell what we do. Nevertheless, autobiographical method invites us to struggle with those determinations. It is that struggle and its resolve to develop ourselves in ways that transcend the identities that others have constructed for us that bonds the projects of autobiography and education" (1990b, p. 324). In autobiographical as well as political theory, poststructuralism destabilizes the epistemological ground of contemporary curriculum scholarship.

Dreams, Myth, and Imagination: Mary Aswell Doll
In her commencement address to her alma mater, the Cambridge School (Massachusetts), Mary Aswell Doll, whose son Will and husband (at that time)

Bill [see chapter 9] were seated in the audience [Will about to graduate], told her audience: "This morning I would like to talk about circles, and inner gods and goddesses. The circle's rounded shape is soft, recursive; it curves back upon itself. It is in constant motion; therefore it is dynamic, using its own energy to spiral movement inward, toward reflection" (1991, p. 1). In this passage is captured, in abbreviated language, aspects of Mary Aswell Doll's fifteen-year study of dreams, the inner self, and the imagination. While these subjects have interested students of the curriculum before [for instance, Rugg, 1963], Mary Aswell Doll explored these subjects autobiographically and via interview.

Children's dreams. In a study published in 1988, Doll reported themes she discerned in the dreams of 90 children (ages 4-12). In over half of these dreams, the image of the "monster" was prominent. Often half vegetable, half animal, the monster would appear in the dreamscene suddenly. Not danger but its size and the suddenness of appearance required the dreamer's attention. Indeed, the child was never in danger from the monster. Doll (1988a) explained:

> The monster's metaphoric function in dreams should be taken seriously . . . not because the monster is awful, but because it inspires awe; not because it is problematic but because it gives images to thought. And its presence leads thought down to the springs of memory and imagination. (p. 88)

She concluded that "what was important to the child was that the monster seemed to be the agent by which the child was transported to another world, felt as being *back* or *down* or *in*" (p. 87, emphasis in original).

Doll noted that the image of monster has mythological importance, citing famous mythological monsters (and their combatants) such as Beowulf and Grendel, Hercules and the Nemean lion, David and Goliath. But Doll observed that in the dreams of these children a different, non-combative encounter occurs. In these dreams the monster invites the child to accompany it to its "place." Doll analyzed:

> For in taking the child to his place, the monster is allowing the child to experience the primal mind and to touch base with generative metaphors. And the child's reluctance to slay the beast would seem to indicate an openness to hidden, creative powers of thought. . . . In no dreams did the child kill the monster. (pp. 88, 90)

Etymologically, the French root of monster is "monere," meaning to warn and to remind. In this sense the monster suggests a reminder of what is being forgotten from daily life. The Latin root—"monstrum"—means evil omen, portent, prodigy, suggesting the danger associated with such reminders. Finally, Doll reported that the location of many of these children's dreams are in the world, including the school. In this regard Doll wrote: "Civilization, as Freud knew so well, is the breeding ground for horror" (p. 93). She adds: "Like a thief at the gates, the unconscious slips through the cracks of conscious control" (Doll, M.,1982, p. 198).

For Doll, dreams present a "dialogue with primal thinking" (p. 98). In describing their dreams, children:

> are giving texture to what is on their minds, behind their minds, lurking. As parents and teachers, we should encourage this . . . allowing the images to take shape in drawings and paintings is but another way of objectifying fear, rather than having fear become projected by informed thought. For even the Terrible can be transformed, as the monsters' visits show. (p. 98)

For Mary Aswell Doll, education should not only "lead out," (*educare*); it should "lead in" (1982, p. 201). Such an education of the imagination requires dreaming more deeply in order to discover, or recover, one's inner world (Doll, 1990). [Memory is required as well; see Nixon, 1992.]

A distant daughter. Doll believes that the sphere of the imagination may be more real than everyday experience. To educate the imagination, she writes, one must distantiate oneself from what she terms our "literal" selves. Writing autobiographically may help, oddly it may seem, to achieve this distance. The interweaving of Mary Aswell Doll's scholarship and her life—indicated in her speech at her and her son's alma mater at his commencement—became clear in a 1990 study which includes autobiographical remembrance of her mother and father. Both parents occupy noteworthy places in American literary history:

> I come to my topic autobiographically. I am a distant daughter, who came to know my mother only when my mother was 82 and I was 42. My mother, an extraordinary editor of the 40s and 50s, was much loved by the literati. She had heard Ezra Pound read T. S. Eliot's *The Wasteland* in Paris, had lived downstairs from Truman Capote on Nantucket when he finished his first novel, *Other Voices Other Rooms*; had been one of Eudroa Welty's first editors while fiction editor of *Harper's Bazaar* magazine; and had swum in the nude with Jean Stafford on (pardon the pun) Bear Island, Maine. (p. 3)

While her mother was appreciative of her fellow artists, she had little time for Mary:

> The fact is that I did not live with my mother. She had had a nervous breakdown shortly after I was born. . . . I grew up with my father, and together with my brother, commuted to my editor-mother on alternate weekends. . . . On the week-ends I would have cokes with Truman [Capote] nearby at the Beekman Towers, see Danny Kaye movies with Eudora [Welty]. . . . I tell this story to situate it in the matrix of my unconscious: in my mother, my alma mater. I loved those week-ends and I hated them. (pp. 2 and 3)

In this autobiographical remembrance she situates herself in "my own unconscious matrix, the mother matter out of which I have sprung" (p. 13). Even though Mary Aswell Doll lived with her father, he may have been more distant than her mother. His distance may have resulted from his distance from himself, from his dreamlife, his unconscious. Doll tells us that it may be true that adult men were once as close to their unconscious minds and as freely dreaming as adult women and as children can be now. Doll recalls the Legend of Gilgamesh, a myth older than the Homeric poems, earlier than the transcriptions of the Bible. This legend tells the story of a hero-adventurer who found nourishment in dreams, suggesting that the dreamer-hero is an archetype, expressing a doubled relationship between an outer kindly, civilized self and an inner, wilder self. Doll comments: "The great wisdom of this early epic, to use Jungian terms, is in showing a process of individuation, whereby the haughty one becomes connected with his opposite primal other through material presented to him in dream, thereby making a half person whole" (1990, pp. 10-11). Doll then returns to the memory of her father:

> Through reading this ancient epic I came to understand and appreciate the relationship my editor-father had with his most famous writer, Thomas Wolfe. The two men were opposite in significant ways—my father (Southern, born in early October 1900, Harvard-educated, mother-dominated; editor; conservative) Thomas Wolfe (Southern, born in early October, 1900, Harvard-educated, mother-dominated; writer, drinker, womanizer). . . . The second half of the Gilgamesh epic is really the story of desperate grief and desperate, unrealistic searching. My father was a diminished person after the death of Thomas Wolfe, in 1938, only months after they had met, 2 years before I was born. I grew up with my father's grief. All during my life with my father he was preoccupied, searching for his lost companion, unable to come to terms with the loss of his double, the other more complete half of his self (1990, p. 12).

Dreams and the education of imagination. This search for completion, which Doll undertook here by involving the memory of her parents, is a primary element of an autobiographical curriculum. And dreams become an essential element in such a curriculum. "A curriculum," Doll (1988b) tells us, "that uses dream speech provides a new dispensation for learning about the self and culture" (p. 1). In another place her enthusiasm for dreamwork is stronger. She writes: "Dreams can heal, prophesize, compensate, illuminate. Their power is immense. . . . Dreams can re-mind us of what we need to put back into our minds. If we are, as I propose, to educate the imagination, what better way to this than to dream the dream forward" (1990, pp. 12, 13).

Doll weaves themes of dreams, family, teaching, and death in a 1988 study of her teaching during the time of her brother's dying of AIDS. Her son's school truancy underlines the intensity of this period, a time interrupted by frequent trips across the continent (the family lived in California at the time) to be with her dying brother. In a lyrical voice, Mary Aswell Doll brings us closer to our own experience of death and dying as she narrates her own experience during this period. Writing a story enables her son Will to convert mourning into affirmation of life; for Mary Aswell Doll a dream provides a passage through this labyrinth of emotion. Referring to both the dream and Will's story, Doll observes:

> As teachers we seemed embarrassed to admit to transformation experiences, as if what matters in life is not the subject, not it at all. But this dream seemed the perfect text for the journey assignment. . . . Like Will's story, the dream was a

gift that freed the mind to attend to pain and in that attention to become more authentic in style and tone and voice. (1988b p. 11)

Such authenticity, one surmises, can come only through dwelling in one's experience, admitting the experience of death as well as of life. Doll's dwelling in experience of her brother's death brings her understanding that:

> Death indeed highlights life. Life is not as organized as a set curriculum would have us believe. Nor is death as end-stopped as we fear. We are all on journeys, destinations unknown. What better opportunity for students to begin to come to terms with life than by writing about the dyings they have experienced along the way? . . . We need death in our lives so as to define our living. (pp. 13-14)

"Sleep well." In her commencement address to the Cambridge School, Doll notes that she has stood there before. She is, as we noted, a graduate of the Cambridge School, as will her son be this day. Both she and Will lived in the same dormitory room, separated by a generation. She tells the audience: "The very fact that I stand before you today is a repetition. I lived my first year on campus in White Farm, just as Will did. On the second floor, as Will did. First in the room at the top of the stairs in the hallway, like Will. Then in the room directly to the left of the stairs, like Will" (1991, p. 3). Repetitions are an essential feature of education understood autobiographically. Themes are repeated, sometimes in different form; dreams repeat "problems" and issues until the dreamer manages to "solve" them, to move through them. Doll invites her listeners to think about their lives as circular:

> Lives, I suggest, can be linear or they can be circular. I invite you graduates to consider the journey on which you are about to embark—out from school and into the world—not only as a linear adventure, single points pointing outward only—but as a circle, points looping dynamically from within: your outer journey roundly connected to the spiral of your inner self, the center geyser of your being. (1991, p. 2)

Concluding her commencement address Doll seems to repeat, in summary form, the conclusion of her scholarship. Reminding her listeners that dreams represent the reality of their lives, and that lives are circular, themes repeated, and passages revealed, Doll bids good-bye: "And so, dear graduates, I bid you go your way, sleep well, and remember these lines from T. S. Eliot: 'We shall not cease from exploration, and the end of all our exploring/Will be to arrive where we started/ And know the place for the first time'" (quoted in Doll, 1991, p. 7).

III
Feminist Autobiographical Theory

> [Stories of educational experience] help us to negotiate the tension between the individual and community, a tension never resolved or resolvable because of the fact of difference, a tension which indeed is the subtext of all educational narratives.
>
> (Jo Anne Pagano, 1990, p. 12)

Our narrative of community thus contains multiple accounts [which represent] one way of challenging the ahistorical and essentialized selves that our stories tend to create.

(Janet L. Miller, 1990a, p. 7)

The relationship between autobiography and feminist theory is evident in the work of several important feminist scholars (see Grumet, 1978, 1980, 1981, 1987, 1988b, 1991; Krall, 1982, 1988a; Miller, 1979b, 1980, 1982a, 1983a, 1987a, 1987b, 1987c, 1990a; Pagano, 1988a, 1990; Reiniger, 1989; Witherell & Noddings, 1991; Benstock, 1988; also racial theory: see Williams, 1991; Gates, 1992, p.42). Feminist curriculum theory not only often includes discussion of autobiography and educational practice; it utilizes autobiography as a research tool. Certain scholars (Grumet, 1988b; Miller, 1988; Pagano, 1988a, 1990) share their individual experiences of schools and universities, of the learning process, and report these autobiographically. Such depictions are intersubjective rather than solitary in nature; these accounts constitute a "discourse of affiliation" (Pagano, 1990, p. 11). In feminist autobiographic curriculum theory message and method, public and private, institution and individual, abstract and concrete are all interconnected. [Feminist and gender scholarship is the subject of chapter 7; we discuss feminist theory here in so far as it influences the effort to the understand curriculum as autobiographical and biographic text.]

Between public and private. In the work of Madeleine R. Grumet (1988b) the passage between public and private is a major motif. She writes:

For data we turned to autobiographical accounts of educational experience. For methods of analysis we turned to psychoanalytic, phenomenological, and feminist theories. As we study the forms of our own experience, not only are we searching for evidence of the external forces that have diminished us; we are also recovering our own possibilities. We work to remember, imagine and realize ways of knowing and being that can span the chasm separating our public and private experience. (Grumet, 1988b, p. xv)

In Grumet's work we find an intricate weaving of autobiography with psychoanalysis, phenomenology, and feminist theory.

Despite the sophistication of her scholarship—perhaps due to that sophistication—her autobiographical work has met with criticism. She recalls:

When I first started working with narrative in the early 1970s, I was busy justifying it to the psychometricians. That defense mounted, I turned to answer the Marxists who identified autobiography with bourgeois individualism, a retreat to interiority by those unwilling to don their leather jackets and storm the barricades, or at least picket General Dynamics. (Grumet, 1991, p. 67)

Grumet's theory established her by the late 1980s as a—perhaps the—major figure in both feminist and autobiographical scholarship (Grumet, 1988b; Pinar, 1988f; *Cambridge Journal of Education*, 1990). Her first project, nearly twenty years earlier, was to rescue autobiography from "its association with the self, the alias that has given subjectivity a bad name" (Grumet, 1981, p. 16). She was at pains to elucidate both the social character of the self and its reflexive structure.

In "The Politics of Personal Knowledge" (originally presented at the Symposium on Classroom Studies of Teachers' Personal Knowledge, held at the Ontario Institute for Studies in Education in 1985), Grumet clarified the role of storytelling in autobiography. Stories, she wrote, must be grasped reflexively. To clarify this concept, she cited Alfred Schutz, the social phenomenologist: "Meaning does not lie in experience. Rather, those experiences are meaningful which are grasped reflectively. The meaning is the way in which the Ego regards its experience. The meaning lies in the attitude of the Ego toward that part of its stream of consciousness which has already flowed by" (Schutz, quoted in Grumet, 1991, pp. 69-70). While telling stories is important, a method of listening is required as well: "A method of receiving stories that mediates the space between the self that tells, the self that is told, and the self that listens: a method that returns a story to the teller that is both hers and not hers, that contains herself in good company" (Grumet, 1991, p. 70). To foster self-reflexive storytelling Grumet encouraged her students—often practicing teachers—to write multiple accounts of one educational experience. Often she asked for three narratives which functioned to "splinter the dogmatism of a single tale" (Grumet, 1991, p. 72). In multiple accounts of the same experience the writer brackets out conventional and perhaps restrictive categories of explanation, "taken-for-granted" understandings of experience. Grumet warns that storytelling is "risky business." Self-disclosure can entail risk, but telling our stories to researchers and/or teachers complicates the relationship. This complication may represent a drawback of autobiographical methods (Graham, 1991).

Safe places. Autobiography is considerably more than the "interpretation of lived experience" (Schubert, 1986a, p. 33). Autobiography is inextricably social and political. Grumet (1988b) observed: "Knowledge evolves in human relationships," (p. xix) a view shared by Miller (1990a) and Pagano (1990). Knowledge develops via conversations among members of communities. The process involves "creating spaces and finding voices" (Miller, 1990a). The gender dimension of autobiographical understanding is explicit in this scholarship:

> We need to re-create safe places, even in schools, where teachers can concentrate, can attend to their experience of children and of the world, and we need to create community spaces where forms that express that experience are shared. The process of creating those spaces will be as important as the spaces themselves. (Grumet, 1988b, p. 90)

That process is political in nature.

The concept of space is a feminist notion which can be linked to Virginia Woolf's famous idea of a "room of one's own." That is, feminist self-understanding and transformation requires lived spaces in which the corrosive power of misogyny can be weakened or avoided altogether. Such a space is not necessarily a solitary one, as Woolf's notion implied. Indeed, group process has been a significant feature of "consciousness-raising" in the feminist movement since the 1960s. Janet Miller (1990a) describes the significance of these spaces for educators and researchers struggling to challenge the status quo:

> Our narrative of community thus contains multiple accounts of our individual and collective processes as we work to become challengers in our educational contexts. These multiple episodes are one way of challenging the ahistorical and essentialized selves that our stories tend to create; they are one way to diminish the coherence and logical development with which we tend to infuse the stories that we tell. (p. 7)

A discourse of affiliation. Relatedly, Jo Anne Pagano describes women's communities as communities of exiles, formed to discuss stories of women's experience in a "discourse of affiliation" (Pagano, 1990, p. 11). In such settings the power of autobiography is compelling:

> As narratives having the instructive force of myth, stories of educational experience, the texts which we make of our lives in classrooms, teach us what it means to be knowing creatures, what it means to know ourselves as selves. They teach us about the relationships between cognition and emotion, between reason and passion, between mind and body, between epistemology and politics. Finally, they help us to negotiate the tension between the individual and community, a tension never resolved or resolvable because of the fact of difference, a tension which indeed is the subtext of all educational narratives. (Pagano, 1990, pp. 11-12)

In one sense Pagano is sketching a feminist and autobiographical notion of identity, as we saw in chapter 6 a term of increasing importance to the field at large.

For instance, research practices themselves disclose the influence of autobiographical and feminist scholarship. That influence is evident in the following observation of Deborah Britzman (1992b), who writes:

> Research methodology has evolved to enable students to study their biographies and practices. If we can extend this idea to the murky world of identity, and provide spaces for student teachers to rethink how their constructions of the teacher make for lived experience, then I think students . . . will be better able to politically theorize about the terrible problem of knowing thyself. . . . Students may come to understand knowing thyself as a construction and eventually, as a socially empowering occasion. (p. 43)

As we will see in chapter 13, teacher education as well is being influenced by autobiographical discourses.

Meaning-making communities. Carol Witherell and Nel Noddings (1991) have stressed the importance of community in sharing individual experience. Their narrative model of education includes several elements:

that we live and grow in interpretive, or meaning-making communities; that
stories help us find our place in the world; and that caring, respectful dialogue
among those engaged in educational settings—students, teachers, administrators—serve as the crucible for our coming to understand ourselves, others and
the possibilities life holds for us. (Witherell & Noddings, 1991, p.10)

Autobiography is, then, inherently social. Particularly for those whose
effort to understand curriculum as an autobiographic and biographical text is
informed by feminist theory, the presence of community is powerful indeed.
Others working autobiographically but without a gender emphasis, such as
Richard Butt and Danielle Raymond (forthcoming), emphasize the social
character of autobiography, as we shall see. Taken socially, autobiography
can be understood as creating a space between ego and non-ego, as well as
expressing their intersections. Such a space may require solitude. In an
autobiographical voice, Miller (1993a) argues, as an academic and as a
woman, for a notion of solitude that acknowledges and enables her to
participate in her attachments to others and to the work that symbolizes
those attachments.

The Middle Passage: Grumet and Miller
In an essay published in 1978, Grumet specified the relations among autobiography, *currere*, and curriculum criticism (or evaluation). Grumet criticized
the language of mainstream curriculum practice, language typified by
"intended learning outcomes," "socialization," "the disciplines of knowledge," and "learning environments." Such concepts "obliterate all that is
personal in favor of what is general. The outside is favored over the inside in
curriculum work in the United States" (1978, p. 278). Contesting Huebner's
1976 dictum that the only function remaining for curriculum is "the making
present of content to persons" (quoted in Grumet, 1978, p. 278), Grumet
argued that it is "persons who are made present through the contact with
curriculum" (Grumet, 1978, p. 278). For her curriculum is the process of
persons coming to form. Autobiography is the method by means of which
curriculum can be so employed (Grumet, 1978). Grumet employed the
notion of figure and ground to contrast technological and aesthetic ways of
understanding experience. What distinguishes the former from the latter is
"the relationship of the product—the figure—to the situation from which it
comes—the ground" (Grumet, 1978, p. 279). The aesthetic function of
curriculum, Grumet suggests, "replaces the amelioration of the technologuc
function with revelation" (p. 280).

    Within experience, then, meaning is the relationship between situation
and action. Grumet argues that it is the curriculum which provides new
experience for the student, which stands out against the ground of ordinary
experience, both revealing and transforming it. The new experience then
tends to "sink onto the ground of ordinary experience," creating a new but
now familiar situation. The curriculum becomes, in this scheme, "the middle
passage or way," that passage in which movement is possible from the familiar to the unfamiliar, to estrangement, then to a transformed situation. The

curriculum leads to transformation in the way the situation is experienced. Grumet acknowledges that such movement is hardly guaranteed, as she illustrated in her depiction of a complex curricular event [the 1976 University of Rochester Theatre Festival; see chapter 11 for a description of this event].

A middle way. In her *Bitter Milk: Women and Teaching* (1988b) autobiographical and feminist theory are interwoven in a highly sophisticated curriculum theory. In exploring "what teaching means to women" (Grumet, 1988b, p. xi), Grumet describes teaching and curriculum as a middle way between public and private:

> They [women] go back and forth between the experience of domesticity and the experience of teaching, between being with one's own children and being with the children of others, between being the child of one's own mother and the teacher of another mother's child, between feeling and form, family and colleagues. (p. xv)

Via autobiography Grumet details these movements, and the lived experience of women as women, mothers, and teachers. Autobiography becomes a means of disclosing the experience of women that has been banished from curriculum discourses. It allows lived experience to be revealed and expressed, unlike mainstream educational research which in its obsession with measurement obliterates subjectivity.

Public and private, separate and connected. In her "Reading Women's Autobiographies: A Map of Reconstructed Knowing," Anita Plath Helle describes the distinction between public and private in her discussion of separate and connected knowing, based on the work of Carol Gilligan (1982). In separate knowing the speaker articulates a public language. In their "performances they address their message not to themselves or intimate friends but to an audience of relative strangers" (Gilligan, quoted in Helle, 1991, p. 54). In contrast is the voice of connected knowing. According to Helle, this form of knowing "is attuned to creating continuity between the so-called private language of self reflection and the formal designs of public speech" (p. 54). There is a gender element here: although connected knowing is not an exclusively feminist approach, as Gilligan (1982) suggested more women tend toward connected knowing than do men. Men tend toward separate knowing (Helle, 1991). In this context Helle discusses women's autobiographical writing. Reading autobiographies of marginalized women requires a more subtle attunement to multiple differences (Helle, 1991). Such reading might support feminist pedagogy by encouraging connectedness and multiplicity. For certain feminist theorists writing and reading autobiography provides a means of connecting public and private worlds in multiple ways. It becomes one aspect of "making a place fit for women to live in" (Pagano, 1990).

Janet L. Miller's concept of passage exhibits both feminist and autobiographical elements. She has described autobiographically the struggles of a woman scholar in academe, making explicit the frustrations, confusions, and tensions within schools (1983a). In a recent study, Miller (1992a) examined her sixth grade classroom and her former teacher Mr. Brucker, as she reconstructs and examines the construction of her identity as a young student. She reflects on these influences on her subsequent work as a woman teacher. Here autobiography permits a vivid account of the lived experience of women scholars struggling to overcome patriarchal obstacles. Miller (1990a) has also described, as we noted in chapter 7, the labor of five classroom teachers and their university professor as they examine together the possibilities and dilemmas of collaborative inquiry in education. In this work the multiple and changing voices of individual teachers are clearly articulated in Miller's autobiographical account. Like Grumet, Miller also views this collaborative process of finding a passage or middle way. At the conclusion of the study she reported: "We now view our collaborative researching efforts as a point of mediation, a balancing place from which to launch our next questions, to oppose our persistent interruptions, and to explore new points of dissonance" (p. 147).

The roots of this research are evident in Miller's work ten years earlier. In her 1979 "Women: The Evolving Educational Consciousness," Miller (1979b) discussed what she characterized as a dichotomy between the public and private (she designated these as the professional and private self). In this work there surfaces a search for connection between the two realms. Miller suggested that teacher education could profit from creating connections between private and public worlds. She then set out on a search to formulate a curriculum theory that would permit such linking and bonding, and it is a search which led her to the important statement that is *Creating Spaces and Finding Voices* (1990a).

The sound of silence breaking. In "The Sound of Silence Breaking: Feminist Pedagogy and Curriculum Theory" (1982a), Miller provided a summary of feminist curriculum scholarship and suggests possible future directions. Of interest to us in this chapter is her concern with the personal and public: "Pedagogy, which attends to the authentic concepts of teachers and students sharing their lives together forces an articulation of identity as well as of problems which are inherent in that articulation of the personal and the public" (p. 10). This movement between the private and the public, autobiography and feminist theory, is continued in Miller's "The Resistance of Women Academics: An Autobiographical Account" (1983a). In an evocative and autobiographical voice, Miller spoke to the dilemma of women working in academe. It is a dilemma both political and psychological, a dilemma of the private and the public. The male-identified character of academic work functions to move women to self-alienation. Miller made clear that self-reflective study of educational experience allows feminist research to move through the psychopolitical labyrinth that is the university, preserving the feminist scholar's and teacher's nurturant capacities while encouraging autonomy, independence, and a critical posture: "I still give of myself in a teaching situation, but I give in an informed sense of my functions as a teacher rather than as an obligatory enactment of myself as others have conceived me" (Miller, 1983a, pp. 106-107).

Miller demonstrated that autobiographic reflection and insight contribute both to resistance and emancipation for women in schools. In feminist theory, then, autobiography is one means to find passages between private and public, a way to express shared knowledge with a community of scholars. Miller's work questions the taken-for-granted relationship between the researcher and the researched. Framed by feminist concerns regarding possible impositional and hierarchical construction and interpretations of others' identities in the research process, Miller's *Creating Spaces and Finding Voices* points to problems and issues inherent within unequal power relationships in collaborative research. In so doing, Miller's work represents an important effort to understand curriculum autobiographically.

Autobiographical Reclamations of the Self: Grumet and Reiniger

In her "Feminism and the Phenomenology of the Familiar" (1988b), Madeleine Grumet discussed autobiography as a way of understanding curriculum. She discussed her earlier work with Pinar and the initial efforts in the early 1970s to formulate autobiographical method. Grumet was concerned with those interpretative methods she employs to understand educational experience, a consistent theme in her work. In this essay she interpreted her students' autobiographical writing through the lens of feminist theory:

> So it is the shadow of the experience of teaching that we pursue here, hoping that as we catch a glimpse of its distortions and of the ground on which it falls, mingling the human figure with its roots, cracks, curbs, and stairwells, we shall address what is hidden in autobiographical accounts of teaching. And because so many teachers are women working in the shadows cast by the institutions of the public world and the disciplines of knowledge, I read their narratives to draw our life worlds out of obscurity so we may bring our experience to the patriarchal descriptions that constitute our sense of what it means of know, to nurture, to think, to succeed. (Grumet, 1988b, p. 61)

She reminds those women who are teaching to achieve a fuller sense of human possibility and agency to read the "shadows of their stories to recover intentionality" (p. 74). Implied here is that to understand curriculum and teaching with complexity requires understanding them autobiographically. Students of curriculum must not only write accounts of their educational experience, but also search these accounts with a feminist lens, seeking always the shadows of experience.

Gyn/Ecology. Another illustration of scholarship which employs feminist theory as a lens to interpret autobiography is Meredith Reiniger's "Autobiographical Search for Gyn/Ecology: Traces of Misogyny in Women's Schooling" (1989). Here Reiniger argued that to understand curriculum and schooling we must understand it autobiographically and from within a feminist perspective. The feminist perspective Reiniger endorsed and employed was that of Mary Daly, particularly her *Gyn/Ecology: The Metaethics of Radical Feminism* (1978): "I am provided with data. The analysis of that material will allow me in-sight that dis-covers female-defined self in a male-designed existence. Exposed, the power of the patriarchy can be unpowered" (Reiniger, 1989, p. 9). Like Grumet and Miller, Reiniger claimed that autobiographical method can assist women in the project of reclaiming the self, and in "a repudiation of the male lens through which we have seen the world, through which we have become objects, a repudiation of patriarchal scholarship" (Reiniger, 1989, p. 11).

Reiniger employed journal-writing in her research. She understood that merely recording educational experience is insufficient; autobiographical writing must be shared (see Pinar & Grumet, 1976; Grumet, 1978; Miller, 1990a). This call for community is a common and important thread in the autobiographical theory of curriculum. Reiniger believes that in journal-writing there is a possibility to counteract the dehumanization of schools as described by Pinar (1975a): "Perhaps the journals can provide the one area in which confirmation of the individual is possible, in which there is time and space for a teacher to give a 'genuine reply to one's being'" (Pinar, 1975a; in Reiniger, 1989, p. 26). In her research Reiniger linked journal writing, autobiography, and feminist theory. She suggested that "journal writing becomes a method of personal dis/covery and of an intellectual challenge while it is also the analysis of our past and the synthesis of our future" (Reiniger, 1989, p. 26). Regressive and synthetical steps of the method of *currere* are incorporated in Reiniger's use of journal-writing.

Discovering the (gendered) self. To understand misogyny in school, Reiniger employed both the journals of her women students and her own autobiographical writing. These writings represent a twofold process which aimed to free women from the tyranny of a misogynist world. This two-step process, according to Daly (1978), is seeking and sharing. Autobiography supports both steps. The regressive moment in autobiographical remembrance allows for the search for lost experience; the readers who constitute one's community allow for sharing of experience. Reiniger's appropriation of Daly's theory recalls the psychopolitical dimensions of feminist work elaborated by Miller (1983a). Reiniger concluded that the process of autobiography is a process of discovering the (gendered) self in the curriculum: "Writing can provide a haven, that solitude with the self. The seeking of self is the curriculum of Gyn/Ecology" (Reiniger, 1989, p. 81).

Autobiography has become an important method of feminist research and theory. At the same time, feminist theory has enlarged our knowledge of autobiographical theory and practice, including the meaning of community, collaboration, voice, and the middle passage. Autobiographical work would appear to be profoundly congruent with feminist theory and political practice.

IV
Studying Teachers' Lives

We need . . . to know more about teachers' lives.
(Ivor F. Goodson, 1989a, p.138)

The educational importance of this work is that it brings theoretical ideas about the nature of human life as lived to bear on educational experience as lived.
(F. Michael Connelly & D. Jean Clandinin, 1990, p. 3)

The secret of teaching is to be found in the local detail and the everyday life of teachers; teachers can be the richest and most useful source of knowledge about teaching; those who hope to understand teaching must turn at some point to teachers themselves.
(William Ayers, 1992, p. v)

The way biography brings together experience, thought, acting, theory, practice, research development and self education, and the way it makes research relationships among insiders and outsiders more collaborative, gives biography, as an epistemology, tremendous integrative, synergistic, and emancipatory potential.
(Richard Butt, Danielle Raymond, & L. Yamagishi, 1987, p. 88)

This sector of autobiographical and biographical research is comprised of four streams: teachers' collaborative autobiography [Butt and Raymond], personal practical knowledge [Clandinin and Connelly], teacher lore [Schubert and Ayers], and studying teachers' lives [Goodson]. Interest in teachers' lives and lived experienced has intensified in recent years (Abbs, 1974; Butt, 1984, 1985b, 1990, 1991; Butt & Raymond, 1986, 1987, 1988, 1992; Butt et al., 1986, 1988, 1992; Clandinin, 1985, 1986; Clandinin & Connelly, 1987a, 1987b, 1988, 1990, 1992; Connelly & Clandinin, 1987, 1988a, 1988b, 1990, 1991; Diamond, 1991; Elbaz, 1981, 1983, 1991; Goodson, 1981a, 1983, 1992a; Goodson & Cole, 1993; Miller, 1990a; Schubert, 1991b; Schubert & Ayers, 1992; McDonald, 1992). The autobiographical scholarship on teacher development, teacher thinking, and teacher knowledge [see also chapter 13] may represent what Thomas E. Barone (1992b) has called for the field to produce: "The time is right for additional accessible, compelling, and morally persuasive storybooks about schools and schoolpeople. . . . [with] educational researchers themselves crafting this literature, rather than abandoning this task to talented noneducator journalists" (p. 20). In his historical study, Philip Jackson (1992a) cited the work of Connelly and Clandinin particularly as illustrative of the movement in the contemporary field toward practitioners, a movement inspired in part by an interest in supporting teachers' voices.

"Looking at teaching from the inside." In her "Research on Teachers' Knowledge: The Evolution of a Discourse," Freema Elbaz situated this voluminous

research on teacher knowledge within the context of the movement to understand curriculum as autobiographical text. Taken as a whole, Elbaz asserted that the primary focus of this research is "looking at teaching from the inside" (Elbaz, 1991, p. 2). We see this focus in each of the four streams of scholarship which study teachers' lives. For instance, in the burgeoning literature on teacher lore (Schubert 1987, 1991a), an inner focus is evident as well. Schubert explains:

> we use lore to specifically delineate that knowledge which has guiding power in teachers' lives and work. We are moving beyond viewing knowledge as concepts to include the values, beliefs, and images that guide everyday work of teachers (a pervasive notion of experiential knowledge). (Schubert, 1991b, p. 224)

In research on teachers' lore and personal practical knowledge, teachers are asked to report their experiences autobiographically. Goodson's (1992a) study of teachers' lives and Butt and Raymond's scholarship on collaborative autobiography also exhibit this interest in life history and lived experience. Clearly, the autobiographical and biographical are interwoven throughout this work. We review these four now to see how autobiographical/biographical research has recast our understandings of teachers and teaching.

Collaborative Autobiography: Richard Butt and Danielle Raymond

The voluminous and important work of Richard Butt (1983, 1984, 1985a, 1985b, 1989, 1990, 1991) represents a major effort to understand teacher thinking via biography and autobiography. Butt's work intersects with that of Connelly and Clandinin (1987) on personal practical knowledge; however there are differences (Elbaz, 1991).

Richard Butt strives to understand biography and autobiography as educational praxis. One theme is the significance of personal experience in schools; a second is the importance of not only writing about this personal experience, but the necessity of sharing this autobiographical work with others. We noted the role of community in this stream of autobiographical work as well as in the feminist strand of autobiographical research. Butt employs autobiography to help teachers examine their lived experience of the curriculum (Butt & Raymond, 1987, 1988, 1992).

In their "Arguments for Using Qualitative Approaches in Understanding Teacher Thinking: The Case for Biography" (1987), Butt and Raymond discuss the potential uses of biography as a method by means of which we might more fully understand how teachers think, feel, and act. Citing Berk's (1980) careful study of educational biography, Butt and Raymond defined biography as "a disciplined way of interpreting a person's thought and action in the light of his or her past" (Berk, 1980, cited in Butt & Raymond, 1987, p. 63). That which is pertinent to understanding our lives, Butt and Raymond assert, must be included in this effort to understand teacher thinking, a view Ivor Goodson takes as well, as we shall see momentarily.

There is also a notion here that to understand our lives and our experience of curriculum, we must interpret and share that experience. The concept of "collective biography" is formulated to point to the appropriateness of reporting and analyzing teachers' shared or common experience. Butt and Raymond claim that in this process of interpreting individual and collective biographies one might blend qualitative and quantitative aspects of educational experience:

> The irony, from my vantage point in education, is that collective biography, in its moderate form, illuminates the synergy and the complementarity of using both qualitative and quantitative approaches. This consists in thorough investigation of the quality of individual experience which undergirds warranted quantitative analysis of evident commonalities across individual lives. (Butt & Raymond, 1987, pp. 64-65)

Collaboration in autobiographical and biographical praxis is imperative in Butt's view. The researcher who collects the data of experience must work in a "close and continuous collaboration with the teacher" (p. 69). Teachers need to be seen as "co-researchers/co-developers of classrooms" (p. 70). This idea of collaboration and of teachers as co-researchers is shared by the other major scholars working in this area, including, as we have seen, Janet L. Miller (1990a), F. Michael Connelly and D. Jean Clandinin (1988a, 1988b, 1990), William Schubert (1987), and William Ayers, (1992). Butt and Raymond emphasize the importance of collaboration also, contrasting it with "uncollaborative autobiography." Biographic data would include "conversations, interviews, observations, video and audiotapes, field notes, stimulated recall, 'stream of consciousness' journals, and logs" (p. 82). It is the interpretation of this data that is most problematic, a view shared, as we saw earlier, by feminist curriculum theorists (Grumet, 1988b; Miller, 1983a; Pagano, 1990).

Biography over phenomenology. Butt and Raymond have argued for the primacy of biographical understanding over phenomenological understanding. They cite three reasons to support their case: 1) the case for phenomenology has already been well made; 2) biographical understanding tends to be omitted in orthodox phenomenology; and 3) the unique characteristics of biography are better suited to understanding teaching and the curriculum (Butt & Raymond, 1987). Biography accentuates the power of the "conscious and the unconscious, of the past over the present" (Butt & Raymond, 1987, p. 76), in contrast with phenomenology's "preoccupation with the present" (Butt & Raymond, 1987, p. 76). Butt and Raymond conclude this study of biography by restating that this focus and mode of curriculum research permits research conducted "in the middle" of the qualitative and quantitative methods:

> besides teaching, biography (especially the collective biography) can utilize ancillary quantitative approaches to truth claims. The way biography brings together experience, thought, acting, theory, practice, research development

and self education, and the way it makes research relationships among insiders and outsiders more collaborative, gives biography, as an epistemology, tremendous integrative, synergistic, and emancipatory potential. (Butt & Raymond, 1987, p. 88)

Autobiographical praxis vs. personal practical knowledge. In a second major statement, Butt, Raymond, and Yamagishi (1988) distinguished autobiographical praxis from the research on personal practical knowledge conducted by Connelly and Clandinin (1987, 1988a, 1988b). The major distinction lies in the notion of breath. Butt et al. (1988) assert: "it is out of the whole cultural ecological breath of context interacting with the intentionality of living, working, and acting that each teachers' unique knowledge is expressed in the present" (p. 102). In autobiographical praxis we observe a search for a unity of experience. Such a full account would include "the whole story not just fragments derived from what is most obvious in action" (p. 117). Butt, Raymond, and Yamagishi argue for including all that the person has undergone, all that is the self. Human experience becomes reduced, they allege, in research on personal practical knowledge. In that work unity occurs in "the present as a person brings past experience to bear to make present action meaningful" (Elbaz, 1991, p. 4). Like Goodson, Butt and his collaborators seem to regard the focus on "practical knowledge" as crowding out, somehow, a focus upon the "personal."

For Butt autobiography conveys how teachers' knowledge is held, formed, and how it can be studied and understood. Autobiographic praxis refers to conceptualizations of teachers' knowledge. Praxeology refers to the meanings and understandings of human action. Butt characterizes his methodology (by means of which he studies teachers' knowledge) as autobiographic praxeology. This methodology permits the researcher to study teachers' knowledge, including "the process of how it has been and is being elaborated, how it is expressed through autobiographic inquiry" (Butt, et al., 1988, p. 120). Butt asks four basic questions: "What is the nature of my working reality? How do I think and act in that context and why? How, through my worklife experience and personal history, did I come to be that way? How do I wish to become in my professional future?" (Butt, et al., 1990, p. 257).

Butt returns to the importance of collaboration in the interpretation of experience. Butt views the teacher as a coresearcher, permitting an enhanced understanding of the "nature, sources and evolution of professional knowledge that they possess and use" (Butt, et al. 1988, p. 150). Those understandings achieved collaboratively by teachers in this process—autobiographical praxeology—enable us to begin to understand the curriculum as experienced by teachers. Butt's accomplishment consists in part of his formulation and refinement of a methodology to generate autobiographical "data" regarding teachers' experience, a methodology whose epistemological underpinnings he had developed earlier (1983). Butt (1991) believes that in interpreting and reconstructing our past, present, and future, we move beyond what we thought before through action. In exploring these notions through acting them out, we are able to rehearse the possibility of transformation.

Personal Practical Knowledge: F. Michael Connelly and D. Jean Clandinin
The research of D. Jean Clandinin, F. Michael Connelly, and Freema Elbaz (Clandinin, 1985, 1986; Clandinin & Connelly, 1987a, 1987b; Connelly & Clandinin, 1987, 1988a, 1988b, 1990, 1991; Elbaz, 1981, 1983, 1991) presents a view of knowledge and theory as residing in the "heads" of real teachers (Britzman, 1991, p. 50). This work has been promoted particularly through *Curriculum Inquiry* (of which Connelly is editor), which has featured a "Personal Practical Knowledge Series." A newsletter, *Among Teachers: Experience and Inquiry* has been published as a joint project of the Centre for Teacher Development at the Ontario Institute for Studies in Education, and the Faculty of Education, University of Alberta. [We saw in chapter 8 that the University of Alberta's Department of Secondary Education is the North American center for phenomenological studies. D. Jean Clandinin's appointment is to the faculty of the Department of Elementary Education.] Clandinin, Connelly, and Elbaz propose that teachers routinely enact theories of teaching and learning in their daily classroom activity. Such theories may be implicit; they constitute "personal practical knowledge." Personal practical knowledge is conceived to be that combination of theory and practical knowledge born of lived experience. Deborah Britzman (1991) characterizes such knowledge as "contextual, affective, situated, flexible and fluid, aesthetic, intersubjective, and grounded in the body" (Britzman, 1991, p. 50). Clandinin defines the concept as follows:

> By "knowledge" in the phrase "personal practical knowledge" is meant that body of convictions, conscious or unconscious, which have arisen from experience . . . and which are expressed in a person's actions. The actions in question are all those acts that make up the practice of teaching, including its planning and evaluation. Personal practical knowledge is knowledge which is imbued with all the experiences that make up a person's being. Its meaning is derived from, and understood in terms of, a person's experiential history, both professional and personal. (Clandinin, 1985, p. 362)

This last statement would seem to contest criticisms by Butt and Goodson that research on "personal practical knowledge" does not focus upon the personal.

A variety of methods. Studies of personal practical knowledge conducted by Clandinin, Connelly, and Elbaz provide narrative accounts of teachers' lived experience. Narrative is defined as "the making of meaning from personal experience via a process of reflection in which storytelling is the key element and in which metaphors and folk knowledge take their place" (Connelly & Clandinin, 1988b, p. 16). Narrative accounts portray how teachers come to understand their lives in classrooms. They suggest that teachers work and struggle to achieve meaning and understanding. They labor to make sense of their worlds. To do so they report their experience by a variety of methods, including journal records, interview transcripts, observations, story telling, letter writing, autobiographical writing, class plans, newsletters, and other writing (Connelly & Clandinin, 1990, p. 5). Narrative is defined as a "reconstruction of experience" (p. 245). The three key terms are "collaborative research, ethics of participation and the concept of negotiation. Where we had originally seen these terms as being functionally discrete, we now see them as bound together by the notion of the negotiation of narrative. . . . Relationships are joined . . . by the narrative unities of our lives" (Clandinin & Connelly, 1988, p. 281). Discussing differences and similarities of "personal practical knowledge" with the work of Pinar and Grumet (1976), Berk (1980), and Butt (1984), Connelly and Clandinin (1987) explained:

> The emphasis on personal knowledge of classrooms highlights one of the principal differences between narrative and biography. The primary focus in autobiography and biography . . . is on method. . . . The purpose of method is to reveal something about individual persons. . . . In contrast, the emphasis in narrative, at least as defined in the study of personal practical knowledge, is on how people know classrooms. Method is subsidiary. (p. 136)

Time and place. How does the researcher structure this data? Quoting Eudora Welty, Connelly and Clandinin note that time and place are the two points of reference by which the novel organizes experience, an organization found in the writing of narrative experience as well. They note: "Time and place become written constructions in the form of plot and scene respectively. Time and place, plot and scene, work together to create the experiential quality of narrative" (1990, p. 8). Scene and plot are to be distinguished from interpretation; they are points of organization of "the thing itself" (p. 8). Connelly and Clandinin explain how they proceed:

> In our work, especially in teaching but also in research, instead of asking people at the outset to write a narrative we encourage them to write a chronology. We avoid asking people to begin by writing biographies and autobiographies for the same reason. People beginning to explore the writing of their own narrative, or that of another, often find the chronology to be a manageable task whereas the writing of a full-fledged autobiography or narrative, when one stresses plot, meaning, interpretation, and explanation, can be baffling and discouraging. . . . In the end, of course, it is of no real theoretical significance what the writing is called because all chronicles are incipient narratives and all narratives reduce to chronicles as one pursues the narrative, remembers and reconstructs new events, and creates further meaning. For inquiry, the point is that a heartfelt record of events in one's life, or research account of a life, does not guarantee significance, meaning, or purpose. (1990, p. 9)

Connelly and Clandinin note that narrative accounts may seem to freeze experience, but that narrative research discloses that as stories are retold, understandings change. Autobiographical researchers narratively discover the phenomenon of the "multiple I," that is, that the self is "plurivocal" (Barnieh, 1989, quoted in Connelly & Clandinin, 1990, p. 9). They note: "in the writing of narrative, it becomes important to sort out whose voice is the dominant one when we write 'I'" (p. 9). For instance, the narrative researcher's "I" becomes less distinct in collaborative moments; it reasserts itself during the writing:

> The question of who is researcher and who is teacher becomes less important as we concern ourselves with questions of collaboration, trust, and relationship as we live, story, and restory our collaborative research life. . . . The researcher moves out of the lived story to tell, with another another kind of story. (Connelly & Clandinin, 1990, p. 10)

Connelly and Clandinin add that they work with participants throughout the writing, so that the process of narrative inquiry remains collaborative throughout.

Teacher's experience as curriculum discourse. Clandinin and Connelly (1990) emphasize the practical character of their narrative inquiry:

> Our own work, perhaps more prosaically "practical" than most, is to rethink curriculum and teaching in terms of a narrative inquiry which draws on classroom observation and participant observation of the practical, along with the bringing forward of personal experience in the form of stories, interviews, rules, principles, images, and metaphors. (p. 245)

In defending their focus upon the teacher, they write:

> We assume that in the curricular event, it is teachers that reproduce or revolutionize social structures, communicate or reinterpret curriculum context, and cooperate with, or act in opposition to, the nature of their student charges. In short, we propose to entertain the consequences of adopting a teacher topic for curriculum discourse. (p. 246)

As we saw earlier in this chapter, other autobiographical/biographical scholars (for instance, Grumet, Ayers, and Salvio) focus upon the student as well as the teacher.

Connelly and Clandinin distinguish their research program from other, more theoretical efforts, and from efforts to understand curriculum as political text [see chapter 5], which they decry as ideological, by emphasizing the practical. They insist: "what is at stake is less a matter of working theories and ideologies and more a question of the place of research in the improvement of practice and how researchers and practitioners may productively relate to one another" (1990, p. 12). Quoting Eisner, Connelly and Clandinin assert that narrative inquiry is part of a movement on researchers' part "to go back to the school, not to conduct commando raids, but to work with teachers" (Eisner, 1988, p. 19). Interesting in this regard is that both Connelly and Eisner are both Ph.D. graduates of the University of Chicago, where, you will recall, Joseph Schwab promoted the cause of the practical arts [see chapter 4].

Connelly and Clandinin (1991) refer to their field as "narratology" (p. 121), and observe that "because it focuses on human experience, perhaps because it is a fundamental structure of human experience, and perhaps because it has a holistic quality, narrative is exploding into other disciplines"

(p. 121). Because narrative inquiry "may be sociologically concerned with groups and formation of community" (p. 122), Connelly and Clandinin (1991) cite Goodson's (1988b) work on teachers' life histories but wish to "maintain a distinction between biography/autobiography and life history" (p. 122). Inquiry, they suggest, has shifted from the question "what does it mean for a person to be educated?" to "how are people, in general, educated?" (p. 123). Connelly and Clandinin argue that individual psychology has been displaced, and with it, the tradition they associate with Pinar and Grumet.

Narrative inquiry moves toward constructing "a caring community: when both researchers and practitioners tell stories of the research relationships, they have the possibility of becoming stories of empowerment" (p. 126). To contribute to a "shared" perspective, they include "field notes of shared experience," "journal records," "interviews," "letter writing," "storytelling," and, lastly, "autobiographical and biographical writing" (pp. 128-132). "Good" narrative must go beyond reliability, validity, and generalizability: "A 'plausible' one tends to 'ring true'. . . . Thus, while fantasy may be an invitational element in fictional narrative, plausibility exerts firmer tugs in empirical narratives" (p. 136). Scene and plot continue to be important elements of narrative, but, more importantly, is what they term "the restorying quality of narrative" (p. 139). This is described as "the task of conveying a sense that the narrative is unfinished and that stories will be retold and lives relived in new ways . . ." (p. 139). In a section on "risks, dangers and abuses of narrative" (pp. 141-142), they perceptively note that the "intersubjective quality of the narrative" (p. 141) needs to be emphasized: "To dismiss criticisms of the personal and interpersonal in inquiry is to risk the dangers of narcisissm [sic] and solipsism" (p. 141). This is linked to their second warning, the "Hollywood plot" and its happy ending (p. 142). Narrative must look to the future, which is another element of "restorying: The third thing to do with the story follows from this. The person returns to present and future considerations and asks what the meaning of the event is for them and how they might create a new story of self which changes the meaning of the event, its description, and its significance for the larger life story the person may be trying to live" (p. 144). This phase sounds similar to Pinar's notion of the synthetical moment in autobiographical practice (1994; Pinar & Grumet, 1976).

Commentary. Personal practical knowledge has provoked considerable commentary. Mark Johnson (1989) characterized personal practical knowledge as an emerging orientation that focuses on the many ways that teachers' understandings of their world affect how they structure classroom experience and interact with students, parents, colleagues, and administrators. Johnson argued that personal practical knowledge research contributes significantly to models of cognition, meaning, understanding, and knowledge. These models represent nonpropositional, pre-reflective dimensions of meaning that emphasize spatio-temporal dimensions, perceptual interaction, and bodily movements. To examine these dimensions of experience requires new models of reflection, and personal practical knowledge may represent just such a new territory for curriculum inquiry.

Also reviewing the personal practical knowledge project, John Willinsky (1989)—whose scholarship we examine in chapters 5, 6, and 14—worried that personal practical knowledge "needlessly isolates them [teachers] with their personal sense of, and thus their responsibility for, the state of things. The act of teaching is de-institutionalized" (p. 256). Personal practical knowledge labors "to recover and reconstruct what might be characterized as this Romantic conception of the lost unity of the self "(p. 257). Further, Willinsky expressed concern that:

> personal practical knowledge risks a complacency . . . risks becoming more therapeutic and reassuring than diagnostic or critical. . . . I have pressed for re-inserting the teacher within the realities of the personal, practical ideologies of power in educational systems as part of the researcher's contribution to the collaborative process. I have asked that the subject be considered as more dynamic, if less successfully coherent, in making a life out of the social formations of classrooms. (p. 262)

We suspect that Willinsky's criticism would be dismissed by Connelly and Clandinin as merely ideological.

Teacher Lore: William Schubert and William Ayers

William H. Schubert (1991b) is the primary author of this stream of research. The Teacher Lore Project, housed at the University of Illinois at Chicago, has been funded in part by the Chicago Area School Effectiveness Council (CASEC). Schubert defines teacher lore as:

> the study of the knowledge, ideas, perspectives, and understandings of teachers. In part it is inquiry into the beliefs, values, and images that guide teachers' work. In this sense, it constitutes an attempt to learn what teachers learn from their experience. (Schubert, 1991b, p. 207)

Like Richard Butt, William Schubert invokes the concept of praxis to refer to the blend of theory and practice embedded in teachers' work. Teacher lore research aspires to disclose "the experiential knowledge that informs their teaching or the revealed stories about their practical experiences" (Schubert, 1991b, p. 208). By this definition teacher lore closely resembles the "personal practice knowledge" that Clandinin and Connelly study.

Schubert identifies two basic origins of teacher lore. The first is related to curriculum development [see chapter 13]. Schubert regards curriculum as developed "by teachers in their daily interactions with students. . . . It can be better understood as such [when] teachers are approached for their experiential insights" (Schubert, 1991b, p. 210). [You will note that Schubert's view of curriculum development here seems very much in keeping with Jackson's (1992a), namely that the space of curriculum development has moved over the last 70 years from the public to the private domain.] The second origin of teacher lore resides in the study of such experiential insights, including personal constructs and theories of action. Schubert regards this area as an unstudied realm in curriculum, despite its apparent proximity to the research into "personal practical knowledge" conducted by Clandinin, Connelly, and Elbaz. Schubert situates the teacher lore project in the Deweyan tradition [see chapters 2 and 3], citing particularly Dewey's *Democracy and Education* (1916) and *The Sources for a Science of Education* (1929). Schubert points out that Dewey characterizes teachers as "creators of knowledge and theory [that] can illuminate an understanding of curriculum, teaching and the educative process" (p. 214). Consequently, Schubert regards as essential to teacher lore research reflective conversations with teachers, analyzing the process of knowing, the notion of teaching as a moral craft [Tom, 1984], teachers as connoisseurs [Eisner, 1985a, 1985b], the reasoning of teachers, political impediments to praxis, and the spiritual character of teaching [see chapter 12]. These questions—and their Deweyan rationale—constitute the theoretical base of the teacher lore project. [Clandinin and Connelly also cite Dewey as precedent to their formulation of narrative inquiry (Clandinin & Connelly, 1990). Robert Graham (1991) regards Dewey as foundational to all auto-biographical work.]

Schubert characterizes the findings of the Teacher Lore Project as of two types. The first type is literature review, the review of pertinent bodies of knowledge to discover "insights into teachers' stories, experiential knowledge, modes of everyday inquiry, and sources of meaning and direction" (p. 219). A second type includes what he terms primary studies, i.e. research with teachers directly, via interviews and observations. A number of Ph.D. dissertations exploring teacher lore have been completed at the University of Illinois at Chicago (Melnick, 1988, Hulsebosch, 1988, 1992; Millies, 1989; Jagla, 1989; Koerner, 1989). Research studies which have been published as of this writing include Schubert, Weston, Ponticell, & Melnick, (1987); Ponticell, et al., (1987) and a book reporting the first three years of the teacher lore project (Schubert & Ayers, 1992). Schubert (1991b) emphasizes the necessity of a "community of affiliation":

> Through these efforts we hope to encourage the continued consideration of both the reflective process and the context of teachers' experiential repertoires of knowledge and values that give meaning and direction to their work. We hope, too, that teacher lore is increasingly acknowledged as a legitimate form of educational inquiry, one that engages collaborative efforts of teachers, scholars, and interested others to interpret praxis in ways that would not be possible without serious dialogue, conversation, and sharing. (p. 223)

This strand of autobiographical research, with its emphasis upon reflexivity and lived experience, shares with the work of Clandinin, Connelly, Goodson, Butt and Raymond a commitment to explore the lived experience of teachers. As has the work of Clandinin, Connelly, Goodson, Butt, and Raymond, the work of Schubert and Ayers continues to attract attention of scholars and practitioners (Ponder, 1990). We will report examples of teacher lore in chapter 13 in the section on teacher development [in-service teacher education].

Biographical Studies: Ivor F. Goodson

As early as 1981, Ivor F. Goodson (1981a) promoted the use of life history as source and method for the study of schooling. In life history Goodson saw a "dynamic model of how syllabuses, pedagogy, finance, resources, selection, the economy and the like all interrelate" (p. 176). And this model of interrelation would disclose activity at the "preactive and interactive levels" (p. 177), an apparent if unacknowledged reference to the 1967 Duncan/Frymier essay presented at the Ohio State Curriculum Theory Conference [see chapter 3]. Ten years later, in a book written with Rob Walker, Goodson (1991) restates his enthusiasm for life history and narrative in the conduct of educational research. The use of life history and narrative would constitute a fundamental reconceptualization of educational research, research that then would express "the teacher's voice" (p. 139). Central to educational research is the importance of communicating the teacher's voice, so that it may be "heard loudly, heard articulately" (1991, p. 139). Such work would build on the "teacher as researcher" idea, especially as that phrase was elaborated by John Elliott and Clem Adelman during 1973-1975 at the University of East Anglia (U.K.).

For Goodson, as for Butt, Raymond, Schubert, Ayers, Connelly and Clandinin, articulating teachers' lives is essential to understanding teachers' practices. Goodson (Goodson & Walker, 1991) argues: "To the degree that we invest our 'self' in our teaching, experience and background therefore shape our practice" (p. 144). Considerations of class, gender, and ethnicity are important, but teachers' lives are unique, even idiosyncratic, and cannot be reduced to broad social forces. Goodson (Goodson & Walker, 1991) contrasts his interest in life history with Clandinin and Connelly's focus upon "personal practical knowledge." He judges their efforts as "innovative" and "interesting" (p. 140). Further, the inclusion of "personal" in a study of "practical knowledge" points to the importance of "biographical perspectives." However, he has a reservation:

> But again the person is being linked irrevocably to practice. It is as if the teacher *is* her or his practice. For teacher educators, such specificity of focus is understandable but I wish to argue that a broader perspective will achieve more. . . . In short, what I am saying is that it does not follow logically or psychologically that to improve practice we must initially and immediately focus on practice. Indeed, I . . . argue the opposite point of view. (p.141)

Goodson proceeds to suggest that locating teachers' classroom practice at the heart of action research highlights the most "exposed and problematical aspects of the teachers' world at the center of scrutiny and negotiation" (p. 141). In terms of political and personal strategy, Goodson regards doing so as a mistake. He asserts: "A more valuable and less vulnerable entry point would to be examine teachers' work in the context of teachers' lives" (141). Why he regards teachers' private lives as making teachers less vulnerable, requiring them to feel less exposed, is not clear. While Grumet, Pinar, Butt, and Raymond would seem to agree that the lives of teachers and students are essential to the study of the experience of education, none of these autobiographical theorists has argued so on strategic grounds. All scholars who understand curriculum as autobiographical/biographical text might be in agreement, however, with Goodson's observation that: "work in this area begins to force a reconceptualization of models of teacher development. We move in short from the teacher-as-practice to the teacher-as-person as our starting point for development" (Goodson & Walker, 1991, p. 145). Clearly, the work of Ivor F. Goodson and other autobiographical scholars has reconceptualized our understanding of studying teachers and teaching.

V
Conclusion: Not Pruned from the Disciplines

> I become nervous when the study of narrative is pruned from the humanities disciplines of history, philosophy, and literature in which it is rooted and is grafted on to social science disciplines committed to generalized description, typology and prediction.
>
> (Madeleine R. Grumet, 1990b, p. 324)

The effort to understand curriculum as autobiographical and biographical text emerged in the 1970's as an alternative to the conceptual-empirical and quantitative social science research dominating education at that time. This work has weathered attacks from both psychometricians and from Marxists to emerge as one of the major contemporary strands of curriculum scholarship. The effort to understand curriculum autobiographically has spawned important curriculum scholarship, such as dialogue journals and autobiographical and biographical teacher research. It has been employed in provocative and insightful ways by feminist theory as well.

As we saw in chapter 4, tension between political and autobiographical theorists characterized the 1970s. While the two camps have generally ignored each other during the 1980s, Jean Clandinin and Michael Connelly have recently criticized what they term sociopolitical analysis, suggesting that this dispute is only dormant. They write that their narrative inquiry allows a return "upward" to the "whole," a return "from the technical rationalists' reduced world of skilled practice" (Clandinin & Connelly, 1990, p. 243). Technicism is not the only "downward" flight from the whole, however. So, according to Clandinin and Connelly, are efforts to understand curriculum as political text:

> There is another retelling of the story "downward" to the whole from a paradigmatic sociopolitical analysis. Just as reductionism makes the whole into something lesser, sociological and political analysis can also make the whole lesser through the use of abstraction and formalism. (1990, p. 243)

Additionally, Clandinin and Connelly criticize the effort to understand curriculum as political text as treating "the teacher as an unconscious reproducer of inequitable social structures" (p. 246).

Perhaps most autobiographical/biographical scholars would agree that the effort to understand curriculum as political text has functioned to erase the individual and his or her experience in a fascination with abstractions such as "cultural reproduction." Most would also agree that cultural reproduction occurs, but that it can be best understood as its expresses itself in the concrete lives of existing individuals. Thus autobiographical/biographical scholarship claims that it understands curriculum as political text as well, as at least one recent collection of essays testifies (McLaughlin & Tierney, 1993). There is no either/or choice here; the individual is social and society is comprised of individuals. In this regard, Grumet (1990b) asserts:

> Narratives of educational experience challenge their readers and writers to find both individuality and society, being and history and possibility in their texts. It is a brave company of educators who forsake simplistic polarities of individual and society to write, to read and to do scholarly work these ways. It challenges feminists to encode the body and the idioms of meaningful lived relations without abandoning the disciplines of knowledge. It challenges teachers to listen to stories and to hear their resonance in the distant orchestration of academic knowledge. And it invites all of us, no matter how wide our disillusion, to notice how existence quickens us with joy surpassing despair. (p. 323)

Commenting on the explosion in autobiographical/biographical scholarship, Grumet has expressed her concern that autobiography might be severed from those academic disciplines she believes to be inextricably interwoven with it. Additionally, she worries about over-generalization from lived experience and a simultaneous sentimental refusal to analyze this lived experience. For Grumet, autobiography is understood as a middle way.

> As the interest of educational researchers and policy-makers has been drawn to the experience of teachers, both to the process of illumining their expertise and to the project of strengthening their voices in the negotiations that determine educational policy, autobiographical writing has been included in many projects and research studies. Although such writing cannot be owned by an particular discipline or group of disciplines, I become nervous when the study of narrative is pruned from the humanities disciplines of history, philosophy, and literature in which it is rooted and is grafted on to social science disciplines committed to generalized description, typology and prediction. I fear that studies designed to investigate "teacher thinking," for example, abuse the creative and transformative character of thought by reserving that function for the researcher. On the other hand a failure to engage in some analysis of the autobiographical texts beyond celebration and recapitulation leads to a patronizing sentimentality. It consigns the teacher's tale to myth, resonant but marginal because it is not part of the discourse that justifies real action. (Grumet, 1990b, p. 324)

Autobiographical work is a political, intellectual project devoted to transformation, not only of the field, but of its participants. This dimension of this work is underlined by some. In noting that constructions of race, class, and gender intersect autobiographical remembrance, Naomi Norquay reminds scholars that the point of this work is not merely knowledge accumulation. It is change: "This also makes problematic the tendency for life history research to simply use memories of experience to explain classroom practice, without exploring the possibility of using memories as a springboard for change" (Norquay, 1990, p. 292). What began in the early 1970s as solitary work to elucidate the relations among the knower and the known has grown explosively to a multi-dimensional study of students, teachers, and that reconstruction of their lived experience known as curriculum. It is an exciting and vital sector of contemporary scholarship. In these respects, however, it is not alone. Antedating autobiography in the field is the effort to understand curriculum as aesthetic text. To this crucial discourse we turn next.

Chapter 11

Understanding Curriculum
as Aesthetic Text

The aesthetic function of curriculum replaces the amelioration of the technological function with revelation.

(Madeleine R. Grumet, 1978, p. 280)

The task of the critic is to perform a mysterious feat well: to transform the qualities of painting, play, novel, poem, classroom or school, or act of teaching and
learning into a public form that illuminates, interprets, and appraises the qualities that have been experienced.

(Eiliot W. Eisner, 1991a, p. 86)

If the uniqueness of the artistic-aesthetic can be reaffirmed, if we can consider
futuring as we combat immersion, old either/ors may disappear. We may make
possible a pluralism of vision, a multiplicity of realities. We may enable those
we teach to rebel.

(Maxine Greene, 1988b, p. 295)

I
Introduction: Not the Singing of Hymns

Considerable scholarship supports the notion that curriculum *is* aesthetic
text. In the school, however, the aesthetic dimensions of curriculum tend to
be underemphasized. This has been the case historically. For instance, during
the nineteenth century in the United States, when music—other than the
singing of hymns—was introduced into the schools, a storm of protest
ensued. Music, said the protesters, would take away time from the three R's
(Tanner & Tanner, 1990). The marginalization of the arts continues to the
present day (Egan, 1985). Even in educational research it is underemphasized, despite its acknowledged importance, even to the research on classrooms (Uhrmacher, 1989; Hunter, 1993).

Reflecting on children's dance, Susan W. Stinson (1985b) has made a point
of more general significance: "Curriculum exists only as it comes through
persons" (p. 17). For Stinson, and for other students of the effort to understand curriculum as aesthetic text, this is an aesthetic not autobiographical
realization. That is, the curriculum comes to form as art does, as a complex
mediation and reconstruction of experience. In this regard curriculum can

be likened to any art form, including, for instance, dance (Stinson, 1986). An aesthetic model for curricular thought and action would rest upon the principle of developing experience: "the point is not to do away with substantive principles and rules and recipes, but to transform our use of them by reflectively relating them to developing experience" (Knitter, 1986, p. 265).

What is at the base of understanding curriculum aesthetically? The prominent philosopher of education, Maxine Greene (1988b), has written in this regard: "aesthetic experiences, as I have suggested, involve us as existing beings in pursuit of meanings" (p. 293). She continued: "If the uniqueness of the artistic-aesthetic can be reaffirmed . . . old either/ors may disappear. We may make possible a pluralism of visions, a multiplicity of realities. We may enable those we teach to rebel" (p. 295). On many occasions (1973, 1975b, 1988a, 1988b, 1991a, 1991b), Greene has memorably made the case that the arts challenge empty formalism, didacticism, and elitism. Those shocks of awareness to which encounters with the arts can provoke persons leave us less submerged in the everyday, and more likely to wonder and to question. An important art educator, Karen Hamblen (1986), has explained that studying art—insofar as it indicates universal associations and relationships— reveals what it means to be human at a particular time and place. Hamblen observes: "we now occupy a global aesthetic village" (p. 41).

While the work reported in this chapter is related to scholarship in art education, the emphasis here is not upon methods of teaching art nor upon other scholarly areas typically associated with art education: for instance, history of art, and philosophy of art. [For a recent history of art education see Efland, 1993.] In this chapter you will be introduced to research and scholarship which employs the arts to understand curriculum. Rather than focusing on the teaching of art more effectively, more appropriately, and more creatively, we will focus upon that scholarship which illumines the aesthetic dimensions of curriculum generally. This distinction does not always hold hard and fast; the scholars whose work you will study sometimes have reputations in art education. While the research here intersects with that in art education proper, our interest in this chapter is to present work which will assist the understanding of curriculum as aesthetic text.

Streams of scholarship. Nearly thirty years ago Dwayne E. Huebner identified aesthetic language as an important language alternative to what was then the Tylerian mainstream (Huebner, 1966b). Aesthetic language developed fairly extensively during the three decades that followed Huebner's essay. Currently, the effort to understand the aesthetic character of curriculum has several streams. First, the significance of the arts to the general curriculum has been sketched. This work responds in part to the compartmentalization of curriculum into distinct disciplines, a phenomenon which has had the effect of marginalizing the arts. This result becomes especially unfortunate during difficult economic times when art programs are often the first victims of budget-cutting. This area of scholarship works to establish the centrality of the arts to the curriculum. The work of Harry Broudy has been important here. Next, the aesthetic notions of knowledge acquisition and of thinking have been elucidated in order to suggest frameworks—frameworks contrasting with those associated with mainstream social and behavioral science—for understanding the curriculum. In this section—aesthetic knowing and inquiry—the scholarship of José Rosario, Elizabeth Vallance, and Thomas Barone has been central. Twentieth-century conceptions of art, articulated by the artists themselves, have been linked with conceptions of curriculum, and in the next section we examine these. The work of Ronald Padgham has been the major contribution in this category. Fifth, the relation of art to society has been studied to provide an aesthetic agenda for curriculum, and to make explicit the politics of art. Landon Beyer's scholarship has been primary here. Sixth, notions associated with the arts have been utilized to provide conceptual tools for understanding teaching and curriculum. The most important work in these areas has been done by Elliot W. Eisner, Elizabeth Vallance, and Margo Figgins. Seventh, we review scholarship elaborating the relations between theater and curriculum, focusing on the work of Madeleine R. Grumet and, again, Margo Figgins. Finally, we sketch scholarship that points to a postmodern notion of curriculum as aesthetic text, pointing here to the work of jan jagodzinski [sic], Daiyo Sawada, and Karen A. Hamblen.

II
Significance of the Arts: Broudy, Beyer, and Hamblen

[Art] intercepts every shade of expressiveness found in objects and orders them in a new experience of life.

(John Dewey, 1934b, p. 104)

Recent research discounts traditional rationales for the inclusion of the arts in the school curriculum. In an era when slogans such as "back to the basics" and "minimum competencies" determine the content of school programs, art has been viewed as marginal information, more appropriately taught and learned in museums than in schools. Instruction in the arts proper—music, painting, etc.—is more economically located outside schools, or so suggest many budget-cutting committees. A contemporary rationale for the importance of the arts discounts both these disputed rationales. Instead, it focuses upon the centrality of the imagination to aesthetic experience, and the consequent relations among imagination, language, thought, and feeling (Langer, 1957; Egan, 1992). The distinguished philosopher of education Harry Broudy (1988) argues that historically and theologically the material of the imagination—the image—precedes "the word", i.e. concepts. Thus using a phenomenological epistemology, Broudy suggests that the cultivation of the intellect—the capacity to generate, analyze, and synthesize concepts—necessarily requires cultivation of the imagination. For instance, language is a system of symbols, often imagistic in character. Those children without a rich store of images are less able to decode concepts and articulate perceptions. In this way aesthetic literacies can be regarded as essential to linguistic literacies. They are foundational to social intelligence as well (Greene, 1978).

Historical/cultural primacy of the image. Since language and thought are intersecting categories, Broudy argues that the capacity to decode aesthetic clues—the elements of an image—is central to the capacity to think, especially during a historical period in which "reality" is thoroughly imagistic. Others too have made this general argument. For instance, Edward Milner (1987) linked the visual and the verbal in the notion of "transvestite." Social and cultural historian Christopher Lasch (1984) documented the primacy of the image in twentieth-century advanced societies. Indeed, for Lasch, this primacy contributes to an erosion (or "minimalization") of the individual self, making academic (as well as any public) achievement psychologically problematic (Lasch, 1984; Pinar, 1988b). Broudy dwells on the political use of the image and the urgency of educating students to decode such usage. In part, this issue is one of distinguishing truth from falsehood, and it leads him to discuss the relation of the image to human feeling. Broudy argues that education in the arts can permit students to become analytically discriminating in their apprehension of images and more sensitive to its emotional veracity or manipulation.

Landon Beyer (1985) concurs that the arts speak to morality and politics. Art objects make accessible realities inexpressible through other orders of representation. Indeed, certain realities may be politically suppressed; their aesthetic representation and consequent decoding suggest crucial aspects of understanding curriculum as aesthetic text. John Dewey (1934b) expressed another aspect of this "revelatory" function of art:

> Art throws off the covers that hide the expressiveness of experienced things; it quickens us from the slackness of routine and enables us to forget ourselves by finding ourselves in the delight of experiencing the world about us in its varied qualities and forms. It intercepts every shade of expressiveness found in objects and orders them in a new experience of life. (p. 104)

Karen Hamblen (1990) has noted that advocates of cultural literacy, such as E. D. Hirsch and William Bennett (Secretary of Education under President Reagan), present culture as a single weave, a singular standard that precludes the legitimacy, if not the existence, of other cultural possibilities. Hamblen examines how cultural literacy can come to mean a particular form of aesthetic literacy and how that literacy is rationalized. Relying on critical theory [see chapter 5], Hamblen suggests that cultural literacy should take the form of ethnoaesthetic studies of art and culture wherein the value systems of different aesthetic systems are examined, analyzed, and contrasted. In this view, art is contextualized culturally and historically. Hamblen believes that ethnoaesthetic approaches most closely approximate the means and the goals of a critical consciousness of aesthetic meanings.

III
Aesthetic Knowing and Inquiry: Rosario, Vallance, and Barone

[Aesthetic inquiry] rarely helps us to predict our reactions to other curricular events, focusing instead on the particular. It is partly this abstention from seeking generalizable rules that contributes to its maverick identity within educational research circles.

(Elizabeth Vallance, 1991, p. 162)

Imagination is the capacity to think of things as possibly being so; . . . it is not distinct from rationality but is rather a capacity that greatly enriches rational thinking.

(Kieran Egan, 1992, p. 43)

An aesthetic epistemology. The arts curriculum not only provides students with an aesthetic literacy crucial to the development of thought and feeling in an imagistic world. It provides a theory of knowing divergent from those associated with mainstream educational psychology, and divergent as well from certain strands of pragmatism, associated with the work of John Dewey, now expressed to some extent in the work of Schwab, Reid, and Walker [see chapters 2 & 3]. José Rosario (1988) has explicated Harold Rugg's [see chapter 2] aesthetic theory of knowing, comparing and contrasting it with Dewey's. The latter's classic formulation appears in *How We Think* (Dewey, 1910). [For a more complete view of Dewey's aesthetic theory, see Dewey, 1934b, and, perhaps, his poetry (Jackson, 1989).] In that 1910 work, rational deliberation is constituted by five sequential cognitive steps. These are:

1. suggestions, in which the mind leaps forward to a possible solution;
2. an intellectualization of the difficulty or perplexity that has been felt (directly experienced) into a problem to be solved, a question for which the answer must be sought;
3. the use of one suggestion after another as a leading idea, or hypothesis, to initiate and guide observation and other operations in collection of factual material;
4. the mental elaboration of the idea or supposition as an idea or supposition (reasoning, in the sense in which reasoning is a part, not whole, of inference); and
5. testing the hypothesis by overt or imaginative action. (quoted in Rosario, 1988, p. 344)

Rugg's challenge to Dewey. Rosario argues that Harold Rugg was among the first to challenge Dewey's formulation. As a social reconstructionist, Rugg was committed to schools' rebuilding the American social order. In this effort he ascribed to aesthetics a central role, writing in the 1940s that "the discoveries of the American esthetic frontier since 1890" must comprise "the life and program of the coming school of the mid-twentieth century" (Rugg, quoted in Rosario, 1988, p. 344). These "discoveries" were not those made by social and behavioral scientists studying creative process. Instead they were those aesthetic experiences articulated by practicing artists themselves. The most compelling conclusion of these experiences:

have been the cumulative confirmation of one hypothesis: there are other modes of human response than that of the experimental method of knowing. [Indeed] the psychological stress on intelligence and the acts of problem-solving thinking and habit has long closed our minds to the true role of the expressive acts of men. (Rugg, quoted in Rosario, 1988, p. 345)

Rugg is led, then, to reformulate Dewey's five-step model of thinking and knowing in a decidedly aesthetic mode (a twentieth-century fine arts mode):

There is, first of all, that urge to create—hazy, intangible, it may manifest itself as a vague restlessness. There is, second, the illuminating flash of insight which suddenly reveals to the artist a conception, perhaps indefinite, of the meaning toward which he is groping. There is, third, the mastery of the necessary techniques. And there is fourth, a long grueling enterprise of the integrative process itself—the tenacious grip on application of the necessary techniques in shaping and reshaping the work as it develops; the successive stages of ruthless self-criticism; the rigorous sense of dissatisfaction with the work as it progresses; the insistence upon unsparing exactitude, precision; the constant polishing and changing. (Rugg, quoted in Rosario, 1988, p. 345)

A meditative quality. Rosario identifies a "meditative" quality in Rugg's formulation absent in Dewey's 1910 description of problem-solving. Rosario finds Dewey's conception "overly calculative," requiring the individual to exercise conscious control over the many variables of the problem. In contrast, Rugg's view "implies a giving of oneself to concentration, a quiet waiting . . . for significant meaning to emerge and be known" (Rosario, 1988, p. 346). There is a phase in which conscious control is suspended; calculation is absent. Rugg believed this process was descriptive for science as well as for art. While we do not know if Rugg knew Heidegger's work [see chapter 8], Rugg's theory acknowledges a Heideggerian appreciation for the "meditative" moment in cognition. [Other scholars have emphasized the "communal" dimension of aesthetic experience; see Stinson, 1988.]

Rugg's aesthetic theory of knowing would form the framework for a curriculum theory "appropriate to a revolutionary culture." Rugg believed that:

We are living in one of these recurring cycles in the history of thought when many old conceptions are outmoded, have served their tentative usefulness; some have actually been disproved. New horizons loom before us, comparable to those faced by Kepler, Galileo, and Newton, and we listen now to new physical theorists, new behavioral theorists, and new expressional artists. (Rugg, quoted in Rosario, 1988, p. 350)

Rugg's view also anticipated those of contemporary curriculum theorists, including the political interests of Apple, Giroux, and Wexler [see chapter 5], and those of Landon Beyer, who insists upon the primacy of art as political text [see Beyer, 1987, 1988a, 1988b; Jagodzinski, 1979, 1992; Stinson, 1985a, 1985b]. Rugg's views foreshadowed as well current interest in the "new paradigm" elaborated by physics and other disciplines exhibited by William E. Doll, Jr. (1988, 1993a), and Ronald E. Padgham (1983, 1988a, 1988b). [As we saw in chapter 9, Doll comes to his understanding of "paradigm" shift via Piaget. Padgham comes to his position via twentieth-century "modernist" painters, as we shall see in this chapter.]

Rosario sketches implications of Rugg's aesthetics for curriculum organization. He suggests that Rugg's work implies that traditional curricular areas would be interwoven through the primacy of imagination and aesthetic knowing. The current organization of curriculum into discrete disciplines, without attention to epistemological parallels among them, results in children believing that aesthetic knowing and aesthetic experiences generally inhere only in the arts and humanities. Identifying and exploring the aesthetic moment in all disciplinary forms of knowing would underline a common cause and process in knowledge production and acquisition [see also Franklin, E., 1989].

Aesthetic inquiry. Extending work she published in 1977 (and which we will review later in this chapter), Elizabeth Vallance (1991) discussed, in a less historical but more synoptic way, the character of aesthetic inquiry. A doctoral graduate of Stanford University where she studied with Elliot Eisner, Vallance traced educational aesthetics from the work of Huebner (1966b), Greene (1967, 1968), and Eisner (1967, 1969), but it is Eisner (1977, 1985a, 1985b), she tells us, who developed aesthetic inquiry "as a regular tool for understanding curricular problems" (p. 157). Few investigators, she noted, employ the term "aesthetic inquiry" but all "refer at least tacitly to the investigator's aesthetic response to the [curricular] event" (p. 158). Contrasting aesthetic inquiry with quantitative research, Vallance made two qualifications:

1) aesthetic inquiry has the same *purposes* as traditional experimental research: it seeks to help the researcher—and others—to see the qualities of a curriculum that help account for students' *and* educators' reactions to it; 2) but aesthetic inquiry in today's educational climate is *neither necessary nor sufficient*; it is, however, highly *desirable*. (pp. 160-161)

Aesthetic inquiry, Vallance continued, "rarely helps us to predict our reactions to other curricular events, focusing instead on the particular. It is partly this abstention from seeking generalizable rules that contributes to its maverick identity within educational research circles" (Vallance, 1991, p. 162).

Vallance (1991) listed ten items of comparison between art and curriculum: 1) both are products of human construction; 2) both are means of communication between originators (curriculum developer or artist) and an audience (students or museum goers); 3 both are transformations of knowledge; 4) both are products of a problem-solving process; 5) both depend for their meaning on an encounter with an audience; 6) both provide situations in which the audience's response is invited and demanded; 7) both provide boundaries to the audience's experience; 8) both can stimulate strong reactions; 9) both can be situated in a tradition of history and style; and 10) both invite criticism and assessment.

While standards have been established for experimental educational research, "we do not expect any two art critics to see the same things in an art exhibition and indeed would feel cheated if they did—we expect different critics to produce different insights and to help us see the work in as many informative ways as possible" (p. 167). There are standards of art criticism, of course, and Vallance characterizes them as "structural corroboration" (p. 167), i.e. the structure must support the interpretation. The second is referential adequacy: "the criticism must tell 'the truth' in its account of the work" (p. 168). She calls for "fresh, jargon-free language," "good writing," and "both the large perspective of the big picture and a sensitivity to telling detail" (pp. 168-9). Vallance's essay is a useful introduction to understanding curriculum as aesthetic text.

Critical storytelling. Another important scholar in this area, Thomas E. Barone, incorporates aesthetic notions of curriculum into his research on narrative and critical storytelling. Barone has worried that curriculum scholars have insulated themselves from the various constituencies in the field, from practitioners, and from the public at large, a concern shared, as we saw in chapter 5, by Jesse Goodman. Barone (1992a, 1992b, 1992c) wants to promote an alternative way of speaking, reading, and writing—which he terms "critical storytelling" in educational inquiry—for the purpose of enlisting more allies to support those who work in schools. Such an effort means "acquiring a public voice" and affirming the narratives of practitioners. Barone (1993a, 1993b) contends that educational reform must begin with curriculum specialists deconstructing their own texts. Barone (1993b) tells us:

> When we are, when we *can be*, strong readers, we participate in a dismantling of that hierarchy of writers over readers which Derrida so deplored. Indeed, as Agger notes: "Strong reading is most likely to become writing, hence political practice where the readers are writers themselves (and where writers read). The two practices are inseparable: one's writing is always silent dialogue, where one's reading intends to start and extend dialogues, thus forming *communities*." Agger's (1990) notion of a discursive community is a vigorous one, more robust, it seems to me, than that which flows from, say, Barthes' (1975) definition of a work of literature as a closed system of meaning with its own "galaxy of signifiers." *That* kind of communication is a weaker, more bounded sort, perhaps occasionally "beautiful" or "aesthetic" (in the classical sense of those terms), but seldom disturbing or transformative. (pp. 1-2)

Barone wants to move the reform debate away from the realm of a closed system to a strong discursive community where the curriculum will be "disturbing" and "transformative." Particularly, Barone (1993a) insists that students must be empowered to participate in this process when he calls for "breaking the mold" of education by creating the "new American student as strong poet." In Barone's scholarship we see an intersection of the efforts to understand curriculum as institutional, political, and aesthetic text.

Strong poets participate in critical storytelling. To further explicate his proposal, Barone contrasts critical storytelling with two other alternatives.

The first is the traditional discourse that honors the hierarchy of producers over consumers of mass media, popular magazines, trade books, and journals. Barone (1993b) argues:

> Much of this writing is modernist, narrowly pragmatic in its focus, even while exhibiting what Habermas calls "comprehensibility" and "sincerity." It is generally accessible. . . . Nevertheless, this discourse is "distorted" (Habermas) by power and ideology in its uncritical acceptance of the prevailing assumptions about how schools operate. (p. 3)

The second alternative presented by Barone is "critical theory as popular educational discourse." He laments the invisible power configurations, norms, values, and interests of much educational literature, and along with poststructuralists, supports analytical and theoretical languages that attempt to deconstruct such configurations. Barone proposes a third approach, his "critical storytelling," wherein the voices of students and teachers find public support through narrative. In fact, in an attempt to "disturb" the field, Barone (1993b) announced that he would take a sabbatical "to abandon theory in order to fashion for members of the public, stories about the lives of schoolpeople that will invite them into extending the conversation. I want, that is, to strengthen the understanding of the larger community about matters of education" (p. 5).

Barone challenges others in the field to join in this effort to recover curriculum theory from the grips of behavioral and critical theories that isolate rather than empower students and teachers. This will be accomplished, according to Barone, by working diligently toward "Sartre's goal of telling the stories of the weak and inarticulate" (p. 5). If Barone's earlier efforts in this regard [see *Phi Delta Kappan*, October, 1989] are any indication of the potential of critical storytelling, his proposal to incorporate narrative into aesthetic understanding of curriculum will be significant for the field. The alternative of ignoring narratives is disconcerting (Barone, 1989). He warns:

> Empowering teachers (and students) in this way may require more resources than our society is willing to provide. We will need to reeducate teachers, to reduce their workload, and to purchase material resources to link the local community with the larger one. Thus far, we have lacked the vision and the will to commit the resources necessary to this effort. Instead, we have sometimes resorted to gimmicks to lure our children back to school. In some Florida schools, pizza is offered as an incentive to attend classes. In one Kentucky district, a snazzy car is raffled off as a door prize for students with good attendance. But should such bribery succeed in filling classrooms with warm bodies, will this no longer be a nation at risk of losing the hearts and wasting the minds of its young people? I think not. (p. 151)

Barone's scholarship not only illustrates the employment of aesthetic categories to frame curriculum questions, it is a rare instance of a politically and institutionally engaged scholar working with aesthetic conceptual tools. It is a highly suggestive contribution to the effort to understand curriculum as aesthetic text.

IV
Twentieth-Century Art and Curriculum Theory:
Ronald E. Padgham

> A teacher who communicates to his students nothing but the syllabus laid down by the authorities, using methods he learned at the teachers' training college, can be compared to the dispenser of pills made up according to prescription, who can never be a true physician.
>
> (Johannes Itten, quoted in Padgham, 1988a, p. 369)

During the twentieth century, art (especially painting) moved from a photographic portrayal of reality to the rendering of imagined realities. For one scholar this movement holds important consequences for curriculum theory. Ronald Padgham (1988a) observed the epistemological shift Rugg had noticed earlier. Rather than a dualistic worldview in which the individual and the world are unconnected, the twentieth-century view of reality stresses relationality. Indeed, art historian Werner Haftmann asserted that objective reality is a construction of human consciousness. A number of contemporary artists have lost interest in discrete units of the objective world; as Haftmann expressed it, the artist is no longer interested in the static conception of reality that is the noun, e.g., tree, flower, stream. Now the artist explores "the dynamic verbs behind them [the nouns]: to grow, to flower, to flow" (Haftmann, quoted in Padgham, 1988a, pp. 360-361). Similarly, the curricularist *qua* aesthetician is preoccupied with the senses in which the curriculum is a verb, not a noun (Mann, 1975).

Padgham concludes that the contemporary artist no longer relies on his senses to apprehend and copy reality "out there." Rather, reality is created in a fundamental sense within the artist himself. Now reality is a synthesis of the known, the felt, the remembered. Reality is an integration of past, present, and future. Padgham (1988a) sketches correspondences between this worldview and that expressed in strands of contemporary curriculum theory. For instance, he notes that Maxine Greene explains that knowledge and meaning are not static concepts to be acquired in any simple manner; rather, they are dynamic concepts constantly altering according to the student's vantage point. Padgham compares this view to that embedded in Cubism, an early twentieth-century art movement in which the reality of the object painted could be portrayed only by painting multiple perspectives of it. The reality of an object can be apprehended only via multiperspectival representations.

Time. Padgham suggests that the temporal aspects of Cubism, i.e. the fusion of past, present, and future, corresponds to Dwayne Huebner's (1967) study of time and curriculum. Relying on a Heideggerean theory of time, Huebner wrote that "the very notion of time arises out of man's existence, which is an emergent. . . . Human life is . . . a present made up of a past and future brought into the moment" (quoted in Padgham, 1988a, p. 362). [See chapter 8 for a review of Huebner's conception of curriculum as concern for temporality.] The curricularist must honor this view of time by designing curricula which "encourage the moment of vision, when the past and future are the horizons of the individual's present so that his own potential for being is grasped." Such a curriculum would be explicitly multiperspectival and stimulate students' awareness of their capacity for transcendence, both of themselves and of the world (Huebner, 1967, quoted in Padgham, 1988a, pp. 362-363).

Like the Cubists, Futurists painted objects from multiple points of view, both spatial and temporal. Futurists proclaimed that through art one could transcend history and culture; they were, in this sense, "modernists" *par excellence*. Their art would produce a heightened state of reality for those viewers who would then be provoked to recall and re-experience what they remembered, felt, heard, saw, imagined, and thought when contemplating an object. Experience is thus heightened in multi-sensory ways. Padgham notes that, in like fashion, Maxine Greene argued that the curriculum must stimulate activities of "perceiving, judging, believing, remembering, imagining" (Greene, quoted in Padgham, 1988a, p. 364), in order for the student to develop her or his cognitive and perceptive capacities.

Significance of self. In the curricular emphasis upon the concept of "self" Padgham observes a correspondence between twentieth-century art and contemporary curriculum theory. Herbert Read sees in the conscious cultivation of the self the basis for cultural renewal. Educator-architect Walter Gropius emphasized the significance of self as the beginning point in the education of an artist. Describing the curriculum of the German Bauhaus, Gropius wrote that the chief function of the preliminary course "is to liberate the individual by breaking down conventional patterns of thought in order to make way for personal experiences and discoveries which will enable [the student] to see his own potentialities and limitations" (Gropius, quoted in Padgham, 1988a, p. 369). Johannes Itten, responsible for the preliminary course Gropius describes, focused on two major possibilities inhering the curriculum. One is the possibility of self-exploration and self-discovery for both student and teacher; the second is the support for intuition and spontaneity as the core of teaching method and learning style. Itten insisted:

> The most precious moments in a student-teacher relationship, when the teacher succeeds in lighting an intellectual spark in a student as he gets through to his innermost being, can never be repeated. . . . Knowledge of human nature—intuitive knowledge of human nature—appears to me to be a gift essential to the true educator, who needs to recognize and be able to develop the natural talents and temperaments of those in his charge. A teacher who communicates to his students nothing but the syllabus laid down by the authorities, using methods he learned at the teachers' training college, can be compared to the dispenser of pills made up according to prescription, who can never be a true physician. (Itten, quoted in Padgham, 1988a, p. 369)

Autobiographical method. Padgham compares the autobiographical work of William Pinar to that of Gropius and Itten at the Bauhaus. Pinar's early scholarship (1972-1977) focused on the self-alienating and self-fragmenting impact of conventionally "objectivist" and mechanistic curricula, curricula which permitted few opportunities for dialogue, self-exploration, and spontaneity. As we have seen, Pinar developed an autobiographical method—the regressive, progressive, analytic, synthetic method—by means of which the mature student works to locate his or her current intellectual interests in his or her life history, research by means of which the student might hope to discover himself or herself more fully and thereby enliven one's intellectual life. The method promised to portray the complexity of the relations among the "knower and the known," among student, teacher, and curriculum, a curriculum reconceptualized from a "course of study" to *currere*, the "running of the course." Utilizing the method of *currere* the student re-experiences his or her past, imagines his or her future, analytically locates both accounts in his or her present, amplifying it multi-perspectivally and temporally. In this way, Padgham asserts, Pinar's curriculum method and theory resemble those of Cubism and Futurism.

The Basic Course developed by Itten for the Bauhaus offered several means by which students might explore and become more fully conscious of their experience. One such means was the use of physical exercises before painting classes, events which Itten believed might help students to experience the present more completely, including one's bodily presence in the present moment. Another such means was the use of meditation just before beginning to draw or paint, reminiscent of Rugg's interest in the educational potential of such activity. Padgham compares these aspects of the Bauhaus curriculum to those aspects of dance and theater used by Madeleine Grumet in her elaboration of Pinar's method of *currere* [see the forthcoming section in this chapter]. Padgham (1988a) concludes by suggesting that "form" and "content" have been fused in contemporary painting. In "traditional" curriculum theory, he asserts, form and content were kept as separate as were self and world in the modernist paradigm. In autobiographical versions of contemporary curriculum theory content and form are conjoined.

V
Art and Society: Landon E. Beyer

It is in seeing the ability of aesthetic experience to transform lived experience, the given of social interaction and meaning, and the facts of political consciousness that a revolutionized educational and social life may become possible.

(Landon Beyer, 1985, p. 397)

Art and the effort to understand curriculum as aesthetic text have social and political dimensions. These dimensions imply a critique of so-called "attitude theories" of aesthetic experience. In these theories art is viewed as an autonomous domain, thoroughly distinct from interests, involvement, and commitments. This general view is expressed succinctly by art critic Clive Bell, when he wrote that:

> to appreciate a work of art we need bring with us nothing from life, no knowledge of its ideas and affairs, no familiarity with its emotions. Art transports us from the world of man's activity to a world of aesthetic exaltation. For a moment we are shut off from human interests; our anticipation and memories are arrested; we are lifted above the stream of life. (Bell, quoted in Beyer, 1988b, p. 382)

What is the response of critical theory? Philip Wexler and Tony Whitson (1982) wrote:

> High culture collects the silences, incompletenesses, and contradictions of social relations and the frustrations they produce, and then marks them off as a separate and distinct compartment of reality. What is repressed and unrealized in everyday life gets transferred to a special domain, where frustration and contradiction are resolved—symbolically. (p. 35)

Art as political text. Landon Beyer (1988b) also criticizes Bell's view, arguing that a) abstracting aesthetic experience from personal, social, and political events with which it might be associated impoverishes aesthetic experience; b) attitude theories result in "contentless" experience, focussed only on presentational features of the art object or work; and c) the evaluation of art objects is limited when only formal, surface features (e.g., shading, brush stroke, symmetry) constitute legitimate content for analysis. Beyer finds a compelling alternative to aesthetic theory as articulated by Bell in the aesthetic theory of Karl Marx. Marx's interest in aesthetics was stimulated by his reaction against censorship, an issue which for Marx raised the more general and complex matter of the status of literature (and art) in bourgeois society. In capitalist economies literature became reduced to commodity status, reducing the writer to tradesperson and writing a means of economic survival. To remain faithful to its aesthetic nature, Marx insisted, literature must be written "organically," not as a means of capital accumulation. Marx viewed the Prussian government's attempt to reintroduce and enforce state censorship in 1842 as class warfare. He viewed the government as representing the ruling class, the press the mass of people. Because it tended to result in dullness of style, Marx taunted the government's effort to censor, writing:

> Every dewdrop in the sun glitters in an infinite play of colors, but the light of mind is to produce only one; only the official color, no matter in how many individuals and in which objects it may be refracted. The essential form of mind is brightness and light, and you want to make shadow its only appropriate manifestation. It is to be dressed only in black, and yet there are no black flowers. The essence of mind is always truth itself, and what do you make its essence? Restraint. Only a good-for-nothing holds back, says Goethe, and you want to make the mind a good for nothing? (Marx, quoted in Beyer, 1988b, p. 385)

In a free society, according to Marx, literature identifies and expresses the fundamental historical and social trends of the time, and does so in ways which make vivid actual material conditions. Beyer outlines the implications of this Marxian aesthetic for curriculum.

Curriculum changes. Criticizing both *The Paideia Proposal* and *A Nation at Risk* as reproducing a classical, socially decontextualized view of aesthetic appreciation, Beyer (1988b) posits aesthetic experience as a material production and as a lived experience, requiring several curriculum changes within educational institutions. First, Beyer argues that the distinction between the "fine arts" and the "popular arts" (or crafts) is a spurious one. The separation of the former into museums and galleries reinforces art as apart from the daily life. Relatedly, the production of crafts tends to be viewed as unartistic, certainly not as "high art." Second, the isolation of the arts in schools, their characterization as elective and frill, must end. Third, Beyer (1988b) calls for attention to the communicative significance of the arts: "While works of art can be regarded from a number of vantage points, it is their capacity to communicate a particular point of view, set of values, or perspective on the world that is most telling if we are to realize their social and ethical connotations" (p. 395). Fourth, the social content of aesthetic objects must be elucidated. Students need to learn to decode issues of race, class, and gender embedded in particular art objects; they need to learn to express more ethical visions of these matters via aesthetic production. Fifth, Beyer reaffirms Rugg's interest in the fundamental, multi-disciplinary nature of aesthetic experience and knowing. He calls for investigations of the aesthetic dimensions of language arts, the humanities, social studies, and the natural sciences. Finally, Beyer (1988b) calls for more attention to the aesthetic dimensions of teaching and evaluation, acknowledging the contributions made by Elliot Eisner and Maxine Greene. He views the aim of these proposals as:

> the reintegration of aesthetics into social life, the rejuvenation of the aesthetic image so that its social, ethical, and political import may become manifest. . . . In the end, this process will necessitate and help evolve a revised education and social order within which the arts—as perhaps the highest forms of human achievement—can flourish. (pp. 396-397)

This would not seem to be the view of the Getty Foundation, which has sponsored [but did not originate; Eisner, 1990b, p. 425] a major revision of art curriculum in the schools. In that revision, four categories of art are identified: art production, art history, art criticism, and aesthetics, so-called disciplined-based art education. Kerry Freedman and Thomas Popkewitz (1988) argue that the result of the Getty work is a technical conception of social practice. Such a conception distorts art, because: "art education and curriculum are only understandable by interrelating school history with a concern for social, economic, cultural and intellectual history" (p. 403). However, making art technical is not only a problem with the Getty-sponsored work

(Arnstine, 1990; for other responses see Broudy, 1990; Eisner, 1990b; Swanger, 1990). For instance, Robert Bullough, Jr., Stanley L. Goldstein, and Ladd Holt (1984) examined the AIE program (Art is Elementary), which they found ignored the distinctiveness of art, while trying to make it fit in a technical curriculum mold. Such curriculum molds seem to overwhelm the distinctiveness of a specific discipline or field. We suspect Beyer would agree.

VI
The Art of Curriculum and Teaching:
Eisner, Vallance, and Figgins

> Criticism is the art of disclosing the qualities of events or objects that connoisseurship perceives. Criticism is the public side of connoisseurship. One can be a connoisseur without the skills of criticism, but one cannot be a critic without the skills of connoisseurship.
>
> (Elliot W. Eisner, 1985a, p. 223)

Perhaps the best-known formulation of the significance of the arts and aesthetic knowing for curriculum and teaching is that of Elliot W. Eisner (1967, 1969, 1971a, 1971b, 1972a, 1972b, 1975, 1976, 1977, 1979, 1984, 1985a, 1985b, 1988, 1990a, 1990b, 1991a, 1991b, 1992a, 1992b, 1993). In particular, Eisner's use of aesthetic notions for teaching and evaluation have attracted international attention (Knitter, 1986). [Eisner's work has been translated into Japanese, Spanish, and Norwegian; it has appeared in several European, South American, and African countries.] Here we review and discuss his views concerning the artistry of teaching (for Eisner the distinction between curriculum and teaching is blurred) and the imagery and epistemology of his influential view of curriculum evaluation. A fuller description and discussion of the procedures of Eisnerian curriculum evaluation appear in chapter 13.

Eisner (1985b) identifies four senses in which teaching can be considered an art. First, there is the sense in which a teacher is sufficiently accomplished in his or her craft, that for the student as well as the teacher, the classroom is an aesthetic experience. Second, teachers—as do painters, dancers and so on—make judgments during the teaching process based on qualities discerned during the course of the process. Pace, tone, and tempo are among the qualitative features of teaching that are selected and re-selected by the teacher as she "reads" or decodes students' responses. Third, artistry in teaching requires routines or repertoires upon which the individual teacher calls. Eisner affirms a tension and a balance between automaticity and inventiveness. Fourth, teaching like art achieves ends sometimes unanticipated at the start, but which are desirable, even welcomed. Eisner distinguishes between craft and art, the former a process through which skills are employed to achieve predetermined outcomes, the latter a process in which skills are utilized to discover ends through action. Teacher-artists avoid a freezing of their "pedagogical intelligence" into mechanical and routinized behaviors by allowing for the unanticipated and the creative (Eisner, 1985b).

Connoisseurship. Connoisseur and connoisseurship are terms associated with the arts [where they have been contested; see Greene, 1973, p. 291]. Dewey's biographer Robert Westbrook (1991) has noted: "The appreciation of art required cultivated taste. . . . Critics had the privilege of fostering the communication between the arts and audience, but more often than not, Dewey complained, they arrested it" (p. 395). Madeleine R. Grumet (1989a) has admitted that she has worried that "Eisner's standard of connoisseurship is vulnerable to an elitist interpretation and application" (p. 225). These dangers acknowledged, Eisner's use of the terms seems indisputably progressive in the context of behavioral and bureaucratic notions of curriculum, teaching, and evaluation.

Eisner borrows the terms of connoisseur and connoisseurship to devise the concept of educational criticism. The concept of connoisseurship derives from the Latin *cognoscere*, to know. Eisner (1991a) notes that in the visual arts to know requires the capacity to see, not merely to look. Criticism refers to the process of enabling others to see those qualities of art that the connoisseur is able to see. Thus, criticism is the public disclosure of these situations; according to Eisner it exhibits three aspects: the descriptive, the interpretive, and the evaluative (Eisner, 1985a, 1985b).

Connoisseurship suggests qualitative knowing or an example of epistemic seeing, i.e. the order of knowledge secured through sight. Eisner (1991a) explains: "My emphasis on seeing should be regarded as a shorthand way of referring to all of the senses and the qualities to which they are sensitive" (p. 68). He distinguishes further between primary epistemic seeing, which depends upon an awareness of the particular, and secondary epistemic seeing, which refers to seeing the particular as a member of a larger set or category. The connoisseur is said to appreciate excellence, which is to say: "to experience the qualities that constitute each [say wine, a book, or a school] and to understand something about them. It also includes making judgments about their value" (1991a, p. 69).

Eisner (1991a) employs the notion of ecology to suggest the interconnectedness of various aspects of schooling which the educational connoisseur might consider. He lists five aspects or dimensions: 1) the intentional, referring to goals or aims, 2) the structural or organizational features of the school, 3) the curricular dimension, 4) the pedagogical, and 5) the evaluative dimension. The educational connoisseur studies these five dimensions of schooling via direct observations of teachers and classroom life, via interviews, as well as from examination of instructional materials, student work, teacher-made tests, bulletins from school administrators, homework assignments and so on. Eisner (1991a) points out that:

> My main aim, however, is not to construct a laundry list of potential data sources for educational connoisseurship, but rather to underscore the point that whatever is relevant for seeing more accurately and understanding more deeply is fair game. (p. 82)

Educational criticism. Connoisseurship is a private act of appreciation. When the connoisseur becomes a critic, he or she makes this private act public:

> The task of the critic is to perform a mysterious feat well: to transform the qualities of a painting, play, novel, poem, classroom or school, or act of teaching and learning into a public form that illuminate, interprets, and appraises the qualities that have been experienced. (Eisner, 1991a, p. 86)

In this sense criticism is an act of reconstruction of that experience; it becomes an "argued narrative" (p. 86). As such, there will always be alternative interpretations; there is no one-to-one correspondence between educational criticism and the event or experience it seeks to illumine. Eisner (1991a) elaborates four dimensions of educational criticism: description, interpretation, evaluation, and thematics. While the first three are self-evident, the last term may need additional comment. Thematics refers to the task of educational criticism in the identification of a broader theme or idea in a particular situation: "The theme, embedded in the particular situation, extends beyond the situation itself" (1991a, p. 103). We report additional scholarship regarding Eisner's concept of criticism [see, for instance, Uhrmacher, 1989], especially as it pertains to curriculum evaluation, in chapter 13.

Theoretical issues. One scholar supportive of the Eisner approach notes that empathy—one aspect of coming to appreciate an educational situation—might conceal as well as reveal (Pinar, 1988c). Empathy can be understood as prerequisite for understanding the intentions of others. It invites one to participate in those intentions, intentions which can function as self-rationalizing, self-forgiving, indeed self-deceiving ideas. Empathizing with another, if it means losing one's distance from the other, one's sense of a critical edge, might lead to collusion. Pinar suggests that the educational critic might be careful not to lose his or her critical distance in the effort to empathetically understand.

Pinar focused upon the imagery Eisner employs to describe the work of the educational critic. Eisner describes this work as "rendering the essentially ineffable qualities constituting works of art into a language that will help others to perceive the work more deeply. In this sense, the critic's task is to function as a midwife to perception" (Eisner, 1979, p. 19). Pinar notes that the image of midwife implies a presence (the unborn child in the image, understanding in the analogy) discernible yet not visible, not yet brought to form, to birth. This imagistic understanding of present yet not visible is indicated as well in the preceding sentence (in the quoted passage above) by the use of the word "ineffable." Pinar suggests that ineffable represents hyperbole, as it means indescribable, incapable of being expressed in words. If Eisner intended ineffable in a literal sense, the work of the critic would be impossible. Perhaps, Pinar speculated, Eisner is thinking of a second, less common meaning of the word. This second definition is: ineffable—not to be uttered, as in taboo. Such a definition is highly provocative, as it suggests a political dimension to educational criticism.

"Whole, bright, deep with understanding." Pinar suspects that Eisner's definition of connoisseur as one who attends to the "happenings of educational life in a focused, sensitive, and conscious way" is incomplete. Pinar asks: how does one achieve such a focus, sensitivity, and consciousness? He suggests: autobiographical practice may be helpful:

> But in another sense autobiographical work, because it focuses upon the self and its history, slows down movement, makes it stay, so it becomes more visible, its detail discernible. It is like a blow-up in a photographic sense. A character in Virginia Woolf's *The Years* seeks to see the same: "There must be another life, here and now, she repeated. This is too short, too broken. We know nothing, even about ourselves. We're only just beginning, she thought, to understand, here and there. She held her hand hallowed; she felt that she wanted to enclose the present and future, until it shone, whole, bright, deep with understanding. (Pinar, 1988c, p. 151; Woolf, quoted in Pinar, 1988c, p. 151)

Applications. Anticipating the 1991 essay we summarized earlier, Elizabeth Vallance (1977) identified seven applications of aesthetic criticism to the study of curriculum. [Vallance refers to painting as a paradigmatic instance of art.] First, curriculum and art both represent processes of human construction; they are, in Vallance's word, "artifactual." Second, both curriculum and art can be viewed as a mode of communication between the curriculum-maker or artist and an intended audience. Third, both represent transformation of the knowledge and vision of the curriculum-maker and the artist into forms perceived to be accessible to the intended audience. Fourth, both curriculum and art are products of problem-solving processes, and in this sense share aspects of "deliberation" articulated by Walker (1971) and Reid (1978) after Schwab. Fifth, the meaning of both resides in the encounter between audience and artifact. Sixth, the forms of both curriculum and art construct boundaries or frames around the experience of the audience. Seventh, both curriculum and art reside in specific historical and stylistic traditions. Eighth, both curriculum and art elicit judgment and criticism (Vallance 1977).

A phenomenological response. Vallance's essay provoked a thoughtful response from Canadian scholar Walter Werner, a Ph.D. graduate of the University of Alberta. Werner (1980) examined editorial criticism in curricular analysis related to Eisner's notion of educational criticism. Working phenomenologically, Werner noted that:

> *krisis*, the Greek root from which the word criticism is derived, means "judgment." This judgment is in the sense of "radical"—"that which is connected with the root" (Latin *radix*). In other words, radical criticism is a judging of the roots or foundations of something. (p. 143)

Werner quoted Vallance (1977): "The language of art criticism is a vehicle for communicating these experiences. It is a bridge between the critic's perceptions of the work and the reader. In the end, then, it is the experiential quality of the materials, and not the language per se, that matter. It is the experiential quality of the materials that will color the student's encounter with them." Against this view he wrote:

> Editorial criticism differs somewhat from Vallance's approach in emphasis and form and may usefully broaden the basis for making curricular judgments. She emphasizes the experiences that a set of materials may provide students, and her use of evocative portrayal tries to clarify the reader's own impressions of these experiences. In contrast, the editorial critic teases out embedded assumptions and values within the material to portray the author's editorial perspective. (p. 145)

Then Werner turned to what he termed Hugh Munby's (1979) "impressive (and broader) example of criticism" [which] addresses the question: "Of what should a curriculum consist?" (1979, p. 246). Munby (1979) had written:

> In this light, I believe the role of the critic, as Vallance conceives it, ought to be broadened so that we assume responsibility for doing more than disclosing salient features and providing analysis. When the materials warrant it, critics should applaud or condemn and contemporaneously illustrate the basis of their judgments. They should attend to the practitioner's judgments too, and rebuff or support them as appropriate. (p. 249)

After quoting Manby, Werner (1980) moved to establish the functions of editorial criticism:

> First and foremost, criticism aims to uncover the underlying perspectives embodied in curricular phenomena, their "deep structure" that often remain hidden in the everyday world of schools. Second, criticism aims to uncover the underlying relationships between the document and its social context. Third, criticism seeks to determine the possible implications that these underlying perspectives and relations have for the classroom. (pp. 148-149)

Finally, Werner (1980) explained: "Editorial criticism is a deliberate attempt to redact an interpretive statement about curricula. Its success will be measured, at least partly, by the degree of our own self-consciousness in making arguments such as this one and in developing and carrying out our curricular criticisms" (p. 154).

Curiously, Vallance (1980a) replied by pointing out that Werner is a theoretician, sidestepping the important questions Werner had raised:

> Curricularists, I have observed, seem to be trained in either of two camps. The first (and more common) is the practically minded camp. . . . The practical curricularists work with how-to-do-it skills. . . . The second camp has a decidedly theoretical bent—its students worry about the conceptual bases of curriculum, the societal and philosophical foundations of education, the research questions implied by current curricular practice, the merits of various evaluation models, and the relationship of theory to practice. The theorists are harder to locate, but they seem to turn up in research-oriented graduate schools and sometimes in federally funded think tanks. As a theorist currently housed at a land-grant

institution, I find the contrasts between the two perspectives to be unremittingly visible. (p. 155)

Here Vallance was implying that Werner's concerns are of interest to the theoretician only. As we have seen, in the contemporary field practice *is* theoretical.

Advocacy for the arts takes many forms. Recently the *Harvard Educational Review* printed the proceedings of a symposium entitled "Art as Education" [*Harvard Educational* Review, Vol. 61, No. 1, 1991, pp. 25-87]. Maxine Greene (1991a) introduced the special issue, which focused on classroom teaching and featured classroom teachers, as evident from the titles. Karen Gallas (1991) described the "Arts as Epistemology: Enabling Children to Know What They Know"; Judith Wolinsky Steinbergh (1991) wrote: "To Arrive in Another World: Poetry, Language Development, and Culture;" Victor Cockburn (1991) suggested "The Uses of Folk Music and Songwriting in the Classroom;" and V. A. Howard (1991) admitted that "And Practice Drives Me Mad; or the Drudgery of Drill." Other scholarship has attempted to infuse art and creativity across the curriculum (Poole, 1980) and elaborate a notion of congruence between "the educator's interior character and personal beliefs to her public, social character and professional commitments" (Shuchat-Shaw, 1980, p. 178).

Freinet. Krystyna Nowak-Fabrykowksi (1992) describes the work of Celestin Freinet (1896-1966), a French educator and creator of teaching methods and techniques based on the creative work of students. In addition to his theoretical work Freinet founded, in 1928 in Cannes, the Cooperative of Secular Education which brought together teachers willing to introduce his techniques in their education practice. In 1935 he opened an experimental school which still operates in Venice. A "Freinet teacher" should recognize the individual values and potential of children and base his or her teaching upon these. Further, the Freinet teacher feels the need for emotional links with the students; she or he creates opportunities for children to show their strongest points. Sounding not unlike the child-centered American progressives of the 1920s, Freinet teachers base the curriculum on the child's activities and design situations where children can experiment. Above all, the Freinet teacher does not follow routines. Fifty years after its first appearance in 1920, Freinet's theory is still practiced in thirty-eight countries. In Canada, the "Mouvement Freinet" was introduced in 1966 in Quebec. However, the movement died after ten years due to organizational problems. Still, a few Quebecois teachers make use of Freinet's methods. Nowak-Fabrykowksi (1992) tells us that Freinet's principal idea is that schools should reinforce the positive traits of a child's personality by giving the child possibilities for creative work.

Talkhard. Perhaps the most creative recent work on teaching as artistry has been done by Margo A. Figgins and Michael Ebeling at the University of Virginia who view acts of creation as central to their enactment of critical pedagogy (Figgins & Ebeling, 1991). In their "Toward a Discourse of Hardtalk: The Electronic Conference as a Means of Creating and Reflecting on Class as a Text," they describe a sustained dialogue among students in a course in language pedagogy taught by Figgins. The dialogue occurred within the context of a private, on-line electronic conference created for this course. The name and notion of the conference, *Talkhard*, were derived from a recent popular film entitled "Pump Up the Volume." As the instructor, Figgins was interested in the film's story of a pirate radio program whose anonymous disk-jockey uses the anonymity of radio air waves to enable himself and his phone-in listeners to "talk hard" about the deceptions and inequities they experience at the high school which they attend. Intrigued by this concept, Figgins conceived the electronic conference as an analogous vehicle for empowering her own students to speak out. The process involves students adopting a persona early in the semester which they assume each time they log in and speak to other members of the class who are also speaking through personae. By speaking through fictional identities, it is assumed that students can talk and respond to others with imagination and honesty and, as a result, with greater sense of possibility. As they do this, they are at the same time creating a text together which they can later interrogate for its meaning and its aesthetic qualities.

This ongoing research constitutes a remarkable synthesis of research and pedagogy wherein student voices help chart the course of and provide existential texts for the class. The students' texts suggest both possibilities and limitations of the electronic conference as a means of privileging student voice and students' meaning-making processes. The dialogue ranged from one student's self-revelation ("I can pretend to [take a position], argue the point, but in my cold, little heart of hearts, I really don't give a shit about positions in the *right* and *wrong* scheme of things. I'm a nihilist"); to another student's regulatory castigation ("I think when we get used to it we can gain some great insight by everyone getting a chance to talk without intimidation. . . . [And] I hope we can respect each other's anonymity and not attack each other personally; I think that would defeat our purpose"); to yet another student's suggestion for improving class discussion ("I'd like to suggest to Margo and Michael that we get to see some of the videotape of ourselves in the process of 'breaking down' during discussion. Just five minutes or so. What our goal should be is . . . to start talking about language and stop talking about talking!") Figgins & Ebeling, 1991, p. 12).

The richness of story, contention, and speculation that develops through *Talkhard* demonstrates the aesthetic pleasure in which Figgins' brand of pedagogy and research is rooted, an element she considers essential to students' willingness to engage in sustained, unswerving looks at the meaning of their own experience. As Figgins notes: "It's pretty hard to invest in your own pain" (quoted in Ebeling, 1992, p. 165). When students adopt personae and "talkhard," the pain of self-revelation is balanced by the pleasure, even delight, in rendering their insights in artful ways, e.g., creating dramatic scripts or writing poems. This delight and pleasure guarantees engagement and invention—a process Figgins describes as both playful and problematic. What begins in pleasure leads to tension and struggle, but ultimately discovery.

Perhaps almost as remarkable as the pedagogy/research itself was the conference presentation of the work, which was performed in strikingly artful ways. This accomplishment is implied in their written text:

> We see the Bergamo Conference as the next step in the evolution of *Talkhard* as a technique of and device for critical pedagogy. We have in mind a presentation which represents the harassing, seductive, iconoclastic, and disquieting nature of the *Talkhard* space—a messy, painful, and hopeful place where irreverence is allowed to do its work and their experience of pedagogy is reflected on by students who need not negotiate the power relations of the traditional classroom in order to speak. This presentation is our attempt to revisit the possibilities of this kind of forum. We invite you to eavesdrop, imagine yourselves into the conversation, and speculate about what this space could mean and be for you and your students. (Figgins & Ebeling, 1991, p.1)

Talkhard and her theatrical/pedagogical performances follow from theoretical research Figgins conducted earlier on the centrality of the poem as an aesthetic form in the teaching of English. In that research Figgins (1987) asserted the importance of the poem in cultivating individual subjectivity and imagination, which, she argued, are increasingly subverted by mass communication technology. Figgins drew on the work of teaching poets for whom the poem is an essential way of knowing about the self and the world.

The pedagogical model which resulted rested on two premises: that the poem embodies the attributes of both interior monologue (unuttered speech) and logical argumentation (formal rhetorical modes); and by its synthesis of the particular and the universal, the poem includes more of the self and the world than do other modes of discourse. The model articulates four levels of study: 1) exploration and enjoyment of poetry, 2) study of the poem's language and the poet's craft (sound, rhythm/meter, story, image/descriptive language, metaphor/figurative language, syntax, and line) i.e. those components which contribute to the poem's non-discursive character, enrich one's reading and writing of poems, and empower one's linguistic imagination in other discourse modes as well, 3) encounters with other literary genres and traditions, wherein the poem functions as a bridge between the student's word/world and the frequently unfamiliar, and therefore less accessible, words and worlds represented in other literature, and 4) writing in a variety of modes across the entire discourse spectrum. Finally, the model, with the poem as its organizing center, is appraised with the aims of the language and personal growth model recommended at the 1966 Dartmouth Conference (Figgins, 1987).

Clearly, this research shifts the curriculum emphasis toward unconscious thought processes and the feelings that are interwoven in students' cognitive assertions. The logic of the disciplines gives way to a heightened appreciation of the uncertainties which release and shape new meaning, with the consequence of empowering students to become creators of language and literature. Two strands—experience and theory—interweave throughout this work, which includes studying actual student poems through work in the Virginia Artists-in-Education program, and observing teacher orientations to reading and writing poetry. Her research, in which she extrapolated that process inherent in the language and personal growth model and employed it to critique existing paradigms, led to her discovery of the missing link between the student's interior and exterior worlds: the poem. [The centrality of poetry in curriculum theory is shared by Edward Milner (1980, 1981, 1982a) whose poetry illumined a range of topics, from professional conferences to curricular issues concerning the gifted and handicapped.] Figgins's research is an exciting and sophisticated illustration of the effort to understand curriculum as aesthetic text.

VII
Curriculum as Theater: Grumet, Figgins, Norris, and Steinberg

Drama should have a central role in the curriculum field.
(Robert Donmoyer, 1991a, p. 91)

Like the poem, theater has been viewed by several scholars as a central metaphor for curriculum (Simon & Dippo, 1980; Willis & Schubert, 1991; Starratt, 1990; Craig, 1984; Potter-Tomfohr, 1993; Doyle, 1993). Robert Donmoyer (1991a) argued: "images are the raw material for thought. . . . Theatre and cinema provide very rich raw material for thinking about educational phenomena and issues" (p. 99). Perhaps more extensively than any other theorist, Madeleine R. Grumet has interwoven curriculum and theater, drawing on the work of Polish theater director and theoretician Jerzy Grotowski to illustrate an important sense in which curriculum is theater. Grotowski directed the Theater Laboratory in Poland, a research institute he founded in 1959. Grotowski judged twentieth-century theater as a mausoleum of dead conventions and empty forms. In his book *Toward a Poor Theater*, Grotowski (1968) described the education of the actor as a *via negativa*, an eradication of psychological blocks. Grotowski employed physical, non-verbal exercises in training actors to overcome their resistance to and blockage of experience. Once the "life mask" or persona is stripped away, the actor can act with full consciousness to reclaim it, knowing now what ends it serves and what it conceals (Pinar & Grumet, 1976).

Autobiographical study of the hidden curriculum. Grumet likened this work to the scrutiny Michael Apple called for in his study of the "hidden curriculum" [see chapter 4]. Apple suggested that students should study their own experience in schools in order that they might be molded to the shapes of the masks they wear there. Apple wrote:

> It might we wise to consider engaging students in the articulation and development of paradigms of activity within their everyday lives at school. Such

involvement could enable students to come to grips with and amplify crucial insights into their own conditionedness and freedom. (Apple, quoted in Grumet, 1976c, p. 70)

The method of *currere* intends, Grumet pointed out, to provide opportunities for such involvement. Autobiographical reflection can expose the genesis of assumptions and commonsensical attitudes of students and teachers. The process of "bracketing," the analytic moment in the method, does not remove the student from the school, but rather moves him or her closer to his or her life. Bracketing allows one to see through the structures of "objectivity" to that preobjective and prereflective domain on which they rest. The point of such work is twofold: to provide portraits of educational experience as lived, and in so doing to recover the intentionality of the auto-biographer (Grumet, 1976c).

Conscious embodiment of action. This interest in recovering intentionality is not limited to the autobiographical reflection that is the method of *currere*. Grumet employed theater, particularly improvisational dance and acting exercises and scene production, to bring students back to a conscious sense of their own bodies, feelings, thoughts, and words. An actor's training, in Grotowski's sense, brings one out of one's preoccupations and habitual responses so that one might be more fully present, more fully conscious behind and in his or her words. So present, the actor or student is said to be directed by his or her own intentionality and aware of the specific and concrete situation within which he or she acts. Grumet drew the parallel between theater and autobiography, noting that "as autobiography is postre-flection, reflective self-representations reflected on; theater is prereflective, preceding the reflective self-representation in actions requiring an immedi-ate, non-verbal response" (Grumet 1976c, p. 80).

Teaching as acting. Grotowski's training demands that actors challenge those limitations associated with self-as-object. Consequently, Grotowski's theater is a theater of cruelty for the actor who blocks her or his inclinations, suppresses one's preferences, or dissolves one's identity into one's work. The production of the play is the form around which the discipline is forged, and it is the material production which prevents Grotowski's training from dete-riorating into a kind of masochistic self-indulgence. In parallel fashion, Grumet employed scene production in order that the challenge to self-as-object may find justification in the creation of a physical form. Later, Grumet asked her students to examine their participation in academic disciplines, especially their efforts to teach them, as like forms.

Another type of acting exercise Grumet (1976c) employed is the transfor-mational exercise, in which one person receives a gesture or sound from another, then mirrors it or responds to it in some way. Then the gesture is extended, transforming it into a gesture of one's own, which is then brought to another. This exercise requires receptivity and concentration to the inten-tion and gesturing of another, acknowledging the other's specificity both in mirroring the gesture received and transforming it into a gesture of one's own. As Grumet uses the exercise, students are participating in phenomeno-logical acts that parallel the psychosocial dynamics of the teacher and student as they attempt to speak to each other in the classroom. As students mirror each other's gestures, they imitate each other's actions, immerse themselves in each other's perspectives and intentions. As a gesture is extended and transferred to another, its essential character is amplified and intensified. In transforming a gesture, the student identifies his or her own intentionality, and becomes conscious of his or her own inclinations. If the transformation occurs at the moment it is passed to another, the transformation reflects the specific relationship of initiator and recipient. Because the gestures are word-less, the phenomenology of the relationship is laid bare. In so doing students begin to see, as Grumet phrased it, "the dialectics of both theater and educa-tion: one and many, activity and passivity, leading and following, freedom and contingency, abstraction and particularization, self and others, giving and taking, assimilation and accommodation" (Grumet 1976c, p. 82).

Intensity, spontaneity, authenticity, and discipline. Grumet argued that the consideration and rehearsal of teaching methods and techniques are hope-lessly hypothetical because they lack temporal and spatial facticity. Theater exercises, such as the transformational ones, refer to themselves, rather than to an imagined place and time. They are presentational rather than represen-tational symbols. They do not stand for someplace, someone else, separated and estranged from the present. Instead, their referents are to the immediate experience—as lived—of the student-participants. Grumet (1976c) noted: "In this immediacy self-as-place is present and palpable and prior to self-as-object or agent" (p. 83). Like Grotowski's actor, Grumet's teacher works to identify and dissolve that which blocks "his [sic] resistance, his reticence, his inclina-tion to hide behind masks, his halfheartedness, the obstacles his body and his intellect place in the way of his creative act, his habits and even his good manners" (Grotowski, quoted in Grumet, 1976c, p. 83). If this work is successful, spontaneity is achieved. Even so, expression is disciplined within the structure of teaching and the social conventions of the school. Grumet's teacher is not trained to perform a "set of tricks," but rather to maintain an "idle readiness, a passive availability," that keeps her attuned to her students, to subject matter, ready to respond to both. The training of a teacher for the "poor curriculum," the curriculum of intensity, spontaneity, authenticity, and discipline, must be training to study oneself. In this regard, curriculum as theatrical text is a variation of *currere*.

Figure/Ground in *Currere*:
The 1976 University of Rochester Theater Festival

Another aspect of curriculum as aesthetic text is explored in Grumet's study of *currere* and the 1976 University of Rochester Theater Festival. Theoreti-cally, Grumet's interest was the study of the figure/ground relationship embedded in curriculum. Grumet (1978) wrote: "I intend to examine curriculum as a moving form, to catch it at the moment that it slides from being the figure, the object and goal of action, and collapses into the ground for action" (p. 277). Grumet (1978, p. 276) introduced this study by quoting the protagonist of Jean-Paul Sartre's (1964) novel *Nausea:*

> Some of these days,
> You'll miss me honey.

Listening to these lines on a scratched disc, Roquentin waits in an ugly café for the vocalist to sing and the saxophonist to play, the beer in his glass warming. The melody is modest; its interest for Roquentin is not its musicality as much as its relationship to the situation it surpasses:

> I think about a clean-shaven American with thick black eye-brows, suffocating with the heat, on the twenty-first floor of a New York skyscraper. The sky burns above New York, the blue of the sky is inflamed, enormous yellow flames comes and lick the roofs; the Brooklyn children are going to put on bathing drawers and play under the water of a fire-hose. The dark room on the twenty-first floor cooks under a high pressure. The American with the black eye-brows sighs, gasps and the sweat rolls down his cheeks. He is sitting, in shirtsleeves, in front of his piano, he has a taste of smoke in his mouth and vaguely, a ghost of a tune in his head. "Some of these days." (Sartre, quoted in Grumet, 1978, pp. 276-277)

Figure becomes ground. The song and the figure silhouetted against the intense heat of a New York summer day now falls back into the ground that is the fictional city of Bouville, transfigured into the ground for the action of Roquentin. "Some of These Days," once a figure, transfigures Roquentin's situation, and not in an ideational sense only. It is not limited to Roquentin's decision to forsake history for fiction; it is sensory and palpable: "I feel something brush against me lightly, and I dare not move because I am afraid it will go away . . . . I am like a man completely frozen after a trek through the snow who suddenly comes into a warm room" (Sartre, quoted in Grumet, 1978, p. 277). Roquentin's response expresses Sartre's existential aesthetic: "For us man is characterized above all by his going beyond a situation and by what he succeeds in making of what he has been made—even if he never recognizes himself in objectification" (Sartre, quoted in Grumet, 1978, p. 277).

A spectatorial curriculum? Grumet observed that Dwayne Huebner, in his 1976 address to Division B of the American Educational Research Association "calls upon curricularists to clear the stream and to attend to the course of study" (quoted in Grumet, 1978, p. 278). "Course of study" refers to both the syllabus and the environment. The student engagement with these, however, is that of "an enthralled spectator." Huebner concluded: "If curriculum has any meaning left today, it is in the identification and the making present of content to persons" (Huebner, quoted in Grumet 1978, p. 278). Grumet replied: "I am afraid that in his eagerness to reclaim the stream, Huebner has pulled out the swimmers along with the algae and sent them to sit upon the banks. There they sit and wait for the curriculum to reach them" (Grumet, 1978, p. 278). In contrast, as aesthetic text curriculum is a medium through which persons are made present, in the Grotowskian sense: "Curriculum is the process of persons coming to form, not content." Only in "idealized isolation" is curriculum content primary. The "gaze" of the student transfigures the surface of the syllabus into a reflection of images of the student's situation. It is the student and his or her experience, not the syllabus, which is made present. Grumet argued that: "The student's response to the curriculum reveals his possibilities for action within the particular domain of experience—natural, social, aesthetic—that the curriculum as content symbolizes" (1978, pp. 278-279).

Succumbing to what is; imagining what is not (yet). In considering the curriculum as both figure and ground, a third form, the relation between the two, emerges. This form is to be filled with human action. Sartre had written: "The most rudimentary behavior must be determined both in relation to the real and present factors which condition it and in relation to a certain object still to come which it is trying to bring into being" (Sartre, quoted in Grumet, 1978, p. 279). This third form—Grumet termed it a double vision—suggests a structure of curriculum which is simultaneously aesthetic and technological. She noted that both interests are concerned with making things. The distinction between the two involves the relationship of the product (the figure) to the situation from which it derives (the ground). Grumet insisted that the products of technology, including that extension of technology into curriculum—the Tyler Rationale and all its offspring—are designed to conform to the requirements of the existing situation:

> The ameliorative approach of current [curriculum] theory, which fabricates curriculum to meet the needs of the situation, is, in its eagerness to address reality, succumbing to the technological intention to produce the pieces that will fit most comfortably into the whole. (Grumet, 1978, p. 280)

In contrast, while aesthetic interest requires the production of artifacts which address the original or existing situation, its products function to create anew—or reconceptualize—that situation. The aesthetic interest not only satisfies the demands of an existing ground but posits a new ground and a new figure distinguishable from the old gestalt by their unity, what Dewey (1934b) termed their "pervasive quality." Curriculum as aesthetic text functions as an agent of disclosure, in which new possibilities, hitherto unperceived in the ground of their daily experience, are revealed to students. It is this transformational possibility that distinguishes curriculum as aesthetic text from curriculum as technological text.

Dewey, Piaget, Sartre. Grumet (1978) traced the recent history of the aesthetic interest. She noted that John Dewey conceived of inquiry ecologically, as a complex interaction of the biological organism and the environment. More specifically, inquiry for Dewey was a response to an indeterminate situation, a state of disequilibrium. To bring the situation to equilibrium, a resolution is required. Dewey wrote:

> Inquiry, in settling the disturbed relation of organism-environment (which defined doubt) does not merely remove doubt by recurrence to a prior adaptive integration. It institutes new environing conditions that occasion new problems. What the organism learns during the process produces new powers that make new demands upon the environment. In short, as special problems are resolved, new ones tend to emerge. There is no such thing as a final settlement, because every settlement introduces the conditions of some degree of new unsettling. (Dewey, quoted in Grumet, 1978, p. 281)

Like Piaget, Dewey attributed disequilibrium to the arbitrariness of nature. Not until the development of his aesthetic theory did Dewey treat disequilibrium as an issue belonging to the cultural order rather than the natural order. On this matter Dewey, like Sartre, acknowledged that the cultural order—Grumet reminds us that the cultural order is the order of curriculum—cannot be reduced or collapsed into the natural order. An aesthetic product, unlike a natural or technological one, is not shaped solely to the specification of an external natural imperative; instead it contains both a new figure and a new ground. In the "state of nature," the human being is, in Dewey's words, "pulled and pushed about, overwhelmed, broken to pieces, lifted on the crest of the wave of things, like anything else" (Dewey, quoted in Grumet, 1978, p. 282). The state of nature is precisely what disgusts Roquentin in *Nausea*. Bouville is the ground, the root of the chestnut tree is "knotty, inert, nameless" (Sartre, quoted in Grumet, 1978, p. 283).

Grumet theorized that while meaning cannot be found in the natural order, it cannot be found in any self-evident fashion in the sphere of the possible. She pointed out that Roquentin, in fleeing the natural order and the "bad faith" of the bourgeoisie, fails to create meaning by writing the biography of a seventeenth-century nobleman. He cannot ignore his experience by substituting stories about another's. To "find" or create meaning, existence must be integrated with the possible. Dewey:

> First, then, art is solvent union of the generic, recurrent, ordered, established phase of nature with its phase that is incomplete, going on, and hence still uncertain, contingent, novel, particular . . . a union of necessity and freedom, a harmony of the many and one, the sensuous and the ideal. (quoted in Grumet, 1978, p. 284)

The technological and the aesthetic, the actual and the possible. Grumet outlined the three elements of curriculum as "existential aesthetic" text:

> 1) Curriculum is an aesthetic as well as technological product, belonging both to the cultural and natural order. As a product of aesthetic activity it creates and encompasses both figure and ground. 2) Curriculum, by providing a new gestalt, stands out against the ground of daily experience, both revealing and transforming it. 3) Curriculum once presented, tends to sink into the ground of daily experience, to mingle with it and become confused with the natural

order. This aesthetic critique requires that we acknowledge that curriculum is the world of meanings that we have devised and that as teachers and students we assume responsibility for it and for the action that it admits. (Grumet, 1978, p. 286)

Grumet noted that this view is contrary to an "idealized" view that conceives of aesthetic forms apart from mundane experience. [In this respect her view intersects with Beyer's.] She pointed out that Sartre required that the culture discloses possibilities for meaning and action within daily existence. For instance, Roquentin imagines his readers referring from the novel back to the existence from which it originated: "Antoine Roquentin wrote it, a red-headed man who hung around cafés." This is the same process of reference that typified his experience of the song "Some of These Days." Rosario [see also Rosario, 1988, this chapter] acknowledged this figure/ground relationship in his discussion of Heidegger's aesthetic: "The created object sets forth the world from which it comes, against which it rests. The truth disclosed in a world of art is a tension, a conflict between an unconcealed entity and a concealed background within an 'open' field" (Rosario, quoted in Grumet, 1978, p. 287). When curriculum is examined discrepancy is sought, "a lid that won't quite fit the pot and lets a little steam escape to tell us what's cooking inside. Discrepancy," Grumet suggested, "is a result of the movement of experience from the familiar to the strange, and our subsequent awareness of the relation between the two" (Grumet, 1978, p. 287). [This notion is similar to the one Maxine Greene (1973) elaborates in *Teacher As Stranger*.]

Grumet (1978) takes *currere* as requiring the claiming of an actual situation. Roquentin so claims, as he remains in Bouville. He focuses on his own situation, including the stains on the mirror in the café, the smell of tobacco, the nausea engendered by the facticity of things. Grumet noted that:

estrangement rests upon the familiar. We cannot be estranged from something that we have never known. In order to reap the disclosure that lies dormant within our curricular forms, we must claim them in our familiar, daily experience and then estrange ourselves from them. (Grumet, 1978, p. 288)

Currere asserts that the situation has depth as well as breath. The figure/ground analogy requires a third perspective, one born in time and (lived) space. The method of *currere* investigates the relation of figure and ground, subject and object, student to curriculum. Unlike the narcissism and reification Grumet associated with values clarification, self-concept and cognitive or learning style research, *currere*, by naming the relation between the knower and known, the student to her or his studies, loosens the frame of that structure rather than intensifying it. For this reason Grumet decides to employ *currere* with students in the 1976 University of Rochester Theater Festival.

Curriculum as encompassing both figure and ground. Grumet worked with the Director of Theater at the University of Rochester, Stefan Rudnicki. Like Grotowski, Rudnicki was not content to produce plays that merely entertained the audience. Like Grotowski, he wanted his plays to challenge the "communal myths" of the audience. He approved Grumet's interest in using autobiography to challenge the students' personal myths as well. Grumet explained:

> Throughout the festival, the curriculum, whether or not it was Shakespeare's Richard III, a mime workshop, or a seminar, was conceived first as a critical mirror reflecting the student's experience of both the natural and cultural order, and then as the ground for his action within either or both of those domains. (Grumet, 1978, p. 290)

This relation of teaching and learning to the curriculum parallels Grotowski's notion of the relation of theater to its dramatic literature:

> The strength of great works really consists in their catalytic effect; they open doors for us, set in motion the machinery of our self-awareness. For both the producer and actor the author's text is a sort of scalpel enabling us to open ourselves, to transcend ourselves, to find what is hidden within us. . . . For me, a creator of theater, the important thing is not the words but what we do with these words, what gives life to the inanimate words of the text, what transforms them into "the Word." (Grotowski, quoted in Grumet, 1978, pp. 290-291)

The autobiographical methods of *currere* provided a means for students to claim and examine their own experience of his and others' words, requiring them to acknowledge and cultivate their own responses to those words.

The relation between form and experience. Rudnicki and Grumet conceived of the play as a form. The pedagogical task was to discover the relation, both communal and individual, between that form and the experience of the Festival participants. That relation would constitute a "third" form, one encompassing both the figure—the curriculum—and the ground—the participants' experience. A weekly seminar provided for discussion of the group's associations with the plays. As well, the instructors introduced other associations. For instance, Eric Bentley's transcripts from the McCarthy hearings were played as a context for *Richard III*. These were not presented to force a consensus, but rather to underline the group's associations. Grumet (1978): "I thought of this identification of contexts as a gathering of experience along a horizontal axis, a drawing out of intersubjective association lodged within the shared social and cultural experience of the group" (p. 293).

In counterpoint to this group effort to make the text familiar was the method of *currere*, designed to situate the plays and the seminar within the life history and present lived experience of the Festival participants. Grumet (1978): "I thought of the autobiographical process as strung out along a vertical axis of educational experience, and it was this process that I nurtured most closely" (p. 293). *Currere* is introduced, Grumet tells us, in order to protect students from the curriculum. Like other students, these students might lose themselves to the forms of the plays and their characters. Further, as an educator one wants students to come to their own forms, not one determined by others, fictive or actual.

Critical reflection for transfiguration. The point of the autobiographical writing, Grumet suggested, was not to disclose startling episodes. One assumes that the autobiographical depiction of academic experience will be mundane and only occasionally extraordinary. The point is found in the interpretation of mundane events, a significance that emerges as the events are described and analyzed. The point was not to excite a voyeuristic reader, but to reveal and perhaps alter the present assumptions and intentions of the reader. The ambition of *currere* is to provide students with the process and tools of critical reflection they must know in order to meaningfully transfigure their situations, whatever those situations might be. Students then might create another objectivity from the objectivity transfigured. It is the same ambition Brecht holds for the theater: "He [the spectator] will be received in the theater as the great 'transformer' who can intervene in the natural processes and the social processes, and who no longer accepts the world but masters it" (Brecht, quoted in Grumet, 1978, p. 298)

Knowledge of the body. Grumet (1978) made use of mime to provide a "physical, prereflective analog to the written, reflective work of *currere*" (p. 305). Gestures and other movements of the mime were not mere replications. Rather, they became expressions of continuity, both of situation and action. Grumet suggested: "The givens of the physical world, the hardness of a floor . . . and the givens of our bodies, their capacities for torsion, stretch, balance, were fused by our intentions into meaningful actions" (p. 305). Even a simple movement "required total awareness of the contributions of the natural and cultural orders to behavior" (p. 305). Movements empty of intention and feeling were lifeless and boring; gestures filled with intention but oblivious to its surroundings and the mechanics of its performance were imprecise, sometimes confusing. Grumet noted the link with *currere*:

> If *currere* was to reveal our conceptual inclinations, intellectual and emotional habits, mime would reveal the knowledge that we have in our hands, in our feet, in our backs, in our eyes. It is knowledge gathered from our preconceptual dialogue with the world, knowledge that precedes our utterances and our stories. (Grumet, 1978, p. 305)

The mime work seemed important to students, Grumet reports. Its physical difficulty and the discipline, practice, and concentration required challenged the theater workshop participants. Excerpts from student journals illustrate their experience:

> While doing the warmups and exercises today I realized what discipline it must take to work at this constantly, as Bob [Berky, the mime teacher] does. I have regimented other physical exercises, but this stretching and straining is really taxing.
> I want to find a way to act that allows my body to be used correctly but still allows me to fly.
> Tonight in mime I was told that I did a particular exercise well. Further attempts were not good at all. Suddenly the idea popped into my head—I was trying to reproduce instead of recreate.

This loosening up really came to me last Friday night, when Bob had us doing that walk, and falling forward and catching ourselves. I really got into it for a while, and suddenly I felt like I was performing a mime movement. I don't know how it looked, but it sure felt great. And then I was having a blast, just breaking into laughter a few times from sheer enjoyment. I guess a lot of it was just surrendering to an idea finally and following it.

Stop! Where are you? Hold on to a point. Move around it, feel, see it, hold it. Be there!

Be a tiger . . . so, sit down. Eyes closed. Think. Back to old movies, the zoo. Pan in. See him breathe. Feel his hot breath on my face. Feel the texture of his fur and the way it changes on different parts of his body. Pan in closer. Swing around. I am seeing what he is seeing. My feet slide neatly, snugly into his. My legs follow. My torso and arms follow suit. Only our heads are separate. A tiger with two heads . . . and one human. Finally, our eyes merge. We take in a breath through our extended black nostrils. But isn't this my daily routine?

This aspect of being a mime and/or an actor is rather frightening in a way. It's hard to contemplate spending years in pain, always asking the body to do a little bit more than last time, and going on even when the pain is great. It's a matter of self-discipline, of course. Right now I seem to still need someone standing over me, telling me to go on when I want to stop.

I'm not getting up in the morning. The morning, the early sun, the dawn is my strength. The Festival is Delilah; mime the scissors; I'm Samson. (quoted in Grumet, 1978, pp. 306-307)

In her responses Grumet cautioned students not to lose themselves to the mime work or to the mime teacher, Bob Berky. To one journal entry Grumet replied: "It may be useful, if you have the occasion, to think further about what it is that your relation with Berky has done for you? How can *you* do what *he* does for you for *yourself?*" (p. 308). Grumet characterized her response as introducing a space of estrangement in the student's immersion in the curriculum, in this instance the mime work.

She distinguished "estrangement" from phenomenological "distancing" or "bracketing." These latter concepts denote the phenomenological practice of suspending the "natural attitude," the habitual, common-sense experience of others and events to apprehend reality definitively. Grumet recalled Heidegger's quarrel with Husserl, the former's contention being that Husserl's phenomenological reflection tended toward idealism, too removed from "lived experience." Grumet noted that phenomenological distancing functions to *know* the actual by way of the possible: "The essential form (*eidos*) of a phenomenon, whether it was an emotion of fear or the tree outside the window, would be reached when imagination had stripped it of all its contingent characteristics, leaving it only with what was essential to its identity" (1978, p. 308).

A teacher's vulnerability. In contrast, Grumet (1978) continued, "estrange-ment" investigates the possible rather than the actual, functioning to lift the subject from one's immersion from the latter so that one might realize the former in one's present activity. The process of *currere* utilizes estrangement in this sense of suspending the familiar by focusing upon it. In the Theater

Festival *currere* created a tension between the familiar and the strange, and some students, for a time, resisted it. Grumet identified the space between the two as the ground of development and growth, but she noted that resistance can be the first moment of "occupying" that ground. She acknowledged her vulnerability to students' resistance: "although I often wish I could just place 'Some of These Days' on the phonograph, attribute its limitations to scratches on the record, the dullness of the needle, lecture on the history of jazz, and leave it at that" (p. 313). Elaborating, Grumet wrote:

> The response of the student to *currere* was my Bouville. It was my situation and in order to transform it, I, too, had to claim it and then estrange myself from it in order to create a new curriculum. This case study of *currere* is part of that process. It is invested with Roquentin's own aspirations, voiced as he waits for the train that will take him from Bouville to Paris, where he hopes to write his book: "A book. Naturally it would be only troublesome, tiring work, it wouldn't stop me from existing or feeling that I exist. But a time would come when the book would be written, when it would be behind me, and I think that a little of its clarity might fall over my past." (Grumet, 1978, p. 314; Sartre, quoted in Grumet, 1978, p. 314)

Grumet's study of *currere* and theater represents one of the most provocative studies in this sector of the field. While theoretically sophisticated, Grumet's work also illustrates the central elements of so-called action research, i.e. research that engages students and teachers actively while including self-reflexive strategies which are then reported to the scholarly community. Grumet's (1978) work represents an exemplary case of contemporary research to understand curriculum as aesthetic text.

Reclamations

In a rather different but also strikingly original use of theater, Margo Figgins, whose *Talkhard* pedagogy we examined earlier in the chapter, collaborates with her students in scripting and performing educational theater derived from an autobiographical project. The project joins the autobiographical text of an artist with the student's own biographic situation, creating a dialectic through which points of tension and connection are exposed and then explored dramatically. An example of this work was *Reclamations*, an original theater performance presented to the Bergamo Conference on Curriculum Theory and Classroom Practice, on October 21, 1989, in Dayton, Ohio. The script existed originally in the form of journal entries developed from a response process described by William Pinar in "The Abstract and the Concrete in Curriculum Theorizing" (Pinar, 1981b, 1994), a process which Figgins adapted for engaging students in actively reclaiming the lived sense of the self for their practice as classroom teachers.

In the program for this beautiful and moving performance, Figgins and her students describe the reclamatory process in this way:

> expressive writing, particularly journaling and poetry writing, has the effect of liberating a very particular kind of energy—the energy of the self. How might

that energy be harnessed to sustain the tenuous balance one must keep between learning and teaching? We have combined autobiography, the discourse of the self, with the journal to create a vehicle for dialectical relationship. The "I" of the autobiographical text . . . and the "I" of the student teacher have entered into a dialogue as a way for the student teacher to engage in that very essential work of the self from which such balance derives. . . . Our problem has been how to develop an honesty about ourselves and a consciousness which will help us to relate to students who are not enfranchised by our culture in the way that we have been, and help to support us together as we seek an education which liberates the self to discover its own voice and make its own meaning. . . . Following our performance, we invite your comments, in the hope that we can extend the process of the reclamation of the self to include all of those around us. Our belief is that this is where all learning begins—in the creative acts of the self. (Figgins, 1989, p. 3)

A year later Figgins presented another original theater performance at the Bergamo Conference, entitled "Inside the Cage, Making Love with the Beast: A Dramatic Performance of Research into Perceptions and Experience of First World Critical Pedagogy" (Ebeling & Figgins, 1990). This drama portrayed the multiple realities of students and teacher as they spoke about their different experiences in a language pedagogy course they shared together. These experiences ranged from one student's mistrust of her classmates ("I don't think [people in class] were critically evaluating the texts and philosophies. . . . They were operating in a vacuum"); to another student's need for a clearly established source of authority and knowledge ("Margo was the teacher and she knew more than I did and I wanted her to [know more]. . . . I needed [her] to sort of direct me and verify what I did, what I said as being correct"); to yet another student's discovery of a powerful voice capable of giving forceful shape to his experience ("Being given the opportunity to write in a way I'd never written before and to draw on feelings that they usually don't draw on in a traditional classroom . . . was amazing. I felt like for the first time that I came into contact with a different part of myself"). In the program for presentation, Figgins and Ebeling described this theatrical event as an:

> attempt to draw critical theory up through the viscera of experience in order to bring to you voices of First World critical pedagogy in all their fear, frustration, and passion. This is an invitation to envision new paradigms for investigating and understanding acts of critical pedagogy—to join us inside the cage. (Ebeling & Figgins, 1990, p. 3)

For Figgins, the metaphor of the beast serves to portray that part of the self in need of reclamation—that which has resisted domestication and is therefore still able to surprise and subvert habitual acts of mind. For Figgins, then, theater is a means to a palpable evocation of the self, in her words, "a self whose voice is disruptive, irreverent, and dissenting, a voice which creates ambivalence and demands response, the voice we need to hear in order to resist the next small death that comes when we give over to what has always been" (Ebeling & Figgins, 1992, p. 2).

Collective Creation

Figgins's theater pieces exhibit many of the features of the "collective creation," a dramatic genre which is said to rest between creative dramatics and performance. The participant actors may or may not have a theatrical background; they work together to explore social and autobiographic assumptions regarding educational issues. These student-actors write their own scripts by studying theoretical texts, their own life histories and the life histories of others. Through the translation of theory and histories into dramatic form the participants create the opportunity to reconceive their present stance as they negotiate with one another the meanings of their scenes. This work is enhanced via improvisational role-playing as the participants free themselves from the traditional restraints of "appropriate behavior" and explore elements of their personalities under the protection of "assumed roles." The potential is that educational theater of this kind can lead participants to look into the mirrors created by the roles they produce and discern those reflections of self which often go unnoticed (Norris, 1990a, 1990b, 1990c, 1990d, 1991a, 1991b, 1992, 1993a, 1993b, 1993c).

Joe Norris has worked with this genre for the past ten years in junior and senior high schools, and at the university level. The process could be characterized as both psychodrama and sociodrama wherein many points of view are brought to the surface and then questioned. Such work allows the participants to voice their lived experience, and perhaps politicize that experience through performance. In *Some Authorities as Co-Authors in a Collective Creation Production*, Norris (1989) described both the process and the product emphasizing the political relationships between the teacher/director and the students, and among the students themselves. Videotaped appendices show the teacher and students at work and the theatrical products they collectively produced.

Extending the dramatic collective, Shirley R. Steinberg develops the community notion of the social theater by inviting the audience to break their silence by entering into the performance, thereby changing the curriculum of the theatrical experience each time the piece is produced. Steinberg's (Steinberg & Berry, 1995) *In Process Collective* is fluid, ambiguous, and tentative, expressing central themes of the contemporary effort to understand curriculum.

VIII
Mind, Body, and the Postmodern:
Jagodzinski, Hamblen, Sawada, and Blumenfeld-Jones

> The development of creativity is "soul-making" because it is bringing to play all
> of the visions of the pantheon of Gods which make us up.
> (Ronald E. Padgham, 1988b, pp. 143-144)

What makes a critique postmodern? Wanda T. May (1989) answers it is when meanings are dispersed and deferred throughout symbol systems. May concludes: "Written texts—such as curriculum guides—dupe us into believing that meanings are fixed and stable" (p. 9). jan jagodzinski's [sic] research—which we also noted in chapter 9—would seem to qualify. jagodzinski locates the bifurcation of mind and body within the arts in the eighteenth century. During the absolutist rule of Louis XIV the "artist" replaced the "artisan," accompanied by the slogan *l'art pour l'art* [art for art's sake]. For jagodzinski, since that time sensuous knowledge has been separated from the body and relegated in the art object to be displayed in a museum gallery. There, he tells us, ripped from the soil of its germination, art is studied, categorized, and examined from a distance. jagodzinski works to restore the fusion between feeling (body), mind (cognition), and soul (spiritualism) which were separated during the growth of modernism and the rise of the bourgeois class (jagodzinski, 1992). So understood, the aesthetic problematic is not limited to debates internal to art but extend to curriculum as a whole.

The body's recollection of being. School curricula continue to be laced by the legacy of the Enlightenment, a male-dominated vision in which bifurcations between mind and body, male and female, thought and feeling result in the "disappearance" of the latters and the distortion of the formers. jagodzinski (1989) argues that the aesthetic dimension, as he elaborates it, might provide a source of knowledge constituting an anthropological a priori to transcend the contemporary patriarchal knowledge. He theorizes that six layers of aesthetic experience, layers having both anthropological and physiological roots, can comprise a post-Enlightenment state of [aesthetic] being. These six layers, jagodzinski claims, are part of the arch-writing on the body, part of the body's recollection of being. They are states of the body which inform experience. jagodzinski acknowledges the danger of essentialism in such a postulation; he insists that his categories are framed by history and lived experience. These layers [which we reported in more detail in chapter 9] or, as he alternately characterizes them, "ontological realms," and their relation to the curriculum, are the following:

1. *Line*: lived experience of directionality—making the Grade
2. *Color*: lived experience of the mood—the Period
3. *Texture*: the lived experience of home room—Familiarity
4. *Size*: the lived experience of scale
5. *Mass*: the lived experience of gravity
6. *Space*: the lived experience of the cosmos [see chapter 9].

These six dimensions of aesthetic feeling manifest through the body and mind. They can be experienced as a posture, or a gesture against the world informed by that world. Each sphere or level presents the teacher with ethical and political choices. For jagodzinski, the aesthetic, the ethical, and the political are intertwined. Curriculum as an aesthetic text represents a political and moral commitment in constant antagonism with reality. Aesthetic experience becomes, in jagodzinski's extraordinary scholarship, a transvaluation and a call to action.

Other postmodern scholarship focuses on the relationship between contemporary art and modernity. Karen A. Hamblen (1983) has suggested that modern fine art is a vehicle for understanding western modernity: "it is the asocial, self-referential character of much modern fine art that makes it very much part of a society which gives legitimation to decontextualized experiences" (p. 10). Like Beyer, Hamblen (1983) regards art as social experience:

> As a synthetic, self-referenced language system, modern fine art is part of the larger information society. . . . The understanding of modern art requires expert knowledge. . . . In modern art, the values of modernity are writ large. . . . Disciplinary specialization, the isolation of experience from context, the credence given to discipline-specific language codes, an emphasis on innovation and individual freedom, etc. are all part of the legitimating structure of modern society. (p. 14)

Perhaps illustrative of Hamblen's view that art is rooted socially is an essay by Daiyo Sawada (1989), entitled "Aesthetics in a Post-Modern Education: The Japanese Concept of Shibusa." Sawada wrote:

> The irregularity of forms, the openness to nature, the roughness of textures, and the naturalness of daily life are all aspects of *shibusa*, the adjectival form of which is shibui. . . . Shibusa may be described as having seven qualities: simplicity, implicitness, modesty, silence, naturalness, roughness and normalcy. (p. 2)

Sawada explained: "In shibui education, subjects would not be separated out for individual glorification; knowledge would constitute the everyday epistemology of the everyday experiences of the everyday student who does not leave life behind when entering school" (p. 9).

In the scholarship of jagodzinski, Hamblen, and Sawada we see a movement away from the Cartesian emphasis upon thought and a concomitant alienation from sensuous experience. The movement appears toward the body. We can see that the body is privileged in the theater work of Grumet and Figgins. And it becomes an explicit focus in the scholarship of Donald Blumenfeld-Jones.

Dance. The work of Donald Blumenfeld-Jones emerged at the University of North Carolina at Greensboro where he received the M.F.A. degree in dance and the doctoral degree in curriculum theory. [The University of North Carolina at Greensboro, you will recall, is well-known in the curriculum field: James B. Macdonald taught there during his path-breaking work in the 1970s [see chapter 4], David Purpel and Svi Shapiro conducted their important research on morality and values [see chapter 12] and Kathleen Casey works in feminist theory and autobiography at the same institution.] Integrating dance and curriculum theory, Blumenfeld-Jones has reported the voices of young women dance students, collaborating with Susan Stinson and J. van Dyke (1990). As a result of that and more recent work, he has proposed a creative dance curriculum with three purposes:

1) to understand and critique how such curricula conceptualize the relation between creativity and control, 2) to critique the educational value of control in general, and 3) to develop a method for exploring how curricular language both reveals and hides educational values. (p. 1)

Dance curricula, and we might add, curriculum as dance, suggests a way out of the apparent obsession with control and prediction of outcomes in school practice. He reviews Margery Turner's (1957) *Modern Dance for High School and College* which espoused such humanistic educational values as democracy, individuality, and creativity. Turner (1957) noted: "Too often the emphasis is placed on physical control [in dance] by means of coordination and strengthening exercises. These exercises carry little expressive values in themselves" (p. 167). Blumenfeld-Jones employs Turner's book in autobiographically working through his own experience with dance education. He writes:

My own experience in dance confirms this lack of trust. As a dance student I was taught to find constant dissatisfaction with both my ability to perform movement and with my body. I was taught to suspect my physical inclinations which were said to be fraught with misapprehension and wrong understandings. . . . I was taught . . . to distance myself from my body, to make it into a fixable object, to see it not as "my body" but as "a body" in need of correction. . . . The majority of dancers become desiccated by the call for control because, I suppose, their at-homeness in their bodies is not strong enough to resist the teaching of their teachers. In one sense the valuing of skillful control becomes a trap which prevents the development of creativity. (in press, a, pp. 16-19)

Blumenfeld-Jones argues that control and creativity are dialectical opposites. Unlike Turner (1957), he sees no educational role for control in the cultivation of creativity. Creativity requires freedom, and freedom implies community or cooperation. Creativity, he concludes, flourishes in communion, not via control. For Blumenfeld-Jones, understanding curriculum as aesthetic text requires our commitment to creativity, communion, and cooperation in educational practice.

IX
Conclusion: Imagination and Wonder

My comments thus far have been intended to free the aesthetic form from the province of the arts alone and to recognize its presence in all human formative activity.

(Elliot W. Eisner, 1985c, p. 28)

To understand the role of the imagination in the development of the intellect, to cultivate the capacity to know aesthetically, to comprehend the teacher and his or her work as inherently aesthetic: these are among aspirations of that scholarship which seeks to understand curriculum as aesthetic text. It is an effort not aimed at reducing uncertainty and achieving universal truth. Rather, as Dewey reminded us, "art departs from what has been understood and ends in wonder" (quoted in Westbrook, 1991, p. 395).

Like art, such curriculum theory permits students and teachers a distance from their everyday functional existence. Such distance invites an aesthetic transformation that demystifies the taken-for-granted, the naturalized understanding of knowledge and the world (Marcuse, 1978). Maxine Greene rightly observed that encounters with the arts do not in themselves guarantee such "wide-awakeness" (Greene, 1978, 1988a, 1988b). Encounters with the arts can, however, open spaces which require reflection and reformulation. The arts, and curriculum experienced aesthetically, provoke questioning that supports sense-making and the understanding of what it is to exist in the world (Greene, 1978). This undertaking, in Greene's words, must allow a turning back to the stream of consciousness, to the contents of one's experience, and a critical grasping and transformation of the moment. The task is to see colors for the first time, each time. The task is to experience "color" as a verb, not a noun. The task is for the teacher to be a verb, not a noun, and to express such an intensity of perception and feeling to her or his students. To understand the curriculum as aesthetic text questions the everyday, the conventional, and asks us to view knowledge, teaching, and learning from multiple perspectives, to climb out from submerged perceptions, and see as if for the first time.

Chapter 12

Understanding Curriculum as Theological Text

Education is a subject which cannot be discussed in a void: our questions raise other questions, social, economic, financial, political. And the bearings are on more ultimate problems even than these: to know what we want in education we must know what we want in general; we derive our theory of education from our philosophy of life. The problem turns out to be a religious problem.
(T. S. Eliot, 1952, p. 132)

To ignore theological language today, however, is to ignore one of the more exciting and vital language communities.
(Dwayne E. Huebner, 1975d, p. 259)

I
Introduction: Historical Background

The history of American education is linked intimately with religious movements and controversies. From the colonial period to the present time, various churches have influenced debates about American education. Despite the constitutional separation between church and state, a concept that has been understood differently by different Supreme Courts, there has been a keen curricular interest in the matters associated with religion. Those educational issues which are intertwined with the concept of morality have especially engaged parents, students, and educators. Of course, teachers, students, and administrators (Joseph, 1988) do not shed their personal beliefs and values upon entering school buildings. Yet, traditional curriculum theory has tended to ignore these subjects [see Richards & Short (1981) for a brief review]. Kathleen Casey observed:

> The ethical, moral, and religious (in the broadest sense) dimensions of educa-
> tion have never been, and indeed cannot be, excluded from our schools. Yet,
> rather than acknowledge the sharply conflicting interpretations of morality
> which characterize our heterogeneous society, much of American education
> theory, policy, and practice is silent on the subject. (Casey, 1991, p. 23)

We break this silence by reviewing efforts to understand curriculum as theological text. This subject is broader and more complicated than church/ school relations, and includes discussions of morality, ethics, values, hermeneutics, cosmology, and religious beliefs. We employ the notion of theology as an umbrella term for summarizing and simplifying the complexities of this subject.

From the earliest establishment of schools in the "new world," religious groups and churches exercised pivotal roles. Of course, some immigrants came to North America to escape religious persecution in Europe. Once here, several factors encouraged local religious involvement in schools. Guthrie and Reed (1986) report five reasons for such involvement. First, the states held legal authority over education. Second, resistance to centralized authority meant that responsibility for education tended to shift to locales, enabling relatively small groups to exert influence over local institutions. Third, during the eighteenth and much of the nineteenth century, transportation and communication were slow and tedious, sharpening regional differences. Fourth, schools were financed by private fees and community taxes (in that order until the public system was established in the nineteenth century when taxes became the major and often only source of school funding). Finally, since mobility was limited and economic organization was local (rather than national and multinational as in the present time), most students remained in their home communities to work, supporting intergenerational continuity. Because many colonists had fled religious persecution in Europe and were deeply religious, local churches comprised an integral, often central element of early American community life.

Colonial education. The educational perspective of the early colonists was based on the assumption that the family was responsible for education. Since the dominant colonial culture was English, the social policy established by the House of Tudor—which emphasized the role of the family in the education of children—became the norm. The Royal Injunctions of Henry VIII (1536) required fathers, mothers, masters, and governors, to "bestow on their children and servants, even from their childhood, either to learning or to some other honest exercise, occupation, or husbandry" (quoted in Guthrie & Reed, 1986, p. 21). This family orientation to education was harmonious with the religious sentiments during the colonial period. The first American educational ordinances were enacted by the Massachusetts colonial legislature, then called the General Court, in 1642. These statutes reaffirmed the primacy of the family's responsibility for providing instruction for literacy and vocational training for children. If a family failed to so provide, the public was held responsible to place the child in a suitable apprenticeship. Subsequently, similar compulsory education laws were enacted by all the New England and Middle Atlantic Colonies (Cremin, 1970).

"Old Deluder Satan Law." In 1647, the Massachusetts General Court enacted the first legislation referring to schools. This legislation required all towns of fifty or more families to provide a teacher of reading; those of one hundred families were required to provide a Latin grammar school. This legislation became known as the "Old Deluder Satan Law," as its explicit purpose was to ensure that everyone in the Commonwealth was able to read and understand the principles of religion and capital law, thereby combating

moral evil and social unrest. While examples such as the "Old Deluder Satan Law" make clear the religious character of early American education, later legislation shifted control of the schools from churches to local governmental bureaucracies and to lay boards. Lay people joined church personnel in supervising educational practice. The shift from church to state control of education was slow yet visible. For example, in 1789, the Massachusetts General Court codified in law many educational practices that had evolved in that state. With respect to control and supervision of the schools, this legislation stated:

> And it shall be the duty of the minister or ministers of the Gospel and the selectman (or other such persons as shall be specifically chosen by each town or district for that purpose) of the town or districts to use their influence and best endeavors, that the youth of their respective town and districts, do regularly attend the schools appointed . . . and once in every six months at least . . . to visit and inspect the several schools in their respective town and districts. (Cremin, 1951, p. 130)

While this 1789 legislation illustrates the prominence of church leaders in early American education, it indicates as well that control of the school was to be shared with lay officials. In fact, teacher certification rested with "selectmen" rather than solely with church officials. Madeleine Grumet (1988b) argued that the "Old Deluder Satan Law" compensated for a marked decline in religious fervor and commitment. American schools have often, she noted, contradicted prevailing social tendencies. For instance, Grumet cited the ideology of American schooling as democratic, egalitarian, and an avenue of upward social and economic mobility, as contradictory of the efforts of upper middle and upper classes to retain their class privilege via a conservative school system. Racial integration via busing contradicted racial antagonism and separatism in society; William Bennett's (1987) *James Madison High School* and other "great books" curricula contradict our culture of transience, video, and ever-changing technology.

Religious pluralism and struggle over the curriculum. Despite the religious foundations of education in New England, lay and governmental influence over the schools grew. Outside New England, the diversity of religious faiths prevented the same order of uniform influence the Puritans enjoyed in Massachusetts. The combination of growing secular control and religious diversity prevented the establishment of a national curriculum or national common school. Still, colonial education was typified by strong religious influences, contradicted by culture and government. The struggle over the school curriculum has continued to the present time. Herbert Kliebard (1986) observed:

> The outcome of the struggle for the American curriculum was an undeclared, almost unconscious, detente. At one and the same time, the curriculum in the twentieth century has come to represent a reasonably faithful reflection of the intellectual resources of our culture and its anti-intellectual tendencies as well;

it serves to liberate the human spirit and also to confine it; it is attuned to the well-being of children and youth and also contributes to their disaffection and alienation from the mainstream of social life; and it represents a vehicle for social and political reform as well as a force for perpetuating existing class structure and for the reproduction of social inequality. (pp. 269-270)

This struggle is rooted in the colonial period during which time various religious groups vied with each other and with the growing secular government over the character of school curriculum.

Despite the struggle among religious groups for control of the colonial school, a kind of religious hegemony had evolved by the beginning of the nineteenth century. The Christian, and more specifically Protestant majority (with its various denominational expressions), exercised dominance. This dominance of an Anglo-Protestant culture was accompanied by intolerance of minority religions, including Roman Catholic, Jewish, and Native American religions. One consequence of this intolerance was the creation of sectarian schools, by far the largest of which was the Catholic parochial system.

The nativist reaction. The arrival of Irish Catholic, Jewish, and other immigrants in large numbers during the late eighteenth and early nineteenth century sparked a strong reaction in the "native" majority culture, i.e. those immigrants who had preceded these groups. Resistance to, including fear of, Roman Catholics was particularly vocal. In 1837, petitions from 97 electors in Washington County, New York, were sent to Congress demanding that laws be passed to restrict the citizenship of the new arrivals. The petition read:

Your Memorialists view with deep concern the great influx of Roman Catholics into this country from the various nations in Europe, and their admission to citizenship while they retain their principles, as eminently threatening our civil and religious liberties. Popery . . . prepares and breaks the mind for political servitude—it is a system of superstition which is the firmest foundation of civil tyranny—a religion whose very spirit as well as practice is persecuting, sanguinary, and encroaching. Against Roman Catholics, as men, we have no hostility. Against their religion we ask no legislation, offensive or defensive; we leave it to be combated by the appropriate weapons of education and religious institutions; but against political principles interwoven with their religion, we do ask legislative defense. (Haynes, 1990, p. 79)

Despite this hostility, the Roman Catholic population grew from about 30,000 to more than 300,000 by 1820. The fear was that these "foreign-born" would bring with them antidemocratic and "absolutist" ideas from Europe, including an unquestioning allegiance to the Pope. Such an allegiance, it was feared, would override allegiance to the government of the United States (Haynes, 1990). The irony of this fear of "foreign-born" by, in many cases, other foreign-born was lost on the Americans. President John Adams reflected the view of the religious majority when he wrote in 1821 that "a free government and the Roman Catholic religion can never exist together in any nation or country" (in Leonard & Parmet, 1971, p. 24). Irrational anti-Catholic sentiment continued throughout the nineteenth and twentieth centuries and was visible in the 1960 presidential campaign of John F. Kennedy.

Protestant virtue, Catholic vice. Famous inventor Samuel F. B. Morse in his *Foreign Conspiracy Against the Liberties of the United States* (1835) and prominent Protestant clergyman Lyman Beecher in his *A Plea for the West* (1834) reflected the "nativist" fear that Catholics were gaining ground in the American West. Beecher exhorted Americans to "save the West" for Protestantism and resist what he feared would be a union of church and state should Catholics take control (Haynes, 1990). Twentieth-century Catholic historians view the anti-Catholicism of the nineteenth century as a major factor in the creation of Catholic parochial education. One comprehensive history is Harold A. Buetow's *The Catholic School: Its Roots, Identity and Future* (1988). He comments on anti-Catholicism during the nineteenth century:

> During the decades before the Civil War, the popular Puritan hope for the Kingdom of God on earth led to desires for reform. One of the areas of reform was schooling. The most vocal educational crusader at the time was Horace Mann (1796-1859). Dedicated to eliminating sectarian religion from government schools, he was equally convinced that the schools must instill the historical Protestant virtues. William H. McGuffey (1800-1873), through his millions of reading books, helped shape the national mind in forging an ever closer bond between schooling and Protestant virtues. The same could be said of the enormously popular works of instruction written by two New England ministers, Samuel G. Goodrich (1793-1860), known as Peter Parlet, and the prolific Jacob Abbot. Most of these works contained anti-Catholic prejudices. (Buetow, 1988, p. 23)

The reaction of the Catholic hierarchy to the charged political atmosphere of nineteenth-century U.S. society was critical in the formation of the Catholic parochial school system. Catholic bishops viewed American society, and its public schools, as hostile to Catholicism. This view was underlined by the Eliot School controversy (1859). This case involved a Catholic family who protested a public school regulation that required that their son attend Protestant services and read a Protestant version of the Bible. The parents sued the school but lost the case. The Eliot decision stood until the Edgerton-Wisconsin decision (1890) permitted Catholics to absent themselves from Protestant services in public schools.

Horace Mann vs. Orestes Brownson. Perhaps representative of the early struggle to define the role of religion in American education was the debate in the 1840s between Unitarian Horace Mann, superintendent of public schools in Massachusetts and defender of the common school, and Catholic Orestes Brownson, editor of the *Boston Quarterly Review* and opponent of the common school. Mann promoted "nonsectarian" public schools, but his intent was to promote morality based on nondenominational Christianity. Mann (1848) wrote: "In this age of the world, it seems to me that no student of history, or observer of mankind, can be hostile to the precepts and the doctrines of the Christian religion, or opposed to any institutions which expound and exemplify them" (p. 102). In "Morality, Religion, and the Public Schools," Joseph Newman (1980) contends that Mann naively believed that the answer to the problem of religion and the curriculum lay in removing specific religious doctrines from the schools while retaining a common, nonsectarian Christian creed as the basis for morality. Brownson and other Catholics objected because religious education would be left in the hands of the local majority, threatening the religious beliefs of the minority religions. Brownson proposed instead that public funds be used to support parochial schools, a practice widely accepted before the rise of the common schools. Newman (1991) summarizes this debate:

> Brownson's vision of publicly funded sectarian schools clashed with Mann's vision of moral and religious commonality. Sectarian schools were divisive, Mann argued. . . . Mann became alarmed as still other disputes over commonality broke out, making the possibility seem remote indeed. (p. 134)

The debate between Mann and Brownson was never settled, and it contains the seeds of a continuing debate in our time.

Councils of Baltimore. Beginning in 1829, anti-Catholic sentiment was addressed by the Catholic Church's Councils of Baltimore. A Pastoral Letter, issued in 1837, outlined expressions of this sentiment, but counseled Catholics to be patient, remain loyal to civil government, and attend to religious duty. The Letter called for Catholic publications and the expansion of Catholic higher education as well. However, it was not until the First Plenary Council of Baltimore (1852) that the Catholic Bishops urged the establishment of parochial schools. By 1884, when the third and final Plenary Council of Baltimore was held, the Catholic Church in the United States was increasing by approximately 2 million members each year. Again the Council urged the establishment of parochial schools and the creation of a Catholic university. [The University of Notre Dame was established in 1842 as a private Catholic University; Catholic University of America was established some forty years later as a church-owned institution of higher learning.] Additionally, a Catholic Catechism (*The Baltimore Catechism*) was prepared for both parochial school students and for those Catholic children who attended public schools. The Bishops set a goal of placing every Catholic child in a Catholic school. These policy directives represented efforts to protect the religious education of Catholic youth in a hostile society. They led to a proliferation of Catholic schools which, at their peak, enrolled approximately 6 million students in 13,000 schools by 1965 (Convey, 1992, p. 53). By 1984, the numbers had declined but remained impressive: 7,937 elementary schools, 1,464 secondary schools, 225 colleges and universities, 200 seminaries, four million students, and 160,000 teachers (McBride, 1984). In 1990, Catholic elementary and secondary schools enrolled 2.5 million students in 8,719 schools. This represents 50% of the total private school enrollment in the United States (Convey, 1992, p. 53).

UnAmerican? Catholics were often accused of separatism and unAmerican-ism as a consequence of their educational successes. In 1922, for instance, the state of Oregon passed legislation to outlaw nonpublic schools on the grounds they were undemocratic. The American Protective Association, a local organization, and the Ku Klux Klan had lobbied in favor of this legisla-tion, which would have abolished Catholic schools. In 1925, the Sisters of the Holy Names of Jesus and Mary sued the state of Oregon over this legislation. In Pierce v. Society of Sisters [268 U.S. 510; 455 S. Ct. 571 (1925)] the Supreme Court awarded the nuns victory and permitted the continuation of nonpublic schools. Illustrative of other court cases which indicate the continued resistance to Catholic schools are two: in Evenson v. Board of Education [300 U.S. 1; 67 S. Ct. 504 (1947)] the State of New Jersey was authorized to provide bus transportation for parochial students, and in Aguilar v. Felton [473 U.S. 402, 87 L. Ed. 2d 290 (1985)] federal compen-satory education programs were restructured; however, they continued to provide instruction to private school students.

II
Contemporary Concerns

> I am much afraid that schools will prove to be the great gates of hell unless they diligently labor in explaining the Holy Scriptures, engraving them in the hearts of youth.
>
> (Martin Luther, quoted in Reese, 1982, p. 9)

No prayer in school. The latter part of the twentieth century has seen a decline in anti-Catholic sentiment in the U.S. and an enlarged discussion of private and parochial education. While Catholic school enrollment declined in recent decades, overall private school enrollment has increased to eleven percent (11%) of the nation's elementary and secondary students in the 1980s. Joseph W. Newman (1990) reports: "During the 1980s the trend in enrollment was toward private schools, a trend that private schools hope will continue" (p. 278). Growing rapidly have been non-sectarian academies and non-denominational Christian schools, not a few of which represented responses to federally mandated desegregation in the South. Many Protes-tants—who decades before had accused Catholics of separatism—now rushed to establish their own, separate schools. In addition to racism, many of the independent religious academies were established in response to the removal of prayer and other religious activities from the public schools. In 1962, in the case of Engle v. Vitale [370 U.S. 421(1962)], the Supreme Court held that the New York Public Schools' daily classroom recitation of a nondenomina-tional prayer composed by the state government violated the establishment clause of the U.S. Constitution. The following year, in the case of the School District of Abington Township v. Schempp [374 U.S. 203 (1963)], the Supreme Court held unconstitutional, again under the establishment clause, a Pennsylvania statute requiring at least ten Bible verses be read aloud to students without comment at the start of each school day. It also found unconstitutional a Baltimore policy requiring the recitation of the Lord's Prayer at the start of each school day.

The Lemon Test. In both of these latter cases the decisions were based on a three-part test employed by the Court to determine whether laws, policies, and practices related to religion in the public sector were constitutional. Although not formalized until 1971 in Lemon v. Kurtzman [403 U.S. 602 (1971)], the courts ruled that government law or practice was constitutional if it met all three of the following tests: 1) the government act that bears on religion must reflect a secular purpose, 2) it may neither advance nor inhibit religion as it primary effect, and 3) it must avoid excessive government entanglement with religion. This test (known as the Lemon Test, from the case name) is a guide for courts in their review of religious activities in the curriculum. From the time this test was first used in Engle (1962) until it was formalized in Lemon (1971), it has affected not only specific legal decisions but a more general perception of public education in the United States. Ultra right-wing and fundamentalist groups rightly claim their influence on religion in public schools has been undermined by these cases (Provenzo, 1990).

Other fundamentalist concerns. As we have seen, the increase in the number of nonpublic schools and other alternative educational programs (for instance, home schooling) can be associated with legal and governmental developments regarding the practice of religion in the public schools. The issue of prayer in the school has been a powerful force; sex education has proven to be another. Illustrative of the fundamentalist position on this issue is Barbara Morris' *Change Agents in the Schools.* Morris alleged: "The purpose of sex education is to eradicate Christian values and Christian behavior relating to sexual activity and to replace them with Humanist values and behavior" (Morris, 1979, p. 143). Also illustrative is Tim LaHaye's (1983) *The Battle for the Public School* which argued that sex education represents a catastrophic failure from the Christian perspective. This issue has been addressed by several courts, including Citizens for Parents Rights v. San Mateo Board of Education [124 Cal. Reptr. 68 (1968)], a case in which parents protested sex education classes, arguing that their children had been pressured informally to attend these courses, thereby infringing upon their religious freedom. The lower court ruled: "A mere personal difference of opinion as to the curriculum which is taught in our public schools system does not give rise to a constitutional right in the private citizen to control exposure to knowledge" (cited in Provenzo, 1990, p. 70).

Court decisions such as Citizens for Parental Rights highlight the continuing conflict between public school curriculum and the values, especially the religious values, of individuals attending public schools. There have been hundreds of court cases dealing with school prayer, sex education, creation science, and censorship. Perhaps one of the most widely reported series of cases in the 1980s unfolded in Mobile, Alabama. Beginning with the Mobile v. Bolden [466 U.S. 55 (1980)] voting rights case, followed by the Wallace v.

Jaffree [472 U.S. 38 (1985)] school prayer case, and concluding with the Smith v. Board of School Commissioners (1987) secular humanism textbook case, the struggle over the American curriculum—and in particular the role of religion in that curriculum—is evident. In his "Organized Prayer and Secular Humanism in Mobile, Alabama's Public Schools," Joseph Newman (1991) shows how local culture, political leadership, religious tradition, and social mores all contribute to a testing of the constitutional separation between church and state. The fundamentalist position is clear on this issue; there *is* no separation. For instance, Henry Morris wrote: "There is no boundary or dichotomy between spiritual truth and secular truth; *all* things were created by God and are being sustained by Him" (Morris, 1978, p. 10). Also typical is the following, written by Onalee McGraw in her *Family Choice in Education*:

> Value-free schooling is impossible because ultimately all educational endeavors must emanate from a world view that is either transcendent or humanistic. All concepts of the meaning of knowledge and of what is worth knowing must of necessity flow from religious and philosophical beliefs. (cited in Provenzo, 1990, p. 94)

Clearly, the school curriculum is now scrutinized carefully by religious groups concerned over values embedded in it. In particular, textbooks that omit the Judeo-Christian tradition in American history, literary works that contain nonjudgmental portrayals of morality, and courses that encourage critical thinking and self-reflection rather than "trust in God," have all come under attack. Some religious groups contend that these values represent a religious belief system called "secular humanism." The Bible and/or church doctrines are viewed as the only legitimate source of understanding religious truth, and for many fundamentalist sects, political, economic, and social truth as well. Joseph Newman (1991) summarizes this position: "The cumulative effect of public education on students is subtle but powerful, fundamentalists conclude. By persuading students that they are in charge of their own destiny, public schools are promoting the religion of secular humanism. From the fundamentalist point of view, Christian schools that teach submission to God's will offer a clear alternative" (p. 285).

Absolutist, intolerant, exclusive? During the 1980s there was a growing realization that the concept of a value-neutral curriculum would be rejected by large segments of the American population, court decisions and the U.S. Constitution notwithstanding. From nineteenth-century Catholics to twentieth-century fundamentalists, many Americans insist that the education of their children be religious. To avoid a breakdown of the public sphere altogether or the complete avoidance of controversial subjects (such as sex education) in public schools, reasonable and reflective educators have worked to strike a balance among impartiality, tolerance, and religious liberty. Christian concerns regarding the value content of public school curriculum are legitimate; concerns regarding their religious freedom are understandable. Fundamentalists are correct when they criticize school textbooks for underrepresenting the significance of religion in American life (Provenzo, 1990). Religious groups are protected under the First Amendment of the U.S. Constitution. However, in expressing their concerns and protecting their freedom, these groups have no constitutional or educational right to force their religious views upon others. Historian Eugene Provenzo writes:

> The public schools should not deal with the ultra-fundamentalists as a threat to public education, but simply as another special interest group in the culture. Accommodation, compromise and empathy are essential to both sides. In dealing with the ultra-fundamentalist perspective we must avoid countering with a version of the ultra-fundamentalist perspective, i.e. being absolutist, intolerant, and exclusive. The ultra-fundamentalists have the right to promote their beliefs and to maintain their rights, but not to impose their vision of culture and education on the majority of American schoolchildren. (1990, p. 98)

Provenzo's balanced view will be difficult to maintain given the religious conflict and rivalry that has intensified the competition among private, parochial, and public schools in the 1990s.

National Council on Religion and Public Education. An organization which promotes moderation in this contentious sphere of religion and public education is the National Council on Religion and Public Education. Founded in 1971, NCRPE has provided resources for teaching religion in public schools which are designed to be constitutionally permissible and academically sound. NCRPE assists teachers and school districts in meeting the challenges of this subject by disseminating curriculum materials related to public education religion studies, including the publication of a journal, *Religion and Public Education.* Recent issues have featured topics such as "Religiously Diverse Students in the Schools" (Spring/Summer 1989), "The Supreme Court Ruling on Religious Clubs in Public Schools" (Winter, 1990), "Secular Humanism" (Summer, 1988), "Women, Religion, and Education" (Summer, 1987), and "Theological Dimensions of the School Curriculum" (Spring, 1993).

Other projects and publications devoted to religious tolerance and education include the National Endowment for the Humanities' funding (in 1976-77) of elementary and secondary curriculum units on religion. Sample lessons included "Black Tribal African Religions," "Russian Iconography," "Siddhartha: An Introduction to Buddhism and Hinduism Yesterday and Today," and "Special Time in Families." The largest professional curriculum organization, the Association for Supervision and Curriculum Development (ASCD; see chapters 3 and 4) in its May 1987 issue of its monthly journal, *Educational Leadership,* discussed issues concerning religion in the public schools. Editor Ron Brandt set the tone by defending public education from those he characterized as "neo-Puritans." Brandt reminded educators that dogmatism is irreconcilable with the most basic tenets of education. He argued that religion must be taught impartially so as to protect the intellectual freedom of students. Among the points discussed in this issue of *Educa-*

tional Leadership were separation of church and state, religious freedom, and textbook controversies (Brandt, 1987). Acknowledged is that: "It is the classroom teacher who will bear the burden of curricular selectivity. Teachers will have to become amateur theologians to determine what might offend the beliefs of their students" (Hulsizer, 1987, p. 16). ASCD, NEH, and NCRPE have all exhibited an interest in teaching religion and values in the public school curriculum in ways which avoid religious prejudice and jealousy.

Our deepest differences. Former U.S. Commissioner of Education and President of the Carnegie Foundation for the Advancement of Teaching, Ernest L. Boyer, has directed a group of educators associated with the Williamsburg Charter Foundation (1988) in the development of a comprehensive curriculum which aspires to circumvent the minefield of controversies concerning religion and public education. This curriculum, historical in character, is entitled "Living with Our Deepest Differences: Religious Liberty in a Pluralistic Society" (Boyer, 1991). ASCD has published a somewhat similar curriculum entitled "Religion in American History: What to Teach and How" (Haynes, 1990). The ASCD curriculum makes use of historical documents to demonstrate the important role religion has played in American history. The curricular point of view is indicated by the following:

> America has shifted from the largely Protestant pluralism of the 18th century to a pluralism that now includes people of all faiths and a growing number of people who indicate no religious preference. If we are to continue to live together as one nation of many faiths, it is a matter of some urgency that students develop a strong commitment to the First Amendment principles of religious liberty and a clear understanding of the role religion plays in history and society. (Haynes, 1990, p. x)

Among the documents ASCD employs to communicate this understanding are: letters from President George Washington to Jewish congregations (1790); letters from President Thomas Jefferson to the Danbury Baptist Association (1802); a letter from an African American Church to the Freedmen's Bureau (1867); a press release from President Theodore Roosevelt on religious discrimination (1908); and a memorandum from William O. Douglas to Hugo Black on school prayer (1962). Also included in this curriculum are recommendations made by the American Association of School Administrators (AASA). These include the promotion of teacher training and sensitivity in this area, understanding of First Amendment considerations, and attention to developmental issues in the design—and in particular the sequencing—of curriculum materials (Haynes, 1990).

More than any other curriculum material in school classrooms, the textbook tends to represent the totality of the school curriculum for many parents and other lay observers such as politicians [see the section on textbooks in chapter 13 for elaboration of this point]. Of course, too many teachers and administrators also limit their concept of curriculum to that information printed in textbooks. Given this conflation of curriculum with textbooks, it is unsurprising that debates over religion in the public school classrooms have focused on textbooks. Debates over textbooks are debates over power (Apple & Christian-Smith, 1991); efforts to shape the religious dimensions of the curriculum are also political power struggles.

Mozert v. Hawkins County, Tennessee. Illustrative of this focus is the widely reported Tennessee textbook case [Mozert v. Hawkins County, 765 (1985)] which addressed the question of the proper balance between a school board's authority to prescribe a curriculum and the rights of individual parents to protect their children from books and ideas they consider religiously objectionable. The parents in the Mozert case asserted that their First Amendment right to free exercise of religion had been violated by the requirement that their children read textbooks expressing ideas and values they regarded as contrary to their religious beliefs. Included in these ideas and values to which they objected were: a) the advocacy of humanistic moral values, b) an anti-Christian bias, c) promotion of one world government, d) false ideas of death, and e) feminist views favored over concepts of the traditional role of women. In fashioning a judgment, the district judge did not grant the plaintiffs' request that the school board be ordered to provide alternative reading classes with different textbooks, because it was judged that such a directive would impose undue educational and administrative hardships on the school system. Such a directive might also violate the establishment clause by tailoring reading instruction to the plaintiffs' religious beliefs. In an effort to accommodate the plaintiffs' rights and the school board's interests, the judge decreed that the plaintiffs' children would have a choice of remaining in standard reading classes or leaving these reading classes to study reading privately, outside the public schools (Sendor, 1988).

Promoting secular beliefs? The U.S. Court of Appeals for the Sixth Circuit reversed the district court judge's decision. However, this Court shared the view that the free exercise clause protects citizens from being coerced to affirm ideas in conflict with their own values. But the Court also ruled that the free exercise clause does not protect people from mere exposure to such beliefs. The children were ordered back to the public schools for reading instruction (Sendor, 1988). In *Legal Guide to Religion and Public Education* (1988), Benjamin Sendor summarized the textbook controversies:

> Although most litigation about religious objections to materials or method have involved only the free exercise clause, two interesting cases illustrate a different strategy used by some students and parents: challenging materials or methods under the establishment clause. In these cases the challengers have argued that the materials or methods in question violated the establishment clause by promoting secular humanist beliefs. (Sendor, 1988, p. 40)

Despite a variety of court cases regarding textbooks, in 1990 the California State Board of Education approved social studies textbooks that had been protested by a variety of ethnic and religious groups. The new textbooks (Houghton Mifflin Company's K-8, and an 8th grade book by Holt, Rinehart, and Winston) include in-depth discussions of world religions. *Education Week* reported that spokespersons for minority religious groups complained of omissions, inaccuracies, and misrepresentations in the textbooks. Former California State Superintendent of Instruction Bill Honig concluded: "The most important thing is we got a strong book. We showed in a pluralistic state with some heavy political attacks, we still could adopt a strong book" (Viadero, 1990, p. 18). These recent controversies represent, in a sense, a microcosm of the national debate over religion in the public school curriculum. The textbook becomes one of the most visible objects on which to focus the debate.

Religion and civic education. The role of the public or common school in promoting democratic values has been endorsed by educational and political leaders for more than one hundred years. Proponents of including the teaching of religion in American history classrooms also contend that the social studies curriculum is a central place to teach civic values. Among proponents are organizations such as the Center for Civic Education (CCE) and the Council for the Advancement of Citizenship (CAC), both of which provide curricular materials. Both groups insist that civic education involves the study of morality. Indicative of this view is the following statement from *Religion and Public Education*:

> In recent years, the public philosophy, the shared moral vision that binds us together as a people, diverse yet one, has been significantly diluted and this development has adversely affected moral education in the public schools. Consequently, to the extent that there is a problem with moral education in the United States today, it fuels the "values problem" in the public schools. (United States Catholic Conference, 1987, p. 338)

This statement was adopted by the United States Catholic Conference in 1987, demonstrating the movement of the marginalized Catholic minority of the nineteenth century to the mainstream of American society by the 1980s.

Both the Center for Civic Education and the Council for the Advancement of Citizenship have made recommendations regarding the teaching of civic values in the school curriculum. The curriculum must be based upon the common bond of humanity shared by all people of every race, creed, and color. Teachers are regarded as transmitters of our cultural legacy and heritage. School communities of students, teachers, administrators, staff, and parents constitute a moral community conscious of the impact they make upon one another. A major goal of the school curriculum, in their view, is to build a community dedicated to traditional democratic values and civic responsibilities. While focusing upon ethnicity, Arthur Schlesinger, Jr. represents this general view:

> The growing diversity of the American population makes the quest for unifying ideals and a common culture all the more urgent. In a world savagely rent by ethnic and racial antagonism, the U.S. must continue as an example of how a highly differentiated society holds itself together. (Schlesinger, Jr., 1991a, p. 21)

The three c's. As we have seen, former U.S. Secretary of Education, William Bennett, has been one visible proponent of a common core curriculum. During the 1980s he urged America's schools to emphasize the three c's: character, content, and choice. According to Bennett: "Common culture—common values, common knowledge, and a common language—are essential to sharing dreams and to discussing differences. There are some things that we must all learn together" (Bennett, 1986, p. 23). Common to whom is a question Bennett leaves unanswered.

Other conservatives endorsed this concept of core curriculum, arguing that such a curriculum is a prerequisite to realize a common political vision (Finn, Ravitch, et al., 1985). In *Cultural Literacy*, E. D. Hirsch (1987) argued that America's literacy problems derive from students' ignorance of our common culture, not from failing to acquire reading skills. Both Hirsch and Bennett believed that a fact-based civic curriculum would recreate a common American culture and lead to greater productivity in the economic sector. Undersecretary of Education Gary Bauer went even further:

> The most important values that our public schools must teach, I believe, are the fundamental principles that are the basis of our free society and democratic government. In our effort to identify values that can be taught in public schools, we should attempt to discover a common body of ethical knowledge that, even if it has religious origin, serves the purpose of maintaining and strengthening devotion to our country. (Bauer, 1986, p. 26)

A civic religion? It is unsurprising, then, that the concept of a common curriculum struck some as having religious connotations. For instance, Christine Shea characterized the core curriculum proposal as a new form of civic religion. She argued that:

> within these appeals for a common core curriculum is a subtle cry for a new kind of civic religion—a civic religion that supposedly blends the Judeo-Christian moral code, the patriotic fervor of traditional democratic beliefs, with a facts-based, skills-oriented curriculum. (Shea, Kahane, & Sola, 1989, p. 21)

Clearly, education which purports to promote civic awareness and responsibility through a core curriculum has its skeptics. Just as fundamentalists decried the absence of traditional religious values and the substitution, in their judgment, of "secular humanism," many critics of the core or common culture curriculum regard those efforts as establishing a civic religion.

The need for civic, moral, and value education to redress social decay and spiritual turmoil is disputed on the political left as well as right. For instance, calls for curricular cohesion and common values are viewed by curriculum theorists on the left as vehicles for continued oppression of racial, gendered, and religious minorities. Such critics point out that the "core" is advocated by governmental officials and education establishment bureaucrats, and is in the service of economic productivity, not the emancipation of oppressed groups. Illustrative of this view is the collection of essays entitled *The New*

Servants of Power, edited by Christin Shea, Ernest Kahane, and Peter Sola (1989). Maxine Greene summarized the collection in her foreword:

> [The book] is in many ways unique in its critique of the educational reform movement of the late 1970s to the late 1980s. [It] breaks unapologetically through the mystifying claims that the reforms intend to reconcile equity and excellence. Fascinating material is presented on the differences among the various elites: those preoccupied with military dominance and those concerned about trilateral management of a global economy; those interested in using schools to repair character deficiencies and those interested in using them to upgrade competence and skills. [The book] sheds a new and sometimes lurid light on what the reform reports actually imply when it comes to learning to learning minimal competency skills and the requirements for the dead-end jobs awaiting perhaps the majority of our youth. (Greene, in Shea, 1989, pp. ix-x)

Greene goes on to raise a crucial question: from where does the so-called consensus in moral education derive? For some it is embedded in the enduring truths of democracy and traditional religious values. Others disagree. Stuart A. McAninch (1989) denies that the school curriculum ought to preserve and promote a cohesive political community by preparing youth for "responsible" citizenship. Such a conservative curriculum disables those who would fight injustice and oppression in American society. A truly core curriculum, he argues, would undermine individual liberty and thus corrode democratic and religious values (McAninch, 1989).

Schools of choice–an appropriate alternative? The intensity and complexity of debates regarding religion in the public school curriculum lead some to conclude that "choice" represents the only possible resolution of the issue, and of the wider crisis in public education. Many states and local school districts are experimenting with "choice." So called "magnet" schools have been designated, some open to all students, others to those who meet prerequisites. Some "magnet" schools are discipline-linked, such as schools for the arts or schools for science and mathematics; others are open to students who have excelled. Several states have experimented with voucher plans and tuition tax credits whereby funding for educational services is directed to the school of choice through each student's family (Fiske, 1991). A few school districts have begun contracting with private companies and private schools to provide educational services, for instance, the Milwaukee Public Schools.

Government financial support of private and parochial schools has been a contested issue since before the common school era. In the 1980s the Reagan administration proposed tuition tax credits to reduce a family's federal income tax obligation based on the number of children in private elementary and secondary schools, with a maximum family income of $50,000 for eligibility. Some states, for example Louisiana, have passed legislation to provide state income tax credits for all school age children. Proponents of tuition tax credits argue that parents of children who attend private and religious schools have a double tax burden because they pay tuition as well as taxes for public schools. Opponents argue, much as did Horace Mann, that all citizens receive benefits from public education. Additionally, the tax credit would only serve to reward those who currently choose to send their children to private schools, thereby depleting resources that could be available to support the majority of children who attend public schools. Proponents counter that without incentives such as tax credits, families of private and parochial school students will be less inclined to support additional funding for public schools, perhaps creating gridlock in the political realm. A more complete analysis of this volatile issue can be found in Thomas James and Henry Levin's (1983) *Public Dollars for Private Schools: The Case of Tuition Tax Credits.*

Some concepts of choice provide students and parents choices limited to the public schools. Even these plans have been greeted with skepticism by those who claim that the value systems of specific interest groups are promoted inappropriately by choice options. In 1990 ASCD published *Public Schools of Choice,* a book which sought to clarify the debate regarding various choice programs. Three general justifications for choice are identified. One is characterized as "reaction to the present." Choice proponents in this category point to student underachievement, bureaucratic unresponsiveness, and the failure of past reform efforts in their justification for parental choice. Another category of justification is "a means for desegregating schools." Proponents in this category argue that choice allows poorer families to select schools that richer families now select by moving into neighborhoods with exceptional schools or by paying to send their children to highly regarded private schools. Presumably, a voucher plan would permit minority parents to choose these alternatives, once available only to the upper middle class and the wealthy. Opponents counter that such plans have resulted in segregation in the past. A third category cited in the ASCD study is called "choice as a catalyst for change." These proponents insist that variety, options, self-direction, flexibility, and responsiveness will be the primary benefits of choice. Choice will address individual and family needs in faster, more responsive ways. ASCD summarized its position:

> The mission of ASCD is to develop quality education for all students. Our values include balance in the curriculum, self-direction, equity, and cultural pluralism, each of which relates directly to public schools of choice. What's more, many of our members are affected by state or local choice policies. They are facing questions of whether to implement choice and how to achieve equity if they do. (ASCD 1990a, p. vii)

Cheated in a system that excludes God? Since the concept of choice is integral to the idea of a democratic society and to a free-market economy, and because choice implies a sense of power, freedom, variety, and quality, it is likely that the concept will remain a focal point of school reform in the 1990s. Many of those who espouse the concept regard choice as an inalienable right and a moral issue. What for some is a bureaucratic effort to revitalize a moribund public school system [see the section on school reform in chapter 13] becomes for others a constitutional issue of religious freedom. Many parents who regard religion as the paramount feature of their lives would embrace choice as providing them the means to follow their conscience. Speaking for many fundamentalists, a Christian school headmaster provided a rationale for parents seeking choices outside the public school system:

> Children are cheated in a school system that excludes God. By law, the public schools cannot teach the whole truth about life, and, by deliberate design, textbook companies and teacher unions have purged God from texts and lesson plans. . . . The Scriptures are clear. Public schools are a mission field for Christian teachers and administrators, but they're not suitable schooling environments for children of Christian parents. (Wackes, 1991, p. 2)

Such a perspective conveys educational choice as a religious idea and moral imperative.

Private schools superior? In *Public and Private Schools,* commonly referred to as the *Coleman Report,* James Coleman and associates (1981) concluded that private schools—and most of these were religious schools—are closer to the America ideal of the common school than are public schools. In comparing school systems, Coleman explained that private schools appear to have teachers who are more committed to seeing that students learn, spend more time on academic subjects, demand stricter discipline, assign more homework, enjoy greater support from parents, and, although they do not safeguard students rights as carefully as do public schools, the students themselves feel they are treated more fairly. Coleman's original report, and his *High School Achievement: Public, Catholic, and Private Schools Compared* (Coleman et al., 1982), was acclaimed for its comprehensive and authoritative research; it also aroused considerable criticism, especially regarding the finding that students in private schools consistently outperformed public school students. Another study found that graduates of private schools, Catholic or not, are much more likely to enter college (Falsey & Heyns, 1984). In "How Valid Are Coleman's Conclusions?," Donald Erickson (1985) argued that public and private school students are not comparable groups; consequently, Coleman's conclusions are invalid. He challenged Coleman to direct future research to the more important question of assuring quality and equity for all students.

The impact of communities. James Coleman, Thomas Hoffer, and Sally Kilgore (1981, 1982) have injected several new elements into the religious and educational debate. Specifically, they have argued that a "functional community" is created by Catholic and other religious schools. Even though students do not necessarily live in the same neighborhood, the families transmit similar values from generation to generation within the church and school community. Coleman (1981) conceded that a few public schools are capable of creating "value communities" composed of "people who share similar values about education and childrearing but who are not a functional community" (p. 10). However, he concluded that most public schools are grounded in no community at all, and that arbitrary attendance zones militate against the development of either functional or value communities. Indeed, most public schools have lost their base of community support (Coleman, 1981, 1982).

Coleman responded to his critics in the 1987 publication entitled *Public and Private High Schools: The Impact of Communities* which reported follow-up studies of the 1,105 high schools studied in his earlier report. Here he focused upon the role of school-community relationship to explain the superior performance of students in Catholic and other private, mostly religious, schools. Why are religious schools—apparently inegalitarian in character—so effective? Coleman concluded:

> The evidence presented in this book indicates that functional communities with intergenerational closure constitute social capital that is of widespread value for young persons in high school. Furthermore, the evidence indicates that this social capital is particularly valuable for young persons from families in which the social capital or the human capital of the parents is especially weak. (Coleman, 1987, p. 231)

Coleman (1987) continued by arguing that Catholic schools are the most effective at increasing "human capital," which economists define as the skills and capabilities that make people productive. The movement of Catholic immigrants from poverty to mainstream American life is based on this principle. Joseph W. Newman (1990) comments on Coleman's conclusions:

> Some students come from families in which human capital is lacking—their parents may be poorly educated and unemployed. Yet some families that lack human capital may have an abundance of social capital, which "exists in the relations between persons." Families with social capital are close.... Some families, of course, lack both human capital and social capital, while other families have both. Still other families have human capital but lack social capital. The parents may be well educated, for example, but spend no time with their children. Coleman points out that social capital exists in communities as well as families. (p. 282)

From this perspective, families or individuals who share the same church or same religious values can more ably sustain one another. This leads to the conclusion that functional communities surrounding Catholic schools and other religious schools can supply social capital to students who lack it at home.

Social capital. Coleman admits that previous research contradicted his conclusion. How then, he asks, can he conclude that social capital, especially for disadvantaged students, is a positive factor in private schools? Why do the Catholic schools in his study contradict the inegalitarian nature of previous theoretical positions? Coleman suggests: "Our conjecture is that a functional community based on a single dimension of religious association is different, in just those respects that relate to inegalitarianism, from a functional community that encompasses all arenas of social and economic life" (1987, p.

232). In part, his conclusion is due to the egalitarian ethic of religion itself and, in part, to the abstraction of a single arena of activity from the total fabric of social and economic life. This abstraction permits a student to escape the statistical effects of the family based on the totality of its activities. Coleman views this to be an instance of "role-segmentation" of modern social life which is important in inhibiting the inheritance of the parents' status by the child. Therefore, the social capital of the religious school community becomes a unique factor in the greater level of success of private school students in religious schools, especially those from disadvantaged backgrounds. Coleman challenged superintendents and principals in all schools to use his findings to increase social capital for students, especially since the social capital available to children outside of the school has eroded in recent years. When families are intact and communities exhibit extensive social capital, public education can work well. However, for disadvantaged students, Coleman found that private religious schools enjoy a greater success rate. This factor of social capital is the key element

Fundamentalist schools. In addition to theological issues, social and economic forces outside the school are sometimes cited for an intensified interest in religious [especially Protestant] schools in the 1980s. Susan D. Rose suggested that social uncertainty and economic decline function to intensify certain groups' interest in social stability and theological certainty. She reported an ethnographic study of two groups of evangelicals and their schools, Lakehaven, a working-class fundamentalist Baptist congregation, and Covenant, a middle-class, independent Charismatic fellowship. Rose (1988) explained:

> Both the people at Covenant and Lakehaven are engaged in a symbolic crusade. They are struggling to achieve a greater sense of personal and social coherence in a world that appears chaotic and unpredictable. . . . They want Christianity to have a more powerful influence in contemporary society. It is no longer a question of manifest destiny, of how to spread Christianity to other countries, but primarily of how to restore America to a Christian nation. (p. 170)

In Rose's view, the Christian school movement represents an "experiment in cultural production as well as social reproduction" (p. 203). That is, in a cultural sense these Christian schools are expressions of these groups' efforts to provide a haven in an uncertain world and to transmit conservative Christian values to their young. Rose suggests, however, that these groups and their schools are also unknowingly reproducing the American social structure while producing their own community. Rose concluded that problematical as the social exclusivity of the Lakehaven and Covenant fellowships may be, these church/school communities may imply a basis for understanding social relationships between school and society. Educating the young must take place in a social setting which is accompanied by community building.

The gates of hell. William Reese (1982) notes that evangelical Protestants in particular have always had considerable influence upon the nation's public school system:

> From the Great Awakening of the colonial period, to the resurgence of revivalism in the nineteenth century, to the religious movements of modern America, evangelical Protestants have linked personal salvation, social order, and national destiny with the fate of common schooling. (p. 9)

He (1982) locates this relations among religion, society, and the nation in the Protestant Reformation:

> "I am much afraid," wrote Martin Luther in the sixteenth century, "that schools will prove to be the great gates of hell unless they diligently labor in explaining the Holy Scriptures, engraving them in the hearts of youth. I advise no one to place his child where the Scriptures do not reign paramount." (quoted in Reese, 1982, p. 9)

Evangelicals and fundamentalists have taken Luther's concern very much to heart.

In his study of the Christian private school movement, David C. Lisman (1991) reflected on the resurgence of Christian fundamentalism [see also Peshkin, 1983]. Approximately 22 percent of Americans eighteen and older consider themselves to be "born-again Christians." These individuals accept the Bible as the infallible word of God. In the mid-1980s a survey sponsored by the Committee Against Censorship of the National Council of Teachers of English of librarians in school systems across the country revealed a decided increase in local critics of schools. Lisman (1991) acknowledged: "Currently, the Christian school movement represents one million children, 20 percent of the total private school population. . . . Although representing a small percentage of the total school population, the symbolic significance of this movement cannot be underestimated" (p. 378).

John Willinsky (1989) observed that in light of the continuing challenges which schools and libraries face from those who would restrict on moral grounds the literary curriculum of the young, it is important to recall the original arguments in public education for making literature a central curricular element, arguments which hinged on literature's ability to form the soul, to restore a lost community.

Home schooling has grown dramatically, spurred largely by "new-right Christians" who see public schools as ignoring or in fact hostile to their basic values and rights (Kincheloe, 1993b, pp. 50-51). Home schooling advocates have enjoyed tremendous success in pressuring state legislatures around the country to pass home schooling laws. While for some economics appears to be a factor in the decision to home school—some parents cannot afford private tuition and will not send their children to public school—others prefer to educate their children themselves (Garland, 1991).

Waldorf schools. Another instance of religious schools grounded in a tradition quite different from fundamentalist schools is that of the Waldorf schools. Founded in Stuttgart, Germany in 1919 by Emil Molt, director of the Waldorf Astoria Company, these schools grew out of a concern with the devastation in central Europe following World War I. Molt envisioned new modes of thought which might enable Europeans to transcend those social and political currents which led to mass destruction and upheaval. His hope was to develop those capacities in children that would enable them, as adults, to transform society. Molt enlisted the support of Rudolf Steiner in order to develop a form of education which might support his vision. Steiner's first major work, *The Philosophy of Freedom,* had appeared in 1894 and established the foundation for his worldview which he named anthroposophy. Anthroposophy is defined as the ability to transmit not only technical knowledge, but also those understandings which help students to study life itself.

The curriculum of the contemporary Waldorf school emphasizes the inner development of the child, the unity of all branches of knowledge, and schooling as art which supports the development of the whole person, including spirit, body, and soul. The spiritual dimensions of the Waldorf schools express the aspiration to transcend the ravages of contemporary life, including the destruction of the human spirit and the natural environment by modern industrial society: "The rapid spread of Waldorf education in this century is more than a social fact: it is a testament to the power of an ideal and the striving of men and women who are working for the development of the human being, the transformation of society, and the renewal of the earth" (Trostli, 1988, p. 51). The Waldorf school movement is another visible example of understanding curriculum as theological text.

The future? Religion has played a highly significant role in the "struggle for the American curriculum" (Kliebard, 1986). This role cannot be ignored by curriculum scholars or by prospective and practicing educators. While historically religion has been a divisive force in American education, perhaps it need not necessarily be so. The curriculum as theological text emerging in the twenty-first century may well be different from the conservative-to-fundamentalist spectrum of beliefs, rooted as these are in appeals to supernatural revelation which often contradict history and science. The emerging curriculum may also be different from those liberal theological perspectives which avoid contradicting contemporary historical and scientific knowledge but often seem to put a religious gloss over secularism's nihilistic and relativistic views of human experience. Theology has often been ignored during the twentieth century because both the premodern conservative and modern liberal approaches have seemed irrelevant in the world of contemporary society, history, and science. The scholarly project to understand curriculum as theological text which is developing now might challenge the modern worldview of salvation by material progress and scientific technology, a salvation seriously imperiled by ecological limits (Lasch, 1991). Such a challenge would not be accomplished by an appeal to antiscientific authoritarianism.

Religion and its study—theology—have often been ignored in the effort to understand curriculum, in part due to the field's adherence to "scientific management" [see chapters 2 and 3] and, more recently, a preoccupation with Marxism [see chapter 5]. It may be that understanding curriculum as theological text can result in a new consensus on the teaching of religion, a view within which the variety of religious groups, atheists, and agnostics may all find their beliefs protected and respected. Scholarship in this vein has begun; we report it now.

III
Moral and Ethical Dimensions:
Huebner, Purpel, Oliver and Gershman

If education truly encounters religion (as opposed to tucking it into the school curriculum), education would take on a diversity of forms with qualities I have called *rooted and reverent*.
(Gabriel Moran, 1981, p. 162)

While the last quarter century has not been the best of times morally . . . it surely has been a golden age for the study of moral education.
(Barry Chazan, 1992, p. 3)

A great concern of the last several decades, moral and spiritual values, is misplaced. That very focus is unfortunate, because it assumes there is something special that can be identified as moral or spiritual. This assumption is false. Everything that is done in schools, and in preparation for school activity, is already infused with the spiritual.
(Dwayne Huebner, 1993, p. 11)

The work of several curriculum theorists in the 1970s established the foundation for a renewed interest in morality and ethics in education in the 1990s (Dixon, 1980; Jarrett, 1980). James Macdonald and Dwayne Huebner can be regarded as pioneers of the theological and spiritual dimensions of curriculum during the beginning phases of Reconceptualization [see chapters 3 and 4]. Huebner argued that ethical and aesthetic language regarding schooling had been limited, inconsistent, and of much lower priority than other discourses. He lamented:

How [can] one plan educational futures via behavior objectives when the mystical literature emphasizes the present moment and the need to let the future care for itself? . . . I am convinced that the curriculum person's dependency on scientific thought patterns . . . has broken his linkage with other great and important intellectual traditions of East and West which have profound bearing on the talking about the practice of education. (1975a, p. 215)

Huebner continued by foreshadowing future research in these forgotten (by the curriculum field) traditions. He wrote: "Classroom activity which is socially significant because of heightened technical efficiency might have greater personal significance . . . if the aesthetic and ethical categories were also used to value the activity . . . for further search and eventual research" (1975b, p. 228). Huebner promoted a moral vision of education that included "ethical rationality" where the human situations existing between student and teacher, student and other beings in the world, and the student and the beauty of the phenomenal world, are seen as primary. James Macdonald (1975b) also argued against the traditional structures of curriculum research that excluded the ethical dimension of education. In the 1970s Macdonald began to explore curriculum from a "utopian impulse for justice, equity, and fairness." He wrote:

> Education [is] a moral enterprise rather than simply a set of technical problems to be solved within a satisfying conceptual scheme. . . . Thus, the struggle for personal integration, educational integrity, and social justice go on, necessitating a constant revaluation of oneself, one's work and one's world—with the hope that with whatever creative talent one possesses will lead toward something better that we may all share. (p. 4)

In addition to Huebner and Macdonald, Philip Phenix (1975) made a significant contribution to this moral discourse with his exploration of transcendence and curriculum. Also, William Pinar's 1975 characterization of post-critical scholarship in curriculum as a move away from obsessive criticism of the status quo toward concern for transcendence and consciousness, toward the creation of a new order which respects spirituality, theology, and autobiography, helped point to the moral discourses in the 1990s. Cleo Cherryholmes (1988b) criticized structuralism for its separation of ethics and action, and in this chapter we include reports of efforts to link ethics and morality to the project to understand curriculum.

Lawrence Kohlberg's (1981) *Essays on Moral Development* and his earlier works on education and moral development (1970), as well as Carol Gilligan's (1982) influential revision of Kohlberg's scheme, were widely read by practitioners as well as researchers, and have had a dramatic impact on moral discourses. Kohlberg's moral development scheme from the preconventional level through the conventional to the postconventional principled level, along with the stages of human development devised by Piaget and Erikson, significantly influenced James Fowler, considered by many as a central figure in the psychology of religion. In *Stages of Faith: The Psychology of Human Development and the Quest for Meaning*, Fowler (1981) proposed six stages to describe the passage of life in the quest for meaning: 1) the intuitive, imitative faith of childhood, 2) mythic-literal faith, 3) synthetic-conventional faith, 4) individuative-reflective faith, 5) conjunctive faith, and 6) universalizing, self-transcending faith of full maturity. Fowler interviewed Christians, Jews, agnostics, and atheists as part of his sociological, theological, and ethnographic scholarship. Reminiscent of Dewey's study of religion, Fowler's work does not equate faith and morality with religion in the early phases. Rather, "human faith" is seen as a way of learning and constructing the meaning of life. Fowler, paralleling the concept of *currere* in curriculum studies, wrote: "more verb than noun, faith is the dynamic system of images, values, and commitments that guide one's life. It is thus universal; everyone who chooses to go on living operates by some basic faith" (1981, p. 1).

Gabriel Moran's ethics. Educator and theologian Gabriel Moran (1981), along with other scholars (Noddings, 1989), raised several concerns about the developmental models of Kohlberg and Fowler [including methodological biases and theological naiveté, (p. 88)]. Moran (1981) proposed in *Interplay: A Theory of Religion and Education* that moral education must move beyond developmental theories to holistic models rooted in justice and ethics. Moran presented a four-part solution to global ethical dilemmas through a process of religious education that is attentive to productive and meaningful work, an organic family/community with a vision for a united world, attention to the issue of food where starvation becomes intolerable, and finally an ecological vision of a new and transformed earth (pp. 145-154). Moran (1981) wrote:

> If education truly encounters religion (as opposed to tucking it into the school curriculum), education would take on a diversity of forms with qualities I have called *rooted and reverent*. Education would have roots in the earth, the body, and the family. . . . Education can be reconceptualized to include family life, daily work, and contemplative quiet. Education would be centered on how people are living and would be concerned with improving the main forms in which people learn the art of living. (p. 162)

Political morality. While Moran and Fowler represent the theological and psychological dimensions of scholarship on moral education, political scholars also support a moral vision. As we saw in chapter four, Michael Apple (1975b) argued that "Education is ultimately a moral activity and as such it cannot be understood without recourse to, and thus must be held accountable to, ethical principles and obligations of justice and responsibility to other persons" (p. 89). Alex Molnar (1975) also explored the significance of the spiritual in moral and ethical issues: "Like a good deal of analysis preferenced in Marxism-Leninism, [a political focus on student rights] fails to account for the significance of the spiritual dimension in human affairs" (p. 166).

The 1970s were, as we saw in chapter 4, a time of ferment in the field of curriculum theory. The scholars introduced here are representative of the variety of voices supporting an understanding of curriculum from moral and ethical viewpoints. As we continue, we will explore the more recent scholarship on moral education which have emerged from this moral and theological understanding of curriculum established by Macdonald, Huebner, Phenix, Pinar, Kohlberg, Gilligan, Fowler, Moran, Apple, and Molnar in the 1970s.

Contemporary discourses. Barry Chazan (1985), philosopher of education at the Hebrew University of Jerusalem and author of *Contemporary Approaches to Moral Education: Analyzing Alternative Theories*, noted that prior to the 1970s moral education was neglected in philosophic and educational circles, resulting in ethical relativism and malaise. However, the 1980s saw the emergence of a significant number of theories and programs of moral education which began in the 1970s [as recorded in Chazan's (1973) earlier work, *Moral Education*, with the distinguished philosopher of education Jonas Soltis]. In both texts, the authors compare the major theories of moral education, including: 1) the tension between the social and the individual, 2) moral principles, 3) reason in ethics, 4) content and form, 5) action/praxis, 6) the conception of the morally educated person, 7) "indoctrination" of moral education, 8) the role of the teacher, and 9) pedagogy. Chazan and Soltis established a foundation for moral education from the perspective of French sociologist Emile Durkheim, who proposed that educators should neither preach nor indoctrinate. Rather, moral education should serve as a directive and guide for moral living. However, Chazan also acknowledged that many educators oppose moral education. He wrote:

> The anti-moral education tradition encompasses the broad spectrum of views on the nature of morality that we find in classical and contemporary thought. Thus, some perspectives see morality in exclusively individualistic terms, whereas the socialists start with social assumptions that are extremely close to Durkheim and Dewey. Tolstoy assumes the integral connection between religion and morality, whereas Ferrer disavows any such connection. . . . Hence, there is no one underlying conception of morality that characterizes the history of ethics and moral education. (Chazan, 1985, pp. 100-101)

Chazan concluded that the anti-moral education movement, as well as the diversity of approaches by those who promote moral education, demonstrates the complexity of the emerging ethical debates. The task of contemporary education is not solely academic, he cautions, rather: "The moral failures of the twentieth century and the moral wrestlings of the contemporary young person clearly indicate that the issues of moral education are far from being resolved" (p. 119). At the conclusion of his book, Chazan turns to John Dewey (1975) to provide a clearer perspective on the moral and ethical challenges of the global society where morality develops within the context of the interaction between individuals and social settings, teachers and students (p. 104). The work of Dewey, along with Kohlberg and Durkheim, suggests to Chazan that there is hope of "better introducing our young to the mysteries and majesty of the moral sphere" (p. 119).

What will stimulate moral education in the future? Chazan (1992) writes:

> In the years to come, moral education theory . . . will be fueled by the moral dilemmas and the moral prisons of the world. Some of these moral prisons periodically open, and a few of the morally oppressed are released. But until all the moral prisons of the world have been opened and all the beleaguered released, the task of moral education has only just begun. (p. 22)

Macdonald, Purpel, Shapiro. Some of the most important work on theology and morality has been and is currently being done at the University of North Carolina at Greensboro. This can be credited in no small measure to the influence of James B. Macdonald, who taught at the University until his death in 1983. H. Svi Shapiro and David E. Purpel have edited the useful collection *Critical Social Issues in American Education: Toward the 21st Century* (1993). Additionally, Purpel wrote *The Moral and Spiritual Crisis in Education: A Curriculum for Justice and Compassion in Education* (1989). Shapiro's Ph.D. Student, Sue Books, now a professor at Knox College (Illinois), has also contributed to the dialogue on moral education in her "Literary Journalism as Educational Criticism: A Discourse of Triage" (1992b). The work of these three scholars is suggestive perhaps of emerging moral educational discourses. Shapiro's social moral perspective, Purpel's moral and spiritual view, and Books' concept of triage from a holistic curriculum perspective are all on the cutting edge of discourses in the 1990s. Briefly, we review this work now.

David Purpel's (1989) book *The Moral and Spiritual Crisis in Education: A Curriculum for Justice and Compassion in Education* identified two competing voices in educational theory: the enormous cultural, political, and economic crisis of the present age and the growing body of scholarship in all fields of study that challenges existing canons and proposes new paradigms. Purpel's self-assigned task is daunting. He seeks to develop a liberating discourse regarding the relationships among society, culture, and education to reduce the probability of social disaster. Additionally, he seeks to move beyond the critical pedagogy focus on empowerment to a moral and religious discourse. Purpel tells us there is an urgency not only to be critical but to seek affirmation, commitment, and advocacy, a view not unlike Pinar's "post-critical" category in *Curriculum Theorizing: The Reconceptualists* [see chapter 4]. Purpel reflects here the perspective of all those theorists who are engaged in theological issues, challenging the curriculum field to explore theological discourses for the amplification of our understanding of curriculum as profoundly human and spiritual.

In the first two chapters Purpel examines what he terms "American anti-intellectualism," calling for the inclusion of moral and religious dimensions in educational discourse. He proposes a moral and religious framework that represents a:

> vision that speaks to meaning, purpose, and ultimacy. It is a framework that borrows from two ancient traditions, the Socratic and the Prophetic, and two current movements, Liberation Theology and Creation Theology. The major emphasis, however, is on Prophecy, conceptualized as the voice that in Walter Brueggemann's phrase combines "energy and criticism" and a consciousness which, says Abraham Heschel, "has the ability to hold God and man in a single thought." Prophecy holds us to our deepest commitments, chides us when we do not meet them, and provides hope for us when we think we cannot. (quoted in Purpel, 1989, p. xi)

Purpel concludes the book with an application of this vision to the curriculum in order to facilitate "love, justice, community, and joy" with compassion. He urges that these themes "permeate the entire spectrum of educational activities—hidden, overt, planned, implicit, or otherwise" (p. 123), and he insists that the school be seen as an opportunity for the growth and learning of all persons within the educational community.

Purpel supports democratic community building in schools, not unlike the work of Henry Giroux and Paulo Freire, who wrote an introduction to Purpel's text. Purpel (1989) writes:

> Much of our culture teaches us not the skills of community building but rather of individual competition. We know that democratic communities do not simply happen and that their growth is certainly not inevitable. Democratic communities need constant nurturance and attention to remain dynamic and responsive. . . . Educators have a responsibility to determine those skills of practice that are critical to the defense and growth of our political and moral commitments. (pp. 127-128)

Purpel then calls upon educators to speak out about the inadequacy of the technical aspects of the profession as well as the inadequacy of cultural institutions and accept the responsibility "to make clear statements on the moral and spiritual dimensions of various educational polices and practices" (p. 130).

Critics of Purpel's work, including Paula M. Salvio (1992) [see chapter 10], argue that religion should be viewed as a social rather than metaphysical phenomenon. Salvio is concerned that Purpel's use of the religious framework reduces the search for meaning and moral education to a "monadic, rational pursuit which fails to capture the complexity of interactions between language, tradition, emotion, imagination, and memory" (p. 90). While she might be right, Salvio's criticism points to a problem faced by scholars who attempt to incorporate religious language and theology into their research: namely, the assumption that an uncritical acceptance of patriarchal, rational, and scholastic methodology is inherent in theological dialogue. Purpel rejects such an uncritical stance. However, the volatile history of religion and education discussed at the beginning of this chapter often prevents contemporary critical analysis from the theological perspectives from being heard.

Henry Giroux and Paulo Freire acknowledge this debate in their introduction to Purpel's book. They write: "There is a volatile debate in social theory taking place over what constitutes the relationship among knowledge, power, desire, and subjectivity" (in Purpel, 1989, p. xiii). Giroux and Freire support Purpel's moral and spiritual perspective in this debate. They critique postmodern social theories and poststructuralism [see chapter 9] for insufficiently addressing the central issue of how identities and subjectivities are constructed within different moral experiences and relations. Critics have failed, they contend, to develop "a substantive ethical discourse and public morality that is necessary for overcoming existing forms of exploitation and subjugation" (p. xiv). In supporting Purpel's moral discourse, Giroux and Freire hope that the debate over the reform of public schooling in the U.S., which has emphasized character education and moral fundamentalism due to the dominance of conservative voices such as William Bennett and Chester

Finn, Jr., will take a turn toward new principles of democratic community and social responsibility.

Social responsibility. The need for a renewal of moral education is found in the critique of contemporary moral philosophy in Alasdair MacIntyre's (1981) *After Virtue* and the critique of intellectual and moral confusion in American society in Allan Bloom's (1987) *The Closing of the American Mind.* Curriculum scholars have responded to these critiques by calling for community, solidarity, and social responsibility as in Henry Giroux's (1992c) [see chapter 5] "Educational Leadership and the Crisis of Democratic Government," John P. Miller's (1988) *The Holistic Curriculum,* Alex Molnar's (1987) *Social Issues and Education: Challenge and Responsibility,* and Svi Shapiro and David Purpel's (1993) *Critical Social Issues in American Education.* What we see in these works is a common concern for a vision of education that can shape a democratic society rooted in justice, social responsibility, creativity, interdependence, multiculturalism, and community solidarity. The moral imperatives of curriculum research are clearly expressed.

Svi Shapiro and David Purpel's (1993) collection of essays entitled *Critical Social Issues in American Education* advances the dialogue on moral theology to a concern for the ethical dimensions of education to provide:

> a focus for thinking about education in the context of a society that . . . is faced with a range of critical, sometimes catastrophic, issues and problems such as poverty and growing social injustice, racism and sexism, and other forms of exclusion; the depersonalization of social and political life; the moral and spiritual decay of the culture; and the ecological deterioration of the planet. (p. xiii)

The moral imperative of curriculum is therefore not only to address these issues and problems but to move beyond their narrow and sometimes superficial treatment in the school curriculum. Shapiro and Purpel (1993) insist: "For education to become a humanly vital, ethically responsible endeavor, infused with a serious commitment to democratic values, we must understand its connection to [these] urgent and pressing issues" (p. xiii). Yet, educators face a tradition of presumed political indifference and ethical neutrality. Shapiro and Purpel (1993) write:

> Many of the students we have taught find disturbing, even shocking, our efforts to connect deliberately the work of teachers to an ethically committed, politically charged pedagogy. This linkage flies in the face of many teachers' best liberal instincts about the moral neutrality of what is taught and the impartial role of teachers. (p. xiv)

Shapiro and Purpel respond to this problem by pointing to the substantial body of literature that underlines the notion that curriculum is a moral, social, spiritual, and political enterprise. Albeit there are, as in the culture at large, conflicting demands and values: "the free-market economy versus democratic and egalitarian values; the assertion of cultural differences versus community; social justice and responsibility versus individual freedom; and moral commitment versus truth or knowledge" (p. xv). Evident in the work of Shapiro and Purpel is a challenge to the curriculum field and to the teaching profession to move beyond illusions of moral neutrality.

In _A Discourse on Triage_, Sue Books (1992b) employs Tracy Kidder's (1989) _Among Schoolchildren_ and Samuel Freedman's (1990) _Small Victories_ to illustrate the educational implication of accepting the notion that the world is "rigged" and that some students are always going to be "winners" and that others are perennial "losers." Books is committed to a theological foundation for educational practice that permits us to move beyond ideological rhetoric. She employs the military and medical concept of triage—a system designed to produce the greatest benefit for the most likely to survive battlefield casualties by giving them full medical treatment and not using scarce resources on those who are not likely to survive—as a metaphor for the current state of American education. In reference to the statistics documenting inequality, Books (1992a) asserts: "I see in these numbers evidence of a dangerous social Darwinist consciousness that takes for granted that some people can, and maybe should, be forgotten, abandoned, or destroyed—because they are simply inferior" (p. 3). Books challenges critical educators particularly to move beyond a limited political and aesthetic language to a theological discourse that offers hope. She concludes that:

> while radical critics here [in the U.S.] often affirm the same faith in transformative possibility that Freire affirms, a larger narrative in (or with) which to sustain that faith is missing. Radical educational theory and criticism in this country are not bereft of ideals, but those ideals tend to be expressed in a political or aesthetic language and not in a religious or spiritual one, which, I believe, leaves us with a far-too-shallow discourse of hope. (1992a, pp. 20-21)

Sue Books provides a strong argument for engaging theology for constructing a more comprehensive and profound language of hope within the realm of moral religious traditions.

The moral basis of process education. Donald Oliver and Kathleen Gershman investigated the moral and spiritual dimensions of teaching and learning from a different perspective, that of process philosophy and process theology. Oliver and Gershman (1989) argued in their _Education, Modernity, and Fractured Meaning: Toward a Process Theory of Teaching and Learning_ that it is morally dangerous to remove people from the occasions of which they are a part. Process theology implies a moral vision of intimacy, community, balance, and connection. While this view is similar to Purpel's call for community and Books' aversion to triage, Oliver and Gershman expand moral community to include a deep involvement with the occasions of which educators are a part. They reject hierarchy and "a morality of principles, dialectics, personalities, and objects [as] intrinsically morally dangerous" (p. 152). They continue: "The core of immorality comes about when we are distanced from or disconnected from thoughts, actions, and impulses of which we, in fact, are a part" (p. 152). Oliver and Gershman are adamant that we cannot understand the environment in which we all participate unless we overcome the dangerous immorality of hierarchy and compartmentalization in institutions, especially schools and classrooms. They concluded: "The morality of process suggests that we share, in some degree, the diversity of humanity and the diversity of our natural environment in which we all have a common being" (p. 153).

Goodlad's moral dimensions of teaching. Another illustration of intersections between theological and traditional curricular concerns can be found in John I. Goodlad's (1990b) *The Moral Dimensions of Teaching.* Goodlad [see chapters 3, 4, and 13] links educational reform to moral issues, arguing—with contributors to this collection of essays—that all questions of educational reform are rooted in moral questions.

> What are public schools for in a democratic society? Whose interests are served and whose should be served in a system of compulsory education? What is the nature of the relationship between the interests of the individual, the family, the community, the state and society? Are there reasoned answers to these and like questions, or is there just an assortment of value positions each as "good" as the other? Or, to put it another way, are there not fundamental normative positions derived from moral ethical argument that serve to ground appropriate answers to crucial educational questions such as these? We are all agreed that the answer to the last question is yes, and their arguments, taken as a whole, spin a web of normative intrigue from the reconceptualization and reconstruction of professionalism in teaching, to the proper role and function of American public education, to the inherent moral and ethical relationship between those who teach and those who are taught. (Goodlad, 1990b, p. xi)

The search for answers to these questions is evident also in several recent efforts—a number of them conservative—to understand anew the curriculum ethically and morally (Jeffcoate, 1981; Wynne & Ryan, 1993; Snarey & Pavkov, 1992; Johnston, 1992; Lickona, 1992; Swartz, 1992; Strom, Sleeper, & Johnson, 1992; Beedy, 1992; Mosher, 1992; Howard & Kenny, 1992; Power & Higgins, 1992; Sadowsky, 1992; Farrell, 1987; Howe & Miramontes, 1992, Sockett, 1993; Jackson, Boostrom, & Hansen, 1993).

A totalizing public sphere? Historically, the discourses on curriculum and religion tended to be limited to specific denominational concerns regarding curricular issues such as school prayer, sex education, censorship, and related organizational issues such as funding formulas for parochial schools, voucher and choice plans, as well as general constitutional issues concerning the separation of church and state. Historically, these debates can be understood as constituting ideological struggles for political control of the school curriculum (Arons, 1983; Whitson, 1988b; Newman, 1991). On the right some have attempted to use church/state separation as justification for supporting denominational or special interest group influence. Illustrative of this view is the following:

> Without a complete separation of school and state, the governing process of American schooling has been increasingly undermined by unresolvable value conflict, and individual freedom of belief, expression, and political participation have been hobbled. . . . When government imposes the content of schooling it becomes the same deadening agent of repression from which the framers of the Constitution sought to free themselves. (Arons, 1983, p. 189)

On the left we hear this view repudiated. James Anthony Whitson [see chapter 5] characterized Arons' position as "an adventure in monopolis. . . . Only in Arons' dogmatic Wonderland is the realm of freedom confined to a private sector threatened by a monopolistic, totalizing public sphere" (Whitson, 1988b, p. 106). Arons, he concluded, is submerged in a "crude social Darwinism."

Time, place and voice. While historically the discourse on curriculum as theological text has been characterized by debates and disputes, mainstream curriculum scholars—Whitson is an exception—have tended to look the other way. In a 1984 (published in 1988) essay entitled "Time, Place, and Voice," William Pinar lamented that the right has wrapped itself in the mantle of religion and morality. In successfully identifying its political causes with transcendent rationales, the right—by the time of Reagan's landslide re-election in 1984—had successfully undermined traditional understandings of the separation of church and state. He argued that the left has tended toward secular experience, ignoring the Church due to its history of racism, sexism, militarism, and colonialism. Pinar pointed out that within the Christian Church movements are underway—black liberation and feminist theologies, for instance—which challenge this legacy, and which are, in general ways, in keeping with the agenda of the left, i.e. concerns for social, racial, gender, and economic justice. He continued that fundamentalists misunderstand Christianity, and that progressive educators must join with progressive churchpeople, including theologians, to resist the continuing threat from the right. He wrote:

> The traditional argument regarding the separation of church and state has broken down in our time. Perhaps it was always only partially descriptive. It is unmistakable now, however, that religious groups—mostly on the right and far right—are very actively involved in redefining the nature of the state, and of the public sphere generally. Unless those who are theologically informed speak out against the television preachers and self-promoters, against the demagogue disguised as preacher, the debates concerning the nature of the public sphere will be excessively influenced by the right and the far-right. (Pinar, 1988b, p. 275)

The conditions which provoked Pinar's concern in 1984 remain in the 1990s. The far-right remains vocal. For instance, while speaking to an audience of "Christian Coalition Republicans" on September 11, 1993, Patrick Buchanan lashed out against "multiculturalism" and criticized those who argue for equality of the world's many cultures. Buchanan reportedly said: "Our culture is superior. Our culture is superior because our religion is Christianity and that is the truth that makes men free" (Buchanan, 1993, p. A7).

Curriculum as theological text. In his 1984 essay Pinar found congruences between certain strands of homiletical work—the teaching of preaching—and certain strands of curriculum research, namely the autobiographical, the feminist, and the political. Just as the successful sermon can be seen as a blending of the minister's "witness" and the congregation's faith, curriculum understood as theological text can be regarded as involving a blend of the teacher as individual and the class as a community. Pinar explained:

> The notion of *blended force,* implying that the "personal witness" arises from a communal experience of time and place, experience animated by both the human and the divine, brings the self out of its obsessive self-absorption into a social and public sphere. . . . To become present among ourselves, not as atomized, acquisitive individuals posturing for individual gain but as individuated beings giving our shared experience form and reality through our words and actions, to become so present, the self allows its circumference to extend into its own past and into what is metaphysically transcendent. (Pinar, 1988b, p. 271)

For Pinar, autobiography is one means to achieve this "expanded" sense of self which allows the teacher to move beyond a mechanical concept of teaching and an informational sense of the curriculum to educational experience with authentically religious aspects.

Conclusion. We have seen in this section that an essential aspect of the project to understand curriculum is to understand that curriculum is also a moral and ethical project, grounded theologically. Moral and ethical issues had been abdicated to the extreme right wing; they are now being reclaimed as essential to the reconceptualized effort to understand curriculum, a project that is hermeneutical in its acknowledgment of its political, theological, practical, and spiritual dimensions. In the middle ages, theology was "queen of the sciences." From that zenith it was banished from the liberal arts curriculum, relegated to divinity schools. Respectable academics would not incorporate theological discourse in mainstream scholarship, victims of the Enlightenment bifurcation of truth from faith, knowledge from ethics, thought from action. These polar opposites are rewoven into one whole in contemporary curriculum theory. Those who pursue these issues still travel a risky path. As Slattery (1993) has noted, those curriculum scholars who employ moral, spiritual, and theological discourses face hostility from both secular critics and from traditional scholastic theologians. Finally, radical critics resist theological dialogue, victims too of an Enlightenment epistemology, as Bowers has shown. However, their own project to reclaim the public sphere, and in so doing, reclaim education, may require theological legitimation. Contemporary advances in ethics, cosmology, liberation theology, and hermeneutics, as we will see shortly, all contribute to this legitimation of the theological in contemporary curriculum discourse.

IV
Hermeneutics

The returning of life to its original difficulty is a returning of the possibility of the living Word. It is a return to the essential generativity of human life, a sense of life in which there is always something left to say, with all the difficulty, risk, and ambiguity that such generativity entails. Hermeneutic inquiry is thus concerned with the ambiguous nature of life itself
(David W. Jardine, 1992a, p. 119).

As we saw in chapter 8, hermeneutics, as derived from the phenomenological philosophers Martin Heidegger and Edmund Husserl, acknowledges that discourse is an essential constituent element of textual understanding. Understanding sets free what is hidden from view by layers of tradition, prejudice, and even conscious evasion. Hermeneutic interpretation, for Heidegger, was moving toward such understanding. While the influence of the hermeneutic tradition in chapter 8 was on the development of the effort to understand curriculum as phenomenological text, our focus here is on relevant theological foundations of hermeneutics and the development of related contemporary curriculum discourses in the hermeneutical tradition.

Hermeneutics, in its broadest formulation, is the theory of interpreting oral traditions, other verbal communications, written texts, and aesthetic products. Theologically it refers to the criteria for textual interperetation in order to establish normative religious and legal community practices. The Greek *Hermeneuein* (to interpret) refers to Hermes, the messenger of the Greek gods who explained the decisions of the gods to humans. More specifically, hermeneutics is concerned with understanding religious texts, canonical scriptures, and non-canonical writing within their own historical, cultural, and social milieux. The difficulty of such interpretive tasks is immense, some would contend impossible, because the worldviews of contemporary societies are far removed from ancient cosmologies in which the original text was produced. Hermeneutics, then, represents a concern for the process of understanding the meaning of text.

Biblical hermeneutics. Early Greek and Jewish thinkers were concerned with appropriate interpretation of the Torah, the prophets, and the wisdom literature of the Hebrew Scriptures. The allegorical method was employed to understand linguistic and grammatical components of scriptural texts to appropriate this meaning within the wider spiritual framework of the time (Jeanrond, 1988). Werner Jeanrond (1988) explained: "Philo of Alexandria united the Jewish and Greek hermeneutical traditions and developed the thesis that an interpretation should disclose the text's spiritual sense on the basis of an explanation of the text's literal sense" (p. 462). This concept of hermeneutics expanded with the influence of Christian interpreters who sought to confirm their belief in salvation in Jesus Christ. Hebrew scriptures were interpreted in the light of the Christian faith in Jesus, arguing that the promises to Israel were fulfilled:

The first major Christian hermeneut, Origen, emphasized the need for both ways of text-interpretation: the historical-grammatical (literal) sense and the spiritual sense (further distinguished in moral application and allegorical-mystical assessment) need to be understood by every interpreter of sacred Scriptures. (Jeanrond, 1988, p. 462)

Following Origen, Augustine developed his philosophy of language where the "sign" points to the "thing." Thomas Aquinas, author of the *Summa Theologiae*, became the definitive authority on textual interpretation. Since the thirteenth century, Aquinas was presumed to support the literal interpretation as the accurate bearer of theological truth. Jeanrond (1988), echoing centuries of Thomistic theology, wrote:

According to Aquinas, appropriate interpretation is the task of dogmatic theology while exegesis concentrates on the purely philological task of preparing the text for theological understanding. Since the Council of Trent (1545-1563), the ultimate decision on the criteria and the validity of results of biblical interpretation remained the prerogative of the teaching office (Magisterium) of the Roman Catholic Church. (p. 463)

Recent revisions of Aquinas. A major controversy concerning the status of Thomistic hermeneutics has occurred in the 1990s. Matthew Fox, a Dominican priest [until his removal in 1993] as was Aquinas, published in 1992 a new interpretation of the works of Thomas Aquinas entitled *Sheer Joy: Conversations with Thomas Aquinas on Creation Spirituality*. Fox had already been silenced for one year by Rome prior to the publication of this book, primarily as the result of an ongoing debate with Cardinal Joseph Ratzinger over the doctrinal purity of Fox's "creation spirituality" and "original blessings." In his work, Fox emphasizes a cosmological dimension of Christ and all of creation with the ontological goodness of human beings, rather than their sinfulness, as primary. Fox (1992) relies heavily on the hermeneutical interpretation of Hebrew and Christian scriptures to support his theology. And now, with the publication of *Sheer Joy*, Fox has produced a hermeneutical narrative study which reevaluates, and possibly replaces, seven centuries of Christian hermeneutics in the Thomastic tradition.

Fox begins by claiming that Thomas Aquinas was not a Thomist. Fox (1992) asserts: "I descholasticize Aquinas by interviewing him. . . . I . . . ask him *our* questions and allow him access to *our* pressing issues in spirituality. This is important because the questions that preoccupied his thirteenth-century contemporaries are of course not always the issues that concern us" (p. 2). Fox explains that his interview method is designed to uncover the "person behind the analytic mind" (p. 2) so as to interpret the meaning of philosophical categories such as "God" or "moral life" for contemporary society. Fox offers new interpretations of Aquinas' biblical commentaries to move beyond the scholastic methodology that typified Aquinas' other works. Fox (1992) writes: "Following the inner logic of the biblical text, he [Aquinas] is free to make connections, let his creative genius work, and allow his heart as well as his head to speak. Here his passion often comes tumbling out—especially when he is speaking of his favorite love, wisdom" (p. 3).

Fox is working to move beyond the modern era's fix on hermeneutical interpretation as mechanistic and literalistic: "Enlightenment prejudices have often been employed in interpreting Aquinas over the centuries" (p. 7). Fox terms his creation spirituality "postmodern" (p. 7), in a constructive rather than deconstructive sense. He continues to employ a hermeneutical method to recover premodern wisdom embedded in the Biblical treatises written by Thomas Aquinas in the thirteenth century and bring those insights to a contemporary, postmodern cosmology. Fox (1992) concludes:

> Some Thomists, while frequently rejecting much of Descartes and modern philosophy in argumentation, in fact, have often succumbed to rationalist tendencies in vigorous attempts to prove Aquinas was "scientific" and respectably rational. In doing so they have often limited themselves to the scholastic texts of Aquinas and the linear thinking of scholasticism. I believe Aquinas deserves—and we today require from Aquinas—a nonlinear celebration of his amazingly mystical *and* intellectual thought. (p. 12)

As students of curriculum, we can see in Matthew Fox's interpretation of Aquinas' Biblical commentaries a hermeneutical process that seeks to reevaluate scholastic theology. This is the hermeneutics of a double-edged sword that offers fresh insights for some but anxiety for others. Regardless of the ways that the work of Matthew Fox will be judged by scholars in years to come, he has intensified the debate over Biblical interpretation. For students of curriculum, Fox's work offers suggestive parallels to issues of text interpretation, and in particular, underlines the religious origins and present uses of hermeneutics.

Protestant Reformation. While the literalistic practice of Biblical interpretation in the Thomistic scholastic tradition continued to dominate through the Protestant Reformation, the emphasis on the scriptures during the Reformation promoted reading and understanding biblical texts by individual believers rather than papal officials. Thus, the Protestant Reformation had the effect of deemphasizing the interpretation of scripture by the Roman Magisterium. Following the Enlightenment, hermeneutics was reevaluated by Friedrich Schleiermacher (1768-1834) who rejected all formal, extra-textual authorities as illegitimate imposition on individual acts of understanding. Schleiermacher's work discredited special theological or legal hermeneutics:

> Rather, *every* written text must be understood both in terms of its individual sense (psychological understanding) and in terms of the linguistic procedures through which this sense is achieved (grammatical understanding). Hermeneutics is now understood as the art of understanding the sense of the text. Allegorical interpretation is ruled out, the text must be allowed to speak for itself. (quoted in Jeanrond, 1988, p. 463)

Schleiermacher's work paved the way for contemporary developments in hermeneutical understanding.

Paul Ricoeur (1981) contended that a movement of deregionalization began with the attempt to extract a general problem from the activity of interpretation which is each time engaged in different texts, and "the discernment of this central and unitary problematic is the achievement of Schleiermacher" (p. 45). Before Schleiermacher a philology (historical linguistic study) of classical texts and a literalistic exegesis (critical analysis) of sacred texts predominated. After Schleiermacher, it became clear that the hermeneutical process requires that the individual interpreter must discern the operations which are common to the two traditional branches of hermeneutics—philology and exegesis.

The hermeneutical circle. Awareness of historical conditions came to dominate hermeneutical understanding during the nineteenth century. Interpreters were now understood to move within a hermeneutical circle that required the specification of historical conditions in textual interpretation. During the twentieth century, Hans-Georg Gadamer called attention to preunderstandings which underpinned interpretation. Gadamer terms the conditions and the perspectives of interpreters their "horizons" and the act of understanding the sense of a text "the fusion of horizons." Through this fusion of horizons the interpreter enters the tradition of the text, and shares in the text's particular representation of truth. Gadamer's hermeneutics has been criticized primarily for "his refusal to allow for methodological controls of the act of interpretation" (Jeanrond, 1988, p. 463).

In his important work *Hermeneutics and the Human Sciences*, Paul Ricoeur (1981) argued that the first understanding of the sense of the text must be validated through some explanatory procedures to ensure the sense of the text. Ricoeur contended that the movement from a structuralist science to a structuralist philosophy is bound to fail. John Thompson (Ricoeur, 1981), translator of Ricoeur, explains: "For structuralism, insofar as it precludes the possibility of self-reflection, can never establish itself as a philosophy. 'An order posited as unconscious can never, to my mind, be more than a stage abstractly separated from an understanding of the self by itself; order in itself is thought located outside itself'" (Ricoeur, 1981, p. x). A genuinely reflective philosophy must nevertheless be receptive to the structuralist method, specifying its validity as an abstract and objective moment in the understanding of self and being. This forms one of the principal guidelines for Ricoeur's recent work on language and interpretation.

Ricoeur's interest evolved, in part, from his initial efforts to formulate a concrete ontology infused with the themes of freedom, finitude, and hope at the Sorbonne as a graduate student with Gabriel Marcel in the 1930s (Marcel, 1963, 1967). However, Ricoeur became intent on discovering a more rigorous and systematic method than he found in Marcel. The phenomenology of Edmund Husserl provided this method, and in turn led to the development of a reflective philosophy disclosing authentic subjectivity for understanding human existence. At the same time, Ricoeur was convinced that necessity and freedom were integral aspects of that existence. Finally, he turned to the problem of language and here he engaged hermeneutics. Ricoeur (1981) explains:

> I propose to organize this problematic [the historicity of human experience and communication in and through distance] around five themes: (1) the real-ization of language as a *discourse*; (2) the realization of discourse as a *structured work*; (3) the relation of *speaking to writing* in discourse and in the works of discourse; (4) the work of discourse as the *projection of a world*; (5) discourse and the work of discourse as the *mediation of self-understanding*. Taken together, these features constitute the criteria of textuality. (p. 132)

Ricoeur moves the hermeneutical process beyond theological understanding to a more general level of human understanding. His work has influenced a number of contemporary curriculum scholars, including William Reynolds (1989) [see chapter 8].

Ricoeur's theory of hermeneutical understanding was judged as politically naive by contemporary German philosopher Jurgen Habermas (1970). Habermas insisted that "only a critical and self-critical attitude toward inter-pretation could reveal possible systematic distortions in human communica-tion and their impact on our interpretive activity" (quoted in Jeanrond, 1988, p. 463). In its contemporary form, hermeneutics is faced with three interre-lated concerns: understanding, explanation, and critical assessment. The latter implies that a community of interpreters must work to unmask ideolog-ical distortions, limited "objective" interpretations, and analysis of the textu-ality of the text. These developments in hermeneutics in the nineteenth and twentieth century from Schleiermacher and Dilthey, to Heidegger and Husserl, to Gadamer and Ricoeur, and most recently Habermas have confronted theologians with a difficult dilemma: either engage philosophers in debates over the nature of hermeneutics in a mutually critical correlation [as proposed by David Tracy, 1981] or remain committed to a formalist, extra-textual hermeneutics of scripture as provided by direct divine inspira-tion and/or ecclesiastical authority. Other theologians propose dialogue with philosophers to make use of the philosophical development of hermeneutics to enhance Biblical and religious interpretation, including the identification and correction of possible ideological distortions in the understanding of the Christian faith, especially if the methodology included a wide spectrum of contributors to the development of a renewed faith-praxis in the Church.

Just as theology is being challenged to enter in the "hermeneutic circle" and to be open to new methodologies, so, too, the curriculum field faces similar challenges. There remain curriculum specialists at work today who would seek to return to the security of a traditional authority, the curricular magesterium that has provided legitimation for the paradigm of curriculum development (Hlebowitsh, 1993). Hermeneutics has influenced those who seek to understand curriculum phenomenologically as well as others who seek political and autobiographical understanding. Originally confined to scriptural interpretation, hermeneutics now engages all those involved in the project of understanding. For example, this tradition was discussed in a recent book on curriculum inquiry. Nelson Haggerson (Haggerson & Bowman, 1993) works to recover theological hermeneutics (primarily the realm of what he terms the mytho-poetic, the cosmological, and the narrative), while engaging the philosophical hermeneutics of Ricoeur, Gadamer, and Heidegger. Haggerson's scholarship has promoted the importance of qualitative and interpretive research throughout the 1980s, and it appears that in the 1990s he is part of an intensification of interest in hermeneutics in the field. Haggerson and Bowman (1993) bring to contemporary curriculum debates what Tracy (1981) has brought to theology, a mutually critical correlation between hermeneutics as understanding, explanation, and critical assessment from the multiple viewpoints of theology and the human sciences.

V
Liberation Theology: Kincheloe and Slattery

If faith is a commitment to God and human beings, it is not possible to live in today's world without a commitment to the process of liberation.
(Gustavo Gutierrez, 1968, p. 64)

The reconceptualization of curriculum and theology is a process of conscientizing and liberating; it is an autobiographical journey and a spiritual phronesis.
(Patrick Slattery, 1992b, p. 21)

A Latin American movement. One of the most important and controversial developments in contemporary theology is the Liberation Theology movement which began in Latin America in the 1960s [see chapter 14]. This movement is associated with—some would say indebted to—Paulo Freire and other educators working in Latin America [see chapters 5 and 14]. It emerged as a response to the massive poverty in South and Central America, the oppression of indigenous populations during colonial period, and the socio-economic repression of poor and marginalized peoples in modern times. Liberation Theology professes a "preferential option for the poor" and it addresses social issues that affect the poor within a Christian vision of reality, particularly the Roman Catholic tradition of social justice as promulgated in Vatican documents such as *Gaudium et Spes* (Flannery, 1975), and the general Conferences of Latin American Bishops from Medellin, Columbia in 1968 to Santo Domingo, Dominican Republic in 1992, as well as Biblical imperatives of the prophets. Theological studies by scholars such as Uruguayan Jesuit Juan Luis Segundo (1973), Brazilian Franciscan Leonardo Boff (1979), Basque Jesuit Jon Sobrino (1985) of El Salvador, and the most prominent Liberation Theologian, Peruvian Gustavo Gutierrez, author of *A Theology of Liberation: History, Politics and Salvation* (1973), have all contributed to the development of Liberation Theology. The work of Gutierrez and other theologians was challenged and condemned by many within the Roman curia and by right-wing governments and wealthy landowners in Latin America.

As has been the case historically when new theological developments challenge the *Sitz im Laben* (worldview) of institutional churches, several liberation theologians have also been "silenced." Additionally, Archbishop Oscar Romero of El Salvador, one of a number of bishops who actively supported Liberation Theology in the 1970s, was assassinated in 1980. However, the attempts to silence the liberation movement, whether with papal bulls or with bullets, have only strengthened the resolve of the *communautes de base* (basic ecclesial communities). The intense debates over the theological and social foundations of Liberation Theology are evident in the numerous publications from the left and right. The scholarship of Gustavo Gutierrez and the response of the Vatican congregation reveal many parallels to the current debates between critical scholars and those entrenched in a bureaucratic or "banking" (Freire, 1968) model of education.

Liberation and the Reconceptualization. An important step was taken at the 1992 Bergamo Conference on Curriculum Theory and Classroom Practice to begin to link Liberation Theology and the reconceptualized field of curriculum. Papers on Liberation Theology were presented by Joe Kincheloe (1992b) ["Liberation Theology and the Attempt to Establish an Emancipatory System of Meaning"] and Patrick Slattery (1992b) ["Liberation Theology and Postmodern Pedagogy"]. Additionally, Peter McLaren and Thomas Oldenski responded to these papers, employing notions of critical pedagogy. McLaren reported on his travels in Latin America, and Oldenski reviewed his research in inner city Catholic schools in East St. Louis, Illinois. Oldenski's research is reminiscent of Jonathan Kozol's (1991) documentation of the economic and social plight of East St. Louis public schools in his *Savage Inequalities.* However, Odenski's work seeks to incorporate the theological dimensions by examining religious schools, using the methodology [see below] of Liberation Theology.

Kincheloe's emancipatory research. Joe Kincheloe introduced the possibility of Liberation Theology informing postmodern pedagogy and emancipatory research methodologies by suggesting that theology could serve as a grounding for a critical system of educational ethics. Kincheloe (1992) argued:

> As it attacks the modernist cult of objectivism, Liberation Theology lays the groundwork for an emancipatory system of meaning on which a critical pedagogy can be built. In its refusal to accept history as a record of what has prevailed, i.e., the record of the established and successful—Liberation Theology exposes the fact that the conquered and defeated have received the short end of the historical stick, that the unfulfilled dreams of the commoners have not found their way into the "official story." Pedagogically, this exclusion contributes to oppression when students from subjected groups are taught the science and culture of the dominant society without this knowledge passing through a filter constructed by a historically grounded self-consciousness. (p. 1)

Slattery and autobiography. Patrick Slattery linked Kincheloe's proposal for historically grounded self-consciousness and Liberation Theology with

Pinar's (Pinar & Grumet, 1976) four autobiographical moments described in *Toward a Poor Curriculum*. Slattery (1992b) explained the link:

> Personal and global salvation emerging from a commitment to justice and humanization is the proleptic vision of Liberation Theology. It offers an understanding of time, history, and hope which parallels contemporary curriculum discourses such as the method of *currere* developed by William Pinar. It is interesting that Pinar, like Gutierrez, begins his commentary on *currere* paraphrasing Freire's (1968) *Pedagogy of the Oppressed*. The human vocation, Freire, Pinar, and Gutierrez insist, is humanization; the vision of pedagogy is a dialogical relationship with students; the goal of pedagogy is to cultivate thought and action in praxis. Pinar (Pinar & Grumet, 1976) contends: "The method of *currere*, regressive-progressive-analytical-synthetical in procedure, is a systematic attempt to reveal . . . individual life history and the historical movement. Because its motive and aim are humanization, I see it as consonant with Freire's pedagogy. I see it as complementary to explicitly political efforts" (pp. 106-107). In Liberation Theology, human life in its entirety is seen as an encounter with God's salvific grace. There is a regressive moment in this encounter: a baptism in the death of the historical Jesus, where one enters into the past, meditates on it, submerges oneself in its waters, but does not succumb to its despair. In the progressive movement, the future enters into the historical present revealing the glory of resurrection. The analytical movement is the awareness that religious praxis is also my praxis. Thus, eternity (past, present, and future) become embedded in human existence through grace. Finally, in the synthetical moment, the fullness of time is recognized and celebrated. Thus, spirituality becomes an autobiographic movement which allows the individual to become present to shared experiences of humanity. (pp. 20-21)

The challenge of Liberation Theology for postmodern pedagogy is to recognize that present solutions to social and educational problems cannot be addressed outside of the context of an autobiographical relationship with the past and the future. Pinar (1988b) explains:

> By remaining, perhaps unknowingly, integrated with one's past and simultaneously being extended into an experience of God, one is capable of being fully present in the sensory here and how, not estranged from it, hiding behind a "persona" concocted to defend against the human other. (p. 275)

Here Pinar, like Moltmann, Gutierrez, and other theologians, explains that the proleptic experience of the future entering into the present and reclaiming the past is essential for human development, authentic praxis, social reform, and ultimately an experience of transcendence. It is also the basis of Slattery's constructive postmodern pedagogy and the development of the self-consciousness proposed by Kincheloe. Slattery (1992b) concluded: "The reconceptualization of curriculum and theology is a process of conscientizing and liberating; it is an autobiographical journey and a spiritual phronesis" (p. 21).

Liberation Theology can expand the dialogue with those who believe that critical pedagogy has appropriated the language of empowerment, hope, and eschatology from theology, stripped it of its spiritual, cosmological, and autobiographical imperatives, and converted critical theory into an empty political ideology. The Vatican curia of the Catholic Church has concluded that Liberation Theology has done this same thing by reducing faith to Marxist revolution and materialism. This reductionist view of both critical pedagogy and Liberation Theology is a common critique by traditionalists in both curriculum theory and in theology.

Five frames of analysis. There are five frames of reference that permeate Liberation Theology and postmodern pedagogy, as elaborated by Slattery (1992b). First, Liberation Theology emerged within the context of 100 years of Roman Catholic social encyclicals, beginning with *Rerum Novarum* in 1891 which legitimated theological reflection on social justice issues. Liberation Theology must not be mistaken as simply a political or social ideology. Rather, it is rooted in an overwhelming religious experience of justice. The encyclicals of the twentieth century have challenged the global community to explore the question of justice and freedom in society. Pope Leo XIII's 1891 encyclical addressed the condition of human labor and the political implications of human dignity. It also addressed the pressing problems of industrialization and the oppression of workers. However, the most influential encyclical on Liberation Theology was the Vatican II document *Gaudium et Spes* in 1965 which described the church in its relationship to the world. This document defined human existence socially and referred to the social dimension of sin, a most significant theological articulation.

Some would contend that the social encyclicals emerged out of the guilt of institutional religion for its complicity in centuries of oppression of indigenous cultures. Even a recent Guatemalan bishops' pastoral letter contends that "the Catholic church committed grave errors and sins [when] Christianization was confused with Westernization" (Indian Pastorals, 1992). Others argue that the encyclicals express an authentic commitment to social justice. Of course, the encyclicals alone do not explain the entire history of social justice positions of the Roman Catholic Church in the twentieth century: for example, the relationship between the papacy and Mussolini, the Lateran Treaty of 1929, the Concordat of 1931, the condemnation of Action Francaise by Pius XI in 1914 (published in 1926), the rise of the Catholic Worker Movement, the reaction of the church to Hitler during world War II, Pope John Paul II's criticisms of Liberation Theology and silencing of theologian Leonardo Boff, and the forced removal of clerics from political office around the world, all offer additional perspectives on the complex and sometimes contradictory positions of the Catholic church on social justice issues.

The second frame. While the influence of European theologians such as German Jesuit Karl Rahner and German Lutheran Jurgen Moltmann, especially in the renewal of eschatology, is important to understanding Liberation Theology, the Latin American context is ultimately most significant in the development of this movement. Theologians contend that there have been two important transformations in the history of Christianity: first when the church ceased to be a Jewish sect in the second century and began developing a European identity, and second when theology ceased to be Eurocentric following the Second Vatican Council's recognition of a "world church" in the 1960s and began developing a global consciousness. The emergence of the global church supported the birth of Liberation Theology.

The third frame. The commitment to a "preferential option for the poor" by Liberation theologians is intimately related to Paulo Freire's critical pedagogy, particularly as expressed in his "Conscientizing as a Way of Liberating" (1971). This relationship between theology and pedagogy has informed critical postmodern scholars and helped offset egocentric ideological struggles for intellectual dominance. Ideological entrapment is avoided with authentic deference to the theological rootedness of the human experience within unique socio-historical and cultural milieux. There are two ways that dominant theories and theologies can both become destructively ideological, according to Rosemary Radford Ruether in "Christology and the Latin American Liberation Theology." Ruether (1983a) explains:

> One [destructive approach] is by directly identifying Christ and the church with the social hierarchies of [the status quo] system and by making God the author and vindicator of it. The second way is indirect through divorcing religion from life, body from soul, Christian hope from human hope. In this way the message of liberation is alienated and direct to a never-never-land beyond the stars which has no concrete implications for the world. (1983a, pp. 26-26)

The "preferential option for the poor," which is the foundation of Liberation Theology, must not, according to Ruether and other theologians, be sacrificed on the altar of any ideology.

The fourth frame. The Vatican reaction to the work of Liberation theologians reflects a desperate attempt on the part of some institutional clerics to cling to traditional Eurocentric systematic theology. However, it also reflects a genuine concern on the part of others that the Christian Gospel as a message of freedom and liberation not be restricted to an earthly materialism. While the Vatican document *Instructions on Certain Aspects of the "Theology of Liberation"* (Sacred Congregation, 1984) is characterized by some as unduly worried about the influence of Marxist thought on the development of Liberation Theology, it does offer the following clarification:

> This warning [about Marxist thought] should in no way be interpreted as a disavowal of all those who want to respond generously and with an authentic evangelical spirit to the "preferential option for the poor." It should not at all serve as an excuse for those who maintain an attitude of neutrality and indifference in the face of the tragic and pressing problems of human misery and injustice. It is, on the contrary, dictated by a certitude that the serious ideological deviations which it points out tend inevitably to betray the cause of the poor. . . . More than ever the church intends to condemn abuses, injustices, and attacks against freedom . . . especially for the poor. (Sacred Congregation, 1984, pp. 4-5)

The fifth frame. The Vatican reaction to Liberation Theology offers an opportunity for students of curriculum to reflect on the resistance of educational bureaucrats, right-wing politicians, and liberal philanthropists. This reflection can lead to refinements and advancements in our understanding of curriculum generally, and in political theory more narrowly. Additionally, it may point to the inclusion of theology in any comprehensive understanding of curriculum. Liberation Theology might also create a broader base of acceptance for the reconceptualized field with the public at large, increasing the possibility of authentic democratic educational reform in the United States. This is similar to the hope of Liberation theologians, including Jon Sobrino (1985). In his *Spirituality of Liberation: Toward Political Holiness*, Sobrino wrote:

> I speak of "political Holiness" and of "Liberation with Spirit." The intuition is the same. Spirit and practice must join hands. Without spirit, practice can always degenerate. Without practice, spirit will remain vague, sidelined, even alienating. [This] ought to be sufficient to allay suspicions concerning [Liberation] theology. . . . There can be no honest denial that Latin American theology is concerned with spirituality [as] a basic dimension of theology. It is precisely the application of theory to practice. (1985, pp. ix-x)

It is noteworthy in this regard that curriculum theorist James B. Macdonald had concluded that "the act of theorizing is an act of faith, a religious act. . . . Curriculum theory is a prayerful act" (cited in Schubert, 1992a, p. 60). Alfred North Whitehead (1929) also insisted that "the essence of education is that it be religious" (p. 14). It is this commitment to a spirituality and a practice of liberation that is integral to liberation theology and critical postmodern theory in the effort to truly effect a "preferential option for the poor" in society, in the churches, and in the schools.

Liberation Theology methodology. While Liberation Theology is not a unified theoretical field, Gutierrez's methodology is representative of the threads that hold the tapestry together. His early work presents an analysis of the human condition in Latin America and explores theological and Biblical teachings that apply to these conditions in order to reevaluate Christian principles in light of poverty and oppression in Latin American culture. His methodology incorporates the social sciences: economics, history, sociology, and political theory. This is done not only to explain the social milieu of Latin America, but also to concretize the ethical consequences of the response to social injustice. On a deeper structural level, Gutierrez challenges previous theological understandings that have failed to address social oppression. In particular, he emphasizes that sin and salvation are not confined to individual personal realities but also to social structures (Gutierrez, 1973, pp. 36-37). Like all Liberation theologians, Gutierrez reveals an explicit commitment to the poor with a call for social action for liberation of the poor. This praxis, he insists, is at the heart of the corporate responsibility of the church. Social theories emerge from praxis and are generated in the theological context. Finally, Gutierrez claims that his methodology is connected to Marxism only incidentally and not intrinsically. Marxism is used by some, but not all, Liberation theologians in much that same way that some social scientists in Europe and North America use it as a vehicle to analyze society. While some Liberation theologians use Marxist language, one scholar concludes that "no Liberation Theologian has incorporated an integral Marxist vision of reality which would be incompatible with Christian faith" (Haight, 1988, p. 573). To emphasize, the connection between Liberation Theology and Marxism is not seen as intrinsic; it stems from the Latin American situation of poverty and oppression which first Marxism and now churches are both addressing.

Gutierrez comments. Gutierrez (1968) reflected on Liberation Theology in "Toward A Theology of Liberation" when he wrote:

> Theology is a progressive and continuous understanding . . . of an existential . . . commitment to history concerning the Christian's location in the development of humanity and the living out of faith. Theology is a reflection, a re-flecting that comes after action. Theology is not first; the commitment is first . . . Theology, therefore, will accompany that pastoral activity of the church—that is, the presence of the church in the world. . . . If faith is a commitment to God and human beings, it is not possible to live in today's world without a commitment to the process of liberation. (pp. 63-64)

The Vatican responds. In 1983 the Vatican Congregation for the Doctrine of Faith published a scathing attack on the theology of Gustavo Gutierrez which included the following charges:

> The urgent attention focused on the scandal of the masses of Latin America and the uncritical acceptance of the theology of this situation explain the seductiveness of the theology of Gustavo Gutierrez. . . . Because of its "scientific" character, Gutierrez accepts the Marxist conception of history, which is a history of conflict, structured around the class struggle and requiring commitment on behalf of the oppressed in their struggle for liberation. . . . As an excuse for eliminating every "dualism," the author proposes a dialectical relationship between liberation-salvation and liberation-politics. Although he does not admit it, he falls into a temporal messianism and reduces the growth of the kingdom to the increase in justice. . . . The influence of Marxism is clear both in the understanding of truth and the notion of theology. Orthodoxy is replaced by orthopraxy, for truth does not exist except within praxis—that is, in the commitment to revolution. . . . Therefore, the objective is to make of Christianity a means of mobilizing for the sake of the revolution. By its recourse to Marxism, this theology can pervert an inspiration that is evangelical: the consciousness and the hopes for the poor. (Hennelly, 1990, pp. 349-350)

These statements are based on the assumption that there is *not* a political function of theology *nor* a social construction of knowledge and religious dogmas. In the Vatican declaration, theologians are advised that divine revelation is separate from the social context. The Vatican's charges did not go unanswered. The renowned theologian Karl Rahner came to the defense of Gutierrez in a letter written to Cardinal Juan Ricketts of Lima, Peru in 1984.

Rahner defends the orthodoxy of Gutierrez's theology and argues that the social sciences are essential but not normative to the development of theology [Hennelly, 1990, p. 351).

Gutierrez expands the dialogue. The tone of Gutierrez himself, in an interview with the Peruvian newspaper *La Republica* on September 14, 1984, demonstrates a commitment to justice and clarity in his response to the Vatican.

> I believe that being a Christian in Latin America today means proclaiming in action and in word, the message of life—precisely in the face of the reality of the premature and unjust death of so many of this continent's people. . . . It also means having the courage to examine the underlying causes of the painful, incredible situation of violence in which we are living. . . . I admit that this [Marxist analysis found in Liberation Theology] is one of the central criticisms. It is necessary to be very clear on this point: to deal with the poverty—the inhuman poverty—lived by the great majority of the inhabitants of our country, and to shed the light of the gospel upon it, we must attain the most exact understanding available of the causes of this situation of poverty. In theology, the contemporary social sciences must be used critically, just as any working tool must. . . . Theology must go to its own sources, but out of its grounding in faith. It cannot disdain anything that will allow it to more fully understand the situation of those to whom the gospel must announced. (cited in Hennelly, 1990, pp. 419-420)

Questions. The ongoing discourses on Liberation Theology and the dialogues between Gustavo Gutierrez and the Vatican raise the following questions: is Liberation Theology primarily a political project? Is it primarily a religious movement? A revolutionary critique? An ideological construct challenging economic boundaries? A campaign for social and religious literacy? Is Liberation Theology an existential project disconnected from religious salvation, or does it engender an eschatological sense of the eternal in the present struggle for justice? Can Liberation Theology inform contemporary curriculum theory, or is it empty denominational religious rhetoric destined to disappoint curriculum scholars as well as the poor? Of course, this final question is our central concern, and several scholars have affirmed the role of Liberation Theology in curriculum discourse (cf. Purpel, Shapiro, Books, Slattery, Kincheloe, Oldenski, and McLaren, among others). Indeed, scholarship of the 1990s concludes that Liberation Theology can inform and enrich our critical understanding of curriculum if it develops a comprehensive and global worldview in the development of a liberatory praxis. Ultimately, the theology of liberation is a commitment to hope that leads to praxis. Likewise, much reconceptualized curriculum theory is also committed to hope—a hope rooted in democratic reform, social justice, and liberatory praxis.

A new cosmology. Liberation Theology is committed to a vision of history, time, and hope that recognizes that the cosmos is created in freedom and empowered by grace. Liberation Theology recognizes a continuity among life, death, and resurrection. Salvation is neither disconnected from the present by relegating it to an extra-terrestrial experience after death, nor is it objectified in a concrete materialism that refuses to recognize the lure of the future toward transcendence. Rather, salvation is understood as a proleptic event where the past and the future, while retaining their unique identity, exist as integrally embedded in the experience of the present moment. This dimension of Liberation Theology is its most important contribution to the advance of a socio-historical theology of emancipation: a future that is accessible to the marginalized who have been denied their birthright of freedom and hope. Liberation Theology argues that human action must contribute to the ultimate end of things, otherwise, creative human freedom and even human existence in the present is ultimately meaningless. Additionally, it insists that the exercise of human freedom establishes a continuity between the values of social justice in Latin America and salvation at the end-time. Gutierrez (1968) writes: "I emphasize that the work of building the earth is not a preceding stage, not a stepping stone, but already the work of salvation" (p. 71). He also establishes the relationship between creation and salvation where "creation is included in the process of salvation, which is God's self-communication" (p. 71). For Gutierrez and Liberation theologians, this self-communication is grace, and it has the power to transform both the individual and society, unlike modern fundamental theology that divorces the individual from the world because grace is only a protective shield guarding the believer from natural evil. In contrast, Gutierrez (1968) concludes:

> To labor to transform this world is to save it. As Marx has clearly seen, work as a humanizing element normally tends through this transformation of nature to construct a society that is more just and worthy of human beings. . . . Every offense, every humiliation, every alienation of human labor is an obstacle to the work of salvation. (p. 72)

The "already" and the "not yet." Just as most curriculum theorists now acknowledge that the Reconceptualization has occurred, so, too some theologians contend that Liberation Theology has become the norm for all theology. This is true, they insist, despite the conservative entrenchment of Pope John Paul II and his cautions about Liberation Theology in his visits to Latin America in the 1980s and 1990s. A careful reading of recent Vatican encyclicals, analysis of the Pope's role in the rise of the Solidarity movement in his native Poland and the fall of communism in Europe, and finally, the international travels of the pope, all demonstrate the powerful impact of Liberation Theology, even on a vocal critic such as John Paul II. Jesuit theologian Roger Haight (1988) contends that this:

> represents the completion of the cycle of the mandate of Vatican II, that is, for the inculturation of its teachings at the periphery in the local churches and, [today] the reappropriation of what was learned there at the center, i.e., by the Vatican. Liberation Theology is now the universal theology of the Roman Catholic church. (p. 576)

In both spheres—theology and curriculum theory—reconceptualizations have occurred. The former reconceptualization is reflected in the fact that Liberation Theology is a socio-theology that is held together by the proleptic understanding of the fullness of the "already" and the "not yet" proposed by Ernst Bloch (1970) and the God of the future drawing us "ahead" rather than "upward" as explained by Jurgen Moltmann (1967, 1969). It is rooted in the ancient irony of many eastern religious traditions where one must lose one's life or empty one's self in order to find peace, harmony, freedom, or, in western terms, salvation.

The foregoing discussion of Liberation Theology illustrates one linkage reconceptualized curriculum theory might make with theology. The traditional separation between church and state in the United States has functioned to keep theological considerations out of curriculum theory, effectively ceding religious bases for moral arguments to right-wing fundamentalists. In its linkage of theology and politics, Liberation Theology parallels important elements of reconceptualized curriculum theory, and in the future, may significantly influence its contours.

VI
Eschatology, Cosmology, and Feminist Theology:
Slattery, Mitrano, and Noddings

This fuller quality of ontological knowledge requires that we have available a range of living metaphors within culture—not only the machine metaphor that dominates the modern paradigm but also the metaphors of organic life and transcendent dance.
(Donald W. Oliver & Kathleen W. Gershman, 1989, p. 3)

An eschatological curriculum. Traditionally, theology has turned to the study of final or apocalyptic events—eschatology—to attempt to explain phenomena of destruction, decadence, and death. Faced with sin and irredeemable evil in the physical world, theologians turned to the idea of a heaven as justifying suffering in this life. Marxist analysis attacked this theology for perpetuating injustice and tolerating oppression. Justice delayed was justice denied. John Dewey also challenged traditional theology; he distinguished between "religion" and the "religious" in *A Common Faith* (1934a), and he criticized the churches for having abandoned their prophetic voice. [In fact, in a 1908 piece entitled "Religions and Our Schools," Dewey called for a moratorium on religious instruction, until a narrow supernaturalism was abandoned; see Westbrook, 1991, p. 418.] The concept of the future and utopian visions is at the heart of these critiques of traditional eschatology. Recent developments in eschatology have been employed by Patrick Slattery to rethink the idea of curriculum as theological text and address the concerns of Dewey and critical theorists. Slattery reports that contemporary eschatology rejects the traditional bifurcation of time and space into here and hereafter and reconceives the future as the directive property of the present: "The future enters into the present as a persuasive and directive force encouraging individuals to overcome evil. . . . This framework allows proleptic eschatology to provide hope and liberation in the midst of evil in the world" (Slattery, 1989, p. xii).

In his *Toward an Eschatological Curriculum Theory,* Slattery (1989) posits important parallels between contemporary theology and curriculum theory. In both fields he finds themes of transformation, emancipation, relatedness, and temporality. The modernistic conception of the isolated individual, captured in measurable time and space, unable to establish authentic relationships of intimacy and care, unable to affect the future, has given way to psychoanalytic (Pinar, 1991) and postmodern (Lather, 1991; Pinar & Reynolds, 1992a; Doll, 1993a) views of the past as present. Slattery outlines a postmodern vision in which the individual person, in relation to others and connected to a meaningful past and to an emerging future, is essential for social transformation and global survival (Slattery, 1989, 1992a, 1992b).

A vision of liberation and hope. Out of this framework for eschatological theology, Slattery (1992b) identifies parallels with the themes of the Reconceptualization of curriculum studies. Slattery concludes that the emphasis in contemporary theology on processes of transformation, emancipation, liberation, relatedness, and time offer significant support to certain strands of contemporary—and reconceptualized—curriculum studies. In both fields, the view of past experience as an integral part of present reality represents a shift away from the presentism of a modernistic perspective. The latter isolates the individual in quantifiable time and space, unable to establish relationships and incapable of affecting the future course of events. In contrast, a postmodern vision regards the individual in relation to others, connected to a meaningful past and an emergent future, capable of influencing not only individual transformation, but social change and global survival as well. Slattery's eschatological curriculum theory challenges curricularists to move well beyond the Tylerian understanding of curriculum as the development of institutional programs, and beyond the traditional apocalyptic understanding of eschatology as only the last events at the end of time. He challenges the field to move toward a new vision of curriculum rooted in liberation and eschatological hope.

Process philosophy. The eschatological dimension is also evident in the work of those scholars who approach the study of curriculum from the process philosophy associated with the contributions of Alfred North Whitehead, Charles Hartshorne, and Henri Bergson. A national organization, the Association of Process Philosophy of Education (APPE), meets biannually to investigate process issues and the curriculum. Additionally, the journal *Process Studies* is published by the Center for Process Studies at the School of Theology at the Claremont Colleges in southern California. As do eschatological studies, process philosophy of education investigates a notion of time that is durational (Bergson, 1946; Huebner, 1967; Heidegger, 1962), proleptic (Whitehead, 1929, 1933; Slattery, 1989, 1992a), and cosmological (Davies, 1990; Oliver & Gershman, 1989; Doll, 1993a). Durational time is essential to process perspectives that seek to reintegrate a fragmented curriculum and become transformative (LePage, 1987). Whitehead (1929) wrote about the importance of reverence in understanding the aims of education, and he concluded that "the foundation of reverence is this perception, that the present holds within itself the complete sum of existence, backwards and forwards, that whole amplitude of time which is eternity" (p. 14). Wrestling with the concepts of time and eternity is a central task of process philosophy and theology.

Premodern theology promoted a futuristic eschatology which reserved salvation to life after death. This theology of the "delayed Parousia" was of particular concern to John Dewey (1934a). Dewey believed that this notion of the future caused churches to lose their prophetic calling for society. The response of modernity to the parousia has been the rejection of religion and spirituality in favor of a realized eschatology which locates all hope in present experience disconnected from any meaningful past or immanent future. Marxist philosophy and critical theory correctly recognized the economic and social abuses that can result from adherence to a premodern eschatology, but too often Marxist traditions have rejected any theological perspective at all. Ernst Bloch (1968, 1970, 1986) attempted to reconcile Marxism and eschatology, and contemporary curriculum theorists explore hope from multiple perspectives.

However, it is proleptic eschatology and process philosophy, particularly as expressed in the theology of Jurgen Moltmann and Carl Peter, the philosophy of Alfred North Whitehead, Charles Hartshorne, Ernst Bloch, John Dewey, Henri Bergson, and Eric Fromm, and the curriculum theory of James B. Macdonald, Dwayne E. Huebner, and Patrick Slattery that expose the futility of futuristic and realized eschatologies. Process philosophy and eschatology both recognize the integral relationship between the past, present, and future, and also the impossibility of hope without a future that is related to the present. Whitehead (1933) commented:

> The doctrine of the immanence of past occasions in the occasions which are the future, relative to them, has been sufficiently discussed. . . . The past has an objective existence in the present which lies in the future beyond itself. But the sense in which the future can be said to be immanent in occasions antecedent to itself, and the sense in which contemporary occasions are immanent in each other, are not so evident in terms of the doctrine of the subject-object structure of experience. It will be simpler first to concentrate upon the relation of the future to the present. (chapter XII, section I, p. 191)

Whitehead continued by explaining that the future exists in relation to the present, a concept apparently lost in mass culture in contemporary society. It is especially evident at graduations when students are told that they are "the future of the world."

The delayed parousia of theology became a dominant metaphor for education, career choices, and democratic living. This is clearly a major factor in the fragmentation which is so firmly embedded in mainstream academic psychology. Whitehead warned: "Cut away the future, and the present collapses, emptied of its proper content. Immediate existence requires the insertion of the future in the crannies of the present" (chapter XII, section I). [In his *The Minimal Self: Psychic Survival in Troubled Times*, Christopher Lasch (1984) makes a similar point working from a different tradition.] In what sense is the future embedded in the present? Whitehead explained that the future is immanent in the present by reason of the fact that the present bears in its own essence the relationships which it will express in the future. The present "thereby includes in its essence the necessities to which the future must conform. The future is there in the present, as a general fact belonging to the nature of things" (1933, chapter XII, section III, p. x). As we are seeing, the theological dimension of the "nature of things" is of profound significance in understanding curriculum.

Feminist theology and curriculum. Writing in 1979, Barbara Mitrano (1979b, 1979c) [see chapter 7] contended that feminist theologians and curriculum theorists have much in common. Both are interested in lived experience and social transformation, concepts which ought not to be denuded of spiritual content. Mitrano (1979c) explained:

> Another part of the reason I believe the feminist voice needs to be made clearer in curriculum theory lies in the insight which it can bring to the areas of spirituality and community. The feminist example has shown that contact with Self is indeed a spiritual, educational experience which leads to community and social action. Feminist experience in women's studies courses has yielded new insight into a mutual concern of feminists and reconceptualists; that the content of courses be congruent with the lived experience of those who constitute the meaning of that experience. Since women have for so long been silent because of their disembodiment from their Selves, their understanding of fragmentation and madness goes very deep. (p. 219)

Mitrano's call for links between feminist theology and curriculum theory is evident in the work of, among others, Mary Daly (1973, 1978), and by Denise Lardner Carmody (1991) who calls for an alliance among feminism, religion, and education. Additionally, Mary Elizabeth Moore (1989) has included a feminist perspective in her *The Art of Teaching from the Heart: The Heart of the Matter* in which she calls for a process-oriented approach to teaching rooted in reverent relationships.

Nel Noddings' [see also chapters 7 and 13] important scholarship (1981, 1984, 1985, 1986, 1989, 1992a, 1992b) also speaks to feminist theological concerns. In *Caring: A Feminine Approach to Ethics and Moral Education*, Noddings (1984) proposed an ethics based on caring grounded in receptivity, relatedness, and responsiveness. Noddings' approach differs from traditional, rationalistic ethics. It differs as well from those traditional theological conceptions of human nature that begin in sinfulness and depravity. Noddings' ethic of caring in this sense parallels Matthew Fox's creation spirituality discussed earlier. Noddings argues that moral education should begin with care for other human persons rather than with rationality, a view other feminist theologians share. However, Noddings cautions that her educational philosophy is feminist only in the sense that "all of humanity can participate in the feminine ethic" she develops:

> As in development of the ethic itself, I shall refrain from the use of jargon often associated with moral education. I shall not . . . discuss "stages" of moral development and . . . I shall not dwell on moral reasoning. Is my view, then, "affectivist?" I shall reject that label, although both the ethic and the resulting recommendations for moral education rest on a foundation of affective relation. I reject the label because such labels are often affixed simplistically, and the notion arises that one who insists on recognizing the affective base of morality must, therefore, minimize the role of cognitive activity. One cannot dismiss thinking and reasoning from ethical conduct, and I have made no attempt to do this. It is a matter of emphasis and of origin. When I have recognized the affective "I must," I must think effectively about what I should do in response to the other. I do not respond out of blind sentiment, but I put my best thinking at the service of the ethical affect. If I exclude cognition, I fall into vapid and pathetic sentimentality; if I exclude affect—or recognize it only as an accompaniment of sorts—I risk falling into self-serving or unfeeling rationalization. . . . I shall accept the label "feminine" but only if we understand that all of humanity can participate in the feminine as I am describing it. (pp. 171-172)

In a more recent work entitled *Women and Evil*, Noddings (1989) investigates traditional theological and psychological understandings of the relationship between women and evil. Rooted in women's experience, Noddings' describes her project: "Through the use of examples I attempt to draw out the logic of situations in which we face evil and to probe for the underlying commonalities in our experience with evil. What we will find is a pervasive fear of pain, separation, and helplessness" (1989, p. 3). Noddings insists that evil must be examined phenomenologically rather than through the lens of traditional moralistic pronouncements which often branded women as evil or especially suspectible to evil. Ironically, women have also been exalted as possessing maternal goodness, often framed as a madonna or goddess. Noddings explains: "The paradox is resolved when we realize that the dichotomous view of women as evil (because of her attraction to matters of the flesh) and good (because of her compassion and nurturing) served as a means of control" (p. 3). Women perceived themselves as good when they lived lives of obedience and service, a psychology that made women especially vulnerable to patriarchal education.

Noddings addresses the central theological problem in her opening chapter when she poses the dilemma of theodicy: if God could have prevented evil and did not, then God is malevolent; if God would have prevented evil but could not, then God is impotent; if God could not and would not, then why "God"? (p. 17). Other contemporary theologians have wrestled with this question and, like Noddings, have explored this dilemma by challenging traditional Aristotelian, Augustinian, and Thomistic views of deity. Notable are Rosemary Radford Ruether (1983b) in her *Sexism and God-Talk: Toward a Feminist Theology*, David Ray Griffin (1976) in *God, Power, and Evil*, and S. Paul Schilling (1977) in *God and Human Anguish*. As Patrick Slattery (1989) in *Toward an Eschatological Curriculum Theory*, acknowledged: "If a new way of living for decent human survival is to be developed, if an emancipatory view of education is to be accepted, and if postmodern view of curriculum are to be understood and assimilated, then the issue of evil and human suffering must be addressed" (p. 76).

A new theodicy which views evil in the context of "God's bounded power and unbounded love" (Schilling, 1977) is evident in the writings of contemporary theorists working to understand curriculum as theological text. Additionally, Noddings, like other scholars, proposes that this new theodicy is supported by a feminine perspective on evil which had been suppressed by traditional theology for centuries. Noddings concludes:

> Education has—at least in modern times—been guided by optimism and notions of progress (notions that are, I think, peculiarly masculine). Perhaps we should now consider an education guided by a tragic sense of life, a view that cannot claim to overcome evil (any more than we can overcome dust) but claims only to live sensitively with as little of it as possible. Even as I write this, I realize that the expression "tragic sense of life" will not quite work. It has been used to describe experience that is essentially male, and it points to the male hero who strives courageously with or against a deity—a god good or evil but often aloof or absent. The sense of sadness is right, but the response is wrong. It includes the notion Ricoeur endorsed: "Man enters into the ethical world through fear and not through love." We cannot deny that fear inspires some ethical thinking, but so does love. The desire to be like a loving parent is a powerful impetus toward ethical life, and so is the desire to remain in loving relation. A woman's view has to find new language or at least to modify language as it seeks expression. It should not be articulated as mere opposition, but rather as a positive program for human living. From this perspective, in agreement with those who adopt a tragic sense of life, life is at bottom sad. All the more reason for us to give and take what joy we can from each other. (pp. 244-245)

Noddings' (1989) assertion of the presence of love and joy in a tragic world is a powerful statement of feminist theory which extends substantially our understanding of curriculum as theological text.

Curriculum and cosmology. Contemporary cosmology is regarded as having three elements: 1) science, the story of origins, revealed via myths and scientific data; 2) mysticism, responses of amazement and awe to the cosmos; and 3) art, expressions of our responses to the cosmos which inform and transform our cultural institutions, including education and religion (Gentry-Akin, 1990). Traditional scientific cosmology understood the universe as a random collection of particles acted upon by blind forces. Ilya Prigogine characterized this conventional cosmology as a system in which God is reduced to mere archivist, turning the pages of a cosmic history book already written by mechanical forces. Contemporary cosmology bestows upon human beings dignity, a dignity lacking were the universe an incidental accident in the cosmos (Davies, 1990).

In work we mentioned earlier in a discussion of the moral basis of process education, Donald W. Oliver and Kathleen Waldron Gershman (1989) proposed contemporary cosmology as a basis for curriculum. They wrote that a "comparative cosmological curriculum" is inextricably linked to deep images and metaphors which not only influence how we describe the world but even what we actually apprehend, perceive, and bring to conscious expression. Oliver and Gershman (1989) explained:

> Technical knowing refers to adaptive, publicly transferable information or skills; ontological knowing refers to a more diffuse apprehension of reality, in the nature of liturgical or artistic engagement. In this latter case we come to know with our whole body, as it participates in the creation of significant new occasions, occasions which move from imagination and intention to critical self-definition, to satisfaction, and finally to perishing and new being. This fuller quality of ontological knowledge requires that we have available a range of living metaphors within culture—not only the machine metaphor that dominates the modern paradigm but also the metaphors of organic life and transcendent dance. (p. 3)

In this view teaching becomes a kind of dance in which participants (teachers and students), knowledge (curriculum), and movement (setting) come together in a common transcendent occasion.

The Ecozoic Age. Angela Lydon, a professor at Xavier University in New Orleans, is another curriculum theorist working in the area of cosmology. In her study *Cosmology and Curriculum: A Vision for an Ecozoic Age*, Lydon (1992) linked cosmology and curriculum, emphasizing ecology and the mytho-poetic imagination, the latter concept associated with the work of James B. Macdonald and Nelson Haggerson. Lydon employed the notion of an Ecozoic Age, which she defined as an emerging geological period during which the general relationship between humanity and the earth will be harmonious. Ecologically and educationally, Lydon believes that the earth is evolving toward a period of creativity, beyond contemporary expressions of dominance, survival, and struggle. Lydon's work is influenced by the work of Thomas Berry, noted historian of culture. Like Berry, she proposes an integrative moment of theory ("insight") and praxis ("creative action") which is contextualized within a vision of "human-earth" relationality. An interesting feature of Lydon's work is the analysis of original art work by students in early childhood education classes. The students studied by Lydon responded to cosmological poetry and stories read aloud by the teacher as part of the language arts curriculum. The artistic creations composed by the students revealed intuitive understanding of the ecozoic cosmology proposed by Lydon.

VII
Conclusion: Between the Ideal and the Actual

It is this *active* relation between ideal and actual to which I would give the name "God".

(John Dewey, 1934a, 1968, p. 51)

Those who understand curriculum as theological text understand education as wedded to the most profound issues of the human heart and soul. Postmodern theologian David Ray Griffin identifies these as "the human self, historical meaning, and truth as correspondence" (Griffin, 1989, p. xiii). Other theological issues include those mystical-ecological yearnings for union with the source of life, the nature of morality in an evil world, and those mythico-imaginative longings of the human spirit. Curriculum as theological text invites students to explore "divine reality, cosmic meaning, and enchanted nature" (Griffin, 1989, p. xiii). Rather than impose denomination-specific dogma, postmodern theology seeks to uncover layers of mystical experience, individual insight, and harmony with creation. Curriculum as postmodern theological text understands that the dogma of fundamentalist denominations seeks to eliminate doubt, uncertainty, and struggle while stifling creative and social competence. Even theoretical wings of scientific fields such as physics understand that we live in a world that cannot be completely predicted or predetermined (Hawking, 1988; Davies, 1988, 1992; Doll, 1993a). Curriculum as a postmodern theological text invites us to a search for truth wherein our destination remains unknown.

Curricular issues. As issues of ethics and morality begin to concern those academicians who have seen their work as value-free, theological and religious subjects may move back from the margins. Medicine and business are two fields which have in recent years incorporated ethics and morality into their curricula. Those interested in theology and religion are concerned that these subjects be taught not strictly as secular topics. For instance, Maureen Muldoon (1990) observed:

> It appears that the field of business ethics is developing an agenda which does not draw in a significant way on the field of religious studies. . . . [Religious studies] can contribute significantly to the understanding of what people hold to be of ultimate worth for themselves and others. . . . It provides the larger framework for the day-by-day practice of business. (p. 252)

The possible reluctance some educators may experience regarding the introduction of religious issues was expressed by Clive Beck (1985), who argued that schools must be very careful to respect people's religious commitments. The function of religious education is to develop students' religious and spiritual life but not redirect it. The curriculum "should help people find the religious truth that is appropriate for them and their family and community" (p. 269). Leonard J. Waks (1985) regarded Beck's (1985) position as "functionalist," arguing that the ends of religion must be conceived in distinctively religious terms. He insisted:

> And we will require religious practices that are demonstrably useful in assisting a linkage with the mystery, and the living of a life that derives from it, a life transcending narrow personal, social, religious, and national boundaries, and materialist values such as greed and domination. These requirements establish the problems and priorities for religion and religious education at this time. (p. 276)

In *The American Religion: The Emergence of a Post-Christian Nation,* Harold Bloom (1992) argued that there is an American religion which masks itself as Protestant Christianity but has ceased to be Christian. This religion is experiential in nature, celebrates knowing rather than believing, and achieves freedom in solitude. Ralph Waldo Emerson, suggested Bloom, is the theologian of this American religion. Despite these controversies (or perhaps due to them), E. Wayne Ross (1992) is among those who believe that teaching about religion in the public school should be encouraged: "This dialogue must be fostered if we are to avoid both the blind patriotism of a civic religion and the absolutism of the religious right while advancing a democratic vision within an increasingly pluralistic society" (p. 214). Schools are in fact adding religious studies to their curricula, according to the *New York Times,* a move supported by both liberals and conservatives (March 19, 1989). The one curricular rule may be: "If religious liberty is to be protected, it must protect the liberties of minorities as well as majorities, the freedom of conscience of all religious groups—as well as those who profess no religion" (Green, 1992, p. 223).

Just as the history of curriculum thought can be portrayed as tumultuous movements of creation, crisis, and transformation, so too can the effort to understand curriculum as theological text be characterized as a processive movement of body, mind, and spirit in the spiral of procreation, death, and resurrection. The significance of such a ritual is embedded in Native American experience. A Pueblo priest and clan chief, Santiago Rosetta, advises that "spirit" plays as important a role in human wellness and illness as do mind and body. As a medical student, Carl Hammerschlag recalls meeting Santiago in the Santa Fé Indian Hospital. Hammerschlag writes:

> Santiago tried to teach me if you are going to dance, you have to move. You can't watch the dance; you can't listen to it or look at it. You have to do it to know it. He told me that he could teach me his steps, but I would have to hear my own music. (Hammerschlag, 1988, p. 10)

From this perspective body, mind, and spirit are interrelated. The "wholeness" of this view contradicts the modern experience of fragmentation and isolation and suggests a new theological perspective from which to explore curriculum.

Chapter 13

Understanding Curriculum
as Institutionalized Text

Regulation, bureaucratization, and centralization would equalize education by standardizing it, delegate decision making to experts, and Americanize a diverse population.

(David Tyack, 1993, p. 3)

At an institutional level, curriculum discourse serves primarily to define or typify schooling.

(Walter Doyle, 1992, p. 486)

The approach [to curriculum development] is almost entirely bureaucratic.

(David Pratt, 1987b, p. 28)

I appreciate that there are some teachers who simply ignore all the guff, and get on with inspiring children with poetry or mathematics, fascinating them with learning and scholarship, riveting their attention to scientific and other forms of inquiry, and provoking and nurturing imaginative and critical treatment of worthwhile subject matter.

(Robin Barrow, 1990, p. 158)

Teaching itself is a victim of bureaucratization.

(William Ayers, 1992, p. 260)

Many contemporary curriculum discourses focus upon the school. What is distinctive about the effort to understand curriculum as institutional text? Understanding curriculum as institutionalized text suggests understand-ing curriculum as it functions bureaucratically [see Kliebard, 1975b]. Questions within this discourse include: Does the curriculum work? How can it fit the institution? Will the school function more smoothly and efficiently? How do we measure success? Understanding curriculum as institutional text is, fundamentally, an ameliorative approach linked explicitly to the everyday functioning of the institution. The point of curriculum development in the traditional field was to make incremental improvements. However, in the reconceptualized field the focus of curriculum development scholarship and research has diversified somewhat. Now understanding has also become an issue. However, generally speaking, institutional maintenance or improve-ment remains a paramount reason for this genre. Even so, it is remarkable to what extent the Reconceptualization has occurred even in this vestige of the traditional field. To an extent we would not have observed during the pre-

1970 period, much contemporary research on curriculum development aims toward understanding, not toward bureaucratic reform.

In traditional synoptic texts, the categories which comprise this chapter once comprised the entire book. Including these categories in one chapter reflects the paradigmatic shift of the 1970s. As Jackson (1992a) and the Tanners (1990) have noted, the space in which curriculum development can occur has been reduced. For subject matter specialists, especially specialists in mathematics and the sciences, opportunities remain. However, for those generalists whose responsibility it is to attend to the overall curriculum, including the relations among individual subjects as well as the relations of the curriculum to the person and to society, the institutional domain of opportunity has indeed shrunk. While a sizable segment of the field continues to define its raison d'etre as serving the schools and those who must live in them, even that relationship has been redefined. The traditional role of the "expert" which implied a relationship of "theory" *into* "practice" has been altered to a smaller, more modest role of consultant, as we discussed in chapter one [see also Jackson, 1992a]. The consultant does not inform his or her clients what the curriculum shall be; he or she responds to issues and problems that the clients themselves have articulated. The consultant attempts to work with clients on their own ground, negotiating and collaborating rather than stipulating, even across government agencies (Cushman, 1992a). Teacher participation, even "empowerment," is encouraged. Even business leaders involved in contemporary school reform have acknowledged that the "teacher-proof" idea of the 1960s National Curriculum Reform Movement is empty. For instance, the Assistant Secretary of Education in the Bush administration, David Kearns, the former CEO of Xerox Corporation, admitted as much. At a conference on school reform funded by a Japanese corporation and the Los Angeles, California, Chamber of Commerce, Kearns, said: "You cannot restructure a system and end-run all the people that are currently involved in it" (quoted in California Public Affairs Forum, 1991b, p. 34).

Despite its shrinking position in the field, we are not suggesting that the institutional function of the field is unimportant. It will continue to be an important area of curriculum scholarship, but as Jackson (1992a) implies, perhaps less important if the opportunity to influence schools continues to diminish and the institution of the public school becomes increasingly locked in the gridlock of the more than occasionally conflicting interests of politics, business, and government. That is not to suggest that we believe that university specialists should suffer diminished influence over curriculum matters in the school. On the contrary, we believe that curriculum specialists should have more influence over the practice of schooling. Perhaps in the future, to an extent not possible today, we will join colleagues in economics, business, law, and other fields in advising politicians regarding informed practice in the sphere of education. As for now, politicians assert control over education, and as scholars our task is to understand what we observe. We should be clear that observation and understanding are not only the "remains" of a wider, more vital, practice-oriented field. Indeed, the case can be made that one reason we lost our influence in the practice of schools is exactly because the field was too practice-oriented in the past, not sufficiently grounded in thoughtful scholarship and research. The result was ahistorical, atheoretical, bandwagon rhetoric (Kliebard, 1970). Without question the fields mentioned earlier—economics, for instance—have extensive research bases, not that these bases have "solved" the continuing problems of economic life. However, extensive and sophisticated research fields are absolute prerequisites to thoughtful intervention in the public sphere.

While the work described in the previous chapters escapes or at least tries to escape institutionalization, we must acknowledge plainly that it is institutionalization and bureaucratization against which theory seeks to differentiate itself. Further, some contemporary scholarship is not institutionalized, not because it does not want to be, but because it represents political views out of favor for a generation. If, for instance, socialists or feminists or artists were somehow swept into national office in the U.S., many of those associated with the corresponding discourses would no doubt rush to Washington, D.C. and to positions in the U.S. Department of Education, seeking to stipulate the curricular terms of school life by whatever institutional means available to them.

The research in these areas that comprises understanding curriculum as institutional text has changed significantly over the past twenty years, roughly the period of Reconceptualization of the field. While the interests of these domains of scholarship we describe in this chapter have tended to remain focused on the school as institution, the themes and forms these interests take are sometimes congruent with various themes of the theoreticians. Of course, many whose work is reported here are both theoreticians *and* practitioner-oriented, for instance, Elliot Eisner in the area of curriculum evaluation. Eisner's skepticism regarding behaviorism and the Tylerian system of curriculum development, as we noted in chapter 3, represented an important theoretical element in the breakdown of the Tylerian paradigm. However, Eisner's interests have long been focused on the schools, and secondarily on the nature of the field in which he works. His influence, as we shall see, has been even greater in the evaluation field, not in terms in what occurs in schools (although there are some signs this is changing), but in terms of having influenced the scholarly discourse on evaluation. Eisner is an unusual scholar with a commitment to institutional improvement and to theory development. In both intellectual and generational terms, Eisner has one foot planted in the traditional curriculum development paradigm, and the other in the reconceptualized field of theory.

The categories of this chapter are linked explicitly with the school as institution. Curriculum development, a concept and activity which used to define the totality of the curriculum field, has been explicated in its various aspects. Even today, the concept has been reconceived as less hierarchical and more collaborative in nature. Recent research seems less focused on developing new "how-to's" of curriculum development, more on *describing* curriculum development or making it responsive to new problems (Longstreet & Shane,

1993), new ideas (Pratt, 1982) or research (Klein, 1983), or accessible to remote regions (Parrett, 1983). In this chapter we have followed loosely the Tylerian sequence, assuming for organizational purposes only that policy determines objectives (which, we learn from the research, is not necessarily so), after which curriculum is planned and designed, then implemented, including its embodiment in materials and technology, and lastly supervised and evaluated. In this sequence, teaching tends to be reduced to implementation. We include a discussion of teaching as it is linked to curriculum, with attention to teacher education (pre-service and in-service, the latter now conceived as "teacher development"), and school textbooks. Following the review of pedagogy will be a brief discussion of curriculum and students. The chapter concludes with a brief review of the extracurriculum, an overlooked area which is, despite its prefix, very much wedded to the school as institution. All areas are reviewed primarily from the point of view of contemporary curriculum theory.

The chapter is organized around general categories. Curriculum development as a general category is understood to have the following aspects: 1) curriculum policy, 2) school reform, 3) curriculum planning, design, and organization, 4) curriculum implementation, 5) curriculum technology, 6) curriculum supervision, and 7) curriculum evaluation. Included in the second general category, that of teachers and teaching, as they are related to curriculum, are 1) pedagogy, 2) pre-service teacher education, 3) teacher development, and 4) textbooks. Concluding this chapter are reports on two additional areas: curriculum and students, including the extracurriculum.

These categories reflect institutional, bureaucratic concerns. Interests in life history, in politics, in the lived or phenomenological experience of those in schools are often present—that is the legacy of the Reconceptualization—but they are in service of institutional interests, i.e. teacher development, preparing teachers, evaluating programs, and so on. Studies of ideas independent of institutional concerns, about profound human aspirations for meaning, excitement, and joy, as we described in the preceding chapter for instance—while sometimes given a rhetorical acknowledgment—tend to be absent in the effort to understand curriculum as institutional text. For traditionalists, the institutional dimensions of curriculum comprised the entire field, and, as we noted in chapter one, comprised it in the main traditional synoptic textbooks. Our commitments rest with other sectors of curriculum scholarship; we have not tried to disguise these. In the name of comprehensiveness, however, we attend now, as completely as space permits, to the effort to understand curriculum as institutional text.

PART ONE
CURRICULUM DEVELOPMENT

Basically, what is needed is a way of understanding institutions as the necessary context for curriculum deliberation and curriculum action.
(William A. Reid, 1988, p. 15)

What authorizes curriculum developers to be curriculum developers is not only their expertness in doing tasks of curriculum development, but more so a deeply conscious sensitivity to what it means to have a developer's touch, a developer's tact, a developer's attunement that acknowledges in some deep sense the uniqueness of every teaching situation. . . . To raise curriculum planning from being mired in a technical view is a major challenge to curriculum developers of this day.

(T. Aoki, 1986b, p. 10)

As we noted, curriculum development is a generic term which includes policy, design, implementation, technology, supervision, and evaluation. Borrowing from Decker Walker (1979), we can say that:

the one term "curriculum development" covers at least three distinguishable enterprises: *curriculum policy making*, the establishment of limits, criteria, guidelines, and the like with which curricula must comply, without developing actual plans and material for use by students and teachers; *generic curriculum development*, the preparation of curriculum plans and material for use potentially by any students or teachers of a given description; and *site-specific curriculum development*, the many measures taken in a particular school or district to bring about curriculum change there. (p. 269)

Some scholars attend to curriculum development generally, although as we have seen, this concept has declined in significance to the field. The major divisions of the section on curriculum development will report work in the three areas Walker identified: curriculum policy, curriculum planning and design (generic curriculum development), curriculum implementation (site-specific curriculum development), although boundaries among these areas are blurred. Additionally, we will report briefly on aspects of curriculum development Walker omits, including technology in the curriculum, curriculum evaluation, and supervision. In theory as well as in practice, these domains are not entirely distinguishable, procedurally or conceptually.

I
Curriculum Policy:
Elmore, Sykes, McNeil, Page, and Shulman

The legacy of reform is the bureaucratic state.
(William Lowe Boyd, 1979, p. 122)

In their recent review of research on curriculum policy, Richard Elmore and Gary Sykes (1992) report that such research "is anything but a well-organized, distinctive field of inquiry" (p. 185), characterizing the body of work on government involvement in curriculum as "loosely organized, both topically and conceptually" (p. 185). They identify three sources of policy research: 1) disciplinary research applied to curriculum, especially by the fields of sociology, history, and political science, 2) evaluation of government-sponsored interventions thought to be of curricular significance, and 3) that public policy research which is focused on curriculum issues. Curriculum theory itself attends to policy issues, such as Whitson's (1991a) important study of Supreme Court cases affecting censorship and related curriculum issues [see chapter 5].

Policy follows as well as precedes events. Elmore and Sykes (1992) define curriculum policy "as the formal body of law and regulation that pertains to what should be taught in schools" (p. 186). Research on curriculum policy investigates how regulatory events occur, including what these events require of the curriculum. They note that policy often follows interventions rather than precedes them, as they would in a rational model. Indeed, policies often function as rationales for political interventions already made.

Curriculum policy functions on many levels as organizations of authority. For instance, policy sets standards and procedures for government—federal, state, and local—dealings with each other and with schools. Policy stipulates relationships among various interests, for instance, as in collective bargaining laws and contract negotiations among school boards, administrators, and teachers. Policy stipulates or at least structures relationships between "clients" and schools, as in the establishment of mechanisms for parental participation in school policy-making or in writing guidelines for school choice. Another level of policy functioning is financial and organizational, such as in the provision of financial and governance hierarchies for elementary and secondary schools, for community colleges and post-secondary vocational schools, state college, and universities (Elmore & Sykes, 1992). Curriculum policy tends to focus more on issues of content in the school subjects, as well as ideological responses to one traditional curriculum question: what knowledge is of most worth? [see chapter 2; Spencer, 1860]

Two concepts. In all of these levels and domains of policy, two concepts of policy are operative. One regards policy instrumentally, as a form of goal-directed behavior designed to achieve predetermined ends. This view dominates the research literature in policy analysis, and those studies of curriculum policy which prescribe protocols for effective decision-making in curriculum (Walker, 1990). In addition to this instrumental view, policy can also viewed as a result of political negotiation among various constituencies. This concept of policy, sometimes characterized as a "garbage can" view, regards policy research as laying bare the politics of curriculum decisions (Boyd, 1979; Kirst & Walker, 1971). Both concepts appear to ascribe considerable rationality to the process of policy-making (Elmore & Sykes, 1992).

A less deterministic picture. An alternative to these two concepts has emerged from recent research on policy making. This third view contains elements of the previous two; however, it communicates a less deterministic picture. Here policy making is comprised by a series of problems, solutions, various constituencies, resource bases, and, most certainly, various consequences. Such a view is hardly depicting policy-making as a rational process, either as instrumental intervention or analyzable negotiation. Instead, "problems and solutions flow in more or less independent streams, and they converge, often in random ways, around critical events" (Elmore & Sykes, 1992, p. 190).

Policy making, according to John Kingdon, is said to be comprised of three "process streams:"

> First, various problems come to capture the attention of people in and around government. . . . Second, there is a policy community of specialists—bureaucrats [planners, evaluators, budget analysts, legislative staff], academics, interest groups, researchers—which concentrates on generating proposals. They each have their pet ideas or axes to grind; they float their ideas up and the ideas bubble around in these policy communities. . . . Third, the political stream is composed of things like swings of national mood, vagaries of public opinion, election results, changes of administration, shifts in partisan or ideological distributions [of decision makers], and interest group pressure campaigns. (Kingdon, 1984, pp. 92-93; quoted in Elmore & Sykes, 1992, p. 190)

Such a view—Kingdon terms it "policy primeval soup" (1984, p. 122)—reflects a familiar image of how policy gets made in the present-day United States.

Policy now. Elmore and Sykes (1992) suggest that "understanding curriculum policy, then, involves understanding the parallel processes by which policy and curriculum are elaborated in teaching practice" (p. 192). The simplest model, they assert, is a "top-down" one in which curriculum flows from an authoritative source through the medium of the school, including patterns of teaching practice, resulting in certain effects on students. Policy analysts offer multiple explanations of this policy "flow." While some analysts regard policy as impacting practice in important ways, others argue it tends to enjoy minor influence in the day-to-day life of schools. Some analysts insist policy mandates have favorable consequences for school life; others argue they have negative effects. Research on the policy-practice relationship yields a mixed picture (Elmore & Sykes, 1992). We will look briefly at four views: one which argues that policy has great influence on practice, a second which regards the influence of policy as contradictory, a third which conceives of policy as inconsequential, and a fourth which regards teachers as rightfully influencing the implementation of policy. The first of these, that policy has had a strong influence on curricular practice, is termed hyperrationalization.

Hyperrationalization. The view that policy has had increasingly greater influence on practice is associated with the work of Arthur Wise (1979). Wise regarded this influence as negative, as regulating and thereby constraining the options of teachers in the name of efficiency and effectiveness. This increasing regulation of the school was described as:

> hyperrationalization . . . an effort to rationalize beyond the bounds of knowledge, [which] involves imposing means which do not result in the attainment of ends or the setting of ends which cannot be attained, given the available means—imposing unproven techniques, on the one hand, and setting unrealistic expectations on the other. (Wise, 1979, p. 65)

Elmore and Sykes summarize this view: "When policies are based on logic, but divorced from the reality of teaching . . . hyperrationalization results" (1992, p. 193). Such a view fails to acknowledge the complexity and uncertainty of teaching (Jackson, 1968, 1986, 1992c). In Wise's view policy exercises considerable, if unfortunate, influence on curriculum and teaching (Elmore & Sykes, 1992).

Contradictions of control. A second view of the policy-practice relationship is communicated in the work of Linda McNeil (1986). In her *Contradictions of Control,* McNeil argued that public schools are caught in a contradiction between those goals associated with social efficiency (illustrated by tracking and grading) and broader educational goals (which are socially inclusive). She regarded this fundamental contradiction as a result of a school system required to prepare citizens for democratic life and for technical roles in a complex, stratified economy. She attributed the recent decline in test scores and other ostensible measures of quality as rooted in the triumph of the social efficiency view, which has trivialized the curriculum. Further, the most recent wave of school reform—preoccupied with issues such as test scores and teacher certification—failed to acknowledge the basic contradiction of American schools, and in so doing, functioned to increase the alienating pressure on students to perform (McNeil, 1986; Elmore & Sykes, 1992). McNeil's study reveals that policy rooted in political ideology (in this instance, the conservative agenda of the Republican Party) that fails to take into account the history and character of the American public school, is condemned to intensify rather than ameliorate the contemporary educational crisis in America.

Policy exercises little influence? A third view suggests that policy exercises little influence on teaching practice and curriculum as enacted. Due to constraints of various kinds and from different sources, teachers must modify the policy mandates they receive to fit the situations in which they find themselves. Elmore and Sykes (1992) report:

> Clients are classified according to stereotypes to make interactions with them more manageable . . .routines and simplifications . . . are the policies the public receives. A teacher's classification of students according to academic ability significantly influences the type of knowledge those students receive. For those students, the teacher's coping mechanisms constitute the policy that governs access to knowledge. (p. 194)

In this view, associated with the work of Michael Lipsky (1980), curriculum policy mandates showed little influence on the daily lives of many students. Teachers' heavy workloads result in major modifications of curriculum policies in order to fit the conditions of the work place, i.e. the classroom.

Policies = laws; teachers = judges? The mainstream view is that teachers rightfully exercise some discretion over the implementation of curriculum policy. The traditional and overlooked idea of academic freedom suggests precisely that, namely that teachers must enjoy the privilege of teaching what they regard as important in ways they regard as appropriate. While granted to a variable extent to university professors, such freedom has not tended to dominate the literature on instruction. Lee Shulman (1983) expressed succinctly one view of this complicated matter:

> policies are very much like laws and teachers like judges. Educational systems are organized to permit the design of policies and their interaction in the court of the classroom. Teachers must understand the grounds for competing demands on their time, energy and commitment. They must be free to make choices that will cumulate justly in the interests of their students, the society, and humanity. (pp. 501-502)

This is a balanced view of the policy-practice relationship, one which grants considerable discretion to the teacher but which acknowledges the various constituencies to which the teacher is responsible.

A curriculum policy issue: Tracking. One example of an important curriculum policy issue is tracking. From the point of view of efficiency and increased academic productivity, there is a commonsense argument that students need to be tracked according to academic performance and ability. However, an important study of tracking shows this curriculum policy and design issue to be considerably more complicated than common sense would indicate.

Reba Page (1991) studied two high schools to understand in detail how curriculum differentiation—that is, tracking—affected teachers and students. Page (1991) began the study by noting that traditional studies of curriculum differentiation have revealed contradictory findings:

> Even for academic achievement, the dependent variable most often considered, the impact of tracking is inconclusive. Depending on the study consulted, its effects may be positive . . . insignificant . . . or mixed. . . . The effects of tracking on other outcome variables, such as self-esteem or life chances, are equally contradictory. (p. 9)

Empirical research, then, fails to establish how tracking functions in the school lives of those who experience it. Page located her study in the interpretative, qualitative tradition.

Page's questions. Page asked the following questions. What does it mean to be a teacher or a student in classrooms designated as lower-track? What is the character of the school subject that is taught and learned in lower-track classrooms? How do the roles of teachers and students become differentiated from those of teachers and students in so-called regular classrooms, and: "How are the particular meanings that individuals in classrooms generated . . . related to stable, socially consequential precepts of difference, based on academic ability, age, race, or social class, which democratic schools are supposed to ameliorate?" (p. 11). What did Page conclude? She located tracking in culture and in American democratic life:

> Tracking is a cultural lightning rod. The persistent oscillations in the research literature, the polemical rhetoric of policy, and the pervasive, ambivalent, and too frequently negative versions of curriculum indicate that the issue grounds serious, complicated struggles over who we are and how we will live together. . . . To ask whether schools should (or should not) differentiate curriculum is the wrong question and to look to research results for unassailable direction is a misguided expectation. To argue universal policies and standards is to disregard multivocal humanity, the mediating influence of schools, and our prerogatives and responsibilities as persons who make meaningful choices. (1991, p. 252)

Reba Page's view is rooted in an effort to understand curriculum as institutional text which links school, individual experience, and public life. While Page's interest here is understanding, implied in her conclusion is a preference for what McNeil termed the civil as opposed to social efficiency goal of schooling. Page (1990c) found in a study of a lower-track curriculum in a college preparatory high school that lower-track lessons combined elements of the standard, routinized, remedial curriculum with the school's more typical liberal regular-track curriculum. The combination resembled a game of chance: it provided and legitimated school knowledge that is trivial, knowing as guessing, and academic success or failure that is primarily a matter of luck. As such, Page (1990c) concluded that this lower-track curriculum communicates the view that: "failure in schools and society . . . is 'nobody's fault'—and nobody's responsibility" (p. 277).

In tracking, Page is arguing, we see the dilemmas, paradoxes, and ambiguities of American culture, e.g., that the individual and the community are not opposites, but are indeed dependent upon each other. They are mutually constitutive. When specific expressions of curriculum differentiation—such as tracking—are examined, we can see how the complex forces we link with communities, individuals, and the culture are concretized in specific institutional practices. By moving away from simple assessments of heterogeneous vs. homogeneous grouping, Page is reconceptualizing tracking as an institutional expression of complex and contradictory cultural demands. Only through deliberation, she believes, can educators appreciate the complexity of tracking questions, and take responsibility for their decisions.

While Page (1989, 1990a, 1990b, 1990c, 1991) is not endorsing a heterogeneous grouping over homogeneous tracking (or vice versa), others do take specific positions. For instance, the Coalition of Essential Schools, a Brown University centered coalition for school reform, led by Theodore Sizer, recommends heterogeneous grouping. We will review the work of the Coalition in the next section on school reform. Suffice to say now that a spokesperson for the coalition, Kathleen Cushman, judged: "Heterogeneous grouping . . . is central to the Coalition's vision" (Cushman, 1992b, p. 1).

II
School Reform: Sizer and Cheney

Historical amnesia allows curriculum reconstruction to be presented as curriculum revolution.

(Ivor F. Goodson, 1989a, p.137)

The stories teachers tell about the bureaucratization and unprofessional treatment they face daily will be heard. And when they are, the right-wing house of educational cards will collapse.

(Joe L. Kincheloe, 1992a, p. 231)

The reform reports of the 1980s share a strong nationalism, an unwavering millennial vision, a continuing assumption about possessive individualism, and a belief in the efficiency of the market.

(Thomas S. Popkewitz, 1991, p. 164)

The modern state, for reasons having to do with its structural commitment to the existing order in the distribution of power and statuses, is basically unable to implement major reforms.

(H. Weiler, 1989, p. 304)

One important example of curriculum policy as instrumental action is surely the conservative agenda for school reform. Perhaps the opening volley was the *Paidea Proposal*, published in 1982, followed by *A Nation at Risk* in 1983. These reports accused American schools of decline, a lack of vision, even incompetence. The sense of alarm came this time not from military competition, as in 1957 [see chapter 3], but from economic competition with Japan and Germany [see chapter 14]. Soon to follow were conservative curriculum proposals by Allan Bloom (1987) and E. D. Hirsch (1987). These conservatives tended to malign the history of curriculum theory. For instance, Herbert Kliebard (1987) observed that Hirsch misunderstands Dewey while reducing curriculum to a list. Despite misunderstandings, the 1980s belonged to conservatives, both in government and in education. In addition to a reassertion of a Eurocentric core curriculum in the universities was the notion that American elementary and secondary schools should be more like American business. Various business-school coalitions have been formed at national, state, and local levels. Illustrative of this view is Denis P. Doyle, Senior Research Fellow at the Hudson Institute who asserted: "The only group in America that can bring this off successfully is the American business community. They are the stakeholders with the most to gain and the most to lose because of bad schools" (1991, p. 18).

We have observed the stake of business in American schools from their inception [chapters 2 and 3]. Pinar (1992a, 1994) suggests that the issue is a phony one, that Republicans were attempting to deflect criticism from the political and corporate spheres, displacing them onto the educational one. Other studies document the political character of the business/education alliance (Shea, Kahane, & Sola, 1989). As in the case of improving business productivity, conservative educational reforms have focused on minimizing schools' reliance on its human "infrastructure." In this regard, Linda Darling-Hammond (1988) characterized the reforms initiatives of the 1970s as attempts to make curriculum "teacher proof." Not unrelatedly, many of the state-mandated curriculum reforms of the 1980s reflected the attitude of state legislatures, which in general regarded teaching as a standard set of techniques that can be applied to everyone, everywhere (Tanner & Tanner, 1990). As Canadian curriculum theorist Terry Carson has observed, the conservative tendency is to meet new challenges by turning back to the old values and standards that have declined. Conservatives relocate social and cultural problems onto the school, which cannot contain or manage these economic, social, and political crises. "But," Carson (1990c) reminds us, "the children and teachers who dwell in the schools in their infinite variety and possibility are the ones who wish to strive for an education of the quality that produces a better world" (p. 25).

There *are* examples of school experimentation that occur outside a right-wing/business model, for instance the Harmony School in Bloomington, Indiana (Goodman, 1992), the experiments in the Chicago Public Schools (Ayers, 1992), and the Alex Taylor Community School, an example of an urban community school (Hart, 1992; Ramsankar & Hart, 1992). Perhaps the best known example of school reform that is not linked to right-wing politics is the Coalition for Essential Schools (CES), housed at Brown University. Theodore Sizer (1984, 1989) is the architect of this important national movement, which received $50 million of the $500 million gift to public education by Walter Annenberg (*New York Times*, 1993). The Coalition for Essential Schools' *Re: Learning* unites the CES with the Education Commission of the States (ECS) to work with people in several parts of the education system. Fifty Coalition schools support the value of CES principles as a framework for local school redesign. These principles of school redesign include: 1) an intellectual focus, 2) simple goals (students should master a limited number of essential skills and areas of knowledge), 3) universal goals (goals should apply to all students; school practice should be tailored to meet the needs of every group of students), 4) personalization, 5) concept of student-as-worker, 6) diploma by "exhibition," 7) tone (fairness and unanxious expectation), 8) staff (teachers as generalists), and 9) budget (total student load of 80 or fewer per teacher, substantial time for collective staff planning, competitive staff salaries) (Sizer, 1989). Publications of the Coalition for Essential Schools suggest the character of this reform as well. Illustrative Coalition publications include Patricia A. Wasley's (1990a) "Trusting Kids and their Voices: A Humanities Teacher in the Midst of Change," her (1990b) "A Formula for Making a Difference," and her (1990c) "Stirring the Chalkdust;" Joseph P. McDonald's (1991a) "Three Pictures of an Exhibition," his (1991b) "Dilemmas of Planning Backwards," his (1991c) "Exhibitions: Facing Outward, Pointing Inward," and his (1991d) "Steps in Planning Backwards;" Jody Brown Podl and Margaret Metzger's (1992) "Anatomy of an Exhibition;" and Marshall A. Cohen's (1991) "An American Teacher's View of British Assessment Practices." There is an informality, even a playfulness, in these sensible publications which emphasize the non-bureaucratic, creative, and reasonable character of the reform work of the Coalition for Essential Schools.

Cheney's proposals. A recent example of conservative school reform [see also Ravitch & Finn, 1987] was the report of Lynne Cheney (1987), former Director of the National Endowment of the Humanities under President Bush. Her attacks on the education establishment were far-ranging and familiar to the student of curriculum history. From attacks on teacher education to textbooks, Cheney challenged the emphasis upon research in American research universities, decrying the de-emphasis upon teaching such a division of labor requires. She pointed out that community college instructors are paid less than research university professors, even though the former spend more time in classrooms. Cheney endorsed school choice, saying bluntly that in such a scheme "that unsuccessful schools that no one wants to attend will either reform or be forced to close" (1990, p. 21). Her policy recommendations included:

- parents should be able to choose the school their child attends;
- prospective teachers should be able to choose paths to certification different from the traditional one;
- teachers in the schools should have abundant opportunities to study the subjects they teach. In-service training, in particular, should provide alternatives to studying pedagogy in isolation from subject matter;
- those involved in textbook selection need alternatives to the mechanical criteria commonly used to select textbooks. They should make use of textbook reviews done by scholars and teachers in the field to inform their choices. Schools should be encouraged to use alternatives to textbooks: stories, speeches, documents, and other authentic materials;
- we need alternatives to the SAT . . . to tell us what students know and are able to do and how our schools are performing. (1990, pp. 50, 51)

While many within the business community and not a few among the professional education community regarded many or all of these recommendations as reasonable, others responded quite negatively. Henry A. Giroux and Peter McLaren [see chapters 5, 6, and 9] are illustrations of the latter. Giroux and McLaren (1992) focused upon former President Bush's *America 2000* plan as illustrative of conservative school reform proposals.

America 2000. President Bush's education reform initiative was called the *America 2000*, among the goals of which were that "every child will start school ready to learn; the high school graduation rate will increase to 90 percent; competency will be demonstrated in five core subjects in grades 4, 8, and 12; American students will be ranked first in the world in both math and science; every American adult will be a literate and responsible citizen; and every school will be liberated from drugs and violence" (America 2000, 1991; quoted in Giroux & McLaren, 1992, p. 99). Henry A. Giroux and Peter McLaren (1992) criticized these goals as "highly generalized" (p. 99). "More specifically," they continued:

> *America 2000* can be understood as a wider ideological and political attempt by conservatives to divest government service agencies in favor of the private sector, consolidate wealth among affluent groups, and construct a privatized market system which enshrines individualism, self-help, management, and consumerism at the expense of the values which reflect the primacy of the ethical, social and civil in public life. (Giroux & McLaren, 1992, p. 100)

They noted that celebrated conservatives such as E. D. Hirsch and Chester Finn are associated with *America 2000*; they pressure school systems to adopt a national curriculum. Perhaps worst of all, in their view, *America 2000* is:

> rooted in a notion of pedagogy that presupposes that the solution to the problems of American schooling lie in the related spheres of management and efficiency rather than in the realm of values and politics. Similarly, teachers are increasingly being asked to adopt pedagogical models dominated by the dictates of technique, implementation, "what works!" and measurement. (Giroux & McLaren, 1992, p. 104)

America 2000 "represents a direct assault on the issue of cultural difference" (p. 106) in its language of consensus and uniformity.

All agree: Restructure. From the right and left there is agreement, however, on the need for significant change, or, in the jargon of the day, on "restructuring." Restructuring and decentralization both followed from effective schools research (Common, 1983). What is restructuring?

> Restructuring may refer to specific changes within a school (e.g., block scheduling or arranging for one set of teachers to stay with a group of students as long as they are in the school) or to systematic changes (e.g., eliminating major central office units or privatizing formerly centralized functions, such as the delivery of staff development courses). (Hill & Bonan, 1991, p. 6)

For some, restructuring may refer to "school-based management," another reform of the 1980s.

What is school-based management? The simple definition is that SBM is a governance plan in which authority and responsibility for the functioning of individual schools are shared between the central office and the school-site officials, all of whom are to work as professional, collaborating colleagues, rather than supervisors and subordinates (Clift, Veal, Johnson, & Holland, 1990). There is the notion as well that restructured schools would take greater responsibility for teacher education, dedicated to practice-based research (Levine, 1992). According to Linquist and Mauriel (1989), the three fundamental elements of SBM are decentralization, collaborative decision-making, and advocacy of the school district. In general terms, the model is borrowed from trends in the corporate sector (Peters & Waterman, 1982). However, it is consonant with school reform initiatives associated with the so-called "second wave" (1980s) of reform movement:

> [It] is distinguished not by chronology, but by an exciting and markedly different agenda, including: the individual school as the unit of decision making; development of a collegial, participatory environment among both students and staff; flexible use of time; increased personalization of the school environment with a concurrent atmosphere of trust, high expectations, and sense of fairness; a curriculum that focuses on students' understanding what they learn—knowing "why" as well as "how"; and an emphasis on higher-order thinking skills for all students. (Michaels, 1988, p. 3)

The first wave had focused on raising standards, increasing accountability, lengthening school days, and in general intensifying the rigor of school practice (Michaels, 1988). Opinion on the possible efficacy of the second wave—and SBM in particular—ranges from judging it an elusive, cyclical, and largely symbolic gesture (Malen et al., 1990) to the only real hope for true reform (Shanker, 1990). Unless a historical perspective is maintained, a third wave may simply recapitulate earlier errors. As Daniel and Laurel Tanner (1990) have noted:

> Curriculum improvement is approached by each new group of reformers as though the problems they are trying to solve have never been recognized before. As a result, there is a failure to build on curriculum work done in the past. The continuity between past and present has too often been a tale of repeated mistakes. (p. 30)

Decentralization: Hans Weiler and David Tyack

Curriculum decentralization has attracted international attention (Silva, 1993; Pinar, 1993b; Han, 1993). In 1993, decentralization was the subject of an international seminar sponsored by UNESCO in Santiago, Chile and chaired by Juan Casassus. Hans Weiler (1993), one of the most perceptive students of decentralization (and school reform generally), argues that decentralization advocacy ordinarily takes the form of one of three arguments: the redistribution argument, referring to the sharing of power; the efficiency argument, linked to a faith in the cost-effectiveness of the educational system through a more efficient deployment and management of resources; and third a cultures of learning argument, pointing to the decentralization of educational content.

Three arguments. Regarding the first argument—the sharing of governance power—Weiler (1993) characterizes the situation in the United States as more complex than in other countries in that four somewhat contradictory tendencies have developed more or less simultaneously. First, significant concentration of authority at the state level (mostly at the expense of the local level) has occurred during the last decade or so, primarily as a function of shifts in the financing of education. Second, there has occurred a further weakening, throughout the Reagan and Bush administrations, of the already modest role of the federal government in educational policy, especially in terms of resource allocation. Third, there appears to be a continuing trend toward further decentralization in the movement for school-site management. Accompanying this movement toward decentralization is a campaign for a national curriculum and a standardized national achievement tests (Weiler, 1993).

Regarding the second [or efficiency] argument, Weiler (1993) understands the issue as requiring calculations concerning a favorable trade-off between loss of economies of scale, on the one side, and enhanced efficiency in the use of resources (presumably due to a leaner bureaucracy), on the other. Weiler believes that there is some initial evidence that the balance does indeed come out in favor of a more decentralized structure (Weiler, 1993, p. 63).

The third argument involves the congruence between local cultures and curriculum structure, content, and delivery. As postmodern political theorist Joe Kincheloe (1993b) observes: "One aspect of this postmodern valuing of difference involves a growing appreciation for local cultures with their diversity of forms of human patterning" (p. 69). Language as well as racial and regional differences can be acknowledged and, some would say, appropriated, for educational and—for Weiler—state legitimation purposes. [See Tierney, 1993, pp. 140-141 for comments on cultural separatism; see also Kincheloe & Pinar, 1991]

Weiler (1993) provides what he terms an "interim assessment" of decentralization debates:

1. The notion of decentralization as redistribution of power seems largely incompatible with the modern state's manifest interest in maintaining effective control and discharging some of its key functions with regard to economic production and capital accumulation.
2. Decentralization as a means of enhancing the efficiency of educational governance, both by generating additional resources and by using available resources more effectively, seems to have some potential, especially where the utilization of resources is concerned, but it also appears to rest on the premise of a real division of authority, which seems, on closer examination, difficult to uphold.
3. The notion of decentralizing the contents of learning as means of recognizing and accommodating the diversity and importance of different cultural environments in one society is generally considered meaningful and valid. At the same time, however, it encounters the conflicting claims of different conceptions of knowledge, which contrast a kind of learning that is more geared to the specifics of cultural contexts with the national and international universalities of dealing with modern systems of technology and communication. (p. 66)

Skepticism. Others worry that insufficient attention is paid to decentralization structures and procedures. For instance, Dan Lewis (1993) implies that the privatization of education (which he links with other forms of privatization such as corrections facilities) carries risks that are obscured in the heat of debate. Lewis writes:

> Reformers . . . push resistant bureaucracies and entrenched politicians to open up the governing process, but they do not explore how the new arrangements work. We must deinstitutionalize the way we think about school reform. (p. 99)

Martin Carnoy (1993) insists that social inequities can only be exaggerated through privatization and decentralization schemes. Compensatory efforts in a decentralized structure amount to "a pipe dream" (p. 189). Economist Clair Brown expresses skepticism that: "decentralization as a sole strategy in education should not be expected to have any direct impact on learning, although it may have a direct impact on the working conditions of teachers" (p. 228). Brown's skepticism is broader still, suggesting that the general arguments made between quality of education and economic growth may be exaggerated: "Improvement in the education provided by high schools will not by itself strengthen the weak labor market or raise the returns on high school graduates' investment in schooling" (Brown, 1993, p. 229).

Historical perspective. The distinguished historian of education David Tyack provides a historical perspective. Tyack (1993) observes that debates regarding "restructuring" and "choice" and "national standards" are recent rhetorical episodes in a long series that date back a century and a half. Despite the duration of this interest, Tyack (1993) insists that little is known about how differences in governance affect the heart of education, the classroom curriculum. He fears that governance is not self-evidently linked with the classroom. This is a position shared by others (Elmore, 1993; Brown, 1993).

Tyack reminds us: "In the Progressive Era, for example, business leaders wanted to centralize control of schools, emulating the consolidation of vast corporations; today they urge 'restructuring' or decentralization, citing business in each case as a guide to reform in schooling" (Tyack, 1993, pp. 1-2.). Tyack points out that during the nineteenth century, public schools—called "common schools"—were primarily decentralized institutions, especially in rural America: locally supported and controlled. In early decades of the twentieth century, educational reformers insisted that the centralization of authority and the use of experts would support a standardized accountability that was absent in a more fragmented and localized system. Tyack (1993) summarizes: "Regulation, bureaucratization, and centralization would equalize education by standardizing it, delegate decision making to experts, and 'Americanize' a diverse population" (p. 3). Here Tyack is observing that bureaucratization was in part in the service of cultural homogeneity. Today we find decentralization arguments employed by marginalized groups in the U.S.—such as African-Americans and right-wing Christians (Tyack terms these so-called Christian schools as "paradigm cases of grass-roots institutions" (p. 10)—to affirm cultural heterogeneity, as Weiler (1993) notes.

For Tyack, the fundamental problem with centralization/decentralization arguments are finally located in the vision of education that they communicate. He reminds us that the great American philosopher of education "John Dewey believed that the family, not the firm, should be the prototype of the school" (Tyack, 1993, p. 14). Tyack concludes:

> The belief systems underlying much of current American educational reform seem impoverished and incomplete in comparison with earlier ideologies. As Mann, Dewey, and King would have perceived, such statements as *A Nation at Risk* and *America 2000* (U.S. Department of Education, 1991) narrow both the sense of purpose and the measure of success in U.S. education. These recent manifestos have moved away from the tradition of a broad-based conception of democratic citizenship, revealed in action. They substitute the aim of economic competitiveness, to be certified by higher test scores. Such a narrowing of purpose omits much that is of value from the discussion of educational policy and constricts the historical vision of the common school. The ideology of competition may resonate among current opinion shapers and may create a temporary sense of public urgency, but is it a lasting and generous conception of educational purpose? (pp. 25-26)

Many believe that the public schools are overbureaucratized, overcentralized, and glacier-like in their capacity to enact dramatic reform. Decentralization in the U.S. is primarily (but by no means exclusively) a conservative ideological movement in conformity with recent Republican policies (under Presidents Reagan and Bush) of privatization of several sectors of institutional infrastructure, such as correctional facilities. Rather than focusing upon the democratic character of local control, or its congruence with the cultural and political goals of marginalized ethnic and social groups (including gays, lesbians and other women, the homeless as well as African-Americans [see, for instance, Foster, 1993b] and other marginalized ethnic groups), decentralization rhetoric has focused upon the benefits which will presumably derive from competition among independent schools which, also presumably, will be more likely to serve the interests of a diverse population. So framed, it is clear that decentralization is a political movement, with multiple (sometimes contradictory) motives and perhaps insufficient educational and curriculum rationale elaboration. As Weiler (1993) has observed:

> Both centralization and decentralization ultimately have to do with the exercise of power, and there is always the possibility that the power that decentralization gives away with one hand evaluation may take back with the other. Reconciling the two may well turn out to be an exercise in contradiction. (p. 78)

Editors of a new collection of essays on decentralization, Jane Hannaway and Martin Carnoy (1993), emphasize a different point: "The main point is that for any reform to improve instruction, it must ultimately be focused on instruction and must affect instruction" (p. 233). Policy analyst Richard

Elmore reports: "Indeed, research on centralization and decentralization in American education is characterized by the virtually complete disconnection between structural reform and anything having to do with classroom instruction or the learning of students" (p. 35). Further: "Policy debates about centralization and decentralization are unlikely to produce any improvements in schooling" (Elmore, 1993, p. 50). As we will see at the conclusion of this section, the tendency toward skepticism regarding decentralization extends to school reform in general, at least for Hans Weiler.

Curriculum in Restructured Schools:
D. Tanner, McNeil, Cuban, Kirst and Meister, Weiler

What will characterize school curriculum in restructured schools? As opposed to greater curriculum differentiation, i.e. more homogeneous tracking, at least one student of the contemporary school reform movement believes that the coming curricula with "be characterized by both greater complexity and greater cohesion" (Murphy, 1991, p. 52). Murphy (1991) predicts seven curricular changes and six "threads" of flexible curricular organization, one of which echoes Page's (1991) study and one which recalls Cheney's (1990) conservative recommendations. The seven curricular changes include:

> 1) expanded use of a core curriculum, 2) an increase in the interdisciplinary nature of content, 3) emphasis on depth of coverage, 4) use of more original source materials, 5) enhanced focus on higher order thinking skills, 6) expanded methods of student assessment, and 7) additional teacher choice. (Murphy, 1991, pp. 52-53)

The six organizational threads include:

> 1) flexible use of space, 2) less regimented scheduling patterns, 3) nontraditional grouping patterns within classes, 4) more flexible instructional arrangements, 5) less emphasis on self-contained classrooms, and 6) less use of age grouping patterns. (p. 67)

The success of restructuring may ultimately hinge on the detachment of college entrance requirements on the composition of the high-school curriculum. That is, authentic curricular reform may require the curricular separation between high schools and colleges and universities. Recall that the linkage between college and high-school curricula was first established by the Committee of Ten in 1893 [see chapter 2]. When the thirty progressive schools were permitted to conduct curriculum experimentation without concern for college admission requirements, students clearly benefited [for a review of the Eight-Year Study, see chapter 3]. Restructuring may require addressing this question (Westbury, 1988)—and the related one of mission (Reynolds, 1990)—once again. Others see the fundamental question of school reform in cultural terms. Michelle Fine (1991), studying the politics of an urban high school, argued that reform represents the reclaiming of the public sphere. She called for an image of the public sphere, and of school that is filled "with energy, complexity, and contradiction; rich in bodies, voices, and critique; boiling with tensions; simmering in creativity; and organized through democracy—a fully democratic sphere" (p. 228). Despite the basic agreement on the necessity of school reform, the second wave may be over. One observer of the reform scene suggested that "1986 may have seen the peak year, and that 1987 has seen the first signs of a turning-away from education reform" (Westbury, 1988, p. 293). The $500 million-dollar donation made by Walter Annenberg during December, 1993 suggests that Westbury's judgment may be premature.

School choice. Various plans supporting school choice have been debated, from allowing parents to choose schools within the public system to a voucher system which would allow all parents to choose public or private schools [see chapter 12 for further discussion of choice plans]. In a study of alternative schools (in which she regards them as models for emulation not replication), Mary Anne Raywid (1983) observed: "Finally, they [alternative schools] respond to a message that recurringly rouses the consciousness of educators and public alike: Americans will have educational choice. If the public sector does not provide it, they will seek it elsewhere" (p. 196). One plan betting on Raywid's conclusion is Christopher Whittle's Edison Project, headed by Benno Schmidt, former Yale University President. [Also working on the project is Chester Finn, former assistant to Education Secretary William Bennett.] Whittle's company plans to create a chain of 1,000 for-profit K-12 schools. He is skeptical of school restructuring: "Trying to reform schools is like trying to renovate a house while you're still in it" (quoted in Tompkins, 1993). Whittle has already developed Channel One, a twelve-minute current events program shown daily to students in 400,000 classrooms nationwide, which has been criticized for showing candy and tennis shoe ads. Whittle Communications Corporation is said to have earned $100 million from Channel One.

Schools stay the same? Writing nearing twenty years ago about the future of the secondary school, Eisner (1975) observed: "Much of what is offered today as new is old wine in new bottles" (p. 137). Despite the anti-education school sentiment accompanying much school reform rhetoric, it is true that many of these changes have all been recommended generally by large segments of the field for some time. Joseph Murphy notes this wave of school reform faces the same institutional conditions faced by previous waves. He observes: "Schooling today looks a good deal as it has in the past. Given the current organizational infrastructure and political culture of schools, education has a tremendous capacity (and need) to deflect improvement efforts and to respond to change in a ritualistic fashion" (1991, p. 94). Business has been employed as a model for schooling since public schooling became common one hundred years ago. It may be that business will be no more effective now than it was then in guaranteeing academic success of students. Even business consultants recommend a role for the federal government. John T. Golle,

Chairman and CEO, Education Alternatives, Inc., advises that "the feds must step in and equalize the disparity in funding" (1991, p. 31). Murphy (1991) cautions against a non-critical adoption by schools of business practices in general.

Daniel Tanner's view of curriculum reform. One prominent curriculum historian judged the reform atmosphere of the post-1960s as decidedly worse than earlier periods: "the negativism toward American public elementary and secondary education in the recent era of sociopolitical retrenchment contrasts sharply with the positive and optimistic attitude that prevailed at midcentury . . . the seventies were an era of retreat" (Tanner, D., 1984, p. 13). Recent commissions and panels, he worried, seem too willing to discard the comprehensive high school (Tanner, D., 1979). Reformers on the left and right alike, he continues, overlook what is right about American education: "American schools, with all their faults, have accomplished more than any other of our social institutions in generating the expectancy of social opportunity for all people" (Tanner, D., 1974, p. 225). Furthermore: "No other nation has made higher education so accessible to such a large proportion of its youth" (Tanner, D., 1982, p. 613).

While Daniel Tanner has sometimes suffered the reputation as a right-wing critic, that is not accurate. He has, for instance, opposed performance contracting (a curriculum fad of the 1960s and early 1970s) as a "contrivance of the industrial-governmental-educational complex" (Tanner, D., 1973), arguing that it is mistaken to assume that the skills of business and industry can be applied to the solution of problems in education. In fact, Daniel Tanner may be regarded as a civic or public intellectual, a public spokesperson for the curriculum field, as he has published in a number of non-specialized journals. He has been a champion of a centrist position, avoiding what he regards as excesses on both the left and the right.

Contradictions of reform. Linda McNeil (1987) has worried over the disparity between teachers' expressed concerns for individual differences and their tendency, at least in heterogeneous classes, to teach as though those differences did not exist or were not meaningful. She noted:

> most of the recent U.S. reports on educational reform seem to be reinforcing an aggregate model of instruction . . . . This paper suggests a model for a research methodology which can help illuminate those student differences teachers actually operationalize in their instruction (p. 105)

That model is ethnography, the tools of which, she argued, are very useful in going "behind educationists' jargon and bringing into the open the lived culture of the school as it relates to teachers' treatment of the varieties of students in their classes" (p. 120). Why is this important to school reform? McNeil replied (1987): "Student alienation is often brought about by aggregate instructional forms which assign passive roles to students that allow very little attention to student differences. This pattern requires reforms that are not aimed at greater standardization" (p. 120).

Determinants of curriculum change and stability. Larry Cuban (1979) has listed a number of determinants of curricular change. They include broad social, economic, and political movements, corporate industrialism, progressivism, cold war and national defense, political-legal decisions, state and federal laws, court decisions, influential groups, publishers, foundations, professors, professional associations, internal groups, and influential individuals (such as Dewey, Harris, Thorndike, Bobbitt, Tyler). Determinants of curricular stability include external forces such as the social functions of schooling, accrediting and testing agencies, textbooks, state and federal laws and agencies, and internal forces such as organizational rationality and loose coupling (i.e. a curriculum guide may not show up in classroom; when it does pupils may not listen). Cuban regards the teacher as a source of both change and stability. These determinants for change and stability appear evenly balanced. Can change occur?

Reforms that have endured; reforms that have not. Given the conservative character of schools, to what extent is curricular, and broadly, school reform possible? In a 1985 study, two students of school reform listed educational reforms that have endured, and reforms that have not. Among those reforms that have lasted are the following: 1) graded school, 2) consolidation of rural elementary schools, 3) abolishing ward school boards and cutting the number of trustees' positions on central urban boards, 4) Carnegie units, 5) reducing class sizes, 6) raising educational requirements for teachers, 7) school lunch programs, 8) creating vocational courses and tracks in high schools, 9) intelligence and other forms of standardized testing, 10) guidance counselors, 11) adding other specialists to the school staff, 12) movable desks, and 13) teacher aides (Kirst & Meister, 1985, p. 181). To this list we would add advanced placement, the only reform—aside from certain science curriculum initiatives such as BSCS (1993) [Biological Sciences Curriculum Study]—remaining from the Sputnik era.

Among those reforms that did *not* last are: 1) broadcast television in classroom, 2) individually prescribed instruction (IPI), 3) new math, 4) flexible scheduling, 5) team teaching, 6) management and budgeting systems such as Program Planning and Budgeting System (PPBS), Management by Objectives (MBO) and Zero Based Budgeting (ZBB), 7) computer-assisted instruction, 8) state-mandated teacher evaluation systems, 9) merit pay and differentiated staffing, and 10) programmed instruction (Kirst & Meister, 1985, p. 181). There is some evidence, however, that broadcast television, computer-assisted instruction, and state-mandated evaluation systems may return.

One of the more visible conservative experiments of the late 1980s was Boston University's takeover of the Chelsea, Massachusetts, public schools. John Silber, the president of Boston University and recent unsuccessful right-wing candidate for governor of Massachusetts, has been a persistent critic of the "education establishment." He is known particularly to the American curriculum field, having personally intervened in the promotion and tenure case of political theorist Henry Giroux over a decade ago (Jacoby, 1987).

Three years after Boston University assumed management of Chelsea's public schools, what was billed as a reform model for urban education had received poor marks (Marcus, 1992). Scholastic Aptitude Test scores had fallen, teacher absenteeism was up and the dropout rate was still above 50 per cent. University officials blamed budget cuts for many of the setbacks, insisting that their progress should not be judged from test scores. In fact, John Silber, angry at the focus on test scores, called the partnership "a huge success. Somebody ought to go to the classroom and look at what's going go and see the excitement in these kids." (Marcus, 1992, p. A-8). Of course, curriculum specialists have worried for decades about the overreliance on test scores in determining the educational worthiness of any particular school program.

Given the partially conservative character of contemporary school reform and the difficult economic circumstances in which it is proceeding, what kinds of reforms might we predict to have the best chance of lasting in the next few years? Kirst and Meister suggested the following:

[The] environment for school funding will be increasingly competitive. Consequently, lower cost reforms will have a higher probability of being fully implemented. Of reforms that will be implemented, two kinds are most likely to endure: first, reforms that create new organizational structures and new constituencies and, second, reforms that are amenable to easy monitoring, but stay within cost constraints. (1985, p. 184)

Policy, then, seems driven by economic conditions which, when mixed with political agendas and institutional complexities, results, it seems, in institutional inertia or even gridlock. It is as if there is a kind of inability to change because the crosscurrents of change are multiple and sometimes at cross purposes. Add to this problem those internal, bureaucratic resistances to change and we face what Seymour Sarason (1990) has termed the "intractability of schools to educational reform" (p. 147). In this light, the efforts of curricularists to make curriculum planning, design, and organization a rational and orderly process seem compensatory indeed.

One of the most interesting and provocative studies of school reform has an international focus. On the basis of case studies of France and the Federal Republic of Germany (FRG), Hans Weiler (1989) reports that:

the state in advanced industrialized societies has a tendency to maximize the political gain to be derived from designing, and from appearing to implement, educational reforms, while at the same time to minimize the political costs associated with carrying them through. . . . An important part of the political calculus of reform policy, therefore, is to contain and manage these conflicts in such a way as to minimize the resulting threat to the state's authority. (p. 291)

In other words, the state engages in the rhetoric of school reform, and in the formulations of policies and practices of reform that it has little intention to fully actualize, unless such enactment promises only positive political returns on its investment. Weiler (1989) is suggesting that the state enjoys maximum gain by only *appearing* to enact school reform:

> This line of interpretation could be carried a step further by adopting the premise that the modern state, for reasons having to do with its structural commitment to the existing order in the distribution of power and statuses, is basically unable to implement major reforms. (p. 304)

This conclusion leaves educators in the cynical position of suspecting that any school reform initiative from politicians, from the state, must have as its tacit—if not explicit—motive the solidification of political support for the state itself. Educational reform is merely an implement in the state's effort to strengthen its political position.

If the state cannot be trusted to engage in meaningful school reform, where can such reform occur? It may be that educational change must occur at the level of the classroom, barring any significant political realignments in the larger social arena which would permit educators' more direct influence on school curriculum. Even when reform is limited to the institution itself, it is often conservative and self-serving. For instance, Robert Bullough & Andrew Gitlin (1985) argued that "school reform tends to be top down" (p. 219). The rhetoric of theoreticians is not helpful, they asserted: "Passionate pleas of the kind Giroux makes are too often merely inspirational interludes, resonant to be sure, but off the mark. What teacher is likely to listen to a call of this kind?" (p. 221). Meaningful school reform can occur, Bullough and Gitlin (1985) believe, from the "bottom-up." That is, school reform "is, in our view, context-specific. . . . The problem . . . is twofold, that of gaining new eyes and of establishing new roles, neither of which comes easily or quickly" (p. 235). Regarding reform in this micro-sense, other researchers have pointed to overlooked considerations. For instance, in his study of a high school faculty, Charles Bruckerhoff (1988) says that "the point for curriculum theorists is that the faculty culture is an important, if not powerful, feature of the hidden curriculum of the high school" (p. 58). There is no point for reformers to revise the curriculum while ignoring the faculty who must enact it.

III
Curriculum Planning, Design, and Organization: Saylor, Alexander, Lewis, Egan, and Noddings

> A curriculum plan should be seen as an opening up of possibilities that enable learning, rather than as the management of expected outcomes
> (Terrance R. Carson, 1989, p. 55)

> Curriculum planning [cannot be] divorced from its human, social, economic, political, and religious context
> (James B. Macdonald & David E. Purpel, 1987, p. 192)

Quite simply, we are in no position to treat curriculum design as an applied science. . . . Curriculum design is an otiose notion
(Robin Barrow, 1984b, pp. 66-67)

The written curriculum policy presumably proceeds to the planning and design of the curriculum which, when implemented, will institutionalize the policy. While the history of curriculum design is long [see Short, 1986, for an abbreviated history, and Kliebard, 1975d for a sketch of the metaphorical roots of design], perhaps the best-known traditional view of curriculum planning and design is that of J. Galen Saylor, William Alexander, and Arthur Lewis (1981). The topic is venerable enough to have engaged scholars whose work functioned to reconceptualize traditional categories (Macagnoni, 1981; Macdonald & Purpel, 1987). For Saylor, Alexander, and Lewis, the planning and design process is a rational, orderly, and bureaucratic process. As indicated in the table of contents to their *Curriculum Planning for Better Teaching and Learning* (1981, 4th edition), it includes attention to processes and role, to collecting data, and translating these into goals and objectives. After establishing goals, curriculum planners then select an appropriate curriculum design. The table of contents, revealing a highly bureaucratized, rationalized, and sequential protocol for curriculum development, listed the following chapters: 1) Curriculum Planning—an Overview, 2) Processes and Roles in Curriculum Planning, 3) Data for Curriculum Planning, 4) Defining Goals and Objectives, 5) Selecting Appropriate Curriculum Designs, 6) Planning Curriculum Implementation: Instruction, 7) Evaluating the Curriculum, and 8) Curriculum Planning and the Future (Saylor, Alexander, Lewis, 1981).

Curriculum designs. Saylor, Alexander, and Lewis list typical curriculum designs (1981, p. 206). Their Table 5.1 indicates how each curriculum design privileges a certain order of goal, from learning the school subjects and academic disciplines in design number one, to cultivating individual interests, a design we might associate with the child-centered wing of the Progressive Education Movement [see chapters 2 and 3]. Design number 4 might be associated with the political left-wing of the Progressive Movement, such as Counts [see chapter 3]. As Saylor, Alexander, and Lewis point out, no one design is educationally comprehensive. [That is to be expected, given the "two contradictory tendencies—specialization and integration" (Vars, 1982, p. 215).] In columns two and three are listed primary sources for objectives, and the corresponding organization of instruction in the implementation phase.

Which design dominates? Which curriculum design dominates American schooling in our time? As we have seen [chapter 3], since the 1960s the academic disciplines design is the taken-for-granted organization of the school curriculum. Saylor, Alexander, and Lewis (1981) cite the common-sense appeal of the academic disciplines design:

J. Galen Saylor, William Alexander, Arthur Lewis (1981)
Table 5.1 Curriculum Designs

Curriculum designs	Primary Source of Data for Goals and Objectives	Usual Ways to Organize Instruction
1. Subject matter/ disciplines	1. Subject matter to be learned	1. By disciplines (for example, chemistry)
2. Specific competencies/ technology	2. Competencies to be acquired	2. Through instructional designs (for example, learning modules)
3. Human traits/ processes	3. Human traits of learners to be developed	3. Through planned processes (for example, values clarification exercises)
4. Social functions/ activities	4. Needs of society	4. Through community activities or 1, 2, or 3 above (for example, "get out the vote" campaign)
5. Individual needs and interests/activities	5. Needs and interests of the learners	5. Through independent learning activities or 1, 2, or 3 above (for example, learning to paint)

The most characteristic and comprehensive feature of the subject matter/ disciplines design is the relative orderliness of this pattern. The curriculum plan appears neatly divided into subjects, which themselves frequently are subdivided according to school grades and even marking and reporting periods. The Carnegie unit system entrenched this design and a related schedule in the high school with the original definition (1909) of a unit of credit as the study of a subject in high school for one period a day throughout the school year. (pp. 206-207)

Goodlad and Su (1992) suggest that political conditions, rather than intrinsic orderliness, support the popularity of the discipline approach to curriculum design. They argue: "When the nation's welfare appears to be at stake because of the perceived condition of our schools, organizational arrangements that stay close to the academic discipline tend to be in favor" (Goodlad & Su, 1992, p. 327).

There are subsets of organization in the academic disciplines approach to curriculum design (Goodlad & Su, 1992). The first of these is the *single-subject pattern* which emphasizes the logical organization of each academic discipline, with no particular effort to interrelate several disciplines (Hunkins, 1980). A second form of curriculum organized around the academic disciplines is termed *correlational-subject design*. This configuration is designed to build on relationships between and among subject areas. It emphasizes, however, the identities of individual academic disciplines or school subjects. One writer has described this design as "multidisciplinary" (Klein, 1985). Like the correlated-subject pattern, the *fused curriculum* is designed to build on relationships between and among two or more separate disciplines. However, in the fused design the individual identities of academic disciplines tend to blend. Finally, the *broad-field pattern* of curriculum organization creates a unified design across broad domain of knowledge. In this design separate courses in the academic disciplines disappear; subject matter from many different sources is integrated. A commonly acknowledged limitation of this approach is the possibility of a superficial knowledge of the disciplines (Hunkins, 1980).

Other designs influence schooling. Despite the dominance of this curriculum design, other designs listed in the chart operate, although sometimes in the service of the academic disciplines design. For instance, in design number 2, specific competencies have enjoyed influence, especially in the organization of instruction, although they have functioned in the service of learning the academic disciplines. Today the competencies/technology design is supported by an uncritical enthusiasm for technology, especially computers, in the classroom. [We will examine technology and curriculum in a subsequent section of this chapter.] This design has a long tradition in the field, finding its antecedents in the 1920s in the curriculum-as-activity position of Bobbitt and Charters [see chapter 2]. Saylor, Alexander, and Lewis (1981) make a distinction between the social efficiency orientation of the 1920s and its more recent curricular expression:

> there are major differences between the specific-competencies design of Bobbitt and Charters in the 1920s and those of its proponents 60 years later, of whom Popham (1975) is probably the most articulate and prolific writer. In both sets of theories, however, much emphasis is placed on the definition of objectives as the first step in curriculum development . . . But Bobbitt and Charters envisioned performance in far more general terms than do competency-based curriculum protagonists of today. (p. 219)

Another if less well-known example of a bureaucratic model of curriculum is the *Handbook for Evaluating and Selecting Curriculum Materials*, written by Meredith Damien Gall (1981). Gall identified four processes of curriculum materials selection: 1) access: search for materials to meet specific needs, 2) analysis: breakdown and description of the components of a particular set of materials, 3) appraisal: evaluation of the quality and effectiveness of materials, and 4) adoption: selection and purchase. In contrast, other curriculum scholars have thought about the problem of design in broader terms. For instance, in his concept of design as a curriculum matrix, Foshay (1991) argued that it is time for designers to think in terms of larger meanings. Others have worked to combine technical or bureaucratic concerns with broader, humanistic issues. For instance, Pratt (1987a) has viewed curriculum design as a humanistic technology: "I approach these issues as one schooled in educational technology, but committed to the tenets of humanistic education" (p. 150). He noted that "the word 'design' . . . derives from the Latin *designare,* to make a sign. . . . So the word 'design' has a cutting edge which runs back to the design of the first stone tools by protohominids. In its most comprehensive sense, it embraces almost all intentional human activity" (p. 152). Pratt worried that an overreliance on curriculum technology will engender what he terms "cognitive reductionism" (p. 152) and "instrumentalism" (p. 153). He concluded with a call to both camps to come together on the problem of curriculum design:

> The willingness of committed educators of both orientations (humanistic and technological) to enter into informed and open-minded dialogue may hold out the best hope for the future of the curriculum field and for the evolution of schools marked by "practical competence and professional artistry" [Schön, 1983, p. vii]. (p. 160)

[For an elaboration of reflective practice, see Schön, 1991.]

In their *Curriculum Planning for the Classroom,* Connelly, Dukacz, & Quinlan (1980) wrote "for teachers who want to play a stronger, more direct role in planning curriculum and putting it into practice" (p. 1). Underlining its focus on the teacher, a focus Connelly would develop later in the decade into a concept of "personal, practical knowledge" [which we introduced in chapter 10], the three sections of the book are: section 1: sizing up yourself, 2: sizing up others, 3: doing the job. This simple, commonsensical organization of the problem is typical of material written for teachers. Robert S. Zais (1986) regarded the major problem of design as one of confronting encapsulation. Students and teachers are stuck in their own limited perspective—this is what he means by encapsulation—and it is the problem of curriculum design to organize knowledge and experience in order "to liberate students from encapsulation" (p. 19). He explained:

> Encapsulation consists of an interlocking fabric of largely unconscious ideas that distort our concept of reality. . . . [Curriculum] illuminates encapsulation and transmits information concerning "what is real." . . . The critical element is the teacher's way of being with knowledge and people. (p. 22)

These views provide a contrast to the formalized system of curriculum planning and design evident in the traditional approach.

Reservations regarding the influence of behaviorism. Despite their highly rationalized and bureaucratized system, Saylor, Alexander, and Lewis do express reservations regarding the highly behavioral emphasis given curriculum implementation by writers such as Popham (1975). They ask: "Are educational institutions equally effective in achieving both halves of a complete education—learning new behaviors and developing human traits?" (p. 169). Saylor, Alexander, and Lewis appear to answer that question negatively, but only by implication, as they quote approvingly John Goodlad's observation that: "In recent years, we have become almost exclusively preoccupied with, at best, only half of each goal for schooling—the behavioral half" (Goodlad, 1978, p. 276; quoted in Saylor, et al., p. 219). It could be that this reservation about their greatest accomplishment, the nearly complete identification of curriculum with its institutional expression and form, functioned as a "seed" for the "Reconceptualization" of the field in the 1970s.

The new field regards the problem of design and planning rather differently. From a phenomenological perspective for instance, Aoki (1986b) explained that "curriculum as plan . . . [ignores that] teaching is fundamentally a mode of being [and the notion of] curriculum as lived experience" (p. 8). The problem of implementation is not regarded as a bureaucratic problem of enforcement, but rather a problem of dwelling: "in-dwelling in the zone between curriculum-as-plan and curriculum-as-lived experience is not so much a matter of overcoming the tensionality but more a matter of dwelling aright within it" (Aoki, 1986b, p. 9). Esther Zaret (1986) also endorsed "phenomenological curriculum planning" (p. 49); she believed "that it is misleading for someone outside the immediate situation to take on such a task [as curriculum planning]" (p. 51). Wanda May (1986) argued that many alternative and legitimate methods exist in teachers' planning. May called for a "reconceptualization of what curriculum planning is and could be. This would help professionals—neophytes and veterans—develop the sense of agency they deserve" (May, 1986, p. 12).

Futurism and curriculum design: Engle and Longstreet. Saylor, Alexander, and Lewis appear to embrace the interest in futurism that intensified in the 1970s [see also Miel, 1969]. They characterize the proposal developed by Shirley H. Engle and Wilma Longstreet (1978) as "a major curriculum change utilizing future forecasting." For Engle and Longstreet curriculum development must be based on the assumption that:

> the present historical circumstances of accelerating change, multiplying information, and runaway technological production have escaped the control of our democratically oriented society, threatening its survival. . . . Regaining control via systematic use of logical analyses, reflective reasoning, and an increased independence from enculturating processes must take precedence over all other possible functions of schooling. (1978, pp. 234-235)

Engle and Longstreet suggested a "bi-level scenario" in their "values strand" (one of four) of the curriculum. This exercise illustrates the nature of their approach to curriculum development and design. Students would be asked to write a scenario forecasting the future of society based on the collection of data. After the completion of such scenarios, including predictions of the probabilities of their occurrence, students redevelop the scenarios in terms of their own lives: "What might this mean for my life, for what I cherish, for what I hope to be? Subsequently, value questions, applied societally and personally, to the change predicted are explored by students" (1978, p. 255). In "Curriculum for the 21st century," David Pratt (1983) worried that educators teach young people to be like adults while educators ought to be preparing them for the twenty-first century. The interest in futurism has persisted in the field. Longstreet employs it as a central element in her (and Harold Shane's) new synoptic text entitled *Curriculum for a New Millennium* (Longstreet & Shane, 1993).

A Shift in the Field: Kieran Egan
Curriculum design has a also been articulated as a consequence of theory (Egan, 1990a). Kieran Egan's elaborate and sophisticated curriculum design for middle-school aged students is based on "romantic understanding" and expresses Egan's view that stories represent the substance of education (Egan, 1986). [Egan took his Ph.D. with the distinguished philosopher of education Kenneth A. Strike at Cornell University; together (Strike & Egan, 1978) they edited *Ethics and Educational Policy*, a collection in the international library of philosophy of education edited by British philosopher of education R. S. Peters (see chapter 4).] Egan's design represents a significant divergence from the traditional bureaucratized conceptualization of curriculum planning and design.

Saylor, Alexander, and Lewis' conceptualization becomes quickly sensible when one remembers that the first edition appeared in 1954. Public schools were still proliferating in number; curriculum development had not yet been fully standardized by the centralization of the textbook industry. Nor had professors of education been displaced by disciplinary specialists by the Sputnik incident of 1957 and the subsequent funding of university arts and sciences scholars as curriculum developers in the 1960s. The prototypical graduate student of curriculum was probably a teacher aspiring to become a department chair or an associate superintendent for curriculum and instruction. The attention to roles and group processes indicates that Saylor, Alexander, and Lewis envisioned their students as preparing for administrative roles with heavy responsibility for curriculum planning involving diverse constituencies. The highly rationalized and sequential system would function well to deflect special interest groups and to build consensus, or the illusion of consensus, important to the smooth functioning of bureaucratic organizations.

Egan's book reflects the shift in the field during the past forty-five years. While an associate superintendent—aspiring or actual—will still enroll in a graduate course in curriculum, she or he is studying a field that is now a field about ideas, not primarily a field about institutional roles and processes. While Egan's book points to institutional practice and specifically curriculum design, it is a highly theoretical work, a sophisticated instance of contemporary curriculum theory, with a design conclusion. Because the book represents an important shift in the conceptualization of curriculum design, we will review the arguments in some detail. [To study Egan's scholarship more fully, see also Egan, 1988, 1992.]

Romanticism defined. Romanticism is often associated with the nineteenth century. [For other studies linking Romanticism and curriculum theory, see

Willinsky (1987, 1990b, 1990d); Karier, 1990; Martin, 1990; van Manen, 1990; Friedenberg, 1990; Grumet, 1990c; Butt, 1990; Egan, 1990b]. Ralph Waldo Emerson in America, the poets William Wordsworth and Lord Byron in England, philosophers such as Friedrich Nietzsche in Germany, all exhibited Romantic characteristics. Egan (1990a) defines Romanticism as the:

> delight in the exotic, emphasis on individualism, revolt against the conventional, stress on the importance of imagination, intoxication with the sublime in nature, intense inquiry about the self, resistance to order and reason, glorification of transcendent human qualities. (p. 1)

Egan argues that the middle-school years are the appropriate period for the development of romantic understanding in children. Primary romantic understanding is appropriate, Egan tells us, because middle-school students exhibit many of these characteristics anyway. Many children are in a process of differentiating themselves from their families, establishing their own identities, exploring the world outside the home. However, Egan's rationale is based not only on developmental expediency. With Alfred North Whitehead, Egan believes that "during the process of education students should pass through a stage of romance" (p. 16). Egan (1990a, p. 204) notes that in "The Rhythm of Education" Whitehead (1967) discussed a "romantic stage" which lasts from about age eight to twelve. Whitehead wrote: "The stage of romance is the stage of first apprehension. The subject-matter has the vividness of novelty. . . . Education must essentially be a setting in order of a ferment already stirring in the mind" (Whitehead, 1967, 1929, pp. 17-18). Whitehead's process philosophy not only influences Egan's curriculum design, but the work of other curriculum theorists as well. [See Doll, W., 1993a; Oliver & Gershman,1989; see chapters 9 and 12].

Not only Europeans viewed Romanticism as important to the education of the young. The American George Herbert Mead regarded Romanticism not just as a process of self discovery, but a separation as well of the sense of self from the roles played in the world. In this view the "invention" of the "public" self involves also the invention of new roles for people to play or to be (Egan, 1990a). Such self-invention involves the romantic attraction to the imaginative freedom of myth and fantasy, matched with an interest for the particular details of everyday, material reality. A capacity to "re-enchant" the everyday, to bring a sense of the mythic to the mundane, are central features of the romantic life.

Mythic understanding. Egan observes that often the process of education is "described in terms of developments from x to y:"

> from concrete to formal operations, from the simple to the complex, from ignorance to knowledge, "from a social and human center towards a more objective intellectual scheme of organization" (Dewey, 1938). . . . An underlying principle of this [Romantic] scheme is that ideally we leave nothing behind. . . . Romantic understanding, then, should be seen as largely comprising mythic understanding. (1990a, p. 92)

Such understanding suggests the order of intensity of learning one sometimes observes in those with obsessive hobbies. Accompanying such learning is a sense of awe and wonder. Egan is careful to acknowledge that romantic understanding can lead to "vacuous awe" (p. 172) and "cynicism" (p. 173). However, these risks are acceptable because Romanticism is so important. "Romance is," Egan tells us, "the ferment, the excitement without which learning is barren." It is "a mental capacity that we can use to vivify the world and so make it more readily engaging and meaningful" (p. 115).

A curriculum design for romantic understanding. What curricular form would education for romantic understanding take? Egan suggests that a "romantic" curricular design would be one based on narrative and story-telling. This romantic framework is evident in the example of curriculum planning he provides. While his planning protocol is surprisingly Tylerian in character, his organizing concepts are romantic and not behavioral. [Incidentally, in another place, Egan (1988) reviews and restates the objections to the Tylerian, objectives-based procedures of curriculum development, concluding with an alternative procedure based on the story form.]

A Romantic Planning Framework

1. Taking a romantic perspective:
    What images are brought into sharpest focus by viewing the topic romantically? What transcendent human qualities with which students can form romantic associations are prominent and accessible?
2. Organizing the content into a story form:
2.1 Providing access: What content with which students can associate most vividly exemplifies the romantic qualities of the topic?
2.2 Organizing the unit/lesson: What content best articulates the topic into a developing story form, drawing on the principles of romance?
2.3 Pursuing details and contexts: What content can best allow students to pursue some aspect of the topic in exhaustive detail? What perspectives allow students to see the topic in wider contexts?
3. Concluding:
    What is the best way of resolving the dramatic tension inherent in the unit/lesson? How does one bring the romantically important content of the topic to a satisfactory closure that opens to further topics?
4. Evaluating:
    How can one know whether the topic has been understood and the appropriate romantic capacities have been stimulated and developed? (Egan, 1990a, p. 257)

One week. Egan provides a sample of a week's curriculum design based on romantic understanding. The week's activities were designed to teach about medieval castles; the designer is a teacher named Sandy Chamberlain.

Egan ends his theorization of curriculum planning and design by asking: "How can one keep the mind awake, and not have it sink into an ossified slumber? . . . The same problem [Wordsworth] expressed rather more vividly:

Monday	Tuesday	Wednesday	Thursday	Friday
History —the development of the castle in early medieval society; purposes, and responses to social needs and norms.	*Art* —art in castles, study and practice	*Animal and Plant Life* —around the castle; rats and disease; *herbs and healing;* herb gardens.	*History* —castles at the height of their power; numbers and placement around Europe.	*Science* —the physics of undermining a castle's walls.
Math —geometry of castle construction, and defensive angles of fire, etc.	*Music* —as Art above mix two and extend through week. *People Past and Present* —hierarchies of Kings, Barons, Minstrels, Jesters, etc.	*Logic* —the logic of aggression and deterrence in castle; in castle dominated societies.	*Art and Music* —extend Tuesday's work; world of the minstrel, songs and instruments.	*History* —the decay of castles and their destruction in order to build the towns around them.
Language —folk tales about castles; effects of castle life on our language	*History* —Increasingly sophisticated castles as technology of attacking escalated.	*Language* —medieval castle games and their rhymes.	*People Past and Present* —minstrels and artists	*Language* oral and literate influences on cultural life of castles.
People Past and Present —famous people in the development of castles; major builders and planners.	*Technology of Familiar Things* —the wheel and its uses in castles, drawbridges; supplies, etc.	*People Past and Present* —functionaries in castle life, the jobs that kept the daily life going.	*History* —the growth of villages and towns around castles.	*People Past and Present* —toolmakers in the castles.
Science —building walls; using catapults and other weapons.	*Ideas* —justice in medieval castle culture.	*Science* —dynamics of drawbridges, moats, and their maintenance. *Technology of Familiar Things* eating utensils and their development; toilets in castles.	*Science* —instruments for measuring time in castles.	*Ideas* —feudal protectionism. *Celebrate* —constructed model castle, medieval songs, stories, and games. (Egan, 1990a, pp. 246-247)

Making and doing: construction of a model castle continues through the week.

'And custom lie upon thee with a weight,/Heavy as frost, and deep almost as life!'" (quoted in Egan, 1990a, p. 286). Egan acknowledges that the socialization of education permits us to proceed relatively smoothly in society:

> [yet] if we are not careful, that weight of convention and custom seeps through our whole lives, heavy as frost, and that distinctive Western enterprise we call education is frozen at the start and cannot get adequately underway. Wordsworth's and Romanticism's answer, which I am drawing on, is for the middle-school years a particular energetic kind of understanding which begins to build rational thought through the activity of our romantic imagination. (1990a, p. 286)

Egan's thoughtful elaboration of a curriculum design based on romantic understanding is a strong example of theory-driven curriculum design.

Caring: Nel Noddings

Another thoughtful, theory-inspired curriculum design is entitled *The Challenge to Care in Schools: An Alternative Approach to Education*, written by Nel Noddings (1992a), whose feminist theory we have reviewed in chapters 7 and 12. In this volume Noddings makes a significant contribution to the concept of curriculum design. She begins by distinguishing her view from the dominant design emphasis upon the academic disciplines. She explains:

> My argument against liberal education is not a complaint against literature, history, physical science, mathematics, or any other subject. It is an argument, first, against an ideology of control that forces all students to study a particular, a narrowly prescribed curriculum devoid of content they might really care about. Second, it is an argument in favor of greater respect for a wonderful range of human capacities now largely ignored in schools. Third, it is an argument against the persistent undervaluing of skills, attitudes, and capacities traditionally associated with women. (p. xii)

She then reconceives the design problem rather dramatically. Instead of asking questions regarding the academic disciplines, or society, or developmental psychology, Noddings advises the following course:

> We will pretend that we have a large heterogeneous family to raise and educate. . . . How shall we educate them? . . . I will suggest education might best be organized around centers of care: care for self, for intimate others, for associates and acquaintances, for distant others, for nonhuman animals, for plants and the physical environment, for the human-made world of objects and instruments, and for ideas. (p. xiii)

Importantly, the curriculum designer is not a bureaucrat, or even a theoretician; she is a mother:

> Much of the time I will speak as the actual mother of a heterogeneous family, and I will draw freely on personal experience to illustrate my points. Indeed, one of my points will be that we cannot separate education from personal experience. Who we are, to whom we are related, how we are situated all matter in what we learn, what we value, and how we approach intellectual and moral life. (p. xiii)

The basis of her design perspective established, Noddings goes on to criticize incremental reform: "Tinkering with the standard curriculum I will argue, is futile, but drastic change may contribute to a new environment in schools" (p. 3). Next, she rejects any rigid notion of common learnings, insisting that: "There are few things that all students need to know, and it ought to be accepted for students to reject some material in order to pursue other topics with enthusiasm. Caring teachers listen and respond differentially to their students" (p. 19). The concept of caring, on which she has been working for fifteen years, is located partly in the phenomenological tradition:

> Finally, we must consider Heidegger's deepest sense of care. As human beings, we care what happens to us. . . . For adolescents these are among the most pressing questions: Who am I? What kind of person will I be? Who will love me? How do others see me? Yet schools spend more time on the quadratic formula than on any of these existential questions. (p. 20)

If caring is established as the central element of this curriculum design, the primacy of maternal experience is evident: "Women have learned to regard every human encounter as a potential caring occasion" (p. 24). Noddings quotes Ellsworth (1989), Grumet (1988b), and Martin (1984, 1985) in scolding the Marxists: "An increasing number of feminists point out the folly of trying to redistribute either monetary or cultural wealth without addressing the basically evil value structure that undergirds structures of domination" (p. 33).

Noddings argues that there are centers of care and concern in which all people share and in which the capacities of all children must be developed. Further, education should nurture the special cognitive capacities or "intelligence" of all children, and in so doing will want to utilize a scheme of multiple intelligences resembling that suggested by Howard Gardner (1983). Next, she emphasizes that a focus on the centers of care and the development of capacities:

> must be filtered through and filled out by a consideration of differences that are associated with race, sex, ethnicity, and religion. Finally, my arguments draw on . . . maternal interests. . . . Our parental interests inevitably guide the choices we make in all the other categories and, indeed, the categories themselves. (p. 62)

Noddings' quotes approvingly Sizer's (1984) advice to shift to interdisciplinary work so students can concentrate on problems instead of rigidly compartmentalized subjects or disciplines. Concluding her design theory is a section on "Getting Started in Schools," in which she writes:

> We need to give up the notion of an idea of the educated person and replace it with a multiplicity of models designed to accommodate multiple capacities and interests of students. We need to recognize multiple identities. . . . Education should be organized around themes of care rather than the traditional disciplines. (Noddings, 1992a, p. 173)

Noddings' important book incorporates recent efforts to understand curriculum as feminist, phenomenological, and institutional text, weaving a compelling and novel curriculum design.

Noddings' concept of caring is highly developed theoretically. It has, as well, a commonsensical appeal. For instance, in a *New York Times* story:

"Rochester Asks Teachers for 'Extra Mile'" (February 19, 1988), it is reported that every teacher and administrator in a particular school would take personal responsibility for a group of twenty or so students for several years, an idea close to what Noddings has advocated. The reporter notes that:

> adding this element of personal responsibility might help end the failure of the schools to educate poor inner-city children. This program of establishing long-term relationships among students, teachers, and administrators clearly seems to align with the care orientation. (Johnston, 1992, p. 83)

In like fashion, Dobson, Dobson, & Koetting (1983) suggest that the curriculum be judged according to "the extent to which the person has the capacity to be loving" (p. 39). Also thematically linked to Noddings' notion of parental caring in schools is George Willis' (1989) "Reflections on Performance, Pedagogy and Parenting." Robert Starratt, whose work we reported in chapters 4 and 11, has written also of the centrality of care and concern:

> Students progressing through a curriculum of sympathetic learning move from knowing and appreciating fellow students in their own classroom, to sharing and celebrating their own cultural background and that of their fellows in the school, to appreciating several cultures different from those familiar in their own setting, to reflecting on and experiencing the sense of the human family, to having concern for those in distress. (Starratt, 1989, p. 279)

A number of scholars, then, have looked to care as the theoretical element of curriculum design. No scholar has done so more comprehensively, however, than Nel Noddings (1992a).

Types of curriculum organization. Whether planning a curriculum for caring or for business efficiency, curriculum design and organization are intersecting terms. Skilbeck's definition of organization is perhaps broader than that of design. He writes that curriculum organization is:

> the manner in which the elements that constitute the curriculum of an educational system or institution are arranged, interrelated, and sequenced. These elements comprise such general factors as teaching plans and schemes, learning materials, equipment and plant, the professional expertise of the teaching force, and the requirements of assessment and examination bodies. (1985, p. 129)

Goodlad and Su (1992) summarize the traditional elements of curriculum design and organization, which include: 1) scope, 2) continuity, 3) sequence, 4) and integration. *Scope* refers to the breath of the curriculum, that is, the curriculum viewed horizontally "across, for example, the array of courses offered by a secondary school in a given year to those taken or to be taken by a given student" (p. 330). In contrast, continuity and sequence are said to be principles of vertical organization, i.e. the school's or a student's curriculum viewed over time, perhaps the duration of a K-12 school experience. *Continuity* is thus said "to assure students' revisitation of a theme or skill; *sequence*, to build on what preceded" (Goodlad & Su, 1992, p. 330). Sequence refers not just to the repetition of a theme or skill (i.e. continuity), but rather to "the deepening of it, so each success encounter builds on the preceding one" (Goodlad & Su, 1992, p. 330; Leonard, 1950).

Conceptions of curriculum sequence. A classic statement of sequence is associated with Smith, Stanley, and Shores (1950) [see chapter 3]. They identified four sequential approaches to curriculum design and organization: 1) from the simple to the complex, 2) a successive identification of prerequisites, 3) teaching from the part to the whole, and 4) the chronological. In a related scheme, Leonard (1950) identified the following arrangements of sequence: 1) time or chronological order, 2) logical order, 3) difficulty, 4) geographical expansion, and 5) the developmental unfolding of the child. In a more recent study, Armstrong (1989) summarized the four most commonly used approaches: 1) *A chronological approach* in which facts and other curricular elements are sequenced from past to present or present to past. The curricula of history and English literature are commonly organized chronologically. 2) *A thematic approach*, in which factual material is organized thematically, and then taught sequentially. Armstrong lists elementary school language arts programs as an example of a school subject taught thematically. Others might include drama, creative writing, and poetry. 3) *A part-to-whole approach* arranges topics and units in a sequence in which more simple concepts and operations precede more complex ones. Mathematics and foreign languages are commonly sequenced in this fashion. 4) *In the whole-to-part approach,* general information is presented first, providing an overview of the material to be learned. After the overview is grasped, more specific information illustrating general principles is presented. Geography is an example of a school subject commonly organized in this way. The final traditional element of curriculum design and organization is *integration.* This curricular principle functions to interweave curricular elements such as concepts, skills, and values so that they are mutually reinforcing (Goodlad & Su, 1992; Aceland, 1967). Of course, the "location" of ultimate integration is the individual student, a fact that led one wing of the field to study autobiography and biography to portray the individual's integration of curricular experience [see chapter 10].

The Core Curriculum: Goodlad and Su
One of the more durable curriculum designs has been the concept of the core curriculum. Goodlad and Su (1992) define the core curriculum concept as "a specification of those fields deemed essential for all students (usually geared to college admission requirements), most often mathematics, science, English, and social studies" (p. 338). They note that much contemporary debate over the secondary school curriculum emphasizes the question of how much of this curricular core should be required of all students (Adler, 1982; Powell, Farrar, & Cohen, 1985; Sizer, 1984; Goodlad & Su, 1992).

While the contemporary conception of the core curriculum locates the academic disciplines at the curricular center, conceptions of a core curriculum in the 1940s and 1950s located the core at the center of students' needs and the problems of society (Alberty, 1947; Harap, 1952; Goodlad & Su, 1992). Students were to consult the academic disciplines after an "organizing center" of interest had been chosen, ordinarily through a process in which student choice played a major role (Bossing, 1949; Goodlad & Su, 1992). Goodlad & Su (1992, p. 339, emphasis added) list a series of quoted passages which illustrate these prior concepts of the core curriculum.

The emphasis upon the development of a unified program of studies . . . has resulted in the organizing of a common core of experiences drawing content from all the major areas of human living, a curriculum which disregards subject matter lines and which is generally required of all pupils a substantial part of each day (Brown, *1938*, p. 210).

The core program then is made up of those educational experiences which are thought to be important for each citizen in our democracy. Students and teachers do not consider subject matter to be important in itself. It becomes meaningful only as it helps the group to solve the problems which have been selected for study (MacConnell, *1940*, p. 25).

A core represents the sum total of personal youth problems and the problems of social significance encountered by youth. It exists without relation to subject lines and is organized around problems (Smith, *1945*, p. 164).

The term core has come to be applied in modern education to those types of experiences thought necessary for all learners in order to develop certain behavior competencies considered essential for effective living in our democratic society (Bossing, *1949*, p. 394).

A true core curriculum attacks the problems common to all youth. It is a functional approach to harmonizing the concerns of youth, on the one hand, with the demands of society, on the other, without unduly emphasizing one or neglecting the other (Burnett, *1951*, p. 97).

The core curriculum may be regarded as those learning experiences which are fundamental for all learners because they are drawn from their common individual and social needs as competent citizens of a democratic community (Kessler, *1956*, p. 43).

Goodlad and Su comment:

All of these comments are a far cry from the core curriculum frequently proposed for high school students after the publication of *A Nation at Risk* (National Commission on Excellence in Education, 1983): a core of courses in the fields of the natural sciences, the social studies, mathematics, and English required for admission for college. (1992, p. 339)

As Goodlad and Su have noted, in times of perceived national emergency, the organization of the curriculum tends toward a traditional academic disciplines design. Even the durable concept of "core curriculum" has been recast as a school-subject centered design.

IV
Curriculum Implementation:
Snyder, Bolin, Zumwalt, and Fullan

Change is a process, not an event.
(Michael Fullan, 1982, p. 41)

The solemn truth is that at present some attempts at curriculum implementation involve little more than a poor plan, drawn up with the meticulous detail of a plan for a rocket, but serving no discernible educational end.
(Robin Barrow, 1984b, p. 225)

Three Major Approaches

In a recent review of research on curriculum implementation, Snyder, Bolin, and Zumwalt (1992) list three major approaches. The first, possibly the most common, is termed the "fidelity perspective," by which they mean a focus on: "1) measuring the degree to which a particular innovation is implemented as planned and 2) identifying the factors which facilitate or hinder implementation as planned" (p. 404). The assumption here is that successful curriculum implementation is characterized by fidelity to the original plan. This is the traditional conception of curriculum implementation. Previously, in a related example, Mauritz Johnson (1974) had elaborated "a PIE technical model: planning, implementation, evaluation" (p. 375). Despite his loyalty to a "scientific" elaboration of curriculum planning, Johnson acknowledged that:

Some decision-making processes relating to curriculum are essentially political in nature and more often follow a strategy of "disjointed incrementalism" than the rational, formal methods implied by the model discussed here. But political decisions need not be devoid of rationality. (Johnson, 1974, p. 384)

Also acknowledging the politics of curriculum implementation, Louise Berman (1988) argued for normative inquiry in curriculum (NIC). In NIC the emphasis is upon values and ethics, as contrasted with a primarily analytic approach. A normative approach would still encounter the difficulties of curriculum implementation: "Yet in many communities never have teachers had so little curriculum decision-making power. . . . In doing the tough work associated with NIC, perhaps we will develop curriculums consonant with the problematic nature of life in a democracy" (Berman, 1988, p. 292). Whether working normatively or analytically, the fidelity approach to curriculum implementation tends to limit our appreciation for teaching as a creative and autonomous sphere of activity.

The fidelity approach. Snyder, Bolin, and Zumwalt (1992) list the assumptions underlying the fidelity approach to curriculum implementation. First, it is assumed that the curriculum is developed by experts outside the classroom. Second, change is conceived to be a linear process in which teachers implement the curricular innovations developed by experts. Third, the curriculum is then evaluated to determine if planned objectives have been met. Implementation is considered successful when teachers enact the curriculum plan as stipulated. Typically, an implementation scale and/or checklist is developed in order to assess the degree of implementation. The fidelity approach was the most common perspective in curriculum implementation according to a research review study conducted by Fullan and Pomfret in 1977, involving 12 of 15 studies reviewed. Illustrative of implementation studies from a fidelity perspective include Gross, Giacquinta, and Bernstein's (1971) study of implementation in an inner city elementary school, work by Hall and Loucks (1976) [considered by Fullan and Pomfret (1977) as "the most sophisticated and explicit conceptualization" (p. 335)], and more recently, studies of the National Diffusion Network (NDN) which typify a large-scale modified "research, development, and dissemination" (RD&D) approach (Crandall et al., 1983; Huberman, 1983; Snyder, Bolin & Zumwalt, 1992).

The mutual adaptation approach. The second major approach to curriculum implementation is termed "mutual adaptation." This approach is defined as: "that process whereby adjustments in a curriculum are made by curriculum developers and those who actually use it in the school or classroom context. This implies a certain amount of negotiation and flexibility on the part of both designers and practitioners" (Synder, Bolin & Zusswalt, 1992, p. 410). As Fullan notes, "change is a process, not an event" (1982, p. 41).

The term "mutual adaptation" emerged from the 1970s Rand Study headed by Berman and McLaughlin. McLaughlin suggested that the nature of the projects required that implementation be a mutually adaptive process between the client and the institution, i.e. that specific project goals must be concretized over time by the participants themselves (McLaughlin, 1976). Other illustrative research on curriculum implementation investigated an open space school whose faculty were asked to promote individualization and humanization (Smith & Keith, 1971). More recent research (Popkewitz, Tabachnick, & Wehlage, 1981) investigated how underlying ideological assumptions influenced curriculum implementation.

Factors affecting implementation. Using Fullan's scholarship (1982) as a framework, Snyder, Bolin, and Zumwalt (1992) list fifteen factors affecting implementation.

The first four are related to the characteristics of change:
1. Need and relevance for the change, including the perceived need by the implementors. The greater the recognized need for change, the greater the likelihood of implementation.
2. Clarity of the goals of curricular innovation. Again, the greater the understanding of goals and what is to be gained by innovation, the greater the degree of implementation.
3. Complexity, referring to the difficulty and extent of change required: "The greater the complexity in innovations with differentiated components incre-

mentally introduced, the greater the degree of implementation." (Snyder, Bolin, Zumwalt, 1992, p. 416)
4. Quality and practicality, referring to the quality and availability of materials.

Six factors refer to characteristics at the level of the school district.
5. The history of the district's attempts at innovation. If the district's previous history is favorable, the more likely is implementation of future projects.
6. The adoption process, suggesting that the higher the quality of planning, the greater the likelihood of successful implementation.
7. District administrative support. The more support, the more likely is successful implementation.
8. Staff development and participation. Again, the predictable relationships appear to apply.
9. Time-line and information systems (evaluation). When the timing of events is guided by a shared understanding of the implementation process, the greater the likelihood of implementation success.
10. Board and community characteristics, and again the predictable relationships appear to hold.

The next three school-level factors are pertinent as well.
11. The role of the principal, suggesting that the greater the active support of the principal, the greater the likelihood of implementation success.
12. Teacher-teacher relationships, suggesting that the greater the degree of collegiality, trust, and open communication among teachers, the greater the likelihood of successful implementation.
13. Teacher characteristics and orientations, suggesting that the greater the degree of teacher efficacy, the greater the degree of implementation.

Finally, two so-called external factors affect implementation.
14. Government agencies, suggesting that the greater the congruence among local needs, reform elements, and subjective realities, the greater the degree of implementation.
15. External assistance, suggesting that the greater the integration with the local district, the greater the likelihood of implementation. (Snyder, Bolin, Zumwalt, 1992, pp. 416-417)

A third approach: Curriculum enactment. The third approach to curriculum implementation is characterized as curriculum enactment, an approach used less frequently than fidelity and mutual adaptation. From this perspective, the:

externally created curricular materials and programmed instructional strategies at the heart of the fidelity and mutual adaptation perspectives are seen as tools for students and teacher to use as they construct the enacted experience of the classroom. (Snyder, Bolin, Zumwalt, 1992, p. 418)

Snyder, Bolin, and Zumwalt (1992) cite the Denver Curriculum Project [see chapter 2] as an early instance of the enactment approach to implementation. Additionally, they discuss three illustrative studies: 1) *The Eight Year Study* (Aikin, 1942), 2) *Beyond Surface Curriculum* (Bussis, Chittenden, and Amarel, 1976), and 3) *Contexts of Curriculum Change: Conflict and Consonance* (Paris, 1989).

The Eight-Year Study. The Eight-Year Study was the most comprehensive study of curriculum experimentation at the high school level ever undertaken. [For a review of the Eight-Year Study, see chapter 3.] Suffice to say in the context of curriculum implementation, two findings were noteworthy:

> 1) the important characteristics of both of the more effective schools were: their willingness to undertake a search for valid objectives; organizing curricula and techniques and setting them in motion in order to attain the objectives; and finally measuring the effectiveness of curricula and techniques by appropriate evaluation devices. These are basic processes; their utility in any type of school is demonstrated (Chamberlin, et al., 1942, p. 182; quoted in Snyder, Bolin, Zumwalt, 1992, p. 422), and 2) uniformity would be neither necessary nor desirable in school practice. (Aikin, 1942, p. 123; quoted in Snyder, Bolin, Zumwalt, 1992, p. 422)

Beyond the surface curriculum. Like Connelly and Clandinin (1991), Bussis, Chittenden, and Amarel (1976) acknowledge the teacher—along with the child—as the central figure in curriculum development. They argue that if educational change is to occur, changes in teacher thinking must occur: "Neither a stimulus nor a curriculum can be psychologically relevant entities apart from a person's interpretation of them" (p. 13). Implementation becomes characterized as a change in the thinking of teachers; therefore, the study's "major emphasis is on a theoretical analysis of teachers' understandings" (p. 3).

Change at the individual level. Michael Fullan (1985) has suggested what is necessary for change to occur at the individual level. While some of the following characteristics overlap with the previous list of general factors affecting implementation, these focus upon the process of individual teachers changing their thinking, a view that Bussis, Chittenden, and Amarel would seem to agree is essential to successful curriculum implementation. Fullan (1985) wrote:

> To summarize, a change at the individual level is a process whereby individuals alter their ways of thinking and doing (e.g., teaching in this case): 1) change takes place over time; 2) the initial stages of any significant change always involve anxiety and uncertainty; 3) ongoing technical assistance and psychological support assistance are crucial if the anxiety is to be coped with; 4) change involves learning new skills through practice and feedback—it is incremental and developmental; 5) the most fundamental breakthrough occurs when people can cognitively understand the underlying conception of and rationale to "why this new way works better;" 6) organizational conditions within the school (peer norms, administrative leadership) and in relation to the school (e.g., external administrative support and technical help) make it more or less likely that the process will succeed; and 7) successful change involves pressure, but it is pressure through interaction with peers and other technical and administrative leaders. (p. 396)

Fullan's view seems consonant with that of Diane L. Common (1983), who argued that:

> The centralizing of curriculum decision-making along with increased bureau-cratization of school operation typify this [dominant] model [which frames the] teacher as user rather than creator of curriculum ideas and materials. . . . The implementation of curriculum innovations is, in effect, a struggle for the power to determine classroom practice. (p. 203)

Democratizing this power may be a prerequisite for reform. Authentic curriculum change may require research "into the nature of language of practitioners and how that language can be used to express new conceptions of school practice" (Olson, 1982, p. 95).

Conflict and consonance. Cynthia Paris (1989) has promoted the "enactment perspective." Her assumptions—generally congruent with reconceptualized curriculum theory—include:

1. Curriculum knowledge includes situated knowledge, created in practice when teachers engage in the ongoing processes of teaching and learning in class-rooms.
2. Curriculum change is a process of individual growth and change in thinking and practice rather than an organizational procedure of design and imple-mentation.
3. Teachers' work with curriculum, whether creating and adapting their own curricula or responding to curricula created and imposed by others, is shaped in response to their perceptions of their contexts. (1989, pp. 2-3)

Paris' perspective is consonant with research conducted in by those working to understand curriculum as phenomenological [see chapter 8] and autobio-graphic text [see chapter 10] and with those who have reconceptualized in-service education as teacher development [see later this chapter].

"Change" replaces "implementation." From these three assumptions, Paris (1989) ethnographically studied curriculum change, rather than curriculum implementation (which implies a fidelity approach). She studied five elemen-tary teachers for two years as they worked to create and adapt a word-processing curriculum. Paris locates curriculum change in the "multiple and often conflicting contexts that include ongoing practices, histories, and dominant ideologies of organization and individuals, and interprets the influence of these contexts from the meaning perspectives of the partici-pants" (Paris, 1989, p. 23). In this study the process of curriculum change involved the conflict and consonance between the fidelity approach to curriculum implementation shared by the district-level administrative team and the curriculum enactment approach to curriculum change shared by the teachers. In this case, the building principal acted to deflect the perspective of the district administrative team, allowing the teachers to work from their enactment perspective. However, the two perspectives came into conflict, resulting in wasted time, energy, and resources. Paris wrote:

> At points of conflict, teachers' energies were needlessly wasted "managing" to conduct their work within and around constraints and conflicts and to cope with the anger and frustration they engendered. Efforts were blocked, ideas

sacrificed, and goals compromised at the points of conflict that could not be "managed" or, in the teachers' words, "gotten around." (1989, p. 2)

Despite this conflict, Paris reported that the five teachers in the project were able to create their own curriculum for teaching work processing, including the use of word processing to extend the ongoing curricula (Paris, 1989; Snyder, Bolin & Zumwalt, 1992).

Another model of change has been developed at the University of Texas at Austin which appears to be an example of the enactment perspective. Called the Concerns-Based Adoption Model (CBAM), this research summarized the following: 1) change is a process, not an event [cf. Fullan, 1982, p. 41]; 2) change is accomplished by individuals; 3) change is a highly personal experience; 4) change involves developmental growth; 5) change is best understood in operational terms; and 6) the focus of facilitation should be on individuals, innovations, and the context (Hord, Rutherford, Huling-Austin, & Hall, 1987).

Decision-making. In the sphere of the classroom, curriculum implementation and change occurs as teachers make decisions. For example, decision-making can be the heart of social studies curriculum, and central to the curriculum as a whole (Engle, 1960; Engle & Longstreet, 1971). From a fidelity perspective, the teachers' decisions are generally in the realm of "how to," i.e. how to deliver the curriculum most efficiently and effectively to the students in classrooms. From the perspective of mutual adaptation, the teacher's role amplifies, and her or his decisions are understood to reshape the curriculum as planned according the dictates of the local classroom situation. From the enactment perspective, teachers' decisions are necessary for there to be a curriculum at all, as it is the curriculum enacted that makes a curriculum at all (Snyder, Bolin, Zumwalt, 1992). The distinction between the two ends of the implementation continuum—fidelity at one end, enactment at the other—is not unlike the distinction Caswell made in the 1930s between curriculum making and curriculum development [see chapter 3]. Curriculum development is that which makes "curriculum ideas come alive in the classroom" (Foshay, 1989), requiring negotiation (Common, 1983). In a Caswellian sense, then, fidelity approaches to curriculum implementation represent curriculum making, and enactment approaches to curriculum implementation represent curriculum development (Snyder, Bolin, Zumwalt, 1992).

V
Technology: Saettler, Bereiter, Scardamalia, and Bowers

The essential task of educational technology . . . is to focus on how learners use their knowledge and constructions to understand what they are taught.
(Paul Saettler, 1990, p. 319)

Our position is that the field of instructional computing is still young and evolving. The computer has an important role in instruction *alongside* the teacher, the book, and other instructional media.

(Stephen Alessi & Stanley Trollip, 1991, pp. 2-3)

Technology creates the illusion of immediate success, based on that which the eyes can see here and now.

(Ellis A. Joseph, 1983, p. 64)

The Greek word for technology is *techne*, translated as art, craft, or skill. Plato regarded *techne* and *episteme* (translated as systematic or scientific knowledge) as closely related. For Aristotle, *techne* was the systematic use of knowledge for intelligent human action. Broadly understood, then, technology refers to any system of practical knowledge; it is not restricted to hardware. One contemporary definition says that technology is: "any systematized practical knowledge, based on experimentation and/or scientific theory, which enhances the capacity of society to produce goods and services, and which is embodied in productive skills, organization, or machinery" (Ely, 1983, p. 2).

Technology has influenced curriculum and especially instructional design. The development and employment of hardware has been secondary to the employment of technological schemes for instruction and learning. Behavioral psychology epitomized this technological view of education in the 1960s, but it was soon eclipsed by Piagetian developmental psychology in the 1970s, which was then eclipsed by cognitive psychology and cognitive science. In this latter formulation, the emphasis upon behavior and developmental stages, evident in the behavioral and Piagetian approaches, was replaced with an emphasis upon the: "organization, processing, and storage of information by the learner. . . . From the cognitive view, educational technology should be focused on activating the appropriate learning strategies during the instructional process rather than merely initiating behavioral responses" (Saettler, 1990, p. 14). Bereiter and Scardamalia (1992) note that, contrary to common belief, cognitive scientists to not believe that the computer is an adequate model of the mind.

More recent if unconventional views incorporate fields outside cognitive psychology and cognitive science. Psychotechnology involves the management and control of psychological processes of the student, and may draw upon biofeedback, meditation, music, and yoga. Other scholars in the field have begun to explore fields well-known to curriculum theorists, such as qualitative research and hermeneutics [see chapters 8 and 12] (Messer, et al., 1988; Hlynka & Belland, 1991). A full review of technological influences is outside the scope of this introductory textbook. For a comprehensive history of educational technology see, for example, Paul Saettler's *The Evolution of American Educational Technology* (1990). In this section we will review briefly major aspects of this history, and list recent developments as well as reservations regarding the uncritical embrace of educational technology by some curriculum scholars.

Visual Instruction

The interest in visual curriculum and incorporating emerging visual technologies—such as film, slides, interactive videos, hypercards, video lessons—in instructional presentations can be said to have distinct historical phases. The first is the school museum movement. The second is the organization of slide libraries. Next is the development of education film, followed by the employment of computers during the past two decades.

School museum movement. Rather than existing solely as storage houses, museums in America have also sought an instructional role. It is not uncommon for museums to employ educational specialists to organize displays with an eye to teaching, rather than a random collection of objects. [For instance, Elizabeth Vallance, whose work we have reviewed in chapters 1 and 11, has worked for the St. Louis Art Museum.] Educational directors of museums enjoy responsibility for a wide range of school-museum and general public educational activities, including guided tours, lectures, cooperative programs with public and private schools, as well as arranging for temporary loans of single specimens made to libraries, schools, individuals, as well as other museums.

The school-museum history is a long one; at the opening of the Metropolitan Museum in New York City in 1880, museums were characterized as instruments for the social and educational progress of the American people (Saettler, 1990). Under the impetus of the U. S. commissioner of education, William Torrey Harris, a former superintendent of schools in St. Louis [see chapters 2 & 7], the St. Louis Educational Museum became the first administrative unit for instructional media in an American public school system in 1905. Thirty years earlier, in his annual report, Harris had written: "every lesson should be given in such a way as to draw out the perceptive powers of the pupil by leading him to reflect on what he sees or to analyze the object before him" (Harris, 1875, p. 164). The Reading (Pennsylvania) and Cleveland (Ohio) Educational Museums were the second and third school museums established, in 1908 and in 1909 respectively.

Rationale for visual instruction. From the earliest days, the rationale for visual instruction rested upon the notion that visual materials could function as an antidote for verbalism. One of the first statements of the rationale was written by the National Education Association (NEA), which stated in 1886:

> The objects of thought used in teaching are the *real object*, which is the material object in relation with the senses, or the mental object distinctly in consciousness; the *model*, which represents, in the solid, the form, color, size, and relative position of the parts of the object; the *picture*, which imperfectly represents on a surface the appearance of the object in position, form, color, and relative position of parts; the *diagram*, which represents on a surface the sectional view of the object; the *experiment*, which shows the action and effects of physical forces; *language*, as an object of thought, in the formation of words . . . and the *book*, how to read and use books. (NEA, 1886, p. 274)

This century-old statement of a concrete-to-abstract continuum in cognition and instruction will resurface again and again.

Also illustrative of this concrete-to-abstract notion is a statement by William G. Bagley [see chapter 2], who wrote an introductory section for the first edition of *Visual Education* in 1906. That statement, entitled "Concreteness in Education," reads that "the most effective kind of education is that in which the learner is brought face to face with actual concrete situations," and that education in general is "more closely realized by pictures projected through the stereopticon, by moving pictures, and by stereographs" (Bagley, 1906, ix-x).

This notion of a concrete-to-abstract continuum was reasserted in the second half of the twentieth century by Edgar Dale (1954), who developed a "Cone of Experience." At the bottom of the cone was "direct, purposeful experiences," presumably the most concrete form of experience, and at the top of the cone, "verbal symbols." Categories in-between included, moving from concrete to abstract, "contrived experiences, dramatic participation, demonstrations, field trips, exhibits, motion pictures, still pictures, radio-recordings, and visual symbols." As we noted, the concrete-to-abstract notion also surfaced in the influential work of Jean Piaget, whose work on cognitive development influenced two generations working in early and middle childhood education. Piaget's stage theory began with concrete operations and ended with formal or abstract operations. A similar idea seems to hold in phenomenological epistemology, except that phenomenology privileges direct, unmediated experience over abstract formulation [see chapter 8].

Educational radio. Several public school systems pioneered the instructional use of radio, including Cleveland, Chicago, Detroit, Des Moines, Buffalo, and Rochester. In Rochester, for instance, an inter-institutional collaboration developed, which included the Rochester Civic Music Association, the Rochester Public Library, and the Rochester Museum of Arts and Sciences. Institutions of higher learning that were involved in exploring the educational uses of radio included the Universities of Wisconsin, Kansas, Michigan, and Minnesota, as well as Oregon State University (Saettler, 1990). A promising technological development, radio would enjoy a short life in the history of educational technology.

An illustrative example of the educational use of radio was the Ohio State School of the Air, supported by the state government, private foundation money (the Payne Fund), station WLW in Cincinnati, and private individuals. Despite an auspicious debut on January 7, 1929, the program was disbanded less than a decade after its inception (Saettler, 1990). The first weekly schedule is illustrative:

Weekly Schedule

Monday:	Story plays and rhythmics and health talks, alternating.
	Current events.
	History dramalogs.

Tuesday:	Special features, questions and answer periods. Art appreciation. Civil government, by those who govern.
Wednesday:	Stories for younger pupils. Stories for intermediate grades. Stories for upper grades.
Thursday:	Dramatization of literature for high schools. Geography.
Friday:	No program in deference to the Damrosch [conductor of the New York Symphony Orchestra] lessons in music.

(Saettler, 1990, p. 199)

National schools of the air. National schools of the air were established as well. The first was the RCA Educational Hour, which went on the air on October 26, 1928, and ceased broadcasting in 1942. The second national school of the air was sponsored by the Columbia Broadcasting System (CBS); it began broadcasting on February 4, 1930. Called the American School of the Air, the program broadcast until 1940. An international school of the air was conceived by a radio engineer named Walter Lemmon who had worked on President Woodrow Wilson's peace ship. In cooperation with the Massachusetts Institute of Technology, Mount Holyoke College, Boston University, Harvard University, Brown University, Tufts University and Wellesley Colleges, this program began to broadcast in 1937. Despite these many efforts to promote the educational uses of the radio, educators failed to take a long-term interest in this form of educational technology (Saettler, 1990).

Educational film. Before the advent of the microcomputer, the major item of educational technology was the film. The first use of educational films in schools occurred in 1910. While the New York City Board of Education declined to incorporate film in the curriculum due to expense, and the Boston schools rejected film due to fire hazards which accompanied the early film projectors, Rochester, New York became the first public school system to adopt films for regular instructional use, perhaps due to the presence of the Eastman Kodak Company in Rochester. In fact, not quite twenty years later the Eastman Kodak Company formed Eastman Teaching Pictures, Inc., which produced silent educational films in the areas of geography, general science, and health. The company withdrew from this business in 1944 (Saettler, 1990).

Educational television. As early as 1945, Iowa State College (now University) in Ames applied to the Federal Communications Commission (FCC) for a construction permit to build an educational television studio. On February 21, 1950, WOI-TV began broadcasting. The first educational television stations operating on channels exclusively maintained for education started in 1953. KUHT, licensed by the University of Houston and the Houston Board of Education, became the first noncommercial station [WOI carried advertisements but was nonprofit], broadcasting on May 12, 1953. After the inauguration of these first stations, others followed, and by mid-1955 sixteen channels were in operation. Among these first stations were WQED Channel 13 in Pittsburgh, KQED Channel 9 in San Francisco, WGBH Channel 2 in Boston, WTTW Channel 11 in Chicago (Saettler, 1990). Now characterized as public television, nonprofit television, still serving an important educational function, is available throughout the United States.

While educational television refers to any type of video program broadcast for any serious purpose, instructional television refers to open- or closed-circuit video programs designed to teach specific subject matter. The first instructional television programs were developed at the State University of Iowa during the 1930s. By the mid-1950s, instructional television was not uncommon, especially in large, introductory courses required of all students on state university campuses. Widespread use of instructional television developed in elementary and secondary schools, with more on the elementary than secondary level (Saettler, 1990). Recently, commercial efforts at educational television, for instance Channel One (developed by Whittle Communications), have appeared. Television projects have been underway in the United States ("ThinkAbout", developed by a consortium of American states and Canadian provinces, and "Freestyle"), Canada ("Eureka!" developed by Television Ontario), and the United Kingdom ("Scene" developed by the British Broadcasting System). "Eureka!" exhibits the closest fit with existing school curricula; "ThinkAbout" was designed to extend the curriculum by introducing problem-solving skills; "Freestyle" attempted to teach social problems; "Scene" represented a miscellany of programs not closely related to any particular syllabus or project (Rockman & Burke, 1991). Despite some enthusiasm for these ventures and for the possibilities of instructional television, there were caveats:

> Television is not the medium for total teaching, nor should it be used as an automation device to reduce the cost of education by enlarging the teacher-pupil ratio. Television should be used to provide learning experiences that are not possible under conventional conditions of classroom instruction. (Tanner, D., 1961, pp. 320-321)

And at least one scholar in the area is reserved regarding its future: "When the final chapter of the history of instructional television is written, it may be that, like the slide, film, radio, and teaching machine, television as an instructional medium will fall into general disuse" (Saettler, 1990, p. 388).

Programmed Instruction

B. F. Skinner. Relying on the behaviorist school of psychology, educational technology was developed to program instruction. B. F. Skinner was the most visible in this area. In 1954, at a conference at the University of Pittsburgh, Skinner demonstrated a machine to teach spelling and arithmetic (Skinner, 1954). This work had begun at least twenty-five years earlier. Sidney L.

Pressey, a psychologist on the faculty of Ohio State University, exhibited a device which anticipated modern teaching machines at the 1925 meeting of the American Psychological Association (Saettler, 1990). The programmed instruction movement was short-lived, however, and by 1964 Skinner was expressing concern that teaching machines were not widely understood (Skinner, 1965). By the 1970s most publishers had abandoned the programmed text business as well (Saettler, 1990). Replacing it were other instructional applications of behaviorism, now adjusted to accommodate "individual differences." Typical approaches to the "individualization" of instruction included the Keller (a colleague of Skinner's) Plan, Individually Prescribed Instruction (IPI), Program for Learning in Accordance with Needs (PLAN), and Individually Guided Education (IGE). By the mid-1970s, however, individualized instruction as a movement was on the decline (Saettler, 1990). Its replacement was computer-based instruction.

Computer-based instruction (CBI). Very generally speaking, computer applications can be divided into administration (such as grading, producing assignments, correspondence, record keeping), teaching about the computer, and teaching with the computer. All three are relevant for teaching about the computer (computer literacy and computer science instruction) and for teaching other subject areas *with* the computer (Alessi & Trollip, 1991).

Instructional computer programs, also known as courseware, are referred to by a variety of different terms. Among these are:

CAI—computer-assisted instruction
CBE—computer-based education
CAL—computer-assisted learning
IAC—instructional applications of computers

The five major types of computer-based instructional programs are: 1) tutorials, 2) drills, 3) simulations, 4) games, and 5) tests. The objectives of the *tutorial* include: 1) information is presented and/or skills are modeled, 2) students are guided through initial use of the information or skills, 3) student practices for retention and fluency, and 4) student learning is evaluated. *Drills* are used primarily for the third aspect of the instructional process, providing practice. *Simulation* teaches about some aspect of the world by imitation or replication. Simulations differ from interactive tutorials, which assist students to learn by providing information and using selected question-answer techniques. In a simulation the student learns by in fact performing those activities that are to be learned in a setting that is similar to the real world. Simulations may be employed for any of the four phases of instruction. *Instructional games* are defined broadly, and include such games as "decimal darts," a game which instructs about points on the number line, "how the west was one—three × four" a board game which depicts a race between a stagecoach and railroad engine, "ordeal of the hangman," a vocabulary game. All games involve the following elements:

goals, rules, competition, challenge, fantasy, safety, entertainment. Finally, the computer can be used to design and administer tests or examinations. What is involved in the development of computer-based instruction? First is preparation, then design, followed by flow charting, then storyboarding, programming and supporting materials, and finally, evaluation. Traditional computer-based instruction, that is the tutorial, drill, simulation, or game varieties, tend to embed the instruction within the content of the lesson. Specific instructional techniques are selected and incorporated in the particular content of the lesson (Alessi & Trollip, 1991).

Computer-Assisted Instruction (CAI). Much early work on computer-assisted instruction was done at the International Business Machines Corporation (IBM) in the 1950s. It began its ascent just as programmed instruction declined, during the 1960s, when millions of dollars in federal funds supported its development. However, due to excessive expectations, CAI began to decline. CAI was propped up by additional funding from the federal government, through the National Science Foundation. In 1971 a $10 million grant was awarded to Control Data Corporation (CDC) and Mitre Corporation, to create one national system of CAI. Two approaches to CAI, building on the IBM work, emerged from this project: PLATO, developed in 1959 by Don Bitzer, and TICCIT, developed in 1971 (Saettler, 1990). PLATO enabled computer-based instruction to integrate text and graphics; it provided teachers with one of the first programming environments for computer-based instruction. Less comprehensive than PLATO, TICCIT was created by researchers at MITRE and at the University of Texas at Austin, most prominent of whom was Victor Bunderson [who later moved to Brigham Young University] (MacGregor, 1992). TICCIT project introduced computer-based instruction on mini-computers (Alessi & Trollip, 1991).

Drill and practice. These approaches followed the pioneering work of Richard Atkinson and Patrick Suppes who had developed early applications of CAI in collaboration with IBM. A drill-and-practice system began in 1963 in elementary mathematics and reading. The influence of behaviorist psychology is evident in Suppes' depiction of the teaching process as present-ing exercises (or stimuli) and reinforcing students' responses. The behaviorist protocol is a simple one: tell students they are correct; then present a new exercise. Alternately, tell them they are wrong; tell them the correct response, then re-present the exercise. The teacher's job (assumed by the computer) is to present increasingly more difficult exercises, each building on previous experience, leading finally to knowing the specific body of information (quoted in Solomon, 1986, p. 8). Suppes, Atkinson, and William Estes founded the Computer Curriculum Corporation (CCC) in 1967 to further the development of CAI drill-and-practice materials (Saettler, 1990).

PLATO and TICCIT. PLATO is a second illustration of the drill-and-prac-tice strategy associated with CAI. While Suppes and his colleagues worked at

Stanford University, PLATO, more comprehensive than TICCIT, was developed first at Control Data Corporation, then at the University of Illinois. The project was charged with the development of a comprehensive system of hardware and software that could be widely used in the nation's schools. The third project that reflected the drill-and-practice scheme was TICCIT (Time-Shared, Interactive, Computer-Controlled Information Television) project. The project began focused on elementary school curriculum, but by the late 1970s had refocused on providing CAI for mathematics and English at community colleges. Were these projects successful? Saettler (1990) judges:

> Clearly, the NSF-funded projects PLATO and TICCIT can be considered failures by their own criterion, namely, that of achieving commercial profitability. Their emphasis on technological hardware was misplaced, and they did not solve the basic problem of producing effective instructional hardware. (p. 310)

Artificial intelligence and expert systems. In 1956 Allan Newell and Herbert A. Simon published a description of a computer program that solved problems by simulating rationality or logic. When a computer program imitates the human process of deduction, the program is regarded as *artificial intelligence* (AI). An AI program which solves a problem using a pre-programmed data base consisting of knowledge that human experts, such as physicians and medical personnel, might use, is an instance of an expert system. The CAI system called SCHOLAR, an interactive expert system for teaching facts about South American geography, was the first effort to develop a tutorial system which simulated the ways human teachers worked (Saettler, 1990).

Beginning in 1976 at Stanford University, E. A. Feigenbaum and associates developed artificial intelligence programs in several areas. PUFF diagnosed pulmonary disorders; MYCIN diagnosed blood inflection and prescribed appropriate treatment; DENDRAL enabled chemists to make accurate guesses regarding the molecular structure of unknown compounds; META-DENDRAL was designed to compose its own rules for explaining basic sets of data. In 1979, the MYCIN program was utilized to develop a teaching program called GUIDON. Another CAI program was SOPHIE, which taught problem-solving skills to engineers.

Model building and microworlds. The LOGO project, based not on behaviorism but on Piagetian psychology, was designed to provide a microworld for young children so that they might study mathematics. This microworld, called mathland, was developed by Seymour Papert (1980). The LOGO system may point to more sophisticated CAI systems in which the computer might be employed within a humanistic educational tradition. Despite these developments, difficulties in CAI remained. O'Shea and Self (1983) pointed to four: 1) the reaction of those involved, 2) materials which are not well designed, 3) technical problems, such as cost and reliability, and 4) evaluation, in trying to decide whether what has been done was educationally worthwhile (O'Shea & Self, 1983, pp. 217-218). Clancey (1987), whose

GUIDON program is perhaps the most advanced of existing programs in its interaction with the learner, suggested that "it may be another five years before questions about completeness, usefulness, and reliability of AI-based instructional programs are even meaningful" (p. 245). Five years have now passed and the verdict is still out.

More recently the use of computers in the classrooms has been expanded beyond their functions as tutors in computer-assisted instruction (CAI). There is heightened interest in interactive video, which is computer-based instruction augmented by a video peripheral for high quality visual and aural presentations. Interactive video, artificial intelligence, and computer-managed instruction are three aspects of computer-based instruction that may become increasingly utilized in the future (Alessi & Trollip, 1991). There is also a growing interest in integrating computers into the mainstream curriculum. How is this integration accomplished? Salomon (1991) advises that: "The designers of a curriculum [must] take into consideration computers' unique possibilities, whereas the use of computers comes to serve the curriculum rather than its own purposes" (p. 89). An example might be the study of ecology, which now can be presented in its complex interrelationships among numerous variables, thanks to the computer (Salomon, 1991).

AI incorporated into CAI. Bereiter and Scardamalia (1992) note that the incorporation of artificial intelligence (AI) into computer-assisted instruction (CAI) represents a more profound shift than many perhaps appreciate. They suggest that the incorporation of AI into CAI represents a shift from programs that store answers to exercise programs that actually represent the knowledge required to do the exercises (Clancey, 1987). In conventional or simulation "drill and practice" CAI, the program cannot be said to "know" the subject it intended to teach (as a geometry textbook cannot be said to know geometry) (Bereiter & Scardamalia, 1992). AI-based or so-called intelligent tutoring systems, such as SCHOLAR, can be said to "know." Bereiter and Scardamalia cite Anderson's geometry tutoring program (Anderson, Boyle, & Yost, 1985; Glaser & Bassock, 1989), which they believe "knows" geometry in so far as it represents principles and procedures that enable it to prove theorems which have not been presented to it before. Intelligent tutoring systems make the computer a highly active agent in the educational process (Bereiter & Scardamalia, 1992).

Other developments in this area include a project designed to develop, implement, and evaluate a computer-assisted thinking skills curriculum at the secondary level, described by S. Kim MacGregor (1990). Evaluation of the project's first year indicated positive outcomes for critical thinking, social studies achievement, self-esteem, and attitude toward school. Among her recommendations are the following "curriculum principles: integrate computer activities into the existing curriculum; eliminate boundaries between content areas; provide collaboration among students" (MacGregor, 1990, p. 127). Despite such potential, the politics of institutional reward must be favorable, or else innovation can be undermined (Olson, 1989a). Relatedly, another study found that unless educational researchers and practitioners have the appropriate and necessary support, microcomputers may be used in traditional ways in classrooms (Sirotnik, Goldenberg, & Oakes, 1986).

Problems. There are several problems involved in the incorporation of computers into the curriculum. One is the simple availability of computers. Their cost means they are distributed differentially, and that economic variation may mean that CBI may function to widen the general gap between wealthy and economically disadvantaged students (Passow, 1987). When schools are able to purchase computers, typically money is available for only a few; they are often placed in a central laboratory. Despite their physical absence from individual classrooms, teachers are expected to employ computers in their teaching. Incorporating computers into the curriculum is extremely difficult when computers are located in a different room, must be scheduled ahead of time, and often are too few in number to accommodate an entire class. A second problem involves courseware, which is usually purchased at district level. However, acquisition procedures are often not well formulated, and it is not unusual for funds to be spent on courseware teachers do not or cannot use. A third problem concerns computer literacy. There are more than a few teachers who cannot use the computer themselves. And even those who are computer literate find the availability of courseware limited. A negative aspect of both the IBM Secondary School Computer Education Program and the Apple Classroom of Tomorrow project, for example, is that the priority has been on providing schools with an abundance of hardware. Insufficient funding or effort has been provided for courseware. Perhaps the most serious problem is that the presence of computers alters the need for traditional academic skills and hence is affecting the roles of teachers. Finally, computer-based instruction always runs the risk of providing poor instruction at great cost. Alternately, CBI also holds potential for making instruction more efficient (Alessi & Trollip, 1991).

Questions raised. Generally, educators' interest in computers and their curricular possibilities has been unwaivering. Information has been made available to them by professional organizations [see, for instance, Grady & Gawronski, 1983]. However, several thoughtful observers of the scene have expressed concern for what can seem an excessive enthusiasm for computers. For instance, Douglas Sloan has noted that the current wave of enthusiasm for the use of computers in the schools is uncritical. He observed:

American educators have made no concerted effort to ask at what level, for what purposes, and in what ways the computer is educationally appropriate and inappropriate, in what ways and to whom we can count on its being beneficial or harmful. The overall picture has been one, instead, of educators vying to outdo one another in thinking of new ways to use the computer in all manners and at every level of education possible. Professional responsibility demands more. (Sloan, 1985, p. 1)

C. A. Bowers (1988, 1993) [see chapter 5] has been concerned that human experience may be distorted to coincide with computer capability, rather than computers being employed to extend and enlarge human intelligence and capability. Bowers (1988) observed:

> In effect, a twentieth-century view of knowledge involves using the microcomputer as a powerful and legitimate tool of the teacher and students. But it means subordinating the machine to the complexity of the human experience rather than amplifying only those aspects of experience that fit the logic of the machine. (1988, p. 46)

In a recent work, Bowers (1993) notes that insofar as computers embody the conceptual framework (and by consequence the ideology) of these experts who devise them, the technology itself can be viewed as reproducing a specific ideological orientation. Further, Bowers believes that this ideology is based on fundamental misconceptions regarding the nature of the individual, the nature of knowing (including intelligence), and more specifically how individual empowerment relates to social progress. More generally, Bowers is concerned that the metaphor of an "Information Age," which he regards as the most recent expression of this ideological orientation, functions to hide the moral and spiritual character of the ecological crisis, a concern shared by other scholars as reported in chapter 12. Bowers continues by arguing that the proponents of educational computing bring all the essential elements of the liberal canon into the "future is now" argument, which include: 1) that individual autonomy and rational empowerment are dependent upon data, 2) that change is linear and progressive, 3) a naive anthropocentricity, and 4) a tendency to universalize the assumptions of liberalism by equating them with modernization. Bowers also worries about the model of thinking that Artificial Intelligence portrays. He points to the metaphorical character of thinking which indicates that a new experience cannot be understood on its own terms. However, he asserts that AI depends upon thinking of the new in terms of the familiar. Additionally, he points to the violence of video games. Bowers (1993) concludes by insisting that the real crisis of our time is not the lack of data or computer literacy, but rather the lack of moral and spiritual development that takes account of the interconnectedness of all life, a view anticipated twenty years earlier by James B. Macdonald (1974).

A more sanguine view of the impact of technology generally and of computers more specifically is expressed by Chen and Oren (1991; see also Hlynka, 1989). It is a view that Sloan and Bowers would perhaps wish to share:

> Curriculum, as a dynamic mediating interface between public knowledge and the learner, would, as a result, represent knowledge in a nonlinear mode. Knowledge representation would become flexible and the cognitive load amenable to change during the learning process. Knowledge would be conveyed via multimedia devices, organization would be modular and defined by bits, frames, and slots, while instruction would be constantly monitored. (p. 136)

In this vein, one computer specialist asserted: "Computers are open-ended, nonlinear extensions of 'our central nervous system,' and as such the uses of computers can produce nonlinear results" (Zamora, 1983, p. 6). In contrast, Salomon argued: "Given computers' diversity, it becomes evident that neither the computer itself, nor even a particular kind of software in and of itself, are likely to affect learning in any profound way" (1991, p. 89). Other observers of CAI and software development generally are more optimistic (Kamil, 1991). Parker Rossman (1992) foresees computer networks, electronic organizations of knowledge, electronic textbooks, and a myriad of ways students might use computers and related technology to enhance their educational experience. At the heart of his discussion is a vision of an emerging worldwide electronic university in which students, faculty, and research libraries will be connected electronically across continents. Clearly, however, the possibilities of computers in the classroom present a mixed picture at this point.

What is the future? Landauer (1988) believes that "by 2020 a good portion of the cognitive tasks now performed by people will be capable of performance by machine" (p. 19). This prediction requires much technology development, at least if we take seriously Stefik's sober judgment of AI technology's accomplishments to date. Stefik (1986) judged: "AI technology, as it now exists, does not function in an important way as a knowledge medium in our society. Its influence has been far less important to the creation and propagation of knowledge than the secondary roads in France" (p. 40). Yet he saw, in the future, "an information network with semi-automated services for the generation, distribution, and consumption of knowledge" (pp. 34-35) that would be somewhat like a highway system in its cultural impact. Such an information network would support cultural diffusion and stimulate a variety of unforeseeable initiatives by virtue of the increased flow and interaction of knowledge (Bereiter & Scardamalia, 1992).

Summary. Two observers suggest that as important as technology is and can be to education, it leaves unexamined the classic curriculum question of what knowledge is of the most worth. Instead it focuses on how worthwhile knowledge can be organized and learned:

> Curriculum as technology . . . focuses on process. It is concerned with the technology by which knowledge is communicated and learning is facilitated. Again, it is concerned with the "how" rather than the "what" of education. The function of curriculum is to find efficient means to a set of predefined and, usually, rather simple ends. The focus is on the practical problem of efficiently packaging and presenting the material to the learner, but not on the individuality of the learner or the content. The technologists claim to be developing a value-free system. (Goodlad & Su, 1992, p. 335)

Bowers (1988, 1993), among others (Aoki, 1987b), dispute the technologists' claim, arguing that the values of the computer programmers as well as the models of thinking inherent in such programs represent powerful value statements regarding the nature of education.

Technology Education

Industrial arts. One contemporary expression of technology education originated in industrial arts education. During the past fifteen years or so, industrial arts curricula have been reconceived as technology. Indeed, the phrases "industrial arts" or "shop" may soon disappear altogether from the secondary school curriculum. Illustrative of this shift is the Jackson's Mill Industrial Arts Curriculum Symposium, which met in the United States from 1979 to 1981. Its members tried to translate the debate about the future of industrial education into contemporary curriculum designs. The Symposium decided to appropriate technology by stipulating it as one of the two central objects study for industrial arts programs—industry being the other one (Fensham, 1992). An official statement of technology, which incorporates industrial arts, reads: "Technology is considered as the knowledge and study of human endeavors in creating and using tools, techniques, resources, and systems to manage the human-made and natural environments, to extend human potential, and the relationship of these to individuals, society and the civilization process" (Hales & Snyder, 1982). This shift from industrial arts to technology is reflected in the new name of the industrial arts professional association, now the International Technology Education Association (Fensham, 1992). Reconceived as technology education, it is possible that: "from here [the curricular space reserved for industrial arts], technological ideas can infuse the rest of the curriculum" (Lewis & Gagel, 1992, p. 136).

Scriven's and Layton's proposals. A second model for technology education originates not in industrial arts, but in philosophy and history. Michael Scriven (1987) argued for a technology education separate from science and which is grounded instead in history, epistemology, and pedagogy. Peter J. Fensham (1992) notes that Scriven goes considerably further than many other scholars by identifying the use, adaptation, and evaluation of technologies as the central targets for technology education. Scriven argued what most citizens need is knowledge, confidence, and experience of employing a wide range of modern technologies, the ability to adapt them to their own particular purposes, and to compare technologies that claim to be competitors for similar tasks. Another proposal is based on the history of technology and science (Layton, 1987; Fensham, 1992). This technology education proposal argues that there is a uniqueness to technological knowledge which is precisely its intimate link to concrete practice. Technology is now said to be so central to human behavior that Layton argues that a moral component is an essential element of the curriculum of technology education. Fensham (1992) notes that the report of the Technology Panel of Project 2061 exemplifies Layton's claim that technology is autonomous (Rutherford & Ahlgren, 1990).

A curriculum about technology. A sample curriculum of technology is one mandated by New York State by the end of grade 8 (Todd, 1987; Fensham, 1992). The 10 curriculum modules for use in grades 7 or 8 are listed as: 1) getting to know technology, 2) what is needed for technology, 3) how people use technology to solve problems, 4) what must be known about systems and subsystems, 5) how technology affects people and the environment, 6) choosing appropriate resources for technological systems, 7) how resources are processed by technological systems, 8) controlling technological systems, 9) using systems to solve problems, and 10) technology and you: interests, decisions, and choices (Todd, 1987; Fensham, 1992).

The area of vocational education has recently labored to incorporate technological and academic content with vocational preparation, evidenced by a recent publication of the National Center for Research in Vocational Education at Western Illinois University (Grubb, Norton, Davis, Lum, Plihal & Morgaine, 1991). One curriculum proposal that has followed from this curriculum development work is the "2+2 tech prep" proposal which is intended to address access for the "neglected majority." The program title refers to the last two years in high school plus two years at a community college that yields an associate degree. The "2+2 tech prep" is designed to provide students with academic, technical, and/or professional preparation for careers in the work place by linking secondary, post secondary (community college and university) and business and industry (Molina, 1992).

Project 2061. In other developments in this area, the American Association for the Advancement of Science (AAAS) has developed its Project 2061 to support science education in the schools. The Project 2061 Technology Panel has stated that technological literacy is a subset of scientific literacy. The Panel posed the following question: is the goal of technological literacy to be attained through the teaching of technology as a separate subject, or through a reflection of the technological across the range of school subjects? Their answer is that technological literacy must be viewed in the context of the changing nature of the general or core curriculum, and changing conceptions of the nature and content of literacy generally.

STS. These are questions that intrigue those who are associated with the movement with science education known as STS (Science/Technology/Society) [see DeBoer, 1991, pp. 178-179). Originating with James Gallagher's (1971) call for "A Broader Base for Science Teaching," the Science/Technology/Society (STS) movement within science education challenged the 1960s structures-of-the-disciplines approach which had so successfully undermined curriculum theory in favor of single-subject matter emphases. STS stresses the social significance of science and technology. Gallagher (1971) argued that: "for future citizens in a democracy, understanding the interrelations of science, technology, and society may be as important as understanding the concepts and processes of science" (p. 337). [Others associated with STS include Roger Bybee (1979, 1985a, 1985b; Bybee & Welch, 1972; Bybee,

Harms, Ward & Yager (1980), Paul Hurd (1970, 1986), and Robert Yager (1984, 1986, 1987).]

A decade later Hofstein and Yager (1982) argued for the organization of the science curriculum around social issues, including those science issues related to the personal needs of citizens:

> Information is needed regarding controversial areas such as abortion and family planning; use of energy in homes; planning for proper food preparation and use; care and maintenance of the body; stress and mental health; life style and its effects upon others; pollution rights and responsibilities; disease prevention and cure. (p. 545)

[Others argue for the inclusion of philosophy and history of science in the teaching of science; see, for instance, Matthews, 1991; Wandersee, 1990a.]

Opponents within the science education community protested a reorganization of the curriculum around social issues. For instance, Kromhout and Good (1983) did not object to teaching social issues in the sciences, especially as these might encourage students to study science in itself. However, they did worry that a fundamental reorganization of the science curriculum, as STS proponents wanted, represented a flight from science, and had to be resisted. The response from curriculum theory has been limited and mixed (Wraga & Hlebowitsh, 1991; Cummins, Good, & Pinar, 1989).

Current state of technology education: Fluid. Clearly, an explosion in technology applications for the classroom and in technology education generally has occurred, just as applications exploded with the advent, in turn, of educational radio, film, slides, and television. The use of computers in classrooms offers many possibilities and raises many questions. Some have regarded technology as a rescue from the "ingrown, closed system" of curriculum theory (Pratt, 1978, p. 149). Perhaps Peter J. Fensham (1992) summarizes best the current state of the technology education: "Technology education as a component of the curriculum in its own right is far too new for its major influences to be identified in any adequate way. . . . The situation with technology education at the moment is still very fluid" (p. 815). Without question, scholars must continually evaluate the practices and potentials of technology. As Shirley Grundy (1991) has observed: "the computer can enrich the learning experiences of children, [but] it has not demonstrated that such learning is more worthwhile than traditional print-based experiences" (p. 54). Clearly, technology in the curriculum must be critically evaluated, not uncritically embraced. Evaluation, a specific component of the curriculum development process, represents another important area in the effort to understand curriculum as institutional text. Before examining the evaluation literature, let us review an area that in the traditional field was considered central. That specialization and its status are indicated in the name of the traditional professional association: the Association for Supervision and Curriculum Development (ASCD).

VI
Supervision:
Sergiovanni, Smyth, Garman, and Haggerson

At the turn of the century, when American educational administration began
its development in earnest, the "respected source" which socialized the field's
leaders could be considered our Protestant theology, a theology which predis-
posed us to think of extra-temporal concerns, of essences rather than acciden-
tals, and of glancing at the center rather than the circumference.
(Ellis A. Joseph, 1988, p. 50)

What is called for in a postmodernist rendition is that the educator (teacher,
counselor, or administrator) be a "performing artist," rather than a "narrator"
of the specific text of the organization of the school.
(Spencer J. Maxcy, 1991, p. 134)

Supervision merely serves to help the teacher to become a student of her own
work.
(Madeleine R. Grumet, 1979a, p. 255)

We quickly arrive at the abandonment of the notion of supervision.
(Richard L. Butt, 1985b, p. 21)

The evolving relationship between supervision and curriculum has been
established in several synoptic textbooks, including such works as *Emerging
Patterns of Supervision: Human Perspectives* (Sergiovanni & Starratt, 1971),
Supervision for Improved Instruction (Lewis & Miel, 1972), *Supervision in Educa-
tion: Problems and Practices* (Tanner & Tanner, 1987), *Supervision for Today's
Schools* (Oliva, 1989), and *The Central Office Supervisor of Curriculum and
Instruction: Setting the Stage for Success* (Pajak, 1989). As Common and Grim-
met (1992) have observed:

> The relationship between curriculum and supervision is a fragile one; its nego-
> tiation can proceed from the exercise of legal-rational authority and procedural
> correctness, or it can proceed through mutual reflection and reconstruction.
> The former leads to estrangement, the latter to rapprochement. The choice is
> ours, researchers and practitioners alike. (p. 225)

The function of supervision as a vehicle for curriculum development has
been an integral part of supervision textbooks for decades. For example, an
emphasis on the leadership role of the supervisor in guiding curricular practices is found in *Supervision: A Guide to Practice* (Wiles & Bondi, 1980). The
traditional view of this area is that a competent supervisor is needed as much
as competent professors; the "future of education depends on a successful
and well-supervised student teaching program" (Anderson, Major, & Mitchell,
1992, p. 152). Others agree: "supervision is important to teacher education"
(Zimpher & Howey, 1987, p. 126). As the history of ASCD indicates, the
political relationship between curriculum and supervision has not always

been an easy one [see chapter 4]. The relatively new ASCD *Journal of Curriculum and Supervision* attempts to bridge this gap.

What is supervision? Acheson and Gall (1987) explain that:

> Curriculum supervision is a process, a distinctive style of relating to teachers. For this process to be effective, the clinical supervisor's mind, emotions, and actions must work together to achieve the primary goal of clinical supervision: the professional development of the preservice or inservice teacher. (pp. 3-4)

A clinical supervisor observes, supports, and guides the preservice or inservice teacher. There are three phases: the planning conference, classroom observation, and the feedback conference [see Acheson & Gall, 1987, pp. xiii, 3-4].

Historical notes. Among several historical reviews of supervision (Bolin, 1987), the Tanners' (1987) and Jeffrey Glanz's (1990) are among the most useful. Daniel and Laurel Tanner (1987) trace supervision to lay assessment in colonial times by "selectmen" and later by state superintendents, the most noteworthy of whom was the first professional supervisor, Horace Mann [see chapters 2 and 12]. The certification of teachers and teacher training programs intensified the interest in supervision of instruction in the late 1800s, and this led ultimately to the emergence of modern professional supervision in the twentieth century with central office supervisors and site principals being designated as instructional leaders. Daniel and Laurel Tanner (1987) conclude that the evolution of the role of supervisor has always been tied to educational leadership of curriculum and instruction:

> Supervision evolved with the total American educational system, including teacher education and the professional administration of schools. Good teaching was at the very center of the ideal public school. . . . Teacher training was the major responsibility of supervisors well into the twentieth century. (p. 26)

While the professionalization of supervisors of curriculum and instruction occurred during the twentieth century, Daniel and Laurel Tanner (1987) identify two fundamental principles guiding the development of the contemporary supervision field: improving the quality of teaching and learning and integrating supervision and curriculum development as a single complementary process. They credit Hilda Taba (1962) with developing the definitive statement on the traditional relationship between supervision and curriculum development and, thus, with initiating the dramatic expansion of subject-area specialists and training programs for supervisors. Daniel and Laurel Tanner promote the application of scientific methods to the problems encountered by teachers in their day to day work so that professional supervisors and subject-area specialists may overcome what they see as the three remaining obstacles to curriculum development: 1) the lack of time for supervision, 2) negative attitudes by teachers toward supervision, and 3) inappropriate business management models imposed upon schools. A prescriptive plan for addressing these obstacles, for designing and developing curriculum, and ultimately, for evaluating school improvement is the emphasis of the recent work in supervision by the Tanners. However, their proposal is also critical of methods of supervision that do not promote cooperative, democratic-participative opportunities for teachers. Daniel and Laurel Tanner (1987) argue:

> Educational problems cannot be solved by focusing on instruction apart from curriculum. Yet this faulty premise of dualism between curriculum and instruction has been promulgated in inspectional supervision, production supervision, and most recently, in clinical supervision. As a consequence, the responsibility of the teacher is primarily the delivery of instruction in connection with a curriculum that is predetermined at a higher judgmental level. A holistic problem-solving model of supervision, as opposed to a segmental model which divides instruction from curriculum, is . . . the most effective path to educational improvement. (p. 185)

Jeffrey Glanz (1990), himself a school principal at the time he wrote "Beyond Bureaucracy: Notes on the Professionalization of Public School Supervision in the Early 20th Century," appears to regard supervision as less benign than do the Tanners: "Supervision, as an integral component of the school bureaucracy, perpetuated bureaucratic mandates, such as standardizing curriculum and controlling teacher behavior" (1990, p. 151). He notes that before 1900 superintendents acted as supervisors. During the first decade of the twentieth century, the growth and bureaucratization of school systems meant a dramatic increase in supervisory personnel. Between 1906 and 1910 the number of supervisors increased 68.8 percent while the number of teachers increased only 18.1 percent (Glanz, 1990, p. 154). Replacing superintendents as supervisors first were principals and then a new cadre of administrative personnel: the professional supervisor. While increased supervision was defended as promoting professionalization, Glanz cites Corwin (1970) to distinguish between bureaucratization and professionalization: "Bureaucracy, by its nature, requires a high degree of standardization, with a stress on uniformity in both rules and conduct. . . . Professionalization, however, is marked by a low degree of standardization" (Glanz, 1990, p. 162).

Evaluation an important aspect of supervision: Oliva. Echoing the Tanners' integrated model of curriculum and supervision is Peter F. Oliva's (1989) model in the text *Supervision for Today's Schools*, now in its third edition. Oliva insists, as do Daniel and Laurel Tanner, that the primary role of the supervisor is to provide leadership in three interrelated projects: improvement of instruction, curriculum development, and staff development. Summative dimensions of teacher evaluation, such as assessment instruments, career ladders, accountability procedures, teacher testing, and comprehensive appraisals by administrators and supervisors are justifiable, according to Oliva, only if extensive formative processes have been utilized to improve instruction and develop curriculum first. Otherwise, evaluation of instruction is reduced to a management and personnel function. Oliva reviews succinctly the problems inherent in linking supervision of curriculum and instruction with personnel evaluation. However, even after having exposed the drawbacks, he concludes:

> Administrators [must] make their ratings of teachers as fair and objective as possible. If a teacher is found to be deficient in some way, it is the administrator's [and supervisor's] responsibility to recommend and monitor measures that may assist the teacher in overcoming the deficiencies. (1989, p. 542)

Despite the critical analysis of managerial evaluation, Oliva concludes that summative evaluation is integral to the process of supervision of curriculum and instruction. This is a recurring theme in many synoptic textbooks employed in supervision courses.

The theater analogy. Edward Pajak (1989) contends that central office supervisors must shift the burden of summative evaluation to site-based administrators so as not to compromise the supervisor's informal working relationships with teachers in curriculum development and instructional improvement. Pajak (1989) employs the metaphor of a theatrical direction—a metaphor we saw linked to teaching in chapter 11—to describe the preferred role of supervisors when he writes:

> Curriculum development, from a theatrical perspective, is especially interesting because it involves nothing less than writing and rewriting the "script" that is followed by teachers during their classroom performances. The practice of involving teachers in this process disperses the function of "author" to the "actors" themselves and contributes further to the character-driven quality of teaching. Thus, as "director," the supervisor is allowed access "backstage" and may help teachers individually and collectively plan with "scripting" and "staging" their lessons. (p. 207)

The I-B-F model. Pajak attempts to reconceive the role of the central office supervisor of curriculum and instruction so as to reduce the emphasis on formal classroom observations and evaluations. He promotes the "Image-Behavior-Feedback" model (Hill, 1968) over the popular clinical supervision model of preconference, observation, and postconference (Goldhammer, 1969; Cogan, 1973; Hunter, 1980) because I-B-F allows the teacher to construct meaning in the classroom. In this model, the need for growth and change is not imposed by the supervisor. Pajak (1989) writes:

> I-B-F supervision is compatible with the backstage metaphor of supervision because it emphasizes the teacher's construction of an image to be projected and the supervisor's role in helping the teacher to enact that image successfully. In effect, the supervisor helps the teacher to interpret and bring to life the script that the teacher has written for a particular lesson . . . similar to the functions performed by the theatrical direction. (pp. 210-211)

Pajak's theatrical vision of the role of the supervisor attempts to move the field beyond the Tanners' integrated model of supervision and curriculum development and beyond Oliva's conceptual model of universally applicable generic skills of supervision.

These three textbooks (Tanner & Tanner, 1987; Oliva, 1989; Pajak, 1989) provide examples of contemporary approaches to supervision of curriculum and instruction. While the view of the purpose of the supervisor is different in each of the three textbooks, the function of central office supervision and role segmentation of the various participants remain integral to the perspective of each scholar. Additionally, the linkage between supervision and curriculum is evident throughout the literature on supervision.

Supervision in transition. There is a movement among supervision scholars in the 1990s to reject the "top-down" approach to supervision and transcend the norms and structures presented in much contemporary literature. The 1992 ASCD Yearbook, entitled *Supervision in Transition* (Glickman, 1992), insists that educational leadership and supervision must be shared, decentralized, and empowering for teachers in order to be effective. Contributors to the yearbook promote peer-coaching, teacher mentors, collegial support, and peer assistance models of supervision with explicit suggestions for teachers to assume decision-making leadership roles. Glickman (1992) writes:

> As the educational system struggles with "restructuring" and organizational shifts, the old bureaucratic style of supervision is in flux. Teachers, who are the ultimate experts in curriculum and instruction, must be involved in the planning and delivery of instruction. They are the best judge of effective instructional strategies. (p. v)

This emphasis on the classroom teacher's leadership role in supervision represents a dramatic shift away from the inspection, production, and clinical models of supervision.

Clinical supervision. Clinical supervision is an approach to supervision of curriculum and instruction which has been prominent since its inception by Morris Cogan in the 1950s and its development by Robert Goldhammer (1969) in the 1960s. The professional status of teachers has been inextricably linked to this model of supervision for decades [see Garman, 1986a]. One study has found that a recent adaptation of clinical supervision by Madeline Hunter [which at least one scholar denies bears any resemblance to the spirit of clinical supervision (Smyth, 1991)] has been adopted by the majority of districts in Pennsylvania (Garman, 1987). Noreen Garman and Helen Hazi (1988) document the frustration experienced by many teachers who complain of being "Hunterized" by their school districts. They write:

> We cannot ignore the bad news contained in the comments of Pennsylvania teachers. In order to gain resources, privileges, and rewards, one must first be cooperative and compliant with the district initiated program. One must be willing to be Hunterized. A teacher in a Hunterized district has little chance to follow his or her career interests or to join with a small group of colleagues in a common project. The resources and the rewards are clearly tied to the MH/CS model. Moreover, if a teacher chooses another direction, he or she runs the

risk of being labeled a dissident—or worse, a deviant malcontent. That teacher's evaluation could eventually suffer. Few teachers are willing to risk these consequences. . . . They see evaluation as a way of rewarding compliance. (Garman & Hazi, 1988, p. 672)

Clinical supervision is designed to allow for interaction, planning, and collaboration between supervisors and teachers. However, the research of Garman and Hazi demonstrates that clinical models often reinforce bureaucratic and inspectional evaluative procedures that can suppress creative teaching: "'Research says' is an invocation that administrators have discovered to persuade teachers to adopt a particular model of teaching for the purpose of legitimizing their evaluations" (Hazi & Garman, 1988, p. 7). Rather, a person cannot be said to be a clinical supervisor until he or she appreciates that "the teacher-supervisor relationship stands for ethical conduct as it is lived out in important choices. . . . When he/she . . . can . . . sort out the nontrivial from the trivial in order to bring meaning to educational endeavors" (Garman, 1982, p. 52). Features of authentic supervision include: 1) an inquiry approach to observation (i.e., no model of certainty about teaching), 2) self-confrontation as part of making judgments, and 3) congruence (collaboration). In a phrase, supervisors should work to empower teachers (Garman, 1986a). Empowerment has become an important concept in the supervision literature, and Noreen Garman has provided leadership in this movement.

Peer coaching/cognitive coaching. In an effort to incorporate the collaborative dimensions of clinical supervision and overcome the limitations of its evaluative functions, new models have emerged in the 1990s that emphasize teacher "empowerment." Mutually supportive relationships are encouraged in peer coaching models which have emerged to address three problems: 1) the vocal opposition of many teachers to clinical supervision, 2) dwindling resources available for supervision, and 3) shifting job responsibilities of central office supervisors. Participative-democratic models of education have also contributed to the emphasis on peer mentoring and coaching in the supervision of curriculum and instruction.

Wanda May and Nancy Zimpher (1986) posit three positions in supervision: positivism, phenomenology, and critical theory. They assert: "We need a theory of practice" (p. 97), by which they mean an eclectic theory: "To reduce such complexity to a single frame of reference or to mask our enterprise beyond moral recognition jeopardizes the rich and serious nature of our task" (p. 99). Sergiovanni (1987) also argues for the need to build "practice models." He notes that the current state of knowledge generation and model building in supervision and teaching is patterned after the physical sciences [what May and Zimpher have termed positivism], but in fact these areas belong more properly to "the domain of the cultural sciences" (p. 221). Sergiovanni (1987) does not want to abandon science, "merely redirect it" (p. 222). In another study, Sergiovanni (1989) identifies two dangers in the scholarly study of supervision and teaching: danger of "poetism" (p. 93) and the danger of "scientism" (p. 95). For supervision to advance, there is a "need for a new metaphor" (p. 103). He believes the notion of "craft" will suffice:

> the metaphor of craft has the best possibility for helping us think about teaching and learning in a fashion that brings together both scientific and poetic dimensions while diminishing the dangers of lapsing into scientism or poetism. (Sergiovanni, 1989, p. 104)

Pajak (1989) points to another direction, to a recent interest in psychoanalysis: "In summary, recent interest among psychoanalysts in the process of self-formation and its relationship to teaching and supervision can help us better understand the personal and interpersonal dynamics involved in these activities. . . . The metaphor of supervision as teaching, guided by self psychology, highlights growth and development instead of control or remediation" (Pajak, 1989, p. 131). In another study, Lawrence Stenhouse (1983) recalls his work with the British Humanities Curriculum Project, 1967-1972, [reported in his 1971 article (Stenhouse, 1971)] concluding, after twenty-five years of curriculum development work, that "managerial and research support are needed, [although] they are subordinate to the development of, and hence to the judgment of, teachers and students" (p. 211). To a considerable extent, Stenhouse's conclusion seems to convey the mainstream wisdom of the contemporary supervision field.

Effective schools. Teacher empowerment and autonomy is also acknowledged by those interested in the promotion of "effective schools." The single most important factor in such schools, according to this research, is a "strong" principal. Yet, this strong leadership must support teacher autonomy:

> Strong supportive school leadership by the principal mainly is the most important content factor of effective schools. Strong cultures permit principals to realize the main focus of effective schools while permitting much teacher autonomy. Effective principals promote strong cultures but also have roles of instructional leadership, internal change agent, program improver, and systematic problem solver. (Downer, 1991, p. 323)

Some may see a tension between a "strong principal" and teacher empowerment, but those in the "effective schools" movement do not.

Empowerment and voice. Horizontal evaluation is an illustration of an "empowerment approach" to the supervision of curriculum. "Communication analysis," "historical perspective," and "challenge statements" are used along with a consideration of alternative practices to enhance and deepen dialogue among teachers. Gitlin and Price (1992) report that: "In traditional administrative evaluation, teachers have little or no say in determining the standards for good teaching; instead, they are forced to behave in ways that at best reflect only one notion of good teaching" (p. 63). They argue that teacher empowerment is a necessary aspect of the contemporary school.

Inspectional and managerial supervision and evaluation represent bureaucratic rituals in which teachers "put on a show" to achieve a positive assessment. Teachers need to work together to appraise situations and consider a wide array of problems, concerns, and alternative strategies for curriculum enhancement. In this horizontal model teachers "participate in at least three evaluation 'laps' in which each lap allows both participants to be observer and teacher" (Gitlin & Price, 1992, p. 68). Teacher empowerment has expanded the notion of supervision to include a notion of voice [see chapters 5, 7 and 10], especially for those who sense that supervision is in part a gendered process: "Such an expanded role for teachers includes a moral discourse that focuses on the aims of education and confronts the historical limits of those working in what is often referred to as a woman's profession" (Gitlin & Price, 1992, p. 73). While concepts of teacher empowerment and voice are not discussed in traditional supervision textbooks such as Oliva's (1989), they tend to be regarded as central to the supervision process in emerging models (Glickman, 1992). Another emerging model may involve discourse analysis. In Patricia Holland's (1989) review of the literature on the supervisory conference for the past twenty years, she concludes that assumptions about the supervisory conference have remained remarkably consistent over this period. Holland believes the field of supervision suffers from too much theory and not enough research, although she does cite "discourse analysis" as promising.

A postmodern shift? Several contributors to the 1992 ASCD yearbook contend that recent changes in supervision models reflect a postmodern shift in the field. They also seem to suggest that the term instructional supervision itself has even outlived its usefulness. Glickman (1992) summarizes:

> Over the past decade, school supervision has been in the midst of swirling, transitional views. One view of supervision—as a district-based, inspector-type function carried out by line supervisors who understand generic processes of effective teaching—has gained ascendancy. A shifting view of supervision as a school-based collegial process, based on reflection, uncertainty, and problem-solving, has been finding acceptance in schools that are recasting the roles and responsibilities of teachers. A further area of shifting views has been from an emphasis on pedagogy to a focus on the interaction of content (subject knowledge) and instruction. These transitions in supervision have created volatile issues, tugging at the security of people's professional lives, and changing previous organizational structures. (pp. 2-3)

These shifting conceptions of supervision include a challenge to many traditional methodologies in the area. For instance, they challenge the behavioral approach to teacher induction and evaluation initiated by many states in the 1980s (French et al., 1990). These states adopted low-inference evaluation instruments that only required observation and tallying of specific behaviors in an effort to be objective. [See, for example, the Florida Beginning Teacher Program described in Darling-Hammond, 1992]. Darling-

Hammond (1992) contends that "when evaluation is made 'evaluator-proof' in this way, the supervisor's job is simplified, as supervision can focus only on the search for and the production of these behaviors" (p. 16). Sergiovanni (1984) and other critics of state-mandated supervision programs contend that this approach is typical of the reductionism that is symptomatic of the "web of primitive scientism" in which educational supervision seems trapped:

> Examples of reductionism in the supervision and evaluation of teaching would be the reducing of complex patterns of human interaction to tallies on a data collection schedule and reducing the phenomenon of student response to teaching to the timing of specific student task behaviors. (1984, p. 355)

The irony of this approach to so-called objective data collection as a method of supervision [and of curriculum research, as we saw in chapter 1] is that it establishes its own preconceived methodological bias with many of its own internal limitations. For example, behaviors which are found to be effective in one learning environment may be counterproductive when used in different circumstances. Researchers such as Griffin (1985), Darling-Hammond (1986), and Peterson and Kauchak (1982), among others, have contributed to the growing body of literature that challenges this objectivistic, data-collection approach to supervision. There is a developing interest as well in "cognitive perspectives on educational leadership" (Hallinger, Leithwood, & Murphy, 1993).

Are supervisors business managers? Another challenge to the mainstream methodologies in the supervision area is found in the ongoing debate surrounding a proposal to model curriculum supervision after a business management system used in the insurance industry (Duffy, 1990). Duffy proposed that supervisors should act like managers in order to promote efficient results in the educational marketplace. A number of scholars have taken exception to this proposal (Glickman, 1990; Hazi, 1990; Pajak, 1990). Others have continued the discussion started by Duffy by expanding the business management model and establishing a critique of emerging research methodologies in the supervision area. Jean Hills (1991), for example, offered a critique that identifies apparent ambiguities in the work of "Garman, Grimmett and Crehan, Blumburg, Sergiovanni, and Holland" (p. 1). Hills asserted:

> All of these authors reject . . . science as either misplaced, inappropriate, or unproductive for studying human interaction generally and supervisory behavior specifically—and well they might reject parts of it. [However,] they justify their antirationalist positions by appealing to aspects of the very form of science they reject. (pp. 3-4)

Hills concluded that while hermeneutic and interpretive studies are not to be discredited, the rational-scientific approach to supervision is not to be discarded.

A quick fix? Nelson Haggerson (1991) raised important questions concerning the nature of supervision. What is the role of the supervisor, especially in evaluation? How do we improve instruction? And most controversially, who determines how to improve instruction? Haggerson identified three stakeholders in the debate: university scholars, entrepreneurs, and field supervisors. He criticized the entrepreneurs for offering a "quick fix" to the problems of supervision with products that are promised to be "scientific" and "research-based." Practitioners in the field have tended to accept the entrepreneurs, while scholars question the validity of this so-called scientific research. In response to Hills' critique of these scholars, as seen above, Haggerson explained:

> Most of the authors discussed here have concluded that instructional supervision is not a science; it is a practice. Interpretive inquiry into the meaning of instructional supervision as a practice differs from cognitive-technical-rational inquiry into instructional supervision as a science. . . . For the most part, [they] have determined that interpretive inquiry is most suitable for explicating and understanding practice. (p. 15)

Haggerson continued by presenting a hermeneutic process of understanding the role of supervision in contemporary educational practice that challenges educators to develop holistic awareness. This is accomplished when supervisors and researchers use stories, stream-of-consciousness journals, portfolios, and poetry to represent knowledge and understanding. Haggerson debated conflicting conceptions of supervision and the enhancement of professional growth and renewal (Garman, Glickman, Hunter, & Haggerson, 1987).

Supervision grounded in hermeneutics and phenomenology. Perhaps no scholar has considered more carefully the significance of hermeneutics for supervision than Noreen Garman (1990). Relying on Husserl and Ricoeur, Garman has outlined the "embedded theories in the taken-for-granted events of clinical supervision" (p. 212). She points to the need for a language for teaching (1984) in order to "articulate supervisory practice" (p. 212). Much of contemporary supervisory practice, she notes, "is now tailored to meet administrative convenience and is couched in 'scientism' rather than sound supervisory practice based on moral justification" (p. 212). Garman's hermeneutic approach requires a suspension of the administrative interest for the sake of "generating hermeneutic knowledge" (p. 212). She observed:

> If the "clinic" is the instructive mode implying a place and time where people practice (or rehearse) to become more skillful and scholarly about their work, then the participants agree, for that special period, to become learners—to bracket the experience of clinical supervision so that the events can be put into textual form, reviewed, inquired about, and set into perspective. . . . We make a commitment of time, a commitment to looking at the ordinary with an extraordinary sensibility, a commitment to letting go of our ego and equilibrium for a while, and a commitment to certain methods and actions associated with reflection and inquiry. (Garman, 1990, pp. 212-213)

Garman's employment of hermeneutics as the basis for supervisory inquiry and practice, implying as it does the primacy of a moral vision of supervision, may be her greatest contribution to the field. It may rival in significance the seminal contributions of Thomas Sergiovanni and John Smyth, the two scholars often regarded as the most important in the area of supervision.

Feminist theory speaks to supervision. James Joseph Scheurich and Patti Lather (1991) have responded to Jean Hills by advancing a view of supervision that incorporates the voices of feminists, critical theorists, critical post-modernists, and advocates of cultural epistemological orientations. Scheurich and Lather criticized Hills' endorsement of mainstream science with its emphasis upon researcher-subject separation, empirical verification, and cause-and-effect order relationships. They challenged those in the supervision area to move beyond these mainstream, and for them discredited ideas, and they join Garman in proposing as replacements models of interpretation grounded in hermeneutics, constructionism, and phenomenology. They wrote:

> The scholarly work on supervision is divided between those who incorrectly are trying to create a science, applied or not, and those who correctly are trying to create loosely defined theories of practice. Anyone who might be trying to take something other than these two positions or who wants to do something different presumably does not exist. (1991, p. 27)

For instance, excluding feminist theory in the discourse on supervision ignores gender stratification in schools, including the effects of gender issues on supervisory relations. They argued that neither interpretivism nor positivism is free from gender considerations. Scheurich and Lather (1991) concluded:

> Therefore, dichotomous paradigmatic maps of positivism and interpretivism are not innocent. In fact, following [John H.] Stanfield, who argues that whites can forget that they are white while blacks cannot forget they are black, this exclusionary dichotomy is itself a function of the privilege of those drawing the maps. Because of their socially privileged position, they can forget or not know that their map of reality makes some groups of people and some positions invisible and that this constructed invisibility reproduces the broader social maldistribution of power, resources, and pain by class, race, and gender. Our act of compulsion in this response [to Hills] is to re-map, but always, provisionally, the paradigmatic territory to include especially those groups and positions marginalized, exploited, and oppressed in our society. (pp. 29-30)

The work of Scheurich and Lather is illustrative of recent scholarship—some of it imported from curriculum theory—which challenges the supervision area to incorporate political, racial, and gender discourses. This work leads to questions about clinical and mainstream supervision. This new set of questions allies supervision with the empowerment of teachers:

> To what extent are the practices of clinical supervision just in treating teachers as capable of participating fully in the determination of their own destiny? To

what extent is the process of clinical supervision practical in enabling teachers to discover aspects of their own teaching through action? To what extent is clinical supervision realistic in acknowledging the nature of school and classroom life? (Smyth, 1991, pp. 347-348)

The production, inspection, and clinical models of supervision continue to be challenged and revised by a number of scholars in the 1990s, with so-called empowerment models, such as peer coaching, as possible replacements. Spencer Maxcy (1991) outlined a postmodern concept of administrator:

> What is to be called for in a postmodernist rendition is that the educator (teacher, counselor, or administrator) be a "performing artist," rather than a "narrator" of the specific text of the organization of the school. . . . Postmodernism divests the self of subjectivity and generates a tension between nihilism and authoritarianism. (p. 134)

It may well be that the scholarly discourses on supervision are being reconceptualized, and in ways which parallel contemporary curriculum theory.

In their *Culturally Responsive Teaching and Supervision: Handbook for Staff Development*, C. A. Bowers and David J. Flinders (1991) have argued that traditional supervision is based on an old industrial model. Further, it is based on mistaken assumptions about how people best work together, ignoring the important fact that cultural traditions are necessary to maintain a sense of community and personal identity. They bring to their culturally responsive model the realization that the ecological crisis is central to any educational endeavor in our time. Supervision must acknowledge changes in basic areas of understanding, such as the acknowledgement that language is metaphorical rather than narrowly representational and literalistic. Instead of regarding the classroom as a complicated machine, we should regard the "classroom as an ecology of language and cultural patterns" (p. viii). For Madeleine Grumet (1979a, 1989a), the issue of supervision is less cultural and more autobiographical. Grumet has suggested that the teacher become his or her own supervisor: "The teacher who can be the critic of her own assumptions can welcome the diversity in her students' experiences without defensiveness or denial" (1989a, p. 21).

In Britain. Shaw (1987), a British researcher, regards management studies, one subset of which would be supervision studies, as ascendant in the effort to understand curriculum as institutional text. He argues:

> My contention is that curriculum studies and management studies are displacing educational psychology and sociology from the dominant position which they occupied and are moving steadily towards the center of the stage in undergraduate, post-graduate and in-service courses for teachers [in the UK]. (p. 205)

Shaw's British location is clearly evident when he links curriculum with the work of Hirst, Peters and White [see chapter 4], philosophers of the curriculum who have enjoyed little influence in the United States. Also true to the British model of curriculum, and evoking the concept most associated with Schwab, Shaw concludes: "In short, a deliberative element is as much at the heart of management as it is at the heart of curriculum-making" (p. 212). He is indebted to William A. Reid [see chapter 4] when he writes: "A common concern for the practical and a revised view of how theory relates to their activities is coming to characterize the domains of both curriculum and management: theory as tool and as inquiry, not as idealized practice or guide to specific activity. Both seek to solve their problems via action" (p. 216).

VII
Curriculum Evaluation:
Scriven, Stake, and Eisner

The curriculum, whether it deals with the nature of work, time, metaphorical thinking, poverty, or ways of knowing, should be judged, in part, on the basis of whether it helps the student understand how the content area relates to the broader, overarching belief system of the culture that influences the existential questions faced in the course of everyday life.

(C. A. Bowers, 1984, p. 80)

Formal evaluation exercises are vastly overrated. If half the time and energy expended on them were expended on thinking about curriculum, we might be getting somewhere.

(Robin Barrow, 1984b, p. 251)

Evaluation defined. Since the 1960s, George F. Madaus and Thomas Kellaghan (1992) tell us, curriculum evaluation has experienced enormous growth, as has assessment in school classrooms. Evaluation, like all major terms in the curriculum field, enjoys multiple definitions (Madaus, Scriven, & Stufflebeam, 1983; Murphy & Torrance, 1987; Stufflebeam & Shinkfield, 1985; Worthen & Sanders, 1987; English, 1988; Weiss, 1989), but Madaus and Kellaghan report that it is Ralph Tyler's definition of 1949 [see chapter 3] that has enjoyed "considerable influence" (1992, p. 120): "The process of evaluation is essentially the process of determining to what extent the educational objectives are actually being realized by the program of curriculum and instruction" (Tyler, 1949, pp. 105-106; Madaus & Kellaghan, 1992, p. 120). Dissatisfaction with the Tylerian definition led, in the 1970s, to a variety of evaluation approaches. Indeed, the 1981 Joint Committee on Standards for Educational Evaluation defined evaluation broadly as "the systematic investigation of the worth or merit of some object (program, project, or materials)" (p. 12). Evaluation is the broad category while assessment is subsumed within it. Within assessment is measurement, the most narrow form or subset of evaluation.

Despite the variety of approaches to evaluation, the term has become increasingly important in political debates regarding the progress of education in the United States and worldwide [see chapter 14; Fuhrman & Malen,

1991]. The term "educational indicator" (developed to parallel existing terms such as "economic indicators" and "social indicators") has been employed to summarize the current condition of the educational system nationwide (Johnstone, 1981; Oakes, 1986). Presumably, weaknesses and progress in student achievement in individual subject areas are detected and reported. Such evaluation reports can be expected to become even more important as national political pressure builds to increase test scores of American students (Madaus & Kellaghan, 1992). Specific information regarding student achievement, as measured by standardized examinations, is housed in the National Center for Education Statistics (1985). Such data will probably be increasingly employed by politicians who use measures of educational decline or progress to advance their own agendas.

Early history. Madaus and Kellaghan (1992) report that the first recorded instance of evaluation occurred in Europe in 1444 in a contract between town officials and the town schoolmaster. This contract stipulated that the schoolmaster's salary would vary according to the achievement of pupils in the school, as measured by an oral examination. This contract is the earliest [with the exception of the Chinese mandarin civil service examinations; see chapter 14] reference to the use of assessment instruments, examinations in this instance, to evaluate teachers' performance. This concept of linking student achievement to teacher remuneration turned out to be a durable one, resurfacing in eighteenth-century Ireland (Burton, 1979), in ninteenth-century Great Britain (Bowler, 1983; Montgomery, 1967; Sutherland, 1973), Ireland (Coolahan, 1975; Madaus, 1979), Australia (Hearn, 1872), and Jamaica (Gordon, 1968). Recent variations of the idea include the perfor-mance-contracting movement of the 1960s (Levine, 1971), present-day efforts to link merit pay to the test scores of students (Lerner, 1981), and proposals to remunerate those students who score well on tests (Hughes, 1979; Laffer, 1982). Despite critics, such as Matthew Arnold in nineteenth-century England (Madaus & Kellaghan, 1992), the idea that learning is labor to be rewarded financially has persisted. Today this notion is one of payment by results (Bowler, 1983; Barone, 1989; see chapter 11).

Twentieth century. Evaluation in general and testing in particular accom-panied the social efficiency movement in the field [see chapter 3]. Many school systems began to make surveys of rates of expenditure, dropout rates, promotion rates, and tests of achievement in the various basic skill areas, such as arithmetic, spelling, and writing (Madaus & Stufflebeam, 1984). Such tests functioned also as curriculum evaluation, although during the 1920s a shift occurred, one from employing tests to evaluate curricula to employing tests to assess teachers and school systems as a whole (Madaus & Kellaghan, 1992). Another shift occurred a decade later, as tests were employed primar-ily to make assessments of the progress of individual students, including to assign grades, to diagnose learning problems, and to track [see curriculum differentiation in the curriculum policy section of this chapter] (Cronbach, 1983). Following World War II, standardized tests became more available and more frequently used to measure student progress. Also during this period, Tyler popularized the notion and practice of objectives (Madaus & Stufflebeam, 1989; Tyler, 1949) [see chapter 3]. In the post War period, taxonomies were developed, designed to assist educators in the writing of objectives (Bloom, et al., 1956; Krathwohl, Bloom, & Masia, 1964) [see chapter 3]. While the Tyler rationale for curriculum development advanced a triangle of educational concerns—objectives, learning experiences, evaluation—by the 1960s it became a rationale for test development (Bloom, 1950, 1966, 1969; Bloom, Hastings, & Madaus, 1971; Madaus & Kellaghan, 1992). While Tyler regarded evaluation as derived from curricular objectives, by the 1960s many considered that it was the test itself that came to determine the curriculum (Travers, 1983).

While historical antecedents are important, and particularly the seminal influence of Tyler's rationale (Walberg, 1970), the contemporary field of curriculum evaluation is sometimes dated from 1967, with the appearance of Michael Scriven's "The Countenance of Educational Evaluation" (Popham, 1975). [This is the same Scriven, educated as a philosopher of science, whose proposal for technology education we reported in the previous section.] Popham's dating seems consistent with the annotated bibliography (Fraser, 1989); thirty-nine book titles listed were published after 1967. Why the sudden expansion of the field in the late 1960s? Most commentators link it with the governmental need to evaluate the massive curriculum projects associated with the "curriculum reform movement" of the early 1960s sponsored by the Kennedy administration (Fraser, 1989) [see chapter 3].

Formative and summative, description and judgment. Barry Fraser (1989) lists three papers written during the late 1960s as seminal in the development of curriculum evaluation. In addition to the Scriven paper mentioned above, papers by Robert Stake (1972) and Elliot Eisner (1967, 1969) have proven to be of lasting significance. Scriven's paper has been characterized by Guba and Lincoln (1981) as "the single most important paper on evaluation written to date" (p. 9). Another student of the area noted that the Scriven article was cited at least 160 times (Smith, 1980). What was so important about this paper? In it Scriven introduced a distinction between "formative" and "summative" evaluation, the former category suggesting evaluation intended to inform revisions in practice and the latter suggesting judgments, say, for personnel files. Scriven argued that the former is as important to the evaluation process as the latter. Additionally, he argued that the intrinsic worthiness of curricular goals must be examined, not simply taken for granted. Intrinsically worthwhile curricular goals must be pursued, he seemed to imply, regardless of the how well they are achieved. In a later paper, Scriven (1973) argued for evaluation not tied to curricular objectives, i.e. a goal-free evaluation in which all consequences of the curriculum should be investigated, not just those intended by those writing objectives. In this model, the concept of evaluation is broadened to include transactions, antecedents, and contingencies (Fraser, 1989). Robert Stake's important 1967 paper also functioned to broaden the concept of evaluation by criticizing mainstream evaluation specialists for viewing the educative process "with a microscope rather than with a panoramic viewfinder" (p. 536). Further, Stake distinguished between description and judgment as the two "basic acts of evaluation" (1967, p. 525).

Eisner. As we noted earlier [see chapter 3], Elliot Eisner [see chapters 1, 4, 11] played an influential role in setting the stage for the 1970s Reconceptualization by challenging mainstream, so-called "scientific" ideas of curriculum development. He challenged also mainstream ideas of evaluation. In two widely read papers (1967, 1969), Eisner criticized the role of objectives in curriculum development evaluation. His 1967 paper, entitled "Educational Objectives: Help or Hindrance," was cited 52 times in the literature (Smith, 1980). Eisner's criticism was that objectives as commonly conceived failed to take into account several of the most educational significant aims, i.e. curiosity and inventiveness. Such aims, if expressed in objectives, could be written metaphorically, not behaviorally or operationally. Additionally, Eisner (1969) introduced the concept of "expressive" objectives to represent those educationally important consequences which had not been indicated in advance. Expressive objectives refer to those encounters in which students learn rather than those behaviors which students simply "do" (Eisner, 1969, 1971a; Fraser, 1989). Eisner's contribution to evaluation is enormous; we shall report his late 1970s and 1980s work on educational criticism momentarily.

The 1970s and 1980s. The growth of scholarly writing on evaluation was dramatic during these two decades. Rather than report a large number of individual contributions, we will emphasize two organizing themes. These themes are: 1) distinctions drawn between qualitative and quantitative methods of evaluation, and 2) the discipline undergirding particular models and methods of evaluation. Much literature during these two decades argued that qualitative approaches ought to be included with quantitative methods (Willis, 1978), an argument which, from the point of view of the early 1990s, appears to have prevailed, as we have seen in chapters 1 and 4 (Gage, 1989). The other major category of literature during these decades focuses on the discipline underlying a particular model of evaluation, for instance science and social science (methods involving statistics and control groups) and nonscientific disciplines (such as the law, arts, journalism, literary criticism) (Fraser, 1989). In postpositivist evaluation (Donmoyer, 1991b) for example, curriculum evaluation is conceived as the negotiation of meaning (Donmoyer, 1990b), in which epistemological issues are paramount (Donmoyer, 1985). Jon Nixon (1990) writes: "The new paradigm is fundamentally concerned with issues of value" (p. 645). Perhaps Louise Berman (1986) summarizes this shift when she (1986) argued that:

> the focus on the measured curriculum . . . has frequently ruled out much teaching of human experience that is not measurable. . . . To deal with aspirations, hopes, and dilemmas, students need a rich, invigorating, and problematic

curriculum. Such an unmeasured curriculum can help students to better deal with the unmeasurable elements of life. (p. 45)

Quantitative vs. Qualitative Methods

Despite the general, if not vague, definitions of these concepts, and their functions as umbrella terms of convenience, they have become widely accepted in the literature. In 1979, the distinction was drawn between quantitative and qualitative methods in the following way. Quantitative research referred to the use of the techniques of randomized experiments, quasi-experiments, multivariate statistical analyses, sample surveys, and so on. In contrast, qualitative methods included ethnography, case studies, in-depth interviews, and participant observation. In the 1970s, methodological tolerance was an idea, not the reality. In the lead issue of a new journal, *Evaluation Quarterly*, Rossi and Wright (1977) asserted: "There is almost universal agreement among evaluation researchers that the randomized controlled experiment is the ideal model for evaluating. . . . If there is a Bible for evaluation, the Scriptures have been written by Campbell and Stanley" (p. 13).

Criticism of quantitative evaluation. In addition to Eisner's criticism (1971a) of the dominance of quantitative methods and the "scientific" mind-set, Hamilton (1976) advanced five criticisms of quantitative evaluation. His first criticism intersected Eisner's, namely that quantitative evaluation directs attention away from important aspects of educational programs which are not easily measured. Second, Hamilton noted that the interests of the evaluator and curriculum developer can conflict when the evaluator works to tighten experimental control by discouraging redevelopment in programmatic midstream. Third, quantitative evaluation tends to emphasize the interests of administrators and researchers rather than the practical questions of interest to teachers. Fourth, unplanned consequences are ignored in favor of intended outcomes. Finally, quantitative evaluation tends to overlook that consensus on curricular aims is unlikely (Hamilton, 1976; Fraser, 1989).

British writers were insistent in their criticism of quantitative evaluation. Significant publications included those by Parlett and Hamilton (1972), Jenkins, et al. (1979), and Hamilton, et al. (1976). What should complement or replace quantitative models? British writers have advanced models termed illuminative evaluation (Parlett & Hamilton, 1972) and the case study approach (MacDonald & Walker, 1975; Norris, 1977; Simons, 1980). In the United States, Eisner (1979) advanced educational criticism, as did George Willis (1978). Robert Stake (1972, 1975) advocated responsive evaluation, Egon Guba and Yvonna Lincoln advanced naturalistic evaluation (1981; Guba, 1978), and Smith (1978) and Stake and Easley (1978) advocated the case study approach. Action research could be said to have been formulated during this period (Russell, 1993).

Illustrative of these qualitative approaches is illuminative evaluation, developed by Parlett and Hamilton. In their description of this concept, we see the interests of qualitative researchers in investigating modalities of educational experience not easily measured. They wrote:

> The aims of illuminative evaluation are to study the innovative program: how it operates; how it is influenced by the various school situations in which it is applied; what those directly concerned regard as its advantages and disadvantages; and how students' intellectual tasks and academic experience are most affected. It attempts to discover and document what it is like to be participating in the scheme, whether as teacher or pupil; in addition to discern and discuss the innovation's most significant features, recurring concomitants, and critical processes. (Parlett & Hamilton, 1972, p. 9)

By the 1990s qualitative inquiry generally and qualitative curriculum evaluation specifically had achieved legitimation in the field. No longer would responsible scholars assert that the quantitative approach is the only legitimate form of evaluation. A shift from the quantitative to the qualitative is evident (Eisner & Peshkin, 1990). One reviewer of the field judged: "Evaluation is now less concerned with responding to prespecified problems than with discovering and articulating the problems that are pressing upon participants" (Nixon, 1990, p. 644). Another formulation of recent shifts in evaluation concerns teacher-directed evaluation, the implications of which are "similar to those involved in a shift from authoritarian to progressive classrooms" (Beattie, 1986, p. 70). In evaluation as well as in the curriculum field more broadly, a reconceptualization has occurred.

Disciplinary Foundations
Several scholars of evaluation pointed out during the late 1970s and early 1980s that the methods of quantitative evaluation relied exclusively on the methods of scientists, and that other fields, other disciplines—such as law, art, journalism—might be appropriate sources for developing models and methods of evaluation (Smith, 1978; Worthen, 1978; Fraser, 1989). A project in the late 1970s at the Northwest Regional Education Laboratory led to the publication of two books influential in the exploration of non-scientific disciplinary foundations for curriculum evaluation. These books were *Metaphors for Evaluation: Sources for New Methods* (Smith, 1981a) and *New Techniques for Evaluation* (Smith, 1981b).

The law as disciplinary foundation for curriculum evaluation. During the 1970s several scholars advanced what they termed adversary or judicial evaluation models based on the law as a metaphor (Owens; 1973; Wolf, 1979). In the practice of law were found several methods which might be helpful in curriculum evaluation. Among these are the use of expert testimony, cross-examination, and the weighing of conflicting evidence (Fraser, 1989). One merit of judicial evaluation is that:

> the law, as a metaphor, offers many important concepts (fact-finding, adversarial proceedings, cross-examination, evidentiary rules and procedures, structured deliberations, etc.) that . . . add a certain dimensionality lacking in more

conventional forms of social inquiry. In contrast to more "scientific" methodologies, which generally exclude human testimony and judgment . . . the "legal"
model places a premium on these forms of evidence. (Wolf, 1979, p. 21)

Of course, the law is not a perfect parallel to curriculum evaluation. The
social protocol of the courtroom appears ritualistic and inappropriate.
Curriculum as "indicted" is an inappropriate model as well. Fraser added:
"Having a prosecution and defense can lead to excessive polarization and
shift attention away from points of agreement and middle ground" (1989, p.
124). Sensitive to this problem, Popham and Carlson (1977) suggested involving interested parties in both sides of a particular case.

Journalism as disciplinary foundation for curriculum evaluation. Egan Guba
(1979, 1981) proposed investigative reporting as a model for curriculum
evaluation. Like a reporter, a curriculum evaluator might be required to
defend the report should it present a damaging picture of the curriculum; or
the evaluator might face ethical dilemmas, as when subjects withhold information or misrepresent situations, or when a reporter might be tempted to
breach ethical principles in order to secure necessary information. Like a
reporter, the interview might be a central event in curriculum evaluation, as
when a subject's testimony might be crucial to understanding and making
judgments regarding a particular curricular event; and, an evaluator may use
legal means to require testimony by unwilling subjects. Finally, like a
reporter, the curriculum evaluation specialist understands that the findings
of an investigation must take the form of a story well told, with a keen appreciation of the audience for the story (Guba, 1979, 1981; Fraser, 1989).

Art as a disciplinary foundation for curriculum evaluation. A third major
disciplinary foundation for contemporary curriculum evaluation is art. The
foremost spokesperson of this approach is Elliot W. Eisner. Eisner's ideas on
curriculum evaluation began to appear in the early 1970s and have culmi-
nated, at least at the time of this writing, with the second edition of *The
Educational Imagination: On the Design and Evaluation of School Programs*
(1985a) and *The Enlightened Eye* (1991a). Because Eisner's work has been
especially influential, we will consider his contributions in a separate section.

The Artist as Curriculum Evaluator: Eisner
Elliot W. Eisner, a professor of art as well as of education at Stanford University, has borrowed the concepts of "connoisseurship" and "criticism" from
the arts to broaden and refocus the concept and practice of curriculum evaluation. The two concepts are intimately interrelated, as we noted in abbreviated fashion in chapter 11. Eisner explains: "Connoisseurship, generally
defined, is the art of appreciation. It is essential to criticism because without
the ability to perceive what is subtle and important, criticism is likely to be
superficial or even empty" (1985a, p. 219). The distinction between the two
concepts is in function: to act as a connoisseur is to appreciate; to act as a
critic is to disclose. Eisner explains further: "Connoisseurship is a private

act. . . . It does not require either a public judgment or a public description" (1985a, 219).

The educational connoisseur. Like a connoisseur of, say, fine wine, or of opera, the educational connoisseur must have enjoyed years of study and appreciation. Still, Eisner cautions us, mere frequency of observations of classrooms is insufficient to guarantee the ability to make insightful judgments. What is required as well is, first, the ability "to attend to happenings of education life in a focused, sensitive, and conscious way" (1985a, p. 221). Second, the educational connoisseur must be able to compare what he or she has seen with past observations, "to discuss what he sees so that perceptions can be refined, to identify events not previously perceived, and to integrate and appraise what has been seen" (1985a, p. 221). At Stanford University, Eisner reports, such work proceeds by direct observation of classrooms and by the careful viewing of videotapes. He finds that:

> Over time, descriptive language becomes less mechanical, more incisive, and increasingly literary or poetic as students try to get at the essence of what is occurring. To talk about essences and significance in the observation of educational events requires, of course, not only a sensitivity to the emerging qualities of classroom life, but also a set of ideas, theories, or models that enable one to distinguish the significant from the trivial and to place what one sees in an intelligible context. . . . The essence of perception is that it is selective; there is no value-free mode of seeing. (1985a, 221-222)

Like tasting hundreds of wines or attending many musical performances, the educational connoisseur perceives and discusses his or her perception with other connoisseurs in order to refine perceptions, and to situate these perceptions in the pertinent context. For classroom observation, such a context might involve comparing a particular class to other classes in the same subject taught to the same age-level students. More subtly, such contextualization might involve understanding what the teacher and students are attempting to do, and appreciating to what extent the class succeeds on its own terms. Or, should it be judged a failure, the connoisseur would explore whether or not the class was an interesting failure. As in art, an interesting failure must be appraised more favorably than an uninteresting success.

Such judgments the connoisseur renders in the writing of educational criticism. What do critics do? On what do they base their criticism? Eisner answers these questions by defining the term:

> Criticism is the art of disclosing the qualities of events or objects that connoisseurship perceives. Criticism is the public side of connoisseurship. One can be a connoisseur without the skills of criticism, but one cannot be a critic without the skills of connoisseurship. (1985a, p. 223)

What is required is the translation of what one observes, the visual mode, into language, into a discursive mode. Eisner settles on the concept of rendering to convey the process of criticism, a view of the process not unlike the epistemological stance associated with phenomenology, a view poststructuralism rejects. Eisner writes: "What critics do or should try to do . . . [is] to create a rendering of situation, event, or object that will provide pointers to those aspects of the situation, event, or object that are in some way significant" (p. 224). The educational critic allows us to appreciate what was important about a particular educational event by rendering that significance in language.

The evaluative aspect of educational criticism. Eisner notes that the point of educational criticism is to improve the educational process. Improvement requires, he reminds us, a conception of what is important. For Eisner, the following questions are the important ones to ask:

> Are the children being helped or hindered by the form of teaching they are experiencing? Are they acquiring habits of mind conducive to further development or are these habits likely to hamper further development? . . . Questions such as these require the use of educational criteria. The critic, unlike the social scientist who has no professional obligation to appraise the educational value of a culture or group, has this obligation as part of his or her work. (1985a, pp. 235-236)

To answer these and other questions by the educational critic, three aspects of educational criticism must be attended to: description, interpretation, and evaluation (1985a, p. 237).

Examples of educational criticism. Eisner (1985a) includes examples of educational criticism, with the following titles: "Playing the School System: The Low Achiever's Game" by Barbara Porro, "Things of Use and Things of Beauty: The Story of the Swain County High School Arts Program" by Thomas Barone, "Honors: An Educational Criticism" by James Marshall, "Portrait of a Ceramics Class: Control and Freedom in a Delicate Balance" by Lorna Catford, and "An Educational Psychologist Goes to Medical School" by Stuart J. Cohen. Several other examples have appeared. For instance, Dorothy Huenecke (1992) performed an "artistic criticism" of "Writing to Read," an IBM program for kindergarten and first grade students, which she judged negatively. Thomas E. Barone has reflected on the process of criticism (1982; 1987b, 1990a, 1990b); in another study he employed educational criticism to evaluate the fine arts program in a black elementary school (Barone, 1987a). Gail McCutcheon was a early exponent of criticism (1979; 1982). Robert Donmoyer (1980) has contributed to this literature as well. The 1979 edition of *The Educational Imagination* included Donmoyer's educational criticism of Miss Hill's fourth grade classroom. Donmoyer's interesting criticism suggests that the issue of empathy is central to the practice of Eisnerian educational criticism.

In his criticism, entitled "School and Society Revisited: An Educational Criticism of Miss Hill's Fourth-Grade Classroom" (in Eisner, 1979, pp. 229-240), Donmoyer reported that the teacher reminds him, initially, of the television character "Mary Hartmann" (an unfavorable comparison for those unfamiliar with this 1970s television character). As he came to know her, he viewed her mechanical and routinized teaching more a function of the school. Outside the classroom, Donmoyer found her spontaneous and humane. She became for him a Jekyll-and-Hyde character (Donmoyer in Eisner, 1979). There is a difficult issue here, as Pinar (1988c) noted in his analysis of connoisseurship. Granted, empathy is necessary in order to understand the intentions of others. However, empathy invites the observer to identify with those intentions, a process which can function in rationalizing and obscuring ways. Unacknowledged, this danger results in the critic's complicity with another's legitimations, even delusions. The critic, as suggested in Eisner's image of the midwife, must not relinquish her independent judgment even as she empathizes. For empathy can conceal while it reveals (Pinar, 1988c).

Quasi-mystical? Pinar is clearly appreciative of Eisner's approach. Other critics, however, are less favorable (Sadler, 1985; Alexander, 1986; Pagano & Dolan, 1980). Writing in 1980, Jo Anne Pagano and Lawrence Dolan complained:

> The vagueness of his [Eisner's] presentation, the almost quasimystical character ascribed to "connoisseurship" leaves us with no public forum for the adjudication of the validity of the connoisseur's observations and consequent praises or complaints. . . . This kind of criticism smacks of the same kind of ideological imperialism as that of the quasi-empirical approach. (1980, p. 374)

Others insist that the major assumptions of Eisner's model are themselves problematic. These assumptions include: 1) that education is like a fine art, 2) that educational evaluation is, therefore, like art criticism, and 3) that an educational evaluation which employs artistic language can be rigorous and relatively error-free (Alexander, 1986). Despite such criticism, Eisner's model and practice of curriculum evaluation remains highly respected and heuristic for the field. A recent review of research on curriculum evaluation (Madaus & Kellaghan, 1992) lists Eisner's approach as one of the five major approaches to qualitative evaluation.

Eisner (1985b) describes his view as "a personal, autobiographical view of educational evaluation" (p. 1). [For Eisner's autobiographical reflection on the arts, see Eisner 1991b.] Eisner insists that educational evaluation is an educational enterprise, not primarily an administrative one. It has the processes of classroom life as its major focus. "In short," Eisner (1985b) tells us:

> in both the construction of educational means (the curriculum) and the appraisal of its consequences, the teacher would become an artist, for criticism itself when carried to its height is an art. This, it seems to me, is a dimension to which curriculum theory will someday have to speak. (p. 37)

Clearly, curriculum theory has been reconceived, thanks in part to the work of Eisner and his students (such as Barone, Donmoyer, McCutcheon, Vallance, and others). They have argued persuasively that there is much to be learned about classrooms, teaching, and the character of student work by seeing first-hand what the curriculum as enacted looks like. Such accounts need to be written by "connoisseurs" whose literary prose illuminates its subtleties. Educational criticism can be supplemented by reading those scores that students received on standardized tests or that teachers secured on observation schedules ticked off by impartial observers. Eisner (1985b) acknowledges: "No single form representation will do justice to everything" (p. 252).

In a recent work, Eisner (1993) suggests that the term "evaluation" has become dated, replaced by "assessment." Drawing on his earlier work, Eisner (1993) develops eight criteria which, he argues, are appropriate for creating and appraising authentic assessment. These are:

> 1) The tasks used to assess what students know and can do need to reflect the tasks they will encounter in the world outside schools, not merely those limited to the schools themselves. 2) The tasks used to assess should reveal how students go about solving a problem, not only the solutions they formulate. 3) Assessment tasks should reflect the values of the intellectual community from which the tasks are derived. 4) Assessment tasks need not be limited to solo performance. 5) New assessment tasks should make possible more than one acceptable solution to a problem and more than one acceptable answer to a question. 6) Assessment tasks should have curricular relevance, but not be limited to the curriculum as taught. 7) Assessment tasks should require students to display a sensitivity to configurations or wholes, not simply to discrete elements. 8) Assessment tasks should permit the student to select a form of representation he or she chooses to display what has been learned. (pp. 226-231)

These criteria acknowledge, Eisner believes, the diversity of response to "common experiences" (p. 232). Indeed, he continues: "It is precisely in the diverse of response . . . that our cultural lives are enriched" (p. 232). He notes that such interpretative assessment cannot easily be quantified, and may thereby be difficult for the public to accept. Eisner (1993) concludes: "I can only hope that with responsible and articulate interpretation, authentic assessment will be understood and valued by the public at large. If it is, assessment will not only contribute to better schooling for children, it will contribute to a broader, more generous conception of education itself" (p. 232).

Conclusion

Critical approach to evaluation. One other major approach to curriculum evaluation merits mention here, a strand of scholarship Madaus and Kellaghan (1992) characterize as "critical/emancipatory" [see chapter 5]. The critical approach is said to represent the most radical departure from the mainstream tradition in curriculum evaluation (Coomer, 1986). Gitlin and Goldstein (1987) argued for a dialogical approach, in which they asked: "How can we encourage the conditions necessary for teachers to enter into a dialogue aimed at understanding?" (p. 27). In their view, understanding becomes "the aim of evaluation" (Gitlin & Goldstein, 1987, p. 18). Acknowledging that most schemes attempt to control teachers' conduct, horizontal evaluation, as Gitlin and Goldstein conceived it, attempts to "promote change by empowering teachers. Teachers are given the opportunity to reexperience the ordinary and therefore to act on a critical accounting of practices and aims as opposed to acting out of habit" (Gitlin, 1989, p. 322). In other work that might typify this category, Greenfield (1982; see also Greenfield, 1980, 1986; Johnson, 1990) outlined an anarchistic theory of organization which recognized the individual as the fundamental building block in social reality. Madaus and Kellaghan note that this approach, associated with the work of Jurgen Habermas and critical theory [see chapter 5], is sufficiently marginal that other surveys of qualitative work fail to include it (Smith, 1987; Jacob, 1987). Such omissions are themselves political. As we noted in chapter 1, comprehensiveness has been one casualty of the "paradigm wars." The critical/emancipatory approach was in evidence at the 1988 Stanford University Conference on Qualitative Inquiry in Education, co-sponsored and published by Teachers College Press (Eisner, & Peshkin, 1990). As is the case with the field of curriculum generally, qualitative approaches have gained important ground, even in the area of curriculum evaluation, at least in the sphere of theory. In theory, postmodernism is making an appearance in curriculum evaluation (Russell & Willinsky, 1993), as it has in supervision.

Practice is another matter, of course. Positivists have not disappeared completely from the field. Madaus and Kellaghan note:

> It should not be concluded from our attention to qualitative methods that they now dominate the evaluation scene. Such is far from the case. There is still a strong view that methods derived from the physical sciences and used widely in educational research provide the strongest basis for drawing inferences about cause-effect relationships. (1992, p. 134)

To escape the bureaucratic power of testing. While quantitative methods have not been adequate, and probably will never be [see chapters 1 and 8 for reviews of pertinent issues] adequate to the establishment of cause-effect relationships among curriculum, teaching, and learning, such new models of curriculum evaluation will probably be forthcoming. Madaus and Kellaghan (1992) are not sanguine:

> More than new forms of assessment and evaluation, however, will be needed to escape the bureaucratic power of testing. If the new forms are used for the same purposes as the systems they are designed to replace, and without attention to underlying systemic reasons for such problems as poor student achievement, it would appear that the new modes will eventually be open to corruption in the way the older ones were. (pp. 147, 148)

Understanding curriculum as institutional text implies the realization that certain forms of educational practice function to maintain the institution as it is, requiring perhaps incremental improvements, but all done in the name of institutional maintenance. Despite the promise of evaluation expressed in the work of Elliot Eisner, the mainstream practice of curriculum evaluation appears to function primarily as bureaucratism, i.e. as a conservative social practice designed to maintain the institution as it is. The rhetoric politicians employ is of course quite different. That rhetoric is about "change," as we saw in the section of this chapter on curriculum policy. But the politicians' insistence on largely ignoring the most interesting orientation the field has developed, i.e. Eisner's connoisseurship, implies that political rhetoric regarding school reform is only that, political rhetoric.

PART TWO
CURRICULUM AND TEACHERS

If teaching is going to be good work, we have to be able to get beyond the simplistic, teacher-proof curriculums, standardization of evaluation, and an excellence read as conventionality.

(Shirley Steinberg, 1992a, p. 72)

Where is the teacher in curriculum talk?

(Terrance R. Carson, 1990c, p. 21)

Instruction does not make the man [sic].

(Robert McClintock, 1971, p. 205)

After the curriculum has been developed, that is, after the phases of policy, planning, design, implementation, embodiment in material form (including in print and/or technological forms), then supervised and evaluated, what is still missing in the effort to understand curriculum as institutional text? It is the experience of teaching and learning. In classrooms teachers and students encounter the materials that have been developed, and it is in this encounter that curriculum becomes mediated and symbolic social experience. In classrooms, as Philip Wexler (1990, 1992) might say, curriculum becomes a social practice. To sketch the relation between curriculum and teachers, we move to a brief discussion of pedagogy, then to selected discourses on teacher education and development, and finally to a brief review of textbooks, one major medium through which the teacher/student encounter occurs.

VIII
Pedagogy: Doyle, Shulman, Jackson, and Cuban

Teachers generally see themselves as being fairly autonomous—as being in control of what is taught and how it is taught—but when it comes to actual practice, they tend to depart very little from a single approach: standing in front of a class—telling, explaining, or lecturing.

(Daniel & Laurel Tanner, 1990, p. 308)

But one thing is certain: there do not appear to be sufficient data for a theory of instruction in any specific, coherent and worthwhile sense.

(Robin Barrow, 1984b, p. 134)

Instruction did not suffice; it left too little room for human doubt, inquiry, uncertainty, the search for self.

(Robert McClintock, 1971, pp. 171-172)

If teaching is a text, then it is a fast and evanescent one, authored serially minute by minute.

(Joseph P. McDonald, 1992, p. 17)

Separate but interrelated. In Walter Doyle's (1992) review of research at the intersection of curriculum and pedagogy, an area he has been studying for some time (Doyle & Carter, 1984), he characterizes the two domains as "separate but interrelated" (p. 486). Doyle defines pedagogy as the "how" of schooling, "the human interactions that occur during actual teaching episodes" (486). The major topics of pedagogy have included motivation, communication, feedback, and accessibility. Doyle continues:

> Given this distinctiveness, it is not surprising that a considerable amount of work in each domain has gone on as if the other did not exist. At the same time, a curriculum is intended to frame or guide teaching practice and cannot be achieved except during acts of teaching. Similarly, teaching is always about something so it cannot escape curriculum, and teaching practices, in themselves, imply curricular assumptions and consequences. It is difficult, therefore, to avoid stumbling on curriculum when one is trying to understand teaching, or commenting on pedagogy when one is deliberating about curriculum. (p. 486)

Understood institutionally, curriculum and pedagogy do appear to be separate domains, and their relationship is often construed as linear (Doyle, 1992). Institutionally, curriculum defines the knowledge to be taught; pedagogy is conceived of as the delivery system (Beauchamp, 1961; Foshay & Foshay, 1980). This view has a history (Kliebard, 1986). As we saw in the section on implementation, teaching is commonly characterized as the means by which curriculum is implemented. Teaching came to function as a means of administrative control over the education of American youth. In contrast to the history of the curriculum field, teaching as a field remained closer to psychology. This meant, in the 1930s, that research on teaching became infused by the behavioral psychology of Thorndike and Judd [see chapter 3]. Research on teaching shared in the growing prestige of psychology as the core discipline of educational research. By the 1980s, findings from research on teaching became a source of authority independent from curriculum for prescribing and controlling quality in teaching practice (Doyle, 1992). Put bluntly, much of research on teaching has been concerned with how to get teachers to do what others (usually administrators) want them to do (Richardson, 1990). Teaching is viewed largely as a process of disciplining and controlling students so that they can learn what the experts have stipulated

(Doyle, 1992). In this institutional view of teaching, the curriculum becomes invisible (Dunkin & Biddle, 1974; Doyle, 1992).

Depsychologizing of teaching. In recent years, however, this view has changed. No longer is teaching viewed exclusively as applied psychology. The "depsychologizing" of teaching has invited multidisciplinary research, including work grounded in anthropology, sociology, and linguistics (Cazden, 1986; Doyle, 1978; Erickson, 1986). Some have attempted to elaborate a view of pedagogy and learning grounded in critical theory, especially the work of Jurgen Habermas (Young, 1988). Additionally, curriculum tends to be viewed as an important aspect of teaching (Shulman, 1986a). Ben-Peretz (1990) links the two as inseparable: "To sum up: teachers are encouraged to see their major role in the partnership of curriculum development as that of informed and creative interpreters who are prepared to reflect on their curriculum and to reconstruct it" (p. xv). Others, however, disagree on this point: "teaching is unlike curriculum development" (Martin-Kniep & Uhrmacher, 1992, p. 262)

Another view of teaching comes from those working to understand curriculum as deconstructed text. Clermont Gauthier (1992) does not regard pedagogy as either science or an art. Rather, teaching is better understood as an exercise in persuasion aimed at courting the student's consent in order to win the learning game. That teaching exists in the middle between science and art means that "the way we write when we are concerned with pedagogy will differ significantly from the way we write when we are concerned with art or science" (Gauthier, 1991, p. 246). Political theory influences research on teaching as well. The hidden curriculum concept [see chapter 5] has its parallel in the teaching literature, i.e. hidden pedagogy, and it is just as contested (Denscombe, 1982; Hatton, 1987; see chapter 5).

The situatedness of learning. Doyle (1992) reviews work in two important areas of teaching research: so-called content pedagogy and pedagogical content knowledge. Content knowledge refers to "attempts by cognitive scientists to understand knowledge representations and comprehension processes in various subject matter domains" (Doyle, 1992, p. 497). These attempts are founded in attention to the learner's viewpoints or "paradigms" as they relate to comprehension of a particular unit of content (Marton, 1989). "The ultimate aim," Doyle tells us, "is to generate content-specific theories of how people handle particular contents, rather than general psychological theory applicable across content domains" (1992, p. 497). This research tends to appreciate the "situatedness" of learning (Lave, 1988; Lave & Wagner, 1991; Whitson, 1992b; St. Julien, 1992; Kincheloe & Steinberg, 1993), which argues that:

> Learning viewed as situated activity has as its central defining characteristic a process that we call legitimate peripheral participation. By this we mean to draw attention to the point that learners inevitably participate in communities of practitioners and that the mastery of knowledge and skill requires newcom-

ers to move toward full participation in the sociocultural practices of a community. (Lave & Wagner, 1991, p. 29)

Or, relatedly, "situations might be said to coproduce knowledge through activity" (Brown, Collins, & Duguid, 1989, p. 32). The situatedness of learning is evident in one study of representational abilities of children, which indicates that "adults are analogically part of the process of development" (Jardine & Morgan, 1987, p. 217). [The emphasis upon "situatedness" replaces earlier emphases upon, for instance, concept formation; see Vygotsky, 1962; Miel, 1962, p. 82. The notion of apprentice had been developed twenty year earlier by Robert McClintock, 1971, p. 190 ff.]

Of the research on content pedagogy, Doyle (1992) concludes that it:

mirrors the traditions of educational psychology in that knowledge about psychological processes is used as a basis for thinking about and designing instructional procedures and for psychologizing the content to be taught. The work today [however] reflects richer conceptions of subject matter. (pp. 497-498)

As a result of this shift in research toward curriculum, psychology is no longer the exclusive discipline upon which teacher research is grounded: linguistics, philosophy, anthropology, cognitive science, and other disciplines are pertinent. These developments acknowledged, however, Doyle still judges this category of research on teaching as "largely pedagogical, rather than curricular" (p. 498). Also evident, he remarks, "is the almost complete lack of a classroom perspective" (p. 498) in this research.

Pedagogical content knowledge. The second major category of research on teaching Doyle (1992) reviews is "pedagogical content knowledge." Lee Shulman is the most visible researcher in this area, which attends to the subject matter of teachers and, more specifically, to the knowledge teachers require to convey subject matter to students. Shulman defines pedagogical content knowledge as that capacity of the teacher "to transform the content knowledge he or she possesses into forms that are pedagogically powerful and yet adaptive to the variations in ability and background presented by the students" (1987, p. 15). In this regard, Shulman writes that a teacher must:

understand the structures of subject matter, the principles of conceptual organization, and the principles of inquiry that help answer two kinds of question in each field: what are the important ideas and skills in this domain? How are new ideas added and deficient ones dropped by those who produce knowledge in this area? That is, what are the rules and procedures of good scholarship or inquiry. (1987, p. 9)

Knowing physics or history is insufficient for success in the classroom. Other knowledge is required. This other knowledge is characterized as pedagogical content knowledge, which is a concept which intersects with the notions of "teacher lore" (Schubert & Ayers, 1992) and "personal practical knowledge" (Clandinin & Connelly, 1992). All three concepts seem to suggest that in addition to knowing one's discipline or school subject, other knowledge is required:

> What is also needed is knowledge of the most useful forms of representation of those ideas, the most powerful analogies, illustrations, examples, explanations, and demonstrations—in a word, the ways of representing and formulating the subject that make it comprehensible to others. . . . Pedagogical content knowledge also includes an understanding of what makes the learning of specific topics easy or difficult: the conceptions and preconceptions that students of different ages and backgrounds bring with them to the learning of those most frequently taught topics and lessons. (Shulman, 1986b, pp. 9-10)

Pedagogical content knowledge, then, is understood to be that knowledge which allows a teacher "eventually to lift the curriculum away from texts and materials [and] to give it an independent existence" (Doyle, 1992, p. 499). Like content pedagogy research mentioned earlier, research on pedagogical content knowledge suggests that in the foreseeable future the study of teaching will be increasingly grounded in classroom experience (Doyle, 1992). Other researchers point to the knowledge the teacher brings to the classroom: "The single factor which seems to have the greatest power to carry forward our understanding of the teacher's role is the idea of teachers' knowledge" (Elbaz, 1983, p. 11).

Shulman's model. The concept of pedagogical content knowledge is embedded in a larger view of teacher education and its knowledge base. Shulman (1987) elaborates the following categories of teacher education's knowledge base: 1) content knowledge (i.e. the academic disciplines), 2) general pedagogical knowledge, with special reference to those broad principles and strategies of classroom management and organization that appear to transcend subject matter, 3) what Shulman terms curriculum knowledge, with particular knowledge of the materials and programs that serve as "tools of the trade" for teachers, and 4) pedagogical content knowledge, that special mix of content and pedagogy that is uniquely the province of teachers, their own particular form of professional understanding which includes a) knowledge of learners and their characteristics, and b) knowledge of educational contexts, ranging from the workings of the group or classroom, the governance and financing of school districts, to the character of communities and cultures, and c) knowledge of educational ends, purposes and values, and their philosophical and historical grounds.

Shulman cites here four major sources for what he terms the teaching knowledge base: 1) scholarship and research in content (academic) disciplines; 2) the materials and settings of the institutionalized educational process (i.e., school curricula, textbooks, school organizations and finance, and the structure of the teaching profession); 3) research on schooling, social organization, learning, teaching and human development, and the other social and cultural factors that affect what teachers can do; and 4) "the wisdom of practice itself" (p. 8). Drawing on Fenstermacher (1978), Shulman argues that "the goal of teacher education . . . is not to indoctrinate or to train teachers to behave in prescribed ways, but to educate teachers to reason soundly about their teaching as well as to perform skillfully" (p. 13). We reprint Shulman's (1987, p. 15) model of pedagogical reasoning and action here.

A Model of Pedagogical Reasoning and Action

Comprehension

Of purposes, subject matter structures, ideas within and outside the discipline

Transformation

Preparation: critical interpretation and analysis of texts, structuring and segmenting, development of a curricular repertoire, and clarification of purposes

Representation: use of a representational repertoire which includes analogies, metaphors, examples, demonstrations, explanations, and so forth

Selection: choice from among an instructional repertoire which includes modes of teaching, organizing, managing, and arranging

Adaptation and Tailoring to Student Characteristics: consideration of conceptions, preconceptions, misconceptions, and difficulties, language, culture, and motivations, social class, gender, age, ability, aptitude, interests, self concepts, and attention

Instruction

Management, presentations, interactions, group work, discipline, humor, questioning, and other aspects or active teaching, discovery or inquiry instruction, and the observable forms of classroom teaching

Evaluation

Checking for student understanding during interactive teaching
Testing student understanding at the end of lessons or units
Evaluating one's own performance and adjusting for experiences

Reflection

Reviewing, reconstructing, reenacting and critically analyzing one's own and the class's performance and grounding explanations in evidence

New Comprehensions: Of purposes, subject matter, students, teaching, and self. Consolidation of new understanding and learnings from experience

Shulman (1987) concludes his discussion of his model of pedagogical content knowledge by noting:

> An emphasis upon pedagogical content knowledge would permeate the teacher preparation curriculum. . . . We must achieve standards without standardization. We must be careful that the knowledge-base approach does not produce an overly technical image of teaching, a scientific enterprise that has lost its soul. (p. 20)

While enjoying a generally favorable reception in the teacher education field, Shulman's work has been criticized (Henderson, 1988) by a few curriculum specialists. Apparently critical of Shulman's scheme of a knowledge base in teacher education, William Ayers (1988) outlined an "alternative teacher education program," identifying five areas as foundational: a) autobiography, b) inquiry, c) reflection, d) critique, and e) community. Other scholars praise Shulman's work, as we will in see the next section (Beyer, Feinberg, Pagano, Whitson, 1989).

The practice of teaching. Another major statement on the nature of teaching comes from Philip Jackson (1986) who has carefully reflected on the "practice of teaching." That teaching is more complex than commonly regarded is one of his main themes. He begins his study by questioning the public assumption that everyone knows how to teach, as long as the subject matter is known. Knowing what to teach and knowing how to teach are quite different matters, he points out. With John Dewey, Jackson (1986) acknowledges that there are teachers who do wonderful work but do not conform to any specific methodology: "These naturally endowed teachers, we are asked to believe, are the ones who get by and even excel without formal training" (p. 9). That such individuals exist raises the question: are there any formal laws or rules of teaching? Being fair, impartial, and caring are all commonsensical attributes of a good teacher, he points out. However, common sense is insufficient:

> There is an additional point that must be inserted here. It is that common sense, when it speaks imperatively is not always of one voice. It tells us to be prudent and cautious, but it also advises us to strike while the iron is hot. It tells us to be gentle in our dealings with the young, but it also warns us not to spare the rod, for fear of spoiling the child. (p. 12)

Clearly, it is necessary to go beyond common sense, and to do so may require a more complex understanding of the teacher's existential circumstances. He looks for the "epistemic superstructures" (p. 17) within which the what and how take place.

Jackson (1986) delineates three assumptions of the teaching act: "1) the presumption of a public, 2) the presumption of ignorance, and 3) the presumption of a shared identity" (p. 24). Jackson is convinced that teachers can never be sure of any of these, the third being most dangerous. He concludes that only individual teachers can decide how much they can gain from teacher education programs: "In the final analysis, teachers themselves must judge" (p. 30). Jackson expresses concern over the lack of certainty regarding the results of one's teaching. He reviews what he terms the "quartet of 'classic' strategies" employed by teachers to discover what students know or do not know: 1) observing students in order to look for visual and auditory signs of involvement, 2) arranging for the report of self-perceived difficulties, 3) on-the-spot questioning for evidence of understanding, and 4) examining for the acquisition and retention of knowledge and skills after instruction is finished or during intervals when it has been temporarily suspended. Knowledge takes form in the individual over time and each form is unique: "Therein lies the fate of all who teach—from here to eternity, uncertainties galore" (p. 72).

In the face of such uncertainty, how can we judge what is "real teaching?" He draws three conclusions: first, he insists there is no such thing as a behavioral definition of teaching and there never can be. The second is closely related to the first: our attempt to say when a person is or is not teaching is always an act of interpretation, a view not dissimilar from that of Eisner's. The third conviction, one that follows from the first two, denies the possibility of our ever arriving upon an enduring or universal definition of what it means to teach. Acknowledging that, Jackson identifies three basic approaches to teaching: "the generic, the epistemic, and the consensual" (p. 89). He examines and rejects each approach, although he seems to privilege the consensual. Jackson (1986) asserts: "To put the argument in a nutshell, there is no such thing as 'genuine' teaching. There is only an activity that people call teaching, which can be viewed from a variety of critical perspectives" (p. 95). Consequently, one must ask: does it make sense to imagine progress in teaching? Yes, Jackson answers, qualifiedly. Jackson refuses to take either a progressive or traditional position:

> In sum, to be genuinely true to their calling, all teachers must be partially conservative and partially liberal in outlook. Though the historical drift of the profession, at least in recent years, may seem to have been in one direction only—toward a more liberal interpretation of teaching—the health and future development of teaching depend upon most teachers' maintaining a balanced view of both the means and ends of pedagogy. (p. 114)

Jackson (1986) does see "two distinguishably different ways of thinking about education" (p. 116): the mimetic and the transformative, the former being learning by imitation, the latter changing how the learner feels and perceives. In the Socratic tradition, the teacher is perceived as artist or creator. There is no formula here, but Jackson mentions 1) personal modeling, 2) "soft" suasion, and 3) the use of narrative. He says, incidentally, that Socrates himself was more "content-oriented" than is generally understood. Transformation, akin to psychoanalysis, often encounters "the well-known phenomenon of *unintended consequences*" (p. 128). The mimetic tradition is ascendant, due to the power of science (supported by technology), including educational psychology. Today teachers find themselves reduced to data in a giant "bureautechnocracy" (p. 142).

In the Rosa Sachs Memorial Lectures presented at Teachers College, Columbia University, in the fall of 1990, Jackson (1992d) turns his attention to "untaught lessons," that is, the influence that teachers have on their students and well as the influences teaching has on those who teach. In these lectures Jackson employs autobiography, literary criticism, and ethnography to explore the effects of teaching: "This synchronous intermingling of past, present, and future is precisely what happens, I argued, when one reflects on one's prior teaching and tries to figure out what one has learned from it or what remains to be learned" (1992d, pp. 92-93). In what Pinar (1994; Pinar & Grumet, 1976) characterizes as the regressive moment in autobiographical reflection, Jackson (1992c) notes:

> We change our mind about our teaching past . . . and in so doing we re-create it. We also surprise ourselves from time to time by dredging up memories that have long been dormant, for so long sometimes they may even seem brand new. In this way we continue to refurbish the past, to *realize* it, one might say. (p. 93; emphasis in original)

There is an extensive literature on teaching, little of it as thoughtful as Jackson's. Indeed, much of it is "bureautechnocratic," in Jackson's term. Such researchers would characterize their work as "scientific." Rosenshine & Stevens (1986) concluded, for example, that the major functions or components of systematic instruction are known. Sharing that confidence in a "scientific" concept of teaching have been Nathan Gage and Madeline Hunter, although, they "draw on art to fill gaps" (Zahorik, 1987, p. 277). The perspectives on teaching with currency in the reconceptualized curriculum field are those of teaching as artistry and transformation. The instructional repertoire produced by the "scientific" community, from standardized examinations, bureaucratically-imposed instructional models to teacher-proof curricula, "all help to hinder the teacher's ability to utilize or implement a more orchestral perspective on teaching and learning. . . . In the final analysis, it is the teacher's own skill and insight that act as the final arbiter of what is taught and how it is taught" (Hlebowitsh, 1990, p. 159).

As we saw in chapter 11, the major work in elaborating teaching as art is that of Elliot Eisner and others, including Louis Rubin (1985, 1991), Alan Tom (1984), who emphasizes teaching as a moral craft, Lawrence Stenhouse (1988), and Nelson Haggerson (1985; Haggerson & Bowman, 1993). Stenhouse (1988), for instance, observed: "The artist is the researcher whose inquiry expresses itself in performance of his or her art rather than (or as well as) in a research report. . . . Educational knowledge exists in, and is verified or falsified in, its performance" (p. 51). In his "Curriculum as Figurative Language: Exalting Teaching and Learning Through Poetry," Haggerson (1985) urged us to explore personal meaning. The notion of "reflective practitioner" has also become of interest to those working on problems of teaching, a concept that can be linked to the earlier work of James B. Macdonald (Henderson, 1988) and to the work of Donald Schön (1983, 1991). Acknowledging his debt to Nel Noddings and Elliot Eisner, James G. Henderson (1992) identified three key characteristics of reflective practice: 1) an ethic of caring, 2) a constructivist approach to teaching, and 3) artistic problem-solving, that is when [teachers] understand that quality education involves judgment, imagination, and flexibility. Henderson described what he terms constructivist teaching, which asks the questions: 1) what is the relationship between what I am trying to teach and students' past experience, and 2) what is the relationships between what I am trying to teach and my students' personal purposes? For some, like Jackson (1986) and Sergiovanni (1984, 1987) in supervision, some mix of science and art is preferable. Such a synthetical model, many believe, "appears to have a better chance for improving teaching" (Zahorik, 1987, p. 284).

Others emphasize the interconnectedness of factors:

> When we view a teaching perspective as a dynamic complex of beliefs and assumptions about a wide range of aspects, any change to one part of that system will affect, and will be affected by, the other parts of the system. Successful efforts to help teachers change, then, will have to consider the whole teaching perspective. (Trumbull, 1987, p. 60)

Relatedly, Kaufman (1988) asks us to attend to the "ecological contexts of student, colleague, and profession" (p. 85). Many point to the importance of practice (Gideonse,1988), of collegial interaction (Flinders, 1988), of forming a community of intellectuals and school practitioners in the search for a sophisticated practice congruent with teacher professionalism (Sockett, 1989).

More in a phenomenological vein, William Reinsmith (1992) discusses teaching as presence and encounter. Referring to phenomenological philosopher of education David Denton (1974), Reinsmith (1992) points to teaching as a way of being in the world: "More concretely, teaching is a way of being present to students which establishes, should they be receptive, a specific engagement" (p. 12). Reinsmith then goes on to provide models and modes of teaching, moving from teacher-centered to student-centered forms. For example, the first is a presentational model (teacher as disseminator/transmitter; lecturer/dramatist). The second is what he terms an initiatory mode (teacher as inducer/persuader; inquirer/catalyst). The third is a dialogic mode (teacher as dialogist). Moving toward the student-centered end of the spectrum, he describes the elicitive mode (teacher as facilitator/guide; as witness/abiding presence), and finally an apophatic mode in which the teacher becomes a student. Teacher as student might avoid the problems of teacher as expert (Welker, 1991). This latter concept of pedagogy has been remarkably durable over the history of teaching.

History of teaching. Larry Cuban (1983) has asked how teachers have taught, and the answer he provides is a historical one [see also Grumet, 1988b]. Consulting descriptions of 1200 classrooms and 6000 teachers, Cuban was able to produce composite sketches of mainstream teaching during several periods during the past century. "At the turn of the century," he begins, "the prevailing form of teaching was teacher-centered. . . . Classes were taught in a whole group. Teacher talk dominated verbal expression during class time" (1983, p. 163). During the next period—1920s and 1930s—in urban schools in cities such as Denver, New York City, and Washington, D.C., and rural schools across the nation, Cuban found that the majority of elementary teachers continued to use pedagogical practices that emphasized large-group instruction, recitation, seatwork, and little student mobility. There were, he reports, a substantial number of teachers [especially in New York City where the Activity Program (1934-1941) was underway, and in Denver where successive school administrations nurtured progressive approaches, but elsewhere as well] who experimented with the rearrangement of their classroom furniture, with variegated grouping of children for instruction, with the use of projects that encouraged students to express themselves and move around freely in the classrooms. Cuban found some progressive practices were used and others were not, showing up without a predictable pattern in both rural and urban schools. Although Cuban reports that progressive teachers were never a majority in any setting he studied, these teachers did represent substantial minorities in various districts. What did Cuban find in secondary schools? "If there appeared to be modest changes in elementary classrooms, that didn't seem to be the case at the high school level. . . . What occurred in most high school classrooms were mere traces of progressive practice" (Cuban, 1983, p. 164).

Progressive teaching. Cuban (1983) did find exceptions, as we would expect given the influence of the Eight-Year Study (1933-1941). For example, Denver's five high schools which participated in the Eight-Year Study established experimental classes in each of its schools. Cuban reports that never more than one-quarter of the student body and faculty were involved in these progressive educational experiments; their classes were quarantined in a separate wing of the building. The last vestiges of the curriculum changes that grew out of the Eight-Year Study in Denver had disappeared by 1954, a time when the "life adjustment movement" was under sustained attack by conservatives such as Bestor [see chapter 3].

By the beginning of World War II, Cuban tells us, the common patterns of instruction included the following: 1) employing the entire class as the primary teaching vehicle, 2) use of the question-answer format, 3) a teacher monopoly of classroom talk, and 4) a general reliance upon the textbook which has been basically undisturbed, except for those progressive experiments mentioned earlier.

Teaching after 1965. Cuban then moves to the years after 1965 when another reform impulse resulted in new ideas, additional money, and new faces into public schools across the country. Informal education, open classrooms, and alternative schools were among the innovations tried to varying extents in different locations. What were the results? These efforts at innovation:

> produced a composite portrait of schoolteaching not unlike that of previous generations: teachers talking most of the time to the entire class, listening to student answers, assigning portions of the text to the class for homework—the meat-and-potatoes of instruction. (1983, p. 164)

The last period, the present one, Cuban surveys begins in 1975. Since that date, he reports that the dominant pattern has continued to be teacher-centered instruction with some small percentage of elementary teachers developing hybrid versions of what twenty years ago were characterized as open classrooms. In high school classrooms, little variation from the dominant teaching pattern is discernible. Cuban (1983) concludes that:

a dominant core of teaching practices has endured since the turn of the century in both elementary and high school classrooms. These practices (teaching the whole group, reliance upon a textbook, rows of desks, question-answer framework for carrying on dialogue, etc.) persisted over time, in different settings, in spite of changes in teacher education and the knowledge that students bring to school and major social and cultural movements. (p. 175)

In sum, the institutional practices of teaching have changed little in one hundred years.

IX
Pre-service Teacher Education: The Holmes Group

Reliance on technical knowledge and skill in professional teacher education leaves student teachers ill prepared to think about schooling in a context-sensitive and socially constructive way and to consistently execute their practice accordingly.
(Andreas Dick, 1992b, p. 365)

If critically reflective teacher education is to make a difference, it must help students not only to see and understand current social and educational dynamics but also help them understand how they may overcome them by redefining teaching as centrally concerned with moral commitment and action.
(Landon E. Beyer, 1991, p. 214)

A reconceptualized teacher education curriculum must challenge its students to investigate the locus of community power and demystify social relations.
(James T. Sears, 1985, p. 69)

For many years, those interested in the education of prospective teachers have been well aware of the conservative power of schools and the importance of pre-professional experience to enable prospective teachers to critically engage established teacher practices (Dewey, 1904; Rugg, 1952). The quality of the school curriculum is very much dependent upon the quality of teachers, and the quality of teachers is very much dependent upon the quality of their pre-professional educational experience (Borrowman, 1965; Koerner, 1963; Conant, 1963). John Goodlad (1990a) has argued extensively that teacher education must be a higher national priority. Relying on the scholarship of Herbert Kliebard (1986), Kenneth Zeichner and Daniel Liston (1990) identify four traditions of reform in American teacher education: academic, social efficiency, developmentalist, and reconstructionist. They acknowledge that most existing teacher education programs represent some mixture of the four traditions: "we hope to encourage conversation across as well as within particular traditions" (p. 16). For example, the rhetoric of teacher education reform recently has been decidedly developmentalist [see

Darling-Hammond, Griffin, Wise, 1992]. This developmentalism has been, however, justified in the name of academic excellence and social efficiency, which presumably would have the consequence of socially reconstructing the American nation.

The significance of teacher education for education generally is not, you might guess, only an American notion. Globally, the preparation of teachers continues to be regarded as crucial to a country's well-being (Foshay, in Leavitt, 1992, p. viii). Examining teacher education internationally, Leavitt (1992) identifies eight major issues in teacher education: 1) recruitment, 2) content of preservice programs, 3) governance and quality control (local and centralized), 4) research, 5) professionalism, 6) theoretical vs. applied teacher education programs, and 7) in-service education. Among the global trends Leavitt (1992) identifies are the following: 1) with a few exceptions, teacher education is being increasingly brought under the province of universities; 2) increasingly heterogeneous student population makes teaching more complex; 3) recruitment of teachers is a worldwide problem; 4) teacher education models are less imported from other countries, and more indigenous to local culture; and 5) innovations and other revisions are supported, including technology.

Robin Barrow's summary criticism of mainstream educational practice applies to conventional teacher education. Indeed, we might say that it is the acceptance of many, if not all, of these criticisms that has set the stage for rethinking teacher preparation. Barrow's (1990) criticisms included: 1) an unheeding commitment to the tenets of faculty psychology [see chapter 2], 2) a presumption that mental qualities are skills, 3) a presumption that ideas can be understood divorced from their historical and cultural setting, 4) a presumption in favor of materialistic and technocratic values, 5) a presumption that values are relative, and 6) a presumption that the scientific mode is the most developed and the best mode of inquiry.

Conventional teacher education programs are also acknowledged to inadequately prepare teachers for urban settings specifically: "working-class and especially underclass students are educationally disadvantaged. . . . We [must] provide improved preparation that helps teachers learn to deal with the problems [of teaching such students]" (Ornstein & Levine, 1989, p. 22). To redress these inadequacies and to make teacher education generally more rigorous, several certification agencies have developed "knowledge base frameworks for teacher education." These criteria include the following: a) it must include knowledge derived from all relevant scholarly traditions, b) it must present competing views of teaching and schooling, c) it must show relationships between technical and normative aspects of teaching, d) it must be useful and accessible to practitioners, and e) it must encourage reflective practice (Valli & Tom, 1988). Applying these criteria to documents produced by AACTE (American Association of Colleges for Teacher Education), NCATE (National Council for Accreditation of Teacher Education Standards), NASDTEC (National Association of State Directors of Teacher Education & Certification), to teacher preparation programs at the University of Wisconsin and at Michigan State University, and to Shulman's conception of knowledge base, Valli and Tom (1988) found that to some extent all must be judged as inadequate by the above criteria. Many reform proposals focus upon teacher education as essential to the larger project of school reform (Sizer, 1984; Goodlad, 1984; Boyer, 1983). Relying on his concept of "multiple intelligences," Howard Gardner (1991) underlined the necessity of teachers to become introspective, flexible, and self-disciplined. Current efforts to reexamine and reconceptualize teacher education have raised awareness of the importance of teachers' curriculum knowledge base (Ariav, 1991).

In contrast, conservatives tend to locate the problems of teacher education in the "education establishment." Unsurprisingly, their proposals call for reducing the size of this "establishment," including the creation of stream-lined avenues for entry into the classroom, avenues which would bypass conventional teacher education requirements (Cheney, 1990). Zumwalt (1991) described and compared three alternative certification programs, one in Los Angeles, another in New Jersey, and a third in Connecticut. These are designed to provide "short-cuts" to teacher employment, bypassing institu-tionalized regulations regarding teacher certification. Professional teacher educators express reservations regarding these "short-cuts." Regarding the New Jersey plan and other "fast-track" programs, Judith Shulman (1989) has cautioned: "The alternate routes into teaching . . . are not blue highways, but 'blue freeways.' They attempt to achieve their ends at the fastest pace possi-ble. Designers of these route would be well advised to navigate very carefully; speeding on such roads can be dangerous" (p. 7). Shulman believes that mentors can be especially helpful to those who move directly into classrooms without moving through teacher preparation programs in the universities.

The Holmes Group. Teacher education institutions have themselves sug-gested a basic restructuring of teacher education. One major proposal for the reform of teacher education is a series of recommendations advanced by the Holmes Group. The Holmes Group is a consortium of invited research universities, headed by Michigan State University's Judith E. Lanier. In abbreviated form, the goals of the Holmes Group included:

1. To make the education of teachers intellectually more solid.
2. To recognize differences in teachers' knowledge, skill, and commitment, in their education, certification, and work. If teachers are to become more effective professionals, we must distinguish between novices, competent members of the profession, and high-level professional leaders.
3. To create standards of entry to the profession—examinations and educational requirements—that are professionally relevant and intellectually defensible.
4. To connect our own institutions [research universities] to schools.
5. To make schools better places to work. (Holmes Group, 1986, p. 4)

At a number of those universities which have adopted these goals, the undergraduate education curriculum was dropped. A bachelor's degree in a relevant field in the arts and science was required; education courses were moved to the fifth, Masters-degree year. Clinical faculty who would spend much of their time in schools were hired, working with the new teacher candidates and with revision of school curricula. Those schools selected to work closely with research university education faculty would be designated "professional development schools" (Holmes Group, 1990). Included in this revised and expanded relationship between the school and the university might be an extended "practice" teaching or internship experience, one which would attempt to overcome the most common barrier to effective practice teaching, namely the lack of opportunity for student teachers to address personal concerns about their teaching, a problem complicated by the poorly defined supervisory role of associate or supervising teachers (Duquette, 1991).

A reconceptualization of teacher education? The Holmes proposals have generated critique. One prominent scholar has characterized the Holmes reports as "an assertive and defensive reaction" (Popkewitz, 1991, p. 131). Some on the educational left have worried that an emphasis upon Masters students would further reduce the number of minority students in teacher preparation, although the Holmes Group has officially denied such charges (Holmes Group, 1990). Other curriculum theorists have made a more complicated response (see Grumet, 1989b; Shaker, & Kridel, 1989; Beyer, 1989; Schubert, 1989b). One theorist expressed a qualified endorsement of the Holmes proposals, sensitive to concerns regarding minority enrollment and to the theoretical commitments held by many scholars who participated in the Reconceptualization of the field. Pinar (1989) reminded those whose work reconceptualized the curriculum field during the 1970s that: "The theoretical apparatus is now in place for a curricular reconceptualization of teacher education. If schools are to be the 'second site' of reconceptualization, teacher education will be an important instrument" (p. 9). A framework for employing certain ideas associated with Reconceptualization of the field in the 1970s had, in fact, been developed, and had found traditional undergraduate teacher education programs weak (Mulder, 1983).

Holmes is an improvement on traditional teacher education? Pinar (1989) reminded critical scholars in the field that traditional teacher education, which the Holmes proposals would presumably replace, could be characterized as pseudo-scientific. Such programs, claiming to be "practice-oriented," emphasized a narrow vocationalism over the cultivation of professional judgment or serious consideration of curriculum questions (Ginsburg, 1986). Provided teacher education programs are grounded in serious study in the arts, humanities, sciences, and in curriculum theory, Pinar argued that professional judgment and "wisdom" are appropriate aspirations for the prospective teacher. The distinction between academic vs. vocational or technical curriculum is well expressed, Pinar suggested, in the following catalog statement, taken from the University of Michigan Law School Announcement.

> The Law School is very much a professional school. But it is distinctly not a vocational school. Students are not trained to perform many, or even most, of the tasks that its graduates may be called upon to perform as lawyers, and should not expect to be fully prepared to deliver a wide range of legal services on the day of graduation. Students may acquire or begin to develop some practical or technical skills and may gain confidence in their ability to perform as lawyers. Our practice-oriented courses and clinics provide, however, only an introduction to skills and a framework for practice which can only be defined through years of experience. The majority of our graduates join law firms where numerous opportunities exist for skill development under supervision of experienced practitioners who share with the novitiate responsibility for the quality of service rendered. Michigan, more than many other law schools, seeks to provide students with the intellectual and theoretical background with which an attorney can undertake a more reflective and rewarding practice. *It is felt that too much haste or emphasis on vocational skills, without a broader and more critical view of the framework in which lawyering occurs, runs the risk of training technicians instead of professionals.* (quoted in Pinar, 1989, p. 15, emphasis added)

Interdisciplinarity important. Pinar (1989) acknowledged that for some the Holmes Group proposals implied too sharp a split between undergraduate liberal arts and a graduate teacher preparation program. Pinar agreed that graduate study in education must not be severed from the undergraduate liberal arts curriculum. Rather, the fifth and graduate year of study must enhance and surpass the experiences and understandings that students have accumulated during these pre-education years. Pinar worried that the Holmes courses may simply restate the usual disciplinary work of traditional courses, i.e. courses in educational psychology, sociology, philosophy, separated from "methods" and curriculum. Holmes graduate courses ought to be interdisciplinary rather than disciplinary. For instance, replacing a typical child development and psychology course might be an interdisciplinary course on the "Experience of Childhood," with readings from the history and phenomenology of childhood, fiction [see also, Wear, 1989], political analyses of family, children, schooling, as well as developmental psychology. Pinar insisted that non-European knowledge as well as material from marginalized classes and groups must be included, replacing the traditional "social engineering" or Tylerian emphasis.

An autobiographical element? To provide an opportunity to integrate fifth-year readings and experience, the student might maintain a journal in order to address both phenomenological and gender-related experience (Grumet, 1988b), a journal which would be read by the student's "mentor." This person, trained in autobiography and journal work (Meath-Lang, 1990a, 1990b, see chapter 10; Figgins & Ebeling, 1991, Figgins, 1992, see chapter 11), would help the student reflect upon and analyze his or her experience.

Regarding the closer working relationship between universities and schools that are integral to the Holmes programs, Pinar (1989) warned:

> Closer links to the schools ought not to be viewed uncritically. The powerful press of daily life in the school can function as a kind of "black hole" into which theory disappears. . . . While we are friends with our colleagues in the schools . . . we must maintain a respectful distance from them. We cannot advise or educate those with whom we have thoroughly identified. For teacher educators, the school must remain an object of study as well as a site for success. (1989, p. 11)

Pinar and Grumet have not been alone in promoting a place for autobiography in teacher education courses, apart from the debates over the Holmes proposals. Other scholars have pointed to autobiographic issues of lived experience and voice as central to the process of teacher education [for a recent review see Elbaz, 1991]. In developing "Models for Understanding Pre-service and Beginning Teachers' Biographies," J. Gary Knowles (1992) notes that teacher role identity is an important but traditionally overlooked concept in teacher development. By failing to address life history in teacher preparation programs, teachers are more likely to teach as they were taught. In addressing life history issues, D. Jean Clandinin (1989) argues that the support of beginning teachers "must be characterized by features that allow for the reflective reconstruction of the novice's narrative of experience" (p. 139). [See Clandinin et al. (1993) for additional studies of narrative and collaboration in teacher education.]

Relatedly, Deborah Britzman (1989) has insisted that "teacher educators [must] rechart the boundaries of curriculum, teaching, and learning to encompass the struggle for voice" (p. 160). Britzman believes that ethnography can be used as a means for enabling pre-service teachers to become critics of their own teaching experience (Britzman, 1989). Others have noted that through examination of one's own text, one moves toward self-reflexivity:

> Through the careful analysis of our language, we have become aware of subtle influences on our thinking. . . . We have come to realize that the expectation for a resolution of the issues we have raised must remain unsatisfied, that we must learn to live with the tension that arises from the uncertainty of unanswered questions. This is the nature of reflective practice. (Oberg & Artz, 1992, pp. 154-155)

Phenomenologist Terry Carson regards the issue this way:

> Reflectivity in teacher education means that we hope that students will become aware of themselves becoming teachers. As they record and recall the difficulty of becoming teachers, they come to accept that there are many roads the journey might take and that the journey is never over. As teacher educators we have responsibility to help sustain students in their difficulty by encouraging their conversations and by helping to build in our classrooms the contexts that will support them. (Carson, 1991, p. 142)

As we saw in chapter 10, the process of self-reflection is not always solitary; indeed, it is often collaborative (Trousdale & Henkin, 1991; Bennison, Jungck, Kantor & Marshall, 1989) and inextricably linked with political, gender and racial issues (Foster, 1993a; McLaughlin, 1993a, 1993b; Gumport, 1993; Tierney, 1993b).

There are signs that the Holmes movement has lost some momentum, and that in particular a number of research universities have declined to move teacher preparation to the graduate level. Even so, there have been definite advances in enacting the Holmes proposals. For instance, a literature has begun to appear regarding the establishment of so-called "professional development schools" in which university and college professors would work more closely with teachers and students. See, for example, Winitzky, Stoddart, and O'Keefe's (1992) "Great Expectations: Emergent Professional Development Schools," Rushcamp and Roehler's (1992) "Characteristics Supporting Change in a Professional Development School," Dixon and Ishler's (1992) "Professional Development Schools: Stages in Collaboration" Clark and LaLonde's (1992) "A Case for Department-based Professional Development Sites for Secondary Teacher Education" and Abdal-Haqq's (1992) "Professional Development Schools: An Annotated Bibliography of Selected ERIC Resources." This last reference as well as a recently published collection of essays edited by Linda Darling-Hammond (1994) might be one place to begin for the student interested in pursuing the Holmes Group's promotion of "professional development schools." Despite the growing literature regarding this aspect of the Holmes agenda, the prospects of fundamental teacher education reform—such as proposed by the Holmes Group—are mixed, at best (Weiler, 1993).

The experience of Holmes students in professional development schools might suitably be chronicled by careful case studies (Shulman, J., 1992a, 1992b). See, for instance, Robert V. Bullough, Jr., et al. (1991) in which six beginnings teachers are followed, focusing on their metaphors of teaching with which they begin their experience. Bullough and his colleagues found that three left the school in frustration, and three others adapted to institutional conditions, reexamining their metaphors. Studies of the continuities and discontinuities between prospective teachers in teacher education programs and their initial professional experience would concretize more theoretical debates regarding theory and practice. [For annotated bibliography of teacher education program evaluation, see Ayers & Berney, 1990.]

Teachers as professionals. In their *Teachers as Professionals*, Landon Beyer, Walter Feinberg, Jo Anne Pagano, and James A. Whitson (1989) argued for a conception of "educational studies as field of moral action" (p. 132). They noted that like the Carnegie and other recommendations, the Holmes proposals presume that improving the quality of teaching will result necessarily in improving the quality of education. What is the status in the Holmes reform of the undergraduate major in the arts and sciences? They answer: "The academic major is good-in-itself but good-for-nothing; it is however, a necessary *foundation* for the study of teaching" (p. 4). Such a concept of the undergraduate major represents a bifurcation of liberal and professional studies. Such a separation:

> rests on a mistake regarding the nature of practice. . . . Central to our project . . . is developing a notion of practice in which liberal and professional studies are part of the same existential project, a notion of practice that does not hang it on the coattails of theory, and a notion of practice in which it is at once foundational and derivative. (p. 6)

Beyer, Feinberg, Pagano, and Whitson point to the work of Lee Shulman as escaping this simplistic conception of theory and practice. His view, they suggest, portrays teaching as a reasoned activity requiring a depth of knowledge. That knowledge, in the Shulman scheme, undergoes continual transformation as it becomes the object of its own reflection. Shulman implicitly denies the forced separation between thought and action and between content and method preserved in most reform proposals. Beyer, Feinberg, Pagano, and Whitson (1989) insist that: "Teaching is essentially social, moral, and political. . . . In professional education, the aim is something that we will call practical competence" (p. 19). What does this mean? They wish to link dialogically thought and action, content and method, theory and practice. In this view liberal study is itself a profession, not just a foundation to be forgotten in the fifth year of professional teacher preparation. Informed by hermeneutics, they identify a distinct competence ("phronesis") for practical (as opposed to technical or instrumental) judgment and action. Teachers as professionals must exhibit the competence to assist in the praxis of progressive reinterpretation of their clients' projects and interests. Praxis refers to the conduct of social life, with its profound political and ethical dimensions, "to a mode of knowing in which knowing is a form of social conduct, in which it is an enactment of social relations" (p. 18). For Beyer, Feinberg, Pagano, and Whitson (1989), "education is a liberal discipline" (p. 20).

Post-Formal thinking. Joe Kincheloe (1993b) and Shirley R. Steinberg (Kincheloe & Steinberg, 1993; Kincheloe, Steinberg, & Tippins, 1992) have elaborated a "post-formal expansion of inquiry-oriented teacher education" (Kincheloe, 1993b, p. 197), a view informed by political theory and a critical postmodernism [see chapters 5 and 9]. Kincheloe identifies four features of such a view: 1) teacher educators are profoundly conscious of the role of power in all dimensions of teaching and professional education; 2) they labor to "uncover the deep structures that shape education and society" (p. 197); 3) they "encourage desocialization via ideological disembedding" (p. 197), that is, elucidate how hyperreality [see chapter 9] shapes the lives of students and teachers; and 4) they support community-based groups to contest entrenched political and business elites. Kincheloe (1993b) argues: "Grounded on a conception of solidarity with the oppressed and the excluded, teacher education seeks to connect with democratic organizations dedicated to a cultural politics of emancipatory change" (p. 196). Here Kincheloe's affinity with Giroux and McLaren is explicit.

Kincheloe (1993b) also focuses upon the student in teacher education programs. He lists six principles upon which "post-formal" teacher education would be grounded: 1) prospective teachers would develop the capacity to design situations in which students might learn about the world via their own efforts; 2) prospective teachers would learn to comprehend critical constructivism, that is, "that the world is socially constructed and shaped by human action or inaction" (p. 210); 3) students would come to view themselves in relation to the world and consider how they might communicate this relationality to their students; 4) prospective students would engage in "rewriting the world, in the making of a new history, in the revitalization of a democracy dissipated by the postmodern condition" (p. 210); 5) students would confront and contest the myths which subjugate them and their future students; and 6) prospective teachers learn to decode the world and become "post-formal thinkers and critically reflective practitioners" (p. 211). Kincheloe's synoptic and suggestive work illustrates how contemporary curriculum theory is reshaping the thematic contours of traditional institutional concerns such as pre-service teacher education.

X
In-service Teacher Education:
Aoki, Hargreaves, Fullan, and Jackson

> The best hope for improvement in educational practice is the enhancement of teachers as autonomous and reflective beings.
> (Nel Noddings & D. Scott Enright, 1983, p. 182)

Traditionally termed "staff development" (Griffin, 1983; Beegle & Edelfelt, 1977), in-service teacher education represents opportunities for further development for practicing teachers (Miel, 1968b). One example of a statewide effort is the North Carolina Center for the Advancement of Teaching, which has sponsored seminars which "are designed as a means by which teacher participants can reexamine, refine, and in some cases reconstruct their existing philosophical world views" (Shea, 1992, p. 15). In-service education today seems to acknowledge that "it is significant to understand how teachers see their worlds" (Munby, 1986, p. 197; see also Russell & Munby, 1991). Further, as Duckworth (1986) proposes, many scholars now regard teachers as significant participants in theoretical and pedagogical discussion on the nature and development of human learning. In the forward to a recent publication of the British Columbia Teachers Federation, entitled *Voices of Teaching,* in which teachers reflect on their experience as teachers, Aoki's (n.d.) notes:

our authors have been mindful of the habitual way in which we understand the vocation of teaching as jobs. . . . [These teachers] have sought ways of attunement that will allow them to hear, even faintly, the call of the calling. [They] offer us narratives of some moment in their experiences of teaching, thereby opening themselves to the lived meanings of teaching. (p. 1)

In sharp contrast to this phenomenological view of teaching, traditional staff development tended to focus upon instructional skills and strategies. Contemporary work—what is termed by many as teacher development—focuses more broadly on the teachers' lives:

Teachers teach in the way they do not just because of the skills they have or have not learned. The ways they teach are also grounded in their backgrounds, their biographies, in the kinds of teachers they have become. . . . Teacher development, teachers' careers, teachers' relations with their colleagues, the conditions of status, reward and leadership under which they work—all these affect the quality of work they do in the classroom. (Hargreaves & Fullan, 1992, pp. ix-x)

Hargreaves and Fullan (1992) identify three major areas of teacher development: 1) knowledge and skill development, 2) self-understanding, and 3) ecological change, including peer coaching and collaborative change. For some scholars, gender considerations cut across all three areas (Robertson, 1992). All the major strands of teacher development scholarship are said to acknowledge the complexity of teachers' work (Lieberman & Miller, 1992). One student of teacher development observes: "Indeed, teaching is increasingly seen as an intellectual activity in the sense that successful practice rests fundamentally on interpretation, problem-solving, and reflection rather than simply on mastery of an assortment of teaching skills" (Carter, 1992, p. 121). Another writes:

The general point that underlies this is that teachers' interpretations of their teaching tasks (their current frames, that is) are likely to be based on a strategy for dealing with what they see as institutional imperatives, a strategy all the more powerful because it is shared. If changes in teaching are to take place, the teachers' frames must change. (Barnes, 1992, p. 31)

Nearly all agree that teachers' professional choices are influenced by numerous factors, but the classroom is where reform will succeed or not (Hawthorne, 1992).

Jackson's "way of art." Philip Jackson (1992b), whose *The Practice of Teaching* (1986) we examined earlier, has listed four ways to contribute to teacher development. The first he describes as "know-how" or technique, simply telling teachers how to teach, or if they already know, how to teach more effectively. The second contribution would be to improve the conditions in which teachers work, including supporting the independence or autonomy of teachers as professionals. A third way involves helping teachers come to terms with the demands of teaching, which Jackson characterizes as "the way of role accommodation" (1992b, p. 65). He notes that this way involves "the use of journals, autobiographies, and diaries . . . as well as 'support groups' within schools and the kind of 'buddy' system that pairs up experienced and novice teachers"(1992b, p. 65). The fourth way Jackson terms "the way of art" (p. 66), because this "mode of development . . . is closely analogous to what happens when someone encounters a work of art and is deeply affected by it" (1992b, p. 66). In this experience "we say that our horizons have been broadened, that our awareness has been extended. We see *more* than we did" (1992, p. 66, emphasis in original). This order of experience allows teachers to understand more deeply what it is they do (Jackson, 1992b).

Concepts of teacher development. Other scholars interested in teacher development focus on "teachers as designers in self-directed professional development" (Clark, 1992), "classroom-based teacher development" (Thiessen, 1989, 1992), life and career cycle research (Huberman, 1992), the reframing of experience (Russell & Munby, 1991), collaborative research (Louden, 1992; Miller, 1990a; Butt, Raymond, McCue, & Yamagishi, 1992; Shannon & Meath-Lang, 1992; Erickson, 1991; see Ladwig, 1991, for a dissenting opinion on collaboration), on deliberation (Mulder, 1991; Zeuli & Buchmann, 1988), construct theory (Oberg, 1987), the "cultures of teaching" (Hargreaves, 1992), and upon experience and teachers' lives (Goodson, 1992a; Butt, Townsend & Raymond, 1990; Oberg & Underwood, 1992), including teacher identity (Britzman, 1992b). Autobiography may be ideally suited to the purpose of elucidating the perspectives of teachers and students (Solas, 1992). It is this latter category of teacher development that Clandinin and Connelly (1987a, 1987b) endorse as important, not only to teacher development efforts generally, but to understanding teacher thinking more specifically. To the major varieties of this stream of teacher development, with roots in efforts to understand curriculum as autobiographic and biographic text [see chapter 10], we turn next.

Teacher Lore: Schubert and Ayers
Conceptually related to the "collaborative autobiography" of Richard Butt and Danielle Raymond (1992), the "personal practical knowledge" project of D. Jean Clandinin and F. Michael Connelly (1987a), and those calls for the study of teachers lives associated with the work of Ivor F. Goodson (1992a), is the teacher lore project housed at the University of Illinois in Chicago (Schubert, 1989c, 1991b), described as autobiographical practice in chapter 10. Schubert (1992b) defines teacher lore as including "both what I have gained from other teachers for my own teaching and what I can offer other teachers from my experience" (p. 9). This project takes as its basic assumption, as William Ayers notes, that:

> The secret of teaching is to be found in the local detail and the everyday life of teachers; teachers can be the richest and most useful source of knowledge about teaching; those who hope to understand teaching must turn at some point to teachers themselves. (Schubert & Ayers, 1992, p. v)

Schubert and Ayers link their work with what they term the "enlightened action research" (1992, p. vii) associated with Ann Lieberman, Stephen Kemmis, and Robin McTaggart, as well as that line of teacher-oriented research known as the teacher-as-researcher movement associated with the work of Lawrence Stenhouse in Great Britain. A third line of research Schubert and Ayers acknowledge as informing the teacher lore project is that of Schön and Zeichner, a line which "implicitly respects teachers as people who reflect in action" (1992, p. viii). Schubert and Ayers acknowledge the work of Elliot Eisner and his students as well [see evaluation section, this chapter, and chapters 1, 3, 4, and 11]. They acknowledge as well that Connelly and Clandinin have recently begun to advocate the sharing of stories and ideas, i.e. "personal practical knowledge," among teachers through a newsletter entitled *Among Teachers* (1992, p. viii). Finally the work of Madeleine Grumet, William F. Pinar, and Richard Butt is acknowledged (p. viii). Schubert and Ayers note that the teacher lore project "fits within these streams or traditions, sometimes overlapping several of them, drawing insights from many, and hopefully contributing to each in some fashion" (1992, p. viii).

Questions. The questions asked by those interested in teacher lore include: "Why are teachers so often invisible and silent even in their own worlds? . . . What gives meaning and direction to the lives of teachers?" (1992, p. ix). Schubert and Ayers are "convinced that conscientious teachers reflect seriously on their work" (p. ix). How is teacher lore defined? Schubert (1992b) writes that:

> I am quite content with the fluid image of teacher lore. I want to resist the usual expectation that the academic should always develop a theoretical framework. I fear that such a framework would do to deep inquiry what a lesson plan too often does to teaching—namely, separate learning from spontaneity. (1992b, p. 9)

Janet L. Miller, whose autobiographical and collaborative theory has been reviewed in chapters 7 and 10, regards the project as interested especially in "the intuitive, the informal, the spontaneous and subjective" dimensions of teaching (Miller, 1992a, p. 14). She writes: "Lore is what we know to be similar in our teaching experiences, even as we tell our stories to point to the differences among us" (Miller, 1992a, p. 14).

Alice and "special moments." Illustrative of the work of the teacher lore project is a study of the relationship between a teacher's life and teaching by Palma Millies (1992). Millies reports the reflections of Alice, a teacher in her sixties, for whom time is a central theme. For Alice, "special moments" in life become important, and when she teaches, she often points to these "moments" in literature, especially in poetry. Such moments have served as a focal point for her teaching. Alice observes:

> I feel sincerely that life is made up of beautiful moments. But not majestic events. Waiting for that in life, you're going to wait a long time. But if you can

find little pauses . . . just something to bolster you up for the next day, then you always have the wherewithal to deal with whatever is coming. (Millies, 1992, p. 30)

At the same time, Millies reports that Alice feels that time has been elusive for her. Alice reflects that:

Time cheats us of savoring things; we can experience it but we can't savor it. An experience of a child or of young womanhood or your maturity. You can't savor anything; it's gone before you even knew you had it. . . . To go back and savor, to really enjoy it, I think that's a common resentment of a lot of women, but I don't know about men. Women have all those pressures; we keep hearing them say, "I need some time for myself; some quality time." There just aren't enough minutes in a day for that quality time. (quoted in Millies, 1992, p. 31)

Millies believes that Alice's "lore" is not fixed and unchanging. Her life interest in time, and in particular, important moments, expressed itself in her teaching. Millies reports "through Alice I saw a strong connection between a teacher's mental life and the curriculum" (1992, p. 40). More generally, she concluded that "reflection is a means for teachers to participate consciously and creatively in their own development" (Millies, 1992, p. 40).

A second study illustrative of teacher lore research is Mari E. Koerner's (1992) "Teachers' Images: Reflections of Themselves." Koerner reports that one teacher named Sophie, reflecting on the community of her classroom, regards that which is best about teaching is:

interacting in a classroom and receiving interest, excitement, communication back. . . . It's not the other extreme of being too loose where everybody's talking out and running around. It's somewhere in between there, where we can have a mutual respect. They respect me. . . . I respect them. We have a good healthy communication. They know they're there to learn. They know I'm there to teach—it's like that. That's when it's good. (Koerner, 1992, p. 48)

Koerner reports how another teacher, Toni, describes what she terms the "flow" in her classroom:

So it's a job that I think is kind of exciting because I can go in there and when I'm really down. . . . I have to psych myself up. . . . Those are the days that I get pleasantly surprised because all of a sudden there's a flow. You and the children are moving together toward a common vision. I don't even like to say goal, it's like a vision. We're just all on the same mind set. . . . And that's the neatest feeling every time. I love that sense of flow, that just everything pulls together that day. (Koerner, 1992, p. 49)

What makes a "bad" day for a teacher? Koerner reports that for another teacher named Bob:

There are a lot of . . . extraneous things that can make it a bad day . . . like the fire drills. People pull the fire alarm, or things happen. You try to get started.

But the buses are late. The kids are coming in and then . . . there's a crisis in the next class a kid comes in, sprains his ankle, somebody's drugged out. . . . So it's kind of like you never get out of low gear. . . . I think a bad day is when situations arise that prohibit that something wonderful from happening, something good from happening. (Koerner, 1992, pp. 50-51)

Why are teachers held in such low regard by much of the public? Koerner explored this question with several teachers. She reports that one teacher named Bill believes that teachers are held in low regard because their work is considered low-priority. Why would teaching be regarded a low priority? Bill believes it is due to society's devaluation of children and women. After teaching for twenty-five years, another teacher, named Judy, has also come to believe that education is not a top priority in the United States. Judy observes:

We don't get the money to fund materials that we should get. We don't get the money to fund education we should. I feel that the people in the United States know enough to have one of the best school systems . . . in the world. But we do more to hurt the children. It took me a long time to realize that educating children was not number one. Sometimes, maybe education is number two, or number three, or number four. (Koerner, 1992, p. 53)

Liz, another teacher, notes:

And they pay grown people to hit a ball with a little stick and they pay millions and millions of dollars. . . . I guess there's a skill involved. But they get a lot of money. And then you have teachers who are preparing your children. We as teachers, we could do a lot of damage. But then we're paid so little. . . . The low pay [of teachers] is maddening and demoralizing to these experienced teachers. (Koerner, 1992, p. 54)

How is this accumulation of teacher lore important? Koerner concludes that: "Teachers need to become aware of their own thoughts and perceptions, their own images of teaching, as well as of images others hold about teachers, if they are to shape a future more whole and more hopeful than today" (1992, p. 59). Virginia Jagla (1992) reports that her study of teacher lore has led her to conclude:

It is only through emotional involvement with students, subject matter, and the environment that we are able to formulate ideal teaching. Teachers' everyday use of imagination and intuition is necessary for *educare*, authentic teaching. Genuine education, leading from darkness to light, is accomplished with the brilliant flame of intuition, the passionate blaze of imagination, the luminous kindling of caring, and the radiant glow of love. (p. 78)

Studying Teachers' Lives: Goodson

In addition to the teacher lore project, teachers' lives have been studied in a number of ways. There have been studies of teachers' personalities (Smith, Kleine, Prunty, & Dwyer, 1992), histories of teachers, living (Munro, 1992; Casey, 1992; see also chapter 10) and deceased (Nelson, 1992). There has been "during the past decade a renaissance of research based on life-history method" (Measor & Sikes, 1992, p. 209). Part of the credit for this remarkable phenomenon must be given to Ivor F. Goodson, who, as we saw in chapter 10, has vigorously promoted studying the lives of teachers. In a recent theoretical exposition of issues involved in this project, Goodson (1992a) notes:

> The teacher's life operates at a number of intersections. First, there is the personal intersection for . . . a life is lived on two levels . . . the *surface* and the *deep*. . . . Second, the life operates at the intersection of context, as in issues of race and gender. Third, the teacher's life operates at the intersection of life as experiences and life as text. . . . The life account should be produced in a way which achieves as much harmony as is possible across these levels. (pp. 236-237)

Goodson then identifies what he terms "levels" across which life history data can be collected:

> 1) From the teachers' own accounts, but also from more detached research studies, it is clear that the teachers' previous *life experience and background* help shape their view of teaching and essential elements in their practice. 2) The teacher's life style both in and outside school and his/her latent identities and cultures impact on views of teaching and on practice. 3) The teacher's *life cycle* is an important aspect of professional life and development. 4) The teacher's *career stages* are important research foci. 5) Beyond major career stages there are *critical incidents* in teachers' lives and specifically their work which may crucially affect their perceptions and practice. 6) Studies of teachers' lives might allow us to [see the individual in historical context]. (pp. 243-244)

Goodson might agree with Andreas Dick (1992a), who writes: "Biography-taking that is ethnographic in its purpose wishes to examine the present rather than to uncover the past" (p. 2). "The central message," Dick (1992a) continues, "is that the study of student teachers and experienced teachers—experiencing the curriculum of teaching and the everyday pedagogy jointly in an ethnographic process—must be grounded in teaching events and in the biography of both of them" (p. 10).

Case methods in teacher education. Studying teachers' lives allows teachers' voices to be heard. Utilizing autobiographic/biographical research, this work appears to make use of case methods, an approach recently articulated by Judith and Lee Shulman (Shulman, J., 1992b). [See also Shulman, J., 1991; Carter & Unklesbay, 1989; and Yonemura, 1991.] Lee Shulman explains that case studies, which are third-person accounts, draw their data from case reports, which are first-person accounts. These first-person accounts "are diaries, personal letters, student work samples, videotapes, observer's notes" (Shulman, L., 1992, p. 19). He goes on to explain that "teaching cases are original accounts, case reports or case studies that have been written or edited for teaching purposes" (Shulman, L., 1992, p. 19).

There are disadvantages to this order of research material, according to Shulman. He reports that such methods are: 1) expensive and time-consuming to produce and "demanding to field test," 2) difficult to teach well, 3) inefficient, 4) episodic, discontinuous, and 5) may be susceptible to overgeneralization (Shulman, L., 1992, pp. 26-27). Despite these disadvantages, Lee Shulman would seem to agree with Judith Shulman: "I will argue that teacher-written cases can and should serve as important part of the curriculum in preservice, inservice, and graduate teacher education, as a way of understanding the wisdom of practice from the 'insider's' perspective" (Shulman, J., 1992a, p. 132).

Teacher Thinking and Development: Kincheloe, Smyth, Britzman, Carlson
As we saw before, Joe Kincheloe (1993b) has argued on behalf of a view of teacher thinking informed by political theory and critical postmodernism. Kincheloe's view represents another reconceptualization of in-service teacher education or teacher development. [Earlier in the chapter we reviewed the implications of Kincheloe's post-formal thinking theory for pre-service teacher education.] He terms such a teacher a "post-formal practitioner" (p. 201), and such a practitioner engages in thinking that is: 1) inquiry-oriented, 2) socially contextualized and conscious of power, 3) committed to remaking the world, 4) engaged in the art of improvisation, 5) dedicated to universal participation, 6) concerned with critical self-reflection and social analysis, 7) committed to democratic self-directed education, 8) sensitive to pluralism, 9) committed to action, and 10) attentive to affective dimensions (Kincheloe, 1993b, pp. 201-203). Kincheloe laments that mainstream teacher education reform during the past decades has failed to incorporate these elements.

In somewhat related work that draws upon life history as well as critical theory, Smyth (1989) formulated what he termed "a critical pedagogy of classroom practice." Smyth begins by criticizing the focus on teaching skills characteristic of most in-service teacher education. Smyth characterizes his work as "an attempt . . . to develop a politicized counterdiscourse" (p. 484). He develops three questions: 1) Describing: what do I do? 2) Informing: what is the meaning behind my teaching? 3) Confronting: how did I come to be this way? 4) Reconstructing: how might I do things differently? (p. 486). He believes that

> it is possible to contest the apparently commonsense bureaucratic way of construing schools and to posit in its place more democratic and informed ways of thinking and working. . . . Through exploring the notion of a critical pedagogy, I have sought to provide a rationale and some general principles by which teachers *themselves* might begin to move beyond questions of technical competence and thereby challenge the rules, roles and structures within which teaching occurs. (Smyth, 1989, p. 499)

Toward what ideal? Teacher development, whatever its methods, aspires to improve teaching. Toward what ideal? Gary Griffin (1987) believes that "the ideal teacher is a knowledgeable, well-organized, and consistent classroom leader who interacts with students, colleagues, and patrons purposefully and effectively" (p. 255). What is necessary in order to improve teaching, toward realization of this or other ideals? Deborah Britzman (1992a) identifies four conditions that provide good teaching: "First, teachers need opportunities to move beyond their isolation from one another and their isolation from the community" (Britzman, 1992a, p. 78). "A second condition," Britzman continues, "is that teachers have the time and space to continue their education in ways they determine" (p. 79). A third condition "concerns carefully linking those just entering the profession to those already there in ways that value the contributions of the newly arrived and the experienced teachers" (p.79). A fourth condition "involves extending the present boundaries of learning and teaching" (p. 79). Dennis Carlson (1992a) would link these conditions with forms of social and political organization, expressing the hope that:

> should the various groups which have been disempowered by basic skills reforms (in ways that are related to their class, gender, and race) articulate their different concerns as part of a common movement to challenge bureaucratic state discourse and practice in education, it might yet become possible to build a new democratic-progressive "voice" and movement for change that looks beyond crisis management and mismanagement towards crisis resolution. (p. 272)

Perhaps summarizing these issues, Linda Darling-Hammond (1985) argued that the "most critical issue facing American education today is the professionalization of teaching. Professionalization involves not only the status and compensation accorded to the members of an occupation; it involves the extent to which members of that occupation maintain control over the content of their work and the degree to which society values the work of that occupation" (p. 205). Studying teachers' lives through the variety of means formulated by those contemporary theorists whose work we have reviewed here would make an important contribution to such professionalization.

The Critical Thinking Movement: Ennis and L. Tanner

The Institute for Critical Thinking. A movement to incorporate critical thinking in teaching and learning has appeared in recent years, institutionally located at the Institute for Critical Thinking [founded in 1986] at Montclair State College in New Jersey. As of this writing, Wendy Oxman-Michelli is Director; Mark Weinstein is Associate Director. A yearly conference is sponsored, as is a journal *Inquiry: Critical Thinking Across the Disciplines.* Scholars from various disciplines in the humanities, social sciences, sciences, and the arts labor to establish a theory and practice of critical thinking to be taught across the academic disciplines. Critical thinking has been summarized as: "leading students to an appreciation of the role of good reasons in their own thinking, both in the specialized contexts of their college courses, and with application to their future learning and to their roles as citizens" (Siegel, 1988; Weinstein & Oxman-Michelli, 1989). Seminars and workshops are held regularly on the Montclair State campus, involving as of September 1991 over two hundred university faculty. Titles of representative faculty workshops and seminars include: critical thinking in global education, creative writing in mathematics, science and computer science classrooms, maleness and masculinity, the pedagogy of critical thinking (Institute for Critical Thinking, 1991).

Illustrative of scholarship published by the Institute in *Inquiry* is John A. White's (1992) elaboration of "Dialectic: The Role of Discussion in Education." In this article White traces the history of the word "discussion" from the ancient Greeks, noting that the dialectic is no more effective than monologue as a method of education, at least in terms of ethics. White insists: "Dialectic will not ensure ethicality. The great bad men of history could argue as forcefully and successfully as the good" (1992, p. 22). Another article published in *Inquiry* examines questions and questioning, written by Matthew Lipman, Founder and Director of the Institute for the Advancement of Philosophy for Children, also at Montclair State. [The two Institutes collaborate.] Lipman (1992) notes that questions must be structured carefully in order to provoke critical thinking.

There has been established a National Council for Excellence in Critical Thinking (NCECT) among the affiliated centers of which are the Institute at Montclair State. A related organization is the Foundation for Critical Thinking, a nonprofit corporation located in Santa Rose, California. The Foundation for Critical Thinking works cooperatively with the Center for Critical Thinking and Moral Critique at Sonoma State University (California), the National Council for Excellence in Critical Thinking Instruction, PBS Adult Learning Satellite Service, The College Board, and other research centers, institutes, and public institutions, to publish and disseminate a variety of critical thinking resources. Illustrative of publications supported by the Foundations is *Critical Thinking: Shaping the Mind of the 21st Century* (1992), produced by the Foundation and the Center for Critical Thinking and Moral Critique. In *Critical Thinking* appears a "Critical Thinking, Problem Solving and Communication Skills Essay Exam" (p. 13), which we reproduce here, to provide a concrete illustration of this work.

Directions

This test is designed to assess your critical thinking, problem solving, and communication skills. Your answer will be judged for its clarity, relevance, consistency, logic, depth, coherence, and fairness. More specifically, the reader will be asking the following questions:

1. Is the question at issue well stated?
2. Does the writer cite relevant evidence, experiences, and/or relevant information essential to the issue?
3. Does the writer clarify key concepts when necessary?
4. Does the writer show a sensitivity to what he or she is assuming or taking for granted?
5. Does the writer develop a definite line of reasoning, explaining well how he or she is arriving at his or her conclusions?
6. Is the writer's reasoning well-supported?

7. Does the writer show a sensitivity to alternative points of view or lines of reasoning?
8. Does the writer show a sensitivity to the implications and/or consequences of the position he or she has taken?

Issue #1 Ecology
Issue #2 Politics
Issue #3 Morality. (Foundation, 1992, p. 13)

Theoreticians of the movement. The distinguished philosopher of education Robert Ennis is usually credited as stimulating the current interest in critical thinking, in an article he wrote for *The Harvard Educational Review* in 1962 entitled "A Concept of Critical Thinking." He originally defined critical thinking as "the correct assessment of statements" (p. 8; quoted in Thayer-Bacon, 1992, p. 3). In 1985 Ennis revised his definition of critical thinking, in response to criticism, to "reasonable reflective thinking that is focused on deciding what to believe or do" (Ennis, 1987, p. 10; quoted in Thayer-Bacon, p. 4). Barbara Thayer-Bacon (1992) tells us that for John McPeck, another major theorist of the movement, critical thinking is a subset of rational thinking. Rational thinking is "the intelligent use of all available evidence for the solution of some problem" (McPeck, 1981, p. 12; quoted in Thayer-Bacon, 1992, p. 4). Harvey Siegel (1988) argued that to seek reasons one has to recognize and commit oneself to principles, for principles are required in order to determine the pertinence and strength of reasons. Ennis (1962, 1987) emphasized skills, Siegel (1988) focused on rationality, and McPeck (1981) pointed to critical thinking being domain specific rather than as generally applicable. Richard Paul called attention to the possibility of degrees or levels of critical thinking. Thayer-Bacon (1992) characterizes her interest in critical thinking somewhat differently: "My desire is to encourage self-awareness as part of the development of critical thinking skills" (p. 7). Thayer-Bacon links the notion of caring (Noddings, 1984) to critical thinking (Thayer-Bacon, 1993). Richard Paul (1992) summarized the notion of critical thinking:

> Critical thinking as an educational ideal extends far beyond the conception of critical thinking as a course of study, and even beyond critical thinking seen as a set of skills and dispositions. As an educational ideal, critical thinking is an image of the ends of education: students who are rational and autonomous, who can apply critical thinking in their courses of study and in their lives as members of a social and political community. The exploration of the idea involves such fundamental concerns as the nature of rationality, the forms of education, and an analysis of the societal and historical contexts within which thoughtful teaching and learning occurs. (p. 1)

The issue of context is underlined by some working in the area:

> education aimed at critical thinking must be concerned with developing a particular content and context as opposed to focusing merely on skills. [Critical

thinking] is not itself an ethically neutral conception of intellectual and social life. The full realization of critical thought depends upon the existence of communities of inquirers and honest and forthright communication within and among these communities. (Hostetler, 1991, p. 11)

Others have also endorsed a contextualist view of critical thinking (Blatz, 1989), a point made rather differently by Robin Barrow (1990):

the literature on critical thinking tends to ignore the question of what innate factors may be necessary prerequisites of becoming a critical thinker, and to concentrate on the question of what we can do to develop it. . . . The error consists in failing to see that critical thinking is context bound. (pp. 80-81)

Additionally, Barrow is skeptical of something generalizable called critical thinking. He writes: [regarding critical thinking] we must avoid talking as if there were some mono-skill, like using a spade, which has to be acquired or developed, and may then be put to use in a variety of circumstances" (1984b, p. 131). [For a useful review of debates within the critical thinking movement, see Weinstein, 1993.]

Criticism of the critical thinking movement. Robin Barrow is not the only critic of critical thinking [see also Kaplan, 1991]. For instance, Laurel Tanner points to the faddish and ahistorical character of the "critical thinking" movement, quoting two spokespersons for the movement: "Perhaps never before in the history of educational practice has there been a greater push to teach children to think critically" (Sternberg, 1985, p. 194, quoted in Tanner L., 1985, p. 417), and "The field of critical thinking is more vibrant than ever" (Norris, 1985, p. 40; quoted in Tanner, L., 1985, p. 417). Quoting Hudgins' and Edelman's (1986) definition of critical thinking "as the disposition to provide evidence in support of one's conclusions and to request evidence from others before accepting their conclusions" (p. 333; quoted in Tanner, L., 1985, p. 472), Tanner (1985) acknowledges that critical thinking so conceived might be valuable. However, it should not be identified with Dewey's conception of the reflective process in which thinking resulted in plans of action for problem-solving, including the actual testing of the plans, with the goal of improving actual conditions. In contrast to Dewey's conception of thinking, Laurel Tanner (1985) suggests that the contemporary critical thinking movement is canned and packaged.

Logical games? Tanner (1985) argues that, in the contemporary version of critical thinking, typical problems are predetermined, not arising out of actual situations, and so critical thinking is closer to involving logic, not behavior. She quotes Adler (1986) approvingly: "The programs in critical thinking now being advocated from coast to coast are minuscule and over-simplified versions of the much more rigorous course in logic that I taught in college. And they will be just as ineffective. . . . Nor will they train teachers to think critically" (p. 10; quoted in Tanner, L., 1985, p. 473). Tanner (1985) implies that aspects of the critical thinking movement do not escape commercial motives. She notes that Sternberg (1986) asserts that problem solving can be taught through "performance components"—problem-solving tasks—such as encoding, mapping (relating one rule to another rule on the basis of a higher order rule), application, etc. She suggests that "Sternberg's interest in analogical reasoning is not surprising, for he is author of a manual on how to pass the Miller Analogies Test" (Tanner, L., 1985, p. 473).

Reread Dewey. How can the ahistorical character of the movement be corrected, and in so doing, alter what Tanner judges as the excessively logical character of the movement's conception of critical thinking? She writes:

> Somewhere a teaching method lies waiting—waiting to be used to teach critical thinking. . . . It can be found in an old book: Dewey's *Democracy and Education* (1916). If we follow Dewey, critical thinking is motivated by a problem. It must be a genuine problem—the pupils' own problem. Neither a simulated problem nor a practice problem intended to help pupils perform well on reasoning items would qualify. (Tanner, L., 1985, p. 471)

Tanner emphasizes that the important point is that Dewey's conception of critical thinking requires that the curriculum be based on the way problems are in fact solved, through scientific method, rather than playing with words, i.e. logic. Dewey would insist that critical thinking occurs in actual settings when actual problems are being solved:

> Critical thinking had been one of the dominant themes in the progressive curriculum reforms earlier in the century. The trouble with the recent efforts in teaching thinking skills was that a mechanical-segmental approach was often taken—as if thinking could be taught as a separate skill subject rather than in relationships extending throughout the curriculum. (Tanner & Tanner, 1990, p. 46)

XI
Textbooks: Venezky, Elson, and Doyle

> The major function of creative curriculum materials is to amplify the teacher's skills, not to constrain them.
>
> (Elliot W. Eisner, 1990a, p. 64)

In a recent review of research on textbooks, Richard L. Venezky (1992) lays out the following framework for textbook studies. He notes that a textbook functions both as a *cultural artifact* and as a *surrogate curriculum*. He employs the term *intertextuality* to refer to a textbook's relationship to preceding textbooks, and the term *validation* to refer to processes of legitimation. Historically, Venezky identifies three major attempts to study the general character of textbooks and their use in schools. The first was published in the Thirtieth Yearbook of the National Society for the Study of Education, which focused exclusively on the preparation and selection of textbooks (Whipple, 1931; Venezky, 1992). In general, textbooks were praised in this early publication (Venezky, 1992). A second effort proceeded under the leadership of Lee

Cronbach at the University of Illinois as the Text Materials Study, summarized in *Text Materials in Modern Society* (Cronbach, 1955). A third effort has been published as *Textbooks and Schooling in the United States* (Elliott & Woodward, 1990). A bimonthly bulletin in which textbooks are reviewed is available from the California Textbook League (1992, 1993).

Control of textbook content. Venezky (1992) cites three sources for control of textbook content: a) federal and state government, b) publishers, and c) society. Venezky suggests that the influence of federal and state governments has been relatively weak. He writes: "Almost by default, the primary influence over textbook content has been left to two groups: the publishers and society, as represented both by broad social movements and by special interest groups that act directly upon the schools and publishers" (Venezky, 1992, p. 444). Textbooks are profitable, grossing over $2 billion a year (Squire & Morgan, 1990). The question that is raised is the extent to which textbooks are a function of business as opposed to educational interests. Goodlad (1979) has argued business exercises a strong influence: "In fact, it is fair to say that the ends and means of curricula frequently are determined by publishers and not by the elected representatives of the people, although the process is a cyclical one, with the identification of who is influencing being exceeding difficult" (Goodlad, 1979, p. 34). Little is known about how the textbook industry operates, despite fine conjectures (Apple, 1986; Luke, 1988; Venezky, 1992). One well-known curriculum specialist expressed considerable concern regarding the business of curriculum development:

> publishers and educators alike are caught up in the bureaucratization of curriculum to the point that programs are seen as more important than people. That is, the emphasis on programs [represents] an inappropriate and ineffective way to comprehend and respond to the multiple realities of individual differences that exist among both students and teachers in the schools. (Frymier, 1987, p. 151)

It is true that throughout the history of the United States, textbooks have reflected mainstream and conservative political interests (Venezky, 1992). For instance, a typical textbook of the 1920s mirrored the xenophobia, even racism, common among conservative and mainstream politicians during that period (Selden, 1988). *The First Book in United States History* informed its readers:

> Immigrants that came from the Northern countries of Europe are of a class that make good citizens. . . . But since the War of Succession most of the immigrants coming to this country have been from the lower classes of Eastern and Southern Europe, and they give much trouble. They are for the most part very ignorant. . . . They have no respect for law or government. In fact, many of them would like to see the government of the United States destroyed. (cited in Venezky, 1992, p. 445)

This example confirms that not only during this period did ethnic, racial, and religious intolerance find its way in American textbooks, but also that there have not been corrective measures taken to prevent intolerance from expression in textbooks. Racial bias has been documented particularly (Bierstedt, 1955; Banks, 1969; FitzGerald, 1979).

History textbooks. History textbooks have come under close scrutiny. For example, issues of class have been distorted in many textbooks. Jean Anyon (1979) studied 17 secondary school American history textbooks, finding that the majority were unsympathetic to the labor movement. The conditions of workers were ignored, and a generally negative view of labor was presented. In addition to class, nationalism has been treated uncritically in many history textbooks for most of this century (American Council on Education, 1949; Bagley & Rugg, 1916; Bierstedt, 1955; Walworth, 1938; Venezky, 1992). FitzGerald (1979) commented: "There are no polluters: there is only the pollution which we are struggling against. And what I call the natural disaster theory of history" (p. 55). More recently, however, an improvement in history textbook impartiality has been noted:

> We happily note a reversal of an apparent trend to water down school history. . . . The United States of America is presented in a positive light by all of the textbooks studied. At the same time, these books do not tend to obscure recognizable blemishes on the story of our nation's continuing progress. (Davis, Ponder, Burlbaw, Garza-Lubeck, & Moss, 1986, p. 9)

Citizens action groups. Special interest groups, usually on the political right, have been influential in the ideological content of textbooks. Their success illustrates the vulnerability of schools to political pressure (Sieber, 1968; Venezky, 1992). Constitutional issues, including Supreme Court decisions regarding textbooks and censorship issues in particular, have been carefully reported and analyzed by Tony Whitson (1988a, 1991a, 1991b). One of the most famous cases occurred in Kanawha County, West Virginia, where conservative parents fought to keep "humanism," "socialism," and other threats to their fundamentalist beliefs out of school textbooks (Moffett, 1988; England, 1988; Watras, 1983). Their victory, and others like it, have had the effect of tightening a conservative noose around an already conservative textbook industry. Commenting on another issue (that of school reform), one professional association has noted: "A danger arises when a minority group works aggressively to impose its beliefs on a slumbering—or misled—majority" (Willis, S., 1992. p. 4).

Right-wing attacks. More systematic lobbying has been conducted by organizations such as Norma and Mel Gabler's Educational Research Analysts, which works across the United States against the a wide range of subjects they find objectionable, including profanity, sexual references, nonstandard English, women in nondomestic roles, socialism, criticism of the United States (especially its founders), and criticism of religion (DelFattore, 1986; Venezky, 1992; Whitson, 1988b). Such attacks have their historical antecedents, perhaps the most prominent one of which is the case of Harold

Rugg [see chapters 2 & 3], who wrote social studies textbooks based on ideas of social justice. Richard Venezky (1992) tells the story:

> In the middle 1920s he [Rugg] signed a contract with Ginn & Co. for a social studies series that was to be developed from his survey and assessment work. From the time that the first volume of *Man and His Changing Society* was published (1929) until 1939, 1,317,960 copies of the various texts were sold, along with 2,687,000 workbooks (Kliebard, 1986). The series was the first to treat such topics as the slave trade, urban blight, and poverty with candor, but its restrained treatment of the free enterprise system was what fired the National Association of Manufacturers and the Hearst newspaper chain into national campaigns of opposition. Primarily through the efforts of these groups, the series was driven out of the schools by the early 1940s (Tanner, 1988). Rugg's defense of the series in 1941 came too late and was read by too few to overcome the damage that already had been done. (Rugg, 1941; Venezky, 1992, p. 447)

Another set of social studies textbooks under the direction of Paul Hanna, *Building America*, was also driven out of existence by accusations by the rightwing that the textbooks were un-American and sympathetic to communism (Tanner, 1988; Venezky, 1992) and anti-Christian.

Biology textbook controversies. A 1895 biology textbook was the first to mention the theory of evolution, while many textbooks ignored the subject (Skoog, 1979, 1984; Rosenthal & Bybee, 1987; Venezky, 1992). In 1920 the state of Oklahoma outlawed textbooks which mentioned evolution, and soon after the state of Tennessee forbade the teaching of evolution generally (Venezky, 1992). Following that law was the famous Scopes trial held in Dayton, Tennessee, in 1925. A high school teacher, John Thomas Scopes, had agreed to test the Tennessee law banning the teaching of evolution. William Jennings Bryan, three-time Democratic candidate for President, argued for the Tennessee statute, while Clarence Darrow defended Scopes. The prosecution won the case, only to have the decision reversed at the state courts on a technicality. The statute forbidding the teaching of evolution remained on the books (Venezky, 1992).

Other states forbid the teaching of evolution. Not long after the Scopes trial, Mississippi and Arkansas passed similar legislation, forbidding the teaching of evolution. The Arkansas law, known as the Rotenberry Act, reached the Supreme Court in 1968, at which time it was judged unconstitutional to forbid the teaching of evolution in public schools and universities (De Camp, 1969). Tennessee responded in 1973 with a law requiring that equal instructional time be given to the Genesis version of human creation. The California Board of Education had taken a similar position in 1969. The "equal-time" Tennessee law was declared unconstitutional and repealed in 1975. The California Board reversed itself as well (Venezky, 1992). Currently, those who object to the teaching of evolution are not primarily residents of Appalachia (as in the case of Kanawha County, West Virginia) but residents of areas such as southern California and urban Texas (Nelkin, 1976). The growth of right-wing influence, starting with the election of Richard Nixon to the Presidency in 1968, has been largely uninterrupted, and textbook series—such as MACOS [an anthropology-based social studies curriculum; see chapters 3 and 4]—which were not sufficiently sensitive to the special ideological interests of the right-wing, have suffered (Conlon & Dow, 1975).

Right wing lobbying groups (for instance, the Heritage Foundation, Save Our Children, Parents Who Care, Concerned Women for America) have been fought by several primarily left-of-center groups that lobby for equitable treatment of subjects in textbooks. The People for the American Way, the National Association for the Advancement of Colored People (NAACP), the National Organization for Women (NOW), and the American Civil Liberties Union (ACLU) have all been active in various power struggles over the content of school textbooks (Venezky, 1992).

Central tendency theory. One major type of textbook analysis is characterized by Venezky as the "central tendency theory," which he identifies with the work of Ruth Elson. In her study of nineteenth century textbooks, Elson reviewed over 1,000 textbooks in various school subjects for grades 1 to 8. She wrote:

> The schoolbooks delineated for [an American child] an idealized image both of himself and of the history that had produced the admitted American type. They were a compendium of ideas popularly approved at the time, and they offer an excellent index of concepts considered "proper" for the nineteenth century America. (Elson, 1964, p. vii)

And because nineteenth-century textbooks did not compete with television, movies, and other twentieth-century forms of popular culture, they were more reflective of mainstream attitudes as well as influential in reinforcing these attitudes and beliefs. Cremin (1980) also asserted that textbooks during the first century after the Revolution "played a significant role in articulating and shaping the attitudes, values, tastes, and sensibilities of the American people" (p. 70).

Other studies of nineteenth-century textbooks are those of Garfinkle (1954), who studied textbooks published during the period 1783 (the publication of Webster's spelling book) until 1860, and Mosier (1947), who studied the famous McGuffey Readers (1830-1879). Both studies concluded that after 1840 readers reflected the conservative interests of merchants and industrialists. Education was viewed as a means of social control, an idea advanced by the political scholars of the 1970s and 1980s (Franklin, 1988a, 1988b). Reviewing the findings of these studies of early textbooks, Venezky (1992) points to the contemporary textbook and the images they portray:

> In summary, the latent content of textbooks from the middle of the 17th century until the last decade of the 19th century was, with some deviations, regulated by society's idealized image of itself, including its expected future

and its ennobling past. This image was, however, primarily of a white, Protestant nation, in which men were strong and noble, and women supportive and caring. . . . With the shift to silent reading for comprehension, and with the change in child psychology to a nurturing view, society's adult images were sublimated to the needs and interests of the child. . . . With the introduction in the 20th century of a culturally diverse literature, a clear image of adult American society and of the child's role in it was no longer available and has not reappeared. (Venezky, 1992, pp. 451-452)

Walter Doyle (1992) observes that in addition to historical research, the contemporary study of textbooks has tended to focus on the economic and political conditions in which they are produced (Cherryholmes, 1988a; Apple, 1986, 1990a; FitzGerald, 1979; Willinsky, 1990a), their linguistic and instructional characteristics (Anderson & Armbruster, 1984; Beck & McCaslin, 1978; Beck, McKeown, and Gromoll, 1989; Durkin, 1981; Meyer, Greer, & Crummy, 1987; Osborn, 1984; Westbury, 1990), and their relationship to tests and assessment (Armbruster, Stevens, & Rosenshine, 1977; Freeman, et al., 1983). Despite the multitude of influences on textbooks, Doyle (1992) notes that teachers still exercise considerable influence on their use in classrooms. He writes: "Teachers . . . appear to exercise independent control over the curriculum as it is enacted by using texts and other material selectively in the service of their own curricula" (p. 496).

One longitudinal study of teacher preparation at a large midwestern university concluded that strong teachers avoid following too closely textbooks and relying exclusively on teacher guides. Strong teaching, it is suggested, may mean creating one's own lessons and materials (Ball & Feiman-Nemser, 1988). It may mean on occasion abandoning the single course textbook in favor of a combination of eclectic texts, fiction, and journals. Strong teaching might also mean resisting pressures to censor pertinent material. In this regard, James Moffett (1990) notes two powerful forces that suppress texts: one force is religious and the other is commercial. He observes as well that schools censor too by over-controlling what students read and write. Censorship, he suggests, is a kind of not wanting-to-know—agnosis—which operates within the individual and throughout a culture. It is this force that must be opposed: "Only a culture that transcends itself will survive itself" (Moffett, 1990, p. 15; see also van Brummelen, 1991). The matter of textbooks is an especially important one, for as Jack Frymier (1986) has observed:

the essence of schooling revolves around what young people do in school. What they do, by and large, is work with curriculum materials—hour after hour, day after day. Such materials are the substance of schooling. Do we want to try to improve the quality of life in schools? If so, we must increase the quantity and improve the quality of curriculum materials that students work with every day. [We should] . . . help students develop and grow rather than control their behavior. (p. 63)

PART THREE
CURRICULUM AND STUDENTS

In sum, virtually no research has been done that places student experience at the center of attention.

(Frederick Erickson & Jeffrey Shultz, 1992, p. 467)

We must come to know how students view their worlds if we want to teach them.

(William H. Schubert & Ann Lynn Lopez Schubert, 1981, p. 249)

Students comprise the themes of research in several sectors of curriculum scholarship, especially in the phenomenological and autobiographical/biographical traditions [chapters 8 and 10]. However, in a recent systematic review of "students' experience of the curriculum," Frederick Erickson and Jeffrey Shultz (1992) note: "Neither in conceptual work, nor in empirical research, nor in the conventional wisdom and discourse of practice does the subjective experience of students as they are engaged in learning figure in any central way" (p. 466). Perhaps not in a central way, but students have occupied important "places" in curriculum discourses from the beginning. As Erickson and Shultz point out, that "place" has tended to be a passive one, as their portrait of the curriculum as "school lunch" indicates.

XII
School Lunch: Frederick Erickson and Jeffrey Shultz

There is no established relationship between teacher behavior and student achievement.

(R. Heath & M. Nielsen, 1974, p. 483)

[Students] try to believe in what is most real despite what must seem at times like an overwhelming conspiracy to silence their inner worlds.

(John M. Rankin, 1992, p. 43)

Frederick Erickson and Jeffrey Shultz (1992) employ the image of "school lunch" to convey what they see as the mainstream view of curriculum and pedagogy in relation to the student. In this image the teacher's job is to take packages of "mind-food" from the freezer (the written curriculum), thaw and prepare them (instruction), and monitor students' eating until the food is gone (classroom management for maximization of time on task) (Erickson & Shultz, 1992). This view of the student's role in contemporary education is similar to that of Freire's (1968), in which the student is viewed as the repository of banking deposits (i.e. information). In both images the student is passive, and the teacher's role is sharply circumscribed. Erickson and Shultz (1992) note:

The emphasis, both in preparing and serving the lunch, appears to be to stimulate consumption and monitor its short-term nutritional effects, which are called outcomes. If certain students repeatedly refuse to eat the normal lunch, or eat it very slowly, they are served specially wrapped packages of the same food, chopped a bit more finely (remedial instruction). . . . If the students continue to be slow in consuming their lunch or refuse to eat it at all, they are taken away to another lunchroom (special education). (p. 467)

Traditional educational interest in students seems limited to their performance on examinations.

Curricular engagement. Erickson and Shultz (1992) argue that at the moment of engagement with a classroom task, there are at least two aspects at work, one they term a "social relational aspect," the other a "subject matter aspect" (p. 468). Despite research, primarily conducted by cognitive psychologists, which provides analysis of the logical operations required by the student to complete any given task, still missing is what Erickson and Shultz characterize as the "problem space" (p. 468), i.e. the cognitive structure of the task as perceived (Posner, 1982a, 1982b; Erickson & Shultz, 1992). Bearing on this cognitive structure, yet separate from it, is that aspect of "social relations and social meaning" (Erickson & Shultz, 1992, p. 468). Included in this latter category are considerations such as the teacher-student relationships, the peer relationships of those who observe the student working on tasks, and the "location" of the task in the "trajectory of the student's purposes in learning" (p. 468), which could be considered a somewhat narrower version of Pinar's (1994) notion of "biographic function." Erickson and Shultz (1992) summarize:

Depending upon the learner's purposes, the emotional content of relations with other persons in the scene, the cultural familiarity of oral discourse routines by which the task is being manifested in classroom talk, and a myriad of other features of social relations that can bear on accomplishing a classroom task successfully, the task itself becomes a fundamentally different entity depending upon its situation in social relations. (p. 469)

Here the significance of context is underlined. It appears that behavior cannot be understood unless it is situated and framed contextually, a point of which curriculum theorists have become acutely aware.

Students' engagement with curriculum is audienced. For Erickson and Shultz (1992), to understand student experience, the essentially social character of learning has be taken into account. Following Jackson (1968), they note that "the engagement of students with curricular tasks is audienced" (p. 469). The gaze of other students may encourage competition and competence, or withdrawal and passivity, and all points in-between. The potential attention of the teacher cuts many ways, sometimes encouraging, sometimes intimidating, always mediated by the gaze of other students, which can turn an encouraging, supportive teacher gaze into an opportunity declined. Erickson and Shultz (1992) write:

Teacher attention is only one among a number of fundamental processes in classrooms that are likely to influence the educational experience of students. Another process, equally pervasive, is the social and cultural organization of classroom trust and legitimacy. This is an issue in relations among students, and it seems to be an especially fundamental issue in relations between teachers and students. (p. 470)

Erickson and Shultz (1992) report research from the anthropology and history of education. In traditional societies, they note, individual rather than group instruction is often the norm. In such societies, the emphasis is upon learning rather than teaching. To illustrate these points, Erickson and Shultz draw upon Okakok's (1989) account of learning in the Inupiat of Alaska's North Slope:

Parents often stand back and let a child explore and experience things, observing the child's inclinations. If a child shows an aptitude for skills that the parents don't possess, they might arrange for their child to spend time with an expert, or an adult may ask to participate in the education of the child. Thus, many adults in the community have a role in the education of our children. (Okakok, 1989, p. 414; Erickson & Shultz, 1992, p. 471)

Erickson and Shultz note that among the Inupiat learning occurs amidst the activities of everyday life, rather than in special places such as schools. Additionally, what is taught to the child, what the child is encouraged to learn, is tailored to his or her particular gifts and talents. Citing several historical studies (Hogan, 1988; Katz, 1987; Katznelson & Weir, 1985; Zelizer, 1985), Erickson and Shultz (1992) observe that many forces account for the character of our educational lives.

Erickson and Shultz distinguish between studies of students' engagement with the so-called manifest curriculum and the implicit or "hidden" curriculum. Regarding the former, they report the research of Vivien Johnston (1987), who surveyed students' responses to curricular content:

An open-ended question asked pupils to reflect on what they thought they had learned while using the microcomputer. Nearly one-third (31 percent) were unable to comment on the learning outcomes, possibly because they rarely consciously articulate this to themselves or others, since they are neither used to controlling their own learning activities nor to subsequently reviewing what they have done and achieved. (Johnston, 1987, p. 50; Erickson & Shultz, 1992, p. 474)

Another major category of research on student response is in the area of science education, which has focused on students' "misconceptions" of science and scientific phenomena (Shymansky & Kyle, 1988). However, this category of research is interested in students' experience as a means of improving the teaching of science. Consequently, this research is judged not to be especially "enlightening regarding student experience of subject matter" (Erickson & Shultz, 1992, p. 474).

Resistance theory and students. Erickson and Shultz (1992) report resistance theory [see chapter 5] as another example of research on student response to the curriculum. In this category of scholarship, however, students' engagement with specific subject matter is secondary to their negotiation of social relationships, especially in terms of class, gender, and race. As we have seen, resistance theory suggests that students [and teachers] manipulate the social system of the school in order to accomplish their own objectives. Such studies, for Erickson and Shultz, represent a subset of a larger set of studies which focuses on students' alienation from school. Among those who have focused on this issue are Giroux (1983a) and Pinar (1975a). Peter R. Grahame and David W. Jardine (1990) have examined "deviance" and "resistance" by exploring "disruptive behavior" as play and playfulness: "we also view it as fruitful to regard the myriad of activities glossed as 'resistance' . . . as practices with their own distinctive organization. They can also be seen as knowledge-constitutive practices, or alternatively, knowledge-avoidance practices" (p. 301).

Other scholars have attempted, in their pedagogy and research, to address issues of alienation and resistance. For instance, in their "Toward a Discourse of Hard Talk: The Electronic Conference as a Means of Creating and Reflecting on Class as a Text," Margo Figgins and Michael Ebeling described a sustained dialogue among students in a course in language pedagogy as taught by Figgins at the University of Virginia. Ebeling and Figgins provided a space in which students could speak and respond to others with imagination, a sense of possibility, directness, and honesty (Figgins & Ebeling, 1991; see chapter 11).

An anthropology of alienation. Alienation is also a theme of anthropological research in the schools. Among the research Erickson and Shultz (1992) report in this category are that of Delgado-Gaitan (1988) who found that students drop out of school due to boredom with school work and perceived abuse by school staff, Gibson's (1982) study of differential success rates of males and females due to differential gender expectations, Rueda and Mehan's (1986) study of strategies employed by students with learning disabilities to construct identities which communicate that they are competent, Fordham's (1988) study of the negative reactions of a number of students to African-American peers who did well academically and who spoke standard English, and Deyhle's (1986a, 1986b) and Gilmore's (1983) studies of students' employment of non-school-sanctioned activities in order to compensate for their academic failures.

Sociolinguistic research. Erickson and Shultz also report a series of sociolinguistic studies which emphasize that student experience is culturally variable. [Surveys of this area have been conducted by Cazden (1988) and by Cazden & Hymes (1972).] Hawaiian students in elementary grades have been found to progress more rapidly when permitted to interact in culturally appropriate ways, i.e. when overlapping speech is permitted rather than the customary "one speaker at a time" rule (Au, 1980). Native American students and their teachers have found embarrassing public reinforcement of the behavior of individual students whose antipathy to comparison with others makes even teachers' praise an uncomfortable experience (Dumont, 1972; Erickson & Mohatt, 1982, and Philips, 1983). Erickson and Shultz conclude:

[Sociolinguistic research] raises the strong possibility that for some students, especially for those who fare least well in schools organized according to current standard practice, the medium of cultural interactional style is strongly implicated in the messages of subject matter content and of personal identity work that students interpret and manifest as they experience school and classrooms on a daily basis. (1992, p. 475; see chapter 6)

XIII
Becoming Somebody: Philip Wexler and Nancy Lesko

Each student contributes to his own self-production by the interactional labor that he performs.

(Philip Wexler, 1992, p. 10)

A recent and highly suggestive study of student experience is Philip Wexler's (1992) ethnographic research on school life and identity, entitled *Becoming Somebody*. [See chapter 5 for a review of Wexler's participation in the effort to understand curriculum as political text.] With the assistance of Warren Crichlow, June Kern, and Rebecca Martusewicz, Wexler (1992) represents the "different lifeworlds and . . . dynamic organizational economies that generate and sustain diverse understandings and aspirations" (p. 8) in three upstate New York high schools. Wexler observes: "Each student contributes to his own self-production by the interactional labor that he performs" (p. 10). One schools is urban; one is middle-class; one is working class.

Working class high school: Nobody cares. In the working-class high school Wexler studied he found that the "disciplinary apparatus" (p. 21) related to student identity. A student reported:

It's a vicious circle, 'cause once the kids start bumming out on the teachers or the curriculum, or whatever, then they skip classes, or whatever, and then they have to come down harder on them, which makes the kids hate them more, which makes them come down harder and harder and pretty soon it gets out of control. And that's why two hundred people a day get called down for referral. (p. 21)

Wexler concludes that "the 'vicious circle' is confirmation of negative or 'rad identity' by the apparatus" (p. 21), i.e. the school personnel begin to assume that these students are "troublemakers." Other student identities, i.e. jocks, are also both self-produced and conferred by others. These forms of collective identity, i.e. "rads" and "jocks" are, in Wexler's view, "*compensatory reactions to an interactional relational lack*" (p. 34, emphasis in original). Because "authentic, organic interactional processes" (p. 34) have succumbed to "institutionalized" modes of interaction, working class students' experience that "nobody cares" (p. 35). Teachers are not to blame, in any simple sense, as they are caught up in their own institutional distortions of self-production and identity. Wexler (1992) notes that: "Teachers see the student groups and image making process of becoming somebody. They see it from the vantage point of their own histories, and their own struggles for self confidence, inside the moving apparatus" (p. 38). What all this adds up to is what Wexler terms the "likewise principle" (p. 40). He quotes a student: "So, it's likewise, you know. Teacher doesn't want to teach the kids who don't want to learn. Kids don't want to learn because they don't like the teacher" (p. 40).

The professional middle class: Success without society. In what he characterizes as a "professional middle class" high school, Wexler found that social control was also a major issue. However, in this location, social control was primarily conceived in terms of "self-control." Self-control is a prerequisite for success in this college-bound school where many students expect to attend Ivy-league colleges and universities. Certainly their parents expect them to attend. All this adds up to pressure, which helps produce particular ideas of strength and identity. One student reports:

> Well, what I mean when I say strong personality—I mean you have to have a strong personality to be able to handle the pressure because sometimes it gets really intense . . . there's always the pressure to be well-rounded so, oh, you have to do this so you can get into college and you have to do that so you can get into college. (p. 56)

The pressure to succeed, Wexler observes, leads, for some, to a sense of "failure and inadequacy" (p. 63). It leads, as well, to the absence of a "social center" (p. 65), no sense of society or of a collective enterprise. This absence makes easier the middle class, professional striving for individual success. He concludes: "Professionalism is accomplished at Penbroke, but at the price of the society in which it must be embedded" (Wexler, 1992, p. 73).

The urban under-class: I am somebody. Student experience at the urban under-class high school Wexler studied is, at best, a "testing ground in self-determination" (p. 76), and at worst, "a battle to defend against . . . an assault on the self" (p. 76). Wexler regards the entirety of interactional life at this high school, from peer relations to interactions with teachers and administrators, shaped "by the tenuous character of self value . . . a self-sensitivity born of fragility and uncertainty" (p. 76). One student reported:

> I am going full speed ahead and am not going to look at nothing that I left behind. Whatever I left behind—leave it alone. I am not going to look back towards it. I am going to go towards the future where I can get things happening, get brand new things. You have got to struggle to get what you want. (p. 78)

This sense of struggle is pervasive, Wexler suggests; it is always about self-affirmation or self-deprecation. Respect is possible in a myriad of ways, from academic achievement, to dressing, dancing, and fighting. Wexler asserts that "self respect is . . . under assault" (p. 80).

Wexler concludes that in different ways, the self is under assault in each of the three high schools he studied, a subset of "macrostructural historical and socioeconomic processes" that become institutionally enacted with the organization of school life "as a dynamic for controlling and dampening self expression for the sake of population control" (p. 126). For the students, Wexler regards this process as a "social emptying of the self," against which the students fight (p. 126). One "strategy" is withdrawal from official school life and an intensification of peer experience. However, this "strategy" is doomed to fail. Wexler concludes: "The struggle for self activates powerful and expressive peer networks that decentralize the self, as the best, though ironically, self-defeating form of self defense" (Wexler, 1992, p. 127).

Wexler's study is a convincing and provocative account of students' class-variable experience of contemporary school curriculum. It is also an excellent example of a theoretically-informed ethnographic study, one in which the phenomenological experience of students is explicated theoretically. It is a study which contributes significantly not only to our understanding of curriculum and students, but to our understanding of the ethnographic research form itself.

Symbols and identity: Nancy Lesko. Another suggestive ethnographic study of student experience is Nancy Lesko's (1988a) *Symbolizing Society: Stories, Rites and Structure in a Catholic High School,* which Philip Wexler (1988b) [her Ph.D. professor when they were at Wisconsin] introduces by saying that it "is among the first in a new genre of social analysis in education. It is post critical" (p. ix). In this study Lesko (1988a) argues that we "must rethink the relation between public and private . . . a new view must strive to conceive of individuals and society as inextricably linked" (p. 9). In studying a Catholic high school—St. Anne—Lesko found that "religious traditions simultaneously contain authoritarian, emancipatory, and egalitarian potentials" (p. 17). In order to portray their experience of the school, Lesko draws upon the structuralist tradition in cultural and symbolic anthropology, emphasizing forms of thought, ritual, myth: "In adopting structuralism to analyze a school I have tried, by examining cultural structures in the context of social relations and individual action and feelings, to minimize the tendency to abstract and reify structure" (p. 29). For instance, she identifies a theme of caring, and its limits (expressed as concerns about favoritism). Among students she identifies the "rich and populars," "burn-outs," and "apathetics." [These basic groups sometimes had subgroups; for instance, the "apathetics" included the "mellows."] The "rich and popular" are concerned about "being in everything", and consequently, not unlike Wexler's professional middle-class high school students, they suffered fragmented selves, fragmented friends. Lesko (1988a) looks for organizational "resolutions" of various tensions, for instances of the caring/contest contradiction. In school life at St. Anne, she found that certain rituals were helpful, i.e. homecoming preparations (Court Day), homecoming spirit assembly, all-school mass:

the conscious collective rituals and ideology of a Catholic school maintained the structural conflict and provided students with opportunities to explore the productive dialogue between the "public" good and individual development. The school's rituals, its code for conduct, and its relational and interpretive principles in interaction with students' codes for conduct in friendship, sexuality, and school members maintained the "public" as an idea and as a reality. (p. 138)

Lesko (1988a) concludes:

At each level of research and practice, we must strive to conceive of schools as creations of human actions with meaning and potential beyond the surface. We must interpret schools, not just report surface characteristics, and we must view aspects of school in relation to other aspects, and in relation to social and cultural configurations. . . . We must consider schools as sites of identity-creation as well as of training and competition. . . . Both the contest and caring views of schools need to be preserved; the tension between them is productive, just as is the tension between public and private welfare. Those are the lessons of St. Anne's private school for public education and scholarship on schooling. (pp. 147-148)

Perhaps the undertheorization and underinvestment in research regarding students' experience of curriculum is nearing an end, given the significant studies we have reported here. Additionally, William Schubert has extended his interest in "teacher lore" to include "student lore." In order to support research in this area, the State University of New York Press has established a book series. From the announcement we read: "Student Lore: The Educational Experience of Students in School and Society" will publish "portrayals . . . of ways in which non-school experiences (such as home, family, non-school organizations from scouting to street gangs, peer culture, mass media, vocations, and avocations) shape the experiences of young persons." We might expect theory reported in this series to derive from biographical/autobiographical, ethnographic, empirical and interpretative, critical and phenomenological sources and stories.

XIV
The Extracurriculum: Laura Berk

Neither leadership nor membership in academic and vocational clubs brings with it the same kind of visibility and social prestige, both within the school and in the surrounding the community, that accrues from athletic participation, a factor that undoubtedly contributes to the allure of athletic pursuits found repeatedly in studies of high school social life.
(Laura Berk, 1992, p. 1007)

[Michael Jordan's] big black body—graceful and powerful, elegant and dark—
. . . is still the symbolic carrier of racial and cultural desires to fly beyond limits

and obstacles, a fluid metaphor of mobility and ascent to heights of excellence secured by genius and industry.

(Michael Eric Dyson, 1994, p. 126)

Extracurricular activities. More commonly, the extracurriculum refers to those activities and events sponsored by the school which occur outside the formal school curriculum. Extracurricular opportunities include sports, music (such as marching band, orchestra, and chorus), student publications (such as newspapers and yearbooks), drama, debate, student government, student clubs (such as future farmers, future teachers, etc.), and assemblies. Sometimes these activities have been viewed negatively, or as unconnected to the academic curriculum. A more neutral set of terms, including the third curriculum, the informal curriculum, and most recently co-curricular activities has been developed (Berk, 1992). This final term has been espoused by those educators and other students and practitioners of curriculum who regard these activities as an essential aspect of school experience.

More social than cognitive. Generally in the domain of secondary school education, extracurricular activities can be distinguished from mainstream curricular activities. The extracurriculum tends to be more social than cognitive in nature and more organized by students than by teachers, except in athletics. Additionally the extracurriculum tends to occur outside regular class hours, and participation—unlike in the school subjects—tends to be voluntary (Berk, 1992). Extracurricular activities tend to be regarded as one of the lasting innovations of the early twentieth century, alongside the comprehensive high school, vocational education, and compulsory school attendance (Spring, 1986; Violas, 1978). These innovations—often associated with the 1918 *Cardinal Principles of Secondary Education* [see chapter 2]—represent a diversification of school curriculum, with greater attention to the social needs of students as well as academic requirements of colleges and universities.

Japanese developments. Not only the Americans were interested in the development of extracurricular activities. At mid-century, Japanese educators became interested in after-school activities. After World War II, extracurricular activities were increasingly regarded as important to the development of democratic sensibilities. However, one scholar suggests that pre-War authoritarian tendencies remain in contemporary Japanese extracurricular activities (Rohlen, 1983). Additionally, Japanese after-school offerings tend to enjoy less faculty involvement than their American counterparts, as well as less student participation, due, perhaps, to the stresses many Japanese students suffer preparing for university entrance examinations (Rohlen, 1983; Berk, 1992). [For further discussion of Japanese education, see chapter 14.]

The importance of athletics. In her review of research related to the extracurriculum, Laura Berk (1992) reports that over half of all student participation in the extracurriculum is in the athletic/sports category, with an additional 3 to 4 per cent involved indirectly through cheerleading and pep clubs. Far fewer numbers of students are involved in school subject-related activities, despite the fact that the number of these is greater than non-school subject related activities. Berk (1992) concludes:

> Neither leadership nor membership in academic and vocational clubs brings with it the same kind of visibility and social prestige, both within the school and in the surrounding community, that accrues from athletic participation, a factor that undoubtedly contributes to the allure of athletic pursuits found repeatedly in studies of high school social life. (p. 1007)

Not surprisingly perhaps, athletic accomplishment has also been studied as a form of cultural iconicity (Dyson, 1994).

The extracurriculum is understudied. Berk reports a 1985 Gallup Poll of public attitudes toward public school life. Eighty per cent of those polled asserted a favorable view of extracurricular activities, a result which duplicated a poll conducted a decade earlier. When adults in the 1978 Poll were asked "What subjects that you studied or experiences you gained in high school have you found to be most useful in later life?" extracurricular activities ranked fourth behind English, mathematics, and commercial subjects such as bookkeeping and typing (Gallup, 1978, reported in Berk, 1992, p. 1023). Clearly, scholarly attention to the extracurriculum does not parallel the level of public support. Given findings which link student athletic participation with lower incidence of court-recorded crime, with higher levels of self-esteem and identity development, and with possibly favorable attitudes toward political participation in the American system, scholars in the curriculum field may wish to devote more attention to this understudied area.

XV
Conclusion

> The theory-practice connection is no better served than when it is lived. . . . Our challenge is to create a community that educates all of us, those in the university and those in the schools, a community that expands our relationships with one another and, in so doing, our knowledge and our effectiveness.
> (Ann Lieberman, 1992, p. 11)

> At root, technocratic thinking is driven by a vision of control and standardization.
> (David Hamilton, 1989, p. 153)

It is clear from our review of scholarship in the area of curriculum development and pedagogy that these areas too have been reconceptualized. The shift is partly thematic and partly functional. The work we reported in this chapter remains focused on the curriculum in schools, that is, curriculum as an institutional phenomenon. However, in contrast to the traditional field's rather exclusive focus on devising schemes for improving the procedures of curriculum development, much contemporary scholarship labors to *under-*

stand how curriculum is developed, from the domain of policy, to planning and implementation, to teaching, and to evaluation and supervision. Consequently, it has been appropriate to rename this sector of scholarship. No longer can the traditional designation of "curriculum development" comfortably apply. Rather, scholarship in this area can now be characterized as laboring to understand curriculum as institutional text. As the size of this chapter makes clear, this work remains important to many scholars. Whether the sector will continue to shrink in future decades depends in part upon the politics of school reform. Will the role of arts and sciences faculty change? Will curriculum theory become sufficiently prestigious to be permitted a powerful role in policy and practice? How these questions are answered will determine to a considerable extent the future of this sector of curriculum scholarship. Even if curriculum specialists are returned to positions of influence, it may be that the institutional interest is a fundamentally mistaken one. This would seem to be the implication of the Canadian curriculum theorist Robin Barrow:

> My point has never been that as a matter of fact teachers are wiser and more to be trusted than school boards, administrators, or researchers. It is that the nature of education is such that a great deal of the research on which people base their curriculum and policy decision is misconceived, and consequently misleading, and that what it is best to do in a classroom depends a great deal on particular situations and people, and cannot readily be encompassed in general rules. . . . But once we have agreed that we ought to be teaching literature in a particular kind of way, the details, such as whether to read *Anne of Green Gables* or *The Wind in the Willows*, and whether to adopt instruction or discussion, are best left to individuals to decide in the light of what they know about themselves, their class of children, and other things going on in a particular school. I am skeptical, not only of the claim that we know a great deal that is specific about the rules of good teaching, other than what we can establish by reasoning, but also of the idea that there are many such rules to be known. (Barrow, 1990, p. 157)

From the American school classroom we depart for a quick world tour before concluding our journey toward understanding curriculum.

Chapter 14

Understanding Curriculum
as International Text

Internationalization [is] . . . tantamount to global ethics and solidarity.
(Bengt Thelin, 1992, p. 10)

I
Introduction: Politics and Research

While many scholars [for instance, see Schubert, 1991a; Rogan & Luckowski, 1990)] have called for attention to international dimensions of curriculum study, as of this writing not one major synoptic textbook has devoted a chapter on the subject. This omission is somewhat understandable, given that the effort to understand curriculum internationally is too large and too complex an undertaking to be surveyed comprehensively in a synoptic textbook. Despite this problem, some attention to these matters is necessary. Clearly the field has a serious interest here. For example, there is a professional association for curriculum specialists interested in international issues: the World Council for Curriculum and Instruction (Overly, 1988), which interested students may wish to join. Our intention in this chapter is to introduce these important elements of the project to understand curriculum, review prominent developments, and include sources for further study. Understanding curriculum internationally cannot be reduced to summaries of national developments and programs, themselves extensive and complicated enough to require separate volumes.

Of course, curriculum developments are not sealed air-tight within national boundaries. Just as economic, political, and ecological phenomena increasingly ignore national boundaries, so do educational issues. For example, recently there has been an expansion of "whole language" programs in the United States that integrate language arts and reading throughout the curriculum with an emphasis on experience and inquiry rather than on drill. The "whole language" approach finds its roots in the language arts curricula of New Zealand where children learn to decode words in context as they read (Burns, 1991). During this century school curricula have become somewhat standardized worldwide, suggesting that a single concept of contemporary society may be moving toward global dominance. This phenomenon of curricular similarity is not restricted to, say, developed countries, where one might expect some degree of standardization.

Curricular differences between developing and developed countries are not as great as one might expect (Raymond, 1991), a phenomenon supported by the use of expatriate teachers, especially in so-called developing countries (Abdulmalik & Chapman, 1992).

The following brief summaries of selected national curriculum development efforts are intended to be suggestive only. For those students who wish to pursue this subject, please refer to more comprehensive studies such as the *International Encyclopedia of Curriculum* (Lewy, 1991), the annual survey of international educational events in the *Comparative Educational Review* (see, for example, volume 35, number 2, May 1991), *Curriculum Research in Europe* (Hameyer, Frey, Haft, and Kuebart, 1986), *Asian Programme of Educational Innovation for Development* (APEID, 1980), *Curriculum Development in East Asia* (Marsh & Morris, 1991), *African Curriculum Organization*, (ACO, 1983) and the *Encyclopedia of Comparative Education and National Systems of Education* (Postlethwaite, 1988). See as well *Curriculum Perspectives* and *The Journal of Educational Thought* for commentary on curriculum issues in Australia and Canada, respectively.

We also recommend Ivor F. Goodson's (1983) Falmer Press book series on the history of school subjects. While not international studies specifically, these studies make clear how the school subjects are intertwined with the political, social, and intellectual histories of the countries where they were taught. As Goodson (1992b) explains:

> Studying school subjects then provides us with a window on the wider educational and political culture of a country. The accumulation of such studies will also aid comparative study of global cultures: they are in fact the necessary precursor of comparative study. We need detailed local and historical studies of how common subject labels override different patterns of knowledge formation and institutionalized practice. (p. 25)

Goodson's series and scholarship contribute significantly to our understanding of these issues.

Research perspective and paradigms. Studying curriculum internationally is conducted in seven different traditions of research: 1) descriptive studies which delineate components of an educational system and the correlation among the components (for instance, a study of the organizational structure of nonformal curriculum in Central America); 2) analytical studies which not only describe components of an educational system, but seek as well to specify cause-and-effect relationships, that is, to judge why the system functions as it does (for instance, a study of the educational remnants of colonialism in the Pacific Islands); 3) interpretive studies which attempt to demonstrate relationships unrecognized before (such as a study linking von Humboldt's and Dewey's educational theories to the development of German schools); 4) evaluative studies that assess formal goals and how closely educational systems achieve those goals (for instance, a study of students' mathematics achievement in several nations); 5) predictive studies that involve description, analysis of causal factors, and assessment of past and present trends in a prediction of what is likely to occur in the future (for instance, a study of expected impact of oil price changes on educational expansion in Arab States); 6) a planning model or organizational scheme which specifies significant elements of an intended educational operation (for instance, designing literacy programs in developing nations); and 7) theoretical studies which analyze curriculum according to its political, economic, racial, gender, historical, or social consequences (for instance, a study of social class competition for admission to higher education institutions in Argentina) (Thomas, 1990, pp. 9-12; see also Raissiguier, 1993). The diversity of research orientation and of theme underline the complexity of understanding curriculum internationally.

Political uses of international comparisons. A wide range of educational planners, consultants, professors, and students have an interest in the international dimensions of curriculum. Businesses with international trade interests, global industrial entities, missionaries and religious organizations, political scientists, and foreign aid agencies all monitor international educational developments. Politicians and governmental officials utilize educational trends and issues to promote specific agenda within their own spheres of influence. For instance, the publication of *A Nation at Risk: The Imperative for Educational Reform* (NCEE 1983) in the United States rationalized aggressive educational reform based on the argument that student achievement in the United States was deficient when compared to students in other nations, particularly economic competitors Japan and Germany. Such international comparisons fueled a decade of political rhetoric and educational reform in the United States. [As we saw in chapter 3, such arguments have been used before: the Sputnik event in 1957 prompted national curriculum reform in the early 1960s.] Whether educational systems are legally decentralized (despite nationalizing influences such as testing and funding that tend to undermine local autonomy), as in the United States or Great Britain, or highly centralized (despite local adaptations that tend to undermine the goals of the centralized bureaucracy), as in Mexico, Greece, and France, information regarding curriculum and other aspects of education is valued by the various stakeholders in the educational arena.

Primary sources. As scholars conduct studies to uncover artifacts and textbooks which illuminate global curriculum projects, they stress the importance of primary sources. American trained scholars from other countries sometimes avoid using primary sources in native languages when researching U.S. relations with their own countries. Often, they rely on secondary English sources exclusively (Schoonover, 1991, 1992). Two examples of this phenomenon include Geir Lundestad's *America, Scandinavia, and the Cold War: 1945-1949* (1980) and Alex Roberto Hybel's *How Leaders Reason: U.S. Intervention in the Caribbean Basin and Latin America* (1990). The problem becomes acute when English-speaking scholars limit their international research to secondary English sources and decline to accept research positions and fellowships abroad. While many Third World countries encourage students to attend European and American universities, the reciprocal number of First World students who study outside their countries is small. Several countries have recently established special programs to attract students from North America and Great Britain in an effort to counter this trend [see, for instance, Japan's efforts as cited in Shive, 1991]. This matter illustrates a tendency toward ethnocentrism in the First World, especially English-speaking, nations. The significance of employing primary sources in the study of education internationally must be emphasized.

Afrocentrism. In addition to the use of primary source material to explore international trends and issues in education, primary source material has been recommended to emphasize the international origin and character of American culture. For instance, as we observed in chapter 6, there is a growing movement in the United States to reevaluate African history and its influence on Western, and specifically, American history (Keita, 1991; Asante, 1987). Many believe that: "African people for 500 years have lived on the intellectual terms of Europeans. The African perspective has finally come to dinner" (Begley, Chideya, & Wilson, 1991, p. 42). Others—including liberals such as Arthur Schlesinger, Jr. (1991a, 1991b)—oppose this reevaluation: "I regard blacks as part of American culture, not African culture" (quoted in Begley, et al., 1991, p. 44). Certain American schools' curriculum are being revised according to a new-found appreciation for African history and its role in the West (*Newsweek,* September 23, 1991). The importance of African history generally and the international character of the American population underlines the significance of studying curriculum internationally.

The politics of the textbook. One feature of a growing internalization of school curriculum is evident in Third World countries. In nations where resources are limited, textbooks produced for the major markets—Europe and North America—tend to be used. Such textbooks do not tend to reflect the culture and history of these countries where they have been distributed. Yet, in many poor countries foreign textbooks have become the primary curricular material. Such phenomena may be viewed as representing colonial and neo-colonial domination (Altbach & Kelly, 1988). Textbooks used worldwide tend to be written in the major world languages (English, French, German, Russian, and Spanish) and produced by the major multinational publishers (located in Great Britain, the United States, Germany, and France). A peripheral industry in India and China provides for domestic publishing in those countries; a few countries such as Mexico and Egypt publish a limited number of textbooks which are exported to small Third World nations in their regions (Altbach, 1991).

Peripheral nations are not necessarily all in the Third World. Canada, for example, has been concerned about its cultural autonomy and has worried about "Canadian content" in its textbooks. Despite steps to protect its intellectual integrity, it is subject to major foreign influences from the United States and Britain as well as from France. The 1988 Canadian-American free trade treaty, which is similar to a much more far reaching pact implemented in 1992 in Western Europe, and the North American Free Trade Agreement (NAFTA) among Canada, Mexico, and the United States in 1993, will also have significant implications for Canada's intellectual marketplace (Altbach, 1991). Clearly, sometimes the textbook influences the production of national cultures beyond its nation of origin.

Debates are raging in many countries over the impact of imported curricular materials, especially films and other media that are available globally via satellite, and popular culture, especially music, clothing, and lifestyles, that are beginning to transcend national borders. [See chapter 5 for a discussion of popular culture.] The Islamic response to Western media and popular culture is one of particular interest, as was evident during the 1989 military operation in Saudi Arabia, Iraq, and Kuwait. The clash there was not only political and military; it was religious, cultural, gendered, and economic. Live media coverage of the War in Iraq/Kuwait heightened the sense of global convergence as well as international differences [see McLaren & Hammer, 1992; chapter 9].

II
Educational Outcomes

Because schools had been the traditional source for supplying staff to the bureaucracies, the schools themselves began to introduce examinations, in part, at least, as a means of preparing students for the official examinations.

(W. Cummings, 1990, p. 91)

Examinations worldwide. One issue which is at the heart of understanding curriculum as international text is comparative educational evaluation, especially the validity and reliability of examinations compared internationally. Despite theoretical objections, testing and quantitative evaluation continue to spread globally, as every aspect of international educational research is somehow linked with evaluation. Another way of studying the curriculum internationally—in addition to perusal of curriculum discourse country by country—is to study an educational topic across nations. In the following paragraphs we will suggest such a study by looking briefly at examinations. Our questions include: how did examinations and evaluations become so central in curriculum planning and educational policy? What are national variations of evaluation procedures? What are the implications of the reliance on evaluation and examination as the primary means of judging educational accomplishment?

Origins of examinations. As we saw in chapter 13, examinations and educational evaluation have long been integral aspects of the institutionalized curriculum. Rigorous forms of evaluating educational achievement are believed to have been developed first in China by the Sui emperors 589-613 CE [the new form of AD, i.e. rather than BC/AD; scholars and theologians now say "Before Common Era" (BCE) and "Common Era" (CE)] who were intent upon establishing control over an entrenched aristocratic system

(Miyazaki, 1981). Sui leaders recognized the prestige of the Confucian heritage and they decided to test candidates for official government positions according to their knowledge of this heritage. They reasoned that this method would allow those with natural ability to enjoy equal opportunity with the aristocracy. China's emphasis upon written forms of examinations contrasts with the classical Greek and Judeo-Hebraic traditions wherein knowledge was developed through disciplined conversation and argumentation (Nakayama, 1984). For example, the measure of proof in Plato's dialogues was success in convincing a group of peers of the soundness of a particular viewpoint (Cummings, 1990). Debates concerning the relative validity of these two general approaches to evaluation continue today internationally (Boorstin, 1983). For example, national systems of testing at various ages to limit educational advancement are commonplace. National tests have been proposed in the United States as part of *America 2000* and in England as part of a new national curriculum. In contrast to this macrotrend, a few programs, such as St. John's College (Maryland and New Mexico), continue to emphasize the "great books" and dialogues.

Examinations in the West. The rhetorical tradition first developed in early Greece and the Mediterranean region gave rise to many forms of oral examinations. In Europe, most final school examinations include an oral component. The interview is a major dimension of the admission process to the prestigious English universities, as it is to prestigious American universities and colleges. Indeed, throughout the seventeenth century, evaluations in the West relied almost exclusively on oral examinations (Cummings, 1990).

It has been suggested that Prussia was the first European nation to rely on written assessments for the selection of public officials, this during the nineteenth century (Amano, 1990). Another account (Montgomery, 1967) suggests that the British East India Company so admired the Chinese examination system that it decided to introduce a similar examination procedure for the selection of its personnel. Cummings (1990) adds:

> especially from this period [the nineteenth century], the examinations for entry into the professions became more rigorous, and often the state played some role in the administration of exams. Because schools had been the traditional source for supplying staff to the bureaucracies, the schools themselves began to introduce examinations, in part, at least, as a means of preparing students for the official examinations. (p. 91)

Many contemporary examination procedures and patterns can be traced to these nineteenth century developments. The international emphasis on examinations highlights the importance of understanding curriculum internationally. Such an emphasis may exaggerate tendencies toward standardization of curriculum worldwide, implying cultural homogeneity and bureaucratism.

The implications of the reliance on standardized testing are widely discussed in the literature [see, for example, Kellaghan & Madaus, 1991;

Binkley, et al., 1991]. Particularly, it is noted that countries vary widely in the methods they use to measure student achievement, including the types of tests utilized, grade levels tested, and comprehensiveness of the sample test groups. Ornstein and Levine (1993) report that countries "also differ in the degree to which tests are used to make final decisions about students' placement and careers, and the extent to which improving testing is seen as a means of reforming schooling" (p. 590). Ornstein and Levine (1993) review the work of a team of analysts who surveyed student testing practices in seventeen industrialized countries to determine whether or not the data collected from the examinations were valid for international comparisons. They report: "Team members concluded that assessment practices vary so greatly that the resulting data are mostly incomparable" (p. 590; see also Westbury, 1992, later this chapter). In the 1990s, it is not universally accepted that examinations and the comparative international data resulting from examinations are valid and comparable. However, examinations continue to proliferate, and curriculum policy and practice continue to be driven in many countries by the results of examinations.

Kellaghan and Madaus (1991) identified several potential problems associated with national tests or other "external examinations" administered across school districts or across national boundaries: 1) external examinations restrict the curriculum; objectives and materials that are not tested tend to be excluded from or neglected in instruction; 2) costs of examining practical and oral skills are sufficiently high that they tend to be left untested; 3) it is extremely difficult if not impossible to prepare external examinations that conclusively assess such aspects of student performance as determination and adaptability in executing projects; and 4) external examinations in effect determine much of the curriculum and circumscribe the professional role of teachers (p. 89; also cited in Ornstein & Levine, 1993, p. 592). Kellaghan and Madaus (1991) are currently studying testing practices in England and Wales where a national curriculum has been established that is assessed partly through a national testing system. Initially, the testing system is reported to have the positive effect of establishing and communicating national standards. However, Kellaghan and Madaus also report "dizzying" challenges face teachers (cited in Ornstein & Levine, 1993, p. 592).

The English national curriculum. Maggie MacLure and John Elliot of the Centre for Applied Research in Education at the University of East Anglia, United Kingdom, reported on the British efforts to establish a national curriculum at the annual meeting [1992] of the American Educational Research Association. In a paper entitled "Packaging the Primary Curriculum: Textbooks and the English National Curriculum," they analyzed mathematics and science textbook schemes for elementary schools in light of the move toward a centralized national curriculum in England and Wales. MacLure and Elliot (1992) wrote:

> The introduction of the national curriculum has, in itself, been a traumatic event in the professional lives of many teachers. . . . The new curriculum

compartmentalizes knowledge, breaking down each subject into an array of components and subcomponents, described at ten "levels" which purport to encapsulate a developmental progression in each subject, over the eleven years of compulsory education from 5 to 16. (p. 1)

The national curriculum will have the effect, they contend, of diminishing the teaching profession, supporting a return to the "basics," and the emergence of a role for publishers as the "new curriculum technologists" (1992, p. 12). MacLure and Elliot show how the bureaucratic curriculum cycle unfolds: from testing, to a national curriculum, to the professional status of teachers, to the production of textbooks and curricular materials that prepare the students for testing. It is a bureaucratic not a hermeneutic circle.

III
Global Education

Today we are witnessing the rise of a civilization quite without precedent in human history—a civilization founded on science, technology, and machinery, possessing the most extraordinary power, and rapidly making the entire world into a single great society.

(George S. Counts, 1932, p. 9)

A new phase of evolution seems to be approaching, similar to the Copernican revolution—namely, the realization that this world was not created for humans, but that humans were created as living, perceiving, active units of earth itself in a cosmic process of evolution that is yet to be fully understood. We are discovering that the whole Earth is a living globe, a planet alive, of which we are intimate parts, not detached and separate.

(Robert Muller, 1989, p. 286)

Historical antecedents. Marcus Aurelius, Roman emperor and philosopher (161-180 CE), maintained that he was a citizen of the world, not just of Rome (Ozmon & Craver, 1990). This view can be found in the writings of many contemporary educational writers as well, including George S. Counts [1889-1974; see chapter 3] and Theodore Brameld [1904-1987]. Counts' major statement—*Dare the Schools Build a New Social Order?*—was written after returning to the United States from a trip to the Soviet Union in 1930. As Counts witnessed the deepening social crisis which accompanied the Great Depression (a condition he regarded as inexcusable), he worked to awaken educators to their investment in social and cultural reconstruction. As we saw in chapter 3, Counts' central thesis was that modern science, technology, and industrialization had created social inequalities which education must labor to correct. He asserted the primacy of this political agenda to his colleagues in the Progressive Education movement:

If Progressive Education is to be genuinely progressive, it must emancipate itself from the influence of this class [the upper middle class], face squarely and courageously every social issue, come to grips with life in all of its stark reality, establish an organic relation within the community, develop a realistic and comprehensive theory of welfare, fashion a compelling and challenging vision of human destiny, and become less frightened than it is today at the bogies of *imposition* and *indoctrination*. . . . Today we are witnessing the rise of a civilization quite without precedent in human history—a civilization founded on science, technology, and machinery, possessing the most extraordinary power, and rapidly making the entire world into a single great society. (Counts, 1932, p. 9; also quoted in Ozmon & Craver, 1990, pp. 167, 191)

Educational philosopher and fellow reconstructionist Theodore Brameld expressed a similar view:

We must forego narrow nationalistic bias and embrace the community in a worldwide sense. This will involve world government and world civilization in which peoples of all races, all nations, all colors, and all creeds join together in the common purpose of a peaceful world united under the banner of international order. (quoted in Ozmon and Craver, 1990, p. 168)

The global education movement of the present day shares this vision.

Global models. Global education communicates those problems and issues which cut across national boundaries. Particularly, global educators are interested in the interconnectedness of systems—ecological, economic, political, technological, religious, cultural, and educational. One widely accepted definition of global education states: "Global education involves perspective-taking: seeing things through the eyes and minds of others—and it means the realization that while individuals and groups may view life differently, they also have common needs and wants" (Hanvey, quoted in Tye, 1991, p. 5). Like Counts and Brameld, Robert Hanvey and Kenneth Tye encourage an interdisciplinary approach that emphasizes current events, worldwide concerns, cross-cultural exchanges, cooperative programs, and international order.

One of the most widely recognized global education programs in the United States is the Iowa Global Education Association (IGEA) which grew out of the model United Nations program of the early 1970s and the ongoing meetings of global educators at Las Palomas de Taos in New Mexico in the 1980s. The result was the publication of *Iowa Connection*, a newsletter for global educators, and *A Guide for Integrating Global Education Across the Curriculum* (Svengalis, 1989). The Iowa global education curriculum proposes five basic themes: 1) global interdependence, 2) human resources, values, and culture, 3) the global environment and natural resources, 4) global peace and conflict management, and 5) change and alternative futures. The Iowa program was reviewed in *Educational Leadership* by Anita DeKock and Craig Paul (1989) who offered an enthusiastic endorsement of the practical application of global education in the Iowa Public Schools.

United Nations' curriculum. The United Nations also entered the international curriculum discourse of the 1970s and 1980s, under the influence of the political and educational leadership of many nations, developing and publishing *A World Core Curriculum* in 1982 (Muller, 1984). The world core curriculum was an outgrowth of the global crises of the 1970s and the urgent concern for a school curriculum to address pressing international issues of the day. The proposed curriculum has four components, as reported by Robert Muller (1989):

> Simply stated, its objectives are to give the children 1) a good picture of the home into which they are born, 2) a correct picture of the family into which they are born—namely, the human family with its great variety of natural and cultural common features and infinite diversity, 3) an accurate picture of the time flow into which they are born, and 4) a sense of their important, personal, and miraculous lives in this wondrous creation, with the physical, mental, sentimental, and spiritual qualities, and the role they can play to further humanity's progress during their life on earth. (p. 284)

The United Nations' curriculum exhibits a distinctive global perspective on the place of individuals and societies in the human community.

Because the lack of instructional time is often cited as an obstacle to incorporating global education into the traditional school curriculum, integration of global education with existing school subjects is a typical approach. Literature and language arts classes are considered especially suitable for such curricular integration. Traditional physical education, home economics, art, and social studies classes can be internationalized, via emphasis upon international cuisine, arts, sports and customs (Tye, 1991). [Other scholars worry that "food and festival" emphases perpetuate first-world colonialism, as we will see momentarily (Willinsky, 1993b, in press).] The object is to promote international understanding and cooperation that might lead eventually to cultural and social reconstruction:

> It is my position that a deliberate and conscious effort to implement global education will ease the inevitability of international belligerence and promote global understanding. People tend to fear and attack what they do not understand. Enhancing international understanding and information-sharing will be more likely to sustain world peace. (Hellinger, 1991, p. 4)

A global village. With increasing numbers of immigrant children in many First World nations, expanded opportunities for education in South Africa, Eastern Europe, and the republics of the old Soviet Union, increased English as a Second Language (ESL) instruction in the United States, and the effects of mass media on an ever "shrinking" world community, the international classroom is a reality, whether intended or acknowledged as such. Global education aspires to provide models of this interconnectedness, interdependence, and interrelationship of world cultures in an educational effort to promote cooperation and progress.

Diane Ravitch, the controversial historian of education, asserts that "we have much to gain by learning about other cultures and . . . they have much to gain by learning about ours. Learning about other people does not require us to relinquish our values" (Ravitch, 1989, pp. 20-21). Others [see, for instance, Kenneth Tye, 1991] argue that changes in educational programs, state guidelines, and textbooks should place more emphasis on world cultures, world history, and geography. Tye contends that few programs "deal with the concept of global systems in a manner that might shed light on what a Japanese industrialist has called the 'borderless world economy' or global environmental concerns such as depletion of the ozone layer, acid rain, or pollution of the oceans" (1991, p. 73).

In her *The Meaning of International Experience for Schools*, Angene Hopkins Wilson (1993) suggests the following guidelines for schools which wish to adopt a global or international perspective in the curriculum: 1) the school mission statement should include the goal that students will gain a global perspective as an integral part of their education for citizenship in the twenty first century; 2) the leadership of superintendents and administrators, including principals and curriculum supervisors, is essential; 3) employment policies should encourage internationally experienced persons for all positions in the school, and personnel policies should encourage summer and sabbatical study–travel and exchange [see Burn, 1993, for institutional case studies of study abroad]; 4) ten percent of the high-school student body should be involved in international exchange each year; 5) an International Studies magnet school or program and at least one world language which is not the traditional French, German, or Spanish should be available in each medium-sized and large school system, and otherwise on a regional or state basis; and 6) extracurricular and co-curricular activities should involve both internationally and non-internationally experienced students in issues and service (Wilson, 1993, pp. 132-134).

Critics of global education. International cooperation and global alliances do not enjoy universal acceptance, either on the left (cf. Willinsky) or particularly among fundamentalist religious leaders and conservative politicians with isolationist views. Perhaps typical of these critics is Gary H. Kah, author of *En Route to Global Occupation: A High Ranking Government Liaison Exposes the Secret Agenda for World Unification* (1991). In this thorough and copiously referenced work, Kah claims global education is a part of a master plot to create a "New World Order" with economic, political, and religious motivations. The co-conspirators Kah claims to identity include the Freemasons, New Age religious and philosophical communities, the World Constitution and Parliament Association (WCPA), the Trilateral Commission, the United Nations, and its affiliated World Bank and World Court. With the support of a shadow government in the United States, these organizations are prepared, according to Kah, to eliminate geopolitical boundaries and create a world government. Kah and similar critics of international education contend that global education supports these efforts to create a world order, an order presumably devastating to the United States and its allies, such as Great Britain.

These critics of global education have successfully challenged curricular materials in several states in the late 1980s and early 1990s. In Minnesota, for instance, attorney and parent Katherine Kerstein of St. Louis Park prepared an exhaustive report charging that biased views regarding Central America were included in Minnesota's global education program. The Association for Supervision and Curriculum Development (ASCD) reported: "She charged that the state has drawn upon a radical left-wing advocacy group . . . to provide schools with teacher training and materials on Central American issues" (O'Neil, 1989, p. 5). Kerstein's allegations were supported by Lynne Cheney, director of the National Endowment for the Humanities [see chapter 13]. Bob Erickson, director of the Global Studies Resource Center, defended the program as balanced because materials available in the resource center included a variety of ideological perspectives, including U.S. State Department documents.

Similar controversies erupted in several Colorado school districts in 1989. The National Council of Teachers of Social Studies (NCTSS) dismissed the Colorado attacks as "sweeping generalizations from only a few pieces of instructional material" (O'Neil, 1989, p. 4). However, the NCTSS report failed to convince critics such as writer Andre Ryerson. Ryerson (cited in O'Neil, 1989) states: "Never in the history of the United States have the public schools been conceived as a licit vehicle for one political segment of the population to convert the children of another" (p. 4). Susan Alexander, executive director of Educators for Social Responsibility in Cambridge, Massachusetts, countered that the materials reviewed by Ryerson "are out of print and would not be reprinted without revision" (cited in O'Neil, 1989, p. 4). Such controversies will no doubt continue.

Survival of the species. Despite the objections by critics in Colorado and Minnesota, as well as by individual writers such as Gary Kah and Andre Ryerson, implementation of global education programs with world history, world culture, and geography as the centerpieces of the curriculum have proceeded. Global educators contend that this view may be vital not only for a well-rounded curriculum, but also for the very survival of the human species. The ecological, economic, political, and social interdependence of global societies contributes to a sense of urgency in articulating an international curriculum in schools. Robert Muller (1989) describes the situation in this way:

> A new phase of evolution seems to be approaching, similar to the Copernican revolution—namely, the realization that this world was not created for humans, but that humans were created as living, perceiving, active units of earth itself in a cosmic process of evolution that is yet to be fully understood. We are discovering that the whole Earth is a living globe, a planet alive, of which we are intimate parts, not detached and separate. (p. 286)

Transcending traditional fears of foreign cultures and ideologies in order to encourage global understanding is a first step in the realization of an internationalized curriculum. With this perspective in mind, we now turn to specific countries to highlight international curriculum developments.

IV
Japan

> If I had $1,000 for every time a Japanese teacher has described her practices to me mentioning John Dewey, I'd be a wealthy person.
>
> (C. Lewis, quoted in Chira, 1992, p. E5)

We begin our review—which we emphasize is suggestive and impressionistic, not comprehensive, as we noted at the outset—with Japan [see Beauchamp (1991) for one introduction]. There has been obsession in the United States with comparing American education with Japanese education (Feinberg, 1993). The 1983 report of the National Commission on Excellence in Education (NCEE), *A Nation at Risk,* intensified this tendency by emphasizing comparative analysis of international programs. For instance, the report cautions that in many industrialized countries "it is not unusual for academic high school students to spend 8 hours a day at school, 220 days per year" (NCEE, 1983, p. 5). The report goes on to compare the typical school day in Japan, England, and other countries with a typical six-hour day for 180 days in the United States. The rationale for these comparisons is to bolster American economic competitiveness internationally, although the length of the American school day and school year did not seem to affect the American economy adversely during earlier, more prosperous times (1945-1970). Yet, the report asserts:

> Citizens know intuitively what some of the best economists have shown in their research, that education is one of the chief engines of a society's material well-being. Citizens also know in their bones that the safety of the United States also depends principally on the wit, skill, and spirit of a self-confident people, today and tomorrow. (NCEE, 1983, p. 4)

One astute scholar has pointed out how conservatives have used the Japan-U.S. educational comparisons for their own political ends in the United States (Feinberg, 1993).

Japanese education. Comparisons of U.S. with Japanese education can be found in numerous educational journals and in popular literature. A Louisiana newspaper editorial is typical:

> A Gallup poll last summer found that 58 percent of respondents in Louisiana favored more time in school for students. At the Lafayette Parish School Board, some officials think extending the school year by 20 days is a good idea. Others disagree. Those favoring a longer school year from the current 180 days point to the competition: Japan's school year is 243 days, West Germany is 226 to 240, and South Korea's is 220 days. Students in these countries far surpass their American counterparts. The United States, in fact, ranks near the bottom in quantity—and quality—of education. (*Lafayette Sunday Advertiser,* 1991, p. 6)

Such comparisons both speak to and create a popular impression that educational systems can be assessed, as we noted earlier, by comparing quantified outcomes. Despite the educational problems associated with such comparisons, popular interest in them has reached a high level in the early 1990s.

This interest is also evident in scholarly journals as well. Comparative studies of schooling in the United States and Japan appear regularly. Interesting for us is "Comparing American and Japanese Achievement: Is the United States Really a Lower Achiever," by Ian Westbury who, with Neil Wilkof, had edited the collected essays of Joseph Schwab [see chapter 4]. Westbury (1992) contends that the emphasis on comparative national standards based on cross-national achievement studies [such as data from the International Association for Evaluation of Educational Achievement and the International Assessment of Educational Progress] may excite political and public interest; however, the data cannot be regard as valid for comparative analysis. Westbury contends that the focus on the undifferentiated variable of "country" as a unit of analysis is not reliable; other more important factors must be considered, casting doubt on the current state of comparative analysis. Westbury's detailed analysis of the curriculum and achievement of students in grades 7/8 algebra and grade 12 calculus in both countries indicates that the apparently lower achievement of American students is a result of curricula that are not well matched to the test in the United States. However, when the curricula of Japan and the U.S. are both comparable to the assessment instrument, the achievement of students in both countries is comparable. Westbury's (1992) study underlines the complexity of comparative educational analysis. It also underlines the impact of examinations on curriculum. [For a discussion of Westbury's study, see Baker, 1993a, 1993b; Westbury, 1993.]

Japanese system superior? Another typical comparison of the Japanese and American systems was published in the *National Review,* with the title "Why Johnny Can't Read, but Yoshio Can" (Lynn, 1988). This editorial complains that American schools are expected to enforce racial integration, foster social progress, and keep kids off the streets, but Japanese schools are expected to teach. Again, the results of achievement tests are used to conclude that the Japanese educational system is superior to the American and European educational systems. The author of the editorial, Richard Lynn, concludes:

> There can be no doubt that American schools compare poorly with Japanese schools. In the latter there are no serious problems with poor discipline, violence, or truancy; Japanese children take school seriously and work hard. Japanese educational standards are high, and illiteracy is virtually unknown. (1988, p. 40)

Negative assessments of Japanese education are in the minority, but they do exist (Schoolland, 1990).

The factors that are often attributed to Japan's educational success are threefold: a strong national curriculum stipulated by the central government, strong incentives for students, and the stimulating effects of competition between schools. Lynn notes that the curriculum in Japan is a national one, developed by the Department of Education. Included are Japanese language and literature, mathematics, science, social studies, music, moral education, and physical education. Periodically, the Department of Education requests advice on the curriculum from representatives of the teaching profession, industry, and trade unions. Syllabi are composed to specify in detail the subject matter that has to be taught at each grade level. These syllabi are issued to the school principals, who are then responsible for ensuring that the stipulated curriculum is taught in every school (Lynn, 1988).

However, some believe that school success in Japan, and in Asia generally, was "made in America." Susan Chira (1992) reports that:

> A growing number of scholars . . . show . . . that [Asian schools] are run on the very principles American educators endorse but usually fail to practice. Chinese and Japanese elementary school children, they report, have less drill, more time for play, and more opportunity to solve problem creatively than their American peers. (p. E5)

It is true that regimentation applies to Asian high schools; elementary schools are a different matter. John Dewey, still shunned by American politicians and business leaders, is remembered positively in the East: "If I had $1,000 for every time a Japanese teacher has described her practices to me mentioning John Dewey, I'd be a wealthy person," said Catherine C. Lewis of the University of California at San Francisco (quoted in Chira, 1992, p. E5). Certainly, the institutional conditions for teaching are more favorable in Japan and Asia. Asian teachers rarely teach more than four hours a day, leaving ample time to confer on lesson plans, meet individually with students, and grade homework. Additionally, teachers' salaries in Japan are 2.4 times higher than the national per capita income, compared to 1.7 times higher in the United States. Two other items in Chira's (1992) report may surprise Americans: Asian children reported feeling less stress than American students. Children are more relaxed and attentive, perhaps in part because they have a short recess after each class. Secondly, Asian children are typically not divided into high- or low-ability groups, a practice widely denounced in the United States for dooming children on the low track to low expectations [see also the research of Page and McNeil on this subject, reported in chapter 13].

Courtesy and reform. Other authors point to additional factors to account for perceived Japanese educational superiority. Merry White, author of *The Japanese Educational Challenge* (1987), contends that Japanese culture and childrearing support learning and performing at high levels. Japanese culture is based on courtesy. In a relatively small, densely populated country (an average of over 800 people per square mile) a tradition of polite conduct is necessary, according to White, in order to survive in such crowded conditions. Japanese children are expected to obey social customs and perform well in schools (White, 1987). White concludes her book by suggesting that schools in the United States must provide tougher standards, reform and centralize the school curriculum, improve teachers' pay and working conditions and, ultimately, set a priority for education and a concern for the improvement of the lives of children above all else.

Japan avoids large military expenditures. Since the end of World War II the Japanese have banned nuclear weapons and have refused to arm the military for international conflicts. Not until 1991 did the question of military rearmament occupy the serious attention of the Japanese parliament. The Japanese have invested heavily in manufacturing, technology, and education. While all other First (and Third) World nations were spending large percentages of their GNP on weapons research and military defense, Japan invested in the non-military economic sector and has emerged as the global leader economically and to a lesser extent, politically. A comparison of education funding between Japan and the U.S. highlights this differential pattern of national investment: "Japan spends 10 percent of its gross national product on education; America spends 6.8 percent and is busily reducing that figure" (Troy, 1985, p. 469).

Abbreviated history of Japanese education. Over the past one hundred and fifty years, two major changes in Japan's educational goals have occurred as a result of Western cultural and military invasions. The first change occurred in the mid-nineteenth century when Japan's policy of political, economic, and cultural isolationism ended when the West arrived. For more than two centuries prior to the mid-1800s, Japan had been governed feudally, with a ruling shogun and his samurai warriors. Separate schools were conducted for sons of rulers and sons of commoners, while daughters were kept home to learn domestic skills. Schools for the ruling samurai class included Chinese Confucian literature, calligraphy, history, self-discipline, and the martial arts. Schools for commoners taught reading, writing, calculating with an abacus, and moral precepts. Although formal education was moderately widespread, it was far from universal (Ministry of Education, 1980).

Universal primary schooling. When the emperor was restored as the head of government in 1867 after the collapse of the Tokugawa Shogunate, the new leaders sought help from the West to renovate Japan's military, economic, and educational establishments. A commission proposed radical educational reforms based on the education systems of Europe and North America. The Meiji government decided that the function of schools would shift from Confucian scholarship to more practical knowledge and skills. The plan included providing universal primary schooling for boys and girls and expanded opportunities for students in secondary institutions. By the mid-1890s, 46 percent of primary-age children were in school. By 1906 the figure had risen to 97 percent and by 1916 to 99 percent (Ministry of Education, 1980).

Before World War II. Before the second World War, the goals of Japanese education had been directed toward strengthening the national identity and increasing industrial output and military capabilities. R. Murray Thomas (1990) describes these goals:

> Throughout these years, a growing spirit of national pride and ambition became evident among Japan's educational aims. An Imperial Rescript on Education issued in 1890 identified the development of national identity as a prime goal of education. A Royal Message on the Enhancement of National Spirit in 1923 urged the creation of a vigorous spirit of national glory, of prosperity founded on industrial production, and of strong soldiers. (p. 35)

By the 1920s, the elementary school curriculum in Japan included Japanese language, arithmetic, geography, moral development, drawing, music, physical education, and handicrafts. By the 1930s, greater stress was placed in secondary schools on citizenship and vocational training, with the addition of compulsory classes in civic virtue and industrial arts. Some contend that the school curriculum was being viewed as an essential instrument for achieving the political aim of the military leaders who dominated governmental policy before World War II. The purpose was the construction of the Greater East Asia Coprosperity Sphere, uniting all territories from Korea to Indonesia to form an immense commercial empire under Japanese rule. This dream ended with the defeat of Japan in 1945, at which time nationalistic courses were dropped from the school curriculum by the American interim government. At the conclusion of American military occupation in 1952, certain post-war curriculum innovations were retained while others were altered. Most notably, morality and national identity courses were reinstated, reflecting educational ideals rooted in deep-seated cultural values that could not be erased by military occupation (Thomas, 1990).

By the early 1960s, a weekly moral conduct course was required in all compulsory schools, guided by a Ministry of Education manual of essays and stories emphasizing moral qualities. This movement was viewed with alarm by many Japanese. One observer wrote:

> Many intellectuals viewed the events with alarm and criticized the move of the Ministry as another step backwards in Japan's ultra-right past when morals had been a course that aimed to indoctrinate youth into chauvinistic and authoritarian values. Most Japanese, however, did not share the fear and, on the contrary, appeared to feel that Japanese youth needed greater aid from the schools in developing stronger characters. They also saw the need for the schools to aid in reversing the rising trend of juvenile delinquency. (Kobayaski, 1968, p. 112)

The Japanese experience is one clear example of curriculum that is influenced by the broader context of social-political history and cultural values. The curriculum is hardly an artifact isolated from the larger social and political context. In the Japanese instance we observe a society which 150 years ago voluntarily imported educational objectives from the West so as to enhance its process of industrialization and modernization. In the twentieth century, political leaders placed greater emphasis upon patriotism, national identity, and national self-interest. Military defeat brought unwelcomed changes in the Japanese curriculum, changes which faded after the Americans departed in the 1950s.

Comparative studies of Japan and the U.S. Among the many comparative studies of United States and Japanese education, the research of Robert D. Hess and Hiroshi Azuma (1991) is perhaps representative. As do many researchers, Hess and Azuma uncovered significant differences in cultural support for schooling in the two countries. Using the Developmental Expectations Questionnaire (Hess, Kashiwagi, Azuma, Price, & Dickson, 1980) to measure parent expectations for preschool age children, the researchers found that Japanese parents tend to stress the development of adaptive dispositions to school while Americans attempt to make the learning experience more appealing. Hess and Azuma contend:

> Teachers can deal with the adverse conditions intrinsic in schooling by promoting adaptive dispositions or can mitigate their impact by using techniques that engage the student and make the learning situation more appealing, or both. Some cultures—in this discussion, Japan—seem to be particularly concerned about developing adaptive dispositions in students. Other cultures focus more on modifying the classroom environment. We suggest that international discrepancies in achievement arise in part from differences in the relative emphasis on these strategies. (1991, p. 2)

The interaction of student characteristics and teacher strategies is seen to create different classroom climates and differential rates of academic achievement.

While studies of Japanese and United States education are common due to economic competition between the two countries, comparative education research is by no means limited to Japan. Comparative studies of multinational systems are reported by Dogan and Pellassy (1984), Ragan (1987), Theisen (1984), Postlethwaite (1988), and Arnove (1980), among others. These studies indicate the continuing influence of comparative research on educational policy and practices in the United States. Next, we turn to a another national educational system which has captured the attention and, for some, the envy of political and educational leaders in the United States.

V
Germany

> To will the essence of the German university is to will science, in the sense of willing the spiritual historical mission of the German people as a people that knows itself in its State. Science and German destiny must, in this will to essence, achieve power at the same time.
> (Martin Heidegger, 1933, p. 7)

> And they will not be free again for the rest of their lives.
> (Adolph Hitler, December 4, 1938)

American educational and economic competition with Germany is second only to competition with the Japanese. Prior to the reunification of East and West Germany in 1991, comparative studies focused on the Federal Republic of Germany (West Germany). In the German-speaking countries (Austria, Switzerland, Liechtenstein, and Germany) from the seventeenth to the middle of the twentieth century, questions concerning aims, content, methods, and materials for education were focused on the concept of didactics. The German concept of *didaktiken* emphasizes that disciplinary knowledge is a major source for curriculum development. Theories of teaching and instruction in German-speaking countries have taken precedence over systematic planning and evaluation of learning programs. With the introduction of the concept of curriculum in the mid-twentieth century (with specified objectives and evaluation criteria), an interest in systematically developed learning aids has emerged. Although the terms "curriculum" and "didactics" are sometimes used interchangeably, there is a historical emphasis on what is worth teaching rather than the goals of instruction (Frey, 1986; Klafki, 1971). Didactic and curriculum theories significantly influence educational planning in German-speaking countries in the 1990s (Wulf, 1991).

Early German theorists. Curriculum theory in Germany can be traced to the writing of seventeenth century theorists Wolfgang Ratke (1571-1635) and Johann Amos Comenius (1592-1670) who both contended that it is possible to teach anyone anything. In the *Didacitica Magna* (1657), Comenius held that curricular content and goals could be derived from a preordained divine plan (*ordo rerum*). His curriculum and teaching strategy was designed to mirror the fundamentals of the divine plan. According to Comenius, learning proceeds sequentially [not unlike "mastery teaching" in the U.S.; see Hunter, 1982] at the pace indicated by students' abilities. For the first time, the pedagogical focus shifted to the individual (Schaller, 1962).

The Age of Enlightenment accompanied new ways of seeing the world, including an evolution of curriculum theory in Germany. French philosopher Jean-Jacques Rousseau (1712-1778) exerted influence in Germany as well as in France, focusing educational theory upon the "natural" needs and predispositions of the young person. Rousseau's emphasis (in *Emile*) upon the individual student and his or her social milieu was extended in the work of German philosophers of education Johann Fredrich Herbart (1776-1841) and Wilhelm von Humboldt (1777-1835), figures influential not only in Germany and throughout Europe, but in the United States as well [see chapter 2]. Founder of the Berlin University, Humboldt promoted general education in the classics to enable the individual to become independent of the constraints of his or her social milieu. Herbart developed an educational and curricular theory based on the idea of "instruction as education" (*Erziehender Unterricht*), an idea rooted in morality. The Herbartian aim was to introduce young people to those ethical principles exemplified by the moral conduct of the great figures of the past. Herbartian formal stages of education consisted of educational analysis, synthesis, association, system, and method. These stages became widely accepted during the nineteenth century as ways of organizing curriculum units and teaching plans. One author contends that these criteria are still discernible in contemporary curriculum development, in its emphasis on goals, analysis, and evaluation (Asmus, 1968/1970). As we noted in chapter 2, a number of Americans traveled to Germany during the nineteenth century to study Herbartianism, returning to introduce it to American educators.

Twentieth century developments. The European Educational Reform Movement (*Reform Padagogik*) of the early twentieth century in Germany returned to Rousseau's child-centered philosophy and rejected Herbart's curriculum theory. Attempts to implement rigid Herbartian principles gave way to several reform movements: 1) the work-oriented education movement (*Arbeitsschulbewegung*), 2) the experience-oriented education movement (*Erlebnispadagogik*), and 3) the group and project-oriented education movement (*Gruppen- und Projektpadagogik*). In general, the various movements associated with the European Educational Reform Movement promoted greater emphasis upon the needs of the individual child in processes of curriculum planning (Rohrs, 1980).

National Socialism. During the period of National Socialism under Adolph Hitler, educational reform collapsed. One analyst describes the period:

> During the period of National Socialism, curriculum development and classroom methods largely served as tools for indoctrination into the National Socialist ideology. After the war, educational and curricular theory returned to the lines of thinking which had previously been established in the Weimar Republic. (Wulf, 1991, p. 232)

During the period of the Third Reich (1933-1945), German youth were subjected to total control through educational indoctrination, exemplified in the words of Hitler: "And they will not be free again for the rest of their lives" (Hitler, speech in Reichenberg, December 4, 1938, quoted in Burleigh and Wipperman, 1991, p. 207). An entire generation of Germans was forced to comply with the curricular policies imposed by Hitler, including, for example, mandates that all students received several hours of physical exercise each day. Burleigh and Wipperman (1991) report that:

> Hitler justified his [physical education] policy by remarking that an "excessive emphasis upon purely intellectual development and the neglect of the physical education . . . leads to the onset of sexual imagings" (*Mein Kampf*, p. 277). The premature "satisfaction of the senses" was especially dangerous because it could lead young men to consort with prostitutes, and hence to run the risk of contracting syphilis. This was bad enough, for according to Hitler, the "struggle against syphilis, and its cause, prostitution, was among the most important tasks facing humanity." But worse, and most dangerous of all, was the "fact" that behind prostitution and syphilis lurked "the Jew." (p. 199)

During the period of National Socialism, curriculum was directed by the Reich Minister for Education and Science, a post occupied by the former grammar school teacher Bernhard Rust. Burleigh and Wipperman (1991) comment:

> In one of the [many] struggles over areas of competence which characterized the regime, Rust succeeded in curtailing the influence of the Hitler Youth within schools. The latter threatened to undermine not only the authority of teachers—a trend incidentally encouraged by the pseudo-Nietzschean anti-intellectualism propagated by the regime itself—but also the requirements of employers for a reasonably well-educated workforce. (p. 208)

Many of the curricular changes mandated by Hitler took years to develop, and in some cases new subjects like "racial science" never produced consistent or comprehensive textbooks and other materials to replace the books destroyed in 1933. Therefore, full implementation was not achieved before the end of National Socialism in 1945. In the case of liberal arts subjects such as German or history, the problems were fewer, given that these subjects were already infused by nationalist-ethnocentric and anti-democratic ideas. The dramatically increased number of hours and general curricular importance attached to sports and racial science did create serious dilemmas. Burleigh and Wipperman (1991) observe:

> A mark of "5" (on a German scale of 1 to 5) in sport meant not being allowed to take the exams leading to university admission. The introduction of compulsory studies in "racial science," from 13 September 1933, was complicated by both the virtual absence of appropriate textbooks on the subject and the obvious illogicality of what was to be taught. Teachers took it upon themselves to make extracts from the works of Hans F. K. "Rassen" Gunther, and to introduce cranial measuring into the classroom. Since the most prominent "racial scientists" often contradicted each other, mistakes in this field were unavoidable. A grammar school, Zehlendorf in Berlin, which reported proudly that in "racial studies" it taught "the concept of race, the origins of races, the physical characteristics and origins of the different races in the German racial mixture" (Wipperman, *Das Berliner Schulwesen*, p. 65) was courting racial-ideological disaster. The problems set in subjects like mathematics could also be used to subliminally implant the racial-social goals of the regime in the minds of the young. (pp. 213-214)

Contemporary developments. Three main streams of curricular thought had developed by the mid-1960s in Germany. The information theory position (*Informationstheoretische Position*) treated learning as a process of management and control of information. The learning process was viewed as the input, storage, processing, and retrieval of information. Although many have regarded this position as useful in curriculum development, it had a minor impact on the educational system in the Federal Republic of Germany. The second major curriculum position was that of learning theory (*Lerntheoretische Position*) which focused attention on classroom instruction in order to identify sociocultural and anthropological variables (so-called situation variables) and variables such as goals, objectives, themes, methods, and media (so-called decision variables). These variables were to direct the development of curriculum units (Heimann, et al., 1972).

The most influential contemporary position in Germany has been the educational theory position (*Bildungstheorewtische Position*), formulated by Herman Nohn (1879-1960), Erich Weniger (1894-1961), and continued in the 1970s by Wolfgang Klafki. The two major components of this position are content (or topical relevance) and methods of teaching. Proponents of the "educational theory position" emphasize the importance of social forces, government administrations, political parties, religious groups, unions, and centers of learning in determining curriculum content. This position calls for reconciling the differences between society's educational demands and individual needs. Klafki rejects all solely content-oriented educational theories which maintain that education is exclusively a process of imparting knowledge. Klafki also rejects process-oriented theories which maintain that learning takes place solely via the acquisition of techniques and skills. Klafki argues in favor of "*Kategoriale Bildung*," an integration of criteria for the specification of goals, content, and processes in learning, where classroom planning aims to create environmental reality open to the individual and an individual open to the reality of his or her environment (1964). Klafki's work is related, in its emphasis on social and political forces, to the critical theory associated with the Frankfurt School [see chapter 5].

Trends and issues. In the 1990s, Western European countries, including Germany, have formed an alliance called the Council for Cultural Cooperation in the Council of Europe. There appears to be general agreement among member states that educational reforms should be directed at assuring a broad general education, including mastery of the mother tongue, one or two other foreign languages, mathematics, history, geography, civics, and science/technology (Tarrow, 1991). Additionally, a five-year foreign language program for the European community, LINGUA, was funded for 1990-1994. This program stresses the in-service training of foreign language teachers and educational exchange students. Most Western European countries are moving toward greater democratization of education, including greater access to schooling, from preschool through university levels. Tarrow reports that as German-speaking areas opt for tracking, dialogue about comprehensive versus diversified secondary schooling has grown. There is strong opposition to early selection and to attempts to attach higher social prestige to vocational education (Tarrow, 1991). These debates, as well as others concerning education in Germany, will be influenced by economic and political issues associated with the reunification of Germany, as well as by LINGUA and other language programs, the proceedings of the Council of Europe, and the Council for Cultural Cooperation, by the European Common Market, by the appearance in 1992 of Neo-Nazism among some young Germans, and by other geopolitical and economic developments in Europe in the 1990s.

VI
The People's Republic of China

The more we know of Chinese art, Chinese literature, and of Chinese philosophy of life, the more we admire the heights to which that civilization attained.
(Alfred North Whitehead, 1925, p. 6)

Moreover, the Chinese leadership is more tolerant to the influx of Western
ideologies. However, the crackdown on the pro-democracy movement in June
1989 and the subsequent leadership change have swung the political pendulum
back to the Stalinist model of central planning and tight political control.
(Julian Leung Yat-ming, 1991, p. 81)

The Chinese civilization is held in respect and even awe worldwide. Some
would ascribe this to the immensity of the population, most to the impressive
contributions made by the Chinese people over the centuries. Alfred North
Whitehead summarized this respect succinctly:

> The more we know of Chinese art, Chinese literature, and of Chinese philoso-
> phy of life, the more we admire the heights to which that civilization attained.
> For thousands of years, there have been in China acute and learned men [and
> women] patiently devoting their lives to study. Having regard to the span of
> time, and to the population concerned, China forms the largest volume of civi-
> lization which the world has seen. (1925, p. 6)

Our most brief review of contemporary Chinese curriculum must be framed
by an awareness of the immensity of the thousands of years old contribution
made by Chinese civilization, a contribution which continues today.

The direction of contemporary education in the People's Republic of
China was established during the fourteen-year period commencing with the
Long March of the communists in Shanxi province in 1934-1935 and ending
with communist control in mainland China in 1949. The Yan'an government
formulated three distinctive views on appropriate curriculum for China: 1)
the curriculum should serve the needs of a mass society; 2) the curriculum
should be saturated with political education reflective of Marxist-Leninist-
Maoist thought; and 3) the curriculum should emphasize the connection
between education and productive labor (Connell & Lizhong, 1991).

Contemporary curriculum developments in China can be organized into
three phases: 1) curriculum reorganization in the 1950s and 1960s; 2)
curriculum intensification during the Cultural Revolution, 1966-1976; and 3)
post-Cultural Revolution modernization, 1977-1990. The impact of the
violent repression of the 1989 student demonstrations in Tiananmen Square
and the subsequent imprisonment of reform leaders is still unfolding. The
official Chinese curriculum today (1993) retains a strong interest in political
education rooted in socialism, support for the people's democratic dictatorship, leadership by the Communist Party, and the continuing influence of

Marxist-Leninist-Maoist thought (sometimes called the "four basic principles"). However, as demonstrated at Tiananmen Square in 1989, not all students accepted the official curriculum. We will review briefly salient features of each phase.

Curriculum reorganization in the 1950s and the 1960s. Prior to 1949, two political factions vied for the control of China: the Nationalists (Kuomintang Party) and the Communists (Chinese Communist Party). In 1949 the Nationalists retreated to the island of Taiwan after a military defeat at the hands of the Communists. The Communists were now free to establish a People's Republic on the mainland and implement their educational goals of producing thoroughly dedicated adherents of Marxism (called the politically *red* citizens), and highly skilled, diligent workers (called vocational *experts*) [see T. H. Chen, 1981, pp. 121-152]. Secondary educational goals, such as extending literacy in the population where over 80 per cent of those over age 10 were illiterate, were often used to promote the primary political goals. For example, considerable efforts were made to simplify (as well as politicize) the reading materials used in primary schools and to introduce a simplified phonetic system.

During the period following the "Liberation of 1949," the whole school curriculum was gradually pruned of traditional elements to make room for courses in skills and trades at all grade levels. Mathematics and science were emphasized, and in 1954 an agreement regarding scientific and cultural cooperation with the Soviet Union was signed. For the next six years Soviet textbooks and methods influenced Chinese education. The Russian language vied with English as the most popular foreign language in secondary schools. A concerted effort to expand production and specialization, known as the "Great Leap Forward," attempted to produce persons who were "red and expert." Significant instructional time was devoted to productive work, and small factories were even established in some schools. One observer describes the period:

> Between 1949 and the mid-1960s, Chinese officials occasionally altered the emphasis between the red aspect and the expert aspect in both formal and nonformal educational programs. . . . There was clearly a need to prepare skilled scientists and engineers to implement China's socialist modernization program, so the stress in the education system was on producing experts. However, concern over a decline in political fervor led to the Great Leap Forward in 1958 and a consequent shift in the field of education to the red component. Economic problems intensified with the Great Leap [and] led to a retrenchment, and in the 1960s the educational system shifted to an emphasis on expertise. (Thomas, 1990, p. 41)

Despite the reform initiatives by Mao Zedong in the People's Republic of China in the 1950s and the shifting emphasis on "red" and "expert" citizens, there was evidence in many schools of a continuation of traditional practices by teachers whom the reconstruction had not touched (Thomas, 1990). It was the ensuing Cultural Revolution which began the more significant upheaval of the educational establishment in China.

The Cultural Revolution of 1966-1976. In 1966, Mao Zedong introduced the Great Proletariat Cultural Revolution aimed at rooting out the elements of anti-revolutionary revisionism which were perceived to be widespread enough in the schools to endanger the Marxist ideal of a classless society governed by peasants and workers. During this period, institutions of higher learning were closed, courses were shortened, intellectuals were discredited, office and intellectual workers were sent to the countryside to work with peasants, formal entrance examinations were eliminated as Communist Party connections rather than academic aptitude determined educational advancement, and efforts were made to raise the educational level of peasants and workers so as to provide easier access to higher education. The school curriculum at both primary and secondary levels consisted of a balanced general education in language, mathematics, social science, art, physical education, and productive work. The object of general education was to produce the new socialist who would be loyal to the people and the Party without personal ambition, conscious of class and ready to engage in class struggle, and imbued with a scientific and industrious attitude [see Mao Zedong, 1967].

In summary, the curriculum represented an intensification of the objectives and aspirations of the revolutionaries of 1949 which sought to provide an education pertinent to the mass society of China in the modern age without developing a minority bourgeois social class and intellectual elite. Ultimately, the goal was to insure that socialist consciousness would pervade the People's Republic of China. Several years later, however, even the Communist Party's Central Committee condemned the Cultural Revolution for bringing "domestic turmoil and catastrophe to the party, the state, and the whole people" (Kwong, 1988, p. 1). After Mao's death in 1976, there was a reevaluation of the political agenda of the Cultural Revolution and the social, educational, and economic upheaval it had produced in the 1970s.

After the Cultural Revolution. Following the death of Mao Zedong and the overthrow of the "Gang of Four," many educational policies and practices began to emerge (or re-emerge) as the Cultural Revolution was gradually repudiated. For instance, formal examinations, particularly for admission to higher education, were restored. The emphasis on vocational education and factory productivity was lessened. Elite "key" schools (both primary and secondary) were founded, leading to the designation of existing institutions as "key" universities and technological colleges. Specialized technical secondary schools were established. Diplomas and academic titles were restored. Theoretical and practical studies were included in the curricula. Deng Xiaoping (1979) outlined the principles of education:

[It is necessary] to improve the quality of education by insisting on higher standards of knowledge by raising our science and culture to a higher level, [and insisting that education keeps pace with the modernization of China] and with the requirements of national economic development. (p. 10)

This speech marked the beginning of an ongoing discussion of the relation of economics and education, similar to that already well underway in developed nations.

Science and mathematics were emphasized in the Deng Xiaoping era with the issuing of new national syllabuses and textbooks for the primary and secondary levels in 1978-1979. Observers have noted:

For the 1980s, education was identified even more with production and economic development, but the objective was approached by an emphasis on the need to develop scientific and technological understanding, and on the necessity to produce intellectual cadres who could apply their knowledge to the advancement of the nation's technology. Hence, the development of "key" schools with preferential treatment and a new emphasis on a search for talent and the specific cultivation of intellectuals. (Connell & Lizhong, 1991, p. 230)

In the 1990s, then, the curriculum in China maintains a lively interest in political education, but China is slowly experimenting with scientific and technological applications in certain schools. The tension between the "red" and "expert" continues to dominate the educational policies and practices in the People's Republic of China, but economic concerns have begun to influence contemporary curricular emphases. This is documented in an insider's view of educational development and problems in China since the economic reforms of 1978 by Jing Lin (1993) in *Education in Post-Mao China*. This recent study examines the issue of political socialization through curriculum and compares the curriculum in use during the Cultural Revolution with that in use throughout China in the 1980s. [For an American view, associated with critical pedagogy, see Epstein, 1989]. China's curricular practices have a history of upheaval and reorganization. As China emerges from the effects of the Tiananmen Square prodemocracy movement and massacre of students in 1989, it will be important to observe the direction China takes in the near future, especially given that the "uprising" began in the universities. Additionally, American-Chinese relations will have potentially significant impact on education, especially on exchange programs. Previous antagonisms between China and the United States from 1949 until the Open Door Policy of the 1970s impeded not only diplomatic relations, but educational and cultural relationships as well. Gerald Gutek (1993) reports that "since the crushing of the prodemocracy movement, there has been a renewed emphasis on ideological conformity" (p. 20). Predictably, curriculum development is textbook dominated, top-down, and bureaucratic (Lai, 1991). Thus, the tension between Communist ideological commitments and the need to prepare experts for the modernization of China in a global society continues to be a central feature of curriculum in China in the 1990s.

VII
Africa

The notion of people's education has acquired wide political currency in South Africa. To ordinary black South Africans, it describes a promised liberation from an inferior and disabling education system.

(Johan Muller, 1987, p. 1)

Everything in South Africa reduces to black and white.

(Frank Smith, 1993, p. 5)

The educational, social, and cultural diversity of the nations of the African continent, coupled with that political instability that regularly alters the geopolitical landscape, would appear, at first glance, to make a description of curriculum developments and discourses in African countries impossible. Additionally, as the twentieth century draws to a close, Africa—especially in sub-Saharan countries—contends with problems which have been partially addressed and alleviated to some extent in industrialized, northern nations: widespread famine, escalating populations, land distribution controversies, explosive racial and ethnic rivalries, religious intolerance, long-term drought, poverty-stricken nomadic tribes, and apartheid. These problems became dramatically evident in Somalia in 1992, precipitating United Nations and United States intervention in December, 1992. Especially tragic is the economic stagnation following centuries of colonial subjugation by the Portuguese in Gambia and Mozambique, the Germans in the Union (now Republic) of South Africa and Namibia, the Italians in Ethiopia and Libya, the British in Ghana (Gold Coast), Zimbabwe and Zambia (formerly Rhodesia), Uganda, Kenya, and Tanzania, the French in Guinea, Ivory Coast, Morocco, and Niger, and Belgium in Zaire (Belgian Congo). The litany of colonialism, political upheaval, independence, civil wars, economic devastation, and starvation on the African continent is overwhelming. Nonetheless, it is only a part of the African story.

Ancient civilizations. Centuries before colonial domination, various African cultures flourished. These cultures produced achievements in art and architecture (such as the pyramids in Egypt), agriculture (irrigation along the Nile and Congo rivers), archeology (fossil discoveries in Tanzania, the "Lucy" humanoid skeleton in Ethiopia, and tombs in Egypt), culture (Phoenicians in the Carthaginian Empire in Tunisia, Moors in Algeria, and Bantu tribes in Angola and Zimbabwe), history (Solomon and the Queen of Sheba in Ethiopia), hunting (Bushmen of Botswana), religion (Coptic Christian church of Egypt in 4th century CE and tribal rituals and mythology of nomadic societies), and higher education (El Karaocrine, the oldest university in Morocco). The contributions of ancient African civilizations are indisputably significant in the evolution of global societies and world cultures.

It is noteworthy that Western culture, especially Greek culture, was preserved in the great library of Alexandria in Egypt during the reign of Ptolemy II (265-246 BCE). Daniel J. Boorstin (1992) describes this period:

A wily and aggressive monarch, [Ptolemy II] expanded his fathers' realm up the Nile, along the Red Sea, and into northern Arabia. . . . Alexander the Great, according to legend, had imagined a great library in his namesake city. The Ptolemies made his vision a reality, when their royal library became the first ample repository of the West's literary inheritance. . . . This library would preserve a reliable text of every work in Greek and a representative collection in other languages. (pp. 47-48)

While Alexander the Great and his successors, the Ptolomies, were among early conquerors on the African continent, it was there that Greek culture was preserved and became the seedbed of the ancient Greek Renaissance of Hellenistic culture. Here also the Hebrew Bible was translated into Greek (the Septuagint). Boorstin (1992) concludes that Greek culture eventually became mingled and subsumed in the widening stream of Christianity, in no small measure as a result of the library, museum, and research center established in Alexandria.

Educational impact of colonialism. In analyzing the decimation of African culture in the past two hundred years and the problems of illiteracy on the continent [see Thomas, 1990, p. 229], several educational scholars have linked contemporary African educational struggles with colonialism (Hellinger, 1991). Egypt, for example, can be described as a country with an atmosphere in which thirteenth century spirit and twentieth century technology intermingle. With fewer than 5% of adult Egyptians attaining educational levels to qualify for university admission, it is not difficult to understand the absence of support for schooling among the majority of Egyptian citizens. More than 60% of adult Egyptians cannot read and write; many parents prefer to put their children to work rather than have them spend time in schools (Hellinger, 1991). Despite the dignified and remarkable history of ancient Egypt and the civilization it produced, many modern Egyptians live in poverty. It is also interesting to note that Egyptian art and artifacts have been excavated by colonial powers during the past two centuries. Museums in Great Britain and the United States have been prime beneficiaries of the export of Egyptian cultural artifacts. Several educational critics contend that colonial domination has not only looted and decimated Egyptian and other African cultures, but has also stripped these cultures of the capacity to rebuild and educate their communities (Hellinger, 1991; Thomas, 1990). R. Murray Thomas (1990) described the repression of educational opportunities in the East African nations of Kenya and Tanzania (formerly Tanganyika and Zanzibar) following their independence in the 1960s:

These newly freed East African nations reflected political and economic initiatives of the British Parliament and private industries. During colonialism, their education systems functioned primarily for the benefit of the colonial rulers rather than for Africans. Operating under the colonial motto that the "masters' children were to remain masters in the government," the colonial rulers determined the level and type of education that Africans would receive. The educational system that was developed by the British government clearly reflected racist, segregationist policies, with Europeans trained as supervisors and leaders and Africans trained as servants and laborers. (Cheru, 1987, p. 34; Kahama, et al., 1986, p. 177; Thomas, 1990, p. 244)

Although missionary schools did exist, they differed little from government schools, since neither was linked to comprehensive African development or to the enhancement of indigenous cultures. Indeed, many Africans believed that the missionary schools actually cooperated with European settlers by providing a second rate education intended to force Africans into roles as laborers. This is most pronounced in homelands created within national borders, such as Lesotho which is surrounded by the Republic of South Africa, where laborers are exploited for mining (Andambi, 1984; Cheru, 1987; Rono, 1988; UNESCO, 1987; Holmes, 1985). Lesotho gained independence from Britain in 1966, and by 1980 the country began to make economic and educational progress partly due to the leadership of the prime minister, Chief Leabua Jonathan. However, by 1980 "at least 150,000 Lesotho citizens worked as migrant laborers in South African mines, almost a quarter of the work force. Another 50,000 are employed in South African factories and farms" (Burns, 1980, p. F-2).

East Africa. Critics suggest that the limitations of educational efforts in East Africa are often the result of the attempted direct transfer of features of northern nations that are unsuitable in the African setting. This is particularly visible in the economic dependence of East Africa societies upon northern nations. If educational progress is to be achieved in East Africa, it will be necessary to correct this dependency relationship, replacing it with relationships of economic, social, and political interdependence. Thomas notes:

> Because Kenya and Tanzania are still in a state of national and educational development, they can profit in the future from examining closely features of Western education that foster inequalities and thereby more readily avoid adopting such features. A reexamination of traditional and emerging East Africa educational goals and practices may provide new paradigms that build bridges between socioeconomic conditions and educational institutions that can lead to boulevards of equity. (Thomas, 1990, p. 220)

One way to examine educational practices and life in East Africa involves reading the accounts of the many Western and northern teachers who have volunteered to work in countries such as Ethiopia, Somalia, Kenya, and Tanzania. For instance, one American missionary educator writes in 1991 from Meki, Ethiopia the following account:

> The absence of persistent beggars in Meki is in striking contrast to the capital city of Addis Ababa where swarms of destitute, crippled, blind, and homeless

victims of the war surround you on the streets. It breaks your heart to see the mass of mangled humanity trying to survive on handouts. Particularly sad are the children, many of them injured, deformed, or blind, and all of them filthy and ragged. The seventeen years of civil war have left a generation of abandoned, unanchored, helpless people trying to eke out an existence in the streets in a city with little work, an unsure government, and a bleak future. It adds up to a situation of concentrated wretchedness. (Porter, 1991, p. 1)

This same missionary describes a lesson in his school in Ethiopia:

> Some 2000 mothers with babies come to our nutrition center. We have them divided into groups and set a day for each so we can see all of them once every 30 days. Most of them walk (a very few ride donkeys), some from 8-10 miles away. They must later return home not only with their babies on their backs, but also with a supply of grain, beans, and sometimes vegetable oil. Before they get their rations, we do our teaching. Here are the points of this month's lesson: 1) Animals spread germs and should not live in the house. If they do, clean out the manure everyday. 2) Dishes need to be cleaned before use. 3) Bad food should not be thrown on the floor. 4) Many sicknesses come from feces. Do not let the children use the floor as a toilet. . . . I like what I am doing, but I cannot be sure that it is of any great worth. . . . We just hope that the nutrition center personnel, the AIDS educators, or one of the school's teachers [will make a difference]. (Porter, 1991, p. 3)

In discussing curriculum in African schools, it is important to recall that in many cases basic nutritional, health, and medical instruction is the most that teachers and missionaries can offer. David Court (1989) reminds us of this salient feature of African curriculum when he reports that even in the midst of educational advancements in some parts of the continent: "It is salutary to remember the numbers of those children in countries grappling with famine, such as Sudan and Ethiopia, or the children in refugee camps, escaping from the war-torn, destabilized zones of Mozambique and Angola. For these children, physical survival is the only preoccupation, and education of any kind is no more than a distant aspiration" (p. 183).

Leadership in higher education. Despite the tremendous economic and social problems facing the peoples of the African continent, progress toward comprehensive educational advancement continues to be made, led, in part, by the outstanding research universities on the continent. These universities contribute to the ongoing process of educational reform. For instance, the University of Dar Es Salaam and Brandeis University created an innovative science camp for teacher preparation in 1988. Additionally, the University of Botswana sponsored an international symposium on educational research in southern Africa in 1989. In South Africa, where the persistent problem of inequality of educational opportunities for racial and ethnic groups is starkly visible, integration is slowly proceeding in the English-speaking universities of Cape Town, Natal, Rhodes, and Witwatersrand where the four universities estimated black enrollments between 20 and 25 percent of the total student population (Dorsey, 1990). In some cases, however, progress is controversial.

In 1989, for instance, the University of Zimbabwe, for the first time in its thirty-two year history, was closed as a result of student protests and the destruction of university property. The contentious character of educational policy in African higher education continues into the 1990s.

The World Bank Report. The 1988 report of the World Bank on African education (entitled *Education in Sub-Saharan Africa: Policies for Adjustment, Revitalization, and Expansion*) proposed sweeping educational changes. David Court (1989) reports that the proposals include the following: 1) increased "cost sharing" that would find new ways of financing postprimary education and increase funding for primary education; 2) expansion and diversification of higher education; 3) a recognition that individual nations can no longer aspire to provide all formal education, and that education would occur as much outside as inside any national system; and 4) a renewal of science education and basic science literacy so that Africa will be able to enter a new era of scientific and technological independence (Court, 1989).

Many observers contend that African nations have made progress toward acceptance of the World Bank's Report and implementation of the proposals. It has been reported that the use of microcomputers has increased dramatically, restructuring of primary and secondary education has occurred, and undergraduate and graduate programs in agriculture have been strengthened. For example, Paul-Albert Emoungu (1991) reported:

> Various nations have created working groups (Cote d'Ivoire), commissioned existing educational bodies (Kenya), or created special commissions (Madagascar, Congo) as forums that prepare national adjustment policies and strategies to implement them within the [World] Bank's recommendations framework. Within this framework, African policymakers are addressing the difficult issue of resource transfer from higher education to primary education and proposed efficiency measures like cost-sharing. (p. 385)

Additionally, countries like Botswana and Zimbabwe have begun the process of instituting curriculum changes that place greater emphasis on the acquisition of scientific, technical, and agricultural knowledge, as recommended by the World Bank. The Department of Educational Foundations at the University of Zimbabwe reports that "these changes were designed to enable school-leavers to become either more employable in the formal sector of the economy or to develop entrepreneurial skills that would allow them to become self-employed after leaving school" (Dorsey, 1990, p. 289). This has led to an increased emphasis on vocational specialization after the first nine years of a common curriculum. It is hoped in many nations that curriculum reform will help ease unemployment, expand industry and scientific technology, and revitalize agriculture.

Rate of return on education. The rate of return on education by various regions of the world is an economic and political issue debated extensively by many scholars [see, for instance, Cohn & Geske, 1990]. It is not appropriate here to review the empirical evidence regarding rate of return on education.

However, in light of the importance of this issue internationally, and because the World Bank report spoke to the issue, we mention the following points. First, the majority of rates of return on education are high and compare favorably with most alternative forms of investment. Specifically concerning Africa, Psacharopoulous (1985) expresses the view that "underinvestment exists at all levels of education, especially in Africa. This proposition is supported by evidence that the social returns to education in the region are well above any plausible social discount rate used in project evaluation" (p. 591). Additionally, it is clear that rates of return are generally highest at the primary level where the World Bank report on African education recommended cost sharing. Finally, it is clear that rates of return from private education are higher than rates of return from public education. The divergence is especially pronounced in developing countries in Africa. In support of the World Bank recommendations, Psacharopoulous (1985) proposes a general decrease in government subsidies for higher education, thereby releasing resources for greater investment in primary education.

Prospects for the future: The case of Nigeria. Continuing our impressionistic review of educational developments on the African continent, we look to the future from the vantage point of one country. Nigeria's curriculum history is inextricably linked to its social and political history. Its disparate peoples existed for centuries as part of the great West African Empires as independent ethnic groups without geopolitical boundaries or common nationalities. Over 250 ethnic languages are spoken in Nigeria today. Islamic, Christian, and indigenous communities create a multicultural society that contributes to the complexity of curriculum in Nigeria's schools.

Prior to the sixteenth century, the traditional Nigerian curriculum was informal and functional, designed to prepare individuals for community life and social interaction. The curriculum of West Africa emphasized the verbal transmission of culture through rituals, dance, demonstrations, initiations, and ceremonies. Subject matter included the practical skills of farming, fishing, cooking, weaving, and dance. Local history, legends, poetry, proverbs, and stories were also an integral part of this socialized curriculum.

The arrival of Islam in West Africa in the eighth century, CE, brought with it a new curriculum designed around the principles and rules of interpretation of Islamic Law. Koranic schools spread in Nigeria and gradually infused the study of logic, arithmetic, algebra, rhetoric, law, and theology into the curriculum. Christian religious and educational traditions came to Nigeria in the sixteenth century, CE, with the arrival of merchant traders, especially from Portugal. W. H. Watkins and Y. Byo (1991) review the curriculum of this period and conclude:

> For 300 years missionaries established outposts of Christian education in Nigeria. Their curriculum was aimed at the training of teachers who would propagate Christianity. Devastated by the slave trade, raw material extraction, poverty, and fossilized social relations, Nigeria was ravaged by European colo-

nization. During this period, educative systems stagnated at the feet of commercial plunder. (p. 237)

With political independence in 1960, a movement to create an indigenous Nigerian curriculum began. The new government emphasized modernization and attempted to create a curriculum to support technological advancement. Subjects such as mathematics, history, English, geography, music, art, physical training, religious instruction, and nature study were included in the curriculum. By the mid-1960s Nigeria expanded science and technology into the curriculum. Curriculum projects such as the "Entebbe Mathematics" project, the "Nuffield Mathematics" project (from Great Britain), and the "Integrated Social Studies" project funded by Western agencies are a few examples of curriculum development for primary and secondary schools.

In 1969, a National Curriculum Conference was convened with representatives from a broad spectrum of Nigerian society. After years of preparation, a National Policy on Education (1977) was published. Among its goals were "a free and democratic society; a just and egalitarian society; a united, strong, and self-reliant nation; a dynamic economy; and a land of bright and full opportunities for all citizens" (Watkins & Byo, 1991, p. 238). The challenge for Nigeria, as well as for other countries in Africa, is to produce curricula and educational systems that will help them reach these goals. Nigerian economic difficulties and ethnic divisiveness will make this labor a monumental task (Ezeomah, 1986).

Additionally, Nigeria faces a turbulent problem of unfulfilled expectations. Independence in 1960 created a euphoric atmosphere in which national planners placed great faith in the powers of formal education to contribute to economic growth and development. While formal schooling has made significant contributions to national development, the pace has been unbalanced, according to Gerald Gutek (1993). He observes:

> More students completed secondary and higher education than could be absorbed into the economy. This led to the problem of the "educated unemployed," individuals who had completed secondary or even higher education but could not find jobs. . . . The problem of "educated unemployability" was aggravated by simultaneous inflation and recession in the 1970s, a condition that might be repeated in the 1990s. (p. 214)

Gutek (1993) concludes that Nigeria should be commended for using national curriculum planning and educational infrastructure improvement to meet the needs of a growing population eager for more educational opportunities following national independence. However, social and economic problems have limited the ability of Nigeria to respond successfully to the economic and educational needs of the populace.

South Africa. Change cannot occur too quickly in this state of racial apartheid. The racist white governments of South Africa have maintained educational apartheid, although there is evidence that the political conditions are changing so that educational apartheid will be dismantled. Beverly Lindsay (1992) writes:

> If educational apartheid is to be dismantled, concrete innovative policies and practices must be initiated—rather than the perpetuation of ingenious methods of stagnation which characterize the legislative and educational policies of the White South African government. This necessitates the clear recognition for a constitutional change leading to a new government with a unitary system of education with equal provision for all students. In the interim and during a transitional period, local school administrators and structures can play pivotal roles in moving toward effective schooling in a post-apartheid period. (p. 86)

Johan Muller (1987) describes one movement to dismantle the present system, a movement which began at the initiative of Soweto parents. It emerged in the "Year of Remembrance," ten years after the Soweto uprising:

> The notion of people's education has acquired wide political currency in South Africa. To ordinary black South Africans, it describes a promised liberation from an inferior and disabling education system. Conversely, the state considers it a threat to law and order that must be curtailed. . . . To the National Education Crisis Committee (NECC), its patron organization, it has become the focus of an increasingly complex strategy of contestation and challenge. (Muller, 1987, p. 1)

For many, the evolution of this movement can be understood as a shift from "liberation first, education later" to "education for liberation" (p. 6). During this transition period urban black education is degenerating even as education in the rural areas is accelerating sharply. This is a unique situation, quite different from other countries where popular education movements have been successful. Guinea Bissau and Zimbabwe, for instance, both have large uneducated peasantries in the countryside: "The converse will soon be true in South Africa" (p. 7). Muller (1987) tells us that the movement for education is a true grass-roots movement:

> The strongest element in the people's education prospectus is likely to be the insistence on "process." Politically, this has meant an emphasis on grassroots participation by student and youth groups and by civic and street committees. Academics and universities need to be brought more systematically into this process too. . . . A further implication of the focus on process is that the teaching packages will have to be learner-driven "learning packages" which can be used even where there is no knowledgeable teacher or tutor in charge. (p. 9)

Muller (1987) concludes: "It is certain that the NECC will continue in 1987 to contest the limits of state restrictions, and the state will continue its efforts to keep the lid on popular initiatives. It is likely to provide a stern test of the resilience of people education for people's power" (p. 10). We conclude our abbreviated review of African curriculum where we began, in the midst of turmoil and change. [For a North American's account of issues of power and language in South Africa, see Frank Smith's (1993) *Whose language? What power?*] Of course, such issues are not isolated in Africa. As we proceed, we will continue to encounter crisis in the global educational community.

VIII
Latin America

New themes have surfaced in the formal curricula of the region [Latin America]. Environmental concerns ranging from the Amazon forest to drought-stricken altiplano in Bolivia have been recognized as important curricular issues, as have concerns for drug use and the politics of its production.
(T. O'Connor, 1991, p. 395)

The history of curriculum in Latin America shares much in common with that of South Africa and Nigeria in particular and Africa in general. Poverty, colonialism, war, genocide, political upheaval, revolution, and economic turmoil are common from Argentina to Columbia in South America, from Panama to Mexico in Central America, and from Haiti to Cuba in the Caribbean. As we shall see, social upheaval in Latin America contributes significantly to its curriculum discourses and developments. In 1991 Terence O'Connor reported that:

Educational trends [in Latin America] continue to be driven by political, economic, and social conditions. Educational research, major conferences, and experimental programs were still found throughout the area; however, these efforts were overwhelmed by the increased stresses created by political and economic restructuring that has marked nearly every Latin American country in the last few years. In 1989 and 1990, the pressure of restructuring pressed educators to confront a changing role of government toward national educational policy. Educators at every level are being forced to reexamine basic questions such as public support for schools, the position of teachers, the purposes of literacy, and the future of university scholarship. The last year [1990] saw Latin America move deeper into a period of potentially profound transition.
(O'Connor, 1991, p. 393)

The current period of transition in Latin America is the major factor influencing curriculum development and discourse in this part of the global community (Silva, 1993).

Paulo Freire. One of the most prominent contemporary leaders worldwide has been the brilliant and internationally acclaimed Brazilian educational theorist Paulo Freire [see chapter 5 for his influence upon American political theorists]. Working from a complex perspective rooted in liberation theology [see chapter 12], Marxism [see chapter 5], and phenomenology [see chapter 8], Freire viewed the problems of education as inseparable from political, social, and economic problems. His original and widely praised work, *Pedagogy of the Oppressed* (1968, 1970), presented a "problem-posing" pedagogy as an alternative for the prevalent "banking pedagogy." Freire's pedagogy was most effective in helping Brazilian peasants to read, and it has been of great interest to teachers and theorists worldwide (Nunes, 1992; see also Lima,

1992). His literacy projects in Brazil teach people not only to read and write, but to decode themselves and their "submersion" in the political status quo. Peasants examine critically the situation in which they find themselves and are encouraged to take the initiative in acting to transform that social reality that has denied them meaningful civic participation.

Freire jailed and exiled. The work of critical theorists such as Freire has been attacked by political conservatives due to its intellectual ties to Marxism and its proposals for radical social change. Moderates also view this work with suspicion because they believe that educational inquiry and practice should be free from ideology and values. They insist that theory and practice should remain in the realm of scientific inquiry, safely insulated from social conflict and political allegiances. Paulo Freire's work with Brazilian peasants was so threatening to the conservative political establishment that he was jailed immediately after the military coup in 1964. After his release, he was forced to leave the country. He traveled first to the United States where he taught at Harvard; then, he settled in Switzerland. He returned to Brazil after democracy was restored in the early 1980s. Coming full circle, Freire was appointed Secretary of Education for Sao Paulo province—the most populous in Brazil—after the electoral triumph of the Workers' Party in Sao Paulo in 1988. Without question Paulo Freire is one of the great figures of our time (McLaren & Leonard, 1993).

The politics of illiteracy. Freire's recent work—with Donald Macedo—examines the implications of high levels of illiteracy. In their *Literacy: Reading the Word and Reading the World* (1987), Freire and Macedo suggest that illiteracy represents not only a curricular problem, but also a problem of social justice. The illiteracy crisis in Latin America, as well in much of the global community, undermines democratic institutions and social progress as illiterate citizens sometimes lack the skills to promote their own economic and political causes. Freire concludes that illiteracy threatens the very fabric of societies by undermining principles of justice and democracy.

While Freire's work hardly enjoys universal acceptance—especially the propertied classes and dominant political parties in Brazil have been critical—it has, nonetheless, brought the social crisis of contemporary Latin America very much into the heart of the international curriculum dialogue. His "problem-posing" pedagogy has spread throughout Latin American schools, in agricultural co-ops, and in religious "communautes de base" [base communities] in the Catholic church. Liberation theology, a religious movement among Latin American Catholic theologians and lay leaders (Hennelly, 1990) is indebted to the work of Paulo Freire [see chapter 12]. Freire's manuscript "Conscientizing as a Way of Liberating" (1971) is considered as one of the important philosophical foundations of liberation theology [see Hennelly, 1990, pp. 1-5]. Freire's emphasis upon praxis—that is, action *and* reflection—has influenced thinking beyond the Latin American community. This is evident in the comparative educational literature. For instance, a recent collaborative effort by Cyril Poster (England) and Jurgen Zimmer

(Germany) entitled *Community Education in the Third World* (1992) utilizes Freire's notion of praxis throughout the book. Freire's influence is traced through Mexico, Costa Rica, Central America, and South America, as well as in several African countries, in the development and support of community education for literacy, justice, and social change. In Africa, for example, is the "animation rurale" which has been employed for over two decades in Senegal and Niger to establish a local organization structure for educational, economic, and political development (Moulton, 1983).

Democratization. Partly in response to three decades of influence by critical theorists, liberation theologians, and educators such as Paulo Freire, Latin American countries have moved toward greater democratization. Most observers agree that recent years have seen a strengthening of freedom of expression and a more active public participation in policy debates. This has been particularly evident in Argentina, Brazil, Chile, Colombia, and Nicaragua [after 1989]. Unfortunately, these recent political reforms have left most underlying causes of unrest throughout the region unchanged. In all Latin American countries, the gap between a small elite and the impoverished masses remains dramatic. The elite enjoy luxuries and privileges, including educational opportunities for private academies and foreign boarding schools, that are denied to the majority.

Contemporary patterns of inequality in Latin America were established hundreds of years ago during the European colonization of the region. The dominant colonial power was Spain, of course, although Portugal, the Netherlands, Britain, and France were also players. Prior to the arrival of Europeans in the sixteenth century, CE, various native peoples inhabited what became Latin America, including the Incas, whose sophisticated civilization flourished in what is now Ecuador, Peru, and Bolivia. Much of the indigenous population either disappeared during the colonial period or intermarried with the Spanish-Portuguese population to create what is called the mestizos. The descendants of the Spanish, other Europeans, mestizos, African slaves, and native populations form the unique Latin American cultures of the 1990s.

The great inequalities in the distribution of wealth in the population led to the emergence of Marxist movements throughout Latin America. This has been especially evident in Cuba and Nicaragua, where attempts were made to establish more equitable economic systems with varying degrees of success. Additionally, peasants, farmers, and even governments have turned to the lucrative drug trade, and cocaine has become a major source of income for thousands from Peru to Bolivia to Colombia.

"Slash and burn." One ominous consequence of economic, social, and political exploitation in Latin America has been ecological damage. The "slash and burn" destruction of the Brazilian rain forest is a well-known example. Extreme poverty in Brazil—aggravated by an intolerable level of foreign debt—has prompted zealous efforts to convert the Amazonian rain forest for agricultural and other economic purposes. The international

community has been alarmed by the massive dimensions of deforestation, an event which underlines the interconnectedness of all peoples. This fact has not been lost on the Brazilians and other Latin Americans. One observer reports: "New themes have surfaced in the formal curricula of the region. Environmental concerns ranging from the Amazon forest to drought-stricken altiplano in Bolivia have been recognized as important curricular issues, as have concerns for drug use and the politics of its production" (O'Connor, 1991, p. 395). In 1992, the largest international United Nations conference ever held took place in Rio de Janeiro, Brazil, to discuss the ecological crisis facing the global community. This "Earth Summit"—attended by diplomats from 180 countries—called attention to the deteriorating ecological conditions of the globe. The Summit ratified several curricular proposals, challenging the world educational community to increase awareness of the global crisis.

Nonformal education. Three models of education for systematic teaching and learning—formal, informal, and nonformal—have been identified by Coombs and Ahmed (1974). Formal education is characterized as the institutionalized, chronological, and hierarchically structured educational system. Informal education refers to the lifelong process of daily experience through which the person acquires knowledge and self-understanding. Coombs and Ahmed defined nonformal education as any organized and systematic educational activity outside the framework of the formal school system designed to provide selected educational opportunities to specific population groups of any age. This third model has found wide acceptance in Latin America. Nonformal education began in the 1970s in an effort to extend educational opportunities to youth and adults who were either unserved or poorly served by formal school systems. Nonformal education has demonstrated considerable utility in responding to societal problems involving health, nutrition, unemployment, and food production. For many Latin Americans nonformal education is the only means of job training, health and safety instruction, community organization, and social development available to them (Nunes, 1992).

Nonformal education varies from country to country. Cuba, for example, under the leadership of Fidel Castro, and Chile, under the rule of Augusto Pinochet, have restricted nonformal educational programs to those that enhance the political goals of the state (Thomas, 1990). R. Murray Thomas tells us:

Since such control is so dominant, schools and nonformal education programs tend to complement one another. Even when the state does not monopolize nonformal education, however, it may be a major sponsor of such activity, thereby extending the government's influence beyond the formal school. Such a complementary effort may foster common, society-wide lifestyles, political ideology, and nationalism as important values for the welfare of the society as a whole. In the United States, for example, such organizations as the Boy Scouts and baseball Little League are national efforts operating with the explicit support and approval of the national congress. (Thomas, 1990, p. 153)

While nonformal education may be restricted by totalitarian regimes so that competing cultural, political, or economic doctrines are prohibited [for example, in Chile, South Africa, Rumania, Cuba, and the Soviet Union in the 1980s (Thomas, 1990, p. 153)], it can also extend important opportunities for basic learning to populations unable to access formal educational systems. Literacy rates are often higher in these countries than in neighboring nations.

Conclusion. As we cautioned at the outset, the preceding sketches of educational systems and curricular practices found in selected regions of the global community offer a very limited and introductory view. It is essential to realize that no single or monolithic scheme or "master narrative" can summarize curriculum in any given country. Certainly our review of American curriculum discourses points to the complexity of understanding curriculum in even one nation. No study of the American curriculum scene, however, would be complete without acknowledgement of our interconnectedness with all peoples of the globe, ecologically, politically, spiritually, economically, and educationally. We hope these sketches will encourage you to pursue international studies as an integral part of your study of curriculum.

It is, of course, important to realize as well that the extreme problems of poverty and education characteristic of the Third World are not isolated there. As Jonathan Kozol (1991) has reminded us in his *Savage Inequalities: Children in America's Schools*, conditions in American inner cities approach those of the Third World. Additionally, it is necessary for American students of curriculum to appreciate the significant technological, cultural, and educational advancements made by Third World nations, for instance that of nonformal education (Lewy, 1991) and contemporary literature (Gonzales-Echeuarria, 1985) in Latin America. There is much for all nations and regions to learn from each other. The days of hegemonic superiority of a few nations are past. Curriculum of the twenty-first century will increasingly reflect the internationalization of curriculum, and hopefully greater global cooperation and respect (Blumenfeld-Jones, in press a, b). In the final section of this chapter we will review selected discourses which suggest that such a global perspective is indeed emerging.

IX
Selected Contemporary Discourses:
Carson, Willinsky, Gutek, and Thelin

This new Soviet history text no longer lauds Stalin as a hero of the Soviet people but tells us about his forced labor camps, purges, and responsibility for the deaths of 20 million of his own people. [Russian] students reading the text find the role of the Communist Party diminished.

(G. Gutek, 1993, p. 124)

In this section we highlight selected contemporary discourses emerging in the international educational community in order to provide glimpses of a growing internationalization of curriculum theory, inquiry, and practice. In the following review of selected curriculum research it will become clear that curricular concerns transcend national, geopolitical, and cultural boundaries. There is an emerging revolution in the global community, which expresses itself in educational research as well as in political upheaval. Some would characterize the present period as an epochal shift to a postmodern world [see chapter 9; also Jencks, 1987; Griffin, 1988a, 1988b; Giroux, 1991; Aronowitz & Giroux, 1991, Doll, W., 1993a]. This evolving global community is seen as multilayered and diverse. Jencks (1987) describes the postmodern world as moving from mass production to segmented production, from centralized authority to decentralized pluralism, from few styles to many, from consistent patterns to kaleidoscopic sensibilities, and from exclusion to inclusion. The eclectic pluralism of postmodernism aspires to weave the discontinuous worlds of modern global societies into a complex whole. So, too, the eclectic nature of these international curriculum discourses we review here attempt to link the apparently disconnected systems of national curricular practices into a sometimes harmonious, sometimes cacophonous whole. While the idea of postmodernism is not intrinsic to the following discourses (indeed, certain aspects of postmodernism are rejected by many scholars), it does allow us to perceive the interconnectedness of cultural traditions, the utilization of multinational research, and interrelationship among contemporary curriculum theory and practice.

The globalization of reform strategy. Our first example of international curriculum discourse comes from the 1992 meeting of the American Educational Research Association, held in San Francisco. In a symposium entitled "The Globalization of a Reform Strategy: The Role of the Market in School Reform," Geoff Whitty (University of London) and Tony Edwards (University of Newcastle upon Tyne) presented a paper entitled "School Choice Policies in Britain and the USA: Their Origins and Significance." These British scholars argue that there is considerable interest in transatlantic comparisons of education reform. They discuss the apparent convergence of problems facing British and American school systems, the impact of societal frames of reference, and actual solutions proposed in both countries. Additionally, they uncover evidence of direct policy exchange between the two countries through shared policy networks and argue for a clearer conceptualizing of the relationships between the accounts of micro-politics (i.e. local) of policy networks and macro-level (i.e. national) explanations of policy change (Whitty & Edwards, 1992).

The focus of the Whitty and Edwards study centers upon the Thatcher government's 1980 and 1986 Education Acts which removed restrictions by local educational authorities (LEAs) on parental choice programs. The 1988 Education Reform Act continued the decisive break with the so-called "social democratic consensus" that characterized most education policy in Britain since 1944. Whitty and Edwards argue that the 1988 Education Reform Act in Britain with its emphasis on "standards, freedom, and choice" will make the present configuration of formal schooling largely unrecognizable by the mid-1990s. Proponents of the 1988 Act presume that curriculum will follow structural diversity, as "monopoly" provisions had suppressed consumer demand and created uniformly mediocre schools. Parental choice, including the establishment of sectarian schools, was seen as the key element in producing more specialized and differentiated schools and equality in opportunity in the 1988 Act. However, Michael Barber (1992) asserts: "It is already accepted that the government's ill-conceived National Curriculum and assessment plans are foundering. We must do something else" (p. 454).

A social market. The similarities between the Education Act in Britain and those educational reform proposal in the United States during the same decade (1980s) are examined by Whitty and Edwards. While the apparent parallels are attributed by some to a short-term ascendancy of "new right" ideas in Britain and the United States under Margaret Thatcher and Ronald Reagan respectively, these scholars prefer to attribute the similarities to the idea of a social market. They cite the work of Stevens (1991) which supports this concept by demonstrating that similar policies have been pursued by governments of various ideologies in Australia, New Zealand, Eastern Europe, and Japan. The apparent shift away from narrow national industrial bases toward a multinational and finance-based world economy might support such proposals on a global scale.

   Whitty and Edwards do not find implausible the diverse support for school choice programs among the "new right," black communities, disillusioned white liberals, and former student radicals of the 1960s in the United States (Moore, 1990) and white ethnic minorities and the Thatcher government in Britain (Phillips, 1988). Such alliances may appear paradoxical at first glance, but less so if the postmodern setting is seen as a pluralist, pragmatic, and restless set of partially differentiated social orders (Whitty & Edwards, 1992, p. 5). Some would contend that this is an example of a rejection of "master narratives," whether they be conservative, liberal, or Marxist. Whitty and Edwards cautiously analyze this conclusion and promote a postmodernity that celebrates "difference" and "heterogeneity" rather than "distinction" and "hierarchy." They point out that the imposition of a National Curriculum in England contradicts the reliance on market forces and choice: "The discourse of National Curriculum, especially in subjects like history, is essentially that of the European Enlightenment—a master narrative that differentiates cultures on a hierarchical basis and sees social progress largely in terms of assimilation into European culture" (Whitty & Edwards, 1992, p. 6). Finally, despite the forging of alliances, there exist tensions among proponents of choice plans. Additionally, a variety of applications of these plans can be found from nation to nation.

   The research of Geoff Whitty and Tony Edwards contributes not only to the examination of the issue of school choice programs in Great Britain and the United States but to the emerging global education reform debate. As they note, the Thatcher-Reagan proposals of the 1980s have been felt in Australia, New Zealand, Japan, and in other European countries [see, for example, Dale, 1992, for further discussion of this phenomenon]. It appears that not only ecological matters seep through national borders; curricular matters do also.

Curriculum and international leadership. In another comparative study, Benjamin C. Duke (1991), chair of the graduate faculty of education and professor of comparative education at the International Christian School (Tokyo), reviewed the educational methods and environments that are shaping future leaders and the ways that attitudes and perceptions affect the political and economic future of nations, regions, and the international community as a whole. Duke draws upon the expertise of leading comparative educational scholars in the three countries he studies: Joseph Lauwerys (University of London), George Bereday (Teachers College, Columbia University), and Masunori Hiratsuka (Director of the National Educational Research Institute, Tokyo). Duke surveyed over 3,000 secondary students in Japan, Britain, and the United States to document national educational approaches and to determine the values, character traits, and perceptions that the various curricular approaches are designed to mold. He reports striking differences between what he calls the more innovative British and American curricular models and the more traditional and unchanging Japanese methods which stress preparation for exams. Duke concludes that Japan is educating leaders who will encourage harmony and consensus but will be unable to provide the bold, creative leadership required to deal with its superpower responsibilities. The Japanese curriculum offers little to encourage active student participation in the educational process, according to Duke. Ironically, the American and British reform efforts to emulate the Japanese emphasis on testing and examinations with a move toward a national curriculum, ignore their implications for the cultivation of creative leadership.

Educational freedom in Eastern Europe. Under a contract with the U. S. Office of Educational Research and Improvement, Charles L. Glenn produced a report in 1992 on recent educational developments in Eastern Europe. The stunning political developments in Eastern Europe in the early 1990s were a distant dream when Polish educator Wojciech Starzynski wrote: "How good it would be to break the monopoly of the Communists in education" (cited in Glenn, 1992, p. 1). Glenn traces the nature of the Communist education system in various Eastern European countries. He documents sources of resistance to state schooling and the emerging initiative to break the state monopoly. After a review of government responses to new educational initiatives, Glenn addresses the question of the character of these new independent Eastern European schools. He describes these schools in some detail. The emergence of new schools and alternative curriculum paradigms in Poland in the early 1990s, following the collapse of Communist domination, serves to illustrate Glenn's research.

Glenn discovered that more than 200 new independent schools had been formed in Poland between 1990 and 1992. These schools are deliberately small (130 of the new schools enroll fewer than 100 students) in order to provide alternative forms of education from the state schools established by the Communists. Only nine of the schools in Glenn's study had more than 200 students. These small independent schools had been formed by well-educated (but not exclusively wealthy) parents often with the support of the Catholic church. However, the new independent schools studied were not like the parochial schools in the American tradition. The educational interests of the religious hierarchy in Poland—where civil society is intimately related to the Catholic Church [as well as indebted to the Church in many ways for the success of the Solidarity movement of the 1980s]—were found by Glenn to be directed toward religious instruction in the state schools rather than in the establishment of a separate Catholic school system. [See chapter 12 to contrast this scenario to the early development of the Catholic school system in the United States, where Roman Catholics were an unwelcome and indigent minority.]

The curriculum of the emerging independent schools in Poland was explored by Glenn in dialogue with Polish educators such as Julian Radziewicz who described the purpose of the schools as follows:

> [In the new independent schools] there are 10-15 children in each class. These children and their teachers should be less unhappy than pupils and teachers in state schools in classes of 40. They should be less tired, less nervous, less collectivized, less stupefied. These children will be brought up according to Christian principles. The teachers, used to crowds of noisy children, are suddenly astonished to find that, within a few days, they know so much about each child that they can work with every one individually. Although they are working according to the state curriculum for elementary schools they will soon have to work out new methods of . . . teaching, not known by a system that must cope with mass instruction. (Radziewicz, 1990, p. 9; also cited in Glenn, 1992, p. 72)

An additional feature of these schools is an emerging interest in establishing a distinctly Polish character to the curriculum which includes supporting solidarity in a group and a tolerance for dissimilarity. The curriculum in these schools cannot be characterized as uniform or regimented. For example, Glenn reports that the First Civic High School in Warsaw restructured the curriculum so that the traditional subjects were organized into four integrated blocks: humanities, natural sciences, math/physics, and physical/psychological development. Additionally, four hours of sports were required and electives in extra languages and computer science were available. Also noteworthy was the fact that students concentrated on one integrated block daily without interruption (Glenn, 1992).

Charles Glenn reports that the curriculum model in First Civic High School is not a nationally mandated program. Rather, it is designed to meet the needs of one specific educational community. A very different curriculum plan has been developed by Aleksander Nalaskowski (1990), professor of psychology in the Pedagogical Institute of the Copernicus University in Torun. Nalaskowski founded an "Inventic" secondary school which he describes:

> [The emphasis in the Inventic school is on the] teacher's inventiveness in his [or her] own development and thereby in the development of the students, and the students' inventiveness in shaping their own lives and relations with others. . . . We simply should not admit the thought of uncreative education. Is development without creativity possible. . . . A traditional school teaches how to use and work for things that already exist. However, true creativity means looking for something that does not exist yet. (Nalaskowski, 1990, p. 13; also cited in Glenn, 1992, p. 75)

The contrast between Nalaskowski's "Inventic" curriculum and the integrated curriculum blocks in the First Civic High School, as well as other models reported by Charles Glenn, all demonstrate an emerging educational freedom in Eastern Europe, specifically Poland. The monopoly of the Communists over education has indeed been broken, and the possibilities for freedom and opportunity have appeared. While the influence of the Communist regime has left a mark on the curriculum in Poland and on other countries comprising Eastern Europe, changes are clearly underway. Educational researchers such as Charles Glenn make a useful contribution to our understanding of the school curriculum in Europe by depicting the vitality, struggle, creativity, and uncertainty in the emerging postmodern, postcommunistic countries of Eastern Europe.

The Commonwealth of Independent States. The transformation of the former Soviet Union into the Commonwealth of Independent States (a loosely structured confederation by 11 of the 15 former Soviet republics) in 1991 is one of the most stunning political developments of the century. The Glasnost (openness), Perestroika (restructuring), and *novoe myshlenie* (new foreign policy) introduced by Soviet President Gorbachev in the 1980s provided support for democratic reform (demokratizatsiia) carried forward by his "successor" Russian President Boris Yeltsin in 1992. Today the members of the CIS are in the throes of profound social, political, and economic change, and any analysis of contemporary educational reforms must be reported conditionally and cautiously. Gorbachev's glasnost has allowed many assumptions about Soviet education, politics, and society to be reevaluated in light of new information. A new Soviet textbook entitled *The History of the U.S.S.R.* was published in 1990 in order to present a more accurate portrayal of the Soviet Union from the time Communists seized power following Lenin's Bolshevik revolution in 1917 until the glasnost of the 1980s. Gerald Gutek (1993) describes the book:

> This new Soviet history text no longer lauds Stalin as a hero of the Soviet people but tells us about his forced labor camps, purges, and responsibility for the deaths of 20 million of his own people. Students reading the text find the role of the Communist Party diminished. The Soviet decision to send troops into the war in Afghanistan, in which 15,000 died, is interpreted as "considerably

undermining the credibility of the Soviet Union and its peaceful intentions." (p. 124)

This 1990 textbook dramatically demonstrates that the era of ideological uniformity that had marked Soviet education has been challenged. The 1990s will be a time to judge whether these challenges will support further reform and democratization.

Studies of Soviet education. George S. Counts (1957, 1959) constructed an analysis of Soviet education which revealed a total system of ideological formation. In his work he asserted that the Communist Party Central Committee was the actual educational decision-maker and that the governmental bureaucracy merely implemented Party decisions. In a more recent history of the Russian Revolution, Richard Pipes (1990) provides an analysis of the Bolsheviks' attempts to employ ideology to reshape human nature. In the work of both Counts and Pipes we are reminded of the interrelationship between curriculum and political ideology of the Marxist-Leninist Soviet government in the twentieth century. Gutek (1993) has identified five major educational goals of the Soviet regime:

> Reflecting the sense of a unified educational purpose, the goal of general education (*obshchcee vospitanie*) was the well-rounded, harmonious development of students in five major areas: intellectually [a scientific and materialistic outlook], morally [eradicating traditional values of religion, bourgeois sentimentality, and family loyalty in order to create a new consciousness that the working class was destined to create a new society in Marx's dialectic], polytechnically [instilling a sense of socially useful technical labor], aesthetically [utilizing media and art as nonformal education for the support of Soviet ideology] and physically [a sound body to accomplish the ideological aims of education]. (p. 128)

In an interview published in *Educational Leadership*, Robert F. Byrnes, a professor of Russian history, echoes Gutek, Counts, and Pipes. He contends that the control of the Community Party leaders on education was absolute: "They see education as they see the army, the press, or any other institutions of Soviet Society that might strengthen the system. Party leaders thus strive to improve the skills and technical ability of the Soviet population, making their economy stronger and their military force more powerful" (1989, p. 87). Specifically concerning school curriculum, Byrnes provided this telling example of the Central Committee control: "I talked with a Minister of Education, who said that at that hour in every 4th grade across the Soviet Union, every youngster was studying geography and that he or she was probably on page 27 of the same textbook" (p. 87).

Contemporary issues. In light of this very abbreviated introduction to Soviet education, perhaps we can now begin to appreciate the emerging discourses in the new republics. One example of scholarship in the post-communist era is that of Grigory Dmitriyev (1991), who presented a paper entitled "Democratic Changes in Education Under Gorbachev" at the Conference on

Democracy and Education held at the University of Chicago in November, 1991. At this meeting Dmitriyev reported on the following results of democratic reform:

> Abolishment of the Communist Party control over education; decentralization of school management; involvement of teachers, parents, and students in the process of making decisions about schools; more opportunities for teachers to select the curriculum; wider range of schools for students to choose from (profiles, gymnasiums, lycées); and freedom to open parochial schools. (p. 1)

These changes, obviously, would have been impossible in previous years. Dmitriyev (1991) also presents a realistic appraisal of these democratic reforms. He identifies resistance to change, severe political exchanges between "conservatives and democrats," financial constraints resulting from the shift from a centrally planned economy to a market economy, inexperience with political democracy, and the inability of various factions to dialogue, as among the major obstacles to educational growth and change. Despite perestroika, he concludes, "little in the way of school democratization has been implemented" (p. 3). Interestingly, Dmitriyev links the struggles for democratic reform of education in the former Soviet republics with similar issues in Western nations: "Speaking at the second European Conference on School Democratization sponsored by UNESCO and the Ministry of Education of Portugal (February, 1990), Professor Roland Meighan of the University of Birmingham (U.K.) discussed the public's growth of dissatisfaction with the authoritarian school climate in his country" (p. 2). Additionally, Dmitriyev (1991) reports that Americans who participated in the 1990 USA-USSR Summer Institute on School Democratization and Social Responsibility also displayed concerns about the tough "hierarchical power of the principal and the lack of students' choices in their schools" (p. 2). Dmitriyev and other participants in this ongoing USA-USSR Institute [although the future of the Institute is uncertain as of this writing] agreed in 1990 that the development of democratic skills and behavior could best be achieved in all countries by promoting the internationalization of the following across the school curriculum: critical thinking, decision-making, cooperative learning, simulations, and conflict resolution. These abilities and activities were not proposed as separate courses, but rather, as integral elements of all courses. Dmitriyev's paper provides a glimpse into the problems of post-Soviet education, as well as serving as a challenge to Western nations to redouble their efforts toward democratization.

The international classroom: Canada and the world. Terrance Carson, a curriculum scholar at the University of Alberta whose work we have reported in earlier chapters, provides our next example of international curriculum research. Carson has written extensively about teacher education (1990c, 1991, 1992a, 1992b, 1992c), peace education [see chapter 5], and phenomenological topics [see chapter 8]. Here we report his study of "The International Classroom" (1990b). Carson contends that Canadian classrooms have become international, not because of any plan but due to the circumstances of the present age. Canadian classrooms have become internationalized for several reasons: television has brought global events into Canadian homes and classrooms, new immigrants have arrived from Vietnam, El Salvador, Rumania, and Lebanon who speak neither of the official Canadian languages (English and French), and as a result, ESL (English as a Second Language) programs have proliferated throughout Canada. Carson asks two significant questions regarding the emerging international classroom: how are we to respond to the cultural "other" who is already in our midst, and how will we learn to live humanely in a world that is in a period of transformation? This double issue of the globe in the classroom and the classroom in the globe reveals that the local school becomes a focus of international curriculum experience. Carson contends that teacher education programs must encourage educators to interpret and act in accordance with the daily realities of their own classrooms rather than perpetuate an overreliance on the authoritative voice associated with the modern age. He concludes his study by juxtaposing a postmodern classroom that moves from difference to identity through the development of an ecumenical and ecological peace culture against the modern classroom that moves from difference to standardization through the development of an "ego-logical" war culture. He asserts that:

> linking the global with the local gives reason to hope that education will help to build a just and peaceful future. . . . Understanding the global in our midst promises cross-cultural communication with dignity and solidarity. Understanding the past and present in the context of the project of building a common future holds out the hope of a humane international order. (p. 14)

Carson's call to incorporate an understanding of past and present global relations of domination and injustice into classrooms so as to contribute to the possibility of a humane international order in the future is a challenge echoed by other Canadian educators. David G. Smith (1991b) of the University of Lethbridge, for instance, calls for an "international narrative practice" that encourages the development of a curriculum where cultural stories are told internationally so that teachers and students can come to more clearly recognize their common global humanity. [See the discussion of eschatology and liberation theology in chapter 12 for somewhat similar curricular challenges.]

However, mainstream school reform in Canada may be ignoring the recommendations of these important scholars. In his discussion of "The Emerging Agenda for Canadian High Schools," Ken Osborne (1992) tells us that Canadian schools have been criticized in much the same fashion as have American schools, with a similar reform agenda, i.e. a return to the basics and nation-wide testing:

> Essentially, the new agenda consists of giving schools more of what made them sick in the first place. . . . The new agenda . . . intends to rely on control and

mandated revision from without. To what extent it will be successful, given the decentralized and diffuse nature of Canadian education policy making, remains to be seen. (p. 378)

Post-colonial curriculum? Writing "Of Literacy and the Curriculum in Canada," John Willinsky (1992a) argues that literacy education in Canada ought "to afford the young a means of not only mastering the skills of reading and writing, but of exploring and participating in the world of text" (p. 278). Willinsky's (in press) most recent scholarship exhibits postmodern influences, evident in his recent call for a *"post-colonial supplement* designed to create a little space in the curriculum for thinking about the implications of five centuries of a global imperialism" (p. 3). He characterizes the position of the tourist as indicative of the colonial gaze of the Westerner; he wishes "to consider the possibilities from interrupting that gaze, from turning it inward, to its manner of representing self and other" (p. 3). To do so Willinsky refers to the work of Said (1990a, 1990b), Spivak (1990), and Bhahba (1990a, 1990b) in pointing to a post-colonialism that, unlike poststructuralism, "is not so easily implicated in the commercialized production values that currently link postmodern corporate architecture and rock videos; nor is it caught up in a post-structural indeterminacy of meaning" (p. 3). Willinsky (in press) continues: "As I would cultivate it within the educational setting, the post-colonial supplement is intended to develop critical and historically sensitive readings of how the curriculum and its textbooks continue to work within global structures of thought" (p. 3). Acknowledging Roger Simon's characterization of 1992 as a "decolonizing event" (1992b, 1993) and criticizing the *National Geographic* magazine as a "colonizing vision" (p. 4), Willinsky (in press) calls for a "moral economy of *representation*" (p. 5, emphasis in the original) in which the colonial and voyeuristic gaze of the tourist can be broken. The "first supplementary step for educators and students" is to turn their "attention of asking 'who are they?' and 'what do they mean?' to 'who are we?' and 'what do we mean by this study?'" (p. 5). [It is a move not unlike Walter Feinberg's (1993), who examines debates regarding Japanese-American education as efforts to revise the American identity.] In so asking we must address "the multiplicity of voices that are silenced within each of us" (p. 8). Relatedly, "we need to question how it is we want to be known and how it is that we come to know others" (p. 15). [For another statement on postcolonialism and curriculum, see Giroux, 1993b.]

Willinsky (1992c) regards the fundamental questions of education for those living around the Pacific region as linked with issues of colonialism and multiculturalism. For instance, a Pacific cultural literacy would not parallel Hirsch's (1987) notion of literacy, which Willinsky regards as nationalistic. In contrast to Hirsch's nationalism, a pacific cultural literacy would exhibit a "postcolonial and global perspective" (p. 10). He suggests: "The prospect of a Pacific cultural literacy is part of finding the region as a new world for educational co-operation, imagination, inquiry and exchange" (p. 10). The American reader may ask why does it appear that Canadian scholars—such as

Carson, Smith, and Willinsky—are taking leadership in the effort to understand curriculum as international text? Terrance Carson attributes the emergence of international humanitarian themes in the curriculum research of Canada to the fact that Canadians have long prided themselves on living in a peace-loving and tolerant country. Carson concedes, however, that the military clashes with native peoples at Meech Lake and Oka in the summer of 1990 reminded all Canadians that they cannot remain complacent as global transformations impact Canada. The struggle for a postmodern, ecumenical, and ecological peace culture proposed by Carson will require bold curriculum initiatives in the classrooms of Canada and new teacher education programs in Canadian universities. Other countries are well-advised to follow the Canadians toward realization of this international curriculum vision.

Of course, the Canadians have long fought cultural colonization by the United States. As Canadian curriculum historian George Tomkins (1981) noted:

> The considerable Americanization of Canadian curricula since the mid-1950s, a process which undermined the old imperial curriculum in anglophone Canada, provoked a reaction in the form of demands for more Canadian content. . . . At the same time, the Canadian curriculum has continued to manifest its traditional dependent and derivative character. (p. 165)

The recommendations of Carson, Smith, and Willinsky point to the possibility of a very different era in Canadian curriculum history.

A curriculum for ecology. We mentioned ecological concerns in chapter 5. A growing body of scholarship exists which insists that education globally must address the catastrophic impact of human activity on the soil, air, and water of the planet. The much publicized book by U.S. Vice President Albert Gore (1992), *Earth in the Balance: Ecology and the Human Spirit,* links the nations of the world to the shared ecological crisis of "strategic" events. Unlike local or regional pollution problems, Gore contends that certain ecological events threaten the survivability of all global inhabitants. These ecological crises, like international political and military conflicts, are of strategic significance to all global communities. The elevation of the ecological debate to national and international forums, illustrated by the Gore book and the 1991 United Nations' Earth Summit in Rio de Janeiro, create a sense of urgency for the development of appropriate educational materials.

An interesting proposal has been presented by Gerald L. Gutek (1993) in his book *American Education in a Global Society: Internationalizing Teacher Education.* While the central thesis of the book concerns the need to create an international dimension to teacher education programs in order to address the relations among education, global economics, multicultural issues, national security, and the rise of regionalism, Gutek concludes his book with a chapter on the importance of the biosphere in the international curriculum. He writes: "Human activities, especially related to industrial productivity and energy use, are conducted on a scale of such magnitude that they are impacting the ecology, climate, and the environment of our biosphere. . . . The earth as a biosystem is under great stress" (1993, p. 255). Gutek lists seven issues that must be included in the international curriculum and addressed by all national policymakers: 1) depletion of the ozone layer, 2) the developing potential of a global warming trend, 3) air pollution, 4) acid rain, 5) transportation and the disposal of hazardous waste, 6) deforestation of tropical rain forests, and 7) protection of endangered species. Like many other educators, Gutek calls for an international effort to address these serious problems using school curriculum as a focal point for consciousness-raising. He contends: "Consciousness-raising, a goal of many educational programs, is particularly important in our relationships to the environment. Ultimately, such a consciousness comes to bear on the continuation of life on the planet. Immediately, it determines the quality of life" (1993, p. 257). Sounding similar themes to cosmologists [see chapter 12], Gutek proposes an extension of the concept of nation-space to include an international environment of plants, animals, natural resources, and shared behavior by all humanity. Not unlike social reconstructionists such as George S. Counts, Gutek (1993) proposes a "broadened view of citizenship [that] brings a sense of advocacy in which an individual is interested enough and motivated to work for laws and their enforcement in his or her own country that will protect . . . the environment" (p. 258). Ecological problems become educational problems; the curriculum is "biospheric"—a place where solutions can be imagined and planned. In the internationally-focused ecological proposals of Gerald Gutek and many other educators, such as C. A. Bowers (1993), curriculum is elevated to a level of global strategic importance.

X
Conclusion: Education for Global Survival

Contrary to the grim portrait often painted of American education, a new report finds that compared to other industrialized nations, the United States does a reasonably good job of educating its citizens and preparing them for work.

(San Francisco Chronicle, December 9, 1993, p. A-1)

We conclude these impressionistic sketches of contemporary international discourses with a call issued by Bengt Thelin, former Director of Education of the Swedish National Board of Education, for education to accept full responsibility in addressing global survival issues. In a recent paper, Thelin (1992) promotes a curriculum that will address issues such as ecology, peace and war, overpopulation, refugees, and global issues. He investigates these from a Swedish perspective, a country also experiencing demographic changes that are impacting education. For example, Thelin reports that ten percent of the population is now immigrant, and in some communities up to fifty percent of school children come from families with at least one immigrant parent (p. 1). Sweden's political neutrality on global political issues became a matter of debate as Sweden applied for membership in the European Common Market in the early 1990s. Thelin remarks in this regard: "A membership [in the ECC] might imply, later on, political and also military commitments. A real crucial question from a traditional Swedish point of view!" (1992, p. 2). Likewise, Thelin reports that educational policy in Sweden is undergoing review. While there have been several reform movements since the end of World War II, there has been general political agreement in Sweden that the educational system would provide equal opportunity for all individuals, thus resulting in a strong centralized educational governance structure with centrally issued curricula. In 1992 Thelin reports that a decentralization movement is beginning to surface.

Out of the unique cultural, social, and educational milieu of Sweden, Bengt Thelin argues for a stronger emphasis in education on issues concerning the future and destiny of humanity. He presents an analysis of several models and strategies for incorporating his vision into the curriculum in Sweden. He reviews his own work to develop peace education programs in the 1980s. The National Board of Education (NBE) adopted a "positive concept" of peace education that defines peace as not only the absence of open, armed violence, but as well the absence of structural violence (i.e. economic, cultural, and political oppression). Thelin reports that "this positive peace concept is in great accordance with the goals and guidelines of the Swedish centrally issued curricula, although there does not exist any causal connection between them" (p. 7). The development of a peace education curriculum in Sweden may seem unnecessary for a non-aligned state. Thelin argues that Sweden's proximity to the nuclear stockpiles of the former Soviet Union and Eastern Europe as well as concerns regarding a nuclear catastrophe encouraged the development of a peace curriculum which could be described as a "mini variant of the foreign policy of the country" (p. 7).

This peace education curriculum was published in 1985 (English translation, 1986) and was employed primarily to prepare teachers. The publication, Thelin contends, provided this previously unknown subject with an official and authoritative voice. In order to strengthen the initiative, the cooperation of international humanitarian organizations such as Amnesty International, UNICEF, Save the Children, the Red Cross, and the United Nations was solicited. One outgrowth of this successful curriculum in Sweden was the publication in 1988 of "An Action Programme for Internationalisation of Education" by the National Board of Education. It included an appeal for stronger attention in the curriculum generally to issues such as peace, human rights, and the environment. Thelin concludes: "The term internationalization was used as more or less tantamount to global ethics and solidarity" (1992, p. 10).

The work of Bengt Thelin and other educators in Sweden in the development of a peace education curriculum, as well as the work of Carson, Smith, Willinsky, and others in Canada, indicates that curriculum in the 1990s is becoming internationalized. It becomes clear that students of curriculum must attend to international issues as they struggle to understand curriculum in the present historical period. Understanding curriculum as international text, however, is not only important because of possible utilitarian applications to American curriculum problems [see Feinberg, 1993]. Studying international issues is intrinsically important. It must not be reduced to a scholarly version of American nationalism and neocolonialism. Nor must international studies be employed only to make domestic political points, as many have done to criticize American schooling. After all, a recent study finds that the American school system compares favorably with those of other nations (*San Francisco Chronicle*, 1993). As Westbury has shown, international comparisons are very difficult to make. Our simple hope is that the preceding sketches of both national systems and contemporary international discourses function as an invitation to students to explore the emerging literature in international curriculum studies and to pursue this area as an integral aspect of their undergraduate and graduate studies in curriculum.

SECTION IV
CONCLUSION: POSTSCRIPT

Chapter 15

Understanding Curriculum: A Postscript for the Next Generation

The field is no longer moribund; the field is no longer arrested. There is turbulence now.
(William F. Pinar & Janet L. Miller, 1982, p. 222)

The mood is invitation, and humbleness, and deep search, first, for the germ of life in oneself and, then, in [humankind].
(Ross L. Mooney, 1967b, p. 211)

An awareness of and sensitivity toward many environments–physical, psychological, social, and spiritual–are integral parts of postmodern proposals which inform . . . curriculum.
(Patrick Slattery, 1989, p. 156)

The time is certainly right for curriculum change. So in an era of crisis and complaint, we are cautiously optimistic and hopeful.
(William E. Doll, Jr., 1983c, p. 109)

The next century is ours.
(Jacques Daignault, 1992a, p.196)

I
Introduction

You're back. It has been a long journey, we realize, these past fourteen chapters. You were introduced to many, and sometimes complex, ideas. You heard a very large number of individuals speaking in their own voices. These ideas and voices required you to shift your ground many, many times, so that you could appreciate what these ideas were about, what these voices were saying, and why. And you thought curriculum was what the district office required you to teach, or what the state education department published in scope and sequence guides, or, if you are yet to teach, a list of books you were to read. As you know now, curriculum incorporates those literal and institutional meanings, but it is by no means limited to them. What you know now is that curriculum is a highly symbolic concept. It is what the older generation chooses to tell the younger generation. So understood, curriculum is intensely historical, political, racial, gendered, phenomenological, autobiographical, aesthetic, theological, and international. Curriculum becomes the site on which the generations struggle to define themselves and the world.

Curriculum is a extraordinarily complicated conversation. Curriculum as institutional text is a formalized and abstract version of conversation, a term we usually use to refer to those open-ended, highly personal, and interest-driven events in which persons encounter each other. That curriculum has become so formalized and distant from the everyday sense of conversation is a profound indication of its institutionalization and its bureaucratization. Instead of employing others' conversations to enrich our own, we "instruct" students to participate in others'—i.e. textbook authors'—conversations, employing others' terms to others' ends. Such social alienation is an inevitable consequence of curriculum identified with the academic disciplines as they themselves have been institutionalized and bureaucratized over the past one hundred years. Over the past twenty years the American curriculum field has attempted to "take back" curriculum from the bureaucrats, to make the curriculum field itself a conversation, and in so doing, work to understand curriculum. We invite you to participate in that conversation.

Without wishing to pre-empt the aims of your instructor who may have assigned this textbook, we appealed to you directly in chapter one not to regard this textbook as a catechism to be memorized and recited. We appealed to you to regard this textbook as the field appears to be suggesting that we—teachers and students—regard the school curriculum: as a provocation to reflect on and to think critically about ourselves, our families, our society. The point of the school curriculum is not to succeed in making us specialists in the academic disciplines. The point of school curriculum is not to produce accomplished test-takers, so that American scores on standardized tests compare favorably to Japanese or German scores. The point of the school curriculum is not to produce efficient and docile employees for business. The point of the school curriculum is to goad us into caring for ourselves and our fellow human beings, to help us think and act with intelligence, sensitivity, and courage in both the public sphere—as citizens aspiring to establish a democratic society—and in the private sphere, as individuals committed to other individuals. As feminist theory has shown, the two spheres are distinguishable in concept only. Once we shift the point of the curriculum away from the institutional, economic, and political goals of others, once we "take it back" for ourselves, we realize we must explore curriculum as a historical event itself. That is, as soon as we take hold of the curriculum as an opportunity for ourselves, as citizens, as persons, we realize that curriculum changes as we reflect on it, engage in its study, and act in response to it, toward the realization of our ideals and dreams. Curriculum ceases to be a thing, and it is more than a process. It becomes a verb, an action, a social practice, a private meaning, and a public hope. Curriculum is not just the site of our labor, it becomes the product of our labor, changing as we are changed by it.

This has been a backward-looking book in one sense. We wanted that. We wanted to link the field that exists now with the field that existed then. The curriculum field has been suffering a kind of identity crisis, and we wanted to help resolve that, by pointing to the continuities, as well as discontinuities, between the traditional and reconceptualized field. We hope we have, however modestly, succeeded. We hope that you, the student, can see how the complex, sometimes highly theoretical field that exists now, evolved out of a more "practical" and bureaucratic field that existed until just twenty years ago. We also hope that by emphasizing the history of the field, and the history of the contemporary discourses, that you have come to appreciate that all fields of study have histories, all evolve, all suffer "paradigm" breaks, and all proceed in directions they might not have, had those who devoted their careers to these fields not existed. We hope you realize, then, that the American curriculum field is not a thing; it is not finished. Rather, the curriculum field, like other academic disciplines, is a conversation. And we hope you will consider joining it. In summary terms, what can we say about that conversation today?

II
The Curriculum Field Today:
Problems and Possibilities

Few of us have the courage to follow our thoughts wherever they might lead. We all fear the dark at some level of our being.
(Philip W. Jackson, 1994, p. 24)

Eurocentric analysis is viewed as linear. Rooted in empiricism, rationalism, scientific method and positivism, its aim is prediction and control. . . . African epistemology, on the other hand, is circular . . . and seeks interpretation, expression, and understanding without preoccupation with verification.
(William H. Watkins, 1993, p. 331)

Such a language would be . . . one that grows in the middle.
(Ted Aoki, 1993, p. 99)

From paradigmatic unity to particularism. We have seen how the field has moved from a paradigmatic unity—the Tylerian rationale—to particularism—the various contemporary discourses. The situation today is particularistic and even balkanized, but not the bland eclecticism that emerged after the struggle between social efficiency and progressivism in the second and third decades of the twentieth century. This proliferation of discourses can be traced to the vacuum created by the collapse of the Tyler rationale. In this vacuum scholars went to other fields as sources of new theory. This move away from curriculum as institutional text must be termed an astonishing success. The dying patient on which Schwab, Huebner, and Pinar commented from 1969 to 1978 has been profoundly revived due to the transfusions of important ideas from other fields. Yet, now that the patient is revived, there is another problem. How can we take the patient off the IV? That is, how do we encourage autonomy and self-sufficiency, which is not to say a new isolationism or self-importance. To change images, like a strong economy, the field must import—as well as export—important ideas to maintain dynamism. In the 1970s, in order to "jumpstart" the economy of curriculum studies, ideas were imported from European fields. Now that the economy is thriving, it is time to begin to generate domestic ideas, without becoming protectionist. Indeed, it is clear that ideas from curriculum are being exported to other fields, including (and the following list is suggestive not comprehensive) early childhood education (Jardine, 1988a; Swadener & Kessler, 1991; Kessler, 1991; Charlesworth, et al., in press), educational administration (Giroux, 1992b; Maxcy, 1991), science education (Jacknicke & Rowell, 1984; Good, 1992; Roscoe & Jacknicke, 1993), mathematics education (Frankenstein, 1983; Gordon, 1983), at-risk students (Donmoyer & Kos, 1993), special education (Warner, 1991, 1992; Szepkouski, 1993), teacher education (Giroux & McLaren, 1986; Gordon, 1986; Beyer, 1989, Grumet, 1989b; Pinar, 1989; Shaker & Kridel, 1989; Schubert, 1989b; Beyer, Feinberg, Pagano, & Whitson, 1989; Block, 1993), curriculum evaluation (Eisner, 1985a, 1985b, 1991a), English education (Giroux, 1992c; Hurlbert & Totten, 1992), social studies education (Stanley, 1992b), language education (Edelsky, 1991; Walsh, 1991), reading (Block, forthcoming; Grumet, 1988a, 1988b; Hunsberger, 1988, 1992), higher education (Tierney, 1993a), and teacher development (Hargreaves & Fullan, 1992), as well as to humanities disciplines such as cultural studies (Grossberg, 1993; Edgerton, 1992; Giroux & McLaren, 1993) and literary theory (Leitch, 1992; see especially chapter 8 which reviews the history of the Centre for Contemporary Cultural Studies at the University of Birmingham).

Distance from the school. The current interest in becoming closer to practitioners may be an indication just how far apart from practice (i.e. the procedural) we have moved. Indeed, in the 1970s, when Pinar first called for the field to distance itself from the school and from teachers, he was in one sense merely acknowledging what he observed to be the case—that education professors were distant from teachers. In general, it was clear in the 1970s that teachers were skeptical of education professors. The expert-client relationship characteristic of the traditional field had failed. For many, undergraduate preservice teacher courses seemed intellectually lightweight at best—silly and arrogant at worse. True, Pinar observed that a minority of graduate courses were tolerable to students, and a fewer number still were considered exciting. But what was clear, even in the 1970s, was that most teachers did not regard us as friends, and certainly not as experts. Suggesting that the field move away from the school as the institution was merely acknowledging what was the case.

If there was ever a "paradise lost" of teacher-professor relations (during the first decades of this century?), no doubt it expressed a client-expert relationship. Not until we reconceive our role as strictly consultants and collaborators, as many working in the area of teacher development today are laboring to do, can this inequality and concomitant alienating consequences of distrust and misunderstanding be lessened. John Dewey wanted "experts" consigned to an "advisory role," as democratic education would require. Further, Dewey insisted that expertise must be subordinated to "fully participatory, deliberative, democratic politics" (Westbrook, 1991, p. 188), recalling the emphasis upon "deliberation" the Schwabian wing of the contemporary field has emphasized.

If teachers have been skeptical of the contributions education professors might make to school improvement, colleagues in arts and sciences, many politicians, and even the general public have been, at times, downright contemptuous. No matter that we education professors were even less responsible for the crisis in the schools than teachers themselves. Just as the students' achievement (or lack thereof) cannot be completely attributable to public school teachers, the failure of teachers cannot be laid entirely at the feet of university and college teacher educators. None of us teachers—at any level—is primarily responsible for how our students turn out; the process of education, interwoven as it is with family, history, and culture, is much too complicated to follow in a linear-causal fashion from the efforts of any one group. Furthermore, as Philip Wexler has suggested, identity formation in a "semiotic society" may occur largely outside school where the popular culture is imagistic, not print-based, as in schools. If Wexler is right, and education in an authentic sense now occurs outside school, and only incidentally inside, then the responsibility of educators is commensurately reduced further.

In the university. Where does this leave curriculum theorists? We are left in the university, a place of scholarship and teaching, where, instead of wringing our hands over lost influence in the schools and rejection by teachers and policymakers, we might commit ourselves to understanding what curriculum is, has been, and might be. It bears repeating that this does not mean fleeing from "practice," turning our backs on teachers, pretending to be like arts and sciences professors, as many educational foundations professors have pretended in the past. We curriculum theorists must still offer friendship and colleagueship to teachers; we must offer teachers our expertise as they request (and as circumstances permit it to be offered and to be accepted). We can offer politicians and policymakers that expertise but we ought not be surprised and certainly not deflated when they decline to employ it. After all, their interests in the schools are not necessarily educational, rather political and economic. We curriculum theorists must be firm that we are not responsible for the ills of public schools, especially given that our advice regarding how they can be improved, indeed transformed, has been and is so consistently ignored. Just as the field of economics is not to blame for the ills of the American economic system, or just as the field of political science is not responsible for the sorry state of the American political system, the field of curriculum is not primarily responsible for the condition of the schools. Or, as Bruce Kimball (1986), asks in regard to the liability of teacher education programs: "[what if] departments of art or music . . . were held responsible for the aesthetic sensibilities of American popular culture?" (p. 21). That is not to say we university teachers have not had a hand in the present dilemma, via teacher education (both pre- and in-service), but hardly our whole bodies.

In order to advance. Further, in our insistence that we must fix the schools (which cannot be fixed in any case, given present political and economic conditions and given that politicians will not let us try), an insistence that will only function to devalue our stock further, we undermine the only way we might develop the sophisticated understanding which—should the school establishment and politicians ever attend to our advice—might indeed help in significant ways. Such understanding must be grounded in educational experience (not necessarily schooling), but it must not remain there. Like physics or art, curriculum as a field cannot progress unless some segment of the field explores phenomena and ideas that perhaps few will comprehend and appreciate, certainly not at first and perhaps never. Our field will not progress beyond a certain primitive point unless we support a sector of theory—such as the work of Jacques Daignault—that perhaps most in the field cannot understand initially. Imagine physics progressing if scholars in that discipline were limited to work which beginning students readily understood. Imagine art progressing unless forms of painting and dance were supported which, initially, very few could appreciate. In any field there must be a sector of advanced work; otherwise, a field cannot advance.

Of course, the theoretical wing of a field must not pretend that its work is inherently superior to that which is institutional (or "applied," if we take the theory-practice relationship on a conventional continuum), but neither should the theory wing of a field be subjected to anti-intellectual tirades about "making a difference" in the schools or "improving practice" [see, for instance, Sears, 1992b]. The theoretical wing of the field must not be ignored, as several synoptic textbooks continue to do. For books claiming to be surveys of the field to ignore the theory wing—or significant segments of it—is simple irresponsibility. If there were a professional society of curricularists, authors of such books would be expelled. Obviously, this is not to say books must not be written which reject particular theoretical positions, only those which ignore them.

The near-term future. How should the field progress in the near term? We would answer, "pretty much as it is." That faction of the field dealing with curriculum as institutional text is probably still too large, but conditions will continue which will reduce its size. One hopes it may never disappear altogether. Curriculum theory must not be collapsed into discourse. To understand educational experience requires being in the political, racial, aesthetic, spiritual, gendered, global, and phenomenological world. There must continue some extension toward schools as institutions as they are, as thankless and sisyphus-like this work often seems. However, the next generation of curriculum scholarship might move away from its sources in "parent" disciplines, such as phenomenology and poststructuralism, and away from the school, toward exploration of concepts indigenous to curriculum, independent of institutional agendas.

Toward autonomy. However, the next generation's movement away from present sources to develop conceptual and methodological autonomy must not be in order to mimic the other disciplines, which, after all, regularly borrow from each other. Nor must a move toward autonomy be made simply in order to be considered a "mature" discipline, as such a title would be merely honorific. Rather, the field will move toward conceptual and methodological autonomy because staying near our sources pulls us toward a posture of "application" or "implications for curriculum." To understand curriculum further we must capture its internal dynamics and moments, i.e. its movements (flashes, raptures, intensities) of educational experience, so that curriculum does not appear to reside apart from the ideas which elucidate it. Such work does not imply a rejection of ideas conceived in other disciplines; it means that such work will not proceed in a linear causal manner from source to application. Rather, our work with sources will mirror the mediations and transformations that characterize educational experience.

Contemporary discourses transitional. Much of the work reported in this textbook, we can say, exhibits, in the context of this discussion of the field's next step, a transitional character. Having rejected the narrow instrumentalism of the Tyler period, the field has moved toward theory, and intelligently enough, employed some of the most current and sophisticated theory available at the time, ideas from social theory, phenomenology, feminist theory, and so on. This phase is not played out yet, but perhaps nearly so, as we see a proliferation of studies that are in their conceptual structure, similar, and close to their sources, like pressure building on a fault line. A "leap" or shift in conceptual "plates" may be forthcoming, when not only themes but conceptual structures will change, and we think it is possible that this "hybrid" theory will come, to change images, through cross-fertilization.

Several sectors of curriculum scholarship reported here exhibit porous borders already. For instance, feminist theorists would insist their work is profoundly political, and prominent political scholars have been moving rapidly away from class into race and gender. Their current boundaries result from being close to the parent disciplines which themselves are boundaried. As well, a certain loyalty to the parent discipline is a likely concomitant to immature appropriations of them. The transitional character of these sectors as well as the coming hybridization is implied by the current breakdown of borders associated with the sectors we have reported here, although this is still generally in an early stage. For instance, Giroux's notion of bordercrossings (1992a) might apply here, in one sense, that is, of moving easily across borders that before seemed to employ customs agents. For true hybridization to occur, however, the identity of the traveler must fuse with those with whom he or she travels and visits.

Giroux's work may further illustrate this point. He can be said to have moved from a nearly exclusive political emphasis to concerns for curriculum as racial and gendered text, but these later aspects seem to be, in the context of his opus, "add-ons." That is, the basic theses do not seem to have changed much from the "language of possibility," struggling for a more democratic public sphere, resistance to the status quo, and so on. Giroux seems to have "added on" concerns for race, gender, and postmodernism in his most recent writing, leaving intact his core theme of "critical pedagogy." We make this observation not as a criticism of Giroux—both his importance to the field and his achievement are indisputable—but to offer a specific example of how the work of Giroux's generation, which is to say, the work which functioned to reconceptualize the field in the 1970s, may not take us to the next generation of scholarship. While Giroux's generation may have taken the field through the violence of a paradigm shift, a contribution of which those of us in that generation might feel justifiably proud, we will not, most likely, be the ones to take the field to the next step. That next step probably will not constitute another paradigm shift, but a maturing conceptually and methodologically toward independence and autonomy, and away from the parent disciplines.

One example of this next stage might be hinted at by thinking about theory and ethnography. For many mainstream scholars theory now seems to some to be separated from schools. Ethnography, fashionable even among mainstream scholars in the early 1990s, claims to describe what occurs in schools. For these mainstream scholars, then, theory is considered to be stripped of practice, but ethnography seems stripped of theory. Many of us realize that this is not true, but there is on the surface a commonsense appeal to this binary distinction. Our point here is that in the next stage of the field's development we might see theory which is very much explicit in depictions of school life, and we might see explicit depictions of school life in theory. Wexler's (1992) *Becoming Somebody* [see chapter 13] and the work of Margo Figgins [see chapter 11; also Ebeling, 1992] are current examples of possible moves in this direction.

Philip Jackson, as we saw in chapter 1, presents the field as currently moving in two directions, one pointing toward practitioners and the other pointing away. It is not an either/or choice, of course. The fact is that the contemporary field is moving in both directions simultaneously, as this text-book makes clear. As we suggested earlier, the move closer to practitioners may be compensatory, but it is important and it is to be supported. In the next generation of work it may be merged with some strands of work in the theory wing. In a certain sense, this movement within the contemporary field represents a "second wave" (Pinar, 1988f, p. 13) of Reconceptualization, however modest its program of action and intervention.

History important. The current and growing emphasis upon the history of the field is important; we hope it will continue and intensify. Recent publications by curriculum historians such as Craig Kridel (1989), Herbert Kliebard

(1986, 1992a), Larry Cuban (1984/1993), Daniel and Laurel Tanner (1990), Daniel Tanner (1991), Ivor Goodson (1983), and O. L. Davis (1976, 1986) highlight this important emphasis in the contemporary field. Organizations such as the Society for the Study of Curriculum History (Kridel & Tanner, 1987) perform a significant service in institutionalizing this interest. Departments of Curriculum and Instruction ought to hire at least one historian, in addition to several theoreticians, to join with those whose work is close to schools. An American Curriculum Studies Association might be formed to monitor the professional interests of the field so that the field receives appropriate institutional support for curriculum history and theory.

The institutional sector recedes. To understand curriculum comprehensively requires understanding curriculum as institutional text. Because the topics and functions of this sector of the field tended to be opponents in the 1970s decade of struggle for Reconceptualization, it has been somewhat difficult to write completely impartially about these areas. It is quite important here to distinguish between our own research programs and theoretical commitments, and what the field is saying, and where we think the field ought to move. First, we suspect there will always be an institutional sector of the field, partly, as Goodlad and Su (1992) suggest, because the categories of curriculum development, design, and evaluation are time-honored. Unlike Goodlad and Su, however, clearly we do not see a simple reassertion of the traditional wing in the aftermath of the Reconceptualization. Curriculum as institutional text is a smaller "nation" than before; it has ceded considerable territory to the contemporary discourses, as the simple distribution of pages in this textbook makes clear.

There has been a second change as well in the effort to understand curriculum institutionally. To a striking extent, the very nature of this sector has changed, and changed in ways sometimes closely consonant and sometimes identical with the themes and programs of the reconceptualized field. For instance, Elliot Eisner has advanced a rationale for curriculum evaluation remarkably free of previous schemes' bureaucratic and pseudo-scientific elements. The notions of "educational criticism" and "connoisseurship," as he himself acknowledges, rest comfortably in the Deweyan and Schwabian traditions, intersecting but diverging discourses. Also indicative of this change is the groundbreaking work of Lee Shulman, as well as the work of F. Michael Connelly and D. Jean Clandinin, which takes seriously the complex uses of knowledge by both teachers and students, and suggests strategies for acknowledging and supporting these in curricular and school practice generally.

Overlapping efforts. The next stage of the field, as we have suggested, will require that scholars not only read their own discourses, including new source material for that discourse, but material outside their sector as well. The careful reader of this textbook will have noticed overlapping ideas in several discourses. For instance, within the autobiographical/biographical sector, efforts to develop "personal practical knowledge," "teacher lore," and "collaborative autobiography" overlap. Hermeneutics is significant to several sectors of curriculum research, especially the phenomenological and theological (Pinar & McKnight, in press). Illustrative of overlapping across discourses might be Shulman's notion of "pedagogical content knowledge," Daignault's "passage," and Grumet's "middle way." Poststructuralism may function like a virus for political scholarship, undermining its present structure and function. Racial scholarship may well become an integrative sector in which political, feminist, phenomenological, poststructuralist, aesthetic, theological, and international elements are recombined and synthesized into a sophisticated, autonomous theory of curriculum. The point here is to build on what has been done already. At this point in the field's development we risk balkanization, building nearly identical fiefdoms which do not contribute to a "common faith" or to movement in the field as a whole. Perhaps we need a "United Nations" of scholarship sectors to formalize dialogue across discourse borders.

III
What Is the Field Saying?

The outbreak of crime and violence is a symptom of lives not lived deeply enough. . . . At the end of the twentieth century we are in a boundary situation. We can transform ourselves, or not.
(Mary Aswell Doll, 1994, p. 15)

Emancipatory pedagogy is the freeing of one's mind to explore the essence and influence of the African-American race through the world, and the ability to pass on that information as a foundation upon which to build.
(Beverly M. Gordon, 1993, p. 278)

Liberatory education can help us create a *dialogue across differences.*
(Elizabeth Ellsworth, 1990a, p. 12)

It is not possible to answer this question in summary fashion. To attempt it is to risk composing a "masternarrative," creating the illusion that we, or any observer, stands apart from the field, and can distill the complex discourses we have reported into a single narrative. Theory is not such a narrative. In the reconceived field, theory is intended to undermine such pretensions to definitiveness and universality. Bowers is right when he observes: "In the hands of liberal-technicist educators, theory has become the talisman for centralizing authority over the decision-making process and increasing the efficiency of control and predictability. We all are quite clear that an 'objective' position is in principle impossible" (Bowers, 1984, pp. 14-15). With this acknowledgement of our "positionedness," we think it is possible to make a very general statement regarding what the reconceptualized field of curriculum might be saying.

No longer arrested. The place to begin a summary statement is that the field is no longer arrested. When that allegation was made—first by Schwab in

1969, then by Huebner in 1975, and by Pinar in 1978 that the field was moribund and arrested, respectively—the traditional field was in place. However, the Tylerian paradigm was collapsing, from both internal difficulties which Kliebard, Huebner, Eisner, Macdonald, and others made clear in the 1960s and 1970s, and by external developments, such as the National Curriculum Reform Movement of the 1960s, as well as the changing political terrain of schools and departments of education, as we described in chapters 3 and 4. The fact that a generation of curriculum professors remained in place whose careers were invested in a paradigm that had collapsed made for a crisis in the field. Naturally, this generation was not about to say, "Oh, it's over, is it? Okay. Here, take the microphone." Nor did we rebels—would-be revolutionaries—ask for the microphone politely. As perhaps in any paradigm shift, emotions intensified and overstatements were made, all around, as chapter 4 reminds us.

A relatively rapid shift. Despite these excesses, the field made a relatively rapid reconceptualization [10 years approximately is our estimate for the shift to have occurred], and as this textbook indicates, the reputations of the major scholars associated with the too-broad [see Hlebowitsh, 1992] concept of "traditionalists" remain in tact. Even Tyler himself, who has not always been treated completely fairly, remains an enormous figure, whose shadow is very much cast still today. Of course, the field is today hardly "one happy family." Even during periods of so-called "normal science," when a paradigm is securely in place and faces no insurmountable challenges from within or destabilizing circumstances externally, differences in viewpoint bring tensions and even acrimonious disputes, as the controversies in the political sector [chapter 5] or the theological sector [see chapter 12], for example, indicate. Other disputes occur across discourse borders, as feminist critiques of political and poststructuralist scholarship illustrate. Other sectors seem relatively free of significant criticism, either internally or externally, as the phenomenological movement indicates. There are signs that the phenomenological movement is extending beyond its own borders to influence scholarship in other sectors, for instance, Aoki's work with teacher voice [see chapter 13], Carson's phenomenological revision of curriculum implementation [see chapter 8], his political efforts to promote peace education [see chapter 5], and his interest in international and global education [see chapter 14]. The theological and international sectors too often tend to be ignored. So, what does this somewhat smooth although dynamic situation tell us, very generally speaking?

We do not wish to homogenize the distinctiveness of the various individual discourses. For example, political scholars should press toward activism. Yet, while respecting tendencies toward "extremism" in individual discourses, we must realize that no one discourse offers final answers to curriculum questions. We may wish a comprehensive theory of curriculum, but it cannot pretend to be a "totalizing" one. We can avoid totalization by realizing that such a comprehensive theory is, to borrow McCarthy's (1990) term, nonsynchronous, not merely additive, i.e, two parts political, two parts race, one part theology. Rather, we might appreciate that according to time, place, and voice—which include our individual institutional situations—we enact various elements of a comprehensive point of view, we become infused by them as it were, and in Deweyan fashion, move our practical situations forward. Unlike Lasch (1991), we believe progress is possible, despite the often illusory nature of progress, its contentiousness, persisting ethical, moral, and political dilemmas associated with the concept, and its technological dangers. We believe in—and accept theological grounding for—a moral view of humankind that asserts the primacy of human study, teaching, and understanding.

We now understand the curriculum to be even more complex than our predecessors understood it to be, certainly much more complicated than most politicians and many colleagues in arts and sciences realize. In this respect, we are in the odd position of knowing much more than other groups who act as stakeholders in the curriculum, but, in real political terms, we are the least politically powerful group to be able to act on that knowledge. Perhaps that is one price of understanding, although one would hope not, for it is those working in educational institutions who suffer most as a result.

Textbooks are the beginning. It is an understatement to observe that curriculum is not simply those materials made by experts or by textbook writers; textbooks are the beginning. That second clause might sound flippant, perhaps arrogant. Of course, what is recorded as human knowledge in books and on computer discs is of unspeakable importance. That is not in question here. What is in question is what the reconceived field has studied: what has been made, what is made, what can be made, what might be made of human knowledge in our time, for our ends, given the great political, racial, aesthetic, and gender issues of our day? There is no devaluation of the "tradition" when we use the simple and bureaucratic word "textbooks." Tradition and textbooks are the ground against which, in honor of which, all curriculum study can be said to occur and proceed. It is we who live now, and those coming to live after us, who become the figure in this gestalt. The curriculum question becomes: what do we make of this knowledge, which is to say, what do we make of the world, what do we make of ourselves?

Movement. From different traditions toward different ends each of the contemporary discourses points to an understanding of curriculum in terms of movement, even, we might say, velocity, knowledge prompting questioning that moves the student (a broad category to include the teacher and scholar as well as the student) from one "location" to another, a location we hope as educators is more intellectually complicated, more developmentally mature, more passionate and compassionate. This movement may be like skating on the frozen surface of facts, generalizations, theories, but it may also create the sense of intellectual space being extended, enlarged, and multiplied so that intelligence itself may be mulitiplied as well as "sharpened." In this view, curriculum is not only particles moving through space, but it is the space in which the particles move, and the velocity and intensity of movements. The passages are intellectual and bodily, and they are relational, gendered, racial, political, and phenomenological. Some would term such movement cosmological (Oliver & Gershman, 1989). Velocity and intensity decrease and cosmology becomes obscure when curriculum becomes encrusted with ideology, with politics, with the bureaucratism of institutions so that the "free play of the signifier," that is, the free movement of ideas, is reduced. To the extent the curriculum reproduces or resists a status quo, it is "lifted out" of its passages, and bores crevices in the mind, creating ruts and rituals that decrease movement, and produce inauthentic knowing and static, bureaucratic knowledge. Similarly, teaching for tests subverts the movement of curriculum, recapitulating the recitation of the nineteenth century faculty psychology and classical curriculum.

This is not to say that velocity and intensity imply an anarchy of teaching and learning, although "chaos" as a concept in curriculum has achieved legitimacy (Doll, W., 1993a). It does suggest, however, that the organizing designs of the curriculum are only superficially in the books we read and the lectures we give and the small group discussions in which we participate. The organization of curriculum occurs in the lives of educators and students, involving political, racial, gendered, phenomenological, autobiographical, aesthetic, theological, international configurations as well as institutional ones. School curricula are discursive formations and configurations of facts, feelings, etc., which reflect the temporality, historicity, and provisionality of knowledge. Curriculum designs and organizations are a little like kaleidoscopic configurations of what we know, traces of what we have forgotten and suppressed, distributed through the echoes and shadows of life history, popular culture, and laced with desire. Put another way, Bowers (1984) has observed:

> Existential choice is thus expanded in proportion to the complexity of the symbolic code the individual acquires. A complex symbolic world provides the means for choosing among different interpretational schemes, as well as imagining future possibilities that would result from different scenarios. . . . What cannot be imagined cannot be chosen. (p. 47)

Then and now. Like Dewey, Bode (1927) spoke about the psychological (as opposed to logical) organization of subject matter. Bode made a compelling if "folksy" (Bullough, Jr., 1981, p. 4) defense of Deweyan progressivism. These were the heydays—the late 1920s and the 1930s—of curriculum construction. In his introduction to the 1927 edition of Bode's *Modern Educational Theories*, Bagley spoke of the receptiveness of schools to professional, presumably, university-originated ideas of curriculum making. The questions he asked are still, to a degree, questions regarding what knowledge is of the most worth, but he located the answers in the organization of subject matter, the construction of curriculum. That was taken-for-granted. There was opportunity on a grand, public scale.

Today the location of opportunity is different. There is little construction to do on the scale and in the senses that Dewey, Bol Bode argued over. Today public curriculum construction is located in multinational textbook conglomerates, in state textbook adoption committees, in district or ministry curriculum guidelines. The era of local construction of curriculum materials, certainly at the secondary level, is over. Where curriculum can be constructed now is in the "lived space" of the classroom, in the lived experience of students and teachers. In such space and in such experience, the knowing teacher and student can find passages from what is given (indeed, mandated) to the what might be, "a middle way" between strict adherence to the facts and to participation in flights of fancy, a "midpoint" between the idiosyncrasy and spontaneity of chaos and intimacy, and the predictable formalism of bureaucratic officialdom. Passages, middle ways, and midpoints can be discussed via the "pedagogical content knowledge" of a self-knowing teacher, a teacher who knows that her or his pedagogical obligation is not to deliver someone else's mail (not a little of it "junk" mail at that), but, with his or her students, to compose our own correspondence (cf. Figgins & Pinar, 1993) regarding the knowledge the textbook publishers and district curriculum guidelines have decreed.

The return of Dwayne E. Huebner. Another perspective on the historical shifts in the field became available in a recent and important paper by Dwayne E. Huebner (1993; see chapters 3 and 4.) More than fifteen years after leaving Teachers College, Columbia University and the curriculum field for the Divinity School at Yale University and the field of religious education, a 70-year old Dwayne Huebner returned to curriculum theory by composing a paper focused on the spiritual in curriculum. Huebner's paper was in response to an invitation to speak in New Orleans to a seminar on spirituality and curriculum, sponsored by three near-by universities, organized by William E. Doll, Jr. In a powerful reading, Huebner returned to many of the themes that had preoccupied him—and the field—over a life-span. Huebner appreciates that the problem of the field remains one of language (Huebner, 1966b; see chapters 3, 4, 8, and 11):

> How can one talk about education, specifically, curriculum, and also talk about the spiritual? The problem is one of language. . . . Thanks to Macdonald, Pinar, Apple, and a variety of other curriculum writers who stand on their shoulders, we no longer have the horrendous hegemony of technical language (drawing primarily on learning theory and ends/means structures) usurping discussion of education. (p. 1)

Huebner acknowledges that, while not dominant in the scholarly field, technical language remains embedded in the schools, i.e. in the talk of schoolpeople. To some extent he blames the field he left for the present predicament of educators, lost in the technical, pseudo-scientific language of bureaucratic legitimation which erases not only the spiritual but the imagination as well. In a "we" that includes educators and especially educational psychologists, he reminded us that: "We have forgotten or suppressed that imagination is a foundation of our givens" (1993, p. 1). Evoking a notion of educational journey that he had employed over two decades ago (1975a), he dismissed once again the language of educational psychology, and especially that of learning theory: "'Learning' is a trivial way of speaking of the journey of the self" (p. 4). It is this pseudo-scientific and profoundly distorting language that had led Huebner to become skeptical of mainstream research: "Several years later I began to question the educator's dependency on the research enterprise" (p. 1). In part, it is the pretense of certainty of the social and behavioral sciences fields that is so reprehensible. It is awareness that there is a "beyond" to our knowledge that is the beginning of the theological: "It is a 'moreness' that takes us by surprise when we are at the edge and end of our knowing" (p. 2). What other damage has technical language done as he looks back at thirty years? In language which reminds us of Robert McClintock's strong essay on study published in that memorable 1971 issue of *Teachers College Record* [see chapter 4; also McClintock, 1971; Jennings, 1971] Huebner (1993) observed:

> Similarly, the significance of the word "study" has been destroyed. Students study to do what someone else requires, not for their own transformation, a way of "working" on their own journey, or their struggle with spirit, the otherness beyond them. Just as therapy is work—hard work—but important for the loosening of old binds and discovering the new self; so too should education as study be seen as a form of that kind of work. (p. 8)

From students and study, Huebner moves to teachers and teaching. Sounding not only theological but phenomenological (cf. Aoki 1992a, 199b; Aoki & Shamsher, 1993), Huebner (1993) reminded the audience that: "teaching is a vocation. . . . A vocation is a call" (p. 8). Indeed, the vocation of teaching, he continued, involves three aspects: "Three voices call, or three demands are made on the teacher. Hence the life that is teaching is inherently a conflicted way of living. The teacher is called by the students, by the content, and by the institution within which the teacher lives. . . . Spiritual warfare is inherent in all vocations" (1993, p. 9). Given such complexity of this calling, Huebner (1993) understands that: "The pain of teachers, unable to respond to the call of some students, is often too much, and they seek relief by hardening their hearts" (p. 10). How can teachers respond to the demands of their profession? Huebner (1993) tells us:

> It is also quite clear to me, that it is futile to hope that teachers can be aware of the spiritual in education unless they maintain some form of spiritual discipline. This needs to be of two kinds. Given the inherent conflicts involved in teaching, and the inherent vulnerability of their vocation, teachers need to seek out communities of faith, love, and hope. . . . The second discipline is a disciplining of the mind, not in the sense of staying on top of all the educational research and literature, but in the sense of developing an imagination that has room for the spiritual, such that when you look out over the educational landscape you see not only what is there and recognize your call to respond with

love, truth and justice; but so you can also see the principalities and powers, the ideals and the spiritual possibilities hidden behind all of the forms and events that are taken for granted. (p. 11)

Here Huebner has pointed to the center of understanding curriculum, especially as theological text. He enables us to appreciate that finally our struggle to teach and to study with others and with God is precisely that: a call for labor, for discipline, sustained by faith, love, and hope. The effort to understand curriculum as theological text is not a separate specialized sector of scholarship; it is call to live with others morally and transcendentally: "The need is not to see moral and spiritual values as something outside the normal curriculum and school activity, but to probe deeper into the educational landscape to reveal how the spiritual and moral is being denied in everything" (Huebner, 1993, p. 11). In seeing how the moral is denied we glimpse how we might work toward its realization.

Dwayne E. Huebner returned to the curriculum field November 20, 1993, on the campus of Loyola University in New Orleans, but it was clear he had not left us. As our abbreviated and simplified reports of his work in this textbook make clear, he and a very few others—such as his friend and colleague James B. Macdonald—helped create the world we inhabit now and labor to recreate as educators and theoreticians. His generative influence has been evident in many discourses, including the political, the phenomenological, and the aesthetic as well as the theological. Huebner may have left the field partly in grief over what has happened in the schools, and partly because he was unable to find solace in the emerging scholarly field which his own work had made possible. His own journey has been remarkable, highly significant for an entire field of study. As he retires in spring 1994, Huebner remains one of the most important minds the field of curriculum has known.

Changed and still the same. In these ideas we see how the field has changed and how it has stayed the same. No longer are we asking and acting upon our answers to the fundamental curriculum question—what knowledge is of most worth?—by constructing curriculum materials. We answer the question via our own discursive "moves" with our students and with ourselves. These moves, the field is suggesting, are complicated, but they can be passages away from the curriculum as literal, as institutional, as officially decreed. These moves are political, racial, gendered, autobiographical, phenomenological, aesthetic, theological moves, deconstructed moves, and moves away from the provincialism of the United States of America toward global and international understanding. The reconceived field of curriculum understands that its raison d'etre is seeking answers to fundamental questions—including what knowledge is of most worth?—and, in this one specific sense, in the struggles of the 1970s the reconceptualists were reasserting a past that had been allowed to be forgotten. In seeking to answer these questions, curriculum development as a paradigmatic organizing concept and activity has been largely abandoned. The field still seeks to befriend its constituency in the schools and, to a lesser extent, in the government, but having been largely abandoned by the latter, segments of the field have redoubled their efforts toward the former, in programs called "teacher lore," "personal practical knowledge," and "collaborative autobiography." As well, the field has created a theoretical wing to ensure that it does not again collapse on the social surface of existing bureaucratic institutions, as it did in the triumph of Bobbitt and Tyler that became the traditional field.

IV
Conclusion

> The prism hangs in my study window, swaying slighting with the spring breeze. It turns, and I watch new patterns emerge in the crystal planes as blooming forsythia meld into green branches. I see that I cannot turn the prism for others in a complete or constant manner, just as I cannot possibly view all the patterned colors detailed by its movement. I struggle with the story of my own teaching, knowing that this is only half the telling and that even this half is refracting only scenes, slight segments of the process of teaching and thinking about curriculum. Still, some students, as they leave our class, speak of never being able to think about curriculum in quite the same ways again.
>
> (Janet L. Miller, 1990b, p. 95)

> Theory is the result of our desire to create a world we can understand.
>
> (Elliot W. Eisner, 1985c, p. 29)

We have portrayed the field as it is today, a field just recently reconceptualized, animated, filled with a thousand voices. It is a vital and energetic field, not one smooth and neatly subdivided as, for instance, academic psychology. As William A. Reid (1992) writes, reflecting on the shift in the 1970s: "Yet, fifteen years on, there still seems to be little agreement about what the 'reconceived' field should be like" (p. 193). That is true. There remains little agreement. Cherryholmes (1988a) thinks there will not be, that the character of curriculum is controversy. However, we do not regard that as a terrible problem.

A more serious problem, we believe, is the apparent inability of the various sectors to speak to each other, to move into an independent "middle" from their various "corner" positions, and to develop a literature on curriculum at some distance from sources in other disciplines. These issues of disciplinary sources and the field's autonomy are not new. Fifteen years ago Pinar wrote:

> What is crucial for reconceptualists . . . is to remember that these [European] traditions are sources for the Reconceptualization. We must use their insights to create our own. We are Americans not Europeans; we are curricularists not philosophers or psychoanalysts. We must avoid the temptation to uproot insights from these traditions and "apply" them to the educational issues of our time. Such work is by definition derivative and distorting, involving as it does reduction of complex issues to conceptual systems created in other times, on other soil, for other purposes. To become scholars of phenomenology or of Marxist theory first and curricularists second is to betray our historical calling.

These origins are important; I do not demean them. But they are origins only, and we must create our own intellectual and practical discipline, independent of its sources, sensitive and responsible to our present. (1979a, pp. 97-98)

Being sensitive and responsible to our present is one typification of the educator's challenge, inviting us to do the order of educational labor laid out by each of the contemporary discourses. In the accomplishments that understanding such work may bring, we move toward independence. Pinar wrote:

> We must take seriously our responsibility to face the educational issues of our time, both in their surface forms as well as in their deeper theoretical significance, a significance we must identify. This means being willing to speak in our own voices, with words which while clearly related to established theoretical traditions, strictly speaking belong to no one discipline. Almost as a kind of by-product we must be willing to attempt what our predecessors and contemporaries may have wished but never achieved. We must make curriculum studies . . . into an autonomous discipline, with its own distinctive research methods and theoretical emphases. Of course, these methods and emphases will bear significant relation to the traditions from which they originated. However, they will not be identical or reducible to them. (1979a, p. 99)

In remaining loyal to our sources, the contemporary reconceptualized field may be placed in danger of being torn apart by tendencies toward "particularism" or "localisms" in the contemporary discourses, not unlike the nationalisms which we have seen in world politics in the early 1990s. The field is threatened by being taken too far to the left by the Marxists; by focusing too narrowly on gender by certain feminist theorists; by focusing too narrowly on phenomenological pedagogy by phenomenologists; by focusing too righteously on the Western Judeo-Christian contribution by theological scholars; by focusing too preciously on art by those who understand curriculum as aesthetic text, and too exclusively on life history by the autobiographers. What the next generation might explore is a political phenomenological understanding of curriculum, influenced by gender analysis, autobiographical theory, situated internationally in a multiracial global village. This is not to suggest a bland eclecticism, i.e. understanding curriculum as political, racial, etc. etc. etc. The various dimensions of curriculum must be interrelated non-synchronously rather than as parallel aspects (McCarthy, 1990; see chapter 6).

Believing that "curriculum is essentially public and institutional in character" (p. 172), William Reid (1992) asks: "Could curriculum inquiry reintegrate the new-found humanism of the reconceptualists with the insistence on the public nature of curriculum as subject matter which we find in the tradition which they sought to replace?" (p. 174). We believe that the answer the field makes to Reid's question is yes, a qualified yes. We cannot share without modification Reid's insistence that "curriculum is intrinsically and historically an institutional conception" (p. 174). Historically yes; intrinsically no. We see work—autobiography, for instance—that is not identified with institutional interests. We do agree with Reid (1992) that "those interested in curriculum inquiry should, in the 1990s, be taking stock both of what the work of the last 20 years has achieved, and what it has failed to achieve. The limitations of 'traditional' approaches has been exposed" (p. 177). We disagree that "on the other hand, we have not, as yet, equipped ourselves with criteria for understanding how far the various kinds of experiments in which we are engaging might, in combination with elements of the more established schools of thought, contribute to a 'reconceived' tradition of curriculum inquiry with a distinct and coherent character" (p. 177).

We believe this textbook demonstrates that the field has evolved to exhibit a "distinct and coherent character." Like no other specialization in education, influenced as it is by the humanities, arts, and social theory, curriculum is a hybrid interdisciplinary area of theory, research, and institutional practice. True, it is balkanized and particularized; there are problems of cross-discourse communication. Clearly, however, the contemporary curriculum field *is* distinctive and coherent. The problem is consolidation, and this Reid (1992) understands. As we opened this textbook with his question for the 1990s, so we close it: "Whether the 1990s will be indeed prove to be a period of consolidation and integration, based on broadly humanistic approaches . . . remains to be seen. It would be a worthy agenda" (p. 177). We agree.

One effort at consolidation and integration is the scholarship of Peter S. Hlebowitsh whose reconsideration of the Tyler Rationale in light of the Reconceptualization we reported in chapter 4. In another essay, Hlebowitsh (1992) suggests that Dewey's work can provide one line of thematic continuity between the traditional and reconceptualized fields. A renewed appreciation (Schubert, 1987) for this line could help mend the fractured identity of the contemporary field, thus supporting a moment of consolidation and integration. Hlebowitsh (1992) suggests that the distinction between procedure (linked with Bobbitt) and method (as conceived by Dewey) is the thematic line that links the reconceptualized field with aspects of the traditional one. He writes:

> The difference between procedure and method in the curriculum is the difference between Bobbitt and Dewey; it is also the difference between Bobbitt and a number of "traditionalists," including Tyler, Taba, and the Tanners (to mention three generations of curriculum scholars). Method is in the spirit of Dewey's pragmatism; it is the thread with which the divided nature of *curriculum scholarship may begin to receive mending*. (Hlebowitsh, 1992, p. 82, emphasis added)

[Hlebowitsh's most recent work (1993) seems to have forsaken the project of mending.]

Understanding curriculum. What we teachers and students make of what is given to us is in large measure determined by our willingness to explore the questions implicit in the various discourses reported in this volume. Just as it is not enough for teachers to work with a model of teaching in which they simply transmit a body of knowledge or a set of skills to students, just as it is not enough for students to regard learning as reproducing such content and such skills, so it is not enough for curricularists to view the object of their study as "out there," waiting to be described and represented to teachers as formulae and recipes. What is required is more profound understanding of curriculum. By understanding curriculum we do not mean the ultimate and definitive representation of what is there already, waiting for the right words. Nor do we mean that educational experience can be collapsed into discourse and become simply the object our practice forms. Rather, understanding curriculum implies remaking both experience and its discursive representations so that we see the past and present more clearly, and where our seeing might lead us. Thanks to political scholarship we are clear that we must see the curriculum as an ideological document which both expresses and requires particular forms of labor embedded in the reproduction of power. We understand that to resist politically means linking forms of the curriculum with the larger society, with analysis of the "selective tradition," with cultural capital made available to different populations differentially. To understand curriculum politically leads us to racial and gender investigations (and they lead back to politics), as both sets of representations function to distribute knowledge and power differentially. Phenomenological, aesthetic, autobiographical, and theological experience both expresses political privilege and undermines it. International understandings of curriculum help us to bracket the taken-for-granted, and the intertextual understanding of curriculum that the reconceptualized field offers can lead us to ask, with greater complexity and sophistication, the traditional curriculum questions: what knowledge is of most worth? What do we make of the world we have been given, and how shall we remake ourselves to give birth to a new social order? What John Dewey said in reference to philosophy might be said in reference to the contemporary curriculum field:

> A [curriculum theory] which was conscious of its own business and province would then perceive that it is an intellectualized wish, an aspiration subject to rational discriminations and tests, a social hope reduced to a working program of action, a prophecy of the future, but one disciplined by serious thought and knowledge. (Dewey, quoted in Westbrook, 1991, p. 147)

Here Dewey unites self-realization and society (Westbrook, 1991), two of the major currents in contemporary curriculum scholarship. An intellectualized wish expressed as a social practice, thoroughly theorized and subject to rigorous critique which functions to reformulate the wish, re-expressed as practice: a moving form, that is understanding curriculum today.

V
Prologue

Curriculum is our memorial to an old intentionality. Remembered, resymbolized, a former relation to the world is reviewed and then arranged for someone else. . . . What curriculum theory strives to return to the reception of curriculum is the reflexive moment that was there in its creation.
(Madeleine R. Grumet, 1990c, p. 193)

Any discussion of curriculum reform must address issues of representation as well as issues of unequal distribution of material resources and power outside the school door.

(Cameron McCarthy, 1993b, p. 291)

That's how a textbook might end, is it not? A summary statement in which 3200 references are incorporated, requiring, it is true, notching up the level of abstraction, but summing it up in the process. Doesn't work, does it. Even summoning the grand ghost of Dewey isn't enough. [We are not trying exhume Dewey for the 1990s; see, for instance, Paringer, 1990; Doll, W., 1993b). Why? Charles Ives doesn't sound like Aaron Copeland. Unlike the Grand Canyon, curriculum is not a thing of nature, but of culture [Kieran Egan (1992) reminds us that: "our culture *is* our nature" (p. 118, emphasis added).] And culture is contentious. Furthermore, we are arguing over what to tell the children (and what not to tell them). We are reinventing the world, although we manage often to present it in schools as a museum piece, something dead to be revered or at least memorized. In this book we have worked to present the sound of silence breaking (in Janet Miller's memorable phrase; Miller, 1982a), of the cacophony that occurs when everybody is moved into the same room. No one note—no matter how abstract, how melodious—can capture what is multiple, contradictory, contentious. A modest aspiration, perhaps, but we find ourselves in a field where most pretend theirs is the only discourse worthy of study. Now that everyone is in the same room, what is next?

While the field may always be cacophonous, we think the scholars in the field might choose to be kinder to each other, might acknowledge each other's presence more frequently and more respectfully. As you can see, a number of people are working on similar problems, inspired by similar traditions, aspiring to like ends. There is no reason why these people might not work together a bit more. The curriculum field, it has been pointed out, is a disciplinary community (Pagano, 1981), and there is much to be gained if we started acting a bit more like one. Feminist theory might represent a model that is more genuinely collaborative.

We are not suggesting, of course, that the field requires more order, that its diversification is a problem. On the contrary, we call for collaboration, conversation, and disciplinary autonomy to increase the complexity of the field. We agree with Henry Louis Gates, Jr., who, writing in regard to his own field of African-American Studies, endorses critical inquiry: "We are scholars. For our field to grow, we need to encourage a true proliferation of ideologies and methodologies, rather than to seek uniformity or conformity" (1992, p. 126). Like Gates, we seek growth and proliferation. Our hope is that this book supports that movement.

You can see that this field is very much a conversation, despite the efforts of some to pretend others do not exist. It is a conversation that invites your participation. Unlike more mature fields, curriculum theory remains, relatively speaking, open. You needn't search for a niche, for some small area that has not yet been explored. The new, reconceptualized field—the contemporary field—of curriculum theory is hardly more than a generation old, and the frontier is all around us. You might find that inviting. It is a field where your interests can be pursued. From our point of view, the most important motive for entering a field is that it is interesting, that it appeals, that one's interests can be supported and developed.

Perhaps the most exciting areas may be ones we have not identified in this book. They may be areas—hybrid ones—that will evolve out of existing sectors, across discourses, identifying areas of focus and specialization of which we cannot conceive at this time. Because the field is relatively young, somewhat unstable, still quite open, such work may find warmer welcomes than it would in a more conservative and mapped field. As you have seen, the conversation in the field shifted rather dramatically just twenty years ago, and it might shift again, in a direction we cannot foresee at this time. This is the excitement of working in the curriculum field. And it is the promise of excitement not of prudence that we think should inform your choices regarding graduate study in education. We invite you to join us. The next moment is yours.

References

Abbs, P. (1974). *Autobiography in education*. London, England: Heinemann.

Abdal-Haqq, I. (1992). Professional development schools: An annotated bibliography of selected ERIC resources. *Journal of Teacher Education*, 43 (1), 42-45.

Abdulmalik, H. & Chapman, D. (1992). *Teacher nationality and classroom practice in the Republic of Yemen*. Paper presented to the annual meeting of the American Educational Research Association, San Francisco, CA.

Aceland, R. (1967). *A move to the integrated curriculum*. Exeter, England: University of Exeter.

Acheson, K. & Gall, M. (1980, 1987). *Techniques in the clinical supervision of teachers: Pre-service and in-service applications*. [2nd edition: 1987.] New York: Longman.

Adams, N. (1992). *Redefining Scarlett: Making meaning from the myths*. Baton Rouge, LA: Louisiana State University, Department of Curriculum and Instruction, unpublished paper.

Adler, M. (1982). *The paideia proposal*. New York: Macmillan.

Adler, M. (1986, March). Critical thinking programs: Why they won't work. *Education Digest*, 9-11; originally published in *Education Week*, 6 (September 17), 28.

African Curriculum Organization (ACO). (1983). *Aspects of education and curriculum development*. Ibadan: Institute of Education.

Aggleton, P. (1987). *Rebels without a cause? Middle class youth and the transition from school to work*. London: Falmer.

Agger, B. (1990). *The decline of discourse*. New York: Falmer.

Aikin, W. (1942). *The story of the eight-year study: With conclusions and recommendations*. New York: Harper & Brothers.

Albertini, J. & Meath-Lang, B. (1986). An analysis of student-teacher exchanges in dialogue journal writing. *JCT*, 7 (1), 153-201.

Alberty, E. (1967). Toward a framework for curriculum development. *Theory into Practice*, 6 (4), 204-208.

Alberty, H. (1947, 1953). *Reorganizing the high school curriculum*. New York: Macmillan.

Alberty, H. & Alberty, E. (1962). *Reorganizing the high school curriculum*. New York: Macmillan.

Alcoff, L. (1988). Cultural feminism vs. post-structuralism: The identity crisis in feminist theory. *SIGNS: A Journal of Women in Culture and Society*, 13, 405-436.

Alcoff, L. & Porter, E. (Eds.). (1993). *Feminist epistemologies*. New York: Routledge.

Alcott, L. (1896, 1930). *Little women.* New York: Grosset & Dunlap.

Alessi, S. & Trollip, S. (1991). *Computer-based instruction: Methods and development.* [2nd edition]. Englewood Cliffs, N.J.: Prentice-Hall.

Alexander, H. (1986). Eisner's aesthetic theory of evaluation. *Educational Theory,* 36 (3), 269-270.

Alexander, W. (1964). *Changing curriculum content.* Washington, DC: Association for Supervision and Curriculum Development.

Alexander, W. (1967). *The changing secondary school curriculum.* New York: Holt, Rinehart & Winston.

Allan, K. & Miller, M. (1990, Summer). Teacher-researcher collaboratives: Cooperative professional development. *Theory into Practice,* XXIX (3), 196-202.

Allen, D. (1992). *Schools for a new century: A conservative approach to radical school reform.* New York: Praeger.

Allen, J., Bonner, K. & Moore, M. (1984). The child prodigy. *Phenomenology + Pedagogy,* 1 (3), 319-334.

Allen, R. (Ed.) (1987). *Channels of discourse: Television and contemporary criticism.* Chapel Hill, NC: University of North Carolina Press.

Allen, W. (1993). Response to a "white discourse on white racism." *Educational Researcher,* 22 (8), 11-13.

Allgeier, E. & Allgeier, A. (1984). *Sexual interactions.* Lexington, MA: D. C. Health.

Altbach, P. (1991). Textbooks: The international dimensions. In M. Apple & L. Christian-Smith (Eds.), *The politics of the textbook* (242-258). New York: Routledge.

Altbach, P., & Kelly, G. (Eds.). (1988). *Textbooks in the third world.* New York: Garland.

Altbach, P., & Kelly, G. & Weis, L. (Eds.) (1985). *Excellence in education: Perspectives on policy and practice.* Buffalo, NY: Prometheus Books.

Althusser, L. (1971). *Lenin and philosophy and other essays.* [Trans. B. Brewser] New York: Monthly Review Press.

Amano, I. (1990). *Education and examinations in modern Japan.* Tokyo, Japan: University of Tokyo Press.

American Association of Colleges for Teacher Education (1973). No one model. *Journal of Teacher Education,* 24, 264-265.

American Council on Education (1949). *Intergroup relations in teaching materials: A survey and appraisal.* Washington, DC: American Council on Education.

American Council on Education, American Youth Commission (1940). *What the high schools ought to teach: The report of a special committee on the secondary school curriculum.* Washington, DC: The Council.

Ammons, M. (1969). Communication: A curriculum focus. In A. Frazier (Ed.), *A curriculum for children* (105-122). Washington, D.C.: ASCD. [Also reprinted in R. Hyman (Ed.) (1973), *Approaches in curriculum.* Englewood Cliffs, NJ: Prentice Hall.]

Andambi, M. (1984). *The launching of the 8-4-4 educational system.* Nairobi, Kenya: Kenyatta University College, Bureau of Educational Research.

Anderson, D., Major, R., & Mitchell, R. (1992). *Teacher supervision that works: A guide for university supervisors.* New York: Praeger.

Anderson, J. (1978, Winter). Northern foundations and the shaping of southern black rural education, 1902-1935. *History of Education Quarterly,* 371-396.

Anderson, J. (1988). *The education of blacks in the south 1860-1935.* Chapel Hill, NC: University of North Carolina Press.

Anderson, J., Boyle, C., & Yost, G. (1985). The geometry tutor. In A. Joshi (Ed.), *Proceedings of the ninth international conference on artificial intelligence* (1-7). Los Altos, CA: Morgan Kaufman.

Anderson, T. & Armbruster, B. (1984). Content area textbooks. In R. Anderson, J. Osborn, & R. Tierney (Eds.), *Learning to Read in American schools: Readers and Content Texts* (193-226). Hillsdale, NJ: Erlbaum.

Anderson, V. (1965). *Principles and procedures of curriculum improvement.* New York: Ronald Press.

Angelou, M. (1969). *I know why the caged bird sings.* New York: Random House.

Angelou, M. (1976). *Singin' and swingin' and gettin' merry like Christmas.* New York: Bantam Books.

Angus, D. (1981). A note on the occupational backgrounds of public high school students prior to 1940. *Journal of the Midwest History of Education Society,* 9, 158-183.

Angus, D. (1988). Conflict, class, and the nineteenth century public high school in the cities of the midwest. *Curriculum Inquiry,* 18 (1), 7-31.

Anyon, J. (1979). Ideology and United States history textbooks. *Harvard Educational Review,* 49 (3), 361-386.

Anyon, J. (1988). Schools as agencies of social legitimation. In W. Pinar (Ed.), *Contemporary curriculum discourses* (175-200). Scottsdale, AZ: Gorsuch Scarisbrick.

Anyon, J. (1992). *The retreat of Marxism and socialist feminism: Postmodern theories in education.* Newark, NJ: Rutgers University, Department of Education, unpublished manuscript, 38 pp.

Aoki, T. (1974). A response [to W. James Popham's "Curriculum design: The problem of specifying intended learning outcomes"]. In J. Blaney, I. Housego, & G. McIntosh (Eds.), *Program Development in Education.* Vancouver, British Columbia, Canada: University of British Columbia, Centre for Continuing Education, Publications Division.

Aoki, T. (1977a). On being and becoming a teacher in Alberta: A Japanese Canadian experience. *RIKKA* (Toronto), (4).

Aoki, T. (1977b). Theoretic dimensions of curriculum. *Canadian Journal of Education,* (2) 1.

Aoki, T. (1978). Curriculum approaches to Canadian ethnic histories in the context of citizenship education. *The History and Social Science Teacher,* (13) 2.

Aoki, T. (1979). *Toward a curriculum in a new key*. Curriculum, Media and Instruction Occasional Paper No. 2. Edmonton, Alberta, Canada: University of Alberta, Faculty of Education, Department of Secondary Education.

Aoki, T. (Ed.). (1981). *Rethinking education: Modes of enquiry in the human sciences*. Edmonton, Alberta, Canada: University of Alberta, Faculty of Education, Department of Secondary Education.

Aoki, T. (1983a). Experiencing ethnicity as a Japanese Canadian teacher: Reflections on a personal curriculum. *Curriculum Inquiry*, (13), 3.

Aoki, T. (1983b). Curriculum implementation as instrumental action and practical action. *Curriculum in Canada, Volume IV*. Vancouver, British Columbia, Canada: University of British Columbia, Centre for the Study of Curriculum and Instruction.

Aoki, T. (1984a). Competence in teaching as instrumental and practical action: A critical analysis. In E. Short (Ed.), *Competence: Inquiries into its meaning and acquisition in educational settings* (71-79). Landham, MD: University Press of America.

Aoki, T. (1984b). *Understanding situational meanings of curriculu in-service acts: Implementing, consulting, in-servicing*. Monograph No. 9. Edmonton, Alberta, Canada: University of Alberta, Faculty of Education, Department of Secondary Education.

Aoki, T. (1984c). Towards a reconceptualization of curriculum implementation. In D. Hopkins & M. Wideen (Eds.), *Alternative perspectives on school improvement*. London, England: Falmer.

Aoki, T. (1984d). Whose culture? Whose heritage? Ethnicity within Canadian social studies curriculum. In J. Mallea & J. Young (Eds.), *Cultural diversity and Canadian education: Issues and innovations*. Ottawa, Ontario, Canada: Carleton University Press.

Aoki, T. (1986a). Interests, knowledge and evaluation: Alternative approaches to curriculum evaluation. *JCT*, 6 (4), 27-44.

Aoki, T. (1986b, April/May). Teaching as in-dwelling between two curriculum worlds. *The B.C. Teacher*, 8-10.

Aoki, T. (1987a). In receiving, a giving: A response to the panelists' gifts. *JCT*, 7 (3), 67-88.

Aoki, T. (1987b). Toward understanding "computer application." *JCT*, 7 (2), 61-71.

Aoki, T. (1987c). The educated person. Vancouver, British Columbia, Canada: *The BC Teacher*, (67), 1.

Aoki, T. (1987d). Principals as managers. Vancouver, British Columbia, Canada: *The BC Teacher*, (66), 3.

Aoki, T. (1987e). The dialectic of mother language and second language: A curriculum exploration. *Canadian Literature: A Quarterly of Criticism and Review*. Vancouver, British Columbia, Canada: University of British Columbia.

Aoki, T. (1988a). Toward a dialectic between the conceptual world and the lived world. In W. Pinar (Ed.), *Contemporary curriculum discourses* (402-416). Scottsdale, AZ: Gorsuch Scarisbrick.

Aoki, T. (1988b). *What is it to be educated?* Paper presented at Convocation I. Lethbridge, Alberta, Canada: University of Lethbridge.

Aoki, T. (1988c). *Bridges that rim the Pacific.* Washington, DC: National Council for the Social Studies.

Aoki, T. (1988d). What is to ask: What is critical in curricular scholarship? *Elements: A Journal of Elementary Education.* Edmonton, Alberta, Canada: University of Alberta, Department of Elementary Education.

Aoki, T. (1989a). Thoughts from the threshold. In F. Hultgren & D. Coomer (Eds.), *Alternative modes of inquiry in home economics research* (315-321). Peoria, IL: Glencoe Publishing Co.

Aoki, T. (1989b). The ear and the eye: Beyond the metaphor of disembodied seeing in curriculum talk. In B. Hanley & G. King (Eds.), *Rethinking music education in British Columbia* (1-7). Victoria, BC: Department of Arts in Education, University of Victoria.

Aoki, T. (1989c, March). *Layered understandings of curriculum and pedagogy: Challenges to curriculum developers.* Presented at the symposium Empowering Teachers as Curriculum Developers, sponsored by the Alberta Teachers Association, Edmonton.

Aoki, T. (1989d). Revisiting the notions of leadership and identity. In C. Kobayashi & R. Miki (Eds.), *Spirit of redress: Japanese Canadians in conference.* Vancouver, British Columbia, Canada: JC Publications.

Aoki, T. (1989/1990). Beyond the half-life of curriculum and pedagogy. Alberta Teachers Association, *FINE.*

Aoki, T. (1990a). Themes of teaching curriculum. In J. T. Sears & J. D. Marshall (eds.), *Teaching and thinking about curriculum: Critical inquiries* (111-114). New York: Teachers College Press.

Aoki, T. (1990b). The sound of pedagogy in the silence of the morning calm: Towards post-metaphysical pedagogy. In *Korean studies, cross-cultural perspectives, papers of the sixth international conference.* Seoul, Korea: Academy of Korean Studies.

Aoki, T. (1990c, January/February). Inspiriting the curriculum. *The ATA Magazine,* 37-42.

Aoki, T. (1990d). Sonare and videre: Questioning the primacy of the eye in curriculum talk. In G. Willis & W. Schubert (Eds.), *Reflections from the heart of educational inquiry: Understanding curriculum and teaching through the arts* (182-189). Albany, NY: State University of New York Press.

Aoki, T. (1991a). *Inspiriting curriculum and pedagogy: Talks to teachers.* Edmonton, Alberta, Canada: University of Alberta, Faculty of Education, Publication Services.

Aoki, T. (1991b). Layered understandings of orientations in social studies program evaluation. In J. Shaver (Ed.), *Handbook of research on social studies teaching and learning.* Washington, DC: National Council for the Social Studies.

Aoki, T. (1991c). Five curriculum memos and a note for the next half-century. *Phenomenology + Pedagogy*, (9). [Special issue, 50th anniversary of the Faculty of Education, University of Alberta.]

Aoki, T. (1992a). *Teachers narrating/narratives teaching*. Victoria, British Columbia, Canada: Ministry of Education and Ministry Responsible for Multiculturalism and Human Rights, Province of British Columbia.

Aoki, T. (1992b). Layered understandings of teaching: The uncannily correct and the elusively true. In W. Pinar & W. Reynolds (Eds.), *Understanding curriculum as phenomenological and deconstructed text* (17-27). New York: Teachers College Press.

Aoki, T. (1993a). In the midst of slippery theme-words: Toward designing multicultural curriculum. In T. Aoki & M. Shamsher (Eds.), *The call of teaching* (87-100). Vancouver, British Columbia, Canada: British Columbia Teachers' Federation.

Aoki, T. (1993b). The child-centered curriculum: Where is the social in pedocentrism? In T. Aoki & M. Shamsher (Eds.), *The call of teaching* (67-76). Vancouver, British Columbia, Canada: British Columbia Teachers' Federation.

Aoki, T. (1993c). Legitimating lived curriculum: Towards a curricular landscape of multiplicity. *Journal of Curriculum and Supervision*, 8 (3), 255-268.

Aoki, T. (Ed.).(n.d.). *Voices of teaching*. Monograph, Volume 1. Program for Quality Teaching. Vancouver, British Columbia, Canada: British Columbia Teachers' Federation.

Aoki, T. & et al. (Eds.). (1985). *Understanding curriculum as lived: Curriculum Canada VII*. Vancouver, British Columbia, Canada: University of British Columbia, Faculty of Education, Centre for the Study of Curriculum & Instruction.

Aoki, T. & Werner, W. (Eds.). (1978). *Identifying evaluation tasks: A case study of the Amerindianization project*. Vancouver, British Columbia, Canada: University of British Columbia, Centre for the Study of Curriculum and Instruction.

Aoki, T. et al. (Eds.). (1978). *Canadian ethnicity: The politics of meaning*. Vancouver, British Columbia, Canada: University of British Columbia, Centre for the Study of Curriculum and Instruction.

Aoki, T. & Shamsher, M. (Eds.). (1991). *Voices of teaching*. Volume 2. Program for Quality Teaching. Vancouver, British Columbia, Canada: British Columbia Teachers' Federation.

Aoki, T. & Shamsher, M. (Eds.). (1993). *The call of teaching*. Vancouver, British Columbia, Canada: British Columbia Teachers' Federation.

Appel, S. (1992). *Psychoanalysis and the "new" sociology of education: Positioning subjects*. Rochester, NY: University of Rochester, Graduate School of Education and Human Development, unpublished Ph.D. dissertation.

Appiah, A. (1985). The uncompleted argument: Du Bois and the illusion of race. *Critical Inquiry*, 12 (1), 21-37.

Appiah, K. (1992). *In my father's house: Africa in the philosophy of culture*. New York: Oxford University Press.

Apple, M. (1975a). The hidden curriculum and the nature of conflict. In W. Pinar (Ed.), *Curriculum theorizing: The reconceptualists* (95-119). Berkeley, CA: McCutchan.

Apple, M. (1975b). Autobiographical statement. In W. Pinar (Ed.), *Curriculum theorizing: The reconceptualists* (89-93). Berkeley, CA: McCutchan.

Apple, M. (1979a). Curriculum and reproduction. *Curriculum Inquiry*, 9 (3), 231-252.

Apple, M. (1979b). *Ideology and curriculum*. London, England: Routledge.

Apple, M. (1979c). On analyzing hegemony. *JCT*, 1 (1), 10-27.

Apple, M. (1980). Analyzing determinations: Understanding and evaluating the production of social outcomes in the schools. *Curriculum Inquiry*, 10 (1), 55-76.

Apple, M. (1981). Reproduction, contestation and curriculum: An essay in self-criticism. *Interchange*, 12 (2-3), 27-46.

Apple, M. (1982a). *Education and power*. New York: Routledge & Kegan Paul.

Apple, M. (Ed.). (1982b). *Cultural and economic reproduction in education: Essays on class, ideology, and the state*. New York: Routledge & Kegan Paul.

Apple, M. (1982c). *Work, gender and teaching*. Curriculum Praxis Series, Occasional Paper No. 22. Edmonton, Alberta, Canada: University of Alberta, Faculty of Education, Department of Secondary Education.

Apple, M. (1982d). Curriculum form and the logic of technical control. In M. Apple (Ed.), *Cultural and economic reproduction in education: Essays in class, ideology and the state* (247-274). London: Routledge and Kegan Paul.

Apple, M. (1983). *Teaching and women's work: A comparative historical and ideological analysis*. Curriculum Praxis Series, Occasional Paper No. 25. Edmonton, Alberta, Canada: University of Alberta, Faculty of Education, Department of Secondary Education.

Apple, M. (1985a). There is a river: James B. Macdonald and curricular tradition. *JCT*, 6 (3), 9-18.

Apple, M. (1985b). Old humanists and new curricula: Politics and culture in the *Paideia Proposal*. *Curriculum Inquiry*, 15 (1), 91-106.

Apple, M. (1986). *Teachers and texts: A political economy of class and gender relations in education*. New York: Routledge & Kegan Paul.

Apple, M. (1987a). Producing inequality: Ideology and economy in the national reports on education. *Educational Studies*, 18 (2), 195-220.

Apple, M. (1987b). Will the social context allow a tomorrow for tomorrow's teachers? *Teachers College Record*, 88 (3), 330-337.

Apple, M. (1988a). Social crisis and curriculum accords. *Educational Theory*, 38 (2), 191-201.

Apple, M. (1988b). The politics of pedagogy and the building of community. *JCT* 8(4), 7-22.

Apple, M. (1989). Regulating the text: The socio/historical roots of state control. *Educational Policy*, 3, 107-123.

Apple, M. (1990a). *Ideology and curriculum* (2nd. ed.). New York: Routledge & Kegan Paul.

Apple, M. (1990b). The text and cultural politics. *The Journal of Educational Thought*, 24 (3a), 17-33.

Apple, M. (1990c). The politics of pedagogy and the building of community. *JCT*, 8 (4), 7-22.

Apple, M. (1992a). Education, culture, and class power: Basil Bernstein and the neo-Marxist sociology of education. *Educational Theory*, 42 (2) 127-145.

Apple, M. (1992b, October). The text and cultural politics. *Educational Researcher*, 21 (7) 4-11.

Apple, M. (1993). *Official knowledge: Democratic education in a conservative age.* New York: Routledge.

Apple, M. & Christian-Smith, L. (Eds.). (1991). *The politics of the textbook.* London, England: Routledge.

Apple, M. & Jungck, S. (1990, Summer). You Don't Have to Be a Teacher to Teach This Unit: Teaching, Technology and Gender in the Classroom. *American Educational Research Journal*, 27 (2), 227-251.

Apple, M. & Ladwig, J. (1989, December 20). Educators reel from decade of right-wing attacks. *The Guardian*, p. 9.

Apple, M. & Teitelbaum, K. (1986). Are teachers losing control of their skills and curriculum? *Journal of Curriculum Studies*, 18 (2), 177-184.

Apple, M. & Weis, L. (Eds.). (1983). *Ideology and practice in schooling.* Philadelphia, PA: Temple University Press.

Apple, M. & Wexler, P. (1978, Winter). Cultural capital and educational transmissions. *Educational Theory*, 28, 34-43.

Aptekar, L. (1989). Picaresque tragedies: The "abandoned" children of Columbia. *Phenomenology + Pedagogy*, 7, 79-92.

Arac, J. (Ed.) (1986). *Postmodernism and politics.* Minneapolis, MN: University of Minnesota Press.

Ariav, T. (1991). Growth in teachers' curriculum knowledge through the process of curriculum analysis. *Journal of Curriculum and Supervision*, 6 (3), 183-200.

Armbruster, B., Stevens, R., & Rosenshine, B. (1977). *Analyzing content coverage and emphasis: A study of three curricula and two tests.* Technical Report No. 26. Urbana, IL: University of Illinois, Center for the Study of Reading.

Armstrong, D. (1989). *Developing and documenting the curriculum.* Boston, MA: Allyn & Bacon.

Arnove, R. (1980). Comparative education and world system analysis. *Comparative Education Review*, 31 (1), 48-62.

Arnstine, D. (1990). Art, aesthetics, and the pitfalls of discipline-based art education. *Educational Theory*, 40 (4), 415-422.

Aronowitz, S. (1989). Working-class identity and celluloid fantasy. In H. Giroux & R. Simon (Eds.), *Popular culture: Schooling and everyday life* (197-218). Granby, MA: Bergin & Garvey.

Aronowitz, S. (1990). *The crisis in historical materialism: Class, politics and culture in marxist theory.* Minneapolis, MN: University of Minnesota Press.

Aronowitz, S. (1993). Paulo Freire's radical democratic humanism. In P. McLaren & P. Leonard (Eds.), *Paulo Freire: A critical encounter* (8-24). London & New York: Routledge.

Aronowitz, S. & Giroux, H. (1985). *Education under siege: The conservative, liberal and radical debate over schooling.* South Hadley, MA: Bergin & Garvey. [2nd edition published in 1993 as *Education still under siege.*]

Aronowitz, S. & Giroux, H. (1987). Ideologies about schooling: Rethinking the nature of educational reform. *JCT,* 7 (1), 7-38.

Aronowitz, S. & Giroux, H. (1991). *Postmodern education: Politics, culture and social criticism.* Minneapolis, MN: University of Minnesota Press.

Arons, S. (1983). *Compelling belief: The culture of American schooling.* New York: McGraw Hill.

Asante, M. (1987). *The Afrocentric idea.* Philadelphia, PA: Temple University Press.

Asanuma, S. (1983). *The autobiographical method in Japanese education: The writing project and its application to social studies.* Paper presented to the Bergamo Conference on Curriculum Theory and Classroom Practice, October 19, Dayton, OH.

Asanuma, S. (1986a). The autobiographical method in Japanese education: The writing projects and its application to social studies. *JCT,* 6 (4), 5-26.

Asanuma, S. (1986b). *Phenomenological curriculum theories in North America.* Madison, WI: University of Wisconsin, School of Education, Department of Curriculum and Instruction, unpublished Ph.D. dissertation.

Asian Programme of Education Innovation for Development (APEID). (1980). *National strategies for curriculum design and development.* Bangkok: UNESCO/APEID.

Asmus, W. (1968/1970). *Johan Friedrich Herbart.* Heidelberg: Quelle & Meyer.

Association for Supervision and Curriculum Development. (1961). *Balance in the curriculum.* [1961 yearbook]. Washington, DC: ASCD.

Association for Supervision and Curriculum Development. (1962). *Perceiving, behaving, becoming: A new focus for education.* [1962 Yearbook]. Washington, DC: ASCD.

Association for Supervision and Curriculum Development. (1964). *Individualizing instruction.* [1964 yearbook]. Washington, DC: ASCD.

Association for Supervision and Curriculum Development. (1987a). *Religion in the curriculum.* Alexandria, VA: ASCD Press.

Association for Supervision and Curriculum Development. (1987b, May). Religion in the public schools. *Educational Leadership,* 44 (8), 3-32.

Association for Supervision and Curriculum Development. (1990). *Public schools of choice.* Alexandra, VA: ASCD Press.

Association for Supervision and Curriculum Development. (1993, January). Chicago conference in '69 seen as a turning point . *ASCD Update,* 4-5

Assor, A. & Gordon, D. (1987). The implicit learning theory of hidden-curriculum research. *Journal of Curriculum Studies,* 19 (4), 329-339.

Astin, H. & Bayer, A. (1973). Sex discrimination in academe. In A. Rossi & A. Calderwood (Eds.), *Academic women on the move.* New York: Russell Sage Foundation.

Atkins, E. (1988a). Reframing curriculum theory in terms of interpretation and practice: A hermeneutical approach. *Journal of Curriculum Studies,* 20 (5), 437-448.

Atkins, E. (1988b). The relationship of metatheoretical principles in the philosophy of science to metatheoretical explorations in curriculum. *JCT,* 8 (4), 69-86.

Atkins, E. (1991). Solitude and irony: A private vision and public position. In J. Erdman & J. Henderson (Eds.), *Critical Discourse on Current Curriculum Issues* (188-204). Chicago, IL: Mid-West Center for Curriculum Studies.

Atkinson, T. (1974). *Amazonian odyssey.* New York: Music Sales Corporation.

Au, K. (1980) Participation structures in a reading lesson with Hawaiian children: Analysis of a culturally appropriate instruction event. *Anthropology and Education Quarterly,* 11 (2), 91-115.

Ausubel, D. (1959). Viewpoints from related disciplines: Human growth and development. *Teachers College Record,* 60, 245-254.

Ausubel, D. (1968). *Educational psychology: A cognitive view.* New York: Holt, Rinehart & Winston

Ayers, J. & Berney, M. (1990). *Teacher education program evaluation: An annotated bibliography and guide to research.* New York & London, England: Garland Publishing, Inc.

Ayers, W. (1988). Fact or fancy: The knowledge base quest in teacher education. *Journal of Teacher Education,* XXXIX (5), 24-31.

Ayers, W. (1990). Small heroes: In and out of school with 10-year-old city kids. *Cambridge Journal of Education,* 20 (3), 269-278.

Ayers, W. (1992, Summer). The shifting ground of curriculum thought and everyday practice. *Theory Into Practice,* XXXI (3), 259-263.

Ayers, W. (1993). *To teach: The journey of a teacher.* [Foreword by H. Kohl.] New York: Teachers College Press.

Bagley, W. (1905). *The educative process.* New York: Macmillan.

Bagley, W. (1906). Concreteness in education. *Visual Education.* Meadville, PA: Keystone View Co.

Bagley, W. & Kyte, G. (1926). *The California curriculum study.* Berkeley, CA: University of California Press.

Bagley, W. & Rugg, H. (1916). *The content of history as taught in the seventh and eighth grades: An analysis of typical school textbooks.* Champaign, IL: University of Illinois School of Education Bulletin, (16), 5-59.

Baker, D. (1993a). Compared to Japan, the U.S. is a lower achiever ... Really: New evidence and comment on Westbury. *Educational Researcher,* 22 (3), 18-20.

Baker, D. (1993b). A rejoinder. *Educational Researcher,* 22 (3), 25.

Baker, E. & J. Popham (1973). *Expanding dimensions of instructional objectives.* Englewood Cliffs, NJ: Prentice-Hall.

Bakhtin, M. (1986). *Speech genres and other late essays*. [Edited and translated by V. McGee, et al.] Austin, TX: University of Texas Press.

Baldwin, J. (1956/1988). *Giovanni's room*. New York: Laurel.

Baldwin, J. (1971). Author's notes, Blues for Mister Charlies. In Glassner, J. & Barnes, C. (Eds.), *Best American plays*. New York: Crown.

Baldwin, J. (1985). The fire next time. In James Baldwin, *Price of the ticket*. New York: St. Martin's/Marek.

Ball, D. & Feiman-Nemser, S. (1988). Using textbooks and teachers' guides: A dilemma for beginning teachers and teacher educators. *Curriculum Inquiry*, 18 (4), 401-423.

Banks, J. (1969). A content analysis of the American blacks in textbooks. *Social Education*, 33, 954-957, 963.

Banks, J. (1981). *Multiethnic education: Theory and practice*. Boston, MA: Allyn & Bacon.

Banks, J. (1987). *Teaching strategies for ethnic studies*. Boston, MA: Allyn & Bacon.

Banks, J. (1991). Social studies, ethnic diversity, and social change. In C. Willie, A. Garibaldi & W. Reed (Eds.), *The education of African-Americans* (129-147). New York: Auburn House.

Banks, J. (1993). The canon debate, knowledge construction, and multicultural education. *Educational Researcher*, 22 (5), 4-14.

Barbanel, J. (1993, January 25). Syracuse U. plans link to new high school. *The New York Times*, B12.

Barber, M. (1989). Edmund Perry, the distribution of knowledge, and the looking glass of race. *Phenomenology + Pedagogy*, 7, 218-231.

Barber, M. (1992, September/October). An entitlement curriculum: A strategy for the nineties. *Journal of Curriculum Studies*, 24 (5), 449-455.

Barnes, D. (1992). The significance of teachers' frames for teaching. In Russell, T. & H. Munby (Eds.) *Teachers and teaching: From classroom to reflection* (9-32). London, England: Falmer.

Barnes, H. (1987). Conceptual basis for thematic teacher education programs. *Journal of Teacher Education*, 38 (4), 13-18.

Barnieh, Z. (1989). *Understanding playwriting for children*. Calgary, Alberta, Canada: University of Calgary.

Baron, D. (1979). A case study of praxis. *JCT*, 1 (2), 46-53.

Barone, T. (1982). The Meadowhurst experience: Phases in the process of educational criticism. *JCT*, 4 (1), 156-170.

Barone, T. (1987a). On equality, visibility, and the fine arts program in a black elementary school: An example of educational criticism. *Curriculum Inquiry*, 17 (4), 421-446.

Barone, T. (1987b). Educational platforms, teacher selection, and school reform: Issues emanating from a biographical case study. *Journal of Teacher Education*, 38 (2), 12-17.

Barone, T. (1989). Ways of being at risk: The case of Billy Charles Barnett. *Phi Delta Kappan*, 71 (2), 147-151.

Barone, T. (1990a). Using the narrative text as an occasion for conspiracy. In E. Eisner & A. Peshkin (Eds.), *Qualitative inquiry in education: The continuing debate* (395-326). New York: Teachers College Press.

Barone, T. (1990b). Response to the commentary by Miles and Huberman. In E. Eisner & A. Peshkin (Eds.), *Qualitative inquiry in education: The continuing debate* (358-363). New York: Teachers College Press.

Barone, T. (1992a). On the demise of subjectivity in educational inquiry. *Curriculum Inquiry*, 22 (1), 25-38.

Barone, T. (1992b). A narrative of enhanced professionalis m: Educational researchers and popular storybooks about schoolpeople. *Educational Researcher*, 21 (9), 15-24.

Barone, T. (1992c). Interview, November 25, 1992. Researcher urges colleagues to use "storytelling" techniques: A conversation with Thomas E. Barone. *Education Week*, 12 (12), 6-7.

Barone, T. (1992d). Beyond theory and method: A case of critical storytelling. *Theory into Practice*, 31 (2), 142-146.

Barone, T. (1993a, in press). Breaking the mold: The new American student as strong poet. *Theory into Practice*, 32 (3).

Barone, T. (1993b, in press). Acquiring a public voice: Curriculum specialists, critical storytelling, and educational reform. *JCT*, 10 (1).

Barone, T. (1993c, in press). Curriculum, control, and creativity: An examination of curricular language and educational values. *JCT*.

Barritt, L., Beekman, T., Bleeker, H., & Mulderij, K. (1984). Analyzing phenomenological descriptions. *Phenomenology + Pedagogy*, 2 (1), 1-17.

Barrow, R. (with R. Woods).1975). *Introduction to philosophy of education.* London, England: Methuen.

Barrow, R. (1976a). *Common sense and the curriculum.* Hamden, CT: Linnet Books.

Barrow, R. (1976b). *Plato and education.* London, England: Routledge & Kegan Paul.

Barrow, R. (1978a). *Radical education.* Oxford, England: Martin Robertson.

Barrow, R. (1978b). *The Canadian curriculum.* London, Ontario, Canada: University of Western Ontario.

Barrow, R. (1980). *Happiness.* Oxford, England: Martin Robertson.

Barrow, R. (1981a). *The philosophy of schooling.* Brighton, England: Wheatsheaf.

Barrow, R. (1981b). *Educational and curriculum theory.* Vancouver, British Columbia, Canada: University of British Columbia.

Barrow, R. (1982a). *Injustice, inequality and ethics.* Brighton, England: Wheatsheaf.

Barrow, R. (1982b). *Language and thought.* London, Ontario, Canada: University of Western Ontario.

Barrow, R. (1984a). Does the question "what is education?" make sense? *Educational Theory*, 33 (3 &4), 191-196.

Barrow, R. (1984b). *Giving teaching back to teachers: A critical introduction to curriculum theory.* Totowa, NJ: Barnes & Noble.

Barrow, R. (1990). *Understanding skills: Thinking, feeling, and caring.* London, Ontario, Canada: The Althouse Press, University of Western Ontario, Faculty of Education.

Barrow, R. & Milburn, G. (1986). *A critical dictionary of educational concepts: An appraisal of selected ideas and issues in educational theory and practice.* New York: St. Martin's Press.

Barth, F. (Ed.). (1969). *Ethnic groups and boundaries: The social organization of cultural difference.* London, England: George Allen & Unwin.

Barth, R. (1972). Open education. In D. Purpel & M. Belanger (Eds.), *Curriculum and cultural revolution* (424-454). Berkeley, CA: McCutchan.

Barthes, R. (1975). *The pleasure of the text.* [Trans. by R. Miller]. New York: Hill & Wang.

Barton, L. & Walker, S. (Eds.). (1981). *Schools, teachers, and teaching.* London, England: Falmer.

Barton, L. & Walker, S. (Eds.). (1984). *Social crisis and educational research.* Dover, NH: Croom Helm Ltd.

Barton, L., Meighan, R., & Walker, S. (Eds.). (1980). *Schooling, ideology and the curriculum.* Sussex, England: The Falmer Press.

Bateman, D. (1974). The politics of curriculum. In W. Pinar (Ed.), *Heightened consciousness, cultural revolution, and curriculum theory: The proceedings of the Rochester conference* (54-68). Berkeley, CA: McCutchan.

Bath, S. (1987). Emancipatory evaluation: Themes of Ted Aoki's orientation to curricular evaluation. *JCT,* 7 (3), 51-66.

Bath, S. (1988). *Justice in evaluation: Participatory case study evaluation.* Edmonton, Alberta, Canada: University of Alberta, Faculty of Education, Department of Secondary Education, unpublished Ph.D. dissertation.

Baudrillard, J. (1981). *For a critique of the political economy of the sign.* St. Louis, MO: Telos Press.

Baudrillard, J. (1983). *In the shadow of the silent majorities.* Semiotext(e).

Baudrillard, J. (1988). *Jean Baudrillard: Selected writings.* [Edited by M. Poster (Ed.) Stanford, CA: Stanford University Press.

Bauer, G. (1986, Fall). The moral of the story: How to teach values in the nation's classrooms. *Policy Review,* 24-27.

Bauman, Z. (1978). *Hermeneutics and social science.* New York: Columbia University Press.

Beattie, C. (1986). The case for teacher directed curriculum evaluation. *JCT,* 6 (4), 56-73.

Beattie, C. (1989). Action research: A practice in need of theory? In G. Milburn, I. Goodson & R. Clark (Eds.), *Re-interpreting curriculum research: Images and arguments* (110-120). London, Ontario, Canada: The Althouse Press.

Beauchamp, E. (Ed.). (1991). *Windows on Japanese education.* New York: Greenwood Press.

Beauchamp, G. (1961). *Curriculum theory: Meaning, development and use.* Wilmette, IL: The Kagg Press.

Beauchamp, G. & Beauchamp, K. (1967). *Comparative analysis of curriculum systems.* Wilmette, IL: The Kagg Press.

Beauchamp, L. & Parsons, J. (1989). The curriculum of student teacher evaluation. *JCT*, 9 (1),125-171.

Beck, C., Berneier, N., Macdonald, J., Walton, T. & Willers, J. (1968). *Education for relevance: The schools and social change.* Boston, MA: Houghton Mifflin.

Beck, C. (1985). Religion and education. *Teachers College Record*, 87 (2), 259-270.

Beck, F. (1992). *Women and community.* Paper presented to the Bergamo Conference, Dayton, OH.

Beck, I. & McCaslin, E. (1978). *An analysis of dimensions that affect the development code-breaking ability in eight beginning reading programs.* Pittsburgh, PA: University of Pittsburgh, School of Education, Learning Research and Development Center.

Beck, I., McKeown, M., & Gromoll, E. (1989). Learning from social studies texts. *Cognition and Instruction*, 6 (2), 99-158.

Beck, R., Cook, W. & Kearney, N. (1973). *Curriculum in the modern elementary school.* Englewood Cliffs, NJ: Prentice-Hall.

Beecher, L. (1834, 1977). *A plea for the west.* New York: Arno Press.

Beedy, J. (1992). Athletic development and personal growth. In A. Garrod (Ed.), *Learning for life: Moral education theory and practice* (154-176). Westport, CT: Praeger.

Beegle, C. (1974). Reactions of a group leader. In W. Pinar (Ed.), *Heightened consciousness, cultural revolution, and curriculum theory: The proceedings of the Rochester conference* (138-142). Berkeley, CA: McCutchan.

Beegle, C. & Edefelt, R. (Eds.). (1977). *Staff development, staff liberation: A report of a conference.* Alexandria, VA: ASCD.

Beegle, C., Bentley, M. & Bash, J. (1987). Beyond 1986: Education for survival. *JCT*, 7 (2), 126-146.

Begley, S., Chideya, F., & Wilson, L. (1991, September 23). African dreams. *Newsweek*, CXVIII (13), 42-50.

Behar, L. (1994). *The knowledge base of curriculum: An empirical analysis.* Lanham, MD: University Press of America.

Beineke, J. (1989). A progressive at the pinnacle: William Heard Kilpatrick's final years at Teachers College Columbia University. *Educational Theory*, 39 (2),139-149.

Belenky, M., Clinchy, B., Goldberg, N., & Tarule, J. (1988). *Women's ways of knowing: The development of self, voice, and mind.* New York: Basic Books.

Bell, D. (1973). *The coming of post-industrial society.* New York: Basic Books.

Bell, R. (Ed.). (1971). *Thinking about the curriculum.* Bletchley, Bucks, England: The Open University Press.

Bellack, A. & Kliebard, H. (Eds.) (1977). *Curriculum and evaluation.* Berkeley, CA: McCutchan. [Sponsored and prepared by the American Educational Research Association.]

Bem, S. (1975). Sex role adaptability: One consequence of psychological androgyny. *Journal of Personality and Social Psychology*, 31 (4), 634-643.

Benham, B. (1981). Curriculum theory in the 1970s: The reconceptualist movement. *JCT*, 3 (1), 162-170.

Bennett, K. (1991). Wrenched from the earth. In J. Kincheloe & W. Pinar (Eds.), *Curriculum as social psychoanalysis: The significance of place* (99-120). Albany, NY: State University of New York Press.

Bennett, W. (1986). *What works: Research about teaching and learning.* Washington, DC: U.S. Department of Education.

Bennett, W. (1987). *James Madison high school: A curriculum for American students.* Washington, DC: U.S. Department of Education.

Bennison, A., Jungck, S., Kantor, K. & Marshall, D. (1989). Teachers' voices in curriculum inquiry: A conversation among teacher educators. *JCT*, 9 (1), 71-106.

Ben-Peretz, M. (1990). *The teacher-curriculum encounter: Freeing teachers from the tyranny of texts.* Albany, NY: State University of New York Press.

Benstock, S. (Ed.). (1988). *The private self: Theory and practice of women's autobiographical writing.* Chapel Hill, NC: University of North Carolina Press.

Bereiter, C. & Scardamalia, M. (1992). Cognition and curriculum. In P. Jackson (Ed.), *Handbook of research on curriculum* (517-542). New York: Macmillan.

Berger, C. (1985, April). The erosion of professional schools: The right blend in a time of decline. *The Journal of Educational Thought*, 19 (1), 24-28.

Bergson, H. (1946). *The creative mind: An introduction to metaphysics.* New York: Philosophical Library.

Bergson, H. (1955). *An introduction to metaphysics.* New York: Macmillan.

Berk, L. (1980). Education in lives: Biographic narrative in the study of educational outcomes. *JCT*, 2 (2), 88-154.

Berk, L. (1992). The extracurriculum. In P. Jackson (Ed.), *Handbook of research on curriculum* (1002-1044). New York: Macmillan.

Berlak, A. (1989). *Dilemmas of schooling.* New York: Routledge, Chapman & Hall.

Berlak, A. (1994). Antiracist pedagogy in a college classroom: Mutual recognition and a logic of paradox. In R. Martusewicz & W. Reynolds (Eds.), *Inside out: Contemporary critical perspectives in education* (37-60). New York: St. Martin's Press.

Berliner, D. (1984), The half-filled glass: A review of research on teaching. In P. Hosford (Ed.), *Using what we know about teaching* (57-77), Alexandria, VA: ASCD.

Berlowitz, M. (1984). Multicultural education: Fallacies and alternatives. In M. Berlowitz & R. Edari (Eds.), *Racism and the denial of human rights: Beyond ethnicity* (129-136). Minneapolis, MN: Marxism Educational Press.

Berlowitz, M. & Edari, R. (Eds.). (1984). *Racism and the denial of human rights: Beyond ethnicity.* Minneapolis, MN: MEP Publications.

Berman, E. (1980). Educational colonialism in Africa: The role of American foundations 1910-1945. In R. Arnove (Ed.), *Philanthropy and cultural imperialism: The foundations at home and abroad* (179-201). Boston, MA: G. K. Hall.

Berman, L. (Ed.). (1967). *The humanities and the curriculum.* Washington, DC: ASCD.

Berman, L. (1968). *New priorities in the curriculum.* Columbus, OH: Merrill.

Berman, L. (1985). Perspectives and imperatives: Re-searching, rethinking , and reordering curriculum priorities. *Journal of Curriculum and Supervision,* 1 (1), 66-71.

Berman, L. (1986). Perception, paradox, and passion: Curriculum for community. *Theory Into Practice,* XXV (1), 41-45.

Berman, L. (1988). Problematic curriculum development: Normative inquiry in curriculum. *Journal of Curriculum and Supervision,* 3 (4), 271-295.

Berman, L. (1990). Toward a continuing dialogue. In J. Sears & D. Marshall (Eds.), *Teaching and thinking about curriculum* (280-286). New York: Teachers College Press.

Berman, L. (1991). Louise's voice. In L. Berman, F. Hultgren, D. Lee, M. Rivkin, S. Roderick, *Toward curriculum for being: Voices of educators* (137-138). [In conversation with Ted Aoki. Foreword by C. Stimpson.] Albany, NY: State University of New York Press.

Berman, L., Hultgren, F., Lee, D., Rivkin, M., Roderick, S. (1991). *Toward curriculum for being: Voices of educators.* [In conversation with Ted Aoki. Foreword by C. Stimpson.] Albany, NY: State University of New York Press.

Berman, P. & McLaughlin, M. (1976). Implementation of educational innovation. *Educational Forum,* 40 (3), 324-370.

Bernal, M. (1991). *Black Athena.* New Brunswick, NJ: Rugters University Press.

Bernstein, B. (1975, 1977). *Class, codes and control: Towards a theory of educational transmissions.* (2nd edition, volume 3). London, England: Routledge & Kegan Paul.

Bernstein, R. (1976). *Restructuring of social and political theory.* New York: Harcourt Brace Jovanovich.

Bérubé, M. (1991, October). Just the fax, ma'm: Or, postmodernism journey to decenter. *Village Literary Supplement,* 99,13-17.

Best, S. & Kellner, D. (1991). *Postmodern theory.* New York: Guilford Press.

Bestor, A. (1953). *Educational wastelands: The retreat from learning in our public schools.* Urbana, IL: University of Illinois Press.

Beyer, L. (1979a). Aesthetic theory and the ideology of education institutions. *Curriculum Inquiry,* 9 (1),13-26.

Beyer, L. (1979b). Cultural forms as therapeutic encounters. *Curriculum Inquiry,* 9 (4), 349-359.

Beyer, L. (1983). Philosophical work, practical theorizing, and the nature of schooling. *JCT,* 5 (1), 73-91.

Beyer, L. (1985). Aesthetic experience for teacher preparation and social change. *Educational Theory,* 35 (4), 385-397.

Beyer, L. (1986a). The reconstruction of knowledge and educational studies. *Journal of Education,* 168 (2), 113-135.

Beyer, L. (1986b). The parameters of educational inquiry: A review of understanding education by Walter Feinberg. *Curriculum Inquiry*, 16 (1), 87-114.

Beyer, L. (1986c). Critical theory and the art of teaching. *Journal of Curriculum Studies*, 1 (3), 221-232.

Beyer, L. (1987). Art and society: Toward new directions in aesthetic education. *JCT*, 7 (2), 72-98.

Beyer, L. (1988a). *Knowing and acting: Inquiry, ideology and educational studies*. London, England: Falmer Press.

Beyer, L. (1988b). Art and society. In W. Pinar (Ed.), *Contemporary curriculum discourses* (380-399). Scottsdale, AZ: Gorsuch Scarisbrick.

Beyer, L. (1989). Reconceptualizing teacher preparation: Institutions and ideologies. *Journal of Teacher Education*, XXXX (1), 22-26.

Beyer, L. (1990). Curriculum deliberation: Value choices and political possibilities. In J. Sears & D. Marshall (Eds.), *Teaching and thinking about curriculum* (121-137). New York: Teachers College Press.

Beyer, L. (1991). Schooling, moral commitment, and the preparation of teachers. *Journal of Teacher Education*, 42 (3), 205-215.

Beyer, L. & Apple, M. (1988). *The curriculum: Problems, politics and possibilities*. Albany, NY: State University of New York Press.

Beyer, L. & Wood, G. (1986). Critical inquiry and moral action in education. *Educational Theory*, 36 (1), 1-8.

Beyer, L., Feinberg, W., Pagano, J. & Whitson, J. (1989). *Preparing teachers as professionals: The role of educational studies and other liberal disciplines*. New York: Teachers College Press.

Bhabha, H. (1990a). DissemiNation: Time, narrative, and the margins of the modern nation. In H. Bhabha (Ed.), *Nation and narration*. New York: Routledge.

Bhabha, H. (1990b). Interrogating identity. In L. Appignanesi (Ed.), *The real me: Postmodernism and the question of identity*. London, England: Institute of Contemporary Arts, ICA Documents 6.

Bierstedt, R. (1955). The writers of textbooks. In L. Cronbach (Ed.), *Text Materials in Modern Education* (96-126). Champaign, IL: University of Illinois Press.

Billett, R. O. (1970). *Improving the secondary school curriculum: Guide to effective curriculum planning*. New York: Atherton Press.

Binkley, M., Guthrie, J., & Wyatt, T. (1991). *A survey of national assessment and examination practices in OECD countries*. Lugano, Switzerland: OECD Press.

Birney, C. (1885). *Sarah and Angelina Grimke*. Boston, MA: Lee & Shepard.

Bishop, L. (1967). *Collective negotiation in curriculum and instruction*. Washington, DC: ASCD.

Blackburn, R. & Mann, M. (1979). *The working class in the labor market*. London, England: Macmillan.

Blackham, H. (1965). *Reality, man and existence*. New York: Bantam.

Blatz, C. (1989). Contextualism and critical thinking: Programmatic investigations. *Educational Theory*, 39 (2), 107-119.

Bleich, D. (1978). *Subjective criticism*. Baltimore, MD: Johns Hopkins University Press.

Bleich, D. (1988). *The double perspectives: Language, literacy, and social relations*. New York: Oxford University Press.

Bleth, M. (1993). *Metaphor and thinking: The college experience*. [Edited by G. Johansen.] Landham, MD: University Press of America.

Bloch, E. (1970). *A philosophy of the future*. New York: Herder & Herder.

Bloch, E. (1986). *The principle of hope*. Oxford, England: Blackwell.

Block, A. (1988). The answer is blowin' in the wind: A deconstructive reading of the school text. *JCT*, 8 (4), 23-52.

Block, A. (1992). *Anonymous toil: A re-evaluation of the American radical novel in the twentieth century*. Lanham, MD: University Press of America.

Block, A. (1993, June 27-July 1). *My Lord I have not the skill: On the relation between theory and practice*. Paper presented to the International Conference on Teacher Education, Tel-Aviv, Israel.

Block, A. (1994). Marxism and education. In R. Martusewicz & W. Reynolds (Eds.), *Inside out: Contemporary critical perspectives in education* (61-78). New York: St. Martin's Press.

Block, A. (forthcoming). *Occupied reading*. New York: Garland.

Block, A. & Reynolds, W. (1991). *I was lost, but now am found: Curriculum as grace*. Paper presented to the Bergamo Conference on Curriculum Theory and Classroom Practice, Dayton, OH.

Bloom, A. (1987). *The closing of the American mind*. New York: Simon & Schuster.

Bloom, B. (1950). *Problem-solving processes of college students*. Chicago, IL: University of Chicago Press.

Bloom, B., et al. (1956). *Taxonomy of educational objectives: Cognitive domain*. New York: David McKay.

Bloom, B. (1966). The role of the educational sciences in curriculum development. *International Journal of Educational Sciences* 1 (1), 5-16.

Bloom, B. (Ed.) (1969). *Taxonomy of educational objectives*. New York: D. McKay Co. Inc.

Bloom, B. (1976). *Human characteristics and school learning*. New York: McGraw Hill.

Bloom, B., Hastings, T. & Madaus, G. (1971). *Handbook of formative and summative evaluation of student learning*. New York: McGraw-Hill.

Bloom, B., Madaus, G. & Hastings, T. (1981). *Evaluation to improve student learning*. New York: McGraw-Hill.

Bloom, H. (1992). *The American religion: The emergence of the post-Christian nation*. New York: Simon & Schuster.

Bloom, L. & Munro, P. (1993a, April). *Conflicts of selves: Interpretation and women's personal narratives*. Paper read to the annual meeting of the American Educational Research Association, Atlanta, GA.

Bloom, L. & Munro, P. (1993b). *Conflicts of selves: Non-unitary subjectivity in women's life history narratives.* Ames, IA: Iowa State University, College of Education, unpublished manuscript.

Blumenfeld-Jones, D. (in press, a). Curriculum, control, and creativity: An examination of curricular language and educational values. *JCT.*

Blumenfeld-Jones, D. (in press, b). Democracy education and human rights. *Education in Asia.*

Blumenfeld-Jones, D., Stinson, S. & Van Dyke, J. (1990). An interpretive study of meaning in dance: Voices of young women dance students. *Dance Research Journal,* 22 (2), 13-22.

Blundell, V., Shepherd, J. & Taylor, I. (Eds.). (1993). *Relocating cultural studies: Developments in theory and research.* London & New York: Routledge.

Boals, K. (1976). The politics of cultural liberation: Male-female relations in Algeria. In B. Carroll (Ed.), *Liberating women's history: Theoretical and critical essays.* Champaign, IL: University of Illinois Press.

Boateng, F. (1990). Combating deculturalization of the African-American child in the public school system: A multicultural approach. In K. Lomotey (Ed.), *Going to school: The African-American experience* (73-84). Albany, NY: State University of New York Press.

Bobbitt, F. (1911, November). A city school as a community art and musical center. *Elementary School Teacher,* 12 (3), 119-126.

Bobbitt, F. (1912, February). The elimination of waste in education. *Elementary School Teacher,* 12 (6), 259-271.

Bobbitt, F. (1915a). High school costs. *School Review,* 23 (8), 505-534.

Bobbitt, F. (1915b). *What the schools teach and might teach.* Philadelphia, PA: William F. Feel Company.

Bobbitt, F. (1918). *The curriculum.* New York: Houghton Mifflin.

Bobbitt, F. (1922). *Curriculum making in Los Angeles.* Chicago, IL: University of Chicago Press.

Bobbitt, F. (1924). *How to make a curriculum.* Boston, MA: Houghton Mifflin.

Bobbitt, F. (1926). *Curriculum investigations.* Chicago, IL: University of Chicago Press. [Reprinted 1927]

Bobbitt, F. (1934). Questionable recommendations of the commission on the social studies. *School and Society,* 40, 201-108.

Bode, B. (1927). *Modern educational theories.* New York: Macmillan.

Bode, B. (1938). *Progressive education at the crossroads.* New York: Newson & Company.

Boff, L. (1979). *Jesus Christ liberator: A critical Christology for our time.* [Trans. by Patrick Hughes.] Maryknoll, NY: Orbis.

Bolin, F. (1985). Dialogue or anti-dialogue. *JCT,* 6 (2), 80-116.

Bolin, F. (1987). On defining supervision. *Journal of Curriculum and Supervision,* 2 (4), 368-380.

Bollnow, O. (1989a). The pedagogical atmosphere. *Phenomenology + Pedagogy,* 7, 5-11.

Bollnow, O. (1989b). The pedagogical atmosphere: The perspective of the child. *Phenomenology + Pedagogy,* 7, 12-36.

Bollnow, O. (1989c). The pedagogical atmosphere: The perspective of the educator. *Phenomenology + Pedagogy*, 7, 37-63.

Bollnow, O. (1989d). Ceremonies and festive celebrations in the school. *Phenomenology + Pedagogy*, 7, 64-78.

Bond, H. (1934). *The education of the negro in the American social order*. New York: Prentice Hall.

Bond, H. (1939). *Negro education in Alabama: A study in cotton and steel*. Washington, DC: Associated Publishers.

Bond, H. (1959). *The search for talent*. Cambridge, MA: Harvard University Press.

Bond, H. (1972). *Black American scholars: A study of their beginnings*. Detroit, MI: Balamp Publishing.

Bond, H. (1976). *Education for freedom: A history of Lincoln University*. Princeton, NJ: Princeton University Press.

Books, S. (1992a, October). *Critical authority as a terrain of struggle: What is gained and what lost in the struggle on this terrain?* A paper presented to the Bergamo Conference on Curriculum Theory and Practice, Dayton, OH.

Books, S. (1992b). Literary journalism as educational criticism: A discourse on triage. *Holistic Education Review*, 5 (3), 41-51.

Boorstin, D. (1983). *The discoverers*. New York: Random House.

Boorstin, D. (1992). *The creators: A history of the heroes of the imagination*. New York: Random House.

Boostrom, R., Jackson, P. & Hansen, D. (1993, Fall). Coming together and staying apart: How a group of teachers and researchers sought to bridge the "research/practice gap." *Teachers College Record*, 95 (1), 35-44.

Borrowman, M. (Ed.). (1965). *Teacher education in America: A documentary history*. New York: Teachers College Press.

Bossing, N. (1949). *Principles of secondary education*. Englewood Cliffs, NJ: Prentice Hall.

Bowers, C. (1969). *The progressive educator and the depression: The radical years*. New York: Random House.

Bowers, C. (1980). Curriculum as cultural reproduction: An examination of the metaphor as carrier of ideology. *Teachers College Record*, 82 (2) 267-290.

Bowers, C. (1981). Orthodoxy in Marxist educational theory. *Discourse*, 1 (2) 54-63.

Bowers, C. (1984). *The promise of theory: Education and the politics of cultural change*. New York: Longman.

Bowers, C. (1986). The dialectic of nihilism and the state: Implications for an emancipatory theory of education. *Educational Theory*, 36 (3), 225-232.

Bowers, C. (1987). *Elements of a post-liberal theory of education*. New York: Teachers College Press.

Bowers, C. (1988). Teaching a nineteenth-century mode of thinking through a twentieth-century machine. *Educational Theory*, 38 (1), 41-46.

Bowers, C. (1991a). Some questions about the anachronistic elements in the Giroux- McLaren theory of a critical pedagogy. *Curriculum Inquiry*, 21 (2), 239-252.

Bowers, C. (1991b). Critical pedagogy and the "arch of social dreaming:" A response to the criticisms of Peter McLaren. *Curriculum Inquiry*, 21 (4), 479-487.

Bowers, C. (1993). *Against the grain: Critical essays on education, modernity, and the recovery of the ecological imperative.* New York: Teachers College Press.

Bowers, C & Flinders, D. (1991). *Culturally responsive teaching and supervision: A handbook for staff development.* New York: Teachers College Press.

Bowers, C., Housego, I., & Dyke, D. (Eds.). (1970). *Education and social policy* (169-179). New York: Random House .

Bowler, R. (1983). *Payment by results: A study in achievement accountability.* Boston, MA: Boston College, unpublished doctoral dissertation.

Bowles, S. & Gintis, H. (1976). *Schooling in capitalist America: Educational reform and the contradictions of economic life.* New York: Basic Books.

Bowles, S. & Gintis H. (1980). Contradiction and reproduction in educational theory. In L. Barton, R. Meigham & S. Walker (Eds.), *Schooling, ideology and the curriculum* (51-65). London, England: Falmer.

Bowman, A. & Haggerson, N. (1990). Empowering educators through the processes of enfolding and unfolding curriculum. In J. Sears & D. Marshall (Eds.), *Teaching and thinking about curriculum* (48-60). New York: Teachers College Press.

Boyd, W. (1979). The changing politics of curriculum policy making for American schools. In J. Schaffarsick & G. Sykes (Eds.), *Value Conflicts and Curriculum Issues* (73-138). Berkeley, CA: McCutchan.

Boyer, E. (1983), for the Carnegie Foundation for the Advancement of Teaching. *High school: A report on secondary education in America.* New York: Harper & Row.

Boyer, E. (1991). *Living with our deepest differences: Religious liberty in a pluralistic society.* Princeton, NJ: Carnegie Foundation for the Advancement of Teaching.

Brameld, T. (1971). *Patterns of educational philosophy: Divergence and convergence in culturological perspective.* New York: Holt, Rinehart, & Winston.

Brandt, R. (1987, May). Defending public education from the new puritans. *Educational Leadership*, 44 (8).

Brannon, R. & David, D. (Eds.). (1976). *The forty-nine percent majority: The male sex role.* Reading, MA: Addison Wesley Publishing Co.

Braverman, H. (1974). *Labor and monopoly capital: The degradation of work in the twentieth century.* New York: Monthly Review Press.

Bridges, T. (1991). Multiculturalism as a postmodernist project. *Inquiry: Critical Thinking Across the Disciplines*, 7 (4), 3-7.

Brimelow, P. (1985). Competition for public schools. In B. Gross & R. Gross (Eds.) *The great school debate: Which way for American education?* (345-353). New York: Simon & Schuster.

Brinkhaus, C. (1991). *Education systems in Europe.* Lafayette, LA: University of Southwestern Louisiana, College of Education, unpublished manuscript.

Britzman, D. (1989). Who has the floor? Curriculum, teaching, and the English student teacher's struggle for voice. *Curriculum Inquiry,* 19 (2), 143-162.

Britzman, D. (1991). *Practice makes practice: A critical study of learning to teach.* Albany, NY: State University of New York Press.

Britzman, D. (1992a). Teachers under suspicion: Is it true that teachers aren't as good as they used to be? In J. Kincheloe & S. Steinberg (Eds.), *Thirteen questions* (73-80). New York: Peter Lang.

Britzman, D. (1992b). The terrible problem of knowing thyself: Toward a poststructural account of teacher identity. *JCT,* 9 (3), 23-46.

Britzman, D. (1994). *Is there a queer pedagogy? Or, stop reading straight.* North York, Ontario, Canada: York University, Faculty of Education, unpublished paper.

Britzman, D., et al. (1993). Slips that show and tell: Fashioning multiculture as a problem of representation. In C. McCarthy & W. Crichlow (Eds.), *Race, identity, and representation in education* (188-200). New York: Routledge.

Brod, H. (1990, March 21). Scholarly studies of men: The new field is an essential complement to women's studies. *Chronicle of Higher Education,* B2-B3.

Brodkey, L. & Fine, M. (1988). Presence of body, absence of mind. *Journal of Education,* 170 (3), 84-99.

Brodribb, S. (1988). *Nothing matters: A critique of post-structuralism's epistemology.* Toronto, Ontario, Canada: University of Toronto, unpublished doctoral dissertation.

Brodribb, S. (1992). *Nothing mat(t)ers: A feminist critique of postmodernism.* North Melbourne, Australia: Spinifex Press.

Brooks, J. & Brooks, M. (1993). *In search of understanding: The case for constructivist classrooms.* Alexandria, VA: ASCD.

Broudy, H. (1988). Aesthetics and the curriculum. In W. Pinar (Ed.), *Contemporary curriculum discourses* (332-342). Scottsdale, AZ: Gorsuch Scarisbrick.

Broudy, H. (1990). DABE: Complaints, reminiscences, and response. *Educational Theory,* 40 (4), 431-435.

Broudy, H. (1991). The role of art education in the public school. In G. Willis & W. Schubert (Eds.), *Reflections from the heart of educational inquiry: Understanding curriculum and teaching through the arts* (60-73). Albany, NY: State University of New York Press.

Broudy, H., Smith, B. & Burnett, J. (1964). *Democracy and excellence in American secondary education.* Chicago, IL: Rand McNally.

Broverman, I., et al. (1970). Sex role stereotypes and clinical judgments of mental health. *Journal of Consulting and Clinical Psychology,* 34, 1-7.

Brown, C. (1993). Employee involvement in industrial decision making: Lessons for public schools. In J. Hannaway. & M. Carnoy (Eds.). *Decen-*

tralization and school improvement: Can we fulfill the promise? (202-231). San Francisco, CA: Jossey-Bass Publishers.

Brown, J., Collins, A. & Duguid, P. (1989). Situated cognition and the culture of learning. *Educational Researcher, 18* (1), 32-42.

Brown, R. (1973). *Knowledge, education and cultural change: Papers in the sociology of education.* London, England: Tavistock Publications.

Brown, R. (1991). *Toward a phenomenology of curriculum: The work of Max Van Manen and T. Tetsuo Aoki.* Baton Rouge, LA: Louisiana State University, Department of Curriculum and Instruction, unpublished Ph.D. dissertation.

Brown, T. (1988). How fields change: A critique of the "Kuhnian" view. In W. Pinar (Ed.), *Contemporary curriculum discourses* (16-30). Scottsdale, AZ: Gorsuch Scarisbrick.

Brown, W. (1938, May). The core is not all of the curriculum. *Curriculum Journal, 9,* 210.

Brubaker, D. & Brookbank, G. (1986). James B. Macdonald: A bibliography. *Journal of Curriculum and Supervision, 1* (3), 215-220.

Bruce K. (1986) *Orators and philosophers: A history of the idea of liberal education.* New York: Teachers College Press.

Bruckerhoff, C. (1988). Escape from the classroom routine: How collegial relations sponsor relief for teachers. *JCT, 8* (2), 43-59.

Bruckerhoff, C. (1994). School routines and the failure of curriculum reform. In R. Martusewicz & W. Reynolds (Eds.), *Inside out: Contemporary critical perspectives in education* (79-98). New York: St. Martin's Press.

Bruner, J. (1960). *The process of education.* New York: Vantage.

Bruner, J. (1966). *Toward a theory of instruction.* New York: Norton.

Bruner, J. (1971, September). The process of education revisited. *Phi Delta Kappan, 53,* 18-21.

Bruner, J. (1983). *In search of mind: Essays in autobiography.* New York: Harper & Row.

Bruner, J. (1986). *Acts of meaning.* Cambridge, MA: Harvard University Press.

Bruner, J. & Weisser, S. (1991). The invention of self: Autobiography and its forms. In D. Olson & H. Torrance (Eds.), *Literacy and orality* (129-148). Cambridge, England & New York: Cambridge University Press.

Bryson, M. & de Castell, S. (1993a). En/gendering equity: On some paradoxical consequences of institutionalized programs of emancipation. *Educational Theory, 43* (3), 341-355.

Bryson, M. & de Castell, S. (1993b). Queer pedagogy: Praxis makes perfect. *Canadian Journal of Education, 18* (3), 285-305.

BSCS (1993). *Developing biological literacy: A guide to developing secondary and post-secondary biology curricula.* Colorado, CO: BSCS [Biological Sciences Curriculum Study].

Buchanan, P. (1993, September 12). Speech to the Christian coalition in Washington, D.C. Reported by the Associated Press in "Buchanan defends anti-abortion stance." *Lafayette Sunday Advertiser,* A7.

Buetow, H. (1988). *The Catholic school.* New York: Crossroads.

Buhle, M. & Gordon, A. (1976). Sex and class in colonial and nineteenth century America. In B. Carroll (Ed.), *Liberating women's history: Theoretical critical essays.* Urbana, IL: University of Illinois Press.

Bulhan, H. (1985). *Frantz Fanon and the psychology of oppression.* New York: Plenum Press.

Bull, J. (1974). High school women: Oppression and liberation. In J. Stacey, S. Bereaud, & J. Daniels (Eds.), *And Jill came tumbling after: Sexism in American education.* New York: Dell.

Bullock, H. (1967). *A history of Negro education in the south: From 1619 to present.* Cambridge, MA: Harvard University Press.

Bullough, Jr., R. (1979a). Curriculum theory: A brief sketch of three historical strands. *Impact,* 14 (3), 5-9.

Bullough, Jr., R. (1979b). Persons-centered history and the field of curriculum. *JCT,* 1 (1), 123-135.

Bullough, Jr., R. (1981). *Democracy in education–Boyd H. Bode.* Bayside, NY: General Hall, Inc., Publishers.

Bullough, Jr., R. (1982). Teachers and teaching in the nineteenth century: St. George, Utah. *JCT,* 4 (2), 199-206.

Bullough, Jr., R. (1988). *The forgotten dream of American public education.* Ames, IA: Iowa State University Press.

Bullough, Jr., R. & Gitlin, A. (1985). Schooling and change: A view from the lower rung. *Teachers College Record,* 87 (2) 219-237.

Bullough, Jr., R., Goldstein, S., and Holt, L. (1981). *Human interests in the curriculum: Teaching and learning in a technological society.* New York: Teachers College Press.

Bullough, Jr., R., Goldstein, S. & Holt, L. (1982). Rational curriculum: Teachers and alienation. *JCT,* 4 (2), 132-143.

Bullough, Jr., R. & Goldstein, S. & Holt, L. (1984). Technical curriculum form and American elementary school art education. *Journal of Curriculum Studies,* 16 (2), 143-154.

Bullough, Jr., R., Knowles, J. & Crow, N. (1991). *Emerging as teacher.* New York: Routledge.

Burch, R. (1989). On phenomenology and its practices. *Phenomenology + Pedagogy,* 7, 187-217.

Burke, M. (1985). The personal and professional journey of James B. Macdonald. *JCT,* 6 (3), 84-119.

Burleigh, M. & Wipperman, W. (1991). *The racial state: Germany 1933-1945.* Cambridge, England: Cambridge University Press.

Burnett, L. (1951, February). Core programs in Washington State junior high schools. *School Review,* 59, 97-100.

Burn, B. (Ed.). (1993). *Integrating study abroad into the undergraduate liberal arts curriculum: Eight institutional case studies.* Westport, CT: Greenwood Press.

Burns, B. (1991, December 2). In New Zealand, good reading and writing come "naturally." *Newsweek,* 53.

Burns, J. (1980, July 19). Life and times of 2 African mini-states. *San Francisco Chronicle*, F-2.

Burns, R. & Brooks, G. (Eds.). (1970). *Curriculum design in a changing society*. Englewood Cliffs, NJ: Educational Technology Publishers.

Burt, E. (1985). *Curriculum and resistance in the public sphere: Language, community and responsibility*. Curriculum Praxis Monograph Series, No. 6. Edmonton, Alberta, Canada: University of Alberta, Faculty of Education, Department of Secondary Education.

Burton, E. (1979). Richard Lowell Edgeworth's Education Bill of 1779: A missing chapter in the history of Irish education. *Irish Journal of Education*, 13 (1), 24-33.

Burton, W. (1974). *Personal correspondence*. [Cited in Miller, J., 1979a.]

Bussis, A., Chittenden, E. & Amarel, M. (1976). *Beyond surface curriculum: An interview study of teachers' understandings*. Boulder, CO: Westview Press.

Butler, J. (1990). *Gender trouble: Feminism and the subversion of identity*. London, England: Routledge, Chapman & Hall.

Butt, R. (1980). Against the flight from theory: But towards the practical. *JCT*, 2 (2), 5-11.

Butt, R. (1983). *The illucidatory potential of autobiography and biography n understanding teachers' thoughts and actions*. Paper presented to the Bergamo Conference (Ohio, U.S.A.) and to the First International Symposium of the International Study Association on Teacher Thinking, Tilburg University (Holland).

Butt, R. (1984). Arguments for using biography in understanding teacher thinking. In R. Halkes & J. Olson (Eds.), *Teacher thinking: A new perspective on persisting problems in education* (95-103). Lisse, Holland: Swets & Zeitlinger.

Butt, R. (1985a). Appropriate multicultural pedagogy and its implementation in the high school. A paper presented at an Invitational Symposium "Teaching Methods for a Multicultural Society," Queens University, Kingston, Ontario, Canada, May 1-4.

Butt, R. (1985b). Curriculum: Metatheoretical horizons and emancipatory action. *JCT*, 6 (2), 7-24.

Butt, R. (1986). Preface. In T. Aoki & K. Jacknicke (Eds.), *Curriculum Canada VI: Understanding curriculum-as-lived*. Vancouver, British Columbia, Canada: Canadian Association of Curriculum Studies and the Centre for Curriculum and Instruction.

Butt, R. (1988). *Educating ourselves beyond racism*. A brief submitted to Alberta's Multicultural Commission. Lethbridge, Alberta, Canada: University of Lethbridge, unpublished manuscript.

Butt, R. (1989). An integrative function for teachers' biographies. In G. Milburn, I. Goodson & R. Clark (Eds.), *Re-interpreting curriculum research: Images and arguments* (146-159). London, Ontario, Canada: The Althouse Press.

Butt, R. (1990). Autobiographic praxis and self education: From alienation to authenticity. In J. Willinsky (Ed.), *The educational legacy of romanticism* (257-286). Waterloo, Ontario, Canada: Wilfrid Laurier University Press.

Butt, R. (1991). In the spotlight of life: Dramatic expression as emancipatory pedagogy. In G. Willis & W. Schubert (Eds.), *Reflections from the heart of curriculum inquiry: Understanding curriculum and teaching through the arts* (267-276). Albany, NY: State University of New York Press.

Butt, R., & Cremin, L. (1953). *A history of education in American culture.* New York: Henry Holt & Company.

Butt, R., & Raymond, D., (1986) Personal, practical and perspective: Influences on a teacher's thoughts and actions. In J. Lowyck (Ed.), *Teacher thinking and professional action* (306-327). Leuven, Belgium: University of Leuven.

Butt, R. & Raymond, D. (1987). Arguments for using qualitative approaches in understanding teacher thinking: The case for biography. *JCT,* 7 (1), 63-69.

Butt, R. & Raymond, D. (1988). Biographical and contextual influences on an "ordinary" teacher's thoughts and actions. In J. Lowyck, C. Clarke, & R. Halkes (Eds.), *Teacher thinking and professional action.* Lisse, Holland: Swets & Zeitlinger.

Butt, R. & Raymond, D. (1992). Studying the nature and development of teachers' knowledge using collaborative autobiography. *International Journal of Educational Research,* 13 (4), 402-449.

Butt, R. & Raymond, D. (forthcoming). Arguments for using qualitative approaches in understanding teacher thinking: the case for biography. In I. Goodson, (Ed.), *Understanding teachers' lives.* London, England: Routledge.

Butt, R., Raymond, D. & Yamagishi, L. (1987). Autobiographic praxis: Studying the formation of teachers' knowledge. *JCT,* 7 (4), 87-164.

Butt, R., Raymond, D., & Yamagishi, L. (1988). Autobiographic praxis: Studying the formation of teachers' knowledge (notes 1 & 2). *JCT,* 7 (4), 87-164.

Butt, R., Raymond, D., McCue, G. & Yamagishi, L. (1986). Individual and collective interpretations of teachers' biographies. *Resources in education* (E.R.I.C. microfiche; ED 269853).

Butt, R., D. Raymond, G. McCue & L. Yamagishi (1992). Collaborative autobiography and the teachers' voice. In Ivor F. Goodson (Ed.), *Studying Teachers Lives* (51-98). New York: Teachers College Press.

Butt, R., Townsend, D., & Raymond, D. (1990). Bringing reform to life: Teachers' stories and professional development. *Cambridge Journal of Education,* 20 (3), 255-268.

Bybee, R. (1979). Science education and the emerging ecological society. *Science Education,* 63, 95-109.

Bybee, R. (1985a). The restoration of confidence in science and technology education. *School Science and Mathematics,* 85, 95-108.

Bybee, R. (1985b). the Sisyphean question in science education: What should the scientifically and technologically literate person know, value, and do—as a citizen? In R. Bybee (Ed.), *Science/technology/society* (79-93). Washington, DC: National Science Teachers Association.

Bybee, R. & Welch, D. (1972). The third force: Humanistic psychology and science education. *The Science Teacher*, 39 (8), 18-22.

Bybee, R., Harms, N., Ward, B. & Yager, R. (1980). Science, society and science education. *Science Education*, 64, 377-395.

Byrnes, R. (1989, December/January). Contemporary education in the U.S.S.R.: A conversation with Robert F. Byrnes. [Harold G. Shane, interviewer]. *Educational Leadership*, 46 (4), 86-88.

California Public Affairs Forum (1991a). *Rebuilding America's Education Foundation*. Sponsored by the California Chamber of Commerce, Bay Area Council, and Hitachi, Ltd.

California Public Affairs Forum (1991b). *Education Reform: America's New Frontier*. Sponsored by the California Chamber of Commerce, the Los Angeles Area Chamber of Commerce, and Hitachi, Ltd.

California Textbook League (1992, 1993). *The textbook letter: A national report on schoolbooks and schoolbook affairs*. Sausalito, CA (PO Box 51): California Textbook League.

Callahan, R. (1962). *Education and the cult of efficiency*. Chicago, IL: University of Chicago Press.

Callan, E. (1982). Dewey's conception of education as growth. *Educational Theory*, 32 (1), 19-27.

Cambridge Journal of Education (1990). Special issue: *Biography and Life History in Education*, 20 (3).

Campbell, D. & Stanley, J. (1963). *Experimental and quasi-experimental designs for research*. Chicago, IL: Rand McNally.

Caputo, J. (1987). *Radical hermeneutics: Repetition, deconstruction and the hermeneutic project*. Bloomington, IN: Indiana University Press.

Carby, H. (1989, Winter). The canon: Civil war and reconstruction. *Michigan Quarterly*, 35-43.

Carby, H. (1993). Encoding white resentment: Grand Canyon—A narrative. In C. McCarthy & W. Crichlow (Eds.), *Race, identity, and representation* (236-247). New York: Routledge.

Carlson, D. (1982a, October). *Formulating a critical ethnographic account of school culture and everyday life*. Paper presented at the fourth annual Conference on Curriculum Theory and Classroom Practice, Airlie, Virginia.

Carlson, D. (1982b). Updating individualism and the work ethic: Corporate logic in the classroom. *Curriculum Inquiry*, 12 (2), 125-160.

Carlson, D. (1982c). An ontological grounding for curriculum: Learning to be in-the-world. *JCT*, 4 (2), 207-215.

Carlson, D. (1986). Teachers, class culture, and the politics of schooling. *Interchange*, 17 (4), 17-36.

Carlson, D. (1987). Teachers as political actors: From reproductive theory to the crisis of schooling. *Harvard Educational Review*, 57 (3), 283-307.

Carlson, D. (1991). *Alternative discourses in multicultural education: Towards a critical reconstruction of a curricular field.* Paper presented to the Bergamo Conference on Curriculum Theory and Classroom Practice, Dayton, OH.

Carlson, D. (1992a). Education as a political issue: What's missing in the public conversation about education? In J. Kincheloe & S. Steinberg (Eds.), *Thirteen questions* (263-274). New York: Peter Lang.

Carlson, D. (1992b). *Teachers and crisis: Urban school reform and teachers' work culture.* New York & London, England: Routledge.

Carlson, D. (1992c). Ideological conflict and change in the sexuality curriculum. In J. Sears (Ed.), *Sexuality and the curriculum* (34-58). New York: Teachers College Press.

Carlson, R. (1972). Understanding women: Implications for personality theory and research. *Journal of Social Issues,* 28, 17-32.

Carmody, D. (1991). *The good alliance: Feminism, religion, and education.* Lanham, MD: University Press of America.

Carnoy, M. (1993). School improvement: Is privatization the answer? In J. Hannaway. & M. Carnoy (Eds.). *Decentralization and school improvement: Can we fulfill the promise?* (163-201). San Francisco, CA: Jossey-Bass Publishers.

Carnoy, M. & Levin, H. (1985). *Schooling and work in the democratic state.* Stanford, CA: Stanford University Press.

Carr, W. & Kemmis, S. (1986). *Becoming critical: Education, knowledge and action research.* London, England: Falmer.

Carroll, B. (Ed.). (1976). *Liberating women's history: Theoretical and critical essays.* Urbana, IL: University of Illinois Press.

Carroll, D. (1978). A review of *Of Grammatology by Jacques Derrida. Clio,* 7 (3).

Carroll, J. (1963, May). A model of school learning. *Teachers College Record,* 64, 723- 733.

Carson, T. (1984). *A hermeneutic investigation of the meaning of curriculum implementation for consultants and teachers.* Edmonton, Alberta, Canada: University of Alberta, Faculty of Education, Department of Secondary Education, unpublished Ph.D. dissertation.

Carson, T. (1987). Teaching as curriculum scholarship: Honoring Professor Ted Tetsuo Aoki. *JCT,* 7 (3), 7-10.

Carson, T. (Ed.). (1988). *Toward a renaissance of human ity: Rethinking curriculum and instruction.* Edmonton, Alberta, Canada: World Council for Curriculum & Instruction.

Carson, T. (1989, May/June). Beyond curriculum management. *The ATA Magazine,* 52-56.

Carson, T. (1990a). What kind of knowing is critical action research? *Theory into Practice,* XXIX (3), 167-173.

Carson, T. (1990b, September). *The international classroom.* Paper presented at the annual conference of the Canadian Educational Association, St. John's Brunswick.

Carson, T. (1990c, January/February). Hearing the voices of teachers. *The ATA Magazine,* 21-25.

Carson, T. (1991). Pedagogical reflections on reflective practice in teacher education. *Phenomenology + Pedagogy,* 9,132-142.

Carson, T. (1992a). Remembering forward. In W. Pinar and W. Reynolds (Eds.). *Understanding curriculum as phenomenological and deconstructed text* (102-115). New York: Teachers College Press.

Carson, T. (1992b). Questioning curriculum implementation: Scenes from a conversation. *JCT,* 9 (3), 71-96.

Carson, T. (1992c, May/June). Re-visioning the nineties: Some thoughts on the urgency for educational change. *The ATA Magazine,* 20-22.

Carson, T., Connors, B., Ripley, D., & Smits, H. (n. d.). *Creating possibilities: An action research handbook.* Edmonton, Alberta, Canada: University of Alberta, Faculty of Education, Department of Secondary Education.

Carter, K. (1992). Creating cases for the development of teacher knowledge. In T. Russell & H. Munby (Eds.). *Teachers and teaching: From classroom to reflection* (109-123). London, England: Falmer.

Carter, K. & Unklesbay, R. (1989). Cases in teaching law. *Journal of Curriculum Studies,* 21 (6), 527-536.

Casey, K. (1990). Teacher as mother: Curriculum theorizing in the life histories of contemporary women teachers. *Cambridge Journal of Education,* 20 (3), 301-320.

Casey, K. (1991). Teachers and values: The progressive use of religion in education. *JCT,* 9 (1), 23-69.

Casey, K. (1992). Why do progressive women activists leave teaching: Theory, methodology and politics in life-history research. In I. Goodson (Ed.), *Studying teachers lives* (187-208). New York: Teachers College Press.

Casteel, J. & Stahl, R. (1975). *Value clarification in the classroom: A primer.* Pacific Palisades, CA: Goodyear Publishing Co., Inc.

Castenell, Jr., L. (1990). The new south as curriculum: Implications for understanding southern race relations. In J. Kincheloe & W. Pinar (Eds.), *Curriculum as social psychoanalysis: The significance of place* (155-166). Albany, NY: State University of New York Press.

Castenell, Jr., L. (1992). Introduction: Politics and the schools. *Educational Foundations,* 6 (2), 3-5.

Castenell, Jr., L. & Pinar, W. (1993). Introduction. In L. Castenell, Jr., & W. Pinar (Eds.), *Understanding curriculum as racial text: Representations of identity and difference in education* (1-30). Albany, NY: State University of New York Press.

Caswell, H. (1934). Practical application of mechanistic and organismic psychologies to curriculum making. *Journal of Education Research,* 23 (1), 16-24.

Caswell, H. (1978, November). Persistent curriculum problems. *The Educational Forum,* 43, 99-110.

Caswell, H. & Campbell, D. (1935). *Curriculum development.* New York: American Book Company.

Caswell, H. & Campbell, D. (Eds.). (1937). *Readings in curriculum development.* New York: American Book Company.

Caswell, H. (1950). *Curriculum improvement in the public schools.* New York: Teachers College Press.

Caws, P. (1988). *Structuralism: The art of the intelligible.* Atlantic Highlands, NJ: Humanities Press International, Inc.

Cazden, C. (1983). Can ethnographic research go beyond the status quo? *Anthropology and Education Quarterly,* 14, 33-41.

Cazden, C. (1986). Classroom discourse. In M. Wittrock (Ed.), *Handbook of Research on Teaching* (432-463). [Third edition.] New York: Macmillan.

Cazden, C. (1988). *Classroom discourse: The language of teaching and learning.* Portsmouth, NH: Heinemann.

Cazden, C., John, V. & Hymes, D. (Eds.). (1972). *Functions of language in the classroom.* New York: Teachers College Press. [Reprinted by Waveland Press, 1982.]

Celis 3rd, W. (1992, September 2). Schools reopen in town that made them close. *New York Times,* A8.

Chamberlin, D., Chamberlin, E., Drought, N., & Scott, W. (1942). *Adventures in American education. Vol. IV: Did they succeed in college?* New York: Harper & Brothers.

Charlesworth, R., Hart, C., Burts, D., & DeWolf, M. (in press). *Advances in early education and day care.*

Charters, W. (1909). *Methods of teaching developed from a functional standpoint.* Chicago, IL: Row, Peterson & Company.

Charters, W. (1923). *Curriculum construction.* New York: Macmillan.

Chazan, B. (1985). *Contemporary approaches to moral education: Analyzing alternative theories.* New York: Teachers College Press.

Chazan, B. (1992). The state of moral education theory. In. A. Garrod (Ed.), *Learning for life: Moral education theory and practice* (3-24). Westport, CT: Praeger.

Chazan, B. & Soltis, J. (Eds.). (1973). *Moral education.* New York: Teachers College Press.

Chen, D. & Oren, A. (1991). Knowledge technology and curriculum theory. In A. Lewy (Ed.), *International encyclopedia of curriculum* (131-137). Oxford, England: Pergamon Press.

Chen, T. (1981). *Chinese education since 1949–academic and revolutionary models.* New York: Pergamon.

Cheney, L. (1987). *American memory: A report on the humanities in the nation's public schools.* Washington, DC: National Endowment for the Humanities.

Cheney, L. (1990). *Tyrannical machines: A report on educational practices gone wrong and our best hopes for setting them right.* Washington, DC: National Endowment for the Humanities.

Cherryholmes, C. (1980). Social knowledge and citizenship education. *Curriculum Inquiry,* 10 (2), 115-142.

Cherryholmes, C. (1988a). An exploration of meaning and the dialogue between textbooks and teaching. *Journal of Curriculum Studies,* 20 (1), 1-21.

Cherryholmes, C. (1988b). *Power and criticism: Poststructural investigations in education.* New York: Teachers College Press.

Cheru, F. (1987). *Independence, underdevelopment, and unemployment in Kenya.* Lanham, MD: University Press of America.

Chesler, P. (1978). *About men.* New York: Simon & Schuster.

Chiarelott, L. (1983a). The role of experience in the curriculum: An analysis of Dewey's theory of experience. *JCT,* 5 (3), 29-40.

Chiarelott, L. (1983b). The role of experience in the curriculum: Application of Dewey's theory of experience. *JCT,* 5 (4), 22-37.

Childs, J. (1931). *Education and the philosophy of experimentalism.* New York: The Century Co.

Childs, J. (1938, November). Dr. Bode on "authentic democracy." *Social Frontier,* 15 (39), 40-43.

Chinese Education (1984, Summer). China's keypoint school controversy 1978-1982. 17 (2).

Chira, S. (1992, April 26). Made in America: Asia's school success. New York: *New York Times,* E5.

Chodorow, N. (1978) *The Reproduction of Mothering.* Berkeley, CA: University of California Press.

Chodorow, N. (1979). Feminism and difference: Gender, relation, and difference in psychoanalytic perspective. *Socialist Review,* 9 (4), 51-69.

Christian-Smith, L. (1987). Gender, popular culture, and curriculum: Adolescent romantic novels as gender text. *Curriculum Inquiry,* 17 (4), 365-406.

Christian-Smith, L. (1988). Romancing the girl: Adolescent romance novels and the construction of femininity. In L. Roman & L. Christian-Smith, *Becoming Feminine* (76-101). Philadelphia, PA: Falmer.

Ciardi, J. (1960). *How does a poem mean?* Boston, MA: Houghton Mifflin.

Cixous, H. (1976). The laugh of the Medusa. *Signs: Journal of Women in Culture and Society,* 1 (4), 875-893.

Cixous, H. (1986). *Inside.* [Trans. by C. Barko.] New York: Schocken Books.

Cixous, H. & Clement, C. (1986). *Newly born woman.* [Trans. by B. Wing.] Minneapolis, MN: University of Minnesota Press.

Clancey, W. (1987). *Knowledge-based tutoring: The GUIDON program.* Cambridge, MA: MIT Press.

Clandinin, J. (1985). Personal practical knowledge: A study of teachers' classroom images. *Curriculum Inquiry,* 15 (4), 361-385.

Clandinin, J. (1986). *Classroom practice: Teachers images in action.* London, England: Falmer.

Clandinin, J. (1989). Developing rhythm in teaching: The narrative study of a beginning teacher's personal practical knowledge of classrooms. *Curriculum Inquiry,* 19 (2), 121-141.

Clandinin, J., Davies, A., Hogan, P. & Kennard, B. (Eds.). (1993). *Learning to teach, teaching to learn: Stories of collaboration in teacher education.* New York: Teachers College Press.

Clandinin, J. & Connelly, M. (1987a). Teachers' personal practical knowledge: What counts as 'personal' is studies of the personal. *Journal of Curriculum Studies*, 19 (6), 487-500.

Clandinin, J. & Connelly, M. (1987b). Inquiry into schooling: Diverse perspectives. *Journal of Curriculum and Supervision*, 2 (4), 295-313.

Clandinin, J. & Connelly, M. (1988). Study teachers' knowledge of classrooms: Collaborative research, ethics, and the negotiation of narrative. *The Journal of Educational Thought*, 22 (2A), 269-282.

Clandinin, J. & Connelly, M. (1990). Narrative, experience and the study of curriculum. *Cambridge Journal of Education*, 20 (3), 241- 254.

Clandinin, J. & Connelly, M. (1991). Narrative and story in practice and research. In D. Schon (Ed.), *The reflective turn: Case studies in and on educational practice* (258-281). New York: Teachers College Press.

Clandinin, J. & Connelly, M. (1992). Teacher as curriculum maker. In P. Jackson (Ed.), *Handbook of research on curriculum* (363-401). New York: Macmillan.

Clark, C. (1992). Teachers as designers in self-directed professional development. In A. Hargreaves & M. Fullan (Eds.), *Understanding teacher development*. New York: Teachers College Press.

Clark, R. & LaLonde, D. (1992). A case for department-based professional development sites for secondary teacher education. *Journal of Teacher Education*, 43 (1), 35-41.

Cleaver, E. (1968). *Soul on ice*. New York: McGraw-Hill.

Clement, J. (1923). *Curriculum making in the secondary schools*. New York: Henry Holt & Company.

Clifford, G. (Ed.). (1962). *Psychology and the science of education: Selected writings of Edward L. Thorndike*. New York: Teachers College Press.

Clifford, G. (1968). *The sane positivist: A biography of Edward L. Thorndike*. Middletown, CT: Wesleyan University Press.

Clifford, G. (1987). Gender expectations and American teachers. *Teacher Education Quarterly*, 14 (2), 6-1.

Clift, R., Veal, M., Johnson, M., & Holland, P. (1990). Restructuring teacher education through collaborative action research. *Journal of Teacher Education*, 41 (2), 52-62.

Cockburn, V. (1991). The uses of folk music and songwriting in the classroom. *Harvard Educational Review*, 61 (1), 71-79.

Cogan, M. (1973). *Clinical supervision*. Boston, MA: Houghton Mifflin.

Cohen, M. (1991). An American teacher's view of British assessment practices. Studies on Exhibitions, No. 2. Providence, RI: Brown University, Coalition for Essential Schools.

Cohen, S. (Ed.). (1974). *Education in the United States: A documentary history*. (Vols. 1-5). New York: Random House.

Cohn, E. (1979). *The economics of education*. Cambridge, England: Ballinger.

Cohn, E. & Geske, T. (1990). *The economics of education*. [Third edition.] New York: Pergamon Press.

Coleman, J. (1976). Athletics in high school. In R. Brannon & D. David (Eds.), *The forty-nine percent majority: The male sex role.* Reading, MA: Addison Wesley.

Coleman, J. (1989, November). Schools and communities. *Chicago Studies, 28* (3), 232-244.

Coleman, J. & Hoffer, T. & Kilgore, S. (1981). *Public and private schools.* Washington, DC: National Center for Education Statistics.

Coleman, J. & Hoffer, T. (1987). *Public and private high schools: The impact of communities.* New York: Basic Books.

Coleman, J., Kilgore, S., & Hoffer, T. (1982). *High school achievement: Public, Catholic and private schools.* New York: Basic Books.

Collins, P. (1993). It's in our hands: Breaking the silence on gender in African American studies. In L. Castenell, Jr. & W. Pinar (Eds.), *Understanding curriculum as racial text: Representations of identity and difference in education* (127-142). Albany, NY: State University of New York Press.

Collins, R. (1993). Responding to cultural diversity in our schools. In L. Castenell, Jr. & W. Pinar (Eds.). *Understanding curriculum as racial text: Representations of identity and difference in education* (195-208). Albany, NY: State University of New York Press.

Collins, S. (1974). *A different heaven and earth.* Valley Forge, PA: Judson Press.

Comer, J. & Haynes, N. (1990). Helping black children succeed: The significance of some social factors. In K. Lomotey (Ed.), *Going to school: The African-American experience* (212), Albany, NY: State University of New York Press.

Comer, J. & Haynes, N. (1991). Meeting the needs of black children in public school: A school reform challenge. In C. Willie, A. Garibaldi & W. Reed (Eds.), *The education of African-Americans* (67-71). New York: Auburn House.

Common, D. (1983). Power: The missing concept in the dominant model of school change. *Theory Into Practice,* XXII (3), 203-210.

Common, D. & Grimmett, P. (1992). Beyond the war of the worlds: A consideration of the estrangement between curriculum and supervision. *Journal of Curriculum and Supervision,* 7 (3), 209-225.

Conant, J. (1959). *The American high school today.* New York: McGraw Hill.

Conant, J. (1963). *The education of American teachers.* New York: McGraw-Hill.

Conlon, J. & Dow, P. (1975). Pro/con forum: The MACOS controversy. *Social Education,* 39, 388-396.

Connell, W. & Lizhong, Z. (1991). People's Republic of China. In A. Lewy (Ed.), *The international encyclopedia of curriculum* (228-230). New York: Pergamon.

Connelly, M. & Clandinin, J. (1987). On narrative method, biography and narrative unities in the study of teaching. *The Journal of Educational Thought,* 21 (3), 130-139.

Connelly, M. & Clandinin, J. (1988a). *Teachers as curriculum planners: Narratives of experience.* New York: Teachers College Press.

Connelly, M. & Clandinin, J. (1988b). Narrative meaning: Focus on teacher education, *Elements*, 19 (2), 15-18.

Connelly, M. & Clandinin, J. (1990). Stories of experience and narrative inquiry. *Educational Researcher*, 19 (4), 2-14.

Connelly, M. & Clandinin, J. (1991). Narrative inquiry: Storied experience. In E. Short (Ed.), *Forms of curriculum inquiry* (121-154). Albany, NY: State University of New York Press.

Connelly, M., Dukacz, A., & Quinlan, F. (Eds.) (1980). *Curriculum planning for the classroom*. Toronto, Ontario, Canada: OSIE Press.

Convey, J. (1992). *Catholic schools make a difference: Twenty-five years of research.* Washington, DC: National Catholic Educational Association.

Cook, R. & Doll, R. (1973). *The elementary school curriculum.* Boston, MA: Allyn & Bacon, Inc.

Cook, T. & Reichardt, C. (Eds.). (1979). *Qualitative and quantitative methods in evaluation research.* Beverly Hills, CA: Sage.

Coolahan, J. (1975). *The origins of the payment by results policy in education and the experience of it in the national and intermediate schools of Ireland.* Dublin, Ireland: Trinity College, Dublin, unpublished masters thesis.

Coombs, P. & Ahmed, M. (1974). *Attacking rural poverty: How nonformal education can help.* Baltimore, MD: Johns Hopkins University Press.

Coomer, D. (1986). Reformulating the evaluation process. In K. Sirotnik & J. Oakes (Eds.), *Critical perspectives on the organization and improvement of schooling* (163-204). Boston, MA: Kluwer-Nijhoff.

Cornbleth, C. (1991). *Curriculum in context.* London, England: Falmer.

Cornett, J. (1990, Summer). Utilizing action research in graduate curriculum courses. *Theory into Practice*, XXIX (3),185-195.

Corrigan, P. (1989). State formation and classroom practice: Once again "on moral regulation." In G. Milburn, I. Goodson, & R. Clark (Eds.), *Re-interpreting curriculum research: Images and arguments* (64-84). London, Ontario, Canada: The Althouse Press.

Cortes, C. (1986). The education of language minority students: A contextual interaction model. In California State Department of Education (Ed.), *Beyond language: Social and cultural factors in schooling language minority students* (3-33). Los Angeles, CA: California State University, Evaluation, Dissemination, and Assessment Center.

Corwin, R. (1970). *Militant professionalism: A study of organizational craft in high schools.* New York: Appleton-Century-Crofts.

Cottrell, D. (1987). The instructional climate at Teachers College, 1930-1945. *Teaching Education*, 1 (2), 25-26.

Counts, G. (1922). *The selective character of American secondary education.* Chicago, IL: University of Chicago Press.

Counts, G. (1926). *The senior high school curriculum.* Chicago, IL: University of Chicago Press.

Counts, G. (1927) *The social composition of boards of education.* Chicago, IL: University of Chicago Press.

Counts, G. (1930). *The American road to culture: A social interpretation of education*. New York: John Day Co.

Counts, G. (1932). *Dare the schools build a new social order?* New York: John Day Co.

Counts, G. (1934). *The social foundations of education*. New York: Scribners.

Counts, G. (1957). *The challenge of Soviet education*. New York: McGraw-Hill.

Counts, G. (1959). *Kruschev and the Central Committee speak on education*. Pittsburgh, PA: University of Pittsburgh Press.

Court, D. (1989). Sub-Saharan Africa. *Comparative Education Review*, 33 (2), 282-283.

Courtney, R. (1986). Islands of remorse: Amerindian education in the contemporary world. *Curriculum Inquiry*, 16 (1), 43-64.

Cousins, N. (1987). T.C. in the thirties. *Teaching Education*, 1 (2), 22-24. Reprinted from W. First (Ed.), (1969), *University on the heights*. New York: Doubleday.

Coward, R., Jr. (n.d.). Cultural collision in urban schools. In M. Belok & R. Shoub (Eds.), *Sex, Race, Ethnicity and Education*, 1 (1,2), 208-215.

Craig, T. (1984). *The experience of active imaging: The Jungian and the dramatic perspectives*. Curriculum Praxis, Occasional Paper No. 29. Edmonton, Alberta, Canada: University of Alberta, Faculty of Education, Department of Secondary Education.

Crandall, D. et al. (1983). *People, policies, and practices: Examining the chain of school improvement*. Andover, MA: The Network.

Crary, R. (1969). *Humanizing the school: Curriculum development and theory*. New York: Alfred A. Knopf.

Cremin, L. (1951). *The American common school*. New York: Teachers College Press.

Cremin, L. (1955, March). The revolution in American secondary education, 1893-1918. *Teachers College Record*, 56, 295-308.

Cremin, L. (1961, 1964). *The transformation of the school: Progressivism in American education 1876-1957*. New York: Vintage.

Cremin, L. (1965). *The genius of American education*. New York: Random House.

Cremin, L. (Ed.). (1969). *The national Herbart society yearbooks 1-5, 1895-1899*. New York: Arno Press.

Cremin, L. (1970). *American education: The colonial experience 1607-1786*. New York: Harper & Row.

Cremin, L. (1971). Curriculum-making in the United States. *Teachers College Record*, 73 (2), 207-220. Reprinted with Cremin's autobiographical statement in W. Pinar (Ed.) (1975), *Curriculum theorizing: The reconceptualists* (19-35). Berkeley, CA: McCutchan.

Cremin, L. (1976). *Public education*. New York: Basic Books.

Cremin, L. (1980). *American education: The national experience 1783-1876*. New York: Harper Colophon Books.

Cremin, L. (1988). *American education: The metropolitan experience, 1876-1980*. New York: Harper & Row.

Crichlow, W. (1985). *Urban crisis, schooling, and black youth unemployment: A case study.* Rochester, NY: University of Rochester, Graduate School of Education and Human Development, unpublished manuscript.

Crichlow, W. (1990, October). *Theories of representation: Implications for understanding race in the multicultural curriculum.* Paper presented to the Bergamo Conference, Dayton, OH.

Crittenden, B. (1991). Comparing liberal and marxist theorists. *Curriculum Inquiry,* 21 (3), 387-392.

Cronbach, L. (1955). *Text materials in modern education.* Champaign, IL: University of Illinois Press.

Cronbach, L. (1983). Course improvement through evaluation. In G. Madaus, M. Scriven, & D. Stufflebeam (Eds.), *Evaluation models: Viewpoints on education and human services evaluation* (101-115). Boston, MA: Kluwer-Nijhoff.

Crowley, S. (1989). *Deconstruction.* Champaign, IL: NCTC.

Cuban, L. (1979). Determinants of curriculum change and stability, 1870-1970. In J. Schaffarzick, & G. Sykes, (Eds.). *Values conflicts and curriculum issues: Lessons from research and experience* (139-196). Berkeley, CA: McCutchan.

Cuban, L. (1982). Persistence of the inevitable: The teacher-centered classroom. *Education and Urban Society,* 1 (26-41).

Cuban, L. (1983, Summer). How did teachers teach, 1890-1980. *Theory into Practice,* XXII (3), 159-165.

Cuban, L. (1984/1993). *How teachers taught: Constancy and change in American classrooms 1890-1980.* New York: Longman.

Cuban, L. (1990). Reforming again, again, and again. *Educational Researcher,* 19, 3-13.

Cuban, L. (1992). Curriculum stability and change. In P. Jackson (Ed.), *Handbook of research on curriculum* (216-247). New York: Macmillan.

Cubberley, E. (1920). *The history of education.* Boston, MA: Houghton, Mifflin.

Cubberley, E. (1934). *Public education in the United States.* Boston, MA: Houghton Mifflin.

Culler, J. (1976). *Structuralist poetics: Structuralism, linguistics, and the study of literature.* Ithaca, NY: Cornell University Press.

Culley, M. & Portuges, C. (Eds.) (1985). *Gender subjects: The dynamics of feminist teaching.* New York: Routledge.

Cummins, C., Good, R. & Pinar, W. (1989). *The hidden curriculum with the teaching of science and its relationship to current science education goals.* Paper presented to the annual meeting of the American Educational Research Association, San Francisco, CA.

Cummings, W. (1990). Evaluation and examination. In R. Thomas (Ed.), *International comparative education* (87-106). Oxford, England: Pergamon.

Cunningham, B. (1979). *Teaching as being: The right to personhood.* Occasional paper no. 6. Edmonton, Alberta, Canada: University of Alberta, Faculty of Education, Department of Secondary Education.

Curtis, B. (1989). Curricular change and the "Red Readers:" History and theory. In G. Milburn, I. Goodson, & R. Clark (Eds.), *Re-interpreting curriculum research: Images and arguments* (41-63). London, Ontario, Canada: The Althouse Press.

Cushman, K. (1992a, March). Essential schools and state systems: How is the climate changing? *Horace*, 8 (4), 1-8.

Cushman, K. (1992b). Essential schools' "universal goals:" How can heterogeneous grouping help? *Horace*, 8 (5), 1-8.

Daignault, J. (1983). Curriculum and action-research: An artistic activity in a perverse way. *JCT*, 5 (3), 4-28.

Daignault, J. (1984). *Curriculum: Beyond words with words.* Rimouski, Québec, Canada: University of Québec, unpublished manuscript.

Daignault, J. (1986). *Semiotics of educational expression.* Rimouski, Québec, Canada: University of Québec, unpublished manuscript.

Daignault, J. (1987, October). *Autobiography of a style.* Paper presented to the Bergamo Conference on Curriculum Theory and Classroom Practice, Dayton, OH.

Daignault, J. (1988). *The language of research and the language of practice: Neither one nor the other: Pedagogy.* Rimouski, Québec, Canada: University of Québec, unpublished manuscript.

Daignault, J. (1989). *Curriculum as composition: Who is the composer?* Rimouski, Québec, Canada: University of Québec, unpublished manuscript.

Daignault, J. (1992a). Traces at work from different places. In W. Pinar & W. Reynolds (Eds.), *Understanding curriculum as phenomenological and deconstructed Text* (195-215). New York: Teachers College Press.

Daignault, J. (1992b, October). *Serenity.* Paper presented to the Bergamo Conference, Dayton, OH.

Daignault, J. & Gauthier, C. (1982). The indecent curriculum machine. *JCT*, 4 (1), 177-196.

Dale, E. (1954). *Audiovisual methods in teaching.* [Rev. ed.] New York: Dryden Press.

Dale, M. (1986). Stalking a conceptual chameleon: Ideology in marxist studies of education. *Educational Theory*, 36 (3), 241-257.

Dale, R. et al. (Eds.). (1976). *Schooling and capitalism.* London, England: Routledge & Kegan Paul.

Dale, R. (1992). *National reform, economic crisis and "New Right" theory: A New Zealand perspective.* Paper presented to the annual meeting of the American Educational Research Association, San Francisco.

Daly, M. (1973). *Beyond God the father: Toward a philosophy of women's liberation.* Boston: Beacon Press.

Daly, M. (1978). *Gyn/Ecology: The metaethics of radical feminism.* Boston, MA: Beacon Press.

Daniels, A. (1975). Feminist perspectives in sociological research. In M. Millman & R. Kanter (Eds.), *Another voice: Feminist perspectives on social life and social science.* Garden City, NY: Anchor Press, Doubleday.

Daniel, D. (1991). *Teaching as hermeneutics.* Edmonton, Alberta, Canada: University of Alberta, Department of Educational Psychology, unpublished Ph.D. dissertation.

Darling-Hammond, L. (1985). Valuing teachers: The making of a profession. *Teachers College Record,* 87 (2), 205-218.

Darling-Hammond, L. (1986). A proposal for evaluation in the teaching profession. *Elementary School Journal,* 86 (4), 531-551.

Darling-Hammond, L. (1988). Accountability and teacher professionalism. *American Educator,* 12 (4), 8-13, 38-43.

Darling-Hammond, L. with Sclan, E. (1992). Policy and supervision. In C. Glickman (Ed.), *Supervision in transition.* Alexandria, VA: ASCD.

Darling-Hammond, L. (Ed.). (1994). *Professional development schools: Schools for developing a profession.* New York: Teachers College Press.

Darling-Hammond, L. & Snyder, J. (1992). Curriculum studies the traditions of inquiry: The scientific tradition. In P. Jackson (Ed.), *Handbook of research on curriculum* (41-78). New York: Macmillan.

Darling-Hammond, L., Griffin, G., & Wise, A. (1992). *Excellence in teacher education: Helping teachers develop learner-centered schools.* Washington, DC: National Education Association.

da Silva, T. & McLaren, P. (1993). Knowledge under siege: The Brazilian debate. In P. McLaren & P. Leonard (Eds.), *Paulo Freire: A critical encounter* (36-46). London & New York: Routledge.

Davies, P. (1988). *The cosmic blueprint: New discoveries in nature's creative ability to order the universe.* New York: Simo n & Schuster.

Davies, P. (1990, May/June). Cosmogenesis. *Creation,* 6 (3), 10-13.

Davies, P. (1992). *The mind of God.* New York: Simon & Schuster.

Davis, B. (1994a). Mathematics teaching: Moving from telling to listening. *Journal of Curriculum and Supervision,* 9 (3), 262-283.

Davis, B. (1994b). *Listening to reason: An inquiry into mathematics teaching.* Edmonton, Alberta, Canada: University of Alberta, Department of Secondary Education, unpublished Ph.D. dissertation.

Davis, Jr., O. (Ed.). (1976). *Perspectives on curriculum development 1776-1976.* Washington, DC: ASCD.

Davis, Jr., O. (1986). ASCD and curriculum development: The later years. In W. van Til (Ed.), *ASCD in retrospect: Contributions to the history of the Association for Supervision and Curriculum Development* (83-93). Alexandria, VA: ASCD.

Davis, Jr., O., Ponder, G., Burlbaw, L., Garza-Lubeck, M., & Moss, A. (1986). *Looking at history: A review of major U.S. history textbooks.* Washington, DC: People for the American Way.

Davis, T. (n.d.) *Beyond the scared and the profane: Landscape photography and the sense of place.* Austin, TX: University of Texas at Austin, American Civilization Program, unpublished manuscript.

de Beaugrande, R. (1988). In search of feminist discourse: The "difficult" case of Luce Irigaray. *College English,* 50, 253-272.

de Beauvoir, S. (1974). *The second sex.* New York: Vintage Books.

DeBoer, G. (1991). *A history of ideas in science education.* New York: Teachers College Press.

DeBoer, P., et al. (1993). *Educating Christian teachers for responsive discipleship.* Landham, MD: University Press of America.

Debord, G. (1990). *Comments on the society of the spectacle.* New York & London: Verso.

De Camp, L. (1969). End of the monkey war. *Scientific American* 200,15-21.

de Castenell, S. (1988). Teachers and texts: A political economy of class and gender relations in education: A review. *Educational Studies,* 19 (3-4), 338-349.

Deem, R. (Ed.). (1980). *Schooling for women's work.* London, England: Routledge & Kegan Paul.

Deever, B. (1991, April 2-3). *The Panopticon of tracking: Desegregation and curriculum change in a southern school, 1968-1972.* Paper presented to the Society for the Study of Curriculum History Annual Conference, Chicago, IL.

DeGarmo, C. (1895). *Herbart and the Herbartians.* London: Heinemann.

DeKock, A. & Paul, C. (1989, September). One district's commitment to global education. *Educational Leadership,* 47 (1), 46-49.

Deleuze, G. & Guattari, F. (1977). *Anti-oedipus: Capitalism and schizophrenia.* New York: Viking.

DelFattore, J. (1986). Contemporary censorship pressures and their effects on literature textbooks. *ADE Bulletin* 83, 35-50.

Delgado-Gaitan, C. (1988). The value of conformity: Learning to stay in school. *Anthropology and Education Quarterly,* 19 (4), 354-381.

Delgado-Gaitan, C. (1990). *Literacy for empowerment.* New York: Falmer.

Delpit, L. (1988). The silenced dialogue: Power and pedagogy in educating other people's children. *Harvard Educational Review,* 38 (3), 280-298.

DeMocker, S. (1986). *A trail of desire: Aspects of relationship with nature.* Rochester, NY: University of Rochester, Graduate School of Education and Human Development, unpublished doctoral dissertation.

Deng Xiaoping. (1979). Speech at the national educational work conference. *Chinese Education,* 12 (1), 5-10.

Denscombe, M. (1982). The 'hidden pedagogy' and its implications for teacher training. *British Journal of Sociology of Education,* 3 (3), 249-265.

Dentler, R. (1991). School desegregation since Gunnar Myrdal's *American dilemma.* In C. Willie, A. Garibaldi, & W. Reed (Eds.), *The education of African-Americans* (27-50). New York: Auburn House.

Denton, D. (Ed.). (1974). *Existentialism and phenomenology in education.* New York: Teachers College Press.

Derman-Sparks, L. (1989). *Anti-bias curriculum: Tools for empowering young children.* Washington, DC: National Association for the Education of Young Children.

Derrida, J. (1972). Discussion: Structure, sign and play in the discourse of the human sciences. In R. Macksey & E. Donato (Eds.), *The structuralist controversy* (247-272). Baltimore, MD: Johns Hopkins University Press.

Derrida, J. (1976, 1967). *Of grammatology.* [Trans. by G. Spivak.] Baltimore, MD: Johns Hopkins University Press. [Originally published in French, 1967.]

Derrida, J. (1981). *Positions.* Chicago, IL: University of Chicago Press.

Derrida, J. (1986). The last word in racism. In H. Gates, Jr. (Ed.), *Race, writing and difference.* Chicago, IL: University of Chicago Press.

de Saussure, F. (1959). *A course in general Linguistics.* New York: McGraw Hill.

Descombes, V. (1980). *Modern French philosophy.* New York: Cambridge University Press.

Deutelbaum, W. & Morris, A. (1983). The anti-pedagogical pedagogues. *JCT*, 5 (3), 143-147.

Dewey, J. (1897). My pedagogic creed. *The School Journal,* 54 (3), 77-80.

Dewey, J. (1899). *The school and society.* Chicago, IL: University of Chicago Press.

Dewey, J. (1902). *The child and the curriculum.* Chicago, IL: University of Chicago Press.

Dewey, J. (1904). The relation of theory to practice in education. Third Yearbook of the National Society for the Scientific Study of Education, *The relation of theory to practice in the education of teachers* (9-30). Bloomington, IN: Public School Publishing Co.

Dewey, J. (1910). *How we think.* New York: D. C. Heath.

Dewey, J. (1916). *Democracy and education.* New York: Macmillan Company. [Reprinted 1966, the Free Press].

Dewey, J. (1929). *The sources of a science of education.* New York: Liveright.

Dewey, J. (1931). *The way out of educational confusion.* Cambridge, MA: Harvard University Press.

Dewey, J. (1934a, 1968). *A common faith.* New Haven, CT: Yale University Press.

Dewey, J. (1934b). *Art as experience.* New York: Minton Balch.

Dewey, J. (1938). *Experience and education.* New York: Macmillan.

Dewey, J. (1939). *Intelligence in the modern world: John Dewey's philosophy.* [Edited by J. Ratner.] New York: Random House.

Dewey, J. (1959). *Dewey on education: Selections.* [Edited by M. Dworkin.] New York: Teachers College Press.

Dewey, J. (1964). *John Dewey on Education: Selected Writings.* [Edited by R. Archambault.] Chicago, IL: University of Chicago Press.

Dewey, J. (1975). *Moral principles in education.* Carbondale, IL: Southern Illinois University Press.

Dewey, J. & Dewey, E. (1915). *Schools of tomorrow.* New York: E. P. Dutton.

Deyhle, D. (1986a). Break dancing and breaking out: Anglos, Utes, and Navajos in a border reservation high school. *Anthropology and Education Quarterly,* 17 (2), 111-127.

Deyhle, D. (1986b). Success and failure: A micro-ethnographic comparison of Navajo and Anglo students' perceptions of testing. *Curriculum Inquiry,* 16 (4), 365-390.

Diamond, C. (1991). *Teacher education as transformation.* Philadelphia, PA: Open University Press.

Diawara, M. (1993). Black studies, cultural studies, performative acts. In C. McCarthy & W. Crichlow (Eds.), *Race, identity, and education* (262-267). New York & London, England: Routledge.

Dick, A. (1992a, April). *Ethnography of biography: Student teachers reflecting on "life-stories" of experienced teachers.* Paper presented to the annual meeting of the American Educational Research Association, San Francisco, CA.

Dick, A. (1992b). Putting reflectivity back into the teaching equation. In F. Oser, A. Dick & J-L. Patry (Eds.), *Effective and responsible teaching: The new synthesis* (365-382). San Francisco, CA: Jossey-Bass Publishers.

Dicker, M. (1990, Summer). Using action research to navigate an unfamiliar teaching assignment. *Theory into Practice,* XXIX (3), 203-208.

Diop, C. (1991). *Civilization or barbarism.* Brooklyn, NY: Lawrence Hill Books.

Diorio, J. (1985). Contraception, copulating domination, and the theoretical barrenness of sex education literature. *Educational Theory,* 35 (3), 239-254.

Dixon, G. (1980). Taking moral education seriously. *JCT,* 2 (1), 203-208.

Dixon, P. & Ishler, R. (1992). Professional development schools: Stages in collaboration. *Journal of Teacher Education,* 43 (1), 28-34.

Dmitriyev, G. (1991, November). *Democratic changes in education under Gorbachev.* Paper presented to the Conference on Democracy and Education, University of Chicago, Chicago, IL.

Dobson, R., Dobson, J. & Koetting, J. (1983). Toward a process definition of curriculum: Human existence to formative evaluation. *Journal of Humanistic Education,* VII (2), 37-40.

Dobson, R., Dobson, J. & Koetting, J. (1987). Looking at, talking about, and living with children. *JCT,* 7 (2), 11-125.

Dogan, M. & Pellassy, D. (1984). *How to compare nations.* Chatham, NJ: Chatham House.

Doll, M. (1982, Winter). Beyond the window: Dreams and learning. *JCT,* 4 (1), 197-201.

Doll, M. (1986). The monster in children's dreams: Night alchemies. *Journal of Mental Imagery,* 10 (2), 53-60.

Doll, M. (1988a, Spring). The monster in children's dreams. *JCT,* 8 (4), 89-99.

Doll, M. (1988b, October). Connections and disconnections in the classroom: Night thoughts. Paper presented to the Bergamo Conference, Dayton, OH.

Doll, M. (1990, October). *Educating the imagination: A curriculum proposal.* Paper presented to the Bergamo Conference, Dayton, OH.

Doll, M. (1991, June). *Dancing the circle.* Commencement Address, The Cambridge School, Cambridge, MA.

Doll, M. (1992, October). *Teaching as erotic activity.* Paper presented to the Bergamo Conference, Dayton, OH.

Doll, M. (1994, April). *My body, my self: The alma materia of knowing.* Paper presented to the annual meeting of the American Educational Research Association, New Orleans, LA.

Doll, R. (1989). *Curriculum improvement: Decision making and process.* Boston, MA: Allyn & Bacon. (Previous editions: 1986, 1982, 1978, 1974, 1970, 1964).

Doll, Jr., W. (1980). Play and mastery: A structuralist view. *JCT,* 2 (1), 209-226.

Doll, Jr., W. (1983a, Summer). A re-visioning of progressive education. *Theory into Practice,* XXII (3), 166-173.

Doll, Jr., W. (1983b). Curriculum and change. *JCT,* 5 (2), 4-61.

Doll, Jr., W. (1983c). Practicalizing Piaget. *JCT,* 5 (4), 92-110.

Doll, Jr., W. (1986). Prigogine: A new sense of order, a new curriculum. *Theory Into Practice,* XXV (1), 10-16.

Doll, Jr., W. (1988). Curriculum beyond stability: Schon, Prigogine, Piaget. In W. Pinar (Ed.), *Contemporary curriculum discourses* (114-133). Scottsdale, AZ: Gorsuch Scarisbrick.

Doll, Jr., W. (1989). Foundations of a post-modern curriculum. *Journal of Curriculum Studies,* 21, 243-253.

Doll, Jr., W. (1990). Teaching a post-modern curriculum. In J. Sears & D. Marshall (Eds.), *Teaching and thinking about curriculum* (39-47). New York: Teachers College Press.

Doll, Jr., W. (1993a). *A post-modern perspective on curriculum.* New York: Teachers College Press.

Doll, Jr., W. (1993b). Curriculum possibilities in a "post-future." *Journal of Curriculum Supervision,* 8 (4), 277-292.

Doll, Jr., W. (in preparation). Ghosts and the curriculum. In W. Doll, Jr., N. Gough & W. Schubert (Eds.), *Curricular visions.* New York: Teachers College Press.

Donmoyer, R. (1980). The evaluator as artist. *JCT,* 2 (2), 12-26.

Donmoyer, R. (1985, December). The rescue from relativism: Two failed attempts and an alternative strategy. *Educational Researcher, 13-*20.

Donmoyer, R. (1987a). Why case studies? Reflections on Hord and Hall's three images. *Curriculum Inquiry,* 17 (1), 91-101.

Donmoyer, R. (1987b). Beyond Thorndike/beyond melodrama. *Curriculum Inquiry,* 17 (4), 353-363.

Donmoyer, R. (1989, Spring). Theory, practice, and the double-edged problem of idiosyncrasy. *Journal of Curriculum and Supervision,* 4 (3), 257-270.

Donmoyer, R. (1990a). Generalizability and the single-case study. In E. Eisner & A. Peshkin (Eds.), *Qualitative Research in Education* (175-200). New York: Teachers College Press.

Donmoyer, R. (1990b, March). Curriculum evaluation and the negotiation of meaning. *Language Arts,* 67 (3), 274-286.

Donmoyer, R. (1990c). Curriculum, community, and culture: Reflections and pedagogical possibilities. In J. Sears & D. Marshall (Eds.), *Teaching and thinking about curriculum* (154-171). New York: Teachers College Press.

Donmoyer, R. (1991a). The first glamourizer of thought: Theoretical and autobiographical ruminations on drama and education. In G. Willis & W. Schubert (eds.), *Reflections from the heart of educational inquiry: Understanding curriculum and teaching through the arts* (90-106). Albany, NY: State University of New York Press.

Donmoyer, R. (1991b, August). Postpositivist evaluation: Give me a for instance. *Education Administration Quarterly,* 27 (3), 265-296.

Donmoyer, R. & Kos, R. (1993). *At-Risk students: Portraits, policies, programs, and practices.* Albany, NY: State University of New York Press.

Dorsey, M. (1990). Sub-Saharan Africa. *Comparative Education Review,* 34 (2), 289-290.

Doty, A. (1993). *Making things perfectly queer.* Minneapolis, MN: University of Minnesota Press.

Douglas, A. (1988). *The feminization of American culture.* Garden City, NY: Doubleday.

Downer, D. (1991). Review of research on effective schools. *McGill Journal of Education,* 26 (3) (Fall), 323-331.

Doyle, C. (1993). *Raising the curtains on education.* Westport, CT: Bergin & Garvey.

Doyle, D. (1991). *Rebuilding America's Education Foundation,* a forum organized by the California Public Affairs Forum, sponsored by the California Chamber of Commerce, Bay Area Council, and Hitachi, Ltd. Quoted on p. 18.

Doyle, W. (1978). Paradigms for research on teacher effectiveness. In L. Shulman (Ed.), *Review of Research in Education,* 5 (163-198). Itasca, IL: Peacock.

Doyle, W. (1992). Curriculum and pedagogy. In P. Jackson (Ed.), *Handbook of research on curriculum* (486-516). New York: Macmillan.

Doyle, W. & Carter, K. (1984). Academic tasks in classrooms. *Curriculum Inquiry,* 14 (2), 129-149.

Draper, E. (1936). *Principles and techniques of curriculum making.* New York: D. Appleton-Century Company.

Dreeben, R. (1968). *On what is learned in school.* Reading, MA: Addison-Wesley.

Dreeben, R. (1976). The unwritten curriculum and its relation to values. *Journal of Curriculum Studies,* 8 (2), 111-124.

DuBois, W. (1903). *The souls of black folk.* New York: Signet.

DuBois, W. (1919). Opinion of W. E. B. DuBois. *Crises,* 18, 9.

Duckworth, E. (1986). Teaching as research. *Harvard Educational Review,* 56 (4), 481-495.

Duckworth, E. (1987). *The having of wonderful ideas and other essays.* New York: Teachers College Press.

Duckworth, E. (1991). Twenty-four, forty-two, and I love you: Keeping it complex. *Harvard Educational Review,* 61, 1-24.

Duffy, F. (1990). Supervising for results: A case study from the business world. *Journal of Curriculum and Supervision,* 6 (1), 31-38.

Duke, B. (1991). *Education and leadership for the twenty-first century: Japan, America, Britain.* New York: Praeger.

Dumont, Jr., R. (1972). Learning English and how to be silent: Studies in Sioux and Cherokee classrooms. In C. Casen, V. John, & D. Humes (Eds.), *Functions of Language in the Classroom* (344-369). New York: Teachers College Press. [Reprinted by Waveland Press, 1985).

Duncan, J. & Frymier, J. (1967). Explorations in the systematic study of curriculum. *Theory into Practice,* VI (4), 180-199.

Dunkel, H. (1969a). *Herbart and education.* New York: Random House.

Dunkel, H. (1969b). What is at stake: Value conflicts and crises. In. A. Frazier (Ed.), *A curriculum for children* (58-71). Washington, DC: ASCD.

Dunkel, H. (1970). *Herbart and Herbartianism: An educational ghost story.* Chicago, IL: University of Chicago Press.

Dunkin, M. & Biddle, B. (1974). *The nature of teaching.* Glenview, IL: Scott, Foresman.

Duquette, C. (1991, Fall). The evaluation of practice teaching: A revised approach. *McGill Journal of Education,* 26 (3), 345-355.

Durkin, D. (1981). Reading comprehension instruction in five basal reader series. *Reading Research Quarterly,* 16 (4), 515-544.

Duroche, L. (1989). Gender, class, and power in the academy: Reflections on anti-sexist male gender studies and its institutional obstacles. *Men's Studies Review,* 6 (4), 1-9.

Dyson, F. (1988). *Infinite in all directions.* New York: Harper & Row.

Dyson, M. (1994). Be like Mike? Michael Jordan and the pedagogy of desire. In H. Giroux & P. McLaren (Eds.), *Between borders: Pedagogy and the politics of cultural studies* (119-126). New York: Routledge.

Eagleton, T. (1983). *Literary theory: An introduction.* Minneapolis, MN: University of Minnesota Press.

Eakin, P. (1985). *Fictions in autobiography: Studies in the art of self-invention.* Princeton, NJ: Princeton University Press.

Earle, W. (1972). *Autobiographical consciousness.* Chicago, IL: Quadrangle.

Ebeling, M. & Figgins, M. (1990, October). *Inside the cage, making love with the beast: A dramatic performance of research into perceptions and experience of first world critical pedagogy.* Presentation to the Bergamo Conference on Curriculum Theory and Classroom Practice, Dayton, OH.

Ebeling, M. & Figgins, M. (1992, October). *Knowing-in-action: An interactive inquiry into first world critical pedagogy and beyond.* Presentation to the Bergamo Conference on Curriculum Theory and Classroom Practice, Dayton, OH.

Ebeling, M. (1992). *Knowing-in-action: A naturalistic inquiry into first world critical pedagogy.* Charlottesville, VA: University of Virginia, Curry School of Education, unpublished doctoral dissertation.

Ebert, T. (1991). Writing in the political: Resistance (post) modernism. *Legal Studies Forum,* XV (4), 291-303.

Edelfelt, R. & Smith, E. (1978) (Ed.). *Breakaway to multidimensional approaches: Integrating curriculum development and inservice education.* Washington, DC: Association of Teacher Educators.

Edelin, R. (1989). Curriculum and cultural identity. In *Infusion of African and African-American content in the school curriculum*: Proceedings of the First National Conference.

Edelsky, C. (1991). *With literacy and justice for all: Rethinking the social in language and education.* London, England: Falmer.

Edgerton, S. (1991). Particularities of "otherness:" Autobiography, Maya Angelou, and me. In J. Kincheloe & W. Pinar (Eds.), *Curriculum as social psychoanalysis: The significance of place* (77-97). Albany, NY: State University of New York Press.

Edgerton, S. (1992). *Cultural studies and the multicultural curriculum.* Baton Rouge, LA: Louisiana State University, Department of Curriculum and Instruction, unpublished Ph.D. dissertation.

Edgerton, S. (1993a). Love in the margins. In L. Castenell, Jr., & W. Pinar (1993) (Eds.) *Understanding curriculum as racial text: Representations of identity and difference in education* (55-82). Albany, NY: State University of New York Press.

Edgerton, S. (1993b). Toni Morrison teaching the interminable. In C. McCarthy & W. Crichlow (Eds.), *Race, identity, and representation in education* (220-235). New York: Routledge.

Edgerton, S. (1993c). *Re-membering the mother tongue(s): Toni Morrison, Julie Dash, and the language of poetry.* Paper presented to the Bergamo Conference on Curriculum Theory and Classroom Practice, Dayton, OH.

Edsall, T. & Edsall, M. (1991, May). Race. *Atlantic Monthly*, 53-86.

Edwards, R. (1991, Fall). Theory, history, and practice of education: Fin de siécle and a new beginning. *McGill Journal of Education*, 26 (3), 237-266.

Efland, A. (1993). *A history of art education: Intellectual and social currents in teaching the visual arts.* New York: Teachers College Press.

Egan, K. (1978). What is curriculum? *Curriculum Inquiry*, 8 (1), 65-72.

Egan, K. (1982). On the possibility of theories of educational practice. *Journal of Curriculum Studies*, 14 (2).

Egan, K. (1985). Imagination and learning. *Teachers College Record*, 87 (2), 155-166.

Egan, K. (1986). *Teaching as storytelling: An alternative approach to teaching and curriculum in the elementary school.* London, Ontario, Canada: The Althouse Press.

Egan, K. (1988). *Primary understanding: Education in early childhood.* London & New York: Routledge.

Egan, K. (1990a). *Romantic understanding: The development of rationality and imagination, ages 8-15.* New York & London, England: Routledge.

Egan, K. (1990b). Recapitulating romanticism in education. In J. Willinsky (Ed.), *The educational legacy of romanticism* (287-305). Waterloo, Ontario, Canada: Wilfrid Laurier University Press.

Egan, K. (1992). *Imagination in teaching and learning.* Chicago, IL: University of Chicago Press. [Published in Canada by the Althouse Press, London, Ontario. References are to this edition.]

Eisner, E. (1967). Educational objectives: Help or hindrance. *School Review,* 75, 250-260.

Eisner, E. (1969). Instructional and expressive objectives: Their formulation and use in curriculum. In W. Popham, E. Eisner, H. Sullivan, & L. Tyler (Eds.), *Instructional objectives. A.E.R.A. monograph series on curriculum evaluation, no. 3.* Chicago, IL: Rand McNally.

Eisner, E. (1971a, May). How can you measure a rainbow? *Art Education,* 24, 36-39.

Eisner, E. (Ed.). (1971b). *Confronting curriculum reform.* Boston, MA: Little, Brown & Co.

Eisner, E. (1972a). *Educating artistic vision.* New York: Macmillan.

Eisner, E. (1972b). Emerging models for educational evaluation. *School Review,* 80, 573-590.

Eisner, E. (1975). The future of the secondary school: A viewpoint. *Curriculum Theory Network,* 5 (2), 127-138.

Eisner, E. (Ed.). (1976). *The arts, human development, and education.* Berkeley, CA: McCutchan.

Eisner, E. (1977). Implications of the new educational conservatism for the future of the arts in education. In E. Eisner (Ed.), *The arts, human development, and education* (213-226). Berkeley, CA: McCutchan.

Eisner, E. (1979, 1985a). *The educational imagination: On the design and evaluation of school programs.* New York: Macmillan.

Eisner, E. (1984). No easy answers: Joseph Schwab's contributions to curriculum. *Curriculum Inquiry, 14* (2), 201-210.

Eisner, E. (1985b). *The art of educational evaluation: A personal view.* London, England: Flamer.

Eisner, E. (1985c). Aesthetic modes of knowing. In E. Eisner (Ed.), *Learning and teaching the ways of knowing: Eighty-fourth yearbook of the National Society for the Study of Education* (23-36). Chicago, IL: University of Chicago Press.

Eisner, E. (1988, June/July). The primacy of experience and the politics of method. *Educational Researcher,* 17 (5), 15-20.

Eisner, E. (1990a, Fall). Creative curriculum development and practice. *Journal of Curriculum and Supervision,* 6, (1), 62-73.

Eisner, E. (1990b). Discipline-based art education: Conceptions and misconceptions. *Educational Theory,* 40 (4), 423-430.

Eisner, E. (1991a). *The enlightened eye: Qualitative inquiry and the enhancement of educational practice.* New York: Macmillan.

Eisner, E. (1991b). What the arts taught me about education. In G. Willis & W. Schubert (Eds.), *Reflections from the heart of educational inquiry: Understanding curriculum and teaching through the arts* (34-48). Albany, NY: State University of New York Press.

Eisner, E. (1992a). Objectivity in educational research. *Curriculum Inquiry,* 22 (1), 9-15.

Eisner, E. (1992b). Are all causal claims positivistic? A reply to Francis Shrag. *Educational Researcher,* 21, (5), 8-9.

Eisner, E. (1993). Reshaping assessment in education: Some criteria in search of practice. *Journal of Curriculum Studies,* 25 (3), 219-233.

Eisner, E. & Peshkin, A. (Eds.) (1990). *Qualitative inquiry in education.* New York: Teachers College Press.

Eisner, E. & Vallance, E. (Eds.) (1974). *Conflicting concept ions of curriculum.* Berkeley, CA: McCutchan.

Elam, S. (Ed.). (1964). *Education and the structure of knowledge.* Chicago, IL: Rand McNally.

Elbaz, F. (1981). The teacher's "practical knowledge": Report of a case study. *Curriculum Inquiry,* 11 (1), 43-71.

Elbaz, F. (1983). *Teacher thinking: A study of practical knowledge.* London, England: Croom Helm.

Elbaz, F. (1991). Research on teachers' knowledge: The evolution of a discourse. *Journal of Curriculum Studies,* 23 (1), 1-19.

Elbaz, F. & Elbaz, R. (1988). Curriculum and textuality *JCT,* 8 (2), 107-131.

Eliot, T. (1952). Modern education and the class. In *Social Criticism.* London, England: Penguin.

Elliott, D. & Woodward, A. (Eds.) (1990). *Textbooks and Schooling in the United States. Eighty-Ninth yearbook of the National Society for the Study of Education, Part I.* Chicago, IL: National Society for the Study of Education.

Ellison, R. (1952). *Invisible man.* New York: Vintage.

Ellsworth, E. (1984). Incorporation of feminist meanings in media texts. *Humanities in Society,* 7 (1& 2), 65-75.

Ellsworth, E. (1986). Elicit pleasures: Feminist spectators and *Personal Best. Wide Angle,* 8 (2), 45-58.

Ellsworth, E. (1987a). Educational films against critical pedagogy. *Journal of Education,* 169, (3),32-47.

Ellsworth, E. (1987b). Media interpretation is a social and political act. *Journal of Visual Literacy,* 8 (2), 27-38.

Ellsworth, E. (1987c). The place of video in social change: At the edge of making sense. *Frame/Work,* 1 (2), 26-34.

Ellsworth, E. (1987d). Fiction as proof: Critical analysis of the form, style, and ideology of educational dramatization films. *Proceedings of selected research paper presentations at the 1987 convention of the Association for Educational Communications and Technology, sponsored by the research and theory division.* Atlanta, GA.

Ellsworth, E. (1988). Educational media, ideology, and the presentation of knowledge through popular cultural forms. *Curriculum and Teaching,* 3 (1 & 2), 19-31.

Ellsworth, E. (1989). Why doesn't this feel empowering? Working through the repressive myths of critical pedagogy. *Harvard Educational Review,* 59 (3), 297-324.

Ellsworth, E. (1990a). Educational films against critical pedagogy. In E. Ellsworth & M. Whatley (Eds.), *The ideology of images in educational media* (10-26). New York: Teachers College Press.

Ellsworth, E. (1990b, August). The question remains: How will you hold awareness of the limits of your knowledge. *Harvard Educational Review,* 297-324.

Ellsworth, E. (1991). I pledge allegiance: The politics of reading and using educational films. *Curriculum Inquiry,* 21 (1), 41-64. Reprinted in C. McCarthy & W. Crichlow (Eds.), *Race, identity, and representation in education* (201-219). New York & London, England: Routledge.

Ellsworth, E. (1992, February). Teaching to support unassimilated difference. *Radical Teacher.*

Ellsworth, E. (1993). Claiming the tenured body. In D. Wear (Ed.), *The center of the web: Women and solitude* (63-74). Albany, NY: State University of New York Press.

Ellsworth, E. (1994). Representation, self-representation, and the meanings of difference: Questions for educators. In R. Martusewicz & W. Reynolds (Eds.), *Inside out: Contemporary critical perspectives in education* (99-108). New York: St. Martin's Press.

Ellsworth, E. & Miller, J. (1992). *Working difference in education.* Paper presented to the Bergamo Conference on Curriculum Theory and Classroom Practice, Dayton, OH.

Ellsworth, E. & Whatley, M. (Eds.) (1990). *The ideology of educational media: Hidden curriculum in the classroom.* New York: Teachers College Press.

Elmore, R. (1993). School decentralization: Who gains? who loses? In J. Hannaway. & M. Carnoy (Eds.). *Decentralization and school improvement: Can we fulfill the promise?* (33-55). San Francisco, CA: Jossey-Bass Publishers.

Elmore, R. & Sykes, G. (1992). Curriculum policy. In P. Jackson (Ed.), *Handbook of research on curriculum* (185-215). New York: Macmillan.

Elshtain, J. (1981). *Public man, private woman: Women in social and political thought.* Princeton, NJ: Princeton University Press.

Elson, R. (1964). *Guardians of tradition: American schoolbooks of the nineteenth century.* Lincoln, NB: University of Nebraska Press.

Ely, D. (1983, Spring). The definition of educational technology: An emerging stability. *Educational Leadership, 10,* 2-4.

Emoungu, P. (1991). Africa. *Comparative Education Review,* 35 (2), 385-386.

England, D. (1988). A case study—of censorship? Or of the censored? *JCT,* 8 (3), 205-211.

Engle, S. (1960). Decision making: The heart of social studies instruction. *Social Education,* 24, 301-306.

Engle, S. & Longstreet, W. (1971). Exploring the meaning of the social studies. *Social Education,* 35, 280-288.

Engle, S. & Longstreet, W. (1978). Education for a changing society. In J. Jelinek (Ed.), *Improving the human condition: A curricular response to critical realities.* Washington, DC: ASCD.

Engle, S. & Ochoa, A. (1988). *Education for democratic citizenship: Decision making in the social studies*. New York: Teachers College Press

English, F. (1988). *Curriculum auditing*. Lancaster, PA: Technomic Pub. Co., Inc.

Ennis, R. (1962). A concept of critical thinking. *Harvard Educational Review*, 32 (1), 81-111.

Ennis, R. (1987). A taxonomy of critical thinking dispositions and abilities. In J. Baron & R. Sternberg (Eds.), *Teaching thinking skills: Theory and practice* (9-26). New York: W. H. Freeman.

Entwistle, N. (Ed.) (1990). *Handbook of educational ideas and practices*. London: Routledge.

Epstein, I. (1989). Critical pedagogy and Chinese education. *JCT*, 9 (2), 69-98.

Erdman, J. (1990). Curriculum and community: A feminist perspective. In J. Sears & D. Marshall (Eds.), *Teaching and thinking about curriculum* (172-186). New York: Teachers College Press.

Erickson, D., Sullivan, D. & Thomas, G. (1985). How valid are Coleman's conclusions? In B. Gross & R. Gross (Ed.), *The great school debate: Which way American education?* (462-465). New York: Simon & Schuster.

Erickson, F. (1986). Qualitative methods in research on teaching. In M. Wittrock (Ed.), *Handbook of research on teaching* (119-161). [Third edition.] New York: Macmillan.

Erickson, F. (1992) Why the clinical trial doesn't work as a metaphor for educational research. *Educational Researcher*, 21 (4), 9-11.

Erickson, F. & Mohatt, G. (1982). The cultural organization of participation structures in two classrooms of Indian students. In G. Spindler (Ed.), *Doing the ethnography of schooling* (132-174). New York: Holt, Rinehart & Winston.

Erickson, F. & Shultz, J. (1992). Students' experience of the curriculum. In P. Jackson (Ed.), *Handbook of research on curriculum* (465-485). New York: Macmillan.

Erickson, G. (1991). Collaborative in inquiry and the professional development of science teachers. *The Journal of Educational Thought*, 25 (3), 228-243.

Essien-Udom, E. (1962). *Black nationalism: A search for an identity in America*. New York: Dell.

Estrada, K. & McLaren, P. (1993). A dialogue on multiculturalism and democratic culture. *Educational Researcher*, 22 (3), 27-33.

Evans, M. (Ed.). (1993). *Schooling for the postmodern world*. Belle Meade, NJ: Apple.

Ezeomah, C. (1986). The development of a special type of curriculum for the nomads of Nigeria. *JCT*, 6 (4), 45-55.

Fafunwa, A. (1974). *History of education in Nigeria*. London, England: Allen & Unwin.

Fahlman, L. (1984). *Toward understanding the lived-world of Lebanese Muslim students and their teachers*. Edmonton, Alberta, Canada: University of

Alberta, Faculty of Education, Department of Secondary Education, unpublished Ph.D. dissertation.

Falsey, B. & Heyns, B. (1984, April). The college channel: Private and public schools reconsidered. *Sociology of Education*, 57, 111-122.

Fanon, F. (1963). *The wretched of the earth*. New York: Grove Press.

Fanon, F. (1967). *Black skin, white masks*. New York: Grove Press.

Fanon, F. (1970). *A dying colonialism*. Harmondsworth, England: Pelican.

Farrell, J. (1987). Cultural differences and curriculum inquiry. *Curriculum Inquiry*, 17 (1), 1-8.

Favaro, B. (1981). *Recasting a program in teacher education from a critical perspective*. Curriculum Praxis Series, Occasional Paper No 19. Edmonton, Alberta, Canada: University of Alberta, Faculty of Education, Department of Secondary Education.

Favaro, B. (1982). *Re-searching the meaning of consulting in continuing teacher education through phenomenological and critical inquiry orientations*. Edmonton, Alberta, Canada: University of Alberta, Faculty of Education, Department of Secondary Education, unpublished Ph.D. dissertation.

Featherstone, J. (1968, March 2). A new kind of schooling. *The New Republic*, 158 (9).

Featherstone, W. (1950). *A functional curriculum for youth*. New York: American Book Company.

Federbush, M. (1974). The sex problems of school math books. In J. Stacey, S. Bereaud, & J. Daniels (Eds.), *And Jill came tumbling after: Sexism in American education*. New York: Dell.

Feinberg, P. (1985). Four curriculum theorists: A critique in light of Martin Buber's philosophy of education. *JCT*, 6 (1), 5-164.

Feinberg, W. (1983). *Understanding education*. New York: Cambridge University Press.

Feinberg, W. (1993). *Japan and the pursuit of a new American identity*. New York: Routlege.

Felman, S. (1982). Psychoanalysis and education: Teaching terminable and interminable. In B. Johnson (Ed.), *The pedagogical imperative: Teaching as literary genre* (21-44). New Haven, CT: Yale University Press.

Fensham, P. (1992). Science and technology. In P. Jackson (Ed.), *Handbook of research on curriculum* (789-829). New York: Macmillan.

Fenstermacher, G. (1978). A philosophical consideration of recent research on teacher effectiveness. In L. Shulman (Ed.), *Review of research in education, vol. 6* (157-185). Itasca, IL: Peacock.

Fenstermacher, G. (1980). The nature of science and its uses for education: Remarks on the philosophical import of Schwab. *Curriculum Inquiry*, 2 (2), 191-206.

Feyereisen, K., Fiorino, A., & Nowak, A. (1970). *Supervision and curriculum renewal: A systems approach*. New York: Appleton Century-Crofts.

Figgins, M. (1987). *A center that will hold: A rationale and model for placing the poem at the center of the secondary English curriculum*. Charlottesville, VA: University of Virginia, Curry School of Education, unpublished doctoral dissertation.

Figgins, M. (1989, October). *Reclamations.* An original theater piece presented to the Bergamo Conference on Curriculum Theory and Classroom Practice, Dayton, OH.

Figgins, M. (1992). *Autobiography in teacher education: An act of reclamation.* Charlottesville, VA: University of Virginia, Curry Memorial School of Education, unpublished manuscript.

Figgins, M. & Ebeling, M. (1991, October). *Toward a discourse of hard talk: The electronic conference as a means of creating and reflecting on class as a text.* Presentation to the Bergamo Conference on Curriculum Theory and Classroom Practice, Dayton, OH.

Figgins, M. & Pinar, W. (1993, October). *Dancing behind the mirror: A Performance of letters.* Presentation to the Bergamo Conference on Curriculum Theory and Classroom Practice, Dayton, OH.

Fillmore, L. & Meyer, L. (1992). The curriculum and linguistic minorities. In P. Jackson (Ed.), *Handbook of research on curriculum* (626-658). New York: Macmillan.

Finkelstein, J. & Williams, R. (1979, October). Letter to the editor. *Educational Researcher,* 8 (9), 24-25.

Fine, M. (1991). *Framing dropouts: Notes on the politics of an urban public high school.* Albany, NY: State University of New York Press.

Finn, C., Ravitch, D., & Roberts, R. (Eds.). (1985). *Challenges to the humanities.* New York: Holmes & Meier.

Firestone, S. (1972). *The dialectic of sex.* New York: Bantam.

Firth, G. (1986). ASCD and supervision: The later years. In W. vanTil (Ed.), *ASCD in retrospect: Contributions to the history of the Association for Supervision and Curriculum Development* (69-79). Alexandria, VA: ASCD.

Firth, G. & Kimpston, R. (1973). *The curricular continuum in perspective.* Itasca, IL: F. E. Peacock.

Fischer, C. (1989). The child's world of play and pain. *Phenomenology + Pedagogy,* 7, 106-114.

Fisher, E. (1974) Children's books: The second sex, junior division. In J. Stacey, S. Bereaud, & J. Daniels (Eds.), *And Jill came tumbling after: Sexism in American education.* New York: Dell.

Fiske, E. (1991). *Smart schools, smart kids.* New York: Simon & Schuster.

FitzGerald, F. (1979). *America revised: What history textbooks have taught our children about their country, and how and why these textbooks have changed in different decades.* New York: Vintage.

Flannery, O. P., A. (Ed.). (1975). Gaudium et spes: Patorla constitution on the church in the modern world, 1965. In *Vatican Council II: The conciliar and post couciliar documents (study edition)* (903-1001). New York: Costello Pub. Co.

Flax, J. (1990). *Teaching fragments: Psychoanalysis, feminism and postmodernism in the contemporary west.* Berkeley, CA: University of California Press.

Flexner, A. (1923). *A modern college and a modern school.* New York: Doubleday.

Flinders, D. (1988). Teacher isolation and the new reform. *Journal of Curriculum and Supervision,* 4 (1), 317-329.

Flinders, D., Noddings, N., & Thornton, S. (1986). The null curriculum: Its theoretical basis and practical implications. *Curriculum Inquiry*, 16 (1), 33-42.

Fonow, M. & Marty, D. (1992). Teaching college students about sexual identity from feminist perspectives. In J. Sears (Ed.), *Sexuality and the curriculum* (157-170). New York: Teachers College Press.

Ford, G. & Pugno, L. (1964). *The structure of knowledge and the curriculum.* Chicago, IL: Rand McNally.

Fordham, S. (1988). Racelessness as a factor in black students' school success: Pragmatic strategy or pyrrhic victory? *Harvard Educational Review*, 58 (1), 54-84.

Foshay A. (1970). *Curriculum for the seventies: An agenda invention.* Washington, DC: National Education Association (CSI).

Foshay, A. (1987). Hollis Leland Caswell: An appreciation. *Teaching Education*, 1 (1), 76-79.

Foshay, A. (1989). Hollis Caswell: The legacy. *Curriculum Studies Newsletter* (3-4). AERA: Division B and the George Washington University.

Foshay, A. (1991). Foreword. In D. Tanner, *Crusade for democracy: Progressive education at the crossroads* (ix-x). Albany, NY: State University of New York Press.

Foshay, A. & Foshay, A. (1980). Curriculum development and instructional development. *Educational Leadership*, 38 (8), 621-626.

Foster, M. (1993a). Self-portraits of black teachers: Narratives of individual and collective struggle against racism. In D. McLaughlin & W. Tierny (Eds.), *Naming silenced lives: Personal narratives and the process of educational change* (155-175). New York: Routledge.

Foster, M. (1993b). *Savage inequalities*: Where have we come from? Where are we going? *Educational Theory*, 43 (1), 23-32.

Foucault, M. (1970). *The order of things: An archaeology of the human sciences.* New York: Vintage.

Foucault, M. (1972). *The archaeology of knowledge.* [Trans. M. Smith.] New York: Pantheon.

Foucault, M. (1973). *Madness and civilization: A history of insanity in the Age of Reason.* [Trans. by R. Howard.] New York: Vintage.

Foucault, M. (1978). *The history of sexuality: Vol. 1. An introduction.* [Trans. R. Hurley.] New York: Vintage.

Foucault, M. (1979). *Discipline and punish: The birth of the prison.* [Trans. A. Sheridan.] New York: Pantheon.

Foucault, M. (1980). *Power/knowledge.* New York: Pantheon.

Foucault, M. (1986a). *The history of sexuality: Vol. 2. The use of pleasure.* [Trans. R. Hurley.] New York: Pantheon.

Foucault, M. (1986b). *The history of sexuality: Vol. 3. The care of the self.* [Trans. R. Hurley.] New York Pantheon.

Foundation for Critical Thinking (1992, Fall). *Critical Thinking: Shaping the Mind of the 21st Century.* Sonoma, California: The Foundation for Critical Thinking and the Center for Critical Thinking and Moral Critique, 1 (1).

Fowler, J. (1981). *Stages of faith: The psychology of human development and the quest for meaning.* San Francisco, CA: Harper and Row.

Fox, M. (1992). *Sheer joy: Conversations with Thomas Aquinas on creation spirituality.* San Francisco, CA: Harper.

Frankenstein, C. (1966). *The roots of the ego: A phenomenology of dynamics and structure.* Baltimore, MD: The Williams & Wilkins Company.

Frankenstein, M. (1983). Critical mathematics education: An application of Paulo Freire's epistemology. *Journal of Education,* 163 (4), 315-339.

Franklin, B. (1977). Career Education and self concept: A Meadian perspective. *Teachers College Record,* 78, 285-297.

Franklin, B. (1979). Self control and the psychology of school discipline. *JCT,* 1 (2), 238-254.

Franklin, B. (1980). From backwardness to L.D.: Behaviorism, systems theory, and the learning disabilities field historically reconsidered. *Journal of Education,* 162 (4), 5-22.

Franklin, B. (1986). *Building the American community: The school curriculum and the search for control.* Philadelphia, PA & London, England: Falmer.

Franklin, B. (1988a). Self control and the psychology of school discipline. In W. Pinar (Ed.), *Contemporary curriculum discourses* (31-49). Scottsdale, AZ: Gorsuch Scarisbrick.

Franklin, B. (1988b). Whatever happened to social control? The muting of coercive authority in curriculum discourse. In W. Pinar (Ed.), *Contemporary curriculum discourses* (80-90). Scottsdale, AZ: Gorsuch Scarisbrick.

Franklin, B. (1989, Spring). On the death of Hollis Caswell. *Curriculum Studies Newsletter,* AERA, Division B, 1-2.

Franklin, E. (1989). Thinking and feeling in art: Developing aesthetic perspectives of preservice teachers. *JCT,* 9 (2), 55-68.

Fraser, B. (1982). *Annotated bibliography of curriculum evaluation literature.* [In collaboration with K. Houghton.] Jerusalem: Israel Center, Ministry of Education and Culture.

Fraser, B. (1989). An historical look at curriculum evaluation. In C. Kridel (Ed.), *Curriculum History* (114-128). Landham, MD: University Press of America.

Fraser, D. (Ed.). (1962). *Current curriculum studies in academic subjects.* Washington, DC: National Education Association.

Fraser, N. (1994). Rethinking the public sphere: A contribution to the critique of actually existing democracy. In H. Giroux & P. McLaren (Eds.), *Between borders: Pedagogy and the politics of cultural studies* (74-98). New York: Routledge.

Frasher, R. & Walker, A. (1975). Sex roles in early reading textbooks. In E. Maccia, M. Estep, & T. Shiel (Eds.), *Women and education.* Springfield, IL: Charles C. Thomas.

Frazier, A. (1957). Organization and management of the research process. In A. Foshay & J. Hall (Eds.), *Research for curriculum improvement* (228-248). Washington, DC: ASCD.

Frazier, A. (Ed.). (1963). *New insights and the curriculum.* [1963 yearbook.] Washington, DC: ASCD.

Frazier, A. (Ed.). (1969). *A curriculum for children.* Washington, DC: ASCD.

Frazier, A. (1970). Here and now: Points of decision for a new curriculum. In R. Leeper (Ed.), *A man for tomorrow's world* (28-44). Washington, DC: ASCD.

Frazier, A. (1976). *Adventuring, mastering, associating.* Washington, DC: ASCD.

Frazier, N. & Sadlek, M. (1973). *Sexism in school and society.* New York: Harper & Row.

Freedman, K. & Popkewitz, T. (1988). Art education and social interests in the development of American schooling: Ideological origins of curriculum theory. *Journal of Curriculum Studies,* 20 (5),287-405.

Freedman, S. (1990). *Small victories: The real world of teachers.* New York: Harper & Row.

Freeman, D., et al. (1983). Do textbooks and tests define a national curriculum in elementary school mathematics? *Elementary School Journal,* 83 (5), 501-513.

Freire, P. (1968, 1970). *Pedagogy of the oppressed.* New York: Seabury.

Freire, P. (1971, March). Conscientizing as a way of liberating. *Contacto.* [Also in A. Hennelly (Ed.), (1990), *Liberation Theology.* Maryknoll, NY: Orbis Books.].

Freire, P. (1985). *The politics of education: Culture, power and liberation.* [D. Macedo, trans.] South Hadley, MA: Bergin & Garvey.

Freire, P. (1993). Foreword. [Trans. D. Macedo.] In P. McLaren & P. Leonard (Eds.), *Paulo Freire: A critical encounter* (ix-xii). London & New York: Routledge.

Freire, P. & Macedo, D. (1987). *Literacy: Reading the word and reading the world.* South Hadley, MA: Bergin & Garvey.

Freire, P. & Macedo, D. (1993). A dialogue with Paulo Freire. In P. McLaren & P. Leonard (Eds.), *Paulo Freire: A critical encounter* (169-176). London & New York: Routledge.

Freire, P. & Shor, I. (1987). *A pedagogy for liberation: Dialogues for transforming education.* South Hadley, MA: Bergin & Garvey.

French, R., Holdzkom, D., & Kuligowski, B. (1990, April). *Teacher evaluation in SREB states. Stage I: Analysis and comparison of evaluation systems.* Paper presented at the annual meeting of the American Educational Research Association, Boston, MA.

Frey, K. (1986). European traditions of curriculum research. In U. Hameyer, K. Frey, & F. Kuebart (Eds.), *Curriculum research in Europe* (11-16). Lisse, Netherlands: Swets & Zeitlinger.

Friedan, B. (1963/1981). *The feminine mystique.* New York: Dell.

Friedenberg, E. (1962). *The vanishing adolescent.* New York: Dell.

Friedenberg, E. (1965). *Coming of age in America.* New York: Vintage.

Friedenberg, E. (1990). Romanticism and alternatives in schooling. In J. Willinsky (Ed.), *The educational legacy of romanticism* (175-187). Waterloo, Ontario, Canada: Wilfrid Laurier University Press.

Friedman, M. (1993). *Taking control: Visualizing education.* Westport, CT: Praeger.

Frye, N. (1957). *Anatomy of criticism.* Princeton, NJ: Princeton University Press.

Frymier, J. (Ed.) (1973). *A school for tomorrow.* Berkeley, CA: McCutchan.

Frymier, J. (1977). *Annehurst curriculum classification system.* W. Lafayette, IN: Kappa Delta Pi.

Frymier, J. (1986). After thirty years of thinking about curriculum. *Theory Into Practice,* XXV (1), 58-63.

Frymier, J. (1987). A study of children's interests in words. *Journal of Curriculum and Supervision,* 2 (2), 128-151.

Frymier, J. & Hawn, H. (1970). *Curriculum improvement for better schools.* Worhington, OH: Charles A. Jones.

Frymier, J., Wilhour, J. & Rasp, A. (1973). In J. Frymier (Ed.), *A school for tomorrow* (87-128). Berkeley, CA: McCutchan.

Fuhrman, S. & Malen, B. (Eds.). (1991). *The politics of curriculum and testing.* London, England: Falmer.

Fujita, M. (1985). Modes of waiting. *Phenomenology + Pedagogy,* 3 (2), 107-115.

Fujita, M. (1987, October). *Dialogical approach to lived meaning.* Paper presented at the Bergamo Conference on Curriculum Theory and Classroom Practice, Dayton, OH.

Fulbright, E. & Bolmeier, E. (1964). *Courts and the curriculum.* Cincinnati, OH: W. H. Anderson Company.

Fullan, M. (1982). *The meaning of educational change.* New York: Teachers College Press.

Fullan, M. (1985). Changes processes and strategies at the local level. *The Elementary School Journal,* 85 (3), 391-420.

Fullan, M. & Pomfret, A. (1977). Research on curriculum and instruction implementation. *Review of Educational Research,* 47 (1), 335-397.

Fuss, D. (1989). *Essentially speaking: Feminism, nature and difference.* New York: Routledge.

Gadamer, H-G. (1960/1975). *Truth and method.* New York: Crossroad.

Gadamer, H-G. (1976). *Hegel's dialectic.* [Trans. P. Smith.] New Haven, CT: Yale University Press.

Gadamer, H-G. (1980). *Dialogue and dialectic: Eight hermeneutic studies on Plato.* [Trans. P. Smith.] New Haven, CT: Yale University Press.

Gage, N. (Ed.). (1963). *Handbook of research on teaching.* Chicago, IL: Rand McNally.

Gage, N. (1972). *Teacher effectiveness and teacher education.* Palo Alto, CA: Pacific Books.

Gage, N. (1989, October). The paradigm wars and their aftermath. *Educational Researcher,* 4-10.

Gagné, R. (1965). *The conditions of learning.* [Second edition, 1977]. New York: Holt, Rinehart & Winston, Inc.

Gagné, R. (1974). *Essentials of learning for instruction.* Hinsdale, IL: Dryden Press.

Gagné, R. & Briggs, L. (1974). *Principles of instructional design.* [Second edition]. New York: Holt, Rinehart & Winston.

Gaines, E. (1972). *The autobiography of Miss Jane Pittman.* New York: Bantam.

Gall, M. (1981). *Handbook for evaluating and selecting curriculum materials.* Boston, MA: Allyn & Bacon.

Gallagher, J. (1971). A broader base for science teaching. *Science Education,* 55, 329-338.

Gallas, K. (1991). Arts as epistemology: Enabling children to know what they know. *Harvard Educational Review,* 61 (1), 40-50.

Gallup, G. (1978, September). The 17th annual Gallup Poll of the public's attitude toward the public schools. *Phi Delta Kappan,* 67, 33-45.

Gardner, H. (1983). *Frames of mind: The theory of multiple intelligences.* New York: Basic Books.

Gardner, H. (1989). *To open minds.* New York: Basic Books.

Gardner, H. (1991). *The unschooled mind: How children think and how schools should teach.* New York: Basic Books.

Garfinkle, N. (1954). Conservatism in American textbooks, 1800-1860. *New York History,* 35, 49-63.

Garibaldi, A. (1991a). Blacks in college. In C. Willie, A. Garibaldi & W. Reed (Eds.), *The education of African-Americans* (93-99). New York: Auburn House.

Garibaldi, A. (1991b). Abating the shortage of teachers. In C. Willie, A. Garibaldi & W. Reed (Eds.), *The education of African-Americans* (148-158). New York: Auburn House.

Garland, G. (1991, September 29). Home schooling highlights. Baton Rouge, LA: *Sunday Advocate,* 8A.

Garman, N. (1982). The clinical approach to supervision. In T. Sergiovanni (Ed.), *Supervision of teaching* (35-52). Alexandria, VA: ASCD.

Garman, N. (1984). *Languages of teaching for supervisory practice.* Pittsburgh, PA: University of Pittsburgh, School of Education, unpublished manuscript.

Garman, N. (1986a). Clinical supervision: Quackery or remedy for professional development. *Journal of Curriculum and Supervision,* 1 (2), 148-157.

Garman, N. (1986b). Reflection, the heart of clinical supervision: A modern rationale for professional practice. *Journal of Curriculum and Supervision,* 2 (1), 1-24.

Garman, N. (1987). *Madeline Hunter/clinical supervision survey of Pennsylvania's 500 school districts.* Pittsburgh, PA: University of Pittsburgh, School of Education, unpublished manuscript.

Garman, N. (1990). Theories embedded in the events of clinical supervision: A hermeneutic approach. *Journal of Curriculum and Supervision,* 5 (3), 201-213.

Garman, N. & Hazi, H. (1988, May). Teachers ask: Is there life after Madeline Hunter? *Phi Delta Kappan,* 669-672

Garman, N., Glickman, C., Hunter, M. & Haggerson, N. (1987). Conflicting conceptions of supervision and the enhancement of professional growth and renewal: Point and counterpoint. *Journal of Curriculum and Supervision,* 2 (2), 152-177.

Garrod, A. (Ed.). (1992). *Learning for life: Moral education theory and practice.* Westport, CT: Praeger.

Gaskell, J. (1986). The changing organization of business education in the high school: Teachers respond to school and work. *Curriculum Inquiry,* 16 (4), 417-437.

Gates, Jr., H. (1985). Introduction to "race," writing, and difference. *Critical Inquiry,* 12 (1), 1-20.

Gates, Jr., H. (1990). Critical remarks. In D. Goldberg, (Ed.), *Anatomy of Racism* (319-332). Minneapolis, MN: University of Minnesota Press.

Gates, Jr., H. (1992). *Loose canons: Notes on the culture wars.* New York: Oxford University Press.

Gauthier, C. (1986, October). *Postmodernism, desire and education.* Paper presented to the Bergamo Conference on Curriculum Theory and Classroom Practice, Dayton, OH.

Gauthier, C. (1991). Science, pédagogie et art: Des ressemblances et des différences. *The Journal of Educational Thought,* 25 (3), 246-274.

Gauthier, C. (1992). Between crystal and smoke: Or, how to miss the point in the debate about action research. In W. Pinar & W. Reynolds (Eds.), *Understanding curriculum as phenomenological and deconstructed Text* (184-194). New York: Teachers College Press.

Geer, J., Heiman, J. & Leitenberg, H. (1984). *Human sexuality.* Englewood Cliffs, NJ: Prentice-Hall.

Genet, J. (1978). *The blacks: A clown show.* New York: Grove Press.

Gentry-Akin, D. (1990, May-June). Cosmology: A context for living. *Creation,* 6 (3), 4-5.

Gergen, K. (1991). *The saturated self.* New York: Basic Books.

Gibson, M. (1982). Reputation and respectability: How competing cultural systems affect students' performance in school. *Anthropology and Education Quarterly,* 13 (1), 3-28.

Gibson, R. (1986). *Critical theory and education.* London: Hodder and Stroughton.

Gibson, R. (1991). Curriculum criticism: Misconceived theory, ill-advised practice. In D. Hlynka & J. Belland (Eds.), *Paradigms regained: The Uses of illuminative, semiotic and post-modern criticism as modes of inquiry in educational technology.* Englewood Cliffs, NJ: Educational Technology Publications.

Gideonse, H. (1988). Practice-oriented inquiry and teachers: Justifications and implications for school structure. *Journal of Curriculum and Supervision,* 4 (1), 65-76.

Gilchrist, R. (1963). *Using current curriculum developments: A report.* Washington, DC: ASCD.

Giles, H., McCutchen, S., & Zechiel, A. (1942). *Exploring the curriculum.* New York: Harper & Brothers.

Gilligan, C. (1982). *In a different voice: Psychological theory and women's develop-ment.* Cambridge, MA: Harvard University Press.

Gilmore, P. (1983). Spelling "Mississippi": Recontextualizing a literacy-related speech event. *Anthropology and Education,* 14 (4), 235-236.

Ginsburg, M. (1986). Reproduction, contradictions and conceptions of curriculum in preserve teacher education. *Curriculum Inquiry,* 16 (3), 283-309.

Giroux, H. (1980a). Beyond the correspondence theory: Notes on the dynam-ics of educational reproduction and transformation. *Curriculum Inquiry,* 10 (3), 225-248.

Giroux, H. (1980b). Dialectics of curriculum theory. *JCT,* 2 (2), 27-36.

Giroux, H. (1981a). *Ideology, culture and the process of schooling.* Philadelphia, PA: Temple University Press.

Giroux, H. (1981b). Hegemony, resistance, and the paradox of educational reform. *Interchange,* 12 (2-3), 3-26.

Giroux, H. (1981c). Toward a new sociology of curriculum. In H. Giroux, A. Penna & W. Pinar (Eds.), *Curriculum and instruction: Alternatives in educa-tion* (98-108). Berkeley, CA: McCutchan.

Giroux, H. (1981d). Pedagogy, pessimism, and the politics of conformity: A reply to Linda McNeil. *Curriculum Inquiry,* 11 (3), 211-222.

Giroux, H. (1983a). *Theory and resistance in education: A pedagogy for the opposi-tion.* South Hadley, MA: Bergin & Garvey.

Giroux, H. (1983b). Theories of reproduction and resistance in the new soci-ology of education: A critical analysis. *Harvard Educational Review,* 53 (3), 261-293.

Giroux, H. (1985a). Toward a critical theory of education: beyond a marxism with guarantees—A response to Daniel Liston. *Educational Theory,* 35 (3), 313-319.

Giroux, H. (1985b). Thunder on the right: Education and the ideology of the quick-fix. *Curriculum Inquiry,* 15 (1), 57-62.

Giroux, H. (1986, Spring). Radical pedagogy and the politics of student voice. *Interchange,* 17 (1), 48-69.

Giroux, H. (1987). Liberal arts, public philosophy, and the politics of civic courage. *Curriculum Inquiry,* 17 (3), 331-335.

Giroux, H. (1988a). *Schooling and the struggle for public life.* Minneapolis, MN: University of Minnesota Press.

Giroux, H. (1988b). *Teachers as intellectuals: Toward a critical pedagogy of learn-ing.* South Hadley, MA: Bergin & Garvey.

Giroux, H. (1988c). Border pedagogy in the age of postmodernism. *Journal of Education,* 170 (3), 162-181.

Giroux, H. (1988d). Liberal arts, teaching, and critical literacy: Toward a definition of school as a form of cultural politics. In W. Pinar (Ed.), *Contemporary curriculum discourses* (243-263). Scottsdale, AZ: Gorsuch Scarisbrick.

Giroux, H. (1989). Rethinking education reform in the age of George Bush. *Phi Delta Kappan,* 70 (9), 728-730.

Giroux, H. (Ed.). (1991). *Postmodernism, feminism, and cultural politics: Redrawing educational boundaries*. Albany, NY: State University of New York Press.

Giroux, H. (1992a). *Bordercrossings*. New York: Routledge.

Giroux, H. (1992b). *Educational leadership and the crisis of democratic culture*. University Park, PA: Pennsylvania State University, University Council of Educational Administration (UCEA).

Giroux, H. (1992c). Educational leadership and the crisis of democratic government. *Educational Researcher*, 21 (4), 4-11.

Giroux, H. (1992d). Textual authority and the role of teachers as public intellectuals. In M. Hurlbert & S. Totten (Eds.), *Social issues in the English classroom* (304-321). Urbana, IL: NCTE.

Giroux, H. (1993a). *Living dangerously: Multiculturalism and the politics of difference*. New York: Peter Lang.

Giroux, H. (1993b). Paulo Freire and the politics of postcolonialism. In P. McLaren & P. Leonard (Eds.), *Paulo Freire: A critical encounter* (177-188). London & New York: Routledge.

Giroux, H. & McLaren, P. (1986). Teacher education and the politics of engagement: The case for democratic schooling. *Harvard Educational Review*, 56 (3), 213-238.

Giroux, H. & McLaren, P. (1989). *Critical pedagogy, the state, and cultural struggle*. Albany, NY: State University of New York Press.

Giroux, H. & McLaren, P. (1992, April). America 2000 and the politics of erasure: Democracy and cultural difference under siege. *International Journal of Educational Reform*, 1 (2), 99-110.

Giroux, H. & McLaren, P. (Eds.). (1993). *Between borders: Pedagogy and the politics of cultural studies*. New York: Routledge.

Giroux, H. & Purpel, D. (Eds.). (1983). *The hidden curriculum and moral education: Deception or discovery?* Berkeley, CA: McCutchan.

Giroux, H., Simon, R., et al. (1989). *Popular culture, schooling, and everyday life*. South Hadley, MA: Bergin & Garvey.

Giroux, H., Penna, A., & Pinar, W. (Eds.). (1981). *Curriculum and Instruction: Alternatives in education*. Berkeley, CA: McCutchan.

Gitlin, A. (1989). Educative school change: Lived experiences in horizontal evaluation. *Journal of Curriculum and Supervision*, 4, (4), 322-339.

Gitlin, A. (1990). Educative research, voice, and school change. *Harvard Educational Review*, 60 (4), 443-466.

Gitlin, A. & Goldstein, S. (1987). A dialogical approach to understanding: Horizontal evaluation. *Educational Theory*, 37 (1), 17-27.

Gitlin, A. & Myers, B. (1993). Beth's story: The search for the mother/teacher. In D. McLaughlin & W. Tierney (Eds.), *Naming silenced lives: Personal narratives and the process of educational change* (51-69). New York: Routledge.

Gitlin, A. & Price, K. (1992). Teacher empowerment and the development of voice. In C. Glickman (Ed.), *Supervision in transition* (61-74). Alexandria, VA: ASCD.

Gitlin, A., Siegel, M., & Boru, K. (1988). *Purpose and method: Rethinking the use of ethnography of the educational left.* Paper presented at the annual meeting of the American Educational Research Association, New Orleans, LA.

Glanz, J. (1990). Beyond bureaucracy: Notes on the professionalization of public school supervision in the early 20th century. *Journal of Curriculum and Supervision,* 5 (2), 150-170.

Glaser, R. & Bassock, M. (1989). Learning theory and the study of instruction. *Annual Review of Psychology,* 40, 631-666.

Glasser, W. (1969). *Schools without failure.* New York: Harper & Row.

Glatthorn, A. (1984). *Differentiated supervision.* Alexandria, VA: ASCD.

Glazer, N. & Moynihan, D. (Eds.). (1975). *Ethnicity: Theory and experience.* Cambridge, MA: Harvard University Press.

Glenn, C. (1992). *Educational freedom in Eastern Europe* [first draft]. Report prepared under contract (43 3J47 000875) with the Research Division, Office of Educational Research and Improvements/Programs for the Improvement of Practice.

Glickman, C. (1985). *Supervision of instruction: A developmental approach.* Boston, MA: Allyn & Bacon.

Glickman, C. (1990). Right question, wrong extrapolation: A response to Duffy's "Supervising for Results." *Journal of Curriculum and Supervision,* 6 (1), 39-40.

Glickman, C. (Ed.). (1992). *Supervision in transition: 1992 Yearbook of the Association for Supervision and Curriculum Development.* Alexandria, VA: ASCD.

Goldberg, D. (Ed.). (1990). *Anatomy of racism.* Minneapolis, MN: University of Minnesota Press.

Goldhammer, R. (1969). *Clinical supervision: Special methods for the supervision of teachers.* New York: Holt, Rinehart & Winston.

Goldman, R., Weber, W. & Noah, H. (1971). Some economic models of curriculum structure. *Teachers College Record,* 73 (2), 285-303.

Golle, J. (1991). *Rebuilding America's education foundation,* a forum organized by the California Public Affairs Forum, sponsored by the California Chamber of Commerce, Bay Area Council, and Hitachi, Ltd.

Gomez, J. (1993). Black women heroes: Here's reality, where's the fiction? In L. Castenell, Jr. & W. Pinar (Eds.), *Understanding curriculum as racial text* (143-152). Albany, NY: State University of New York Press. Also (1986), *The Black Scholar* (March/April), 8-13.

Gonzales-Echeuarria, R. (1985). *The voice of the masters: Writing and authority in modern Latin American literature.* Austin, TX: University of Texas Press.

Good, R. (1991, October). *Constructivism's many faces.* Paper presented at the Bergamo Conference on Curriculum Theory and Classroom Practice, Dayton, OH.

Good, R. (1992, September). Notes from Bergamo. *Journal of Research in Science Teaching,* 29 (7), 635-636.

Goodlad, J. (1964). *School curriculum reform in the United States.* New York: Fund for the Advancement of Education.

Goodlad, J. (1966). *School, curriculum and the individual.* Waltham, MA: Blaisdell Publishing Company.

Goodlad, J. (1975). *The dynamics of educational change: Toward responsive schools* [Introduction by Samuel G. Sava.] New York: McGraw Hill.

Goodlad, J. (1978, March). On the cultivation and corruption of education. *The Educational Forum, 22,* 276.

Goodlad, J. (1979). *Curriculum inquiry: The study of curriculum practice.* New York: McGraw-Hill.

Goodlad, J. (1984). *A place called school.* Highstown, NJ: McGraw-Hill.

Goodlad, J. (1990a). *Teachers for our nation's schools.* San Francisco, CA: Jossey-Bass.

Goodlad, J. (1990b) *The moral dimensions of teaching.* San Francisco, CA: Jossey-Bass.

Goodlad, J. & Klein, F. (1974). *Looking behind the classroom door.* Worthingon, OH: Charles A. Jones Publishing Co.

Goodlad, J. & Su, Z. (1992). Organization of the curriculum. In P. Jackson (Ed.), *Handbook of research on curriculum* (327-344). New York: Macmillan.

Goodlad, J., Von Stoephasius, R. & Klein, M. (1965). *The changing school reform.* New York: Fund for the Advancement of Education.

Goodman, J. (1987). Masculinity, feminism, and the male elementary school teacher. *JCT,* 7 (2), 30-60.

Goodman, J. (1988). The disenfranchisement of elementary teachers and strategies for resistance. *Journal of Curriculum and Supervision,* 3 (3), 201-220.

Goodman, J. (1991a). Critical curriculum theorizing: Towards a discourse of imagery. In J. Erdman & J. Henderson (Eds.), *Critical discourse on current curriculum Issues* (47-76). Chicago, IL: The Mid-West Center for Curriculum Studies.

Goodman, J. (1991b). Redirecting sexuality education for young adolescents. *Curriculum and Teaching,* 6 (1), 12-22.

Goodman, J. (1992). *Elementary schooling for critical democracy.* Albany, NY: State University of New York.

Goodman, J. & Kelly, T. (1988). Out of the mainstream: Issues confronting the male profeminist elementary school teacher. *Interchange,* 19 (2), 1-14.

Goodson, I. (1981a). Life history and the study of schooling, *Interchange,* 11 (4).

Goodson, I. (1981b). Becoming an academic subject: Patterns of explanation and evolution. *British Journal of Sociology of Education,* 2 (2), 163-180.

Goodson, I. (1983). *School subjects and curriculum change.* London, England: Falmer. [2nd edition: 1987; 3rd edition: 1993, with foreword by Peter McLaren.]

Goodson, I. (1984). Subjects for study: Towards a social history of curriculum. In I. Goodson & S. Ball (Eds.), *Defining the curriculum: Histories and ethnographies* (25-44). London, England: Falmer.

Goodson, I. (1988a). *International perspectives in curriculum history.* Boston, MA: Routledge & Kegan Paul.

Goodson, I. (1988b). *The making of curriculum: Collected essays*. Philadelphia, PA: Falmer.

Goodson, I. (1989a). Curriculum reform and curriculum theory: A case of historical amnesia. *Cambridge Journal of Education*, 19 (2), 131-141.

Goodson, I. (1989b). "Chariots of fire": Etymologies, epistemologies and the emergence of curriculum. In G. Milburn, I. Goodson, & R. Clark (Eds.), *Re-interpreting curriculum research: Images and arguments* (13-25). London, Ontario, Canada: The Althouse Press.

Goodson, I. (1991). Teachers' lives and educational research. In I. Goodson & R. Walker (Eds.), *Biography, identity and schooling* (137-149). London, England: Falmer.

Goodson, I. (1992a). Sponsoring the teachers' voice: Teachers' lives and teacher development. In A. Hargreaves & M. Fullan (Eds.), *Understanding teacher development* (110-121). New York: Teachers College Press.

Goodson, I. (1992b). Study school subjects. *Curriculum Perspectives*, 12 (1), 23-26.

Goodson, I. & Cole, A. (1993). Exploring the teacher's professional knowledge. In D. McLaughlin & W. Tierny (Eds.), *Naming silenced lives: Personal narratives and the process of educational change* (71-94). New York: Routledge.

Goodson, I. & Walker, R. (1991). *Biography, identity and schooling: Episodes in educational research*. London, England: Falmer.

Gordon, B. (1986). The use of emancipatory pedagogy in teacher education. *Journal of Educational Thought*, 20 (2), 59-65.

Gordon, B. (1993, 1985). Toward emancipation in citizenship education: The case of African-American cultural knowledge. In L. Castenell, Jr. & W. Pinar (Eds.), *Understanding curriculum as racial text: Representations of identity and difference in education* (263-284). Albany, NY: State University of New York Press. [Also (1985) in *Theory and Research in Social Education*, 12 (4), 1-23.]

Gordon, D. (1988). Education as text: The varieties of educational hiddenness. *Curriculum Inquiry*, 18 (4), 425-449.

Gordon, I. (Ed.). (1968). *Theories of Instruction*. Washington, DC: ASCD.

Gordon, M. (1983). Conflict and liberation: Personal aspects of the mathematics experience. In H. Giroux & D. Purpel (Eds.), *The hidden curriculum and moral education* (361-383). Berkeley, CA: McCutchan.

Gordon, M. & Weingarten, I. (1979). Communication or communiqué: Towards a theory of practice. *JCT*, 1 (2), 65-77.

Gordon, S. (1968). *Reports and repercussions in West Indian education 1835-1933*. London, England: Ginn.

Gore, A. (1992). *Earth in the balance: Ecology and the human spirit*. Boston, MA: Houghton Mifflin.

Gore, J. (1989, October). *The struggle for pedagogies: Critical and feminist discourses as "regimes of truth."* Paper presented at the Conference on Curriculum Theory and Classroom Practice, Dayton, OH.

Gore, J. (1990). Pedagogy as "text" in physical education teacher education: Beyond the preferred reading. In D. Kirk & R. Tinning (Eds.), *Physical education, curriculum and culture: Critical studies in the contemporary crisis* (101-138). London, England: Falmer.

Gore, J. (1991). On silent regulations: Emancipatory action research in preservice teacher education. *Curriculum Perspectives*, 11 (4), 47-51.

Gore, J. (1993). *The struggle for pedagogies: Critical and feminist discourses as regimes of truth.* New York: Routledge.

Gore, J. (1994). Enticing challenges: An introduction to Foucault and educational discourses. In R. Martusewicz & W. Reynolds (Eds.), *Inside out: Contemporary critical perspectives in education* (109-120). New York: St. Martin's Press.

Gotz, I. (1983). Heidegger and the art of teaching. *Educational Theory*, 33 (1), 1-9.

Gotz, I. (1987). Camus and the art of teaching. *Educational Theory*, 37 (3), 265-276.

Gough, N. (1989a). *Becoming ecopolitical: Some mythic links in curriculum renewal.* Paper presented at the annual meeting of the American Educational Research Association, San Francisco, CA.

Gough, N. (1989b). From epistemology to ecopolitics: Renewing a paradigm for curriculum. *Journal of Curriculum Studies*, 21 (3), 225-242.

Gough, N. (1991). Narrative and nature: Unsustainable fictions in environmental education. *Australian Journal of Environmental Education*, 7, 31-42.

Gough, N. (1993). Environmental education, narrative complexity and postmodern science/fiction. *International Journal of Science Education*, 15 (5), 607-625.

Gough, N. (1993). *Laboratories in fiction: Science education and popular media.* Geelong, Australia: Deakin University Press.

Gough, N. (1994). Narration, reflection, diffraction: Aspects of fiction in educational inquiry. *Australian Educational Researcher*, 21 (3), 1-18.

Gough, N. (1994). Playing at catastrophe: Ecopolitical education after poststructuralism. *Educational Theory*, 44 (2), 189-210.

Gouldner, A. (1970). *The coming crisis of western sociology.* New York: Basic Books.

Grabiner, G. (1983). Juridical subjectivism and juridical equivocation in the Bakke decision. *JCT*, 5 (3), 55-73.

Grabiner, G. & Grabiner, V. (1987) The self-determined educator and the expansion of the "labor-education" thesis. *JCT*, 7 (1), 39-61.

Grady, M. & Gawronski, J. (Eds.). (1983). *Computers in curriculum and instruction.* Alexandria, VA: ASCD.

Grafton, A. & Jardine, L. (1986). *From humanism to the humanities: Education and the liberal arts in fifteenth- and sixteenth century Europe.* London, England: Duckworth.

Graham, P. (1967). *Progressive education from arcaddy to academe: A history of the progressive movement.* New York: Teachers College Press.

Graham, R. (1989). Autobiography and education. *Journal of Educational Thought*, 23 (2), 92-105.

Graham, R. (1991). *Reading and writing the self: Autobiography in education and the curriculum*. New York: Teachers College Press.

Graham, R. (1992). *Currere* and reconceptualism: The progress of the pilgrimage 1975-1990. *Journal of Curriculum Studies*, 24 (1), 27-42.

Grahame, P. & Jardine, D. (1990). Deviance, resistance, and play: A study in the communicative organization of trouble in class. *Curriculum Inquiry*, 20 (3), 283-304.

Gramsci, A. (1971). *Selections from the prison notebooks of Antonio Gramsci.* [Edited and trans. Q. Hoard & G. Smith.] New York: International Publishers.

Gramsci, A. (1975). *Selections from cultural writings.* [Edited D. Forgacs & G. Smith; trans. W. Boelhomer.] London, England: Lawrence & Wishart.

Grannis, J. (1972). The school as a model of society. In D. Purpel & M. Belanger (Eds.), *Curriculum and cultural revolution* (146-165). Berkeley, CA: McCutchan.

Grant, C. & Sleeter, C. (1986). *After the school bell rings*. Philadelphia, PA: Falmer.

Grant, G. (1988). *The world we created at Hamilton high*. Cambridge, MA: Harvard University Press.

Grant, L. (1984, April). Black females' "place" in desegregated classrooms. *Sociology of Education*, 57, 98-111.

Gray, D. (1985). An old humanist's reply to Apple. *Curriculum Inquiry*, 15 (3), 320-323.

Green, G. (1922). *Psychoanalysis in the classroom.* [Introduction by W. McDougall.] New York & London: G. P. Putnam's Sons, the Knicker-bocker Press.

Green, Jr., R. (1992). Religion and education: What role should religion play in the public schools? In J. Kincheloe & S. Steinberg (Eds.), *Thirteen questions* (215-224). New York: Peter Lang.

Greenberg, J., Bruess, C. & Sands, D. (1986). *Sexuality: Insights and issues*. Dubuque, IA: Wm. C. Brown.

Greenall-Gough, A. (1991). Greening the future for education: Changing curriculum content and school organization. *Journal of Curriculum Studies*, 23 (6), 559-571.

Greenall-Gough, A. & Robottom, I. (1993). Towards a socially critical environmental education: Water quality studies in a coastal school. *Journal of Curriculum Studies*, 25 (4), 301-316.

Greene, J. (1991, October 13). This school is out. *New York Times Magazine*, 32-69.

Greene, J. (1992). The practitioner's perspective. *Curriculum Inquiry*, 22 (1) 39-45.

Greene, M. (1965a). *The public school and the private vision: A search for American in education and literature*. New York: Random House.

Greene, M. (1965b, February). Real toads and imaginary gardens. *Teachers College Record*, 66, 416-424.

Greene, M. (1967). Higher dignity. *Teachers College Record*, 69, 271-276.

Greene, M. (1968). Art, technique, and the indifferent gods. *Teachers College Record*, 70, 256-261.

Greene, M. (1971). Curriculum and consciousness. *Teachers College Record*, 73 (2), 253-269. [See also Greene, 1975b.]

Greene, M. (1973). *Teacher as stranger*. Belmont, CA: Wadsworth.

Greene, M. (1974). Cognition, consciousness, and curriculum. In W. Pinar (Ed.), *Heightened consciousness, cultural revolution, and curriculum theory* (69-84). Berkeley, CA: McCutchan.

Greene, M. (1975a). Autobiographical statement. In W. Pinar (Ed.), *Curriculum theorizing: The reconceptualists* (295-298). Berkeley, CA: McCutchan.

Greene, M. (1975b). Curriculum and consciousness. In W. Pinar (Ed.), *Curriculum theorizing: The reconceptualists* (299-317). Berkeley, CA: McCutchan.

Greene, M. (1978). *Landscapes of learning*. New York: Teachers College Press.

Greene, M. (1979, October). Letter to the editor. *Educational Researcher*, 8 (9, 25.

Greene, M. (1980). Response to P. Jackson. *Curriculum Inquiry*, 10 (2), 172-175.

Greene, M. (1988a). *The dialectic of freedom*. New York: Teachers College Press.

Greene, M. (1988b). The artistic-aesthetic and curriculum. *Curriculum Inquiry*, 6 (4), 283-296.

Greene, M. (1991a). Texts and margins. *Harvard Educational Review*, 61 (1), 27-39.

Greene, M. (1991b). Blue guitars and the search for curriculum. In G. Willis & W. Schubert (Eds.), *Reflections from the heart of educational inquiry: Understanding curriculum and teaching through the arts* (107-122). Albany, NY: State University of New York Press.

Greene, N. (1990). *Pier Paolo Pasolini: Cinema as heresy*. Princeton, NJ: Princeton University Press.

Greenfield, T. (1980). The man who comes back through the door in the wall: Discovering truth, discovering self, discovering organizations. *Education Administration Quar terly*, 16 (3), 26-59.

Greenfield, T. (1982). Against group mind: An anarchistic theory of education. *McGill Journal of Education*, 17 (1), 3-11.

Greenfield, T. (1986). The decline and fall of science in educational administration. *Interchange*, 17 (2), 57-80.

Greer, G. (1970). *The female eunuch*. London, England: MacGibbon & Kee.

Greer, C. (1972). *The great school legend*. New York: Viking.

Gress, J. & Purpel, D. (Eds.). (1978). *Curriculum: An introduction to the field*. Berkeley, CA: Mutchan.

Gress, J. (Ed.). (1988). *Curriculum: An introduction to the field*. Berkeley, CA: McCutchan.

Griffin, A. (1993). *Romanticism reconsidered: The implications of organicism in educational reform.* Baton Rouge, LA: Louisiana State University, Department of Curriculum and Instruction, unpublished Ph.D. dissertation.

Griffin, D. (1976). *God, power, and evil.* Philadelphia, PA: Westminister Press.

Griffin, D. (1988a). (Ed.). *The reenchantment of science: Postmodern proposals.* Albany, NY: State University of New York Press.

Griffin, D. (1988b). *Spirituality and society: Postmodern visions.* Albany, NY: State University of New York Press.

Griffin, D. (1989). *Varieties of postmodern theology.* Albany, NY: State University of New York Press.

Griffin, D. (1990). *Sacred interconnections: Postmodern spirituality, political economy, and art.* Albany, NY: State University of New York Press.

Griffin, G. (Ed.). (1983). *Staff development: Eighty-second Yearbook of the National Society for the Study of Education, Part II.* Chicago, IL: University of Chicago Press.

Griffin, G. (1985). Teacher induction: Research issues. *Journal of Teacher Education, 36* (1), 42-46.

Griffin, G. (1987). Clinical teacher education. *Journal of Curriculum and Supervision, 2* (3), 248-274.

Grinberg, J. (1994). From the margin to the center: Teachers' emerging voices through inquiry. In R. Martusewicz & W. Reynolds (Eds.), *Inside out: Contemporary critical perspectives in education* (121-137). New York: St. Martin's Press.

Gross, N., Giacquinta, J. & Bernstein, M. (1971). *Implementing organizational innovations: A sociological analysis of planned educational change.* New York: Basic Books.

Grossberg, L. (1993). The formations of cultural studies: An American in Birmingham. In V. Blundell, J. Shepherd & I. Taylor (Eds.), *Relocating cultural studies: Developments in theory and research* (21-66). London & New York: Routledge

Grotowski, J. (1968). *Towards a poor theater.* New York: Simon & Schuster.

Grubb, W., et al. (1991). *"The cunning hand, the cultured mind": Models for integrating vocational and academic education.* Macomb, IL: Western Illinois University, National Center for Research in Vocational Education, Materials Distribution Service.

Grumet, M. (1976a). Existential and phenomenological foundations. In W. Pinar & M. Grumet, *Toward a poor curriculum* (31-50). Dubuque, IA: Kendall/Hunt.

Grumet, M. (1976b). Psychoanalytic foundations. In W. Pinar & M. Grumet, *Toward a poor curriculum* (111-146). Dubuque, IA: Kendall/Hunt.

Grumet, M. (1976c). Toward a poor curriculum. In W. Pinar & M. Grumet, *Toward a poor curriculum* (67-88). Dubuque, IA: Kendall/Hunt.

Grumet, M. (1978). Songs and situations. In G. Willis (Ed.), *Qualitative Evaluation* (274-315), Berkeley, CA: McCutchan.

Grumet, M. (1979a). Supervision and situation: A methodology of self-report in teacher education. *JCT, 1* (1), 191-257.

Grumet, M. (1979b). *Conception, contradiction and curriculum.* Paper presented to the Airlie Conference, Virginia. [Also, *JCT*, 1981, 3 (1), 287-298.]

Grumet, M. (1980). Autobiography and reconceptualization. *JCT*, 2 (2), 155-158.

Grumet, M. (1981). Restitution and reconstruction of educational experience: An autobiographical method for curriculum theory. In M. Lawn, & L. Barton (Eds.), *Rethinking curriculum studies.* London, England: Croom Helm.

Grumet, M. (1983). My face in thine eye, thine in mine appears: The look of parenting and pedagogy. *Phenomenology + Pedagogy*, 1 (1), 45-57.

Grumet, M. (1985). The work of James B. Macdonald: Theory fierce with reality. *JCT*, 6 (3), 19-27.

Grumet, M. (1987). The politics of personal knowledge. *Curriculum Inquiry*, 17 (3), 319-329.

Grumet, M. (1988a). Bodyreading. In W. Pinar (Ed.), *Contemporary curriculum discourses* (453-473). Scottsdale, AZ: Gorsuch Scarisbrick.

Grumet, M. (1988b). *Bitter milk: Women and teaching.* Amherst, MA: University of Massachusetts Press.

Grumet, M. (1988c). Women and teaching: Homeless at home. In W. Pinar (Ed.), *Contemporary curriculum discourses* (531-540). Scottsdale, AZ: Gorsuch Scarisbrick.

Grumet, M. (1989a). Word worlds: The literary reference of curriculum criticism. *JCT*, 9 (1), 7-23.

Grumet, M. (1989b, January-February). Generations: Reconceptualist curriculum theory and teacher education. *Journal of Teacher Education*, XXXX (1), 13-18.

Grumet, M. (1989c). Feminism, and the phenomenology of the familiar. In G. Milburn, I. Goodson, & R. Clark (Eds.), *Re-interpreting curriculum research: Images and arguments* (87-101). London, Ontario, Canada: The Althouse Press.

Grumet, M. (1990a). Voice: The search for a feminist rhetoric for educational studies. *Cambridge Journal of Education*, 20 (3), 277-282.

Grumet, M. (1990b). Retrospective: Autobiography and the analysis of educational experience. *Cambridge Journal of Education*, 20 (3), 321-326.

Grumet, M. (1990c). The theory of the subject in contemporary curriculum thought. In J. Willinsky (Ed.), *The educational legacy of romanticism* (189-209). Waterloo, Ontario, Canada: Wilfrid Laurier University Press.

Grumet, M. (1990d). On the daffodils that come before the swallow dares. In E. Eisner & A. Peshkin (Eds.), *Qualitative inquiry in education: The continuing debate* (101-120). New York: Teachers College Press.

Grumet, M. (1991). Curriculum and the art of daily life. In G. Willis & W. Schubert (Eds.), *Reflections from the heart of educational inquiry: Understanding curriculum and teaching through the arts* (74-89). Albany, NY: State University of New York Press.

Grumet, M. (1992). Existential and phenomenological foundations of autobiographical method. In W. Pinar & W. Reynolds, *Understanding curriculum as phenomenological and deconstructed text* (28-43). New York: Teachers College Press.

Grumet, M. & Pinar, W. (1992, December). *Doublereading.* Paper presented to the annual meeting of the Modern Language Association, New York.

Grundy, S. (1991). A computer adventure game as a worthwhile educational experience. *Interchange, 22* (4), 41-55.

Guba, E. (1978). *Toward a methodology of naturalistic inquiry in educational evaluation.* Los Angeles, CA: University of California, Center for the Study of Evaluation.

Guba, E. (1979). *Investigative reporting.* Research on evaluation program paper and report series. Portland, OR: Northwest Regional Educational Laboratory.

Guba, E. (1981). Investigative reporting. In N. Smith (Ed.), *New techniques for evaluation.* Beverly Hills, CA: Sage.

Guba, E. (1992). Relativism. *Curriculum Inquiry, 22* (1), 17-22.

Guba, E. & Lincoln, Y. (1981). *Effective evaluation: Improving the usefulness of evaluation results through responsive and naturalistic approaches.* San Francisco, CA: Jossey-Bass.

Gundem, D. (1992). Notes on the development of Nordic didactics. *Journal of Curriculum Studies, 24* (1), 61-70.

Gumport, P. (1993). Fired faculty: Reflections on marginalization and academic identity. In D. McLaughlin & W. Tierny (Eds.), *Naming silenced lives: Personal narratives and the process of educational change* (135-154). New York: Routledge.

Gunn, J. (1982). *Autobiography: Towards a poetics of experience.* Philadelphia, PA: University of Pennsylvania Press.

Gusdorf, G. (1980). Conditions and limits of autobiography. In J. Olney (Ed.), *Autobiography: Essays theoretical and critical.* Princeton, NJ: Princeton University Press.

Gutek, G. (1993). *American education in a global society: Internationalizing teacher education.* New York: Longman.

Guthrie, J. & Reed, R. (1986). *Educational administration and policy: Effective leadership for American education.* Englewood Cliffs, NJ: Prentice-Hall.

Gutierrez, G. (1968). Toward a theology of liberation. In A. Hennelly (Ed.), *Liberation theology: A documentary history* (62-76). Maryknoll, NY: Orbis.

Gutierrez, G. (1973). *A theology of liberation: History, politics, salvation.* Maryknoll, NY: Orbis Books.

Gutmann. A. (1987). *Democratic education.* Princeton, NJ: Princeton University Press.

Guttchen, R. & Bandman, B. (Eds.). (1969). *Philosophical essays on curriculum.* New York: J. B. Lippincott.

Gwynn, J. (1943, 1950, 1960). *Curriculum principles and social trends.* New York: Macmillan.

Gwynn, J. & Chase, J. (1969). *Curriculum principles and social trends.* New York: Macmillan.

Habermas, J. (1970). *Knowledge and human interests.* Boston, MA: Beacon.

Habermas, J. (1979). *Communication and the evolution of society.* [T. McCarthy, trans.] Boston, MA: Beacon Press.

Habermas, J. (1981). Modernity versus postmodernity. *New German Critique* (22), 3-14.

Habermas, J. (1990). Remarks on the discussion. *Theory, Culture and Society,* 7 (4), 127-132.

Hacker, A. (1990, November 22). Trans-national America. *New York Review of Books,* 37(22), 19-24.

Hacker, A. (1992). *Two nations: Black and white, separate, hostile, unequal.* New York: Scribners.

Haggerson, N. (1985). Curriculum as figurative language: Exalting teaching and learning through poetry. *Illinois School Research and Development,* 22 (1), 10-17.

Haggerson, N. (1986). Reconceptualizing professional literature: An aesthetic self-study. *JCT,* 6 (4), 74-97.

Haggerson, N. (1988). Reconceptualizing inquiry in curriculum: Using multiple research paradigms to enhance the study of curriculum. *JCT,* 8 (1), 81-102.

Haggerson, N. (1991). Another contribution to the discussion: A response to Hills' "Issues in research on instructional supervision." *Journal of Curriculum and Supervision,* 7 (1), 13-25.

Haggerson, N. & Bowman, A. (Eds.). (1993). *Informing educational policy and practice through interpretive inquiry.* Lancaster, PA: Technomic Publishers.

Haight, R. (1988). Liberation theology. In J. Konomchak, M. Collins, & D. Lane (Eds.), *The new dictionary of theology* (570-576). Wilmington, DE: Michael Glazier.

Hale-Benson, J. (1990). Visions for Children: Educating black children in the context of their culture. In K. Lomotey (Ed.), *Going to school: The African-American experience* (212), Albany, NY: State University of New York Press.

Hales, J. & Snyder, J. (1982, Feb. 6-10 & March 6-10). Jackson's Mill industrial arts curriculum theory: A base for curriculum derivation. Parts 1 & 2. *Man, society, technology.*

Hall, B. (1973). *Value clarification as learning process: A guidebook of learning strategies.* New York: Paulist Press.

Hall, J. & Lewis, A. (1925). The Denver program. *National Education Association: Addresses and Proceedings.* Washington, DC: National Education Association.

Hall, S. (1883). The contents of the children's minds. *Princeton Review,* 11, 249-272.

Hall, S. (1923). *Life and confessions of a psychologist.* New York: D. Appleton.

Hall, S. & Loucks, S. (1976). *A developmental model for determining whether or not the treatment really is implemented.* Austin, TX: University of Texas, Research and Development Center for Teacher Education.

Hallinger, P., Leithwood, K. & Murphy, J. (Eds.). (1993). *Cognitive perspectives on educational leadership.* New York: Teachers College Press.

Hamblen, K. (1983). Modern fine art: A vehicle for understanding western modernity. *The Bulletin of the Caucus on Social Theory and Art Education*, 3, 9-16.

Hamblen, K. (1986). Artistic commonalities and differences: Educational occasions for universal-relative dialectics. *Visual Arts Research*, 12 (2) 41-51.

Hamblen, K. (1990). Beyond the aesthetic of cash-culture literacy. *Studies in Art Education*, 31 (4), 216-225.

Hamerow, T. (1993). Disturbing echoes of old arguments about ethnic experience. *The Chronicle of Higher Education*, XXXIX (48), A36.

Hameyer, U., Frey, K., Haft, H. & Kuebart, F. (Eds.). (1986). *Curriculum research in Europe*. Lisse, Netherlands: Swets & Zeitlinger.

Hamilton, D. (1976). *Curriculum evaluation*. London, England: Open Books.

Hamilton, D. (1989). *Toward a theory of schooling*. London, England: Falmer.

Hamilton, D. (1990). *Curriculum history*. Geelong, Victoria, Australia: Deakin University Press.

Hamilton, D., et al. (Eds.). (1976). *Beyond the numbers game: A reader in educational evaluation*. London: Macmillan.

Hammer, R. & McLaren, P. (1991). Rethinking the dialectic: A social semiotic perspective for educators. *Educational Theory*, 41 (1), 23-46.

Hammer, R. & McLaren, P. (1992). The spectacularization of subjectivity: Media knowledge, global citizenry and the new world order. *Polygraph*,5, 46-66.

Hammerschlag, C. (1988). *The dancing healers: A doctor's journey of healing with native Americans*. San Francisco, CA: Harper & Row.

Hampden-Turner, C. (1968). *Radical man*. Garden City, NY: Anchor Books, Doubleday.

Han, Jong-Ha (1993, November). Curriculum and decentralization in Korea. Paper presented to the International Seminar on Curriculum and Decentralization, Santiago, Chile.

Hannaway, J. (1993). Decentralization in two school districts: Challenging the standard paradigm. In J. Hannaway, & M Carnoy (Eds.), *Decentralization and school improvement: Can we fulfill the promise?* (135-162). San Francisco, CA: Jossey-Bass Publishers.

Hannaway, J. & Carnoy, M. (Eds.). (1993). *Decentralization and school improvement: Can we fulfill the promise?* San Francisco, CA: Jossey-Bass Publishers.

Hanvey, R. (1976). *An attainable global perspective*. Denver, CO: Center for Teaching International Relations.

Harap, H. (Ed.). (1937). *The changing curriculum*. New York: D. Appleton-Century Company.

Harap, H. (1952). *Social living in the curriculum: A critical study of the core in action in grades one through twelve*. Nashville, TN: George Peabody College for Teachers.

Harbo, T. (1983). The curriculum field today: A Scandinavian view. *Theory Into Practice*, XXII (3), 231-234.

Hargreaves, A. (1992). Cultures of teaching: A focus for change. In A. Hargreaves & M. Fullan (Eds.), *Understanding teacher development* (216-240). New York: Teachers College Press & Cassell (U.K).

Hargreaves, A. & Fullan, M. (Eds.). (1992). *Understanding teacher development.* New York: Teachers College Press & Cassell (U.K.).

Harlan, L. (1983). *Booker T. Washington: The wizard of Tuskegee 1901-1915.* New York: Oxford University Press.

Harmon, W. (1972). The nature of our changing society: Implications for schools. In D. Purpel & M. Belanger (Eds.), *Curriculum and cultural revolution* (4-63). Berkeley, CA: McCutchan.

Harré, R. & Secord, P. (1972). *The explanation of social behavior.* Oxford, UK: Basil Blackwell & Mott.

Harris, A. (1970). The second sex in academe. *American Association of University Professors Bulletin,* 56, 283-295.

Harris, W. (1875). *Twenty-first annual report of the board o f directors of the St. Louis Public Schools.* St. Louis, MO: St. Louis Public Schools.

Harris, W. (1898). *Psychological foundations of education: An attempt to show the genesis of the higher faculties of the mind.* New York: D. Appleton.

Harris, W. (1969). *Report on the committee of fifteen on elementary education.* New York: Arno Press.

Harrison, E. (1984). *Social worlds: British Columbia social studies curriculum unit "developing the tropical world" as reflected through the writings of George Herbert Mead and Alfred Schutz.* Edmonton, Alberta, Canada: University of Alberta, Faculty of Education, Department of Secondary Education, unpublished Ph.D. dissertation.

Hart, C. (1992). An introduction to Steven Ramsankar of the Alex Taylor Community School. *Journal of Curriculum & Supervision,* 7 (4), 327-333.

Hartnett, A. & Naish, M. (1987). Multicultural education. *Journal of Curriculum Studies,* 19 (4), 361-370.

Hartshorne, C. (1937). *Beyond humanism: Essays in the philosophy of nature.* Lincoln, NE: University of Nebraska Press.

Harvard University, Committee on the Objectives of General Education in a Free Society. (1945). *General education in a free society: Report of the Harvard committee.* Cambridge, MA: Harvard University Press.

Haskell, M. (1974). *From reverence to rape: The treatment of women in the movies.* New York: Holt, Rinehart & Winston.

Hass, G. (Ed.). (1977). *Curriculum planning: A new approach.* [Second edition.] Boston, MA: Allyn & Bacon.

Hass, G., Bondi, J. & Wiles, J. (Eds.). (1974). *Curriculum planning: A new approach.* Boston, MA: Allyn & Bacon.

Hatfield, B. (1991). *A critical film study of racial representations and social identities embedded in two contrasting films used in a health and family living curriculum on the subject of AIDS.* Baton Rouge, LA: Louisiana State University, Department of Curriculum and Instruction, unpublished Ph.D. dissertation.

Hatfield, B. (1993). 'Til the death do us part: AIDS, race, and representation. In L. Castenell, Jr., & W. Pinar (Eds.), *Understanding curriculum as racial text: Representations of identity and difference in education* (107-123). Albany, NY: State University of New York Press.

Hatton, E. (1987). Hidden pedagogy as an account of pedagogical conservatism. *Journal of Curriculum Studies*, 19 (5), 457-470.

Haubrich, V. & Apple, M. (Eds.). (1975). *Schooling and the rights of children.* Berkeley, CA: McCutchan.

Hayles, K. (1990). *Chaos bound: Orderly disorder in contemporary literature and science.* Ithaca, NY: Cornell University Press.

Haynes, C. (1990). *Religion in American history: What to teach and how.* Alexandria, VA: ASCD.

Hawking, S. (1988). *A brief history of time: From the big bang to black holes.* New York: Bantam.

Hawthorne, R. (1992). *Curriculum in the making: Teacher choice and the classroom experience.* New York: Teachers College Press.

Hazi, H. (1990). The lure of the business world: A response to Duffy's "Supervising for results." *Journal of Curriculum and Supervision*, 6 (1), 49-51.

Hazlett, S. (1979) Conceptions of curriculum history. *Curriculum Inquiry*, 9 (2), 129-135.

Heap, J. (1980). What counts as reading: Limits to certainty in assessment. *Curriculum Inquiry*, 10 (3), 265-292.

Hearn, W. (1872). *Payment by results in primary education.* Melbourne, Australia: Stellwell & Knight.

Heath, R. (Ed.). (1964). *New curricula.* New York: Harper & Row.

Heath, R. & Nielsen, M. (1974). The research basis for performance-based teacher education. *Review of Educational Research*, 44, 463-484.

Heath, S. (1982). Ethnography in education: Defining the essentials. In P. Gilmore & A. Glatthorn (Eds.), *Ethnography and education* (33-55). Washington, DC: Center for Applied Linguistics.

Heath, S. (1983). *Ways with words: Language, life, and work in community and classrooms.* Cambridge, England: Cambridge University Press.

Heath, S. (1986). Sociocultural contexts of language development. In California State Department of Education (Ed.), *Beyond language: Social and cultural factors in schooling language minority students* (143-186). Los Angeles, CA: California State University, Evaluation, Dissemination and Assessment Center.

Heidegger, M. (1933, 1985). The self-assertion of the German University: Address, delivered on the solemn assumption of the rectorate of the University Freiburg. [Trans. by K. Harries.] *Review of Metaphysics*, (38), 467-502. [Reference is to French translation by G. Granel, quoted by J. Derrida (1989,Winter). Of spirit. *Critical Inquiry*, (15), 456-474.]

Heidegger, M. (1962). *Being and time.* [Trans. J. Macquarrie & E. Robinson.] New York: Harper & Row.

Heimann, P., Otto, G. & Schultz, W. (1972). *Unterricht: Analyse und planung.* [*Instruction: Analysis and planning*]. Hanover, Germany: Schrodel.

Held, D. (1980). *Introduction to critical theory: Horkheimer to Habermas.* Berkeley, CA: University of California Press.

Helle, A. (1991). Reading women's autobiographies: A map of reconstructed knowing. In C. Witherell & N. Noddings (Eds.), *Stories lives tell: Narrative and dialogue in education.* New York: Teachers College Press.

Hellinger, W. (1991). *Global education: Educational systems in Syria, Egypt, Israel, and American Jewish schools.* Lafayette, LA: University of Southwestern Louisiana, College of Education, unpublished manuscript..

Henderson, J. (1988). A comprehensive hermeneutic of professional growth: Normative referent and reflective interplay. *JCT*, 8 (3), 147-167.

Henderson, J. (1992). *Reflective teaching: Becoming an educator.* [Foreword by N. Noddings.] New York: Macmillan.

Hennelly, A. (1990). *Liberation theology: A documentary history.* Maryknoll, NY: Orbis Books.

Herbart, J. (1895). *The science of education: Its general principles deducted from its aims.* Boston, MA: D. C. Heath & Company.

Herbart, J. (1901). *Outlines of educational doctrine.* [A. F. Lange, trans.] New York: Macmillan Company.

Herrick, V. (1965). *Strategies for curriculum development: The works of Virgil Herrick.* [Edited J. Macdonald, et al.] Columbus, OH: Charles E. Merrill.

Herrick, V. & Harris, C. (1957). Handling data. In A. Foshay & J. Hall (Eds.), *Research for curriculum improvement* (83-118). Washington, DC: ASCD.

Herrick, V. & Tyler, R. (Eds.) (1950). *Toward improved curriculum theory.* Chicago, IL: University of Chicago Press.

Herron, J. (1987-88, Winter). Detroit: Postmodernism ground zero. *Social Text*, 61-79.

Hertzgaard, M. (1989). *On bended knee: The press and the Reagan presidency.* New York: Schocken Books.

Hess, R. et al. (1980). Maternal expectations for mastery of developmental tasks in Japan and the United States. *International Journal of Psychology*, 15 (4), 259-271.

Hess, R., & Azuma, H. (1991). Cultural support for schooling: Contrasts between Japan and the United States. *Educational Researcher*, 20 (9), 2-8, 12.

Heyser, H. (1992, May 3). Fight begins on how—or if - schools should teach about gays. Baton Rouge, LA: *Sunday Advocate*,10E.

Hicks, E. (1981). Cultural Marxism: Nonsynchrony and feminist practice. In L. Sargent (Ed.), *Women and Revolution* (219-238). Boston, MA: South End Press.

Hicks, W., Houston, W., Cheney, B., & Marquard, R. (1970). *The new elementary school curriculum.* New York: Van Nostrand Reinhold Co.

Hill, C. (1988). *A turbulent, seditious and factious people: John Bunyan and his church 1628-1688.* Oxford, England: Clarendon Press.

Hill, P. & Bonan, J. (1991). *Decentralization and accountability in public education*. Santa Monica, CA: Rand.

Hill, W. (1968). I-B-F supervision: A technique for changing teacher behavior. *The Clearing House*, 43 (3), 180-183.

Hilliard, A., Payton-Stewart, L. & Williams, L. (Eds.). (1990). *Infusions of African and African American content in the school curriculum: Proceedings of the First National Conference, October 1989*. Morristown, NJ: Aaron Press.

Hills, J. (1991). Issues in research on instructional supervision: A contribution to the discussion. *Journal of Curriculum and Supervision*, 7 (1), 1-12.

Hinkel, R. (1993). *Mything and making it*. Paper presented to the Bergamo Conference on Curriculum Theory and Classroom Practice, Dayton, OH.

Hirsch, E. (1987). *Cultural literacy: What every American needs to know*. Boston, MA: Houghton Mifflin.

Hirst, P. (1974) *Knowledge and the Curriculum*. London, England: Routledge & Kegan Paul.

Hirst, P. (1980). The logic of curriculum development. In M. Galton (Ed.), *Curriculum change*. Leicester, England: University of Leicester.

Hitler, A. (1973). *Mein Kampf*. [Trans. R. Manheim. Intro. by D. Watt.] Boston, MA; Houghton Mifflin.

Hlebowitsh, P. (1990). The teacher technician: Causes and consequences. *The Journal of Educational Thought*, 24 (3), 147-160.

Hlebowitsh, P. (1991). Amid behavioral and behavioristic objectives: Reappraising the appraisal of the Tyler Rationale. In J. Erdman & J. Henderson (Eds.), *Critical discourse on current curriculum issues* (80-103). Chicago, IL: Mid-West Center for Curriculum Studies.

Hlebowitsh, P. (1992, Winter). Critical theory versus curriculum theory: Reconsidering the dialogue on Dewey. *Educational Theory*, 42 (1), 69-82.

Hlebowitsh, P. (1993). *Radical curriculum theory reconsidered: A historical approach*. New York: Teachers College Press.

Hlebowitsh, P. & Wraga, W. (1989). The reemergence of the National Science Foundation in American education: Perspectives and problems. *Science Education*, 74, 405-418.

Hlynka, D. (1989). Making waves with educational technology: A deconstructionist reading of Ted Aoki. *JCT*, 9 (2), 27-38.

Hlynka, D. & Belland, J. (Eds.). (1991). *Paradigms regained: The Uses of illuminative, semiotic and post-modern criticism as modes of inquiry in educational technology*. Englewood Cliffs, NJ: Educational Technology Publications.

Hochschild, A. (1975). Inside the clockwork of male careers. In F. Howe (Ed.), *Women and the power to change*. New York: McGraw Hill.

Hocquenghem. G. (1978). *Homosexual desire*. London: Villiers Publications.

Hofstadter, R. (1963). *Anti-intellectualism in America*. New York: Knopf.

Hofstein, A. & Yager, R. (1982). Societal issues as organizers for science education in the '80s. *School Science and Mathematics*, 82, 539-547.

Hogan, D. (1988). The market revolution and disciplinary power: Joseph Lancaster and the psychology of the early classroom system. *History of Education Quarterly*, 29 (3), 381-417.

Holland, P. (1989). Implicit assumptions about the supervisory conference: A review and analysis of literature. *Journal of Curriculum and Supervision*, 4 (4), 362-397.

Holland, P. & Garman, N. (1992). Macdonald and the mythopoetic. *JCT*, 9 (4), 45-72.

Hollingsworth, S. & Miller, J. (1994). Re-writing "gender equity" in teacher research. In S. Hollingsworth & H. Sockett (Eds.), *Teacher research and educational reform*. Chicago, IL: University of Chicago Press.

Holmes Group. (1986). *Tomorrow's Teachers*. East Lansing, MI: The Holmes Group, Inc.

Holmes Group. (1990). *Tomorrow's Schools*. East Lansing, MI: The Holmes Group, Inc.

Holmes, B. (1985). *Equality and freedom in education: A comparative study*. London, England: Allen & Unwin.

Holt, J. (1969). *The underachieving school*. New York: Pitman.

Holt, M. (1978). *The common curriculum: Its structure and style in the comprehensive school*. London, England: Routledge & Kegan Paul.

hooks, b. (1992). *Black looks*. Boston, MA: South End Press.

hooks, b. (1993). bell hooks speaking about Paulo Freire—The man, his work. In P. McLaren & P. Leonard (Eds.), *Paulo Freire: A critical encounter* (146-154). London & New York: Routledge.

Hopkins, L. (1929). *Curriculum principles and practices*. New York: Benjamin H. Sanborn & Company.

Hopkins, L. (1937). *Integration: Its meaning and application*. New York: D. Appleton-Century.

Hopkins, L. (1941). *Interaction: The democratic process*. Boston, MA: D. C. Heath.

Hopkins, L. (1970). *The emerging self in school and home*. New York: Greenwood Press.

Hord, S., Rutherford, W., Huling-Austin, L. & Hall, G. (1987). *Taking charge of change*. Alexandria, VA: ASCD.

Hostetler, K. (1991). Community and neutrality in critical thought: A nonobjectivist view on the conduct and teaching of critical thinking. *Educational Theory*, 41 (1), 1-12.

Howard, R. & Kenny, R. (1992). Education for democracy: Promoting citizenship and critical reasoning through school governance. In A. Garrod (Ed.), *Learning for life: Moral education theory and practice* (210-227). Westport, CT: Praeger.

Howard, V. (1991). And practice drives me mad; or the drudgery of drill. *Harvard Educational Review*, 61 (1), 80-87.

Howard, V. (1992). *Learning by all means: Lessons from the arts*. New York: Peter Lang.

Howe, F. (Ed.). (1975). *Women and the power to change*. New York: McGraw Hill.

Howe, K. & Miramontes, O. (1992). *The ethics of special education*. New York: Teachers College Press.

Howley, A. & Hartnett, R. (1992). Pastoral power and the contemporary university: A Foucaldian analysis. *Educational Theory*, 42 (3), 271-283.

Huber, M. (1981). The renewal of curriculum theory in the 1970's: An historical study. *JCT*, 3 (1), 14-84.

Huberman, A. & Miles, M. (1984). *Innovation up close: How school improvement works*. New York: Plenum.

Huberman, M. (1983). School improvement strategies that work: Some scenarios. *Educational Leadership*, 41 (3), 23-27.

Huberman, M. (1992). Teacher development and instructional mastery. In A. Hargreaves & M. Fullan (Eds.), *Understanding teacher development* (122-142). New York: Teachers College Press.

Hudak, G. (1993). Technologies of marginality: Strategies of stardom and displacement in adolescent life. In C. McCarthy & W. Crichlow (Eds.), *Race, identity, and representation in education* (172-187). New York: Routledge.

Hudgins, B. & Edleman, S. (1986, July/August). Teaching critical thinking skills to fourth and fifth graders through teacher-led small-group discussions. *Journal of Educational Research*, 79, 333-342.

Huebner, D. (1962). Politics and the curriculum. In A. Passow (Ed.), *Curriculum crossroads* (87-95). New York: Teachers College Press.

Huebner, D. (1963). New modes of man's relationship to man. In A. Frazier (Ed.), *New insights and the curriculum* (144-164). Washington, DC: ASCD.

Huebner, D. (1966a). Curriculum as a field of study. In H. Robison (Ed.), *Precedents and promise in the curriculum field* (94-112). New York: Teachers College Press.

Huebner, D. (1966b). Curricular language and classroom meanings. In J. Macdonald & R. Leeper (Eds.), *Language and meaning* (8-26). Washington, DC: ASCD.

Huebner, D. (1967). Curriculum as concern for man's temporality. *Theory into Practice*, 6 (4), 172-179. Reprinted in W. Pinar (Ed.), *Curriculum theorizing: The reconceptualists* (237-249). Berkeley, CA: McCutchan.

Huebner, D. (1968). Implications of psychological thought for the curriculum. In G. Unruh & R. Leeper (Eds.), *Influences in curriculum change* (28-38). Washington, DC: ASCD.

Huebner, D. (1969, February). Language and teaching: Reflections in light of Heidegger's writing about language. Paper presented at the Union Theological Seminary, New York.

Huebner, D. (1970). Status and identity: A reply. In C. Bowers, I. Housego & D. Dyke (Eds.), *Education and social policy* (169-179). New York: Random House.

Huebner, D. (1974). Toward a remaking of curricular language. In W. Pinar (Ed.), *Heightened consciousness, cultural revolution, and curriculum theory* (36-53). Berkeley, CA: McCutchan.

Huebner, D. (1975a). Autobiographical statement. In W. Pinar (Ed.), *Curriculum theorizing: The reconceptualists* (213-215). Berkeley, CA: McCutchan.

Huebner, D. (1975b). Curricular language and classroom meanings. In W. Pinar (Ed.), *Curriculum theorizing: The reconceptualists* (217-237). Berkeley, CA: McCutchan.

Huebner, D. (1975c). Curriculum as concern for man's temporality. In W. Pinar (Ed.), *Curriculum theorizing: The reconceptualists* (237-249). Berkeley, CA: McCutchan.

Huebner, D. (1975d). The tasks of the curricular theorist. In W. Pinar (Ed.), *Curriculum theorizing: The Reconceptualists* (250-270). Berkeley, CA: McCutchan.

Huebner, D. (1975e). Poetry and power: The politics of curricular development. In W. Pinar (Ed.), *Curriculum theorizing: The reconceptualists* (271-280). Berkeley, CA: McCutchan.

Huebner, D. (1976). The moribund curriculum field: Its wake and our work. *Curriculum Inquiry*, 6 (2), 153-167.

Huebner, D. (1985). The redemption of schooling: The work of James B. Macdonald. *JCT*, 6 (3), 28-34.

Huebner, D. (1991, 1963). Notes toward a curriculum inquiry. *Journal of Curriculum and Supervision*, 6 (2), 145-160.

Huebner, D. (1993, November 20). *Education and spirituality*. New Haven, CT: Yale University, The Divinity School, unpublished manuscript. [Presented to the Seminar on Spirituality and Curriculum, November 20, 1993, on the campus of Loyola University in New Orleans, sponsored by Louisiana State, Loyola, and Xaiver Universities.]

Huenecke, D. (1992). An artistic criticism of *Writing to Read*, a computer-based program for beginning readers. *Journal of Curriculum and Supervision*, 7 (2), 170-179.

Hughes, R. (1979, March 15). Education could pay. New York: *New York Times*.

Hulsebosch, P. (1988). *Significant others: Teachers' perspectives on relationships with parents*. Chicago, IL: University of Illinois at Chicago, College of Education, unpublished doctoral dissertation.

Hulsebosch, P. (1992). Significant others: Teachers' perspectives on relationships with parents. In. W. Schubert & W. Ayers (Eds.), *Teacher lore* (107-132). New York: Longman.

Hulsizer, D. (1987, May). Public education on trial. *Educational Leadership*, 44 (8), 12-13.

Hultgren, F. (1985). A hermeneutic approach: Reflecting on the meaning of curriculum through interpretation of student-teaching experiences in home economics. *Journal of Vocational Home Economics Education*, 3 (1) 32-55.

Hunkins, F. (1980). *Curriculum development: Program improvement*. Columbus, OH: Charles Merrill.

Hunsberger, M. (1985a). The experience of re-reading. *Phenomenology + Pedagogy*, 3 (3), 161-166.

Hunsberger, M. (1985b). When child and curriculum meet in reading class. *Reading-Canada-Lecture*, 3 (2),101-108.

Hunsberger, M. (1988). Teaching reading methods. *The Journal of Educational Thought*, 22 (2A), 209-218.

Hunsberger, M. (1989). Students and textbooks: Which is to be the master? *Phenomenology + Pedagogy*, 7, 115-126.

Hunsberger, M. (1992). The time of texts. In W. Pinar & W. Reynolds (Eds.), *Understanding curriculum as phenomenological and deconstructed text* (64-91). New York: Teachers College Press.

Hunter, A. (1991). Review essay of *Social analysis of education: After the new sociology*. *Educational Theory*, 41 (4), 411-420.

Hunter, M. (1980, February). Six types of supervisory conferences. *Educational Leadership*, 37 (5), 408-412.

Hunter, M. (1982). *Mastery teaching*. El Segundo, CA: TIP Publications.

Hunter, W. (Ed.). (1993). A bucket of words: Creative writing about teaching and learning. Special issue of *Journal of Educational Thought*, 27 (1). Calgary, Alberta, Canada: University of Calgary, Faculty of Education.

Hur, S. (1986). *Understanding the meaning of teacher competence: An interpretative study of a teacher education curriculum in Korea*. Edmonton, Alberta, Canada: University of Alberta, Faculty of Education, Department of Secondary Education, unpublished Ph.D. dissertation.

Hurd, P. (1970). *New directions in teaching secondary school science*. Chicago, IL: Rand McNally.

Hurd, P. (1986). A rationale for a science, technology, and society theme in science education. In R. Bybee (Ed.), *Science/technology/society* (94-101). Washington, DC: National Science Teachers Association.

Hurlbert, M. & Totten, S. (Eds.). (1992). *Social issues in the English classroom*. Urbana, IL: NCTE.

Husserl, E. (1962). *Ideas*. [Trans. W. Gibson.] New York: Collier.

Husserl, E. (1964). *The Paris lectures*. [Trans. P. Koestenbaum] The Hague, Netherlands: Martinus Nijhoff.

Husserl, E. (1970). *Cartesian meditations*. [Trans. D. Cairns] The Hague, Netherlands: Martinus Nujhoff.

Hutchins, R. (1936). *The higher learning in America*. New Haven, CT: Yale University Press.

Huxley, A. (1970). *The doors of perception*. New York: Harper & Row.

Hwu, W. (1992, October). *Fording a river without wetting the feet: Displacing the self*. Paper presented to the Bergamo Conference, Dayton, OH.

Hwu, W. (1993). *Toward understanding poststructuralism and curriculum*. Baton Rouge, LA: Louisiana State University, Department of Curriculum and Instruction, unpublished Ph.D. dissertation.

Hybel, A. (1990). *How leaders reason: U.S. intervention in the Caribbean and Latin America*. Cambridge, MA: Blackwell.

Hybel, A. (1993). *Power over rationality: The Bush administration and the gulf crisis*. Albany, NY: SUNY Press.

Hyman, R. (Ed.). (1973). *Approaches in curriculum*. Englewood Cliffs, NJ: Prentice-Hall.

Imber, M. (1982). Toward a theory of curriculum reform: An analysis of the first campaign for sex education. *Curriculum Inquiry*, 12 (4), 339-362.

Indian Pastorals (1992, October). Pastoral letter of the Guatemalan bishops. In the *National Catholic Reporter*, 12.

Inlow, G. (1966, 1973). *The emergent in curriculum.* [Second edition: 1973.] New York: John Wiley & Sons, Inc.

Institute for Critical Thinking (1991). *Announcement.* Montclair, NJ: Montclair State College, Institute for Critical Thinking.

Irigaray, L. (1985a). *Speculum of the other woman.* [Trans. G. Gill.] Ithaca, NY: Cornell University Press.

Irigaray, I. (1985b). *The sex is not one.* [Trans. C. Porter.] Ithaca, NY: Cornell University Press.

Iverson, B. & Waxman, H. (1981). Perspectives on mentorship. *JCT*, 3 (1), 193-201.

Jacknicke, K. (1987). Educational administration as praxiological act. *JCT*, 7 (3), 34-42.

Jacknicke, K. & Rowell, P. (1984). *Reaching for possibilities in science education.* Curriculum Praxis Series, Occasional Paper No. 33. Edmonton, Alberta, Canada: University of Alberta, Faculty of Education, Department of Secondary Education.

Jacknicke, K. & Rowell, P. (1987, March). Alternative orientations for educational research. *Alberta Journal of Educational Research*, XXXIII (1), 62-72.

Jackson, P. (1968). *Life in Classrooms.* New York: Holt, Rinehart & Winston, Inc.

Jackson, P. (1970). The consequences of schooling. In N. Overly (Ed.), *The Unstudied curriculum* (1-15). Washington, DC: ASCD, NEA.

Jackson, P. (1980a). Curriculum and its discontents. *Curriculum Inquiry*, (1), 28-43. Reprinted in H. Giroux, A. Penna, & W. Pinar (Eds.) (1981), *Curriculum and instruction: Alternatives in Education* (367-381). Berkeley, CA: McCutchan.

Jackson, P. (1980b). Response to Maxine Greene. *Curriculum Inquiry*, 10 (2), 175-177.

Jackson, P. (1983). The daily grind. In H. Giroux & D. Purpel (Eds.), *The hidden curriculum and moral education* (28-60). Berkeley, CA: McCutchan.

Jackson, P. (1986). *The practice of teaching.* New York: Teachers College Press.

Jackson, P. (1989). John Dewey's poetry. In C. Kridel (Ed.), *Curriculum history* (99-113). Landham, MD: University Press of America.

Jackson, P. (1990, October). The functions of educational research. *Educational Researcher*, 19 (7), 3-9.

Jackson, P. (1992a). Conceptions of curriculum and curriculum specialists. In P. Jackson (Ed.), *Handbook of research on curriculum* (3-40). New York: Macmillan.

Jackson, P. (1992b). Helping teachers develop. In A. Hargreaves & M. Fullan (Eds.), *Understanding teacher development* (62-74). New York: Teachers College Press.

Jackson, P. (Ed.). (1992c). *Handbook of research on curriculum*. New York: Macmillan.

Jackson, P. (1992d). *Untaught lessons*. New York: Teachers College Press.

Jackson, P. (1994). *Stopping, yet again, to consider Frost's evening traveler*. Chicago, IL: University of Chicago, Department of Education, unpublished manuscript.

Jackson, P., Boostrom, R. & Hansen, D. (1993). *The moral life of schools*. San Francisco, CA: Jossey-Bass.

Jacob, E. (1987). Qualitative research traditions: A review. *Review of Educational Research, 57* (1), 1-50.

Jacobs, M. (1991). *Diary of an ambivalent daughter: A feminist re-visioning of Maxine Greene's discursive landscapes*. College Park, MD: University of Maryland, College of Education, unpublished Ph.D. dissertation.

Jacoby, R. (1987). *The last intellectuals*. New York: Basic Books.

Jaggar, A. (1977). Political philosophies of women's liberation. In M. Vetterling-Braggin, F. Elliston, & J. English (Eds.), *Feminism and philosophy*. Totowa, NJ: Littlefield Adams & Co.

Jagla, V. (1989). *In pursuit of the elusive image: An inquiry into teachers' everyday use of imagination and intuition*. Chicago, IL: University of Illinois at Chicago, College of Education, unpublished doctoral dissertation.

Jagla, V. (1992). Teachers' everyday imagination and intuition. In W. Schubert & W. Ayers (Eds.), *Teacher lore* (61-79). New York: Longman.

jagodzinski, j. (1979). *Towards a New Aesthetic*. Occasional Paper No. 12. Edmonton, Alberta, Canada: University of Alberta, Faculty of Education, Department of Secondary Education.

jagodzinski, j. (1989). *Curriculum as felt through six layers of an aesthetically embodied skin: The arch-writing on the body*. Edmonton, Alberta, Canada: University of Alberta, Faculty of Education, Department of Secondary Education, unpublished manuscript.

jagodzinski, j. (1992). Curriculum as felt through six layers of an aesthetically embodied skin: The arch-writing on the body. In W. Pinar & W. Reynolds (Eds.), *Understanding curriculum as phenomenological and deconstructed Text* (159-183). New York: Teachers College Press.

James, T. & Levin, H. (1983). *Public dollars for private schools: The Case for tuition tax credits*. Philadelphia, PA: Temple University Press.

James, W. (1985). *The varieties of religious experience*. Cambridge, MA: Harvard University Press.

Jameson, F. (1981). *The political unconscious: Narrative as a socially symbolic act*. Ithaca, NY: Cornell University Press.

Jameson, F. (1987, Fall). Regarding postmodernism—A conversation with Fredric Jameson. *Social Text*, 29-55.

Jameson, F. (1991). *Postmodernism and the cultural logic o late capitalism*. Durham, NC: Duke University Press.

Jardine, D. (1987, April). Reflection and self-understanding in Piagetian theory: A phenomenological critique. *The Journal of Educational Thought, 21*(1), 10-19.

Jardine, D. (1988a). "There are children all around us." *The Journal of Educational Thought*, 22 (2A), 178-186.

Jardine, D. (1988b). Reflections on phenomenology, pedagogy, and *Phenomenology + Pedagogy*. *Phenomenology + Pedagogy*, 6 (3),158-160.

Jardine, D. (1988c). Piaget's clay and Descartes' wax. *Educational Theory*, 38 (3), 287-298.

Jardine, D. (1988d). Play and hermeneutics: An exploration of the bi-polarities of mutual understanding. *JCT*, 8 (2), 23-41.

Jardine, D. (1990). On the humility of mathematical language. *Educational Theory*, 40 (2), 181-192.

Jardine, D. (1992a). Reflections on education, hermeneutics, and ambiguity. In W. Pinar & W. Reynolds (Eds.), *Understanding curriculum as phenomenological and deconstructed text* (116-127). New York: Teachers College Press.

Jardine, D. (1992b). *Speaking with a boneless tongue*. Bragg Creek, Alberta, Canada: Makyo Press.

Jardine, D. & Morgan, G. (1987). Analogy as a model for the development of representation abilities in children. *Educational Theory*, 37 (3), 209-217.

Jarrett, J. (1980). Another kind of bias in moral education. *JCT*, 2 (1), 227-237.

Jaspers, K. (1959). *Truth and symbol*. [Trans. J. Wilde, W. Kluback & W. Kimmel.] New York: Twayne.

Jeanrond, W. (1988). Hermeneutics. In J. Komonchak, M. Collins, & D. Lane (Eds.), *The new dictionary of theology* (462-464). Wilmington, DE: Michael Glazier, Inc.

Jeffcoate, R. (1981). Evaluating the multicultural curriculum: Students' perspectives. *Journal of Curriculum Studies*, 13 (1), 1-15.

Jencks, C. (1987). *What is post-modernism?* New York: St. Martin's Press.

Jenkins, D., Kemmis, S., MacDonald, B. & Verma, G. (1979). Racism and educational evaluation. In G. Verma & C. Bagley (Eds.), *Race, education, and identity*. London, England: Macmillan.

Jennings, F. (Ed.). (1971). Curriculum: Interdisciplinary insights. Special issue of *Teachers College Record*, 73 (2).

Jervis, K. & Montag, C. (Eds.). (1991). *Progressive education for the 1990s: Transforming practice*. New York: Teachers College Press.

Jickling, B. (1988). Paradigms in curriculum development: Critical comments on the work of Tanner and Tanner. *Interchange*, 19 (2), 41-40.

Jing, L. (1993). *Education in post-Mao China*. Westport, CT: Greenwood Publishing Group, Inc.

Jipson, J. et. al. (in press). *Positions on imposition: Multiple cultural realities*. Albany, NY: State University of New York Press.

Joffee, C. (1974). As the twig is bent. In J. Stacey, S. Bereaud, & J. Daniels (Eds.), *And Jill came tumbling after: Sexism in American education*. New York: Dell.

Johnson, L. & Pinar, W. (1980). Aspects of gender analysis in recent feminist psychological thought and their implications for curriculum. *Journal of Education*,162 (4), 113-126.

Johnson, M. L. (1974). *Thirty years with an idea*. University, AL: University of Alabama Press.

Johnson, M. (1967, April). Definitions and models in curriculum theory. *Educational Theory*, 17 (2), 127-140.

Johnson, M. (1989). Embodied knowledge. *Curriculum Inquiry*, 19 (4), 361-377.

Johnson, N. (1990). Understanding and administering educational organizations: The contribution of Greenfield's "alternative theory." *Journal of Educational Thought*, 24 (1), 28-38.

Johnston, J. (1974). *Lesbian nation: The feminist solution*. New York: Touchstone Books, Simon & Shuster.

Johnston, K. (1992). Two moral orientations: How teachers think and act in the classroom. In A. Garrod (Ed.), *Learning for life: Moral education theory and practice* (71-85). Westport, CT: Praeger.

Johnston, V. (1987). Attitudes towards microcomputers in learning: 1. Pupils and software for language development. *Educational Research*, 29 (1), 47-55.

Johnstone, J. (1981). *Indicators of education systems*. Paris: UNESCO.

Joint Committee on Standards for Educational Evaluation (1981). *Standards for evaluation of educational programs, projects and materials*. New York: McGraw-Hill.

Jones-Wilson, F. (1991). School improvement among blacks: Implications for excellence and equity. In C. Willie, A. Garibaldi & W. Reed (Eds.), *The education of African-Americans* (72-78). New York: Auburn House.

Jordan, W. (1971). *White over black: American attitudes toward the Negro 1500-1812*. New York: Penguin Books.

Joseph, E. (1983). On the separation of the humanities and technology from each other: A triadic explanation. *JCT*, 5 (4), 58-67.

Joseph, E. (1988). Contributions of theology in educational administration. *JCT*, 8 (1), 37-54.

Joseph, E. (1989). The perfectibility of means and the disregard of ends. *Journal of Teacher Education*, XXXX (1),18-21.

Joyce, B. (1966, 1972, 1986). *Models of teaching*. Englewood Cliffs, NJ: Prentice-Hall.

Joyce, J. (1939). *Finnegan's wake*. New York: Viking.

Judd, C. (1918). *Introduction to the scientific study of education*. New York: Ginn & Company.

Jung, C. G. (1966). *The spirit in man, art and literature*. Princeton, NJ: Princeton University Press.

Jung, C. G. (1968). *Alchemical studies*. Princeton, NJ: Princeton University Press.

Jung, C. G. (1969). *The structure and dynamics of the psyche*. [Trans. R. F. C. Hull.] Princeton, NJ: Princeton University Press.

Kah, G. (1991). *En route to global occupation: A high-ranking government liaison exposes the secret agenda for world unification*. Lafayette, LA: Hunting House Publishers.

Kahama, C., Maliyamkono, T., & Wells, S. (1986). *The challenge for Tanzania's economy*. London, England: James Curry.

Kallos, D. & Lundgren, U. (1979). *Curriculum as a pedagogical problem*. Stockholm, Sweden: Liberlaromedel Lund.

Kamil, M. (1991). Computer software for curriculum. In A. Lewy (Ed.), *International Encyclopedia of Curriculum* (90-92). Oxford, England: Pergamon Press.

Kanpol, B. (1991, August). Teacher group formation as emancipatory critique: Necessary conditions for teacher resistance. *The Journal of Educational Thought*, 25 (2), 134-149.

Kanpol, B. (1992). *Towards a theory and practice of teacher cultural politics: Continuing the postmodern debate*. New Jersey: Ablex.

Kanpol, B. (1993). The pragmatic curriculum: Teacher reskilling as cultural politics. *Journal of Educational Thought*, 27 (2), 200-215.

Kantner, R. (1975). Women and the structure of organizations: Explorations in theory and behavior. In M. Millman & R. Kantner (Eds.), *Another voice: Feminist perspectives on social life and social science*. Garden City, N.Y.: Anchor Books, Doubleday.

Kantor, K. (1983, Summer). The English curriculum and the structure of the disciplines. *Theory into Practice*, XXII, 3, 174-181.

Kantor, D. (1990). Both sides now: Teaching English, teaching curriculum. In J. Sears & D. Marshall (Eds.), *Teaching and thinking about curriculum* (61-74). New York: Teachers College Press.

Kapferer, J. (1986). Curricula and the reproduction of structured social inequalities. *Curriculum Inquiry*, 16 (1), 5-29.

Kaplan, L. (1991). Teaching intellectual autonomy: The failure of the critical thinking movement. *Educational Theory*, 41 (4), 361-370.

Karabel, J. & Halsey, A. (Eds.). (1977). *Power and ideology in education*. New York: Oxford University Press.

Karatheodoris, S. (1984). Language, the unconscious and the formation of a children's joke. *Phenomenology + Pedagogy*, 1 (3), 285-295.

Karier, C. (1967). *Man, society, and education*. Glenview, IL: Scott, Foresman.

Karier, C. (1990). Nineteenth-century romantic and neo-romantic thought and some disturbing twentieth-century applications. In J. Willinsky (Ed.), *The educational legacy of romanticism* (93-113). Waterloo, Ontario, Canada: Wilfrid Laurier University Press.

Katz, M. (1971). *Class, bureaucracy, and the schools: The illusion of educational change in America*. New York: Praeger.

Katz, M. (1987). *Reconstructing American education*. Cambridge, MA: Harvard University Press.

Katznelson, I. & Weir, M. (1985). *Schooling for all: Class, race and the decline of the democratic ideal*. New York: Basic Books.

Kaufman, B. (1988). Ecology of teacher development. *Journal of Curriculum and Supervision*, 4 (1), 77-85.

Kaufman, B. & Kaufman, G. (1980). Reconstructing child development for curriculum studies: Critical and feminist perspectives. *JCT*, 2 (2), 245-268.

Keita, L. (1991). Universal science, technology and critical thinking: An exploration of its possibility in modern Africa. *Inquiry: Critical Thinking Across the Disciplines*, 7 (4), 14-17.

Kellaghan, T. & Madaus, G. (1991, November). National testing: Lessons for American from Europe. *Educational Leadership*, 87-90.

Kelly, A. (1977). *The curriculum: Theory and practice.* London: Harper & Row.

Kelpin, V. (1985). *Ear on the belly: A question of fetal monitors.* Curriculum Praxis Series, Occasional Paper No. 38. Edmonton, Alberta, Canada: University of Alberta, Faculty of Education, Department of Secondary Education.

Kennedy, D. (1991, August). Review essay. *The Journal of Educational Thought*, 25 (2), 160-162.

Kennedy, K. & Hopmann, S. (1992, April). *Curriculum policy structures in federal systems of government: The cases of Australia and Germany.* A paper presented to the annual meeting of the American Educational Research Association, San Francisco, CA.

Kerr, S. (1990, October). Will Glasnost lead to Perestroika? Directors of educational reform in the U.S.S.R. *Educational Researcher*, 19 (7), 26-31.

Kessler, H. (1956, September). Why a core curriculum for a democratic community? *High Points*, 38, 43.

Kessler, S. (1991). Early childhood education as development: Critique of the metaphor. *Early Education and Development*, (2) 2, 137-152.

Kessler, S. & Swadner, B. (Eds.). (1992). *Reconceptualizing the early childhood curriculum: Beginning the dialogue.* New York: Teachers College Press.

Kett, J. (1977). *Rites of passage: Adolescence in America 1790 to present.* New York: Basic Books.

Kickbursh, K. (1986). Curriculum-in-use and the emergence of practical ideology: A comparative study of secondary classrooms. *JCT*, 6 (4), 98-143.

Kickbursh, K. & Everhart, R. (1985). Curriculum, practical ideology, and class contradiction. *Curriculum Inquiry*, 15 (3), 281-317.

Kidder, T. (1989). *Among schoolchildren.* Boston, MA: Houghton-Mifflin.

Kilpatrick, W. (1918). The project method. *Teachers College Record*, 19 (4), 319-335.

Kilpatrick, W. (1925). *Foundations of method: Informal talks on teaching.* New York: Macmillan.

Kilpatrick, W. (1936). *Remaking the curriculum.* New York: Newson & Company.

Kimball, B. (1986). The training of teachers, the study of education, and the liberal traditions. *Educational Theory*, 36 (1), 15-22.

Kimpston, R. & Rogers, K. (1986). A framework for curriculum research. *Curriculum Inquiry*, 16 (4), 463-474.

Kincheloe, J. (1991a). *Teachers as researchers: Qualitative inquiry as a path to empowerment.* London, England: Falmer.

Kincheloe, J. (1991b). Willis Morris and the southern curriculum: Emancipating the Southern ghosts. In J. Kincheloe & W. Pinar (Eds.), *Curriculum as social psychoanalysis: The significance of place* (123-154). Albany, NY: State University of New York Press.

Kincheloe, J. (1992a). Educational reform: What have been the effects of the attempts to improve education over the last decade? In J. Kincheloe & S. Steinberg (Eds.), *Thirteen questions* (227-232). New York: Peter Lang.

Kincheloe, J. (1992b, October). *Liberation theology and the attempt to establish an emancipatory system of meaning.* A paper presented to the Bergamo Conference on Curriculum Theory and Classroom Practice, Dayton, OH.

Kincheloe, J. (1993a). The politics of race, history, and curriculum. In L. Castenell, Jr. & W. Pinar (Eds.), *Understanding curriculum as racial text: Representations of identity and difference in education* (249-262). Albany, NY: State University of New York Press.

Kincheloe, J. (1993b). *Toward a critical politics of teacher thinking: Mapping the postmodern.* Westport, CT: Bergin & Garvey.

Kincheloe, J. & Pinar, W. (Eds.). (1991). *Curriculum as social psychoanalysis: The significance of place.* Albany, NY: State University of New York Press.

Kincheloe, J. & Steinberg, S. (1992). *Thirteen questions.* New York: Peter Lang.

Kincheloe, J. & Steinberg, S. (1993). A tentative description of post-formal thinking: The critical confrontation with cognitive theory. *Harvard Educational Review,* 63 (3), 296-320.

Kincheloe, J., Steinberg, S., & Tippins, D. (1992). *The stigma of genius: Einstein and beyond modern education.* Wakefield, NH: Hollowbrook.

Kincheloe, J., Pinar, W. & Slattery, P. (in press). A last dying chord? Educational and cultural renewal in the American South. *Curriculum Inquiry.*

King, A. & Brownell, J. (1966) *The curriculum and the disciplines of knowledge: A theory of curriculum practice.* New York: John Wiley.

King, J. (1981). Methodological pluralism and curriculum inquiry. *Curriculum Inquiry,* 19 (2),167-174.

King, K. (1971). *Pan Africanism and education: A study of race, philanthropy and education in the southern states of America and East Africa.* Oxford, England: Clarendon Press.

King, N. (1986). Recontextualizing the curriculum. *Theory Into Practice,* XXV (1), 36-40.

Kingdon, J. (1984). *Agendas, alternatives, and public policies.* Boston, MA: Little, Brown.

Kipnis, L. (1988). Feminism: The political conscience of postmodernism? In A. Ross (Ed.), *Universal abandon: The politics of postmodernism* (149-166). Minneapolis, MN: University of Minnesota Press.

Kirk, D. (1988). Ideology and school-centered innovation: A case study and a critique. *Journal of Curriculum Studies,* 20 (5), 449-464.

Kirst, M. & Meister, G. (1985). Turbulence in American secondary schools: What reforms last? *Curriculum Inquiry,* 15 (2), 169-186.

Kirst, M., & Walker, D. (1971). An analysis of curriculum policy making. *Review of Educational Research,* 41 (4), 479-509.

Kiziltan, M., Bain, W., & Canizares, A. (1990). Postmodern conditions: Rethinking public education. *Educational Theory,* 40 (3), 351-369.

Klafki, W. (1964). *Das padagogische problem des elementaren und die theorie der kategorialen bildund.* [*The pedagogical problem of the elementary school and the theory of instructional categories*]. Weinheim: Beltz.

Klafki, W. (1971). Didaktic. In Groothoof, H.-H. & Stallmann, M. (Eds.), *Neues padagogisches lexikon.* Kreutz: Stuttgart.

Klein, F. (1983). The use of a research model to guide curriculum development. *Theory Into Practice,* XXII (3), 198-202.

Klein, F. (1985). Curriculum design. In T. Husen & T. Postlethwaite (Eds.), *International Encyclopedia of Education* (1163-1170). Oxford, England: Pergamon.

Klein, F. (1986). Alternative curriculum conceptions and designs. *Theory Into Practice,* 25 (1), 31-35.

Klein, F. (1989). *Curriculum reform in the elementary school: Creating your own agenda.* New York: Teachers College Press.

Klein, F. (1990). Approaches to curriculum theory and practice. In J. Sears & D. Marshall (Eds.), *Teaching and thinking about curriculum* (3-14). New York: Teachers College Press.

Kliebard, H. (1970). Persistent issues in historical perspective. *Educational Comment,* 31-41. Also in W. Pinar (Ed.) (1975a), *Curriculum theorizing: The reconceptualists* (39-50). Berkeley: McCutchan.

Kliebard, H. (1975b). Bureaucracy and curriculum theory. In W. Pinar (Ed.), *Curriculum theorizing: The reconceptualists* (51-69). Berkeley, CA: McCutchan.

Kliebard, H. (1975c). Reappraisal: The Tyler rationale. In W. Pinar (Ed.), *Curriculum theorizing: The reconceptualists* (70-83). Berkeley, CA: McCutchan.

Kliebard, H. (1975d). Metaphorical roots of curriculum design. In W. Pinar (Ed.), *Curriculum theorizing: The reconceptualists* (84-85). Berkeley, CA: McCutchan.

Kliebard, H. (1977). Curriculum theory: Give me a "for instance." *Curriculum Inquiry,* 6 (4), 257-269.

Kliebard, H. (1979). Systematic curriculum development, 1890-1959. In J. Schaffarzick & G. Sykes, (Eds.). *Values conflicts and curriculum issues: Lessons from research and experience* (197-236). Berkeley, CA: McCutchan.

Kliebard, H. (1981). Dewey and the Herbartians: The genesis of a theory of curriculum. *JCT,* 3 (1), 154-161. Reprinted in W. Pinar (Ed.), *Contemporary curriculum discourses* (66-79). Scottsdale, AZ: Gorsuch Scarisbrick.

Kliebard, H. (1982, January). Education at the turn of the century: A crucible for curriculum change. *Educational Researcher,* 16-24.

Kliebard, H. (1986). *The struggle for the American curriculum 1893-1958.* Boston, MA: Routledge & Kegan Paul.

Kliebard, H. (1987). A century of growing antagonism in high school–college relations. *Journal of Curriculum and Supervision,* 3 (1), 61-70.

Kliebard, H. (1988). Dewey and the Herbartians: The genesis of a theory of curriculum. In W. Pinar (Ed.), *Contemporary curriculum discourses* (66-79). Scottsdale, AZ: Gorsuch Scarisbrick.

Kliebard, H. (1989). Cultural literacy or the curate's egg. *Journal of Curriculum Studies*, 21 (1), 61-70.

Kliebard, H. (1992a). *Forging the American curriculum.* New York: Routledge.

Kliebard, H. (1992b). Constructing a history of the American curriculum. In. P. Jackson (Ed.), *Handbook of research on curriculum* (157-184). New York: Macmillan.

Kliebard, H. & Franklin, B. (1983). The course of the course of study: History of curriculum. In J. Best (Ed.), *Historical inquiry in education: A research agenda* (138-157). Washington, DC: American Educational Research Association.

Klohr, P. (1965, October). Use of the design element in curriculum change. *Educational Leadership*, 23 (1), 25-28.

Klohr, P. (1967a). Problems in curriculum theory development. *Theory into Practice*, 6 (4), 200-203.

Klohr, P. (1967b). This issue. *Theory into Practice*, 6 (4), 165.

Klohr, P. (Ed.). (1967c). Curriculum theory development: Work in progress. *Theory into Practice*, 6 (4), 6-11.

Klohr, P. (1969a, January). Curriculum workers in a bind. *Educational Leadership*, 26, 323-325.

Klohr, P. (1969b). Seeking new design alternatives. In A. Frazier (Ed.), *A curriculum for children* (91-104). Washington, DC: ASCD.

Klohr, P. (1974a). *Curriculum theory: The state of the field.* Columbus, OH: Ohio State University, College of Education, unpublished manuscript.

Klohr, P. (1974b). Reflections on the conference. In W. Pinar (Ed.), *Heightened consciousness, cultural revolution, and curriculum theory: The proceedings of the Rochester conference* (166-173). Berkeley, CA: McCutchan.

Klohr, P. (1980, October). The curriculum theory field—gritty and ragged. *Curriculum Perspectives*, 1 (1), 1-7.

Klohr, P. (1989a). Conversations with Pinar, February 10-13, in Baton Rouge, LA.

Klohr, P. (1989b). Personal papers sent to authors.

Klohr, P. (1992). *The history of the curriculum field: Remarks at Indiana University.* Bloomington, IN: Indiana University, School of Education, unpublished manuscript.

Knitter, W. (1986). Aesthetic experience as a model for curricular thought and action. *Journal of Curriculum Studies*, 18 (3), 257-266.

Knowles, G. (1992). Models for understanding pre-service and beginning teachers' biographies. In I. Goodson (Ed.), *Studying teachers' lives* (99-152). New York: Teachers College Press.

Kobayaski, V. (1968). Japan under American occupation. In R. Thomas, L. Sands, D. Brubaker (Eds.) *Strategies for curriculum change: Cases from 13 nations.* Scranton, PA: International Textbook Company.

Koerner, J. (1963). *The miseducation of American teachers.* Baltimore, MD: Penguin.

Koerner, M. (1989). *Teachers' images of their work: A descriptive study.* Chicago, IL: University of Illinois at Chicago, College of Education, unpublished doctoral dissertation.

Koerner, M. (1992). Teachers' images: Reflections of themselves. In W. Schubert & W. Ayers (Eds.), *Teacher lore* (44-60). New York: Longman.

Kohl, H. (1974). *Half the house.* New York: Dutton.

Kohl, H. (1976). *On teaching.* New York: Schocken.

Kohl, H. (1988). *Thirty-six children.* New York: Plume.

Kohlberg, L. (1966,1972). Moral education in the schools: A developmental view. *School Review,* 74 (1). [Also in D. Purpel & M. Belanger (Eds.), *Curriculum and cultural revolution* (455-478). Berkeley, CA: McCutchan.]

Kohlberg, L. (1970). Education for justice: A modern statement of the Platonic view. *In Moral education: Five lectures* (37-83). [Introduced by N. & T. Sizer.] Cambridge, MA: Harvard University Press.

Kohlberg, L. (1981). *Essays on Moral Development.* San Francisco, CA: Harper & Row.

Kohler III, J. (1982). The confluence of new left and old right persistent criticism of progressive education. *Educational Theory,* 32 (1), 1-8.

Konopak, J. (1989). *Reinventing the public sphere.* Baton Rouge, LA: Louisiana State University, Department of Curriculum and Instruction, unpublished Ph.D. dissertation.

Kovel, J. (1971). *White racism: A psychohistory.* New York: Vintage Books.

Kozol, J. (1991). *Savage inequalities: Children in America's schools.* New York: Crown.

Krall, F. (1979). Living metaphors: The real curriculum in environmental education. *JCT,* 1 (1), 180-185.

Krall, F. (1981). Navajo tapestry, a curriculum for ethno-ecological perspectives. *JCT,* 3 (2), 165-209.

Krall, F. (1982). Indwellings: Reconceptualizing Pan. *JCT,* 4 (1), 217-249.

Krall, F. (1988a). Behind the chairperson's door: Reconceptualizing woman's work. In W. Pinar (Ed.), *Contemporary curriculum discourses* (495-513). Scottsdale, AZ: Gorsuch Scarisbrick.

Krall, F. (1988b). Flesh of the earth, voice of the earth: Educational perspectives on "deep ecology." *JCT,* 8 (1), 55-80.

Krall, F. (1988c). From inside out: Personal history as educational research. *Educational Theory,* 38 (4), 467-479.

Krall, F. (1989, October). *Images and messages from the great goddess.* Paper presented to the Bergamo Conference, Dayton, OH.

Krall, F. (1990). The faceless goddess: Paths to the feminine source. Dedicated to the memory of Ronald Padgham. *Contemporary Philosophy,* XIII (1), 32.

Krall, F. et al. (n.d.). *Telling our stories, finding our place.* Salt Lake City, UT: University of Utah, Department of Educational Studies, unpublished manuscript.

Krathwohl, D., Bloom, B., & Masia, B. (1964). *Taxonomy of educational objectives: The classification of educational goals. Handbook II: Affective domain.* New York: McKay.

Kridel, C. (1979). Castiglione and Elyot: Early curriculum theorists. *JCT*, 1 (2), 89-99.

Kridel, C. (1983). A way of life revisited. *JCT*, 5 (1), 92-95.

Kridel, C. (Ed.). (1989). *Curriculum history: Conference presentations from the society for the study of curriculum history.* Landham, MD: University Press of America.

Kridel, C. (1990a). *The Paul R. Klohr professional papers.* [Compiled by C. Kridel.] Columbia, SC: University of South Carolina, McKissick Museum, the Museum of Education.

Kridel, C. (1990b). Teaching curriculum through an historical-biographical perspective. In J. Sears & D. Marshall (Eds.), *Teaching and thinking about curriculum* (243-258). New York: Teachers College Press.

Kridel, C. (1991). Biographical and archival research in curriculum. *Journal of Curriculum and Supervision*, 7 (1), 100-109.

Kridel, C. (in press). Reconsiderations: The story of the *Eight-Year Study. Educational Studies.*

Kridel, C. & Tanner, L. (1987). The uncompleted past: The Society for the Study of Curriculum History celebrates its tenth anniversary. *Journal of Curriculum and Supervision*, 3 (1), 71-74.

Kris, E. (1952). *Psychoanalytic explorations in art.* New York: International Press.

Kristeva, J. (1977). *About Chinese women.* New York: Urizen Books.

Kristeva, J. (1980). *Desire in language: A semiotic approach to literature and art.* New York: Columbia University Press.

Kristeva, J. (1984). *Revolution in poetic language.* New York: Columbia University Press.

Kristeva, J. (1986). *The Kristeva reader.* [Edited by T. Moi]. New York: Columbia University Press.

Kromhout, R. & Good, R. (1983). Beware of societal issues as organizers for science education. *School Science and Mathematics*, 83, 468-476.

Krug, E. (1960). *The secondary school curriculum.* New York: Harper.

Krug, E. (Ed.). (1961). *Charles W. Eliot and popular education.* New York: Teachers College Press.

Krug, E. (1964). *The shaping of the American high school.* New York: Harper & Row.

Krug, E. (1966). *Salient dates in American education.* New York: Harper & Row.

Kuhn, T. (1962). *The structure of scientific revolutions.* Chicago: University of Chicago Press.

Kundera, M. (1988). *The art of the novel.* [Linda Asher, trans.] New York: Grove Press. [Original work published in 1986].

Kung, H. (1979). *Freud and the problem of God.* [Trans. E. Quinn.] New Haven, CT: Yale University Press.

Kung, H. (1981). *Kung in conflict.* [Edited and trans. L. Swidler.] Garden City, NY: Doubleday.

Kurth-Schai, R. (1992). Ecology and equity: Toward the rational reenchantment of schools and society. *Educational Theory,* 42 (2), 47-164.

Kwong, J. (1988). *Cultural revolution in China's schools: May 1966-April 1969.* Stanford, CA: Hoover Institution Press.

Lacan, J. (1977). *Ecrits: A selection.* London, England: Tavistock.

Ladwig, J. (1991). Is collaborative research exploitative? *Educational Theory,* 41 (2), 111-120.

Lafayette Sunday Advertiser (1991, March 24). Does parish need longer school year? Lafayette, LA: *Lafayette Sunday Advertiser,* 6.

Laffer, A. (1982, June 9). For better schools, pay achievers. *Education Week.*

LaHaye, T. (1983). *The battle for the public schools.* Old Tappan, NJ: Fleming H. Revel.

Lai, A. (1991). Curriculum dissemination in the People's Republic of China. In C. Marsh & P. Morris (Eds.), *Curriculum development in East Asia* (82-105). London, England: Falmer.

Laird, S. (1988). Performing "women's true profession:" A case for "feminist pedagogy" in teacher education? *Harvard Educational Review,* 58, 449-463.

Laird, S. (1991). The ideal of the educated teacher—"reclaiming a conversation" with Louisa May Alcott. *Curriculum Inquiry,* 21 (3), 271-298.

Lang, H. & Meath-Lang, B. (1991). The deaf learner. In S. Foster & G. G. Walter (Eds.), *Deaf Students in Postsecondary Education* (67-89). London, England: Routledge.

Lakomski, G. (1988). Witches, weather gods, and phlogiston: The demise of the hidden curriculum. *Curriculum Inquiry,* 18 (4), 451-463.

Lamm, Z. (1972). The state of knowledge in the radical concept of education. In D. Purpel & M. Belanger (Eds.), *Curriculum and cultural revolution* (124-142). Berkeley, CA: McCutchan.

Landauer, T. (1988). Education in a world of omnipotent and omniscient technology. In R. Nickerson & P. Zodhiates (Eds.), *Technology in education: Looking toward 2020.* Hillsdale, NJ: Laurence Erlbaum.

Langer, S. (1957). *Problems of art.* New York: Charles Scribner's Sons.

Langeveld, M. (1983a). The stillness of the secret place. *Phenomenology + Pedagogy,* 1 (1), 11-17.

Langeveld, M. (1983b). The secret place in the life of the child. *Phenomenology + Pedagogy,* 1 (2), 181-191.

Lankshear, C. (1993). Functional literacy from a Freirean point of view. In P. McLaren & P. Leonard (Eds.), *Paulo Freire: A critical encounter* (90-118). London & New York: Routledge.

La Noue, G. (1971). The politics of education. *Teachers College Record,* 73 (2), 304-319.

Larson, E. (1974). Report on the discussions of group F. In W. Pinar (Ed.), *Heightened consciousness, cultural revolution, and curriculum theory: The proceedings of the Rochester conference* (161-165)). Berkeley, CA: McCutchan.

Larson, R. (1957). Bibliography on curriculum research. In A. Foshay & J. Hall (Eds.), *Research for curriculum improvement* (279-305). Washington, DC: ASCD.

Lasch, C. (1977). *Haven in a heartless world.* New York: Basic Books.

Lasch, C. (1984). *The minimal self: Psychic survival in troubled times.* New York: Norton.

Lasch, C. (1991). *The true and only heaven: Progress and its critics.* New York: Norton.

Lather, P. (1986a). Research as praxis. *Harvard Educational Review,* 56 (3), 257-277.

Lather, P. (1986b). Issues of validity in openly ideological research: Between a rock and a hard place. *Interchange,* 17 (4), 63-84.

Lather, P. (1987). The absent presence: Patriarchy, capitalism, and the nature of teacher work. *Teacher Education Quarterly,* 14 (2), 25-38.

Lather, P. (1989). Ideology and methodological attitude. *JCT,* 9 (2), 7-26.

Lather, P. (1991a). *Getting smart: Feminist research and pedagogy with/in the postmodern.* London, England: Routledge.

Lather, P. (1991b). Deconstructing/deconstructive inquiry: The politics of knowing and being known. *Educational Theory,* 41 (2), 153-173.

Lave, J. (1988). *Cognition in practice.* Cambridge, England: Cambridge University Press.

Lave, J. & Wagner, E. (1991). *Situated learning: Legitimate peripheral participation.* Cambridge, England: Cambridge University Press.

Lawn, M. (1987). The spur and the bridle: Changing the mode of curriculum control. *Journal of Curriculum Studies,* 19 (3), 227-236.

Lawn, M. & Barton, L. (1980). Curriculum studies: Reconceptualism or reconstruction. *JCT,* 2 (1), 47-56.

Lawton, D., et al. (1978). *Theory and practice of curriculum studies.* London, England: Routledge.

Layton, Jr., E., (1987). Through the looking glass from Lake Mirror Image. *Technology and Culture,* 23 (3), 594-607

Leach, M. (1990). Toward writing feminist scholarship into the history of education. *Educational Theory,* 40 (4), 453-462.

Leavitt, H. (Ed.). (1992). *Issues and problems in teachers education: An international handbook.* [Foreword by A. Foshay.] New York: Greenwood Press.

LeCompte, M. (1993). A framework for hearing silence: What does telling stories mean when we are supposed to be doing science? In D. McLaughlin & W. Tierny (Eds.), *Naming silenced lives: Personal narratives and the process of educational change* (9-27). New York: Routledge.

Lee, J. & Lee, D. (1960, 1972). *The child and his curriculum.* New York: Appleton-Century. [Previous editions: 1950, 1940].

Leeper, R. (Ed.). (1965a). *Assessing and using curriculum content.* Washington, DC: ASCD.

Leeper, R. (Ed.). (1965b). *Strategy for curriculum change.* Washington, DC: ASCD.

Lehne, G. (1976). Homophobia among men. In R. Brannon & D. David (Eds.), *The forty-nine percent majority: The male sex role.* Reading, MA: Addison Wesley.

Leitch, V. (1992). *Cultural criticism, literary theory, poststructuralism.* New York: Columbia University Press.

Leonard, I. & Parmet, R. (1971). *American nativism, 1830-1860.* New York: Van Nostrand Reinhold.

Leonard, J. (1950). Some reflections on the meaning of sequence. In V. Herrick & R. Tyler (Eds.), *Toward improved curriculum theory* (70-79). Chicago, IL: University of Chicago Press.

Leonard, J. (1953). *Developing the secondary school curriculum.* [Rev. ed.] New York: Holt, Rinehart & Winston.

Leonard, J. (1983). Mystery and myth: Curriculum as the illumination of lived experience. *JCT,* 5 (1), 17-25.

Leonard, P. (1993). Critical pedagogy and state welfare: Intellectual encounters with Freire and Gramsci, 1974-86. In P. McLaren & P. Leonard (Eds.), *Paulo Freire: A critical encounter* (155-168). London & New York: Routledge.

LePage, A. (1987). *Transforming education: The new 3 R's.* Oakland: Oakmore House.

Lerner, B. (1981). The minimum competency testing movement: Social, scientific, and legal implications. *American Psychologist,* 13 (10), 1057-1066.

Lerner, G. (1986). *The creation of patriarchy.* New York: Oxford University Press.

Lesko, N. (1988a). *Symbolizing society: Stories, rites and structure in a Catholic high school.* New York: Falmer.

Lesko, N. (1988b). The curriculum of the body: Lessons from a Catholic high school. In L. Roman, L. Christian-Smith & E. Ellsworth (Eds.), *Becoming feminine: The politics of popular culture* (123-142). Barcombe-Lewes, England: Falmer.

Lesko, N. (1994). The social construction of "the problem of teenage pregnancy." In. R. Martusewicz & W. Reynolds (Eds.), *Inside out: Contemporary critical perspectives in education* (139-150). New York: St. Martin's Press.

Levine, D. (Ed.). (1971). *Performance contracting in education. An appraisal: Toward a balanced perspective.* Englewood Cliffs, NJ: Educational Technology Publications.

Levine, M. (1992). *Professional practice schools: Linking teacher education and school reform.* New York: Teachers College Press.

Levinson, S. (1982). Law as literature. *Texas Law Review,* 60 (3), 373-403.

Levinson, S. & Mailloux, S. (Eds.). (1988). *Interpreting law and literature.* Evanston, IL: Northwestern University Press.

Levi-Strauss, C. (1972). *Structural anthropology.* [Trans. C. Jacobson & B. Schoepf.] Hammondsworth, England: Penguin.

Lewis, A. & Miel, A. (1972). *Supervision for improved instruction: New challenges, new responses.* Belmont, CA: Wadsworth Publishing Co., Inc.

Lewis, D. (1993). Deinstitutionalization and school decentral ization: Making the same mistake twice. In J. Hannaway, & M. Carnoy (Eds.). *Decentralization and school improvement: Can we fulfill the promise?* (84-101). San Francisco, CA: Jossey-Bass Publishers.

Lewis, M. (1988). The construction of femininity embraced in the work of caring for children—caught between aspirations and reality. *The Journal of Educational Thought,* 22 (2A), 259-268.

Lewis, M. (1990). Interrupting patriarchy: Politics, resistance, and transformation in the feminist classroom. *Harvard Educational Review,* 60 (4), 467-488.

Lewis, T. & Gagel, C. (1992). Technological literacy: A critical analysis. *Journal of Curriculum Studies,* 24 (2), 117-138.

Lewy, A. (Ed.). (1991). *The international encyclopedia of curriculum.* New York: Pergamon Press.

Lickona, T. (1992). Schools and families: Partners or adversaries in moral education? In A. Garrod (Ed.), *Learning for life: Moral education theory and practice* (89-106)). Westport, CT: Praeger.

Lieberman, A. (1992). The meaning of scholarly activity and the building of community. *Educational Researcher,* 21 (6), 5-12.

Lieberman, A. & Miller, L. (1992). *Teachers–their world and their work: Implications for school improvement.* New York: Teachers College Press.

Lima, E. (1992, April). *The form and function of qualitative research in Brazil.* Paper presented to the annual meeting of the American Educational Research Association, San Francisco, CA.

Lincoln, Y. (1992). Curriculum studies and the traditions of inquiry: The humanistic tradition. In P. Jackson (Ed.), *Handbook of research on curriculum* (41-78). New York: Macmillan.

Lincoln, Y. (1993). I and thou: Method, voice, and roles. In D. McLaughlin & W. Tierny (Eds.), *Naming silenced lives: Personal narratives and the process of educational change* (9-27). New York: Routledge.

Lindsay, B. (1992). Dismantling educational apartheid: Case studies from South Africa. *Educational Foundations,* 6 (2), 71-87.

Linn, E., Stein, N., Young, J. with S. Davis (1992). Bitter lessons for all: Sexual harassment in schools. In J. Sears (Ed.), *Sexuality and the curriculum* (106-123). New York: Teachers College Press.

Linquist, K. & Mauriel, J. (1989, August). School-based management. *Education and Urban Society,* 21 (4), 403-416.

Lipman, M. (1991, May). Squaring Soviet theory with American practice. *Educational Leadership,* 48 (8), 72-75.

Lipman, M. (1992). About questions and questioning. *Inquiry,* 9 (2), 10-11.

Lippitz, W. (1983). The child's understanding of time. *Phenomenology + Pedagogy,* 1 (2), 172-180.

Lipsky, M. (1980). *Street level bureaucracy.* New York: Russell Sage Foundation.

Lisman, D. (1991). The Christian private school movement. *Curriculum Inquiry,* 21 (3), 376-385.

Liston, D. (1986). On fact and values: An analysis of radical curriculum studies. *Educational Theory*, 36 (2), 137-152.

Liston, D. (1988). *Capitalist schools: Explanation and ethics in radical studies of schooling*. New York: Routledge & Kegan Paul.

Littleford, M. (1979). Vico and curriculum studies. *JCT*, 1 (2), 54-64.

Littleford, M. (1980). Vico and Dewey: Toward a humanistic foundation for curriculum studies. *JCT*, 2 (1), 57-70.

Littleford, M. (1982). Curriculum theorizing and the possibilities and conditions for social action toward democratic community and education. *JCT*, 4 (2), 144-152.

Littleford, M. (1983). Censorship, academic freedom and the public school teacher. *JCT*, 5 (3), 98-131.

Livingston, D. & contributors (1987). *Critical pedagogy and cultural power*. South Hadley, MA: Bergin & Garvey.

Lobdell, P. (1984). *The Marietta Johnson school of organic education: An historical study*. Auburn, AL: Auburn University, unpublished doctoral dissertation.

Lofstedt, J-I. (1980). *Chinese educational policy*. Stockholm, Sweden: Almqvist & Wiksell.

Lofty, J. (1992). *Time to write: The influence of time and culture on learning to write*. Albany, NY: State University of New York Press.

Lomotey, K. (1989). *African-American principals: School leadership and success*. Westport, CT: Greenwood Press.

Lomotey, K. (Ed.). (1990a). *Going to school: The African-American experience*. Albany, NY: State University of New Press.

Lomotey, K. (1990b). An interview with Booker Peek. In K. Lomotey (Ed.), *Going to school: The African American Experience* (13-30). Albany, NY: State University of New York Press.

Lomotey, K. (1990c). Qualities shared by African-American principals in effective schools: A preliminary analysis. In K. Lomotey (Ed.), *Going to school: The African American Experience* (181-195). Albany, NY: State University of New York Press.

Longstreet, W. & Shane, H. (1993). *Curriculum for the new millennium*. Boston, MA: Allyn & Bacon.

Lopez-Caples, M. (1989). Brief stories and the fictionalization of the self. *Phenomenology + Pedagogy*, 7, 93-105.

Louden, W. (1992). Understanding reflection through collaborative research. In A. Hargreaves & M. Fullan (Eds.) Understanding teacher development (178-215). New York: Teachers College Press.

Lowe, W. (1969). *Structure and the social studies*. Ithaca, NY: Cornell University Press.

Lowe, W. (1974). Some reactions. In W. Pinar (Ed.), *Heightene d consciousness, cultural revolution, and curriculum theory: The proceedings of the Rochester conference* (143-150). Berkeley, CA: McCutchan.

Lucas, T., Henze, R., & Donato, R. (1990). Promoting the success of Latino language-minority students: An exploratory study of six high schools. *Harvard Educational Review*, 60 (3), 315-340.

Luke, A. (1988). *Literacy, textbooks and ideology: Postwar literacy instruction and the mythology of Dick and Jane.* London, England: Falmer.

Lundestad, G. (1980). *America, Scandinavia, and the cold war: 1945-1949.* New York: Columbia University Press.

Lundgren, U. (1979). *School curricula: Content and structure in their effects as educational and occupational careers.* Stockholm, Sweden: Stockholm Institute of Education, Department of Educational Research, Reports on Education and Psychology, No. 2.

Lundgren, U. (1983). *Between hope and happening: Text and context in curriculum.* Geelong, Victoria, Australia: Deakin University Press.

Luttrell, W. (1993). Working-class women's ways of knowing: Effects of gender, race, and class. In L. Castenell, Jr. & W. Pinar (Eds.), *Understanding curriculum as racial text: Representations of identity and difference in education* (153-178). Albany, NY: State University of New York Press. [Also (1989), *Sociology of Education,* 62 (January), 33-46.]

Lydon, A. (1992). *Cosmology and curriculum.* Baton Rouge, LA: Louisiana State University, Department of Curriculum and Instruction, unpublished Ph.D. dissertation.

Lynn, R. (1988, October 28). Why Johnny can't read, but Yoshio can. *National Review,* 40-42.

Lyotard, J-F. (1989). *The postmodern condition: Report on knowledge.* Minneapolis, MN: University of Minnesota Press.

Macagnoni, V. (1981). Zones of potentiality contributing to consciousness: Thrust for curriculum design. *JCT,* 3 (1), 222-231.

MacConnell, C., et al. (1940, March). The core curriculum. *Educational Trends,* 8, 25.

Macdonald, B. & Walker, R. (1975). Case study and the social philosophy of educational research. *Cambridge Journal of Education,* 5 (1), 2-11.

Macdonald, J. (1964). An image of man: The learner himself. In R. Doll (Ed.), *Individualizing Instruction* (29-49). Washington, DC: ASCD.

Macdonald, J. (1967). An example of disciplined curriculum thinking. *Theory into Practice,* 6 (4),166-171.

Macdonald, J. (1974). A transcendental developmental ideology of education. In W. Pinar (Ed.), *Heightened consciousness, cultural revolution, and curriculum theory: The proceedings of the Rochester conference* (85-116). Berkeley, CA: McCutchan.

Macdonald, J. (1975a). Autobiographical statement. In W. Pinar (Ed.), *Curriculum theorizing: The reconceptualists* (3-4). Berkeley, CA: McCutchan.

Macdonald, J. (1975b). Curriculum theory. In W. Pinar (Ed.), *Curriculum theorizing: The reconceptualists* (5-13). Berkeley, CA: McCutchan.

Macdonald, J. (1975c). Curriculum and human interests. In W. Pinar (Ed.), *Curriculum theorizing: The reconceptualists* (283-294). Berkeley, CA: McCutchan.

Macdonald, J. (1981). Theory, practice and the hermeneutic circle. *JCT,* 3 (2), 130-138.

Macdonald, J. (1986). The domain of curriculum. [Foreword by D. Huencke.] *Journal of Curriculum & Supervision.* (1)3, 205-214.

Macdonald, J. (1988). Curriculum, consciousness, and social change. In W. Pinar (Ed.), *Contemporary curriculum discourses* (156-174). Scottsdale, AZ: Gorsuch Scarisbrick.

Macdonald, J. & Leeper, R. (Eds.). (1966). *Language and meaning.* Washington, DC: ASCD.

Macdonald, J. & Leeper, R. (Eds.). (1968). *Theories of instruction.* Columbus, OH: Charles Merrill.

Macdonald, J. & Macdonald, S. (1988). Gender, values, and curriculum. In W. Pinar (Ed.), *Contemporary curriculum discourses* (476-485). Scottsdale, AZ: Gorsuch Scarisbrick.

Macdonald, J. & Purpel, D. (1987). Curriculum and planning: Visions and metaphors. *Journal of Curriculum and Supervision,* 2 (2), 178-192.

Macdonald, J. & Wolfson, B. (1970). A Case against behavioral objectives. *Elementary School Journal* (Dec), 119-128.

Macdonald, J. & Zaret, E. (Eds.). (1975). *Schools in search of meaning.* [1975 yearbook.] Washington, DC: ASCD.

Macdonald, J., Anderson, D. & May, F. (Eds.). (1965). *Strategies for curriculum development: The works of Virgil Herrick.* Columbus, OH: Charles E. Merrill.

MacGregor, S. (1990). Computer-assisted thinking skills instruction: Curriculum principles, teacher preparation, and student outcomes. In A. McDougall & C. Dowling (Eds.), *Computers in education.* North-Holland: Elsevier Science Publishers.

MacGregor, S. (1992). Personal correspondence.

MacIntyre, A. (1981). *After virtue.* Notre Dame, IN: University of Notre Dame Press.

Mackenzie, G. (1964). Curricular change: Participants, power, and processes. In M. Miles (Ed.), *Innovation in education.* New York: Teachers College Press.

MacLure, M. & Elliot, J. (1992, April). *Packaging the pr imary curriculum: Textbooks and the English national curriculum.* A paper presented at the annual meeting of the American Educational Research Association, San Francisco, CA.

Madaus, G. (1979). Testing and funding: Measurement and policy issues. *New directions for testing measurement,* 1, 53-62.

Madaus, G. (1989). The Irish study revisited. In B. Gifford (Ed.), *Test policy and test performance: Education, language, and culture* (63-89). Boston, MA: Kluwer-Nijhoff.

Madaus, G. & Kellaghan, T. (1992). Curriculum evaluation and assessment. In P. Jackson (Ed.), *Handbook of research on curriculum* (119-154). New York: Macmillan.

Madaus, G. & Stufflebeam, D. (1984). Educational evaluation and accountability: A review of quality assurance. *American Behavioral Scientist,* 27 (5), 649-672.

Madaus, G. & Stufflebeam, D. (Eds.). (1989). *Educational evaluation: The classic works of Ralph W. Tyler.* Boston, MA: Kluwer-Nijhoff.

Madaus, G., Scriven, M. & Stufflebeam, D. (1983). *Evaluation models: Viewpoints on educational and human service evaluation.* Boston, MA: Kluwer-Nijhoff.

Mager, R. (1962). *Preparing instructional objectives.* Palo Alto, CA: Fearon.

Magnusson, K. & Osborne, J. (1990). The rise of competency-based education: A deconstructionist analysis. *Journal of Educational Thought,* 24 (1), 5-13.

Malen, G., Ogawa, R. & Kranz, J. (1990). What do we know about school-based management? A case study of the literature - a call for research. In W. Clune & J. Witte (Eds.), *Choice and control in American education: Volume 2. The practice of choice, decentralization and school restructuring* (289-342). Philadelphia, PA: Falmer.

Mander, J. (1978). *Four arguments for the elimination of television.* New York: Morrow.

Mandle, J. (1978, Winter). The economic underdevelopment of the postbellum South. *Marxist Perspectives,* 1 (4), 68-79.

Mann, H. (1848, 1957). Twelfth annual report of the [Massachusetts] board of education. In L. Cremin (Ed.), *The republic and the school: Horace Mann and the education of free men.* New York: Teachers College Press.

Mann, J. (1975). Curriculum criticism. In W. Pinar (Ed.), *Curriculum theorizing: The reconceptualists* (133-148). Berkeley, CA: McCutchan.

Mann, J. & Molnar, A. (1975). On student rights. In W. Pinar (Ed.), *Curriculum theorizing: The reconceptualists* (167-172). Berkeley, CA: McCutchan.

Mao Zedong (1967). *Mao Zedong selected works.* Peking, China: Foreign Language Press.

Marable, M. (1986). *W. E. B. DuBois: Black radical democrat.* Boston, MA: Twayne.

Marcel, G. (1963). *Existential background of human dignity.* Cambridge, MA: Harvard University Press.

Marcel, G. (1967). *Problematic man.* [Trans. B. Thompson.] New York: Herder & Herder.

Marcus, J. (1992, September). Scholastic reform under fire. New Orleans, LA: *New Orleans Times-Picayune,* A-8.

Marcuse, H. (1966). *One-dimensional man: Studies in the sociology of advanced industrial society.* Boston, MA: Beacon Press.

Marcuse, H. (1978). *The aesthetic dimension.* Boston, MA: Beacon Press

Marshall, D. & Sears, J. (1990). An evolutionary and metaphorical journey into teaching and thinking about curriculum. In J. Sears & D. Marshall (Eds.), *Teaching and thinking about curriculum* (15-32). New York: Teachers College Press.

Marsh, C. (1987). Curriculum theorizing in Australia. *JCT,* 7 (2), 7-29.

Marsh, C. (1992). *Key concepts for understanding curriculum.* London, England: Falmer.

Marsh, C. & Morris, P. (Eds.). (1991). *Curriculum development in east Asia.* London, England: Falmer

Martel, A. (n.d.). *On becoming bilingual: Reflections in education.* Curriculum Praxis Monograph Series, No. 4. Edmonton, Alberta, Canada: University of Alberta, Faculty of Education, Department of Secondary Education.

Martel, A. (1987). Ethnicity, language, and culture in the teaching of Professor Ted Aoki: Or, the celebration of double-vision. *JCT,* 7 (3), 43-50.

Martel, A. & Peterat, L. (1988). A hope for helplessness: Womanness at the margin in schools. *JCT,* 8 (1), 103-136.

Martel, A. & Peterat, L. (1994). Margins of exclusion, margins of transformation: The place of women in education. In R. Martusewicz & W. Reynolds (Eds.), *Inside out: Contemporary critical perspectives in education* (151-166). New York: St. Martin's Press.

Martin, J. (1972). The disciplines and the curriculum. In D. Purpel & M. Belanger (Eds.), *Curriculum and cultural revolution* (100-123). Berkeley, CA: McCutchan.

Martin, J. (1984). Bring women into educational thought. *Educational Theory,* 34 (4), 341-354.

Martin, J. (1985). *Reclaiming a conversation.* New Haven, CT: Yale University Press.

Martin, J. (1990). Romanticism domesticated: Maria Montessori and the Casa dei Bambini. In J. Willinsky (Ed.), *The educational legacy of romanticism* (159-174). Waterloo, Ontario, Canada: Wilfrid Laurier University Press.

Martin-Kniep, G. & Uhrmacher, B. (1992). Teachers as curriculum developers. *Journal of Curriculum Studies,* 24 (3), 261-272.

Marton, F. (1989). Toward a pedagogy of content. *Educational Psychologist,* 24 (1), 1-23.

Martusewicz, R. (1988). *The will to reason: An archaeology of womanhood and education.* Rochester, NY: University of Rochester, Graduate School of Education and Human Development, unpublished doctoral dissertation.

Martusewicz, R. (1992). Mapping the terrain of the post-modern subject: Post-Structuralism and the educated woman. In W. Pinar & W. Reynolds (Eds.), *Understanding curriculum as phenomenological and deconstructed text* (131-158). New York: Teachers College Press.

Martusewicz, R. (1994). Guardians of childhood. In R. Martusewicz & W. Reynolds (Eds.), *Inside out: Contemporary critical perspectives in education* (167-182). New York: St. Martin's Press.

Martusewicz, R. & Reynolds, W. (Eds.). (1994). *Inside out: Contemporary critical perspectives in education.* New York: St. Martin's Press.

Marx, K. & Engels, F. (1974). *Karl Marx and F. Engels on literature and art: A selection of writings.* [L. Baxandall & S. Morawski, Eds.] New York: International General.

Maslow, A. (1968). *Toward a psychology of being.* New York: Van Nostrand Reinhold.

Matthews, M. (Ed.). (1991). *History, philosophy, and scie nce teaching.* Toronto, Ontario, Canada and New York: OSIE and Teachers College Press.

Maxcy, S. (1991). *Educational leadership: A critical, pragmatic perspective.* New York: Bergin & Garvey.

May, W. (1986). Teaching students how to plan: The dominant model and alternatives. *Journal of Teacher Education,* 37 (6), 6-12.

May, W. (1989). *What makes a critique of art education "post-modern"?* Paper presented at the annual meeting of the American Education Research Association, San Francisco, CA.

May, W. & Zimpher, N. (1986, Winter). An examination of three theoretical perspectives on supervision: Perceptions of preservice field supervision. *Journal of Curriculum and Supervision,* 2 (2), 83-99.

Mayhew, K. & Edwards, C. (1936). *The Dewey school: The laboratory school of the University of Chicago 1896-1903.* New York: D. Appleton Century. [Reprinted in 1965; New York: Ahterton Press.]

Mazza, K. (1982). Reconceptual inquiry as an alternative mode of curriculum theory and practice: A critical study. *JCT,* 4 (2), 5-89.

McAninch, S. (1989). Civic education reform and the quest for a unified society: A critique of R. Freeman Butt's agenda for civic education. In C. Shea, E. Kahane & P. Sola (Eds.), *The new servants of power* (137-144). New York: Greenwood Press.

McBride, A. (1984, August). Why go to a Catholic school? *St. Anthony messenger,* (1-4).

McCall, A. (1989). Care and nurturance in teaching: A case study. *Journal of Teacher Education,* 40 (1), 39-44.

McCarthy, C. (1988a, August). Rethinking liberal and radical perspectives on racial inequality in schooling: Making the case for nonsynchrony. *Harvard Educational Review,* 58 (3), 265-279.

McCarthy, C. (1988b). Slowly, slowly, slowly, the dumb speaks: Third world popular culture and the sociology for the third world. *JCT,* 8 (2), 7-21.

McCarthy, C. (1990). *Race and curriculum.* London, England: Falmer.

McCarthy, C. (1993a). Multicultural approaches to racial inequality in the United States. In L. Castenell & W. Pinar (Eds.), *Understanding curriculum as racial text: Representations of identity and difference in education* (225-246). Albany, NY: State University of New York Press.

McCarthy, C. (1993b). After the canon: Knowledge and ideological representation in the multicultural discourse on curriculum reform. In C. McCarthy & W. Crichlow (Eds.), *Race, identity, and representation in education* (289-305). New York & London, England: Routledge.

McCarthy, C. & Apple, M. (1988). Race, class and gender in American education: Toward a nonsynchronous parallelist position. In L. Weis (Ed.), *Class, race and gender in American education* (3-39). Albany, NY: State University of New York Press.

McCarthy, C. & Crichlow, W. (Eds.). (1993). *Race, identity, and representation in education.* New York & London, England: Routledge.

McCleary, D. (1993). *The logic of imaginative education.* New York: Teachers College Press.

McClintock, R. (1971). Toward a place for study in a world of instruction. *Teachers College Record*, 73 (20, 161-205.

McCormack, M. (1994). Margaret A. Haley, 1861-1939: A timeless mentor. In R. Martusewicz & W. Reynolds (Eds.), *Inside out: Contemporary critical perspectives in education* (1183-200). New York: St. Martin's Press.

McCutcheon, G. (1979). Educational criticism: Methods and applications. *JCT*, 1 (2), 5-25.

McCutcheon, G. (Ed.). (1982, winter). Theory into Practice: Curriculum Theory. *Theory into Practice*, XXI (1).

McCutcheon, G. (1982). Educational criticism: Reflections and reconsiderations. *JCT*, 4 (1), 171-177.

McCutcheon, G. & Jung, B. (1990). Alternative perspectives on action research. *Theory into Practice*, XXIX (3), 46-153.

McDermott, H. (1977, May). Social relations as contexts for learning in school. *Harvard Educational Review*, 47,198-213.

McDonald, J. (1991a). *Three pictures of an exhibition.* Studies on Exhibitions, No. 1. Providence, RI: Brown University, Coalition for Essential Schools.

McDonald, J. (1991b). *Dilemmas of planning backwards.* Studies on Exhibitions, No. 3. Providence, RI: Brown University, Coalition for Essential Schools.

McDonald, J. (1991c). *Exhibitions: Facing outward, pointing inward.* Studies on Exhibitions, No. 4. Providence, RI: Brown University, Coalition for Essential Schools.

McDonald, J. (1991d). *Steps in planning backwards.* Studies on Exhibitions, No. 5. Providence, RI: Brown University, Coalition for Essential Schools.

McDonald, J. (1992). *Teaching: Making sense of an uncertain craft.* New York: Teachers College Press.

McElroy, L. (1990, Summer). Becoming real: An ethic at the heart of action research. *Theory into Practice*, XXIX (3), 209-213.

McEwan, H. (1992, Winter). Teaching and the interpretation of texts. *Educational Theory*, 42 (1), 59-68.

McEwen, N. (1980). Phenomenology and the curriculum: The case of secondary-school geography. *Journal of Curriculum Studies*, 12 (4), 323-340.

McGee, P. (1993). Decolonization and the curriculum of English. In C. McCarthy & W. Crichlow (Eds.), *Race, identity, and representation in education* (280-288). New York & London, England: Routledge.

McHoul, A. & Luke, A. (1988). Epistemological groundings of educational studies: A critique. *The Journal of Educational Thought*, 22 (3),178-189.

McIntosh, P. (1986). *Interactive phases of curricular re-vision: A feminist perspective.* Working Papers Series No. 124. Wellesley, MA: Wellesley College Center for Research on Women.

McKim, M. (1957). Curriculum research in historical perspective. In A. Foshay & J. Hall (Eds.), *Research for curriculum improvement* (14-40). Washington, DC: ASCD.

McKinney, L. & Westbury, I. (1975). Stability and change: The public schools of Gary, Indiana, 1940-1970. In W. Reid & D. Walker (Eds.), *Case studies* in curriculum change: Great Britain and the United States (1-53). London, England: Rou tledge & Kegan Paul.

McLaren, P. (1985). The ritual dimensions of resistance: Clowning and symbolic inversion. *Journal of Education,* 167 (2), 84-97.

McLaren, P. (1986a). Postmodernity and the death of politics: A Brazilian reprieve. *Educational Theory,* 36 (4), 389-401.

McLaren, P. (1986b). *Schooling as a ritual performance: Towards a political economy of educational symbols and gestures.* Boston, MA: Routledge & Kegan Paul.

McLaren, P. (1987a). The anthropological roots of pedagogy: The teacher as liminal servant. *Anthropology and Humanism Quarterly,* 12, 75-85.

McLaren, P. (1987b). Ideology, science and the politics of Marxian orthodoxy: A response to Michael Dale. *Educational Theory,* 37 (3), 301-326.

McLaren, P. (1987c). Schooling for salvation: Christian fundamentalism's ideology weapons of death. *Journal of Education,* 169 (2), 132-139.

McLaren, P. (1987d). Education as counter-discourse. *Review of Education,* 3 (1), 58-68.

McLaren, P. (1988a). The liminal servant and the ritual roots of critical pedagogy. *Language Arts,* 65 (2), 164-179.

McLaren, P. (1988b). No light but rather darkness visible: Language the politics of criticism. *Curriculum Inquiry,* 18 (3), 313-320.

McLaren, P. (1988c). On ideology and education: Critical pedagogy and the politics of education. *Social Text,* 19/20, 153-185.

McLaren, P. (1989). *Life in schools: An introduction to critical pedagogy in the foundations of education.* New York: Longman.

McLaren, P. (1990). *Capitalist schools: Explanation and ethics in radical studies of schooling, a review.* Oxford, OH: Miami University, School of Education, unpublished manuscript.

McLaren, P. (1991a). Decentering culture: Postmodernism, resistance, and critical pedagogy. In N. Wyner (Ed.), *Current perspectives on the culture of schools* (231-257). Boston, MA: Brookline Books.

McLaren, P. (1991b). Field relations and the discourse of the other. In W. Shaffir & R. Stebbins (Eds.), *Experiencing fieldwork: An inside view of qualitative research* (149-163). Newbury Park, CA: Sage.

McLaren, P. (1991c). Schooling the postmodern body: Critical pedagogy and the politics of enfleshment. In H. Giroux (Ed.), *Postmodernism, feminism, and cultural politics* (144-173). Albany, NY: State University of New York Press.

McLaren, P. (1991d). Critical pedagogy, postcolonial politics and redemptive remembrance. *In learner factors/teacher factors: Issues in literacy and instruction.* [Fortieth Yearbook, National Reading Conference.] Chicago, IL: National Reading Conference, Inc.

McLaren, P. (1991e). The emptiness of nothingness: Criticism as imperial anti-politics. *Curriculum Inquiry,* 21 (4), 459-477.

McLaren, P. (1991f). Critical pedagogy: Constructing an arch of social dreaming and a doorway to hope. *Journal of Education,* 173 (1), 9-34.

McLaren, P. (1992a). Collisions with otherness: "Traveling" theory, post-colonial criticism, and the politics of ethnographic practice—the mission of the wounded ethnographer. *Qualitative Studies in Education,* 5 (1), 77-92.

McLaren, P. (1992b). Collisions with otherness: Multiculturalism, the politics of difference, and the ethnographer as nomad. *The American Journal of Semiotics,* 9 (2-3), 121-148.

McLaren, P. (1993a, January). Multiculturalism and the postmodern critique: Towards a pedagogy of resistance and transformation. *Cultural Studies,* 7 (1), 118-146.

McLaren, P. (1993b). Border disputes: Multicultural narrative, identity formation, and critical pedagogy in postmodern America. In D. McLaughlin & W. Tierny (Eds.), *Naming silenced lives: Personal narratives and the process of educational change* (201-235). New York: Routledge.

McLaren, P. (1994). *Life in schools: An introduction to critical pedagogy in the foundations of education.* [2nd edition.] New York: Longman.

McLaren, P. & Dantley, M. (1990). Leadership and a critical pedagogy of race: Cornel West, Stuart Hall, and the prophetic tradition. *Journal of Negro Education,* 59 (1), 29-44.

McLaren, P. & da Silva, T. (1993). Decentering pedagogy: Critical literacy, resistance and the politics of memory. In P. McLaren & P. Leonard (Eds.), *Paulo Freire: A critical encounter* (47-89). London & New York: Routledge.

McLaren, P. & Hammer, R. (1989, Fall). Critical pedagogy and the postmodern challenge: Toward a critical postmodernist pedagogy of liberation. *Educational Foundations,* 29-62.

McLaren, P. & Hammer, R. (1992). Specularizing subjectivity: Media knowledges and the new world order. *Polygraph* (5), 46-66.

McLaren, P. & Leonard, P. (Eds.). (1993). *Paulo Freire: A critical encounter.* New York: Routledge.

McLaren, P. & Smith, R. (1989). Televangelism as pedagogy and cultural politics. In H. Giroux & R. Simon, et al., *Popular culture, schooling, and everyday life.* So. Hadley, MA: Bergin & Garvey.

McLaughlin, D. (1993a). Personal narratives for school change in Navajo settings. In D. McLaughlin & W. Tierny (Eds.), *Naming silenced lives: Personal narratives and the process of educational change* (95-117). New York: Routledge.

McLaughlin, D. (1993b). Coda: Toward the pathway of a true human being. In D. McLaughlin & W. Tierny (Eds.), *Naming silenced lives: Personal narratives and the process of educational change* (237-239). New York: Routledge.

McLaughlin, D. & Tierney, W. (Eds.). (1993). *Naming silenced lives: Personal narratives and the process of educational change.* New York: Routledge.

McLaughlin, M. (1976). Implementation of ESEA Title I: A problem of compliance. *Teachers College Record,* 80 (1), 69-94.

McLuhan, M. (1962). We need a new picture of knowledge. In A. Frazier (Ed.), *New insights and the curriculum* (55-70). Washington, DC: ASCD.

McMurry, C. (1903). *The elements of general method.* [Rev. ed.] New York: Macmillan.

McMurry, C. & McMurry, F. (1897). *The method of the recitation.* Bloomington, IL: Public School Publishing Company.

McNeil, J. (1976). *Designing curriculum: Self-instructional modules.* Boston, MA: Little, Brown.

McNeil, J. (1977). *Curriculum: A comprehensive introduction.* [2nd edition: 1985]. Boston, MA: Little, Brown.

McNeil, J. (1978). Curriculum—a field shaped by different faces. *Educational Researcher,* 7 (8), 19-23.

McNeil, L. (1981). On the possibility of teacher as the source of an emancipatory pedagogy: A response to Henry Giroux. *Curriculum Inquiry,* 11 (3), 205-210.

McNeil, L. (1986). *Contradictions of control: School structure and school knowledge.* New York: Routledge & Kegan Paul.

McNeil, L. (1987). Talking about differences: Teaching to sameness. *Journal of Curriculum Studies,* 19 (2), 105-122.

McPeck, J. (1981). *Critical thinking and education.* New York: St. Martin's Press.

Mead, G. (1936). *Movement of thought in the nineteenth century.* Chicago, IL: University of Chicago Press.

Mead, G. (1938). *The philosophy of the act.* Chicago, IL: University of Chicago Press.

Measor, L. & Sikes, P. (1992). Visiting lives: Ethics and methodology in life history. In. I. Goodson (Ed.), *Study teachers' lives* (209-233). New York: Teachers College Press.

Meath-Lang, B. (1980). *Deaf students' perceptions of their English language learning: Rationale for an experience-based curriculum model.* Rochester, NY: University of Rochester, Graduate School of Education and Human Development, unpublished doctoral dissertation.

Meath-Lang, B. (1981). "All the things I might not be ...." Issues in communication for curricularists. *JCT,* 3 (1), 232-238.

Meath-Lang, B. (1990a, October). *Teachers responding to the voices of others.* Paper presented at the Bergamo Conference on Curriculum Theory and Classroom Practice, Dayton, OH.

Meath-Lang, B. (1990b). The dialogue journal: Reconceiving curriculum and teaching. In J. Kreeft-Peton (Ed.), *Students and teachers writing together* (3-16). Alexandria, VA: TESOL Publications.

Meath-Lang, B. (1992, October). *Other people's mirrors: Distortion, reflection, and reclamation in biographical curriculum work.* Paper presented to the Bergamo Conference on Curriculum Theory and Classroom Practice, Dayton, OH.

Meath-Lang, B. (1993). The risk of writing outside the margins: A reexamination of the notion of access. In R. Donmoyer & R. Kos (Eds.), *At-risk students: Portraits, policies, programs, and practices* (365-378). Albany, NY: State University of New York Press.

Meath-Lang, B. (in press). A lesser loneliness: Marginalization and the formation of writing communities. *JCT.*

Meath-Lang, B. & Albertini, J. (1989). Authenticity in writing: A reflection on voice, imagination, deafness, and teaching. In A. Martel (Ed.), *To pedagogy and what matters: Texts on authenticity* (7-13). Curriculum Praxis Series, No. 13. Edmonton, Alberta, Canada: University of Alberta, Department of Secondary Education.

Meath-Lang, B., Caccamise, F. & Albertini, J. (1982). Deaf students' views of their English language learning. In H. Hoemann & R. Wilbur (Eds.), *Interpersonal communication and deaf people* (295-329). Washington, DC: Gallaudet College.

Meehan, B. (1993). *Holy women of Russia.* San Francisco, CA: HarperSanFrancisco.

Meeks, L. & Heit, P. (1982). *Human sexuality: Making responsible decisions.* Philadelphia, PA: Saunders.

Megill, A. (1985). *Prophets of extremity.* Berkeley, CA: University of California Press.

Mehan, H. (1978, February). Structuring school structure. *Harvard Educational Review,* 48, 32-64.

Melnick, C. (1988). *A search for teachers' knowledge of the out-of-school curriculum of students' lives.* Chicago, IL: University of Illinois at Chicago, College of Education, unpublished doctoral dissertation.

Melvin, A. (1936). *The activity program.* New York: Reynal & Hitchcock.

Merleau-Ponty, M. (1962). *Phenomenology of perception.* London, England: Routledge & Kegan Paul.

Merleau-Ponty, M. (1963). *The structure of behavior.* [Trans. A. Fisher.] Boston, MA: Beacon.

Messer, S., et al. (1988). *Hermeneutics and psychological theory.* New Brunswick, NJ: Rutgers University Press.

Meyer, L., Greer E., & Crummey, L. (1987). An analysis of decoding, comprehension, and story text comprehensibility in four first-grade reading programs. *Journal of Reading Behavior,* 19 (1), 69-98.

Michaels, K. (1988). Caution: Second-wave reform taking place. *Educational Leadership,* 45 (5), 3.

Michalko, R. (1984). The metaphor of adolescence. *Phenomenology + Pedagogy,* 1 (3), 296-311.

Michener, J. (1987). Reflections on teaching. *Teaching Education,* 1 (1), 10.

Miel, A. (1952). *Cooperative procedures in learning.* New York: Teachers College, Columbia University, Bureau of Publications.

Miel, A. (1962). Knowledge & the curriculum. In A. Frazier (Ed.), *New insights and the curriculum* (71-104). Washington, DC: ASCD.

Miel, A. (1968a). Curriculum design and materials—pressure or release? *Childhood Education,* 44 (7).

Miel, A. (1968b). New patterns of inservice education of elementary teachers. In A. Frazier (Ed.), *The new elementary school*. Washington, DC: ASCD.

Miel, A. (1969). Elements and structure: A design for continuous progress. In A. Frazier (Ed.), *A curriculum for children* (123-136). Washington, DC: ASCD.

Miel, A. & Brogan, P. (1957). *More than social studies*. Englewood Cliffs, NJ: Prentice-Hall.

Mieli, M. (1977). *Homosexuality and liberation: Elements of a gay critique*. London, England: Gay Men's Press.

Milburn, G. (1989). How much life is there in life history? In G. Milburn, I. Goodson, & R. Clark (Eds.), *Re-interpreting curriculum research: Images and arguments* (160-180). London, Ontario, Canada: The Althouse Press.

Milburn, G. (1992). Do curriculum studies have a future? *Journal of Curriculum and Supervision, 7* (3), 302-318.

Miles, M. (1957). Human relations in cooperative research. I n A. Foshay & J. Hall (Eds.), *Research for curriculum improvement* (187-226). Washington, DC: ASCD.

Miller, B. (1993). *The arts and the basis of education*. Lanham, MD: University Press of America.

Miller, J. (1986). Transformation as an aim of education. *JCT, 7* (1), 94-152.

Miller, J. (1988). *The holistic curriculum*. Toronto, Ontario, Canada: OSIE Press.

Miller, J. & Seller, W. (1985). *Curriculum: Perspectives and practice*. New York: Longman.

Miller, J. L. (1977). *Curriculum theory of Maxine Greene: A reconceptualization of foundations in English education*. Columbus, OH: Ohio State University, College of Education, unpublished Ph.D. dissertation.

Miller, J. L. (1979a). Curriculum theory: A recent history. *JCT, 1* (1), 28-43.

Miller, J. L. (1979b). Women and education: The dichotomous self. *Impact, 14* (3), 24-28.

Miller, J. L. (1980). Women: The evolving educational consciousness. *JCT, 2* (1), 238-247.

Miller, J. L. (1982a). The sound of silence breaking: Feminist pedagogy and curriculum theory. *JCT, 4* (1), 5-11.

Miller, J. L. (1982b). Reflections and reciprocal remembrances: A case study of self-concept and the composing process. *Arizona English Bulletin, 25* (1), 194-203.

Miller, J. L. (1982c). Writing and the teaching of writing: Case studies of self-concept and the composing process. *Writing Process of College Students, 2*. Fairfax, VA: George Mason University.

Miller, J. L. (1983a). The resistance of women academics: An autobiographical account. *Journal of Educational Equity and Leadership, 3* (2), 101-109.

Miller, J. L. (1983b). A search for congruence: Influence of past and present in preparing future teachers of writing. *English Journal, 15* (1), 5-11.

Miller, J. L. (1986, Winter). Women as teachers: Enlarging conversations on issues of gender and self-concept. *Journal of Curriculum and Supervision,* 1 (2), 111-121.

Miller, J. L. (1987a). Folded memories and future dialogues: Teaching language arts. *Teaching Education,* 1 (1), 16-18.

Miller, J. L. (1987b). Teachers' emerging texts: The empowering potential of writing inservice. In J. Smyth (Ed.), *Educating teachers: Changing the nature of pedagogical knowledge* (193-205). London, England: Falmer Press.

Miller, J. L. (1987c). Women as teachers/researchers: Gaining a sense of ourselves. *Teacher Education Quarterly,* 14 (2), 52-58.

Miller, J. L. (1988). The resistance of women academics: An autobiographical account. In W. Pinar (Ed.), *Contemporary curriculum discourses* (486-494). Scottsdale, AZ: Gorsuch Scarisbrick.

Miller, J. L. (1990a). *Creating spaces and finding voices: Teachers collaborating for empowerment.* Albany, NY: State University of New York Press.

Miller, J. L. (1990b). Teachers as curriculum creators. In J. Sears & D. Marshall (Eds.), *Teaching and thinking about curriculum* (85-96). New York: Teachers College Press.

Miller, J. L. (1992a) Teachers' spaces: A personal evolution of teacher lore. In W. Schubert & W. Ayers (Eds.), *Teacher lore: Learning from our experience* (11-22). New York: Longman.

Miller, J. L. (1992b). Women and education: In what ways does gender affect the educational process? In J. Kincheloe & S. Steinberg (Eds.,) *Thirteen questions* (151-158). New York: Peter Lang.

Miller, J. L. (1992c). Teachers, autobiography, and curriculum: Critical and feminist perspectives. In S. Kessler & B. Swadner (Eds.), *Reconceptualizing the early childhood curriculum: Beginning the dialogue* (103-122). New York: Teachers College Press.

Miller, J. L. (1992d). Gender and teachers. In N. McCracken & B. Appleby (Eds.), *Gender issues in the teaching of English* (174-190). Portsmouth, NH: Heinemann-Boynton/Cook Publishers.

Miller, J. L. (1992e). Shifting the boundaries: Teachers challenge contempo-rary thought. *Theory into Practice,* 31 (3), 245-251.

Miller, J. L. (1993a). Solitary spaces: Women, curriculum, and teaching. In D. Wear (Ed.), *The center of the web: Women and solitude* (245-252). Albany, NY: State University of New York Press.

Miller, J. L. (1993b). Construction of curriculum and gender. In S. Biklin & D. Pollard (Eds.), *Gender and education* (43-63). Chicago, IL: University of Chicago Press.

Miller, J. L. (1994). Solitary spaces: Women, teaching and curriculum. In R. Martusewicz & W. Reynolds (Eds.), *Inside out: Contemporary critical perspec-tives in education* (201-208). New York: St. Martin's Press.

Miller, J. L. & Pinar, W. (1982). Feminist curriculum theory: Notes on the American field, 1982. *Journal of Educational Thought,* 16 (3), 217-224.

Miller, J. (1979). *History and human existence: From Marx to Merleau-Ponty.* Berkeley, CA: University of California Press.

Millett, K. (1971). *Sexual politics.* New York: Avon Books.

Millies, P. (1989). *The mental lives of teachers.* Chicago, IL: University of Illinois at Chicago, College of Education, unpublished doctoral dissertation.

Millies, P. (1992). The relationship between a teacher's life and teaching. In W. Schubert & W. Ayers (Eds.), *Teacher lore: Learning from our experience* (25-42). New York: Longman.

Millman, M. (1975). She did it all for love: A feminist view of the sociology of deviance. In M. Millman & R. Kantner (Eds.), *Another voice: Feminist perspectives on social life and social science.* Garden City, NY: Anchor Press, Doubleday.

Milner, E. (1980). Airlie: Sacrality, paradigms and the axis mundi. *JCT*, 2 (2), 274.

Milner, E. (1981). Airlie: The ontological bridge. *JCT*, 3 (2), 228.

Milner, E. (1982a). Airlie, 1981. *JCT*, 4 (1), 208.

Milner, E. (1982b). A full curriculum for the gifted handicapped. *JCT*, 4 (2), 216-227.

Milner, E. (1987). Transvestite's return: The syntax exchange of the visual and verbal arts. *JCT*, 7 (2), 99-110.

Ministry of Education (1979). Code of conduct. *Chinese Education* (102-103), 13 (3-4).

Ministry of Education (1980). *Japan's Modern Educational System.* Tokyo, Japan: Ministry of Education, Science, and Culture.

Mishler, E. (1990). Validation in inquiry-guided research: The role of exemplars in narrative studies. *Harvard Educational Review*, 60, (4) 415-442.

Mitchell, J. (1971). *Woman's estate.* New York: Pantheon Books.

Mitrano, B. (1979a). *Feminism and curriculum theory: Implications for teacher education.* Rochester, NY: University of Rochester, Graduate School of Education and Human Development, unpublished doctoral dissertation.

Mitrano, B. (1979b). Self in feminist theology and curriculum theory. *Impact*, 14 (3), 19-23.

Mitrano, B. (1979c, Fall). Feminist theology and curriculum theory. *Journal of Curriculum Studies*, 11 (3), 211-220.

Mitrano, B. (1981). Feminism and curriculum theory: Implications for teacher education. *JCT*, 3 (2), 5-85.

Miyazaki, I. (1981). *China's examination hell: The civil service examination of imperial China.* [Trans. C. Schirokaur.] New Haven, CT: Yale University Press.

Moffett, J. (1988). *Storm in the mountains: A case study of censorship, conflict, and consciousness.* Carbondale, IL: Southern Illinois University Press.

Moffett, J. (1990). Varieties of censorship. *The Journal of Educational Thought*, 24 (3A), 5-16.

Mohr, R. (1989). Gay studies as moral vision. *Educational Theory*, 39 (2), 121-132.

Molina, A. (1991). *Spades, players, and senators: An ethnography of black subcultures in a community college.* Baton Rouge, LA: Louisiana State University,

Department of Curriculum and Instruction, unpublished Ph.D. dissertation.

Molina, A. (1992, April). 2+2 tech prep addressed access for "neglected majority." *South Louisiana College News*, 10.

Molnar, A. (1975). Autobiographical statement. In W. Pinar (Ed.), *Curriculum Theorizing: The Reconceptualists* (165-166). Berkeley, CA: McCutchan.

Molnar, A. (1985). Tomorrow the shadow on the wall will be that of another. *JCT*, 6 (3), 35-42.

Molnar, A. (Ed.). (1987). *Social Issues and Education: Challenge and Responsibility*. Alexandria, VA: ASCD.

Molnar, A. & Zahorik, J. (Eds.). (1977). *Curriculum theory*. Washington, DC: ASCD.

Moltmann, J. (1967). *The theology of hope*. London, England: S.C. M. Press.

Moltmann, J. (1969). *Religion, revolution, and the future*. New York: Charles Scribner's Sons.

Montgomery, R. (1967). *Examinations: An account of their evolution as administrative devices in England*. Pittsburgh, PA: University of Pittsburgh Press.

Mooney, R. (1957). The researcher himself. In *Research for curriculum improvement* (154-186). [1957 ASCD Yearbook.] Washington, DC: ASCD.

Mooney, R. (1961). Creation and communication. In M. F. Andrews (Ed.), *Creativity and psychological health* (37-54). Syracuse, NY: Syracuse University Press.

Mooney, R. (1963). Creation and teaching. In W. P. Street (Ed.), *Creativity and college teaching* (45-62). Lexington, KY: University of Kentucky Press.

Mooney, R. (1965). Nurturing the educational researcher as creative artist. In E. Guba & S. Elam (Eds.), *The training and nurture of educational researchers*. Bloomington, IN: Phi Delta Kappa.

Mooney, R. (1966). Creative integration. *Theory into Practice*, 5 (1), 174-178.

Mooney, R. (1967a, Summer). Creation: Contemporary culture and renaissance. *The Journal of Creative Behavior*, 1, 259-281.

Mooney, R. (1967b). Perspectives on ourselves. *Theory into Practice*, 6 (1), 200-211.

Mooney, R. (1969). Three moments in crisis. *Theory into Practice*, 8:2, 310-311.

Moore, D. (1990). Voice and choice in Chicago. In W. Clune & J. Witte (Eds.), *Choice and control in American education* [Vol. 2]. Basingstoke, England: Falmer.

Moore, M. (1984). Loyalty and education: Principle and practice. *Pedagogy and Phenomenology*, 1 (3), 312-318.

Moore, M. (1989, October 15). The art of teaching from the heart: The heart of the matter. Paper presented to the School of Theology at the Claremont Colleges, Claremont, CA.

Moran, G. (1981). *Interplay: A theory of religion and education*. Winona, MN: St. Mary's Press.

Morgan, R. (1970). *Sisterhood is powerful: An anthology of writings from the women's liberation movement*. New York: Random House.

Morley, F. (1973). *A modern guide to effect K-12 curriculum planning.* West Nyack, NY: Parker Publishing.

Morris, B. (1979). *Change agents in the schools.* Upland, CA: Barbara Morris Report.

Morris, H. (1978). *Education for the real world.* San Diego, CA: Creation Life Publishers.

Morris, W. (1967). *North toward home.* Oxford, MS: Yoknapatawpha Press.

Morris, W. (1981). *Terrains of the heart.* Oxford, MS: Yoknapatawpha Press.

Morrison, H. (1934). *Basic principles in education.* Boston, MA: Houghton Mifflin.

Morrison, T. (1987). *Beloved.* New York: Knopf.

Morrison, T. (1989, Winter). Unspeakable things unspoken: The Afro-American presence in American literature. *Michigan Quarterly*, 1-34.

Morrison, T. (1992). *Playing in the dark: Whiteness and the literary imagination.* Cambridge, MA: Harvard University Press.

Morris, P. (1986). A matrix of describing alternative strategies of curriculum development. *Journal of Curriculum Studies*, 18 (4), 445-448.

Morse, S. (1835). *Foreign conspiracy against the liberties of the United States.* New York: Arno Press [reprinted in 1977].

Mosher, R. (1992). The adolescent as a citizen. In A. Garrod (Ed.), *Learning for life: Moral education theory and practice* (179-209). Westport, CT: Praeger.

Mosher, R. & Purpel, D. (1972). *Supervision: The reluctant profession.* Boston, MA: Houghton Mifflin.

Mosier, R. (1947). *Making the American mind: Social and moral ideas in the McGuffey readers.* New York: King's Crown Press.

Moulton, J. (1983). Development through training. Animation rurale. In J. Bock & G. Papagiannis (Eds.), *Nonformal education and national development* (25-91). New York: Praeger.

Mulder, M. (1991). Deliberation in curriculum conferences. *Journal of Curriculum and Supervision*, 6 (4), 325-339.

Mulder, R. (1983). *A framework for examining reconceptualism and deriving its possible implications for undergraduate liberal arts teacher education.* East Lansing, MI: Michigan State University, College of Education, unpublished Ph.D. dissertation.

Muldoon, M. (1990). Religious studies and the teaching of business ethics. *McGill Journal of Education*, 25 (2), 245-253.

Muller, J. (1987). People's education and the NECC: The choreography of education struggle. *South African Review* 4, 1-10.

Muller, J. (1989). *Social analysis of education: After the new sociology* by P. Wexler: A review. *Perspectives in Education*, 11 (1), 73-79.

Muller, R. (1984). *New genesis.* New York: Doubleday. .

Muller, R. (1989). A world core curriculum. *Social Education*, 53 (5), 284-286.

Munby, H. (1979, Fall). Philosophy for children: An example of curriculum review and criticism. *Curriculum Inquiry*, 9 (3), 229-249.

Munby, H. (1986). Metaphor in the thinking of teachers: An exploratory study. *Journal of Curriculum Studies*, 18 (2), 197-210.

Munby, H. (1987, April). *Metaphorical expressions of teachers' practical curriculum knowledge*. Paper presented to the annual meeting of the American Educational Research Association, Washington, DC.

Munro, P. (1991). Supervision: What's imposition got to do with it? *Journal of Curriculum and Supervision*, 7 (1), 77-89.

Munro, P. (1992, April). Teaching as "women's work": A century of resistant voices. Paper presented to the annual meeting of the American Educational Research Association, San Francisco, CA.

Munro, P. (in press). Continuing dilemmas of life history research. In D. Flinders & G. Mills (Eds.), *Theory and concepts in qualitative research: Perspectives from the field*. New York: Teachers College Press.

Munro, P. & Elliot, J. (1987). Instructional growth through peer coaching. *Journal of Staff Development*, 8 (1), 25-28.

Munro, P. & Jipson, J. (1991). Fictions of the maternal/What's real: The deconstruction of life history as curricular text. In Erdman, J. & Henderson, J. (Eds.), *Critical discourse on curriculum issues* (140-165). Chicago, IL: The Midwest Center for Curriculum Studies.

Murphy, J. (1991). *Restructuring schools: Capturing and assessing the phenomena*. New York: Teachers College Press.

Murphy, L. & Livingstone, J. (1993). Racism and limits of radical feminism. In. L. Castenell, Jr. & W. Pinar (Eds.), *Understanding curriculum as racial text: Representations of identity and difference in education* (179-190). Albany, NY: State University of New York Press. [Also (1985), *Race and Class*, XXVI (4), 61-70.]

Murphy, R. & Torrance, H. (Eds.). (1987). *Evaluating education: Issues and methods*. London, England: Harper & Row.

Musgrave, P. (1979). *Society and the curriculum in Australia*. Winchester, MA: Allen & Unwin, Inc.

Nakayama, S. (1984). *Science in Japan, China, and the west*. [J. Dusenbury, trans.] New Haven, CT: Yale University Press.

Nalaskowski, A. (1990, January/February). Towards the Inventic school. *Education Now*, 7, 13.

Narvaez, A. (1990, January 20). M. Horton, 84, head of school in South that defied racial bias. New York: *New York Times*, 12.

National Center for Education Statistics (1985). *Indicators of education, status and trends*. Washington, DC: United States Department of Education.

National Commission on Excellence in Education (1983). *A nation at risk: The imperative for educational reform*. Washington, DC: United States Department of Education.

National Education Association (NEA) (1886). Reports of committees and discussions. *Proceedings of the National Education Association*. Washington, DC: NEA.

National Education Association (NEA) Committee of Fifteen Report. (1895). *Address and Proceedings*. [Chaired by W. Harris.] Washington, DC: NEA.

National Education Association, Committee of Ten on Secondary School Studies. (1893). *Report*. [Chaired by C. Eliot.] Washington, DC: United States Government Printing Office.

National Education Association. (NEA) (1918). *Cardinal principles of secondary education: A report of the commission on the reorganization of secondary education*. Washington, DC: United States Government Printing Office.

National League for Nursing (1977). *Criteria for the appraisal of baccalaureate and higher degree programs in nursing*. New York: National League for Nursing.

National Society for the Study of Education (NSSE). (1927a). *Curriculum making past and present*. Twenty-sixth yearbook, Part I. [Whipple, editor.] Bloomington, IL: Public School Publishing Company.

National Society for the Study of Education (NSSE). (1927b). *The foundation of curriculum making*. Twenty-sixth yearbook, Part II. Bloomington, IL: Public School Publishing Company.

National Society for the Study of Education (NSSE). (1945). *American education in the postwar period: Curriculum reconstructions*. Forty-fourth yearbook, part I. Chicago, IL: University of Chicago Press.

Nelkin, D. (1976). The science-textbook controversies. *Scientific American*, 234, 33-39.

Nelson, M. (1992). Using oral histories to reconstruct the experiences of women teachers in Vermont 1900-50. In I. Goodson (Ed.), *Studying teachers' lives* (167-186). New York: Teachers College Press.

Nelson, R. & Watras, J. (1981, Spring). The scientific movement: American education and the emergence of the technological society. *The Journal of Thought*, 16 (1), 49-72.

Newell, A. & Simon ,H. (1956). The logic theory machine. *IRE Transactions on Information Theory*, IT-2, 61-69.

Newlon, J. (1923a). *Twentieth annual report of school district number one in the city and country of Denver and state of Colorado*. Denver, CO: Denver School Press.

Newlon, J. (1923b). Attitude of the teachers toward supervision. *NEA Proceedings*. Washington, DC: National Education Association.

Newman, J. (1980, Winter). Morality, religion, and the public schools' quest for commonality. *Review Journal of Philosophy and Social Science*, 4, 18-32.

Newman, J. (1990). *America's teachers: An introduction to education*. New York: Longman.

Newman, J. (1991). Organized prayer and secular humanism in Mobile, Alabama's public schools. In J. Kincheloe & W. Pinar (Eds.), *Curriculum as social psychoanalysis: The significance of place* (45-76). Albany, NY: State University of New York Press.

Newmann, F. & Oliver, D. (1967, 1972). Education and community. *Harvard Educational Review*, 37 (Winter), 61-106. [Also in D. Purpel & M. Belanger (Eds.), *Curriculum and cultural revolution* (205-252). Berkeley, CA: McCutchan.]

New York Times (1993, December 21). A private gift for public education. New York: *The New York Times*, A-14.

Ng, R. (1993). Racism, sexism, and nation building in Canada. In C. McCarthy & W. Crichlow (Eds.), *Race, identity, and representation in education* (50-59). New York: Routledge.

Niece, R. & Viechnicki, K. (1987). Recounting Counts: A review of George S. Counts' challenge and the reactions to "Dare Progressive Education Be Progressive?" *The Journal of Educational Thought*, 21 (3), 149-154.

Nixon, G. (1992). *Autobiographical amnesia*. Baton Rouge, LA: Louisiana State University, Department of Curriculum and Instruction, unpublished Ph.D. dissertation.

Nixon, J. (1990). Curriculum evaluation: Old and new paradigms. In N. Entwistle (Ed.), *Handbook of educational ideas and practices* (637-647). New York: Routledge.

Nkomo, M. (1984). *Student culture and activism in black South African universities*. New York: Greenwood Press.

Noble, D. (1992, April). New American schools and the new world order. Paper presented at the annual meeting, American Educational Research Association, San Francisco, CA.

Noddings, N. (1974). Competence theories and the science of education. *Educational Theory*, 24, (4), 356-364.

Noddings, N. (1979). NIE's national curriculum development conference. In J. Schaffarzick & G. Sykes, (Eds.),*Values conflicts and curriculum issues: Lessons from research and experience* (291-312). Berkeley, CA: McCutchan.

Noddings, N. (1981). Caring. *JCT*, 3 (2), 139-148.

Noddings, N. (1984). *Caring*. Berkeley, CA: University of California Press.

Noddings, N. (1985). In search of the feminine. *Teachers College Record*, 87 (2), 195-204.

Noddings, N. (1986). Fidelity in teaching, teacher education, and research for teaching. *Harvard Educational Review*, 56 (4), 496-510.

Noddings, N. (1989). *Women and evil*. Berkeley, CA: University of California Press.

Noddings, N. (1992a). *The challenge to care in schools: An alternative approach to education*. New York: Teachers College Press.

Noddings, N. (1992b). Shaping an acceptable child. In A. Garrod (Ed.), *Learning for life: Moral education theory and practice* (47-70). Westport, CT: Praeger.

Noddings, N. & Enright, S. (1983). The promise of open education. *Theory Into Practice*, XXII (3), 182-189.

Norquay, N. (1990). Life history research: Memory, schooling and social difference. *Cambridge Journal of Education*, 20 (3), 291-300.

Norris, C. (1982). *Deconstruction: Theory and practice*. London, England: Routledge.

Norris, C. (1991). *What's wrong with postmodernism: Critical theory and the ends of philosophy*. Baltimore, MD: The Johns Hopkins University Press.

Norris, J. (1989). *Some authorities as co-authors in a collective creation production.* Edmonton, Alberta, Canada: University of Alberta, Faculty of Education, unpublished Ph.D. dissertation.

Norris, J. (1990a). An example of collective creation process. [Videotape.] Edmonton, Alberta, Canada: University of Alberta, Instructional Technology Centre.

Norris, J. (1990b). *(Re)visions of old voices: A glance at some research on student authorship.* A paper presented to the American Alliance for Theatre and Education, Minneapolis, MN.

Norris, J. (1990c). *Examples of some dramatic forms used in the collective creation process.* Edmonton, Alberta, Canada: University of Alberta, Instructional Technology Centre.

Norris, J. (1990d). *Examples of the exploration stage of the collective creation process.* Edmonton, Alberta, Canada: University of Alberta, Instructional Technology Centre.

Norris, J. (1991a). *Snapshots of playing together.* [Director and co-author with student company.] Paper/performance presented at the Western Canadian Association for Student Teaching, Regina, Saskatchewan.

Norris, J. (1991b). *Making sense of teaching through drama.* Paper presented to the Bergamo Conference on Curriculum Theory and Classroom Practice, Dayton, OH.

Norris, J. (1992). *Paradise lost.* [Director and co-author with the company No Spare Time.] Paper/performance presented at the Western Canadian Association for Student Teaching, Edmonton, Alberta.

Norris, J. (1993a). *Student teaching: The first frontier.* [Director and co-author with student company.] Paper/performance at the Western Canadian Association for Student Teaching, University of British Columbia, Vancouver, British Columbia.

Norris, J. (1993b). Personal correspondence.

Norris, J. (1993c). *Research skills for drama teachers.* Paper presented to the American Alliance for Theatre and Education, Boston, MA.

Norris, N. (Ed.). (1977). *SAFARI: Theory into practice.* Occasional Publication No. 4. Norwich, England: Centre for Applied Research in Education, University of East Anglia.

Norris, S. (1985, May). Synthesis of research on critical thinking. *Educational Leadership*, 42, 40-45.

Novak, J. (1991). Clarifying with concept maps. *Science Teacher*, 58 (7), 44-49.

Nowak-Fabrykowksi, K. (1992, Winter). Freinet's concept of teachers and theory of teaching. *McGill Journal of Education*, 27 (1), 61-68.

Nunes, M. (1992). *Alternative education and social change in Brazil.* Baton Rouge, LA: Louisiana State University, Department of Curriculum and Instruction, unpublished Ph.D. dissertation.

Oakes, J. (1985). *Keeping track: How schools structure inequality.* New Haven, CT: Yale University Press.

Oakes, J. (1986). *Educational indicators: A guide for policy makers.* Santa Monica, CA: Rand.

Oakes, J., Gamoran, A. & Page, R. (1991). Curriculum differentiation: Opportunities, outcomes, and meanings. In P. Jackson (Ed.), *Handbook of research on curriculum* (570-609). New York: Macmillan.

Oberg, A. (1987). Using construct theory as a basis for research into teacher professional development. *Journal of Curriculum Studies*, 19 (1), 55-65.

Oberg, A. (1990, Summer). Methods and meanings in action research: The action research journal. *Theory into Practice*, XXIX (3), 214-221

Oberg, A. & Artz, S. (1992). Teaching for reflection: Being reflective. In T. Russell & H. Munby (Eds.), *Teachers and teaching: From classroom to reflection* (138-155). London, England: Falmer.

Oberg, A. & Underwood, S. (1992). Facilitating teacher development. In A. Hargreaves (Ed.), *Understanding teacher development* (162-177). New York: Teachers College Press.

O'Brien, E. (1989, November 23). Debates over curriculum expansion continues. *Black Issues in Higher Education*, 6-18, 1-26.

O'Brien, M. (1979). *The idea of the American south*. Baltimore, MD: Johns Hopkins University Press.

O'Connor, T. (1991). Latin America. *Comparative Education Review*, 35 (2), 393-395.

Ogbu, J. (1990). Literacy and schooling in subordinate cultures: The case of Black Americans. In K. Lomotey (Ed.), *Going to school: The African-American experience* (113-131). Albany, NY: State University of New York Press.

Ogbu, J. (1992, November). Understanding cultural diversity and learning. *Educational Researcher*, 21 (8), 5-14.

Ogbu, J. & Matute-Bianchi, M. (1986). Understanding sociocultural factors in education: Knowledge, identity, and school adjustment. In California State Department of Education (Ed.), *Beyond language: Social and cultural factors in schooling language minority Students* (73-142). Los Angeles, CA: California State University, Evaluation, Dissemination and Assessment Center.

Oh, M-S. (1986). *The meaning of morality and moral education: An interpretative study of the moral education curriculum in Korea*. Edmonton, Alberta, Canada: University of Alberta, Department of Secondary Education, unpublished Ph.D. dissertation.

Okakok, L. (1989). Serving the purpose of the education. *Harvard Educational Review*, 59 (4), 405-422.

Oliva, P. (1982). *Developing the curriculum*. Boston, MA: Little, Brown.

Oliva, P. (1989). *Supervision for today's schools*. [Third edition.] New York: Longman.

Oliver, A. (1965, 1977). *Curriculum improvement: A guide to problems, principles, and processes*. [Second edition.] New York: Harper & Row.

Oliver, D. & Gershman, K. (1989). *Education, modernity, and fractured meaning: Toward a process theory of teaching and learning*. Albany, NY: State University of New York Press.

Olney, J. (1972). *Metaphors of self: The meaning of autobiography*. Princeton, NJ: Princeton University Press.

Olney, J. (Ed.). (1980). *Autobiography: Essays theoretical and critical.* Princeton, NJ: Princeton University Press.

Olson, J. (1982). Three approaches to curriculum change: Balancing the accounts. *JCT*, 4 (2), 90-96.

Olson, J. (1989a). Surviving innovation: Reflection on the pitfalls of practice. *Journal of Curriculum Studies*, 21 (6), 503-508.

Olson, J. (1989b). The persistence of technical rationality. In G. Milburn, I. Goodson, & R. Clark (Eds.), *Re-interpreting curriculum research: Images and arguments* (102-109). London, Ontario, Canada: The Althouse Press.

Olson, M. (1989). Room for learning. *Phenomenology + Pedagogy*, 7, 173-186.

Olson, P. (Ed). (1981). Rethinking social reproduction. [Theme issue.] *Interchange*, 12 (2-3).

Omi, M. & Winant, H. (1983). By the rivers of Babylon: Race in the United States. *Socialist Review*, 13 (5), 31-65.

Omi, M. & Winant, H. (1986). *Racial formation in the United States: From the 1960's to the 1980's.* New York: Routledge.

O'Neale, S. (1984). Reconstruction of the composite self: New images of black women in Maya Angelou's continuing autobiography. In M. Evans (Ed.), *Black women writers 1950-1980: A critical evaluation* (25-36). Garden City, NY: Anchros Press/Doubleday.

O'Neil, J. (1989). Global education: Controversy remains but support growing. *Curriculum Update* N1. Alexandria, VA: ASCD.

Ornstein, A. & Hunkins, F. (1988). *Curriculum: Foundations, principles, and issues.* New York: Prentice Hall.

Ornstein, A. & Levine, D. (1983). *Foundations of Education.* [Fifth ed.] New York: Houghton Mifflin.

Ornstein, A. & Levine, D. (1989). Social class, race, and school achievement: Problems and prospects. *Journal of Teacher Education*, XXXX (5), 17-23.

Osajima, K. (1992). Speaking silence. *JCT* 9 (4), 89-96.

Osborn, J. (1984). The purposes, uses, and contents of workbooks and some guidelines for publishers. In R. Anderson, J. Osborn, & R. Tierney (Eds.), *Learning to read in American schools: Readers and content texts.* Hillsdale, NJ: Earlbaum.

Osborn, R. (1974). An all-American small group in search of an electric kool-aid acid theory of curriculum. In W. Pinar (Ed.), *Heightened consciousness, cultural revolution, and curriculum theory: The proceedings of the Rochester conference* (131-137). Berkeley, CA: McCutchan.

Osborne, K., (1992, May-June). The emerging agenda for Canadian high schools. *Journal of Curriculum Studies*, 24 (3), 371-379.

O'Shea, J. (1985). A journey to the midway: Ralph Winfred Tyler. *Educational Evaluation and Policy Analysis*, 7 (4), 447-459.

O'Shea, T. & Self, J. (1983). *Learning and teaching with computers.* Englewood Cliffs, NJ: Prentice-Hall.

Out (1993, September). Dr. "Sodomite." p. 12.

Overly, N. (1970). *The unstudied curriculum: Its impact on children.* Washington, DC: Association for Supervision and Curriculum Development [ASCD], Elementary Education Council.

Overly, N. (1988). WCCI research call. *Journal of Curriculum and Supervision,* 3 (2), 168-171.

Owens, T. (1973). Educational evaluation by adversary proceedings. In E. House (Ed.), *School Evaluation: The Politics and the Process.* Berkeley, CA: McCutchan.

Oxford English Dictionary (OED). Oxford, England: Oxford University Press.

Ozmon, H. & Craver, S. (1990). *Philosophical foundations of education.* [Fourth edition]. Columbus, OH: Charles E. Merrill.

Padgham, R. (1983). The holographic paradigm and postcritical reconceptualist curriculum theory. *JCT,* 5 (3), 132-142.

Padgham, R. (1988a). Correspondences: Contemporary curriculum theory and twentieth century art. In W. Pinar (Ed.). *Contemporary curriculum discourses* (359-379). Scottsdale, AZ: Gorsuch Scarisbrick.

Padgham, R. (1988b). Thoughts about the implications of archetypal psychology for curriculum theory. *JCT,* 8 (3), 123-146.

Pagano, J. (1981). The curriculum field: Emergence of a discipline. *JCT,* 3 (1), 171-184.

Pagano, J. (1988a). The claim of philia. In W. Pinar (Ed.). *Contemporary curriculum discourses* (514-530). Scottsdale, AZ: Gorsuch Scarisbrick.

Pagano, J. (1988b). The nature and sources of teacher authority. *JCT,* 7 (4), 7-26.

Pagano, J. (1990). *Exiles and communities: Teaching in the patriarchal wilderness.* Albany, NY: State University of New York Press.

Pagano, J. (1992). Women and education: In what ways does gender affect the educational process? In J. Kincheloe & S. Steinberg (Eds.), *Thirteen questions* (143-150). New York: Peter Lang.

Pagano, J. & Dolan, L. (1980). Foundations for a unified approach to evaluation research. *Curriculum Inquiry,* 10 (4), 367-381.

Page, R. (1987a). Teachers' perceptions of students: A link between classrooms, school cultures, and the social order. *Anthropology and Education Quarterly,* (18), 77-99.

Page, R. (1987b). Lower-track classes at a college-preparatory high school: A caricature of educational encounters. In G. & L. Spindler (Eds.), *Interpretive ethnography of education: At home and abroad* (447-472). Hillsdale, NJ: Lawrence Erlbaum.

Page, R. (1989). The lower-track curriculum at a "heavenly" high school: "Cycles of prejudice." *Journal of Curriculum Studies,* 21 (3), 197-221.

Page, R. (1990a). Cultures and curricula: Differences between and within schools. *Educational Foundations,* 4 (1), 49-76.

Page, R. (1990b). A "revelant" lesson: Defining the lower-track student. In R. Page & L. Valli (Eds.), *Curriculum differentiation: Interpretive studies in U.S. secondary schools* (17-44). Albany, NY: State University of New York Press.

Page, R. (1990c). Games of chance: The lower-track curriculum in a college preparatory high school. *Curriculum Inquiry*, 20 (3), 249-282.

Page, R. (1991). *Lower-track classroom: A curricular and cultural perspective.* New York: Teachers College Press.

Page, R. (1993). For teachers: Some sketches of curriculum. In P. Phelan & A. Davidson (Eds.), *Renegotiating cultural diversity in American schools.* New York: Teachers College Press.

Page, R. & Valli, L. (Eds.). (1990). *Curriculum differentiation: Interpretive studies in U.S. secondary schools.* Albany, NY: State University of New York Press.

Pajak, E. (1989). *The central office supervisor of curriculum and instruction: Setting the stage for success.* Boston, MA: Allyn & Bacon.

Pajak, E. (1990). Do we need "comparative" supervision? A response to Duffy's "Supervising for Results." *Journal of Curriculum and Supervision*, 6 (1), 41-44.

Papert, S. (1980). *Mindstorms: Children, computers, and powerful ideas.* New York: Harper.

Paringer, W. (1990). *John Dewey and the paradox of liberal reform.* Albany, NY: State University of New York Press.

Paris, C. (1989). *Contexts of curriculum change: Conflict and consonance.* Paper presented to the annual meeting of the American Educational Research Association, San Francisco, CA.

Parker, C. & Rubin, L. (1966). *Process and content: Curriculum design and the application of knowledge.* Chicago, IL: Rand McNally.

Parker, F. (1883). *Talks on teaching.* New York: Kellog's Teachers Library.

Parker, F. (1894). *Talks on pedagogics.* New York: E. L. Kellog.

Parker, W. (1986a). Dorothy's and Mary's mediation of a curriculum invention. *Phenomenology + Pedagogy*, 4 (1), 20-31.

Parker, W. (1986b, Fall). Justice, social studies, and the subjectivity/structure problem. *Theory and Research in Social Education*, XIV (4), 277-293.

Parlett, M. & Hamilton, D. (1972). *Introduction to illuminative evaluation: A new approach to the study of innovatory programs.* Occasional Paper No. 9. Edinburgh, Scotland: Centre for Research in the Educational Sciences, University of Edinburgh.

Parrett, W. (1983). Alaska's rural schools: A unique challenge for responsible curricular development. *JCT*, 5 (3), 41-54.

Passow, H. (Ed.). (1962). *Curriculum crossroads.* New York: Teachers College Press.

Passow, H. (Ed.). (1964). *Nurturing individual potential.* Washington, DC: ASCD.

Passow, H. (1987). *Closing the achievement gap between educationally disadvantaged and other populations.* ERIC document ED282847.

Paul, R. (1992). *Critical thinking: What every person needs in a rapidly changing world.* Sonoma, CA: Sonoma State University.

Pearson, Jr., W. (1991). Black participation and performance in science, mathematics, and technical education. In C. Willie, A. Garibaldi & W.

Reed (Eds.), *The education of African-Americans* (3-6). New York: Auburn House.

Percy, W. (1987). *The thanatos syndrome.* New York: Farrar, Straus, & Giroux.

Pereira, P. (1984). Deliberation and the arts of perception. *Journal of Curriculum Studies,* 16 (4), 347-366.

Perez, L. (1993). Opposition and the education of Chicana/os. In C. McCarthy & W. Crichlow (Eds.), *Race, identity, and education* (268-279). New York & London, England: Routledge.

Peshkin, A. (1983). *Fundamentalist Christian schools.* Paper presented at the annual meeting of the American Educational Research Association, Montreal, Quebec, Canada.

Peterat, L. (1983). *Re-searching the teachers' perspective of curriculum: A case study of piloting a home economics curriculum.* Edmonton, Alberta, Canada: University of Alberta, Faculty of Education, Department of Secondary Education, unpublished Ph.D. dissertation.

Peter, C. (1974, January). Metaphysical finalism in Christian eschatology. *The Thomist,* 38, 125-145.

Peters, R. (1966). *Ethics and education.* London, England: Allen & Unwin.

Peters, R. (Ed.). (1967). *The concept of education.* London, England: Allen & Unwin.

Peters, R. (1975). Education and the educated man. In R. Dearden, P. Hirst & R. Peters (Eds.), *A critique of current educational aims* (1-15). London, England: Routledge & Kegan Paul.

Peters, T. & Waterman, R. (1982). *In search of excellence.* New York: Harper & Row.

Peterson, K. & Kauchak, D. (1982). *Teacher evaluation: Perspectives, practices, and promises.* Salt Lake City, UT: University of Utah.

Phenix, P. (1964). *Realms of meaning: A philosophy of the curriculum for general education.* New York: McGraw-Hill.

Phenix, P. (1971, 1975). Transcendence and the curriculum. *Teachers College Record,* 73 (2), 271-283. [Reprinted in W. Pinar (Ed.), *Curriculum theorizing: The reconceptualists* (321-337). Berkeley, CA: McCutchan.]

Philips, S. (1983). *The invisible culture: Communication in the classroom and community on the Warm Spring Indian reservation.* New York: Longman.

Phillips, D. (1983, May). After the wake: Postpositivistic educational thought. *Educational Researcher,* 12 (5), 4-12.

Phillips, M. (1988, September 9). Why black people are backing Baker. *The Guardian,* 9.

Piaget, J. (1970). *Structuralism.* [Trans. C. Maschler.] New York: Harper & Row.

Piaget, J. (1975). *The child's conception of the world.* New York: Littlefield.

Piaget, J. (1977). *The development of thought: Equilibration of cognitive structures.* [Trans. A. Rosin.] New York: Viking.

Piaget, J. & Garcia, R. (1989). *Psychogenesis and the history of science.* [Trans. H. Feider.] New York: Columbia University Press.

Pierce, C. (1992). *Reasoning and the logic of things: The Cambridge Conference lectures of 1898.* Cambridge, MA: Harvard University Press.

Pilder, W. (1974). In the stillness is the dancing. In W. Pinar (Ed.), *Heightened consciousness, cultural revolution, and curriculum theory: The proceedings of the Rochester conference* (117-129). Berkeley, CA: McCutchan.

Pinar, W. (1972). Working from within. *Educational Leadership,* 29 (4), 329-331.

Pinar, W. (1974a). Mr. Bennett and Mrs. Brown. *The Humanities Journal,* 8 (1), 2-3

Pinar, W. (1974b). *Currere:* Toward reconceptualization. In J. Jelinek (Ed.), *Basic problems in modern education* (147-171). Tempe, AZ: Arizona State University, College of Education.

Pinar, W. (Ed.). (1974c). *Heightened consciousness, cultural revolution and curriculum theory: The proceedings of the Rochester conference.* Berkeley, CA: McCutchan.

Pinar, W. (1974d). *Reply to Burton.* Columbia, SC: University of South Carolina, Museum of Education.

Pinar, W. (1975a). Sanity, madness and the school. In W. Pinar (Ed.), *Curriculum theorizing: The reconceptualists* (359-383). Berkeley, CA: McCutchan.

Pinar, W. (1975b). The analysis of educational experience. In W. Pinar (Ed.), *Curriculum theorizing: The reconceptualists* (384-395). Berkeley, CA: McCutchan.

Pinar, W. (1975c). Search for a method. In W. Pinar (Ed.), *Curriculum theorizing: The reconceptualists* (415-424). Berkeley, CA: McCutchan.

Pinar, W. (Ed.) (1975d). *Curriculum theorizing: The reconceptualists.* Berkeley, CA: McCutchan.

Pinar, W. (1975e). *Currere:* Toward reconceptualization. In W. Pinar (Ed.), *Curriculum theorizing: The reconceptualists* (396-414). Berkeley, CA: McCutchan.

Pinar, W. (1978a). The reconceptualization of curriculum studies. *Journal of Curriculum Studies,* 10 (3), 205-214. [Reprinted in H. Giroux, A. Penna, & W. Pinar (Eds.), *Curriculum and instruction: Alternatives in education* (87-97). Berkeley, CA: McCutchan.]

Pinar, W. (1978b). *Currere:* A Case Study. In G. Willis (Ed.), *Qualitative Evaluation* (316-342). Berkeley, CA: McCutchan.

Pinar, W. (1978c). Life history and curriculum theorizing. *Review Journal of Philosophy and Social Science,* 3 (1), 92-118.

Pinar, W. (1979a). What is the reconceptualization? *JCT,* 1 (1), 93-104.

Pinar, W. (1979b, October). Letter to the editor. *Educational Researcher,* 8 (9), 6.

Pinar, W. (1979c). Notes on the curriculum field 1978. *Educational Researcher,* 7 (8), 5-12.

Pinar, W. (1980a). The field and its journals. *JCT,* 2 (1), 7-11.

Pinar, W. (1980b). The voyage out: Curriculum as the relationship between the knower and the known. *JCT,* 2 (1), 71-92.

Pinar, W. (1980c). Life history and educational experience. *JCT*, 2 (2), 159-212.

Pinar, W. (1980d, Summer). A reply to my critics. *Curriculum Inquiry*, 10 (2), 199-205. [Reprinted in H. Giroux, A. Penna, & W. Pinar (Eds.) (1981), *Curriculum and Instruction: Alternatives in education* (392-399). Berkeley, CA: McCutchan.]

Pinar, W. (1981a). Caring: Gender considerations. *JCT*, 3 (2), 149-151.

Pinar, W. (1981b). The abstract and concrete in curriculum theorizing. In H. Giroux, A. Penna, W. Pinar (Eds.), *Curriculum and instruction: Alternatives in education* (431-454). Berkeley, CA: McCutchan.

Pinar, W. (1981c). Life history and educational experience: Part II. *JCT*, 3 (1), 259-286.

Pinar, W. (1981d). The reconceptualization of curriculum studies. In H. Giroux, A. Penna & W. Pinar (Eds.), *Curriculum and instruction: Alternatives in education* (87-97). Berkeley, CA: McCutchan.

Pinar, W. (1981e). "Whole, bright, deep with understanding." Issues in autobiographical method and qualitative research. *Journal of Curriculum Studies*, 13 (3), 173-188.

Pinar, W. (1982). Gender, sexuality and curriculum studies: The beginning of the debate. *McGill Journal of Education*, 2 (3), 305-316.

Pinar, W. (1983a). Curriculum as gender text: Notes on reproduction, resistance, and male-male relations. *JCT*, 5 (1), 26-52.

Pinar, W. (1983b). The corporate production of feminism and the case of Boy George. Rochester, NY: University of Rochester, Graduate School of Education, unpublished manuscript. [Reprinted in *Autobiography, politics, and sexuality*, Peter Lang Publishing, Inc., in 1994.]

Pinar, W. (1984). *Teaching the text*. Edmonton, Alberta, Canada: University of Alberta, Faculty of Education, Department of Secondary Education Monograph Series.

Pinar, W. (1985). A prayerful act: The work of James B. Macdonald. *JCT*, 6 (3), 43-53.

Pinar, W. (1987). "Unwanted strangers in our own homeland:" Notes on the work of T. Aoki. *JCT*, 7 (3), 11-21.

Pinar, W. (Ed.). (1988a). *Contemporary curriculum discourses*. Scottsdale, AZ: Gorsuch Scarisbrick.

Pinar, W. (1988b). Time, place, and voice: Curriculum theory and the historical moment. In W. Pinar (Ed.), *Contemporary curriculum discourses* (264-278). Scottsdale, AZ: Gorsuch Scarisbrick.

Pinar, W. (1988c). "Whole, bright, deep with understanding." Issues in qualitative research and autobiographical method. In W. Pinar (Ed.), *Contemporary curriculum discourses* (134-153). Scottsdale, AZ: Gorsuch Scarisbrick.

Pinar, W. (1988d). The reconceptualization of curriculum studies, 1987: A personal retrospective. *Journal of Curriculum and Supervision*, 3 (2), 157-167.

Pinar, W. (1988e). Autobiography and the architecture of self. *JCT*, 8 (1), 7-36.

Pinar, W. (1988f). Introduction. *Contemporary curriculum discourses* (1-13). Scottsdale, AZ: Gorsuch Scarisbrick.

Pinar, W. (1989, January/February). A reconceptualization of teacher education. *Journal of Teacher Education*, 9-12.

Pinar, W. (1990). Impartiality and comprehensiveness in teaching curriculum theory. In J. Sears & J. Marshall (Eds.), *Teaching and thinking about curriculum* (259-264). New York: Teachers College Press.

Pinar, W. (1991). Curriculum as social psychoanalysis: On the significance of place. In J. Kincheloe & W. Pinar (Eds.), *Curriculum as social psychoanalysis: Essays on the significance of place* (167-186). Albany, NY: State University of New York Press.

Pinar, W. (1992a, Summer). "Dreamt into existence by others." Curriculum theory and school reform. *Theory Into Practice*, 31 (3), 228-235.

Pinar, W. (1992b). Cries and whispers. In W. Pinar & W. Reynolds (Eds.), *Understanding curriculum as phenomenological and deconstructed text* (92-101). New York: Teachers College Press.

Pinar, W. (1993a). Notes on understanding curriculum as a racial text. In C. McCarthy & W. Crichlow (Eds.), *Race, identity, and representation in education* (60-70). New York & London, England: Routledge.

Pinar, W. (1993b, November). *Curriculum development in the USA: Decentralization and the Politics of School Reform.* Paper presented to the International Seminar on Curriculum and Decentralization, Santiago, Chile.

Pinar, W. (1994). *Autobiography, politics, and sexuality: Essays in curriculum theory, 1972-1992.* New York: Peter Lang.

Pinar, W. & Bowers, C. (1992). Politics of curriculum: Origins, controversies, and significance of critical perspectives. In G. Grant (Ed.). *Review of Research in Education* (163-190). Washington, DC: American Education al Research Association.

Pinar, W. & Grumet, M. (1976). *Toward a poor curriculum.* Dubuque, IA: Kendall/Hunt.

Pinar, W. & Grumet, M. (1981). Theory and practice and the reconceptualization of curriculum studies. In M. Lawn & L. Barton (Eds.), *Rethinking curriculum studies* (20-42). London, England: Croom Helm.

Pinar, W. & Grumet, M. (1988). Socratic *caesura* and the theory-practice relationship. In W. Pinar (Ed.), *Contemporary curriculum discourses* (92-100). Scottsdale, AZ: Gorsuch Scarisbrick.

Pinar, W. & Johnson, L. (1980). Aspects of gender analysis in recent feminist psychological thought and their implications for curriculum. *Journal of Education*, 162 (4), 113-126.

Pinar, W. & McKnight, D. (in press). The uses of curriculum knowledge: Notes on hermeneutics. *International Journal of Educational Research*

Pinar, W. & Miller, J. (1982). Feminist curriculum theory: Notes on the American field. *Journal of Educational Thought*, (16) 3, 217-224.

Pinar, W. & Reynolds, W. (Eds.). (1992a). *Understanding curriculum as phenomenological and deconstructed text.* New York: Teachers College Press.

Pinar, W. & Reynolds, W. (Eds.). (1992b). Appendix, section two: Genealogical notes on post-structuralism in curriculum studies. *Understanding curriculum as phenomenological and deconstructed text* (244-259). New York: Teachers College Press.

Pinar, W. & Reynolds, W. (Eds.). (1992c). Appendix, section one: Genealogical notes on the history of phenomenology in curriculum studies. *Understanding curriculum as phenomenological and deconstructed text* (237-244). New York: Teachers College Press.

Pink, W. (1990). Implementing curriculum inquiry: Theoretical and practical implications. In J. Sears & D. Marshall (Eds.), *Teaching and thinking about curriculum* (138-153). New York: Teachers College Press.

Pipes, R. (1990). *The Russian revolution*. New York: Knopf.

Plantinga, D. (1985). *Dwayne Huebner's curricular language model revisited*. Edmonton, Alberta, Canada: University of Alberta, Faculty of Education, Department of Secondary Education, unpublished master's thesis.

Pleck, J. & Sawyer, J. (1974). *Men and masculinity*. Englewood Cliffs, NJ: Prentice-Hall.

Podl, J. & Metzger, M. (1992). *Anatomy of an exhibition*. Studies on Exhibitions, No. 6. Providence, RI: Brown University, Coalition for Essential Schools.

Podl, J., et al. (1992). *The process of planning backwards*. Studies on Exhibitions, No. 7. Providence, RI: Brown University, Coalition for Essential Schools.

Polakow, V. (1984). Reflections on pedagogy, research and praxis. *Phenomenology + Pedagogy*, 2 (1), 1984, 29-35.

Ponder, G. (Ed.). (1990). Special theme: School culture. *Kappa Delta Pi Record*, 26 (4).

Ponticell, J., Griffin, G., Schubert, W., Henderson, J., Fowler, R., Bacdon, C., & Richardson, O. (1987). *A voice for teachers: Foundational and policy concerns of teachers in an era of educational reform*. Paper presented at the annual meeting of the American Educational Research Association.

Poole, M. (1980). *Creativity across the curriculum*. Sydney, Australia: George Allen & Unwin.

Popham, J. (1970). Probing the validity of arguments against behavioral goals. In R. Kibler, L. Barker & D. Miles (Eds.), *Behavioral objectives and instruction* (115-124). Boston, MA: Allyn & Bacon.

Popham, J. (1975). *Educational evaluation*. Englewood Cliffs, NJ: Prentice Hall.

Popham, J. & Baker, E. (1973). *Classroom instruction tactics*. Englewood Cliffs, NJ: Prentice-Hall, Inc.

Popham, J. & Carlson, D. (1977). Deep dark deficits of the adversary evaluation model. *Educational Researcher*, 6 (6), 3-6.

Popkewitz, T. (1988). What's in a research project: Some thoughts on the intersection of history, social structure, and biography. *Curriculum Inquiry*, 18 (4), 379-400.

Popkewitz, T. (1991). *A political sociology of educational reform: Power/knowledge in teaching, teacher education, and research*. New York: Teachers College Press.

Popkewitz, T. (1992). Cartesian anxiety, linguistic communism, and reading texts. *Educational Researcher*, 21 (5), 11-15.

Popkewitz, T. (Ed.). (1987). *The formation of school subjects: The struggle for creating an American institution*. Philadelphia, PA: Falmer.

Popkewitz, T., Tabachnick, B. & Wehlage, G. (1981). *The myth of educational reform: A study of school responses to a program of change*. Madison, WI: University of Wisconsin Press.

Portelli, J. (1987). On defining curriculum. *Journal of Curriculum & Supervision*, 2 (4), 354-367.

Porter, J., FSC. (1991, December 24). *Brothers: Christian Brothers of the New Orleans-Santa Fé District Newsletter*. XLIII (4). Lafayette, LA: Christian Brothers Press.

Portland Public Schools. *African-American Baseline Essays*. Portland, OR: Portland Public Schools.

Portuges, C. & Culley, M. (Eds.) (1985). *Gendered subjects: The dynamics of feminist teaching*. Boston, MA: Routledge & Kean Paul.

Posner, G. (1979). Curriculum research: Domains of the field. *JCT*, 1 (1), 80-92.

Posner, G. (1982a). A cognitive science conception of curriculum and instruction. *Journal of Curriculum Studies*, 14 (4), 343-351.

Posner, G. (1982b). Cognitive science and a conceptual change epistemology: A new approach to curricular research. *JCT*, 4 (1), 106-126.

Posner, G. (1989). Making sense of diversity: The current state of curriculum research. *Journal of Curriculum and Supervision*, 4 (4),340-361.

Posner, G. (1992). *Analyzing the curriculum*. New York: McGraw Hill.

Posner, G. & Strike, K. (1976). A categorization scheme for principles of sequencing content. *Review of Educational Research*, 46 (4), 665-690.

Posner, G. & Rudnitsky, A. (1986). *Course design: A guide to curriculum development for teachers*. [Third edition; first edition: 1978.] New York: Longman.

Poster, C. & J. Zimmer (1992). *Community and education in the third world*. New York: Routledge, Chapman, & Hall.

Postlethwaite, T. (Ed.). (1988). *Encyclopedia of comparative education and national systems of education*. Oxford, England: Pergamon Press.

Postman, N. (1985). *Amusing ourselves to death: Public discourse in the age of show business*. New York: Penguin.

Potter-Tomfohr, J. (1993). *Teacher fear of sexuality and its impact on drama in the classroom*. Menomonie, WI: University of Wisconsin-Stout, the Graduate College, unpublished M.S. thesis.

Powell, A., Farrar, E., & Cohen, D. (1985). *The shopping mall high school*. Boston, MA: Houghton Mifflin.

Power, C. & Higgins, A. (1992). The just community approach to classroom participation. In A. Garrod (Ed.), *Learning for life: Moral education theory and practice* (228-245). Westport, CT: Praeger.

Pratt, D. (1978). Systems theory, systems technology, and curriculum design. *The Journal of Educational Thought*, 12 (2), 131-152.

Pratt, D. (1980). *Curriculum: Design and development.* New York: Harcourt Brace Jovanovich.

Pratt, D. (1982). A cybernetic model for curriculum development. *Instructional Science,* (11),1-12.

Pratt, D. (1983, Winter). Curriculum for the 21st century. *Education Canada,* 41-47.

Pratt, D. (1987a, December). Canadian curricula. *OPSTF News,* 26-28.

Pratt, D. (1987b). Curriculum design as humanistic technology. *Journal of Curriculum Studies,* 19 (2),149-162.

Prettyman, V. (1915). Ideals of the Horace Mann School for boys. *Teachers College Record,* 16 (1), 11-15.

Prigogine, I. (1980). *From being to becoming: Time and complexity in the physical sciences.* San Francisco, CA: W. H. Freeman.

Pritscher, C. (1982a). A demonstration of making existence explicit and simultaneously monitoring it. *JCT,* 4 (1), 250-256.

Pritscher, C. (1982b). Time as a horizon for a curriculum. *JCT,* 4 (2), 228-235.

Pritscher, C. (1988). Creating new concepts to clarify what is worthy of the name "education." *JCT,* 8 (2), 61-76.

Pritzkau, P. (1959). *Dynamics of curriculum improvement.* Englewood Cliffs, NJ: Prentice-Hall.

Proctor, S. (1970). Education for genuine community. In R. Leeper (Ed.), *A man for tomorrow's world* (3-11). Washington, DC: ASCD.

Pronger, B. (1990). *The arena of masculinity: Sports, homosexuality and the meaning of sex.* New York: St. Martin's Press.

Provenzo, E. (1990). *Religious fundamentalism and American education: The battle for the public schools.* Albany, NY: State University of New York Press.

Psacharopoulous, G. (1985). Returns to education: A further international update and implications. *Journal of Human Resources,* XX (4), 583-604.

Purpel, D. (1981). Humor in the great scheme of things: A response to Elizabeth Vallance. *Curriculum Inquiry, 11 (3), 231-237.*

Purpel, D. (1989). *The moral and spiritual crisis in education: A curriculum for justice and compassion in education.* South Hadley, MA: Bergin & Garvey.

Purpel, D. & Belanger, M. (Eds.). (1972a). *Curriculum and cultural revolution.* Berkeley, CA: McCutchan.

Purpel, D. & Belanger, M. (1972b). Toward humanistic curriculum theory. In. D. Purpel & M. Belanger (Eds.), *Curriculum and cultural revolution* (64-73). Berkeley, CA: McCutchan.

Purpel, D. & Ryan, K. (Eds.). (1976). *Moral education: It comes with the territory.* Berkeley, CA: McCutchan.

Radziewicz, J. (1990, December). Finding a place for children. *Education and Dialogue,* 9.

Raffel, S. (1984). Parental uncertainty as pain. *Phenomenology + Pedagogy,* 1 (3), 335-345.

Ragan, C. (1987). *The comparative method: Moving beyond qualitative and quantitative strategies.* Berkeley, CA: University of California Press.

Raissiguier, C. (1993). Negotiating work, identity, and desire: The adolescent dilemmas of working-class girls of French and Algerian descent in a vocational high school. In C. McCarthy & W. Crichlow (Eds.), *Race, identity, and representation in education* (140-156). New York & London, England: Routledge.

Ramsankar, S. & Hart, C. (1992). Creative curriculum for an inner city: A case study of Alex Taylor Community School. *Journal of Curriculum and Supervision,* 7 (4), 334-348.

Rankin, J. (1992). Objects on the shelf: Transitional objects in a secondary school curriculum. *JCT* 9 (4), 29-43.

Ratner, J. (1939). *Intelligence in the modern world: John Dewey's philosophy.* New York: Random House.

Ratteray, J. (1990). African-American achievement: A research agenda emphasizing independent schools. In K. Lomotey (Ed.), *Going to school: The African-American experience* (197-207). Albany, NY: State University of New York Press.

Ravitch, D. (1989). International studies in the California framework. *Access,* 86-87, 20-21. New York: The American Forum for Global Education.

Ravitch, D. & Finn, C. (1987). *What do our 17-year-olds know? A report on the first national assessment of history and literature.* New York: Harper & Row.

Raymond, C. (1991, March 6). New study finds convergence of school curricula worldwide. *Chronicle of Higher Education,* A8.

Raymond, J. (1979-80, Fall/Winter). Women's studies: A knowledge of one's own. *Union Seminary Quarterly Review,* 39-48.

Raymond, J. (1979). *The transsexual empire: The making of the she-male.* Boston, MA: Beacon Press.

Raywid, M. (1983). Alternative schools as a model for public education. *Theory Into Practice,* XXII (3),190-197.

Read, H. (1958). *Education through art.* London, England: Faber & Faber.

Redefer, F. (1948, May). What has happened to progressive education? *School and Society,* LXVIII, 345-349.

Reese, W. (1982). The public schools and the great gates of hell. *Educational Theory,* 32 (1), 9-17.

Reichardt, C. & Cook, T. (1979). Beyond qualitative versus quantitative methods. In T. Cook & C. Reichardt (Eds.), *Qualitative and quantitative methods in evaluation research.* Beverly Hills, CA: Sage.

Reid, T. (1993). *Toward creative teaching: The life and career of Laura Zirbes.* Columbia, SC: University of South Carolina, College of Education, unpublished doctoral dissertation.

Reid, W. (1975). The changing curriculum: Theory and practice. In W. Reid & D. Walker (Eds.), *Case studies in curriculum change* (240-259). London: Routledge & Kegan Paul.

Reid, W. (1978). *Thinking about the curriculum.* London, England: Routledge & Kegan Paul.

Reid, W. (1980a). A curriculum journal and its field: A question of genre. *JCT,* 2 (1), 12-19.

Reid, W. (1980b). Rationalism or humanism? The future of curriculum studies. *JCT*, 2 (1), 93-108.

Reid, W. (1984). Curriculum, community, and liberal education: A response to the Practical 4. *Curriculum Inquiry*, 14 (1), 103-111.

Reid, W. (1986). Curriculum theory and curriculum change: What can we learn from history? *Journal of Curriculum Studies*, 18 (2), 159-166.

Reid, W. (1988). The institutional context of curriculum deliberation. *Journal of Curriculum and Supervision*, 4 (1), 3-16.

Reid, W. (1992). The state of curriculum inquiry. *Journal of Curriculum Studies*, 24 (2), 165-178.

Reid, W. & Walker, D. (Eds.). (1975). *Case studies in curriculum change.* London, England: Routledge & Kegan Paul.

Reinhold, R. (1991, September 29). Class struggle. New York: *The New York Times Magazine*, section 6, 26-29, 46-47, 52.

Reiniger, M. (1982). *Autobiographical search for gyn/ecology: Traces of misogyny in women's schooling.* Rochester, NY: University of Rochester, Graduate School of Education and Human Development, unpublished doctoral dissertation.

Reiniger, M. (1989). Autobiographical search for Gyn/Ecology: Traces of misogyny in women's schooling. *JCT*, 8 (3), 7-88.

Reinsmith, W. (1992). *Archetypal forms in teaching.* New York: Greenwood Press.

Reynolds, W. (1981). *English teaching and ideology.* Rochester, NY: University of Rochester, Graduate School of Education and Human Development, unpublished manuscript.

Reynolds, W. (1983, October). *Curriculum theory, epistemes, formula and familiarity: A critique of the present discourse in curriculum theory.* Paper presented at the Bergamo Conference on the Curriculum Theory and Classroom Practice, Dayton, OH.

Reynolds, W. (1988). Freedom from control: Toward an abolition of teacher materials and minimum competence tests. *JCT*, 7 (4), 65-86.

Reynolds, W. (1989). *Reading curriculum theory: The development of a new hermeneutic.* New York: Peter Lang.

Reynolds, W. (1990). The mission of schools: Participation and empowerment. *Teaching and Learning*, 5 (1), 27-37.

Reynolds, W. (1993). *The curriculum of curiosity or a curriculum of compassion: Bait fishing or shadow casting.* Paper presented to the Bergamo Conference on Curriculum Theory and Classroom Practice, Dayton, OH.

Reynolds, W. & Block, A. (1994). Curriculum as making do. In R. Martusewicz & W. Reynolds (Eds.), *Inside out: Contemporary critical perspectives in education* (209-221). New York: St. Martin's Press.

Reynolds, W. & Martusewicz, R. (1994). The practice of freedom: A historical analysis of critical perspectives in the social foundations. In R. Martusewicz & W. Reynolds (Eds.), *Inside out: Contemporary critical perspectives in education* (223-238). New York: St. Martin's Press.

Rice, J. (1893a). *The public school system of the United States.* New York: Century. [Reprinted in 1969; New York: Arno Press.]

Rice, J. (1893b). The public schools of Chicago and St. Paul. *The Forum*, 15, 200-215.

Rice, J. (1912). *Scientific management in education.* New York: Hinds, Noble & Elredge.

Rice, S. (1993). Teaching and learning through story and dialogue. *Educational Theory*, 43 (1), 85-97.

Rich, A. (1975). Toward a women centered university. In F. Howe (Ed.), *Women and the power to change.* New York: McGraw Hill.

Rich, A. (1976). *Of woman born: Motherhood as experience and institution.* New York: Norton.

Richards, R. & Short, E. (1981). Curriculum inquiry from a religious perspective: Two views. *JCT*, 3 (2), 209-222.

Richardson, V. (1990). Significant and worthwhile change in teaching practice. *Educational Researcher*, 19 (7), 10-18.

Rickover, H. (1959). *Education and freedom.* New York: E. P. Dutton.

Rickover, H. (1963). *American education–a national failure: The problem of our schools and what we can learn from England.* New York: E. P. Dutton.

Ricoeur, P. (1974). *The conflict of interpretations: Essays in hermeneutics.* [Edited D. Ide.] Evanston, IL: Northwestern University Press.

Ricoeur, P. (1981). *Hermeneutics and the human sciences.* [Trans. & edited J. Thompson.] Cambridge, England: Cambridge University Press.

Rippa, S. (1988). *Education in a free society: An American history.* [Sixth edition.] New York: Longman.

Rizvi, F. (1993). Children and the grammar of popular racism. In C. McCarthy & W. Crichlow (Eds.), *Race, identity, and representation in education* (126-139). New York: Routledge.

Robertson, H. (1992). Teacher development and gender equity. In A. Hargreaves & M. Fullan (Eds.), *Understanding teacher development* (43-61). New York: Teachers College Press.

Robinson, F. & Hedge, H. (1982). *Curriculum design for improved learning: A systematic approach.* St. Catherines, Ontario, Canada: Ontario Institute for Studies in Education, Niagara Centre-Curriculum Process Centre.

Robinson, F., Ross, J. & White, F. (1985). *Curriculum development for improved instruction.* Toronto, Ontario, Canada: Ontario Institute for Studies in Education.

Robison, H. (Ed.). (1966). *Precedents and promise in the curriculum field.* Washington, DC: ASCD.

Roby, P. (1973). Institutional barriers to women students in higher education. In A. Rossi & A. Calderwood (Eds.), *Academic women on the move.* New York: Russell Sage.

Rockman, S. & Burke, R. (1991). Television: Classroom use. In A. Lewy (Ed.), *International Encyclopedia of Curriculum* (93-101). Oxford, England: Pergamon Press.

Roderick, J. (1984). *Perspectives on self as teacher: Cracks in the technocratic.* Curriculum Praxis Series, Occasional Paper No. 28. Edmonton, Alberta, Canada: University of Alberta, Faculty of Education, Department of Secondary Education.

Rogan, J. (1991). Curriculum texts: The portrayal of the field. Part II. *Journal of Curriculum Studies,* 23 (1), 55-70.

Rogan, J. & Luckowski, J. (1990). Curriculum texts: The portrayal of the field. Part I. *Journal of Curriculum Studies,* 22 (1), 17-39.

Rogers, C. (1972). Interpersonal relationships: U.S.A. 2000. In D. Purpel & M. Belanger (Eds.), *Curriculum and cultural revolu tion* (411-423). Berkeley, CA: McCutchan.

Rogers, D., Noblit, G., & Ferrell, P. (1990, Summer). Action research as an agent for developing teachers' communicative competence. *Theory Into Practice,* XXIX, (3),179-184.

Rohlen, T. (1983). *Japan's high schools.* Berkeley, CA: University of California Press.

Rohrs, H. (1980). *Die Reformpadagogik: Ursprung und verlauf in Europa.* [*Pedagogical reform: Origin and Courses in Europe*]. Hanover, Germany: Schrodel Hermann.

Roman, L. (1993). White is a color! White defensiveness, postmodernism, and anti-racist pedagogy. In C. McCarthy & W. Crichlow (Eds.), *Race, identity, and representation in education* (71-88). New York: Routledge.

Roman, L. & Christian-Smith, L. (Eds.). (1988). *Feminism and the politics of popular culture.* London, England: Falmer.

Roman, L. & Apple, M. (1990). Is Naturalism a Move Away from Positivism? Materialist and Feminist Approaches to Subjectivity in Ethnographic Research. In E. Eisner & A. Peshkin (Eds.), *Qualitative Inquiry in Education: The Continuing Debate* (38-73). New York: Teachers College Press.

Romer, N. (1992). Building campus community to challenge bigotry and support multi-culturalism. *JCT,* 9 (4), 97-103.

Rono, P. (1988, March). *Education reforms in Kenya in the independence period.* Paper presented at the annual conference of Comparative and International Education Society, Atlanta, GA.

Rorty, R. (1979). *Philosophy and the mirror of nature.* Princeton, NJ: Princeton University Press.

Rorty, R. (1989). *Contingency, irony and solidarity.* New York: Cambridge University Press.

Rorty, R. (1991, May 20). A paradigm for intellectuals: A review of Robert B. Westbrook's *John Dewey and American Democracy. The New Leader,* 13-15.

Rosario, J. (1979). Aesthetics and the curriculum: Persistency, traditional modes, and a different perspective. *JCT,* 1 (1), 136-154.

Rosario, J. (1988). Harold Rugg on how we came to know: A view of his aesthetics. In W. Pinar (Ed.), *Contemporary curriculum discourses* (343-358). Scottsdale, AZ: Gorsuch Scarisbrick.

Roscoe, K. & Jacknicke, K. (1993). *An experience of curriculum change: Science, technology, and society.* Paper presented to the Bergamo Conference on Curriculum Theory and Classroom Practice, Dayton, OH.

Rose, S. (1988). *Keeping them out of the hands of satan: Evangelical schooling in America.* New York: Routledge.

Rosenau, P. (1992). *Postmodernism and the social sciences: Insights, inroads, and intrusions.* Princeton, NJ: Princeton University Press.

Rosenblatt, L. (1938). *Literature as exploration: The transactional theory of literary work.* New York: Appleton-Century.

Rosenshine, B. & Stevens, R. (1986). Teaching functions. In M. Wittrock (Ed.), *Handbook of research on teaching* (376-391). New York: Macmillan.

Rosenstock, S. (1984). *The educational contributions of W. W. Charters.* Columbus, OH: The Ohio State University, College of Education, unpublished Ph.D. dissertation.

Rosenthal, D. & Bybee, R. (1987). Emergence of the biology curriculum: A science of life or a science of living? In T. Popkewitz (Ed.), *The formation of the school subjects* (123-144). New York: Falmer.

Ross, E. (1992). Religion and education: What role should religion play in the public schools? In J. Kincheloe & S. Steinberg (Eds.), *Thirteen questions* (209-214). New York: Peter Lang.

Rossi, P. & Wright, S. (1977). Evaluation research: An assessment of theory, practice, and policies. *Evaluation Quarterly*, 1, 5-51.

Rossman, P. (1992). *The emerging worldwide electronic university: Information age global higher education.* Westport, CT: Greenwood Press.

Roszak, T. (1970). Educating contra naturam. In R. Leeper (Ed.), *A man for tomorrow's world* (12-27). Washington, DC: ASCD.

Rousseau, J. (1955). *Emile.* [Trans. by B. Foxley.] New York: Dutton.

Rubin, G. (1975). The traffic in women: Notes on the "political economy" of sex. In R. Reiter (Ed.), *Towards an anthropology of women.* (157-210). New York: Monthly Review Press.

Rubin, L. (Ed.). (1977). *Curriculum handbook: The disciplines, current movements, and instructional methodology.* Boston, MA: Allyn & Bacon.

Rubin, L. (1985). *Artistry in teaching.* New York: Random House.

Rubin, L (1991). The arts and an artistic curriculum. In G. Willis & W. Schubert (Eds.), *Reflections from the heart of educational inquiry: Understanding curriculum and teaching through the arts.* (49-59). Albany, NY: State University of New York Press.

Rud, Jr., A. (1993). Breaking the egg crate. *Educational Theory*, 43 (1), 71-83.

Rud, Jr., A. & Oldendorf, W. (Eds.).(1992). *A place for teacher renewal: Challenging the intellect, creating educational reform.* [Foreword M. Greene.] New York: Teachers College Press.

Rueda, R. & Mehan, H. (1986). Metacognition and passing: Strategic interactions in the lives of students with learning disabilities. *Anthropology and Education Quarterly*, 17 (3), 145-165.

Ruether, R. (1983a). Christology and the Latin American liberation theology. In *To change the world: Christianity and cultural criticism* (25-26). New York: Crossroads.

Ruether, R. (1983b). *Sexism and God-talk: Toward a feminist theology.* Boston, MA: Beacon Press.

Rugg, H. (1929-1932). *Man and his changing society.* [The Rugg social science series of the elementary school course, vols. 1-6.] Boston, MA: Ginn.

Rugg, H. (1941). *That men may understand: An American in the long armistice.* New York: Doubleday, Doran.

Rugg, H. (1952). *The education of teachers.* New York: Harper & Brothers.

Rugg, H. (1963). *Imagination.* New York: Harper & Row.

Rugg, H. & Schumaker, A. (1928). *The child-centered school: An appraisal of the new education.* New York: World Book Company.

Rugg, H. & Withers, W. (1955). *Social foundations of education.* New York: Prentice-Hall.

Rushcamp, S. & Roehler, L. (1992). Characteristics supporting change in a professional development school. *Journal of Teacher Education,* 43 (1), 19-27.

Russell, N. (1993). *Personal correspondence.* Vancouver, British Columbia, Canada: University of British Columbia, Faculty of Education, Centre for the Study of Curriculum and Instruction.

Russell, N. & Willinsky, J. (1993). *Fourth generation educational evaluation: Pushing a postmodern paradigm.* Vancouver, British Columbia, Canada: University of British Columbia, Faculty of Education, Centre for the Study of Curriculum & Instruction, unpublished manuscript.

Russell, T. & Munby, H. (1991). Reframing: The role of experience in developing teachers' professional knowledge. In D. Schon (Ed.), *The reflective turn: Case studies in and on educational practice* (164-189). New York: Teachers College Press.

Rutherford, F. J. & Ahlgren, A. (1990). *Science for all Americans.* New York: Oxford University Press.

Ryan, J. (1989). Disciplining the Innut: Normalization, characterization, and schooling. *Curriculum Inquiry,* 19 (4), 379-403.

Sacred Congregation for the Doctrine of the Faith (1984). *Instructions on certain aspects of the "theology of liberation."* Boston, MA: Daughters of St. Paul Publishers.

Sadler, D. (1985). The origins and functions of evaluative criteria. *Educational Theory,* 35 (3), 285-297.

Sadowsky, E. (1992). Taking part: Democracy in the elementary school. In A. Garrod (Ed.), *Learning for life: Moral education theory and practice* (246-258). Westport, CT: Praeger.

Saettler, P. (1990). *The evolution of American educational technology.* Englewood, CO: Libraries Unlimited, Inc.

Said, E. (1979). *Orientalism.* New York: Vintage Books.

Said, E. (1990a). Yeats and decolonization. In T. Eagleton, F. Jameson, and E. Said (Eds.), *Nationalism, colonialism, and literature* (69-98). Minneapolis, MN: University of Minnesota Press.

Said, E. (1990b). In the shadow of the west: Edward Said. In R. Ferguson, W. Olander, M. Tucker, & K. Fiss (Eds.), *Discourses: Conversations in postmodern art and culture* (93-104). [P. Mariani & J. Crary, interviewers.] Cambridge, MA: MIT Press.

Said, E. (1993). The politics of knowledge. In. C. McCarthy & W. Crichlow (Eds.), *Race, identity, and education* (306-314). New York & London, England: Routledge.

Salomon, G. (1991). Computers in the classroom. In A. Lewy (Ed.), *International encyclopedia of curriculum* (88-90). Oxford, England: Pergamon Press.

Salvio, P. (1990). Transgressive daughters: Student autobiography and the project of self-creation. *Cambridge Journal of Education,* 20 (3), 283-290.

Salvio, P. (1992). Review of *The moral and spiritual crisis in education. Journal of Curriculum Studies,* 24 (1), 89-91.

Sand, O. (1958). *Curriculum study in basic nursing.* New York: Putnam.

San Francisco Chronicle (1993, December 9). U.S. earns fair marks in education: Report says it compares favorably with other nations (pp. A1, A23). San Francisco, CA: *San Francisco Chronicle.*

Sanger, J. (1990, Summer). Awakening a scream of consciousness: The critical group in action research. *Theory into Practice,* XXIX (3),174-178.

Sapon-Shevin, M. & Goodman, J. (1992). Learning to be the opposite sex: Sexuality education and sexual scripting in early adolescence. In J. Sears (Ed.), *Sexuality and the curriculum* (89-105). New York: Teachers College Press.

Sarason, S. (1990). *The predictable failure of educational reform.* San Francisco, CA: Jossey-Bass.

Sartre, J-P. (1964). *Nausea.* New York: New Directions.

Sartre, J-P. (1965). *What is literature?* [Trans. B. Frechtman.] New York: Harper & Row.

Sartre, J-P. (1968). *Search for a method.* New York: Vintage.

Sartre, J-P. (1972). The artist and his conscience. In B. Lang & F. Williams (Eds.), *Marxism and art.* New York: David McKay.

Sartre, J.-P. (1980). Existentialism and humanism. In B. Porter (Ed.), *Philosophy: A literary and conceptual approach* (481-492). New York: Harcourt Brace.

Sarup, M. (1989). *An introductory guide to post-structuralism and post-modernism.* Athens, GA: University of Georgia Press.

Sauvé, V. (1991). *Windows of meaning in Adult E.S.L.: Teacher meanings in a special basic E.S.L. program for adult immigrants with little formal education.* Edmonton, Alberta, Canada: University of Alberta, Department of Secondary Education, unpublished Ph.D. dissertation.

Sawada, D. (1989, April). *Aesthetics in a post-modern education: The Japanese concept of shibusa.* Paper presented to the annual meeting of the American Educational Research Association, San Francisco, CA.

Sawhill, I., Reich, R. & Thurow, L. (1991, October). *Lectures.* Recall C-Span.

Saylor, G., & Alexander, W. (1954, 1966, 1974). *Curriculum planning for schools.* New York: Holt, Rinehart, & Winston.

Saylor, G., Alexander, W., & Lewis, A. (1981). *Curriculum planning for better teaching and learning.* [Fourth edition. Previous editions: 1954, 1966, 1974]. New York: Holt, Rinehart & Winston.

Schaffarzick, J. (1979). Federal curriculum reform: A crucible for value conflict. In J. Schaffarsick & G. Sykes (Eds.), *Value conflicts and curriculum issues* (1-24). Berkeley, CA: McCutchan.

Schaffarzik, J. & Hampson, D. (Eds.) (1975). *Strategies for curriculum development.* Berkeley, CA: McCutchan

Schaffarsick, J. & Sykes, G. (Eds.). (1979). *Value conflicts and curriculum issues.* Berkeley, CA: McCutchan.

Schaller, K. (1962). *Die padagogik des Johan Amos Comenius und der anafang des padagogischen realismus im 17 Jahrhundert.* [*The pedagogy of Johan Amos Comenius and the rise of the pedagogy of realism in the 17th century*]. Heidelberg, Germany: Quelle & Meyer.

Scheffler, I. (1974). *Four Pragmatists.* New York: Humanities Press. [Also published in 1986 by Routledge in New York.]

Scheler, M. (1980). *Problems of a sociology of knowledge.* Boston, MA: Routledge & Kegan Paul.

Scheurich, J. (1993a). Toward a white discourse on white racism. *Educational Researcher, 22* (8), 5-10.

Scheurich, J. (1993b). A difficult, confusing, painful problem that requires many voices, many perspectives. *Educational Researcher, 22* (8), 15-16.

Scheurich, J. & Lather, P. (1991). Paradigmatic compulsions: A response to Hills' "issues in research on instructional supervision." *Journal of Curriculum and Supervision, 7* (1), 26-30.

Schilling, (1986). Knowledge of liberal education: A critique of Paul Hirst. *Journal of Curriculum Studies, 18* (1), 1-16.

Schilling, P. (1977). *God and human anguish.* Nashville, TN: Abingdon.

Schlesinger, Jr., A. (1991a, July 8). The cult of ethnicity, good and bad. *Time,* 138 (1),12-24.

Schlesinger, Jr., A. (1991b). *The disuniting of America.* New York: Whittle Direct Books.

Schmitt, E. (1993, September 2). Arms for jobs and country. *The New York Times,* A 1.

Schon, D. (1983). *The reflective practitioner: How professionals think in action.* New York: Basic Books.

Schon, D. (Ed.). (1991). *The reflective turn: Case studies in and on educational practice.* New York: Teachers College Press.

Schonhammer, R. (1989). The walkman and the primary world of the senses. *Phenomenology + Pedagogy, 7,* 127-144.

Schoolland, K. (1990). *Shoguns's ghost: The dark side of Japanese education.* South Hadley, MA: Bergin & Garvey.

Schoonover, T. (1991, October). *It's not what we say, it's what we do.* Paper presented at the symposium Rethinking the Cold War Conference, University of Wisconsin, Madison.

Schoonover, T. (1992, February). An analysis of Alex Hybel's social theory. Review of *How leaders reason: U.S. intervention in the Caribbean Basin and Latin America. International History Review,* XIV (1), 139-143.

Schrag, F. (1992a). In defense of positivist research paradigms. *Educational Researcher,* 21 (5), 5-8.

Schrag, F. (1992b). Is there light at the end of this tunnel? *Educational Researcher,* 21, (5), 16-17.

Schubert, W. (1980a). *Curriculum books: The first eighty years.* Landham, MD: University Press of America.

Schubert, W. (1980b). Recalibrating educational research: Toward a focus on practice. *Educational Researcher,* 9 (1), 17-24.

Schubert, W. (1981c, January). Knowledge about out-of-school curriculum. *Educational Forum,* 185-198.

Schubert, W. (1986a). *Curriculum: Perspective, paradigm, and possibility.* New York: Macmillan.

Schubert, W. (1986b). Curriculum research controversy: A special case of a general problem. *Journal of Curriculum and Supervision.* (1) 2, 132-147.

Schubert, W. (1986c). *The synoptic character of curriculum knowledge.* Curriculum Praxis Series, Occasional Paper No. 40. Edmonton, Alberta, Canada: University of Alberta, Faculty of Education, Department of Secondary Education.

Schubert, W. (1987, Fall). Educationally recovering Dewey in the curriculum. *Current Issues in Education* 7, 1-32 .

Schubert, W. (1989a). Thoughts on the future of the Society for the Study of Curriculum History. In C. Kridel (Ed.), *Curriculum history* (19-23). Landham, MD: University Press of America.

Schubert, W. (1989b). Reconceptualizing and the matter of paradigms. *Journal of Teacher Education,* XXXX (1), 27-32.

Schubert, W. (1989c). Teacher lore: A neglected basis for understanding curriculum and supervision. *Journal of Curriculum and Supervision,* 4 (3), 282-285.

Schubert, W. (1990). The question of worth as central to curricular empowerment. In J. Sears & D. Marshall (Eds.), *Teaching and thinking about curriculum* (211-227). New York: Teachers College Press.

Schubert, W. (1991a). National systems of education. In A. Lewy (Ed.), *The international encyclopedia of curriculum.* New York: Pergamon Press.

Schubert, W. (1991b). Teacher lore: A basis for understanding praxis. In C. Witherell & N. Noddings (Eds.), *Stories lives tell: Narrative and dialogue in education.* New York: Teachers College Press.

Schubert, W. (1992a). On mentorship: Examples from J. Harlan Shores and others through lenses provided by James B. Macdonald. *JCT,* 9 (3), 47-69.

Schubert, W. (1992b). Our journeys into teaching: Remembering the past. In W. Schubert & W. Ayers (Eds.), *Teacher lore* (3-10). New York: Longman.

Schubert, W. & Ayers, W. (Eds.). (1992). *Teacher lore: Learning from our own experience*. New York: Longman.

Schubert, W. & Posner, G. (1980). Origins of the curriculum field based on a study of mentor-student relationships. *JCT*, 2 (2), 37-67.

Schubert, W. & Schubert, A. (1981). Toward curricula that are of, by, and therefore for students. *JCT*, 3 (1), 239-251.

Schubert, W. & Schubert, A. (1982). Teaching curriculum theory. *JCT*, 4 (2), 97-111.

Schubert, W, Schubert, A. & Herzog, L. (1986, April). *Curriculum books, 1980-86: Bibliography and discussion*. Paper presented at the annual meeting of the American Educational Research Association, San Francisco, CA.

Schubert, W., Schubert, A. & Schubert, H. (1986, Summer). Familial theorizing and "literatures" that facilitate it. *Journal of Thought*, 21 (2), 61-73.

Schubert, W., Weston, N., Ponticell, J. & Melnick, C. (1987). *Teacher lore project: The first year*. Panel presentation to the Bergamo Conference, Dayton, OH.

Schubert, W., Lopez-Schubert, A., Herzog, L., Posner, G. & Kridel, C. (1988). A genealogy of curriculum researchers. *JCT*, 8 (1), 137-184.

Schuster, M. & van Dyne, S. (1985). *Women's place in the academy: Transforming the liberal arts curriculum*. Totowa, NJ: Rowan & Allanheld.

Schultz, D. (1984). *Human sexuality*. [Second edition]. Englewood Cliffs, NJ: Prentice-Hall.

Schutz, A. (1967). *The phenomenology of the social world*. [Trans. G. Walsh & F. Lehnert. Introduction G. Walsh.] Evanston, IL: Northwestern University Press.

Schwab, J. (1964a). Problems, topics, and issues. In S. Elam (Ed.), *Education and the structure of knowledge* (4-47). Chicago, IL: Rand McNally.

Schwab, J. (1964b). Structure of the disciplines: Meanings and signficances. In G. Ford & L. Pugno (Eds.), *The structure of knowledge and the curriculum* (1-30). Chicago, IL: Rand McNally.

Schwab, J. (1964c). The structure of the natural sciences. In G. Ford & L. Pugno (Eds.), *The structure of knowledge and the curriculum* (31-49) Chicago, IL: Rand McNally.

Schwab, J. (1970). *The practical: A language for curriculum*. Washington, DC: National Education Association. [Also (1969) University of Chicago *School Review*; in (1972) in D. Purpel & M. Belanger (Eds.), *Curriculum and cultural revolution* (79-99); in (1977) in A. Bellack & H. Kliebard (Eds.), *Curriculum and evaluation* (26-45). Berkeley, CA: McCutchan. Citations here are to Bellack & Kliebard reprint.]

Schwab, J. (1978). *Science, curriculum and liberal education: Selected essays, Joseph J. Schwab*. [Edited I. Westbury & N. Wilkof.] Chicago, IL: University of Chicago Press.

Schwab, J. (1983, Fall). The practical 4: Something for curriculum professors to do. *Curriculum Inquiry*, 13, 239-266.

Schwager, S. (1987, Winter). Educating women in America. *Signs*, 12 (2), 333-373.

Schwartz, B. & Disch, R. (1970). *White racism*. New York: Dell.

Schwartz, E. (1991, September 22). The radicalism of a liberal: A review of Robert B. Westbrook's *John Dewey and American democracy*. New York: *The New York Times*, Section 7, 48-49.

Schwartz, J. (1979a). Review of Carbone's *The Social and educational thought of Harold Rugg. JCT*, 1 (1), 258-262.

Schwartz, J. (1979b). The world of Harold Rugg and the question of objectivity. *JCT*, 1 (2), 100-238.

Scobey, M. & Graham, G. (Eds.). (1970). *To nurture humaneness: A commitment for the 70s*. Washington, DC: ASCD.

Scott, J. (1991, September 11). Liberal historians: A unitary vision. *Chronicle of Higher Education*, XXXVIII (3), B1-B2.

Scriven, M. (1967). The methodology of evaluation. In R. Tyler, R. Gagne, & M. Scriven (Eds.), *Perspectives of curriculum evaluation*. A.E.R.A. monograph series on curriculum evaluation, no. 1. Chicago, IL: Rand McNally.

Scriven, M. (1972). Education for survival. In D. Purpel & M. Belanger (Eds.), *Curriculum and cultural revolution* (166-204). Berkeley, CA: McCutchan.

Scriven, M. (1973). Goal-free evaluation. In E. House (Ed.), *School evaluation: The politics and the process*. Berkeley, CA: McCutchan.

Scriven, M. (1987). *The rights of technology in education: The need for consciousness raising*. A paper for the Education and Technology Task Force. Adelaide, South Australia, Australia: Ministry of Education and Technology.

Seamon, D. (1989). Phenomenology + Pedagogy: A "Repository for the Romantic and the Nostalgic?" *Phenomenology + Pedagogy*, 7, 257-262.

Searles, W. (1982). A substantiation of Macdonald's models in science curriculum development. *JCT*, 4 (1), 127-155.

Sears, J. (1983, Spring). Sexuality: Taking off the masks. *Changing Schools*, 11, 12-13.

Sears, J. (1985). Rethinking teacher education: Dare we work toward a new social order. *JCT*, 6 (2), 24-79.

Sears, J. (1987a). Peering into the well of loneliness: The responsibility of educators to gay and lesbian youth. In A. Molnar (Ed.), *Social Issues and Education* (79-100). Alexandria, VA: ASCD.

Sears, J. (1987b). *Developing a Sense of Difference among Gay and Lesbian Children in the Deep South: The Difference between Being Queer and Being Different*. Paper presented at the 1987 Bergamo Conference, Dayton, OH.

Sears, J. (1988a, Fall). Growing up gay: Is anyone there to listen? *American School Counselors Newsletter*, 26, 8-9.

Sears, J. (1988b, April 7). *Attitudes, experiences, and feelings of guidance counselors in working with homosexual students: A report on the quality of school life for southern gay and lesbian students*. Paper presented at the annual meeting of the American Educational Research Association, New Orleans, LA. [ERIC Document Reproduction Service No. ED 296-210.]

Sears, J. (1989a, Fall/Winter). Playing out our feelings: The use of reader's theater in anti-oppression work. *Empathy*, 2, 33-37.

Sears, J. (1989b). *Personal feelings and professional of prospective teachers toward homosexuality and homosexual students*. Paper presented at the annual meeting of the American Educational Research Association. [ERIC Document Reproduction Service No. ED 312 222.]

Sears, J. (1989c, Spring). The impact of gender and race on growing up lesbian and gay in the south. *NWSA Journal*, 1 (3), 421-456.

Sears, J. (1990a). *Growing up gay in the south*. New York & London, England: Haworth Press.

Sears, J. (1990b, April). *On conducting homosexual research*. Paper presented at the annual meeting of the American Education Research Association, Boston, MA.

Sears, J. (Ed.). (1992a). *Sexuality and the curriculum*. New York: Teachers College Press.

Sears, J. (1992b, Summer). The second wave of curriculum theorizing: Labyrinths, orthodoxies, and other legacies of the glass bead game. *Theory into Practice*, XXXI (3), 210-218.

Sears, J. & Marshall, D. (Eds.). (1990). *Teaching and thinking about curriculum: Critical inquiries*. [Foreword N. Noddings]. New York: Teachers College Press.

Sears, P. & Feldman, D. (1974). Teacher interactions with boys and with girls. In J. Stacey, S. Bereaud & J. Daniels (Eds.), *And Jill came tumbling after: Sexism in American education*. New York: Dell.

Segal, L. (1990). *Slow motion: Changing masculinities, changing men*. New Brunswick, NJ: Rutgers University Press.

Seguel, M. (1966). *The curriculum field: Its formative years*. New York: Teachers College Press.

Selden, S. (1985). Education policy and biological science: Genetics, eugenics, and the college textbook, c. 1908-1931. *Teachers College Record*, 87 (1), 35-51.

Selden, S. (1988). Biological determinism and the normal school curriculum: Helen Putnam & the N.E.A. Committee on Racial Well-Being, 1910-1922. In W. Pinar (Ed.), *Contemporary curriculum discourses* (50-65). Scottsdale, AZ: Gorsuch Scarisbrick.

Senese, G. (1991). Warnings on resistance and the language of possibility: Gramsci and a pedagogy from the surreal. *Educational Theory*, 41 (1), 13-22.

Sendor, B. (1988). *A legal guide to religion and public education*. Topeka, KS: National Organization on Legal Problems of Education.

Serbin, L. & O'Leary, K. (1975). How nursery schools teach girls to shut up. *Psychology Today*, 9, 56-58.

Sergiovanni, T. (1976). Toward a theory of clinical supervision. *Journal of Research and Development in Education*, 9 (22), 20-29.

Sergiovanni, T. (1984). Expanding conceptions of inquiry and practice in supervision and evaluation. *Educational Evaluation and Policy Analysis*, 6 (4), 355-365.

Sergiovanni, T. (1987). The metaphorical use of theories and models in supervision: Building a science. *Journal of Curriculum and Supervision*, 2 (3), 221-232.

Sergiovanni, T. (1989). Science and scientism in supervision and teaching. *Journal of Curriculum and Supervision*, 4 (2), 93-105.

Sergiovanni, T. & Starratt, R. (1971). *Emerging patterns of supervision: Human perspectives*. [Later editions: 1979, 1983, 1988]. New York: McGraw-Hill.

Segundo, J. (1973). *The shift within Latin American theology*. Toronto, Ontario, Canada: Regis College Press.

Serres, M. (1983). *Hermes: Literature, science, philosophy*. Baltimore, MD: Johns Hopkins University Press.

Sewall, G. (1983). *Necessary lessons: Decline and renewal in American schools*. New York: The Free Press.

Shaker, P. (1990). Foundations of education as a curriculum laboratory. In J. Sears & D. Marshall (Eds.), *Teaching and thinking about curriculum* (228-242). New York: Teachers College Press.

Shaker, P. & Kridel, C. (1989). The return to experience: A reconceptualist call. *Journal of Teacher Education*, XXXX (1), 2-8.

Shane, H. (1977). *Curriculum change: Toward the 21st century*. Washington, DC: National Education Association.

Shanker, A. (1986, October 26). Power vs. knowledge in St. Louis: Professionals under fire. *New York Times*.

Shanker, A. (1990). The end of the traditional model of schooling—and a proposal for using incentives to restructure our public schools. *Phi Delta Kappa*, 71 (5), 244-357.

Shannon, N. & Meath-Lang, B. (1992). Collaborative language teaching: A co-investigation. In D. Nunan (Ed.), *Collaborative Language Teaching and Learning* (120-140). Cambridge, England: Cambridge University Press.

Shapiro, H. (1981). Functionalism, the state, and education: Towards a new analysis. *Social Praxis*, 98 (3/4), 5-24.

Shapiro, H. (1982a). Shaping the educational imagination: Class, culture and the contradictions of the dominant ideology. *JCT*, 4 (2), 153-165.

Shapiro, H. (1982b). The making of conservative educational policy: Middle-class anxieties and corporate profitability in the 1980's. *Urban Education*, 17 (2), 233-252.

Shapiro, H. (1983a). Class, ideology and the basic skills movement: A study in the sociology of educational reform. *Interchange*, 14 (2), 14-24.

Shapiro, H. (1983b). Schools, work and consumption: Education and the cultural contradictions of capitalism. *The Journal of Educational Thought*, 17 (3), 209-220.

Shapiro, H. (1984a). Choosing our educational legacy: Disempowerment or emancipation. *Issues in Education*, II (1), 11-22.

Shapiro, H. (1984b). Crisis of legitimation: Schools, society, and the declining faith in education. *Interchange*, 15 (4), 26-39.

Shapiro, H. (1986a). Curriculum alternatives in a survivalist culture: Basic skills and the 'minimal self.' *New Education*, 8 (2), 3-14.

Shapiro, H. (1986b). Schooling and the left: Policy alternatives for education and the economy in the 80's. *The Journal of Educational Thought*, 20 (2), 77-89.

Shapiro, H. (1987). Educational theory and recent political discourse: A new agenda for the left. *Teachers College Record*, 89 (2), 171-200.

Shapiro, H. (1988a). Beyond the sociology of education: Culture, politics, and the promise of educational change. *Educational Theory*, 38 (4), 415-430.

Shapiro, H. (1988b). Education and democracy: Constituting a counter-hegemonic discourse of educational change. *JCT*, 8 (3), 89-122.

Shapiro, H. (1988c). Education and the language of politics: Towards an agenda for radical change. *Educational Policy*, 2 (3), 251-263.

Shapiro, H. (1989). *Pedagogy in a time of uncertainty: Post-modernism and the struggle for community*. Greensboro, NC: University of North Carolina at Greensboro, School of Education, unpublished manuscript.

Shapiro, H. (1990). *The end of radical hope? Postmodernism and the challenge to radical pedagogy*. Greensboro, NC: University of North Carolina at Greensboro, School of Education.

Shapiro, H. & Purpel, D. (Eds.) (1993). *Critical social issues in American education: Toward the 21st century*. New York: Longman.

Sharp, R. (1980). *Knowledge, ideology and the politics of schooling: Towards a marxist analysis of education*. London, England: Routledge & Kegan Paul.

Shaw, K. (1987). Curriculum, management and the improvement of education: Forging a practical alliance. *Journal of Curriculum Studies, 19* (3), 203-218.

Shea, C. (1992). NCCAT's search for a teacher renewal philosophy: An historical account. In A. Rud, Jr. & W. Oldendorf, (Eds.), *A place for teacher renewal: Challenging the intellect, creating educational reform* (1-24). [Foreword M. Greene.] New York: Teachers College Press.

Shea, C., Kahane, E., & Sola, P. (1989). *The new servants of power: A critique of the 1980's school reform movement*. New York: Greenwood Press.

Shive, G. (1991). East Asia survey of events, 1990. *Comparative Education Review*, 35 (2), 386-389.

Shor, I. (1986). *Culture wars: School and society in the conservative restoration 1969-1984*. New York: Routledge & Kegan Paul.

Shor, I. (1987a). *Critical teaching and everyday life*. [Third printing]. Chicago, IL: University of Chicago Press.

Shor, I. (Ed.). (1987b). *Freire for the classroom: A sourcebook for liberatory teaching*. Portsmouth, NH: Boynton/Cook.

Shor, I. (1993). Education is politics: Paulo Freire's critical pedagogy. In P. McLaren & P. Leonard (Eds.), *Paulo Freire: A critical encounter* (25-35). London & New York: Routledge.

Shor, I. & Freire, P. (1987a). *A pedagogy for liberation: Dialogues for liberatory teaching.* Portsmouth, NH: Boynton/Cook Publishers.

Shor, I. & Freire, P. (1987b). What is the dialogical method of teaching? *Journal of Education,* 169, 11-31.

Short, E. (1973). Knowledge production and utilization in curriculum. *Review of Educational Research,* 43 (3), 237-301.

Short, E. (1985). Organizing what we know about curriculum. *Curriculum Inquiry,* 15 (3), 237-243.

Short, E. (1986). A historical look at curriculum design. *Theory Into Practice,* XXV (1), 3-9.

Short, E. (1990). Challenging the trivialization of curriculum through research. In J. Sears & D. Marshall (Eds.), *Teaching and thinking about curriculum* (138-153). New York: Teachers College Press.

Short, E. (Ed.). (1991). *Forms of curriculum inquiry.* Albany, NY: State University of New York Press.

Short, E. (1992). Beginning the conversation: Critical analysis of the 1992 handbook of research on curriculum. *Journal of Curriculum and Supervision,* 8 (1), 1.

Short, E., Willis, G. & Schubert, W. (1985). *Toward excellence in curriculum inquiry: The story of the AERA special interest group on creation and utilization of curriculum knowledge: 1970-1984.* State College, PA: Nittany Press.

Showalter, E. (1990). *Sexual anarchy: Gender and culture at the fin de siecle.* New York: Viking.

Shuchat-Shaw, F. (1974). The listeners. In W. Pinar (Ed.), *Heightened consciousness, cultural revolution, and curriculum theory: The proceedings of the Rochester conference* (156-160). Berkeley, CA: McCutchan.

Shuchat-Shaw, F. (1979). Congruence: The relation of curriculum to instruction. *Impact,* 14 (3), 15-18.

Shuchat-Shaw, F. (1980). The meanings of congruence. *JCT,* 2 (1), 178-202.

Shulman, J. (1989). Blue freeways: Traveling the alternative route with big-city teacher trainees. *Journal of Teacher Education,* XXXX (5), 2-8.

Shulman, J. (1991). Revealing the mysteries of teacher-written cases: Opening the black box. *Journal of Teacher Education,* 42 (4), 250-262.

Shulman, J. (1992a). Teacher-written cases with commentaries: A teacher-researcher collaboration. In J. Shulman (Ed.), *Case methods in teacher education* (131-154). New York: Teachers College Press.

Shulman, J. (Ed.). (1992b). *Case methods in teacher education.* New York: Teachers College Press.

Shulman, L. (1983). Autonomy and obligation: The remote control of teaching. In L. Shulman & G. Sykes (Eds.), *Handbook of teaching and policy* (484-504). New York: Longman.

Shulman, L. (1984). The practical and the eclectic: A deliberation on teaching and educational research. *Curriculum Inquiry,* 14 (2), 183-200.

Shulman, L. (1986a). Paradigms and research programs in the study of teaching: A contemporary perspective. In M. Wittrock (Ed.), *Handbook of research on teaching* (3-36). [Third edition.] New York: Macmillan.

Shulman, L. (1986b). Those who understand: Knowledge growth in teaching. *Educational Researcher*, 15 (2), 4-14.

Shulman, L. (1987). Knowledge and teaching: Foundations of the new reform. *Harvard Educational Review*, 57 (1), 1-22.

Shulman, L. (1992). Toward a pedagogy of cases. In J. Shulman (Ed), *Case methods in teacher education* (1-32). New York: Teachers College Press.

Shymansky, J. & Kyle, Jr., W. (1988). A summary of research in science education—1986. *Science Education*, 72 (3), 249-402.

Sieber, S. (1968). Organizational influences on innovative roles. In T. Eidell & J. Kitchel (Eds.), *Knowledge production and utilization in educational administration* (120-142). Eugene, OR: Center for Advanced Study of Educational Administration, University of Oregon.

Siegel, H. (1988). *Educating reason*. London, England: Routledge.

Silberman, C. (1970). *Crisis in the classroom: The remaking of American education*. New York: Random House.

Silin, J. (1992). School-based HIV/AIDS education: Is there safety in safer sex? In J. Sears (Ed.), *Sexuality and the curriculum* (267-283). New York: Teachers College Press.

Silva, E. (1993, November 3-5). *Trends and challenges on curriculum decentralization in Latin America*. Santiago, Chile: Regional Office for Education in Latin America and the Caribbean [OREALC], UNESCO.

Silvers, R. (1984). Teaching phenomenology. *Phenomenology + Pedagogy*, 2 (1), 18-31.

Simon, R. (1987, April). Empowerment as a pedagogy of possibility. *Language Arts*, 64 (4).

Simon, R. (1992a). *Teaching against the grain*. South Hadley, MA: Bergin & Garvey.

Simon, R. (1992b, 1993). *Forms of insurgency in the production of popular memories: The Columbus Quincentenary and the pedagogy of counter-commemoration*. Toronto, Ontario, Canada: Ontario Institute for Studies in Education, unpublished paper. Published in 1993 in H. Giroux & P. McLaren (Eds.), *Between borders: Pedagogy and the politics of cultural studies* (127-142). New York: Routledge.

Simon, R. & Dippo, D. (1980). Dramatic analysis: Interpretive inquiry for the transformation of social settings. *JCT*, 2 (1), 109-134.

Simon, R. & Dippo, D. (1986). On critical ethnographic work. *Anthropology and Education Quarterly*, 17 (4), 195-202.

Simons, H. (Ed.). (1980). *Towards a science of the singular*. Occasional Publication No. 10. Norwich (U.K.): Centre for Applied Research in Education, University of East Anglia.

Simpson, E. (1986). A values-clarification retrospective. *Educational Theory*, 36 (3), 271-287.

Simpson, L. (1983). *The dispossessed garden*. Baton Rouge, LA: Louisiana State University Press.

Sirotnik, K., Goldenberg, C., & Oakes, J. (1986). Teachers meeting technology: Computer courseware authoring in schools. *Journal of Curriculum and Supervision*, 1 (4), 316-330.

Sizemore, B. (1990). The Madison elementary school: A turnaround case. In K. Lomotey (Ed.), *Going to school: The African-American experience* (155-180). Albany, NY: State University of New York Press.

Sizer, T. (1984). *Horace's compromise: The dilemma of the American high school.* Boston, MA: Hougton Mifflin.

Sizer, T. (1989). Diverse practices, shared ideas: The essential school. In H. Walberg & J. Lane (Eds.), *Organizing for learning: Toward the 21st century.* Reston, VA: National Association of Secondary School Principals.

Skilbeck, M. (1985). Curriculum organization. In T. Husen & T. Postlethwaite (Eds.), *International encyclopedia of education* (1229-1233). Oxford, England: Pergamon.

Skinner, B. (1954, Spring). The science of learning and the art of teaching. *Harvard Educational Review*, 24, 86-97.

Skinner, B. (1965, July). Review lecture: The technology of teaching. *Proceedings of the Royal Society* 162, 427-443.

Sklar, K. (1976). *Catherine Beecher: A study in American domesticity.* New York: Norton.

Skoog, G. (1979). Topic of evolution in secondary school textbooks 1900-1977. *Science Education*, 63 (5), 621-640.

Skoog, G. (1984). The coverage of evolution in high school biology textbooks published in the 1980s. *Science Education*, 68 (2), 117-128.

Slattery, P. (1989). *Toward an eschatological curriculum theory.* Baton Rouge, LA: Louisiana State University, Department of Curriculum and Instruction, unpublished Ph.D. dissertation.

Slattery, P. (1992a). Toward an eschatological curriculum theory. *JCT*, 9 (3), 7-22.

Slattery, P. (1992b, October 17). *Liberation theology and postmodern pedagogy: Lessons from the debate between Gustavo Gutierrez and the Vatican Congregation for the Doctrine of Faith.* Paper presented to the Bergamo Conference on Curriculum Theory and Classroom Practice, Dayton, OH.

Slattery, P. (1993). Postmodern schooling, curriculum, and the theological text. In M. Evans (Ed.), *Schooling for the Postmodern World.* Bellemead, NJ: Appe.

Slattery, P. (in press). *Curriculum development in the postmodern era.* New York: Garland.

Slattery, P. & Daigle, K. (1992, October). *Curriculum as a place of turmoil: Uncovering the source of anguish in Ernest Gaines' Pointe Coupee and Walker Percey's Feliciana.* Paper presented to the Bergamo Conference, Dayton, OH.

Sleeter, C. (1992a). *Keepers of the American dream: A study of staff development and multicultural education.* London, England: Falmer.

Sleeter, C. (1992b). Resisting racial awareness: How teachers understand the social order from their racial, gender, and social class locations. *Educational Foundations*, 6 (2), 7-32.

Sleeter, C. (1993a). How white teachers construct race. In C. McCarthy & W. Crichlow (Eds.), *Race, identity, and representation in education* (157-171). New York: Routledge.

Sleeter, C. (1993b). Advancing a white discourse: A response to Scheurich. *Educational Researcher*, 22 (8), 13-15.

Sleeter, C. (1994). Resisting racial awareness: How teachers understand the social order from their racial, gender, and social class locations. In R. Martusewicz & W. Reynolds (Eds.), *Inside out: Contemporary critical perspectives in education* (239-264). New York: St. Martin's Press.

Sleeter, C. & Grant, C. (1988). *Making choices for multicultural education: Five approaches to race, class, and gender*. Columbus, OH: Merrill.

Sleeter, C., Gutierrez, W., New, C., Takata, S. (1992). Race and education: In what ways does race affect the educational process? In J. Kincheloe & S. Steinberg (Eds.), *Thirteen questions* (173-182). New York: Peter Lang.

Sloan, D. (1971). Harmony, chaos, and consensus: The American college curriculum. *Teachers College Record*, 73 (2), 221-251.

Sloan, D. (Ed.). (1985). *The computer in education*. New York: Teachers College Press.

Sloane, D. & Sloane, B. (1990). AIDS in schools: A comprehensive initiative. *McGill Journal of Education*, 25 (2), 205-228.

Smith, B., Stanley, W., & Shores, H. (1950, 1957). *Fundamentals of curriculum development*. New York: World Book Co. [1957 revised edition published by Harcourt Brace and World.]

Smith, B. & Orlosky, D. (1975). *Socialization and schooling*. Bloomington, IN: Phi Delta Kappa.

Smith, D. (1983a). Learning to live in the home of language: Hearing the pedagogic voice as poetic. *Phenomenology + Pedagogy*, 1 (1), 29-35.

Smith, D. (1983b). *The meaning of children in the lives of adults: A hermeneutic study*. Edmonton, Alberta, Canada: University of Alberta, Faculty of Education, Department of Secondary Education, unpublished Ph.D. dissertation.

Smith, D. (1988a). Experimental eidetics as a way of entering curriculum language from the ground up. In W. Pinar (Ed.), *Contemporary curriculum discourses* (417-436). Scottsdale, AZ: Gorsuch Scarisbrick.

Smith, D. (1988b). Children and the gods of war. *The Journal of Educational Thought*, 22 (2A), 173-177. [Reprinted from *Elements*, 19 (1).]

Smith, D. (1991a). Hermeneutic inquiry: The hermeneutic imagination and the pedagogic text. In E. Short (Ed.), *Forms of curriculum inquiry* (187-209). Albany, NY: State University of New York Press.

Smith, D. (1991b). *Pedagogy as an international narrative practice*. Lethbridge, Alberta: University of Lethbridge, Faculty of Education, unpublished manuscript.

Smith, D. (1993). *African America students' perceptions of mandatory participation in a remedial program at a historically black university in the South.* Baton Rouge, LA: Louisiana State University, Department of Curriculum and Instruction, unpublished Ph.D. dissertation.

Smith, E. & Tyler, R. (1942). *Adventures in American education, III: Appraising and recording student progress.* New York: Harper & Brothers.

Smith, F. (1993). *Whose language? What power? A universal conflict in a South African setting.* New York: Teachers College Press.

Smith, L. & Keith, P. (1971). *Anatomy of an educational innovation: An organizational analysis of an elementary school.* New York: Wiley.

Smith, L., Kleine, P., Prunty, J. & Dwyer, D. (1992). School improvement and educator personality. In I. Goodson (Ed.), *Studying Teachers Lives* (153-166). New York: Teachers College Press.

Smith, M. (1987). Publishing qualitative research. *American Educational Research Journal*, 24 (2), 173-183.

Smith, N. (1945, April). The core program. *Social Studies*, 36, 164-168.

Smith, N. (1978). *The development of new evaluation methodologies.* Portland, OR: Research on Evaluation Program Paper and Report Series, Northwest Regional Educational Laboratory.

Smith, N. (1980). Classic 1960's articles in educational evaluation. *Paper and Report Series of Northwest Regional Educational Laboratory.* Portland, OR: Northwest Regional Educational Laboratory.

Smith, N. (1981a). *Metaphors for evaluation: Sources for new methods.* Beverly Hills, CA: Sage.

Smith, N. (1981b). *New techniques for evaluation.* Beverly Hills, CA: Sage.

Smith, P. (1988). *Decentering the subject.* Minneapolis, MN: University of Minnesota Press

Smith, S. (1988, April). *Risk and the playground.* Paper presented to the annual meeting of the American Educational Research Association, New Orleans, LA.

Smith, S. (1989). Operating on a child's heart: A pedagogical view of hospitalization. *Phenomenology + Pedagogy*, 7, 145-162.

Smith, S. (1990). The riskiness of the playground. *The Journal of Educational Thought*, 24 (2), 71-87.

Smyth, J. (Ed.). (1986). *Learning about teaching through clinical supervision.* London, England: Croom & Held.

Smyth, J. (1989). A critical pedagogy of classroom practice. *Journal of Curriculum Studies*, 21 (6), 483-502.

Smyth, J. (1991). Problematising teaching through a 'critical' approach to clinical supervision. *Curriculum Inquiry*, 21 (3), 321-352.

Smyth, J. & Garman, N. (1989, Winter). Supervision as school reform: A critical pedagogical perspective. *Journal of Education Policy*, 4.

Snarey, J. & Pavkov, T. (1992). Moral character education in the United States: Beyond socialization versus development. In A. Garrod (Ed.), *Learning for life: Moral education theory and practice* (25-46). Westport, CT: Praeger.

Snedden, D. (1921). *Sociological determination of objectives in education.* Philadelphia, PA: J. B. Lippincott Company.

Snedden, D. (1923). "Case group" methods of determining flexibility of general curricula in high schools. *School and Society,* 17, 287-292.

Snedden, D. (1924). Junior high school offerings. *School and Society,* 20, 740-744.

Snedden, D. (1925). Planning curriculum research. *School and Society,* 22, 259-265, 287-293, 319-328.

Snyder, J., Bolin, F., & Zumwalt, K. (1992). Curriculum implementation. In P. Jackson (Ed.), *Handbook of research on curriculum* (402-435). New York: Macmillan.

Sobrino, J. (1985). *Spirituality of liberation: Toward political holiness.* Maryknoll, NY: Orbis.

Sockett, H. (1989). Research, practice and professional aspiration within teaching. *Journal of Curriculum Studies,* 21 (2), 97-112.

Socket, H. (1993). *The moral base for teacher professionalism.* New York: Teachers College Press.

Solas, J. (1992). Investigating teacher and student thinking about the process of teaching and learning using autobiography and repertory grid. *Review of Educational Research,* 62 (2), 205-225.

Solomon, C. (1986). *Computer environments for children.* Cambridge, MA: MIT Press.

Sontag, S. (1966). *Against interpretation.* New York: Octagon Books.

Sontag, S. (1978). *On photography.* New York: Farrar, Strauss & Giroux.

Spears, H. (1951). *The teacher and curriculum planning.* Englewood Cliffs, NJ: Prentice-Hall.

Spencer, H. (1860). What knowledge is of most worth? Chapter 1 in *Education.* New York: Appleton.

Spivak, G. (1989). Who claims alterity? In B. Kruger & P. Mariani (Eds.), *Remaking history* (269-292). Seattle, WA: Bay Press.

Spivak, G. (1990). *The post-colonial critic: Interviews, strategies, dialogues.* [Edited S. Harasym.] New York: Routledge.

Spodek, B. (1985). Reflections in early childhood education. *JCT,* 6 (3), 54-64.

Spring, J. (1972). *Education and the rise of the corporate state.* Boston, MA: Beacon Press.

Spring, J. (1986). *The American high school 1642-1985: Varieties of historical interpretation and development of American education.* New York: Longman.

Spring, J. (1989). *The sorting machine revisited: National educational policy since 1945.* New York: Longman.

Squire, J. & Morgan, R. (1990). The elementary and high school textbook market today. In D. Elliott & A. Woodward (Eds.), *Eighty-Ninth Yearbook of the National Society for the Study of Education* (107-126). Chicago, IL: National Society for the Study of Education.

Stake, R. (1967). The countenance of educational evaluation. *Teachers College Record,* 68, 523-540.

Stake, R. (1972). *Responsive evaluation*. Urbana-Champaign, IL: University of Illinois, College of Education.

Stake, R. (Ed.). (1975). *Evaluating the arts in education: A responsive approach.* Columbus, OH: Merrill.

Stake, R. & Easley, Jr., J. (1978). *Case studies in science education*. Urbana, IL: Center for Instructional Research and Curriculum Evaluation, University of Illinois.

Stanley, W. (1987). Christopher Lasch as social educator. *Educational Theory*, 37 (3), 229-250.

Stanley, W. (1992a). Socioeconomic class and education: In what ways does class affect the educational process? In J. Kincheloe & S. Steinberg (Eds.), *Thirteen questions* (197-206). New York: Peter Lang.

Stanley, W. (1992b). *Curriculum for utopia: Social reconstructionism and critical pedagogy in the postmodern era*. Albany, NY: State University of New York Press.

Stanley, W. & Nelson, J. (1994). The foundations of social education in historical context. In R. Martusewicz & W. Reynolds (Eds.), *Inside out: Contemporary critical perspectives in education* (265-284). New York: St. Martin's Press.

Starratt, R. (1974). Curriculum theory: Controversy, challenge, and future concerns. In W. Pinar (Ed.), *Heightened consciousness, cultural revolution, and curriculum theory: The proceedings of the Rochester conference* (16-35). Berkeley, CA: McCutchan.

Starratt, R. (1989). Knowing at the level of sympathy: A curriculum challenge. *Journal of Curriculum and Supervision*, 4 (3) 271-281.

Starratt, R. (1990). *The drama of schooling/the schooling of drama*. London, England: Falmer.

Steffere, B. (1975). Run, mama, run: Women workers in elementary readers. In E. Maccia, M. Estep & T. Shiel (Eds.), *Women and education*. Springfield, IL: Charles C. Thomas.

Stefik, M. (1986). The next knowledge medium. *AI Magazine*, 7 (2), 34-46.

Steinberg, S. (1992a). Teachers under suspicion: Is it true that teachers aren't as good as they used to be? In J. Kincheloe & S. Steinberg (Eds.), *Thirteen questions* (67-72). New York: Peter Lang.

Steinberg, S. (1992b). Critical multiculturalism and democratic schooling: An interview with Peter McLaren and Joe Kincheloe. *International Journal of Educational Reform*, 1 (4), 392-405.

Steinberg, S. & Berry, K. (1995). *Re-acting: Drama as an agent for change*. New York: Garland.

Steinbergh, J. (1991). To arrive in another world: Poetry, language development, and culture. *Harvard Educational Review*, 61 (1), 51-70.

Steiner, R. (1894). *The philosophy of freedom. [Die philosophie der freiheit: Grundzuge einer modernen weltanschaung*. Berlin, Germany: E. Felber.]

Stelly, L. (1991). *Multicultural perspectives: The analysis of an urban school district's systemic process*. Baton Rouge, LA: Louisiana State University,

Department of Curriculum and Instruction, unpublished Ph.D. dissertation.

Stenhouse, L. (1971). The humanities project: The rationale. *Theory Into Practice* 10, 154-162.

Stenhouse, L. (1975). *An introduction to curriculum research and development.* London, England: Heineman.

Stenhouse, L. (1980). *Curriculum research and development in action.* London, England: Heinemann Educational Books.

Stenhouse, L. (1983). *Authority, education and emancipation.* London, England: Heinemann.

Stenhouse, L. (1988). Artistry and teaching: The teacher as focus of research and development. *Journal of Curriculum and Supervision*, 4 (1), 43-51.

Sternberg, R. (1985, November). Teaching critical thinking, part 1: Are we making critical mistakes? *Phi Delta Kappan*, 67, 194-198.

Sternberg, R. (1986). *Beyond IQ: A triarchic theory of human intelligence.* Cambridge, England: Cambridge University Press.

Stevens, M. (1991). *Japan and education.* London, England: Macmillan.

Stewart, J. (1984). The legacy of W. E. B. DuBois for contemporary black studies. *Journal of Negro Education*, 53 (4), 296-311.

Stewart, J. (1991). The field and function of black studies. In C. Willie, A. Garibaldi & W. Reed (Eds.), *The education of African-Americans* (159-169). New York: Auburn House.

Stinson, S. (1985a) The social/moral context of the arts curriculum: A critique. *Resources in education*, 20, 170. [ERIC documents reproduction service No. ED 256674.]

Stinson, S. (1985b). Curriculum and the morality of aesthetics. *JCT*, 6 (3), 66-83.

Stinson, S. (1986). Planning the dance curriculum: A process of dialogue. *Drama/Dance*, 5, 36-46, 51-53.

Stinson, S. (1988). Inner process vs. outer result. *Musical America*, 107, 12-13, 52-55.

St. Julien, J. (1992). *Explaining learning: The research trajectory of situated cognition and the implications of connectionism.* Paper presented to the annual meeting of the American Educational Research Association, San Francisco, CA.

St. Maurice, H. (1987). Clinical supervision and power: Regimes of instructional management. In T. Popkewitz (Ed.), *Critical studies in teacher education: Its folklore, theory, and practice.* Philadelphia, PA: Falmer Press.

Stoddart, K. (1989). Unpacking the stash: A preliminary note on creative concealment among children and adolescents. *Phenomenology + Pedagogy*, 7, 163-172.

Stone, J. (1979). Structures and systems. *JCT*, 1 (2), 37-45.

Strasser, S. (1969). *The idea of a dialogic phenomenology.* Pittsburgh, PA: Duquesne University Press.

Stratemeyer, F., Forkner, H., McKim, M. & Passow, A. (1957). *Developing a curriculum for modern living*. [Second edition.] New York: Teachers College Press.

Strickland, C.& Burgess, C. (Eds.). (1965). *Health, growth and heredity: G. Stanley Hall and natural education*. New York: Teachers College Press.

Strickland, D. & Ascher, C. (1992). Low income African-American children and public schooling. In P. Jackson (Ed.), *Handbook of research on curriculum* (609-625). New York: Macmillan.

Strike, K. (1985). A field guide of censors: Toward a concept of censorship in public schools. *Teachers College Record*, 87 (2), 230-258.

Strike, K. (1989). *Liberal justice and the Marxist critique of education*. New York: Routledge & Kegan Paul.

Strike, K. & Egan, K. (Eds.). (1978). *Ethics and educational policy*. London, England: Routledge & Kegan Paul.

Strom, M., Sleeper, M. & Johnson, M. (1992). Facing history and ourselves: A synthesis of history and ethics in effective history education. In A. Garrod (Ed.), *Learning for life: Moral education theory and practice* (131-153). Westport, CT: Praeger.

Stufflebeam, D. & Shinkfield, A. (1985). *Systematic evaluation*. Boston, MA: Kluwer-Nijhoff.

Sturrock, J. (1977). The new model autobiographer. *New Literary History*, 1, 51-64.

Sufrin, S. (1963). *Administering the national defense education act*. Syracuse, NY: Syracuse University Press.

Sullivan, C. (1980). *Clinical supervision: A state-of-the-art review*. Alexandria, VA: ASCD.

Sumara, D. (1992a). Teacher as director: Spotlighting students in whole language classrooms. *Reflections on Canadian Literacy*, 9 (3,4), 189-194.

Sumara, D. (1992b). Bringing life to writing: Katherine Pateson's weird little kid. *Reflections on Canadian Literacy*, 10 (2,3), 73-79.

Sumara, D. (1993). Gay and lesbian voices in literature: Making room on the shelf. *English Quarterly*, 25 (1), 30-34.

Sumara, D. (1994a). *The importance of unmasking: The literary text and the curriculum*. Edmonton, Alberta, Canada: University of Alberta, Department of Secondary Education, unpublished Ph.D. dissertation.

Sumara, D. (1994b). A path laid down while walking: Curriculum development in high school English programs. In T. Gambell & M-C Courtland (Eds.), *Curriculum planning in the language arts K-12*. North York, Ontario, Canada: Captus Press.

Sumara, D. (in press). Of seagulls and glass roses: Teachers' relationships with literary texts as transformation space. *JCT*.

Sumara, D. & Walker, L. (1991). The teacher's role in whole language. *Language Arts*, 68, 276-286.

Sumara, D. & Luce-Kapler, R. (1993). Action research as a writerly text: Locating co-labouring in collaboration. *Journal of Educational Action Research*, 1, 387-396.

Sung, Il Je (1986). *A critical understanding of technology and educational development: A case study of the Korean educational development institute.* Edmonton, Alberta, Canada: University of Alberta, Faculty of Education, Department of Secondary Education, unpublished Ph.D. dissertation.

Sutherland, G. (1973). *Elementary education in the nineteenth century.* London, England: London Historical Association.

Sutherland, H. (1909). Health conditions of the negro in the south: With special reference to tuberculosis. *Journal of the Southern Medical Association,* (6), 405.

Svengalis, C. (Ed.). (1989). *A guide for integrating global education across the curriculum.* Des Moines, IA: State Department of Education.

Swadener, B. & Kessler, S. (1991). Introduction to special issue: Reconceptualizing early childhood education. *Early Education and Development* (2) 2, 85-94.

Swanger, D. (1990). Discipline-based art education: Heat and light. *Educational Theory,* 40 (4), 437-442.

Swartz, E. (1992). Cultural diversity and the school curriculum: Content and practice. *JCT,* 9 (4), 73-88.

Swartz, R. (1992). Teaching moral reasoning in the standard curriculum. In A. Garrod (Ed.), *Learning for life: Moral education theory and practice* (107-130). Westport, CT: Praeger.

Swiderski, R. (1993). *Teaching language, learning culture.* Greenwood, CT: Bergin & Harvey.

Swinerton, E. (1991). *Philippine higher education: Toward the twenty-first century.* New York: Praeger Publishers.

Sykes, G. (1979). Government intervention in the school curriculum: Floating like a bee, stinging like butterfly. In J. Schaffarzick & G. Sykes (Eds.), *Values conflicts and curriculum issues: Lessons from research and experience* (313-330). Berkeley, CA: McCutchan.

Szepkouski, G. (1993). "I'm me own boss!" In D. McLaughlin & W. Tierny (Eds.), *Naming silenced lives: Personal narratives and the process of educational change* (177-197). New York: Routledge.

Taba, H. (1957). Problem identification. In A. Foshay & J. Hall (Eds.), *Research for curriculum improvement* (42-71). Washington, DC: ASCD.

Taba, H. (1962). *Curriculum development: Theory and practice.* New York: Harcourt, Brace & World, Inc.

Talley, W. (1991). Teaching school in the 1890s. *McGill Journal of Education,* 26 (3) (Fall), 267-275.

Talmage, H. (Ed.). (1975). *Systems of individualized instruction.* Berkeley, CA: McCutchan.

Tanner, D. (1961). Needed research in instructional television. *School Review,* 69 (3), 311-321.

Tanner, D. (1966). Curriculum theory: Knowledge and content. *Review of Educational Research,* XXXVI (3), 362-372.

Tanner, D. (1971a). Evaluation of modification of the comprehensive curriculum. *The High School Journal,* 545 (5), 312-320.

Tanner, D. (1971b). *Secondary education: Theory and development.* New York: Macmillan.

Tanner, D. (1972). *Secondary education: Perspectives and prospects.* New York: Macmillan.

Tanner, D. (1973, March). Performance contracting: Contrivance of the industrial-governmental-educational complex. *Intellect,* 361-365.

Tanner, D. (1979, October). Splitting up the school system: Are comprehensive high schools doomed? *Phi Delta Kappan,* 92-97.

Tanner, D. (1982). Curriculum history. In *Encyclopedia of educational research.* [H. Mitzel, Ed.] New York: Macmillan & Free Press.

Tanner, D. (1983). Knowledge divided against itself. *Bulletin of the Atomic Scientists,* 39 (3), 34-38.

Tanner, D. (1984). The American high school at the crossroads. *Educational Leadership,* 41 (6), 4-13.

Tanner, D. (1988). The textbook controversies. In L. Tanner (Ed.), *Critical issues in curriculum, part I, eighty-seventh yearbook of the National Society for the Study of Education* (122-147). Chicago, IL: National Society for the Study of Education.

Tanner, D. (1991). *Crusade for democracy: Progressive education at the crossroads.* Albany, NY: State University of New York Press.

Tanner, D. & Tanner, L. (1975, 1980). *Curriculum development: Theory into Practice.* [Second edition: 1980.] New York: Macmillan.

Tanner, D. & Tanner, L. (1979, June; 1981). Emancipation from research: The reconceptualists' prescription. *Educational Researcher,* 8 (6), 8-12. [Reprinted in H. Giroux, A. Penna, & W. Pinar (Eds.), (1981), *Curriculum and instruction: Alternatives in education* (382-391). Berkeley, CA: McCutchan.]

Tanner, D. & Tanner, L. (1987). *Supervision in education: Problems and practices.* New York: Macmillan.

Tanner, D. & Tanner, L. (1990). *History of the school curriculum.* New York: Macmillan.

Tanner, L. (1982). Curriculum history as usable knowledge. *Curriculum Inquiry,* 12 (4), 405-412.

Tanner, L. (1985). The path not taken: Dewey's model of inquiry. *Curriculum Inquiry,* 18 (4), 471-479.

Tanner, L. & Tanner, D. (1987). Environmentalism in American pedagogy: The legacy of Lester Ward. *Teachers College Record,* 88 (4), 537-547.

Tarrow, N. (1991). Western Europe survey of events: 1990. *Comparative Education Review,* 35 (2), 397-399.

Taubman, P. (1979). *Gender and curriculum: Discourse and the politics of sexuality.* Rochester, NY: University of Rochester, Graduate School of Education and Human Development, unpublished doctoral dissertation.

Taubman, P. (1982). Gender and curriculum: Discourse and the politics of sexuality. *JCT,* 4 (1), 12-87.

Taubman, P. (1986). Gendered texts: A review of gendered subjects: The Dynamics of Feminist Teaching. *Phenomenology + Pedagogy.*

Taubman, P. (1987, April 9.). *Notes on James Baldwin, a native son.* Miles M. Kastendieck Chair of English Address. Brooklyn, NY: Polytechnic Preparatory Country Day School.

Taubman, P. (1990, 1992). Achieving the right distance. *Educational Theory,* 40 (1), 121-133. [Reprinted in W. Pinar & W. Reynolds (Eds.), *Understanding curriculum as phenomenological and deconstructed text* (216-233). New York: Teachers College Press.]

Taubman, P. (1993a). Canonical sins. In L. Castenell & W. Pinar (Eds.), *Understanding curriculum as racial text: Representations of identity and difference in education* (35-52). Albany, NY: State University of New York Press.

Taubman, P. (1993b). Separate identities, separate lives: Diversity in the curriculum. In L. Castenell & W. Pinar (Eds.), *Understanding curriculum as racial text: Representations of identity and difference in education* (287-306). Albany, NY: State University of New York Press.

Taxel, J. (1981). The outsiders of the American revolution: The selective tradition in children's fiction. *Interchange,* 12 (2-3), 206-229.

Taxel, J. (1986). The black experience in children's fiction: Controversies surrounding award winning books. *Curriculum Inquiry,* 16 (3), 245-281.

Taylor, C. (1992). *Multiculturalism and the politics of recognition.* Princeton, NJ: Princeton University Press.

Taylor, F. (1911). *The principles of scientific management.* New York: Harper.

Taylor, P. (1982). Metaphor and meaning in the curriculum: On opening windows on the not yet seen. *JCT,* 4 (1), 209-216.

Taylor, P. & Richards, C. (1979). *An introduction to curriculum studies.* Windsor, England: NFER Publishing Co.

Taylor, W. (1991). *The effects of politics and economics on non-formal educational systems in Argentina, Cuba, Mexico, and Nicaragua.* Lafayette, LA: University of Southwestern Louisiana, College of Education, unpublished manuscript.

Tennov, D. (1976). *Psychotherapy: The hazardous care.* Garden City, NY: Anchor Press, Doubleday.

Tetreault, M. (1985, July/August). Feminist phase theory. *Journal of Higher Education,* 56, 363-384.

Thayer-Bacon, B. (1992, September). Is modern critical thinking theory sexist? *Inquiry,* 10 (1), 3-7.

Thayer-Bacon, B. (1993). Caring and its relationship to critical thinking. *Educational Theory,* 43 (3), 323-340.

Theisen, G. (1984, March). *Comparative educational analysis: The measurement of meaning and the meaning of measurement.* Paper presented at the meeting of the Comparative and International Educational Society, Houston, TX.

Thelen, H. (1960). *Education and the human quest.* New York: Harper & Row.

Thelin, B. (1992, April). *Education for global survival: Reflections based on some Swedish experiences and examples.* Paper presented to the annual meeting of the American Educational Research Association, San Francisco, CA.

Theobald, P. & Snauwaert, D. (n.d.). *The educational philosophy of Wendell Berry.* Unpublished manuscript.

Theobald, P. (n.d.). *Country school and governance: The one-room school experience in the midwest to 1918.* Unpublished ms.

Thiessen, D. (1989). Teachers and their curriculum-change orientations. In G. Milburn, I. Goodson, & R. Clark (Eds.), *Re-interpreting curriculum research: Images and arguments* (132-145). London, Ontario, Canada: The Althouse Press.

Thiessen, D. (1992). Classroom based teacher development. In A. Hargreaves & M. Fullan (Ed.), *Understanding teacher development* (55-109). New York: Teachers College Press.

Thody, P. (1977). *Roland Barthes: A conservative estimate.* London, England: Macmillan.

Thomas, A. & Sillen, S. (1979). *Racism and psychiatry.* NJ: The Citadel Press.

Thomas, R. (Ed.). (1990). *International comparative education: Practices, issues, and prospects.* Oxford, England: Pergamon Press.

Thomas, R., Sands, L. & Brubaker, D. (Eds.). (1968). *Strategies for curriculum change: Cases from 13 nations* (90-99). Scranton, PA: International Textbook Company.

Thompkins, G. (1993, January 4). Plan to privatize public education draws debate. New Orleans, LA: *New Orleans Times-Picayune,* A-1, A-7.

Thorndike, E. (1904). *An introduction to the theory of mental and social measurements.* New York: Teachers College Press.

Thorndike, E. (1913). *Educational psychology vol. 2: The psychology of learning.* New York: Teachers College Press.

Thorndike, E. (1922). Measurement in Education. In *Twenty First Yearbook of National Society for the Study of Education.* Bloomington, IL: Public School Publishing.

Thorndike, E. (1962). *Psychology and the science of education: Selected writings of Edward L. Thorndike.* [Edited G. Joncich.] New York: Teachers College Press.

Tierney, W. (1993a). *Building communities of difference.* Westport, CT: Bergin & Garvey.

Tierney, W. (1993b). Self and identity in a postmodern world: A life story. In D. McLaughlin & W. Tierny (Eds.), *Naming silenced lives: Personal narratives and the process of educational change* (119-134). New York: Routledge.

Tittle, C. (1974). The use and abuse of vocational tests. In J. Stacey, S. Bereaud & J. Daniels (Eds.), *And Jill came tumbling after: Sexism in American education.* New York: Dell.

Todd, R. (1987). Technology education in the United States: A case study of a state in transition. In K. Riquarts (Ed.), *Science and technology education and the quality of life.* Kiel, Germany: FDR-IPN.

Toffler, A. (1990). *Powershift: Knowledge, wealth, and violence at the edge of the 21st century.* New York: Bantam.

Tom, A. (1984). *Teaching as a moral craft.* New York: Longman.

Tomkins, G. (1981). Foreign influences on curriculum and curriculum policy making in Canada. *Curriculum Inquiry,* 11 (2), 79-88.

Tomkins, G. (1986). *A common countenance: Stability and change in the Canadian curriculum.* Toronto, Ontario, Canada: Prentice-Hall.

Torres, C. (1993). From the *pedagogy of the oppressed* to *a luta continua*: The political pedagogy of Paulo Freire. In P. McLaren & P. Leonard (Eds.), *Paulo Freire: A critical encounter* (119-145). London & New York: Routledge.

Tracy, D. (1981). *The analogical imagination.* New York: Crossroads.

Travers, R. (1983). *How research has changed American schools: A history from 1840 to the present.* Kalamazoo, MI: Mythos Press.

Travers, R. (1987). Apprentice to Thorndike. *Teaching Education,* 1 (1), 46-49.

Trecker, J. (1975). Women in U.S. history high school textbooks. In E. Maccia, M. Estep & T. Shiel (Eds.), *Women and education.* Springfield, IL: Charles C. Thomas.

Tripp, D. (1990, Summer). Socially critical action research. *Theory Into Practice,* XXIX (3), 158-166.

Trostli, R. (1988, Spring). Educating as an art: The Waldorf approach. *Holistic Education Review,* 1 (1), 44-51.

Trousdale, A. & Henkin, R. (1991). Reflection on negotiating curriculum: Praxis in the language arts classrooms. *Teaching Education,* 4 (1), 175-180.

Troy, F. (1985). The day the schools died. In B. Gross & R. Gross (Eds.), *The great school debate: Which way for American education?* (466-470). New York: Simon & Schuster.

Troyna, B. (1984). Multicultural education: Emancipation or containment? In L. Baronton & S. Walker (Eds.), *Social crisis and educational research* (75-97). London, England: Croom Helm.

Troyna, B. & Williams, J. (1986). *Racism, education and the state.* London, England: Croom Helm.

Troyna, B. & Hatcher, R. (1992). *Racism in children's lives: A study of mainly-white primary schools.* London & New York: Routledge.

Troyna, B. & Williams, J. (1986). Multicultural education: Emancipation or containment? In L. Barton & S. Walker (Eds.), *Social crisis and educational research* (75-97). London, England: Croom Helm.

Trumbull, D. (1987). On changing perspective: An examination of teachers' dilemmas. *Journal of Curriculum and Supervision,* 3 (1), 45-60.

Trumbull, D. (1990). Evolving conceptions of teaching: Reflections of one teacher. *Curriculum Inquiry,* 20 (2), 161-182.

Trump, J. & Miller, D. (1972, 1979). *Secondary school curriculum improvement: Meeting the challenges of the times.* [Third edition]. Boston, MA: Allyn & Bacon.

Turner, J. (1971). *Making new schools: The liberation of learning.* New York: David McKay Co.

Turner, L. (1984). *Toward understanding the lived world of three beginning teachers of young children.* Edmonton, Alberta, Canada: University of Alberta, Faculty of Education, Department of Secondary Education, unpublished Ph.D. dissertation.

Turner, M. (1957). *Modern dance for school and college.* Englewood Cliffs, NJ: Prentice-Hall.

Tyack, D. (1974). *The one best system: A history of American urban education.* Cambridge, MA: Harvard University Press.

Tyack, D. (1993). School governance in the United States: Historical puzzles and anomalies. In J. Hannaway. & M. Carnoy (Eds.). *Decentralization and school improvement: Can we fulfill the promise?* (1-32). San Francisco, CA: Jossey-Bass Publishers.

Tyack, D. & Hansot, E. (1990). *Learning together: A history of coeducation in American schools.* New Haven, CT: Yale University Press.

Tye, K. (1991) (Ed.). *Global education: From thought to action.* Alexandria, VA: ASCD.

Tyler, L. (1986). Meaning and schooling. *Theory Into Practice,* XXV (1), 53-57.

Tyler, R. (1934). *Constructing achievement tests.* Columbus, OH: Ohio State University.

Tyler, R. (1949). *Basic principles of curriculum and instruction.* Chicago, IL: University of Chicago Press.

Tyler, R. (1979). Educational improvements best served by curriculum development. In J. Schaffarzick & G. Sykes, (Eds.), *Values conflicts and curriculum issues: Lessons from research and experience* (237-262). Berkeley, CA: McCutchan

Tyler, R. (1987). Charles Hubbard Judd: As I came to know him. *Teaching Education,* 1 (1), 19-24.

U'Ren, M. (1971). The image of woman in textbooks. In V. Gornick & B. Moran (Eds.), *Woman in sexist society.* New York: Basic Books.

Uhrmacher, B. (1989). Visions and versions of life in classrooms. *JCT,* 9 (1), 107-116.

UNESCO (1987). *World education at a glance.* Paris: UNESCO Office of Statistics.

United States Catholic Conference (1987, Fall). Values and virtue: Moral education in the public schools. In *Religion and Public Education,* 16 (3), 337-340.

United States Office of Education (1948). *Life adjustment education for every youth.* Washington, DC: U.S. Government Printing Office.

Unruh, G. (Ed.). (1965). *New curriculum developments.* Washington, DC: ASCD.

Unruh, G. (1975). *Responsive curriculum development: Theory and action.* Berkeley, CA: McCutchan.

Unruh, G. & Leeper, R. (Eds.). (1968). *Influences in curriculum change.* Washington, DC: ASCD.

Urban, W. (1989). The graduate education of a black scholar: Horace Mann Bond and the University of Chicago. In C. Kridel (Ed.), *Curriculum history* (72-88). Lanham, MD: University Press of America.

Urban, W. (1992). *Black scholar: Horace Mann Bond, 1904-1972.* Athens, GA: University of Georgia Press.

Vallance, E. (1977, Summer). The landscape of the "Great Plains Experience:" An application of curriculum criticism. *Curriculum Inquiry,* 7:2, 87-105.

Vallance, E. (1980a). Backward-looking criticism as a forward-looking concept: Response to Walter Werner. *Curriculum Inquiry,* 10 (2), 155-158.

Vallance, E. (1980b). A deadpan look at humor in curriculum discourse. *Curriculum Inquiry,* 10 (2), 179-180.

Vallance, E. (1986). A second look at *Conflicting Conceptions of Curriculum. Theory Into Practice,* Vol. XXV (1), 24-30.

Vallance, E. (1991). Aesthetic inquiry: Art criticism. In E. Short (Ed.), *Forms of curriculum inquiry* (155-172). Albany, NY: State University of New York Press.

Valli, L. (1983). Becoming clerical workers: Business education and the culture of femininity. In M. Apple & L. Weis (Eds.), *Ideology and practice in schooling* (213-234). Philadelphia, PA: Temple University Press.

Valli, L. (1986). *Becoming clerical workers.* Boston, MA: Routledge & Kegan Paul.

Valli, L. & Tom, A. (1988). How adequate are the knowledge base frameworks in teacher education? *Journal of Teacher Education,* XXXIX (5), 5-12.

van Brummelen, H. (1991). The world portrayed in texts: An analysis of the content of elementary school textbooks. *The Journal of Educational Thought,* 25 (3), 202-221.

van Damme, J. (1985). *Curriculum orientation within religious education programs for Catholic secondary schools.* Edmonton, Alberta, Canada: University of Alberta, Faculty of Education, Department of Secondary Education, unpublished Ph.D. dissertation.

van den Berghe, P. (1976). Academic gamesmanship. In R. Brannon & D. David (Eds.), *The forty-nine percent majority: The male sex role.* Reading, MA: Addison Wesley.

van den Berghe, P. (1981). *The ethnic phenomenon.* New York: Elsevier.

van Geel, T. (1979). The new law of the curriculum. In J. Schaffarzick & G. Sykes (Eds.), *Values conflicts and curriculum issues: Lessons from research and experience* (25-71). Berkeley, CA: McCutchan.

van Manen, M. (1973). *Toward a cybernetic phenomenology of instruction.* Edmonton, Alberta, Canada: University of Alberta, Faculty of Education, Department of Secondary Education, unpublished Ph.D. dissertation.

van Manen, M. (1979). Objective inquiry in the structures of subjectivity. *JCT,* 1 (1), 44-64.

van Manen, M. (1980). An interview with a Dutch pedagogue. *JCT,* 2 (2), 68-72.

van Manen, M. (1982). Phenomenological pedagogy. *Curriculum Inquiry,* 12 (3), 283-299.

van Manen, M. (1984a). Practicing phenomenological writing. *Phenomenology + Pedagogy,* 2:1, 36-69.

van Manen, M. (1984b). *"Doing" phenomenological research and writing: An introduction.* Curriculum Praxis Monograph Series, Monograph No. 7.

Edmonton, Alberta, Canada: University of Alberta, Faculty of Education, Department of Secondary Education.

van Manen, M. (1984c). *Action research as theory of the unique: From pedagogic thoughtfulness to pedagogic tactfulness.* Curriculum Praxis Series, Occasional Paper No. 32. Edmonton, Alberta, Canada: University of Alberta, Faculty of Education, Department of Secondary Education.

van Manen, M. (1985). *The tissue of the text: A subtle pedagogy.* Curriculum Praxis Series, Occasional Paper No. 31. Edmonton, Alberta, Canada: University of Alberta, Faculty of Education, Department of Secondary Education.

van Manen, M. (1986). *The tone of teaching.* Richmond Hill, Ontario, Canada: Scholastic-TAB Publications.

van Manen, M. (1988). The relation between research and pedagogy. in W. Pinar (Ed.), *Contemporary curriculum discourses* (437-452). Scottsdale, AZ: Gorsuch Scarisbrick.

van Manen, M. (1989). By the light of anecdote. *Phenomenology + Pedagogy,* 7, 232-256.

van Manen, M. (1990). Romantic roots of human science in education. In J. Willinsky (Ed.), *The educational legacy of romanticism* (115-139). Waterloo, Ontario, Canada: Wilfrid Laurier University Press.

van Manen, M. (1991). *The tact of teaching: The meaning of pedagogical thoughtfulness.* Albany, NY: State University of New York Press.

van Sertima, I. (1990). Future directions for African and African American content in the school curriculum. In A. Hilliard, et. al. (Eds.), *Infusion of African and African American content in the school curriculum: Proceedings of the First National Conference* (87-109). Morristown, NJ: Aaron Press.

van Til, W. (Ed.). (1971). *Curriculum: Quest for relevance.* Boston, MA: Houghton Mifflin Co.

Vars, G. (1982). Designs for general education: Alternative approaches to curriculum integration. *Journal of Higher Education,* 53 (2), 216-226.

Venable, T. (1967). *Philosophical foundations of the curriculum.* Chicago, IL: Rand McNally.

Venezky, R. (1992). Textbooks in school and society. In P. Jackson (Ed.), *Handbook of research on curriculum* (436-461). New York: Macmillan.

Viadero, D. (1990, October 24). Over protests, California board adopts history textbooks. *Education Week,* p. 18.

Violas, P. (1978). *The training of the urban working class: A history of twentieth century American education.* Chicago, IL: Rand McNally.

Voege, H. (1975). The diffusion of Keynesian macroeconomics through American high school textbooks, 1936-70. In W. Reid & D. Walker (Eds.), *Case studies in curriculum change* (208-239). London: Routledge & Kegan Paul.

Vygotsky, L. (1962, 1934). *Thought and language.* [Edited & trans. E. Hanfamann & G. Vakar.] New York & London, England: MIT Press & John Wiley & Sons.

Wackes, K. (1991, April). Which school for your child? *Focus on the Family*, 15 (4), 2-5.

Waks, L. (1985). Fundamentalism and the autonomy of religion. *Teachers College Record*, 87 (2), 271-276.

Walberg, H. (1970). Curriculum evaluation: Problems and guidelines. *Teachers College Record*, 71, 557-570.

Walberg, H. (Ed.). (1979). *Educational environments and effects: Evaluation, policy, and productivity*. Berkeley, CA: McCutchan, 1979.

Walker, D. (1971). A naturalistic model for curriculum development. *School Review*, 80 (1), 51-65.

Walker, D. (1973). What curriculum research? *Journal of Curriculum Studies*, 5, 58-72.

Walker, D. (1975). The curriculum field in formation: A review of the twenty-sixth yearbook of the National Society for the Study of Education. *Curriculum Theory Network*, 4 (4), 263-283.

Walker, D. (1976). Toward comprehension of curricular realities. In L. Shulman (Ed.), *Review of research in education* (4). Itasca, IL: Peacock.

Walker, D. (1979). Approaches to curriculum development. In J. Schaffarzick & G. Sykes (Eds.), *Value conflicts and curriculum issues* (263-290). Berkeley, CA: McCutchan.

Walker, D. (1990). *Fundamentals of curriculum*. New York: Harcourt Brace Jovanovich.

Walker, D. & Soltis, J. (1986). *Curriculum and aims*. New York: Teachers College Press.

Walker, R. & Fisher, R. (1990). Stations. *Cambridge Journal of Education*, 20 (3), 223-240.

Walkerdine, V. (1984). Developmental psychology and the child-centered pedagogy: The insertion of Piaget into early education. In J. Henriques, W. Hollway, C. Urwin, C. Venn & V. Walkerdine (Eds.), *Changing the subject* (153-202). New York: Methuen.

Walkerdine, V. (1985). Science and the female mind: The burden of proof. *PsychCritique*, 1 (1), 1-20.

Walkerdine, V. (1988). *The mastery of reason*. London, England: Routledge & Kegan Paul.

Walkerdine, V. (1992). *Redefining the subject in situated cognition theory*. Paper presented to the annual meeting of the American Educational Research Association, San Francisco, CA.

Wallenstein, S. (1979a). Notes toward a feminist curriculum theory. *JCT*, 1 (1), 186-190.

Wallenstein, S. (1979b). *The reflexive method in curriculum theory: An autobiographical case study*. Rochester, NY: University of Rochester, Graduate School of Education and Human Development, unpublished doctoral dissertation.

Wallenstein, S. (1980). Images of the evolving curriculum. *JCT*, 2 (2), 269-273.

Wallerstein, N. (1988). Interdisciplinary approaches to Paulo Freire's educational theory. *JCT*, 8 (4), 53-68.

Walsh, C. (1991). *Pedagogy and the struggle for voice: Issues of language, power, and schooling for Puerto Ricans.* New York: Bergin & Garvey.

Walum, L. (1977). *The dynamics of sex and gender: A sociological perspective.* Chicago, IL: Rand McNally.

Walworth, A. (1938). *School histories at war.* Cambridge, MA: Harvard University Press.

Wandersee, J. (1990a). On the value and use of the history of science in teaching today's science: Constructing historical vignettes. In. D. Herget (Ed.), *More history and philosophy of science in science teaching* (277-283).

Wandersee, J. (1990b). Concept mapping and the cartography of cognition. *Journal of Research in Science Teaching,* 27 (10), 923-936.

Wankowski, J. & Reid, W. (1982). The psychology of curriculum theorizing: A conversation. *JCT,* 4 (2), 112-131.

Ward, L. (1883). *Dynamic sociology.* New York: D. Appleton.

Ward, L. (1930). *The substance of the sociology of Lester Frank Ward.* New York: Vanguard Press.

Warner, M. (1991). *Objectivity and emancipation in learning disabilities: Holism from the perspective of critical realism.* Paper presented to the Bergamo Conference on Curriculum Theory and Classroom Practice, Dayton, OH.

Warner, M. (1992, April). *Metatheory in special education: Critical pragmatism from the perspective of critical realism.* Paper presented to the annual meeting of the American Educational Research Association, San Francisco, CA.

Warner, N. (1992). *From their perspective: Issues of schooling and family culture of four African American first generation college students.* Baton Rouge, LA: Louisiana State University, Department of Curriculum and Instruction, unpublished Ph.D. dissertation.

Wasley, P. (1990a). *Trusting kids and their voices: A hu manities teacher in the midst of change.* Studies on Teacher Change, No. 2. Providence, RI: Brown University, Coalition for Essential Schools.

Wasley, P. (1990b). *A formula for making a difference.* Studies on Teacher Change, No. 3. Providence, RI: Brown University, Coalition for Essential Schools.

Wasley, P. (1990c). *Stirring the chalkdust.* Studies on Teacher Change, No. 4. Providence, RI: Brown University, Coalition for Essential Schools.

Watkins, W. (1989a). *W. E. B. Dubois: Black social reconstructionist.* Paper presented to the annual meeting of the American Educational Research Association, San Francisco, CA.

Watkins, W. (1989b). Black studies. In T. Husen & T. Postlethwaite (Eds.), *The international encyclopedia of education: Supplementary volume one* (107-110). London, England: Pergamon.

Watkins, W. (1989c). On accommodationist education: Booker T. Washington goes to Africa. *International Third World Studies Journal and Review,* 1, 137-143.

Watkins, W. (1990a). *On the foundations of social reconstructionism: The empiricism of John L. Childs.* Paper presented to the annual meeting of the American Educational Research Association, Boston, MA.

Watkins, W. (1990b). Teaching and learning in the Black colleges: A 130-year retrospective. *Teaching Education,* 3 (1), 10-25.

Watkins, W. (1990c). The social reconstructionists. In T. Husen & T. Postlethwaite (Eds.), *The international encyclopedia of education: Supplementary volume two* (589-592). London, England: Pergamon Press.

Watkins, W. (1990d). W. E. B. DuBois versus Thomas Jesse Jones: The forgotten skirmishes. *Journal of the Midwest History of Education Society,* 18- 305-328.

Watkins, W. (1991). *A curriculum for colored people: The social and educational ideas of Franklin H. Giddings.* Paper presented to the Bergamo Conference on Curriculum Theory and Classroom Practice, Dayton, OH.

Watkins, W. (1993). Black curriculum orientations: A preliminary inquiry. *Harvard Educational Review,* 63 (3), 321-338.

Watkins, W. & Byo, Y. (1991). Nigeria. In A. Lewy (Ed.), *International Encyclopedia of Curriculum* (236-238). New York: Pergamon Press.

Watney, S. (1994). School's out. In H. Giroux & P. McLaren (Eds.), *Between borders: Pedagogy and the politics of cultural studies* (167-179). New York: Routledge.

Watras, J. (1983). Problems in multi-cultural education: The textbook controversy in Kanawha County, West Virginia. *JCT,* 5 (1), 4-16.

Watson, J., et al. (1917). *Suggestions of modern science concerning education.* New York: Macmillan.

Wear, D. (1989). What literature says to pre-service teachers and educators. *Journal of Teacher Education,* XXXX (1), 51-55.

Wear, D. (1991). A reconnection to self: Women and solitude. In J. Erdman & J. Henderson (Eds.), *Critical discourse on current curriculum issues* (168-184). Chicago, IL: Mid-West Center for Curriculum Studies.

Wear, D. (Ed.). (1993). *The center of the web: Women and solitude.* Albany, NY: State University of New York.

Weber, S. (1990). The teacher educator's experience: Cultura l generativity and duality of commitment. *Curriculum Inquiry,* 20 (2), 141-159.

Weedon, C. (1987). *Feminist practice and post-structural theory.* Oxford, England & New York: Blackwell.

Weiler, H. (1989). Why reforms fails: The politics of education in France and the Federal Republic of Germany. *Journal of Curriculum Studies,* 21 (4), 291-306.

Weiler, H. (1993). Control versus legitimation: The politics of ambivalence. In J. Hannaway. & M. Carnoy (Eds.). *Decentralization and school improvement: Can we fulfill the promise?* (55-83). San Francisco, CA: Jossey-Bass Publishers.

Weill, L. (1992). The primacy of the Bachelardian image in the arts and humanities. *JCT,* 9 (3), 97-121.

Weinberg, M. (1991). The civil rights movement and educational change. In C. Willie, A. Garibaldi & W. Reed (Eds.), *The education of African-Americans* (3-6). New York: Auburn House.

Weinstein, G. & Fantini, M. (1970). *Toward a humanistic education: A curriculum of affect.* New York: Praeger.

Weinstein, M. (1993). Critical thinking: The great debate. *Educational Theory,* 43 (1), 99-117.

Weinstein, M. & Oxman-Michelli, W. (1989, November). The faculty development program of the Institute for Critical Thinking. *Inquiry,* 9-13.

Weintraub, K. (1978). *The value of the individual: Self and circumstance in autobiography.* Chicago, IL: University of Chicago Press.

Weis, L. (1983). Schooling and cultural production: A comparison of black and white lived culture. In M. Apple & L. Weis, *Ideology and Practice in Schooling* (235-261). Philadelphia, PA: Temple University Press.

Weis, L. (1985). *Between two worlds.* Boston, MA: Routledge & Kegan Paul.

Weis, L. (Ed.). (1988). *Class, race and gender in American education.* Albany, NY: State University of New York Press.

Weis, L. (1990). *Working class without work: High school students in a de-industrialized economy.* New York: Routledge.

Weis, L. & Fine, M. (1993). *Beyond silenced voices: Class, race, and gender in United States schools.* Albany, NY: State University of New York Press.

Weis, L., et al. (Eds.) (1989a). *Dropouts from school: Issues, dilemmas, and solutions.* Albany, NY: State University of New York Press.

Weis, L., et al. (Eds.) (1989b). Crisis in teaching: Perspectives on current reforms. Albany: State University of New York Press.

Weis, L., Altbach, P., Kelly, G., Petrie, H. & Slaughter, S. (1989). *Crisis in teaching: Perspectives on current reforms.* Albany, NY: State University of New York Press.

Weiss, J. (1989). Evaluation as subversive activity. In G. Milburn, I. Goodson & R. Clark (Eds.), *Re-interpreting curriculum research: Images and arguments* (121-131). London, Ontario, Canada: The Althouse Press.

Weisstein, N. (1971). Psychology constructs the female. In V. Gornick & B. Moran (Eds.),*Woman in sexist society.* New York: Basic Books.

Weldon, J. (1970). *The evolution of curriculum development in the United States as revealed through selected writings.* Carbondale, IL: Southern Illinois University.

Welker, R. (1991). Expertise and the teacher as expert: Rethinking a questionable metaphor. *American Educational Research Journal,* 28 (1), 19-35.

Welty, E. (1977). *The eye of the story: Selected essays and reviews.* New York: Vintage Books.

Werner, W. (1977). *A study of perspective in social studies.* Edmonton, Alberta, Canada: University of Alberta, Department of Secondary Education, unpublished Ph.D. dissertation.

Werner, W. (1980). Editorial criticism in curricular analysis. *Curriculum Inquiry,* 10 (2), 143-154.

Werner, W. (1987). The text and tradition of an interpretive pedagogy. *JCT*, 7 (3), 22-33.

Werner, W. & Rothe, P. (n.d.). *Doing school ethnography*. Monograph Series No. 2. Edmonton, Alberta, Canada: University of Alberta, Department of Secondary Education.

West, C. (1988). Marxist theory and the specificity of Afro-American oppression. In C. Nelson & L. Grossberg (Eds.), *Marxism and the interpretation of culture* (17-33). Urbana, IL: University of Illinois Press.

West, C. (1990). The new cultural politics of difference. *October*, 53, 93-109. Reprinted in C. McCarthy & W. Crichlow (Eds.), (1993), *Race, identity, and representation in education* (11-23). New York and London, England: Routledge.

West, C. (1993). Preface. In P. McLaren & P. Leonard (Eds.), *Paulo Freire: A critical encounter* (xiii-xiv). London & New York: Routledge.

Westbrook, R. (1991) *John Dewey and American philosophy*. Ithaca, NY: Cornell University Press.

Westbury, I. (1988). How should we be judging the American high school? *Journal of Curriculum Studies*, 20 (4), 291-315.

Westbury, I. (1990). Textbooks, textbook publishers, and the quality of schooling. In. D. Elliott & A. Woodward (Eds.), *Textbooks and schooling in the United States: The Eighty-Ninth Yearbook of the National Society for the Study of Education* (1-22). Chicago, IL: NSSE.

Westbury, I. (1992, June-July). Comparing American and Japanese achievement: Is the United States really a lower achiever? *Educational Researcher*, 21 (5), 18-24.

Westbury, I. (1993). American and Japanese achievement. . . . Again: A response to Baker. *Educational Researcher*, 22 (3), 21-25.

Westbury, I. & Wilkof, N. (1978). Introduction. In J. Schwab, *Science, curriculum, and education*. Chicago, IL: University of Chicago Press.

Wexler, P. (1976). *The sociology of education: Beyond equality*. Indianapolis, IN: Bobbs, Merrill.

Wexler, P. (1981). Change: Social, cultural, and educational. *JCT*, 3 (2), 157-164.

Wexler, P. (1982a). Ideology and education: From critique to class action. *Interchange*, 13 (3), 53-68.

Wexler, P. (1982b). Structure, text and subject: A critical sociology of school knowledge. In M. Apple (Ed.), *Cultural and Economic Reproduction in Education* (275-303). London, England: Routledge & Kegan Paul.

Wexler, P. (1983). *Critical social psychology*. Boston, MA: Routledge & Kegan Paul.

Wexler, P. (1987). *Social analysis of education: After the new sociology*. Boston, MA: Routledge & Kegan Paul.

Wexler, P. (1988a). Body and soul: Sources of social change and strategies of education. In W. Pinar (Ed.), *Contemporary curriculum discourses* (201-222). Scottsdale, AZ: Gorsuch Scarisbrick.

Wexler, P. (1988b). Foreword to N. Lesko, *Symbolizing society: Stories, rites and structure in a Catholic high school.* New York: Falmer.

Wexler, P. (1990). Cultural change, science and the university. *Artikkeleita*, 21 (2), 80-90.

Wexler, P. (1992). *Becoming somebody: Toward a social psychology of school.* [With the assistance of W. Crichlow, J. Kern, & R. Martusewicz.] London, England: Falmer Press.

Wexler, P. & Whitson, J. (1982). Hegemony and education. *Psychology and Social Theory* (3), 31-42.

Whatley, M. (1988, 1993). Photographic images of blacks in sexuality texts. *Curriculum Inquiry*, 18 (2), 137-155. [Reprinted in L. Castenell, Jr. & W. Pinar (Eds.), *Understanding curriculum as racial text* (83-106). Albany, NY: State University of New York Press.]

Whipple, G. (Ed.). (1931). *The textbook in American education: The thirtieth yearbook of the National Society for the Study of Education, Part II.* Bloomington, IL: Public School Co.

White, J. (1973) *Towards a compulsory curriculum.* London, England: Routledge & Kegan Paul.

White, J. (1992). Dialectic: The role of discussion in education. *Inquiry*, 9 (2), 1, 18-22.

White, K. (1980). The work of Dwayne Huebner: A summary and response. *JCT*, 2 (2), 73-87.

White, M. (1987). *The Japanese educational challenge: A commitment to children.* New York: The Free Press.

Whitehead, A. (1925). *Science and the modern world.* New York: Free Press.

Whitehead, A. (1929,1967). *The aims of education.* New York: Free Press. London, England: Macmillan.

Whitehead, A. (1933). *Adventures of ideas.* New York: Macmillan.

Whitson, J. (1988a). The politics of "non-political" curriculum: Heteroglossia and the discourse of "choice" and "effectiveness." In W. Pinar (Ed.), *Contemporary curriculum discourses* (279-331). Scottsdale, AZ: Gorsuch Scarisbrick.

Whitson, J. (1988b, Summer). Adventures in monopolis: The wonderland of schooling in Arons' compelling belief. *JCT*, 7 (3), 101-108.

Whitson, J. (1991a). *Constitution and curriculum.* London, England: Falmer.

Whitson, J. (1991b). Defining and confining the curriculum theories of curriculum and instruction from the Supreme Court. In J. Erdman & J. Henderon, *Critical discourse on current curriculum issues* (107-121). Chicago, IL: Mid-West Center for Curriculum Studies.

Whitson, J. (1991c). Post-structuralist pedagogy as counter-hegemonic praxis (Can we find the baby in the bathwater?). *Education and Society*, 9 (1), 73-86). [Page numbers listed in references to this Whitson essay are to the prepublished manuscript.]

Whitson, J. (1992a). Sexuality and censorship in the curriculum: Beyond formalistic legal analysis. In J. Sears (Ed.), *Sexuality and the curriculum* (59-77). New York: Teachers College Press.

Whitson, J. (1992b). *Cognition as a semiotic process: Grounding, mediation, and critical reflective transcendence.* Paper presented to the annual meeting of the American Educational Research Association, San Francisco, CA.

Whitson, J. (1993). Correspondence with W. Pinar.

Whitt, J. (1981). Social action, self reflection, and curriculum theory. *JCT*, 3 (1), 202-210.

Whitty, G. (1985). *Sociology and school knowledge: Curriculum theory, research, and politics.* London, England: Metheun.

Whitty, G. & Young, M. (Eds.). (1976). *Explorations in the politics of school knowledge.* Driffield, England: Nafferton Books.

Whitty, G. & Edwards, T. (1992, April). *School choice policies in Britain and the U.S.A.: Their origins and significance.* A paper presented to the annual meeting of the American Educational Research Association, San Francisco, CA.

Wieder, A. (1988). Possibilities, lost possibilities, no possibilities: Images of middle-class children and lower-class adults. *Qualitative Studies in Education,* 1 (3), 225-238.

Wieder, A. (1992). Afrocentrism: Capitalist, democratic, and liberationist portraits. *Educational Foundations,* 6 (2), 33-43.

Wilcox, B. et al. (1984). *The preparation for life curriculum.* London, England: Croom Helm.

Wiles, J. & Bondi, J. (1980). *Supervision: A guide to practice.* Columbus, OH: Charles Merrill.

Wiles, J. & Bondi, J. (1989, 1984, 1979). *Curriculum development: A guide to practice.* Columbus, OH: Charles Merrill.

Wiles, K. (1963). *The changing curriculum of the American high school.* Englewood Cliffs, NJ: Prentice-Hall.

Wiles, K. (1965). Proposals of Strategies: A Summary. In R. Leeper (Ed.), *Strategy for Curriculum Change.* Washington, DC: ASCD.

Williams, P. (1991). *The alchemy of race and rights.* Cambridge, MA: Harvard University Press.

Williams, R. (1976). *Keywords: A vocabulary of culture and society.* New York: Oxford University Press.

Williams, R. (1982). *John Dewey: Recollections.* Landham, MD: University Press of America. [Reprinted in *Teaching Education,* 1 (1), 11].

Willie, C. (1991a). The social and historical context: A case study of philanthropic assistance. In C. Willie, A. Garibaldi & W. Reed (Eds.), *The education of African-Americans* (7-26). New York: Auburn House.

Willie, C. (1991b). The future of school desegregation. In C. Willie, A. Garibaldi & W. Reed (Eds.), *The education of African-Americans* (51-66). New York: Auburn House.

Willie, C., Garibaldi, A. & Reed, W. (1991). *The education of African-Americans.* New York: Auburn House.

Willinsky, J. (1984). *The well-tempered tongue.* New York: Peter Lang.

Willinsky, J. (1987). The seldom-spoken roots of the curriculum: Romanticism and the new literacy. *Curriculum Inquiry, 17,* (3)267-291.

Willinsky, J. (1989). Getting personal and practical with personal practical knowledge. *Curriculum Inquiry*, 19 (3), 247-264.

Willinsky, J. (1990a). Intellectual property rights and responsibilities: The state of the text. *The Journal of Educational Thought*, 24 (3A), 68-82.

Willinsky, J. (Ed.). (1990b). *The educational legacy of romanticism.* Waterloo, Ontario, Canada: Wilfrid Laurier University Press.

Willinksy, J. (1990c). *The new literacy.* New York: Routledge.

Willinsky, J. (1990d). Lessons from the Wordsworth and the domestic scene of writing. In J. Willinsky (Ed.), *The educational legacy of romanticism* (33-53). Waterloo, Ontario, Canada: Wilfrid Laurier University Press.

Willinsky, J. (1991a). Postmodern literacy: A primer. *Interchange*, 22 (4), 56-76.

Willinsky, J. (1991b). *The triumph of literature/the fate of literacy.* New York: Teachers College Press.

Willinsky, J. (1992a, May-June). Of literacy and the curriculum in Canada. *Journal of Curriculum Studies*, 24 (3), 273-280.

Willinsky, J. (1992b). The politics of the postmodern. *Review of Education*, 14, 343-351.

Willinsky, J. (1992c). Towards a Pacific cultural literacy. *Pacific-Asian Education*, 4 (1), 1-10.

Willinsky, J. (1993a). Lessons from the literacy before schooling 1800-1850. In B. Green (Ed.), *The Insistence of the letter: Literacy studies and curriculum theorizing* (58-74). London, England: Falmer.

Willinsky, J. (1993b). *Race, nation, science: (I'm Chinese).* Vancouver, British Columbia, Canada: University of British Columbia, Faculty of Education, Centre for the Study of Curriculum and Instruction, unpublished manuscript.

Willinsky, J. (in press). After 1492-1992: A post-colonial supplement for the Canadian curriculum. *Journal of Curriculum Studies.*

Willis, G. (1974). Reactions to the conference. In W. Pinar (Ed.), *Heightened consciousness, cultural revolution, and curriculum theory: The proceedings of the Rochester conference* (151-155). Berkeley, CA: McCutchan.

Willis, G. (Ed.). (1978). *Qualitative evaluation: Concepts and cases in curriculum criticism.* Berkeley, CA: McCutchan.

Willis, G. (1979). Phenomenological methodologies in curriculum. *JCT*, 1 (1), 65-79.

Willis, G. (1981). A reconceptualist perspective on curriculum evaluation. *JCT*, 3 (1), 185-192.

Willis, G. (1989). Reflections on performance, pedagogy and parenting. *JCT*, 9 (1), 117-123.

Willis, G. (1991). Phenomenological inquiry: Life-world perceptions. In E. Short (Ed.), *Forms of curriculum inquiry* (173-186). Albany, NY: State University of New York Press.

Willis, G. & Allen, A. (1978). Patterns of phenomenological response to curricula: Implications. In G. Willis (Ed.), *Qualitative evaluation: Concepts and cases in curriculum criticism* (34-71). Berkeley, CA: McCutchan.

Willis, G. & Schubert, W. (Eds.). (1991). *Reflections from the heart of educational inquiry: Understanding curriculum and teaching through the arts.* Albany, NY: State University of New York Press.

Willis, G., Schubert, W., Bullough, R., Kridel, C. & Holton, J. (Eds.). (1993). *The American curriculum: A documentary history.* Westport, CT: Greenwood.

Willis, P. (1981, 1977). *Learning to labour.* Hampshire, England: Gower. [1977 edition published by Saxon House in Farnborough, England.]

Willis, S. (1990, Spring). I want the Black one: Is there a place for Afro-American culture in commodity culture? *New Formations: A Journal of Culture/ Theory/Politics,* 10, 77-98.

Willis, S. (1992, September). Restructuring under fire: Pressure groups object to new practices. *ASCD Update,* 34 (7), 1, 4-5.

Wilson, A. (1993). *The meaning of international experience for schools.* Westport, CT: Praeger.

Wilson, D. (1979). *A critical analysis of teacher education from the perspective of curriculum.* Curriculum, Media, and Instruction Series, Occasional Paper No. 19. Edmonton, Alberta, Canada: University of Alberta, Faculty of Education, Department of Secondary Education.

Wilson, J. (1969). *Moral education and the curriculum: A guide for teachers and research workers.* New York: Pergamon Press.

Wilson, S. (1977). The use of ethnographic techniques in educational research. *Review of Educational Research,* 47 (1), 245-265.

Winitzky, N., Stoddart, T., & O'Keefe, P. (1992). Great expectations: Emergent professional development schools. *Journal of Teacher Education,* 43 (1), 3-18.

Wipperman, W. (1989). Das Berliner Schulwesen in der NS-zeit. Fragen, Thesen und methodische Bemer Kungen (57-73). [The Berlin School System.] In Schmidt, Benno, *Schule in Berlin.* Gestern und heute. Berlin, Germany.

Wisconsin Department of Public Instruction (1986). *A guide to curriculum planning in social studies.* Madison, WI: Wisconsin Department of Public Instruction.

Wise, A. (1979). *Legislated learning.* Berkeley, CA: University of California Press.

Witherell, C. & Noddings, N. (Eds.). (1991). *Stories lives tell: Narrative and dialogue in education.* New York: Teachers College Press.

Witherspoon, R. (1987). The problems of black education. *The Journal of Educational Thought,* 21 (3), 155-161.

Witt, P. (Ed.). (1968). *Technology and the curriculum.* New York: Teachers College Press.

Wolcott, H. (1973). *The man in the principal's office: An ethnography.* New York: Holt, Rinehart & Winston.

Wolcott, H. (1975, Summer). Criteria for an ethnographic approach to research in schools. *Human Organization,* 34 (2), 111-127.

Wolcott, H. (1990). *Writing up qualitative research.* Newbury Park, CA: Sage.

Wolf, R. (1979). The use of judicial evaluation methods in the formulation of educational policy. *Educational Evaluation and Policy Analysis*, 1 (3), 19-28.

Wolfson, B. (1985a). Preface: Special issue in commemoration of James B. Macdonald, 1925-1983. *JCT*, 6 (3), 5-7.

Wolfson, B. (1985b). Closing remarks. *JCT*, 6 (3), 65.

Women on Words and Images. (1974). Look, Jane, look. See sex stereotypes. In J. Stacey, S. Bereaud, J. Daniels (Eds.), *And Jill came tumbling after: Sexism in American education*. New York: Dell.

Wood, G. (1983). Beyond educational cynicism. *Educational Theory*, 32 (2), 55-71.

Wood, G. (1984). Schooling in a democracy: Transformation or reproduction. *Educational Theory*, 34 (3), 219-239.

Wood, G. (1986). Action for democratic education. *Issues in Education*, IV (3), 287-300.

Wood, G. (1988a). Education in Appalachia: Power, powerlessness and the school curriculum. *JCT*, 7 (4), 27-64.

Wood, G. (1988b). Democracy and the curriculum. In L. Beyer & M. Apple (Eds.), *The curriculum: Problems, politics and possibilities* (166-190). Albany, NY: State University of New York Press.

Woods, P. & Hammersley, M. (Eds.). (1993). *Gender & ethnicity in schools: Ethnographic accounts*. London & New York: Routledge and the Open University.

Woolf, V. (1938, 1966). *Three Guineas*. New York: Harcourt, Brace.

Worthen, B. (1978). *Metaphors and methodologies for evaluation*. Paper presented at the annual meeting of the American Educational Research Association, Toronto, Ontario, Canada.

Worthen, B. & Sanders, J. (1987). *Educational evaluation, alternative approaches, and practical guidelines*. White Plains, NY: Longman.

Wraga, W. & Hlebowitsh, P. (1991). STS education and the curriculum field. *School Science and Mathematics*, 91 (2), 54-58.

Wulf, C. (1991). Federal Republic of Germany. In A. Lewy (Ed.), *The international encyclopedia of curriculum* (230-233). New York: Pergamon Press.

Wynne, E. & Ryan, R. (1993). *Reclaiming our schools: A handbook on teaching, character, academics, and discipline*. [Forward James S. Coleman.] New York: Merill (Macmillan).

Yager, R. (1984). The major crisis in science education. *School Science and Mathematics*, 84, 189-198.

Yager, R. (1986). What's wrong with school science? *The Science Teacher*, 53 (1), 145-147.

Yager, R. (1987). Problem solving: The STS advantage. *Curriculum Review*, 26 (3), 19-21.

Yale Report (1828). Original papers in relation to a course of liberal education. *American Journal of Science and Arts*, XV (2), 297-340.

Yat-Ming, J. (1991). Curriculum development in the People's Republic of China. In C. Marsh & P. Morris (Eds.), *Curriculum development in East Asia* (61-81). London, England: Falmer.

Yellin, D. & Koetting, R. (1988). Literacy instruction and children raised in poverty: A theoretical discussion. *JCT*, 8 (4), 101-114.

Yonemura, M. (1991). Glimpses of becoming an early childhood teacher: A teacher educator's perspective. *Curriculum Inquiry*, 21 (4), 397-418.

Young, A. (1993). Toward an understanding of African American ethnicity. In L. Castenell, Jr. & W. Pinar (Eds.), *Understanding curriculum as racial text: Representations of identity and difference in education* (209-222). Albany, NY: State University of New York Press.

Young, M. (Ed.). (1971). *Knowledge and control: New directions for the sociology of education*. London, England: Collier-Macmillan.

Young, R. (1988). Critical teaching and learning. *Educational Theory*, 38 (1), 47-59.

Young, R. (Ed.). (1990). *White mythologies: Writing history and the west*. New York: Routledge.

Zahorik, J. (1987). Teaching: Rules, research, beauty, and creation. *Journal of Curriculum and Supervision*, 2 (3), 275-284.

Zais, R. (1976). *Curriculum: Principles and foundations*. New York: Thomas Y. Cromwell.

Zais, R. (1980). In one era and out another: Anti-school polemics and the sociology of curriculum change. *NASSP Bulletin*, 64, 9-19.

Zais, R. (1986). Confronting encapsulation as a theme in curriculum design. *Theory into Practice*, 25 (1), 17-23.

Zamora, R. (1983). Computer and other literacies. In M. Grady & J. Gawronski (Eds.), *Computers in curriculum and instruction* (6-11). Alexandria, VA: ASCD.

Zaret, E. (1986). The uncertainty principle in curriculum planning. *Theory Into Practice*, XXV (1), 46-52.

Zeichner, K. & Liston, D. (1990). Traditions of reform in U.S. teacher education. *Journal of Teacher Education*, 41 (2), 3-20.

Zelizer, V. (1985). *Pricing the priceless child: The changing social value of children*. New York: Basic Books.

Zeuli, J. & Buchmann, M. (1988). Implementation and teacher-thinking research as curriculum deliberation. *Journal of Curriculum Studies*, 20 (2), 141-154.

Zimpher, N. & Howey, K. (1987). Adapting supervisory practices to different orientations of teaching competence. *Journal of Curriculum and Supervision*, 2 (2), 101-127.

Zirbes, L. (1935). *Curriculum trends: A preliminary report and a challenge*. Washington, DC: Association for Childhood Education.

Zirbes, L. (1959). *Spurs to creative teaching*. New York: Putnam.

Zukav, G. (1986). *The dancing wu li masters: An overview of the new physics*. New York: Bantam Books.

Zumwalt, K. (1988). Beginning professional teachers: The need for a curricular vision of teaching. In M. Reynolds (Ed.), *Knowledge base for the beginning teachers* (173-184). Oxford, England: Pergamon.

Zumwalt, K. (1991). Alternative routes to teaching: Three alternative approaches. *Journal of Teacher Education*, 42 (2), 83-92.

Subject Index

Ability (abilities), 27, 98, 190, 294, 668, 669, 749
Ability grouping, 255
Abode, 422
Abortion, 719
Absence (absences, absent), 289, 328, 356, 386, 435, 458, 463
Absolute difference, 481
Absolute speed, 481, 482
Absolutism (absolutes), 71, 468, 660
Absolutist, 614
Abstract (Abstraction, abstractions), 161,197, 246, 256, 257, 273, 275, 278, 291, 292, 375, 380, 415, 432, 435, 438, 500, 512, 516, 545, 565, 599, 624, 641, 707, 848, 867
Abstract expressionist, 518
Academic, 29, 94, 101, 131, 152, 189, 238, 268, 325, 329, 347, 356, 359, 439, 530, 532, 570, 597, 630, 668, 755, 758, 761, 788
achievement, 787, 809
curriculum, 789
disciplines design, 685, 687
disciplines, 38, 142, 160, 173, 188, 249, 367, 369, 372, 412, 451, 462, 489, 590, 685, 687, 694, 748, 771, 849
excellence, 756
expert (expertise), 284, 344
failure, 784
freedom, 71, 668
journals, 530, 531
rationalism, 21, 29, 30
rationalists, 29
skills, 31, 107
subject, 21
work, 41, 550
Academy, 85, 426
Access, 531, 687
Accessibility, 172, 745
Accommodation, 591
Accommodationism (racial), 320, 321
Accountability, 165, 166, 206, 251, 675, 677, 722
Achievement, 91, 148, 154, 325, 326, 333, 367, 432, 805
Achievement test (tests), 90, 195, 805
Acid rain, 802, 841
Acoustic, 478
Acquisitive, 637
Acting, 478, 553, 555, 590

Action (actions), 15, 22, 23, 30, 41, 48, 64, 92, 139, 181, 195, 213, 261, 265, 272, 285, 289, 301, 309, 310, 313, 348, 355, 379, 383, 416, 419, 436, 491, 505, 548, 554, 557, 581, 590, 592, 595, 597, 628, 630, 634, 649, 731, 732, 762, 766, 770, 827, 848, 854, 866
research journal, 54
research, 52, 54, 140, 289, 491, 563, 599, 736
researcher, 54, 58
Action-full-of-thought, 426
Active occupations, 106, 108
Activism, 323, 399, 857
Activists, 124
Activities, 36, 97, 105, 106, 107
Activity, 27, 28, 33, 34, 105, 115, 226, 282, 442, 624, 628, 694, 747
analysis, 98, 101, 117, 124
curriculum, 155
movement (the), 198
Actors (actor), 64, 214, 278, 590
Actual, 483, 594, 596, 598, 659
Actuality (actual), 251
Actualization, 435
Adaptive (adaptation), 329, 749
Additive, 319, 858
Adjudication (adjudicating), 301
Administering, 389
Administration, 109, 156, 209, 361, 710
Administrative, 143, 148, 166, 237, 252, 253, 530, 703
character, 42, 112
concerns, 78
control, 745
convenience, 74, 77, 88, 729
interest, 34, 77, 204
issues, 77
leadership, 702
organizations, 77
staff, 138
Administrators (administrator), 15, 31, 100, 112, 123, 130, 156, 188, 221, 257, 292, 305, 361, 560, 616, 622, 666, 696, 720, 723, 731, 791
Admission, 797, 816
Adolescent novels, 395
Adolescence (adolescent, adolescents), 93, 99, 287, 363, 395, 401, 409, 442, 457, 462, 463, 465

Adolescent
    development, 30
    female readers, 395
    literature, 395
    pregnancy, 401
Adoption, 687
Adrift, 219
Adult (adults), 97, 100, 105, 126, 138, 332,
    377, 428, 433, 440, 441, 445, 536, 674,
    689, 747, 780, 829
Adult education, 109
Adult-centered school, 122
Adulthood, 431
Adventure, 127
Adventuring, 192
Adversarial, 522
Advertising, 302, 469
Advice, 34, 38, 55
Advocacy, 59, 325, 363, 364, 368, 399, 586,
    631
Aesthetic
    criticism, 55, 62, 584
    epistemology, 571
    inquiry, 571, 573
    knowing, 571, 573, 581
    literacies, 570
    modernity, 507
    of pleasure, 285
    rationality, 179, 180, 181
    theory, 62, 571, 572, 579, 594
Aesthetician, 576
Aesthetics (aesthetic, esthetic), xvi, 5, 19, 25,
    28, 32, 44, 45, 46, 52, 114, 119, 136,
    170, 173, 183, 200, 203, 212, 226, 233,
    236, 373, 376, 403, 405, 406, 415, 417,
    418, 424, 427, 469, 474, 490, 491, 494,
    497, 519, 527, 528, 532, 548, 557, 566,
    567, 568, 570, 571, 572, 573, 574, 575,
    576, 578, 579, 580, 587, 588, 589, 591,
    592, 593, 595, 599, 602, 604, 627, 634,
    638, 836, 847, 852, 856, 862, 864, 866
Affect (affective, affectivist), 155, 165, 166,
    190, 218, 557, 656, 770
Affection (affections), 74
Affective
    education, 189, 227
    objectives, 193
Affiliation, 379, 384
Affiliative needs, 518
Affirmation, 631
Affirmative action, 351
Affirmative political space, 395, 496
Affluence (affluent), 294, 674
African (Africans), 818, 819, 820, 821, 822,
    823
    curriculum, 793, 821, 825, 828
    diaspora, 322
    epistemology, 322, 849
    famine, 255
    history, 341, 795
    slaves, 828

African-American (African-Americans), 128,
    315, 326, 327, 328, 329, 330, 331, 336,
    339, 346, 347, 348, 349, 350, 351, 352,
    353, 354, 356, 507, 678, 784, 856
    church, 616
    culture, 351
    education, 354
    epistemology, 353
    feminism, 311, 314
    feminists (feminism), 353, 401, 508
    history, 351, 352, 353
    intelligentsia, 352
    knowledge, 329, 350
    scholars, 356
    studies, 340, 341, 867
    subjectivity, 354
    traditions, 352
    women, 507, 529
African-European, 349
Afro-American (Afro-Americanness), 351,
    355
Afro-Caribbean, 296
Afrocentric curriculum, 351
Afrocentrics, 322
Afrocentrism (Afrocentric), 320, 322, 351,
    352, 795
After-image, 513
Age, 214, 287, 377, 749
Age-grouping patterns, 679
Age-segregated (age-segregation), 74, 77
Agency, 62, 149, 247, 252, 253, 255, 265,
    270, 281, 282, 283, 301, 302, 306, 312,
    387, 507, 518, 551
Agent (agents), 224, 386
Agentic, 387
Aggression (aggressive), 329, 331, 365
Agnostic, 627
Agreement, 489
Agricultural education, 320
Agriculture (agricultural), 98, 822, 828
Ahistorical (ahistoricism), 12, 42, 50, 69,
    184, 238, 280, 300, 335, 419, 460, 461,
    486, 545, 663, 774
AIDS educators, 821
Aims (aim), 35, 46, 74, 78, 118, 195, 582,
    654, 727, 743, 810
Air pollution, 841
Algebra, 823
Alienation (alienated, alienating), 189, 245,
    260, 275, 288, 305, 313, 355, 460, 518,
    533, 534, 539, 603, 609, 648, 651, 784
All-boy, 399
All-school mass, 788
Allegorical, 638, 640
Alphabet, 73
Already (the), 652
Alternative
    certification program, 757
    expressions, 298
    realities, 222
    schools, 126, 185, 256, 273, 274, 680, 754

teacher education, 750
ways of seeing, 287
Althusserian conception, 246
Altruism, 320, 321
Amazement, 657
Amazon, 829
Amazonian, 828
Amazons, 341
Ambiguity (ambiguous), 198, 638, 670
Ameliorative (amelioration), 199, 364, 548,
　　567, 593, 661, 668, 669
American
　anti-intellectualism, 631
　bicentennial, 199
　child, 779
　Civil War, 316
　civilization, 120, 131
　colonial period, 400, 625
　corporations, 293
　cultural identity, 357
　culture, 328, 670, 795
　curriculum (the), 42, 43, 120, 614, 626
　　audience, 44
　　community, 210
　　discourses, 830
　　field, 10, 12, 13, 14, 22, 23, 39, 48, 70,
　　　72, 139, 187, 205, 310, 373, 682, 848,
　　　849
　　problems, 843
　　studies, 45, 52, 63, 136, 149, 204, 295
　dream, 349, 350, 352
　economy, 49, 804
　education, 177, 183, 189, 606, 608, 610,
　　626, 631, 634, 681, 840, 841
　educational scene, 361
　educational system, 154, 721
　educational technology, 705
　Gladiator jocksniffery, 511
　government, 38
　history, 158, 328, 614, 616, 618, 795
　identity, 317, 327, 328, 330, 345, 347, 353,
　　839
　Indian, 330, 660
　inner cities, 830
　life, 183, 615
　literary criticism, 45
　literary history, 542
　military occupation, 808
　mind, 633
　nation, 328
　national character, 356
　people, 779
　philosophy of education, 81
　political system, 851
　political theory, 216
　politicians, 806
　politics, 49
　population, 614, 795
　prototype, 329
　public, 189, 225, 511
　public schools, 238, 379, 402, 668

religion, 660
research universities, 673
scholars, 52
school children, 615
school classroom, 791
school curriculum, 155, 316, 350
schooling, 608, 636, 843
schools, 672, 681, 805, 838
self, 328, 329, 330
students, 675, 733, 805
studies, 291
worker, 259
American-Chinese relations, 817
Americanize (Americanization), 661, 677,
　840
Americans, 328, 809, 811
Amerindian, 332, 333
Amway enterprise consciousness, 511
Anagrams (anagrammatically), 480, 484, 537
Analog, 597
Analogical reasoning, 775
Analogy (analogies), 423, 461, 483, 748, 749
Analysand, 290, 378, 523
Analysis (analytical, analytic), 32, 36, 47, 60,
　77, 172,197, 212, 271, 272, 299, 344,
　370, 451, 488, 492, 520, 578, 741, 749,
　811
Analyst, 523
Analytic philosophy, 156
Analytic situation, 521
Anarchy (anarchistic), 126, 743, 859
Anatomy, 368
Ancient, 76, 423, 631, 638, 652, 818
Androcentric, 304, 385
Androgyny (androgynous), 366, 476, 525
Anecdote, 430, 438, 439, 445
Angels, 52
Anger, 13, 261
Anglo-American epistemological theories,
　322
Anglo-American philosophy, 205
Anglo-Protestant culture, 609
Anglophone Canada, 840
Angst, 455, 533
Anguish, 340, 455, 657
Animal training, 116
Animals, 841
Anomalies, 501
Anonymity (anonymous), 521, 540
Answer, 435, 453
Antagonisms, 223
Ante-predicative, 447
Anthropocentric (anthropocentricity), 271,
　274, 715
Anthropological (anthropology), 602, 747,
　779, 783, 784, 812
Anthropology, 55, 58, 163, 224, 276
Anthroposophy, 626
Anti-bias, 334, 354, 355
Anti-capitalist, 365
Anti-Catholic, 609, 610, 612

Anti-Christian, 778
Anti-education school sentiment, 680
Anti-imperialist, 365
Anti-intellectualism (anti-intellectual), 153, 608, 631, 852
Anti-Marxist, 505
Anti-moral education, 630
Anti-oppression, 397
Anti-patriarchal, 401
Anti-racist, 331, 332, 334, 357
Anti-revolutionary revisionism, 816
Anti-social, 163, 171
Anti-war, 399
Anticipation, 445, 579
Anticolonialism, 496
Antimetaphysical, 492
Antithesis, 105
Anxiety, 426, 439, 702
Apartheid, 818, 824
Apocalyptic, 652, 653
Apolitical, 221, 222, 384
Appalachian culture, 255
Appalachian fiction, 533
Apparatus, 318
Appearances (appearance), 290, 420, 472
Apperception, 78, 86
Apperceptive mass, 78, 160
Appetites, 472
Application (applications), 74, 79, 207, 231, 299, 461, 479, 488, 582, 584, 648, 775, 832
Applied
    curriculum development, 216
    curriculum research, 216
    knowledge, 161
    psychology, 746
    science, 685
    teacher education, 756
Appraisal, 687
Appreciation, 582, 583, 738
Apprehension (apprehend), 570, 576, 598, 658, 691
Apprenticeship, 607
Appropriation (appropriations), 247, 425, 853
Aptitude, 749
Arch-writing, 490, 491
Arche, 302
Archeology (archeological), 415, 513, 818
Archetype (archetypical), 162, 196
Architect, 220, 538
Architecture (architectural), 437, 490, 494, 513, 538, 818
Archivist, 658
Aristocracy (aristocratic), 535, 796
Arithmatic, 75, 76, 94, 709, 733, 808, 823
Army tank, 191
Arrest (arrested), 187, 231, 518, 519, 847
Art, 35, 57, 97, 150, 169, 385, 408, 418, 427, 568, 569, 570, 572, 576, 578, 579, 581, 594, 602, 603, 605, 626, 657, 705, 737,

738, 739, 746, 752, 764, 765, 814, 818, 824, 852, 864
    appreciation, 708
    criticism, 580, 584, 741
    critics, 574
    curriculum, 580
    education, 568, 580
    exhibition, 574
    historian, 576
    history, 580
    museum, 97
    production 580
Articulation (of school subjects), 77
Artifact (artifacts), 584, 593, 794, 808
Artifactual, 584
Artificial intelligence (AI), 92, 712, 713, 716
Artisan, 602
Artist (artists), 210, 231, 290, 415, 542, 571, 573, 576, 577, 584, 599, 602, 738, 752
Artistic, 29, 50, 567, 658
    criticism, 740
    language, 741
    problem-solving, 752
Artistry, 182, 581, 586, 752
Arts, 32, 50, 51, 52, 62, 65, 109, 152, 153, 162, 164, 176, 183, 201, 220, 249, 332, 451, 482, 489, 567, 568, 569, 573, 580, 582, 586, 604, 605, 620, 735, 757, 758, 761, 851, 858, 865
Aryan, 316
Asexual, 337, 339, 340
Asian schools, 806
Asian-Americans, 315, 330
Asocial, 84, 523, 603
Aspiration (aspirations), 435, 735, 785, 821, 866
Assassinated, 644
Assault, 786, 787
Assemblies, 789
Assembly line, 95
Assessment, 36, 167, 173, 333, 498, 573, 642, 696, 721, 732, 742, 743, 778, 780, 793, 832
    practices, 798
    tasks, 742
Assimilation (assimilationist), 78, 324, 325, 346, 347, 591
Associating, 192
Association, 79
Assumptions, 171, 249, 250, 279, 371, 385, 408, 426, 465, 510, 597, 715, 753
Asymmetry (asymmetrical), 369, 374, 375, 385, 394, 491
At-risk, 322, 850
Atheists, 627
Atheoretical, 12, 50, 54, 212, 221, 229, 231, 238, 419, 663
Athletic (athletics), 154, 363, 365, 788, 789, 790
Atmosphere (atmospheric), 432, 433, 442, 675

Atomization (atomized), 416, 637
Atrophy, 518, 519
Attachment (attachments), 376, 380, 381, 385, 386, 548
Attacks (attack), 176, 370, 461, 466
Attendance, 623
Attending, 431
Attention, 74, 172, 749, 782, 783
Attentiveness, 442
Attitude (attitudes, attitudinal), 102, 106, 127, 324, 327, 337, 407, 694, 713, 779, 833
Attitude theories, 578, 579
Attunes (attune, attunement), 408, 409, 423, 764
Audible silence, 275
Audience, 526, 549, 573, 582, 584, 596, 738
Audienced, 782
Audio-visual materials, 143
Audiotapes, 555
Auditory, 750
Augustinian view, 657
Aural, 513, 531, 713
Australian school curriculum, 229
Authentic assessment, 742
Authentic self, 492, 493, 494, 538
Authentic teaching, 768
Authenticity (authentic), 299, 334, 376, 392, 404, 407, 408, 422, 472, 493, 532, 543, 544, 591, 637, 646, 648
Author (authors), 8, 57, 61, 436, 515, 540
Authoritarian (authoritarianism), 5, 14, 64, 131, 273, 280, 306, 308, 313, 384, 392, 400, 626, 731, 737, 787, 808, 837
Authoritarian populism, 261
Authoritativeness, 310
Authority (authorities), 109, 127, 170, 244, 248, 261, 272, 284, 339, 365, 384, 385, 393, 504, 530, 576, 600, 607, 639, 666, 676, 831, 856
Auto-critique, 61
Autobiographer, 536, 540, 590
Autobiographical/biographical, 55, 216, 261, 263, 312, 514, 515, 523, 535, 559, 564, 565, 769, 855
  curriculum theory, 414
  discourses, 43, 57, 62, 226
  inquiry, 556
  journey, 645
  method (methods), 384, 388, 518, 519, 521, 530, 540, 546, 551, 578, 596
  movement, 645
  narratives, 527, 540
  practice, 493, 517, 532, 552, 560, 584, 765
  praxeology, 556
  praxis, 517, 555, 556
  reclamations, 551
  reflection, 215, 551, 590, 752
  register, 356
  remembrance, 542, 552, 566
  research, 61, 272, 411, 523, 553, 554, 562

researchers, 558
scholars, 516, 564
scholarship, 44, 224, 304, 492, 521, 525, 547, 553
teacher research, 524, 564
theorist (theorists), 537, 564
theory, 372, 376, 417, 515, 517, 532, 549, 552, 864
traces, 537
tradition, 521, 781
understanding, 528, 533, 546, 642
voice, 382, 526, 548
work, 43, 420, 523, 527, 554, 566, 578, 584
writing, 551, 552, 558, 560, 565, 597
Autobiography (autobiographies, autobiographical), xvii, xviii, 4, 16, 32, 43, 46, 61, 64, 218, 223, 227, 238, 243, 256, 287, 289, 290, 291, 302, 355, 370, 375, 381, 384, 385, 388, 389, 395, 402, 403, 415, 416, 420, 424, 475, 478, 493, 495, 506, 514, 516, 517, 518, 521, 522, 524, 526, 527, 532, 533, 534, 535, 536, 537, 538, 540, 541, 544, 545, 547, 548, 549, 550, 551, 552, 554, 558, 560, 564, 566, 567, 578, 589, 596, 599, 600, 604, 628, 637, 644, 645, 646, 697, 731, 741, 750, 751, 759, 760, 765, 766, 847, 862, 864, 866
Automaticity, 581
Automaticization, 189
Automaton, 117
Autonomy (autonomous), 294, 304, 316, 348, 379, 383, 387, 393, 400, 468, 518, 550, 699, 715, 726, 763, 764, 850, 853, 854, 856, 863, 864
Avant garde, 507
Awareness, 124, 170, 282, 443, 459, 470, 522, 577, 582, 765, 829, 861
Awe, 433, 527, 657, 692
Axioms, 60

Baby, 496
Back-to-basics, 238, 569, 838
Back-to-nature, 273
Background, 316, 563, 606, 747, 769
Backlash, 261
Backward, 321
Bad faith, 235, 267, 594
Balance (balanced), 76, 144, 198, 418, 499, 581, 597, 600, 617, 634, 803
Balkanization, 271, 856, 865
Banality, 511
Bandwagon, 177, 214, 663
Banker, 121
Banking (Freire's theory), 644, 781, 826
Baptism, 645
Baptist, 616, 624
Barbarian, 362, 426
Barbecue, 511
Barricades, 309, 310, 545

Base, 245, 246, 251, 267, 269, 276
Baseball, 830
Basic, 320, 830
  ecclesial communities, 644
  science, 169
  skills, 260, 532, 733, 771
Basics, 799
Bathwater, 496
Battle (battlefield), 153, 375, 376, 786
Bauhaus, 577, 578
Beauty (beautiful), 338, 418, 473, 475, 489, 574, 628
Becoming, 172, 446, 459, 528, 785
Beer, 592
Beginning (the), 447
Behaving, 172
Behavior (behaviors), 59, 92, 125, 136, 212, 237, 244, 248, 256, 309, 367, 412, 521, 698, 728, 735, 785, 837, 841
Behavioral, 9, 47, 249, 348, 434, 457, 501, 575, 582, 689, 692, 705, 727, 751
  (behaviorist) psychology, 91, 92, 167, 172, 186, 192, 206, 711
  objectives, 8, 149, 155, 165, 166, 177, 214, 227, 236, 387, 409, 411, 627
  research, 51
  sciences, 36, 50, 89, 151, 212, 213, 569, 861
  scientists, 571
Behaviorism, 91, 92, 168, 184, 200, 688, 710
Behaviorist (behavioristic), 65, 92, 189, 207, 709
Behavioristic offspring, 180
Behavioristic orientations, 183, 199
Behavioral managers, 184
Being, 427, 428, 433, 443, 454, 460, 466, 501, 538, 540, 545, 552, 602, 641, 689, 849
Being-in-relation, 404, 428
Being-in-the-world, 213, 407, 427, 437
Being-toward-death, 447
Beliefs, 407, 489, 554, 561, 753
Believing, 660
Benefits (benefit), 621, 634
Benevolence (benevolent), 284
Between, 481, 491, 501, 512, 545
Bias (biases), 365
Bible (biblical), 93, 62, 640, 642, 648
Bibliographic essay, 7
Bibliographical studies, 43
Bibliography, 61
Bifurcation, 602, 652, 762
Bigotry, 532
Bilingual, 324
Binary (binarisms), 447, 458, 463, 464, 467, 487, 490, 491, 506, 854
Biofeedback, 705
Biographer, 390
Biographic functions (function), 520, 782
Biographic movement, 520
Biographic situation, 406, 520, 599

Biographic themes, 494
Biographical/autobiographical, 788
  praxis, 555
  research, 516, 553
  scholarship, 43
  scholarship, 525
  studies, 563
  teacher research, 564
  understanding, 555
Biography (biographical, biographies), xvii, 55, 61, 213, 274, 328, 413, 416, 429, 515, 516, 518, 520, 524, 531, 532, 537, 540, 545, 547, 548, 553, 554, 555, 556, 558, 560, 563, 564, 599, 697, 760, 765, 769
Biological, 316, 344, 346, 348, 357, 359, 362, 374, 498, 593
Biological determinism (determinations), 94, 373
Biology textbook controversies, 778
Biology, 11, 91, 162, 163, 169, 194, 368, 424, 464, 500
Biosphere (biospheric), 840, 841
Biospheric harmony, 536
Biostatistician, 194
Biosystem, 841
Birth, 63, 70, 71, 583, 647, 866
Birthing, 444
Bisexual, 397
Bits, 715
Bitter, 375, 381, 549
Black, 316, 330, 337, 338, 340, 341, 343, 344, 345, 348, 349, 350, 357, 464, 615, 818, 821, 825
  body, 788
  children, 332
  college men, 326
  colleges, 321
  community (communities), 529, 832
  cultural workers, 357
  culture, 334, 335, 345
  curriculum, 323
    orientations, 316, 319, 320, 509
    theorizing, 319
  education, 320, 321, 825
  educational life, 128
  educational system, 322
  educator, 210, 323
  elementary school, 740
  experience, 319
  feminist theory, 508
  feminist thought, 341
  feminists, 353
  girls, 341
  historians, 12
  history, 350, 351
  ideas, 348
  institutions, 348
  intelligentsia (intellectuals), 322, 323, 340
  liberal education, 321
  liberation theology, 636

men (man), 338, 339, 342, 361
middle-class, 349
nationalism, 320, 321, 322
parents, 326
progress, 321
radicalism (radicals), xviii, 322, 323
school failure, 327
social reconstructionist, 323
students,334
studies, 322, 350
values, 348
women, 338, 339, 341, 342, 343, 344
youth, 349
Black-owned business, 322
Blackness, 464
Blacks, 128, 221, 317, 324, 326, 337, 338,
    339, 340, 346, 730
Blandness, 142
Blended force, 637
Blessed, 444
Blind (blindness), 336, 420, 461, 530, 820
Blocks (blocked, blockage), 290, 378, 523,
    535, 589
Bloodless, 378, 380
Blues (the), 339
Bodies, 477, 575, 590, 680
Bodiless, 384
Bodily movement, 560
Body (the), 61, 74, 218, 222, 361, 366, 376,
    391, 435, 440, 445, 446, 447, 453, 484,
    490, 511, 512, 521, 525, 526, 534, 536,
    537, 547, 557, 565, 578, 591, 597, 601,
    602, 603, 626, 629, 647, 658, 660, 719,
    836
  of curricular writing, 234
  of law, 666
  (bodies) of knowledge, 161, 164, 231, 352,
    562, 865
  of scholarship, 244, 371, 485, 631
  of work, 243, 376
  subject, 434, 454, 455, 456, 459, 513
Bodyreading, 434
Boisterousness, 432
Bolshevik revolution, 835
Bonding, 550
Book (books), 9, 10, 23, 24, 26, 33, 85, 298,
    334, 335, 338, 462, 582, 617, 705, 812,
    867
Bookkeeping, 790
Border pedagogy, 283, 285
Bordercrossings, 311, 401, 508, 853
Borderless world economy, 802
Borders, 286, 853
Bored (boredom, boring), 401, 446, 474, 784
Born-again, 625
Boundaries (boundary), xvii, 22, 145, 148,
    285, 316, 406, 423, 424, 465, 493, 516,
    528, 584, 614, 660, 665, 713, 760, 770,
    853, 856
Bourgeois (bourgeoisie), 251, 257, 274, 294,
    474, 496, 507, 545, 579, 594, 816, 836

Boy Scouts, 839
Boys, 85, 360, 361, 362, 363, 365, 377, 435,
    807
Bracketing (bracket), 62, 406, 407, 414, 424,
    520, 590, 598, 866
Brain, 73
Brazilian, 826, 828
Breakdown (breaking down), 538, 587, 614,
    853
Breaking, 550
Breaks (break), 491, 501
Breath, 172, 556, 595
Bricklaying, 117
Brilliance, 391
British model, 732
Broad-field pattern, 687
Brothers (brother), 384, 543, 544
Browns, 221
Brutalization, 475
Buddhism, 615
Budget, 59, 672
Budget cuts, 683
Bulletins, 582
Bullets, 212, 644
Bureaucracy (bureaucracies, bureaucratic),
    183, 204, 227, 244, 248, 257, 259, 260,
    322, 359, 380, 418, 422, 432, 582, 608,
    621, 644, 664, 676, 677, 685, 687, 688,
    689, 722, 724, 743, 770, 771, 794, 796,
    797, 799, 817, 848, 849, 855, 859, 863
Bureaucrat (bureaucrats), 149, 619, 666, 694,
    848
Bureaucratic (bureaucratized), 16, 20, 46, 54,
    57, 63, 64, 71, 78, 112, 131, 184, 690
  reform, 662
  rituals, 727
  state, 665
Bureaucratism, 744
Bureaucratization, 184, 189, 406, 661, 663,
    671, 677, 703, 722, 776
Bureautechnology (bureautechnocratic), 751
Burn-outs, 787
Business, 27, 30, 31, 102, 124, 125, 153, 199,
    236, 250, 293, 662, 671, 672, 673, 680,
    681, 718, 721, 728, 762, 776, 806, 848
Business school professors, 14
Business/education alliance, 672
Businessmen, 329
Busing (bus, buses), 608, 612, 768
Busywork, 182

Calculations, 676
Calculative, 572
Calculative thinking, 92
Calling, 751, 764, 861
Calls (call), 422, 764
Camouflaged, 490
Canadian, 672, 791, 795, 838, 840
Canadian content, 840
Canadian curriculum, 840

Canon (the) (canons), 23, 286, 287, 315, 328, 330, 335, 398, 631
Canonical sins, 335, 480
Canonical texts, 638
Canonical unconscious, 336
Capacities, 75, 327, 694
Capital, 253, 254, 296
Capital accumulation, 676
Capitalism (capitalist), 120, 220, 244, 266, 267, 271, 304, 318, 351, 358, 427, 473, 474, 496, 512, 579
Care, 344, 653, 656, 694, 695, 696, 779
Career (careers), 517, 654, 798, 849
  education, 249
  ladders, 722
  stages, 769
Caretaking (caretakers), 343, 369, 393, 539
Caring, 258, 259, 369, 380, 381, 389, 390, 427, 434, 485, 523, 524, 548, 655, 694, 695, 696, 752, 768, 773, 788, 848
  community, 560
Caring/contradiction, 787
Carnegie units, 682
Cartesian, 53, 272, 304, 453, 603
Cartesian-Newtonian, 509
Case methods, 769
Case study (studies), 54, 398, 736, 761, 769
Caste system, 160
Castrated, 539
Cataclysm, 42, 159, 186, 187
Catechism, 848
Categories (category), 428, 662, 663, 664, 784
Categorization, 200, 430
Catholic high school, 787
Catholic religious women, 529
Catholicism (Catholic), 529, 609, 610, 611, 612, 614, 618, 622, 623, 639, 643, 644, 646, 651, 787, 788, 827, 834
Causal claims, 53
Causality (causal), 245, 414, 461, 521
Cause/effect, 246, 375, 499, 509, 510, 730, 743
Causes, 222
Cave, 474, 475, 480
Celebrations (celebration), 432, 468, 475
Celebrity, 470
Censorship (censor), 9, 298, 299, 402, 579, 613, 625, 635, 666, 780
Central
  government, 805
  office supervisors (supervisor), 221, 720, 723, 724
  planning, 814
  tendency theory, 779
Centrality, 283, 317, 336, 372
Centralization, 33, 207, 661, 677, 678, 679, 690
Centralized, 794, 798
Centralizing, 703, 856
Centrism, 482

Centrist position, 141, 143, 144, 681
Ceremonies, 432, 823
Certainty, 227, 268, 325, 489, 499
Certification, 721, 756, 757
Chaining, 167
Challenge statements, 726
Change, 6, 24, 38, 54, 164, 165, 192, 202, 203, 252, 255, 272, 274, 321, 373, 418, 500, 566, 621, 682, 689, 699, 700, 702, 703, 704, 715, 723, 800
Change agents, 613
Changes, 35, 39
Chaos, 223, 500, 501, 859, 860
Chaos theory, 498, 500
Chaotic, 478
Character education, 632
Character, 79, 80, 196, 290, 320, 522
Charismatic, 624
Charity, 433
Charts, 85
Chauvinistic, 808
Cheerfulness, 433
Cheerleaders (cheerleading), 363, 789
Chemical Bond Approach Project, 162
Chemistry, 162, 169, 686
Chemists, 712
Child, 26, 52, 78, 80, 84, 85, 92, 103, 105, 106, 107, 122, 126, 132, 143, 149, 155, 178, 185, 190, 197, 222, 332, 336, 339, 347, 377, 380, 407, 428, 429, 430, 432, 433, 439, 441, 442, 454, 522, 549, 586, 611, 624, 625, 673, 697, 750, 767, 780, 783, 811
  care centers, 360
  development, 30, 88, 89, 206, 238, 244
  psychology, 780
  study, 82, 83, 84, 88, 89, 92
Child's place, 440
Child-centeredness (centered), 29, 83, 86, 87, 88, 89, 90, 103, 116, 119, 123, 124, 125, 126, 127, 129, 130, 132, 141, 143, 150, 185, 186, 189, 272, 442, 586, 685, 811
Child-parent bond, 380
Child-rearing, 369, 374, 375, 622
Child-self, 439
Childhood, 189, 290, 362, 429, 431, 454, 533, 607, 628, 759
Childlike, 365
Children, 26, 72, 73, 80, 86, 87, 89, 92, 93, 97, 100, 107, 109, 115, 120, 122, 160, 170, 174, 192,199, 222, 227, 233, 257, 258, 284, 295, 305, 327, 331, 332, 333, 334, 334, 339, 346, 347, 348, 352, 366, 379, 380, 387, 390, 411, 421, 428, 430, 432, 439, 440, 441, 442, 444, 445, 518, 526, 527, 528, 529, 530, 536, 541, 542, 546, 549, 567, 569, 586, 607, 609, 611, 613, 617, 620, 621, 624, 661, 672, 691, 695, 696, 712, 719, 740, 742, 747, 754, 768, 774, 779, 783, 791, 792, 801, 803, 805, 806, 807, 821, 830, 834, 841, 867

Chinese, 814, 815
  Taoism, 492
Choice, 298, 416, 419, 424, 614, 620, 621,
  666, 677, 832
Chorus (choral), 382, 523, 526, 789
Christian (Christians, Christianity), 27, 101,
  102, 377, 399, 472, 534, 609, 610, 613,
  614, 622, 624, 625, 628, 636, 638, 639,
  642, 643, 646, 647, 648, 649, 650
Christian schools, 678
Chronological, 697, 829
Church (churches), 27, 88, 380, 607, 608,
  610, 614, 616, 635, 636, 644, 646, 647,
  648, 649, 652, 654, 660, 819, 823, 834
Church/school relations, 606
Church/state, 635
Churchpeople, 636
Cigarettes, 49
Cinema, 589
Circles, 541
Circular, 371, 467, 544, 849
Circulate, 528
Circus, 220, 266
Cities (city), 84, 90, 96, 99, 103, 120, 208
Citizenry, 145, 153, 244
Citizens (citizen), 49, 95, 99, 102, 131, 171,
  209, 258, 292, 304, 613, 617, 621, 668,
  698, 718, 719, 776, 824, 848
Citizenship, 82, 99, 108, 117, 133, 291, 352,
  353, 609, 618, 620, 678, 802, 808, 841
Civic
  competence, 147
  curriculum, 619
  morality, 139
  religion, 618, 660
  values, 618
  virtue, 808
  workers, 33
Civics (civic), 114, 158, 291, 292, 356, 523,
  618, 619, 670, 681, 813, 827
Civil, 674, 834
  government, 611
  liberties, 128
  rights activist, 128
  rights movement, 184, 187, 277
  rights, 128, 214, 329, 330, 402
  servants, 321
  service examinations, 733
Civilization (civilizations), 304, 380, 541,
  717, 799, 813, 818
Civilize (civilized), 294, 360, 376, 458
Claim (claiming), 384, 386
Clarification, 202, 749
Class (classed), 121, 228, 250, 253, 254, 260,
  261, 264, 265, 268, 278, 284, 294, 306,
  310, 311, 314, 315, 317, 318, 319, 334,
  340, 341, 342, 343, 344, 348, 400, 423,
  472, 503, 524, 535, 563, 566, 580, 730,
  771, 777, 784, 853
Class (monied), 120
Class (ruling), 109, 211

Class (working), 211
Class
  analysis, 289, 294, 295, 303, 308, 309, 354,
    357, 370, 391, 394, 395
  conflict, 309
  consciousness, 264
  differences, 41
  discussion, 587
  domination, 269
  guilt, 308
  identity, 279
  interest, 211
  perspective, 295
  plans (lesson), 558
  privilege, 41, 126, 608
  relations, 293
  size, 682
  structure, 294, 609
  struggle, 304, 309, 649
  system, 222
  warfare, 579
Classical
  age, 481
  curricularists, 108
  curriculum, 72, 73, 77, 84, 86, 103, 105,
    147, 152, 153, 169, 859
  curriculum theory (theorists),70, 72, 75,
    78, 83, 84, 99, 103, 194, 198, 269, 296,
    361
  education, 77
  orientation, 154
  position, 90
  subjects, 74
  thought, 630
  view, 75, 76
Classical/mental discipline, 82, 96
Classicalist, 76, 79, 154
Classicism, 12, 75, 154
Classics, 153, 206, 810
Classification, 155, 286, 475
Classism (classist), 218, 220, 221, 222, 309,
  355
Classless society, 816
Classroom (classrooms), 31, 41, 46, 48, 56,
  59, 64, 77, 109, 111, 134, 169, 171,
  174, 175, 188, 189, 193, 197, 198, 214,
  248, 250, 256, 262, 272, 276, 284, 299,
  305, 309, 334, 337, 341, 353, 360, 364,
  365, 380, 383, 387, 388, 392, 393, 400,
  412, 419, 420, 422, 426, 428, 430, 431,
  441, 472, 479, 502, 531, 532, 546, 547,
  550, 555, 557, 558, 559, 560, 561, 566,
  567, 575, 581, 582, 583, 585, 591, 599,
  612, 616, 618, 627, 635, 668, 669, 677,
  679, 680, 682, 683, 688, 696, 703, 709.
  713, 714, 716, 719, 731, 737, 739, 741,
  742, 747, 748, 753, 754, 757, 760, 764,
  767, 783, 811, 813, 838
  dynamics, 311
  environment, 333, 809
  furniture, 754

Classroom (continued)
  instruction, 812
  management, 748
  meanings, 192
  observation, 721, 723, 739
  organization 748
  performances, 723
  practice, 45, 103, 279, 644, 770
  talk, 754, 782
  task, 782
  teachers, 129, 327
Classroom-based teacher development, 765
Cliché (clichés), 166, 482
Client (clients), 40, 662, 666, 700, 762
Client-expert relationship, 850
Climate, 841
Clinic (clinics), 729, 759
Clinical faculty, 758
Clinical supervision, 721, 722, 724, 725, 729,
  730, 731
Clinical supervisor, 721
Clinical trial, 53
Clock, 502
Closed systems (system), 465, 574
Closeness, 539
Closing, 633
Closure, 394, 433, 499, 501
Clothing, 796
Cloud of knowing, 214
Co-curricular activities, 789, 802
Co-emerge, 437
Coaching, 725
Coalition, 142, 153, 204, 238
Cocaine, 828
Codes (code), 248, 274, 275, 312, 459, 495
Coeducation (coeducational), 360, 361, 362,
  363, 364
Coercion, 251
Cognate field, 224
Cognition, 83, 190, 302, 413, 419, 425, 432,
  509, 547, 560, 572, 602, 707
Cognitive, 116, 164, 190, 271, 366, 417, 451,
  456, 472, 487, 577, 656, 695, 702, 728,
  789
  chains, 252
  coaching, 725
  development, 74, 81, 444, 707
  domain, 155
  level, 160
  perspective, 47
  process orientation, 31
  processes, 21, 29
  psychology, 149, 705
  reductionism, 688
  science, 46, 705, 747
  scientists, 51, 705, 746
  skills, 30
  stages, 457
  steps, 571
  structure, 51, 149, 270, 445, 782
  style, 595

  theory, 307, 509
Cognitive-technical-rational inquiry, 729
Coherence (coherent), 35, 198, 230, 488,
  520, 547, 745, 865
Cohesion, 679
Cold individuals, 190
Cold War, 157, 682
Collaboration (collaborative, collaborating),
  xv, 40, 54, 69, 84, 107, 111, 112, 160,
  258, 289, 335, 382, 384, 386, 391, 400,
  482, 516, 523, 525, 551, 553, 555, 556,
  559, 560, 662, 663, 674, 713, 725, 761,
  766, 867
  autobiography, 516, 553, 554, 765, 856, 863
  change, 764
  communities, 384
  decision-making, 675
  inquiry, 383, 550
  learning, 192
  relationships, 523
  research, 551, 558, 559, 765
Collapse, 294, 308, 849, 857
Colleagues (collegial), 382, 389, 428, 549,
  560, 662, 674, 753, 760, 764, 770, 851,
  858, 862
Collective (collectivist), 5, 69, 118, 124, 148,
  264, 282, 295, 309, 322, 328, 333, 349,
  351, 367, 383, 425, 462, 521, 523, 527,
  547, 555
  bargaining, 666
  biography, 555
  creation, 601
  enterprise, 786
  identity, 258, 472
  memory, 295
  minority identity politics, 327
  mobilization, 277, 278
  self-reflection, 235
  unconscious, 457, 522
College (colleges), 26, 74, 84, 100, 135, 136,
  146, 152, 158, 260, 363, 611, 622, 679,
  786, 789
  admission, 145, 679, 697
  curriculum debates, 191
  entrance requirements, 75, 76, 77, 99,
  134, 137, 679
  professors, 208, 343, 761
College-bound, 786
College-oriented textbooks, 162
College/university curriculum, 76, 196
Colleges of education, 195, 218
Colonial
  domination, 795, 818
  education, 320, 607, 608
  gaze, 839
  period (times), 609, 625, 643, 721, 828
  powers, 819
  rule (rulers), 252, 820
  subjugation, 818
Colonialism (colonial), 321, 350, 636, 793,
  801, 818, 819, 826, 839

Colonization, 305, 321, 828
Colonizer (colonize), 62, 477
Color (colors), 344, 354, 464, 490, 602, 605,
    618, 800
Comfort, 444
Coming to form, 297, 548, 593
Commercial (advertising), 470
Commercial education, 83, 363
Commercial plunder, 824
Commercial subjects, 790
Commercialized production values, 839
Commericialism (commercial), 222, 775,
    780, 808
Commitment (committed), 177, 181, 183,
    220, 227, 416, 487, 532, 579, 631,643,
    645, 648, 649, 663, 669, 729
Commodification (commodity), 180, 296,
    306, 472, 474, 579
Commodities, 472
Commodity reification, 471
Common, 619, 767, 801, 838
  bond, 618
  core curriculum, 619
  culture, 296, 379, 380
  curriculum, 822
  encounter, 442
  experiences, 742
  faith, 45, 856
  future, 838
  ground, 13, 208, 209
  knowledge, 619
  language, 352, 482, 619
  learnings, 198, 694
  man, 132
  order, 230
  schools (school), 72, 83, 84, 610, 611, 620,
    622, 677, 678
  values, 619
Commonplaces, 65, 161, 195
Commonsense (commonsensical), 8, 35, 49,
    77, 99, 156, 244, 276, 343, 407, 454,
    590, 598, 669, 685, 688, 696, 750, 770,
    854
Communal, 351, 355, 356, 371, 387, 572
  register, 356
Communicating (communication), 50, 106,
    108, 174, 182, 192, 195, 199, 211, 274,
    299, 334, 400, 412, 416, 421, 442, 458,
    531, 573, 574, 584, 607, 642, 677, 745,
    767, 772, 774, 838
Communication analysis, 726
Communicative competence, 54, 274, 275,
    276
Communion, 604
Communism, 23, 651, 778
Communistic (communist, communists),
    130, 286, 814, 815, 830, 833, 834, 835,
    836, 837
Communitarianism, 106
Communities of discourse, 170, 171, 198
Communities of exiles, 547

Community (communities), 33, 50, 59, 84,
    87, 97, 106, 107, 109, 112, 118, 127,
    153, 192, 196, 207, 226, 255, 257, 265,
    289, 292, 295, 302, 333, 343, 346, 349,
    362, 382, 385, 386, 387, 392, 395, 418,
    424, 454, 457, 503, 516, 523, 525, 529,
    532, 544, 545, 546, 547, 548, 551, 552,
    560, 575, 601, 618, 623, 624, 631, 632,
    633, 634, 637, 655, 659, 670, 686, 731,
    747, 748, 750, 771, 788, 790, 799, 823,
    828, 829, 861
  (socio-intellectual), 11, 12, 70
  college (two-year), 158, 334, 666, 673, 712,
    718
  education, 828
Comparative
  analysis, 805
  educational evaluation, 796
  educational literature, 827
  methodology, 90, 103
  national standards, 805
  studies (study), 90, 809, 810, 832
Compartmentalization (compartmentalized),
    83, 148, 403, 535, 568, 635, 695, 799
Compassion (compassionate), 426, 631, 656,
    858
Compensatory (compensation), 386, 413,
    474, 677, 683, 771, 854
  education, 612
  reactions, 785
Competency (competencies, competence,
    competent), 167, 200, 249, 313, 328,
    344, 387, 406, 410, 413, 421, 428, 501,
    569, 620, 673, 686, 687, 762, 782, 812
  education, 238, 411
Competition (competitive, competitiveness),
    38, 106, 132, 261, 293, 306, 363, 366,
    367, 400, 711, 782, 788, 805, 810
Complementarity, 372, 555
Completeness, 713
Complex systems, 500
Complexity (complexities, complex), 110,
    213, 218, 233, 236, 270, 275, 291, 302,
    315, 345, 357, 376, 381, 489, 498, 500,
    503, 520, 526, 533, 606, 620, 668, 670,
    679, 680, 691, 697, 700, 725, 764, 805,
    823, 861, 866, 867
Compliant heterosexual identities, 396
Compose, 485
Composer, 481, 485
Composition, 483, 485
Comprehensibility, 575
Comprehension, 73, 746, 749, 780
Comprehensive high school, 681, 789
Comprehensiveness (comprehensive), 13,
    14, 22, 23, 24, 44, 139, 221, 244, 276,
    319, 616, 622, 650, 702, 705, 743, 798,
    800, 804, 857, 858
Compromise, 31
Compulsory, 251, 607, 635, 799, 808
  school attendance, 789

Computation, 190
Computer (computers), 307, 474, 705, 706, 713, 714, 715, 719, 858
capability, 715
literacy, 401, 710, 714
networks, 716
program, 712
programmers, 716
science, 30, 710, 772, 834
specialist, 716
Computer-assisted instruction (CAI), 431, 682, 711, 712, 713
Computer-assisted learning (CAL), 710
Computer-assisted thinking skills, 713
Computer-based instruction (CBI), 710, 711, 713
Computerization, 200
Concealment (concealed), 432, 442, 595
Concentration camp, 150
Concentration centers, 79, 80
Concentration, 79, 81, 86, 87, 572, 597
Concept analysis, 202
Concept formation, 747
Concept learning, 167
Concept mapping, 71, 200
Conception (feminist theory), 374, 375, 376
Conceptions (of curriculum), 14, 20, 25, 29, 31, 33, 34, 63, 97, 105, 119, 181, 182, 184, 212, 230, 390, 401, 569, 577
Concepts (concept, conceptual), 13, 18, 20, 25, 26, 27, 44, 47, 53, 62, 65, 74, 78, 81, 82, 83, 97, 144, 146, 161, 166, 190, 195, 200, 202, 216, 217, 245, 265, 270, 288, 289, 304, 305, 309, 314, 357, 410, 415, 417, 461, 482, 486, 494, 497, 498, 616, 621, 663, 666, 694, 718, 736, 747, 773, 853, 858
autonomy, 62
culture, 217
development, 165
distance, 275
schemes, 165
structures, 853
territory, 51
tools, 160, 209, 210, 248, 282, 569
Conceptual-empiricists (conceptual-empirical), 212, 213, 564
Conceptualization, 447, 690
Concern (concerns), 577, 615, 647, 652, 695, 696, 806
Concerns-based Adoption Model (CBAM), 704
Conclusions, 415
Concrete-operational, 413
Concrete-to-abstract continuum, 707
Concreteness (concrete), 196, 212, 246, 256, 275, 376, 413, 424, 435, 454, 533, 545, 590, 599, 651, 691, 707
Conditioned (conditionedness), 459, 590
Conditions of learning, 167

Conduct, 788
Cone of experience, 707
Conference, xiii, xviii, 52, 147, 159, 164, 168, 171, 179, 181, 192, 201, 207, 208, 210, 215, 216, 218, 219, 220, 222, 223, 226, 229, 231, 239, 253, 374, 417, 519, 563, 588
Conferences, 48, 145, 826
Configurations (configuration, configurative), 285, 373, 392, 403, 460, 575
Conflict management, 800
Conflict, 151, 159, 207, 249, 253, 258, 264, 489, 636, 701, 703, 704
Conformity, 126, 257, 341, 867
Confrontation, 234
Confucian, 797, 807
Confusion (confusions), 532, 549
Congregation, 637, 644
Congruences, 637
Conjunctive faith, 628
Connected (connectedness), 391, 460, 549
Connectionism (connections, connection), 92, 93, 237, 258, 384, 599, 634
Connoisseur (connoisseurs), 582, 584, 738, 739, 741, 742
Connoisseurship, 201, 581, 582, 583, 738, 739, 741, 744
Conscience, 119, 622
Conscientizing (conscientization, conscientizing), 643, 645, 647, 827
Conscious, 281, 426, 460, 518, 541, 555, 557, 665, 739
Conscious collective rituals, 788
Consciousness, 54, 58, 92, 131, 191, 194, 210, 217, 222, 224, 225, 227, 230, 245, 246, 250, 252, 272, 274, 275, 283, 287, 358, 366, 367, 389, 405, 406, 409, 412, 414, 424, 427, 432, 452, 453, 454, 456, 459, 462, 495, 540, 546, 547, 584, 600, 628, 631, 647, 649, 680, 706, 836, 841
Consensual knowledge, 445
Consensual, 751
Consensus, 451, 489, 596, 620, 627, 674, 690, 736, 833
Consequences, 35, 140
Conservatism (conservative, conservatives), 23, 76, 94, 110, 118, 128, 209, 214, 216, 230, 236, 238, 253, 260, 260, 261, 263, 272, 277, 279, 294, 298, 300, 310, 326, 335, 342, 355, 402, 425, 427, 446, 461, 489, 516, 619, 620, 624, 626, 632, 635, 660, 668, 674, 678, 682, 684, 751, 754, 755, 757, 776, 777, 779, 802, 827, 832, 868
curriculum proposals, 671
curriculum theory, 253
educational reforms, 672
school reform, 673
Consolidation, 3, 141, 677, 682, 749, 865

Consonance, 701, 703
Constituency (constituencies), 208, 574, 666, 690, 862
Constitution (constitute), 297, 330, 436
Constitution (phenomenological), 414
Constitutional, 613, 614, 615, 622, 635, 825
Constrained, 459
Constraints, 810
Constructed (construction, constructs), 248, 316, 457, 459, 463, 488, 489, 550, 576, 704
Construction of knowledge, 224
Constructionism, 477, 730
Constructivism, 55, 56, 374, 500
Constructivist teaching, 752
Consultant (consultancies, consultants), 35, 37, 102, 137, 410, 662, 794, 850
Consumer (consumers), 472, 511, 575
Consumer capitalism, 305
Consumerism, 504, 507, 508, 674
Consumption, 394, 472, 473, 781
Contemplation (contemplative), 23, 69, 127, 434, 629
Content, 101, 166, 178, 276, 285, 487, 548, 578, 592, 630, 676, 694, 713, 746, 751, 756, 762, 810, 813, 861, 865
    analysis, 173
    knowledge, 748
    mastery, 532
Contentious, 867
Contentment, 418
Contestation (contested, contestable), 252, 253, 306, 308, 327, 504, 825
Context (contexts), 56, 60, 269, 300, 407, 596, 769, 782
Context-independent, 273
Context-sensitive, 755
Contextualist, 774
Contextualization, 388, 392, 510
Contextualized (contextual), 244, 256, 557
Continental philosophies, 12
Continental philosophy, 358
Contingent (contingency, contingencies), 413, 436, 448, 454, 455, 504, 591
Continuity (continuities), 76, 144, 195, 486, 492, 549, 597, 651, 675, 696, 697, 849
Contract negotiations, 666
Contraction, 159
Contradicting (contradict), 375, 608
Contradiction (contradictions), 223, 247, 253, 261,305, 310, 319, 374, 375, 376, 382, 385, 391, 396, 436, 458, 489, 579, 668, 669, 675, 678, 680, 681
Contradictory, 280, 283, 323, 506, 867
Contrapuntal, 433
Contribution, 217
Control, 124, 153, 180, 207, 212, 213, 233, 250, 251, 254, 261, 287, 375, 382, 390, 417, 470, 499, 502, 518, 541, 603, 604, 608, 668, 689, 694, 776, 838, 849, 856

Controversy (controversies, controversial), 11, 14, 27, 110, 126, 130, 207, 230, 235, 266, 281, 300, 303, 314, 325, 326, 399, 402, 606, 614, 616, 618, 643, 803, 857, 863
Conventional (convention), 419, 421, 425, 428, 430, 489, 605, 628, 657, 693, 757
Conventions (meetings), 208, 209, 211
Conversation (conversations), 12, 70, 234, 266, 330, 359, 364, 382, 385, 386, 402, 421, 426, 427, 433, 490, 540, 546, 555, 562, 575, 639, 755, 760, 797, 848, 849, 867
Conversational analysis, 59, 60
Conversion, 53
Conviction (convictions), 305, 557
Cookbook description, 256
Cool, 371
Cooperation (cooperative), 60, 106, 107, 108, 119, 123, 134, 140, 190, 258, 334, 389, 400, 604, 722, 837
Cooperative professional development, 54
Cooperatives (cooperative), 113, 800
Copernican revolution, 799
Copy (copies), 62, 472, 473, 482, 483, 576
Core curriculum, 79, 113, 353, 618, 671, 679, 697, 698, 718
Core subjects, 675
Corporate
    America, 321
    capitalism, 140
    industrialism, 682
    model, 293
Corporation (corporations, corporate), 96, 292, 375, 672, 675, 677
Corrections facilities, 677, 678
Correlation, 92
Correlation (of subjects), 76, 81, 82, 83, 86, 87, 125, 170
Correlational-subject design, 686
Correspondence, 49, 225, 576, 659, 860
Correspondence theory (theories), 244, 245, 247, 364, 495
Corruption, 743
Cosmic, 799
Cosmological harmony, 499
Cosmological order, 499
Cosmology (cosmologies, cosmological), 62, 499, 500, 606, 637, 638, 639, 640, 643, 650, 652, 658, 859
Cosmos, 169, 657
Cost constraints, 683
Cost-effectiveness, 675
Cost-sharing, 822
Costs (cost), 97, 110, 712, 714
Counter culture (cultural), 184, 187, 210, 358, 363
Counter-hegemony (counter-hegemonic), 251, 254, 312, 313, 393, 496, 497, 506
Counter-indoctrination, 353

Counter-memory, 285, 286
Counter-text, 284, 303
Countercultural ideology, 230, 231, 232
Countertransference, 523
Courage (courageous), 184, 189, 305, 444, 848, 849
Courses (course), 28, 33, 517, 518
    content, 21, 74
    design, 200
    materials, 244, 248
    of study, 26, 198, 578, 592, 773
    proliferation, 164
    structure, 167
    syllabi, 149
Courseware, 710, 714
Court cases (case), 612, 614, 617
Court decisions, 682
Courtesy, 152, 806
Courtroom, 738
Courts (court), 300, 613, 669
Covenant, 389
Craft guilds, 95
Crafts (craft), 343, 538, 580, 581, 705, 726
Craftsman, 95
Crazed, 519
Creation, 69, 182, 201, 225, 460, 485, 501, 639, 659, 660, 866
    science, 613
    spirituality, 639, 640, 655
    theology, 631
Creative arts, 333
Creative concealment, 442
Creative imagination, 440
Creative writing, 206, 342, 439, 697, 772
Creativity (creative), 107, 127, 132, 156, 157, 172, 174, 182, 211, 217, 342, 426, 481, 485, 500, 536, 541, 571, 572, 581, 586, 591, 600, 601, 603, 604, 628, 633, 658, 680, 699, 775
Creators, 230, 236
Credentialed, 519
Creed, 217, 618, 800
Cries, 444
Crime (criminals), 397, 454, 856
Crisis, 11, 43, 44, 62, 63, 124, 141, 159, 160, 174, 176,177, 182, 187, 188, 197, 216, 260, 265, 283, 292, 293, 306, 307, 310, 312, 314, 316, 358, 470, 526, 538, 620, 633, 660, 826, 847, 851, 857
Criteria, 665, 756, 757, 865
Criterion-based testing, 411
Critic (critics), 35, 44, 64, 150, 161, 176, 234, 342, 567, 581, 582, 583, 585, 738, 760, 802
Critical, 54, 64, 65, 262, 270, 297, 304,306, 309, 350, 351, 383, 392, 425, 432, 513, 550, 561, 575, 596, 642, 644, 739, 742, 788
    assessment, 642
    consciousness, 570
    constructivism, 763

constructivist, 58
correlation, 642, 643
curriculum theory, 243
    discourse, 251
    distance, 583
    educators, 634
    ethnographer, 62
    ethnography, 58, 394
    hermeneutics, 58
    incidents, 769
    inquiry, 229, 282, 410, 504, 867
    interpretation, 749
    issues, 201
    knowing, 426
    literacy, 261
    mathematics education, 262
    paradigm, 19
    pedagogy group, 263
    pedagogy, 243, 254, 256, 260, 262, 263, 266, 271, 272, 279, 280, 281, 285, 286, 288, 304, 305,306, 313, 314, 353, 498, 507, 508, 513, 586, 587, 588, 600, 631, 644, 645, 646, 647, 770, 854
    politics, 509
    postmodern theory (theorists), 648, 730, 762, 770
    poststructuralist ethnographic practice, 61
    pragmatism, 489
    praxis, 17
    reconceptualists, 224, 225
    reflection, 597
    reflective practices, 265
    research, 57, 58, 64
    self-reflection, 770
    social consciousness, 248
    social issues, 631
    social science, 504
    storytelling, 259, 574
    tale, 506
    theoretical space, 395, 496
    theorists, 19, 64, 179, 257, 652, 730, 827
    theory, 45, 46, 247, 264, 283, 284, 289, 294, 306, 311, 314, 358, 570, 575, 579, 654, 725, 743, 746, 770, 772, 813
    thinking movement, 771, 774
    thinking skills, 773
    thinking, 282, 614, 713, 771, 772, 773, 774, 775, 837
    voice, 426
Critical/emancipatory, 742, 743
Criticism, 5, 38, 44, 64, 105, 144, 151, 183, 201, 266, 311, 314, 424, 486, 496, 518, 573, 581, 582, 583, 585, 631, 672, 738, 739, 773, 774
Critique, 750
Cross-cultural, 276, 800, 838
Cross-discourse communication, 865
Crossroads, 539
Cruelty, 590
Crystal, 491
Cubism (Cubists), 576, 577, 578

Cult (of the expert, expertise), 58, 506
Cult (of the individual), 76
Cultural
  anthropology, 787
  apartheid, 353
  archetype, 80
  artifact, 775
  assimilation, 333
  attitudes, 221
  autonomy, 795
  break, 451
  capital, 278, 866
  change, 223, 272, 303, 505, 835
  colonization, 840
  commodities, 473
  competence, 323, 324, 325, 347
  configurations, 788
  contexts, 676
  cooperation, 813, 815
  deprivation, 171
  desires, 788
  difference (differences), 285, 291, 325, 633
  diffusion, 716
  diversity, 324, 818
  emancipation, 323, 324
  enrichment, 324
  environments, 676
  episteme, 271
  epochs, 79, 80, 81, 82, 83, 86
  events, 184
  familiarity, 782
  gesticulation, 447
  grammar, 263
  heritage, 151, 153, 154, 178, 324, 618
  heterogeneity, 678
  homogeneity, 678, 797
  iconicity, 790
  identity, 285, 346, 349, 351, 353, 354, 358
  imperatives, 374
  inscription, 61
  isolation, 807
  landscape, 451
  legacy, 618
  lightning rod, 670
  linguistics, 276
  literacy, 153, 296, 330, 570, 619
  logic, 451, 473, 504
  milieu, 333, 647, 842
  modernization, 273
  move (movement, movements), 210, 451,
    755
  mummification, 345
  oppression, 842
  order, 594, 596
  organization, 783
  other, 838
  politics, 262, 284, 296, 763
  practices, 305, 324
  problems, 14, 292, 672
  production, 263, 271, 296, 313, 334
  products, 41, 49

  realities, 209, 309
  reconstruction, 799
  relations, 526, 787
  relationships, 817
  renewal, 290, 577
  representation, 277
  repression, 328
  reproduction, 251, 271, 565
  revitalization, 321, 322
  revolution, 187, 191, 192, 209, 218, 219,
    222, 519, 814, 816, 817
  sciences, 725
  separatism, 676
  shifts, 210
  spaces, 308
  sphere, 219
  struggle, 262
  studies, 262, 850
  tensions, 210
  theorists, 12
  theory, 318
  tradition (traditions), 30, 731
  transformation, 223, 326
  unconscious, 274, 330
  understanding, 323, 324
  values, 808
  vision, 251
  wealth, 695
  workers, 507
Culture (cultures, cultural), 16, 22, 52, 88,
    126, 142, 169, 170, 175, 182, 189,
    183, 207, 210, 217, 218, 222, 227,
    230, 232, 246, 247, 248, 250, 253, 255,
    262, 271, 272, 275, 276, 278, 281, 285,
    290, 294, 296, 303, 308, 323, 327, 330,
    333, 337, 344, 345, 347, 348, 351, 354,
    369, 382, 387, 393, 401, 402, 403, 424,
    450, 452, 457, 458, 461, 469, 472, 490,
    502, 509, 526, 535, 540, 570, 577, 580,
    595, 600, 608, 614, 615, 631, 632, 637,
    638, 652, 657, 658, 669, 731, 740, 748,
    756, 769, 780, 796, 800, 818, , 830,
    867
  bearer, 224
  creator, 224
Culture-epochs theory, 80, 82
Culture-free, 273
Cultures of learning, 675
Cultures of teaching, 765
Curators, 313, 512
Cure, 218, 222
Curiosity, 125, 439, 735
Currere, 414, 415, 416, 420, 493, 502, 515,
    517, 518, 520, 521, 522, 523, 548, 552,
    578, 590, 591, 596, 597, 599, 628, 645
Curricula, 27, 34, 42, 102, 112, 145, 331,
    487, 577, 578, 665, 679, 702, 704, 733,
    776, 816, 824, 826, 842
Curricular, 582, 747
  action, 568
  activities, 107

Curricular (continued)
  advice, 158
  affairs, 35
  aims, 736
  analysis, 584
  approaches, 833
  areas, 163, 164, 172, 173
  ascendancy, 75, 151
  assumptions, 745
  attention, 181
  benefits, 34
  breath, 202
  center, 84, 307, 698
  challenges, 838
  change (changes), 39, 120, 147, 367, 679, 682, 812
  cohesion, 619
  concept, 443
  concerns, 144, 182
  consequences, 745
  content, 265, 783, 810
  continuity, 134
  control, 264
  core, 697
  crisis, 125
  criticisms, 585
  debates (debate), 104, 328, 329, 353
  decision-making, 207
  design, 692
  developments (development), 144, 213
  differences, 783
  discourse, 487
  documents, 324
  element (elements), 625, 697
  emphasis (emphases), 203, 577, 817
  engagement, 782
  event (events), 549, 559, 571, 573, 738
  exclusion, 298
  experience, 697
  experimentation, 142
  experiments, 87, 144
  form (forms), 254, 290, 372, 392, 425, 443, 490, 595, 692
  freedom, 76
  goals, 421, 734, 810
  implications, 171, 336
  inclusion, 298
  initiatives, 165
  innovations (innovation), 136, 700
  integration, 801
  interest, 324
  issues, 31, 56, 253, 301, 589, 635, 659, 829
  judgments, 585
  language, 172, 410, 419,604
  machine, 37
  machinery, 38
  magesterium, 642
  materials, 34, 73, 346, 701, 796, 799, 802
  matters, 63, 236, 833
  meaning, 486
  method, 36

  objectives, 100, 734
  organization, 118, 679
  orientation, 122
  outlines, 490
  phenomena, 237, 585
  philosophy, 115
  point of view, 616
  policies, 811
  practices (practice), 36, 38, 165, 235, 273, 390, 585, 667, 720, 817, 830, 855
  prerogatives, 238
  priorities, 174
  problems, 107, 401, 573, 827
  programs, 375
  projects, 175
  proposals, 154, 829
  question, 116
  reform, 679
  relations, 438
  repertoire, 749
  rule, 660
  schemes, 186
  selectivity, 616
  separation, 679
  significance, 665
  similarity, 792
  sites, 254
  space, 717
  status quo, 39
  strategy, 332
  substructure, 248
  synthesis, 291
  system, 487
  tasks, 782
  terms, 663
  theorist, 213
  theory, 173, 810, 811
  thinking, 97
  thought, 73, 104, 156, 186, 235, 419, 568, 812
  time, 75, 76
  topics, 233
  truce, 323
  values, 36
  view, 184, 217
  workers, 417
Curricularist (curricularists), 10, 26, 27, 32, 44, 92, 101, 144, 148, 158, 173, 177, 180, 184, 204, 208, 210, 211, 213, 235, 237, 246, 288, 371, 372, 373, 391, 401, 451, 493, 495, 576, 577, 585, 592, 653, 683, 852, 863, 866
Curriculum, 3, 11, 15, 16, 18, 19, 20, 23, 24, 25, 26, 27, 28, 29, 31, 33, 34, 35, 39, 43, 45, 46, 47, 49, 50, 55, 56, 58, 62, 64, 65, 69, 70, 74, 77, 79, 80, 81, 82, 83, 84, 85, 87, 93, 96, 97, 100, 102, 105, 106, 107, 111, 116, 117, 124, 127, 137, 142, 145, 147, 148, 151, 153, 155, 156, 160, 162, 164, 166, 169, 170, 171, 174, 176, 177, 178, 180, 182, 183, 188,

190, 191, 192, 194, 195, 196, 197, 198,
199, 201, 202, 203, 204, 207, 212, 213,
215, 216, 218, 220, 222, 223, 226, 228,
232, 233, 238, 239, 243, 244, 249, 251,
253, 258, 261, 264, 267, 270, 271, 274,
276, 280, 282, 285, 286, 287, 288, 289,
291, 297, 299, 302, 303, 304, 313, 315,
319, 321, 328, 330, 332, 334, 337, 345,
346, 351, 357, 358, 359, 371, 374, 375,
376, 378, 387, 388, 389, 390, 392, 394,
395, 396, 397, 399, 402, 404, 406, 409,
415, 417, 418, 421, 426, 427, 430, 433,
434, 436, 443, 446, 450, 451, 452, 463,
464, 476, 478, 480, 482, 483, 484, 485,
486, 487, 489, 490, 492, 493, 497, 498,
499, 500, 501, 502, 503, 507, 511, 514,
515, 517, 518, 523, 528, 531, 532, 533,
540, 544, 545, 548, 549, 551, 552, 554,
555, 559, 561, 562, 566, 567, 568, 569,
573, 574, 575, 576, 577, 578, 580, 581,
584, 585, 586, 589, 591, 593, 594, 595,
596, 598, 599, 601, 602, 604, 606, 608,
611, 613, 614, 616, 617, 618, 619, 621,
626, 627, 631, 635, 637, 638, 640, 643,
645, 647, 650, 652, 653, 655, 657, 659,
660, 661, 662, 663, 664, 666, 668, 670,
675, 679, 685, 689, 690, 694, 695, 696,
700, 703, 704, 709, 713, 714, 715, 717,
718, 719, 720, 721, 722, 723, 724, 724,
731, 732, 738, 741, 742, 743, 744, 745,
746, 752, 759, 760, 765, 767, 781, 782,
784, 785, 787, 788, 789, 791, 792, 794,
795, 796, 797, 798, 803, 805, 806, 808,
812, 814, 816, 821, 823, 824, 826, 834,
835, 836, 837, 838, 839, 840, 842, 843,
847, 848, 851, 853, 854, 855, 856, 857,
859, 860, 862, 863, 864, 865, 866, 867
(college-bound), 146
(null), 27
(overt), 27
(the Chicago), 128
(undergraduate), 128, 194
(unstudied), 27
(unwritten), 27
action, 664
activity, 168
administrators, 156
affairs, 159
analyses (analysis), 368, 487
approaches, 148
artifact, 264, 311
audience, 323
bible, 20, 33
blocks, 835
books, 149, 159
building, 157
center stage, 151
chairperson, 36
change (changes), 39, 42, 54, 145, 164,
165, 175, 178, 183, 191, 203, 207, 237,

240, 580, 665, 682, 689, 701, 703, 754,
847
classification, 192
committees, 487
community, 208
component, 91
conceptions, 184
concepts, 197, 371
conceptualization (conceptualizations), 88,
165, 172, 417
concerns, 75, 143
construction, 15, 74, 98, 100, 101, 111,
117, 119, 121, 122, 124, 150, 198, 860
content, 15, 47, 85, 123, 155, 170, 245,
262, 318, 593, 676, 813
context, 559
core, 79, 108
courses, 3, 69, 157, 159
crisis, 197, 204
criticism, 199, 548
critique, 47
cycle, 799
debates, 11, 72, 73, 127, 158, 181, 191,
269, 643
decentralization, 675
decision-making, 379, 699, 703
decisions, 118, 148, 666
deliberation, 664
delivery, 74, 89, 95, 676
design (designs), 6, 24, 108, 137, 142, 148,
165, 167, 169, 170, 199, 200, 204, 206,
212, 249, 262, 390, 486, 664, 665, 669,
683, 684, 685, 686, 688, 689, 690, 692,
693, 694, 695, 696, 717, 855, 859
designers, 428, 694
developers (developer), 203, 214, 222, 573,
665, 690, 700
development, 3, 6, 9, 10, 11, 13, 14, 15,
16, 17, 18, 19, 20, 23, 24, 32, 33, 34,
36, 37, 38, 40, 41, 46, 63, 65, 71, 86,
89, 99, 101, 102, 112, 119, 139, 140,
141, 142, 143, 147, 148, 149, 153, 154,
155, 157, 158,159, 161, 163, 165, 168,
169, 170, 172, 175, 176,177, 181, 186,
187, 190, 193, 194, 197,199, 200, 204,
207, 208, 210, 212, 213, 224, 229, 231,
232, 236, 237, 313, 397, 500, 501, 535,
560, 642, 661, 662, 663, 664, 665, 685,
687, 689, 692, 700, 702, 704, 719, 720,
721, 722, 723, 724, 746, 776, 790, 791,
803, 811, 812, 824, 855
developments, 164, 173, 826
dialogue, 230, 235, 827
differentiation, 100, 669, 670, 679, 733
diffusion, 167
discourses (discourse), 43, 49, 51, 89, 102,
121, 217, 236, 266, 290, 315, 317, 364,
366, 394, 404, 462, 493, 499, 509, 514,
516, 525, 549, 559, 637, 638, 645, 650,
661, 781, 796, 826

Curriculum (continued)
  discussion, 154
  dissemination, 263, 700
  documentation, 46
  efforts, 112
  emphasis, 84, 167, 588
  enactment, 701, 703
  energies, 35, 193
  enhancement, 727
  enterprise, 42, 69, 421
  evaluation, 6, 15, 16, 17, 44, 45, 47, 183,
    201, 203, 212, 313, 412, 581, 583, 664,
    665, 732, 733, 737, 738, 742, 743, 744,
    850, 855
  evaluator, 738
  experience, 838
  experimentation, 702
  experts, 102, 421
  fabric, 165
  fad, 681
  field, xiii, xiv, xviii, 3, 4, 5, 6, 7, 10, 12, 13,
    14, 17, 19, 24, 25, 30, 35, 41, 44, 49,
    50, 52, 62, 63, 65, 70, 71, 75, 76, 81,
    82, 91, 96, 99, 136, 139, 147, 157, 163,
    172, 174, 176, 179, 182, 184, 186, 187,
    193, 197, 201, 208, 211, 212, 215, 218,
    219, 226, 228, 229, 230, 232, 235, 238,
    243, 244, 252, 271, 316, 317, 358, 364,
    370, 372, 375, 394, 396, 443, 476, 478,
    488, 489, 493, 519, 589, 627, 631, 634,
    642, 663, 688, 732, 737, 745, 790, 848,
    849, 862, 867, 868
  forms, 431
  generalists, 14, 16, 38
  goals, 203
  guidelines, 860
  guides (guide), 149, 602, 682
  historian (historians), 42, 79, 81, 91, 104,
    149, 517, 681, 840, 854
  history, 22, 24, 42, 63, 69, 70, 87, 109,
    124,197, 313, 673, 823, 840, 855
  ideas, 250, 703, 704
  implementation, 6, 19, 47, 155, 212, 410,
    426, 664, 688, 699, 700, 701, 702, 703,
    857
  improvement, 18, 35, 39, 675
  initiatives, 840
  innovations, 703, 808
  inquiry, 19, 51, 201, 229, 230, 388, 561,
    643, 831, 864, 865
  integration, 80, 125, 170
  invention, 431
  issues, xvii, 5, 11, 82, 121, 143, 155, 179,
    201, 208, 666, 793
  knowledge base, 757
  knowledge, 70, 123, 128, 201, 231, 249,
    703, 748
  language, 181, 417, 421
  literature, 176, 200
  maintenance, 203

  maker, 14, 37, 75, 97, 115, 123, 125, 196,
    510, 584
  making, 33, 80, 81, 94, 97, 98, 119, 121,
    122, 149, 191, 236, 704, 732, 859
  management, 249
  manifesto, 159
  materials, 122, 272, 365, 488, 616, 665,
    687, 703, 775, 780, 860, 862
  matrix, 687
  matters, 119, 157, 662
  models (model), 19, 169, 834
  modules, 192
  objectives, 6, 17
  organization (organizations), 15, 17, 47,
    65, 84, 98, 114, 123, 136, 142, 155,
    172, 573, 664, 683, 684, 685, 696, 859
  orientation, 99, 121, 148, 320
  origins, 46
  person, 214, 627
  perspective, 47, 631
  plan (plans), 87, 665, 684, 700, 834
  planners, 685
  planning, 16, 24, 95, 145, 154, 155, 156,
    158, 167, 172, 173, 175, 176, 203, 664,
    665, 683, 684, 688, 689, 690, 692, 693,
    699, 796, 811, 824
  policy, 16, 23, 207, 664, 666, 667, 668,
    669, 671, 685, 733, 744, 798
  policy-making, 207, 665
  politics, 207, 335, 346
  possibility, 15
  practice, 3, 20, 23, 170,199, 215, 256, 402,
    403, 489, 548, 798, 831
  practitioners, 12
  principles, 713
  problems, 5, 139, 156, 165, 168, 171, 196,
    197,199, 202, 204, 206, 843
  procedure, 136
  process, 224
  professionals, 209
  professors, xiv, 37, 38, 57, 156, 857
  projects, 162, 163, 176, 734, 824
  proposals (proposal), 12, 14, 119, 291, 718
  protagonists, 687
  purposes, 15, 46, 47
  question (questions), 51, 56, 76, 80, 201,
    575, 716, 858, 862
  rationale, 678
  reconstruction, 18, 144, 145, 671
  reform (reforms), 15, 18, 37, 39, 86, 103,
    111, 143, 147, 151, 157, 158, 159, 160,
    161, 162, 165, 175, 177, 186, 187, 198,
    200, 201, 207, 298, 327, 402, 681, 734,
    775, 822, 867
  reformation, 368
  relationships, 216, 380
  reorganization, 814
  research programs, 46
  research, 10, 19, 52, 55, 56, 63, 169, 181,
    231, 243, 307, 409, 420, 491, 519, 555,
    637, 793, 831, 840, 856

researchers, 201
revision, 34, 35, 37, 40, 70, 135, 237
revolution, 671
rhetoric, 155
riddle, 30
scene, 149, 830
scholars (scholar), xiv, 12, 42, 60, 126, 140,
    154, 164, 196, 200, 201, 210, 211, 214,
    214, 220, 244, 245, 252, 381, 390, 395,
    397, 530, 574, 636, 637, 642, 650, 687,
    705, 837
scholarship, 12, 42, 51, 62, 78, 141, 187,
    191, 243, 245, 264, 276, 283, 294, 303,
    317, 374, 462, 540, 564, 662, 781, 791,
    852, 865, 866
selection, 74, 76, 168, 170, 202
sequence, 697
specialists, 5, 6, 9, 14, 24, 25, 28, 31, 33,
    34, 35, 36, 37, 38, 39, 63, 96, 118, 142,
    157, 159, 161, 172, 176, 189, 329, 574,
    642, 662, 683, 750, 776, 791
specialization, 100
stability, 207, 682
standardization, 77
structures (structure), 172, 191, 676
students, 48, 201, 450
studies (study), 5, 6, 20, 39, 65, 76, 162,
    167, 191, 197, 201, 202, 204, 219, 226,
    228, 232, 236, 238, 255, 288, 291, 311,
    417, 419, 530, 628, 653, 792, 850, 855,
    858
study, 42, 46, 101
supervision, 664, 728
supervisors, 208, 802
synoptic textbooks, 24,197
synthesis, 83
talk, 744
tasks, 204
teacher, 9
technology, 664, 688
textbooks, 22, 23, 199
texts, 11, 22, 148
theoretician, 321
theories, 46, 221, 238, 253
theorists (theorist), xiii, 6, 14, 87, 119,
    168, 204, 213, 215, 221, 224, 254, 256,
    302, 317, 370, 371, 391, 419, 423, 476,
    480, 498, 525, 572, 627, 648, 651, 654,
    658, 684, 691, 758, 782, 851
theorizing, 148, 180,199, 210, 211, 212,
    215, 219, 224, 226, 437, 476, 493, 517,
    599
theory, xvii, xviii, 9, 10, 19, 20, 30, 31, 39,
    41, 44, 50, 51, 56, 76, 97, 101, 104,
    110, 115, 121, 122, 123, 124, 147, 151,
    155, 156, 159, 160, 168, 170, 172,
    173,177, 179, 181, 182, 183, 184,191,
    192, 196, 201, 202, 204, 205, 218, 219,
    221, 224, 227, 229, 232, 236, 253, 275,
    279, 290, 308, 318, 357, 358, 371, 372,
    374, 375, 380, 381, 389, 392, 396, 402,
    403, 417, 424, 425, 426, 452, 468, 475,
    489, 493, 497, 509, 510, 518, 530, 531,
    550, 563, 572, 576, 589, 603, 605, 629,
    637, 644, 646, 648, 652, 653, 654, 655,
    664, 666, 671, 690, 718, 719, 730, 741,
    758, 810, 811, 831, 852, 855, 860, 866,
    868
thinking, 216, 217
thought, 29, 77, 125, 169, 214, 215, 446,
    500, 660
trends, 143
unification, 100
unit (units), 113, 192, 811, 813
variables, 100, 216
visionaries, 15
work, 37, 42, 43, 675
worker (workers), 172, 183, 226, 233, 260,
    417, 431
writers, 860
writings, 189
Curriculum-as-activity, 687
Curriculum-as-lived experience,428, 689
Curriculum-as-plan, 428, 689
Curriculum-in-use, 47
Customs (custom), 108, 693
Cybernetic, 410
Cyclical, 504
Cynical (cynicism), 469, 508, 684, 692

Daliness (daily), 391, 393, 394, 406, 418,
    420, 442, 533, 580, 594, 595, 603,
    680, 829
Dame schools, 360
Dance curricula, 604
Dance education (educators), 390, 391, 604
Dance, 170, 223, 519, 568, 568, 578, 590,
    603, 658, 823, 852
Dancers, 391, 581
Dancing, 222, 787
Danger (dangerous), 313, 365, 374, 441,
    541, 560, 725, 777
Darkness (dark), 440, 460, 520, 768, 788,
    849
Dasein, 443
Data, 59, 102, 231, 408, 505, 686, 715, 769
    analysis, 59
    base, 712
    collection, 59
    source, 520
Date rape, 393
Daughter, 542
Day-care centers, 27
De-industrialized, 296
De-institutionalized (de-institutionalize), 561,
    677
De-objectify, 276
De-reification, 296
Dead styles, 471
Deaf (deafness), 530, 531

Death (dead), 7, 176, 182, 187, 215, 233, 378, 443, 450, 469, 473, 481, 532, 543, 544, 600, 617, 630, 650, 651, 652, 654, 660
Death of the author, 436
Death of the subject, 468
Debasement, 321
Debates (debate), 23, 53, 82, 102, 147, 155, 159, 162, 177, 203, 237, 283, 311, 375, 394, 421, 477, 491, 524, 602, 611, 616, 617, 620, 632, 644, 760, 774, 789
Decade (decades), 12, 25, 30, 43, 45, 46, 63, 76, 96, 124, 139, 141, 144, 153, 159, 171, 184, 186, 187, 192, 197, 204, 210, 211, 219, 236, 317, 330, 373, 391, 688, 790, 828, 850
Decadence, 652
Decay, 490
Decency, 152
Decentering (decentered), 308, 413, 434, 460, 468, 487, 488, 505, 532
Decentralization, 127, 261, 674, 675, 676, 677, 678, 679, 837, 842
Decentralization/centralization arguments, 678
Decentralized, 724, 794, 831, 839
Decision variables, 813
Decision-making, 18, 170, 174, 204, 352, 661, 666, 699, 704, 837, 856
Decisions, 23, 145, 167, 292, 298
Decline, 294, 295
Decodings (decoding, decode), 490, 570, 580, 581, 792, 827
Decolonization (decolonizing), 326, 839
Deconstruction (deconstruct, deconstructing, deconstructed, deconstructive), 16, 301, 302, 357, 374, 392, 447, 448, 450, 451, 457, 464, 465, 467, 468, 469, 470, 471, 473, 474, 475, 476, 477, 480, 483, 485, 489, 492, 493, 494, 497, 503, 505, 508, 510, 511, 514, 537, 538, 574, 575, 640, 746, 862
Deconstructionism (deconstructionist), 436, 537
Deconstructionist tale, 506
Decontextualized (decontextualism, decontextualizes), 280, 335, 438, 471, 603
Deculturalization, 347, 348
Deduction, 712
Deep (the), 769
Defense (national), 157, 158, 159, 181, 292, 335, 682
Defenses (psychological), 521
Defensive, 526
Defer (deferred), 466, 468, 488, 601
Deference (deferential), 342
Deferral, 467
Definitional issues, 31
Definitional shifts, 25, 27, 28, 41

Definitions, 24, 25, 26, 27, 28, 29, 50, 98, 451, 687
Definitive, 421
Deflect, 526
Deforestation, 829, 841
Deforms (deform), 329, 403, 415
Degendering (degendered), 368, 477
Degenerative (degenerate), 270, 506, 648
Dehumanization, 178, 179, 184, 257, 552
Deity, 657
Deliberation, 35, 36,177, 196, 203, 204, 205, 237, 424, 584, 670, 851
Deliberative, 732
Deliberator, 38
Delimited, 459
Delivery, 722
Demands (demand), 209, 460, 633
Democracy, 83, 84, 87, 100, 102, 104, 106, 108, 116, 117, 118, 124, 129, 131, 169, 255, 257, 352, 508, 513, 562, 604, 680, 698, 718, 775, 827
Democratic, 45, 55, 106, 109, 113, 117, 119, 132, 140, 141, 143, 145, 171, 249, 256, 258, 259, 279, 285, 291, 292, 307, 309, 346, 351, 391, 509, 608, 618, 621, 632, 633, 635, 648, 650, 654, 660, 668, 669, 678, 689, 763, 770, 789, 824, 836, 837, 848, 851, 854
  culture, 292
  dictatorship, 814
  education, 508, 851
  government, 633
  humanism, 272
  public life, 508
  reform (reforms), 835, 837
  revolution, 507
Democratic-participative, 722, 725
Democratic-progressive, 261, 771
Democratization (democratize), 127, 264, 813, 828, 837
Demographic trends, 177, 328
Demonic, 396
Demonized, 305
Demonstrations, 748, 749, 823
Demoralization (demoralizing), 260, 768
Demystification (demystify), 286, 357, 368
Demythologizing, 222
Denaturalizing, 296, 309, 508
Denial, 328, 329, 336, 349, 352
Denominational, 635, 650
Dependency (dependent, dependence), 342, 365, 377, 378, 518, 530, 820
Depersonalization, 179, 291, 633
Depoliticized, 280
Deportment, 139
Depravity, 655
Depression, 134, 139
Depsychologizing, 746
Depth, 144, 438, 463, 468, 472, 492, 595, 679, 762

Depthless, 464, 511
Derridean-Deleuzian, 477
Description (descriptive, describing), 59,
    306, 396, 408, 445, 452, 453, 531, 582,
    583, 663, 735, 739, 740
Desegregation (desegregated,
    desegregating), 331, 341, 366, 612,
    621
Desexualize, 339
Desiccation (desiccated), 519, 604
Design, 18, 24, 33, 155, 159, 171, 180, 181,
    182, 183, 197, 200, 205, 214, 418, 486,
    519, 549, 616, 622, 665, 685, 687, 688,
    689, 694, 711, 738, 744
Designers, 700
Designing, 422, 577
Desire (desires), 61, 205, 280, 305, 336, 338,
    354, 356, 378, 379, 423, 435, 450, 460,
    467, 475, 476, 479, 480, 495, 526, 528,
    632, 859, 863
Desiring, 506
Deskilling, 252, 401
Desocialization, 762
Despair, 219, 223, 252, 253, 455, 477, 565,
    645
Destabilizing (destabilized), 309, 821
Destination, 544, 659
Destiny, 624, 800, 842
Destruction , 652
Destructured, 319
Desubstantialized, 511
Detached individuals, 190
Detached, 400, 799, 803
Detail, 420, 435, 527, 574, 584, 699, 765
Detente, 608
Determinants (of curriculum), 176, 682
Determination, 495
Determinism (deterministic), 247, 274, 666
Detotalization (detotalizing), 374, 512
Devalued (devaluation), 351, 356, 768, 858
Developed countries, 793
Developing countries, 793
Development (growth), 73, 74, 80, 110, 158,
    165, 168, 196, 218, 432, 499, 518, 535,
    599, 747
Development (see curriculum development)
Developmental, 413, 431, 509, 629, 691, 697,
    799
    psychology, 77, 207, 217, 442, 694
    research, 51
    stages, 88, 431
    studies, 169
    view, 192
Developmentalism, 756
Developmentalists (developmentalist), 30,
    755
Deviance (deviant), 253, 784
Devouring, 385
Deweyan, 562, 855, 858
    pragmatism, 287, 446
    progressive emphasis, 184

themes, 321
tradition, 562
Diachronic, 457
Diagnostic, 561
Diagrams, 205
Dialect (language), 348
Dialectic (dialectics, dialectical), 195, 227,
    261, 282, 289, 355, 416, 420, 522, 539,
    604, 634, 772, 836
    analysis, 211, 228
    relation, 225
Dialogist, 753
Dialogue (dialogical), 23, 184, 190, 228, 234,
    256, 279, 294, 299, 334, 340, 382, 394,
    420, 421, 424, 431, 482, 499, 501, 502,
    504, 505, 523, 524, 530, 542, 548, 562,
    578, 587, 597, 633, 645, 650, 660, 688,
    742, 743, 755, 788, 797, 834, 856
Dialogue journals, 516, 531, 532
Dialoguing, 502
Diapers, 470
Diaries, 765, 769
Dichotomy (dichotomies, dichotomous), 105,
    206, 251, 382, 390, 550, 614, 656
Dictatorship, 268
Didacticism, 568
Didactics, 810
Difference (differences), 257, 261, 285, 286,
    299,305, 307, 319, 328, 330, 336, 345,
    348, 351, 354, 356, 358, 369, 380, 385,
    394, 423, 434, 437, 458, 468, 477, 480,
    481, 482, 491, 493, 494, 495, 507, 508,
    512, 544, 547, 616, 619, 669, 681, 695,
    832, 838, 856
Differential schooling funding, 318
Differentiated staffing, 682
Differentiation (differentiated,
    differentiating), 375, 379, 618, 691
Différance, 49, 450, 466
Difficulty, 638, 697, 760
Diffusion (diffuse), 128, 204, 839
Dignity, 233, 397, 423, 525, 658, 838
Digression, 198
Diploma (diplomas), 672, 816
Diplomatic relations, 817
Direction, 132, 490
Directionality, 490
Directness, 784
Director, 723
Disability, 532
Disadvantaged, 174, 324, 380, 623
Disagreement, 489
Discipline (control), 8, 73, 74, 86, 96, 377,
    591, 597, 622
Disciplinary
    autonomy, 867
    communities (community), 386, 867
    foundations, 201, 206, 737, 738
    sources, 863
    specialists, 690
    structure, 159, 160, 162

Discipline (academic subject), xiii, 12, 21, 29, 32, 42, 48, 51, 91, 124, 147, 148, 161, 163, 164, 169, 170, 171, 175, 181, 184, 187, 192, 198, 208, 358, 386, 419, 486, 498, 548, 551, 564, 565, 572, 687, 695, 749, 771, 853, 863, 864
Discipline (rigor), 110, 157
Discipline of curriculum theory, xvii
Discipline-based curriculum development, 176
Discipline-based teaching of science, 195
Discipline-centered orientation, 170, 178, 184
Disclosing (discloses, disclose), 549, 595, 597, 738
Disconfirmation, 519
Discontents, 232, 233, 234, 235
Discontinuity (discontinuities, discontinuous), 319, 404, 486, 492, 831, 849
Discourse, 9, 12, 22, 28, 30, 32, 44, 45, 48, 49, 60, 65, 102, 172, 199, 213, 214, 229, 246, 247, 248, 251, 252, 253, 255, 257, 263, 285, 292, 294, 295, 297, 298, 299, 301, 302, 308, 309, 310, 313, 314, 317, 335, 336, 353, 359, 370, 374, 381, 413, 416, 423, 426, 447, 452, 462, 464, 466, 475, 476, 491, 492, 508, 513, 539, 553, 566, 575, 587, 634, 642, 663, 771, 784, 866, 867
Discourse (field of), 52, 308
of affiliation, 545, 547
of hope, 634
Discourse-practices, 489
Discourses, xiii, xvii, 5, 7, 10, 11, 12, 13, 16, 22, 26, 30, 31, 32, 43, 45, 48, 50, 57, 61, 79, 319, 326, 376, 384, 385, 393, 403, 432, 451, 462, 506, 512, 514, 629, 635, 744, 831, 849, 855, 865, 868
Discovery, 73, 588
Discretion, 669
Discrimination (racial, class), 199, 294, 326, 331, 332, 341
Discursive, 49, 275, 294, 302, 309, 311, 335, 395, 403, 416, 447, 452, 464, 495, 505, 510, 513, 514, 537, 540, 574, 866
fields (field), 50, 308, 309, 477
formations (formation), 357, 463, 536, 859
grid, 476
position, 309
practice (practices), 7, 16, 297, 300, 312, 463, 464, 465, 493, 494, 508, 512, 539
self, 537, 539
shift (shifts), 278, 283, 311, 446, 448
strategies, 17, 450
system (systems), 374, 452, 496
territory, 364, 465
unconscious, 336
Discussion teaching, 194
Discussion, 261, 587, 772, 860
Disease, 338, 719

Disembodied (disembodiment), 428, 655
Disenfranchised, 209
Disequilibrium, 501, 594
Disinformation, 512
Disintegration (disintegrative), 125
Disinvestment, 293
Disjunctions, 253
Disparity, 681
Dispersion (dispersed), 336, 464, 467, 488, 491, 495, 601
Displacement (displaced, displacing), 390, 460, 533, 537
Display, 526
Disposition, 109
Disputation, 325
Disputes, 43, 225
Disruption (disrupt, disruptive), 209, 253, 497, 600, 784
Dissecting, 371
Dissension, 451
Dissent (dissenting), 128, 227, 600
Dissertations (dissertation), 4, 36, 119, 128, 150, 181, 409
Dissipation, 501
Dissolution, 513
Dissolves, 522
Dissonance, 550
Distance (distancing, distances), 375, 414, 415, 416, 418, 438, 466, 478, 479, 480, 520, 522, 527, 539, 542, 605, 760, 850
Distance (right), 480
Distantiation (distantiate), 522, 542
Distortion (distortions, distorted), 263, 291, 551, 575, 642
Distribution (distributive), 247, 684, 867
Distribution controversies, 818
Disturbance, 501
Disturbing, 574
Divergence, 198
Diversification, 822, 867
Diversity (diverse), 48, 224, 259, 308, 309, 316, 340, 346, 354, 357, 397, 608, 618, 635, 661, 676, 678
Dividend, 108
Divine, 637, 642, 649, 810
Divinity schools, 637
Division of labor, 95
Docile, 848
Doctoral
degree, 603
dissertation, 478
graduate, 266, 287, 573
research, 373
student, 140
training, 119
Doctorate, 193
Doctrinal analysis, 300
Doctrinal canon, 295
Doctrine, 232, 301
Document, 256, 585
Document analysis, 59, 60

Documentation, 333
Documents, 50, 70
Dogmatism (dogma, dogmatic), 13, 100, 129, 195, 310, 499, 505, 546, 615, 636
Doing, 404, 407, 427, 428, 659
Domain assumptions, 12
Domestic (domesticity), 343, 403, 807, 850
Domestication (domesticate), 211, 222
Dominance, 204, 368
Dominant (dominating), 65, 246, 249, 253, 287, 306, 319, 348, 368, 395, 422, 477, 534
Domination, 218, 221, 222, 250, 251, 253, 280, 282, 284, 285, 286, 295, 305, 313, 350, 353, 356, 366, 377, 504, 507, 512, 660, 695
Doors of perception, 217
Double consciousness, 350, 356
Double embodiment, 425
Double vision, 593
Doubt, 659, 745
Drama (dramatic), 4, 169, 333, 533, 587, 589, 596, 599, 600, 601, 678, 697, 789
Dramatic collective, 601
Drawing (drawings, draw), 337, 542, 578
Dreams (dream), 188, 309, 342, 349, 381, 423, 440, 449, 466, 493, 516, 522, 540, 541, 542, 543, 619, 644, 848
Dressing, 787
Drill (drills), 586, 710, 711
Drill sequences, 435
Drill-and-practice, 711, 712, 713
Drop-out (drop-outs), 146, 260, 334, 363, 395, 683, 733
Drought, 818, 829
Drug (drugs), 345, 674, 826, 828, 829
Dualism (dualistic), 105, 132, 288, 298, 308, 309, 310, 312, 367, 373, 391, 434, 453, 455, 458, 477, 481, 482, 492, 494, 576, 649
Duration (durational), 378, 381, 523, 653
Dwell (dwelling), 422, 426, 428, 544
Dying, 233, 235, 444, 543, 544
Dysfunctionality, 192

Early childhood, 384, 524, 658, 707
    education, 850
Earth, 288, 490, 629, 658, 799, 801, 829
East (the), 214, 627
Eastern European, 833
Eastern religions, 358
Eastern tradition (traditions), 492, 493, 652
Eccentricity (eccentric), 213
Ecclesiastical, 84, 642
Echoed (echo, echoes), 435, 859
Echolalia, 435
Eclectic, 35, 36, 175, 176, 177, 193, 831
    model, 19, 142
    theory, 725
    traditions, 39

Eclecticism, 141, 849, 864
Ecological, 283, 289, 388, 389, 424, 593, 626, 629, 753, 792, 800, 829, 833, 838, 840
    change, 764
    crisis, 288, 715, 731
    curriculum, 388
    interdependence, 803
    model, 192
    theory, 311
Ecology, 582, 658, 731, 773, 841
Economic, 22, 33, 57, 64, 80, 95, 99, 102, 109, 113, 120, 125, 126, 129, 133, 137, 141, 154, 180, 191, 217, 227, 244, 246, 247, 252, 253, 254, 256, 259, 262, 264, 294, 296, 302,305, 307, 309, 315, 317, 318, 325, 326, 327, 328, 339, 344, 345, 348, 360, 361, 369, 392, 488, 489, 511, 579, 580, 606, 608, 614, 619, 624, 625, 631, 636, 644, 650, 654, 663, 671, 672, 676, 677, 678, 682, 684, 714, 780, 792, 794, 796, 800, 802, 807, 810, 813, 815, 817, 822, 826, 827, 828, 830, 835, 842, 848, 851
    exploitation, 828
    indicators, 733
    interdependence, 803, 820
Economics, 49, 110, 204, 281, 387, 648, 662, 663, 851
Economies of affect, 512
Economies of scale, 158, 676
Economistic, 281, 311
Economists (economist), 623, 677
Economy (economies), 87, 97, 247, 296, 379, 469, 563, 579, 668, 824, 850
Ecopolitical, 288
Ecosystem, 192, 502, 510
Ecozoic age, 658
Ecumenical, 838, 840
Editorial criticism, 584, 585
Educated, 428, 695
Educated mind, 206
Educated woman, 395, 496
Education, 3, 11, 22, 24, 29, 33, 57, 58, 65, 70, 72, 74, 77, 79, 84, 88, 89, 91, 94, 98, 99, 100, 102, 104, 108, 109, 115, 118, 122, 125, 127, 128, 130, 131, 139, 145, 159, 168, 170, 171, 175, 181, 188,191, 192, 193, 195, 200, 205, 208, 210, 226, 237, 247, 251, 255, 260, 261, 264, 269, 272, 275, 276, 277, 278, 279, 281, 294, 298, 299, 300, 301, 302, 303, 326, 349, 358, 362, 364, 366, 368, 371, 373, 385, 411, 433, 434, 443, 453, 478, 481, 482, 483, 485, 486, 488, 491, 500, 501, 515, 518, 522, 535, 537, 540, 542, 544, 547, 550, 562, 564, 574, 575, 586, 600, 606, 607, 608, 615, 621, 627, 628, 629, 632, 634, 648, 654, 655, 657, 660, 662, 671, 672, 673, 676, 677, 678, 690, 691, 692, 705, 707, 714, 717, 720, 727,

Education (continued)
741, 745, 756, 761, 762, 768, 771, 772,
773, 775, 781, 783, 787, 794, 801, 802,
807, 809, 810, 812, 813, 814, 815, 816,
817, 821, 822, 823, 825, 829, 830, 834,
835, 836, 837, 838, 840, 841, 851, 860,
861, 868
(field of), 50, 58, 94, 146, 196, 201, 213,
214, 216, 220, 224, 489, 815
Commission of the States (ECS), 672
departments, 175
editor, 293
establishment, 757
policy making, 838
professors, 14, 111, 152, 850, 851
Educational
accomplishment, 796
achievement, 796, 805
activities, 144
activity (activities), 108, 109, 122, 167, 417,
418, 419, 631
administration, 3, 112, 157, 187
administration, 720, 850
administrators, 428
advancement, 797, 816, 821, 830
aesthetics, 573
affairs, 37
aims, 808
analyses (analysis), 278, 295, 811
apartheid, 825
arena, 794
arguments, 486
assistance, 294
biography, 554
breakthrough, 86
bureaucrats, 648
cards, 671
challenge, 363
change, 837
choice, 622, 680
circles, 629
cliché, 254
climate, 573
community, 632, 834
comparisons, 804
competence, 299
competition, 810
concepts, 46, 206
concerns, 734
conduct, 406
connoisseur, 582, 739
connoisseurship, 582
consciousness, 550
content, 675
context (contexts), 344, 547, 748
crisis, 668
criteria, 740
critic (critics), 740, 819
criticism, 18, 201, 227, 582, 583, 584, 631,
735, 736, 739, 740, 742
crusader, 610

debates (debate), 83, 622
decision-maker, 836
decision-making, 488
demands, 813
development (developments), 409, 517,
817, 820, 823, 828
discourse, 258, 526, 575
diversity, 818
documentaries, 284
dynamics, 755
effectiveness, 297
efforts (effort), 320, 801
end (ends), 699, 748
endeavors, 614, 725
enterprise, 741
environment (environments), 224, 833
establishments (establishment), 807, 816
ethics, 644
evaluation, 734, 741
excellence, 352
exchange, 813, 839
expansion, 794
experience, 33, 185, 204, 211, 213, 233,
333, 372, 380, 383, 391, 394, 414, 416,
491, 493, 517, 520, 521, 527, 540, 544,
550, 552, 553, 565, 590, 637, 655, 698,
716, 737, 755, 783, 788, 852, 853, 866
film (films), 284, 337, 340, 392, 708
foundations, 157
freedom, 833, 835
function, 709
futures, 214, 627
goal (goals), 488, 668, 807, 815, 820, 836
governance, 676, 842
ideal (ideals), 773, 808
ideas, 110, 129
ideology, 287
imagination, 201, 738, 740, 839
impact, 819
importance, 553
improvements (improvement), 207, 722
indicator, 733
indoctrination, 811
infrastructure, 824
innovation, 174
inquiry, 55, 574, 827, 839
institutions, 190, 220, 225, 323, 367, 580,
858
integrity, 628
interests, 776, 834
issues, 57, 83, 99, 323, 395, 601, 792, 863,
864
jargon, 421
journey, 517, 861
knowledge, 89
landscape, 861, 862
language, 421
leaders, 42, 84, 809
leadership, 292, 615, 633, 724, 728, 800,
836
left, 758

level, 290
life (lives), 525, 578, 584, 783
literature, 575, 861
love, 433
marketplace, 728
materials, 46, 840
means, 741
measurement, 194
media, 337
methods, 833
milieu, 842
models (model), 191, 498
movement, 84
museums, 706
narratives, 544
objectives, 34, 97, 118, 136, 155, 165, 166,
    200, 486, 487, 488, 732, 735, 808
operation, 794
opportunity (opportunities), 333, 828, 829
order, 497, 498
orientations, 371
outcomes, 46, 136, 796
perspectives, 257, 288
philosopher, 800
philosophy, 87, 122, 656
planners, 794
poetry, 226
policy (policies), 321, 352, 395, 565, 632,
    676, 678, 690, 796, 809, 816, 817, 822,
    825, 842
policy-makers, 565
politics, 265
potential, 578
practice (practices), 36, 64, 84, 99, 116,
    262, 268, 284, 288, 545, 604, 608, 632,
    634, 729, 743, 756, 763, 774, 809, 816,
    817, 820, 827
practitioners, 272, 714
praxis, 554
problems, 140, 645, 722, 805, 817
process, 46, 273, 275, 433, 519, 713, 833
production process, 245
programs, 174, 220, 736, 802
progress, 706, 805, 820
psychology, 3, 50, 89, 115, 157, 166, 167,
    172, 187, 196, 205, 410, 417, 571, 731,
    747, 759, 861
purpose (purposes), 33, 148, 231, 678,
    748, 836
questions, 635
radio, 707, 719
rationale, 678
realities (reality), 297, 298
reform (reforms), 88, 99, 326, 524, 574,
    620, 635, 648, 678, 681, 794, 807, 813,
    821, 832
reform (reforms), 253, 835
reformer, 78, 131
relationships, 817
renewal, 290
requirements, 682, 757

research, 53, 55, 64, 90, 103, 174, 177,
    364, 406, 409, 414, 549, 563, 567, 571,
    573, 743, 826, 831, 861
researcher (researchers), 53, 318, 482, 553,
    565, 714
retrenchment, 238
right, 615
scholars, 819
services, 620
settings (setting), 58, 839
significance, 486
situation, 583
sociologists, 100
specialists, 706
standards, 805
strategies, 375
struggles, 819
successes (success), 612, 805
supervision, 728
system (systems), 247, 252, 561, 669, 724,
    733, 793, 794, 800, 804, 807, 815, 824,
    830, 842
technology, 688, 704, 705, 708, 709
television, 708, 709
theater, 599
theorist, 114, 272, 318, 826
theory (theorists), 83, 84, 99, 117, 247,
    268, 288, 375, 631, 793, 810, 811, 813
thinking, 57, 205
thought, 126
topic, 796
traditions, 823
upheaval, 816
values (value), 84, 100, 268, 488, 603, 604,
    740, 748
world (worlds), 214, 393
worthiness, 683
writers, 76, 799
Educative
    environment, 182
    process, 96, 123, 528, 562, 735
    research, 256
    systems, 824
Educator (educators), 9, 23, 34, 37, 45, 57,
    60, 80, 91, 92, 127, 149, 156, 163, 181,
    188, 206, 211, 213, 214, 226, 228, 246,
    265, 273, 350, 366, 370, 397, 417, 418,
    419, 422, 430, 432, 507, 527, 530, 547,
    573, 586, 606, 614, 629, 632, 688, 720,
    776, 799, 803, 826, 839, 859, 860, 862
Effective schools research, 674
Effective schools, 702, 726
Effectiveness (effective), 33, 92, 95, 149, 180,
    272, 297, 643, 667, 669, 680, 687, 790
Effects (effect), 35, 115, 148, 667
Efficiency (efficient), 64, 94, 95, 96, 97, 125,
    140, 180, 237, 273, 293, 361, 428, 431,
    473, 474, 481, 667, 671, 675, 676, 822,
    848
Efficiency/production model, 236
Effort, 148, 256

Egalitarian, 307, 322, 608, 624, 633, 787, 824
Ego, 478, 485, 522, 538, 546, 548, 729
Egocentricity, 106
Ego development, 522
Ego stability, 329
Eidetic reduction, 407, 447
Eidetics (eidetic), 419, 421, 440
Eighteenth century (1700s), 321, 499, 602, 607, 609, 616
Eighth century (700s), 823
Either/or, 271, 567, 568
Elective courses, 189
Elective system, 145
Electoral, 321, 322, 827
Electrical engineering, 91
Electronic, 513, 716
  conference, 587, 784
  media, 340, 469, 507
  textbooks, 716
Elementary
  curriculum, 75, 118, 143, 157, 615, 712
  demonstration school, 157
  education, 159, 215, 400, 534, 557
  grades, 80, 122, 522
  mathematics, 711
  reading, 711
  school pedagogy, 84
  school science, 77, 163
  school student, 526
  schools (school), xiii, 39, 73, 75, 77, 84, 85, 90, 102, 110, 143, 152, 175, 188, 257, 360, 611, 666, 671, 682, 700, 709, 806
  social studies, 132, 163
  teachers, 14, 96, 365, 399, 529, 753, 754
Elite, 170, 828
Elitism (elitist), 235, 337, 568, 582
Elliptical, 485
Eloquence, 35
Emancipation (emancipatory), 230, 231, 232, 256, 260, 280, 283, 285, 288, 304, 306, 325, 327, 352, 353, 389, 390, 392, 393, 506, 507, 508, 516, 551, 553, 556, 619, 644, 651, 653, 657, 763, 787, 856
Embedded, 479
Embodiment (embodied), 335, 358, 394, 409, 420, 425, 427, 434, 437, 444, 454, 455, 456, 458, 490, 491, 506, 585, 664, 744
Embryonic, 213
Emotion (emotions, emotionalism), 74, 152, 223, 334, 367, 372, 390, 400, 510, 521, 547, 579, 586, 598, 632
Emotional content, 782
Emotive, 371
Empathy, 58, 387, 390, 397, 583, 740, 741
Empiric (empirical), 100, 165, 173, 212, 213, 216, 266, 267, 405, 448, 560, 741, 788, 822
  investigations, 34
  research, 220

Empirical-analytic, 229, 411, 417
Empiricism, 186, 278, 322, 405, 410, 412, 419, 849
Empirics, 170
Employees, 848
Employment, 72, 260, 326, 400, 802
Empowerment (empowering), 246, 254, 255, 279, 283, 284, 288, 333, 334, 395, 560, 575, 589, 631, 645, 662, 715, 724, 725, 730, 731, 743
Emptiness, 440
Enactment, 312, 551, 586, 683, 703, 704
Encapsulation, 382, 688
Enchanted, 659
Encounter (encounters), 198, 280, 281, 386, 407, 414, 418, 441, 519, 573, 584, 588, 627, 629, 645, 695, 735, 744, 753, 765, 848
Encyclopedia (encyclopedic), xiv, 11, 48, 70, 155, 169
End (ends), 53, 126, 164, 188, 202, 237, 581, 751, 858
End of history, 469
End-time, 651
Endangered species, 841
Energy, 43, 44, 87, 195, 280, 599, 600, 631, 669, 680, 703, 719, 732
Enfleshment, 61, 512, 513
Enforcement, 689
Engagement, 169, 213, 427, 588
Engineering, 18, 30, 169, 226
  theories, 179
  theorists, 180
Engineers, 712, 815
English (the subject), 75, 76, 97, 158, 162, 163, 164, 169, 388, 697, 698, 712, 790, 824
  departments, 7
  education, xviii, 850
  literature, 193, 697
  national curriculum, 798
  primary school, 188
  secondary school, 252
  teachers (teacher), 436, 524
English-speaking nations, 795
English-speaking universities, 821
Enjoyment, 588
Enlightened action research, 766
Enlightened eye, 738
Enlightenment, 71, 74, 271, 325, 326, 450, 452, 460, 461, 469, 504, 602, 637, 640, 810, 832
Enrollments, 30, 146, 187
Entertainment, 711
Entrance examinations, 816
Entrapment, 254
Entrepreneurs (entrepreneurial), 729, 822
Entropy, 474
Entry (ethnographical methodology), 59
Environmental (environment, environments), 22, 51, 80, 92, 94, 171,

190, 213, 215, 217, 272, 288, 292, 472, 473, 593, 622, 635, 694, 717, 718, 768, 813, 826, 833, 841, 842, 847
Environmental crisis, 387
Environmentalism, 104
Epidemic, 340
Epiphenomenal, 318
Episodic, 318
Epistemic, 751
  break, 451
  codes, 61
  seeing, 582
  superstructures, 750
Epistemological (epistemology), 58, 92, 235, 267, 268, 269, 314, 374, 375, 411, 414, 447, 448, 481, 491, 527, 528, 547, 553, 556, 569, 573, 576, 581, 586, 603, 637, 717, 735, 739
  debates, 53
  refugees, 384
Equality, 179, 185, 267, 271, 273, 361, 418, 437, 508, 636
Equalize, 661, 681
Equilibrium, 594, 729
Equity, 288, 328, 372, 383, 620, 621, 622
Equivocity, 467
Erasure, 339
Eros, 61, 195, 433
Erosion, 570
Eroticism, 342
Erudition, 35
Escapes (escape), 491, 526
Eschatological curriculum theory, 657
Eschatological curriculum, 652, 653
Eschatology (eschatological), 62, 470, 645, 650, 652, 653, 654, 838
Essence (essences), 447, 455, 456, 468, 472, 856
Essential schools, 138, 670, 672
Essential structures, 408
Essential themes, 408
Essentialism (essentialized, essentialist), 303, 354, 368, 369, 385, 394, 398, 401, 464, 477, 478, 505, 508, 524, 545, 602
Estrangement, 378, 395, 435, 516, 518, 532, 533, 548, 595, 598, 720
Eternity (eternal), 389, 418, 471, 537, 645, 654
Ethic (ethical), 54, 57, 79, 99,173, 226, 233, 267, 309, 313, 385, 404, 411, 417, 418, 419, 427, 428, 478, 488, 497, 580, 606, 619, 627, 629, 633, 635, 637, 648, 656, 657, 674, 738, 752, 774, 810, 858
Ethical debates, 630
Ethical rationality, 628
Ethical relativism, 163, 535, 629
Ethics, 170, 187, 266, 379, 488, 558, 627, 628, 629, 630, 637, 655, 659, 690
Ethnic (ethnicity), 39, 210, 280, 304, 316, 323, 324, 325, 344, 345, 348, 352, 379, 563, 617, 678, 695, 776, 821, 823, 824

stereotypes, 324
Ethnoaesthetic, 570
Ethnocentricity, 16, 22
Ethnocentrism, 338
Ethnographer, 60
Ethnographers' identity, 59
Ethnographic methodology, 59
Ethnographic research, 61, 62, 394
Ethnographic researcher, 59, 60
Ethnographical, 46, 60
Ethnography (ethnographic), 52, 55, 58, 59, 60, 264, 307, 334, 342, 401, 624, 628, 736, 751, 769, 785, 787, 788, 854
Ethnohistorical, 60
Ethnomethodology, 59, 60
Etymological (etymologically), 408, 520, 521, 541
Eugenics, 94, 104
Eurocentric, 304, 322, 328, 330, 338, 349, 353, 507, 647, 671, 849
European, 329, 330, 352, 353, 646, 647, 811, 823, 828, 833, 837, 850, 863
  humanism, 303
  traditions, 218
European-American, 328, 330, 336, 337, 339, 342, 348, 357, 529
Evaluation, 15, 16,17, 18, 24, 34, 44, 97, 136, 140, 142, 148, 149, 150, 166, 171, 175, 176, 183, 195, 197, 200, 202, 205, 262, 333, 409, 417, 418, 486, 487, 488, 498, 519, 548, 557, 579, 580, 583, 585, 663, 665, 678, 692, 699, 700, 701, 702, 711, 712, 717, 722, 723, 725, 727, 729, 732, 733, 734, 735, 737, 738, 740, 742, 743, 744, 749, 766, 791, 797, 810, 811
  laps, 727
  specialists, 735
Evaluator, 736
Evaluator-proof, 278
Evangelical, 624, 649
Evasion, 448, 638
Events (event), 407, 472, 560, 581, 583, 597, 598, 666, 667, 699, 704, 740, 800
Evidence, 161, 269, 623, 737, 738, 749
Evil, 104, 109, 423, 608, 651, 653, 656, 657, 659, 695
Evil empire (the), 311
Evolution (evolutionary), 69, 89, 143, 169, 334, 424, 499, 778, 799
Evolutionary development, 79
Evolutionary/transformational paradigm, 46
Exactness (exactitude), 440, 572
Examinations, 796, 797, 798, 805
Examples, 748, 749
Excellence, 154, 169, 201, 352, 620, 789
Exchange programs, 817
Excitement, 50, 107, 126, 219, 271, 418, 664, 683, 692, 767, 868
Excluded (the), 763
Excluded middle, 481
Excluded third, 481

Exclusion (exclusions), 319, 357, 379, 393, 494, 633, 831
Exclusive, 371, 430, 614
Executing, 115
Exegesis, 641
Exemplars, 169
Exercise (exercises), 73, 74, 105, 108, 115, 711, 713, 746
Exhibition, 672,673
Exiled, 827
Exiles, 384, 385, 398
Existence (existing), 312, 426, 565, 576, 594, 641, 645, 651, 654, 655
Existentialism (existential), 39, 156, 174, 181, 182, 224, 230, 233, 238, 274, 275, 276, 311, 358, 408, 426, 453, 455, 456, 472, 480, 493, 497, 515, 518, 520, 521, 592, 649, 650, 695, 732, 750, 859
Existing order, 684
Exorcise, 502
Exoticized (exotic), 305, 326, 337, 338
Expansion, 159, 362, 822
Expansionism, 350
Expatriate teachers, 793
Expedient, 371
Expenditure, 94, 733
Experience, xvi, 21, 26, 27, 52, 53, 57, 98, 105, 106, 109, 126, 173, 195, 203, 217, 249, 261, 273, 283, 299, 332, 334, 371, 378, 400, 402, 403, 404, 405, 406, 407, 412, 415, 416, 420, 431, 436, 437, 438, 444, 445, 447, 453, 455, 456, 460, 484, 491, 493, 495, 501, 513, 515, 516, 519, 521, 525, 526, 533, 536, 537, 543, 544, 546, 549, 551, 553, 555, 556, 557, 563, 564, 567, 568, 583, 584, 588, 589, 596, 600, 605, 637, 645, 651, 707, 715, 735, 749, 759, 763, 765, 792
(directed), 27, 98
(educational), 33
(educative), 27
(out-of-school), 27
(planned), 27
(undirected), 27, 98
(unplanned), 27
Experiences, 16, 22, 26, 28
(consummatory), 29
Experiential, 47, 224, 562
knowledge, 554, 561
quality, 585
Experientialist, 21, 104
Experiment (experiments), 132, 133, 137, 144, 228, 256, 481, 672
Experimental, 107, 113, 362, 754
curricula, 519
educational research, 574
eidetics, 420
methods (method), 86, 572
psychology, 83, 89, 90, 92
schools (school), 137, 157, 586
science, 89, 91

Experimentalism, 92
Experimentation, 143, 191, 705
Expert (experts), 40, 102, 284, 603, 661, 677, 699, 700, 712, 715, 815, 817, 850, 851
systems, 712
testimony, 737
Expert/client relationship, 56
Expertise, 815
Expertness, 665
Explanation (explanations), 266, 267, 425, 546, 558, 638, 642, 643, 749
Explicative power, 295
Exploitation (exploited), 228, 268, 295, 304, 632
Exploration, 498, 532, 544, 588
Export, 850
Expresseds, 483, 484, 485, 501
Expressibles, 483, 484, 501, 537
Expressings, 483, 501
Expression (expressional), 301, 435, 636, 828, 849
Expressive objectives, 735
Expressivity (expressiveness, expressive), 367, 569, 570, 572, 604
Exterior, 456, 589
External examinations, 798
External factors (implementation), 701
Externalization (external, externalized), 217, 488, 518
Extra-temporal, 720
Extra-terrestrial, 651
Extra-textual, 642
Extracurricular, 789, 790, 802
Extracurriculum, 664, 788, 790
Extravagance, 432
Écriture feminine, 496

Fable, 425, 460
Face of an era, 463
Facilitator, 753
Facility (building), 110, 175
Facticity, 591
Factory (factories), 95, 96, 192, 816, 820
model, 293
Facts (fact), 9, 75, 78, 84, 96, 105, 218, 411, 458, 460, 655, 858
Faculty, 771
culture, 684
hiring patterns, 318
psychology, 70, 72, 73, 74, 75, 76, 78, 89, 90, 91, 92, 103, 756, 859
Faddish, 774
Fairness, 672
Faith (faiths), 14, 19, 42, 75, 100, 103, 118, 126, 159, 218, 223, 224, 321, 616, 628, 629, 634, 637, 638, 643, 648, 649, 650, 824, 861, 862
Faithful, 51
Fallenness, 447

False
  consciousness, 57
  hope, 489
  identification, 308
  self-system (self), 518, 538
  stability, 494
Falsehood, 570
Falsity, 271
Familiar (the), 230, 415, 548, 551, 595, 598,
  599, 715
Family (families), 27, 80, 94, 147, 252, 332,
  333, 334, 335, 339, 341, 343, 348, 362,
  369, 374, 379, 381, 387, 398, 513, 522,
  527, 529, 532, 549, 607, 614, 615, 620,
  621, 623, 624, 629, 635, 659, 678, 691,
  694, 759, 788, 801, 836, 841, 848, 851
Family planning, 719
Famine, 818, 821
Fantasy (fantasies), 48, 234, 329, 336, 339,
  341, 440, 470, 471, 493, 495, 518, 526,
  560, 691, 711
Far-right, 636
Fascination, 430
Father (fathers), 284, 339, 376, 378, 385,
  435, 443, 505, 528, 543, 607
Father wound, 375
Father/child, 374
Fault lines, 58
Fear (fears), 280, 338, 339, 382, 534, 598,
  600, 808
Fecundity, 500
Federal, 6, 157, 162, 174, 175, 184, 207, 292,
  585, 612, 666, 680, 682, 711, 776
Federalization, 175
Feedback, 745
Feedback conference 721
Feeling (feelings), 124, 166, 189, 195, 198,
  331, 334, 380, 391, 512, 533, 540, 549,
  569, 571, 590, 602, 605
Felt, 520, 577
Female (females), 85, 305, 359, 360, 362,
  365, 366, 368, 369, 377, 379, 384, 387,
  400, 458, 467, 495, 526, 552, 602
Femaleness, 363
Female subject, 495
Feminine (femininity), 359, 361, 363, 379,
  385, 386, 389, 394, 395, 490, 655, 656,
  657
Feminism (feminisms, feminized), 39, 257,
  281, 293, 303, 311, 344, 363, 370, 371,
  373, 374, 375, 391, 476, 477, 496, 497,
  504, 505, 509, 514, 551, 655
Feminist (feminists), xviii, 6, 12, 256, 264,
  304, 340, 341, 363, 366, 371, 382, 385,
  388, 389, 390, 392, 393, 394, 399, 400,
  403, 427, 478, 496, 506, 507, 526, 546,
  547, 551, 552, 554, 637, 656, 663, 695,
  730, 856
  analysis, 359, 373, 375, 392, 394
  autobiographical theory, 544
  autobiography, 516

criticism (critique), 304, 365, 367, 857
curricularists, 381
curriculum analysis, 395
curriculum scholarship, 550
curriculum theorists, 371, 391, 394, 396,
  403, 476, 495, 555
curriculum theory, 372, 375, 545
educators, 368, 386, 496
ethnography, 394
inquiry, 531
materialist epistemology, 394
men, 369, 376
pedagogy, 259, 279, 305, 381, 387, 390,
  400, 478, 550
political theory, 379
psychological thought, 375
research, 390, 504, 550, 552
researcher (researchers), 383, 394
revolution, 359
scholars, 13, 308, 402, 403, 545
scholarship, 12, 387, 545, 547
self-understanding, 546
separation, 508
teacher, 400
teaching, 368, 392, 478
theologians, 656
theology, 636, 652, 655
theorist (theorists), 304, 368, 369, 373,
  381, 382, 387, 388, 532, 853
theorizing, 396
theory, 43, 45, 55, 173, 238, 249, 278, 283,
  284, 307, 311, 312, 317, 364, 368, 371,
  372, 376, 381, 384, 386, 388, 390, 395,
  402, 404, 406, 427, 435, 498, 503, 524,
  525, 545, 548, 549, 550, 551, 552, 564,
  657, 694, 730, 848, 853, 864, 867
thought, 402
voice, 655
writers, 51
Feminization, 305, 400
Ferment, 501, 691, 692
Fervor, 418
Festival, 591, 596
Festive, 432
Fetal monitor, 409
Fetishizing, 336
Fiction (fictional, fictionalized, fictive,
  fictions), 4, 290, 311, 316, 329, 341,
  342, 346, 355, 362, 395, 398, 425, 439,
  458, 460, 471, 479, 481, 494, 495, 504,
  525, 560, 592, 596, 780
Fictional register, 356
Fictive selves, 494
Fidelity approach, 699, 700, 701, 704
Field, 11, 12, 14, 15, 16, 17, 20, 22, 24, 26,
  27, 28, 29, 30, 31, 32, 33, 34, 35, 38,
  39, 40, 43, 44, 45, 46, 47, 50, 51, 52,
  53, 69, 70, 91, 112, 123, 125, 139, 142,
  156, 160, 161, 165, 169, 177, 181, 183,
  186, 187, 189, 211, 215, 219, 220, 223,
  236, 262, 279, 295, 296, 317, 335, 359,

Field (continued)
376, 386, 403, 443, 451, 479, 486, 488,
489, 490, 514, 517, 530, 547, 553, 566,
574, 575, 627, 662, 687, 847, 848, 853,
860, 862, 863, 865, 867, 868
(history of), 12, 13, 43, 96, 133, 849, 852,
854, 855, 856, 857
(of discourse), 52
(of study), 7, 11, 18, 25, 70, 165, 182
(origins of), 42
(state of), 13, 63, 65
(the curriculum), 9, 10, 13, 124, 644
(the traditional), 11, 12, 15, 24
notes, 555
researchers (ethnography), 61
site analysis (ethnography), 61
supervisors, 729
testing (test), 167, 770
trips, 84, 109, 114, 707
Fieldwork, 60, 394
Fifth year (teacher education), 758, 759, 762
Figurative, 536
Figure (figures), 462, 463, 464, 478, 479,
494, 514, 551, 592, 593, 594, 595
Figure/ground (background), 435, 591, 593,
594, 595
Film (films), 284, 302, 307, 340, 469, 471,
587, 706, 708, 709, 719, 796
Finance (financing, financial), 563, 606, 620,
666, 676, 748, 832
Fine arts (art), 226, 580, 603, 741
Finitude, 641
Firm (business), 678
First Amendment rights, 299, 300, 302
First peoples, 349
First world, 468, 600, 795, 801, 807
First-order experience, 411, 412
Fixed, 355, 373, 401, 501, 525, 602
Flashes (flash), 485, 572, 853
Flesh, 61, 444, 447, 656
Flexibility (flexible), 621, 679, 700, 752, 757
Flight, 176, 329, 719
Flowchart, 200, 267
Flowcharting, 711
Flows (flow), 467, 491, 523, 576, 667, 716
Fluid, 557, 719
Flux, 497, 537
Folded, 492
Folkheroes, 351
Folklore, 320
Follow-up procedures (ethnographical
methodology), 59
Food preparation, 719
Food-and-festival events, 326, 801
Football, 363
For-itself (*pour soi*), 453
Forbidden, 386
Force (forces), 44, 78, 243, 250, 283, 492,
657
Forced labor camps, 830, 835
Foreign, 609, 610, 795, 803

debt, 828
language (languages), 75, 158, 162, 164,
169, 213, 482, 813, 815
policy, 328, 835, 842
textbooks, 795
Forlornness, 455
Form (forms), 284, 287, 297, 386, 403, 435,
471, 501, 546, 548, 549, 570, 578, 583,
584, 592, 596, 629, 630, 637, 866
Formal
curriculum (curricula), 440, 512, 829
education, 151, 154, 807, 815, 824
evaluation exercises, 732
features, 579
schools, 829
thinking, 509
Formal-operational (operations), 413, 691,
707
Formalism (formalist, formalized, formalize),
300, 565, 568, 642, 688, 848, 856, 860
Formations (formation), 280, 284, 297, 304,
373
Formative activity, 604
Formative evaluation, 167, 175, 734
Formless foundation, 492
Formlessness, 538
Formulae, 866
Foucauldian, 395, 457, 475, 496, 506, 512,
514
Foundational (foundation, foundations), 452,
458, 461, 462, 463, 468, 477, 500, 502,
506, 508, 570, 584, 762, 856, 861
Foundational discipline, 166
Foundations, 18, 116, 143, 156, 489
(charitable entities), 682
of education, 50
Founding Fathers, 300
Fractured meaning, 634
Fractured, 488
Fragility, 448
Fragmentation (fragmented), 71, 183, 184,
233, 305, 328, 345, 382, 384, 425, 469,
472, 478, 493, 511, 519, 654, 655, 660,
677, 787
Frame (frames), 499, 715
Frame factors, 47
Framework theories, 179
Framework theorists, 180, 216
Frameworks, 24
Fraternity, 418
Free
association, 523
enterprise, 778
expression, 321
floating signifier, 470
market economy, 621, 633
play of desire, 475
schools, 272, 273, 274
society, 580
Freedom, 56, 76, 105, 108, 127, 132, 179,
185, 227, 258, 265, 272, 273, 274, 275,

294, 300, 302, 309, 354, 416, 433, 444, 453, 454, 473, 489, 501, 502, 526, 528, 590, 591, 594, 615, 621, 641, 646, 647, 650, 651, 652, 660, 669, 691, 828, 832, 835
Freedom of speech, 300, 301
Freire's contribution, 263
Freirean ideas, 262
Freirean language, 221
French (the subject), 99, 838
    educator, 586
    feminists, 369, 395, 495, 496
    philosophy, 7, 45, 452, 480
    poststructuralist feminism, 495, 510
    poststructuralists, 395
Freudian, 329, 472
Freudian-based pedagogy, 185
Friends (friend), 760, 787, 850, 862
Friendship, 851
Front-line personnel, 221
Frontier (frontiers), 221, 283, 288, 402, 426
Frustration (furstrations), 127, 549, 579, 600, 703, 761
FTEs (full-time equivalents), 380
Fun, 235, 495
Function, 212, 213
Functional, 101, 142, 143, 145, 147, 153, 279
    communities, 622, 623
Functionalism (racial), 320
Functionalist, 266, 267, 277, 294, 660
Functionality, 151
Fundamentalism (curricular), 144
Fundamentalism (religious), 398, 399, 533, 534, 625
Fundamentalist (religious), 613, 614, 624, 626, 802
Fundamentalists (religious), 329, 614, 619, 636
Funding, 102, 174, 175, 635, 681
Fused curriculum, 687
Fusion, 302, 425, 576, 641
Future, 65, 108, 122, 136, 147, 191, 198, 204, 208, 220, 272, 310, 351, 380, 420, 431, 443, 444, 469, 494, 510, 520, 552, 556, 560, 576, 577, 578, 626, 627, 645, 651, 652, 653, 654, 655, 685, 688, 713, 715, 720, 751, 779, 791, 794, 823, 838, 852, 859, 866
    farmers, 789
    forecasting, 689
    studies, 191
    teachers, 789
Futuring, 567
Futurism, 191, 578, 689
Futuristic, 654
Futurists, 577

Gaia, 490
Galleries, 580
Games (game), 710, 711

Gap (gaps), 49, 56, 460, 480, 483, 497, 752
Garbage can view (policy), 666
Garden, 86
Gay (gays), 398, 402, 477, 678
    activist, 398
    analysis, 359, 370, 376, 397
    knowledge, 482
    liberation, 369, 398
    men, 376, 397
    role models, 396, 397
    studies, 402
    youth, 398
Gaze, 355, 377, 379, 478, 479, 526, 538, 593, 782
Gender (gendered), 8, 16, 39, 43, 44, 51, 55, 57, 61, 62, 64, 79, 236, 250, 254, 256, 260, 264, 265, 278, 279, 280, 284, 285, 287, 289, 290, 294, 304, 305, 307, 314, 315, 317, 318, 319, 328, 329, 334, 340, 341, 342, 343, 344, 346, 348, 350, 357, 358, 359, 361, 362, 363, 365, 366, 368, 369, 371, 372, 375, 381, 382, 386, 387, 388, 389, 390, 392, 393, 394, 395, 397, 398, 399, 400, 401, 403, 424, 427, 472, 475, 476, 478, 496, 503, 524, 525, 532, 535, 545, 548, 563, 566, 580, 619, 636, 730, 749, 759, 761, 764, 768, 771, 784, 794, 796, 847, 852, 853, 854, 858, 859, 862, 864, 866
    analysis (analyses), 4, 268, 364, 370, 371, 373, 375, 376, 385, 387, 396, 399, 400, 403, 864
    essentialism, 369
    identity, 45, 341, 381, 396, 399
    justice, 392
    relations, 372
    research, 303
    stereotyping, 364, 365
    system, 373
    theory, 43, 370, 376
Gendered subjects, 478
Genealogical studies, 43
General education, 145, 158, 194, 353, 810, 813, 836
General science, 169, 708
General track student, 146
Generalist (generalists), 37, 38, 662, 672
Generalizability, 560
Generalization (generalize, general), 52, 53, 56, 78, 79, 150, 156, 168, 367, 411, 415, 521, 548, 565, 858
Generational divide, 32, 219
Generational tensions, 210
Generations (generation, generational), xiv, 6, 11, 13, 15, 16, 45, 48, 88, 92, 127, 138, 141, 164, 180, 184, 191, 205, 214, 215, 357, 537, 622, 663, 811, 847, 853, 854, 864
Generativity (generative), 448, 638, 862
Generic curriculum development, 665
Generic, 594, 665, 724

Genetics, 464
Genius, 789
Genocide, 826
Genre (genres), 11, 24, 63, 70, 139, 190,
  200, 212, 286, 318, 341, 495, 588, 601,
  661, 787
Geographical expansion, 697
Geography (geographic), 32, 41, 52, 76, 84,
  163, 289, 330, 407, 411, 708, 802, 808,
  813, 824, 836
Geometry, 713
Geopolitical, 802, 813, 818, 823
Geostrategic, 293
German, 809, 810, 812, 813, 848
Gestalt, 454, 593, 858
Gesture, 170, 447, 539, 590, 591, 602
Ghost, 306, 502
Gift (gifts), 427, 433, 783
Gifted, 89, 94, 180, 380, 463, 589
Gifted child, 171
Girls, 85, 122, 360, 361, 362, 365, 366, 377,
  395, 399, 435, 807
Girls' schools, 360
Glacier-like, 678
Global
  alliances, 802
  capitalism, 469, 472, 504
  community, 827, 831
  crises (crisis), 801, 829
  cultures, 793
  curriculum projects, 794
  dominance, 792
  economy (economics), 293, 840
  education, 772, 799, 800, 801, 802, 803,
    857
  educational community, 826
  educators, 800, 803
  environment, 800
  ethics, 792, 842
  imperialism, 839
  industrial entities, 794
  interdependence, 800
  models, 800
  structures of thought, 839
  studies, 803
  survival, 841
  themes, 22, 31
  transformations, 840
  understanding, 801, 803
  village, 801
  warming, 841
Globalization, 831
Globes (global), 85, 289, 293, 322, 387, 502,
  568, 620, 629, 630, 645, 646, 647, 650,
  653, 756, 796, 801, 802, 803, 817, 818,
  830, 831, 833, 838, 840, 842, 852
Goal-directed, 371, 666
Goals (goal), 33, 94, 95, 106, 136, 181, 279,
  385, 443, 479, 582, 672, 685, 686, 704,
  711, 758, 807, 810, 811, 813
Goddess, 656

Gods (God), 423, 601, 638, 643, 645, 649,
  656, 657, 659
Good (the), 272, 475, 489, 490, 656, 657
Goodness, 79, 433, 473
Governance, 666, 675, 677, 748, 756
Government (governmental), 57, 84, 106,
  119, 158, 207, 339, 348, 538, 579, 608,
  608, 609, 613, 620, 636, 662, 665, 666,
  667, 671, 674, 701, 776, 797, 808, 813,
  820, 823, 826, 829, 832, 836, 862
Grace, 428, 485, 645, 650, 651, 807
Graceful, 788
Grade levels, 84, 798, 806, 815
Graded schools, 361, 682
Gradedness, 89
Grading (grades), 183, 211, 668, 710, 733
Graduate, 519, 822
  curriculum courses, 54, 850
  school (schools), 5, 133, 585
  student (students), 9, 42, 149, 152, 202,
    257, 523, 641
  study, 150, 430, 868
  teacher preparation (education), 759, 770
  training, 91
Graduation, 673
Graffitied, 469
Grammar (grammatical), 75, 76, 97, 98, 311,
  522, 638, 640
Grand narratives, 312
Grandmother, 533
Gratified, 378
Gratitude, 427, 433
Gravity, 490
Great Awakening, 625
Great books, 153, 194, 195, 269, 285, 608
Greed, 511, 660
Greek, 72, 91, 638, 819
  origins, 59
  rhetoric, 377
Green politics, 283, 288
Gridlock, 662, 683
Gross national profit (GNP), 807
Groundedness (grounded, ground), 275,
  406, 440, 453, 462, 489, 497, 511, 538,
  548, 551, 557, 592, 593, 594, 595, 599,
  650, 663, 748, 764
Group (groups), 280, 289, 355, 383, 412,
  518, 596, 740, 748, 755, 822, 859
  dynamics, 171
  formation, 174
  inquiry curriculum, 190
  instruction, 783
  investigations, 171
  process (processes), 535, 690
  solidarity, 306
  work, 172, 749
Grouping, 318
Growing up, 397, 398
Growth, 56, 108, 126, 168, 172, 195, 196,
  599, 631, 723, 837, 867
Guerrilla, 212

Guidance, 26, 105, 118, 132, 147, 158, 212, 257
Guidance counselors, 147, 397, 398, 682, 720
Guidelines, 197, 666
Guides (guide), 54, 58, 170, 200, 213, 272, 720, 732
Guilt (guilty), 311, 335, 454, 646
Gymnasium (gymnasiums), 73, 109, 837
Gyn/ecology, 551, 552

Habit (habits, habitual), 91, 102, 590, 598, 600, 740, 743
Hallucinatory, 472
Hammering, 492
Handbook, 23
Handicap disability, 334
Handicapped, 589
Handicrafts, 808
Happiness (happy), 485, 536, 537
Happy ending, 560
Hardware, 705, 712, 714
Harmony (harmonious), 65, 106, 433, 652, 659, 769, 831, 833, 836
Hate (hatred), 74, 376
Hawaiian students, 784
Hazardous waste, 841
Healing (heal), 210, 439
Health curriculum, 402
Health, 99, 108, 136, 164, 349, 362, 708, 821, 829
Heart (hearts), 206, 356, 442, 534, 612, 639, 655, 659, 821, 861
Heaven, 652
Heeding, 407
Hegelian, 105
Hegemony (hegemonic, hegemonizing), 53, 62, 248, 249, 250, 252, 255, 262, 266, 269, 271, 276, 277, 287, 302, 304, 313, 367, 496, 830, 860
Heideggerean, 419, 420, 432, 435, 451, 538, 572, 576
Heightened consciousness, 219, 232, 358, 519
Heir, 234
Hell, 612, 625
Helplessness, 427, 656
Heraclitean, 466
Herbartian
  concepts, 81, 82
  curriculum, 86
  formal stages, 810
  ideas, 160
  movement, 81, 82, 83
  theory, 82
Heredity, 89, 94
Heretics, 335
Heritage, 422, 779
Hermeneut, 639

Hermeneutics (hermeneutical), xvi, 4, 46, 48, 54, 62, 194, 196, 289, 290, 301, 302, 358, 404, 410, 422, 423, 424, 426, 427, 432, 438, 448, 502, 606, 637, 638, 639, 642, 705, 728, 729, 730, 856
  circle, 447
  cosmology, 501
  inquiry, 638
Hermeneutical
  circle, 641, 642, 799
  interpretation, 640
  phenomenology, 302, 438
  understanding, 423, 448, 640
Heroism (heroic), 342, 455
Heterogeneity (heterogeneous), 285, 345, 481, 491, 606, 670, 671, 694, 832
Heteroglossia, 298, 299, 302, 325
Heteroglot, 505
Heteroglicity, 467
Heterosexism, 359
Heterosexual (heterosexuality), 61, 349, 365, 368, 373, 376, 396, 463, 476, 477
Heuristic, 181
Hi-fi, 205
Hidden curriculum, 24, 28, 174, 244, 248, 249, 250, 252, 256, 269, 270, 337, 387, 589, 684, 746
Hidden pedagogy, 746
Hierarchical (hierarchy, hierarchies), 217, 245, 257, 366, 367, 371, 391, 436, 466, 551, 574, 575, 634, 635, 663, 832, 837
Hierarchical expert/client relationship, 56
High art, 580
High culture, 283, 469, 507
High school (schools), 72, 76, 83, 85, 93, 99, 102, 120, 143, 146, 152, 158, 175, 188,199, 250, 296, 326, 360, 361, 388, 401, 669, 673, 679, 684, 698, 755, 786, 838
High school social life, 788
High-ability groups, 806
High-school curriculum (curricula), 137, 155, 679
High-school textbooks, 204
Higher education, 150, 611, 681, 794, 816, 818, 821, 822, 823, 824, 850
Higher learning, 366, 707, 816
Higher-order thinking, 675, 679
Hinduism, 615
Historian, 146, 164, 176, 183, 677, 801, 855
Historical
  actors, 294
  amnesia, 511, 671
  analyses, 487
  calling, 863
  conjuncture, 346, 394
  context (contexts), 10, 43, 63, 345, 769, 773
  discourses, 63, 317
  event, 848
  images, 471

Historical (continued)
  meaning, 659
  moment, 278, 411, 538, 645
  perspective, 726
  research, 42, 780
  scholarship, 42, 43, 128
  sedimentation, 450
  sensibility, 263
  shifts, 860
  world, 217
Historicity, 43, 277, 346, 424, 436, 642
Histories (lost), 62
History (historical), xiv, xvi, 4, 6, 7, 8, 11, 12,
    13, 14, 15, 16, 18, 22, 23, 24, 25, 29,
    30, 32, 33, 41, 42, 43, 46, 48, 50, 55,
    58, 65, 69, 70, 76, 79, 80, 82, 84, 85,
    120, 124, 143, 151, 156, 158, 160,
    170,177, 181, 186, 187, 198, 203, 208,
    212, 213, 216, 217, 223, 229, 234, 248,
    262, 266, 271, 273, 276, 281, 290, 291,
    292, 295, 300, 301, 302, 309, 310, 312,
    314, 319, 322, 323, 328, 330, 341, 351,
    352, 354, 356, 359, 366, 368, 371, 386,
    392, 397, 400, 402, 403, 420, 423, 447,
    448, 450, 452, 458, 460, 463, 467, 468,
    469, 470, 472, 473, 475, 476, 481, 488,
    492, 494, 499, 501, 504, 510, 521, 533,
    535, 540, 564, 565, 570, 572, 573, 577,
    580, 584, 592, 599, 602, 606, 610, 616,
    626, 630, 632, 638, 641, 644, 645, 646,
    648, 649, 664, 665, 668, 671, 677, 694,
    697, 705, 707, 717, 720, 747, 756, 776,
    787, 794, 799, 807, 812, 813, 818, 824,
    847, 850, 851, 854
  of art, 568
  of curriculum studies, 121
  of education, 783
  of school subjects, 71, 793
  of science, 4, 717
  of teaching, 753
  of technology, 717
  professor, 153
  textbooks, 777
Hobbies, 692
Holistic (holism, holistic), 224, 368, 399,
    510, 559, 631, 729
  curriculum, 633
Holy, 612
Home (homes), 87, 111, 147, 208, 333, 334,
    339, 347, 362, 380, 394, 421, 440, 529,
    534, 788
  economics, 362, 363, 365, 410, 426
  schooling, 625
Homecoming, 448, 788
Homelessness (homeless), 244, 357, 427,
    511, 678, 820
Homemaker, 153
Homeric poems, 543
Homeroom, 158
Homework, 329, 622, 754, 806
Homiletics (homiletical), 637

Homoeroticism (homoerotic), 339
Homogeneity (homogeneous), 259, 461,
    481, 670, 679
Homogenization, 511
Homophobia (homophobic), 341, 357, 369,
    511
Homosexuals (homosexual, homosexuality),
    339, 347, 349, 359, 363, 369, 370, 371,
    373, 374, 375, 376, 396, 397, 398, 399,
    402, 463, 464, 476, 477, 478
Honesty, 784
Honor, 398
Hope, xviii, 88, 106, 132, 223, 246, 255, 289,
    352, 387, 420, 421, 427, 431, 433, 435,
    444, 481, 489, 626, 631, 641, 645, 647,
    649, 650, 653, 654, 735, 861, 862, 867
Hopeful, 263, 321, 588, 847, 848
Hopelessness, 220
Horizon (horizons), 15, 78, 270, 302, 309,
    355, 389, 406, 411, 412, 415, 425, 428,
    435, 443, 572, 577, 641
Horizontal evaluation, 726
Horizontal, 124, 181, 463, 464, 727
Hormonal, 359
Horror, 541
Hospitalization, 442
Hospitals, 465
Hostage, 209
Hostility (hostile), 282, 314, 609
House of being, 421, 422
Human, 407, 411, 441, 443, 447, 455, 631,
    637, 684
  behavior, 91, 198
  being (human beings), 399, 418, 427, 643,
    658
  capital, 623
  community, 801
  condition, 215, 233, 269, 296, 648
  conduct, 411
  creation, 778
  development, 628, 645, 748
  dignity, 397
  engineering, 91
  environment, 213
  family, 801
  interests, 231, 313, 354
  nature, 89, 91, 92, 148, 272, 288, 394, 401,
    461, 577, 836
  potential, 217, 224, 717
  reality, 49
  relations, 155, 271
  rights, 289, 352, 366, 499, 508, 842
  science research, 438
  science, 439, 504, 641, 643
  sexuality classes, 401
  spirit, 609, 626, 659, 840
  subjects, 213
  survival, 223
  traits/processes, 21, 126, 686
  world, 49
Humane international order, 838

Humanism (humanistic), 3, 21, 29, 77, 89,
    156, 172, 186, 189, 190, 191, 192, 193,
    200, 204, 227, 228, 233, 321, 370, 451,
    455, 456, 459, 461, 464, 475, 604, 614,
    777, 865
Humanist, 460
    curriculum, 77
Humanistic
    education, 222, 688, 712
    moral values, 617
    psychology, 93,178
    technology, 687
    themes, 224
Humanists, 30, 31
Humanitarian, 190, 842
Humanities, 12, 30, 32, 50, 51, 52, 54, 55,
    62, 65, 145, 152, 156, 163, 173, 183,
    203, 213, 220, 369, 495, 519, 540, 564,
    565, 573, 580, 615, 672, 673, 726, 758,
    803, 834, 865
Humanity, 198, 217, 274, 288, 336, 379, 397,
    422, 494, 635, 649, 656, 669, 801, 821,
    842
Humanization, 469, 645, 700
Humanize, 189, 498
Humanizing, 212, 455
Humankind, 225, 389, 498, 847, 858
Humanness, 190
Humiliation, 651
Humility, 313, 409, 527
Humor, 9, 233, 749
Hunterized, 724
Husserlian, 414, 419, 445, 447
Hybrid, 305, 354, 755, 853, 865, 868
Hybridization, 853
Hymns, 567
Hyper-eroticized, 511
Hyper-real space, 471
Hypercards, 706
Hyperrationalization, 667, 668
Hyperreality, 472, 762
Hypertrophy, 518
Hypothesis (hypothesize), 168, 571, 572

I-Thou relationship, 170
Id, 329
Ideal (the), 594, 659, 770
Ideal forms, 480
Idealist (idealistic, idealism), 270, 374, 408,
    414, 434, 453, 455, 460, 461, 598
Idealized, 595, 779
Ideals, 91, 101, 102, 266, 481, 634, 771, 848
Ideas, 7, 10, 19, 29, 78, 110, 127, 133, 160,
    249, 423, 424, 492, 522, 571, 579, 617,
    664, 694, 747, 756, 847, 853
Identification, 223, 268, 278, 435, 596
Identities, 55, 61, 279, 285, 335, 343, 353,
    355, 373, 396, 480, 691, 784, 785
Identity, 12, 62, 69, 123, 147, 230, 261, 274,
    304, 306, 308, 309, 315, 319, 324, 325,

327, 328, 330, 335, 336, 337, 340, 341,
    344, 349, 350, 354, 355, 356, 358, 373,
    378, 394, 422, 423, 424, 426, 466, 476,
    478, 479, 492, 495, 504, 508, 522, 523,
    525, 533, 538, 540, 547, 550, 571, 573,
    590, 598, 651, 769, 785, 786, 838, 849,
    865
    (shared), 750
    formation, 278, 279, 357
    politics, 277, 327
    representation, 342
Identity-creation, 788
Identity-in-motion, 355, 356
Ideological
    conformity, 817
    formation, 836
    hegemony, 245
    imperialism, 741
    mystification, 246
    neutrality, 486, 487, 488
    reductionism, 368
    state apparatus, 246
Ideologist, 321
Ideologue (ideologues), 93
Ideology (ideological, ideologies), 5, 13, 22,
    53, 57, 58, 62, 120, 125, 127, 129, 143,
    171, 185, 216, 226, 227, 244, 245, 246,
    247, 248, 249, 250, 251, 252, 255, 257,
    262, 265, 266, 268, 269, 272, 276, 278,
    281, 282, 283, 284, 286, 288, 296, 298,
    305, 306, 313, 325, 337, 353, 360, 365,
    392, 393, 448, 481, 487, 488, 492, 496,
    513, 559, 560, 575, 634, 635, 642, 647,
    666, 667, 674, 678, 700, 715, 762, 779,
    803, 827, 832, 835, 836, 859, 866, 867
Idiosyncrasy, 52, 56, 860
Idolatry, 335
Ignorance, 284, 326, 329, 344, 691, 750
Illiteracy, 827
Illumination (Illumined), 417, 520
Illuminative evaluation, 736, 737
Image culture, 469
Image industry, 469
Image-Behavior-Feedback (IBF) model, 723
Images (image, imagery, imagistic), 16, 259,
    278, 284, 292, 294, 302, 305, 329, 342,
    346, 470, 471, 472, 473, 479, 490, 507,
    511, 513, 539, 541, 554, 559, 561, 569,
    570, 581, 589, 593, 628, 779, 851
Imaginary (the), 478, 479
Imagination (imaginative, imaginary), 110,
    138,172, 201, 210, 284, 305, 365, 367,
    411, 423, 443, 500, 516, 518, 540, 541,
    542, 543, 569, 571, 573, 588, 604, 632,
    658, 691, 752, 768, 861
Imagining, 593
Imagistic world, 470, 571
Imitation (imitative), 471, 628
Immanence (immanent), 654, 655
Immediacy (immediate), 376, 407, 414, 415,
    430, 431, 444, 494, 527, 591

Immersion, 221, 567
Immigration (immigrants), 14, 33, 345, 346,
    362, 607, 609, 776, 801, 838, 841
Immorality, 634, 635
Imperialism (imperialist), 140, 221, 273, 362,
    839
Imperialistic wars, 222
Impersonal, 377, 456, 497, 529
Implementation (implement, implemented),
    24, 35, 77, 165, 203, 205, 289, 302,
    519, 664, 665, 668, 683, 685, 689, 699,
    700, 701, 702, 704, 744, 791, 822
Implicitness, 603
Import, 850
Imposition (impositional), 125, 127, 390,
    396, 525, 551, 640, 800
Impoverished, 828
Imprinting, 80
Improved instruction, 720
Improvement, 15, 20, 31, 72, 198, 679, 680,
    722, 740, 757
Improvisational (improvisation), 590, 601,
    770
Impulse (impulses), 107, 433, 474, 522, 634
In-between (in-betweens), 395, 480, 496, 782
In-itself (*en soi*), 453
In-sist, 484
Inadequacy, 786
Inauthenticity (inauthentic), 472, 859
Incarnation, 483
Inclusion, 319, 400, 831
Inclusive, 371
Income tax credits, 620
Incomes (income), 326, 372
Incommensurability, 306
Incompleteness (incomplete), 328, 420, 455,
    488, 579
Incorporation (incorporating, incorporated),
    305, 310, 313, 314, 324, 327, 498, 510,
    513, 522, 714
Incremental (increments), 54, 95, 221, 236,
    272, 321, 330, 364, 387, 500, 661, 694,
    744
Incrementalism, 208
Independence (independent), 251, 322, 342,
    383, 387, 764, 818, 854, 864
Independent learning, 686
Independent schools, 678, 834
Independent study, 189
Indeterminacy (indeterminate), 195, 495,
    499, 501, 502, 504, 839
Indifference, 485, 647
Indigenous, 820, 823, 824, 828
Indirect rule, 252
Individual (individuals), 29, 36, 53, 77, 79,
    80, 90, 105, 109, 110, 150, 156, 165,
    175,177, 205, 214, 216, 217, 223, 224,
    225, 272, 282, 291, 292, 301, 319, 321,
    326, 327, 328, 348, 349, 358, 364, 372,
    384, 385, 396, 404, 405, 406, 411, 412,
    416, 418, 420, 426, 427, 428, 431, 437,

453, 458, 459, 475, 476, 488, 498, 500,
    502, 515, 516, 521, 523, 525, 527, 537,
    539, 544, 545, 547, 552, 555, 565, 577,
    588, 603, 623, 630, 635, 637, 653, 669,
    670, 702, 704, 717, 769, 780, 783, 810
development 788
differences, 164, 259, 681, 710
freedom, 603, 633, 636
growth, 703
history, 282
interests/activities, 21
needs, 21, 686, 813
psychology, 560
self, 570
subject, 305
success, 786
Individual-centeredness, 273
Individualism, 127, 132, 217, 257, 273, 306,
    395, 671, 674
Individuality, 5, 126,190, 257, 475, 515, 565,
    604, 716
Individualization (individualize,
    individualized), 89, 103, 113, 190, 192,
    272, 384, 700, 710
Individualized (individualizing) instruction,
    171, 178, 710
Individuals, 10, 24, 27
Individuation (individuate), 217, 518, 528
Indoctrination (indoctrinate), 109, 126, 127,
    129, 131, 163, 353, 630, 748, 800, 808,
    811
Industrial arts (shop), 362, 717
Industrial-governmental-educational
    complex, 681
Industrial-technocratic model, 498
Industrialists, 779
Industrialization, 321, 362, 500, 646, 799,
    808
Industrialized, 683, 818, 841
Industrious, 257, 816
Industry (industrial), 31, 80, 102, 109, 113,
    114, 140, 146, 199, 227, 296, 303, 320,
    357, 626, 718, 789, 795, 806, 808
Indwelling, 689
Ineffable, 583
Inegalitarianism, 623
Inequality (inequalities, inequitable), 275,
    288, 332, 334, 393, 565, 644, 820, 828,
    851
Inextricability, 337
Infancy, 144
Infant, 377, 386
Infantilization, 284, 529
Inferences, 743
Inferential nature of paternity, 374
Inferiority (inferior), 253
    complexes, 127
Infinite, 467
    connection, 491
    regress, 423
Inflation, 824

Inflected, 435
Influence (influences), 35, 43, 45, 79, 91, 93, 104, 110, 118, 129, 130, 140, 144, 149, 155, 161, 163, 175, 178, 183, 184, 195,199, 200, 208, 281, 299, 307, 329, 402, 403, 436, 493, 504, 550, 638, 662, 663, 667, 668, 732, 760, 776, 791, 812, 814, 828, 856, 862
Info-tainment, 474
Informal curriculum, 789
Informal education, 188, 189, 754
Informality, 108, 673
Information, 91,198, 272, 278, 296, 302,306, 469, 470, 474, 492
  age, 715
  networks, 716
  processing, 51
  technology, 511
  theory, 812
Informational, 637
Informational corporatism, 303
Informationalism, 278
Infrastructure, 293, 349, 672
Inheritance, 624
Inhuman, 181
Initiations, 823
Initiative, 138, 365, 825
Injury (injuries), 441,474
Injustice, 227, 332, 349, 485, 489, 534, 620
Innate, 368
Inner, 431, 518, 519, 528, 540, 541, 543, 544, 554
  development, 626
  peace, 485
  time, 405
  world, 440, 542
Inner-city, 696, 700
Innocence, 176, 420, 440
Innovation (innovations), 198, 203, 474, 603, 699, 701, 704, 714, 737, 754, 756, 789
Inquiry, 15, 46, 49, 53, 91, 161,170, 171, 196, 213, 227, 255, 300, 322, 325, 357, 367, 392, 400, 499, 504, 557, 665, 729, 732, 745, 750, 792
Inquiry-guided research, 54
Inscribed, 464
Inservice education, 756
  patterns, 165
  teacher education, 517, 563, 664, 763, 770
  teacher, 9, 721
  training, 37, 813
Inside, 466
Insight (insights), 117, 125, 131, 170, 171, 282, 373, 420, 427, 489, 509, 518, 551, 572, 574, 590, 640, 659, 752
Inspection, 724, 731
Inspectional supervision, 722, 727, 731
Inspiration (inspiring), 311, 661
Instability, 489
Instincts, 107

Institutional (institutionalized, institutionalize), xvi, 4, 5, 6, 8, 12, 16, 20, 30, 32, 33, 42, 43, 44, 45, 50, 51, 55, 57, 64, 69, 77, 78, 92, 142, 203, 204, 214, 236, 277, 278, 279, 282, 292, 306, 319, 350, 363, 387, 421, 426, 440, 490, 518, 574, 575, 646, 661, 662, 664, 670, 680, 683, 685, 689, 690, 695, 719, 731, 743, 745, 790, 791, 829, 847, 848, 855, 858, 862, 864
  authority, 309
  case studies, 802
  center stage, 96
  currency, 6
  curriculum, 441
  distortions, 786
  imperatives, 764
  improvement, 661, 663
  infrastructure, 678
  maintenance, 661, 744
  networks, 357
  overload, 192
  practice (practices), 202, 229, 259, 331, 333, 335, 479, 670, 690, 755, 865
  racism, 311, 329
  reward, 713
  roles, 690
  sexism, 359, 364
  structures, 223
  symbol, 484
  violence, 222
Institutionalization, 303, 366, 474, 663, 848
Institutionalized educational process, 748
Institutionalized modes of interaction, 785
Institutionalized practice, 793
Institutions (institution), 27, 41, 49, 55, 128, 149, 165, 169, 188, 214, 220, 245, 387, 406, 441, 475, 490, 513, 545, 661, 663, 664, 684, 700, 816, 850, 861
Institutions of deprivation, 285
Instruction (instructional), 15, 33, 56, 72, 74, 93, 102, 126, 127, 142, 148, 155, 160, 171, 176, 184, 190, 191, 215, 280, 287, 359, 387, 410, 421, 434, 486, 519, 612, 669, 679, 681, 686, 690, 705, 707, 711, 714, 715, 720, 721, 722, 723, 724, 729, 732, 744, 745, 749, 751, 754, 791, 810, 855
Instruction (large-group), 753
  leaders, 721
Instructional applications of computers (IAC), 710
  behaviorists, 237
  computing, 705
  design, 167, 686
  games, 710
  improvement, 723
  materials (material), 174, 582, 803
  media, 705, 706
  methodology, 192, 334

IAC (continued)
  methods, 72, 76, 77, 85, 166
  models, 752
  objectives, 166, 192,199
  plan, 21
  procedure (procedures), 72, 747
  processes, 57
  program (programs), 33, 713
  schemes, 186
  supervision, 727, 729
  technology, 193
  television, 709
  theory
  time, 815
Instructor, 9
Instrumental action, 428, 671
Instrumental intervention, 666
Instrumental values, 116
Instrumentalism (instrumentality,
    instrumentalist), 116, 209, 227, 410,
    688, 853
Instrumentally (instrumental), 666, 762
Insubstantiality, 455
Insularity, 44
Insurance industry, 728
Integrated model (supervision), 723
Integration, 3, 372, 382, 435, 594
  (curricular), 696, 865
  (psychological), 217, 223
  (racial), 316
Integrative education, 199
Integrative, 170, 553
Integrity, 418, 477
Intellect, 74, 108, 372, 390, 444, 521, 604
  (rhapsodic), 210
Intellectual, 109, 132, 154, 173, 203, 211,
    216, 359, 361, 419, 439, 578
  courage, 446
  debt, 46
  development, 108, 190, 275, 321, 400, 515,
    520, 811
  elite, 88
  freedom, 615
  history, 580
  integrity, 795
  leader, 65
  life, 694, 774
  marketplace, 796
  segregation, 316
  work, 385
Intellectualism, 127
Intellectualization, 571
Intellectualized wish, 866
Intellectuals (intellectual), 61, 131, 151, 262,
    325, 362, 492, 663, 672, 753, 808, 816,
    817, 864
Intelligence, 118, 131, 290, 328, 343, 344,
    416, 444, 535, 572, 695, 715, 848, 858
  test (testing), 90, 682
Intelligent tutoring systems, 713

Intended learning outcomes, 169, 197, 200,
    250, 548
Intended outcomes, 736
Intensification (intensify, intensifying), 401,
    522, 528, 643, 668, 675, 787, 816
Intensified, 591
Intensity (intensities, intense), 414, 467, 477,
    483, 484, 519, 591, 605, 620, 692, 853,
    859
Intention (intentions, intent), 55, 169, 197,
    200, 204, 306, 426, 583, 597, 741
Intentionality (intentional), 274, 356, 406,
    407, 412, 414, 426, 435, 436, 551, 556,
    582, 590, 688, 866
Interacting (interactive), 502, 524, 563
Interaction, 438, 502, 713, 716, 725
Interactional
  labor, 785
  life, 786
  relational lack, 785
Interactionism, 500
Interactive, 190
  model, 19
  videos, 706, 713
Interconnectedness, 582, 715, 753, 800, 801,
    829, 830, 831
Interdependence, 257, 633
Interdisciplinary (interdisciplinarity), 28, 55,
    65, 83, 164, 170, 290, 331, 397, 535,
    679, 759, 865
Interest (interests), 81, 91, 105, 118, 125,
    136, 172, 248, 327, 400, 575, 579, 635,
    767
  groups, 30, 142, 621
Interest-driven, 848
Interesting, 474
Interface, 715
Intergenerational, 234, 607, 623
Interior, 466, 586, 589
Interior life, 336
Interior monologue, 588
Intermediate schools, 93
Internalization (internalize), 270, 336, 356,
    518, 795
Internalized, 222, 249, 372, 382, 388
International, xvii, 22, 23, 32, 45, 46, 55,
    215, 229, 230, 263, 409, 675, 676, 683,
    756, 792, 793, 794, 795, 796, 801, 802,
    809, 821, 828, 829, 833, 838, 840, 841,
    843, 848, 856, 857, 859, 866
  belligerence, 801
  classroom, 801, 837, 838
  community, 833
  comparisons, 794, 798
  conflict, 807
  cooperation, 801
  critique, 120
  curriculum, 803, 832, 840
  curriculum developments, 803
  curriculum discourse, 800

curriculum research, 837
curriculum vision, 840
discourses, 843
economic competitiveness, 6, 102, 154
educational community, 831
educational research, 796
exchange, 802
narrative practice, 838
order, 800
research, 794
slavery, 321
studies, 830
supremacy, 161
trade, 794
understanding, 801
Internationalization (internationalized,
    internationalizing), 22, 792, 801, 830,
    831, 837, 840, 842
Internationalized curriculum, 803
Internship, 36, 758
Interpretation (interpretive), 4, 28, 50, 51,
    60, 62, 63, 64, 181, 194, 204, 205, 255,
    274, 275, 289, 290, 297, 300, 301, 302,
    380, 396, 404, 405, 413, 423, 424, 426,
    427, 437, 448, 454, 465, 471, 478, 492,
    501, 502, 506, 512, 521, 526, 546, 548,
    551, 556, 558, 582, 583, 606, 638, 639,
    640, 641, 642, 684, 702, 728, 730, 740,
    751, 764, 788, 849, 859
Interpreters, 746
Interpretive
    assessment, 742
    community (communities), 524, 548
    inquiry, 229, 404, 405, 729
    research, 643, 669
    studies, 793
Interrupting (interruptions), 393, 550
Intersection, 769
Intersubjective (intersubjectivity), 227, 274,
    275, 306, 335, 377, 407, 412, 427, 439,
    515, 545, 557, 596
Intertextuality (intertextual), xvii, 316, 436,
    466, 775, 866
Intervention (interventions), 207, 259, 663,
    665, 666, 854
Interview (interviews, interviewing), 59, 60,
    505, 541, 555, 558, 559, 560, 562, 582,
    639, 736, 738
Intimacy (intimate), 361, 378, 379, 380, 388,
    435, 527, 539, 634, 653, 799, 860
Intolerance (intolerant), 609, 614, 777
Intoxication, 691
Intrapsychic, 375
Intrasubjective, 227
Introjected, 522
Introspection (introspective), 405, 531, 757
Intuition (intuitive), 179, 180, 214, 405, 577,
    628, 648, 768
Invariable (invariant), 450, 452, 456, 457,
    460, 462, 464, 481
Invariant, 437

Inventic curriculum, 835
Inventiveness, 581, 735
Inventory, 89
Inverted millenarianism, 469
Investigation (investigations), 34, 284, 457
Investment, 684, 799, 823
Invisibility (invisible), 280, 336, 730, 746,
    766
Inwardness (inward), 217
Ironical, 469, 508
Irrationality, 458
Irreducible (irreducibles), 280, 369, 433, 482
Irreverent, 600
Isolation (isolated), 70, 257, 401, 402, 403,
    425, 593, 600, 771
Isolationist (isolationism), 802, 806, 850
Issues, 18, 163, 813, 826, 867

Jails (jailed), 465, 827
Japanese Canadian curricula, 422
Japanese social studies, 521
Japanese, 603, 662, 789, 802, 804, 805, 806,
    807, 808, 810, 848
Japanese-American, 839
Jargon, 428, 681
Jazz, 599
Jewish, 316, 529, 609, 616, 638, 647, 811
Jim Crowism, 361
Job (jobs), 349, 620, 764, 767, 781, 824, 829
Jocks, 785
Joke, 409
Journal records, 558, 560
Journal work, 759
Journal-keeping, 540
Journal-writing, 552
Journalism, 735, 737, 738
Journalist, 188, 222
Journals (journal), xiii, xiv, 13, 36, 48, 88,
    129, 145, 197, 200, 208, 211, 219, 226,
    261, 388, 397, 476, 505, 528, 530, 545,
    555, 575, 599, 729, 765, 780
Journey, 32, 74, 77, 214, 235, 398, 399, 426,
    433, 490, 517, 518, 531, 543, 544, 847,
    861
Joy, 30, 139, 187, 485, 565, 631, 639, 657,
    664, 760, 791
Joyful wisdom, 482
Judeo-Christian, 614
Judges (judge), 299, 301, 668, 669
Judging, 115
Judgment (judgments), 9, 34, 45, 150, 205,
    582, 584, 585, 735, 738, 739, 741
Judicial evaluation model, 737
Jungian, 522
Jungle, 336, 337
Junior high school, 77, 93, 102, 175
Junk mail, 860
Juridical discourses, 462, 463
Jurisprudence, 300
Just society, 131, 244, 260, 334

Justice (just), 109, 179, 214, 226, 267, 286, 288, 292, 301, 409, 477, 508, 509, 629, 631, 632, 645, 646, 649, 650, 651, 652, 827, 828, 838, 862
Justices (Supreme Court), 300
Justification, 266, 635
Juvenile delinquency, 808

Kantian, 457
Key, 228
Keynesian macroeconomics, 204
Kill, 188, 481, 541
Killer, 188
Killing machines, 292
Kindergarten, 86, 740
Kinship, 457
Kiss (kissing), 468,471
Know-how, 764
Knower (the), 364, 566
Knowing, 174, 343, 344, 346, 359, 368, 377, 379, 391, 404, 428, 433, 562, 571, 572, 573, 660, 715, 732, 859, 861
Knowledge, 15, 24, 26, 29, 38, 55, 58, 70, 73, 74, 78, 95, 143, 152, 160, 161, 164, 168, 183, 191, 192, 198, 202, 214, 222, 231, 235, 244, 285, 286, 296, 297, 298, 299, 302, 303, 305, 306, 325, 327, 336, 337, 343, 344, 349, 359, 367, 368, 379, 385, 403, 406, 407, 415, 420, 447, 458, 463, 474, 479, 481, 482, 492, 496, 504, 505, 510, 524, 528, 531, 546, 553, 560, 562, 573, 579, 582, 584, 597, 600, 605, 613, 614, 626, 632, 634, 658, 666, 667, 672, 676, 687, 691, 704, 713, 715, 716, 750, 755, 762, 764, 790, 799, 813, 829, 858, 859, 862, 866
acquisition, 569, 573, 750
base, 748, 749, 750, 756, 757
creation (production), 190, 525
formation, 793
Knowledge-avoidance, 784
Knowledge-constitutive practices, 784
Known (the), 364, 566, 576
Koranic schools, 823

Labor, xvii, 31, 48, 95, 111, 245, 252, 281, 295, 296, 318, 325, 401, 646, 651, 777, 799, 848, 866
Labor market, 222, 250, 318, 325, 677
Labor movement, 228
Laboratory (laboratories), 85, 92, 110, 171, 412, 714, 737
Laboratory school (schools), 107, 132, 135
Laboratory-experimental method, 77
Laborers, 820
Lacanian, 355, 539
Lack, 491
Lads, 254, 268
Laissez-faire, 76, 90, 104, 110

Landscape (landscapes), 291, 373, 472, 507, 538
Language, 7, 9, 10, 32, 48, 49, 60, 76, 178, 182,192, 213, 214, 215, 226, 227, 258, 262, 271, 275, 286, 287, 292, 306, 313, 324, 335, 355, 404, 408, 409, 417, 418, 419, 420, 421, 422, 423, 424, 425, 427, 435, 442, 445, 447, 448, 450, 452, 457, 458, 459, 460, 461, 465, 466, 467, 470, 476, 480, 482, 483, 484, 491, 492, 495, 496, 501, 513, 522, 525, 530, 531, 537, 540, 548, 568, 569, 587, 588, 589, 603, 627, 632, 639, 641, 642, 657, 703, 731, 731, 760, 808, 816, 849, 860, 861
analysis, 182, 205
arts, 580, 658, 792, 801
classes, 531
communities, 606
game, 45, 492
instruction, 75
of possibility, 325, 352, 854
pedagogy, 587, 600, 784
Langue, 458
Latent, 190, 284, 308, 447, 472, 769
Latin, 72, 73, 74, 75, 85, 91, 96, 108
Latin American, 826, 827, 828, 829
Latin grammar school, 84, 607
Latino/Latina, 315, 330, 347
Laughter, 450, 471, 501, 536
Law (laws, legal), 207, 299, 300, 301, 320, 361, 384, 613, 617, 638, 640, 662, 668, 669, 735, 737, 738, 750, 776, 823
Lawyer (lawyers), 121, 299, 759
Lay boards, 608
Lay influence, 608
Layered, 439
Layering, 759
Laziness, 329
Leaders (leader), 142, 770
Leadership, 23, 41, 112, 113, 126, 142, 160, 176, 260, 321, 353, 409, 726, 764, 775, 790, 814, 821
Learners (learner), 144, 149, 237, 686, 704, 713, 715, 746, 748
Learning, 30, 34, 51, 73, 78, 86, 91, 92, 106, 107, 139, 142, 150, 156, 161, 164, 167, 169, 172, 177, 184, 187, 190, 206, 207, 237, 252, 258, 262, 285, 295, 297, 298, 332, 333, 348, 406, 407, 417, 430, 481, 531, 582, 600, 628, 631, 634, 675, 677, 679, 684, 685, 702, 703, 705, 716, 726, 743, 746, 749, 760, 770, 781, 782, 783, 810, 865
activities, 200
difficulty, 206
environment (environments), 171, 397, 400, 548
experiences, 15, 17, 22, 34, 79, 143, 145, 148, 149, 166, 173, 417, 486, 709, 734
materials, 696
modules, 686

objectives, 148, 167
outcomes, 783
packages, 825
problems, 733
process, 175, 545, 715
programs, 810
situation, 809
style, 577, 595
theory, 168, 206, 269, 270, 812, 860, 861
time, 206
Learning-by-doing, 109
Learning-by-rote, 359, 361
Left (the), 44, 233, 261, 294, 317, 326, 619,
    636, 644, 681, 802, 864
Left-of-center, 779
Left-wing, 39, 129, 803
Leftist curriculum theorists, 295
Legacy, 143, 636, 665
Legal rights, 214
Legal-rational authority, 720
Legend (legends), 543, 819, 823
Legislation (legislative), 175, 607, 608, 612,
    778
Legitimacy, 122, 123, 126, 249
Legitimation (legitimations), 275, 418, 474,
    637, 642, 737, 741, 860
Leisure, 97, 99, 189, 394, 513
Lesbian (lesbians), 339, 342, 363, 368, 373,
    374, 397, 398, 476, 477, 478, 678
  role models, 396, 397
Lesson plans (plan), 149, 167, 188, 479, 766,
    806
Lessons (lesson), 137, 167, 248, 692, 711,
    749, 751, 780
Letter writing, 558, 560
Liberal (liberals), 127, 185, 261, 273, 291,
    301, 318, 319, 321, 323, 330, 364, 365,
    366, 633, 660, 670, 715, 751, 832
  arts, 260, 812
  democracy, 504
  developmental ideology, 216
  education, 170, 194, 195, 196, 202, 694
  feminism (feminists), 365, 371
  philanthropists, 648
  realism, 152
  reform, 222
  studies, 762
  theological perspectives, 626
Liberal-technocratic, 272, 273, 274
Liberalism, 261, 270, 272, 320
Liberation (liberating, liberatory, liberative,
    liberate, liberationist), 220, 221, 258,
    262, 304, 305, 351, 352, 354, 389, 477,
    505, 507, 521, 577, 599, 631, 643, 645,
    647, 648, 649, 650, 653, 688, 815, 825
  theologians, 644, 647, 648, 649, 828
  theology, 62, 307, 631, 637, 643, 644, 645,
    646, 647, 648, 649, 650, 651, 652, 826,
    827, 838
Liberatory education, 856
Liberty (liberties), 508, 660

Librarianship (librarian), 101, 112
Libraries (library), 85, 174, 298, 625, 706,
    716, 819
Life, 7, 85, 107, 122, 125, 142, 154, 174,
    182, 189, 227, 262, 274, 283, 295, 320,
    406, 418, 419, 427, 430, 443, 444, 446,
    483, 514, 517, 520, 532, 544, 569, 579,
    590, 603, 626, 628, 638, 651, 652, 659,
    715, 769, 799, 841
  activities, 73
  adjustment, 145, 146, 147, 151, 152, 153,
    154, 155, 159, 357, 372
  experience, 769
  historian, 58
  histories, 55, 535
  history, 58, 392, 413, 515, 517, 521, 525,
    534, 554, 560, 563, 566, 578, 645, 770,
    859, 864
  history data, 769
  (inner), 126
  mask, 589
  problems, 172
  situation, 144, 412
  skills, 250
Life-history method, 769
Lifestyle, 719, 796, 829
Lifeworld (lifeworlds), 406, 407, 408, 422,
    430, 431, 438, 445, 446, 551, 785
Lightness, 490
Lightning, 482
Limitation (limitations), 256
Line, 490, 602
Linear rationality, 217
Linear, 148, 237, 322, 332, 371, 437, 467,
    484, 488, 499, 500, 503, 520, 544, 699,
    715, 745, 851, 853
Linguistic
  analysis, 202
  arabesques, 480
  communism, 53
  idealism, 480
  investigations, 60
  mask, 471
  transformations, 408
Linguistics (linguistic), 4, 299, 448, 457, 458,
    461, 484, 492, 540, 570, 638, 640, 641,
    746, 747
Link, 537
Listening, 334, 391, 425, 431, 431, 546
Literacy (literacies), 61, 230, 260, 287, 314,
    334, 435, 530, 570, 607, 718, 826, 828,
    830, 839
Literal, 536, 638, 847, 862
Literalistic, 640, 731
Literary, 258, 287, 342, 437, 438, 521, 588,
    614, 739, 742
  anthropology, 438
  critic (critics), 182, 233, 423
  criticism, 55, 62, 213, 735, 751
  historian, 535
  journalism, 631

Literary (continued)
  theorist, 290, 351, 535
  theory, 4, 12, 62, 173, 278, 436, 850
Literate, 674
Literature, 4, 6, 76, 79, 82, 84, 86, 164, 169,
  170, 183, 286, 287, 408, 415, 519, 540,
  564, 565, 579, 589, 625, 694, 801, 814
Litigation, 617
Lived, 404, 408, 418, 419, 420, 425, 429,
  430, 445, 520, 521, 529, 540, 590, 599,
  664, 790
  culture, 334
  experience, 62, 64, 246, 358, 370, 378,
    388, 405, 407, 408, 415, 416, 417, 421,
    422, 430, 431, 438, 446, 454, 455, 490,
    501, 522, 523, 524, 527, 530, 546, 547,
    550, 554, 557, 562, 565, 578, 596, 598,
    602, 655, 760
  meaning (meanings), 431, 764
  relation (relations), 428, 565
  situation (situations), 416, 424
  space, 440, 442, 525, 547, 860
  text, 446
  time, 405, 442
  world (worlds), 381, 393, 410, 435
Living universe, 499
Local (the), 291, 300, 311, 312, 387, 502,
  575, 620, 621, 671, 676, 765, 828, 838,
  860
  autonomy, 794
  control, 380, 678
  cultural (cultures), 614, 676, 756
  educational authorities (LEAs), 831
  government, 666
  history, 823
  school, 838
Localisms, 864
Localized, 677
Location (locations), 437, 537, 858, 860
Lockean, 499
Locker room jokes, 396, 397
Logic (logical), 63, 80, 92, 151, 162, 202,
  227, 253, 254, 284,298, 306, 317, 371,
  405, 413, 425, 466, 488, 491, 501, 510,
  588, 656, 668, 689, 715, 774, 775, 859
  analysis, 173
  clarification, 203
  games, 774
  operations, 782
  order, 697
Logicians, 482
Logocentric (logocentrism), 467, 492
Logos (the), 422, 447
Logs, 555
Loneliness (lonely), 214, 397, 402, 440
Longing, 376
Longitudinal study, 780
Look (the), 377, 447, 472, 527
Loose coupling, 682
Loosening, 520, 598
Lord's prayer, 613

Lore, 767
Loss, 435, 472, 511, 518, 532
Lost, 214, 472, 490, 539, 552, 561
Louisiana fiction, 535
Love, 74, 337, 350, 389, 420, 436, 470, 528,
  600, 631, 640, 657, 768, 861, 862
Loving (loved), 174, 479
Low culture, 469
Low status, 365
Low-ability groups, 806
Lower class, 294
Lower schools, 84
Lower track, 669, 670, 806
Loyalty (loyalties), 107, 127, 128, 143, 152,
  308, 409, 853
Luck, 670
Lunchroom, 109
Luxuries, 828
Lyrical, 381, 388, 543

Machine, 92, 498, 652, 658, 715, 716
Machinery, 799
Machinism, 491
Macro-structural, 223, 254, 787
Macrocurricular problems, 186
Macropolitical, 289
Maddening, 768
Madness, 212, 421, 425, 447, 462, 518, 538,
  655
Madonna, 656
Magic, 217
Magnet schools, 620
Maim, 386
Mainstream, 316, 735, 742, 753, 756, 770,
  776, 779, 781, 789, 838, 854
Maintenance, 203
Majority (majorities), 328, 347, 400, 611,
  660, 828
Malaise, 629
Maldistribution, 305
Male (males), 61, 85, 329, 340, 342, 359,
  360, 361, 362, 363, 365, 366, 368, 369,
  376, 379, 385, 387, 392, 396, 399, 400,
  403, 435, 458, 467, 525, 526, 538, 550,
  552, 602
  chauvinism, 222
  discourse, 495
  dominance, 490
  gangs, 363
  homosexuality (homosexual), 369, 399
  identity, 396, 399
  sex roles, 369
  socialization, 399
Male-centered curriculum, 361
Male-identified, 383
Male-male relations, 375, 376
Male-romanticized, 384
Malefic generosity, 392
Maleness, 363, 373
Malevolent, 656

Mammal, 195
Man (men), 77, 206, 221, 266, 280, 294, 306,
    336, 339, 343, 367, 368, 369, 370, 373,
    384, 389, 393, 395, 396, 399, 400, 401,
    407, 476, 490, 549, 626, 780
Management (managers), 95, 220, 227, 249,
    264, 411, 674, 675, 682, 684, 722, 732
Management studies, 731
Management theory, 200
Managerial, 148, 203, 237, 244, 247, 726
  character, 42
  evaluation, 723
  interest, 34, 112
  supervision, 727
Managing curriculum, 18
Manhood, 72
Manifest, 472, 624
Manipulative (manipulation), 116, 365, 481,
    570
Manual labor, 320, 343
Manual skill, 108
Manual work, 343
Manufactured, 305
Manufacturer, 121
Manufacturing, 237, 807
Map (maps), 7, 30, 31, 46, 52, 235, 465, 490,
    491, 511
Mapped, 868
Mapping (Mappings), 28, 31, 32, 41, 170,
    215, 374, 775
Marching band, 789
Marginal (marginality), 317, 319, 336, 351,
    357, 427, 508, 510
Marginalize (marginalized, marginalization),
    231, 249, 286, 287, 296, 312, 325, 327,
    336, 347, 356, 494, 527, 531, 549, 567,
    568, 618, 643, 678, 759
  cultures, 317
  discourses, 285, 306
  students, 531
  traditions, 182
Margins (margin), 4, 337, 357, 427, 448,
    531, 659
Market, 671, 831, 832, 837
Market-logic forces, 319
Marketability (marketable), 158, 473, 474
Marketplace, 349
Marriage (married), 94, 143, 338, 529
Marxian, 105, 245, 247, 266, 537, 580
Marxism (Marxisms), 43, 217, 228, 257, 263,
    268, 270, 272, 283, 288, 291, 295, 304,
    306, 311, 314, 432, 504, 505, 513, 627,
    646, 649, 827
Marxism-Leninism, 228, 629
Marxist (Marxists), 13, 39, 129, 186, 199,
    223, 230, 233, 238, 243, 250, 267, 269,
    270, 271, 273, 276, 308, 309, 315, 318,
    358, 369, 384, 390, 457, 495, 545, 564,
    654, 816, 828, 832, 863, 864
  feminist, 396, 506
  patriarch, 395

Marxist-Leninist-Maoist thought, 814, 815
Masculine ethic of rationality, 366
Masculine, 359, 361, 490, 495, 657
Masculinist, 304, 374, 391, 529
Masculinist epistemology (epistemologies),
    375, 931
Masculinity, 369, 373, 375, 376, 396, 399,
    400, 401, 772
  (cult of), 363
Masculinzed heroic, 389
Masks (mask), 397, 589, 591
Masochism (masochistic), 590
Mass, 490, 602, 814, 834
  communication technology, 588
  culture, 306, 474
  media, 575, 788
  production, 95, 120, 831
  society, 814, 816
Massacre, 393
Masses (the), 458, 492, 649, 828
Mastering, 192
Masternarrative, xiii, 5, 14, 473, 503, 506,
    832, 856
Masters degree, 758
Mastery, 206
  learning, 166, 167, 206, 207
  teaching, 810
Material
  conditions, 265, 284, 512
  constraints, 283
  density, 61
  existence, 246
  processes, 283
  productive forces, 245
  progress, 626
  resources, 867
  wealth, 246
  well-being, 499
  world, 246
Materialism (materialistic, material,
    materialist), 217, 257, 270, 288, 297,
    300, 302, 312, 331, 346, 392, 511, 513,
    575, 590, 646, 651, 660, 691, 744, 756,
    836
Materiality, 309, 436
Materials, 36, 166, 213, 298, 585, 664, 687,
    712, 732, 748, 780, 810
Maternal (maternalism, maternity), 360, 362,
    363, 387, 389, 522, 526, 656, 695
  body, 348
  knowledge, 528
  power, 384
Mathematical, 100, 160, 405, 409, 499
  chaos theory, 498
  literacy, 262
Mathematicians, 159, 164
Mathematics, 6, 74, 76, 99, 144, 158, 162,
    163, 164, 169, 170, 262, 361, 424, 425,
    620, 661, 662, 675, 694, 698, 712, 772,
    790, 813, 815, 816, 824
  education, 16, 262, 850

Mathematics Study Group (SMSG), 162, 163
Mathematization (of human experience), 53, 62, 92
Matriarchal, 388
Maturation, 51
Maturity, 144, 628, 767
Mausoleum, 589
McGuffey readers, 779
Meaning (meanings), 11, 16, 25, 28, 50, 54, 62, 64, 74, 131, 144, 148, 156, 170, 178, 183, 188, 210, 211, 224, 227, 229, 245, 246, 287, 290, 296, 297, 298, 301, 307, 335, 355, 392, 404, 406, 407, 408, 410, 412, 417, 418, 419, 423, 424, 426, 430, 432, 433, 436, 447, 453, 454, 456, 457, 459, 460, 461, 462, 463, 465, 466, 467, 468, 473, 474, 475, 484, 485, 488, 492, 502, 505, 515, 520, 521, 525, 526, 527, 536, 546, 557, 558, 560, 562, 572, 578, 587, 588, 595, 602, 628, 631, 634, 638, 644, 664, 687, 723, 766, 770, 788, 839, 847, 848
Meaning-making communities, 547, 548
Meaningfulness (meaningful), 521, 556, 597, 654, 692, 713
Meaninglessness (meaningless), 183, 418, 470, 472, 651
Means (means-ends), 53, 92, 164, 180,188, 751
Means of production, 13, 129
Measure (measured, measurable), 106, 183, 419, 654, 798
Measured curriculum, 15, 735
Measurement (measurements), 89, 90, 91, 136, 183, 184, 273, 463, 549, 732
Mechanical (mechanistic), 118, 236, 258, 336, 361, 418, 445, 446, 498, 499, 500, 502, 509, 578, 581, 637, 739, 741
Mechanical engineering, 30, 91
Mechanisms, 666, 668
Mechanistic reproduction, 248
Media, 27, 222, 284, 307, 334, 472, 473, 511, 512, 513, 796, 813
  catechism, 513
  literacy, 512, 513
Mediating, 237, 348, 670
Mediation (mediate), 253, 256, 263, 347, 416, 423, 550, 567, 642, 853
Medical, 634, 712, 821
  discourses, 462, 463
Medicine, xiii, 49
Medieval, 692
Meditative (meditation), 424, 520, 572, 705
Medium, 258, 456, 515, 526, 593, 667
Megaparadigmatic, 498, 499
Membership, 790
Memorial, 866
Memorize (memories, memorization), 9, 10, 70, 72, 73, 74, 75, 78, 91, 96, 105, 108, 189, 198, 510, 534, 579, 752, 848, 867

Memory (memories), 58, 74, 85, 91, 124, 263, 295, 328, 351, 454, 481, 535, 541, 543, 566, 632
Men (see man)
Men's liberation, 369
Mending, 865
Mental, 126, 271, 482, 571, 756, 767
  development, 76
  disciplinarians, 91, 147
  discipline, 73, 83, 91, 103, 105, 189
  exercise, 76
  functions, 92
  health, 719
  labor, 254
  powers, 74
  tests, 118
  training, 76
  work, 88
Mentor, 44, 46, 91, 93, 119, 139, 759
Mentorship, 43
Mercantile control, 261
Merchant (merchants), 121, 779, 823
Merging, 538
Merit pay, 682
Meritocratic (meritocracy), 364, 380
Message (messages), 258, 422, 545
Messes, 501
Messianism, 649
Meta-ethical (meta-ethics), 388, 552
Metanarratives (metanarrative), 452, 463, 464, 465, 470, 475, 496, 499
Metaphor (metaphors, metaphoric), 53, 61, 181, 184, 224, 235, 258, 271, 273, 276, 316, 333, 388, 391, 409, 423, 425, 439, 447, 460, 496, 500, 501, 502, 504, 510, 525, 531, 541, 559, 588, 589, 600, 634, 652, 658, 685, 723, 726, 731, 737, 749, 761, 789
Metaphorical thinking, 732
Metaphysical (metaphysics), 49, 301, 309, 418, 448, 468, 499, 501, 637
Methodological territory, 51
Methodological tools, 160
Methodologically (methodological), 55, 58, 98, 115, 173, 212, 218, 226, 257, 267, 367, 371, 423, 438, 556, 629, 641, 728, 853
Methodology (methodologies), 59, 78, 419, 867
Methods (method), 54, 76, 77, 80, 81, 82, 86, 96, 101, 116, 161, 194, 224, 262, 287, 385, 414, 451, 494, 519, 520, 545, 558, 645, 762, 810, 813, 865
Micro-electronic, 504
Microcomputers, 714, 715, 783
Microcosm, 618
Microcurricular problems, 186
Microethnographic, 60
Micropolitical (micropolitics), 289, 512, 831
Micropractices, 61

Microstructural, 254
Microworlds, 712
Middle (the), 142, 144, 422, 482, 746, 849
  ages, 637
  childhood, 707
  class, 61, 266, 280, 342, 360, 392, 534,
    624, 785
  passage, 516, 548, 552
  schools (school), xiii, 77, 401, 690, 691,
    693
  way (the), 422, 549, 550, 565, 860
Middle-range theorizing, 312
Midpoint, 539, 860
Midwestern, 780
Midwife, 583
Militant, 320
Militarism, 636
Military, 154, 161, 162, 199, 292, 293, 620,
    634, 671, 796, 807, 808, 815, 827, 840,
    842
Millennium, 690
Mime, 596, 597, 598
Mimetic, 751
Mind (minds, minding), 70, 73, 74, 75, 78,
    88, 91, 92, 96, 108, 188, 206, 272, 391,
    445, 456, 461, 499, 510, 511, 521, 522,
    534, 542, 547, 579, 600, 601, 602, 660,
    691, 705, 740, 859, 861
Mind-body split, 502
Mind-food, 781
Mindfulness, 441
Minding, 407
Mindless, 447, 534
Minimal self, 655
Minimalization, 570
Minimum competencies, 569
Ministry (ministers), 529, 608, 860
Minorities (minority), 199, 207, 233, 323,
    324, 325, 328, 333, 334, 347, 349, 422,
    609, 611, 618, 660, 758, 777, 816
Mirror (mirrors), 523, 538, 539, 590, 595,
    601
  stage, 539
Mirroring, 591
Misconception (misconceptions), 117, 126,
    749, 783
Miseducation, 331
Misery, 647
Misogyny (misogynist), 365, 388, 547, 551,
    552
Misrepresentation (misrepresentations,
    misrepresent), 11, 24, 391, 618
Mission, 36, 50, 95, 130, 300
Missionary (missionaries), 321, 820, 821, 823
Missiles, 292
Mistreatment, 321
Mistrust, 401
Misunderstanding, 461, 529, 715, 851
Mixed schooling, 360
Mob, 534
Mobility, 789

Mobilization (mobilizing), 354, 423, 649
Model building, 712
Modeling, 518, 523
Models (model), 17, 30, 34, 54, 167, 169,
    205, 322, 393, 463, 468, 564, 644, 705,
    715, 760, 865, 867
Moderation, 615
Modern (modernizing, modernism,
    modernist, modernity), 76, 140, 144,
    176, 179,198, 262, 272, 273, 283, 285,
    288, 305,357, 436, 469, 472, 473, 475,
    498, 499, 500, 501, 502, 504, 507, 508,
    509, 513, 577, 602, 603, 634, 644, 653,
    654, 658, 660, 677, 838
  Language, 75
  philosophy, 640
  state, 671, 676, 684
Modernist curriculum, 502
Modernist political thought, 508
Modernization, 808, 814, 187, 824
Modesty, 603
Modules, 167, 200
Molar problems, 169
Molecular, 336
Moment, 868
Monetary, 695
Money, 161, 292, 343
Monolithic, 308, 316, 326, 344, 376
Monologue, 394, 772
Monopolistic, 636
Monopoly, 832
Monumentalizing, 355
Moods (mood), 432, 847
Moon, 399
Moorings, 470
Moral, 116, 126, 138, 141, 163, 226, 257,
    268, 310, 314, 330, 334, 360, 385, 386,
    424, 497, 602, 606, 608, 622, 627, 630,
    631, 632, 633, 634, 635, 637, 639, 652,
    658, 717, 725, 727, 762, 836, 858, 862
  action, 755
  commitment, 634, 755
  community, 618
  conduct, 808
  craft, 562, 752
  crisis, 631
  critique, 772
  development, 628, 808
  discourses, 628
  economy, 839
  education, 116, 192, 390, 409, 618, 619,
    620, 627, 629, 630, 632, 655, 656, 806
  educational discourses, 631
  education theory, 630
  enterprise, 79, 628
  error, 420
  fiber, 199, 431
  fundamentalism, 632
  judgment, 497
  life, 694
  philosophy, 633

Moral (continued)
   power, 218
   prisons, 630
   reasoning, 656
   reasons, 92
   theology, 633
   value, 79
   vision, 628, 629, 634, 730
Morale, 112
Morality, 244, 273, 409, 424, 570, 603, 606,
   610, 611, 614, 627, 630, 634, 636, 659,
   773, 808, 810
Moratorium, 160, 220
Moribund (morbundity), 35, 63, 176,177,
   187,193, 231, 232, 621, 847, 857
Morning-ness, 433
Morphological, 316
Mortals, 423
Mother (mothers, mothering), 335, 339, 343,
   360, 368, 369, 374, 375, 377, 380, 385,
   386, 390, 528, 533, 537, 538, 539, 542,
   549, 607
Mother tongue, 435, 813
Mother/child, 379
Mother/daughter, 374
Mother/son, 374
Motion pictures, 707
Motivation, 167, 178, 195, 245, 745
Motive (motives), 111, 426
Motor-bike, 205
Movement (in French philosophy), 45
Movement (in the field), 16, 99, 223, 226,
   236, 238, 370, 867
Movement (movements), 490, 493, 658, 858,
   859
Movements (in history), 314
Moving form, 435, 592, 866
Multi-classed, 356
Multi-culture, 335
Multi-disciplinary, 164, 334, 687, 746
Multi-gendered, 356
Multiculturalism (multicultural), 22, 23, 43,
   287, 317, 319, 323, 325, 326, 327, 328,
   331, 332, 338, 342, 343, 345, 352, 354,
   355, 356, 399, 480, 512, 514, 633, 636,
   823, 840
   curriculum theorists, 324
   curriculum, 422
   discourses, 45
   society, 823
Multimedia, 715
Multinational, 469, 809, 831, 832, 860
Multinational publishers, 795
Multiple, 867
   accounts, 545
   discrimination, 167
   identities, 695
   intelligences, 472, 695, 757
   realities, 373, 600, 776
   selves, 472
   sites, 504

   surfaces, 472
   voices, 525, 550
Multiplicity (multiplicities), 325, 345, 464,
   484, 492, 496, 505, 549, 567, 568, 839
Multiracial global village, 864
Multivalent, 308
Multivocal, 670
Multivocally, 526
Mundane, 434, 595, 597, 691
Murder (murders), 188, 470, 480, 485
Muscle, 70, 73, 74, 75, 88, 96
Museum (museums), 309, 573, 580, 602,
   706, 819, 867
Music (musical), 97, 169, 170, 433, 513, 519,
   533, 538, 567, 569, 705, 789, 796, 806,
   824, 852
Music videos, 513
Mutilation, 187
Mutual adaptation approach, 700, 701, 704
Mutual reflection, 720
Mutuality (mutual), 60, 376, 655
Mystery (mysteries, mysterious), 365, 419,
   440, 448, 630, 660
Mystical (mysticism), 217, 232, 371, 405, 406
   442, 516, 640, 657, 659, 741
Mystical literature, 214, 627
Mystical-ecological, 659
Mystify, 493
Myth (myths, mythic, mythological), 253,
   257, 273, 279, 280, 284, 326, 338, 388,
   397, 458, 460, 466, 491, 516, 540, 541,
   543, 547, 596, 657, 691, 787
Myth-making, 494
Mythic understanding, 691, 692
Mythic-literal faith, 628
Mytho-poetic, 388, 643, 658
Mythological paradigm, 46
Mythologize, 221

Naiveté, 460
Naming, 386, 423
Narcissistic (narcissism), 408, 511, 560, 595
Narration, 501
Narrative (narratives), xiii, xiv, 309, 330,
   349, 354, 425, 439, 448, 454, 474, 493,
   501, 506, 526, 527, 528, 535, 545, 547,
   551, 558, 560, 563, 565, 574, 575, 583,
   634, 639, 643, 692, 751, 760, 764, 856
   inquiry, 559, 562, 564
   structure, 473
   studies, 54
   theory, 54
Narratology, 559
Narrator, 720
Nation (nations), 59, 91, 125, 127, 129, 137,
   145, 154,199, 225, 231, 236, 320, 346,
   609, 698, 756, 794, 796, 796, 817, 818,
   830, 832, 833
Nation-state capitalism, 504

National, 16, 22, 33, 102, 155, 159, 160, 162, 176, 177, 180, 184, 208, 210, 211, 221, 265, 359, 362, 364, 402, 616, 625, 660, 663, 667, 671, 676, 805, 822, 830, 840
  borders, 796, 833
  boundaries, 792, 798, 831
  curriculum, 308, 674, 676, 797, 798, 799, 832, 833
  curriculum development, 793
  curriculum planning, 824
  debate, 618
  defense (see defense)
  destiny, 625
  development, 820, 824
  Diffusion Network (NDN), 700
  economic development, 817
  educational policy, 826
  emergency, 698
  glory, 808
  identity, 807, 808, 809
  independence, 824
  per capita income, 806
  planners, 824
  policy, 231
  pride, 808
  schools of the air, 708
  security, 840
  self-interest, 809
  socialism, 811, 812
  spirit, 808
  standards, 677, 798
  supremacy, 6
  tests, 798
Nationalism (nationalisms, nationalistic), 38, 180, 671, 777, 829, 839, 843, 864
Nationalists, 321
Nationality, 279, 823
Nationalizing influences, 794
Native
  Americans (American), 315, 316, 344, 346, 350, 609, 660, 784
  cultural integrity, 347
  culture, 346, 347, 348
  education, 333
  languages, 794
  peoples, 333, 828, 840
Nativist reaction, 609
Natural, 82, 86, 103, 104, 284, 298, 362, 411, 593, 597
  attitude, 274, 406, 407, 598
  environment, 626, 635
  order, 76, 499, 594, 596
  resources, 800, 841
  science (sciences), 11, 145, 580, 698, 834
Naturalist ethic, 267
Naturalistic ethnography, 394
Naturalistic evaluation, 736
Naturalness, 603
Nature, 87, 105, 224, 230, 288, 389, 403, 453, 456, 469, 533, 603, 651, 659, 660, 691, 824, 867

Necessity, 594
Needs (need), 208, 354, 435, 479
Needs assessment, 200
Negation, 304
Negative, 336, 397
Negotiating (negotiated), 502, 525, 662
Negotiation, 204, 220, 255, 258, 274, 396, 490, 558, 666, 700, 784
Negro, 321, 337, 352
Neighborhood (neighborhoods), 332, 356, 441, 621
Neo-
  capitalism, 305
  colonialism (neo-colonial), 61, 221, 795, 843
  conservativism, 291
  Kantian, 461
  Marxist (neo-Marxism), 39, 51, 186, 243, 272, 273, 283, 315, 318, 319, 358, 370, 371, 372, 375, 426, 478, 504
  Nazism, 813
  Nietzschean, 504
  Puritans, 615
  Romantic, 221, 272, 273
  traditionalists, 399
Neologisms, 480
Neurotics, 397
Neutrality (neutral), 177, 181,199, 221, 244, 257, 313, 334, 345, 354, 380, 396, 487, 497, 633, 634, 647, 774, 789
New
  American student, 574
  canon, 336
  curriculum, 798
  curriculum technologists, 799
  field (the), 868
  history, 763
  Left, 529
  literacy, 287
  math, 162, 682
  paradigm, 572, 735
  right, 625, 832
  science, 498
  social order, 866
  social theory, 296
  sociology, 277, 278
  world, 607, 839
  world order, 511, 802
Newsletters (newsletter), 558, 766, 800
Newspaper (newspapers), 470, 778, 789
Newton's world view, 500
Nightmares, 449
Nihilism (nihilist, nihilistic), 301, 302, 312, 481, 482, 483, 485, 497, 504, 587, 626, 731
Nineteen eighties (1980s), 45, 96, 253, 261, 269, 282, 294, 314, 368, 382, 394, 396, 399, 402, 427, 487, 517, 545, 614, 618, 619, 620, 651, 671, 672, 675, 682, 779, 800, 802, 817, 834, 835

Nineteen fifties (1950s), 147, 155, 158, 159, 187, 711, 809, 815
Nineteen forties (1940s), 155, 163, 471, 571, 778
Nineteen nineties (1990s), 41, 212, 311, 396, 402, 636, 651, 725, 735, 737, 805, 810, 824, 833, 836, 842, 864, 865
Nineteen seventies (1970s), 38, 41, 44, 45, 157, 187, 189, 190, 197, 219, 221, 262, 311, 364, 364, 368, 369, 370, 371, 391, 419, 471, 515, 518, 564, 620, 627, 629, 630, 644, 662, 672, 681, 689, 705, 735, 737, 740, 758, 779, 800, 802, 817, 850, 854, 855, 857, 862
Nineteen sixties (1960s), 38, 39, 50, 71, 157, 172, 175, 183, 185, 186,187, 212, 231, 262, 311, 314, 364, 453, 471, 643, 685, 705, 711, 734, 812, 815, 817, 857
Nineteen thirties (1930s), 86, 139, 163, 859
Nineteen twenties (1920s), 33, 124, 733, 778, 859
Nineteenth century (1800s), 70, 71, 73, 74, 75, 77, 85, 95, 105, 152, 153, 154, 186, 194, 320, 360, 361, 362, 460, 470, 476, 567, 607, 609, 609, 610, 614, 618, 642, 677, 690, 721, 733, 779, 797, 807, 811, 859
Nitty-gritty, 214
Noise, 492, 536
Nomads (nomadic), 467, 483
Nomological, 412
Non-
  bureaucratic, 673
  canonical, 335, 638
  dialecticism, 252
  European, 759
  European-American, 328
  fictional, 460
  hierarchical, 504
  impositional, 392
  linear, 488, 500, 510, 640, 715, 716
  meaning, 447
  native, 531
  phallocentric, 368
  political, 297, 298
  racism, 323
  reproducible, 422
  sexist, 400
  structuralist semiotics, 302
  Western, 388
  white, 316
Nondenominational, 610, 612
Nondiscursive, 300, 301, 369, 462, 465, 505, 512, 513, 588
Nondomestic roles, 777
Noneducator journalists, 553
Nonego, 522, 548
Nonformal education, 815, 829, 830, 836
Nonhuman animals, 694
Nonprofit, 708
Nonpropositional, 560

Nonpublic, 612, 613
Nonscientific, 737
Nonsectarian, 610
Nonsense, 484, 491
Nonstandard English, 777
Nonsynchronous identity, 354
Nonsynchronous parallelist position, 264
Nonsynchrony (nonsynchronous, nonsynchronously), 319, 327, 355, 356, 857, 864
Nontraditional grouping patterns, 679
Nonverbal behavior, 60
Nonviolence (nonviolently), 289
Normal, 100
  school (schools), 86, 529
  science, 857
Normalcy, 603
Normalize, 333
Normative, 756
  inquiry in curriculum (NIC), 699
Normative/critical paradigm, 46
Norms, 575
North American culture, 505
North American curriculum studies, 63, 295
Northern corporate interests, 320
Northern nations, 818, 820
Nostalgia, 13, 230, 235, 429, 448, 471, 512, 526
Not yet (the), 652
Not-time, 437
Notes, 483, 485
Nothingness, 460
Nouns (noun), 576, 605, 628
Novel, 594
Novels (novelists), 4, 362, 385, 533, 558, 567
Novelty, 691
Novice, 760, 765
Now, 415, 469, 470, 475, 715
Nuclear
  holocaust, 179
  power, 504
  war, 189
  weapons, 807
Nurturance (nurturant), 374, 384, 389, 403, 460, 550, 632
Nurture (nurturing), 190, 258, 382, 524, 530, 656
Nutrition science, 30
Nutritional, 49, 821

Obedience, 3, 395
Object (objects), 411, 413, 414, 435, 454, 455, 462, 468, 478, 493, 522, 552, 569, 581, 592, 595, 694, 706, 740, 866
Object relations, 522
  theory, 374, 375, 387
Objectification, 180, 377, 592
Objectified knowledge, 427
Objectify (objectifies, objectified, objectifying), 428, 438, 526, 542, 651

Objective subjectivism, 301
Objectives, 17, 33, 34, 36, 37, 64, 98, 100,
    101, 117, 136, 140, 148, 149, 155, 165,
    168, 175, 177, 181, 188,199, 201, 202,
    205, 236, 237, 249, 256, 411, 417, 421,
    443, 479, 486, 519, 664, 682, 685, 687,
    702, 734, 735, 784, 798, 813
Objectivism (objectivist), 302, 432, 578, 644
Objectivity (objective), 53, 57, 64, 76, 91,
    231, 267, 274, 301, 337, 367, 371, 396,
    411, 414, 415, 425, 440, 455, 499, 576,
    590, 597, 641, 691, 728, 856
Obligation, 9, 740
Observation (observations, observable,
    observed), 333, 396, 419, 445, 499,
    562, 662, 723, 727, 739, 742
Obsession (obsessed, obsessive), 188, 434,
    604, 692
Occupation (occupational), 251, 352, 771
Occupation shifts, 41
Oceanic, 460
Oceans, 802
Oedipal crisis, 369, 374
Oedipal drama, 375
Official curriculum, 252, 815
Officialdom, 860
Officials (official), 428, 579, 644, 797
Offspring, 73
Oil price changes, 794
Old Left, 529
Omen, 541
Omissions, 436, 618
One-dimensional, 180, 272
One-room school (structures), 85
Ontogeny (ontogenetic), 79, 80, 88
Ontology (ontological), 275, 420, 447, 519,
    602, 639, 652, 658
Opaque, 460
Open classroom (classrooms), 188, 189, 754
Open education, 188
Open systems, 499
Openness, 433, 484, 501, 502, 506, 541, 603,
    835
Operationalize (operational), 681, 704
Opportunity, 144, 859, 860
Opposite sexed relationships, 365
Opposition (oppositional), 251, 253, 255,
    270, 286, 309, 476, 477, 496, 507
Oppositional canons, 480
Oppositional postmodernism, 512
Oppressed (oppress), 61, 233, 281, 351, 386,
    619, 630, 763, 826
Oppression (oppressive), 33, 184, 220, 244,
    274, 280, 291,305, 308, 311, 313, 316,
    332, 337, 339, 356, 356, 373, 383, 392,
    394, 397, 464, 523, 529, 620, 643, 646,
    648, 649
Oppressor, 518
Optimism (optimistic), 34, 40, 321, 477, 657
Oral, 320, 531, 638, 798
    examination (examinations), 733, 797

reading, 437
Orchestra, 789
Order, 34, 261, 326, 440, 448, 486, 492, 498,
    501, 691, 867
Orderly, 499, 685
    disorder, 500
Ordinary, 428, 429, 548
Ordinary language, 170, 205
Organic, 224, 579, 652, 658, 799
Organism, 594
Organization, 176, 202, 317, 319, 354, 387,
    477, 486, 692, 705, 715, 720, 743, 859
    economies, 785
    resolutions, 787
Organizational, 582, 664, 666, 703, 794
    change, 191
    infrastructure, 680
    rationality, 682
    structures (structure), 683, 793
Organizer, 228
Organizing (organized), 172, 464
    centers, 172, 698
Orientations (orientation), 18, 20, 22, 23,
    29, 30, 31, 42, 46, 142, 151, 153, 229,
    446
Oriented (phenomenologically), 430
Origin (origins), 355, 444, 453, 462, 463,
    464, 465, 468, 490, 502, 657, 796,
    864
Original, 7, 8, 44, 422, 447, 472, 473, 483,
    599
    difficulty, 638
    experience, 49
    nature, 91
Originality, 8, 436
Originary, 447, 467
    experience, 448
    transcendental signified, 302
Orthodoxy (orthodoxies), 255, 256, 267,
    281, 315, 398, 650
Other (the), 191, 294, 304, 305, 308, 315,
    328, 330, 337, 338, 354, 368, 378, 388,
    424, 465, 477, 479, 539, 839
Other people's children, 380, 381
Other-directed (direction), 365, 518
Otherness, 61, 299, 304, 330, 352, 533
Others, 191, 377, 381, 404, 434, 502, 551,
    591, 604
Outcomes, 27, 112, 169, 177, 250, 275, 284,
    604, 669, 684, 781
Outdoor education, 389
Outer, 540
Outer world, 440
Output, 169
Outsiders, 209
Overbureaucratized, 678
Overcentralized, 678
Overdetermined, 521
Overgeneralization, 770
Overpopulation, 841
Overstatements, 857

Overt curriculum, 248
Ozone layer, 802, 841

Pace, 581
Pacific cultural literacy, 839
Pain, 13, 74, 409, 543, 587, 656, 730, 861
Painters, 518, 573, 581
Painting (paint), 483, 542, 567, 569, 576,
    578, 582, 584, 686, 852
Pan-Africanism, 352
Pan-ethic-cultural, 315
Papacy, 646
Parable, 425
Paradigm (paradigms), 12, 13, 15, 17, 18, 19,
    20, 23, 24, 30, 31, 38, 39, 65, 112, 124,
    152, 179,187,193, 201, 210, 211, 230,
    235, 278, 291, 301, 341, 353, 389, 498,
    502, 573, 589, 600, 631, 678, 735, 746,
    793, 820, 857
  shift, 230, 232, 234, 236, 300, 854, 857
  wars, 52, 63, 64, 65
Paradigmatic, 505, 730
  change, 186, 187
  evolution, 239
  shift, xvii, 12, 25, 32, 41, 43, 63, 158, 208,
    451, 662
  unity, 849
Paradox (paradoxes, paradoxical), 219, 253,
    439, 477, 481, 490, 492, 502, 656, 670,
    832
Parallelist position, 318
Paranoid, 231
Parasite, 492
Parent disciplines, 854
Parent-child, 377, 380, 442
Parenting, 375, 377, 696
Parents (parent, parental), 14, 93, 234, 264,
    297, 305, 333, 340, 347, 378, 445, 606,
    613, 617, 621, 622, 623, 666, 779, 786,
    834, 837
Parochial, 379, 529, 610, 611, 612, 621, 635,
    834, 837
Parody, 471
Parole, 458
Part, 697
Part-to-whole approach, 697
Partial (partiality), 280, 305, 420, 455, 506
Participant observation, 59, 60, 343, 736
Participants, 566, 596, 597, 601, 727
Participation, 502, 867
Participatory, 257, 504, 675
Particularism (particularized), 849, 864, 865
Particularity (particular, particularities), 291,
    439, 455, 505, 533, 582
Particularization, 591
Partisan, 330, 667
Partnership, 683
Passage (passages), 29, 222, 377, 450, 459,
    480, 481, 482, 485, 491, 492, 521, 524,
    537, 545, 549, 551, 859, 860

Passion (passions, passionate), 30, 61, 74,
    152, 206, 230, 364, 368, 380, 547, 600,
    858
Passivity (passive), 106, 282, 284, 306, 332,
    342, 365, 375, 380, 782
Past (the), 272, 286, 290, 328, 345, 350, 351,
    379, 415, 420, 443, 444, 445, 448, 470,
    494, 504, 515, 520, 535, 540, 542, 552,
    554, 555, 556, 560, 576, 577, 588, 645,
    651, 654, 675, 751, 752, 769, 780, 793,
    810, 838, 866
Pastiche, 471
Pastoral, 649
Paternalism (paternal), 280, 284, 321, 384,
    385, 522
Paternity, 374
Pathological, 511
Patience, 433
Patina, 490
Patriarchal wilderness, 389, 385
Patriarchy (patriarchal, patriarch), 5, 261,
    284, 304, 308, 330, 339, 357, 358, 364,
    364, 367, 371, 372, 373, 380, 384, 385,
    386, 388, 391, 393, 395, 400, 550. 552,
    602, 632, 656
Patriotism, 261, 660, 808
Patronization, 532
Patterning, 174
Patterns (pattern), 275, 387, 388, 500, 686
Pauperization, 305
Payments by results, 733
Peace, 289, 380, 418, 536, 652, 801, 838,
    841, 842
  education, 283, 289, 842, 857
  movement, 39
Peace-loving, 840
Peasants, 816
Pedagogic interest, 430
Pedagogic unit, 71
Pedagogical
  action, 749
  atmosphere, 432, 433, 442
  content knowledge, 746, 747, 748, 749,
    856, 860
  efficiency, 57
  environment, 396
  innovations, 119
  intelligence, 581
  knowledge, 748
  practice, 533
  reasoning, 749
  reformers, 77
  relationship (relationships), 428, 432, 433,
    444
  research, 439
  significance, 432
  situation, 439
  tact, 431
  textuality, 430
  theorist, 440
  thinking, 72

thoughtfulness, 430
Pedagogue, 280
Pedagogy (pedagogical, pedagogic), 62, 105,
    129, 132, 213, 227, 228, 250, 254, 255,
    260, 261, 262, 265, 284, 289, 368, 369,
    377, 378, 379, 392, 406, 410, 423, 429,
    430, 431, 439, 441, 446, 479, 482, 505,
    507, 513, 526, 532, 563, 582, 587, 588,
    599, 630, 633, 645, 647, 664, 673, 717,
    744, 745, 746, 748, 751, 763, 790, 810,
    826, 835
  of difference, 305
  of possibility, 263
  of remembrance, 263
  of the unknowable, 280
Peer
  assistance model, 724
  coaching, 724, 725, 731, 764
  evaluation, 256
  learning, 334
  mentoring, 725
  networks, 787
  relationships (relations), 782, 786
Peircean pragmatism, 302
Penance, 347
Penetration (penetrations), 254, 268
People (person) of color, 264, 316, 344
People's education, 818, 825
Perceiving (perceive), 172, 174, 519
Perception (perceptions, perceptive), 51, 78,
    405, 412, 453, 455, 456, 570, 577, 583,
    605, 739, 832
Perceptual experience, 217
Perdition, 271
Perennial knowledge, 269
Performance (performances), 90, 98, 105,
    199, 262, 482, 599, 600, 601, 669, 687,
    696, 723, 775
  objectives, 165, 166, 167, 180
Performance-contracting, 681
Performing artist, 720, 731
Periodization (periodizing), 296, 463
Peripheral (periphery), 452, 464, 651
Permanence, 490, 537
Permissiveness (permissive), 126, 320, 522
Persistent life situations, 140, 144
Person-centered humanism, 218
Person-oriented curriculum, 179
Persona (personae), 587, 589
Personal, 19, 55, 61, 102, 124, 148, 150, 227,
    245, 256, 257, 306, 309, 312, 332, 335,
    367, 382, 408, 416, 420, 425, 426, 485,
    499, 515, 516, 518, 527, 540, 548, 550,
    552, 556, 557, 559, 562, 563, 579, 596,
    606, 624, 625, 627, 645, 660, 694, 696,
    704, 731, 741, 752, 769, 785, 848
  commitment orientation, 30
  conduct, 170
  consciousness development, 223
  development, 29, 161
  discovery tier, 190

growth, 192, 215, 334, 430, 588, 589
  histories (history), 55, 556
  humanism, 218
  integration, 628
  interpretation, 59
  knowledge, 170, 400, 546, 558
  liberty, 224
  life, 223
  modeling, 751
  practical knowledge, 55, 177, 517, 553,
      554, 556, 557, 558, 560, 561, 562, 563,
      688, 747, 765, 855, 863
  relevance, 21
  salvation, 625
  struggle, 219
  success model, 30
  witness, 637
Personality (personalities), 109, 116, 206,
    387, 519, 523, 634
Personalization, 672, 675
Personalized education, 189
Personhood, 288, 365
Personification, 336
Personnel, 722, 802
  evaluation, 723
Persons (person), 548, 556, 567, 592, 632,
    662, 848
Perspectives (curriculum), 15, 18, 24, 28, 30,
    446
Persuasion, 36, 746
Perturbation, 500, 501
Pessimism (pessimistic), 220, 251, 259, 261
Pettiness, 388
Ph.D. (the), 215, 690
Ph.D. dissertations (dissertation), 409, 537,
    562
Ph.D. graduate (graduates), 265, 293, 559,
    584
Ph.D. in curriculum, xvii, 36
Ph.D. students, 4
Phallocentric, 376
Phallus (phallic), 386, 495
Pharmacy, 101
Phenomenological
  bracketing, 520
  concept, 412, 443
  critique, 410, 412
  curricularist, 429
  curriculum planning, 689
  curriculum scholarship, 409
  curriculum studies (study), 420, 423
  curriculum theorist, 408
  curriculum theory (theories), 44, 404, 427,
      448, 521
  description, 229, 415, 421, 429, 430, 444
  distancing, 598
  educator, 430
  epistemology, 707
  epoché, 415
  experience, 445, 664
  hermeneutics, 425, 427

Phenomenological (continued)
inquiry, 404, 405
investigator, 408
language, 407, 513
literature, 408
meditation, 443
movement (the), 44, 419, 857
pedagogy, 407, 430, 864
pedagogical theory, 430
philosophers, 638
postmodernism, 491
reduction, 463
reflection, 408, 416, 598
research, 406, 407, 408, 410, 415, 416,
   428, 431, 440, 445, 446
research methodology, 407
researcher, 408, 412
scholars, 410
scholarship, 12, 44, 238, 406, 428, 433,
   434
studies (study), 408, 409, 422, 444, 557
themes, 410, 431, 432
thoughtfulness, 438
tradition, 438, 695, 781
understanding, 445, 446, 448, 555
writing, 408, 439
Phenomenologist (phenomenologists), 6, 44,
   54, 404, 405, 406, 407, 412, 420, 422,
   428, 430, 431, 432, 434, 437, 438, 444,
   445, 453, 456, 536, 546, 760, 864
Phenomenology (phenomenological), xvi,
   13, 16, 32, 39, 44, 46, 47, 50, 54, 55,
   57, 58, 60, 62, 64, 79, 156,173, 179,
   182, 213, 214, 218, 224, 228, 230, 233,
   243, 246, 275, 276, 287, 288, 290, 358,
   370, 371, 372, 376, 381, 402, 404, 407,
   408, 409, 411, 412, 413, 414, 416, 417,
   418, 419, 420, 421, 422, 424, 425, 426,
   427, 429, 432, 434, 435, 437, 438, 446,
   447, 448, 453, 454, 455, 456, 457, 459,
   460, 465, 467, 468, 475, 478, 493, 497,
   513, 514, 515, 521, 531, 538, 545, 551,
   555, 569, 584, 591, 641, 642, 689, 695,
   703, 707, 725, 729, 730, 739, 759, 764,
   787, 788, 826, 837, 847, 852, 853, 856,
   857, 859, 862, 863
Phenotype, 348
Philia, 384
Philology, 641
Philosopher (philosophers), 117, 269, 356,
   406, 407, 423, 447, 480, 642, 690, 799,
   863
of education, 14,191, 202, 203, 230, 372,
   569, 630, 678, 690, 773, 810
of science, 233, 734
of the curriculum 731
Philosophical foundations, 215
Philosophical hermeneutics, 643
Philosophies (continental), 12
Philosophy (philosophical), 23, 51, 55, 62,
   78, 89, 91, 109, 122, 133, 170,

181,183, 194, 202, 205, 206, 212, 213,
   288, 405, 438, 456, 465, 519, 564, 565,
   606, 639, 641, 717, 747, 759, 814
of art, 568
of curriculum, 170, 203
of education, 51, 150, 151, 205, 206
of literature, 183
Phonetic, 815
Phonics, 435
Phonograph, 599
Photocentric, 513
Photographic, 210, 513, 576, 584
Photographs (photography), 284, 291, 337,
   338, 339
Phronesis, 312, 313, 424
Phylogeny (phylogenetic), 79, 80, 88
Physical, 309, 388, 397, 472, 521, 597, 604,
   652, 824, 847
education, 164, 806, 808, 811
exercise, 811
existence, 189
fitness, 147
labor, 320
science (sciences), 91, 158, 162, 163, 694,
   725, 743
survival, 821
world, 60, 170
Physicians, xiii, 33, 121, 712
Physicist, 164
Physics, xiv, 158, 160, 162, 169, 193, 500,
   528, 572, 852
Piagetianism (Piagetian), 45, 705
PIE model, 699
Pilgrimage (pilgrim), 219, 433
Pimp, 338, 340
Pink triangles, 396, 397
Pioneers, 386
Place, 289, 290, 291, 307, 411, 440, 444, 501,
   516, 521, 532, 533, 534, 535, 541, 548,
   558, 568, 636, 637, 858
Plagiarists, 385
Planet, 288, 388, 490, 633, 799, 840, 841
Planned curriculum, 248
Planners, 6, 421
Planning, 24, 115, 155, 203, 673, 685, 699,
   701, 725, 744, 794
conference, 721
Platitude, 166
Plausibility, 560
Play (playing), 86, 98, 108, 423, 441, 463,
   466, 467, 475, 484, 494, 691, 775, 784,
   859
Play (theater), 464, 567, 582, 596
Playfulness (playful), 485, 502, 588, 673, 784
Playgrounds (playground), 59, 440, 441, 442
Pleasure (pleasures), 74, 187, 436, 437, 478,
   587
Pleasure-seeking, 329
Plot, 290, 558, 560
Pluralism (pluralistic), 224, 346, 347, 498,
   504, 567, 568, 616, 618, 660, 770, 831

Plurivocal, 308
Poem (poems), 407, 483, 484, 485, 567, 583, 587, 588, 589
Poet (poets), 210, 691
Poetic theory, 491
Poetism, 725, 726
Poetizing, 406
Poetry (poetic, poetical), 157, 206, 213, 278, 404, 407, 422, 439, 477, 534, 538, 589, 599, 658, 661, 697, 729, 739, 752, 823
Polarization, 127, 738
Polemical, 670
Police, 209
Policing, 363
Policy (policies), 56, 77, 332, 333, 337, 606, 613, 664, 665, 666, 668, 669, 670, 685, 791, 828, 831
  flow, 667
  planning, 59
  primeval soup, 667
  research, 666
Policy-making, 667
Policy-practice relationship, 667, 668, 669
Policymakers, 39, 163, 527, 851
Polish, 834
Political
  action, 211, 225, 275, 310, 393, 497, 511
  activist (activism), 214, 277
  calculus, 683
  change, 835
  codes, 284
  control, 635, 814
  correctness, 287, 398
  costs, 683
  criticism, 225, 304
  culture, 680
  currency, 818, 825
  curriculum scholars, 248
  curriculum scholarship, 262
  curriculum theory, 247, 255, 283, 287, 291, 293, 295, 304, 310, 313, 314, 411
  democracy, 837
  developments, 835
  disengagement, 281
  economy, 264
  education, 264, 356, 814
  events, 184
  exploitation, 828
  history, 823
  holiness, 648
  ideology, 646, 668, 829, 836
  instability, 818
  interdependence, 803, 820
  modernity (modernist), 507, 508
  morality, 629
  neutrality, 842
  opposition, 522
  oppression, 307, 521, 842
  parties, 813
  passivity, 535
  pawns, 376

phenomenology, 864
position, 684
refugees, 384
relations, 526
rights, 214, 317
scholars, 13, 174, 253, 256, 259, 273, 281, 853, 857
scholarship, 12, 51, 221, 222, 269, 270, 277, 281, 283, 295, 866
science (scientists), xiii, 14, 49, 156, 171, 172, 182, 196, 224, 665, 852
sector, 45,199, 297, 313
socialization, 300
sphere, 219
themes, 224
theorist (theorists), 45, 185, 252, 264, 265, 268, 272, 276, 312, 506, 564, 68
theory, 54, 62, 71, 180, 182, 185, 244, 259, 266, 270, 272, 275, 276, 278, 279, 283, 284, 288, 292, 294, 298, 306, 307, 312, 313, 317, 354, 376, 379, 381, 387, 401, 427, 497, 507, 516, 524, 648, 746, 762, 770
upheaval, 826, 831
Political-social, 224
Politically progressive, 296, 507
Politicians, 14, 153, 299, 399, 421, 662, 684, 744, 776, 851, 852, 858
Politicization (politicize), 127, 208, 255, 278, 509
Politicized counterdiscourse, 770
Politicized postmodernism, 44, 513
Politics (political), xvi, 6, 7, 8, 11, 12, 13, 14, 16, 19, 22, 29, 32, 33, 39, 43, 44, 45, 46, 50, 55, 57, 58, 60, 61, 62, 64, 73, 79, 92, 104, 109, 120, 125, 130, 132, 141, 153, 160, 171,181, 182, 187,191, 207, 210, 213, 215, 217, 218, 220, 221, 223, 226, 230, 231, 236, 237, 238, 239, 243, 247, 248, 249, 250, 252, 254, 255, 256, 260, 261, 262, 264, 265, 267, 268, 272, 275, 276, 283, 284, 287, 288, 289, 290, 291, 294, 295, 300, 302, 306, 308, 310, 312, 313, 314, 315, 317, 325, 327, 328, 329, 344, 354, 356, 357, 359, 364, 375, 376, 379, 387, 391, 392, 402, 403, 406, 410, 417, 422, 423, 426, 427, 430, 434, 475, 476, 481, 489, 497, 503, 507, 508, 509, 511, 513, 514, 515, 516, 522, 523, 526, 527, 530, 531, 533, 546, 550, 552, 562, 565, 566, 569, 570, 572, 574, 575, 579, 584, 602, 606, 614, 617, 620, 631, 632, 633, 634, 636, 637, 642, 650, 652, 662, 664, 666, 672, 679, 682, 684, 699, 720, 732, 743, 762, 773, 780, 785, 792, 794, 795, 802, 808, 809, 813, 822, 826, 827, 828, 829, 830, 842, 847, 848, 851, 852, 856, 857, 858, 859, 862, 864
  of difference, 508
Poll, 790, 804
Polluters, 777

Pollution, 719, 777, 802, 840, 841
Poor (the), 72, 120, 221, 233, 334, 643, 647, 649, 650
Poor curriculum, 515, 591, 645
Pope (the), 609, 651
Popery, 609
Popular
 arts, 580
 books, 188
 culture, 141, 283, 284, 285, 286, 296, 303, 304,306, 307, 339, 392, 394, 395, 507, 508, 530, 779, 796, 851, 859
 magazines, 575
 music, 307
 press, 184, 187, 330
Population (populations), 49, 85, 316, 326, 356, 643, 677, 803, 814, 824, 866
Portfolios, 729
Positionedness, 856
Positionings, 384
Positions (position), 462, 539, 791
Positivism, 52, 53, 186, 268, 298, 322, 461, 725, 730, 849
Positivist research paradigms, 53
Positivistic (positivist), 53, 57, 168, 394, 421
Positivists, 743
Possessive individualism, 671
Possibility (possibilities), 15, 18, 265, 286, 289, 310, 427, 428, 435, 494, 507, 526, 545, 551, 638, 784, 849
Possible (the), 594, 598
Post Poststructuralism, 514
Post-
 apartheid, 825
 capitalist, 318
 Christian, 660
 colonial supplement, 839
 communistic (communist), 835,836
 critical reconceptualists, 224, 225
 Cultural revolution, 814
 Darwinian evolutionary theory, 424
 Enlightenment, 602
 feminism, 507
 formal practitioner, 770
 formal teacher development, 770
 formal teacher education, 763
 formal thinkers, 510, 763
 formal thinking, 307, 509, 510, 762, 770
 foundational, 505
 Husserlian, 412
 liberal, 272
 Mao, 817
 Marxist, 505
 Piagetian cognitive theory, 509
 Reconceptualization, 62
 reproduction phase, 295
 secondary, 134, 200, 666
 Soviet, 837
Postcolonialism (postcolonial), 285, 326, 504, 507, 508, 509, 513, 839
Postconference, 723

Postindustrial, 210, 297, 504
Postmodern
 aesthetic, 508
 body, 513
 condition, 470
 critical pedagogy, 305
 critical theory, 510
 cultural landscape, 507
 curriculum, 450, 498, 501, 502
 curriculum discourse, 509
 curriculum theory, 503
 education, 508
 era, 503
 feminist thought, 508
 gender analysis, 396
 paradigm, 498
 pedagogy, 644, 645 646
 period, 469
 perspective, 498
 political theory (theorists), 307, 507, 509, 512, 676
 politics, 44, 296
 scholarship, 603
 space, 472
 theologians, 469
 theorists, 496
 vision, 499, 501
Postmodernism (constructive), 469, 640
Postmodernism (postmodern, postmodernist), xvii, 4, 44, 45, 60, 243, 278, 279, 283, 285, 287, 294, 295, 296, 304,305,307, 308, 310, 311, 312, 325, 354, 357, 394, 395, 396, 400, 450, 451, 452, 468, 473, 474, 475, 485, 493, 496, 497, 498, 499, 501, 502, 503, 504, 505, 506, 507, 508, 509, 510, 511, 512, 513, 514, 569. 601, 640, 647, 653, 659, 676, 720, 727, 763, 831, 832, 835, 838, 839, 840, 847, 854
Postpositivist, 53, 735
Postsecondary, 718
Poststructural (poststructurally), 464, 469, 471, 474, 485, 486, 488, 489, 497, 504
Poststructuralism (poststructuralist), xvii, 4, 5, 7, 9, 13, 32, 43, 45, 48, 49, 50, 54, 55, 57, 61, 62, 217, 226, 229, 238, 254, 261, 262, 263, 267, 268, 278, 279, 281, 283, 293, 295, 296, 297, 301,306, 308, 309, 310, 311, 312, 313, 314, 336, 337, 355, 357, 369, 374, 394, 395, 404, 405, 422, 446, 447, 448, 450, 451, 452, 453, 455, 461, 462, 464, 465, 467, 468, 469, 470, 473, 474, 475, 476, 478, 480, 483, 485, 488, 489, 490, 491, 492, 493, 495, 496, 497, 503, 504, 505, 514, 516, 536, 537, 538, 539, 540, 575, 632, 739, 839, 856, 857
 action research, 491
 curriculum theorists, 491
 pedagogy, 496
 space, 475

Poststructuralists, 6, 8, 447, 461, 463
Posture, 73, 602
Postwar period, 279
Potential (potentiality), 131, 443, 788
Poverty, 174, 179, 244, 276, 305, 511, 633,
    643, 648, 649, 650, 732, 778, 818, 830
Power (powers), 14, 17, 43, 51, 61, 91, 103,
    128,171, 191, 213, 214, 221, 245, 257,
    261, 262, 263, 265, 272, 273, 278, 282,
    285, 291, 294, 295, 302, 303, 306, 308,
    310, 311, 312, 314, 315, 327, 334, 341,
    346, 347, 353, 360, 365, 366, 378, 380,
    382, 385, 392, 393, 422, 427, 433, 450,
    452, 463, 464, 465, 466, 467, 468, 481,
    486, 488, 492, 494, 496, 508, 510, 526,
    528, 547, 575, 617, 620, 621, 632, 657,
    671, 675, 676, 678, 684, 703, 730, 770,
    799, 809, 823, 825, 828, 866, 867
Power elites, 257
Power relations (relationships), 280, 284,
    298, 357, 504, 505
Power structure, 56
Powerful, 474, 788
Practical, 4, 30, 35, 36, 37, 54, 55, 76, 77, 85,
    107, 109, 124, 147, 161, 176, 177, 187,
    192,193, 195,197, 204, 212, 229, 236,
    359, 410, 413, 419, 486, 559, 585, 637,
    798
  activity, 41
  affairs, 220
  arts, 177, 559
  competence, 762
  curriculum inquiry, 55
  discipline, 864
  field, 849
  inquiry, 17, 19
  judgment, 313
  knowledge, 55, 424, 556, 557, 563, 705,
    807
  problems, 204
  reasoning, 424
  research, 56
  subjects, 125
  success, 205
  understanding, 432
  world, 407
Practicality, 34
Practice teaching, 758
Practice, xvi, xviii, 5, 11, 14, 15, 16, 18, 22,
    30, 31, 35, 40, 41, 49, 50, 55, 56, 57,
    58, 112, 118, 144, 165, 173, 175, 197,
    204, 205, 206, 212, 228, 231, 233, 253,
    255, 260, 261, 262, 272, 289, 310, 311,
    312, 374, 390, 413, 424, 426, 428, 438,
    482, 483, 485, 491, 523, 553, 555, 559,
    563, 585, 586, 599, 606, 627, 632, 648,
    662, 663, 665, 688, 703, 711, 720, 725,
    734, 744, 748, 750, 755, 761, 762, 764,
    769, 770, 771, 851, 866
Practices, 35, 220, 402, 451, 475, 613
Practitioner-oriented, 38, 663

Practitioners, xvii, 15, 25, 31, 32, 34, 36, 39,
    40, 54, 62, 201, 205, 212, 213, 221,
    386, 482, 560, 562, 574, 585, 628, 700,
    703, 720, 729, 756, 759, 789, 850, 854
Pragmatic, 220, 302, 446, 575
Pragmatic-hermeneutical, 424
Pragmatism, 489, 507, 571
Praxeology, 556
Praxis, 17, 213, 255, 265, 312, 313, 371, 400,
    406, 426, 496, 562, 630, 645, 648, 827,
    828
Prayer (prayerful), 612, 613, 614, 648, 649
Pre-education, 759
Pre-entry phase (ethnographical
    methodology), 59
Pre-existent, 499
Pre-hermeneutic, 404
Pre-packaged curricula (curriculum), 251,
    401
Pre-professional, 755
Preach (preaching), 630, 637
Preachers, 321
Preactive, 563
Precedents, 179
Precept, 164
Precision, 572
Precollegiate curriculum, 164
Preconceptual, 49, 414, 415, 416, 417, 446,
    447, 459, 597
Preconference, 723
Preconscious, 224
Predestination, 517
Predetermined, 581, 666
Prediction (predictability), 92, 180, 212, 273,
    411, 499, 500, 564, 565, 794, 849, 856
Predictive studies, 793
Prediscursive, 468
Preferential option for the poor, 643, 647,
    648
Pregnancy, 409
Preindividual, 538
Prejudice (prejudices), 306, 318, 324, 335,
    348, 448, 482
Premodern, 499, 504, 640, 654
Preoedipal, 375, 435, 538
Preoperational, 413
Preparation, 79, 107, 151, 154, 189, 320, 775
Prepersonal, 445
Prepredicative, 445
Prereflective, 415, 444, 560, 590, 597
Prerequisites, 697
Preschool, 809, 813
Prescriptions (prescription), 197, 203, 211,
    216, 491, 576
Prescriptive, 56, 99
Presence (present), 431, 437, 458, 463, 467,
    468, 490, 526, 531, 532, 539, 548, 555,
    556, 560, 576, 577, 578, 592, 627, 645,
    651, 654, 655, 675, 753
Present (the), 108, 251, 286, 328, 350, 418,
    420, 423, 428, 443, 444, 445, 470, 471,

Present (continued)
  515, 520, 521, 540, 751, 769, 793, 838,
    864, 866
Presentation, 79, 588, 600
Presentational, 579
Presentism, 535, 653
  Presentness, 431
Preservice, 399, 756
Preservice teacher, 721, 760
Preservice teacher education, 517, 664, 755,
    763, 770
Press (the), 86, 836
Pressure, 56, 668, 702, 780, 786, 853
Prestige, 50, 161, 363
Presubjective, 445
Pretheoretical, 271
Preunderstandings, 408
Preventive medicine, 49
Preverbal, 355
Priest (priests), 88
Primal, 541, 542
Primary education, 822, 823
Primary grades, 80
Primary schools, 331, 332, 360, 815, 817
Primitive, 431, 458, 460
Primordial, 374, 377, 447
Principalities, 862
Principals (principal), 15, 59, 84, 137, 299,
    365, 421, 529, 624, 701, 722, 726, 802,
    837
Principle learning, 167
Principles, 15, 33, 38, 79, 99, 102, 115, 121,
    148, 155, 197, 200, 206, 216, 276, 464,
    486, 559, 568, 634, 713, 773, 823
Priorities (curriculum), 174
Prisoners (prison), 474, 529, 530
Private, 118, 335, 357, 390, 511, 518, 524,
    539, 545, 549, 550, 561, 620, 621, 738,
    787, 828, 848
Private (privatized) sector, 674
Private schools (school), xiii, 110, 121, 135,
    361, 362, 611, 612, 620, 621, 622, 623,
    680, 706
Privatization, 677, 678
Privilege (privileged, privileging), 41, 51, 61,
    120, 245, 353, 461, 467, 479, 506, 539,
    669
Pro-democracy movement, 814, 817
Probability, 92, 411
Problem space, 782
Problem-posing pedagogy, 826
Problem-solving, 8, 37, 164, 167, 169, 220,
    270, 533, 572, 573, 584, 709, 712, 727,
    764, 772, 775
Problematic, 588
Problematize (problematization), 423, 481,
    485, 506, 513
Problems (problem), 163, 189, 195, 222, 265,
    281, 318, 327, 422, 501, 571, 663, 666,
    667, 714, 718, 775, 826, 849, 867
Problems of society, 698

Procedure (procedures, procedural), 18, 20,
    77, 95, 101, 102, 148, 155, 187, 205,
    408, 434, 581, 666, 677, 713, 720, 790
Process, 159, 195, 197, 499, 528, 581, 654,
    655, 699, 704, 813, 848
  education, 634
  philosophy, 634, 653, 654, 691
  philosophy of education, 653
  skills, 168
  streams, 667
  theology, 634
  theory, 634
Process-product, 165
Procreation, 660
Production (means of), 13, 269
Production (produced), 287, 317, 358, 364,
    365, 387, 394, 474, 799, 815, 829
Production supervision, 722, 724, 731
Productive, 623, 814
Productivity, 96, 293, 498, 619, 669
Profane, 291
Profanity, 777
Profeminist men, 399
Profeminist teachers, 400
Profession (professional, professionalized),
    xiii, 6, 9, 10, 24, 27, 31, 46, 72, 80, 81,
    86, 96, 98, 101, 111, 112, 123, 124,
    127, 139, 142, 145, 153, 162, 170, 211,
    223, 237, 277, 292, 313, 314, 323, 365,
    382, 400, 487, 550, 556, 557, 586, 589,
    632, 673, 689, 714, 722, 724, 727, 748,
    755, 757, 762, 770, 798, 799, 859, 861
  academics, 35
  association (associations), 208, 210, 682
  development schools, 758, 761
  development, 765
  expectations, 223
  expertise, 487, 696
  growth, 729
  judgment, 758
  middle class, 786, 787
  reformers, 207
  responsibility, 714
  school, 759
  society, 852
  striving, 786
  studies, 762
Professionalism, 635, 756, 786
Professionalization, 721, 771
Professionals, 759, 761
Professors (professor), 35, 123, 310, 524,
    682, 794
  of curriculum, 208, 211
  of education, 14
Profit, 96, 97
Program (programs), 26, 77, 97, 110, 140,
    155, 197, 207, 475, 713, 732, 855
  evaluation, 166
  of study, 21
Programmed instruction, 682, 701, 709, 710,
    711

Programming, 711
Progress, 13, 27, 42, 74, 88, 129, 136, 140,
    184, 284, 321, 499, 507, 657, 683, 777,
    801, 822, 852, 858
Progressive, 127, 128, 130, 132, 249, 268,
    272, 273, 288, 320, 371, 402, 503, 508,
    509, 520, 578, 677, 682, 715, 737, 754,
    762, 799
  change, 273, 307
  curriculum reforms, 775
  curriculum theorists, 257
  curriculum theory, 272
  dissent, 124
  dream, 222
  education, 126, 187
  educator (educators), 76, 90, 636
  era, 128, 139
  experiments, 86, 111, 113, 203, 754
  ideas, 103, 143
  methods, 110
  moral project, 263
  movement, 86, 103, 108, 110, 117, 121,
    129, 138, 185, 371, 685, 799
  position, 123, 751
  possibilities, 496, 497
  poststructuralism, 278
  reform, 113, 135, 146
  reformer, 121
  schools, 114, 138, 259, 272, 679
  social science, 290
  teaching, 754
  themes, 12
  theoreticians, 119
  thought, 141
Progressive-liberal, 278
Progressives, 104, 125, 186, 586
Progressivism, 86, 89, 103, 121, 123, 124,
    151, 164, 321, 498, 677, 849, 859
Progressivist, 21, 206
Prohibition, 378
Project (projects), 289, 732, 762, 798
  method, 115, 116, 118
Projections (projection), 523, 526, 642
Proleptic, 645, 651, 652, 654
Proletariat, 268, 816
Proliferation, 867
Promiscuous, 212
Promise, 179, 214, 272, 276
Proof (proofs), 161, 325, 448
Propertied classes, 827
Prophecy, 349, 866
Prophet (prophets), 142, 150, 638, 643
Prophetic, 91, 354, 631, 654
Proportion, 499
Proposals, 35
Propositions, 202, 276
Prospectives, 18
Prosperity, 159, 808
Prostitution, 338, 811
Protectionist, 850
Protest, 156, 466, 567

Protestant Reformation, 640
Protestantism (Protestant), 361, 609, 610,
    612, 616, 624, 625, 640, 660, 720, 780
Protocol, 42, 434, 685, 692
Proverbs, 439, 823
Provincialism, 862
Provisionality (provisional), 394, 436, 449,
    859
Provocations (provocativeness), 484, 485
Pseudo-Nietzschean, 812
Pseudo-scientific, 758, 855, 860, 861
Psyche, 217, 222, 368, 452, 456, 511
Psychiatry, 195
Psychic, 291, 477
  malformations, 290
Psycho-political, 353, 357, 383, 552
Psycho-social, 284, 285, 398, 469, 519, 591
Psycho-social development, 74
Psychoanalysis (psychoanalytic), 195, 223,
    224, 263, 275, 282, 290, 304, 310, 328,
    329, 337, 369, 372, 376, 381, 396, 435,
    442, 476, 493, 515, 519, 521, 522, 523,
    538, 545, 653, 726, 751
Psychoanalysts, 233, 863
Psychoanalytic concept, 378
Psychoanalytic theory (theorists, thought),
    39, 358, 387
Psychobiographical, 49
Psychobiological, 101
Psychodrama, 601
Psychodynamics, 377
Psychological, 220, 387, 388, 393, 397, 442,
    513, 528, 550, 656, 847, 859
  discourse, 462
  laboratory, 88
  literature, 197
  study (studies), 34, 200
  theory, 148
  thought, 182
Psychologists, 35, 76, 82, 88, 159
Psychologizing, 747
Psychology, 3, 11, 51, 78, 89, 90, 91, 92, 172,
    196, 287, 476, 519, 535, 560, 628, 656,
    705, 745, 747, 759, 835
Psychometricians, 545, 564
Psychometrics (psychometric), 193, 525
Psychomotor, 155, 165
Psychotechnology, 705
Psychotherapy, 378, 521
Public (publics), 30, 38, 102, 147, 238, 292,
    294, 317, 357, 361, 363, 364, 367, 369,
    375, 390, 472, 479, 499, 511, 513, 522,
    524, 539, 540, 545, 549, 550, 561, 570,
    574, 575, 581, 582, 586, 607, 622, 648,
    739, 742, 750, 768, 787, 790, 826, 828,
    848, 859, 864
  domain, 214
  education, 188, 220, 293, 374, 503, 613,
    614, 615, 617, 621, 624, 672, 788
  expense, 120
  form, 567

Public (continued)
  good, 788
  high school (schools), 76, 120, 623
  intellectual, 681
  life, 214, 261, 282, 292, 670
  official, 539
  opinion, 399, 667
  ownership, 129
  policy, 14, 292, 329
  press, 154
  school curriculum, 27, 613, 618, 620
  school system, 625
  school teachers, 851
  schooling, 632
  schools (school), xiii, 72, 109, 121, 135,
    152, 162, 187, 188, 203, 267, 300, 303,
    360, 362, 529, 611, 613, 614, 615, 618,
    619, 621, 622, 623, 625, 635, 660, 662,
    680, 706, 721, 722, 790, 803, 851
  self, 691
  sphere, 309, 325, 330, 380, 538, 614, 635,
    636, 663, 680
  television, 709
  visibility, 228
  world, 164, 214, 379, 416, 440, 454, 518,
    551
Publishers, 682, 776, 799
Punishment, 333, 339, 347
Puns, 480
Pupils (pupil), 100, 105, 126, 192, 334, 682,
  706, 775, 783
  abilities, 75
  interest, 131
  personnel services, 147
  potential, 92
Pure moods, 432
Purges, 830, 835
Purity, 447
Purpose (purposes), 34, 131,175, 202, 212,
  216, 221, 224, 262, 356, 417, 443, 558,
  631, 678, 749
Purposelessness, 134
Purposive-rational, 275
Puzzle, 428

Qualitative, 554, 555, 581, 643, 669, 735,
  736, 743
  curriculum research, 53
  evaluation, 735, 741
  inquiry, 737, 743
  knowing, 582
  research, 52, 54, 307, 705
  researchers, 737
Qualities, 567, 570, 581, 629
Quality, 87, 621, 622, 677, 701, 761, 804,
  817
  control, 756
  of instruction, 206
  of life, 54, 192, 780, 841
  time, 767

Quantifiable time, 507
Quantification, 89, 92, 184
Quantitative, 64, 89, 418, 424, 540, 555, 564,
  573, 735, 736
  evaluation, 183, 735, 736, 737
  research tradition, 53
  research, 52, 53, 418, 419, 573
  researchers, 53, 516
Quantity, 87, 804
Quarrels, 53
Quasi-practical, 176,193
Queer analysis, 369
Quest, 171,199, 426, 628
Question (questions, questioning), 435, 436,
  453, 568, 606, 749, 772, 783
Question-answer format, 754, 755
Questionnaire, 89
Quick fix, 214
Quiet, 381, 629
Quixotic, 259

Race (racial, racialized), xvii, 5, 8, 16, 21, 23,
  28, 39, 44, 45, 51, 55, 57, 61, 62, 64,
  80, 88, 94, 101, 103, 128, 153, 160,
  173, 187, 210, 254, 260, 261, 264, 265,
  278, 284, 287, 289, 294, 296, 304, 305,
  315, 316, 317, 318, 319, 321, 329, 330,
  331, 332, 334, 335, 336, 339, 340, 342,
  343, 344, 345, 346, 348, 349, 350, 354,
  356, 357, 358, 370, 391, 394, 395, 397,
  398, 400, 423, 424, 427, 464, 472, 475,
  493, 503, 517, 524, 535, 566, 580, 618,
  619, 669, 695, 730, 761, 771, 784, 794,
  812, 821, 847, 853, 856, 858, 859, 862,
  864
  relations, 318, 327
Racecourse, 502
Racial
  agenda, 320
  antagonism, 608, 618
  apartheid, 824
  categories, 316
  classification, 315, 316
  desires, 788
  difference (differences), 318, 533, 676
  differentiation, 140
  discourses, 45
  domination, 327
  experience, 332
  groups, 318, 327
  harmony, 325
  identity, 315, 341, 345, 346, 353, 398
  inequality, 23, 323, 325, 326, 327
  injustice, 511
  integration, 608, 805
  intolerance, 776
  issues, 323, 327
  knowledge, 356
  logic, 316
  miseducation, 331

mixture, 812
oppression, 322, 345
origins, 315
polarization, 323
prejudice, 324, 331
representation, 340
scholarship, 12, 43
science, 812
segregation, 463
separatism, 608
stereotypes, 324, 346
stratification, 342
strife, 318
studies, 812
subservience, 320
theorists,3 18
theory, 296, 315, 316, 317, 323, 357, 399, 545
violence, 534
Racialization, 329
Racialized other, 328
Racially segregated, 320
Racially subordinate subjects, 318
Racism (racist), 23, 218, 220, 221, 222, 244,309, 311, 318, 319, 322, 323, 327, 329, 331, 332, 334, 335, 337, 339, 344, 345, 347, 348, 350, 352, 353, 355, 361, 506, 511, 533, 534, 612, 633, 636, 776
Racist behavior, 332
Racist ideologies, 331
Racist name-calling, 331
Racists, 464
Radical (radicals), 61, 89, 129, 131, 216, 217, 226, 230, 231, 232, 248, 250, 254, 255, 266, 270, 271, 272, 277, 279, 286, 287, 296, 317, 319, 335, 336, 344, 359, 366, 368, 369, 371, 374, 375, 388, 406, 461, 489, 508, 584, 634, 803, 827
   curriculum theory, 243, 253
   feminism (feminists), 364, 366, 369, 552
   homosexual analysis, 476
   homosexuality, 477
   nominalism, 478
Radicalize (radicalizes), 448, 465
Radicalized phenomenology, 467
Radio, 307, 587, 707, 708, 709, 719
Rads, 785
Rage, 529
Rain forest, 828
Rap, 340, 354
Rape (rapist), 338, 339, 341, 393
Rapprochement, 720
Raptures, 853
Rate (rates) of return, 822, 823
Rating scales, 112
Rational
   deliberation, 571
   discriminations, 866
   model, 666
   potential, 181
   thinking, 773

thought (thinking), 273, 435, 460, 571, 694
Rational-scientific approach, 728
Rational/theoretical paradigm, 46
Rationale (rationales), 18, 33, 70, 73, 99, 149, 195, 198, 237, 299, 622, 666, 706, 770
Rationalism, 204, 261, 322, 405, 410, 849
Rationalistic (rationalist), 204, 491, 640, 655
Rationality (rational), 57, 64, 180, 203, 206, 231, 272, 280, 288, 329, 353, 360, 367, 371, 444, 458, 460, 486, 488, 507, 571, 632, 656, 683, 685, 699, 715, 773
Rationalization (rationalize, rationalized), 401, 667, 688, 690
Ravel, 467
Re-conceptualization, 505
Re-experience, 439, 444
Re-present (re-presentation), 468, 470
Re-reading, 437
Reactionary, 266, 277, 278, 289, 291, 314, 496, 497
Reader's theater, 397
Reader-response theory, 287, 436
Readers (reader), 194, 336, 437, 438, 454, 456, 502, 585, 772
Readiness, 115, 137, 257, 591
Reading, 32, 39, 50, 53, 62, 72, 74, 86, 158, 190, 284, 287, 335, 336, 409, 425, 434, 436, 437, 521, 549, 574, 589, 607, 617, 792, 807, 827, 850
   classes, 617
   instruction, 287, 617
   materials, 815
   research, 434
   scores, 380
Real (the), 478
Realism (realist), 300, 512
Realist tale, 506
Realistic, 329
Reality, 49, 53, 62, 305, 306, 310, 320, 333, 356, 398, 406, 412, 417, 422, 424, 439, 453, 455, 456, 457, 459, 461, 463, 464, 465, 466, 468, 471, 472, 473, 475, 486, 503, 511, 537, 570, 576, 598, 602, 659, 688, 799
Reality-centered, 178
Realms of meaning, 170
Reason, 74, 206, 232, 280, 325, 326, 464, 465, 466, 467, 481, 499, 500, 507, 509, 547, 630, 655, 691
Reasonableness, 195
Reasoning, 298, 424, 562, 571, 689, 773
Rebellions (rebel), 345, 536, 567
Rebirths, 444
Receding, 488
Receptivity, 655
Recess, 806
Recession, 824
Recipes, 57, 117, 156, 568, 866
Reciprocity (reciprocal), 60, 255, 377, 378, 392, 396, 414, 415

Recitation, 70, 72, 77, 96, 105, 106, 108, 189, 198, 510, 753, 859
Recited, 848
Reclaiming, 516
Reclamations (reclamation), 599, 600
Recognition, 422, 425, 474, 497
Recollection, 602
Reconceive, 231
Reconceived field, 220
Reconceptualism, 211, 232
Reconceptualist
    discourses, 43
    ideology, 230, 232
    paradigm, 19
    scholarship, 233
    work, 370
    writing, 224, 234
Reconceptualists, 38, 212, 213, 215, 224, 230, 231, 233, 235, 238, 358, 370, 372, 655, 863
Reconceptualization (the), 39, 41, 42, 48, 50, 62, 63, 89, 136, 156, 157, 169, 172, 178, 179, 181, 184, 186, 187, 189, 192, 193, 199, 201, 208, 211, 212, 215, 216, 218, 219, 220, 221, 223, 225, 233, 234, 236, 238, 317, 358, 359, 370, 371, 373, 375, 419, 478, 515, 517, 530, 627, 651, 661, 663, 664, 735, 758, 854, 855, 857, 865
Reconceptualize (reconceptualized), xviii, 10, 13, 16, 119, 187, 201, 211, 221, 223, 226, 228, 230, 236, 313, 530, 653, 757, 854
Reconceptualized curriculum theory, 650, 652, 703
Reconceptualized field, 20, 24, 30, 32, 40, 42, 45, 48, 54, 55, 58, 63,173, 213, 214, 229, 238, 335, 364, 514, 648, 663, 849, 855, 856, 865, 866, 868
Reconceptualized in-service education, 703
Reconceptualized scholarship, 24, 172
Reconceptualizing, 38
Reconstructed knowing, 549
Reconstruction (Civil War), 72
Reconstruction (reconstruct), 720, 746, 816
Reconstruction of experience, 558, 566, 568, 583
Reconstructionism (see also social reconstructionism)
Reconstructionist, 800
Recovery (recover), 435, 447, 542
Recreation (recreational), 97, 125
Recruitment, 756
Recursive, 501, 541
Redemptive remembrance, 513
Redistribution, 676
Reds, 221
Reductionism (reductionist, reductive), 237, 267, 296, 306, 311, 505, 526, 564, 728
Redundancy, principle, 270
Reenchantment (re-enchant), 288, 691

Reference, 49, 434, 460
References, 10, 19
Reflection (reflective, reflecting), 10, 23, 41, 49, 57, 238, 265, 271, 272, 275, 289, 355, 371, 413, 415, 415, 416, 426, 427, 454, 474, 492, 520, 521, 531, 539, 541, 561, 562, 590, 597, 601, 605, 614, 649, 729, 749, 764, 767, 827
Reflective
    action, 171
    practice, 752, 756, 760
    practitioner (practitioners), 752, 763
    thought, 416
Reflexive, 430, 506, 522, 526, 546
    inquiry, 390
    method, 372
    moment, 866
    writing, 61
Reflexivity, 562
Reform, 29, 37, 70, 78, 83, 94, 116, 208, 220, 244, 272, 362, 395, 620, 632, 672, 679, 681, 694, 754, 755, 757, 806, 831
    leaders, 814
    movements, 124, 811
    policy, 683
    reports, 671
Reformation, 18, 151, 220
Reformers, 684
Reformist, 260, 364, 365, 366
    orientation, 42
Reformulation, 605
Refugees, 384, 841
Regime, 812
Regimented, 834
Regimes of discourse, 319
Regimes of truth, 506
Regional characteristics, 398
Regional differences, 607, 676
Regional study centers, 291
Regionalism, 840
Regions (regional), 664, 802, 822, 823, 828, 829, 830, 833, 839
Registers (register), 355, 356, 386, 526
Regression, 522
    equations, 196
Regressive, 508, 520, 552, 578, 645, 751
Regressive force, 400
Regrets (regret), 423, 429
Regulation, 34, 257, 362, 363, 504, 610, 660, 667
Reification (reified), 251, 275, 477, 480, 483, 491, 494, 595, 787
Reinterpretation, 62, 289
Rejuvenations, 432
Relatedness (related), 653, 655, 694
Relating, 172
Relationality (relational), 256, 381, 393, 501, 576, 788, 859
Relations (relation), 315, 319, 369, 422, 526, 596, 662
    of domination, 280, 504

of production, 245
Relationships (relationship), 211, 289, 335, 380, 387, 388, 433, 487, 524, 546, 559, 687, 760
Relativism (relativistic), 53, 301, 502, 535, 626
Relaxation (relaxed), 189, 806
Released time, 191
Relevance, 199
Relevation (relevatory), 258, 567, 570
Reliability, 560, 712
Religion, 45, 55, 170, 183, 316, 398, 606, 607, 609, 611, 613, 614, 615, 616, 618, 622, 624, 625, 626, 627, 628, 629, 630, 632, 636, 637, 652, 654, 655
Religious, 218, 320, 325, 332, 402, 418, 606, 608, 612, 614, 616, 617, 619, 622, 631, 632, 634, 637, 638, 640, 642, 644, 648, 650, 652, 659, 660, 684, 695, 777, 780, 796, 800, 802, 818, 836
    academies, 612
    attitude, 217
    clubs, 615
    discrimination, 616
    education, 183, 629, 660, 860
    experience, 89
    fervor, 608
    freedom, 613, 614, 616, 622
    groups, 607, 609, 614, 615, 617, 618, 627, 636, 813
    hegemony, 609
    hierarchy, 834
    instruction, 824, 834
    intolerance, 776
    leaders, 802
    liberty, 614, 616, 660
    movements, 606
    persecution, 607
    pluralism, 608
    practices, 660
    prejudice, 616
    right, 660
    schools, 622, 623, 624, 626
    tolerance, 615
    traditions, 787, 823
    truth, 614
    tyranny, 534
    values, 619, 620
    workers, 33
Remapped, 286
Remedial, 437, 670, 782
Remembered (the), 576
Remembrance, 263
Renaissance, 176, 182
Renascence, 193
Renewal, 448, 626, 633
Repertoires, 581
Repetition (repetitious), 270, 435, 544, 697
    compulsions, 521
Represent, 11, 17, 23, 24

Representation (representational), xiii, xiv, 15, 16, 180, 205, 245, 245, 287, 296, 305, 306, 327, 335, 336, 340, 342, 344, 346, 348, 384, 394, 405, 452, 457, 463, 466, 470, 473, 482, 483, 503, 511, 512, 570, 641, 715, 731, 742, 746, 748, 749, 839, 866
Repression (repressing, repressed, repressive, repress), 217, 279, 280, 308, 327, 328, 329, 330, 337, 351, 356, 389, 435, 490, 494, 535, 536, 579, 636, 643
Reproduction theorists, 318
Reproduction theory (reproduction), 120, 128, 243, 244, 246, 247, 249, 250, 251, 252, 253, 254, 255, 256, 259, 260, 263, 264, 265, 269, 275, 277, 278, 282, 283, 285, 287, 291, 294, 298, 306, 308, 310, 311, 313, 314, 317, 318, 319, 331, 334, 358, 362, 364, 369, 374, 375, 378, 403, 489, 559, 609, 866
Republicans (Republican), 636, 668, 672, 678
Research, xiii, 4, 5, 12, 13, 18, 19, 24, 25, 35, 51, 52, 55, 56, 57, 60, 61, 62, 63, 65, 91, 140, 148, 151, 157, 173, 182, 203, 227, 235, 255, 256, 270, 284, 297, 332, 333, 340, 367, 383, 390, 392, 396, 406, 421, 428, 438, 482, 483, 491, 504, 505, 507, 515, 516, 531, 553, 554, 556, 558, 559, 574, 578, 587, 588, 600, 622, 663, 664, 666, 679, 700, 748, 769, 775, 781, 783, 788, 792, 793, 861, 865
    development, 553, 555
    literature, 670
    methods (methodology) 52, 391, 415, 681, 728
    on teaching, 745
    paradigms, 46
    programs, 855
    traditions, 55
    universities, 757, 761, 821
Research-based, 729
Research/practice gap, 54
Researched (the), 551
Researcher, 54, 57, 396, 551, 559, 561
Researchers, 56, 430, 547, 628, 720, 791
Resentment, 767
Reservations, 525
Resettling, 386
Resistance postmodernism, 512, 513
Resistance theory (resistance), 247, 248, 251, 252, 253, 254, 255, 259, 260, 262, 264, 265, 268, 270, 273, 275, 277, 278, 281, 283, 285, 294, 304, 306, 308, 312, 313, 314, 341, 342, 344, 345, 346, 352, 375, 382, 393, 433, 477, 504, 505, 550; 551, 589, 591, 599, 609, 691, 784, 854
Resistant, 390, 513, 523
Resistant subjectivity, 513
Resisting (resisted), 282, 308, 310, 311, 334

Reskilling, 252
Resoluteness, 532
Resolution, 439, 594
Resources (resource), 171, 292, 305, 327,
　　346, 621, 666, 676, 730
Respect, 433, 528
Response, 9, 11, 596, 599
Responsibility (responsibilities), 35
Responsibility (responsible), 108, 213, 226,
　　441, 443, 561, 629, 633, 696, 830, 835
Responsive evaluation, 736
Responsive model, 192
Responsiveness, 621, 655
Restlessness, 572
Restoration, 535
Restorying, 560
Restructured schools, 679
Restructuring, 524, 674, 677, 679, 724, 757,
　　835
Results, 15, 144
Resurrection, 444, 645, 651, 660
Retention, 750
Reterritorialized, 286
Retired, 529
Retreat, 50, 254, 311
Retrieval, 447
Retro-fashion, 471
Retrospective (retrospection), 11, 531
Return of the repressed, 310
Revealed, 418
Reverent (reverence), 627, 629, 654, 655
Revisionist liberalism, 272
Revolt, 691
Revolution (revolutionary, revolutionize,
　　revolutionized), 210, 295, 363, 369,
　　392, 466, 559, 572, 578, 646, 649, 650,
　　826, 831
Reward, 333
Rewriting, 408, 723, 763
Rhetorics (rhetoric, rhetorical), 36, 200, 231,
　　261, 275, 278, 314, 588, 664, 670, 683,
　　744, 755, 794, 823
　qualities (quality), 34, 439, 512
　structures, 28
　support, 72
　tradition, 325, 326, 797
Rhythm, 429, 441, 490, 522, 526, 588
Rich (phenomenologically), 430, 474
Rich (richness), 501, 587
Rich (the), 120, 221, 621
Rifle, 212
Right, 271
Right-wing (the Right), 132, 273, 293, 298,
　　326, 512, 613, 636, 637, 643, 648, 652,
　　671, 672, 674, 681, 779
Right-wing attacks, 777, 778
Right-wing Christians, 678
Right-wing/business model, 672
Righteous indignation, 313
Righteousness, 267
Rights, 214, 334, 363, 617, 625

Rigidity (rigid), 223, 365
Rigor (rigorous), 110, 153, 157, 190, 270,
　　405, 406, 411, 415, 438, 451, 501, 502,
　　572, 641, 675, 741, 797
Riot (riots), 209, 210
Ripples, 467
Risk (risks, riskiness), 280, 441, 442, 446,
　　532, 533, 560, 671
Rites, 787
Ritual (rituals, ritualistic, ritualized), 170,
　　257, 262, 267, 270, 333, 432, 534, 660,
　　680, 738, 787, 788, 823, 859
Rock n' roll, 513
Rock videos, 839
Rocket, 699
Role-playing, 601
Role-segmentation, 624
Roles (role), 55, 125, 159, 165, 601, 630, 690
Romance, 152, 365, 691
Roman Catholic, 609, 646, 651
Romance fiction, 395
Romantic individualism, 277
Romantic planning framework, 692
Romantic understanding, 690, 692, 694
Romanticism (Romantic), 186, 216, 561,
　　690, 691, 692, 693
Rootedness (rooted), 424, 627, 629, 647
Rote learning, 78
Rote memorization, 534
Rote methods, 72
Roughness, 603
Routines (routine), 55, 188, 248, 418, 537,
　　570, 581, 586, 668
Routinzation (routinized), 74, 95, 105, 117,
　　118, 313, 314, 581, 670, 741
Rules, 60, 79, 257, 380, 458, 559, 568, 711,
　　722, 750, 770, 823
Ruling class, 252, 579
Rupture (ruptures), 230, 492
Rural, 84, 85, 158, 682, 754
Russian, 815

Sabbatical, 802
Sacred (sacralized), 3, 291, 335, 423, 639
Sadness, 435, 454
Safety (safe), 349, 440, 829
Sainthood, 454
Salvation, 271, 625, 638, 643, 648, 651, 652,
　　654
Sample test groups, 798
Sampling, 102
Sanity, 212, 425, 518
Sartrean, 453
Satellite, 796
Satire, 471
Satisfaction, 109, 811
Saturation, 251
Saussurean, 456, 458, 459
Scale, 490
Scandals, 484

Scene (scenes), 290, 426, 514, 558, 560
    production, 590
Schema development, 51
Schizo-cynicism, 504
Schizophrenic, 469
Scholarly
    allegiance, 233
    disciplines, 32
    discourses, 385
    fields, 24, 49
    journals, 13, 805
    production, 204
Scholars (scholar), 7, 9, 11, 15, 19, 26, 40,
    52, 53, 55, 56, 65, 104, 113, 129, 160,
    162, 165, 179,199, 219, 302, 335, 562,
    575, 791, 854, 867
Scholarship, 10, 12, 13, 23, 24, 25, 28, 30,
    32, 36, 37, 40, 42, 45, 46, 47, 48, 54,
    55, 139, 191, 213, 229, 285, 376, 399,
    451, 515, 629, 661, 663, 790, 854
Scholarship/ the real world, 308
Scholasticism (scholastic), 77, 499, 639, 640
School (schools), xviii, 4, 6, 7, 9, 14, 15, 26,
    30, 31, 32, 33, 35, 36, 37, 39, 40, 46,
    49, 54, 56, 59, 71, 72, 74, 76, 86, 97,
    98, 106, 111, 120, 126,128, 129,
    131,141,143,148, 151, 153, 159,174,
    176, 177, 178, 182,183, 191, 192, 193,
    199, 203, 206, 212, 214, 220, 221, 222,
    227, 230, 236, 238, 244, 245, 250, 254,
    255, 261, 262, 278, 279, 287, 288, 289,
    293, 299, 308, 318, 319, 327, 329, 331,
    333, 343, 345, 353, 355, 365, 366, 372,
    376, 380, 387, 397, 399, 401, 417, 420,
    425, 427, 440, 441,465, 470, 489, 490,
    494, 510, 518, 522, 526, 538, 544,
    545, 551, 552, 553, 567, 582, 583, 603,
    606, 608, 612, 624, 627, 632, 648, 652,
    663, 666, 670, 678, 680, 694, 700, 713,
    720, 754, 757, 760, 784, 785, 787,
    788, 799, 808, 815, 850, 862, 867
    activity, 627
    administrators, 140, 141, 208, 582
    authorities, 300
    board (boards), 103, 120, 617, 666, 682,
        791
    building (buildings), 97, 213, 606
    choice, 666, 673, 680, 832
    climate, 837
    curricula, 36, 162, 222, 602, 748, 792
    curriculum, 20, 31, 33, 64, 70, 74, 75, 82,
        97, 99, 113, 124, 143, 147, 172,199,
        207, 244, 254, 285, 299, 328, 330, 412,
        522, 535, 614, 616, 618, 620, 627, 633,
        679, 684, 685, 787, 795, 801, 808, 815,
        816, 836, 848
    day (days), 109, 675, 804
    democratization, 837
    districts (district), 42, 132, 398, 615, 675,
        701, 748
    establishment, 852

experience, 333, 789
experimentation, 114, 140, 215, 672
funding, 607, 683
grades, 686
history, 777
improvement, 53, 138, 722
knowledge, 251, 275, 285, 317, 323, 515,
    670
leadership, 726
learning, 167
life, 60, 119, 787, 854
lunch, 682, 781
management, 837
materials, 16
milieu, 256
museum movement, 706
officials, 300
organization, 221, 261
organizations, 748
people, 208, 212, 227, 553
personnel, 233
philosophy, 34
plant, 96
policy, 332
population, 259
practice, 57, 94, 604, 672, 675, 702, 703,
    855
practitioners, 41, 753
prayer, 613, 614, 635
principals, 806
program (programs), 207, 221, 683, 738
psychologist, 524
redesign, 672
reform, 12, 29, 96, 282, 293, 298, 331,
    390, 621, 662, 664, 668, 670, 671, 675,
    677, 679, 680, 682, 683, 684, 744, 757,
    791, 831, 838
restructuring, 680
room, 92
routine, 536
staff, 682
structure, 138, 179, 245
subjects (subject), 6, 16, 26, 72, 74, 75, 82,
    83, 87, 95, 107, 142,188, 361, 522,
    666, 685, 687, 748, 793
success, 92, 325, 806
systems (system), 56, 57, 104, 113, 119,
    143, 260, 622
teachers, 534
textbooks, 614, 779
time 437
work, 118, 245
workers, 57
year, 72
School-based
    curriculum chairperson, 35
    curriculum committee chairperson, 36
    curriculum specialist, 35
    management (SBM), 674, 675
    research, 40
School-community relationship, 623

School-site management, 676
Schooling, xviii, 3, 27, 29, 30, 31, 102, 105,
    122, 164, 211, 214, 221, 233, 237, 246,
    248, 255, 260, 263, 266, 283, 319, 325,
    327, 334, 359, 361, 364, 373, 384, 395,
    427, 518, 551, 582, 661, 662, 670, 677,
    679, 680, 687, 689, 689, 742, 748, 755,
    780, 809, 819
Schoolmasters, 57
Schools (experimental), 92
Schools (one-room), 72
Schools (ungraded), 72
Schools of education, 166, 195
School's governance system, 35
Schoolworld, 441
Schwabian, 851, 855
Science (of education), 64, 78
Science (sciences), 6, 18, 32, 76, 82, 84, 85,
    114, 122, 152, 153, 154, 158, 162, 164,
    170, 183, 194, 196, 201, 203, 217, 229,
    270, 283, 288, 290, 303, 412, 413, 451,
    460, 475, 482, 499, 500, 505, 507, 509,
    562, 572, 620, 626, 657, 674, 697, 717,
    718, 725, 729, 730, 746, 758, 761, 799,
    809, 812, 815, 817, 824, 851, 858
  curriculum, 682, 719
  education, 16, 55, 71, 718, 783, 822, 850
  educator (educators), 39, 56, 187
  fiction, 342
  literacy, 822
  scholars, 176
  teacher, 524
  teaching, 718
Science/technology, 813
Scientific, 20, 34, 46, 70, 75, 92, 94, 100,
    102, 103, 110, 111, 115, 119, 123, 125,
    136, 162, 168,173, 178, 182, 184, 206,
    213, 214, 267, 411, 412, 413, 417, 418,
    444, 489, 499, 626, 627, 640, 649, 661,
    699, 729, 735, 738, 749, 752, 756, 775,
    783, 822
  cooperation, 815
  curriculum maker, 140
  curriculum making, 90, 102, 120
  data, 30, 657
  educational research, 64
  experimentation, 42
  faith, 42
  influence, 51
  inquiry, 194, 196, 827
  knowledge, 194, 473
  management, 95, 97, 101, 122, 124, 146,
    627
  Marxism, 272
  method, 107, 117, 121, 125, 149, 322, 424,
    849
  model, 155
  pretensions, 205
  rationalism, 499
  rationality, 504
  status, 50

  technique, 117
  theory, 216
  thinking, 218
  tradition, 51, 64, 65
Scientific/behavioral, 184
Scientism, 142, 184, 201, 218, 220, 270, 726,
    728
Scientist (scientists), 93, 159, 160, 194, 196,
    482, 737, 815
Scientistic curriculum-making, 500
Scope, 33, 125, 144, 167, 168, 172, 696, 847
Scream (screams), 54, 536
Script (scripting), 723
Search, 170, 212, 227, 268, 431, 519, 745,
    847
Seatwork, 753
Second wave, 39, 675
Second-language learners, 530
Second-order experience, 411
Secondary
  curriculum, 198, 615
  education, 99, 159, 409, 534, 557, 816,
    822, 824
  school curriculum, 76, 85, 100, 118, 143,
    151, 170, 697, 717
  school subjects, 93
  school teachers, 15, 200, 365
  schools (school), xiii, 39, 75, 76, 100, 110,
    120, 133, 134, 135, 137, 138, 143, 146,
    147, 152, 158, 203, 611, 666, 671, 709,
    789, 817, 824, 835
Secret margins, 440
Secret place, 409, 439, 440, 441, 442, 444,
    536
Secretarial science, 101
Sectarian, 609, 611, 832
Sectors (sector), xvii, 5, 9, 13, 22, 23, 28, 32,
    37, 43, 44, 45, 48, 51, 63, 238, 262,
    266, 283, 294, 308, 312, 374, 376, 448,
    664, 791, 853, 855, 868
Secular (secularism), 45, 74, 85, 218, 276,
    529, 586, 608, 614, 617, 626, 637, 659
Secular humanism, 504, 614, 619
Security, 433, 442
Sedimentation (sedimented), 281, 282
Seductive, 588
Segmented, 437
Segmenting, 749
Segregation (racial), 321, 345, 350, 361, 621
Seikatsu tsuzurikata, 521
Selection (selected, selecting), 317, 319, 464,
    465, 563, 687, 749, 775
Selective tradition, 251, 264, 866Self, 105,
    127, 156, 178, 187, 191, 218, 222, 225,
    268, 274, 291, 298, 301, 304, 305, 309,
    327, 328, 330, 331, 349, 350, 354, 355,
    357, 358, 371, 381, 388, 391, 414, 415,
    416, 425, 426, 428, 439, 440, 442, 464,
    468, 492, 493, 494, 502, 516, 518, 521,
    522, 524, 528, 533, 536, 537, 538, 541,
    543, 544, 546, 551, 552, 561, 563, 577,

584, 588, 591, 599, 600, 601, 637, 641, 642, 652, 655, 659, 690, 694, 731, 745, 787, 839, 861
Self (minimal), 223
education, 334, 553, 556
value, 786
Self-
absorption, 127, 637
actualization, 29, 30, 172, 178, 190
actualizer, 31
affirmative (affirmation), 526, 786
aggrandizement, 386
alienation (alienating), 274, 383, 550, 578
analysis, 280
as-object, 590
as-place, 591
assertiveness, 342
awareness, 192, 413, 596, 773
communication, 651
concept, 50, 274, 307, 324, 382, 595
confidence, 257, 786
confining, 419
confrontation, 725
conscious agency, 513
consciousness (consciously), 43, 179, 430, 585, 644
constitution, 225
contained classrooms, 679
control, 786
creation, 439, 527
criticism (critical), 247, 252, 253, 392, 572, 642
critique, 290, 393
deceiving, 583
defeating, 787
defense, 787
definition, 214, 475
delusion, 251
deprecation, 786
determination, 339, 379, 387, 393
differentiating, 526
directed teacher development, 765
direction (directed), 106, 518, 621, 770
discipline (disciplined), 598, 757, 807
discovery, 577
educative, 538
effort, 320
employed, 822
encounter, 523, 532
esteem, 348, 669, 713
explicitness, 413
exploration, 577, 578
expression, 787
fictionalization, 439
forgiving, 583
formation (formative), 302, 378, 387, 493, 494, 522, 726
fragmenting, 578
generation, 499, 500
help, 348, 349, 674
identification, 348

image, 245, 333
indulgence, 590
instructional modules, 200
interest, 367
interpretation, 438
invention, 691
knowing, 860
knowledge, 439, 505, 658
love, 518
making, 438
nurturance, 532
organization, 500, 502
possession, 505
presentation, 245, 347, 439
production (produced), 785, 786
profiting, 329
rationalizing, 583
realization, 274, 536, 866
reflection, 56, 156, 290, 334, 372, 416, 427, 510, 521, 614, 641, 761
reflectiveness (reflective), 373, 392
reflexive (self-reflexivity, self-reflexiveness), 257, 261, 392, 406, 434, 528, 539, 546, 599, 760
reliant, 824
remembrance, 534
renewal, 252, 519
report, 410, 416
representation, 351, 590
repression, 337
respect, 787
revelation, 587
righteousness, 308, 310
scrutinizing, 522
sensitivity, 786
serving, 684
sufficiency (self-sufficient), 257, 850
transcending, 628
transformatively, 515
understanding, 56, 225, 290, 328, 413, 425, 444, 472, 534, 642, 764, 829
Selfhood, 171, 382
Selfishness, 105, 115
Semantic clusters, 196
Semantic problems, 194
Semiogenetics, 431
Semiology (semiological), 457, 459, 467
Semiotic orphans, 511
Semiotic society, 851
Semiotics (semiotic), 293, 301, 302, 303, 307, 310, 311, 457, 458, 467, 511, 512, 526
Semiurgical society, 297
Senior high school (see high school)
Sensation, 460
Sense (senses), 206, 434, 460, 467, 334, 484, 811
Sense-making, 493
Sensibility (sensibilities), 472, 779
Sensitivity (sensitive), 114, 324, 325, 484, 533, 574, 584, 665, 739, 773, 848, 864

Sensorimotor, 413
Sensory, 430, 440, 592, 645
Sensual (sensuality, sensuous, sensuously), 436, 494, 519, 594, 602, 603
Sentiment, 18, 359, 361, 416
Sentimental, 130, 565, 801
Sentimentality (sentimentalization), 385, 526, 532, 565, 656, 836
Separate education, 362
Separate identities, 480
Separate lives, 480
Separation (separate), 447, 549, 616, 628, 636, 656
Separatist (separatism), 321, 478, 508, 612
Sequence (sequencing, sequenced, sequential), 33, 144, 167, 168, 200, 500, 519, 616, 690, 696, 697, 847
Serenity, 433, 485
Sermon, 637
Servants, 620
Set of tricks, 591
Sets of relations, 453, 456, 458, 462
Seventeenth century (1600s), 325, 360, 499, 594, 779, 797, 810
Severed, 455
Sex (sexuality, sexual, sexualized), 304, 338, 339, 358, 359, 363, 365, 371, 373, 374, 375, 376, 381, 391, 393, 394, 395, 396, 398, 401, 402, 403, 447, 462, 463, 476, 477, 695, 777, 788
Sex education, 361, 362, 401, 402, 613, 614, 635
Sex education opponents, 402
Sex roles, 369, 387, 476
Sex-role socialization, 365
Sexes, 359, 388
Sexism (sexist), 122, 218, 220, 221, 222, 304, 308, 309, 334, 337, 342, 355, 358, 364, 365, 369, 375, 387, 388, 399, 427, 533, 633, 636, 657
Sexual
   assaults, 338
   differentiation, 464
   discrimination, 365, 366
   double standard, 363
   expression, 463
   grid, 374
   harrassment, 391
   identity (identities), 340, 358, 397, 398
   inequality, 365, 366
   intimacy, 339
   orientation, 280, 397, 398, 402, 472
   politics (political), 341, 364, 374, 476, 477
   power, 338
   prejudice, 366
   stratification, 365
Sexuality education, 401
Sexually dangerous, 337, 338, 339
Sexually transmitted diseases, 338
Shadow (shadows), 212, 475, 551, 859
Sharecroppers, 322

Shared reading, 437
Shibusa, 603
Shift (from quantitative to qualitative research), 52, 53
Shifting, 488
Shifts (in the field), 10, 12, 16, 32, 41, 46, 63, 65, 101, 150, 233, 296, 297, 690, 857
Shop-floor cultures, 252
Short stories, 4, 533
Sight (seeing), 435, 518, 582, 739, 866
Sight words, 435
Sign language, 531
Signal learning, 167
Significance, 59, 357, 558, 569, 577, 615, 629, 660, 740, 831
Significant others, 274, 294
Signification, 296, 512
Signified, 49, 457, 458, 461, 463, 465, 471, 473
Signifier (signifiers), 457, 458, 461, 462, 465, 466, 467, 470, 471, 472, 859
Signifying, 462
Signs (sign), 278, 301, 302, 312, 378, 454, 457, 458, 460, 639
Silence (silent), 234, 249, 287, 340, 346, 381, 382, 386, 391, 393, 531, 532, 536, 550, 603, 766, 867
Silenced (silencing), 644, 646, 839
Silent majority, 214
Silent reading, 780
Simplicity (simple), 603, 691, 697
Simulacrum (simulacra), 468, 471, 473, 482, 483, 511
Simulated, 471, 472
Simulations (simulation), 710, 711, 837
Sin (sins, sinners), 397, 646, 648, 652
Sincerity, 575
Sinfulness, 655
Singing (sings), 340, 407, 435, 567
Single-subject pattern, 686, 718
Singularity (singular), 8, 346, 429
Site (sites), 284, 286, 287, 312, 327, 373, 508, 788, 848
Site-specific curriculum development, 665
Situated knowledge, 703
Situatedness (situated, situate), 227, 257, 263, 533, 694, 746
Situation (situations), 8, 9, 10, 53, 54, 59, 112, 250, 256, 291, 373, 412, 420, 434, 454, 456, 526, 527, 548, 549, 583, 590, 592, 593, 594, 595, 597, 599, 649, 740, 747, 782, 791, 821
   variables, 812
Situational interpretative inquiry, 229
Sixteenth century (1500s), 625, 823
Size, 490, 602
Skepticism (skeptics), 152, 183, 267, 294, 411, 531, 663, 679
Skill development, 171, 759, 764
Skill gaps, 293

Skilled practice, 564
Skillful technicians, 260
Skills (skill), 99, 158, 171, 172, 200, 214, 249,
    251, 279, 341, 356, 434, 581, 620, 623,
    632, 694, 697, 747, 755, 773, 815, 827,
    865, 866
Slave (slaves), 349, 828
    society, 320
    trade, 322, 778, 823
Slavery, 316, 318, 345
Slide libraries, 706
Slides (slide), 706, 709, 719
Slogans (slogan), 171, 183, 214, 469
Slumber (slumbering), 693, 777
Small groups, 211, 219
Small-group work, 69
Smoke, 491
Sniper, 212
Sober, 268, 360
Sociability, 387
Social, 160,199, 227, 243, 246, 250, 258, 272,
    278, 287, 288, 290, 291, 294, 303, 315,
    325, 326, 332, 342, 344, 357, 392, 393,
    398, 422, 426, 427, 447, 456, 473, 512,
    523, 527, 540, 546, 548, 578, 579, 580,
    586, 593, 597, 603, 606, 608, 614, 630,
    631, 633, 638, 645, 650, 660, 674, 678,
    682, 684, 691, 755, 762, 789, 794, 847
    abuses, 654
    action, 148, 228, 387, 472, 648, 655
    adaptation, 21
    agenda, 156
    aims, 109
    alienation, 848
    analysis, 119, 251, 277, 278, 296, 770, 787
    awareness, 107
    behavior, 122
    behaviorist, 21
    capital, 623, 624
    center, 786
    change, 29, 56, 89, 90, 104, 105, 108, 117,
        130,199, 207, 210, 222, 228, 262, 277,
        278, 282, 307, 531, 653, 827, 828,
        835
    class, 245, 277, 398, 669, 794
    coherence, 624
    commitment, 535
    competence, 659
    concern, 215
    conditions, 321, 462, 469
    configuration, 311
    conscience, 423
    construction (constructionists), 357, 368,
        369, 376, 510, 533, 536, 649
    constructivism (constructivist), 253
    context, 29, 292, 585, 649, 808
    control, 51, 252, 779
    crisis, 125, 141,199, 672, 799, 827
    criticism, 119, 281, 285
    customs, 806
    Darwinism, 103, 300, 636

decay, 619
democratic consensus, 831
development, 90, 829
diagnosis, 155
direction, 125
discount, 823
diversity, 818
efficiency, 78, 89, 90, 92, 95, 96, 99, 100,
    109, 110, 117, 118, 121, 122, 123, 125,
    130, 140, 141, 142, 143, 144, 146, 150,
    151, 192, 237, 668, 670, 687, 755, 756,
    849
efficiency curricularists, 124
efficiency educator, 31
emptying, 787
ends, 224
engineering, 9, 20, 74, 92, 126, 236, 274,
    313, 387, 759
engineers, 77
exclusivity, 624
exploitation, 828
factors, 143
forces, 18, 291, 563
formation (formations), 61, 278, 303, 561
foundations, 215
frontier, 129
functions/activities, 21, 122, 131, 686
goals, 148
history, 281, 823
hope, 866
hygiene movement, 401
identity, 358
ideology (ideologies), 127, 237
improvement, 117
indicators, 733
inequality, 609
injustice, 37, 227, 633, 648
inquiry, 738
inscription, 61
intelligence, 570
interaction, 100, 425, 578, 823
interdependence, 264, 820
issues, 114, 719, 799
justice, 307, 397, 529, 628, 643, 646, 650,
    651, 827
market, 832
meaning, 782
meliorists, 31
memory, 263
milieu, 810, 842
mobility, 304
mobilization, 278
modernity, 507
mores, 614
movements (movement), 277, 278, 291,
    303, 314, 416, 755, 776
needs, 75, 85, 90, 100, 108, 789
negotiation, 423
norms, 61
objectives, 127
opportunities, 681

Social (continued)
 order, 126, 129, 130, 131, 132, 171, 255,
  282, 304, 342, 625, 799, 866
 organization, 272, 303, 748, 771, 783
 perspective, 127
 philosophy, 76
 planning, 126, 129
 policy, 199, 321, 607
 practices (practice), 41, 49, 244, 246, 248,
  253, 284, 286, 302, 303, 309, 319, 424,
  512, 580, 848, 866
 prestige, 788, 790, 813
 problems, 106, 127, 129, 139, 140, 169,
  292, 645, 709, 821, 824, 826
 process, 318, 523, 525
 programs, 223
 progress, 118, 706, 715, 805, 832
 psychoanalysis, 290, 291, 328, 532, 533,
  534
 psychology, 119, 297, 414
 readjustment, 118
 reality, 48, 171, 209, 256, 261, 274, 294,
  298, 743
 reconstruction (reconstructionist,
  reconstructionism), 21, 29, 31, 31,
  104, 122, 124, 130, 132, 141, 142, 150,
  171, 186, 216, 228, 243, 244, 312, 313,
  320, 322, 325, 521, 571, 755, 799, 841
 reform, 37, 122, 123, 124, 127, 131, 141,
  161, 288, 322, 323, 352, 680
 reformer, 107
 reintegration, 155
 relatedness, 49
 relational aspect, 782
 relations, 73, 171, 247, 250, 251, 278, 305,
  350, 389, 392, 427, 526, 579, 762, 782,
  823
 relationships, 108, 527, 624
 reproduction, 253, 268
 responsibility, 141, 258, 259, 397, 633, 803
 returns, 823
 role (roles), 368, 376, 396, 416, 526
 sciences (science), 3, 30, 37, 46, 50, 62, 64,
  65, 91, 104, 128, 145, 152, 163,
  173,177,187, 212, 213, 220, 236, 296,
  300, 302, 366, 370, 410, 412, 413, 414,
  424, 500, 521, 564, 565, 648, 650, 816
 scientists (scientist), 35, 58, 88, 423, 571,
  740
 sensitivity, 136
 shifts, 210
 stability, 76, 624
 stratification, 249, 275, 342
 structure (structures), 55, 84, 120, 216,
  224, 265, 312, 318, 459, 559, 565, 624,
  648
 studies education, 850
 studies textbooks, 778
 studies, 132, 144, 150, 158, 162, 164, 291,
  410, 580, 618, 697, 698, 779
 surface, 863
 tendencies, 608
 theater, 601
 theorist (theorists), 290, 313, 512, 648
 theory, 47, 51, 52, 55, 62, 126, 148, 173,
  217, 220, 278, 282, 290, 296, 426, 632,
  853, 865
 totality, 247
 transformation, 263, 306, 312, 373, 427,
  653, 655
 upheaval, 816
 utility, 94, 95
 values, 90, 173, 222
 vision, 127, 128
 welfare, 126
 workers, 33
 world, 60, 88, 164, 274
Social-efficiency movement, 12, 100, 101,
  102, 115, 119, 124, 146, 733
Socialism (socialists), 217, 252, 264, 266,
  277, 286, 295, 369, 663, 777, 816
Socialist feminism, 311
Socialization, 116, 169, 174, 274, 275, 276,
  301, 433, 693
Socially relevant, 125
Societal problems, 190, 274
Society, 3, 24, 29, 30, 38, 60, 72, 74, 99, 104,
  105, 106, 113, 120, 128, 132, 145, 149,
  153, 155, 160, 165, 170, 171, 175,
  178,186, 190, 191, 202, 210, 211, 217,
  220, 227, 237, 243, 244, 247, 255, 257,
  258, 261, 274, 276, 278, 288, 295, 298,
  307, 311, 314, 317, 321, 322, 327, 329,
  348, 358, 364, 368, 370, 399, 401, 423,
  427, 452, 456, 458, 472, 476, 507, 511,
  526, 565, 568, 575, 578, 603, 616, 618,
  619, 620, 624, 625, 626, 630, 631, 633,
  635, 648, 654, 660, 662, 669, 676, 686,
  689, 693, 698, 717, 718, 730, 768, 771,
  776, 779, 786, 787, 788, 799, 813, 836,
  848, 866
 of intimates, 257
Socio-biological, 348
Socio-cognitive theory, 509
Socio-economic, 14, 210, 319, 358, 372, 409,
  411, 787, 820
Socio-historical, 279, 647
Socio-political, 198, 218, 257, 303, 370, 496,
  564, 681
Socio-theology, 652
Sociocultural, 256, 277, 312, 318, 747, 812
Sociodrama, 601
Sociolinguistic, 784, 785
Sociologists, 35, 101, 123, 188, 495
Sociology (sociological), 3, 61, 100, 196, 197,
  224, 258, 276, 296, 369, 374, 476, 559,
  565, 648, 665, 731, 746, 759
 (sociologists) of education, 266, 317
 of curriculum, 243, 370
 of knowledge, 276
Socratic tradition, 751
Software, 712, 716

Solace, 862
Solidarity, 286,306, 342, 376, 380, 389, 529, 633, 651, 792, 834, 838, 842
Solipsism (solipsistic), 455, 502, 516, 523, 560
Solitary (solitariness), 184, 384, 416, 444, 545, 547, 761
Solitude, 389, 391, 427, 433, 440, 519, 537, 552, 660
Solution (solutions), 35, 127, 327, 666, 667
Somatized, 455
Sons (son), 386, 543, 544
Soul, 76, 88, 95, 537, 602, 625, 626, 647, 659
Soul-making, 601
Soul-murdering, 426
Sound (sounds), 381, 382, 435, 493, 550, 590, 867
Sound bites, 474
Source, 7, 720
South African, 820, 825
South American geography, 712
Southern
    culture, 398
    curriculum, 534
    experience, 533
    ghosts, 533, 534
    identity, 398
    literary renaissance, 535
    mass culture, 535
    place, 534
    social boundaries, 535
    studies, 290, 291, 535
    traditions, 534
    writer, 533
Sovereign, 453, 454, 455, 456, 459, 460, 462, 466
Soviet, 133, 830, 835, 836, 837
Soviet satellite, 151, 154, 155, 159, 174
Space (spaces), 20, 37, 40, 196, 226, 336, 373, 381, 383, 384, 393, 395, 430, 431, 435, 440, 441, 443, 447, 448, 471, 474, 475, 477, 480, 482, 483, 490, 524, 530, 546, 547, 548, 550, 552, 588, 599, 602, 652, 653, 662, 664, 700, 770, 839, 858, 859
Space/military race, 6, 154, 157, 159, 162
Spanish, 828
Speaking (speaks), 408, 421, 422, 434, 448, 526, 642
Special education, 524, 782, 850
Special interest, 201, 231, 635
Special moments, 766
Specialist (specialists), 32, 34, 39, 111, 662, 667, 682
Specialization (specialized), 71, 95, 157, 203, 815, 865, 868
Species (the), 803
Species history, 80
Specific competencies, 21
Specificity, 290, 305, 377, 380, 526, 590
Spectacle, 472, 511

Spectacularization (spectacularized), 512
Spectacularizing subjectivity, 511
Spectatorial curriculum, 592
Spectators (spectator), 363, 592, 597
Speculation, 92, 144, 218
Speech (full), 480
Speech, 300, 301, 421, 526, 538, 549
Speed (speeds), 474, 493
Spelling, 86, 320, 709
Spiral, 289, 541, 544
Spirit, 25, 34, 163, 181, 182, 196, 342, 398, 444, 626, 660, 861
Spirit of the age, 463
Spiritual
    crisis, 631
    discipline, 861
    historical mission, 809
    phronesis, 643
    possibilities, 862
    warfare, 861
Spiritualism, 602
Spirituality (spiritual), 74, 82, 110, 189, 228, 230, 233, 259, 332, 391, 562, 614, 619, 626, 627, 628, 629, 631, 633, 634, 637, 638, 639, 645, 648, 654, 655, 715, 830, 847, 852, 860
Spontaneity, 187, 418, 577, 578, 591, 766, 801, 860
Sports, 362, 363, 366, 789, 801, 834
Sputnik era, 682, 690, 794
Stability (stable), 203, 207, 431, 494, 602, 682
Staff development, 37, 342, 674, 701, 722, 731, 763
Staff, 165, 618, 672
Stage (stages), 48, 62, 79, 88, 89, 238, 628, 656, 691
Stage theory, 368, 500
Staging, 45, 482, 723
Stakeholders, 527, 671, 729, 858
Stalemate, 283
Standard, 670
    curriculum, 694
Standardization (standardized, standardizing), 33, 70, 94, 184, 535, 661, 677, 681, 690, 722, 749, 790, 792, 838
    evaluation, 184
    examination (examinations), 733, 752
    national achievement tests, 676
    techniques, 31
    testing (testmakers, tests), 260, 350, 510, 682, 742, 797, 848
Standards, 72, 118, 574, 666, 672, 675, 749, 806, 832
Stars, 399
Starvation, 629, 818
Stasis (static), 231, 477, 499, 859
State (the), 264, 318, 469, 475, 538, 579, 610, 612, 614, 616, 621, 635, 636, 652, 671, 683, 684, 809, 825, 829

1104   *Understanding Curriculum*

State authorities, 300
control, 608
courts, 207, 778
education department, 847
government, 666, 776
laws, 682
legislatures (legislators), 207, 292, 399, 625, 672
legitimation, 676
level, 676
textbook adoption committees, 860
State's authority, 683
State-mandated curriculum reforms, 672
State-mandated teacher evaluation systems, 682
State-of-the-art, 142, 192, 216, 230, 235, 519
State-of-the-field, 165, 231, 232, 233
States, 607
Statistics (statistical), 52, 84, 92, 93, 150, 181, 262, 340, 405, 411, 624, 634, 733, 735
Status (statuses), 316, 387, 684
Status quo, 104, 120, 128, 211, 222, 225, 250, 252, 254, 260, 267, 277, 298, 334, 547, 647, 854
Stereotypes (stereotypic, stereotypical), 290, 339, 342, 354, 668
Stillness, 222, 537
Stimulated recall, 555
Stimulus-response, 91, 92, 115, 164, 711
learning, 167
Stock market, 470
crash, 124
Story (stories), 11, 77, 259, 393, 425, 426, 430, 439, 449, 470, 492, 493, 521, 526, 544, 545, 546, 559, 560, 564, 587, 588, 597, 671, 690, 738, 766, 777, 788, 808, 823
Storyboarding, 711
Storybooks, 553
Storytelling, 259, 494, 527, 558, 560, 692
Strange (the), 595, 599
Strangers, 549
Strategic action, 231
Strategic essentialism, 478
Strategy (strategic), 466, 505, 764, 787
Stratification, 258, 365
Stratified organized compositions, 491
Stream-of-consciousness journals, 555, 729
Street gangs, 788
Streets (street), 285, 310, 332, 338
Strength, 342
Stress, 719, 806
Stretch, 597
Strike (strikes), 210, 309, 310
Strong (phenomenologically), 430
personality, 786
poet, 574
soldiers, 808
teaching, 780
Structural analysis (structuralist analysis), 425, 456, 461, 497

Structural
change, 227
commitment, 684
conflict, 788
corroboration, 574
inequalities, 339
reform, 679
theory of curriculum, 160
Structuralism, 186, 369, 451, 452, 453, 455, 456, 457, 459, 461, 465, 466, 480, 486, 487, 495, 500, 521, 628, 641, 787
Structuralist (structuralists), 195, 282, 306, 461, 478, 480, 488, 497
Structure (structural, structured), 29, 119, 148, 159, 160, 161, 182, 213, 217, 295, 301, 366, 414, 423, 457, 459, 461, 486, 520, 582, 593, 677, 787
Structure (structures) of knowledge, 167, 366, 367
Structures of power, 513
Structure of production, 245
Structure of the disciplines, 47, 160, 161, 162, 163, 164, 173, 175, 178, 179, 183, 186, 188, 189, 195, 196, 718
Structure of thought, 288
Structured learning outcomes, 22
Structured work, 642
Structures, 16, 305, 452, 453, 456, 457, 458, 461, 462, 465, 466, 468, 488, 496, 500, 522, 762, 770
of domination, 695
of everyday life, 432
Structuring, 749
Struggle (struggles), 223, 228, 246, 259, 261, 263, 264, 281, 285, 286, 287, 296, 300, 309, 310, 317, 322, 345, 349, 353, 354, 392, 393, 396, 423, 426, 427, 447, 505, 506, 524, 525, 528, 540, 549, 588, 608, 614, 626, 658, 659, 670, 760, 786, 787, 812, 816, 835, 848, 855
Students (student), xvii, 6, 8, 9, 11, 24, 26, 28, 29, 30, 35, 36, 38, 44, 48, 55, 56, 58, 64, 70, 76, 79, 85, 97, 106, 109, 115, 125, 133, 145, 160, 162, 164, 167, 170, 175, 180, 192, 194, 195, 206, 211, 213, 227, 229, 233, 245, 246, 256, 258, 262, 270, 276, 280, 284, 285, 286, 287, 292, 296, 304, 305, 312, 328, 333, 335, 340, 346, 362, 378, 381, 382, 388, 390, 393, 394, 399, 403, 418, 422, 431, 436, 437, 443, 453, 479, 480, 487, 497, 498, 502, 518, 523, 527, 529, 530, 539, 547, 550, 559, 560, 561, 570, 573, 575, 576, 577, 578, 581, 585, 586, 589, 591, 598, 599, 601, 603, 606, 611, 614, 616, 620, 621, 626, 627, 658, 659, 664, 665, 668, 672, 679, 688, 694, 695, 713, 733, 739, 747, 749, 760, 762, 768, 770, 776, 780, 781, 783, 784, 786, 788, 789, 794, 805, 817, 837, 842, 848, 855, 861, 865
achievement, 733, 743, 781, 798

assessment, 679
autobiography, 528
caprice, 132
characteristics, 809
choice, 698
clubs, 789
demagogues, 231
demonstrations, 814
differences, 681
experience, 262, 522, 527, 781, 783, 784,
    785
failure, 206
groups, 786
identity, 308
journals, 597
lore, 788
movement, 314
newspaper, 299
opposition, 184
performance, 798
poems, 589
population, 177, 756, 821
protest, 196, 199, 822
publications, 789
radicalism (radicals), 277, 832
resistance, 505, 523
response, 784
revolution, 187
rights, 629
teachers (teacher), 540, 547, 600, 758,
    769
teaching, 426
testing practices, 798
understanding, 749
voice, 262, 263, 266, 279, 280, 587
work, 582, 742
Student's world, 588
Student-
    actors, 601
    as-worker, 672
    centeredness (centered), 134, 488, 753
    participants, 591
    teacher relationship, 577
Students
    (beginning), 10, 51, 60, 197, 852
    (of curriculum), 23, 83
    (of education), 148
    (of the field), 12
Students'
    abilities, 810
    alienation, 784
    class variable experience, 787
    codes, 788
    engagement, 782, 783
    experience, 785, 788
    needs, 698
    rights, 227, 228
Studio, 441
Study (studying), 23, 26, 29, 46, 48, 57, 64,
    72, 73, 97, 125, 156, 191, 287, 411,

441, 454, 458, 553, 739, 747, 758, 848,
    858, 861
Style (styles), 284, 471, 526, 537, 538, 543,
    573, 579, 831
Stylistic traditions, 584
Subcultures (subculture), 317, 347
Subject fields, 198
Subject formation, 304
Subject matter, 21, 26, 29, 30, 80, 87, 107,
    125, 172, 250, 427, 428, 434, 518, 661,
    673, 686, 691, 698, 709, 746, 749,
    750, 768, 783, 785, 859, 864
    (area) specialist, 35, 721
    aspect, 782
    specialists, 14, 75, 81, 100, 139, 161, 187,
        195, 662
    structures, 749
Subject position (positions), 304, 462, 477,
    495, 513
Subject-centered, 155, 488, 505
Subject/object, 374, 375, 453, 455, 455, 456
Subjective criticism, 516
Subjective experience, 781
Subjectivity (subjective, subjectivities), 53, 61,
    76, 218, 222, 263, 284, 305, 348, 354,
    358, 377, 384, 407, 411, 414, 415, 434,
    455, 457, 460, 472, 495, 511, 512, 513,
    515, 526, 540, 546, 549, 588, 632, 641,
    731, 766
Subjects (areas of study/teaching), 71, 73,
    77, 86, 160, 662, 686, 687, 799
Subjects (persons), 53, 62, 282, 303, 304,
    305, 313, 408, 411, 413, 414, 454, 455,
    456, 457, 459, 460, 461, 462, 466, 472,
    475, 480, 485, 491, 495, 499, 500, 504,
    507, 522, 539, 595
Subjugation, 536, 532
Sublime, 691
Submerged, 636
Submersion, 827
Submission, 217, 321, 356, 536
Subordinates, 674
Subordination, 341, 393
Subsist, 484
Substance, 462, 472, 690
Substantive structure, 161
Subtracted, 479
Subversive (subverting), 130, 466
Success, 261, 306, 327, 347, 391, 624, 661,
    670, 720, 739, 760, 786
Succumbing, 593
Suffering (sufferers), 73, 305, 316, 326, 340,
    356, 444, 453, 485, 652, 657
Suffocate, 422
Suffrage, 72
Suffragettes, 362
Suggestions, 571
Suicide, 480, 485
Summative evaluation, 167, 175, 723, 734
Summer, 209, 255, 388, 431, 802
    employment, 191

Summer (continued)
  school, 158, 360
Sunday School teachers, 534
Superego, 329
Superexploitation, 318
Superintendency (superintendent), 94, 103,
  111, 112, 113, 142, 618, 624, 721, 722,
  802
Superintendent (associate), 690
Supernatural (supernaturalism), 626, 652
Superstructure, 220, 244, 245, 246, 250, 251,
  258, 267, 269, 276
Supervising teachers, 758
Supervision (supervise, supervised), xiv, xv,
  16, 36, 72, 95, 96, 111, 112, 113, 165,
  172, 190, 208, 224, 236, 397, 409, 523,
  608, 664, 665, 719, 720, 721, 722, 723,
  724, 726, 727, 728, 729, 730, 731, 744,
  753, 759, 791, 803
  field, 721, 726
  literature, 725
  process, 727
  scholars, 724
  studies, 731
  textbooks, 720, 727
Supervisor (supervisors), 127, 142, 208, 421,
  674, 720, 721, 722, 723, 725, 728, 729
Supervisory
  conference, 727
  inquiry, 730
  personnel, 111, 722
  practice, 729, 730
  relations, 730
  role, 758
Supplement, 326
Suppression (suppressed, suppresses), 331,
  570, 590, 861
Surface, 254, 391, 461, 463, 467, 482, 492,
  511, 579, 769, 788, 863
Surface curriculum, 701, 702
Surprise, 490
Surrogate curriculum, 775
Surveillance, 504
Survey, 97, 102, 110, 119, 140, 778
Survival, 388, 655, 657, 658, 803
Suspicion, 492, 827
Syllabus (syllabi), 33, 576, 593, 806, 817
Symbiosis (symbiotic), 375, 386, 511
Symbolic, 11, 16, 60, 170, 275, 290, 295,
  296, 302, 385, 386, 418, 435, 456, 460,
  479, 513, 526, 536, 579, 601, 624, 675,
  788, 847, 859
  (the), 478
  anthropology, 787
  order, 378
  wealth, 246
Symbolics, 169, 170
Symbolizations (symbolize), 375, 461
Symbols, 182, 278, 569, 787
Symphonic, 433
Symptoms, 222, 227, 521

Synchronic (synchronically), 457, 460, 461
Synchronicity, 307
Synergy (synergistic), 555, 556
Synoetics, 170
Synopticon, 195
Synoptics, 170
Syntactical structure, 161
Synthesis (synthetical), 105, 302, 383, 446,
  454, 484, 488, 520, 521, 560, 578, 587,
  603, 628, 753
Syphilis, 338, 811
System approach, 167, 181
System-centered, 258
Systematic, 35, 641, 642
  needs assessment, 200
  planning, 810
  teaching, 829
  theology, 647
Systematization (systematized,
  systematizing), 71, 440, 459, 461, 465
Systems (system), 32, 273, 453, 456, 458,
  459, 460, 461, 462, 468, 474. 718
  approach, 180
  model, 19
  theory, 521

Tabloid, 530
Taboo, 584
Tabulation (tabulated), 92
Tacit, 217, 244
  knowing, 210
  knowledge, 285
Tact (phenomenological), 430, 431, 665
Tactile, 377
Taken-for-granted (the), 406, 413, 424, 432,
  446, 447, 454, 485, 490, 491, 546, 551,
  605, 685, 859, 866
Talent (talents), 158, 190, 783
Talkhard, 586, 587, 588, 599
Taoist (Taoism), 492
Task (tasks), 91, 97, 99, 117, 125, 213, 605
  analysis, 95, 97, 100, 122, 124
Task-master, 111
Taste (tastes), 127, 779
Tax credits, 620, 621
Tax revenues, 292
Taxes, 607, 621
Taxonomy (taxonomies), 71, 155, 165, 166,
  194, 486, 487, 488, 734
Teacher (teachers), xviii, 8, 9, 14, 15, 31, 54,
  56, 67, 68, 64, 76, 77, 78, 79, 84, 103,
  106, 108, 112, 113, 115, 123, 127, 130,
  137, 140, 144, 149, 152, 155, 156, 159,
  175, 188, 192, 194, 196, 197, 200, 208,
  228, 233, 250, 252, 257, 262, 263, 264,
  275, 276, 280, 282, 284, 286, 287, 289,
  292, 302, 309, 321, 335, 342, 343, 346,
  362, 374, 378, 382, 390, 393, 394, 395,
  410, 417, 421, 422, 427, 428, 431, 433,
  441, 453, 478, 479, 483, 487, 497,

498, 500, 502, 510, 516, 518, 523,
530, 531, 538, 542, 549, 550, 552, 554,
557, 560, 561, 562, 564, 575, 576, 581,
582, 591, 599, 605, 606, 611, 615, 616,
628, 630, 658, 661, 664, 665, 666, 669,
671, 688, 695, 696, 699, 702, 721, 722,
723, 725, 731, 739, 742, 744, 746, 757,
762, 763, 766, 768, 769, 776, 780, 783,
785, 786, 791, 798, 799, 812, 826, 834,
837, 842, 848, 851, 855, 861, 865
(beginning), 9, 479, 760
absenteeism, 683
aides, 682
associations, 37
authority, 384
autonomy, 251
behavior, 282, 781
certification, 668
choice, 679
contracts, 85
control, 272
development, 37, 41, 203, 384, 517, 553,
557, 563, 564, 664, 703, 744, 764, 850
education, 9, 35, 167, 262, 324, 331, 371,
384, 389, 410, 432, 517, 547, 550, 664,
674, 720, 744, 748, 750, 755, 756, 757,
758, 760, 763, 837, 838, 840, 850, 852
education field, 750
education institutions, 165, 757
education program evaluation, 761
education reform, 755, 761
education, 9, 35, 167, 262, 324, 331, 371,
384, 389, 410, 432, 517, 547, 550, 664,
674, 720, 744, 748, 750, 755, 756, 757,
758, 760, 763, 837, 838, 840, 850, 852
educator (educators), 100, 343, 563, 757,
760, 762, 851
empowerment, 726, 727
groups, 37
guides, 780
(in-service), 9
induction 272
knowledge, 553, 554
lore project, 766, 768
lore research, 561, 766, 767
lore, 55, 517, 554, 561, 562, 747, 765, 768,
788, 855, 863
planning, 64
preparation, 166, 167,177, 756, 757, 758,
761, 780
professionalism, 753
proof, 672
(prospective), 9, 97
research, 747
resistance, 56, 306
role, 524, 704, 714, 748, 760, 781
strategies, 809
surplus, 177
talk, 377, 526, 753
testing, 722
thinking, 307, 509, 553, 554, 565, 702, 765

topic, 559
training, 97, 101, 150, 522, 721
unions, 622
voice, 263, 524, 563
workforce, 361
Teacher-as-
expert, 753
mother, 530
person, 564
practice, 564
researcher (teachers-as-researchers), 383,
563, 766
student, 753
Teacher-centered, 258, 753, 754
Teacher-colleagues, 36
Teacher-made tests, 582
Teacher-professor relations, 850
Teacher-proof curriculum (curricula), 71,
221, 263, 752
Teacher-pupil relationships, 165
Teacher-researcher, 54, 58, 524, 525
Teacher-student relationship, 782
Teacher-supervisor relationship, 725
Teacher-teacher relationships, 701
Teacher-writers, 532
Teacher/student encounter, 744
Teachers in training, 200
Teachers'
biographies, 760
classroom practice, 563
collaborative autobiography, 553
decisions, 704
experience, 559
images, 767
inventiveness, 835
knowledge, 524, 556, 748, 757
lived experience, 557
lives (life), 553, 554, 563, 564, 765, 768,
769, 771
organizations, 113
pay, 807
performance, 733
personal knowledge, 546
personalities, 768
planning, 689
practice, 563
praise, 785
salaries, 806
stories, 562
understanding, 560, 702
work, 554, 561, 564, 764
working conditions, 807
world, 563
Teaching, 8, 9, 41, 49, 50, 56, 65, 73, 76, 84,
92, 98, 100, 116, 139, 148, 156, 172,
173, 177, 182, 183, 201, 206, 263, 264,
280, 299, 337, 353, 360, 367, 368, 375,
379, 383, 384, 385, 390, 393, 406, 409,
413, 416, 422, 424, 427, 428, 430, 433,
434, 478, 481, 483, 486, 501, 504, 510,
515, 529, 538, 543, 549, 550, 551, 553,

Teaching (continued)
  555, 558, 561, 562, 563, 564, 568, 580,
  581, 583, 590, 596, 600, 605, 616, 618,
  634, 635, 655, 660, 661, 664, 665, 668,
  672, 685, 703, 706, 710, 725, 726, 729,
  740, 743, 744, 745, 746, 748, 749, 750,
  751, 752, 753, 755, 756, 760, 761, 762,
  764, 765, 766, 769, 770, 773, 791, 810,
  858, 863, 865
  machine, 709, 710
  materials, 162
  methods (method), 70, 74, 127, 577, 586
  moment, 501
  of English as a second language (ESL),
    437, 801, 838
  of English, 384, 588
  of science, 783
  practice (practices), 667, 668, 745, 755
  profession, 748, 799, 806
  program, 712, 720
  skills, 764, 770
  strategies (strategy), 200, 392, 393, 810
  techniques, 391, 586
Teaching-learning process, 198
Teaching-to-the-tests, 238
Team, 35, 36
Team teaching, 682
Technical, 8, 32, 50, 57, 61, 64, 108, 155,
  156, 189, 229, 231, 257, 288, 417, 419,
  421, 423, 425, 440, 457, 580, 626, 627,
  632, 658, 665, 687, 702, 712, 749, 755,
  756, 822, 836, 860, 861
  control, 425
  rationality (rationalists), 249, 256, 490, 564
  reason, 181
Technicians, 6, 158, 759
Technicism, 187, 564
Technique (techniques), 81, 120, 121, 145,
  148, 150, 181, 182, 262, 428, 438, 572,
  667, 672, 702, 764
Techno-rationality, 500, 503
Technocratic, 272, 273, 756, 790
  rationality, 237, 270
Technocrats, 358
Technological
  advancement (advancements), 824, 830
  colleges, 816
  efficiency, 474
  literacy, 718
  production, 689
  rationality, 180
  social order, 273
  society, 179, 262
  system of production, 21
  utopia, 126
Technologies of surveillance, 507
Technologist, 233
Technologizing, 406
Technology (technological, technologies),
  xiv, xv, 21, 29, 31, 154, 158, 181, 184,
  198, 217, 367, 409, 451, 469, 473, 474,

  481, 504, 507, 531, 548, 567, 593, 594,
  608, 626, 664, 665, 677, 686, 687, 705,
  715, 716, 717, 718, 744, 756, 799, 800,
  807, 822, 858
  education 717, 719
Televangelism, 284
Television (televised), 209, 302, 307, 469,
  470, 471, 472, 511, 513, 682, 709, 719,
  779
Television preachers, 636
Telos, 302
Temple, 27
Tempo, 581
Tenderness, 485
Tension (tensions), 41, 207, 208, 209, 210,
  224, 285, 291, 319, 416, 426, 439, 454,
  496, 525, 544, 547, 549, 564, 581, 588,
  595, 599, 630, 731, 760, 787, 788
Tensionality, 428, 433, 689, 832
Tenure, 682
Terminology, 166, 204
Terrain (terrains), 50, 254, 308, 314, 369,
  466, 517, 522, 534
Territorialization, 45, 285
Territory, 381, 459, 561
Terror, 470
Terrorism (terrorist), 481, 482, 483, 485,
  503
Test makers, 233
Test scores, 188, 668, 678, 683, 733
Test-taking (test-takers), 333, 848
Testament, 426
Testimony, 738
Testing, 90, 158, 183, 194, 682, 743, 794,
  797, 799
Tests, 8, 463, 582, 710, 711, 733, 780, 798
Text, 3, 7, 10, 11, 17, 23, 28, 32, 33, 41, 43,
  44, 45, 46, 48, 49, 50, 51, 61, 62, 69,
  78, 92, 121, 124, 172, 183, 186, 191,
  194, 203, 221, 235, 238, 239, 243, 246,
  247, 249, 250, 254, 265, 268, 277, 282,
  287, 294, 296, 302, 308, 312, 313, 315,
  316, 317, 329, 335, 337, 345, 346, 349,
  356, 358, 375, 395, 396, 399, 403, 404,
  410, 421, 430, 434, 436, 437, 450, 451,
  452, 456, 465, 466, 475, 480, 488, 497,
  498, 501, 505, 514, 525, 536, 545, 559,
  564, 566, 567, 568, 570, 572, 574, 576,
  579, 587, 589, 591, 593, 599, 600, 626,
  627, 637, 638, 640, 652, 657, 659, 660,
  662, 663, 664, 670, 719, 720, 731, 743,
  744, 745, 746, 765, 769, 792, 796, 838,
  840, 843, 849, 854, 855, 862, 864
  materials study, 776
  (synoptic), 15, 18, 19, 22, 23, 24, 28, 65,
    70, 139, 143, 144, 155, 156, 158, 167,
    169, 175
  (textbook), 33, 41, 54, 78
  world, 425
Text-analogues, 50

Textbook (textbooks), 12, 16, 17, 19, 22, 24, 74, 106, 141, 174, 264, 317, 337, 338, 339, 346, 364, 437, 488, 614, 616, 617, 618, 664, 682, 748, 754, 755, 775, 776, 777, 779, 780, 795, 798, 799, 817, 836, 839, 867
  (transitional), 24
  analysis, 779
  authors, 848
  content, 776
  controversies, 616, 617
  industry, 264, 690
  production, 488
  publishers, 14, 233, 860
  studies, 775
Textbook-recitation approach, 77
Textbooks, xiv, 3, 4, 5, 10, 11, 22, 23, 84, 137, 311, 858
  (synoptic), 5, 7, 10, 11, 13, 16, 17, 24, 46, 48, 63, 176, 197, 370, 462, 792
Texts (textbooks), 53, 264
Textualism (textual), 278, 296, 313, 427, 438, 511, 638
Textualist, 32
Textuality, 214, 295, 312, 497, 512, 642
Texture (textures, textured), 429, 435, 439, 441, 490, 540, 542, 602, 603
Theater, 210, 517, 523, 549, 569, 578, 588, 589, 590, 596, 597, 599, 600, 601, 723
Theatricalized, 384
Thematic, 244, 535, 697, 790
  analysis, 408
  aspect, 223
  cohesion, 211
  continuity, 865
  elements, 218
  heart, 179
  route, 218
Thematics, 583
Thematize, 227
Theme (themes), 212, 220, 221, 224, 583, 813, 855
Theme parks, 471
Theme-words, 422
Theodicy, 656, 657
Theologian (theologians), 388, 616, 629, 636, 642, 643, 645, 646, 656
Theological hermeneutics, 643
Theological naiveté, 629
Theology (theological), xvii, 4, 8, 16, 32, 43, 45, 46, 55, 62, 89,173, 181, 182, 191, 212, 213, 214, 218, 263, 269, 423, 569, 606, 607, 615, 624, 626, 627, 628, 629, 630, 631, 632, 634, 635, 637, 638, 639, 640, 643, 645, 646, 647, 648, 649, 650, 652, 653, 654, 655, 656, 659, 660, 720, 823, 847, 856, 857, 858, 859, 862, 864, 866
Theoretic (the), 35, 193
Theoretical, 4, 5, 6, 15, 20, 40, 43, 47, 62, 99, 114, 118, 125, 141, 150, 168, 175, 176, 186, 187,197, 204, 208, 221, 223, 246, 255, 256, 291, 312, 315, 403, 476, 508, 553, 583, 586, 601, 756, 863
  coalescence, 141
  commitments, 855
  constructs, 54, 165
  eclecticism, 141, 142, 144
  field, 849
  hesitation, 294
  knowledge, 61
  language, 575
  movement (movements), 198, 218, 469
  perspectives, 54, 169
  positions, 56
  problems, 491
  research, 52, 56, 62, 357, 390, 588
  speculation, 220
  stutter, 294
  vanguardism, 506
Theoretician (theoreticians), 44, 215, 221, 585, 663, 684, 694, 855, 862
Theories, 12, 475
Theorists, 34, 116, 204, 370, 631, 813, 826
Theorization, 523, 693
Theorize (theorized), 386, 408
Theorizer, 216
Theorizing, 57, 148, 173, 180, 181, 204, 211, 216, 223, 260, 299, 388, 390, 648
Theory, xiii, 8, 12, 15, 18, 24, 31, 32, 37, 40, 41, 45, 48, 50, 52, 55, 56, 58, 65, 80, 81, 95, 101, 115, 125, 126, 144, 147, 160, 168, 170, 175, 180, 181, 183, 186, 191, 197, 198, 201, 204, 206, 207, 212, 216, 220, 221, 229, 231, 254, 259, 262, 272, 273, 275, 276, 277, 281, 282, 292, 295, 297, 298, 302, 310, 312, 314, 376, 386, 406, 413, 426, 485, 491, 493, 509, 553, 555, 557, 561, 562, 571, 575, 585, 589, 601, 606, 648, 662, 663, 665, 690, 725, 732, 743, 761, 762, 763, 849, 852, 854, 863, 865
  building, 173
  development, 663
Theory-driven, 694
Theory-inspired, 694
Theory-practice relationship, 234, 308, 790
Therapy (therapeutic), 126, 561
Thermodynamics, 500
Thesis (dialectic), 105
Things (thing), 428, 430, 453, 458, 472, 490, 639, 655, 849, 867
Thinking, 8, 9, 81, 86, 116, 126, 140, 148, 149, 172, 180, 210, 238, 276, 391, 404, 418, 428, 438, 481, 482, 483, 488, 494, 510, 551, 569, 572, 633, 675, 703, 760, 775, 863
Third wave, 675
Third world, 295, 296, 315, 344, 794, 795, 807, 828, 830
Third-force psychology, 172, 174, 181, 185, 715

Thirteenth century (1200s), 639, 640, 819
Thomistic theology, 639
Thought, 213, 265, 272, 275, 303, 310, 313,
   404, 436, 480, 481, 482, 491, 541, 553,
   554, 555, 569, 571, 572, 762
Thought-action (thought-full-of-action), 308,
   426
Thoughtfulness (thoughtful), 407, 428, 438,
   663
Threat, 209, 279
Three-tier curriculum, 190
Threshold autobiography, 528
Thwarting, 518
Tiers, 191
Tightrope, 223
Time (temporality, temporal), xiii, 3, 6, 12,
   14, 33, 43, 52, 56, 60, 97, 167, 179,
   181, 182, 196, 198, 214, 276, 280, 332,
   377, 409, 413, 416, 417, 431, 437, 442,
   443, 444, 445, 448, 469, 500, 520, 524,
   532, 533, 535, 552, 558, 568, 576, 577,
   591, 636, 637, 645, 652, 653, 654, 669,
   697, 732, 767, 770, 858, 859
Time on task, 167, 781
Toil, 286
Tolerance (tolerant), 132, 840
Tomorrow, 109, 168, 182, 191, 210
Tone, 409, 543, 581, 615, 672
Tongue, 448, 471
Topical relevance, 813
Topics, 9, 195, 697
Torah, 638
Torsion, 597
Totalitarianism (totalitarian), 137, 220, 830
Totality (totalities), 250, 309, 419, 452, 464,
   465, 477, 478, 616
Totalization, 394, 857
Totalizing, 384, 463, 470, 473, 482, 512, 635,
   636, 857
Touch, 377, 430, 435, 527, 665
Traces (trace_, 388, 390, 436, 467, 482, 485,
   536, 537, 754, 859
Tracking (track), 158, 211, 363, 668, 669,
   733, 813
Trade books, 575
Trade deficit, 154
Trade unionism (unions), 261, 806, 813
Trades, 185
Tradition (traditions), 11, 14, 21, 32, 34, 44,
   50, 55, 63, 124, 148, 196, 205, 214,
   289, 384, 398, 424, 448, 490, 626, 632,
   638, 641, 678, 755, 858, 863
Traditional (the), 230, 474, 498, 617, 642,
   688, 690, 696, 714, 720, 763, 782, 815,
   833, 836, 865
   academic disciplines, 698
   academic skills, 714
   administrative evaluation, 726
   canon (the), 336, 480
   categories, 685

classroom, 379, 600
computer-based instruction, 711
conception (conceptions), 34, 491
concepts, 6, 403
curricular areas, 573
curricular concerns, 635
curricularists, 371
curriculum concepts, 475
curriculum development, 208, 446, 663
curriculum discourses, 486, 514
curriculum field, 12, 15, 24, 39, 40, 313
curriculum question (questions), 666, 866
curriculum specialists, 5
curriculum textbooks, 6
curriculum theory, 205, 373, 485, 578, 606
curriculum thought, 417
curriculum work, 127
curriculum writing, 212
curriculum, 375, 390
disciplines, 169, 695
discourse, 32
education, 70, 87, 280
experimental research, 573
feminine role, 382
field, 11, 20, 24, 41, 42, 43, 48, 62, 69,
   176, 179, 184, 187, 201, 205, 212, 218,
   220, 221, 223, 226, 231, 237, 238, 371,
   395, 516, 661, 790, 850, 863, 865
high school curriculum, 134
mappings, 32
Marxism, 281, 310
paradigm, 24, 30, 193,199, 209, 219
perspectives, 47
physical education, 801
politics, 380
position, 751
practices, 815
role, 214
romantic conduct, 395
school (schooling), 107, 190, 518, 835
school curriculum, 801
socialism, 277
societies, 783
staff development, 764
studies, 372
subjects, 834
synoptic textbooks, 664
teacher education, 758
teaching, 378
textbooks, 22, 24, 46
theology, 657
work, 236
Traditionalism, 273
Traditionalists (traditionalist), 21, 63, 154,
   204, 212, 213, 230, 231, 232, 399, 646,
   865
Tragedy (tragic), 293, 295, 310, 657, 818
Training, 26, 75, 91, 98, 349, 788, 823
Tranquillity, 190
Transaction, 21, 46, 175, 437

Transcended (transcending, transcend), 280, 288, 355, 375, 391, 408, 427, 628, 780, 803
Transcendence (transcendent, transcendentally), 179, 191, 210, 215, 225, 371, 444, 577, 628, 645, 651, 652, 658, 691, 862
Transcendental developmental ideology, 216
Transcendental signifier, 463
Transcendental thought, 218
Transcendentalism (transcendental), 218, 456, 464, 483
Transcendentalists, 362
Transcultural, 463
Transfer value, 31
Transferability, 167
Transference, 378, 379, 479, 523
Transfiguration, 597
Transformation (transformations, transformative, transformed), 46, 50, 61, 69, 124, 225, 247, 259, 260, 261, 262, 272, 278, 282, 283, 302, 313, 318, 354, 356, 364, 368, 374, 393, 395, 423, 433, 498, 499, 500, 501, 527, 540, 543, 547, 557, 566, 568, 573, 605, 626, 651, 653, 654, 660, 751, 752, 762, 835, 853, 861
Transformational, 21, 593
Transformative curriculum, 502
Transformative intellectuals, 260
Transformative practice, 246
Transforming, 591
Transgressing, 528
Transhistorical, 463, 464
Transience, 608
Transition (transitional), 826, 853
Transitional concept, 254
Translation, 739
Transmission (transmissional), 21, 23, 46, 154, 251, 479
Transnational capitalism, 472
Transportation, 607, 612
Transvaluation, 602
Transvestite, 570
Trends, 18, 144, 813
Triage, 631, 634
Tribe, 59
Trivialization (triviality, trivialize), 117, 388, 668, 670
Tropical rain forests, 841
Troublemakers, 785
Truants, 363
True (the), 475, 489
Truism, 271
Trust, 280, 433, 559, 604, 675
Trustees, 682
Truth, 8, 14, 41, 57, 61, 271, 286, 337, 349, 350, 367, 420, 423, 424, 450, 460, 464, 465, 468, 470, 473, 478, 485, 497, 499, 501, 570, 622, 634, 637, 639, 641, 649, 659

Truths, 105
Tuition tax credits, 621
Turbulence, 488, 847
Tutorials (tutorial), 710, 711, 712, 825
Tutors, 713
Twentieth century (1900s), 71, 77, 78, 80, 85, 90, 91, 95, 146, 149, 152, 184, 286, 320, 321, 323, 350, 363, 405, 470, 476, 493, 499, 569, 570, 573, 576, 589, 608, 610, 612, 641, 642, 677, 707, 715, 721, 722, 733, 789, 810, 811, 818, 836, 849, 856
Twenty-first century, 191, 328, 631, 689, 690, 772, 802
Tyler formulation, 198
Tyler Rationale, 15, 17, 19, 20, 36, 38, 42, 127, 149, 151, 156, 175, 177, 180, 187, 188, 199, 233, 237, 417, 419, 486, 499, 501, 593, 734, 849, 865
Tylerian, 653, 664, 692
    emphasis, 201, 205, 759
    field, 44
    mainstream, 212, 568
    paradigm, 178, 212, 663
    tradition, xvii, 487
Typing, 790
Tyranny, 188, 389, 509, 534

Ultimacy (ultimate), 631
Ultimate truth, 470
Ultra-fundamentalists, 615
Ultra-right, 808
UnAmerican (unAmericanism), 612, 778
Uncertainty (uncertainties), 416, 588, 604, 659, 668, 702, 751, 760, 835
Uncommitted, 190, 487
Unconcealed, 595
Unconnected, 208
Unconscious (unconsciously), 246, 273, 278, 281, 282, 290, 304, 328, 329, 372, 390, 413, 426, 459, 460, 478, 479, 480, 504, 518, 521, 522, 539, 541, 542, 555, 557, 588, 641, 688
Unconstitutional, 612, 613, 778
Uncontrollable, 491
Uncoupling, 465
Undemocratic, 129, 612
Underachievement, 621
Underclass, 334, 756
Underemployed, 326
Undergraduate, 761, 762, 843, 850
    education curriculum, 758
    liberal arts, 759
    voices, 527
    women, 527
Underrepresenting, 615
Understanding (understand), xvi, 3, 5, 6, 7, 10, 13, 14, 15, 16, 17, 19, 23, 24, 25, 32, 40, 42, 43, 44, 45, 46, 48, 50, 51, 52, 53, 55, 56, 57, 60, 62, 63, 64, 65,

Understanding (continued)
    69, 74, 81, 122, 124, 131, 159, 160,
    165, 170, 180, 181, 187,198, 201, 203,
    205, 213, 214, 228, 229, 235, 236, 238,
    239, 246, 248, 254, 260, 267, 269, 274,
    275, 283, 291, 292, 294, 299, 302,305,
    307, 315, 316, 318, 328, 335, 337, 342,
    346, 349, 356, 357, 358, 359, 376, 379,
    382, 385, 395, 398, 399, 400, 402, 403,
    404, 409, 412, 413, 420, 423, 424, 425,
    427, 437, 440, 441, 445, 447, 450, 452,
    464, 478, 480, 484, 485, 493, 496, 510,
    514, 518, 520, 521, 524, 525, 526, 527,
    528, 530, 532, 533, 544, 545, 546, 548,
    551, 554, 555, 557, 559, 560, 562, 564,
    566, 567, 568, 570, 573, 574, 575, 576,
    582, 583, 584, 600, 603, 605, 606, 624,
    626, 627, 629, 631, 637, 638, 640, 641,
    642, 643, 649, 650, 653, 654, 655, 660,
    661, 662, 663, 664, 667, 670, 675, 692,
    693, 695, 700, 718, 719, 729, 731, 738,
    739, 743, 744, 746, 748, 749, 750, 759,
    765, 770, 785, 787, 791, 792, 793, 794,
    796, 797, 830, 838, 840, 843, 847, 849,
    851, 852, 855, 858, 862, 863, 864, 865,
    866
Understudied, 790
Undertheorized, 261, 384
Unemployment (unemployed), 113, 326, 623
Unequal, 346, 362, 867
Unfamiliar (the), 230, 236, 548
Unfinished, 422
Unfolded, 492
Unfolding, 98, 216, 448, 467, 470
Unification (of subject matter), 86, 336
Unified design, 687
Unified self, 472
Uniformity, 70, 722, 867
Unifying, 371
Unintended, 751
Union, 264
Unionization, 322
Unions (see trade unions)
Uniqueness (unique), 109, 406, 420, 437,
    456, 485, 568, 665
Unit (units), 139, 141, 145, 692, 697, 746,
    799, 811
United Nations conference, 829
United Nations curriculum, 800, 801
United world, 629
Unity (unities), 70, 79, 461, 464, 468, 476,
    494, 561, 593
Universal theology, 651
Universal truths, 452, 464
Universalistic (universalism), 280, 464
Universality (universal, universals), 291, 353,
    429, 439, 465, 468, 588, 604, 672, 751,
    770, 856
Universalizing, 628
Universe, 274, 423, 499, 501, 658

University (universities), 26, 32, 34, 40, 71,
    94, 303, 470, 545, 601, 611, 666, 679,
    718, 756, 757, 758, 760, 761, 778, 786,
    789, 816, 819, 825, 851, 860
arts and sciences scholars, 690
entrance examinations, 789
professor, 9, 41, 233, 550
scholar (scholars), 63, 208, 729
schooling, 807
University-based curriculum professor, 36
University-based specialist, 35
Unknown (the), 230, 236
Unmeasured curriculum, 736
Unmediated, 522, 707
Unpredictable, 164, 498
Unprofessional, 671
Unravel, 467
Unreflective, 489
Unresponsiveness, 621
Unrest, 828
Unruly (unruliness), 360, 363
Unstable, 491, 868
Untaught lessons, 751
Unthematized, 445
Upheaval, 201, 208
Upper class (classes), 127, 608, 621
Upper middle class, 608, 799
Upper schools, 84
Upward economic mobility, 608
Upward social mobility, 608
Urban, 535, 679, 682, 754, 756, 778, 779,
    825
education, xviii, 260, 683
schools, 85, 529, 679
society, 140
underclass, 786
Urgency, 444, 803
Utilitarian, 98, 154, 843
Utilization, 201
Utopia (utopian), 243, 280, 313, 489, 652

Vacuum, 273, 849
Validation, 54, 59, 216, 267, 775
Validity, 560
Value communities, 622, 623
Value frameworks, 417
Value structure, 695
Value-free, 614, 659, 716, 739
Value-neutral, 614
Valued educational activity, 182, 417
Values (value), 12, 148, 165, 166, 172, 181,
    207, 224, 237, 246, 257, 266, 272, 286,
    296, 300, 327, 348, 361, 392, 407, 462,
    489, 554, 561, 575, 582, 603, 606, 614,
    616, 617, 618, 619, 621, 628, 651, 672,
    697, 699, 735, 779, 801, 827, 832
clarification, 189, 595, 686
strand, 689
Valuing, 174

Variables (variable), 317, 411, 416, 450, 481, 805

Variance, 237

Variant, 100

Variety, 621

Vatican, 643, 647, 648, 649, 651

Velocity, 444, 858, 859

Verb (verbs), 274, 576, 605, 628, 848

Verbal, 570, 638, 753
  association, 167

Verbalism, 706

Verifiability, 91

Verification, 322, 849

Vernacular, 108

Vertical, 124, 181
  organization, 696
  power structure, 56

Veterinary medicine, 101

Victims (victim), 252, 327, 338, 342, 357, 661, 821

Victorian morality, 363

Victory, 485

Video disk cassettes, 472

Video games, 715

Video lessons, 706

Video players, 472

Videos (video), 337, 608, 709, 713

Videotape (videotapes), 218, 555, 587, 601, 739, 769

Villain, 496

Violate, 235

Violence (violent), 217, 341, 363, 393, 481, 485, 650, 675, 715, 842, 854, 856

Virtual, 483

Virtue, 292

Visibility, 144, 149, 283, 311

Vision, 36, 38, 88, 117, 127, 128, 182, 183, 260, 263, 288, 292, 351, 379, 389, 443, 499, 567, 577, 584, 631, 633, 649, 653, 660, 678, 767, 790, 842

Visionary, 217, 489, 491

Visual, 284, 391, 478, 511, 526, 570, 713, 739, 750
  arts, 170, 183, 582
  education, 707
  instruction, 706
  materials, 706
  technologies, 706

Vitality (vital), 485, 606, 835

Vividness, 420, 431

Vivify, 692

Vocabulary, 311, 391, 710

Vocation (vocations), 764, 788, 861

Vocational, 98, 99, 100, 106, 117, 122, 145, 146, 154, 158, 164, 169, 250, 320, 366, 607, 682, 758, 808, 822
  clubs, 788
  education, 718, 789, 813
  experts, 815
  school, 759

Voice (voices), xiii, 4, 5, 14, 218, 236, 249, 256, 268, 286, 291, 292, 298, 305, 308, 309, 312, 334, 353, 354, 381, 382, 383, 384, 386, 390, 391, 393, 407, 422, 426, 433, 444, 458, 508, 516, 521, 524, 525, 526, 528, 529, 530, 532, 539, 543, 546, 550, 552, 600, 631, 636, 637, 672, 726, 750, 760, 770, 839, 863, 864

Voiceless, 431

Void, 606

Volition (volitional), 74, 274, 517, 522

Voting rights, 613

Vouchers (voucher), 191, 635, 680

Voyeurism (voyeuristic), 266, 279, 526, 597, 839

Vulgar Hegelianism, 304

Vulgar interpretation, 246

Vulgar Marxism, 261

Vulgar pragmatism, 261

Vulnerability (vulnerable), 386, 430, 455, 598, 861

Waiting, 431, 445, 446, 572, 766

Wake, 232

Walkman, 442

Wandering, 432

War, 174, 209, 375, 470, 512, 811, 821, 826, 838, 841

Waste (wasting), 96, 102, 115, 490, 575

Watchfulness, 433

Watchwords, 491

Water, 840

Wave, 12

Weak (the), 575

Wealth, 103, 128, 214, 305, 674, 695, 828

Wealthy, 621, 643, 714, 806, 834

Weapons, 180, 807

Weberian, 261

West (the), 214, 538, 627, 807

West (the American), 389, 610

West African, 823

Western
  civilization, 151, 153, 154, 350
  cultural episteme, 271
  cultural tradition, 30
  culture, 285, 338, 460, 819
  discourses, 456
  enterprise, 693
  European, 813
  hemisphere, 409
  history, 795
  ideologies, 814
  logos, 464, 465, 468
  man, 481
  media, 796
  metaphysic, 335
  modernity, 603
  nations, 837
  philosophy, 466

Western (continued)
  popular culture, 796
  reason, 467
  science, 303, 474
  self, 330, 537
  thought, 325, 464, 467, 499
  traditions, 492
  world, 153, 195
Westernization, 646
Whispers (whisperings), 444, 477, 536
White (whites), 61, 221, 266, 280, 316, 317,
    320, 324, 327, 328, 329, 330, 331, 333,
    334, 336, 338, 339, 340, 342, 343, 344,
    345, 346, 348, 349, 353, 354, 360, 392,
    464, 730, 818, 825
  liberals, 832
  men (male), 339, 510
  prejudice, 324
  supremacy (supremacist), 345, 349, 507
  violence, 339
Whiteness, 353
Whole language, 287, 792
Whole, 521, 584, 626, 697
Whole-to-part approach, 697
Whole-word method, 73
Wholeness, 383, 418, 420, 660
Wide awakeness, 373, 409
Wife (wives), 358, 360, 395
Wilderness, 385, 389
Will, 55, 74, 81, 252, 281, 411
Windows (on the soul), 76, 95
Wine, 582, 739
Winter, 389
  schools, 360
Wisdom, 138, 205, 439, 477, 638, 640, 748,
    758, 770
Witchcraft, 474
Withdrawal, 223, 383, 518, 782
Wo(man), 490
Wolf, 481, 482, 499
Woman (women), 77, 85, 101, 206, 221,
    304, 305, 306, 308, 323, 338, 341, 342,
    343, 344, 352, 360, 363, 365, 367, 368,
    369, 373, 374, 375, 379, 381, 382, 384,
    385, 386, 387, 389, 391, 393, 394, 395,
    399, 401, 407, 427, 444, 464, 476, 477,
    478, 490, 524, 526, 529, 530, 542, 548,
    549, 550, 551, 603, 615, 617, 626, 656,
    678, 694, 695, 727, 767, 768, 779, 780
Woman of the Year Award, 157
Womanhood, 767
Womanness, 427
Womb, 490
Women
  academics, 382
  curriculum theorists, 372
  scholars, 550
  students, 552
  teachers, 380, 384, 385, 395, 528, 529, 530
Women's
  authority, 385

autobiography, 549
colleges, 363
conditioning, 383
estate, 396
liberation, 364
moral development, 369
movement, 369, 399
oppression, 364, 496
pedagogical work, 373
rights, 361
self-alienation, 383
self-knowledge, 505
solidarity, 389
studies, 363, 367, 368, 402, 505, 506, 655
voices (voice), 386, 526
work, 390
Women-hating, 388
Wonder, 568, 604, 605, 692
Word (the), 355, 434, 447, 458, 459, 588,
    596, 638, 827
Word-cramming, 87
Word-recitation, 87
Words, 7, 484, 485, 492, 495, 524, 531, 590,
    775, 866
Work, 30, 31, 38, 58, 95, 96, 98, 108, 147,
    212, 213, 225, 232, 254, 276, 296, 341,
    343, 348, 401, 629, 720, 732, 841
  ethic, 110
  lives (life), 395, 556
  status, 372
Workers, 646, 816
Workforce, 293, 812
Working class, 211, 252, 254, 259, 268, 278,
    285, 295, 296, 306, 318, 342, 624, 756,
    785, 836
Working conditions, 677
Working-class
  boys, 252, 268
  high school, 785
  identity, 304
  women, 344
Workload, 575
Workplace (workplaces), 95, 96, 128, 245,
    250, 361, 394, 668
Workshops (workshop), 208, 337, 398, 441,
    597
World, 199, 213, 217, 218, 258, 274, 276,
    283, 291, 310, 337, 344, 377, 399, 400,
    405, 407, 408, 411, 413, 414, 415, 418,
    419, 427, 434, 435, 438, 439, 441, 442,
    444, 447, 453, 455, 457, 459, 469, 472,
    473, 475, 478, 510, 515, 524, 535, 537,
    540, 544, 548, 557, 570, 577, 579, 588,
    597, 602, 605, 618, 628, 647, 653, 672,
    692, 763, 770, 799, 827, 838, 848, 856,
    863
  church, 647
  civilization, 800
  community, 801
  core curriculum, 800
  cultures, 801, 802, 818

economy, 469, 832
educational community, 829
government, 617, 800, 802
history, 802
languages (language), 795, 802
order, 293
peace, 801
politics, 854
religions, 617
unification, 802
World War I, 109
World War II, 79, 125, 130, 137, 142, 173,
    733, 754, 807, 808, 842
Worldliness, 431
Worldview, 299, 442, 499, 500, 509, 576,
    614, 626, 638, 644, 650
Worldwide concerns, 800
Worshipped, 335
Worth, 862, 866
Wounds, 485
Wretchedness, 821
Writable text, 436
Writing, 8, 35, 48, 59, 85, 157, 190, 212,
    287, 347, 408, 434, 436, 438, 439, 475,
    482, 484, 518, 521, 552, 574, 575, 589,
    599, 723, 807
    communities, 531

Wrong, 271
Wu-wei, 492

Xenophobia, 347, 776

Yawn, 454
Yearbooks, 208, 210, 211
Yellows, 221
Yoga, 705
Young (the), 214, 330, 401, 402, 422, 575,
    623, 630, 691, 712, 750, 788, 813
Young minds, 151, 154
Younger generation, 847
Youngsters, 527
Youth, 100, 144, 145, 145, 158, 162,
    174, 199, 254, 293, 303, 317, 324, 325,
    349, 608, 609, 620, 698, 745, 808, 812,
    829
Youthfulness, 234

Zen, 492
Zero-based budgeting, 682
Zone, 428

Name Index

Abbot, Jacob, 610
Abbs, Peter, 517, 553
Abdal-Haqq, I., 761
Abdulmalik, H., 793
Aceland, R., 697
Acheson, K., 721
Activity Program (1934-1941), 754
Adams, John, 609
Adams, Natalie, 533
Addams, Jane, 107
Addis Ababa, 820
Adelman, Clem, 563
Adler, Mortimer, 153, 194, 195, 269, 697, 774
Adorno, Theodor, 248, 281
Afghanistan, 835
Africa (African), 22, 316, 321, 322, 338, 350, 352, 581, 795, 818, 819, 820, 821, 822, 823, 824, 826, 828
African American Church, 616
African Curriculum Organization (ACO), 793
Agger, B., 574
Ahmed, M., 829
AIDS, 338, 340,398, 402, 543, 821
Aikin, Wilford M., 133, 134, 136, 137, 701
Airlie House, xvi, 45, 226, 374
Albertini, John, 516, 530, 531, 532
Alberty, Elsie J., 175, 177, 179
Alberty, Harold, 118, 130, 137, 143, 155, 175, 698
Alcoff, L., 392
Alcott, Louisa May, 361, 362
Alessi, Stephen, 705, 710, 711, 713, 714
Alex Taylor Community School, 672
Alexander the Great, 402, 819
Alexander, H., 741
Alexander, Susan, 803
Alexander, William M., 13, 26, 110, 139, 140, 156, 163, 176, 197, 198, 684, 685, 686, 687, 688, 689, 690
Alexandria, 819
Alfred P. Sloan Foundation, 113
Algeria, 818
Ali, Noble Drew, 321
Allan, K., 54
Allen, J., 409
Allen, R., 283
Allen, W., 354
Allport, Gordon, 174, 178
Altbach, P., 795, 796
Althusser, Louis, 245, 246

Amano, I., 797
Amarel, M., 701, 702
Amazon, 826, 828, 829
America 2000, 673, 674, 797
American Association for the Advancement of Science (AAAS), 159, 717, 718
American Association of Colleges for Teacher Education (AACTE), 324, 756
American Association of School Administrators (AASA), 130, 616
American Civil Liberties Union, 779
American Council on Education, 777
American Educational Research Association (AERA), xiii, 41, 44, 201, 208, 211, 230, 231, 232, 236, 397, 592, 798, 831
American Eugenics Society, 94
American Journal of Psychology, 88
American Journal of Education, xiii, 73
American Psychological Association, 710
Amerindian, 332
Ammons, Margaret, 192, 199
Amnesty International, 842
Andambi, M., 820
Anderson, D., 720
Anderson, J., 320
Anderson, T., 780
Angelou, Maya, 533
Anglo-Saxon, 3, 361
Angola, 818, 821
Angus, David, 120
Annehurst Curriculum Classification System, 192
Annenberg, Walter, 293, 672, 680
Anthony, Susan B., 361
Anthropology Curriculum Study Project, 163
Anyon, Jean, 253, 270, 311, 312, 313, 777
Aoki, Ted (Tetsuo), 44, 228, 229, 316, 404, 409, 410, 411, 412, 420, 422, 425, 426, 427, 428, 433, 437, 448, 531, 665, 689, 716, 763, 849, 857, 861
APEID, 793
Appalachia, 255, 533
Appel, Stephen, 304
Appiah, Anthony, 316, 352
Apple Corporation, 714
Apple, Michael W., xv, 27, 43, 44, 171, 182, 202, 210, 215, 226, 227, 243, 245, 246, 247, 248, 249, 250, 251, 253, 254, 255, 258, 259, 264, 265, 266, 268, 269, 270, 271, 272, 276, 277, 278, 282, 287, 293, 295, 296, 304, 306, 308, 309, 310, 311,

314, 318, 394, 400, 418, 425, 503, 525,
    572, 589, 590, 617, 629, 776, 780, 860
Aptekar, L., 427
Aquinas, Thomas, 639, 640
Arab States, 794
Arabia, 819
Argentina, 794, 826, 828
Ariav, T., 757
Aristotle, 195, 657, 705
Armbruster, B., 780
Armstrong, D., 697
Arnold, Matthew, 733
Arnove, R., 809
Arnstine, D., 581
Aronowitz, Stanley, 249, 250, 253, 260, 281,
    283, 285, 286, 294, 295, 296, 302, 303,
    304, 508, 831
Arons, S., 635, 636
Artificial intelligence (AI), 712, 713, 716
Asante, M. , 322, 795
Asanuma, Shigeru, 426, 521
Ascher, C., 317
Asia, 22, 316, 344, 349, 350, 806
Asmus, W., 811
Association for Supervision and Curriculum
    Development (ASCD), 19, 53, 96, 142,
    143, 162, 163, 172, 173, 178, 190, 208,
    209, 210, 211, 224, 227, 236, 397, 615,
    616, 621, 719, 720, 721, 724, 727, 803
Association of Process Philosophy of
    Education (APPE), 653
Assor, Avi, 270
Astin, H., 367
Asubel, David P., 168
Atkins, Elaine, 391, 422, 424
Atkinson, Richard, 711
Atkinson, Tri-Grace, 366
Atlanta University, 128
Atlantic Monthly, 188
Au, K., 316, 784
Augustine, 657
Aurelius, Marcus, 799
Australia, 229, 733, 832, 833
Austria, 810
Ayers, J., 761
Ayers, William, 516, 525, 526, 527, 553, 555,
    559, 562, 563, 661, 672, 747, 750, 765,
    766
Azuma, Hiroshi, 809

Bacon, Francis, 463
Bader, Edith, 142
Bagley, William C., 96, 121, 707, 777, 859
Bain, W., 503
Baker, D., 805
Baker, Eva, 192
Baker, Houston, 329
Bakhtin, Mikel, 298
Balboa, Vasco de, 350
Baldwin, James, 329, 330, 349, 350

Ball, D., 780
Banff Conference, xvi, 226, 229
Banks, James A., 323, 324, 331, 777
Bannet, Eva Tavor, 458
Bantu (the), 818
Barber, Michael, 832
Barnes, D., 764
Barnieh, Z., 558
Baron, Daniel, 257
Barone, Thomas, 53, 259, 292, 553, 569,
    574, 575, 733, 740, 741
Barritt, L., 408
Barrow, Robin, 37, 46, 64, 168, 173, 190,
    196, 200, 202, 203, 204, 205, 206, 230,
    661, 685, 699, 732, 745, 756, 774, 791
Barrows, Alice, 109
Barth, F., 348
Barth, R., 188
Barthes, Roland, 295, 436, 437, 486, 495,
    574
Barton, Len, 229, 243, 247, 266
Bash, J., 288
Bassock, M., 713
Bateman, Donald R., xviii, 218, 219, 220,
    221, 222, 227
Bath, Stephen, 409
Baudrillard, Jean, 297, 451, 471, 472, 474,
    475, 511
Bauer, Gary, 619
Bauhaus, 577, 578
Bauman, Z., 411
Bay Area, 210
Bayer, A., 367
Beattie, Catherine, 54, 737
Beauchamp, E., 804
Beauchamp, George A., 168, 169, 202, 745
Beck, Clive, 659
Beck, Frances, 392
Beck, I., 780
Beck, R., 198
Beecher, Catherine, 360
Beecher, Lyman, 610
Beedy, J., 635
Beegle, Charles W., 219, 224, 288, 763
Beineke, J., 114, 133
Belanger, Maruice, 191, 192
Belenky, M., 368, 391
Belgium, 818
Bell, Clive, 579
Bell, R., 197
Bellack, Arno A., 143, 156, 173, 176, 199,
    202
Belland, John, 705
Bem, S., 366
Ben-Peretz, Miriam, 746
Benham, Barbara, 212
Benjamin, Jessica, 356
Benjamin, Walter, 248
Bennett, Kathleen P., 533
Bennett, William, 154, 570, 608, 619, 632,
    680

Bennison, A., 761
Benstock, S., 545
Bentley, Eric, 596
Bentley, M., 288
Bereday, George, 833
Bereiter, C., 704, 705, 713, 716
Bergamo Conference, xvi, 211, 226, 229,
    279, 588, 599, 600, 644
Bergman, Ingmar, 444
Bergson, Henri, 653, 654
Berk, Laura, 788, 789, 790
Berk, Leonard, 554
Berky, Bob, 597, 598
Berlak, Ann, 388, 390
Berlin University, 71, 810
Berlowitz, Marvin, 318, 352
Berman, E., 320
Berman, Louise M., 15, 168, 173, 174, 184,
    199, 427, 433, 699, 735
Berman, P., 700
Berney, M., 761
Bernstein, Basil, 243
Bernstein, M., 700
Bernstein, Richard, 424
Bernu, Mark, xvi
Berry, K., 601
Berry, Thomas, 658
Berry, Wendell, 288, 289
Best, S., 450, 451, 472, 474
Bestor, Arthur, 146, 152, 153, 754
Bettleheim, Bruno, 150
Beyer, Landon E., 44, 208, 249, 265, 268,
    278, 308, 516, 569, 570, 572, 578, 579,
    580, 595, 603, 750, 755, 758, 761, 762,
    850
Bérubé, M., 451
Bhabha, H., 839
Bible, 33, 543, 614, 640, 642, 648, 819
Biddle, B., 746
Bierstedt, R., 777
Billett, R. O., 198
Binet, Alfred, 90
Binkley, M., 798
Biological Sciences Curriculum Study
    (BSCS), 162, 163, 682
Birney, C., 320
Bitzer, Don, 711
Black Muslims, 321
Black, Hugo, 616
Blackburn, R., 326
Bleich, David, 436, 516
Bloch, Ernst, 652, 654
Block, Alan A., 286, 287, 303, 434, 475, 850
Bloom, Allan, 96, 153, 154, 269, 633, 671
Bloom, Benjamin, 71, 150, 155, 166, 167,
    206, 486, 487, 488, 734
Bloom, Harold, 660
Blumenfeld-Jones, Donald, 603, 604, 830
Boals, Kay, 368
Boateng, Felix, 331, 347, 348

Bobbitt, Franklin, 10, 11, 14, 26, 27, 31, 33,
    34, 35, 36, 37, 38, 39, 40, 63, 70, 77,
    90, 96, 97, 98, 99, 100, 102, 114, 117,
    118, 119, 121, 122, 124, 125, 130, 140,
    184, 500, 682, 687, 860, 863, 865
Bode, Boyd, 117, 118, 124, 131, 132, 143,
    150, 236, 237, 859, 860
Boff, Leonardo, 643, 646
Bogart, Humphrey, 468, 471
Bolin, Frances, 111, 112, 137, 262, 699, 700,
    701, 702, 704, 721
Bolivia, 826, 828, 829
Bollnow, Otto, 432, 433
Bolshevik revolution (1917), 835
Bolsheviks, 836
Bond, Horace Mann, 12, 128
Bond, Julian, 128
Bondi, J., 11, 18, 19, 21, 23, 48, 198, 720
Bonner, K., 409
Books, Sue, 631, 634, 650
Boorstin, Daniel J., 797, 819
Boostrom, R., 54, 248, 635
Borrowman, M., 755
Boru, K., 256
Bosner, Frederick, 121
Bossing, N., 698
Boston Quarterly Review, 610
Boston University, 682, 683, 708
Botswana, 818, 822
Bourne, Randolph, 109
Bowers, C. A., 13, 129, 185, 199, 255, 265,
    266, 270, 271, 272, 273, 274, 275, 276,
    280, 288, 311, 314, 704, 715, 716, 731,
    732, 841, 856, 859
Bowler, R., 733
Bowles, S., 244, 245, 247, 252, 266, 270, 271,
    318
Bowman, A., 643
Boy George, 375
Boy Scouts, 829
Boyd, William Lowe, 163, 207, 208, 665, 666
Boyer, Ernest L., 616, 757
Boyle, C., 713
Brahe, Tycho, 499
Brameld, Theodore, 122, 130, 228, 799, 800
Brandeis University, 821
Brandt, Ron, 615, 616
Brannon, R., 365
Braverman, H., 95, 365
Brazil (Brazilian), 230, 826, 827, 828, 829
Brecht, 597
Bridges, T. , 310, 325, 326
Briggs, L., 167
Brigham Young University, 711
Brinkhaus, Celeste, xv
Britain, Great (British; see also England), 71,
    94, 152, 168, 202, 203, 205, 206, 243,
    252, 331, 332, 345, 731, 732, 733, 766,
    794, 795, 818, 819, 820, 824, 828, 831,
    832, 833

British Columbia Teachers Federation, 229, 763
British Columbia, 410
British East India Company, 797
British Humanities Curriculum Project, 726
Britzman, Deborah P., 335, 359, 393, 524, 525, 547, 557, 760, 765, 770, 771
Brodkey, L., 391
Brodribb, S., 468
Brogan, P., 46
Brookbank, G., 215, 218
Brooks, G., 198
Brooks, J., 56
Brooks, M., 56
Broudy, Harry, 169, 170, 202, 569, 570, 581
Brown University, 670, 672, 708
Brown v. Board of Education, 300
Brown, Clair, 102, 677
Brown, J., 747
Brown, Norman O., 182
Brown, Robert K., 426, 437
Brown, Theodore, 12
Brown, W., 698
Brownell, John A., 170, 198
Brownson, Orestes, 610, 611
Brubaker, D., 215, 218
Bruckerhoff, Charles, 684
Brueggemann, Walter, 631
Bruner, Jerome, 159, 160, 161, 164, 184, 499, 501
Bryan, William Jennings, 778
Bryson, Mary, 281, 359
Buchanan, Patrick, 636
Buchmann, M., 765
Buetow, H., 610
Bulhan, H., 328
Bull, J., 365
Bullock, H., 320
Bullough, Jr., Robert, 4, 43, 131, 187, 249, 292, 581, 684, 761, 859
Bunderson, Victor, 711
Bunyan, John, 517
Burch, Robert, 408
Burke, Melva, 218
Burlbaw, L., 777
Burleigh, M., 811
Burn, B., 802
Burnett, Joe, 169, 170
Burnett, Lewie W., 698
Burns, J., 820
Burns, R., 198
Burton, E., 733
Burton, William, 210, 225
Bush, George, 292, 366, 662, 673, 676, 678
Bussis, A., 701, 702
Butler, Judith, 359
Butler, Nicholas Murry, 103
Butt, Richard, 40, 221, 334, 335, 516, 523, 548, 553, 554, 555, 556, 561, 562, 563, 564, 691, 720, 765, 766
Bybee, Roger, 718, 719, 778

Byo, Y., 823, 824
Byrnes, Robert F., 836
Byron, Lord, 691

Cable News Network (CNN), 228, 512
Caccamise, F., 530
Cajuns, 347
California Textbook League, 776
Callahan, R., 95
Callan, E., 126, 203
Calvinists, 71, 517
Cambridge Journal of Education, 545
Cambridge School (Massachusetts), 540, 544
Campbell, Carroll, 399
Campbell, Doak, 11, 15, 26, 102, 139, 141, 143
Campbell, Donald, 735
Canada (Canadian), 44, 168, 219, 228, 287, 326, 584, 586, 709, 791, 795, 796, 837, 838, 839, 840, 842
Canizares, A. , 503
Capote, Truman, 542
Caputo, J., 447, 448
Carby, Hazel, 339, 339, 356
Cardinal Principles of Education, 99, 114, 789
Caribbean, 344, 794, 826
Carlson, Dennis, 244, 260, 261, 362, 402, 427, 770, 771
Carlson, R., 367
Carmody, Denise Lardner, 655
Carnegie Foundation, 134, 158, 159, 188, 616, 761
Carnoy, Martin, 250, 270, 677, 678
Carr, W., 54, 58, 289
Carroll, B., 367
Carroll, John, 167
Carson, Terrance R., 52, 54, 283, 289, 409, 410, 426, 672, 684, 744, 760, 830, 837, 840, 842, 857
Carter, K., 764
Carthaginian Empire, 818
Casassus, Juan, 675
Casey, Kathleen, 390, 528, 529, 530, 606, 768
Casteel, J., 189
Castenell, Jr., Louis A., xiv, 23, 323, 327, 328, 329, 330, 338, 349, 354
Castro, Fidel, 829
Caswell, Hollis, 11, 15, 26, 27, 96, 102, 111, 112, 139, 140, 141, 143, 704
Catholic University of America, 611
Cawelti, Gordon, 211
Caws, Peter, 456, 458
Cazden, C., 64, 746, 784
Center for Advanced Study in the Behavioral Sciences, 151
Center for Civic Education (CCE), 618
Center for Critical Thinking and Moral Critique, 772
Center for Process Studies, 653

Center for Research on Women (Wellesley College), 367
Center for the Study of Democratic Institutions, 194
Central America, 643, 793, 803, 826, 828
Centre for Contemporary Cultural Studies (UK), 850
Chamberlin, D., 137, 138, 702
Chamberlin, E., 137, 138
Chamberlin, Sandy, 692
Channel One, 709
Chapman, D., 793
Charlesworth, Rosalind, 850
Charlton, Kenneth, 202
Charters, W. W., 15, 98, 100, 101, 102, 106, 117, 118, 121, 124, 125, 140, 150, 687
Chazan, Barry, 627, 629, 630
Chelsea, Massachusetts, 682, 683
Chen, D., 715
Chen, T. H., 815
Cheney, B., 198
Cheney, Lynne, 673, 679, 757, 803
Cherokee, 316
Cherryholmes, Cleo, 45, 186, 195, 251, 291, 311, 450, 453, 485, 486, 487, 488, 489, 490, 500, 514, 628, 780, 863
Cheru, F., 820
Chesler, Phyllis, 366
Chiarelott, Leigh, 126, 446
Chicago Conference (ASCD, 1969), 208, 210, 239
Chicano, 210
Childs, John L., 116, 117, 133
Chile, 675, 828, 830
China (Chinese), 316, 345, 733, 796, 797, 807, 814, 815, 816, 817
China (Peoples' Republic of), 187, 806
Chira, Susa, 804, 806
Chittenden, E., 701, 702
Chodorow, Nancy, 368, 369, 374, 375, 401
Christian, Barbara, 342
Christian-Smith, Linda, 58, 306, 365, 370, 386, 394, 395, 617
Ciardi, John, 407
Cicero, 25
City University of New York, 152
Civil War, 72, 316, 469, 610, 776
Cixous, H., 369, 495
Clancey, W., 712
Clandinin, D. Jean, 37, 40, 54, 425, 515, 516, 524, 525, 553, 554, 555, 556, 557, 558, 559, 560, 561, 562, 563, 564, 565, 702, 747, 760, 765, 766, 855
Claremont Colleges, 653
Clark, C., 765
Clark, R. J., 761
Clarke, Edward, 362
Clark University, 76, 88, 96, 362
Cleaver, Elridge, 339
Clifford, Geraldine Joncich, 91, 92, 93, 390
Clift, R., 674

Clinical supervision, 724
Coalition for Essential Schools (CES), 138, 670, 672, 673
Cockburn, Victor, 586
Cogan, Morris, 723, 724
Cohen, David, 202, 697
Cohen, Marshall A., 673
Cohen, S., 74
Cohn, E., 822
Cold War (the), 794
Cole, A., 553
Coleman Report, 622
Coleman, J., 365
Coleman, James, 622, 623, 624
Colgate University, 99
College Board (the), 772
Collins, A., 747
Collins, Patricia Hill, 340, 341, 350
Collins, Roger, 346, 347, 348
Collins, S., 371
Columbia, 826, 828
Columbia University, 92, 107, 108, 113, 118, 225
Columbus, Christopher, 350
Comenius, Johann Amos, 810
Comer, James, 331, 351
Commager, Henry Steele, 151
Commission on Current Curriculum Developments (ASCD), 164, 165
Commission on Curriculum Theory (ASCD), 173, 183
Commission on English, 163
Commission on Instructional Theory (ASCD), 173
Commission on the Relation of School to College (PEA), 134
Commission on the Reorganization of Secondary Education, 99, 100
Committee of Fifteen, 71, 75, 76, 77, 82, 84, 89
Committee of Ten, 71, 75, 76, 77, 84, 89, 93, 99, 110, 679
Committee on College Entrance Requirements, 75, 77
Committee on Racial Well-Being (NEA), 94
Committee on the Economy of Time, 94, 97
Common, Diane, 674, 702, 704, 720
Commonwealth of Independent States (the), 835
Communist Party, 9, 814, 815, 816, 833, 834, 835, 836, 837
Computer Curriculum Instruction, 711
Computer-assisted instruction (CAI), 710, 711, 712, 713, 716
Computer-assisted learning (CAL), 710
Computer-based education (CBE), 710
Computer-based instruction (CBI), 710, 714
Conant, James Bryant, 145, 158, 188, 755
Concerned Women for America, 779
Concerns-Based Adoption Model (CBAM), 704

Confucius, 492, 797, 807
Congo, 822
Congo River, 818
Congress, 207
Conlon, J., 779
Connell, W. , 814, 817
Connelly, F. Michael, 37, 40, 54, 425, 515, 516, 524, 525, 553, 554, 555, 556, 557, 558, 559, 560, 561, 562, 563, 564, 565, 688, 702, 747, 765, 766, 855
Connors, B., 54
Control Data Corporation, 711, 712
Convey, J., 611
Cook, R., 191
Cook, W., 198
Coombs, P., 829
Coomer, Donna, 742
Copeland, Aaron, 867
Copernicus University (Torun), 835
Copernicus, Nicolaus, 499, 799, 803
Coptic Christian Church, 818
Cornbleth, Catherine, 244, 256
Cornell University, 690
Cornett, J., 54
Correlation of Studies Subcommittee, 82
Corrigan, Philip, 294
Cortes, Carlos E., 347
Cortes, H., 350
Corwin, R., 722
Costa Rica, 828
Council for Cultural Cooperation, 813
Council for the Advancement of Citizenship (CAC), 618
Council of Europe, 813
Council of Trent, 639
Councils of Baltimore, 611
Counts, George S., 12, 45, 90, 119, 120, 121, 122, 126, 127, 128, 129, 131, 139, 149, 150, 186, 228, 243, 325, 799, 800, 836
Court, David, 821, 822
Courtney, Richard, 332, 333
Cousins, Norman, 133
Coward, Jr., Russell H., 335
Craig, T., 589
Crandall, D., 700
Craver, S., 799, 800
Cremin, Lawrence, 27, 69, 70, 82, 84, 86, 87, 88, 94, 99, 102, 103, 107, 110, 114, 118, 119, 121, 129, 130, 143, 191, 607, 608, 779
Crichlow, Warren, 296, 315, 317, 326, 337, 354, 357, 785
Crittenden, B., 270
Cronbach, Lee, 53, 150, 202, 733, 776
Crosby, Muriel, 209, 239
Cuba, 826, 828, 829, 830
Cuban, Larry, 102, 203, 207, 679, 682, 753, 754, 755, 855
Cubberley, Ellwood, 73, 75, 78, 79, 80
Culler, Jonathan, 452
Culley, M., 368, 478

Cultural Revolution (the), 814, 815, 817
Cummings, W., 796, 797
Cummins, Catherine, 719
Cunningham, B., 428
Curriculum Development Task Force (NIE), 207
Curriculum Inquiry, xiii, 557
Curriculum Journal, 141
Curriculum Perspectives, 793
Curriculum Research Institute (ASCD), 178
Curtis, B., 69
Cushman, Kathleen, 662, 671
Cutright, Prudence, 142

Dahllof, Urban, 202
Dahomeyan, 316
Daigle, Kevin, 535
Daignault, Jacques, 45, 217, 450, 480, 481, 482, 483, 484, 485, 491, 492, 494, 496, 501, 516, 536, 537, 847, 852, 856
Dale, Edgar, 707
Dale, M., 251, 269, 270
Dale, R. 833
Daley, Richard, 209
Dalhousie University, 287
Dall, Catherine, 361
Dalton School, 135
Daly, Mary, 305, 366, 367, 368, 388, 552, 655
Daniel, D., 410
Daniels, A., 366
Dantley, Michael, 318
Darling-Hammond, Linda, 51, 672, 727, 728, 756, 761, 770
Darrow, Clarence, 778
Dartmouth Conference (1966), 588
Darwin, Charles (Darwinian theory, etc.), 79, 88, 89, 94, 103, 424, 634
da Silva, T. , 287
Daughters of Bilitis, 396, 397
David, D., 365
Davies, P., 653, 658, 659
Davis, Brent, 424, 425
Davis, Jr., O. L., 11, 16, 197, 777, 855
Davis, Timothy, 291
De Castell, Suzanne, 281, 359
De Garmo, Charles, 80, 87, 103
Dealey, James Q., 104
de Beauvoir, Simone, 364
de Beaugrande, R., 383
DeBoer, George, 718
DeBord, Guy, 472
Deem, R., 341
Deever, B., 347
De Gama, Vasco, 350
DeKock, Anita, 800
Deleuze, Gilles, 451, 452, 464, 467, 468, 477, 480, 482, 491, 492, 493, 508
DelFattore, J., 777
Delgado-Gaitan, C., 287, 316, 333, 784
Delpit, Lisa, 334

de Man, Paul, 451
DeMicker, Steven, 389
Dendral, 712
Deng, Xiaoping, 816, 817
Denscombe, M., 746
Dentler, R., 331
Denton, David, 753
Denver Curriculum Revision Project, 71, 111, 112, 143, 701
Department of Supervisors and Directors of Instruction (NEA), 142
Derman-Sparks, Louise, 334
Derrida, Jacques, 7, 8, 49, 295, 301, 348, 355, 436, 447, 448, 450, 451, 464, 465, 466, 467, 468, 470, 477, 480, 481, 486, 488, 492, 494, 508, 511, 538, 574
Descartes, René, 456, 499, 509, 603, 640
Descombes, Vincent, 447, 451, 452, 453, 454, 455, 456, 457, 460, 461, 466, 468
Dewey Laboratory School, 107, 115
Dewey, Alice, 107
Dewey, Evelyn, 109
Dewey, John, 8, 14, 26, 40, 45, 79, 81, 82, 83, 84, 86, 91, 94, 100, 103, 104, 105, 106, 107, 108, 109, 110, 115, 116, 117, 118, 119, 121, 124, 125, 126, 127, 128, 129, 130, 131, 132, 133, 134, 141, 149, 150, 151, 152, 153, 164, 175, 177, 184, 189, 194, 195, 198, 202, 237, 275, 321, 446, 499, 501, 523, 562, 569, 570, 571, 572, 582, 593, 594, 605, 628, 629, 652, 654, 659, 678, 682, 691, 750, 755, 774, 775, 793, 804, 806, 851, 855, 858, 859, 860, 865, 866, 867
Deyhle, D., 316, 333, 784
Diamond, C., 553
Diawara, M., 350
Dick, Andreas, 755, 769
Dicker, M., 54
Dickinson, Emily, 402
Dillard University, 128
Dilthey, Wilhelm, 196, 642
Diop, Cheikh Anta, 322
Diorio, J., 401
Dippo, Don, 58, 589
Disch, R., 329
Disney, Walt, 471
Dixon, George, 627
Dixon, P., 761
Dmitriyev, Grigory, 836, 837
Dobson, J., 417, 696
Dobson, Russell, 417, 696
Dogan, M., 809
Doi, James, 218
Dolan, Lawrence, 741
Doll, Jr., William E., xv, xvi, 45, 103, 126, 199, 325, 450, 451, 497, 498, 499, 500, 501, 502, 504, 509, 540, 572, 573, 653, 659, 691, 831, 847, 859, 860, 867
Doll, Mary Aswell, 518, 540, 541, 542, 543, 544, 856

Doll, Ronald C., 11, 18, 19, 21, 22, 23, 48, 70, 191, 239
Doll, Will, 540, 541, 543
Donato, R., 324
Donmoyer, Robert, 52, 53, 54, 56, 589, 735, 740, 741, 850
Dorsey, M., 821, 822
Doty, A., 359
Douglas, William O., 616
Douglas, A., 361
Dow, P., 779
Downer, D., 726
Doyle, C., 589
Doyle, Denis P., 671
Doyle, Walter, 661, 745, 746, 747, 748, 775, 780
Dravidian India, 322
Dreeben, Robert, 27, 248, 269, 270
Drought, N., 137, 138
DuBois, W. E. B., 12, 320, 321, 323, 350, 352
Duckworth, Eleanor, 763
Duffy, F., 728
Duguid, P., 747
Dukacz, A., 688
Duke, Benjamin, 833
Dumont, Jr., R., 316, 785
Duncan, James, 179, 191, 563
Dunkel, H. 79, 80
Dunkin, M., 746
Duquette, C., 758
Durkheim, Emile, 630
Durkin, D., 780
Dutch, 428
Dwyer, D., 768
Dyke, Doris, 199
Dyson, Michael Eric, 789, 790

Eagleton, Terry, 436, 453, 458
Earth Summit (1992), 829
Easley, Jr., J., 736
East Africa, 819
Eastern Europe, 801, 832, 833, 835, 842
Eastman Kodak Company, 708
Ebeling, Michael, 586, 587, 588, 600, 759, 784, 854
Ebert, Teresa, 511, 512
Ecuador, 828
Edefelt, R., 763
Edelin, Ramona, 351, 352, 357
Edelsky, C., 287, 850
Edgerton, Susan Huddleston, xvi, 336, 337, 346, 356, 420, 497, 517, 533, 850
Edison Project, 680
Edsall, M., 330
Edsall, T., 330
Education Reform Act (1988), 831, 832
Education Week, 617
Educational Leadership, 142, 615, 616, 836
Educational Research Bulletin, 150
Educational Researcher, 231, 234, 235

Educational Theory, xiii
Educators for Social Responsibility, 803
Edwards, Ann Camp, 107, 108
Edwards, Tony, 831, 832
Efland, A., 568
Egan, Kieran, 197, 198, 206, 237, 567, 571, 684, 690, 691, 692, 693, 694, 867
Egypt, 818, 819
Eight-Year Study, 110, 111, 133, 135, 136, 137, 138, 144, 148, 149, 150, 151, 157, 679, 701, 702, 754
Eisner, Elliot W., 3, 14, 17, 18, 19, 21, 27, 29, 30, 31, 35, 44, 45, 52, 53, 58, 91, 101, 156, 171, 182, 183, 184, 189, 193, 200, 201, 233, 320, 394, 412, 418, 515, 559, 562, 567, 569, 573, 580, 581, 583, 584, 604, 663, 680, 732, 734, 735, 736, 737, 738, 739, 740, 741, 742, 743, 744, 751, 752, 766, 775, 850, 857, 863
El Karaocrine, 818
El Salvador, 838
Elam, Stanley, 161
Elbaz, Freema, 37, 539, 553, 554, 556, 557, 562, 748, 760
Elbaz, R., 539
Elementary and Secondary Education Act (EESA, 1965), 159, 174
Elementary School Science Project, 163
Eliot, Charles W., 70,75, 76, 110, 153
Eliot School Controversy, 610
Eliot, T. S., 205, 542, 544, 606
Elliott, D., 776
Elliott, John, 563, 798, 799
Ellison, Ralph, 336
Ellsworth, Elizabeth, 266, 279, 280, 281, 284, 285, 303, 304, 305, 311, 312, 337, 340, 358, 384, 386, 388, 391, 392, 506, 508, 528, 695, 856
Elmore, Richard, 23, 163, 665, 666, 667, 668, 679
Elshtain, Jean, 379
Elson, Ruth, 775, 779
Ely, D., 705
Emerson, Ralph Waldo, 133, 660, 691
Emoungu, Paul-Albert, 822
Empathy, 397
Engels, Friedrich, 250
England (English; see also Britain), 154, 189, 691, 733, 795, 797, 798, 804, 827, 832, 838
England, David, 777
Engle, Shirley, 82, 291, 689, 704
English, Fenwick, 732
Enlightenment (Age of), 810, 832
Ennis, Robert, 773
Enright, D. Scott, 763
Entebbe Mathematics Project, 824
Entwistle, Noel, xv
Epstein, I., 817
Erdman, Jean, 392
Erickson, Bob, 803

Erickson, Donald, 622
Erickson, Frederick, 53, 64, 316, 527, 746, 781, 782, 783, 784, 785
Erickson, G., 765
Erikson, Eric, 178, 628
ESL (English as a second language), 437, 801, 838
Essien-Udom, E., 322
Estes, William, 711
Estrada, K., 354
Ethiopia, 818, 820, 821
Europe (European), 316, 795, 796, 797, 820, 828, 833, 850
European Common Market, 813, 842
European Educational Reform Movement, 811
Evaluation Quarterly, 736
Everhart, R., 246
Ezeomah, C., 824

Fafunwa, A., 320
Fahlman, L., 410
Fairhope (Alabama) School of Organic Education, 113
Falmer Press, 71, 793
Falsey, B., 622
Fanon, Frantz, 330
Fantini, Mario, 17, 190, 191
Farrar, E., 697
Farrell, J., 635
Favaro, Basil, 410, 432
Featherstone, J., 188
Featherstone, William F., 153, 154
Federbush, M., 365
Feigenbaum, E. A., 712
Feiman-Nemser, S., 780
Feinberg, P., 212
Feinberg, Walter, 102, 750, 761, 762, 804, 839, 843, 850
Feldman, D., 365
Felman, S., 479
Fensham, Peter J., 717, 718, 719
Fensterhacher, Gary, 748
Ferrell, P., 54
Feyerabend, Paul, 473
Feyereisen, K., 198
Fieldston School, 135
Figgins, Margo A., xiv, 517, 569, 581, 586, 587, 588, 589, 599, 600, 601, 603, 759, 784, 854, 860
Fiji, 322
Fillmore, L., 316, 317
Fine, Michelle, 391, 679
Finkelstein, James, 235
Finn Jr., Chester, 619, 633, 673, 674, 680
Fiorino, A., 198
Firestone, Shulamith, 364, 366
First Amendment, 299, 300
First Civic High School (Warsaw), 834, 835
First Peoples (First Nations), 349

First World (the), 795, 801, 807
Firth, Gerald, 197, 208
Fisher, E., 365
Fisk University, 321
Fiske, Edward, 12, 96, 99, 293, 620
FitzGerald, F., 777, 780
Flamini, Michael, xviii
Flannery, O. P., A., 643
Flax, J., 451
Flexner, Abraham, 110, 114
Flinders, David J., 27, 731, 753
Fonow, M., 402
Fontaine, William T., 352
Ford, G. W., 160
Ford, Gerald, 366
Fordham, S., 784
Foreign Language Program, 163
Forkner, Hamden L., 144
Fort Valley State College, 128
Fortune, 188
Forum, 88, 90
Foshay, Anglea, 745
Foshay, Arthur, 129, 139, 187, 190, 198, 687, 704, 745, 756
Foster, M., 516, 678, 761
Foucault, Michel, 8, 45, 308, 335, 355, 373, 374, 395, 447, 451, 457, 459, 461, 462, 463, 465, 476, 478, 480, 486, 488, 492, 495, 506, 508, 514, 538
Foundation for Critical Thinking, 772
Fowler, James, 628, 629
Fox, Matthew, 639, 640, 655
France (French), 152, 229, 451, 452, 630, 683, 716, 794, 795, 802, 810, 818, 828, 838
Francis W. Parker School, 113, 115, 135, 138
Frank, Jerome, 301
Frankena, William K., 202
Frankenstein, C., 522
Frankenstein, Marilyn, 262, 850
Frankfurt School, 247, 248, 261, 262, 281, 290, 314, 813
Franklin, Barry, 42, 69, 91, 96, 101, 140, 779
Franklin, Benjamin, 85
Fraser, Barry, 734, 735, 736, 737, 738
Fraser, D., 162
Fraser, N., 292
Frasher, R., 365
Frazier, Alexander, 53, 178, 192, 209, 210, 222, 239
Frazier, N., 365
Freedman, Kerry, 580
Freedman, Samuel, 634
Freedmen's Bureau, 616
Freeman, D., 780
Freemasons, 802
Freinet, Celestin, 586
Freire, Paulo, xviii, 221, 230, 254, 262, 263, 272, 273, 280, 287, 366, 392, 634, 643, 644, 645, 647, 781, 826, 827, 828
French, R., 727

Freud, Sigmund, 185, 233, 234, 329, 336, 338, 456, 460, 472, 541, 632
Frey, K., 793, 810
Friedan, Betty, 364
Friedenberg, Edgar, 287, 691
Froebel, F., 86
Fromm, Erich, 174, 178, 189, 654
Frontiers of Democracy, 129
Frye, N., 456
Frymier, Jack, 179, 191, 192, 198, 563, 776, 780
Fuhrman, S., 732
Fujita, Mikio, 431, 445, 446
Fullan, Michael, 699, 700, 702, 704, 763, 764, 850
Fuller, Buckminster, 398
Fuss, Diane, 505

Gabler, Norma and Mel, 777
Gadamer, Hans-Georg, 301, 420, 424, 425, 641, 642, 643
Gage, Nathaniel, 63, 64, 735, 752
Gagel, C., 717
Gagné, Robert M., 167, 202
Gaines, Ernest, 535
Galileo, 499, 572
Gall, Meredith G., 687
Gallagher, James, 718
Gallas, Karen, 586
Gallup Poll, 790, 804
Galton Society, 94
Galton, Francis, 94
Gambia, 818
Gang of Four (China), 816
Garcia, R., 509
Gardner, Howard, 509, 695, 757
Garfinkle, N., 779
Garibaldi, Antoine, 331
Garman, Noreen, xiv, 215, 720, 724, 725, 728, 729, 730
Garvey, Marcus, 321
Gary Plan, 109, 110, 114, 203
Garza-Lubeck, M., 777
Gaskell, J., 250
Gates, Jr., Henry Louis, 313, 314, 316, 317, 336, 351, 514, 545, 867
Gauthier, Clermont, 45, 54, 217, 491, 746
Gawronski, J., 714
General Education Board, 134
Genet, Jean, 454, 464
Gentry-Akin, D., 657
George Peabody College, 142
George School, 135, 138
Germantown Friends School, !35
Germany (German), 80, 81, 84, 152, 229, 433, 671, 683, 691, 793, 794, 795, 802, 809, 810, 811, 812, 813, 818, 828, 848
Gershman, Kathleen W., 627, 634, 652, 653, 658, 691, 859
Geske, Terry, 822

Getty Foundation, 580
Ghana (Gold Coast), 818
Giacquinta, J., 700
Gibson, M., 316
Gibson, M., 784
Gibson, R., 290, 516
Gideonse, H., 753
Gilchrist, Robert, 164
Giles, H., 137
Gilligan, Carol, 369, 391, 549, 628, 629
Gilmore, P., 784
Ginsburg, M., 758
Gintis, Herbert, 244, 245, 247, 252, 266,
    270, 271, 318
Giroux, Henry A., xv, 44, 70, 96, 215, 245,
    246, 247, 248, 249, 250, 251, 252, 253,
    254, 255, 257, 258, 260, 261, 262, 263,
    265, 266, 267, 268, 269, 270, 272, 276,
    277, 278, 279, 280, 281, 282, 283, 284,
    285, 286, 287, 290, 292, 296, 303, 304,
    306, 307, 308, 310, 311, 312, 314, 320,
    339, 353, 354, 400, 401, 496, 497, 498,
    506, 507, 508, 509, 572, 632, 633, 673,
    674, 682, 763, 784, 831, 839, 850, 853,
    854
Gitlin, Andrew, 256, 506, 513, 684, 726, 727,
    742, 743
Glanz, Jeffrey, 69, 70, 113, 721, 722
Glaser, R., 713
Glasnost (the), 835
Glasser, William, 126, 189
Glazer, N., 348
Glenn, Charles L., 833, 834, 835
Glickman, C., 724, 727, 728, 729
Global Studies Resource Center, 803
GNP (gross national product), 807
God, 133, 614, 622, 625, 639, 645, 647, 651,
    656, 657, 659, 862
Goethe, 420, 579
Goldberg, D., 328
Goldenberg, C., 714
Goldhammer, Robert, 723, 724
Goldman, Ralph F., 191
Goldstein, Stanley L., 249, 581, 742, 743
Golle, John T., 680
Gomez, Jewelle, 341, 342
Gonzales-Echeuarria, R., 830
Good, Ronald, 56, 719, 850
Goodlad, John, 27, 28, 65, 163, 165, 192,
    198, 202, 243, 271, 635, 686, 688, 689,
    696, 697, 698, 716, 755, 757, 776, 855
Goodman, Jesse, 256, 257, 258, 259, 292,
    365, 376, 386, 396, 399, 400, 401, 402,
    574, 672
Goodman, Paul, 221
Goodrich, Samuel G., 610
Goodson, Ivor F., 37, 42, 69, 71, 425, 516,
    553, 554, 556, 560, 562, 563, 564, 671,
    765, 769, 793, 855
Gorbachev, Mikhail, 835, 836
Gordon, Beverly M., 331, 352, 353, 856

Gordon, David, 3
Gordon, Ira, 173
Gordon, Marshall, 262, 850
Gordon, S., 733
Gore, Albert, 840
Gore, Jennifer, 496
Gotz, I., 431
Gough, Noel, 283, 287
Gouldner, Alvin, 12, 187
Grabiner, E., 299
Grabiner, V., 299
Grady, M., 714
Grafton, A., 77
Graham, G., 190
Graham, P., 110
Graham, Robert, 212, 237, 515, 521, 522,
    546, 562
Grahame, Peter R., 784
Gramsci, Antonio, 233, 250
Grand Canyon, 867
Grannis, Joseph C., 192
Grant, Carl, 334
Grant, Gerald, 60
Grant, Linda, 341
Grant, Madison, 94
Grant Park, 209, 210
Gray, D., 269
Great Depression, 799
Great Leap Forward (China), 815
Greater East Asia Coprosperity Sphere, 808
Greece (Greek), 794, 797, 819
Green, George H., 304
Greene, J., 63
Greene, Maxine, 156, 183, 184,191, 202,
    219, 230, 234, 235, 373, 405, 406, 409,
    434, 567, 568, 570, 573, 576, 577, 580,
    582, 586, 595, 605, 620
Greenfield, Thomas, 743
Greer, E., 780
Greer, Germaine, 364, 365, 366
Gress, James, 24,197
Griffin, Anne Burford, 362
Griffin, David Ray, 469, 657, 659, 831
Griffin, Gary, 728, 756, 763, 770
Grimke, Sarah, 320
Grimmett, P., 720
Gromoll, E., 780
Gropius, Walter, 577, 578
Gross, N., 700
Grossberg, L., 850
Grotowski, Jerzy, 589, 590, 591, 593, 596
Grubb, W., 718
Grumet, Madeleine R., xiv, 34, 40, 41, 43,
    52, 56, 69, 111, 112, 156, 215, 216,
    230, 291, 304, 358, 360, 361, 363, 364,
    370, 374, 375, 376, 377, 378, 379, 380,
    381, 385, 386, 387, 400, 402, 403, 404,
    405, 409, 412, 414, 415, 416, 420, 434,
    435, 436, 437, 437, 453, 495, 515, 516,
    517, 518, 520, 521, 522, 523, 525, 526,
    528, 530, 540, 545, 546, 548, 549, 550,

551, 552, 555, 559, 560, 564, 565, 567, 578, 582, 589, 590, 591, 592, 593, 595, 596, 597, 598, 599, 603, 608, 645, 691, 695, 720, 731, 752, 753, 758, 759, 766, 850, 856, 866
Grundy, Shirley, 719
Guattari, Félix, 451, 452, 464, 491
Guba, Egon, 53, 734, 736, 738
Guidon, 712, 713
Guinea Bissau, 825
Guinea, 818
Gulf War (see also Iraq), 512
Gumport, P., 761
Gunther, Hans F. K. "Rassen", 812
Gutek, Gerald, 817, 824, 830, 835, 836, 840, 841
Guthrie, J., 607
Gutierrez, Gustavo, 643, 644, 645, 648, 649, 650, 651
Gutmann. A., 132
Gwynn, J. Minor, 143, 144, 155, 175

Habermas, Jürgen, 152, 196, 231, 233, 248, 276, 289, 290, 301, 451, 475, 575, 642, 743, 746
Hacker, Andrew, 326, 348
Haft, H., 793
Haftmann, Werner, 576
Haggerson, Nelson, 46, 388, 643, 658, 720, 728, 752
Haight, R., 649, 651
Haiti, 826
Hale-Benson, J., 331
Hales, J., 717
Hall, B., 189
Hall, G. Stanley, 76, 82, 86, 88, 89, 90, 93, 96, 362
Hall, J., 111
Hall, S., 700
Hallinger, P., 728
Hamblen, Karen A., xiv, 568, 569, 570, 603
Hamerow, T. , 316
Hameyer, U., 793
Hamilton, David, 3, 69, 71, 72, 73, 74, 77, 517, 736, 737, 790
Hammer, Rhonda, 304, 305, 306, 511, 796
Hammerschlag, Carl, 660
Hampson, David H., 197
Han, Jong-Ha, 675
Hand, Harold, 153, 198
Hanna, Paul, 778
Hannaway, Jane, 678
Hansen, David, 54, 248, 635
Hansot, Elizabeth, 359, 360, 361, 362,363, 364, 366
Hanvey, Robert, 800
Harap, Henry, 142, 698
Harbo, T., 230
Hargreaves, A., 763, 764, 765, 850
Harlan, L., 320

Harmon, Willis, 191, 192
Harmony School, 256, 257, 258, 259, 399, 401, 672
Harms, N., 719
Harnett, Richard, 475
Harris, A., 367
Harris, Joyce Braden, 351
Harris, Michael, 351
Harris, William Torrey, 76, 77, 82, 83, 86, 87, 108, 153, 191, 359, 361, 682, 706
Harrison, E., 410
Hart, Charles, 672
Hartmann, Mary, 740
Hartnett, A., 335
Hartshorne, Charles, 653
Harvard Committee on the Objectives of Education in a Free Society, 145
Harvard Educational Review, xiii, 281, 320, 586, 773
Harvard University, 110, 297, 362, 534, 543, 707, 827
Hass, G., 197, 198
Hatcher, Richard, 331, 332, 334
Hatfield, Brenda G., 340
Hatton, E., 746
Hawking, S., 659
Hawn, H., 198
Hawthorne, Richard, 225
Hayles, Katherine, 500
Haynes, C., 609, 610, 616
Haynes, N., 331
Hazelwood v. Kuhlmeier, 299
Hazi, Helen, 724, 725, 728
Hazlett, J. Stephen, 69
Headstart, 324
Heap, J., 435
Hearn, W., 733
Hearndon, Angelo, 322
Hearst (newspapers), 778
Heath, R., 162
Heath, Shirley Brice, 58, 60, 348
Heathcoate, Dorothy, 333
Hebrew University of Jerusalem, 629
Heffernan, Helen, 163
Hegel, G. W. F.,78, 104, 105, 304, 456
Heidegger, Martin, 233, 406, 407, 419, 420, 421, 422, 424, 431, 432, 434, 435, 443, 446, 447, 448, 451, 538, 572, 576, 595, 598, 638, 642, 643, 653, 695, 809
Heimann, P., 813
Held, D., 248, 290
Helle, Anita Plath, 549
Hellenger, Wendy
Hellinger, W., 801, 819
Henderson, James, 750, 752
Henkin, R. , 761
Hennelly, A., 650, 827
Henry VIII, 607
Henze, R., 324
Herbart, Johann Friedrich, 78, 79, 80, 87, 160, 810, 811

Herbartians (Herbartianism), 78, 79, 80, 81, 83, 86, 87, 88, 89, 90, 810, 811
Herbert Club, 81
Heritage Foundation, 779
Hermes, 423, 424, 492, 638
Herrick, Virgil, 147, 148, 172, 181, 215
Hertzgaard, M., 470
Heschel, Abraham, 631
Hess, Robert D., 809
Heyns, B. , 622
Hicks, E. , 319
Hicks, W., 198
Higgins, A. , 635
High School Geography Project, 163
Hill, C., 517
Hill, W., 723
Hilliard, Asa, 322
Hills, Jean, 728, 729
Hiratsuka, Masunori, 833
Hirsch, E. D., 96, 153, 154, 269, 298, 301, 570, 619, 671, 674
Hirst, Paul, 202, 203, 731
Hispanic, 340, 344, 346, 348
Hitler, Adolph, 809, 811, 812
Hlebowitsh, Peter S., 63, 111, 132, 149, 212, 236, 237, 270, 523, 642, 719, 752, 857, 865
Hlynka, D., 705, 715
Hocquenghem, Guy, 369, 375
Hoffer, Thomas, 622
Hofstadter, Richard, 146
Hofstein, A., 719
Hogan, D., 783
Holland (Netherlands), 229
Holland, Patricia, 215, 674, 727, 728
Holmes Group, 757, 758, 759, 760, 761
Holmes, B., 820
Holmes, Oliver Wendell, 133
Holt, John, 184, 221, 222
Holt, Ladd, 249
Holt, M., 198
Holt, Rinehart, and Winston, 617
Holton, John, 43
Homer, 467, 543
Honig, Bill, 618
hooks, bell, 508
Hopkins, L. Thomas, 119, 125
Horace Mann School, 113, 114, 135
Horace Mann-Lincoln Institute of School Experimentation, 140
Hord, S., 704
Horkheimer, Max, 248
Hostetler, K., 774
Houghton Mifflin Company, 617
Housego, Ian, 199
Houston, W., 198
Howard, R., 635
Howard, V. A., 586
Howe, Florence, 366
Howe, K., 635
Howey, K., 720

Howley, Aimee, 475
Hoyle, Eric, 202
Huber, Margaret, 156, 157, 178, 181, 182, 184, 189, 212
Huberman, M., 700, 765
Hudak, Glenn, 336, 395
Hudson Institute, 671
Huebner, Dwayne E., 44, 156, 169, 171, 172, 179, 181, 182, 183, 184, 187,189, 196, 202, 210, 212, 213, 214, 215, 218, 219, 220, 227, 232, 233, 235, 243, 410, 417, 418, 419, 421, 443, 517, 548, 568, 573, 576, 577, 592, 606, 627, 628, 629, 653, 654, 849, 857, 860, 861, 862
Huenecke, Dorothy, 740
Hughes, R., 733
Huling-Austin, L., 704
Hull House, 107
Hulsebosch, P., 562
Hulsizer, D., 616
Hultgren, Francine, 426
Hunkins, Frances, 11, 686, 687
Hunsberger, Margaret, 434, 437, 850
Hunt, Maurice P., 199
Hunter, A., 279
Hunter, Madeline, 723, 724, 729, 752, 810
Hunter, W., 567
Hur, S., 410
Hurd, Paul, 719
Hurlbert, M., 850
Husserl, Edmund, 233, 407, 412, 414, 415, 419, 420, 447, 448, 598, 638, 641, 642, 729
Hutchins, Robert Maynard, 150, 153, 194, 195, 269
Huxley, Aldous, 459
Hwu, Wen-Song, xvi, 481, 482, 483, 484, 492, 493, 503
Hybel, Alex Roberto, 794
Hyman, Ronald T., 198
Hymes, D., 784
Hyppolite, Jean, 456

I-B-F Model, 723
Iaccoca, Lee, 329
Ibo, 316
Illich, Ivan, 185
Illinois State Normal School, 80, 81, 82
Imber, Michael, 401
Indian Pastorals, 646
Individualized Prescribed Instruction (IPI), 710
Individually Guided Education (IGE), 710
Inlow, G., 198
Innut, 333
Inquiry: Critical Thinking Across the Disciplines, 771, 772
Institute for Critical Thinking, 771, 772
Institute for the Advancement of Philosophy for Children, 772

Instructional applications of computers (IAC), 710
International Assessment of Educational Progress, 805
International Association for Evaluation of Educational Achievement, 805
International Business Machines (IBM), 711, 714, 740
International Christian School (Tokyo), 833
International Technology Education Association, 717
Inupiat, 783
Iowa Global Education Association (IGEA), 800
Iowa State University, 94, 708
Iraq, 796
Iraq (War against), 228, 796
Ireland (Irish), 316, 733
Irigaray, Luce, 495
Irish Catholic, 609
Ishler, R. , 761
Islamic, 796, 823
Israel, 638
Italy (Italians), 818
Itten, Johannes, 576, 577, 578
Iverson, B., 43
Ives, Charles, 5, 867
Ivory Coast, 818, 822
Ivy League, 110

Jacknicke, Kenneth, 65, 409, 850
Jackson's Mill Industrial Arts Curriculum Symposium, 717
Jackson, Jesse, 261
Jackson, Michael, 339
Jackson, Philip W., xv, 6, 14, 16, 20, 23, 24, 25, 26, 27, 28, 30, 31, 32, 33, 34, 35, 36, 37, 38, 39, 40, 41, 42, 43, 45, 53, 54, 55, 60, 63, 70, 174, 177, 193, 197, 212, 219, 229, 232, 233, 234, 235, 248, 269, 270, 553, 561, 571, 635, 662, 750, 751, 752, 753, 763, 764, 765, 782, 849, 854
Jacob, E., 743
Jacobs, Mary Ellen, 373
Jacoby, Russell, 682
Jaggar, A., 364
Jagla, Virginia, 562, 768
jagodzinski, jan, 490, 569, 572, 602, 603, 610, 839
Jamaica, 733
James, Thomas, 621
James, William, 89, 116, 133
Jameson, Frederic, 450, 451, 469, 470, 471, 472, 473, 474, 504
Japan (Japanese), 154, 422, 521, 581, 603, 671, 789, 794, 795, 804, 805, 806, 807, 808, 809, 832, 833, 848
Japanese-Canadian, 422

Jardine, David W., 409, 412, 413, 423, 431, 441, 446, 448, 638, 747, 784, 850
Jardine, L., 77
Jarrett, J., 627
Jaspers, Karl, 419
JCT, xiii, xvi, 211, 219, 226, 279, 476
Jeanrond, Werner, 638, 639, 640, 641, 642
Jeffcoate, R. , 334, 635
Jefferson, Thomas, 133, 616
Jencks, C., 469, 831
Jenkins, D., 736
Jennings, Frank, 191, 861
Jesus Christ, 612, 638, 647
Jim Crowism (Jim Crow), 361
Jipson, Janice, 384
Jochannan, Yosef ben, 322
Joffee, C., 365
John Dewey Society, 129, 130
John Paul II, 646, 651
Johns Hopkins University, 88, 114, 199
Johnson, Jr., Mauritz, 15, 19, 46, 169, 200, 202, 699
Johnson, Lee, 371, 375
Johnson, Lyndon B., 174
Johnson, Marietta, 113
Johnson, Mark, 560
Johnson, N., 743
Johnston, Jill, 366
Johnston, K., 635
Johnston, Vivien, 783
Johnstone, J., 733
Joint Committee on Curriculum, 142
Joint Committee on Standards for Educational Evaluation, 732
Jones, Thomas Jesse, 231
Jones-Wilson, F., 331
Jordan, Michael, 788
Jordan, W., 338
Joseph, Ellis A., 606, 705, 720, 758
Journal of Curriculum and Supervision, xiii, 721
Journal of Educational Thought, xiii, 793
Journal of Higher Education, 150
Joyce, Bruce R., 190
Joyce, James, 467, 483, 485
Judd, Charles, 119, 121, 122, 136, 150, 745
Judeo-Christian, 864
Judeo-Hebraic, 797
Jung, B., 54
Jung, Carl, 80, 223, 307, 522, 543
Jungck, S., 401, 761

Kah, Gary H., 802, 803
Kahama, C., 820
Kahane, Ernest, 619, 620 , 672
Kallos, D., 230
Kamil, M., 716
Kanawha County (W.Va.), 777, 778
Kanpol, Barry, 252, 306
Kant, Immanuel, 78, 456, 457
Kantner, R., 366, 367

Kantor, Kenneth, 162, 761
Kaplan, L., 774
Karatheodoris, S., 409
Karier, Clarence, 126, 691
Katz, M., 783
Katznelson, I., 783
Kauchak, D., 728
Kaufman, B., 244, 753
Kaufman, G., 244
Kaye, Danny, 542
Kearney, N., 198
Kearns, David, 662
Keddie, Neil, 202
Keita, L., 795
Keith, P. , 700
Kellaghan, Thomas, 136, 732, 733, 734 , 742, 743, 797, 798
Kellner, D. , 450, 451, 472, 474
Kelly, G., 795
Kelly, Thomas, 376, 400
Kelpin, Vangie, 409
Kemmis, Stephen, 54, 58, 289, 766
Kennedy, David, 426
Kennedy, John F., 39, 610, 734
Kenny, R. , 635
Kent State University, 225
Kenya, 818, 819, 820, 822
Kepler, Johann, 499, 572
Kern, June, 785
Kerstein, Katherin, 803
Kessler, H., 698
Kessler, S., 850
Kett, J., 363
Kickbush, K., 246
Kidder, Tracy, 634
Kierkegaard, Sören, 174
Kilgore, Sally, 622
Kilpatrick, William Heard, 14, 114, 115, 116, 117, 118, 121, 123, 129, 131, 198
Kimball, Bruce, 851
Kimpston, R., 169,197
Kincheloe, Joe L., xviii, 52, 57, 64, 289, 290, 291, 294, 296, 307, 328, 331, 350, 351, 411, 472, 503, 507, 509, 510, 512, 532, 533, 534, 625, 644, 645, 650, 671, 676, 746, 762, 763, 770
King, Arthur R., 170, 198
King, Jean, 235
King, Jr., Martin Luther, 355, 678
King, K., 320
King, Nancy, 56
Kingdom, John, 667
Kingsley, Clarence, 99
Kipnis, L., 505
Kirst, Michael W., 202, 666, 679, 682
Kiziltan, M., 503
Klafki, Wolfgang, 810, 813
Kliebard, Herbert M., 12, 26, 29, 30, 31, 42, 69, 70, 74, 79, 81, 82, 89, 90, 91, 92, 95, 96, 98, 99, 100, 101, 102, 103, 104, 105, 108, 111, 114, 117, 119, 120, 121,

122, 129, 130, 134, 136, 137, 139, 141, 142, 143, 144, 146, 153, 154, 157, 176, 183, 184, 186, 187, 202, 207, 212, 221, 320, 364, 608, 626, 661, 663, 671, 685, 745, 755, 854, 857
Klein, M. Frances, 15, 164, 198, 664, 687
Kleine, P., 768
Klohr, Paul R., xviii, 15, 74, 76, 79, 84, 96, 102, 119, 147, 148, 156, 168, 173, 179, 183, 184, 187, 189, 201, 208, 218, 219, 222, 223, 224, 239
Knitter, W., 568, 581
Knowles, J. Gary, 760
Knox College, 631
Kobayaski, V., 808
Koerner, J., 755
Koerner, Mari E., 562, 767, 768
Koetting, J. Randall, 73, 287, 417, 696
Kohl, Herbert, 185
Kohlberg, Lawrence, 77, 88, 192, 205, 628, 629, 630
Komisar, Paul, 173
Konopak, John, 292
Koranic schools (Nigeria), 823
Korea, 409, 808
Kos, R., 850
Kovel, J. , 329
Kozol, Jonathan, 185, 294, 644, 830
Krall, Florence R., 288, 316, 386,388, 516, 535, 545
Krathwohl, David, 71, 155, 166, 487, 734
Kridel, Craig, xv, 42, 69, 110, 131, 135, 137, 138, 183, 758, 850, 854
Kris, E., 522
Kristeva, Julia, 369, 451, 463, 468, 495
Kromhout, R., 719
Krug, E., 76, 91, 99
Kuebart, F., 793
Kuhn, Thomas, 4, 20, 159, 489, 501
Ku Klux Klan, 612
Kundera, Milan, 501
Küng, Hans, 469
Kuomintang Party, 815
Kurth-Schai, Ruthanne, 288
Kuwait, 796
Kwong, J., 816
Kyle, Jr., W., 783

La Noue, George, 191
Lacan, Jacques, 336, 355, 435, 447, 451, 459, 460, 463, 478, 479, 480, 495, 501, 539
Ladwig, J., 264, 765
Laffer, A., 733
LaHaye, Tim, 613
Lai, A., 817
Laing, R. D., 178, 538
Laird, Susan, 362, 390
Lakomski, Gabriele, 269
LaLonde, D., 761
Lamm, Zvi, 192

Landauer, T., 716
Lang, Harry, 531
Langer, Suzanne, 569
Langeveld, M., 409, 428, 440, 441, 445
Langlinais, Elizabeth, xv
Lanier, Judith E., 757
Lankshear, Colin, 1993
Lao-tze, 492
Larson, Eleanore E., 219
Larson, R., 53
Lasch, Christopher, 88, 126, 223, 273, 292, 330, 470, 588, 570, 626, 655, 858
Lather, Patti, 45, 255, 256, 304, 311, 358, 395, 396, 473, 496, 498, 503, 504, 505, 506, 507, 508, 653, 730
Latin America, 230, 643, 646, 648 , 649, 650, 651, 794, 826, 828, 829
Latin, 25
Lauwerys, Joseph, 833
Lave, Jean, 509, 746, 747
Lawler, Marcella, 140
Lawn, Martin, 229, 251, 252
Lawton, D., 202
Layton, Jr., E., 717
Leavitt, H., 756
Lebanon (Lebanese), 410, 838
LeCompte, M., 516
Lee, Doris, 143, 155, 175, 198
Lee, J. Murray, 143, 155, 175, 198
Lee, Yonghwan, xvi
Leeper, Robert, 164, 173, 178, 179
Leitch, Vincent, 850
Leithwood, Keith, 728
Lemmon, Walter, 708
Lemon Test, 613
Lenin, Vladimir, 228, 629, 814, 815, 835, 836
Leo XIII, 646
Leonard, I., 609
Leonard, J., 697
Leonard, P., 262, 263, 827
LePage, A., 654
Lerner, B., 733
Lerner, Gerda, 367
Lesko, Nancy, 58, 60, 395, 432, 496, 785, 787, 788
Lesotho, 820
Levi-Strauss, Claude, 460, 495
Levin, Henry, 270, 621
Levinas, Emmanuel, 464
Lewis, Arthur, 13, 110, 684, 685, 686, 687, 688, 689, 690, 720
Lewis, Catherine C., 804, 806
Lewis, Dan, 677
Lewis, Magda, 386, 387, 393
Lewis, T., 717
Lewy, A., 793, 830
Liberation Theology, 631, 643, 644, 645, 646, 647, 648, 649, 650, 651, 652, 827, 828
Libya, 818

Lickona, T., 635
Lieberman, Ann, 764, 766, 790
Liechtenstein, 810
Lima, E., 826
Lin, Jing, 817
Lincoln School, 113, 114, 135
Lincoln, Yvonna S., 212, 236, 516, 734, 736
Lindsay, Beverly, 825
Lingua, 813
Linn, E., 391
Linneaeus, Carl, 71
Linquist, K., 675
Lipman, Matthew, 772
Lippitz, Wilfried, 444, 445
Lipskey, Michael, 668
Lisman, David C., 625
Liston, Daniel, 245, 247, 266, 267, 268, 270, 755
Little League (baseball), 830
Littleford, Michael, 252, 298
Livingstone, J., 344, 345, 348
Lizhong, Z., 814, 817
Lobdell, P., 113
Locke, John, 499
Lofty, John S., 532
Logo, 712
Lomotey, Kofi, 331, 356
Long March (the), 814
Longstreet, Wilma, 664, 689, 690, 704
Loomis, A. K., 112
Lopez-Caples, Minerva, 439
Lorge, Irving, 194
Loucks, S. , 700
Louisiana State University, xvi, 229
Loving, Sr., Alvin, 239
Lowe, William T., 219
Loyola University (New Orleans), 862
Lucas, T., 324
Luckowski, Jean, 15, 16, 17, 19, 20, 22, 23, 24, 29, 32, 46, 48, 65, 793
Luke, A., 52, 287, 776
Lundestad, Geir, 794
Lundgren, U., 230
Luther, Martin, 612, 625
Luttrell, Wendy, 343, 344, 391
Lydon, Angela, 658
Lynn, Richard, 805, 806
Lyon, Mary, 360
Lyotard, Jean-Francois, 447, 451, 470, 472, 473, 474, 491, 496, 508, 511

Macagnoni, Virginia, 681
Maccia, Elizabeth S., 173
MacConnell, C., 698
Macdonald, B., 736
Macdonald, James B., 19, 44, 46, 124, 165, 172, 173, 177, 178, 179, 180, 181, 182, 183, 184, 189, 210, 211, 212, 215, 216, 217, 218, 219, 227, 228, 231, 243, 371, 386, 387, 388, 603, 627, 628, 629, 630,

631, 648, 654, 658, 684, 685, 715, 752, 857, 860, 862
Macdonald, Susan Colberg, 371, 386, 388
Macedo, Donald, 287, 827
MacGregor, Kim, xiv, 711, 713
Macherey, Pierre, 295
MacIntyre, Alasdair, 633
MacLure, Maggie, 798, 799
Macmillan, xv
Madagascar, 822
Madaus, George F., 136, 732, 733, 734, 742, 743, 797, 798
Mager, Robert F., 166, 167, 199
Magnusson, K., 238
Major, R., 720
Malcolm X, 321
Malen, B., 732
Malen, G., 675
Man: A Course of Study (MACOS), 132, 163, 207, 779
Management by Objectives (MBO), 682
Mander, Jerry, 468, 470, 471, 473
Mann, Horace, 73, 610, 611, 621, 678, 721
Mann, John Steven, 199, 210, 227, 228, 404, 576
Mann, M., 326
Mannheim, Karl, 196
Mao, Zedong, xviii, 187, 228, 815, 816
Marable, M., 323
Marcel, Gabriel, 641
Marcuse, Herbert, 179, 180, 248, 281, 605
Marquard, R., 198
Marsh, Colin, 229, 793
Marshall, Dan, 761
Martel, Angeline, 409, 422, 427, 437
Martin, Jane Roland, 192, 695
Martin-Kniep, G., 746
Martusewicz, Rebecca, 369, 395, 453, 495, 496, 785
Marty, D., 402
Marx, Karl, 105, 121, 129, 185, 186,199, 217, 223, 225, 226, 227, 228, 233, 238, 243, 245, 246, 250, 251, 257, 261, 263, 266, 267, 269, 270, 271, 272, 273, 274, 276, 281, 283, 288, 289, 294, 295, 303, 308, 309, 310, 314, 315, 318, 358, 372, 375, 390, 391, 395, 400, 432, 456, 457, 460, 468, 478, 504, 505, 537, 545, 564, 579, 580, 627, 629, 647, 649, 650, 651, 652, 654, 695, 815, 826, 827, 828, 832, 836, 864
Mary, 612
Masia, Bertram, 166, 734
Maslow, Abraham, 93, 172, 174, 178, 185, 190, 222
Massachusetts Institute of Technology, 708
Mattachine Society, 396, 397
Matthews, M., 719
Matute-Bianchi, M., 327, 345
Mauriel, J., 675
Maxcy, Spencer J., 720, 731, 850

May, Wanda T., 601, 689, 725
Mayhew, Katherine Camp, 107, 108
Mazza, Karen, 212
McAninch, Stuart A., 620
McBride, A., 611
McCall, Ava, 389
McCarthy, Cameron, xiv, 45, 264, 265, 296, 315, 317, 318, 319, 323, 324, 325, 327, 346, 350, 352, 354, 357, 857, 864, 867
McCarthy, Joseph, 596
McCaslin, E., 780
McClintock, Robert, 191, 744, 745, 747, 861
McCue, G., 765
McCutchen, S., 137
McCutcheon, Gail, 13, 54, 740, 741
McDonald, Joseph, 49, 553, 673, 745
McElroy, L., 54
McEwan, Hunter, 41, 49, 50
McEwen, N., 407
McGee, Patrick, 335
McGill Journal of Education, xiii
McGraw, Onalee, 614
McGuffey, William H., 610
McHoul, A., 52
McIntosh, Peggy, 367, 368
McKeon, Richard, 194, 195
McKeown, M., 780
McKim, Margaret G., 53, 144
McKinney, Lynn W., 203
McKnight, Douglas, xvi, 856
McLaren, Peter, 27, 44, 45, 52, 60, 61, 62, 65, 244, 245, 246, 248, 251, 257, 262, 263, 265, 266, 267, 268, 270, 271, 275, 278, 283, 284, 287, 288, 294, 296, 304, 305, 306, 307, 308, 309, 310, 311, 312, 313, 314, 318, 353, 354, 473, 496, 498, 507, 510, 511, 512, 513, 644, 650, 673, 674, 763, 796, 827, 850
McLaughlin, D., 316, 397, 516, 565, 761
McLaughlin, M., 700
McLuhan, Marshall, 511
McMurry, Charles, 80, 81, 82, 84
McMurry, Frank, 80, 81, 84
McMurry, Linda, 81
McNeil, John, 17, 18, 19, 21, 22, 23, 28, 29, 31, 70, 139,197, 200, 230, 231
McNeil, Linda, 202, 279, 282, 668, 670, 679, 681, 806
McPeck, John, 773
McTaggert, Robin, 766
Mead, George Herbert, 691
Measor, L., 769
Meath-Lang, Bonnie, 516, 518, 530, 531, 532, 759, 765
Mediterranean, 797
Meech Lake, 840
Meehan, Brenda, 391
Megill, Allan, 467, 494
Mehan, H., 784
Meighan, R., 243, 247
Meighan, Roland, 837, 837

Meiji government, 807
Meister, G., 679, 682
Meki, Ethiopia, 820
Melnick, C., 562
Melton Research Center, 196
Mercer University, 114
Merleau-Ponty, Maurice, 233, 407, 411, 412, 415, 425, 430, 434, 435, 447, 453, 454, 455, 513
Messer, S., 705
Metadendral, 712
Metcalf, Lawrence E., 199
Metzger, Margaret, 673
Mexican-American, 327, 347
Mexico (Mexican), 333, 345, 347, 794, 826, 828
Miami University (Ohio), 262, 266
Michaels, K., 675
Michalko, R., 409
Michener, James, 133, 138
Michigan State University, 757
Miel, Alice, 46, 69, 140, 169, 511, 720, 747, 763
Mieli, M., 369
Milburn, Geoffrey, 46, 65
Miles, M., 53
Milken, Michael, 329
Miller Analogies Test (MAT), 775
Miller, D., 198
Miller, Janet L., xiv, 40, 43, 147, 168, 179, 187, 211, 212, 219, 225, 226, 312, 358, 364, 370, 371, 372, 375, 381, 382, 383, 384, 385, 386, 395, 402, 403, 404, 516, 523, 524, 525, 528, 545, 546, 547, 548, 549, 550, 551, 552, 555, 765, 766, 847, 863, 867
Miller, John P., 17, 18, 21, 22, 70, 633
Miller, Kelly, 352
Miller, L. , 764
Miller, M., 54
Millett, Kate, 364, 366
Millies, Palma, 562, 766
Millman, M., 367
Milner, Edward, 570, 589
Minneapolis Department of Supervisors and Directors of Instruction, 127
Miramontes, O., 635
Mishler, E., 54
Mitchell, Juliet, 364, 366, 391
Mitchell, R., 720
Mitrano, Barbara, 364, 371, 372, 373, 652, 655
Mitre Corporation, 711
Miyazaki, I., 797
Moffett, James, 777, 780
Mohatt, G., 316, 785
Mohr, R., 402
Molina, Anthony, 718
Molnar, Alex, 215, 224, 227, 228, 629, 633
Molt, Emil, 626
Moltmann, Jürgen, 645, 646, 652

Montclair State College, 152, 771, 772
Montgomery, R., 733
Mooney, Ross, 53, 156, 157, 179, 182, 847
Moore, D., 832
Moore, M., 409
Moore, Mary Elizabeth, 655
Moors (the), 818
Moran, Gabriel, 627, 629
Morehouse College, 321
Morgan, G., 747
Morgan, Robin, 364, 366
Morley, F., 198
Morocco, 818
Morris, Barbara, 613
Morris, Henry, 614
Morris, P., 793
Morris, Willie, 533, 534
Morrison, Henry, 19, 57
Morrison, Toni, 315, 327, 335, 336, 356
Morse, Samuel F. B., 610
Mosher, R., 635
Mosier, R., 779
Moss, A., 777
Moufé, Chantal, 250
Moulton, J., 828
Mount Holyoke College, 708
Moynihan, Daniel Patrick, 348
Mozambique, 818, 821
Muhammed, Elijah, 321
Mulder, M., 765
Mulder, R., 758
Muldoon, Maureen, 659
Muller, Johan 279, 818, 825
Muller, Robert, 799, 801, 803
Munby, Hugh, 55, 585, 763, 765
Munro, Petra, 384, 390, 526, 528, 768
Murphy, J., 679, 681, 728
Murphy, L., 344, 345, 348
Murphy, R., 732
Murray, Judith Sargent, 360
Museum of Education (University of South Carolina), 43
Musgrave, P., 229
Muslim, 410
Mycin, 712

Naish, M., 335
Nakayama, S., 797
Nalaskowski, Aleksander, 834, 835
Namibia, 818
Nation of Islam, 321
National (Bay Area) Writing Project, 287, 436
National Academy of Sciences, 159
National Association for the Advancement of Colored People (NAACP), 779
National Association for the Education of Young Children, 334
National Association of Manufacturers, 778

National Association of State Directors of
    Teacher Education & Certification
    (NASDTEC), 756
National Board of Education (NBE), 842
National Center for Education Statistics, 733
National Center for Research in Vocational
    Education, 718
National Commission on Excellence in
    Education (NCEE), 698, 804
National Conference on Life Adjustment
    Education, 146
National Council for Accreditation of
    Teacher Education (NCATE), 756
National Council for Excellence in Critical
    Thinking (NCECT), 772
National Council of Teachers of English
    (NCTE), 625
National Council of Teachers of Social
    Studies (NCTSS), 803
National Council on Religion and
.   Publication Education (NCRPE), 615,
    616
National Curriculum (UK), 832
National Curriculum Reform movement,
    159, 163, 187, 662, 734, 857
National Defense Act (1958), 157, 159
National Diffusion Network (NDN), 700
National Education Association (NEA), 75,
    94, 99, 103, 142, 176, 706
National Education Crisis Committee
    (NECC), 825
National Educational Research Institute
    (Tokyo), 833
National Endowment for the Humanities
    (NEH), 615, 616, 673, 803
National Geographic, 839
National Herbart Society, 80, 81, 82, 83, 84,
    87
National Institute of Education, 207
National Organization for Women (NOW),
    779
National Public Radio, 44
National Review, 805
National Science Foundation (NSF), 157,
    158, 159, 162, 163, 711
National Socialism, 811, 812
National Society for the Study of Education
    (NSSE), 77, 81, 83, 111, 112, 113, 121,
    122, 123, 141, 144, 145, 149, 775
National Technical Institute for the Deaf
    (RIT), 530
Naumburg, Margaret, 125, 126
Navajo, 333, 388
Nazi, 150
Neill, A. S., 185
Nelkin, D., 779
Nelson, M., 768
Nelson, R., 90, 92, 102, 117, 118, 126, 132
Neo-Nazism, 813
Netherlands, 828

New American Schools Development
    Corporation (NASDC), 292, 293
New England, 360, 362
New Orleans, 7, 860, 862
New York University, 215
New Zealand, 792, 832, 833
Newell, Allan, 712
Newlon, Jesse, 111, 112, 113, 143, 237
Newman, Joseph, 611, 612, 614, 623, 635
Newmann, Fred, 192
Newsweek, 795
Newton, Isaac, 499, 500, 509, 572
Ng, Roxana, 315
Nicaragua, 828
Niece, R., 127
Nielsen, M., 781
Nietzsche, Friedrich, 274, 430, 448, 460,
    482, 494, 504, 691
Niger, 818, 828
Nigeria, 823, 824, 826
Nile River, 818, 819
Nixon, Gregory, xvi, 516, 542
Nixon, Jon, 737
Nixon, Richard, 366, 779
Nkomo, M., 318
Noah, Harold J., 191
Noble, Douglas, 292, 293
Noblit, G., 54
Noddings, Nel, 27, 149, 207, 368, 380, 386,
    387, 389, 390, 420, 523, 545, 547, 548,
    629, 652, 655, 656, 657, 684, 694, 695,
    696, 752, 763, 773
Nohn, Herman, 813
Nordic countries, 230
Norquay, N., 566
Norris, C., 453, 457, 460, 465, 466
Norris, Joe, 589, 601
Norris, S., 774
North (the), 72, 361
North American Free Trade Agreement
    (NAFTA), 796
North Carolina Center for the Advancement
    of Teaching, 763
Norway (Norwegian), 581
Novak, Joseph, 71
Nowak, A., 198
Nowak-Fabrykowski, Krystyna, 586
Nuffield Mathematics Project, 824
Nunes, M., 826, 829

O'Connor, Terence, 826, 829
O'Hara, Frank, 483, 484
O'Keefe, P. , 761
O'Neale, S., 533
O'Neil, J., 803
O'Shea, James, 142
O'Shea, T., 712
Oakes, Jeannie, 249, 714, 133
Oberg, Antoinette, 37, 54, 765

Ochoa, A., 82, 291
Ogbu, J. , 327, 345, 349
Oh, M-S, 410
Ohio State University, 96, 102, 113, 117,
  118, 129, 130, 136, 137, 142, 149, 150,
  156, 157, 173, 182, 183, 209, 223, 224,
  707, 710
Ohio State University Curriculum Theory
  Conference, 179, 181, 417, 563
Ohio State University Laboratory School,
  135, 157
Ohio University, 255
Oka, 840
Okakok, L., 783
Oldenski, Thomas, 644, 650
Oliva, Peter, 26, 722, 724, 727
Oliver, A., 198
Oliver, Donald W., 192, 627, 634, 652, 653,
  658, 859
Olson, J., 249, 703, 714
Olson, Margaret, 431
Olson, P. , 247, 253
Omi, Michael, 315, 316, 317
Ontario Institute for Studies in Education
  (OISE), 253, 263, 266, 546, 557
Open Door Policy (China), 817
Oregon State University, 707
Oren, A., 715
Orlosky, Donald E., 199
Ornstein, A., 11, 756, 798
Osajima, Keith, 327
Osborn, J., 780
Osborn, Robert L., 219
Osborne, J., 238
Osborne, Ken, 838
Overly, Norman, 27, 792
Owens, T., 737
Oxford University, 168, 206
Oxman-Michelli, Wendy, 771
Ozmon, H., 799, 800

Pacific Islands, 793
Pacific region, 839
Padgham, Ronald E., 226, 230, 236, 569,
  572, 573, 576, 577, 578, 601
Pagano, Jo Anne, 11, 12, 70, 171, 226, 364,
  368, 384, 385, 386, 403, 515, 525, 528,
  530, 544, 545, 546, 547, 549, 555, 741,
  750, 761, 762, 850, 867
Page, Reba, 669, 670, 679, 806
Pajak, Edward, 720, 723, 724, 726
Palm, John, 399
Palto Alto, California, 402
Pan-Africanists (Pan-Africanism), 321, 352
Panama, 826
Papert, Seymour, 712
Parents Who Care, 779
Paringer, W., 867
Paris (France), 452, 514, 542
Paris, Cynthia, 701, 703, 704

Parker, Francis, 75, 76, 83, 84, 86, 87, 88,
  89, 103, 150
Parker, Walter, 292
Parlett, M. , 736, 737
Parmet, R., 609
Parrett, William, 664
Partisan Review, 313
Passow, A. Harry, 140, 144, 171, 714
Paul, Craig, 800
Paul, Richard, 773
Pautz, Anne, xvi
Pavkov, T., 635
PBS Adult Learning Satellite Service, 772
Pearson, Jr., W., 331
Peckham, Earl K., 152
Pedagogical Institute (Poland), 835
Pedagogical Seminary, 88
Peek, Booker, 356
Pellassy, D., 809
Penna, Anthony, 70, 96, 215, 249, 320
Pennsylvania State University, 266
People for the American Way, 779
People v. Hall, 316
Percy, Walker, 535
Pereira, P., 193
Perestroika, 835
Perez, L. , 316
PERT (Program Evaluation and Review
  Technique), 166
Peru, 828
Peshkin, Alan, 52, 58, 394, 625, 737, 743
Pestalozzi, Johann Heinrich, 78, 79, 86
Peter, Car, 654
Peterat, Linda, 410, 422, 427
Peters, Charles, 101
Peters, R. S., 168, 202, 203, 690, 731
Peters, Tom, 675
Peterson, K., 728
Phenix, Philip H., 170, 191, 628, 629
Phenomenology + Pedagogy, xiii
Phi Delta Kappa Symposium (1963), 161
Phi Delta Kappan, 161, 575
Philips, S., 785
Philipines, 322
Phillips, D., 52
Phillips, M., 832
Phoenicians, 818
Physical Science Study Committee (PSSC),
  158, 162, 163
Piaget, Jean, 77, 88, 205, 238, 413, 444, 456,
  498, 499, 501, 509, 573, 594, 628, 705,
  707, 712
Pierce, Charles Sanders, 116, 302
Pilder, William J., 218, 219, 220, 222, 223
Pinar, William F., 4, 10, 13, 23, 34, 39, 41,
  44, 45, 48, 49, 51, 56, 69, 70, 96, 111,
  112, 147, 148, 156, 168, 179, 187, 192,
  199, 204, 210, 211, 212, 214, 215, 216,
  218, 219, 220, 223, 224, 225, 226, 230,
  231, 232, 233, 234, 235, 237, 238, 249,
  255, 268, 269, 271, 278, 288, 289, 290,

291, 293, 295, 304, 320, 327, 328, 329,
330, 338, 349, 350, 354, 364, 370, 371,
373, 375, 376, 381, 389, 396, 397, 402,
403, 405, 406, 409, 411, 415, 416, 420,
425, 437, 443, 444, 450, 451, 493, 494,
495, 513, 515, 516, 517, 518, 519, 520,
521, 522, 523, 532, 535, 538, 545, 552,
560, 564, 570, 578, 583, 584, 589, 599,
628, 629, 631, 636, 637, 645, 653, 672,
675, 676, 719, 741, 752, 758, 759, 760,
766, 782, 784, 847, 848, 850, 854, 856,
857, 860, 863, 864
Pipes, Richard, 836
Pius XI, 646
Plantinga, D. , 213
PLATO, 711, 712
Plato, 420, 474, 480, 482, 483, 501, 705, 797
Pleck, Joseph, 369
Plowden Report, 188, 189
Podl, Jody Brown, 673
Polakow, V., 407
Poland (Polish), 589, 651, 833, 834
Polanyi, Michael, 170, 210, 233
Pollock, Jackson, 448, 518
Pomfret, A., 700
Ponder, G., 562, 777
Ponticell, J. , 562
Poole, M., 586
Popham, W. James, 165, 192, 687, 688, 734,
     738
Popkewitz, Thomas S., 53, 55, 580, 671, 700,
     758
Portelli, J., 26
Porter, E., 392
Porter, J., 821
Portland State University, 265
Portugal, 823, 828, 837
Portuges, C., 368, 478
Portuguese, 818
Posner, George J., 43, 46, 47, 169, 197, 200,
     782
Poster, Cyril, 827
Poster, Mark, 473
Postlethwaite, T., 793, 809
Postman, Neil, 470
Potter-Tomfohr, Joan, 589
Pound, Ezra, 542
Powell, Arthur, 697
Power, C., 635
Pratt, David, 205, 661, 664, 688, 689, 719
Pressey, Sidney L., 710
Price, K., 726, 727
Prigogine, Ilya, 498, 500, 501, 657
Princeton University, 276
Pritscher, Conrad, 52
Pritzkau, P. T., 156
Process Studies, 653
Proctor, Samuel D., 210
Professors of Curriculum, 208
Program Planning and Budgeting System
     (PPBS), 682

Progressive Education, 130
Progressive Education Association, 110, 129,
     130, 133, 134, 140
Project 2061, 717, 718
Project Method (Kilpatrick), 114, 115
Pronger, B., 363
Prosser, Charles, 146
Proust, Marcel, 482
Provenzo, Eugene, 613, 614, 615
Prunty, J., 768
Prussia, 579, 797
Prynne, Hester, 454
Psacharopoulous, G., 823
Ptolemy II, 819
Pueblo, 660
PUFF, 712
Pugno, Lawrence, 160
Punjabis, 345
Puritans, 360, 608, 610, 615
Purpel, David E., 187, 191, 197, 249, 603,
     627, 630, 631, 632, 633, 634, 650, 684,
     685

Québec, 586
Quincy system, 86
Quinlan, F., 688

Radical Caucus (ASCD), 227
Radziewicz, Julian, 834
Raffel, S., 409
Ragan, C., 809
Rahner, Karl, 646, 649, 650
Rainbow Coalition, 261
Raissiguier, C., 794
Ramond, Judith, 368
Ramsankar, S., 672
Rand Corporation, 159, 700
Randolph, A. Phillip, 322
Randolph, Elizabeth S., 224
Rankin, John M., 781
Ratke, Wolfgang, 810
Ratner, J., 131
Ratteray, J., 331
Ravitch, Diane, 619, 673, 801
Raymond, Danielle, 516, 523, 548, 553, 554,
     555, 556, 562, 563, 564, 765
Raywid, Mary Anne, 680
Re: Learning, 672
Read, Herbert, 577
Reagan, Ronald, 30, 238, 255, 259, 366, 470,
     570, 620, 636, 676, 678, 832, 833
Red Cross (the), 842
Red Sea, 819
Redbook (Harvard), 145
Reed, R., 607
Reese, William, 612, 625
Reid, Tony, 142, 157

Reid, William A., 3, 37, 42, 46, 197, 203, 204, 205, 219, 238, 516, 571, 584, 664, 732, 863, 864, 865
Rein, Wilhelm, 80, 87
Reiniger, Meredith, 305, 386, 388, 516, 528, 545, 551, 552
Reinsmith, William, 753
Religion and Public Education, 615, 618
Republic of New Africa, 321
Republican Party, 678
Reynolds, William M., xv, xvi, 4, 43, 44, 45, 49, 226, 238, 278, 295, 303, 373, 396, 409, 422, 425, 426, 450, 451, 642, 653, 679
Rice, Joseph Mayer, 90, 103
Rice, S., 516
Rich, Adrienne, 366, 367, 368, 370
Richards, Colin, 197
Richards, R., 606
Richardson, V., 745
Richter, Jr., Maurice N., 202
Ricketts, Juan, 649
Rickover, Admiral Hyman, 151, 153, 154
Ricoeur, Paul, 425, 434, 435, 641, 642, 643, 657, 729
Riordan, Timothy, 223
Ripley, D., 54
Rippa, S., 8, 73, 74, 78, 79, 91, 92, 99
Robertson, H., 764
Robison, Helen F., 179
Rochester Institute of Technology, 226
Roderick, Jessie, 530
Rodney, Eric, 322
Roehler, L., 761
Rogan, John, 13, 15, 16, 17, 19, 20, 22, 23, 24, 29, 32, 45, 48, 65, 792
Rogers, Carl, 172, 174, 178, 185, 192
Rogers, D., 54
Rogers, J. A., 322
Rogers, K., 169
Rohlen, T., 789
Rohrs, H., 811
Roman, Leslie, 58, 289, 306, 354, 394, 506
Rome, 799
Romer, N., 331
Romero, Oscar, 644
Rono, P., 820
Roosevelt, Theodore, 362, 616
Rorty, Richard, 151, 424, 451, 496, 501
Rosario, José, 69, 119, 569, 571, 527, 573, 595
Roscoe, K., 850
Rose, Susan D., 624
Rosenau, P., 451
Rosenblatt, Louise, 46
Rosenshine, B., 752
Rosenstock, Sheldon, 102
Rosenthal, D., 778
Rosetta, Santiago, 660
Ross, Diana, 339
Ross, E. Wayne, 660

Rossi, P., 736
Rossman, Parker, 716
Roszak, Theodore, 210
Rotenberry Act, 778
Rothe, Peter, 59, 60
Rousseau, Jean-Jacques, 185, 810, 811
Rowell, P., 65, 850
Rubin, Gayle, 367
Rubin, Louis, 192, 752
Rudd, Jr., A., 431
Rudnicki, Stefan, 595, 596
Rudnitsky, Alan N., 46, 197, 200
Rueda, R., 784
Ruether, Rosemary Radford, 647, 657
Rugg, Harold, 25, 74, 105, 114, 119, 121, 122, 129, 130, 132, 139, 149, 228, 243, 322, 325, 443, 541, 571, 572, 573, 576, 578, 580, 755, 777, 778
Rumania, 830, 838
Rush, Benjamin, 360
Rushcamp, S., 761
Russell, Bertrand, 152, 538
Russell, N., 736, 743
Russell, T., 763, 765
Russell, William, 73
Russia (Russian), 795, 815, 830, 835, 836
Rust, Bernhard, 812
Rutgers University, 210
Rutherford, W., 704
Ryan, J., 316, 333
Ryan, R., 635
Ryerson, Andre, 803

Sadlek, M., 365
Sadler, D., 741
Sadowsky, E., 635
Saettler, Paul, 704, 705, 708, 709, 710, 712
Said, Edward, 357, 451, 839
Salomon, G., 713, 716
Salvio, Paula, 527, 528, 559, 632
San Francisco Conference (ASCD, 1970), 208, 209, 210, 239
San Francisco State University, 210
San José State Conference, 160
Sanders, J., 732
Sanger, J., 54
Sao Paulo, 827
Sapon-Shevin, Mara, 365, 402
Sarason, Seymour B., 202, 683
Sartre, Jean-Paul, 152, 174, 217, 233, 267, 434, 438, 453, 455, 575, 592, 593, 594, 595, 599
Sarup, M., 451, 466, 471, 474
Saudi Arabia, 796
Saussure, Ferdinand de, 456, 457, 458, 459, 461, 495
Sauvé, Virginia, 437
Sava, Samuel G., 192
Save Our Children, 779, 842
Sawada, Daiyo, 569, 603

Sawyer, Jack, 369
Saylor, J. Galen, 13, 18, 19, 21, 26, 110, 111, 140, 156, 176, 197,198, 684, 685, 686, 687, 688, 689, 690
Scandinavia, 794
Scardamalia, M. , 704, 705, 713, 716
Schaffarzick, Jon, 163, 197, 202, 207
Schaller, K., 810
Scheffler, Israel, 126, 202
Scheurich, James, 354, 730
Schilling, S. Paul, 657
Schleiermacher, Friedrich, 640, 641, 642
Schlesinger, Jr., Arthur, 618, 795
Schmidt, Benno, 680
Scholar,712
Scholastic Aptitude Test (SAT), 673, 683
Schön, Donald, 501, 688, 752, 766
Schonhammer, Rainer, 442
School-Based Management (SBM), 674, 675
Schoolland, K., 805
Schoonover, T., 794
Schrag, Francis, 53
Schubert, Ann Lynn Lopez, 380, 781
Schubert, Heidi Ann, 380
Schubert, William H., xv, 11, 13, 15, 16, 17, 18, 21, 22, 23, 24, 27, 35, 36, 37, 40, 43, 48, 55, 56, 69, 70, 78, 79, 80, 81, 91, 96, 97, 99, 101, 103, 104, 108, 110, 115, 118, 119, 121, 125, 130, 139, 141, 143, 144, 149, 155, 156, 159, 162, 165, 166, 168, 171, 175, 189, 190, 197, 198, 199, 200, 201, 212, 265, 320, 380, 516, 546, 553, 554, 555, 561, 562, 563, 589, 648, 747, 758, 765, 766, 781, 788, 792, 850, 865
Schutz, Alfred, 233, 407, 412, 546
Schwab, Joseph J., 10, 33, 35, 36, 37, 38, 39, 40, 63, 161, 176, 177, 187, 192, 193, 195, 197, 202, 203, 204, 220, 221, 229, 231, 232, 233, 235, 269, 419, 424, 486, 487, 488, 559, 571, 584, 732, 849, 855, 856
Schwager, S., 360, 361
Schwartz, B., 329
Schwartz, John, 69, 119
Science/Technology/Society (STS) movement, 718, 719
Scobey, M., 190
Scopes Trial, 778
Scott, Joan, 328, 346
Scott, W., 137, 138
Scriven, Michael, 192, 202, 717, 732, 734
Searles, W. , 215
Sears, James T., 310, 376, 386, 396, 397,398, 399, 402, 755, 852
Sears, P., 365
Seeds, Corrine, 79
Seguel, Mary Louise, 69, 79, 80, 81, 91, 92, 93, 100, 101, 103, 141
Segundo, Juan Luis, 643
Selden, Steven, 42, 69, 94, 776

Self, J., 712
Seller, W., 17, 18, 21, 22, 70
Seminole, 316
Sendor, Benjamin, 617
Senegal, 828
Senese, G., 282
Sergiovanni, Thomas, 720, 725, 728, 730, 753
Serres, Michel, 460, 480, 481, 492, 499
Shaker, Paul, 758, 850
Shakespeare, William, 152, 596
Shamsher, M., 861
Shane, Harold G., 191, 664, 690
Shanker, Al, 675
Shannon, N., 765
Shapiro, H. Svi, 249, 294, 603, 630, 631, 632, 634, 650
Sharp, Rachel, 249, 250, 251
Shaw University, 321
Shaw, K., 731
Shea, Christine, 619, 620, 672
Shinkfield, A., 732
Shive, G., 795
Shor, Ira, 249, 262, 280
Shores, J. Harlan, 15, 155, 199, 697
Short, Edmund C., 25, 45, 46, 49, 56, 201, 606, 685
Shuchat-Shaw, Francine, 219, 586, 732
Shulman, Judith, 757, 761, 769, 770
Shulman, Lee, 40, 193, 669, 746, 747, 748, 749, 750, 757, 762, 769, 770, 856
Shultz, Jeffrey, 527, 781, 782, 783, 784, 785
Shumaker, Ann, 105, 114, 119, 132
Shymansky, J., 783
Sieber, S., 777
Siegel, Harvey, 771, 773
Siegel, M., 256
SIG (AERA), Creation and Utilization of Curriculum Knowledge, 201
SIG (AERA), Critical Issues in Curriculum, 201
SIG (AERA), Lesbian and Gay Studies, 397
Sikes, P., 769
Silber, John, 682, 683
Silberman, Charles, 187, 188, 189, 238
Silin, Jonathan, 376, 397, 402
Silva, E., 675, 826
Silvers, Ronald J., 416, 427
Simon, Herbert, 712
Simon, Roger, 58, 262, 263, 283, 284, 286, 304, 589, 839
Simpson, E., 189
Simpson, Lewis, 535
Sioux, 316
Sirotnik, K., 714
Sizemore, B., 327, 331
Sizer, Theodore, 85, 138, 670, 672, 757
Skilbeck, Malcolm, 696
Skinner, B. F., 167, 709, 710
Skoog, G., 778
Slattery, Cheryl Friberg, xv

Slattery, Patrick, xv, 4, 290, 535, 637, 643, 644, 645, 646, 650, 652, 653, 654, 657, 847
Sleeper, M., 635
Sleeping Car Porters Union, 322
Sleeter, Christine E., 331, 333, 334, 342, 343, 354
Sloan, Douglas, 72, 74, 191, 714
Sloane, B., 402
Sloane, D., 402
Small, Albion, 119
Smith, B. Othanel, 15, 147, 148, 155, 161, 169, 170, 173, 199, 697
Smith, David G., 410, 417, 419, 420, 421, 422, 423, 424, 430, 432, 838, 840, 842
Smith, E., 136, 137
Smith, Frank, 818, 825
Smith, Lillian, 188
Smith, M. , 743
Smith, Norville L., 698
Smith, N., 734, 736, 737
Smith, Paul, 281, 282, 304
Smith, Richard, 284
Smith, Stephen J., 440, 441, 442
Smits, H., 54
Smyth, John, 720, 724, 725, 731, 770
Snarey, J., 635
Snauwaert, Dale, 288
Snedden, David, 100, 117, 118
Snyder, Jon, 51, 699, 700, 701, 702, 704
Snygg, Donald, 164
So (the), 338
Sobrino, Jon, 643, 648
Social Frontier, 129, 130, 131
Social Reconstructionists, 104
Society for Curriculum Study, 142
Society for the Study of Curriculum History, 43, 855
Sockett, Hugh, 635, 753
Socrates, 631
Sola, Peter, 619, 620, 672
Solas, J., 765
Solidarity movement, 651
Solomon, C., 711
Soltis, Jonas, 46, 630
Somalia, 818, 820
Sonoma State University, 772
Sontag, Susan, 472
Sophie, 712
Sorbonne, 641
South (the), 72, 289, 290, 291, 320, 361, 397, 398, 463, 533, 535, 543, 612
South Africa, 801, 818, 820, 824, 825, 826, 830
South America (see also Latin America), 828
South Korea, 804
Soviet Union, 6, 9, 133, 151, 154, 801, 815, 830, 835, 836, 837, 842
Soweto, 825
Spain (Spanish), 581, 802, 828
Spears, Harold, 155, 156

Spencer, Herbert, 73, 74, 101, 666
Spivak, G., 478, 505, 839
Spodek, B., 215
Spring, Joel, 74, 91, 99, 157, 174, 175, 789
Sputnik, 154, 159, 690, 794
Squire, J., 776
St. John's College, 797
St. Julien, John, xvi, 746
St. Louis Art Museum, 706
St. Louis Conference (ASCD, 1981), 211
Stafford, Jean, 542
Stahl, R., 189
Stake, Robert E., 53, 202, 732, 734, 736
Stalin, Joseph, 830, 835
Stanfield, John H., 730
Stanford University, 52, 151, 156, 183, 573, 712, 738, 739, 743
Stanley, J., 736
Stanley, William O., 15, 155, 199, 697
Stanley, William B., 82, 116, 122, 129, 130, 186, 228, 243, 281, 283, 291, 294, 296 312, 313, 322, 497, 850
Stanton, Elizabeth Cady, 361
Starratt, Robert, 219, 220, 221, 229, 288, 291, 589, 696, 720
Starzynski, Wojciech, 833
State University of New York at Albany, 169
State University of New York Press, 788
Steffere, B., 365
Stefik, M., 716
Steinberg, Shirley, xviii, 294, 296, 307, 350, 507, 509, 510, 589, 601, 744, 746, 762
Steinbergh, Judith Wolinsky, 586
Steiner, Rudolf, 626
Stenhouse, Lawrence, 37, 203, 726, 752, 766
Stephens College, 101
Sternberg, R., 775
Stevens, M., 832
Stevens, R., 752
Stewart, J., 331
Stier, John, xvi
Stinson, Susan W., 390, 567, 568, 572, 603
Stoddart, Kenneth, 44
Stoddart, T., 761
Stone, Joan, 486
Stonewall, 398
Strasser, S., 438
Stratemeyer, Florence, 144, 198, 202
Strayer, George, 140
Strickland, D., 317
Strike, Kenneth A., 46, 200, 244, 245, 247, 252, 269, 270, 271, 299, 690
Strom, M., 635
Stufflebeam, D., 732, 733, 734
Su, Zhixin, 65, 686, 696, 697, 698, 716, 855
Sudan, 821
Sui emperors, 796, 797
Sullivan, Margaret, xvi
Sumara, Dennis, 437, 438
Sung, Il Je, 409
Suppes, Patrick, 711

Sutherland, G., 733
Svengalis, C., 800
Swadener, B., 850
Swanger, D., 581
Swartz, Ellen, 331
Swartz, R., 635
Sweden (Swedish), 841, 842
Switzerland, 810, 827
Sykes, Gary, 23, 163, 207, 665, 666, 667, 668
Synder, J., 111, 112, 137, 704
Szepkouski, G., 850

Taba, Hilda, 15, 17, 19, 53, 144, 145, 149, 150, 175, 721, 865
Tabachnick, B., 700
Taiwan, 815
Talladega College, 321
Talley, W. , 85
Talmage, H., 198
Tanner, Daniel, 12, 13, 14, 15, 16, 17, 18, 19, 21, 22, 23, 27, 42, 49, 65, 69, 70, 71, 72, 73, 75, 76, 77, 78, 79, 80, 81, 82, 83, 84, 85, 86, 87, 89, 90, 91, 94, 96, 99, 100, 101, 103, 104, 106, 107, 108, 109, 111, 113, 114, 115, 116, 118, 123, 124, 128, 129, 130, 137, 139, 144, 146, 151, 158, 161, 162, 163, 164, 166, 168, 169, 186, 187, 188, 189, 197, 198, 206, 207, 230, 231, 232, 234, 235, 236, 238, 243, 271, 516, 567, 662, 672, 675, 679, 681, 709, 720, 721, 722, 723, 724, 744, 775, 778, 855, 865
Tanner, Laurel, 12, 13, 14, 15, 16, 17, 18, 19, 21, 22, 23, 27, 42, 49, 69, 70, 71, 72, 73, 75, 76, 77, 78, 79, 80, 81, 82, 83, 84, 85, 86, 87, 89, 90, 91, 94, 96, 99, 100, 101, 103, 104, 106, 107, 108, 109, 111, 113, 114, 115, 116, 118, 123, 124, 128, 129, 130, 137, 139, 144, 146, 158, 161, 162, 166, 168, 186, 187, 188, 189, 197, 206, 207, 230, 231, 232, 234, 235, 236, 238, 243, 271, 516, 567, 662, 672, 675, 720, 721, 722, 723, 724, 744, 774, 775, 855, 865
Tanzania, 818, 819, 820
Tarrow, N., 813
Taubman, Peter Maas, xv, 4, 45, 217, 287, 335, 336, 349, 350, 354, 355, 364, 368, 370, 373, 374, 381,401, 476, 477, 478, 479, 480, 485, 501, 517, 538
Taxel, Joel, 334
Taylor, Charles, 106
Taylor, Frederick Winslow, 95, 97, 101, 102, 501
Taylor, Philip, 46, 197
Taylor, Wendy, xv
Teachers College, Columbia University, 91, 96, 112, 113, 114, 116, 129, 132, 133, 139, 140, 149, 152, 156, 157, 171, 173,

179, 181, 183, 190, 191, 193, 202, 223, 227, 751, 833, 860
Teachers College Press, 52, 743
Teachers College Record, xiii, 114, 183,191, 861
Teitelbaum, Kenneth, 251, 264
Temple University, 173
Tennov, D., 367
Tetreault, Mary Kay, 367
Tewa of New Mexico, 333
Texas, 534
Thatcher, Margaret, 831, 832, 833
Thayer-Bacon, Barbara, 773
Theisen, G., 809
Thelen, Herbert, 150, 171
Thelin, Bengt, 793, 830, 841, 842
Theobald, Paul, 85, 288
Thiessen, D., 765
Third Reich, 811, 812
Third World (the), 794, 795, 807, 830
Thirwall, John C., 152
Thody, Philip, 458
Thomas, R. Murray, 794, 808, 815, 816, 819, 820, 829, 830
Thompson, John, 641
Thorndike, Ashley, 152
Thorndike, Robert, 53, 90, 91, 92, 94, 95, 97, 115, 390, 682, 745
Thornston, S., 27
Thurstone, Louis L., 194
Tiananmen Square, 814, 815, 817
TICCIT, 711, 712
Tierney, William, 281, 316, 397, 516, 565, 676, 761, 850
Tippins, D., 762
Title IX (1972 Education Amendment), 366
Todd, R., 718
Tolstoy, Leo, 630
Tom, Alan, 64, 562, 752, 756, 757
Tomkins, George, 69, 840
Torrance, H., 732
Totten, S., 850
Townsend, David, 516, 765
Tracy, David, 642, 643
Travers, Robert, 93, 136, 734
Trecker, J., 365
Trilateral Commission, 802
Tripp, D., 54
Trollip, Stanley, 705, 710, 711, 712, 713, 714
Trostli, R., 626
Trotsky, Leon, 133
Trousdale, Ann, 761
Troy, F., 807
Troyna, B., 326, 327, 331, 332, 334
Truman, Harry S., 157
Trumbull, Deborah, 753
Trump, Donald, 329
Trump, J., 198
Tufts University, 708
Tunisia, 818
Turner, J., 198

Turner, L., 410
Turner, Margery, 604
Tyack, David, 359, 360, 361, 362, 363, 364,
  366, 661, 675, 677, 678
Tye, Kenneth, 800, 801, 802
Tyler, Louise, 304
Tyler, Ralph W., 10, 15, 17, 19, 20, 33, 34,
  36, 37, 38, 39, 40, 42, 44, 102, 119,
  127, 136, 144, 145, 147, 148, 149, 150,
  151, 155, 156, 167, 168, 171, 175, 177,
  178, 180, 187, 188, 194, 195, 198, 199,
  201, 205, 207, 211, 212, 233, 236, 237,
  371, 417, 419, 486, 487, 488, 499, 500,
  501, 568, 593, 663, 664, 682, 692, 732,
  734, 849, 853, 857, 863, 865

U'Ren, M., 365
Uganda, 338, 818
Uhrmacher, B., 567, 583, 746
Underwood, S., 765
UNESCO, 675, 820, 837
UNICEF, 842
United Kingdom (see also Britain and
  England), 37, 202, 229, 345, 563, 709,
  798
United Nations, 800, 801, 802, 818, 829,
  840, 842, 856
United States Air Force, 159
United States Catholic Conference, 618
United States Constitution, 300, 612, 614,
  615
United States Department of Education, 678
United States Office of Education, 146, 159
United States Office of Educational Research
  and Improvement, 833
United States Steel Corporation, 109, 110
United States Supreme Court, 298, 299, 300,
  301, 606, 612, 666, 778
University of Alberta, 44, 228, 229, 289, 409,
  557, 584, 837
University of Birmingham, 203, 837, 850
University of Botswana, 821
University of British Columbia, 229, 287
University of Calgary, 229, 333
University of California, Los Angeles, 79,
  230, 266
University of California, San Francisco, 806
University of Cape Town, 821
University of Chicago, 33, 40, 81, 96, 100,
  107, 108, 113, 119, 128, 136, 148, 149,
  150, 153, 161, 171, 193, 194, 269, 559,
  837
University of Chicago Curriculum Theory
  Conference, 147, 151, 168
University of Colorado
University of Dar Es Salaam, 821
University of Dayton, 226
University of East Anglia, 563, 798
University of Glasgow, 71
University of Heidelberg, 433

University of Houston, 708
University of Illinois (Champaign-Urbana),
  153, 161, 173, 712, 776
University of Illinois at Chicago, 561, 562,
  765
University of Iowa, 113
University of Islam, 322
University of Jena, 79, 80
University of Kansas, 707
University of Konigsburg, 78
University of Leiden, 71
University of Leipzig, 119
University of Lethbridge, 229, 838
University of London, 831, 833
University of Michigan, 107, 707, 759
University of Minnesota, 707
University of Mississippi, 290
University of Natal, 821
University of Newcastle upon Tyne, 831
University of North Carolina at Chapel Hill,
  150
University of North Carolina at Greensboro,
  215, 603, 630
University of Notre Dame, 611
University of Oregon, 265
University of Rhodes, 821
University of Rochester, xviii, 218, 223, 226,
  265, 277, 293, 297, 304, 373, 476, 517,
  519, 549, 591, 595
University of Rochester Conference, xviii,
  192, 216, 218, 219, 220, 223, 229, 519
University of South Carolina, 43, 157, 290,
  399
University of Southwestern Louisiana, xv
University of Texas at Austin, 215, 704, 711
University of Toronto, 266
University of Victoria, 229
University of Virginia, 224, 586, 784
University of Wisconsin at Madison, 43, 96,
  172, 181, 202, 215, 223, 225, 265, 266,
  276, 279, 280, 297, 306, 370, 707, 757,
  787
University of Wisconsin at Milwaukee, 215,
  224
University of Witwatersrand, 821
University of Zimbabwe, 822
Unklesbay, R., 769
Unruh, Glenys, 164, 197, 239
Urban, Wayne, 128
Utrecht School, 438

Vallance, Elizabeth, 14, 29, 30, 31, 187, 201,
  202, 320, 569, 571, 573, 574, 581, 584,
  585, 586, 706, 741
Valli, Linda, 756, 757
van Brummelen, H., 780
van Dammne, J., 410
van den Berghe, P. , 348, 367
van Dyke, J., 603
van Geel, Tyll, 207

van Liew, C. C., 81, 82
van Manen, Max, 44, 54, 228, 229, 405, 406,
    407, 408, 409, 410, 411, 428, 429, 430,
    434, 437, 438, 439, 440, 445, 486, 691
van Sertima, I., 322
van Til, William, 208
Vanderbilt University, 142
Vatican, 643, 644, 646, 647, 648, 649, 650
Vatican II, 646, 651
Veal, M., 674
Venezky, Richard L., 775, 776, 777, 778,
    779, 780
Viadero, D., 618
Victorian morality, 363
Viechnicki, K. , 127
Vietnam, 838
Vietnam War, 184, 209
Violas, P., 789
Voege, Herbert W., 204
von Humboldt, Wilhelm, 793, 810
von Stoephasius, Renata, 164
Vygotsky, L., 747

Wackes, K., 622
Wagner, E., 746, 747
Waks, Leonard J., 659
Walberg, H., 734
Walden School, 113, 125
Waldorf Astoria Company, 626
Waldorf Schools, 626
Wales, 798
Walker, A., 365
Walker, Decker F. , 37, 46, 197, 202, 203,
    206, 207, 571, 584, 665, 666
Walker, Rob, 563, 564, 736
Walker, S., 243
Walkerdine, Valerie, 391, 395, 496, 509
Wallenstein, Sandra, 364, 370, 372, 373,
    381, 516
Wallerstein, N., 262
Walsh, C., 316, 850
Walum, L., 365
Walworth, A., 777
Wandersee, James, 71, 91, 719
Wankowski, J., 516
War on Poverty, 174
Ward, B., 719
Ward, Lester Frank, 103, 104, 105
Warner, M., 850
Washburne, Carleton, 113
Washington, Booker T., 320, 350, 352
Washington, George, 616
Wasley, Patricia, 672
Watergate, 222
Waterman, R., 675
Watkins, William H., 116, 316, 319, 320,
    321, 322, 323, 351, 352, 509, 823, 824,
    849
Watney, Simon, 396

Watras, Joseph, 90, 92, 102, 117, 118, 126,
    132, 777
Watson, John B., 92
Waxman, H., 43
Wear, Delese, 391, 532, 759
Weber, William H., 191
Weedon, C., 392
Wehlage, G., 700
Weider, Alan, 284, 351, 352
Weiler, Hans, 671, 675, 676, 678, 679, 683,
    684, 761
Weill, L., 493
Weimar Republic, 811
Weingarten, Ira, 262
Weinstein, Gerald, 17, 190, 191
Weinstein, M., 774
Weinstein, Mark, 771
Weir, M., 783
Weis, Lois, 249, 253, 255, 265, 266, 296,
    304, 318, 334, 394
Weiss, J., 732
Weisser, S., 160
Weisstein, N., 367
Welch, D., 719
Weldon, J., 69
Welker, R., 753
Wellesley College, 367, 708
Welty, Eudora, 290, 533, 542, 558
Werner, Walter, 59, 60, 409, 410, 584, 585,
    586
West African Empires, 823
West, Cornel, 329, 339, 345, 356, 357
Westbrook, Robert, 103, 107, 109, 110, 128,
    582, 605, 652, 866
Westbury, Ian, 193, 194, 195, 196, 197, 203,
    679, 680, 780, 798, 805, 843
Western Illinois University, 718
Weston, N., 562
Wexler, Philip, 44, 60, 225, 247, 248, 250,
    251, 252, 262, 265, 266, 268, 269, 271,
    276, 277, 278, 279, 281, 291, 293, 296,
    297, 301, 303, 304, 308, 311, 314, 473,
    496, 503, 572, 579, 744, 785, 786, 787,
    851, 852
Whatley, Mariamne, 284, 337, 338, 339
Whipple, G., 775
White, J. P., 203, 731
White, John A., 772
White, K., 213
White, Merry, 806
Whitehead, Alfred North, 501, 648, 653,
    654, 655, 691, 814
Whitman, Walt, 402
Whitson, James A., xiv, 248, 250, 251, 265,
    277, 296, 297, 298, 299, 300, 301, 302,
    325, 402, 466, 496, 504, 579, 635, 636,
    666, 746, 750, 761, 762, 777, 850
Whitt, James, 252
Whittle, Christopher, 680
Whittle Corporation, 709
Whitty, Geoff, 243, 259, 306, 831, 832

Wilcox, B., 145
Wilde, Oscar, 514
Wiles, Jon, 11, 18, 19, 21, 22, 23, 48, 198, 720
Wiles, Kimball, 164, 165, 175
Wilkof, Neil J., 193, 194, 195, 196, 197, 805
Williams, Chancellor, 322
Williams, Eric, 322
Williams, J., 326
Williams, Patricia, 545
Williams, Ray, 235
Williams, Raymond, 251
Williamsburg Charter Foundation, 616
Williard, Emma, 360
Willie, C., 331
Willinsky, John, 186, 266, 285, 287, 326, 357, 451, 508, 561, 625, 691, 743, 780, 801, 802, 830, 839, 840, 842
Willis, George, xv, 43, 56, 69, 183, 199, 201, 219, 404, 405, 589, 696, 735, 736
Willis, Paul, 243, 243, 268, 270, 295, 309
Wilson, Angene Hopkins, 802
Wilson, S., 60
Wilson, Woodrow, 708
Winant, Howard, 315, 316, 317
Winitzky, N., 761
Winnetka Plan, 113
Wipperman, W., 811
Wirt, William, 109, 110
Wirth, Arthur G., 202
Wisconsin Department of Education, 324
Wise, Arthur, 667, 756
Wise, Gene, 199
Witherell, Carol, 545, 547, 548
Withers, W., 322
Wittgenstein, Ludwig, 424
Wolcott, Harry, 54, 58
Wolf, R., 737, 738
Wolfe, Thomas, 543
Wolfson, Bernice, 165, 215
Woman of the Year Award (1948), 157
Wood, George, 255, 262, 268, 270, 278, 308
Woods Hole Conference, 159
Woodson, Carter G., 352
Woodward, A., 776
Woolf, Virginia, 428, 546, 547, 584
Wordsworth, William, 691, 693
World Bank, 802, 822, 823
World Constitution and Parliament Association (WCPA), 802
World Council for Curriculum and Instruction (WCCI), 792
Worthen, B., 732, 737

Wraga, W., 719
Wright, Sewall, 194
Wulf, C., 810, 811
Wundt, Wilhelm, 119
Wynne, E., 635

Xavier University (Louisiana), 658
Xavier University (Ohio), 223
Xerox Corporation, 662

Yager, Robert, 719
Yale Report, 10, 63, 72, 74, 191
Yale University, 351, 680
Yale University Divinity School, 183, 860
Yamagishi, L., 516, 553, 556, 765
Yan'an government, 814
Yat-ming, Julian Leung, 814
Yazoo, Mississippi, 534
Yellin, D., 73, 287
Yeltsin, Boris, 835
Yonemura, M., 769
Yoruba, 316
Yost, G., 713
Young, Alma, 345 , 348, 349
Young, Michael F. D., 202, 243
Young, Robert, 464, 468
Young, R. E., 746

Zacharias, Jerrold, 158
Zahorik, John, 224, 752, 753
Zaire, 818
Zais, Robert S., 18, 19, 21, 27, 70, 197, 688
Zambia, 818
Zamora, R., 716
Zaret, Esther, 210, 211, 689
Zechiel, A., 137
Zehlendorf School, 812
Zeichner, Kenneth, 755
Zelizer, V., 783
Zen, 492
Zero Based Budgeting (ZBB), 682
Zeuli, J., 765
Ziller, Tuikson, 79, 80, 87
Zimbabwe, 818, 822, 824
Zimmer, Jürgen, 827
Zimpher, Nancy, 720, 725
Zirbes, Laura, 118, 142, 157
Zola, Émile, 460
Zumwalt, Karen, 111, 112, 137 , 699, 700, 701, 702, 704, 757